MW00581158

Encyclopedia of
CRIMINOLOGI(
THEOR`

Ro
Emor

Ma
Kent Sta

David P.
Cambridg

VOLUME TWO

Encyclopedia of
CRIMINOLOGICAL THEORY

EDITORS

FRANCIS T. CULLEN
PAMELA WILCOX

University of Cincinnati

⑤SAGE | reference

Los Angeles | London | New Delhi
Singapore | Washington DC

For information:

 SAGE Publications, Inc.
2455 Teller Road
Thousand Oaks, California 91320
E-mail: order@sagepub.com

SAGE Publications Ltd.
1 Oliver's Yard
55 City Road
London, EC1Y 1SP
United Kingdom

SAGE Publications India Pvt. Ltd.
B 1/I 1 Mohan Cooperative Industrial Area
Mathura Road, New Delhi 110 044
India

SAGE Publications Asia-Pacific Pte. Ltd.
33 Pekin Street #02-01
Far East Square
Singapore 048763

Printed in the United States of America.

Library of Congress Cataloging-in-Publication Data

Encyclopedia of criminological theory / edited by Francis T. Cullen, Pamela Wilcox.
    v. cm. – (A SAGE reference publication)
Includes bibliographical references and index.
ISBN 978-1-4129-5918-6 (cloth)
    1. Criminology–Encyclopedias. I. Cullen, Francis T. II. Wilcox, Pamela, 1968–

HV6017.E527 2010
364.01—dc22   2010011183

This book is printed on acid-free paper.

10 11 12 13 14 10 9 8 7 6 5 4 3 2 1

Publisher:	Rolf A. Janke
Acquisitions Editor:	Jim Brace-Thompson
Editorial Assistant:	Michele Thompson
Developmental Editor:	Carole Maurer
Reference Systems Manager:	Leticia M. Gutierrez
Reference Systems Coordinator:	Laura Notton
Production Editor:	Tracy Buyan
Typesetter:	C&M Digitals (P) Ltd.
Proofreaders:	Annie Lubinsky, Rae-Ann Goodwin
Indexer:	David Luljak
Cover Designer:	Bryan Fishman
Marketing Manager:	Amberlyn McKay

Contents

List of Entries

MAHER, LISA: SEXED WORK

Lisa's Maher's *Sexed Work: Gender, Race, and Resistance in a Brooklyn Drug Market* is an ethnographic study of women's participation in a local drug economy—one that begins with the question of how gender and race structure poor women's access to licit and illicit labor markets. Originally published in 1997, it is already considered a classic in the field of feminist criminology because of its rich account of the inner workings of the crack-cocaine market and its sharp theoretical insights regarding social structure and human agency.

The emergence of feminist analyses of crime can be traced to civil rights activism in the 1960s, particularly the second wave of the women's movement. The women's movement raised awareness and offered alternate theoretical perspectives and analyses of various crime-related topics ranging from prostitution to rape. The movement sparked scholarly interest in women's experiences with crime and renewed longstanding debates over gender differences in crime participation. Feminist criminologists challenged positivist explanations that attributed differences in men and women's criminality to biologically essentialist claims about women's weakness and passivity. Instead, feminist research demonstrated that observed gender differences in crime are a function of social factors including labor market participation, opportunity structures, formal and informal social controls, cultural expectations, differential socialization, and prior victimization.

Maher's study takes place during the decade of the 1990s. By this time, criminological research on women offenders had primarily moved in one of two directions. The "victimization" model portrayed women offenders as passive victims of circumstance. Research in this vein suggested that women's crimes are a function of drug addiction, physical and sexual abuse, and/or oppressive social arrangements. In contrast, the "volitional" model emerged in light of the increasing numbers of women arrested and convicted for drug-related crime. In this model, researchers challenged the portrayal of women as passive victims and instead emphasized how women actively strategized their criminal involvements. Several researchers in this model boldly predicted that women's crime would ultimately come to resemble that of men.

Maher's research challenges each of these portrayals. She argues that each perspective is an oversimplification of the relationship between human agency and social structure. By conducting extensive ethnographic research with both women and men in a local drug economy, she is able to demonstrate that neither model is capable of adequately capturing the complexity of women's crime participation. Instead, she argues that economic, cultural, and social structures shape relationships and conditions within local labor markets. Social structures influence the range of choices that individuals have available to them, but they do not determine behavior per se. Maher situates women's decision making within these structures, as well as the intersecting dynamics of race and gender that organize the drug economy in Bushwick, New York.

Ethnographic Context and Discoveries

As a method of data collection, ethnography plays a critical role in criminology. By spending extensive time in a setting and conducting lengthy interviews with research subjects, ethnographers are well-positioned to answer questions of how and why individuals engage in the crimes that they do. Maher's decision to study the drug economy in Bushwick, New York, was driven by at least two sets of concerns. First, a number of quantitative indicators like arrest and self-report data suggested that, in general, women's participation in drug crime was increasing. Some researchers argued that women's greater involvement in drug crime was a sign that the crack-cocaine economy of the 1980s was an "equal opportunity employer" when compared to the heroin market of the 1970s. Maher was curious about the extent to which gender influenced the structure of opportunity in the crack-cocaine market and wondered whether women could be seen as having reached positions of parity with men.

Second, Bushwick was by all accounts a "drug supermarket" in the years that followed the advent of crack-cocaine. By the 1980s, the neighborhood was enmeshed in a vicious cycle of diminishing economic opportunities, declining population, and expanding poverty. It was the poorest neighborhood in Brooklyn with a median household income of just over $16,000 and a high school drop out rate of 80 percent. The majority of its residents were Latino/a, primarily Puerto Rican, Dominican, and Columbian.

Maher spent 3 years collecting ethnographic data and conducting interviews in Bushwick. Over the course of the research project, Maher observed and recorded the lives of more than 200 drug-involved women in three Brooklyn neighborhoods (Flatbush, Williamsburg, and Bushwick). The conclusions offered in *Sexed Work* are drawn primarily from multiple interviews and extensive field observations of 45 women in Bushwick, all of who were street-level drug users. With few exceptions, her subjects' lives were almost entirely structured around their drug use as well as by poverty, racism, violence, and social marginality.

The rapid growth and subsequent contraction of the crack-cocaine market greatly changed the scope and structure of the illicit economy in neighborhoods like Bushwick. Maher's study picks up in the early 1990s, a few years after crack production and distribution peaked nationally. While the drug market in other communities contracted, it became increasingly more concentrated in Bushwick. The intensive police presence that followed actually exacerbated rather than diminished the high levels of violence and economic decline plaguing the community. Nonparticipants in the drug economy continued to move out of the neighborhood as inconvenience and police harassment increased. Legitimate businesses closed or moved and Bushwick became a "world of relentless poverty and resounding lack of opportunity" (1997, p. 20). Drugs, violence, poverty, and AIDS thrived in Bushwick.

Maher's research demonstrates that the drug economy in Bushwickis comprises three distinct yet mutually reinforcing sectors: drug-business hustles, non-drug hustles, and sexwork. The core of the illicit labor market is dominated by drug-business hustles. Drug-business hustles include any activity that is directly linked to the transfer of goods and services related to the use and consumption of drugs. This includes sales and various distribution roles such as serving as a lookout, running a shooting gallery, steering potential customers, and guarding and running drugs. Non-drug hustles are acts that provide revenue to the drug economy even though they are not directly related to buying or selling drugs. Non-drug hustles include activities like robbery, burglary, or shoplifting that are undertaken for the purpose of generating income to buy drugs. The third sector of the labor market included street-level sexwork, in which sexual services are performed in exchange for either money or drugs. Both non-drug hustles and sexwork constitute peripheral sectors of the illicit economy. Neither is well organized, and there is no direct "career path" emerging from either.

Maher discovers that while large numbers of women are present in the general drug economy, they are overwhelmingly confined to the sexwork sector. Few women are present in the primary labor market of drug-business hustles. When they were, they did not work in the more lucrative areas of selling and distributing drugs. Instead, they were more likely to serve in peripheral roles such as "copping" (buying small quantities of drugs for others) or selling small amounts on "risky" corners (e.g., those under police surveillance). Women are similarly underrepresented in the secondary market of street hustles. Instead, they are overwhelmingly clustered in the high-risk, low-status, low-paying world of sexwork. Maher concludes the institutionalized sexism in the criminal underworld is the primary explanation of why women's participation in the drug economy is limited to that of consumer and sexworker. Indeed, male managers refuse to hire and/or promote women in the drug-business hustle because they are invested in gendered and racialized constructions of women as unreliable, untrustworthy, and incapable of effectively mobilizing violence to deter theft and encroachments on sales territory.

Conclusion

Sexed Work challenges a number of popular and academic generalizations about women drug users. Perhaps the most significant contribution of the study is Maher's contestation of a long-standing dichotomy in the literature that casts women criminals as either dependent victims or self-determined, cunning criminals. The women users in Maher's study are neither. She shows that drug-involved and crime-involved women are severely constrained by poverty, drug addiction, and the structure of the street-level drug market. Nonetheless, they weigh their options, think strategically, and consider personal ties in their decision-making processes. Her findings are contrary to the stereotype of crack-addicted women as "willing to do anything" for the drug.

The opportunity structure in the informal economy reflects broader inequalities based on race and gender that help shape legitimate work. Women's roles in the drug economy are severely limited. Women are at the bottom of the hierarchy in the drug market, where high-level sales jobs are almost-exclusively reserved for males. Women struggle to piece together an income from low-paying enterprises and hustles. Race further stratifies women's opportunities and social networks. The drug business is dominated by Dominican males, which has various consequences vis-à-vis white, African American, and Latina women.

Sexwork remains the one occupation dominated by women in Bushwick, as other occupations available to women, such as shoplifting, disappeared with the decline of the legitimate economy.

But the economics of crack also changed the landscape of street-level sexwork. The low cost of crack has driven the going rates for sexual services down and has largely dismantled the pimping structure. At the same time, the spread of addiction has created a new crop of women workers. The public's imagination contributed to the creation of a more demanding clientele and greater risk of violence as "dates" perceive sexworkers as disposable women whose sole concern is acquiring drugs. The increased competition has also contributed to greater isolation among women.

Race and gender converge to produce divisions of labor within sexwork. These divisions are culturally and locally specific. In Bushwick, Latinas are problematized by African American and white women, who blame Latinas for driving down the market rate for sexual services. Black and white women are more likely to have professional histories as sexworkers, while Latinas' participation in sexwork is more directly associated with the crack economy. While white women have an advantage in the sexwork market due to racist perceptions of safety and danger on the part of dates, Maher also suggests that white women are perceived as weak by their African American peers, even as the two groups form loose alliances. The social networks that result from the raced division of labor are crucial to women's survival and income-generating potential, but they also provide a means for sexworkers to establish norms and standards of their work that enable them to maintain a sense of dignity and self-respect.

Maher's study convincingly demonstrates that women's participation in sexwork and the wider drug economy in which it is embedded is a product of both social structure *and* human agency. Women do not choose sexwork over better-paying, less-degrading alternatives. Rather, men's dominance of street economies and their investment in cultural constructions of gender serves to limit women's access to more lucrative forms of illicit work. In this sense, the street economy is analogous to inequalities that are continually reproduced in the formal economy.

Jill A. McCorkel and Brittnie Aiello

See also Adler, Freda: Sisters in Crime; Bourgois, Philippe: In Search of Respect; Messerschmidt, James W.: Masculinities and Crime; Miller, Jody: Gendered Criminal Opportunity; Moore, Joan W.: Homeboys and Homegirls in the Barrio; Simon, Rita J.: Women and Crime; Steffensmeier, Darrell J.: Organization Properties and Sex Segregation in the Underworld

References and Further Readings

Adler, F. (1975). *Sisters in crime*. New York: McGraw-Hill.

Baskin, D., Sommers, I., & Fagan, J. (1993). The political economy of violent female street crime. *Fordham Urban Law Journal, 20*, 401–407.

Belknap, J. (2007). *The invisible woman*. Belmont, CA: Thomson.

Bourgois, P. (1995). *In search of respect: Selling crack in el barrio*. New York: Cambridge University Press.

Britton, D. (2000). Feminism in criminology: Engendering the outlaw. *Annals of the American Academy of Political and Social Science, 571*, 57–76.

Covington, J. (1985). Gender differences in criminality among heroin users. *Journal of Research in Crime and Delinquency, 22*, 329–354.

Fagan, J. (1994). Women and drugs revisited: Female participation in the cocaine economy. *Journal of Drug Issues, 24*, 179–225.

Hagan, J. (1987). Class in the household: A power-control theory of gender and delinquency. *American Journal of Sociology, 92*, 788–816.

Maher, L. (1997). *Sexed work: Gender, race, and resistance in a Brooklyn drug market*. New York: Oxford University Press.

Messerschmidt, J. (1997). *Crime as structured action*. Thousand Oaks, CA: Sage.

Miller, E. (1986). *Street women*. Philadelphia: Temple University Press.

Miller, J. (2000). *One of the guys: Girls, gangs, and gender*. New York: Oxford University Press.

Richie, B. (1996). *Compelled to crime: The gender entrapment of battered black women*. New York: Routledge.

Simon, R. (1975). *Women and crime*. Lexington, MA: Lexington Books.

Smart, C. (1976). *Women, crime, and criminology: A feminist critique*. London: Routledge.

Steffensmeier, D. (1983). Organization properties and sex-segregation in the underworld. *Social Forces, 61*, 1010–1032.

Maruna, Shadd: Redemption Scripts and Desistance

Observers of politics and popular culture are likely familiar with the idea of the habitual offender: the criminal with a long record of past offenses. Political platforms and fictional plot lines often focus attention on the super-predator and the career criminal, dramatizing the notion that crime is intractable and offenders unchangeable. A powerful fact of criminology, however, is that virtually all criminals—including those with long and serious histories of criminal involvement—eventually stop committing crime (Blumstein & Cohen, 1987; Farrington, 1992). This process of abstaining from crime is referred to as desistance.

Although much of criminology is concerned with explaining why people commit crime, or why they continue to commit crime (a process referred to as persistence), there is good reason to ask why people desist from crime. Not only is desistance the most likely outcome, but there is also a strong public interest in understanding the factors that make desistance more or less likely. Annually in the United States, for example, more than 700,000 inmates are released from prison (Sabol & Couture, 2008) and another 2 million are released from probation supervision (Glaze & Bonczar, 2007). As a matter of public safety, it is important to facilitate the process of desistance and avoid official actions that make it more difficult for people to abstain from crime.

In *Making Good: How Ex-Convicts Reform and Rebuild Their Lives*, Shadd Maruna proposes a theory to explain how people with long and serious records of criminal involvement turn their lives around and desist from crime. Maruna's work is identified with a branch of criminology known as life-course criminology, which is concerned with understanding how and why patterns of criminal involvement change over the course of individuals' lives. Maruna proposes that ex-convicts have a lot to explain—to themselves and to others. They need a story that helps make sense of their criminal past and assert convincingly their reform. "[E]x-offenders . . . need a logical self-story to help them deal with their own feelings of culpability, external stigma, and the potential emptiness and void of their lives" (p. 55). Moreover, Maruna suggests that these self-stories are instrumental in shaping behavior. How individuals respond to situations depends in part on interpretations and self-perceptions.

Based on a narrative analysis of the life stories of 20 active offenders and 30 desisting offenders from Liverpool, England, Maruna discovered that the stories interviewees told about themselves followed certain distinguishing patterns. Active offenders told stories that followed a *condemnation script*, a self-narrative characterized by a lack of personal agency, a sense that they had nothing left to lose, and a focus on the pursuit of happiness through consumption and material gain. Desisting offenders, in contrast, constructed a story to redeem themselves of their past and assert a meaningful future, a so-called *redemption script*.

The two groups of interviewees were carefully matched on characteristics related to criminality. In other words, the study participants shared remarkably similar backgrounds and future prospects: both groups were extensively involved in crime (usually from a young age), had poor employment records, struggled with drug and alcohol addiction, grew up in "tough" neighborhoods with few legitimate economic opportunities, experienced physical and emotional abuse, and had spent significant amounts of time incarcerated and under criminal justice supervision. Interestingly, although they confronted similarly bleak prospects for success, the desisters managed to find a "tragic optimism" in their circumstances and an almost zealous hope for their future. In contrast, the active offenders "seemed fairly accurate in their assessment of their situation (dire), their chances of achieving success in the 'straight' world (minimal), and their place in mainstream society ('need not apply')" (p. 9). The sections below takes a closer look at the concept of desistance from crime and provide a fuller explanation of condemnation and redemption scripts. Finally, the entry concludes by briefly exploring how knowledge of how people voluntarily "go straight" can inform efforts to support desistance from crime.

Desistance From Crime

In his book, Maruna relates an old joke: "stopping smoking is easy—I do it every week." This joke aptly illustrates the definitional challenges associated with studying desistance. Some criminologists define *desistance* as an event, like quitting a job. The trouble with thinking about desistance as an event, however, is that crime is not a continuous, uninterrupted activity. In this respect, the criminal career analogy, which suggests that offenders "go

to work" committing crime five days a week or more, is misleading. Offenders are involved in crime sporadically and "stop" committing crime frequently. If an offender does not commit a crime for a year, have they desisted? What about five years? Can we know if they "really" desisted only after they are dead? Other criminologists have conceptualized desistance as a decision, the point at which someone decides to stop committing crime. This definition is also problematic. Like the smoker in the joke above, deciding to desist and actually desisting can be different things.

In Maruna's research, desistance is conceptualized as a process of maintaining crime-free behavior in the face of life's obstacles and temptations. "Desistance might more productively be defined as the long-term abstinence from crime among individuals who had previously engaged in a persistent pattern of criminal offending" (p. 26). Rather than an event or a decision, desistance is a *process*. In turn, this definitional distinction shifts our focus from trying to understand turning points in a person's life (why did they desist?) to instead thinking about *how* people desist from crime. Research by scholars such as Robert J. Sampson and John H. Laub finds that having a meaningful job and a supportive marriage are important structural factors related to desistance. As noted above, Maruna thinks that the answer to how people desist is at least partially explained by differences in how they think about themselves, their past and the future—reading from a condemnation script or a redemption script.

Condemnation Scripts

Contrary to popular portrayals, active offenders in the Liverpool Desistance Study (LDS) were not so much committed to a criminal lifestyle as they were resigned to it. Maruna found that active offenders believed they were doomed to deviance. Their self-stories lacked personal agency and active offenders tended to attribute their criminal involvement to poverty, stigma, and criminal peers. Interestingly, Maruna notes that active offenders tended to have a realistic view of their life prospects and the significant social challenges they confronted. Another distinguishing feature of the condemnation script is a sense of freedom that comes from no longer worrying about succeeding in conventional terms. With nothing to left lose, active offenders were able to find some psychological shelter: "intentionally failing may be less stressful on a person's ego than trying to succeed and failing anyway" (p. 78). A third distinguishing feature of the condemnation script was an emphasis on making the "big score" and finding happiness through consumption and material gain. A surprising number of the active offenders, for example, mentioned that one of their life objectives was to win the lottery. Rather than being motivated by greed, however, the active offenders expressed the desire to share the elusive big score, seemingly in an effort to fill with excitement, drugs, and popularity, an otherwise empty life characterized by a sense of personal failure.

Redemption Scripts

Desisting offenders' self-views are not simply the opposite of those of active offenders'. Indeed, desisting offenders espoused a tragic optimism about their lives, a sense that something uniquely good (redeeming) could come from a criminal past. A central feature of the redemption script is that the self-story asserts the essential goodness of the narrator. When talking about their past, desisting offenders drew a clear distinction between crime and their true selves, psychologically distancing themselves from their crimes and from other criminals. Many maintained that deep down they were *always* a good person. Moreover, they described their criminal involvement as "it," something that happened. Crime was not "them," rather "it was the drugs," or it was the people they were around. Thus, rather than reinventing themselves, desisting offenders re-embraced an earlier identity—not the "new me" but the "real me." Part of this process involved identifying a positive attribute that distinguished themselves from other criminals. For example, they always had a "good heart" or a "good brain."

Whereas active offenders tended to characterize themselves as pawns with little or no control over their future, desisting offenders expressed an exaggerated sense of self-determination, efficacy, and hope for their future. Rather than "burning out," their stories suggested they were "firing up." Their vision of desistance was a comeback story—a story of renewal, gaining strength, and realizing their true selves. This mindset included a belief that they

could beat the odds of The System that keeps people like them trapped in a cycle of crime. As Maruna et al. (2004, p. 227) explain, "by transforming desistance from an acquiescence to authority into a rebellious act, they can simultaneously preserve their identities [as defiant rebels] and change their behavior."

Finally, the redemption script involves a wish to make good and give something back to society as a display of gratitude and possibly cosmic restitution. A common theme of the redemption story is that the bad (the criminal past) had to happen in order to achieve some larger good. The almost zealous desire to make good was illustrated in the frequent telling and retelling of the claim that even if just one person was prevented from going through what they did, a lifetime of waste could be put to use. The desire to give something back to society and make good may allow the former offender to find a moral high ground. As Maruna explains, this framework enabled desisting offenders to cope with the shame and stigma of their past. Defining the past as prologue to a higher calling allowed the desisting offender to announce their criminal history instead of running from it.

Maruna's work makes an important contribution to criminological theory by bringing into focus how offenders desist from crime. Desisting offenders frame their criminal past and law-abiding future with the use of a redemption script. The redemption script includes three important elements: the assertion of a good "core self"; a sense of control over and hope for the future; and, generativity, the desire and effort to give something back, especially to future generations.

Maruna's work may provide direction for efforts to reintegrate former offenders into our communities. If the way people talk and think about themselves and their pasts have implications for their futures, it follows that those who work with and care about former offenders should be careful about the words they use and the stories they tell. Encouraging and supporting those who have been involved in crime to find the good in themselves, take responsibility for their future (not just their past crimes), and to make good, may be instrumental in supporting the process of desistance from crime.

Jody L. Sundt

See also Criminal Career Paradigm; Giordano, Peggy C., and Stephen A. Cernkovich: Cognitive Transformation and Desistance; Moffitt, Terrie E.: A Developmental Model of Life-Course-Persistent Offending; Sampson, Robert J., and John H. Laub: Age-Graded Theory of Informal Social Control; Shover, Neal: Great Pretenders

References and Further Readings

Blumstein, A., & Cohen, J. (1987). Characterizing criminal careers. *Science, 237*, 985–991.

Glaze, L. E., & Bonczar, T. P. (2007). *Probation and parole in the United States, 2006*. Washington, DC: Bureau of Justice Statistics Bulletin, Office of Justice Programs, U.S. Department of Justice.

Farrington, D. P. (1992). Explaining the beginning, progress, and ending of antisocial behavior from birth to adulthood. In J. McCord (Ed.), *Facts, frameworks, and forecasts* (Advances in Criminological Theory: Vol. 3, pp. 253–286). New Brunswick, NJ: Transaction.

Laub, J. H., & Sampson, R. J. (2003). *Shared beginnings, divergent lives: Delinquent boys at age 70*. Cambridge, MA: Harvard University Press.

Maruna, S. (2001). *Making good: How ex-convicts reform and rebuild their lives*. Washington, DC: American Psychological Association.

Maruna, S., Porter, L., & Carvalho, I. (2004). The Liverpool Desistance Study and probation practice: Opening the dialogue. *Probation Journal, 51*, 221–232.

Sampson, R. J., & Laub, J. H. (1992). *Crime in the making: Pathways and turning points through life*. Cambridge, MA: Harvard University Press.

Sabol, W. J., & Couture, H. (2008). *Prison inmates at midyear 2007*. Washington, DC: Bureau of Justice Statistics Bulletin, Office of Justice Programs, U.S. Department of Justice.

Shover, N. (1996). *The great pretenders: Pursuits and careers of persistent thieves*. Boulder, CO: Westview.

Marx, Karl, and Frederick Engels: Capitalism and Crime

Karl Marx and Frederick Engels are the founding fathers of an important paradigm of social theory, known as historical materialism or simply as Marxism. Their work is central to conflict theory and influences a wide range of social and political thought, including some approaches to criminology. Only a few points in their voluminous work deal directly with issues of crime and criminality, yet this has provided a firm, although contested, grounding for Marxist criminology. This entry explains Marx and Engels's conception of how capitalism as a mode of production both defines disorderly populations as criminal, and produces the conditions of disorder that make such criminality likely in the first place. It also discusses their ideas regarding alienation, as the means through which these disorderly conditions result both in criminality and in working class resistance, which is in turn criminalized. Criticisms of Marx and Engels's approach, which argue that it is a form of economic determinism, are also addressed.

The Development of Capitalism and the Criminalization of Poverty

In writing about the origins of the capitalist mode of production, Marx pays particular attention to the process of enclosure in England, which occurred in waves from roughly the 15th to the 19th century. This process transformed common lands into private property, separating the agrarian working population from the lands that had been their primary means of subsistence. This precipitated a massive wave of internal migration, as peasants were forced to seek out alternative ways to provide for themselves and their families. By the 18th century, England was beginning to undergo both an agricultural and an industrial revolution, both of which required waged labor, and this proved to be the main source of income available to displaced peasants. However, this transition was not smooth. There were far more displaced peasants than available jobs in the factories. Further, these factories were often in industrial towns far from where many peasants lived, and thus they required potential wage-laborers to accept entirely new patterns of work and life. As a result, many of the displaced peasants, or vagabonds, resisted this industrial transformation and considered begging and stealing to be a more reasonable alternative to wage-labor. As Marx (1976, p. 896) writes, "these men, suddenly dragged from their accustomed mode of life, could not immediately adapt themselves to the discipline of their new condition. They were turned in massive quantities into beggars, robbers and vagabonds, partly from inclination, in most cases under the force of circumstances."

To control this itinerant and socially disruptive population, the British government used the legal system to define them as criminals. New laws imposed harsh corporeal punishments for begging, stealing, and vagabondage. For example, Marx (1976, pp. 896–897) recounts a law passed by Henry VIII in 1530: "whipping and imprisonment for sturdy vagabonds. They are to be tied to the cart-tail and whipped until the blood streams from their bodies, then they are to swear on oath to . . . 'put themselves to labour.' . . . For the second arrest for vagabondage the whipping is to be repeated and half the ear sliced off; but for the third relapse the offender is to be executed as a hardened criminal and enemy of the common wealth."

The Reserve Army of Labor and the Lumpenproleteriat

Massive waves of unemployment were not limited to capitalism's first emergence out of feudalism, but are, Marx argues, an integral part of the ongoing functioning of capitalism. Capitalism not only requires, but in fact produces an unemployed population, which Marx (1976, p. 791) calls "the industrial reserve army" or the "surplus population." To the extent that capitalism creates this ever-growing population of marginalized people, it creates an ever-increasing potential for criminal activity. Marx sees this surplus population as an unavoidable effect of a profit-maximizing economy that always seeks to minimize labor costs by keeping wages down and by keeping the number of necessary employees to a minimum through technological and organizational advances. As a result of this drive for profits, some portion of those workers who are thrust out of (or never able to enter) the productive sphere find themselves in the "lowest sediment" of the laboring population, the realm of the "lumpenproleteriat," in which Marx includes (1976, p. 797) "vagabonds, criminals, and prostitutes." As a brief aside, not only did Marx and Engels cast aspersions at the lumpenproleteriat, whom they regarded in a morally disdainful fashion, but they also made a connection between these cast-offs and what might be considered the surplus capitalists, or the financial aristocracy, who

were, in Marx's estimation, "nothing but the resurrection of the lumpenproleteriat transported to the heights of bourgeois society" (Marx & Engels, 1976, p. 326).

Engels writes about the criminal activity of the lumpenproleteriat in his work *The Condition of the Working Class in England in 1844*. In this book, which chronicles the abhorrent conditions of working-class life in an industrial town, Engels (p. 132) argues that capitalism leads to a growing demoralization of the working class and therefore to ever more "violent, passionate, irreconcilable" outbursts of energy, which can take the form of criminal activity. Crime is considered to be a symptom of capitalist exploitation and of the demoralization of the laboring population.

This theory of criminality connects to Marx and Engels's broader conception of capitalist alienation, which is centered upon the wage-relation. When a worker takes a wage-labor job, they agree to exchange their labor-power, or capacity to work, for a wage. In order for this exchange to be possible, workers must be in a position to treat their productive capacity as an alienable commodity. Hence, the wage relation is predicated on the alienation of the working population from their productive capacity, both individually and generally. This alienation lies at the core of the capitalist mode of production, and it has a pervasive effect on the subjectivity of all those living within its web.

Engels sees this alienation as a cause of discontent that will either lead to working-class resistance or, in the case of the lumpenproleteriat, to violence and criminal outbursts. It is clear that both Marx and Engels prefer the former over the latter, which they pejoratively discuss as false or pre-political outbursts. For them, according to Paul Hirst, working class organization is productive (as it builds toward positive social change and even revolution) whereas criminality is unproductive (and even, in many instances counterproductive insofar as it can be mobilized against working class struggles). However, both of these outbursts against the prevailing system of private property result, or are made possible by, the same conditions of alienation, where the laboring population is disconnected from its laboring capacity, and hence frustrated and demoralized by its alienation from social production as well as its structural lack of self-sufficiency.

The Criminalization of the Working Class

Marx and Engels believe that capitalist alienation provokes both organized and disorganized forms of resistance, and that it then becomes the responsibility of the capitalist state to keep these expressions of discontent in check. This is accomplished through the legal system, which, along with the state more generally is understood by Marx and Engels to be a set of institutions created and maintained to secure the interests of the ruling class. According to Richard Quinney, this is central to the Marxist conception of crime—that the law itself is a tool of the ruling class.

Both the origins and the ongoing reproduction of capitalist social relations require the working class to accept their exploitation as a natural fact. Writing about 19th-century industrial labor relations in England in *Capital*, Marx shows how the law was used to discipline labor through criminalizing working-class organization. English workers fought for their right to organize collectively, and their employers fought back, using the law to establish limits to the scope and types of organization deemed permissible. Workers fought for legislation that would criminalize overly exploitative and unsafe working conditions, such as limits on the working day, minimum wages, safety standards, and age-minimums, while employers fought for legislation that would limit the effectiveness of working class organization—associating them with criminal anti-establishment activity—and that would minimize the restrictions placed upon their employment practices. Even though Marx understands the state to be, at the most fundamental level, a tool of the ruling class, he also understands how historically, the state is a site of contestation, where struggles to define the limits of wage-labor relations take place.

Economic Determinism or Historical Materialism?

Many criminologists have focused on the connection between Marx and the positivism of social determinists, with their search for objective predictors of criminal behavior (Taylor et al., 1973, p. 216). It is in this vein that Marx and Engels have been labeled economic determinists, as it appears their theory completely attributes the existence of crime to the structural effects of the capitalist economy. While even Marxist criminologists will acknowledge this tendency within Marx and Engels's work, they will also read this as an anomalous dimension of Marx and Engels's broader project, arguing that it is not in line with the far more dialectical methods of historical materialism. Such a dialectical approach would consider the criminal as an individual actor who is both determined by and determinant of his or her material conditions. Hence, in a historical materialist approach to criminology, crime cannot be understood as a completely isolated and subjective phenomenon or as a completely structurally determined effect of economic conditions. It is, in any real historic situation, a combination of the two. As Marx (1963, p. 15) famously writes, "Men make their own history, but they do not make it just as they please; they do not make it under circumstances chosen by themselves, but under circumstances directly encountered, given and transmitted from the past."

Revolution, Resistance, and Criminality

As mentioned above, Marx and Engels were somewhat dismissive of the lumpenproleteriat, or the "dangerous classes" to which they attributed much criminal activity. This population represented a false or pre-political reaction against the capitalist system, and therefore held less revolutionary potential than the more organized resistance of the working class. This is important, insofar as their entire theoretical project was at the same time a political project, aimed at promoting revolution, or the supersession of the entire mode of production, as the only viable means of achieving any truly humane, democratic, and equitable form of society.

Marx and Engels had faith that the end of capitalism would lead to the rise of communism. This transition would entail the "withering away" of the state (Engels, 1969, p. 333), a phrase that has subsequently been interpreted in many different ways. Without a state, are we to presume that there would no longer be a means to regard certain people as criminals, or as transgressing a legal order? Would there be crime in an ideal communist society? Marx and Engels say little about these issues, and they remain an unresolved debate within Marxist criminology today.

Jesse Goldstein

See also Bonger, Willem: Capitalism and Crime;
Capitalism and White-Collar Crime; Currie, Elliot:
The Market Society and Crime; Greenberg, David F.:
Age, Capitalism, and Crime; Spitzer, Steven:
Capitalism and Crime; Taylor Ian, Paul Walton, and
Jock Young: The New Criminology

References and Further Readings

Engels, F. (1950). *Condition of the working class in England in 1844*. London: Allen and Unwin.

Engels, F. (1969). *Anti-Dühring*. Moscow: Progress Publishers.

Hirst, P. Q. (1972). Marx and Engels on crime, law, and morality. *Economy and Society, 1*, 28–56.

Marx, K. (1963). *The 18th Brumaire of Louis Bonaparte*. New York: International Publishers.

Marx, K. (1976). *Capital* (Vol. 1). London: Penguin.

Marx, K., & Engels, F. (1976). *Basic writings on politics and philosophy* (L. S. Feuer, Ed.). London: Fontana.

Quinney, R. (1975). Crime control in capitalist society: A critical philosophy of legal order. In I. Taylor, P. Walton, & J. Young (Eds.), *Critical criminology* (pp. 181–202). New York: Routledge.

Taylor, I., Walton, P., & Young, J. (1973). *The new criminology: For a social theory of deviance*. New York: Routledge.

Taylor, I., Walton, P., & Young, J. (Eds.). (1975). *Critical criminology*. New York: Routledge.

MATSUEDA, ROSS L.: REFLECTED APPRAISALS AND DELINQUENCY

The perspective put forth by Ross L. Matsueda in 1992 essentially posits that delinquency results from an individual's reflected appraisals of oneself. More specifically, Matsueda suggests that individuals whose appraisals of themselves are that of "delinquent" are, in fact, more likely to be delinquent in the future. These reflected appraisals of self as delinquent stem from actual appraisals from significant others as well as from previous delinquent behavior, according to Matsueda.

This theoretical framework regarding the role of reflected appraisals in delinquency, which is reviewed in greater detail below, builds upon the theoretical tradition of symbolic interactionism. This entry thus begins by, first, examining the symbolic interactionist theoretical roots of Matsueda's ideas. The next section explains Matsueda's theory more fully in

light of the interactionist tradition. This exposition of Matsueda's theory is then followed by a section summarizing empirical support for Matsueda's perspective. Limitations of the perspective and directions for future theoretical and empirical work are discussed briefly in a concluding section.

Theoretical Roots

We as humans identify ourselves, think about ourselves, and judge ourselves. The term *self-concept* is sometimes used to describe the fairly stable picture we have of ourselves. For an actor to say "I am this kind of person" or "that kind of person" is a self-appraisal, or an assessment of self. How does this assessment or conceptualization of self occur?

The self-concept has been central throughout the history of symbolic interactionism. The theoretical foundations for self-concept are found in the work of Charles Horton Cooley and George Herbert Mead, most specifically. In the theories of Cooley and Mead, the self would not exist without society. Cooley adopted the view of "self" as the ability to see and recognize oneself as an object. Cooley believed that humans use the gestures of others to see themselves. In this way, the images that people form of themselves are quite similar to reflections from a mirror, or what Cooley describes as a looking glass. The images are similar to a looking glass in the sense that they are provided *to* the individual *by* the reactions of others to their behavior. The notion of "self as object" thus involves how the self is influenced by others' perceptions (actual appraisals) or how an individual thinks others are perceiving him or her reflected appraisals.

Over time, self-perception develops some stability. This stability is what allows us to become knowledgeable about who we are and what we do. Nonetheless, the self-concept is a process and not a fixed entity. Hence, the picture we have of ourselves will change over time and across situations. In other words, because the self is social, it arises in interaction and then changes or remains stable due to interaction. The looking glass, therefore, is a continual process. However, a stable self-conception evolves out of the accumulation of self-images and self-evaluations with reference to specific and then increasingly generalized others.

In sum, Cooley and Meade argue that our understanding of ourselves is primarily a reflection of our perception of how others react to us. Others label and define the self to the actor, and they help the actor understand and situate himself or herself in the environment. Because of the importance of labels of others in self-concept, Cooley's and Meade's symbolic interactionism lies at the heart of what is referred to as *labeling theory*. It is Frank Tannenbaum, however, who is often credited with popularizing the labeling approach by expressing the view that society can produce antisocial behavior by defining an individual as a deviant. Other labeling theorists elaborated on the importance of interaction and interpretation in the production of deviance. One of the more popular theorists was Edwin Lemert, who distinguishes between primary and secondary deviation. According to Lemert, primary deviation is the occasional or situational behavior that is often excused or rationalized by the actor and/or social audience. Primary deviance consists of those deviant acts that do not help redefine the self and public image of the offender. Secondary deviance, on the other hand, is the result of a process between the actor's actions and the societal response to those actions. When the response leads to a deviant label being applied to an individual, it is extremely difficult for the person to escape the classification. The label then emerges as a main or primary identifier for others, which prompts the individual to start seeing himself or herself in terms of the deviant identity (a dramatic redefinition of the self). These are the acts that redefine the offender's self and public image. Thus, acts become secondary deviance when they form a basis for self-concept.

Beyond the influences of Cooley, Meade, Tannenbaum, and Lemert, the work of John W. Kinch is also key to the development of Matsueda's theory. Kinch presented a theoretical model of behaviors that can best be described as a causal chain wherein past behaviors determine actual appraisals of others, which in turn lead to a person's reflected appraisals of self. These reflected appraisals will then determine self appraisals, and finally, lead to future behavior.

Matsueda's Theory of Reflected Appraisals

Matsueda's 1992 research builds on Kinch's work most directly and attempts to specify a more refined symbolic interactionist theory of the self and delinquent behavior. In the tradition of

symbolic interactionism, Matsueda defines reflected appraisals as one's appraisal of self from the standpoint of others. He views one's self as, in part, a reflected appraisal—how an individual thinks significant others are assessing him or her as a result of taking the role of the other and seeing oneself as others do.

Matsueda identifies reflected appraisals of self as a primary variable in explaining future behavior. In brief, significant others such as parents, teachers, and friends label individuals in particular ways (e.g., "troublemaker" or "delinquent"). These appraisals are reflected on and internalized by the individual such that they shape the person's self-concept. As such, they lead to behavior that is consistent with the actual and reflected appraisal.

Matsueda's theory shares both similarities and differences with that of Kinch. First, Matsueda identifies reflected appraisals of self (as opposed to self appraisals, in the case of Kinch's theory) as the main variable for explaining future behavior. Thus, delinquency results primarily from a person's perception of the impressions others form about him or her (reflected appraisals). In Matsueda's theory, as in Kinch's theory, reflected appraisals mediate the relationship between labels of others (actual appraisals) and deviance. However, Matsueda emphasized that reflected appraisals resulted from *selective perceptions* of actual appraisals. As such, reflected appraisals only stem, in part, from actual appraisals, and actual appraisals can affect delinquent behavior above and beyond their effects on reflected appraisals, according to Matsueda.

Matsueda's theory, like Kinch's and other symbolic interactionists, also highlights the importance of prior delinquency. Kinch had proposed that prior deviance affects others' appraisals, which, in turn, affects reflected appraisals. Matsueda accepted that idea, but also suggested that past behavior affects reflected appraisals directly, net of its influence on actual appraisals of others. In addition, Matsueda's conceptualization allows for the possibility that past behavior can have a direct impact on future behavior, above and beyond the effects of reflected appraisals (i.e., non-reflective habit)—a point neglected by Kinch.

Empirical Support

Matsueda used the National Youth Survey (NYS) to test his theoretical perspective. The NYS data are well-suited to examine reflected appraisals because they include questions on labeling, where youths were asked to indicate the extent to which their parents, teachers, and friends would agree with a set of descriptive labels as applied to them (reflected appraisals).

Specifically, the youths were asked, "I'd like to know how your parents, friends, and teachers, would describe you. I'll read a list of words or phrases and for each, will ask you to tell me how much you think your [parents, friends, teachers] would agree with that description of you." The list of descriptive labels included the following 11 items: "well-liked," "needs help," "bad kid," "often upset," "gets along well with others," "messed up," "breaks rules," "has a lot of personal problems," "gets into trouble," "likely to succeed," and "does things that are against the law."

As for delinquency, the NYS provides information on the incidence and prevalence of delinquent behavior among American adolescents (Huizinga and Elliott, 1987). To measure delinquent behavior, the NYS investigators included a delinquency inventory. This inventory was designed to represent the entire range of delinquent acts for which juveniles could be arrested. The NYS self-reported delinquency inventory asks respondents to report the frequency with which they engaged in each of a variety of behaviors during the past year. This delinquency inventory has proven to be a successful tool in a great deal of contemporary research.

Matsueda found that youths' reflected appraisals of themselves were strongly influenced by their parents' independent appraisals of them. So, reflected appraisals were found to be related at least in part to actual appraisals of significant others, just as Matsueda's theory predicts. Furthermore, as also predicted, the "reflected appraisals as a rule violator exert a large effect on delinquent behavior and mediate much of the effect of parental appraisals as a rule violator on delinquency" (Matsueda, 1992, p. 1603). Thus, one of Matsueda's major premises— that appraisals by others affect reflected appraisals, which, in turn, affect crime—found support in this analysis of the NYS data. However, a direct effect of actual appraisals on delinquency remained, even after controlling for reflected appraisals.

Matsueda also found that past delinquent behavior had an impact on youths' reflected appraisals, net of actual appraisals of others, especially when

the appraisals centered on being a "bad kid" or a "rule breaker." In other words, there was a direct link between prior behavior and reflected appraisals that did not operate through actual appraisals. In addition, Matsueda found evidence of a direct link between prior delinquency and subsequent delinquency above and beyond the indirect effect of prior delinquency through reflected appraisals. Thus, he found support for the idea that some delinquency may be due to non-reflective habit.

Finally, Matsueda also found that past delinquency and reflected appraisals explained much of the effects of socio-demographic correlates of delinquency. For instance, he reported that, "age, race and urban residence exert significant total effects on delinquency, most of which work indirectly through prior delinquency, and partially through the rule-violator reflected appraisal" (Matsueda, 1992, p. 1603).

Although Matsueda's framework examined the causes and consequences of reflected appraisals and delinquent behavior, he did not explore possible age-graded factors that may be influencing both reflected appraisals and selective perception, and any subsequent influence on offending. In Michael Patrick Phelan's research (using the NYS), it was found, that for all ages, prior offending was the best predictor of subsequent offending. Of the reflected appraisals, it was the appraisal "bad kid" that shared the strongest relationship with subsequent offending. The dimensions "distressed" and "needs help" also indicated statistically significant positive relationships with offending, while the dimensions "successful" and "sociable" were found to have a negative association with offending. Another important finding of Phelan's work was that the effects of being male or female mattered, but not until age 15.

Conclusion

Limited studies of the role of reflected appraisals in delinquency have shown promising yet inconclusive results. Further, problems have been noted in studying reflected appraisals, with most criticism centering on the inability to adequately test the theory with existing data. More specifically, the data from the NYS do not allow for an assessment of reflective appraisals of specific others. The NYS's operationalization and measurement of reflected appraisals almost assure an inability to find source-specific variation in reflected appraisals. In sum, the NYS leads respondents to think about reflected appraisals in a most general way, not a source-specific manner. Accordingly, the NYS offers no means to analyze the salience and centrality of reflected appraisals.

These shortcomings in the NYS data are significant. What researchers know about reflected appraisals and delinquency is primarily derived from this data source, to be sure, and the extant body of work based on the NYS has provided many useful insights. However, Phelan's analysis suggests that the NYS data offer only a partial explanation of the relationships between identity and delinquency, especially the role of reflected appraisals. What is needed are longitudinal data with better measures of reflected appraisals and offending behaviors.

Michael Patrick Phelan

See also Becker, Howard S.: Labeling and Deviant Careers; Heimer, Karen, and Ross L. Matsueda: A Theory of Differential Social Control; Lemert, Edwin M.: Primary and Secondary Deviance; Tannenbaum, Frank: The Dramatization of Evil

References and Further Readings

Becker, H. S. (1963). *Outsiders: Studies in the sociology of deviance*. New York: Free Press.

Cooley, C. H. (1902). *Human nature and the social order*. New York: Schocken.

Heimer, K., & Matsueda, R. L. (1994). Role-taking, role commitment, and delinquency: A theory of differential social control. *American Sociological Review, 59,* 39–61.

Huizinga, D., & Elliott, D. S. (1987). Juvenile offenders: Prevalence, offender incidence, and arrest rates by race. *Crime and Delinquency, 33,* 206–223.

James, W. (1890). *The principles of psychology* (Vol. 1). New York: Henry Holt.

Kinch, J. W. (1962). Self conceptions of types of delinquents. *Sociological Inquiry, 32,* 228–234.

Lemert, E. (1951). *Social pathology*. New York: McGraw-Hill.

Matsueda, R. L. (1992). Reflected appraisals, parental labeling, and delinquency: Specifying a symbolic interactionist theory. *American Journal of Sociology, 97,* 1577–1611.

Matsueda, R. L., & Heimer, K. (1997). A symbolic interactionist theory of role transitions, role commitments, and delinquency. In T. P. Thornberry (Ed.), *Developmental theories of crime and delinquency* (pp. 163–213). New Brunswick, NJ: Transaction.

Mead, G. H. (1934). *Mind, self and society*. Chicago: University of Chicago Press.

Phelan, M. P. (2003). *Towards a developmental social psychology of crime*. Unpublished doctoral dissertation, University of Kentucky.

Tannenbaum, F. (1938). *Crime and the community*. Boston: Ginn.

MATZA, DAVID: BECOMING DEVIANT

Labeling theory and the broader symbolic interactionist perspective were likely reaching a zenith in 1969 when David Matza published *Becoming Deviant*. Interestingly, this was the same year that Travis Hirschi's *Causes of Delinquency* was published, signaling a significant redirection of criminological thinking away from the phenomenological assumptions of interactionism found in Matza's work.

In *Becoming Deviant*, Matza critiques the contributions of three sociological traditions: the Chicago School, the functionalists, and the neo-Chicagoans. He notes how the contributions of each built upon its predecessors in the development of a naturalistic approach to understanding deviance and criminality. As an alternative to earlier correctional theories that held deviance to be pathological, Matza argued that *only* naturalistic theories of deviance would be able to faithfully render the complexity of deviant lives and lifestyles in their true nature. Viewing deviance as an inevitable and natural element in society offers an approach based on three master conceptions: affinity, affiliation, and signification.

Naturalism

Matza's naturalism—and its emphasis on appreciation of how the actor views his or her own situation—stands in marked contrast to the previous five decades of the dominant correctional perspective found in American criminology.

Correctional theories are concerned with questions of causation and ultimately of getting rid of unwanted phenomena. For Matza, "the stress on the bad consequences of evil phenomena obscured . . . the possibility of evil arising from things deemed good and good from things deemed evil" (p. 22). Evil, or deviant, phenomena are pathological in nature, concrete, objective, and measurable.

Standing in contrast to a correctional approach are naturalistic theories. According to Matza, "naturalism . . . is the philosophical view that strives *to remain true to the nature of the phenomenon under study or scrutiny*" (p. 5, emphasis in the original). Naturalism focuses on the complex diversity of deviance and the deviant subject, requiring criminologists to *appreciate* or empathize with the deviant phenomenon, to consider it from the subject's definition of the situation, ultimately to understand how the world appears to the subject. In contrast to a correctional approach which emphasizes the need to get rid of pathologically deviant phenomena, Matza celebrates the diversity reflected in deviance as a necessary and vital part of society.

Affinity

In the last two-thirds of *Becoming Deviant,* Matza explores how criminologists have dealt with the question of the etiology of deviance. Affinity conceptualizes deviance as being the result of a combination of many possible factors in an individual's background—for example, biological or psychological factors, or cultural or social factors such as urban poverty. People have an affinity to deviance because it reflects an *attractive force* or deterministic notion of contagion. The favorite affinity of sociologists, according to Matza, has been "between poverty and pathology" (p. 96). Individuals do not choose their actions; rather they are objects predisposed or strongly drawn to deviance. According to Matza, however, becoming deviant is not a structurally predetermined process; instead it involves an unfolding of desire and choice.

Affiliation

In contrast to affinity, affiliation emphasizes the process of becoming converted to deviance through making conscious choices. From a correctional perspective, affiliation suggests contagion in which exposure to particular factors lead to deviance. From a humanized naturalistic perspective, affinity produces a simple willingness to act. The consequence of being exposed to the "causes" of deviance is *not* to act; instead the exposure opens the possibility of seeing oneself as the kind of person who *might* engage in a particular act.

Matza explains that the process of making conscious choices involves a subject being willing to try something deviant and, once having tried it, to evaluate the experience and then to choose whether to engage in the act a second time. Using an extensive discussion of Howard Becker's "Becoming a Marijuana User," Matza explores the internal processes or stages in the process of a subject becoming deviant. For Matza, "The *specific* truth of affiliation and its human method of conversion is that the subject mediates the process of becoming *in the terms and issues provided by the concrete matters before him*" (p. 142, emphasis in the original).

Signification

Signification is the final stage in the process of becoming deviant. For Matza, "To signify is to *stand* for in the sense of representing or exemplifying . . . thus, signifying makes its object more significant. . . . To be signified a thief is to lose the blissful identity of one who amongst others happens to have committed a theft. It is a movement, however gradual, towards being a thief and representing theft. . . . [T]hose selected and then cast as thieves come to represent the enterprise of theft" (pp. 156–157). Before a subject can fully engage a deviant identity, the subject must understand the distinction between engaging in a deviant act and being a deviant. The answer to the question "essentially, am I a thief?" involves the subject doing (committing a theft) and being (signified a thief).

This process of building a deviant identity is similar to Edwin Lemert's notion of "secondary deviation" and is fully dependent on the state banning some activities, apprehending those individuals who violate the ban, and then convicting and punishing, often through imprisonment, the identified deviant.

Ban

Contrary to conflict theorists, Matza suggests that social control mechanisms of the state operate primarily to *transform* subjects rather than to *cause* them to become deviant. This transformation is brought about by ban. A primary function of the state includes the identification of both deviant activities and deviants, making them objects of state surveillance and control. Ban identifies and designates acts as deviant and as proper subject matter for state intervention and punishment. Ban acts to produce a moral transformation of activity that, as designated deviant, deters by inculcating an attitude of avoidance in "right-minded" individuals.

For Matza, the most relevant issue regarding the deterrent effects of ban should be focused on the "wrong-minded," those who disobeyed and have tried the deviant activity anyway. Yet, the state will impact the subject even when disobeyed. According to Matza, "Leviathan [the state] bedevils the subject as he proceeds and thus is partly compensated for its gross failure to deter. . . . A main purpose of ban is to unify meaning and thus to minimize the possibility that, morally, the subject can have it both ways. Either he will be deterred or bedeviled" (p. 148). To be bedeviled is to be made a devil in the sense of the subject finding himself or herself in a position of tending toward greater disaffiliation and, consequently, greater involvement in deviance.

Ban leads to further disaffiliation and anticipation of apprehension and penalization. As the subject more fully understands the meaning of ban, choices are made by the "wrong-minded" and continued participation in deviant activity leads to an accommodation to the reality of being deviant. For Matza, such accommodation ultimately leads to further acceptance and adaptation to state control. The subject becomes highly conscious of ban, and knowing that he or she has violated it, becomes self-conscious. Attempting to keep one's deviant activities secret when engaging in them or not, leads the individual to sensing himself or herself as transparent to others. However, being self-conscious of violating ban and feeling transparent, the subject fears being publically identified as the kind of person who engages in deviance.

To the extent that ban "criminalizes" a subject's activities, it is inevitable that to engage in deviance leads the subject down a path inviting discovery, apprehension, and correction. The event of selection through apprehension signifies the individual as deviant through a registration, labeling, defining, or classifying. To be caste with a deviant identity also carries with it a gross exclusion. As Howard Becker suggests, the new stigmatizing deviant identity becomes a master status or the primary perceived status of the individual. The master status determines how other people initially react when they see or meet the person for the first time.

The deviant, who is labeled, convicted, and imprisoned will never be free of the deviant identity: The subject moves from deviant to convict to ex-con. The finished product of signification reflects the success of the state in representing "concentrated evil, or deviation, and pervasive good, or conformity" (p. 197). The state, in its commitment to provide for public order and safety through effective policing and punishment, is vindicated. The benevolence and wisdom of the state is affirmed whether the deviant reoffends and is apprehended again or who has been corrected and reformed, although continuing to be a person who had once been a thief.

Critiques

Matza's phenomenological description of the process of becoming deviant is not without criticism. Deryck Beyleveld and Paul Wiles argue that Matza fails to clearly establish that persons are fully "subjects" and not "objects." That is, Matza suggests both possibilities that "Man is subject" as a metaphysical truth and that "Man has only a partially determined non-free will." Matza never develops "a clear thesis of the nature of causality, the relationship between biological, psychological and sociological factors, and in particular a thesis about man's rationality" (Beyleveld & Wiles, 1975, p. 120). In addition, Ian Taylor, Paul Walton, and Jock Young believe that Matza fails to provide an explanation for why individuals would "find affiliation to deviation attractive" (p. 191) and limits his explanation of the process of becoming deviant to an individualistic phenomenology, never accounting for the effects of collective choice. "*Becoming Deviant* . . . presents us with an essentialist view of deviation. The essence of deviation is its base in an unanalysed and unanalysable existential *Angst*" (Taylor et al., 1973, p. 192, emphasis in the original)

John D. Hewitt

See also Becker, Howard S.: Labeling and Deviant
Careers; Lemert, Edwin H.: Primary and Secondary
Deviance; Matza, David: Delinquency and Drift;
Sykes, Gresham M., and David Matza: Techniques of
Neutralization

References and Further Readings

Becker, H. S. (1963). *Outsiders: Studies in the sociology
of deviance.* New York: Free Press.
Beyleveld, D., & Wiles, P. (1975). Man and method in
David Matza's "Becoming Deviant." *British Journal
of Criminology, 15,* 111–127.
Hirschi, T. (1969). *Causes of delinquency.* Berkeley:
University of California Press.
Lemert, E. M. (1967). *Human deviance, social problems,
and social control.* New York: Prentice Hall.
Matza, D. (1964). *Delinquency and drift.* New York:
Wiley.
Matza, D. (1969). *Becoming deviant.* Englewood Cliffs,
NJ: Prentice Hall.
Matza, D., & Sykes, G. M. (1961). Juvenile delinquency
and subterranean values. *American Sociological
Review, 26,* 712–719.
Sykes, G. M., & Matza, D. (1957). Techniques of
neutralization: A theory of delinquency. *American
Sociological Review, 22,* 664–670.
Taylor, I., Walton, P., & Young, J. (1973). *The new
criminology: For a social theory of deviance.* London:
Routledge and Kegan Paul.

MATZA, DAVID: DELINQUENCY AND DRIFT

David Matza's *Delinquency and Drift*, published in 1964, offers a complex and multilayered critique of what its author considered to be the dominant theories of juvenile delinquency at that time—indeed the dominant themes in criminology since the late 19th century. On one level, the book is a critique and reformulation of the major postwar subcultural theories of delinquency, including the work of Albert Cohen in *Delinquent Boys* and Richard Cloward and Lloyd Ohlin in *Delinquency and Opportunity*. On another level, it represents an affirmation of some of the key themes of control theories of crime and delinquency, which were considerably less prominent in criminology

in the 1950s and early 1960s than they are today. More generally, the work is a critique of what Matza describes as the core assumptions of criminological positivism, and a reaffirmation of some of the principles of the classical theories of Cesare Beccaria and Jeremy Bentham. Matza's (1964, p. 3) aim was not to throw out the positivist framework altogether, but to "incorporate modified versions" of the classical perspective into it. All of these levels are closely related and come together in a densely argued and closely reasoned theoretical analysis.

Explaining Too Much Delinquency: The Critique of Positivism and Subculture Theories

Matza's main purpose in *Delinquency and Drift* is to "question and modify the positivist portrait" of the delinquent (p. 1). He believes that, since the time of Cesare Lombroso, positivism has dominated criminological thinking, even more than it has other branches of social science. "Modern criminology," he writes, "*is* the positive school of criminology" (p. 3, emphasis added). But there are three crucially problematic assumptions in the dominant criminological positivism, all of which represent overreactions against the assumptions of the earlier Classical School.

The first of those problematic assumptions is what Matza calls the "primacy of the criminal actor rather than the criminal law" (p. 3) in the explanation of crime. Modern positivist criminology, unlike the Classical School, looks for the explanation of delinquency in the motivation, character, and background of offenders. Oddly, however, despite its emphasis on the social institutions that influence the delinquent, positivist criminology leaves out one of the most important of them—the law itself. The relationship between legal institutions and delinquency, he argues, is complex, but crucial, since delinquency is, after all, an *infraction*—a violation of law—not simply an *action*. Indeed, committing infractions is the defining characteristic of the delinquent, and delinquency cannot be understood outside of that socio-legal reality. Hence, a key task of *Delinquency and Drift* is to "bring the legal system back in" as a crucial part of the explanation of delinquency.

The second problematic characteristic of positive criminology is its commitment to what Matza calls a "hard" version of determinism—a view that, he argues, has been largely abandoned in most of the rest of social science. Hard determinism assumes that delinquents break the law because they are powerfully compelled to do so by some factor or set of factors—whether those factors are biological, social, or cultural. This leads modern criminology to reject altogether the element of *choice* in the explanation of delinquency, and to embrace a vision of the criminal as entirely "constrained." Against this, Matza poses what he calls a "soft" determinist view. Human beings possess "some leeway of action." The delinquent is not simply pushed around by compelling forces, whether internal or external: "He acts, and his acts are variably free" (p. 11).

Positive criminology, relatedly, views the delinquent as fundamentally different from law-abiding people. That is its third crucially mistaken assumption, for the emphasis on difference, in Matza's view, is both exaggerated and empirically unsupported. Early versions of positivist criminology focused on the delinquent as biologically distinct from everyone else. By the 1960s, those views had been largely discredited. But they had been replaced by an equally problematic *sociological* sense of difference, best represented in those contemporary subcultural theories of delinquency that saw the delinquent as "constrained through an ethical code which makes his misdeeds mandatory" (p. 18). For Matza, the "central idea of the dominant sociological view of delinquency" (p. 19) is that the delinquent has different beliefs, and those beliefs are carried by a distinct and oppositional subculture.

Against this view, Matza offers once again a softer version of the distinctiveness of the beliefs of ordinary delinquents. He does not propose to reject subculture theories altogether, but to modify them in ways that, in his view, better fit what empirical research and common sense observation tell us about the nature of delinquency. He agrees that many delinquents do participate in a subculture of delinquency. But the subculture of delinquency is not a delinquent subculture, and the distinction is crucially important. Delinquents are neither as different from other people nor as committed to delinquency as the dominant theory suggests. Most of the time, delinquent youths are not actually engaging in delinquency. Much of what they do all day long is conventional, as are most of

their beliefs. Moreover, the subculture's hold is usually time-limited. Most delinquents get out of delinquency, sooner rather than later, and the fact that they mature out of delinquency is difficult to square with the idea of powerfully constraining beliefs that impel the delinquent inexorably toward a life of lawbreaking. The delinquent subculture is permeated by conventional values and continually exposed to the influence of conventional adults—most notably parents. As a result, rather than being a distinctively oppositional culture, the subculture's precepts and customs are "delicately balanced between convention and crime" (p. 59).

Matza's critique of subculture theory, however, is not only that it exaggerates the oppositional character of the delinquent subculture, but also that it exaggerates how uniformly conventional the rest of the culture is. The dominant subculture theories, in his view, often seem to assume that the conventional culture is thoroughly Puritan, straight-laced, and unambiguously rejecting of all aspects of delinquency. But Matza argues that the dominant culture is actually far more complex and ambiguous than this. It is shot through with what he calls "subterranean" traditions that support rough and contrary behavior, including a kind of cowboy individualism and disrespect for authority that is not all that different from the defining themes of the subculture of delinquency. Delinquency itself, Matza argues, is a kind of subterranean tradition in American life, and one that is not entirely at odds with, or completely rejected by, the norms of the larger culture.

Drift and Neutralization

The potential delinquent, in short, is caught in between the conventional and the delinquent world. Delinquency is therefore not the result of special compulsions that distinguish the delinquent from others: rather, it involves a release from the ties that often—indeed most of the time—bind youths to the conventional moral order from which they are not nearly so distant as the reigning subcultural theories of delinquency assume. Once those ties are loosened, moreover, youths do not usually fall into a permanent state of delinquency, but are only episodically free from moral constraint. This is the essential meaning of Matza's central conception of *drift*. Drift results when social controls are loosened, but where those who are set loose from conventional controls have also not yet become "agents in their own behalf" (p. 29)—that is, capable of exerting a degree of control over their own destiny. The delinquent, Matza says, is not truly free in this state of drift, because freedom requires that modicum of control and agency. (Note that in stressing this element of agency, Matza is foreshadowing a renewed concern with the idea of agency, as an element of both committing crime and desisting from it, that emerged in criminological theory several decades later.)

This is not to deny the existence of underlying influences that nudge delinquents toward infraction, but those influences may be almost infinite, and their effect is gentle, rather than compelling—a notion that again fits with Matza's embrace of what he calls soft determinism. Many things might nudge youths into delinquency once they have been sufficiently freed from moral constraint; for that matter, many things might nudge them out of delinquency, and indeed usually do. What is constant is the "moral holiday" that permits the drift into delinquency.

Matza acknowledges that the concept of drift bears considerable resemblance to the original meaning of *anomie*. Both refer to a condition of unregulated choice, but Matza prefers to use the term *drift* rather than *anomie*—partly because the latter has taken on confusing multiple meanings since Émile Durkheim originated it at the turn of the century, and partly because he wants to emphasize the "episodic," rather than constant, quality of the moral deregulation that, in his view, permits delinquency (p. 69).

Seen from another angle, drift is a condition that allows the idea of individual choice to come back into the picture, after having been banished by decades of positive criminology. The loosening of moral binds allows youths to choose to transgress, but does not make it certain that they will. Matza emphasizes that in most delinquent behavior there is what he calls an "ineradicable element of choice and freedom" (p. ix)—thus reclaiming a central element of classical theory, but again in a softer variant. He does not deny that some delinquents may indeed be constrained to commit infractions, but not many. The "ordinary" delinquent is one who drifts into delinquency—and also back again. Drift goes in both directions; it is movement between criminal and conventional action. The youth in drift is free to choose delinquency—and also free to choose conventional behavior.

But what causes drift to happen in the first place? How are the ties to the moral order loosened? Here Matza introduces the concept of *neutralization*, an idea developed in the 1950s with Gresham M. Sykes in an influential article called "Techniques of Neutralization: A Theory of Delinquency." "Neutralization," Matza writes, "enables drift. It is the process by which we are freed from the moral bind of the law (p. 176)." Since the delinquent, like everyone else, *usually* adheres to at least some of the legal norms that proscribe infraction, those norms must be neutralized, or nullified, in some way before he or she can be "freed" to break them. Neutralization is not simply the delinquent's after-the-fact rationalization of law breaking: it is an indispensable precondition for it.

What is highly original in Matza's treatment of neutralization is his argument that the law itself, along with other agencies of social control and indeed the modern discipline of criminology itself, contributes to this process of neutralization. In a sense, this argument is a variant of societal reaction theory, but one of a very specific kind. Where most such theories point to the role of labeling or maltreatment by the system in defining and cementing the delinquent in that role, Matza argues in essence that the law and other systems of control facilitate delinquency by helping delinquents to excuse it. The criminal law itself, Matza points out, contains a variety of justifications or exceptions that mitigate its force. The law "contains the seeds of its own neutralization" (p. 61), because it specifies a variety of conditions under which it may be violated, including the absence of intent, self-defense, and insanity.

But neutralization may also be specifically fostered by both the ideology and the routine organization and practices of the youth control system. The modern positivist view of the delinquent, based as it is on the central idea that people are compelled to crime by external forces, matches the view of the subculture of delinquency itself and provides one path toward neutralizing the law's bind. It is an ideology that, by locating the causes of delinquency in the delinquent's parents, their community, the larger society, or even victims, itself becomes a cause of delinquency. These views pervade the juvenile justice system, and, ironically, "are part of the causal nexus culminating in delinquency in that they bolster an otherwise precarious and brittle system of beliefs"—that is, the half-baked but consequential beliefs common to the subculture already (p. 95). Theories of delinquency rooted in hard determinism, then, are in Matza's view not only intellectually untenable but, in a real sense, are causes of the very behavior they seek to explain.

This effect is especially important since, according to Matza, it is precisely the sense of lacking control over their behavior that allows delinquents to drift—that promotes the sense of irresponsibility without which delinquency is unlikely. Matza here introduces the idea of the crucial role of fatalism in the trajectory into delinquency—the youths sense that they are an "effect," rather than a "cause," that they are driven by forces outside themselves. Crime is "extenuated and thus permissible" only when delinquents recall that they are "controlled by external forces" (p. 88) and thereby rendered irresponsible.

This sense of irresponsibility, to Matza, is an indispensable "immediate" cause of drift. But drifting into delinquency is also facilitated by another condition, which he describes as a state of readiness to slide into delinquency once the sense of irresponsibility has been established. This longer-term condition Matza calls the sense of injustice—a feeling that is critical to the loosening of moral bonds because it provides "another and more profound condition of neutralization" (p. 101). The delinquent's sense of injustice—an underlying "simmering resentment"—is fostered by the operation of the justice system itself, because the delinquent often perceives legal authorities as behaving in ways that are arbitrary and often flagrantly unjust.

Crucial to Matza's perspective is the argument that the delinquent's perception of structured injustice is not entirely wrong. It is fostered by certain fundamental features of modern systems of juvenile justice—in particular, the rampant discretion that characterizes those systems, and, relatedly, the vagueness of the principles that guide their decisions about the fate of the youth who come before them. Unlike the legal definitions of offenses themselves, the criteria for judgment in a system of individualized justice, which is a core feature of modern youth control systems,

are diffuse and subjective, relying on the "wisdom" of court officials to weigh a variety of factors in deciding a youth's fate, including many extra-legal characteristics of the youth themselves. This promotes the feeling that the system is inconsistent and arbitrary, and thus feeds the sense of injustice. The wide use of discretion may make the system work reasonably well for those who run it, but to the delinquent it appears as an injustice (p. 132).

The sense of injustice is also fed by the enforcement of status offenses, which, as participants in the subculture of delinquency thoroughly understand, are infractions that apply only to them—and which, moreover, are only sporadically and inconsistently enforced. Activities like drinking, skipping school, and generally being outside of adult control are not merely common within the subculture of delinquency, but are the core of it. Criminalizing them—especially on an inconsistent basis—is thus unsurprisingly a source of resentment.

The Role of Will

The sense of injustice bred by these aspects of the system, then, is a key underlying factor promoting the neutralization that enables the drift into delinquency. But Matza also argues that the process of neutralization alone does not fully explain why the youth chooses to break the law. Neutralization allows infraction but does not compel it. Something else needs to be present—something that does indeed provide the push into delinquency once the bonds to conventional behavior are loosened. Put in another way, the youth must in some sense want to do the crime and be sufficiently freed from constraint to do it. To provide that essential part of the explanation, Matza, again reaching back into classical criminology, introduces the notion of "will." Without will, drift will not result in crime. But in contrast to the classical view, Matza does not suggest that the will to crime is an inherent aspect of human nature that predictably emerges when the "lid" of social control is taken off. Rather, the will to crime is invoked under certain conditions, which Matza labels "preparation" and "desperation."

Preparation means in essence that the youth must feel able to successfully commit the infraction—be prepared for offending in the sense of feeling able to carry it off. Desperation, on the other hand, is a consequence of the mood of fatalism that afflicts the delinquent. According to Matza, the delinquent wills infraction in order to escape the sense of fatalism—the sense of being pushed around—by making things happen. The need to make things happen in this sense is especially urgent because of the fragile sense of masculinity that characterizes the subculture of delinquency. Being manly is a core norm of that subculture, and being at the mercy of external forces or authorities will be regarded as unmanly by both the subculture and the delinquent himself. Breaking the law, even if it means getting caught and suffering the legal consequences, can serve the purpose of making things happen—and thus represents a desperate move on the delinquent's part to restore a sense of himself as cause: an effort to provide "some dramatic reassurance that he can still make things happen" (p. 189).

Conclusion

Delinquency and Drift has remained an influential work in the theory of juvenile delinquency since its publication—a robust record—though many contemporary criminologists may be more familiar with a few of its key concepts, notably neutralization, than with its penetrating critique of contemporary juvenile justice or its subtle analysis of the role of criminal law in crime itself. Part of the reason for this endurance may be that empirical research has tended to support the assertion that many delinquent youths do indeed employ techniques of neutralization to justify their offenses—offering support to Matza's central argument that delinquency may be less a reflection of deep divisions in fundamental values between delinquents and the larger culture than of a process of periodic loosening of moral ties that are mostly shared with law-abiding people. As noted, too, the theme of the importance of the ineradicable element of choice—the zone of at least partial freedom in which relatively unconstrained actors make decisions about the course of action they will take—has resonated in more recent discussions of the importance of agency in understanding individuals' trajectories into, and out of, crime. And still other themes—including the role of fatalism and desperation in

precipitating crime—though less developed, may offer rich opportunities for exploration.

Elliott Currie

See also Beccaria, Cesare: Classical School; Cloward, Richard A., and Lloyd E. Ohlin: Delinquency and Opportunity; Cohen, Albert K.: Delinquent Boys; Matza, David: Becoming Deviant; Matza, David, and Gresham M. Sykes: Subterranean Values and Delinquency; Miller, Walter B.: Lower-Class Culture Theory of Delinquency; Reckless, Walter C.: Containment Theory

References and Further Readings

Currie, E. (2004). *The road to whatever: Middle class culture and the crisis of adolescence*. New York: Metropolitan Books.
Matza, D. (1964). *Delinquency and drift*. New York: Wiley.
Matza, D. (1969). *Becoming deviant*. Englewood Cliffs, NJ: Prentice Hall.
Sykes, G. M., & Matza, D. (1957). Techniques of neutralization: A theory of delinquency. *American Sociological Review, 22*, 664–670.

MATZA, DAVID, AND GRESHAM M. SYKES: SUBTERRANEAN VALUES AND DELINQUENCY

Following their work on the "techniques of neutralization" in 1957, David Matza and Gresham M. Sykes elaborated their perspective on delinquent conduct. It is not enough, they argued in "Juvenile Delinquency and Subterranean Values," to explain how individuals cognitively free themselves from social control—that is, to know "how an impetus to engage in delinquent behavior is translated into action" (p. 713). It also is essential to explain "what makes delinquency attractive in the first place" (p. 713). In the occurrence of delinquent conduct, techniques of neutralization represent the *how* whereas the concept of subterranean values Matza and Sykes explained *why*—"the values and ends underlying delinquency and the relationship of these values to those of the larger society" (p. 713).

The *why* seemed obvious to many—that delinquents were "disturbed" and sought things they should not. But Sykes and Matza dismissed the notion of the disturbed delinquent, pointing to evidence that delinquents were actually conformists most of the time, and were quite capable of feeling guilt and shame for their actions. Rather than some "disturbed" social environment, most were exposed to the same societal pressures that produced nondelinquents. With the techniques of neutralization Sykes and Matza showed how, using culturally acceptable reasons, "normal" individuals could convince themselves that they were not actually doing something wrong. This focus on the *normal*, as opposed to the disturbed, led Matza and Sykes to search for values in the mainstream American value system that could produce delinquency.

Deviant Values?

Drawing on a burgeoning literature on delinquents, particularly the behavior of youths in street gangs, Matza and Sykes (1961) found several "underlying values" that they concluded are entirely consistent with the mainstream American value system. The first of these is a preference or desire for "excitement," an adventurous life filled with "displays of daring" and "charged with danger." Next, delinquents value an ethic of "grandiose dreams and quick success." This contrasted with the notion that one gets ahead through hard work. Better to make one's financial success through the easy score and outwitting one's peers. Finally, the delinquent values a "readiness for aggression" that is often observed in gang violence. The use of aggression, however, is not a pathological drive to create suffering; rather it "is a demonstration of toughness and thus of masculinity."

At first glance, this "cluster of values" appears to represent a disturbed subculture that deviates "from the dominant society," rather than a reflection of conventional American values. Not so, argue Matza and Sykes. In fact, these values appear eerily similar to "the code of the 'gentlemen of leisure' depicted by Thorsten Veblen" (p. 714). Daring and adventure, rejecting the "prosaic discipline of work," a taste for consumption and luxury, and the valuation of masculine endeavors—these are all prototypical of the "leisured elite." It thus appears that non-delinquent members of society's upper classes possess the same values as their lower-class counterparts. The only difference, as Matza and Sykes see it, is the expression of those values in the form of delinquency. All youths, then, subscribe to a similar set of American values; the delinquent's values are no more deviant than the law-abiding youth's values.

Subterranean Values

How then, do these values produce criminal behavior in some, but conforming behavior in others? Here Matza and Sykes show a stunning intuition for a cognitive feature of value systems that will be empirically demonstrated three decades later. Matza and Sykes argue that these values exist in a "system" with other cultural, subcultural, and class-specific values, but that they are often "lurking" just below values with a higher priority. They are "subterranean" in nature and often influenced by other values in the system.

A desire for "adventure," for example, is quite common, but it is often kept in check by the values of the routinized and bureaucratic lives that most people lead. There is an acceptable time and place for thrill-seeking. Delinquents, however, are not checked by the bureaucratic values, and as a result they seek their adventure in places, times, and ways that are considered inappropriate. People who play the stock market or buy lottery tickets are looking for the big score, but these are considered the conventional means by which one seeks easy fortune as opposed to the hustling of delinquent youths. Similarly, expressions of masculinity are ubiquitous throughout the social structure, but it is in the delinquent that the value of masculinity is expressed with less restraint than it is by others.

Delinquents, then, are socialized with values similar to the rest of the society. The only difference is the influence or relative importance of the subterranean values to delinquent youngsters. While most of us value excitement, easy riches, and expressions of aggression, most people are guided by other important values that direct the expression of the subterranean values in conventional ways.

Modern Evidence

Matza and Sykes intuitively offered this view of individual values as part of a system of values where some values are more influential than others and, most importantly in their explanation of delinquency, these value priorities vary across individuals. In the 1970s, Milton Rokeach developed and tested the first general theory of values as cognitive bits of information that help form preferences. He also developed a survey instrument that demonstrated the hierarchical relationship of values within each person. Today, the work of Shalom Schwartz, Ronald Ingleheart, and many others continues to demonstrate the importance of value systems and value priorities on the formation of preferences, decision making, and behavior.

Criminologists continue to link subterranean values to delinquent behavior. Messner and Rosenfeld's *Crime and the American Dream* argues that societies dominated by economic institutions will find that the values of these institutions like the fetishism of money, individualism, and achievement, but lacking the restraining values of civil institutions will experience higher rates of crime than other societies. Mark Konty used Schwartz's value scale to demonstrate that subterranean values in the form of self-enhancement values produce positive evaluations of deviant behavior as well as deviant behavior, a cognitive condition called *micro-anomie*. In both cases, when subterranean values are given highest priority in the value system, delinquency results.

Mark Konty

See also Messner, Steven F., and Richard Rosenfeld: Institutional-Anomie Theory; Miller, Walter B.: Lower-Class Culture Theory of Delinquency; Southern Subculture of Violence Theory; Sykes, Gresham M., and David Matza: Techniques of Neutralization; Wolfgang, Marvin E., and Franco Ferracuti: Subculture of Violence Theory

References and Further Readings

Inglehart, R., Basanez, M., Dietz-Medrano, J., Halman, L., & Luijkz, R. (2004). *Human beliefs and values: A cross cultural sourcebook on the 1999–2002 value surveys.* Buenos Aires, Argentina: Siglo XXI Editores.

Konty, M. (2005). Microanomie: The cognitive foundations of the relationship between anomie and deviance. *Criminology, 31,* 107–132.

Matza, D., & Sykes, G. M. (1961). Juvenile delinquency and subterranean values. *American Sociological Review, 26,* 713–719.

Messner, S. F., & Rosenfeld, R. (2000). *Crime and the American dream.* Belmont, CA: Wadsworth.

Rokeach, M. (1973). *The nature of human values.* New York: Free Press.

Schwartz, S. H. (2006). A theory of cultural value orientations: Explication and applications. *Comparative Sociology, 5,* 137–182.

Sykes, G. M., & Matza, D. (1957). Techniques of neutralization: A theory of delinquency. *American Sociological Review, 22,* 664–673.

Maxson, Cheryl L.: Gang Migration Theorizing

In the late 1980s and the early 1990s, the United States experienced a substantial rise in the incidence of violent crime committed by juvenile offenders. There was also an unprecedented increase in the gang presence in this country. In particular, gang proliferation was escalating. "Gang proliferation" refers to the increase in the number of localities reporting a gang presence. In other words, it is the expansion of gangs in areas that had previously been unaffected. Theory and research on gang migration, or the movement of gangs from one city to another, focuses on whether the proliferation of gangs is caused by gang members moving to new cities. Alternatively, cities may experience a gang problem independent of the occurrence of gang migrants entering their jurisdictions.

Research on the proliferation of gangs has identified two distinct periods of proliferation. Larger cities and mid-size cities experienced gang proliferation at roughly the same period of time, while the proliferation into smaller cities and towns occurred later. Rapid rates of proliferation occurred first in highly populated areas (i.e., population equal or greater to 100,000) in the mid- to late 1980s until 1990. Mid-size cities (i.e., 50,000–99,999 people) experienced growth during the period of 1986 to 1995. The second trajectory of proliferation included small cities and towns (i.e., 25,000–49,999 people). The expansion in these areas occurred in the early to mid-1990s. While gangs had previously been thought of as a "big city" phenomenon, now municipalities of all sizes were confronted with the issue.

Media headlines at the time attributed the pro-liferation of gangs to the migration of members from traditional gang cities (e.g., Los Angeles and Chicago). Gangs were depicted as organizations that were "franchising" their criminal enterprise to burgeoning areas. Numerous reasons for gang movement were offered. Some believed these moves were in responses to over-saturation of tra-ditional gang cities or attempts to avoid laws in certain states. The most common reason, however, was attributed to gangs' connections to the drug trade. Gangs were seen as central players in the distribution of crack cocaine. During this period, they were depicted in the media as highly struc-tured groups that were migrating to new and smaller cities to expand their drug market.

This was in contrast to previous empirical stud-ies that concluded that gangs are more likely to result from local environmental factors as opposed to being formed as "satellite" branches of previ-ously existing gangs. There was also strong research support for the influence of pop culture (e.g., mov-ies, fashion, and music) on local gang activity. In these cases, new gangs adopted the names and/or traditions of well-known gangs like the Crips or the Bloods, but had no actual affiliation with these gangs in other cities.

Most of this previous research was geographi-cally specific. In other words, researchers pin-pointed one or two cities as sites for study/investigation. As an improvement on these previ-ous designs and an attempt to offer a more expan-sive perspective, a team of scholars at the University of Southern California, headed by Cheryl L. Maxson, embarked on a national study of gangs. The goal was to address whether there was evi-dence that widespread gang proliferation was due, all or in part, to gang migration (Maxson, 1998; Maxson et al., 1995).

Gang Migration in the United States

In 1992, Maxson and colleagues conducted a national survey of law enforcement agencies. In total, they mailed instruments to over 1,100 agen-cies around the country. Their sample consisted of all cities with a population of 100,000 or more. In addition, they contacted 900 smaller cities that they deemed to be "likely" environments for street gangs or gang migration. A "likely" city was identified by

suggestions from other jurisdictions and all cities that had established special organization(s) to investigate gangs. After repeated mailings and fol-low-ups, the researchers received over 90 percent participation from the contacted agencies (i.e., over 1,000 cities responding). The researchers described this sample as a "purposive" sample of gang cities as opposed to a full national representation.

In addition, Maxson and colleagues conducted phone interviews with law enforcement officials from 211 cities that reported a moderate level of gang migration (i.e., at least 10 gang migrants in the year 1991). This study also included some interviews with community members and migrant gang members. As is common in this area of research, the authors make a distinction between street gangs and other gangs. Their working defini-tion of "gang" did not include motorcycle gangs, prison gangs, taggers (i.e., groups that concentrate on graffiti), or racial supremacy groups.

First, Maxson and colleagues addressed whether there was any evidence that gangs were migrating to other cities. They found that, of the approxi-mately 1,000 responding cities, 710 had experi-enced some amount of gang migration by 1992. Law enforcement agencies in only three states (New Hampshire, North Dakota, and Vermont) reported having no gang migrants. The areas reporting gang migration were most often in the western United States (44 percent), then the mid-west (26 percent), southern states (25 percent), and least likely in the North East region of the country (5 percent). A vast majority (approxi-mately 80 percent) of cities with over 100,000 people reported migrant gang members. This was not a systematic investigation of all cities in the nation, and as such, the authors could not speak definitively regarding the prevalence of gang migrants in medium and small cities. They did, note, however, that despite this limitation, cities of all sizes did report gang migrants. One important finding was that while the distribution of gang migration was widespread, the depth of the prob-lem was not as extreme. Almost half of the cities (47 percent) reported that they received less than 10 migrant gang members in the previous year. Only 6 percent of cities (n=34) reported over 100 gang migrants in the last year.

The next step for the authors was to investigate whether gang proliferation was due to gang

594   McCarthy, Bill, and John Hagan: Danger and Deterrence

migration. Temporal ordering was of primary importance. If gang migration was the cause of gang proliferation, one would expect the emergence of gangs in a city to follow the arrival of migrating gang members. The authors found that 54 percent of cities had local gangs prior to the arrival of migrant gang members. Only 5 percent of cities report gang migration occurring at least one year prior to the formation of any gangs. The remaining half reported that local gangs and gang migrants occurred in the same year. Over 80 percent of interviewed law enforcement agents disagreed with the idea that gang migration was the cause of their city's gang problem. These findings do not offer support for the notion that gang proliferation is primarily due to the extent of gang migration into those new gang cities. Local gang problems more often precede gang migration than follow it.

What factors led gang members to migrate to different cities? Maxson offers evidence that refutes the claim that the expansion of the drug trade is the primary reason for gang migration. Interviewed officers were asked to choose the primary reason that most gang members moved into their cities. The most common reason cited was that gang members moved to be with their families (39 percent) or other relatives and friends. In total, 57 percent of law enforcement officers chose these social reasons as the primary reason for relocation. Opportunity for criminal behavior was the next most common reason (32 percent) offered for gang member migration. Within these examples, the most commonly cited criminal opportunity was the expansion of drug sales. Lastly, 11 percent of cities reported that the most common reason for gang migration to their cities was gang members being pushed out of their old areas due to law enforcement, court order, or a desire to leave the gang. In light of these findings, the authors argue the reason for gang migration is more likely to be for social reasons than a specific emphasis on criminal motivations.

While a valuable contribution to gang migration theory and research, Maxson's study does suffer limitations. The authors describe it as an exploratory study. First, they rely primarily on law enforcements' assessment of the nature of gangs in their cities. This is one, but certainly not the only, point of view on the subject. Other empirical literature in the area has included data from community members and gang members. In general, the body of research supports the notion that gang members move for social reasons like most people, and not solely with the intention to commit crime. Maxson's study is also cross-sectional. It offers great insight into the time period of late 1980s and early 1990s, but current evaluations of the topic are also valuable.

In conclusion, Maxson and others have strongly refuted the notion that gang migration is the major reason for the gang proliferation in the 1980s and early 1990s. The work does not support the belief that gang members leave their cities in search of new areas to expand their membership. This is not to suggest that gang members never move to expand their criminal enterprises but that the highly organized gang with expanding territories is the rare exception.

Kristy N. Matsuda

See also Cloward, Richard A., and Lloyd E. Ohlin: Delinquency and Opportunity; Klein, Malcolm W., and Cheryl L. Maxson: Street Gang Structure and Organization; Moore, Joan W.: Homeboys and Homegirls in the Barrio; Short, James F., Jr.: Gangs and Group Processes; Thrasher, Frederick M.: The Gang

References and Further Readings

Klein, M. W., & Maxson, C. L. (2006). *Street gangs: Patterns and policies.* New York: Oxford University Press.

Maxson, C. L. (1998). *Gang members on the move: Juvenile justice bulletin.* Washington, DC: U.S. Department of Justice, Office of Juvenile Justice and Delinquency Prevention.

Maxson, C. L., Woods, K. J., & Klein, M. W. (1995). *Street gang migration in the United States.* Unpublished final report, Los Angeles Social Science Research Institute, University of Southern California.

McCarthy, Bill, and John Hagan: Danger and Deterrence

Deterrence theory assumes that individuals have free will, are capable of rationally weighing the

costs and benefits of their actions, and will make decisions that maximize the likelihood of a positive outcome. Previous research has focused on an individual's ability to analyze the benefits of committing crime against the potential formal, informal, and economic costs of being apprehended and punished for their criminal misdeeds. Bill McCarthy and John Hagan contribute to the existing literature on deterrence by suggesting physical danger may be a determining factor in an individual's criminal decision-making process. Specifically, they hypothesize a negative relationship between physical danger and crime wherein the greater the likelihood for physical danger, the less likely an individual will commit crime.

Offenders and Physical Danger

Although many of the characteristics associated with being a perpetrator of crime are also associated with being a victim of crime, victims and offenders are usually studied as separate entities. McCarthy and Hagan bridge this gap and examine offenders who, through their criminal activity, may find themselves victims of physical violence from one or more of McCarthy and Hagan's four sources of physical danger. First, an offender may become the target of physical violence from a victim who is unwilling to surrender one's self or property to the offender. Second, bystanders to a criminal event may intervene, resulting in a physical confrontation. Third, police may use physical force against an offender. Fourth and finally, offenders may be victimized by other criminal offenders.

To date, limited research exists describing the relationship between individual perception of physical danger and criminal decision making. McCarthy and Hagan's 2005 study of prostitution, theft, and drug sales among homeless youths indicates that physical danger is a determining factor in an offender's decision-making process. The direction of the relationship suggests that the more the physical danger, the less likely an individual will commit crime. Similar findings emerged from Eric Beauregard and Benoit Leclerc's study of sex offenders who report the likelihood of resistance from a potential victim and likelihood for bystander involvement are critical factors in the criminal decision-making process. The importance

of capable guardianship is evident in these empirical findings (Cohen & Felson, 1979, p. 588).

Implications for Future Research

McCarthy and Hagan's theory of physical danger and decision making has implications for three additional lines of empirical inquiry. First, Julie Horney and Ineke Haen Marshall suggest that an offender's perception of risk may be shaped by the number of successful crimes committed compared to the number of arrests. This line of reasoning can be applied to the study of physical danger. That is, does an offender's perception of physical harm vary based on the number of crimes committed successfully without sustaining physical injury? Second, does the "resetting effect" extend to physical harm (Pogarsky & Piquero, 2003, p. 95)? Intuitively, one would expect an individual's perception of danger to increase if the individual encounters physical danger. The resetting effect suggests the opposite—that is, an offender's perception of physical danger decreases subsequent to a dangerous encounter because the offender believes the odds of a second dangerous encounter to be extremely low. Third, researchers, such as Greg Pogarsky, Alex Piquero, and Ray Paternoster, have begun to integrate social learning theory into deterrence research. Testing the degree to which vicarious learning experiences may influence one's individual perception of physical danger and criminal decision making will further the deterrence/social learning research agenda.

Conclusion

McCarthy and Hagan's theory and empirical findings support the statement that offenders are rational thinkers and have the capacity to weigh the costs and benefits of their actions. Moreover, McCarthy and Hagan's theory of danger and deterrence is a nod to the past, present, and future of deterrence research in that it incorporates the basic tenets of early deterrence research (free will, calculating costs and benefits), builds on contemporary research that focuses on individual perception and decision making, and outlines a research agenda for the future that integrates sociological, economic, and psychological explanations for danger and decision making.

Brenda Vose

See also Becker, Gary S.: Punishment, Human Capital, and Crime; Gibbs, Jack P.: Deterrence Theory; Nagin, Daniel S., and Raymond Paternoster: Individual Differences and Deterrence; Stafford, Mark C., and Mark Warr: Deterrence Theory

References and Further Readings

Baynard, V. L. (2008). Measurement and correlates of prosocial bystander behavior: The case of interpersonal violence. *Violence and Victims, 23,* 83–97.

Beauregard, E., & Leclerc, B. (2007). An application of the rational choice approach to the offending process of sex offenders: A closer look at decision-making. *Sex Abuse, 19,* 115–133.

Beccaria, C. (1963). *On crimes and punishment.* Upper Saddle River, NJ: Prentice Hall. (Original work published 1764)

Becker, G. S. (1976). *The economic approach to human behavior.* Chicago: University of Chicago Press.

Bentham, J., & Lafleur, L. J. (1948). *An introduction to the principles of morals and legislation.* New York: Hafner. (Original work published 1789)

Cohen, L. E., & Felson, M. (1979). Social change and crime rate trends: A routine activity approach. *American Sociological Review, 44,* 588–608.

Eagly, A. E., & Crowley, M. (1986). Gender and helping behavior: A meta-analytic review of the social psychological literature. *Psychological Bulletin, 100*(3), 283–308.

Horney, J., & Marshall, I. H. (1992). Risk perceptions among serious offenders: The role of crime and punishment. *Criminology, 30,* 575–594.

Jaeger, C. C., Ortwin, R., Rosa, E. A., & Webler. T. (2001). *Risk, uncertainty, and rational action.* London: Earthscan.

Jensen, G. F., & Brownfield, D. (1986). Gender, lifestyles, victimization: Beyond routine activity. *Violence and Victims, 1,* 85–99.

Kleck, G., & DeLone, M. A. (1993). Victim resistance and offender weapon effects in robbery. *Journal of Quantitative Criminology, 9,* 55–81.

McCarthy, B., & Hagan J. (2005). Danger and the decision to offend. *Social Forces, 83,* 1065–1096.

Pogarsky, G., & Piquero, A. R. (2003). Can punishment encourage offending? Investigating the "resetting" effect. *Journal of Research in Crime and Delinquency, 40,* 95–120.

Pogarsky, G., Piquero, A. R., & Paternoster, R. (2004). Modeling change in perceptions about sanction threats: The neglected linkage in deterrence theory. *Journal of Quantitative Criminology, 20,* 343–369.

Pratt, T. C., Cullen, F. T., Blevins, K. R., Daigle, L. E., & Madensen, T. D. (2006). The empirical status of deterrence. In F. T. Cullen, J. P. Wright, & K. R. Blevins (Eds.), *Taking stock: The status of criminological theory* (Advances in Criminological Theory: Vol. 15, pp. 367–395). New Brunswick, NJ: Transaction.

Sampson, R. J., & Lauritsen, J. L. (1990). Deviant lifestyles, proximity to crime, and the offender-victim link in personal violence. *Journal of Research in Crime and Delinquency, 27,* 110–139.

Terrill, W., Leinfelt, F. H., & Kwak, D. H. (2008). Examining police use of force: A smaller agency perspective. *Policing, 31,* 57–76.

Topalli, V., Wright, R., & Fornango, R. (2002). Drug dealers, robbery and retaliation: Vulnerability, deterrence and the contagion of violence. *British Journal of Criminology, 42,* 337–351.

Williams, K. R., & Hawkins, R. (1986). Perceptual research on general deterrence: A critical review. *Law & Society Review, 20,* 545–572.

Wyckoff, R., & Simpson, S. S. (2008). The effects of self-protective behaviors on injury for African American women in domestic violence situations. *Crime, Law, Social Change, 49,* 271–288.

McCorkel, Jill: Gender and Embodied Surveillance

In the 1980s, the United States witnessed unprecedented prison growth. While the numbers of men under correctional supervision increased dramatically, the rate at which women were being locked up outpaced men. The reason for these increases was the result of new policies aimed at getting tough on crime. These get-tough policies included harsher prisons sentences, mandatory sentences for certain offenses, and tougher drug laws. The 1980s were ripe for these get-tough policies given the social context of the prior decades; the country seemed out of control to many in the 1960s and 1970s, and laws were created to deter people from committing crime. Both men and women offenders were targeted with these policies.

Despite the appearance of neutrality with regards to these policies for men and women offenders, Jill McCorkel argues that gender still matters. While supervision and punishment strategies in the get-tough era are based on the assumption that male offenders are rational actors, corrections administrators set up surveillance and punishment mechanisms based on the idea that women offend due to a failure in themselves. Thus, women offenders are both deviant in terms of their gender but also in terms of their criminality. Drawing on Michel Foucault and Joan Acker, McCorkel argues that prisons are gendered organizations and, for women, surveillance and punishment takes a new form.

By the time Ronald Reagan was elected U.S. president in 1980, the country was ready for a leader who was going to get the country "back on track." The 1960s included events such as the civil rights movement, Vietnam War protests, the Attica prison riot and the Kent State student shootings by the police. Liberals believed that the government could not be trusted to be fair, whereas conservatives believed that laws were too soft on crime. This combination led to determinate sentencing policies whereby certain offenses were given specific punishments. In addition, however, more punitive policies were put into place such as mandatory minimum sentences. Mandatory minimum sentences were often imposed for drug offenses, which in turn increased the prison population. Thus, the general feeling of the 1980s was that criminal justice laws should be tougher.

This idea that criminal justice laws should be tougher was not applied only to male offenders. Many thought that females should not be immune from these harsher punishments. Women, too, were being locked up at increasing rates. The same punitive policies were imposed on women prisoners, yet in these prisons, women were often not afforded the same amenities and programs as men. This led many feminists to call this "equality with a vengeance" (Chesney-Lind & Pollock, 1995). McCorkel was interested in how discipline and punishment differed in women's prisons than in men's prisons following this get-tough era.

Foucault and Acker

McCorkel draws on two theorists to frame her study and findings. She builds her study and discussion on several theorists that have presented theories on punishment or gender. First, she discusses Foucault's analysis of penal surveillance and concludes that women's prisons surveillance differs from this. Second, she builds on Acker's idea of

"gendered organizations" and argues that prisons are gendered in that, within the organization, women are treated and thought of as different from men in both criminality and in gender.

In 1977, Foucault published his now famous analysis of prisons and other social organizations, *Discipline and Punish*. In this book, Foucault argues that prisons act as punishment and surveillance mechanisms that control not only inmates' behavior but also their minds. He claims that the architecture of prisons, the Panopticon style whereby prisons are circular with a watchtower in the center, creates the impression that prisoners are always being watched. The guards can see the inmates' every move or the inmates perceive this, yet the inmates cannot see the guards. This fosters a sort of disembodied surveillance, where the inmates do not know who is watching them but they know they are being watched. The goal of this is to control the inmates' behavior.

In 1990, Acker suggested that rather than sexism occurring in the workplace as a result of sexist managers or bosses, sexism is often the product of the larger culture of the organization. By that she means that the organization is based on the idea that there are gender differences and that men are the standard and are the preferred employees. McCorkel draws on this concept of gendered organizations when she conceptualized her ethnographic study of women's prisons.

McCorkel's Study

McCorkel's ethnographic study began in 1994 and ended in 1998. The setting was a medium security prison for women undergoing a shift in punishment strategies by creating a hard-core drug treatment program. McCorkel conducted interviews with 74 women inmates in addition to her participant observation. The drug treatment model was based on the therapeutic community (TC). The main philosophy of TCs is that drug addiction is caused by problematic personality traits and that what is needed is surveillance, discipline and confrontation, and humiliation.

Unlike the surveillance used in Foucault's prisons, surveillance for the women offenders in McCorkel's study was embodied—the women knew who was watching them. Signs were posted around the housing unit that reminded the inmates that they were being watched and they could not escape surveillance. In addition, relationships were controlled, and the women were taught to trust no one. When women did break a rule (even a mundane one), they were confronted in ceremonies where staff and other inmates were present. Thus, discipline manifested itself through confrontation.

Surveillance was also bound up with therapy and diagnosis in the women's prison. The program rested on the assumption that the women were "sick." Women were told they required surveillance because they needed structure due to their chaotic lives and personality deficiencies. According to McCorkel, these surveillance mechanisms allowed the staff to "spy" on the offenders under the guise of determining their diagnoses. The inmate's behavior could then be used to justify her mental health diagnosis. Thus, therapy and diagnosis were used in women's prisons more than men's due to the assumptions that women are sick and men are rational actors who weigh the costs and benefits of their actions.

Conclusion

McCorkel's findings led to her theory of embodied surveillance and gendered punishment. Embodied surveillance is different than Foucault's analysis of surveillance. In Foucault's analysis of (men's) prison, surveillance was a way of getting into the prisoners' heads in order to control their behavior, thus maintaining the order of the prison. However, in the Panopticon-designed prisons, the "watcher" is not known to the inmate. The guards are in the watch tower looking down at the inmates. The inmates cannot see in the watch tower and thus do not know who is watching them or when they are being watched. McCorkel argues that in the equality with a vengeance era in women's prisons, the women inmates are still being watched. However, now they know who is watching them, and thus the surveillance is embodied.

Punishment is gendered according to McCorkel in that it is different from men's prisons. Punishment in women's prisons is tied to therapy and diagnosis. The assumption is that women are "sick" and in need of structure and surveillance. Their punishment is based on hard-core therapy, which includes diagnoses, confrontation, and humiliation.

Dana J. Hubbard

See also Giallombardo, Rose: Women in Prison; Kruttschnitt, Candace, and Rosemary Gartner: Women and Imprisonment

References and Further Readings

Acker, J. (1990). Hierarchies, jobs, bodies: A theory of gendered organizations. *Gender and Society, 4,* 139–158.

Chesney-Lind, M., & Pollock, J. (1995). Women's prisons: Equality with a vengeance. In A. Merio & J. Pollack (Eds.), *Women, law and social control* (pp. 155–176). Boston: Allyn & Bacon.

Foucault, M. (1977). *Discipline and punish*. New York: Random House.

Gartner, R., & Kruttschnitt, C. (2004). A brief history of doing time: The California Institution for Women in the 1960s and the 1990s. *Law and Society Review, 38,* 267–304.

Hannah-Moffat, K. (2004). Losing ground. *Social Politics: State, and Society, 11,* 363–385.

McKim, A. (2008). Getting gut-level. *Gender and Society, 22,* 303–323.

Pollack, S. (2005). Taming the shrew: Regulating prisoners through women-centered mental health programming. *Critical Criminology, 13,* 71–87.

MEDIA VIOLENCE EFFECTS

As media technology has advanced, the issue of media violence and its effects on human behavior has become an important issue of concern for policy makers. The issue of media violence has garnered significant attention from the United States Congress. In 2000, for example, representatives of six different public health organizations (American Medical Association, American Academy of Pediatrics, American Psychological Association, American Psychiatric Association, American Academy of Family Physicians, and the American Academy of Child and Adolescent Psychiatry) signed a joint statement delivered to the Congressional Public Health Summit arguing that "television, movies, music, and interactive games are powerful learning tools and highly influential media" (American Academy of Pediatrics, 2000). The joint statement also asserted that prior research has "point[ed] overwhelmingly to a causal connection between media violence and aggressive behavior in some children."

Claims that violent media consumption has led to an increase in violent and aggressive behavior has not only been presented by representatives of public health organizations. Independent university-based scholars have also argued that the effects of violent media consumption on subsequent aggression and violence are robust. Brad Bushman and Craig Anderson have asserted that in research produced since 1975, the statistical magnitude of the links between media violence and aggression have been "positive and have consistently increased over time" (p. 477). Robert Sege has claimed that "one of the best documented causes of the modern upsurge violence appears to be childhood exposure to television violence" (p. 129). Lastly, in 2003 Anderson et al. suggested that there is "unequivocal evidence that media violence increases the likelihood of aggressive and violent behavior in both immediate and long-term contexts" (p. 81).

The entry first identifies the theoretical mechanisms that scholars have used to connect media violence consumption and subsequent aggression, violence, and criminal aggression. Next, the entry reviews the findings of meta-analytical reviews. A meta-analysis is a statistical method of reviewing literature that reports mean (average) effect sizes of a predictor variable of interest (media violence consumption) on an outcome variable of interest (subsequent criminal or aggressive behavior). The entry reviews meta-analyses that have examined the link between violent media consumption and subsequent aggression and violence. The essay also separately reviews a meta-analysis conducted by Joanne Savage and Christina Yancey; this meta-analysis is treated separately because it is the only published meta-analysis that examined only the effect of media violence consumption on *criminal aggression*. Lastly, conclusions about the link between violent media consumption and aggression, violence, and criminal aggression are summarized.

Theories of Media Violence Effects on Behavior

Theories of the precise mechanisms through which media violence consumption is linked to future aggressive behavior focus on psychological and physiological processes. Many psychologists who have theorized about media violence effects have focused attention on modeling and imitation. Psychologist Albert Bandura suggested that people learn through direct experience and by watching others; thus, media characters who engage in violence serve as violent role models. Rowell Heusmann expanded on Bandura's social learning approach by asserting that when people observe media violence, they develop aggressive cognitive scripts that guide their behavior; in essence, people imitate the actions of characters or individuals they see in mass media by applying these scripts to interactions and circumstances in their own lives. Notably, the theoretical statements by both Bandura and Heusmann suggested a direct causal connection between consuming media violence and future aggression and violence.

Others have suggested a direct causal connection by considering how consumption of media violence impacts human beings physiologically. Scholars using this line of reasoning have argued that when people are exposed to violent images or ideas, there are clear and measurable physiological responses (e.g., increased heart rate and higher blood pressure). And these physiological responses to violence that people experience serve as reinforcements (e.g., something that they enjoy) for future aggressive and violent reactions. D. Zillmann's model of suspense enjoyment argued that when liked characters in a media depiction are victimized or threatened with victimization, such a depiction "arouses dysphoric emotional reactions or empathetic distress" (Hoffner & Levine, 2005, p. 209). Zillmann further noted that most media depictions end, or are resolved, in a way that is satisfying to the viewer (e.g., the offender is caught in the end or the main character survives). The arousal from the suspenseful scenes was viewed as carrying over to, and intensifying, the enjoyment of the positive resolution. Thus, according to Zillman, media violence is reinforced.

In contrast, other psychologically based research studies have suggested that the link between media violence consumption and aggression/violence is not a direct causal connection, but instead media violence consumption serves as a moderating factor for individuals who are already inclined toward aggression and violence. In this approach, consumed media violence simply serves as a behavioral cue for aggressive reactions in individuals

who have pre-existing violent thoughts and tendencies. In essence, individual-level differences are the main factor that creates violent responses, and media violence consumption is one of several different conditions that, if present, could trigger a violent reaction. Bushman, for example, found that individuals classified as having a pre-existing aggressive trait (physical aggression) were more drawn to violent depictions than individuals classified as not having such a trait. Additionally, he found that individuals with a pre-existing aggressive trait were more likely to respond aggressively to stimulus after the individual had been shown media violence than when the individual had been shown innocuous media material. This difference was not observed for people who did not have a pre-existing aggressive trait.

Media Consumption and Aggression/ Violence: Meta-Analytical Reviews

Some meta-analytical reviews of the relationship between violent media consumption and subsequent aggression or violence have suggested a link. However, the studies gathered for these meta-analyses were drawn from a body of research that has been heavily criticized. Three areas of criticism are salient to the current review. First, this area of research has been criticized for its failure to account for competing variables that render the relationship between media violence and subsequent aggression spurious. In other words, if a third variable (such as individual traits and exposure to violence in other contexts) were accounted for, the relationship between media violence consumption and subsequent aggression might disappear or be appreciably reduced (Savage & Yancey, 2008). Second, there is a possible file-drawer effect. The file-drawer effect is the argument that the influence of violent media consumption on subsequent behavior in prior research has been overestimated because researchers and journal editors are less likely to publish the results of studies that find no media violence effects; thus, there is a greater likelihood that studies that produce positive findings become part of the knowledge base when drawing conclusions about media violence effects (Ferguson, 2007). Third, this body of research has been criticized for a failure to adequately define and develop reliable, standardized, and valid measures of aggression (Ferguson, 2007).

Some meta-analyses have attempted to address these methodological issues by accounting for them in the study design. A meta-analysis by Christopher Ferguson considered the influence of the file-drawer effect and different methods of measuring aggression on the media consumption effect. The Ferguson meta-analysis focused on 25 different studies of the effects of violent video game play on aggressive behavior, aggressive thoughts, prosocial behavior, and physiological responses. The analysis found that publication bias had a strong influence on the media violence consumption effect sizes for experimental and nonexperimental research that examined media influence on aggressive behavior and aggressive thoughts. Academic journals have a greater tendency to publish studies that are supportive of a media violence effect and such a tendency produces artificially high media violence effect sizes. The Ferguson meta-analysis also produced results suggesting that studies that use less reliable and less standardized measures of aggression produce higher media violence effect sizes. This study offers credence to the notion that a portion of the media violence effects observed in many studies is the result of publication bias and poor conceptualization of aggression.

Media Consumption and Criminal Aggression/ Violence: Meta-Analytical Reviews

As previously suggested, one of the main problems with existing media violence effects research is inconsistent conceptualization of aggression and violence. This is particularly problematic for the field of criminology because not all aggression and violence is condemned and punishable by the criminal justice system; some forms are socially acceptable. Yet many of the published meta-analyses have not adequately distinguished criminal aggression and criminal violence from other forms of aggression and violence. One notable exception is a recently published meta-analysis by Savage and Yancey.

Savage and Yancey's meta-analysis reviewed 26 independent samples from studies that examined the connection between violent media consumption and subsequent criminal aggression. What is most noteworthy about this meta-analysis is that the authors focused much of their analysis on the media violence effect in studies that utilized a control for various psychological traits that serve as predisposing factors toward criminal aggression (or what some criminologists have referred to as self-control variables). They discovered that these studies produced a very small effect size for media consumption. The authors found that when male and female samples were combined, there was no statistically significant difference in levels of criminal aggression between those exposed to a lot of media violence and those exposed to much less media violence. When males and females were separated, there was a statistically significant difference in level of criminal aggression between high consumers of media violence and low consumers of media violence among males, but not females. Even here, however, the effect was very small and the effect was barely significant. Savage and Yancey noted that the effect size for the male sample was likely exaggerated somewhat because many studies failed to control for relevant competing explanatory factors.

Conclusions on the Effects of Violent Media Consumption

Prior to discussing the research on the effects of violent media consumption, it is important to note that firm conclusions are difficult to establish because the prior research has been less than optimal. As Savage and Yancey note, "there is not one study that reports the comparison we would really like to see to satisfy our curiosity about the media violence–criminal aggression relationship" (p. 786). Savage and Yancey also suggested that an adequate study would be one that uses a measure of serious criminal aggression or crime rates as the outcome variable; in terms of predictor variables, they suggested that an optimal study would be one that has a measure of exposure to violent media, an independent rating of violence in the media under consideration, and controls for pre-existing aggressive traits, social economic status, parent education, parental violence, neglect, and intelligence.

At this point, an optimal study does not exist; thus, the best that can be offered are tentative conclusions. The existing research has produced little evidence suggesting a broad, direct link between media consumption and subsequent aggressive or violent behavior that operates through either psychological or physiological mechanisms. The best available scientific research suggests that many of the claims of special interest groups, asserting a strong link between media consumption and crime and aggression, have been exaggerated and that much of the culture beliefs about this link have been socially constructed. However, there is evidence which suggests that certain people (those with pre-existing aggressive or violent tendencies and males) are more susceptible to behavioral reactions triggered by consumption of violent media. More research needs to be done to establish the nature of the relationship.

Kevin G. Buckler and Steve Wilson

See also Bandura, Albert: Social Learning Theory; Gottfredson, Michael R., and Travis Hirschi: Self-Control Theory; Spector, Malcolm, and John I. Kitsuse: Constructing Social Problems

References and Further Readings

American Academy of Pediatrics. (2000). *Joint statement on the impact of entertainment violence on children.* Congressional Public Health Summit, July 26. Retrieved March 5, 2009, from http://www.aap.org/advocacy/releases/jstmtevc.htm

Anderson, C. A., Berkowitz, L., Donnerstein, E., Huesmann, L. R., Johnson, J. D., Linz, D., et al. (2003). The influence of media violence on youth. *Psychological Science in the Public Interest, 4,* 81–110.

Bandura, A. (1973). *Aggression: A social learning analysis.* Englewood Cliffs, NJ: Prentice Hall.

Bandura, A. (1983). Psychological mechanisms of aggression. In R. G. Green & E. I. Donnerstein (Eds.), *Aggression: Theoretical and empirical reviews: Vol. 1. Theoretical and methodological issues* (pp. 1–40). New York: Academic Press.

Bushman, B. J. (1995). Moderating role of trait aggressiveness in the effects of violent media on aggression. *Journal of Personality and Social Psychology, 69,* 950–960.

Bushman, B. J., & Anderson, C. A. (2001). Media violence and the American public: Scientific facts versus media misinformation. *American Psychologist, 56,* 477–489.

Ferguson, C. J. (2007). Evidence for publication bias in video game violence effects literature: A meta-analytic review. *Aggression and Violent Behavior, 12,* 470–482.

Freedman, J. L. (2002). *Media violence and its effect on aggression: Assessing the scientific evidence.* Toronto: University of Toronto Press.

Grossman, D., & DeGaetano, G. (1999). *Stop teaching our kids to kill: A call to action against TV, movie, and video game violence.* New York: Crown.

Hoffner, C. A., & Levine, K. J. (2005). Enjoyment of mediated fright and violence: A meta-analysis. *Media Psychology, 7,* 207–237.

Huesmann, L. R. (1986). Psychological processes promoting the relation between exposure to media violence and aggressive behavior by the viewer. *Journal of Social Issues, 42,* 125–139.

Paik, H., & Comstock, G. (1994). The effects of television violence on antisocial behavior: A meta-analysis. *Communication Research, 24,* 516–546.

Potter, W. J. (2003). *The 11 myths of media violence.* Thousand Oaks, CA: Sage.

Savage, J., & Yancey, C. (2008). The effects of media violence exposure on criminal aggression: A meta-analysis. *Criminal Justice and Behavior, 35,* 772–791.

Sege, R. D. (1998). Life imitating art: Adolescents and television violence. In T. P. Gullotta, G. R. Adams, & R. Montemayor (Eds.), *Delinquent violent youth: Theory and interventions* (pp. 129–143). Thousand Oaks, CA: Sage.

Wood, W., Wong, F. Y., & Chachere, J. G. (1991). Effects of media violence on viewers' aggression in unconstrained social interaction. *Psychological Bulletin, 109,* 371–383.

Zillmann, D. (1996). The psychology of suspense in dramatic exposition. In P. Vorderer, H. J. Wulff, & M. Friedrichsen (Eds.), *Suspense: Conceptualizations, theoretical analyses, and empirical explorations* (pp. 199–231). Mahwah, NJ: Lawrence Erlbaum.

Zillman, D. (1980). Anatomy of suspense. In P. H. Tannenbaum (Ed.), *The entertainment functions of television* (pp. 133–163). Hillsdale, NJ: Lawrence Erlbaum.

MEDNICK, SARNOFF A.: AUTONOMIC NERVOUS SYSTEM (ANS) THEORY

Sarnoff A. Mednick, who received his Ph.D. in psychology from Northwestern University in 1954, is a well-known scholar with a background in sociobiology and methods of learning. Much of his earlier work focuses on how students interact and efficiently comprehend information in class. Since the initial stages of his career, he has promoted interdisciplinary cooperation, especially among the social and biological sciences. It was this multifaceted approach that led him to concentrate on how biological, environmental, and learning traits all were capable of explaining antisocial behavior for certain members of the general population.

Beginning in the 1970s and continuing into the early 1990s, Mednick's research sought out a series of biological and heritable traits that correlated with criminal behavior. It was his intention to bring to the forefront biological facts from his Danish adoption and schizophrenia studies and merge them with positivistic theories of criminal behavior. His focus, as it is for all modern biosocial criminologists, was not to seek out one specific criminal "gene" or "trait" as the Classical School researchers had done, but rather to uncover more generalized genetic anomalies and assess how they relate to antisocial, and more specifically, criminal behavior.

Mednick's Autonomic Nervous System (ANS) Theory of Crime

Original research from Copenhagen in which Mednick was centrally involved prompted him to develop a socio-biological theory of criminal behavior that focuses on physiological characteristics and, most specifically, on the autonomic nervous system (ANS). Briefly, the autonomic nervous system is the regulatory sector of the central nervous system and is largely responsible for controlling arousal and one's ability to adapt to the surrounding environment. Mednick's construct is a "theory which suggests how autonomic nervous system (ANS) responsiveness may play a role in the social learning of law-abiding behavior" (Brennan et al., 1995, p. 84). The ANS theory assumes that law-abiding behavior is a learned trait (Mednick, 1977). Individuals learn to act in a social manner through proper primary caregiver interaction in childhood, most often through their rearing parents. Parental rearing is conjured to teach the child *passive avoidance,* a learned personality trait that acts as a protective factor in the person's decision-making process.

Passive avoidance is a characteristic that does not develop immediately but rather builds upon itself over multiple stages. The first stage occurs when a child commits an aggressive act and is punished for it by the primary caregiver. At a later time, the child will likely be presented with a situation in which that prior action would be of some use to gain something, but instead the child refrains from the act because he or she has been punished before for the same behavior. ANS theory premises that within this contemplation the youth is overcome with a fear of punishment, causing the normal child to be deterred from the action, which dissipates the fear.

The dissipation of fear is crucial to the ANS theory. If a child experiences a very quick reduction in fear of primary caregiver punishment, the person will be rewarded by a swift reinforcement—not being scared anymore, which in turn reinforces the inhibition of antisocial behavior. However, if the youth is incapable of reducing his or her level of fear of punishment quickly, then there is no significant reinforcing element for refraining from the behavior in the future. The implication is that those individuals who are completely incapable of reducing any fear of punishment will have no inhibiting factors that will restrain them from antisocial behavior and thus cannot learn the notion of passive avoidance.

Operant conditioning clearly is at work within Mednick's fear dissipation notion, which reflects on his background in learning. Mednick points out that fear, whether it is fear of punishment or fear for one's life, is a powerful psychological element that operates through the ANS. One is characterized by having a properly functioning ANS if he or she dissipates fear quickly, thus offering an immediate relaxation. Adversely, someone with a slowly recovering ANS is incapable of reducing this fear and is in no way reinforced, leaving the pathway open for future antisocial behavior of this form again.

Mednick also proposes a method through which the ANS construct can be tested—the common polygraph exam. The polygraph test measures three elements: heart rate, blood pressure, and electrodermal conductance (how much electrical current is carried through the skin). The most typical form of measure implemented to test the theory is by utilizing an electrodermal recovery (EDRec) test.

The EDRec is a timed measure that records the length (in fractions of a second) it takes someone to relax after presented with unpleasant stimuli. The procedure of the test typically requires the administrator to place sensors on the ends of one finger of each hand that measure the conductivity of the electrical currents within one's skin. The participant is then asked to relax while initial readings are taken. The subject is then presented with unpleasant stimuli, which ranges from electric shock, as used by D. T. Lykken, to simply a scenario-based recording to which a person listens, as in Mednick's work. Upon the point in the scenario where there should be a release of built-up fear, the diodes record the amount of time it takes the person's skin conductance to reach the normal levels that were present in the relaxed state.

Therefore, one with a quickly recovering EDRec is deemed to have a properly functioning ANS and thus is theorized to not be biologically predisposed to criminal behavior. However, Mednick (1997, p. 4) predicts that the "slower the recovery, the more serious and repetitive the asocial behavior" will become for an individual. Those marked with slow ANS recovery are also deemed to show *hyporesponsiveness*, a term used to indicate that while their ANS levels do return to normal, it takes more time to do so (also termed *half-recovery*).

ANS theory is purported to best explain the behavior of the 1 percent of the general population that is responsible for nearly half of all criminal convictions. It is these chronic recidivists, Mednick argues, that display the most dangerous form of the ANS—one that either is marked by extreme hyporesponsiveness or complete nonresponsiveness. Mednick (1977, p. 1) hypothesizes, "Most offenders are convicted of having perpetrated only one, two or three relatively minor offenses. These offenders are doubtless instigated by socioeconomic and situational forces." However, those individuals that so frequently return to the courtroom are the individuals that this theory is stated to best explain.

Mednick offers an additional distinct claim in the proposal of the ANS theory of crime. While having a slow EDRec does place someone at risk for criminal activity, this trait can be controlled with proper child-rearing, social learning, and environmental factors. With this point emphasized, Mednick claims that a slow EDRec is a heritable trait that is passed along through a faulty ANS. His central assertion is that "criminal fathers would have children with slow EDRec" at a rate much higher than the general population would (Mednick, 1977, p. 5). To test this, as he emphasizes, longitudinal data are needed.

Evidence Regarding ANS Theory

Given that there are several different elements of the ANS theory (EDRec, hereditary transmission, and learning), it can be argued that many different tests of these elements can garner partial support to the construct. However, there have been more direct tests of the theory, typically yielding mixed results. In 1977, Mednick and colleagues tested electrodermal recovery for fathers and their sons in Copenhagen, hypothesizing that a fast EDRec time would serve as a protective factor on the offspring's criminal behavior. Four groups were created, consisting of criminal father/criminal son, noncriminal father/criminal son, criminal father/noncriminal son, and noncriminal father/noncriminal son. Although "the criminality of the sons and fathers is interdependent" (p. 16), the researchers did find that the criminal son/criminal father group was marked by a fast EDRec, except in the lower-middle and middle classes. This left open the possibility that there could have been a spurious relationship through socio-economic status.

Because this 1977 research by Mednick and colleagues had a small sample size in that it was only a pilot study, it was expanded to represent the entire country of Denmark by Mednick and colleagues in 1984. Criminal conviction and hospital records were gathered on a large cohort of adoptees, their adoptive parents, and their biological parents. Interestingly, the strongest concordance in criminality was between the biological parents and their offspring (24.5 percent of children of criminal biological fathers were convicted) and not between adoptive parents and their adopted children (20 percent of children of criminal adoptive parents were convicted). While this difference is somewhat minute, the authors concluded, "Adoptive parent criminality was not found to be associated with a statistically significant increment in the son's criminality, but the effect of biological parent criminality was" (p. 892). This provides support for the ANS construct's claim that criminality could be passed on genetically. Similar results were found by Mednick and colleagues in 1987.

Other studies have provided positive results for the claims of ANS. Bell and colleagues tested ANS's delayed EDRec hypothesis and found that identical twins consistently had stronger correlations in recovery time than fraternal twins did, indicating that there may be a partial genetic factor in the ANS's ability to return to a normal state. However, the ability to generalize this study should be interpreted cautiously because this finding was observed on measurements of the left hand, but not the right hand. A 1981 study by Mednick and colleagues tested brain wave patterns through an electroencephalogram (EEG), a device that measures brain activity through electrodes placed on the occipital, frontal, temporal, and parietal lobes. Testing a cohort of 11-year-olds to predict their criminality 6 years later, researchers found that alpha brain waves, which affect arousal and are produced by the ANS, were significantly slower for children that would become criminally charged. Overall, findings such as these have been replicated across different cultures and in both laboratory and natural settings, thus lending support to the construct.

Critiques of ANS Theory

However, ANS theory is not without its critics. Mednick has recognized this fact throughout his career as he "has been told to burn data which implicate genetic factors among the causes of crime" (Buikhuisen & Mednick, 1988, p. 6). He also notes that "it should be clear that partial genetic causation need not imply pessimism regarding treatment or prevention" (Mednick, 1987, p. 5) but that rather "a number of environmental mediators have been shown to actually protect the biologically at-risk child against long-term deviant or less than optimal outcomes" (Baker & Mednick, 1984, p. 144).

The most prominent academic critics of Mednick's work are Michael Gottfredson and Travis Hirschi. They note that there are multiple methodological problems with Mednick's research that are potentially severe enough to alter findings. For instance, the authors note that the same participants in Mednick's pilot study were also included in his national sample, indicating that the samples are not independent of each other which "is essential to the interpretation of replication research" (Gottfredson & Hirschi, 1990, p. 55).

Another criticism Gottfredson and Hirschi have is that the measures of the independent variables changed from the pilot to the national study. The measure of parental criminality in the pilot was the biological father's police contact and citations, while in the Denmark sample it is measured by biological parents' (mother's and father's) criminal *convictions*. The authors concluded that by adding criminal mothers into the sample for the national data, Mednick's results are inflated to significance when they should not be. Furthermore, they note that studies that Mednick cites as supportive of his work are seriously methodologically flawed (e.g., Cloninger & Gottesman, 1987; Crowe, 1975).

Conclusion

Despite these criticisms, there has been some support garnered for ANS theory. Evidence has been gathered for the construct across nations and in natural and laboratory designs. In adoption studies, the best predictor of an offspring's criminality is whether their biological parents were criminal, which lends support to the construct's claim that a delayed ANS can be passed on intergenerationally. Brain waves generated by the ANS have been shown to be delayed in children that later became criminal, lending additional support to the ANS construct. Further, a delayed EDRec response has also been demonstrated to predict criminality in middle-class populations. Although it does have critics, it appears that a delayed or stunted ANS response could in fact be a predictor of criminal behavior in certain populations. Due to repeated, supportive findings, it appears that this socio-biological construct is of use to the field, as at some level it does seem to be predictive of criminal behavior.

John Boman

See also Fishbein, Diana H.: Biosocial Theory; Neurology and Crime; Psychophysiology and Crime; Wilson, James Q., and Richard J. Herrnstein: Crime and Human Nature

References and Further Readings

Baker, R. L., & Mednick B. R. (1984). *Influences on human development: A longitudinal perspective.* Boston: Kluwer Nijhof Press.

Bell, B., Mednick, S. A., Gottesman, I. I., & Sergeant, J. (1977). Electrodermal parameters in male twins. In S. A. Mednick & K. O. Christiansen (Eds.), *Biosocial bases of criminal behavior* (pp. 217–225). New York: Gardner.

Brennan, P. A., Mednick, S. A., & Volavka, J. (1995). Biomedical factors in crime. In J. Q. Wilson & J. Petersilia (Eds.), *Crime* (pp. 65–90). San Francisco: ICS Press.

Buikhuisen, W., & Mednick, S. A. (1988). The need for an integrative approach in criminology. In W. Buikhuisen & S. A. Mednick (Eds.), *Explaining criminal behavior: Interdisciplinary approaches* (pp. 3–7). Leiden, the Netherlands: Brill.

Cloninger, R., & Gottesman, I. (1987) Genetic and environmental factors in antisocial behavior disorders. In S. A. Mednick, T. E. Moffitt, & S. Stack (Eds.), *The causes of crime: New biological approaches* (pp. 92–109). Cambridge, UK: Cambridge University Press.

Crowe, R. (1975). Adoptive study of psychopathy: Preliminary results from arrest records and psychiatric hospital records. In R. Fieve, D. Rosenthal, & H. Brill (Eds.), *Genetic research in psychiatry* (pp. 95–103). Baltimore: Johns Hopkins University Press.

Gabrielli, Jr., W. F., & Mednick, S. A. (1983). Genetic correlates of criminal behavior: Implications for research, attribution, and prevention. *American Behavioral Scientist, 27,* 59–74.

Gottfredson, M. R., & Hirschi, T. (1990). *A general theory of crime.* Stanford, CA: Stanford University Press.

Lykken, D. T. (1957). A study of anxiety in the sociopathic personality. *Journal of Abnormal and Social Psychology, 55,* 6–10.

Mednick, S. A. (1964). *Learning.* Englewood Cliffs, NJ: Prentice Hall.

Mednick, S. A. (1977). A biosocial theory of the learning of law-abiding behavior. In S. A. Mednick & K. O. Christiansen (Eds.), *Biosocial bases of criminal behavior* (pp. 1–8). New York: Gardner.

Mednick, S. A. (1987). Introduction: Biological factors in crime causation: The reactions of social scientists. In S. A. Mednick, T. E. Moffitt, & S. Stack (Eds.), *The causes of crime: New biological approaches* (pp. 1–6). New York: Cambridge University Press.

Mednick, S. A., Gabrielli, W. F., & Hutchings, B. (1984). Genetic influences in criminal convictions: Evidence from an adoption cohort. *Science, 224,* 891–894.

Mednick, S. A., Gabrielli, Jr., W. F., & Hutchings, B. (1987). Genetic factors in the etiology of criminal behavior. In S. A. Mednick, T. E. Moffitt, & S. A. Stack (Eds.), *The causes of crime: New biological approaches* (pp. 74–91). New York: Cambridge University Press.

Mednick, S. A., Kirkegaard-Sorensen, L., Hutchings, B., Knop, J., Rosenberg, R., & Schulsinger, F. (1977). An example of biosocial interaction research: The interplay of socioenvironmental and individual factors in the etiology of criminal behavior. In S. A. Mednick & K. O. Christiansen (Eds.), *Biosocial bases of criminal behavior* (pp. 9–23). New York: Gardner.

Mednick, S. A., & Mednick, M. T. (1965). *The associative basis of the creative process* (University of Michigan Cooperative Research Project No. 1073). Ann Arbor: University of Michigan.

Mednick, S. A., & Volavka, J. (1980). Biology and crime. In N. Morris & M. H. Tonry (Eds.), *Crime and justice: A review of research* (Vol. 2, pp. 85–158). Chicago: University of Chicago Press.

Mednick, S. A., Volavka, J., Gabrielli, W. F., Jr., & Itil, T. M. (1981). EEG as a predictor of antisocial behavior. *Criminology, 19*, 219–229.

MENTAL ILLNESS AND CRIME

According to Doris James and Lauren Glaze, over half of the inmates in state prisons and local jails manifest symptoms of mental illness. Specifically, 56 percent of state prison inmates have exhibited symptoms of mental illness within the past year, compared to 45 percent of federal prison inmates and 64 percent of local jail inmates. For female inmates, the rates are even higher. Signs of mental illness were reported for 61 percent of federal female inmates, and 73 percent of state female inmates. These statistics are imperative to understand when one examines the connection between mental illness and crime. Mental illness is an important part of the criminal justice system. The empirical relationship between mental illness and crime, particularly violent offending, has been documented through numerous empirical studies.

This entry assesses the relationship between mental illness and crime through a variety of facets. First, this entry examines mental illness as a criminogenic factor, specifically reviewing some of the empirical studies that have connected mental illness and criminal behavior. Within this section, the theoretical implications of mental illness, particularly as it applies to women, are also considered. Second, this entry then examines how each part of

the criminal justice system—the police, courts, and correctional system—have been affected by mental illness. It also conveys some of the ways that these different parts of the system are coping with mental illness and the challenges that it often presents.

Mental Illness as a Criminogenic Risk Factor

People have assumed for quite some time that there is a link between mental illness and crime. This is documented through decades of public opinion research. Historically, empirical findings have been mixed, with some studies showing no relationship and others showing a small significant correlation. Upon review of the research, it seems that little to no empirical relationship was documented between mental illness and crime or violence until the 1990s. A variety of researchers have since examined this issue in more detail, and most research does support a relationship between mental illness and criminal behavior or violence. Many believe that the results were mixed for so long due to methodological issues with the research that have since been able to be addressed. This section addresses some of the research with regard to the empirical relationship between mental illness and crime, as well as explores some of the theoretical implications of this relationship.

James Bonta, Moira Law, and Karl Hanson conducted a meta-analysis that focused on mentally disordered offenders. These are offenders that suffer from a mental illness and that engaged in some type of behavior that triggered the involvement of the criminal justice system. Bonta et al. examined several individual risk factors for both general and violent recidivism among mentally disordered offenders. With regard to general recidivism, they found that psychosis had effect sizes ranging from −.03 to .06, mood disorders had effect sizes that ranged from −.09 to .01, and antisocial personality disorder had effect sizes that ranged from .11 to .19. The results were similar for violent recidivism, where effect sizes for psychosis ranged from −.07 to −.01, mood disorders effect sizes ranged from −.04 to .06, and antisocial personality disorder effect sizes ranged from .13 to .23. While the effects of psychosis and mood disorders were not found to be statistically significant for either general or violent recidivism, antisocial personality disorder was a robust predictor in both categories. This finding is not surprising when examining the literature with regard to individual risk factors for crime. Don Andrews and Bonta consider antisocial personality disorder to be one of the Big Four predictors of criminal behavior. Bonta et al. also compared the results from this study featuring mentally disordered offenders to another study for nondisordered offenders and found that the results were nearly identical. This held for both general and violent recidivism.

In 2009, Kevin Douglas, Laura Guy, and Stephen Hart conducted another meta-analysis focusing strictly on the relationship between psychosis and violent behavior. According to Douglas et al., "psychosis is a syndrome found in mental disorders such as schizophrenia, delusional disorders, bipolar mood disorder, and some forms of severe depression. This syndrome comprises symptoms reflecting profound disturbances in thought, perception, and behavior" (p. 681). Douglas et al. were concerned about the relationship between psychosis and violence; they only considered violence—whether it be actual, attempted, or threatened—to another person or persons and not self-harm. This meta-analysis consisted of 885 effect sizes from 204 studies of 166 independent data sets. The results indicated that "psychosis was reliably associated with a 49 percent to 68 percent increased likelihood of violence" (p. 692). The average effect size for psychosis ranged from .12 to .16, which is comparable to the findings of antisocial personality disorder and other individual risk factors in Bonta et al.'s meta-analysis of mentally disordered offenders.

While meta-analyses help provide an overall analysis of study results, individual study results are also important to analyze. Eric Silver, Richard Felson, and Matthew Vaneseltine conducted a retrospective longitudinal study examining whether inmates who were formally treated for mental health problems were more likely to be convicted of violent offenses. Particularly, Silver et al. were interested in the relationship between mental illness and conviction of violent crimes such as assault and homicide, which are violent crimes that are typically associated with mental illness. Silver et al. found that the mentally disordered offenders included in the study were more likely to engage in assaultive violence and sexual offenses than in property offenses. This relationship

strengthened even more when they examined individuals who had received mental health services both prior to prison and while in prison. However, while there was a stronger relationship hypothesized, it was also suggested that because these individuals had received mental health treatment both prior to and in prison, they may present more severe symptomology than some of the other mentally ill offenders. Silver et al.'s study was an important contribution to the literature because it showed that mentally ill offenders not only are more likely to engage in violent criminal behavior, but also that they are more likely to engage in sexual criminal behavior.

A number of research studies have also sought to examine the theoretical relationship between mentally ill offenders and violent acts or criminal behavior. Silver (2006) argues that while there has been a documented relationship between mental illness and criminal behavior, particularly violent behavior, there is a lack of a causal mechanism in place. He asserts that the same criminological theories that apply in the general population can also be examined to understand why mentally ill offenders engage in violent behavior. This thought is empirically supported by Bonta et al.'s meta-analysis which showed that the individual risk factors for both general and violent recidivism were nearly identical for general offenders and mentally disordered offenders. Silver argues that the following theories can provide theoretical support for the relationship between mental illness and crime: Ronald Akers's social learning theory, Robert Agnew's general strain theory, Travis Hirschi's social bond theory, Robert Sampson and John Laub's age-graded theory of crime, Marcus Felson's rational choice theory, and Clifford Shaw and Henry McKay's social disorganization theory. While Silver argues that the theoretical support for mental illness and crime can be found in these theories, there is little to no empirical testing of these ideas, which he asserts is an area for future research.

While there is little traditional criminological theory research with regard to mental illness and crime, this topic has been addressed in the growing criminological pathway research for crime with women. Emily Salisbury and Patricia Van Voorhis conducted a quantitative empirical study examining the pathways to offending for women. They examined three different causal models as they

relate to prison admission for women on probation. First, they examined the childhood victimization model, which assumes that the effects of child
abuse and the onset of mental illness occur prior to
the onset of substance abuse. The second model
examined was the relational model. Notably, this
"model temporally begins with intimate relationship dysfunction, which is hypothesized to lead to
reduced levels of self-efficacy and greater likelihood of adult victimization, followed by struggles
with depression/anxiety, and substance abuse"
(p. 546). Their third model was the social and
human capital model, which "investigates how
women's social relationships (with intimate others
and family) produce human capital (educational
achievement, self-efficacy, and fewer employment/
financial needs) to create opportunities to desist
from criminal activity" (p. 547).

Using path analysis, Salisbury and Van Voorhis
found statistical support for all three models. This
study thus highlights the importance of mental illness with regard to women offenders. While it has
been linked to criminal offending and violent
behavior in a variety of empirical studies, the
causal relationship is often unknown. Salisbury
and Van Voorhis are able to articulate the importance of mental illness as a causal relationship
leading to further criminal behavior, particularly
for women. Qualitative research has asserted for
quite some time that mental illness was an important trigger of criminal behavior for women; however, there had been very little quantitative data to
back this idea up. Salisbury and Van Voorhis were
able to demonstrate the theoretical importance of
mental illness as it applies to women.

Mental Illness and the Police

While contacts with the mentally ill make up 7 to
10 percent of all police-citizen encounters, they
take up a significant amount of time. According to
James Janik, mentally ill offenders are most likely
to be arrested because they are engaging in some
type of behavior that is harmful to themselves,
which is not necessarily criminal in nature. When
mentally ill offenders do engage in criminal activity, it is most likely to be of the misdemeanant
nature. Janik notes that they are typically trying to
fulfill some type of personal need. However, mentally ill offenders tend to respond very poorly to

the assertion of authority by the police, and this
can cause a situation that can quickly escalate,
sometimes resulting in physical altercations involving minor offenses. Janik asserts that this easy
escalation of situations may be why the mentally ill
population is more frequently arrested for these
minor offenses compared to individuals who are
not mentally ill. In fact, a 2004 study by Allison
Redlich found that individuals exhibiting signs of
mental illness were 67 times more likely to be
arrested compared to offenders without mental illness for similar offenses.

Due to the special situations that can arise when
dealing with mentally ill offenders, it is often suggested that police officers should receive special
training regarding this population. However, in a
survey conducted by Martha Deane, Henry
Steadman, Randy Borum, Bonita Veysey, and
Joseph Morrissey involving 174 police departments
in cities with populations of 100,000 or more, over
half of the departments (55 percent) had no specialized response for dealing with mentally ill offenders.
In a national survey of police departments, Judy
Hails and Randy Borum found that training hours
dedicated to mentally ill offenders varied from 0 to
41, with the median number of hours being 6.5
(mean = 9.16; mode = 4). However, many departments stated that these hours also included training
on substance abuse and dealing with disorderly and/
or unruly suspects. Conversely, while a minimal
amount of time is sometimes dedicated to training
the entire force, Hails and Borum reported that 32
percent of the departments surveyed had a specialized response for calls that involved mentally ill
individuals. Therefore, while some departments
may not be providing the 16 hours of training on
mentally ill offenders recommended by the Police
Executive Research Forum, specialized units have
been developed in some, which could account for
the lower number of training hours.

As one can see, mentally ill offenders pose a
significant problem for members of the police
force. While they typically are committing minor
offenses, they make up a large percentage of our
nation's jail population. There are several possible
explanations for this phenomenon, which include
the fact that the police are minimally trained to
deal with mentally ill offenders. Second, mentally
ill offenders often agitate the situation which in
turn leads to arrest, and third, many police officers

have limited resources within the community or police department available at their disposal. Mentally ill offenders make up a substantial portion of the criminal population; therefore, it is important to understand some of the obstacles that are faced by the police when dealing with this specialized population.

Mental Illness and the Court System

Once mentally ill offenders enter the court system, historically there was little that could be done. Court officials were often left to attempt to handle mentally ill offenders with very few disposition alternatives or treatment options. However, since the 1990s there has been an emergence of mental health courts in the United States, which can sometimes be used as a diversion program for mentally ill offenders. In 1997, there were just a handful of mental health courts across the United States. Now, the popularity of these courts as an alternative to dealing with mentally ill offenders is growing rapidly. In 2005 and 2006, several researchers (e.g., Redlich et al. and Steadman et al.) estimated that there were more than 100 mental health courts nationwide. Mental health courts were modeled after drug courts and have several distinctive factors. First, there is a separate court docket for all mentally ill offenders in the mental health court. Second, there will be one judge that will preside over the mental health court from the initial hearing through the final disposition. Third, mental health courts require that there be both prosecutors and defense attorneys that are dedicated to the mental health court as they are both vital components. Fourth, both criminal justice officials and mental health professionals work together to form a nonadversarial team approach. Fifth, participation in mental health courts must be voluntary. The defendant has to agree not only to participate in the mental health court, but also in all necessary treatment and services. Sixth, there must be constant monitoring by all of the officials involved in the mental health court. Finally, in order for mental health courts to work, there must either be dismissal of charges (if a pre-adjudication model is followed) or avoidance of incarceration (if a post-adjudication model is followed). This last point is important because it provides a motivator for the individual to complete the mental health court.

Mental health courts provide an important way of dealing with mentally ill individuals through the court system in the United States. As previously stated, many mentally ill offenders are charged with minor offenses, and they will continue to engage in these offenses if the mental illness is not treated. Mental health courts provide a way of addressing the reason that many of these offenders are engaging in criminal behavior. They also may mandate treatment in an effective manner. Individuals who participate in mental health courts are encouraged and rewarded for their continued participation in treatment, while still being closely monitored. Although mental health courts are still a relatively new phenomenon in the United States, Marlee Moore and Virginia Aldigé Hiday's research has indicated that individuals who participate in these courts are less likely to recidivate than offenders who receive traditional penalties. Recidivism statistics have also examined individuals who successfully completed mental health courts compared to those who did not, and findings reveal that both groups have lower recidivism rates, with individuals who successfully completed mental health courts having the lowest rates.

Mental health courts seem to be a promising area regarding court diversion for mentally ill offenders. As discussed earlier, mentally ill offenders make up a significant portion of our incarcerated population, and mental health courts provide a potential way to adequately deal with this population in an effective manner. As funding and research increases in this area, it is expected that this will become a more popular way to deal with this special population.

Mental Illness and the Correctional System

Once mentally ill offenders make it into the correctional system, there are sometimes few options that are available. This causes both the correctional system and mentally ill offenders to suffer unnecessarily. Mentally ill offenders who end up in the correctional system have few treatment options available to them, and correctional officials are often left with very few management alternatives. Because of the large number of mentally ill individuals who are incarcerated throughout the country, institutions are often overwhelmed with the number of individuals who need services and unable to provide adequate services for all of these individuals, according to James and Glaze. While diversion programs, such as mental health courts, help to alleviate the burden on the correctional system, they are still relatively new in nature and limited in availability. However, while options in the correctional field may be limited, there are a number of court cases that have helped establish the right to treatment for mentally ill offenders. In 1977, *Bowring v. Godwin* asserted that prisoners' right to treatment for physical ailments also included psychiatric conditions. In 1980 this was further extended by *Ruiz v. Estelle*, which established that prisons must meet minimal standards of mental health care for all prison inmates. However, although the Supreme Court has asserted that minimum standards of care must be established for prison inmates, this does not always extend to individuals who are on parole or probation.

Various research studies have found that mentally ill offenders have a much higher rate of recidivism following release from prison when compared to non-mentally ill offenders, especially within the first year. Mentally ill offenders are also significantly more likely to be hospitalized within the first year following release from prison. Because of high recidivism rates among mentally ill offenders, correctional officials are faced with unique challenges. While services may be mandated within prison (although minimal in nature), they are not mandated once the inmate is released. Parole supervision can help make sure that individuals are required to continue with mental health treatment through their parole rules and regulations; however, according to Arthur Lurigio, parolees often face unique challenges when trying to gain access to mental health treatment. Many mental health treatment facilities are hesitant to accept individuals who have previously been incarcerated and may deny them treatment. In addition, there is a large presence of co-morbidity within mental health individuals in the criminal justice system. That is, many offenders not only have mental health issues but also have substance abuse issues—a fact that may disqualify many of them from available mental health treatment.

Because of the variety of issues that mentally ill inmates are subject to upon release, detailed re-entry plans are crucial to their continued success in the community, according to Nancy Wolff et al. When reentry programs are successfully put into place, this ensures continued and stable treatment for the mentally ill offender that is crucial with regard to minimizing the potential for relapse. Along with minimizing the potential for relapse, the potential for recidivism also decreases. The Criminal Justice/Mental Health Consensus Project Report highlights the importance for reentry plans for all mentally ill offenders. The Report calls for the inclusion of an "individualized written pre-release plan, provision of a temporary supply of medications for those inmates receiving medication, referrals and linkages to appropriate community mental health providers, and assistance in obtaining necessary financial benefits and housing" (Wolff et al., 2005, p. 25). This reentry plan helps to maximize the success of mentally ill offenders in the community.

Mentally ill individuals in the correctional system are subject to special challenges. While some level of care is mandated in prisons, it is often difficult to enforce in the community. Many of these individuals also face special challenges, especially related to co-morbidity. Although the correctional system is much more likely to have individuals trained to deal with mentally ill offenders, they are still limited by their potential resources. For this reason and many more, it is imperative to have detailed reentry plans for mentally ill offenders prior to release.

Conclusion

This entry has provided a brief overview of the empirical research connecting mental illness to crime and how mentally ill offenders affect each part of the criminal justice system. As this entry has demonstrated, there is an empirical relationship between mental illness and crime, particularly violent crime. This relationship is important not only from an empirical standpoint but also from a theoretical standpoint. While the idea of how the relationship between mental illness and crime can be explained through many of our current criminological theories is still being examined, there has been a documented theoretical relationship between mental illness and future criminal activity with women. Although female inmates may make up a small part of the criminal justice population, as the statistics indicate, mental illness is extremely prevalent within this population.

Mentally ill offenders make up a large part of the criminal justice population. However, the criminal justice system is still struggling with how to deal with this population. Typically, police officers receive little training with regard to mentally ill offenders, and this often leads to higher arrest rates for minor offenses. Once individuals enter the court system, there is often little that the court system can offer, unless there are diversion programs present. The development of mental health courts across the United States has helped to offer more successful alternatives for dealing with mentally ill offenders. However, the problems that mentally ill offenders face also continue into the correctional system. Offenders must receive a minimum level of treatment in prison, but it is often difficult for them to secure treatment services in the community. These challenges are areas that the criminal justice system will have to continue to work on as the understanding of the mentally ill population grows. However, what is important to remember is that this specialized population constitutes a large part of the criminal justice population. Therefore, it is imperative that we find successful ways of dealing with these offenders throughout all the stages of the criminal justice system.

Catherine M. Arnold

See also Alcohol and Violence; Bandura, Albert: Social Learning Theory; Cognitive Theories of Crime; Hare, Robert D.: Psychopathy and Crime; Schizophrenia and Crime

References and Further Readings

Andrews, D. A., & Bonta, J. (2003). *The psychology of criminal conduct* (3rd ed.). Cincinnati, OH: Anderson.

Bonta, J., Law, M., & Hanson, K. (1998). The prediction of criminal and violent recidivism among mentally disordered offenders: A meta-analysis. *Psychological Bulletin, 123*, 123–142.

Deane, M. W., Steadman, H. J., Borum, R., Veysey, B. M., & Morrissey, J. P. (1999). Emerging partnerships between mental health and law enforcement. *Psychiatric Services, 50*, 99–101.

Douglas, K. S., Guy, L. S., & Hart, S. D. (2009). Psychosis as a risk factor for violence to others: A meta-analysis. *Psychological Bulletin, 135*, 679–706.

Hails, J., & Borum, R. (2003). Police training and specialized approaches to respond to people with mental illness. *Crime and Delinquency, 49*, 52–61.

James, D. J., & Glaze, L. E. (2006). *Mental health problems of prison and jail inmates.* Washington, DC: Bureau of Justice Statistics, U.S. Department of Justice.

Janik, J. (1992). Dealing with mentally ill offenders. *FBI Law Enforcement Bulletin, 61*(7), 22–26.

Lovell, D., Gagliardi, G. J., & Peterson, P. D. (2002). Recidivism and use of services among persons with mental illness after release from prison. *Psychiatric Services, 53*, 1290–1296.

Lurigio, A. J. (2001). Effective services for parolees with mental illnesses. *Crime and Delinquency, 47*, 446–461.

Moore, M. E., & Hiday, V. A. (2006). Mental health court outcomes: A comparison of re-arrest and re-arrest severity between mental health court and traditional court participants. *Law and Human Behavior, 30*, 659–674.

Police Executive Research Forum. (1997). *The police response to people with mental illness: Trainers guide.* Washington, DC: Author.

Redlich, A. (2004). Mental illness, police interrogations, and the potential for false confession. *Psychiatric Services, 55*, 19–21.

Redlich, A. D., Steadman, H. J., Monahan, J., Robbins, P. C., & Petrila, J. (2006). Patterns of practice in mental health courts: A national survey. *Law and Human Behavior, 30*, 347–362.

Salisbury, E. J., & Van Voorhis, P. (2009). Gendered pathways: A quantitative investigation of women probationers' paths to incarceration. *Criminal Justice and Behavior, 36*, 541–566.

Silver, E. (2006). Understanding the relationship between mental disorder and violence: The need for a criminological perspective. *Law and Human Behavior, 30*, 685–706.

Silver, E., Felson, R. B., & Vaneseltine, M. (2008). The relationship between mental health problems and violence among criminal offenders. *Criminal Justice and Behavior, 35*, 405–426.

Steadman, H. J., Redlich, A. D., Griffin, P., Petrila, J., & Monahan, J. (2005). From referral to disposition: Case processing in seven mental health courts. *Behavioral Sciences and the Law, 23*, 215–226.

Wells, W., & Schafer, J. A. (2006). Officer perceptions of police responses to persons with a mental illness. *Policing, 29*, 578–601.

Wolff, N., Bjerklie, J. R., & Maschi, T. (2005). Reentry planning for mentally disordered inmates: A social investment perspective. *Journal of Offender Rehabilitation, 41*, 21–42.

MERTON, ROBERT K.: SOCIAL STRUCTURE AND ANOMIE

Robert K. Merton was one of the most distinguished and influential sociologists of the 20th century. Throughout his career, he was a leading figure in the sociology of science, and he made substantial contributions to general sociological theory by developing the paradigm of structural analysis. In the field of criminology, Merton is best known for advancing and popularizing the *anomie perspective* on crime. This perspective highlights the ways in which the normal features of the social organization of American society ironically contribute to high levels of crime and other forms of deviant behavior by producing anomie, a breakdown in the culture. This anomie or cultural breakdown is characterized by a very strong emphasis on the importance of success goals (especially monetary success) and a comparatively weak emphasis on the importance of using the normatively approved means to achieve these goals. Merton further argues that such a strain toward anomie arises when the culture encourages virtually everyone to aspire to lofty goals, while those located at the lower ends of the class hierarchy have limited access to the legitimate means for success. People in such circumstances experience pressures to "innovate"—that is, to substitute technically expedient but often illegal means in the pursuit of their goals.

Merton introduced his initial formulation of the anomie perspective in a brief article titled "Social Structure and Anomie," which was published in the *American Sociological Review* in 1938. He was a little-known instructor at Harvard University at the time, and his article did not create much of a stir at first. This would change dramatically. Over the course of subsequent decades, Merton's arguments as introduced in the initial article and as subsequently elaborated, most significantly in his book *Social Theory and Social Structure*, have inspired an extraordinary volume of empirical studies on crime and deviance, as well as numerous theoretical extensions, exegeses, and critiques. Recently Robert Agnew has attempted to build on Merton's work by explicating more fully the ways in which social

psychological experiences of "strain" link adverse social conditions with crime and delinquency, while Steven Messner and Richard Rosenfeld have highlighted the role of imbalances among major social institutions (economy, family, the polity) in generating anomie. In addition, Merton's ideas about the sociological causes of crime and delinquency have had a profound influence well beyond the academic community. His ideas have informed major policy initiatives that seek to prevent crime by enhancing job opportunities and by providing social services, such as those associated with the Great Society in the 1960s. Moreover, much contemporary discourse about the role inequality of opportunity as a cause of crime continues to be rooted in insights that are traceable to "Social Structure and Anomie."

Social Structure and Anomie and Sociological Theory

Merton's paradigm of social structure and anomie—commonly referred to by Merton and scholars generally by its acronym, SS&A—has a deceptive simplicity surrounding it. As the information scientist Eugene Garfield has observed, much of Merton's work seems "so transparently true that one can't imagine why no one else has bothered to point it out" (quoted in Kaufman, 2003). This quality of Merton's scholarship is attributable in large measure to his mastery of the English language. Merton had the ability to write clear, engaging prose, free of "opaque," "confusing," and "pompous jargon" (Holton, 2004, p. 515). As a result, core elements of his theorizing are easily discerned by the general reader, and they can be summarized quite succinctly, as presented above. However, SS&A can be read at multiple levels. At one level, Merton offers a concise, incisive description of American culture and suggests a few rather straightforward propositions about the relationship between social class position and crime. At a deeper level, SS&A represents an attempt to apply "general theorizing in sociology" to the "specialized theorizing in criminology" (Merton, 1997, p. 518). Indeed, the various themes developed in SS&A cohere into a highly sophisticated sociological analysis of the interconnections between the social organization of society and levels of crime and other forms of deviant behavior, and of the ways individuals make choices among socially structured alternatives.

To appreciate Merton's arguments, it is useful to locate his work in intellectual context. SS&A falls within the more general tradition associated with a founding figure in sociology—Émile Durkheim—who introduced the concept of "anomie" to the sociological community, most prominently in his analyses of suicide. Durkheim assumed that humans have no natural limits on their desires. As a result, people cannot possibly be satisfied in the absence of some type of external restraint. Social norms provide this external restraint by circumscribing the goals that can be legitimately aspired to. Levels of suicide are likely to increase when norms weaken and fail to fulfill this critical function, a condition which Durkheim referred to as anomie. Merton appropriates Durkheim's concept of anomie, reinterprets its meaning somewhat, and places it prominently in the title of his essay.

Merton also shares an overarching objective that motivated much of Durkheim's theorizing. Merton intends to develop a distinctively *sociological* explanation for crime and deviance to serve as an alternative to psychological, and particularly Freudian, explanations that emphasize instinctual impulses and that were popular at the time. In so doing, Merton is essentially making the case for sociology as a scientific discipline that offers a unique perspective on human behavior. The questions addressed in SS&A are thus quintessentially sociological in nature. In Merton's words,

> For whatever the role of biological impulses, there still remains the further question of why it is that the frequency of deviant behavior varies within different social structures and how it happens that the deviations have different shapes and patterns in different social structures. . . . Our perspective is sociological. We look at variations in the rates of deviant behavior, not at its incidence. (1968, pp. 185–186)

Given the nature of the questions under examination, Merton quite naturally turns to sociological concepts to look for the answers. He adopts the general approach in sociology referred to as structural/functionalism and conceptualizes society in terms of a social system. According to this approach, any social system can be described with reference to two fundamental properties: its culture (or culture structure) and its social structure.

Merton does not provide rigorous definitions of either culture structure or social structure in SS&A, but he clarifies their meaning while formulating his explanation for deviant behavior. The key elements of the culture structure are the prescribed goals (or ends) of action and the normatively approved (or institutionalized) means for realizing these goals. The other component of social organization—social structure—refers to patterned social relationships. To illustrate the application of these basic conceptual tools of sociology to the explanation of deviant behavior, Merton focuses his analytic lens on one particular social system—the social system prevalent in the United States in the 1930s. The distinguishing feature of this social system, according to Merton, is *malintegration*—intrinsic tensions between core features of the system. Such malintegration is manifested in two ways: (1) between the main components of the culture and (2) between the culture and the social structure. With respect to the culture, the priority awarded to goals and means is out of balance. The cultural emphasis on the pursuit of goals is exceptionally strong, especially the emphasis on the goal of monetary success. Comparatively less emphasis is placed on the importance of using the institutionalized means to realize these goals. Instead, societal members tend to be governed mainly by "efficiency" norms in the selection of means. People are prone to use whatever means are technically expedient in striving to reach their goals, regardless of whether these means are socially approved of or not. These twin features of culture—the strong emphasis on monetary success goals and the weak emphasis on normative means—are part of the dominant cultural ethos of the society; they are at the heart of the American Dream. Moreover, for Merton (1964, p. 226), the breakdown in the culture associated with the American Dream constitutes the essence of anomie or normlessness: "when a high degree of anomie has set in, the rules once governing conduct have lost their savor and their force."

The second sense in which the social system in the United States exhibits malintegration involves the interrelationships between culture and social structure. Merton underscores the extent to which the cultural goals in American society are universalistic;

they apply to everyone. However, social structure distributes access to the normatively approved means differentially. This is where social class comes into the picture. Opportunities to reach the cultural success goals through legitimate means vary by class position. Specifically, those in the lower classes are not awarded the same chances as those in the higher classes to pursue success in the acceptable ways. It is precisely this disjuncture between features of social structure (inequality of opportunity rooted in the class system) and elements of culture (universal success goals) that undermines the integrity of the culture and leads to anomie. To quote Merton,

> the social structure strains the cultural values, making action in accord with them readily possible for those occupying certain statuses within the society and difficult or impossible for others. The social structure acts as a barrier or as an open door to the acting out of cultural mandates. When the cultural and the social structure are malintegrated, the first calling for behavior and attitudes which the second precludes, there is a strain toward the breakdown of norms, toward normlessness. (1968, pp. 216–217)

Having laid out his analysis of how features of the organization of society can create strains toward anomie, Merton proceeds to consider the ways in which individual actors might respond to their social environment. He sets forth the logical possibilities in the form of a typology of modes of individual adaptation. The respective types are determined by the actor's acceptance of (signified by +) or rejection of (signified by –) the cultural goals and institutionalized means. His types include conformity (+ +), innovation (+ –), ritualism (– +), retreatism (– –), and rebellion (+/– +/–).

The most common mode of adaptation is that of conformity. The actor accepts both the cultural goals and the institutionalized means for pursuing these goals despite any malintegration of the society. Merton maintains that this type of adaptation is actually quite common. If it were not, society would cease to exist in any meaningful sense. The second mode of adaptation is innovation. The innovator aspires to the culturally prescribed goals, especially the goal of accumulating wealth, but is willing to use whatever means are expedient to realize these goals. The applicability of this mode of

adaptation to criminal behavior is readily apparent, given that illegal means (e.g., robbery, theft, drug dealing) may be highly expedient. In the third mode of adaptation, ritualism, the actor abandons the cultural goals but nevertheless continues to adhere to the institutionalized means, essentially "going through the motions." An example would be the low-level bureaucrat who has given up on any chance to rise through the ranks but who nevertheless compulsively follows the rules of the workplace. The retreatist mode of adaptation, in contrast, entails the rejection of both the goals and the institutionalized means. The person adapting in this fashion essentially drops out of society. Drug abuse, alcoholism, and vagrancy are examples of retreatism. Finally, the adaptation of rebellion involves not only rejecting the goals and means of the existing social order but also replacing them with a new set of goals and means. Rebellion constitutes an effort to change the cultural and social structures of society rather than to accommodate to them.

Merton indicates that the likelihood that someone will adapt in a designated way is socially structured, although his account of the linkages is not always very clear. His most explicit and plausible arguments, and those that have generated the most interest in criminology, pertain to innovation. Given that members of the lower classes are confronted most directly with the harsh realities of inequality of opportunity, it is reasonable to anticipate that they will be especially prone to turn to illegitimate means (i.e., to innovate) as they pursue the common cultural goal of monetary success and accompanying high social status. These arguments further imply that rates of criminal behavior should tend to vary inversely with social class position.

In sum, Merton uses the conceptual building blocks of general sociological theory to formulate an original and provocative explanation for the social structuring of crime and other forms of deviant behavior. His explanation is radically sociological in the sense that it is cast in terms of the basic properties of social systems and their interconnections rather than individual propensities. High rates of deviant behavior can be traced to anomie, a cultural imbalance in the emphasis on goals versus means. This cultural imbalance is itself generated by a system disjuncture—an intrinsic incompatibility between goals that are universalistic and inequality in the opportunity to realize these goals. In addition, Merton develops the sociological insight that while people are capable of adapting in varying ways to the social environment, they do so by choosing among socially structured alternatives. Criminal behavior understood as innovation is thus a perfectly understandable (if undesirable) response for those who occupy positions in the social structure where the opportunities to use the legitimate means are limited. The rates of crime should accordingly be comparatively high among the disadvantaged social classes.

Subcultural Extensions

SS&A explains how normal features of the social structure can exert pressures toward crime and other forms of deviant behavior, and the accompanying typology of the modes of individual adaptation sets forth a logically coherent and concise schema for describing possible responses. However, as scholars such as Ian Taylor, Paul Walton, and Jock Young have noted, SS&A does not offer a clear or compelling account of the determinants of *specific* adaptations. For example, assuming comparable exposure to a strain toward anomie, why might people choose the retreatist rather than the ritualist adaptation? There is also a curious sense in which the adaptation to structural pressures is depicted in highly individualistic terms in SS&A, despite Merton's commitment to advancing a sociological explanation for deviant behavior. As Marshall Clinard has observed, it is almost as if each individual confronts and responds to structural pressures in isolation.

Two particularly noteworthy efforts to overcome this limitation of SS&A appeared in the mid-1950s and in 1960—Albert Cohen's *Delinquent Boys: The Culture of the Gang*, and Richard Cloward and Lloyd Ohlin's *Delinquency and Opportunity: A Theory of Delinquent Gangs*. Both works synthesize elements of Merton's anomie perspective with insights about subcultural dynamics. In addition, both scholarly developments grew out of personal contacts with Merton, reflecting what Merton (1997) called their shared "cognitive microenvironments." Cohen had been exposed to lectures on SS&A when he was an undergraduate at Harvard in a course taught by Merton. Cloward wrote his doctoral dissertation under Merton's direction at Columbia.

As indicated in the title of his work, Cohen's primary analytic focus is on explaining juvenile delinquency. He begins with a basic "psychogenic" assumption about motivation, namely, that "all human action—not delinquency alone—is an ongoing series of efforts to solve problems" (p. 50). Cohen further reasons that problems are not distributed randomly. Instead, persons similarly located in the social class system find themselves confronting similar problems. When such persons have effective interaction with others, they tend to develop subcultures as solutions to their shared problems.

Cohen proposes that members of the working class, and especially working-class boys, confront a basic status problem in American society. The dominant values in the culture are those of the middle class, and these are the values that govern the prevailing standards for achievement. In Cohen's words, all youths are judged according to middle-class "measuring rods." Yet working-class boys tend not to fare very well when these measuring rods are applied to them. Following in the spirit of SS&A, Cohen accepts the basic premise that class position determines opportunities. The middle-class home is simply better equipped to train the child to compete for status according to the prevailing standards (p. 94).

Cohen outlines several possible subcultural solutions, but the most important one for understanding juvenile delinquency is the delinquent subculture. The delinquent subculture solves the status problem that is experienced by working-class boys when they are judged by middle-class measuring rods by "providing criteria of status which these children *can* meet" (p. 121, emphasis in the original). These standards of status in the delinquent subculture bear an ironic relationship to middle-class standards—they essentially represent an inversion of middle-class values. "The delinquent conduct is right, by the standards of [the] subculture, precisely *because* it is wrong by the norms of the larger culture" (p. 28, emphasis in the original).

Drawing loosely on psychoanalytic theory, Cohen suggests that the delinquent subculture can thus be understood as a collective reaction formation on the part of working-class boys. These youths have been socialized into middle-class values, and yet they seek to escape the status problems that would result were they to acknowledge the legitimacy of these values by embracing a value system that seems to affirm the opposite. These complex socio-psychological and subcultural dynamics help makes sense out of the peculiar quality of much delinquent activity which, according to Cohen, is "non-utilitarian, malicious, and negativistic" in character rather than rational and goal directed (p. 25).

The other classic subcultural extension of SS&A is Cloward and Ohlin's differential opportunity theory, which is also directed toward explaining juvenile delinquency. Following in the spirit of Cohen, the authors take as their point of departure the premise that delinquency is best understood as a collective, subcultural solution to shared problems. They also remain faithful to the general logic of SS&A by accepting the basic assumption that in American society, members of the lower classes are confronted with structural barriers to achieving the cultural goals of success. The pressures for delinquent behavior can ultimately be traced to problems of adjustment resulting from these unequal opportunities associated with social class position.

Cloward and Ohlin's most distinctive contribution is to expand the conceptualization of opportunity structures by incorporating and building on insights associated with the classic Chicago School in criminology. Whereas Merton directs attention to lack of access to opportunities for achievement in the realm of legitimate activities, Cloward and Ohlin observe that the performance of illegitimate acts also depends on opportunities. They propose that "each individual occupies a position in both legitimate and illegitimate opportunity structures" (p. 150). The collective, subcultural responses to problems of adjustment will accordingly reflect the illegitimate opportunities that are available in the social environment.

Cloward and Ohlin identify three common types of delinquent subcultures that are likely to emerge in disadvantaged areas of large cities: a criminal subculture, a conflict subculture, and a retreatist subculture. The criminal subculture is oriented toward criminal values and the pursuit of material gain through illegal means. The conflict subculture regards the use of violence as the currency of respect and status. The retreatist subculture is characterized by withdrawal from society through the consumption of drugs. The likelihood that the respective subcultures will emerge and persist depends on the available learning and performance structures in the social environment— that is, on the illegitimate as well as the legitimate opportunity structures.

Empirical Assessments and Critiques

The anomie perspective as represented in SS&A and in the subcultural extensions stimulated a large volume of research in the middle decades of the 20th century. The perspective was applied to a variety of forms of deviant behavior, including not only crime and delinquency but also mental disorders, drug addiction, and alcoholism. Some researchers attempted to develop measures of anomie based on indicators of social structural conditions, whereas others directed their efforts to measuring the subjective experience of being in environments with high levels of anomie (this subjective condition was often referred to as anomia). The results of this research failed to support anomie theory in many instances which, combined with theoretical critiques, led to its gradual decline in influence through the 1970s and early 1980s. The perspective has subsequently enjoyed a reversal in fortunes, as scholars have responded to and challenged earlier criticisms.

With respect to theoretical concerns, critics raised questions about the adequacy of Merton's basic conceptual framework and the plausibility of underlying assumptions. Some, such as Edwin Lemert, expressed skepticism that a clear line can be drawn between cultural and social structure in concrete analyses of social phenomena, while others, such as Ruth Rosner Kornhauser, questioned the view that there is in fact a value consensus in American society about the importance of the goal of monetary success. Scholars sympathetic to Merton's approach responded to the latter of these criticisms of SS&A by arguing that the critique is based on an oversimplified rendering of its thesis. Merton does not propose that monetary success is the only success goal. Rather, the proposition at the heart of SS&A is that monetary success enjoys a position of special prominence in the hierarchy of goals in the United States.

With respect to empirical critiques, a good deal of research focused on the commonly derived prediction of an inverse relationship between social class and crime. Interestingly, Merton himself rejected the notion that the validity of his theory depended on an inverse relationship between social class and crime, as he reported in a personal interview with Francis Cullen and Steven Messner. Merton observed that the paradigm of SS&A could explain fraud among scientists who, blocked from much-cherished professional status, sought to innovate by publishing fabricated data. Still, because of his emphasis on differential access to success goals across the class structure, Merton's theory was seen as predicting high rates of crime and deviance among the disadvantaged.

In this regard, an association between neighborhood levels of disadvantage and officially recorded rates of crime and delinquency had been well documented in the early decades of the 20th century by researchers in the Chicago School. The validity of this relationship, however, was questioned in the 1950s as criminologists began to move away from the use of official crime data in favor of the newly developed self-report methodology. In self-report studies, samples of respondents, usually juveniles, are presented with questionnaire items asking about involvement in various forms of criminal and delinquent behavior. Analyses based on self-reported offending typically detected little or no relationship with social class. This led Charles Tittle et al. to conclude in an influential study that the widely held view that crime and delinquency are concentrated in the lower classes is a "myth."

Other researchers urged caution in dismissing a class/crime relationship on conceptual and methodological grounds. One of the limitations of self-report studies is that they typically measure relatively minor forms of offending, especially self-report studies that are focused on juvenile delinquency. The domain of behavior in these studies thus differs from that represented in the official crime statistics, which record very serious offenses (along with some relatively minor offenses). Research that encompassed the more serious forms of illegal behavior in the measurement of self-reported offending tended to find relationships between social class and crime that were more similar to those reported in studies based on official data. A second issue involved the nature of the relationship between social class and crime. Some researchers proposed that high levels of offending

are likely to be observed only among those at the very bottom of the social class hierarchy, and if so, standard socioeconomic status measures that cover the entire range of social classes might fail to detect much of an association because they do not focus on the strategic population. Studies using measures that differentiate the highly disadvantaged from others revealed evidence consistent with the expected association between class and offending.

As noted by J. Robert Lilly et al., critics of the efforts to extend SS&A by incorporating subcultural dynamics have questioned the adequacy of the description of delinquent subcultures. Cohen's claim that the delinquent subculture is oriented toward "non-utilitarian, malicious, and negativistic" activities was criticized as being an exaggerated portrayal. While some delinquent activity reflects these qualities, much delinquency is in fact utilitarian and goal directed. Similarly, Cloward and Ohlin's typology of criminal, conflict, and retreatist subcultures was faulted for implying a degree of specialization that is at odds with reality. Delinquents are typically much more versatile, engaging in activities that cut across the respective subcultural types. As a result of these criticisms, few contemporary criminologists regard the typologies of Cohen and Cloward and Ohlin as faithful descriptions of most delinquent gangs, although there is still considerable appreciation for their accounts of the social processes underlying the formation and persistence of youth subcultures.

A considerable body of literature also accumulated on a social psychological implication derived from SS&A. Researchers formulated an analytic framework to assess strain theory, which was considered to be the individual-level analogue to the social structural arguments advanced by Merton. The principal hypothesis examined was that a perceived discrepancy between aspirations and expectations should be related to levels of offending. More specifically, individuals who aspire to lofty goals but who expect that actual achievements will fall short of these goals should experience strain and exhibit a high degree of criminal and delinquent involvement. Numerous studies implemented this analytic strategy, with results that were often interpreted as being non-supportive of strain theory. However, other researchers identified methodological limitations of these studies and offered more favorable assessments of the accumulated evidence.

Legacy

The renewed interest in the anomie perspective in the late 1980s and early 1990s has led to concerted efforts to refine and elaborate key insights originally put forth in SS&A. At the social psychological level, Robert Agnew has formulated a general strain theory, which enumerates the wide range of sources of strain and identifies conditions that affect the expression of strain in criminal or noncriminal ways. At the macro-level, Steven Messner and Richard Rosenfeld have proposed an institutional-anomie theory, which postulates that anomie and high rates of crime are likely when the institutional structure of society is out of balance, specifically, when the economy tends to take priority over non-economic institutions. These theories are still relatively young and their impact on criminology remains to be determined, but they have stimulated a growing body of empirical research and commentary. In addition, recent efforts to conduct rigorous assessments of Merton's "classic" version of anomie have provided some suggestive support.

Reflecting on the legacy of SS&A in the field of criminology, one cannot help but be impressed by its adaptability and resiliency. Merton often referred to the "evolving" character of SS&A, and the perspective has indeed evolved appreciably over time. Merton himself continued to revise and refine his arguments in response to critical commentary. Others sympathetic to his approach to understanding crime and to sociological theorizing more generally have picked up the baton as well. To be sure, SS&A has been subjected to intense scrutiny and legitimate criticism over the years. Moreover, many contemporary criminologists disagree with specific arguments put forth by Merton. It is nevertheless fair to say that the core insights of SS&A have inspired the sociological imagination of generations of scholars, and this distinctive approach to explaining crime and other forms of deviant behavior continues to enjoy a "living presence" in the discipline at the onset of the 21st century.

Steven F. Messner

See also Agnew, Robert: General Strain Theory; Cloward, Richard A.: The Theory of Illegitimate Means; Cloward, Richard A., and Lloyd E. Ohlin: Delinquency and Opportunity; Cohen, Albert K.: Delinquent Boys; Durkheim, Émile: Anomie and Suicide; Messner, Steven F., and Richard Rosenfeld: Institutional-Anomie Theory

References and Further Readings

Agnew, R. (2006). General strain theory: Recent developments and directions for further research. In F. T. Cullen, J. P. Wright, & K. R. Blevins (Eds.), *Taking stock: The status of criminological theory* (Advances in Criminological Theory: Vol. 15, pp. 101–123). New Brunswick, NJ: Transaction.

Agnew, R. (2006). *Pressured into crime: An overview of general strain theory.* Los Angeles: Roxbury.

Akers, R., & Sellers, S. S. (2004). *Criminological theories: Introduction, evaluation, and application* (4th ed.). Los Angeles: Roxbury.

Baumer, E. P., & Gustafson, R. (2007). Social organization and instrumental crime: Assessing the empirical validity of classic and contemporary anomie theories. *Criminology, 45,* 617–663.

Burton, V. S., Jr., & Cullen, F. T. (1992). The empirical status of strain theory. *Journal of Crime and Justice, 15*(2), 1–30.

Clinard, M. B. (1964). The theoretical implications of anomie and deviant behavior. In M. B. Clinard (Ed.), *Anomie and deviant behavior* (pp. 1–56). New York: Free Press.

Cloward, R. A., & Ohlin, L. E. (1960). *Delinquency and opportunity: A theory of delinquent gangs.* New York: Free Press.

Cohen, A. K. (1955). *Delinquent boys: The culture of the gang.* New York: Free Press.

Cullen, F. T., & Messner, S. F. (2007). The making of criminology revisited: An oral history of Merton's anomie paradigm. *Theoretical Criminology, 11,* 5–37.

Durkehim, É. (1966 [1897]). *Suicide: A study in sociology.* New York: Free Press.

Holton, G. (2004). Robert K. Merton. *Proceedings of the American Philosophical Society, 148,* 506–517.

Kaufman, M. T. (2003, February 23). Robert K. Merton, versatile sociologist and father of the focus group, dies at 92. *The New York Times.* Retrieved October 22, 2008, from http://www.nytimes.com/2003/02/24/nyregion/robert-k-merton-versatile-sociologist-and-father-of-the-focus-group-dies-at-92.html?pagewanted=1

Kornhauser, R. R. (1978). *Social sources of delinquency: An appraisal of analytic models.* Chicago: University of Chicago Press.

Lemert, E. M. (1964). Social structure, social control, and deviation. In M. B. Clinard (Ed.), *Anomie and deviant behavior* (pp. 57–97). New York: Free Press.

Lilly, J. R., Cullen, F. T., & Ball, R. A. (2007). *Criminological theory: Context and consequences* (4th ed.). Thousand Oaks, CA: Sage.

Merton, R. K. (1938). Social structure and anomie. *American Sociological Review, 3,* 672–682.

Merton, R. K. (1964). Anomie, anomia, and social interaction: Contexts of deviant behavior. In M. B. Clinard (Ed.), *Anomie and deviant behavior* (pp. 213–242). New York: Free Press.

Merton, R. K. (1968). *Social theory and social structure.* New York: Free Press.

Merton, R. K. (1997). On the evolving synthesis of differential association and anomie theory: A perspective from the sociology of science. *Criminology, 35,* 517–525.

Messner, S. F., & Rosenfeld, R. (2006). The present and future of institutional-anomie theory. In F. T. Cullen, J. P. Wright, & K. R. Blevins (Eds.), *Taking stock: The status of criminological theory* (Advances in Criminological Theory: Vol. 15, pp. 127–148). New Brunswick, NJ: Transaction.

Messner, S. F., & Rosenfeld, R. (2007). *Crime and the American dream* (4th ed.). Belmont, CA: Thomson Wadsworth.

Stinchcombe, A. L. (1975). Merton's theory of social structure. In L. A. Coser (Ed.), *The idea of social structure: Papers in honor of Robert K. Merton* (pp. 11–33). New York: Harcourt Brace Jovanovich.

Taylor, I., Walton, P., & Young, J. (1973). *The new criminology: For a social theory of deviance.* New York: Harper & Row.

Tittle, C. R., Villemez. W. J., & Smith, D. A. (1978). The myth of social class and criminality: An empirical assessment of the evidence. *American Sociological Review, 43,* 643–656.

MESSERSCHMIDT, JAMES W.: MASCULINITIES AND CRIME

Gender is one of the most stable and pronounced demographic associations with criminality. Men commit the vast majority of most crimes, especially serious crimes. In hindsight, one may wonder why a book placing men's crimes and criminality in the context of their lives *as men* did not appear until 1993. After all, much criminology was done with all-male samples by male researchers. Yet the gendered (or sexed) nature of crime was taken for granted. While some early scholars examined social and cultural structures that would be linked to masculinities concerns by later researchers (e.g., Walter Miller's focal concerns or Albert Cohen's status frustration), at the time they were presented in an a-gendered fashion. As feminist criminology developed in the 1970s, the problem of women's and girls' offending became central for the first time. Early feminist criminologists attacked the discipline as either ignoring the existence of female crime and criminality or dismissing it in stereotypical ways. It took seriously a project of measuring and explaining crimes by women and girls, developing into a theoretically rich and empirically diverse subfield. Women's crime and justice experiences were typically explained by placing women's lived experiences in a gendered context. The next logical step was the application of gender theory to men's lives and offending.

Masculinities and Crime

In *Masculinities and Crime*, James Messerschmidt presents a solid review and critique of existing feminist and criminological theory. He not only takes criminology to task for failing to adequately deal with issues of gender, but he also critiques existing feminist theories for their failures as well (both in and out of a criminological context). He offers up as an alternative to these problematic interpretations his own *theory of structured action* (later a book on its own). Structured action is predicated on two central critiques presented in the book, as well as from Messerschmidt's prior book, *Capitalism, Patriarchy and Crime*. The first emphasis is on what is now often referred to as intersectionality: the idea that "it is necessary to make relevant theoretical links among class, gender and race *without* surrendering to some type of separate systems approach" (1993, p. 62, emphasis added). Clearly all three of these aspects of social structure influence a person's experiences and behavior. But to look only at one and exclude the others means that essential information is missed.

Socialist feminism downplayed race and gender, looking to class systems to explain women's experiences of inequity. Radical feminism, with its sole focus on patriarchy, missed how class systems influence gender inequity. Similarly, emergent black feminists like Patricia Hill Collins and bell hooks criticized feminism for ignoring race and ethnicity.

Structured action theory shows that while each of these elements may vary independently of each other, they work together to create a social context in which social actors perceive, interpret, and project their own actions and the actions of others. All three are important elements in their own right but do not come together without intermixing their effects.

The second foundation is the realization that these structures arise and are replicated through social actors and their actions. This idea comes from sociological symbolic interactionism. For much of the 20th century, social theory had trouble linking two of its main objects of study. At the macro level, sociologists explored how social forces shaped the experiences of various groups in society. Others examined individual-level experiences of social actors and how people interacted with their most immediate social environments and stimuli to produce behavior. Decision making and perception were key foci of this social psychology. Yet, conceptually, these two realms of study were rarely linked together to show how these macro-level forces were working on individual-level perceptions and actions. A strain of sociological thought began developing in the 1960s and 1970s, and was more fully realized in the 1980s and 1990s (in part, due to structured action theory), that resolved this problem by suggesting that individuals cannot exist outside of social structure and social structure does not exist without its (re)creation as embodied in behavior. As Messerschmidt puts it, "social actors maintain and change social structures within any particular interaction, and those social structures simultaneously enable and constrain social action" (1993, p. 63). Conceptually, action and structure are fused together in a dialectical dance of cross-influence. Macro-level forces and trends shape the environments that social actors live in and gain information and other inputs from. Such experiences are internalized and influenced by an individual's specific experiences and worldview. From there, the person acts. Acting in a given way creates patterns of behavior that shape an environment, which is then perceived by other social actors, shaping their behavior, and so on.

In exploring this set of postulates, Messerschmidt brings together numerous strands of work done within symbolic interactionism generally and feminist studies specifically. He draws heavily upon the work of Erving Goffman and Harold Garfinkle,

establishing the mutually reinforcing nature of structure and action. He also explicitly draws on the work of Candace West and others on gender performance. Simply, West and numerous colleagues over the years have demonstrated that individuals enact gender performances based upon their perceptions of audience expectations. As a person is socialized into a set of gender expectations, they enact (or do not) those scripts when in a social situation. This is *doing gender*—the process of conforming one's behavior to a set of specific gender expectations. This view of gendered behavior and relations breaks us conceptually out of the narrow confines of sex role theory (especially the representation of gender as two opposite set of "choices" for behavior). A lifetime of lived experiences composes an individual's gender scripts, whose enactment will vary in various interactions based upon specific audience expectations. Establishing the performative nature of gender is essential to understanding the link between masculinities and crime.

The result of this theoretical situation is the realization that "crime by men is a form of social practice invoked as a resource, when other resources are unavailable, for accomplishing masculinity" (1993, p. 85). To understand male crime one must place that crime commission in the broader context of social life and capital attainment. Men do crime to do masculinity. The enactment of crime becomes a way for men to "do gender." For example, responding to a perceived threat or slight with violence (or even the threat thereof) is a way for men to demonstrate independence, control, and toughness, all key elements of masculinities in most societies. Further, Messerschmidt points out, that the very root of these conflicts often involves masculinity and masculine capital. Terming these interactions "masculinity challenges" in later work, Messerschmidt argues that the reason slights and threats require response is the tentative nature of masculinity and masculine reputations. While femininity is often assumed or bestowed upon women, men have to earn their masculinity in the eyes of others. If presented with a social interaction potentially involving the loss of face (which is almost any interaction), men may find that they have to guard their reputations from others. The core of conflicts are between social actors who are both trying to gain and maintain masculine capital. Violence is a way to do masculinity as it simultaneously

(1) establishes one's ability to draw upon those assets of human bodies and behavior that are typically regarded as masculine (i.e., toughness, strength, courage); (2) prevents one from losing "maleness" in the eyes of one's peers, which would occur if a challenge were ignored; and (3) establishes dominance and power over the other party in the conflict, if successful, through victory. Such an explanation has been frequently used to discuss the gender gap in lethal and non-lethal violence. Men are more likely than women to get into violent disputes and men's disputes (compared with women's) are more likely to cause serious injury or death to combatants. This is a major contribution to understanding the interlinkage of masculinity and crime. However, there is one more theoretical layer to Messerschmidt's structured action theory.

There is no monolithic masculinity or femininity— there is no single way to do masculinity or to do femininity. Men's behavioral performances and demands vary within various structural locations. To explain this variation, Messerschmidt calls on the work of R. W. Connell on hegemony and variations of masculinity. Conceptualizing gender roles and relations as being centrally about power, Connell notes that gender positions are defined not only by what they are but also in opposition to what they are not. Masculinity is defined by femininity and vice versa. Further, within any given social context, there will be plural masculinities and femininities. Connell identifies hegemonic masculinity as the most desired and most empowered form of masculinity within a social milieu. Hegemonic masculinity defines itself in relation to femininities but also in relation to subordinate masculinities. Subordinate masculinities are those ways of being male that are denigrated and unvalued within a social context. The base realization here is that men not only oppress women to maintain their positions of power, but they also oppress other men. Sexuality is an excellent example. Most hegemonic masculinities are compulsorily heterosexual. Heterosexual activity becomes a central way of proving one's maleness. Similarly, heterosexual masculinity is empowered through the denigration and oppression of homosexuality and bisexuality, with men engaging in these acts being typically defined (and treated) as weak and effeminate. This proposition reconnects us with intersectionality and structured action theory is fully laid out. To understand any behavior,

but especially criminal behavior, one must place that behavior squarely within the social interactional context and place social actors within the broader and immediate frames of reference.

Messerschmidt establishes that not only is masculinity constructed in relation to social position and in relation to femininity but also in relation to other masculinities relevant in the social milieu. White men will do masculinity different from black men. Upper-class men do masculinity differently from working-class men. Within each of these intersected milieu, there are several options for masculinity enactment, with general social pressures (and thus social actors) placing greater value upon hegemonic forms of masculinity than subordinate forms. Just as masculinity varies between social contexts, it varies within social contexts. Establishing dominance through, say, success in sports (i.e., "jock" masculinity) is only meaningful when situated in opposition to another masculinity within the same context (i.e., "nerd" masculinity). Social capital can only be gained in interactions through displaying heterosexual sexual conquest if it can be contrasted with others who lack that capital, say, male virgins or homosexuals.

This theoretical positioning allows Messerschmidt to show us that men within certain social positions use crime as a sign of masculinity accomplishment. But because the nature and demands of a specific masculinity depend on the distinct interaction of structural location and social actor performances, men do crimes differently to do masculinities differently. That becomes the central focus of chapter 4 ("'Boys Will Be Boys'—Differently") and chapter 5 ("Varieties of 'Real Men'") of the book, both of which have been widely excerpted and anthologized. Typically, a reader on crime includes an edited version of either of these chapters in their section on gender and crime. They also appear ubiquitously in readers focused on gender and crime, as well as in general books directed at sociology and gender studies courses.

These two chapters explore how varying social contexts—racial and class-based—produce the impulses to crime in the boys and men which inhabit them. Chapter 4 provides discussions of how race and class intersect in the lives of adolescents to produce a wide variety of criminal behavior ranging from street robbery, to gang membership and violence, to petty theft and delinquency to gang rape. Chapter 5 provides focused case studies on specific environments and their ties to crime: urban streetlife subculture and the production of both the pimp and the "badass," workplaces and the production of theft and sexual harassment, and corporate culture and the production of corporate crimes. The value here is not only in the narrowed discussions of specific milieu but the broad scope of discussions. Men dominate almost all crimes, from petty street theft to corporate crimes and crimes of nation-states. In these two chapters, Messerschmidt shows how structured action theory can explain all of these behaviors (something very few other theories of crime can do).

His final chapter of the book goes beyond crime commission to the process of criminalization itself. Through exploring the influence of gender and gendered politics on the behaviors of the state, Messerschmidt explores how masculine dominance and world views within governments and other public institutions shape social control endeavors. His gendered analysis of the regulation of child labor, female sexual "morality," and the nature and functioning of policing and police work highlight that structured action theory is also amenable to the other concerns which arise in the field of criminology—law making and implementation.

Legacy

Landmark as it was, *Masculinities and Crime*, and the ideas within, took time to gain currency within the field, even within a feminist criminology focused on gender issues. In part, this was due to broader tensions and ambivalences within feminist academia overall about gendering the study of men. The field had created itself through critiquing academe's patriarchal biases and was not terribly quick to return to studies focused on men as it could serve to remarginalize the study of women and women's experiences. With the exception of a handful of publications (e.g., a special issue in *The British Journal of Criminology* [Volume 36, issue 3, 1996] and Tim Newburn and Elizabeth Stanko's edited volume on masculinity and crime published in 1994), the idea of exploring the gendered nature of men's crimes was ignored. For example, Kathleen Daly's contribution to Michael Tonry's 1998 *Handbook of Crime and Justice* contained a single paragraph on issues of masculinities and crime,

spending half of it suggesting that studying men's crimes as gendered was a return to the discipline's gender blindness. It was not until Jody Miller and Christopher Mullins's chapter in the 15th volume of the Advances in Criminological Theory series that a survey article either on feminist criminology or upon gender and crime contained a substantial section devoted to the issues of masculinities.

Messerschmidt has continued to elaborate both theoretically and empirically upon the core ideas he presented in this work. Two later books, *Nine Lives* and *Flesh and Blood* not only expand the nuances of structured action theory (e.g., through incorporation of other advances in feminist theory like attention to bodies and bodality) but do so within an empirical context. Both books are grounded in life-history interviews, which allows for complex and situated explorations of how individual social actors' lived experiences and world views show an intersection of situated gender accomplishment and criminality. It also allows for richer development of the theory overall and the refinement that empirical research always brings.

Others have also taken their cue from this book, producing a burgeoning criminology of men as gendered social actors. Little in the way of quantitative work has appeared testing the core theory discussed here, in part due to the difficulties of quantified operationalization of central concepts. However, qualitative researchers have expanded the project laid out here. Many interview and ethnographic based studies have drawn either directly or indirectly on structured action theory to examine the intersection of masculinities and crime by focusing on specific crimes or specific contexts. These works have examined different masculinities in different contexts, showing the richness and wide applicability of Messerschmidt's work. Less has been done with white-collar crime and masculinity; in part this is due to the marginalized nature of white-collar crime studies, but it is also a function of obtaining appropriate data.

Christopher W. Mullins

See also Miller, Jody: Gendered Criminal Opportunity; Miller, Jody: Gendered Social Organization Theory; Steffensmeier, Darrell J.: Organization Properties and Sex Segregation in the Underworld; Steffensmeier, Darrell J., and Emilie Andersen Allan: A Gendered Theory of Offending

References and Further Readings

Connell, R. W. (1995). *Masculinities*. Berkeley: University of California Press.

Connell, R. W. (2002). *Gender*. Cambridge, UK: Polity Press.

Daly, K. (1998). Gender, crime and criminology. In M. Tonry (Ed.), *The handbook of crime and punishment* (pp. 85–108). Oxford, UK: Oxford University Press.

Groombridge, N. (1998). Masculinities and crimes against the environment. *Theoretical Criminology, 2,* 249–267.

Messerschmidt, J. (1993). *Masculinities and crime: Critique and reconceptualization of theory*. Lanham, MD: Rowman & Littlefield.

Messerschmidt, J. (1997). *Crime as structured action: Gender, race, class and crime in the making*. Thousand Oaks, CA: Sage.

Messerschmidt, J. (2000). *Nine lives: Adolescent masculinities, the body, and violence*. Boulder, CO: Westview Press.

Messerschmidt, J. (2004). *Flesh and blood: Adolescent gender diversity and violence*. Lanham, MD: Rowman & Littlefield.

Miller, J., & Mullins, C. W. (2006). Taking stock: The status of feminist theories in criminology. In F. T. Cullen, J. P. Wright, & K. R. Blevins (Eds.), *Taking stock: The status of criminological theory* (Advances in Criminological Theory: Vol. 15, pp. 217–249). New Brunswick, NJ: Transaction.

Mullins, C. W. (2006). *Holding your square: Masculinities, streetlife and violence*. Cullompton, Devon, UK: Willan.

Mullins, C. W., Wright, R. T., & Jacobs, B. A. (2004). Gender, streetlife, and criminal retaliation. *Criminology, 42,* 911–940.

Newburn, T., & Stanko, E. (Eds.). (1994). *Just boys doing business? Men, masculinities and crime*. London: Routledge.

MESSNER, STEVEN F., AND RICHARD ROSENFELD: INSTITUTIONAL-ANOMIE THEORY

It is a well-established fact that crime is substantially more prevalent in some societies than others. Why? What can explain this pattern? These basic questions have stimulated a significant body of criminological theory and research over the past several centuries, and it is the central question to which *institutional-anomie theory* is directed. Institutional-anomie theory refers to a theoretical argument developed by Steven F. Messner and Richard Rosenfeld to account for variation in levels of serious crime across nations and, in particular, to explain why rates of acquisitive crime (e.g., robbery) and lethal violence are especially high in America. Messner and Rosenfeld outlined their explanation in the first edition of *Crime and the American Dream* and elaborated on some of the implications of their argument in subsequent editions of the book. This argument has become widely referenced in the literature as institutional-anomie theory or IAT.

Institutional-anomie theory builds on Robert Merton's classic anomie theory and posits that rates of serious crime, especially robbery and homicide, will be highest in nations characterized both by a cultural imbalance in which there is a strong cultural emphasis on pursuing monetary success goals and weak cultural emphasis on using only legitimate means to pursue such goals, and by an institutional imbalance whereby economic institutions dominate other social institutions in various ways and limit their ability to regulate behavior. In this entry, the origins, core argument, and empirical status of IAT are outlined in more detail. The first section provides a general overview of the components of Merton's anomie theory that are central to IAT. Subsequent sections focus on Messner and Rosenfeld's description of the nature and sources of the cultural orientation they label the American Dream, how this cultural makeup can increase levels of serious crime, and the role that the institutional balance of power plays in the process. The closing sections summarize the state of the existing empirical evidence related to IAT and outline some issues that require additional attention in future scholarship.

Merton's Anomie Theory

The foundation of IAT rests on the shoulders of Merton's anomie theory. Merton's anomie theory is quite general in scope and open to alternative interpretations, but most observers acknowledge that Merton's theoretical argument implies that levels of instrumental crime will likely be higher in societies in which there is a particular type of cultural imbalance, namely a relatively strong cultural emphasis placed on the importance of pursuing monetary success goals and a relatively weak cultural emphasis placed on the importance of using only legitimate means of pursuing monetary success goals. Importantly, Merton noted that the criminogenic tendencies of this type of cultural imbalance are likely to be contingent on individual adaptations to cultural conditions (i.e., whether or not members of society accept or reject cultural messages) and on the distribution of legitimate opportunities for pursuing monetary success goals.

The cultural imbalance highlighted by Merton is also central to Messner and Rosenfeld's IAT. Like Merton, Messner and Rosenfeld suggest that American culture places significant value on material success goals while not emphasizing strongly normative limits on how such goals should be pursued, and they argue that this cultural imbalance is one of the keys to understanding why America tends to exhibit particularly high rates of serious crime, especially robbery and homicide. But Messner and Rosenfeld also extend Merton's theory by integrating ideas from Émile Durkheim, Talcott Parsons, Karl Polanyi, and Karl Marx about the nature, interrelationships, and functioning of various social institutions in taming the criminogenic tendencies of a weakly regulated American Dream.

Messner and Rosenfeld (2007, p. 68) define the American Dream as "a commitment to the goal of material success, to be pursued by everyone in society, under conditions of open, individual competition." They argue that the highly universal cultural orientation that accompanies the American Dream defines personal worth largely in terms of achievement and success in the accumulation of money and wealth, places a high degree of esteem on individual (especially economic) accomplishments, and places relatively little emphasis on the importance of how such accomplishments are realized. Messner and Rosenfeld note that these cultural values have been prominent in America since at least the early 1900s, and are one of the by-products of the distinctive form of capitalism that had emerged in America in the previous century. In essence, American capitalism developed in a context in which noneconomic social institutions were not highly developed, thus giving rise to an imbalanced institutional structure in which economic institutions and imperatives dominated and diluted other institutions (e.g., the family, polity, and schools) and the socialization and social control functions they tend to play in society. According to Messner and Rosenfeld, the dominance of the economy in the institutional sphere and the distinctive value orientations of the American Dream are mutually reinforcing and, together, form a recipe for high levels of serious crime in America.

The American Dream, Anomie, Institutional Imbalance, and Rates of Serious Crime

Messner and Rosenfeld (2007) document in *Crime and the American Dream* that there are substantial differences across nations in the number of homicides and robberies per capita, and that America has exceptionally high rates of both of these crimes. IAT is a general account of why some nations exhibit higher rates of serious crime than others, and specifically why America is "exceptional" with respect to levels of serious crime. Messner and Rosenfeld are quick to point out that the hallmarks of the American Dream—a universal achievement orientation in which individual success is defined largely in terms of the accumulation of money—have yielded a variety of innovations in society. But, as Merton also alluded to, they note that the American Dream can yield some undesirable outcomes as well, including high levels of serious crime. In essence, the American Dream represents a distinctive form of cultural imbalance where the pursuit of economic success goals and realization of economic achievement are strongly valued and encouraged while at the same time there is a relatively weak emphasis on the importance of using legitimate means to satisfy those cultural prescriptions (i.e., high levels of anomie). As Messner and Rosenfeld put it, "The cultural stimulation of criminal motivations derives from the distinctive content of the American Dream." And, "at the same time, the American Dream does not contain within it strong injunctions against substituting more effective, illegitimate means for less effective, legitimate means in the pursuit of monetary success" (2007, p. 84). In essence, they suggest that the cultural values underpinning the American Dream strongly encourage members of society to pursue and achieve monetary success goals through the most expedient means possible.

The anomic cultural imbalance that embodies the American Dream is central to IAT, but according to Messner and Rosenfeld it does not full account for why rates of serious crime in America are exceptionally high. Rather, like Merton, they see the social structure as highly important for shaping the ways in which people respond to the cultural milieu. In many ways, Messner and Rosenfeld provide a much more detailed explication of the social structure than Merton, but they also largely omit from early articulations of their arguments a discussion of the dimension of social structure that is central to Merton's thesis: the stratification system. As Jón Gunnar Bernburg points out, "Messner and Rosenfeld ignore Merton's insight on the role of the unequal distribution of people's objective conditions in translating the anomic ethic into crime and deviant behavior" (p. 738). Messner and Rosenfeld (2006, 2007) have recently acknowledged this omission, and they suggest that integrating it into their theoretical model would yield a more complete explanation. Despite the limited attention they give to the legitimate opportunity structure, though, Messner and Rosenfeld (1994, 2007) integrate ideas from Parsons, Marx, Durkheim, and Polanyi to highlight the potential role that social institutions can play in regulating behavior generally and in countering or mitigating the anomic cultural pressures toward criminal behavior specifically.

Messner and Rosenfeld emphasize the relative strength of economic, political, educational, and familial institutions in the United States, and they suggest that the balance of power between these institutions is both a consequence of and a contributor to the prevailing cultural structure. Perhaps not surprisingly, the institutional arrangement that has accompanied the cultural structure of the American Dream is one in which the economy is particularly dominant, and familial, educational, and political institutions are relatively weak. Building on Parsons's notion that social systems are composed of interrelated social institutions, Marx's insights about how such systems often contain fundamental conflicts between institutions, and Polanyi's arguments about the importance of providing institutionalized protections from the free market economy, Messner and Rosenfeld embed in their anomie theory of crime a significant role for the institutional balance of power.

They highlight the importance of the social institutions of the polity, the family, and education for providing social control over behavior and, specifically, for taming the intense anomic pressures to pursue economic imperatives that are part and parcel to the American cultural structure. In theory, when these social institutions are strong and coordinated, they can play vital roles in regulating behavior both by contributing to and reinforcing the prevailing normative cultural structure and by providing roles that expose people to social controls and social supports. As Messner and Rosenfeld see it, however, the long-standing reality in America is that the dominance of the economy in the institutional structure not only provides an everlasting fuel for the American Dream, but also serves to handcuff the ability of other social institutions to tame the dark side of this cultural prescription (i.e., intense pressure to pursue, and achieve at any cost, visible signs of economic success). The relatively quick and intense development of capitalism in America in a context in which noneconomic social institutions were still evolving and not well prepared to compete with economic institutions set the stage, they say, for an institutional imbalance in which economic norms penetrate other (noneconomic) institutional domains, and in which the independent functions and roles of these other institutions are devalued and increasingly diluted to accommodate economic roles and functions.

Messner and Rosenfeld (2007) provide several examples of how the dominance of the economy in the American institutional sphere has overwhelmed and weakened the potential social control capacity of political, family, and educational institutions. More germane to their theoretical explanation for the exceptionally high rates of serious crime observed in America, however, are the consequences of this process. Specifically, they note that the dominance of the economy in American institutional life has reduced the capacity of noneconomic institutions to "inculcate beliefs, values, and commitments other than those of the marketplace," which in turn has weakened their capacity to "promote allegiance to social rules" and has limited the "social support that they can offer for culturally prescribed behavior" (2007, pp. 85–86). In essence, the dominance of the economy in American life has generated cultural conditions that strongly encourage the pursuit of economic achievements while also weakening the capacity of noneconomic institutions to temper those pursuits or limit the use of illegitimate activities to realize them. According to Messner and Rosenfeld, this combination of cultural arrangement and institutional imbalance has produced a population in America that is more likely than other populations to pursue monetary success goals by any means necessary. More vividly, they suggest that these social and cultural conditions are the main reason why America exhibits rates of robbery and homicide that are substantially higher than those observed in most other nations.

Theoretical Critiques

Since the initial statement of IAT by Messner and Rosenfeld in 1994, three main theoretical critiques have been highlighted in the literature. These critiques question the limited attention devoted in IAT to the distribution of legitimate opportunities for pursuing economic success goals, the relevance of the theory for explaining variation in lethal violence, and the ability of the theory to account for several well-established patterns of serious crime.

With respect to the first critique, as noted earlier, Messner and Rosenfeld largely omit from early articulations of their arguments a discussion of the role of the stratification system in generating crime. They acknowledge this omission in later versions of their argument, however, and also discuss the importance of integrating the stratification system into their conception of the social structure (Messner & Rosenfeld, 2006, 2007). In another critique of the initial statement of IAT, Leonard Beeghley argues that key factors identified in prior research as sources of variation in serious crime rates are ignored or dismissed as unimportant in the theory, most notably racial discrimination, the widespread availability of guns, and the rapid expansion of drug markets. In more recent editions of *Crime and the American Dream* and other writings, Messner and Rosenfeld articulate how these and other well-known crime patterns (e.g., race and gender differences in crime) are consistent with the internal logic of IAT, while also emphasizing the need for additional attention to such issues in future theoretical and empirical examinations.

Finally, some scholars have questioned the relevance of anomie theory for explaining differences in *lethal* criminal violence across social collectivities. Critics have suggested that, while IAT provides a logical explanation for why certain socially structured pressures related to economic goal attainment would yield higher levels of crimes with motives to enhance one's financial circumstances, they do not adequately explain how those pressures would translate into higher levels of lethal criminal violence, except of course for the modest proportion of cases in which money-generating crime turns deadly. Brian Stults and Eric Baumer focus explicitly on this issue and outline an elaborated theoretical model that links the core concepts of IAT to lethal violence through their influence on property crime, drug market activity, and firearm carrying.

Empirical Research

The core linkages implied in IAT rarely have been examined, so it is difficult to draw strong conclusions about the status of existing empirical evidence. Several empirical studies have considered hypotheses related to the arguments outlined in the theory, if not directly relevant to the core causal predictions. For example, in a pioneering empirical test of IAT in 1995, Mitchell Chamlin and John Cochran examined the effect of poverty on property crime rates, and the extent to which that effect is conditioned by the strength of noneconomic institutions. Several subsequent studies have applied similar logic in examining whether the influence of economic inequality on homicide rates across nation-states and other aggregate units (e.g., U.S. counties and cities) is conditioned by noneconomic institutional strength. These studies have advanced understanding of the nature of spatial variation in crime, but they do not speak directly to the core arguments of IAT—whether levels of serious crime are higher in societies with a stronger cultural commitment to monetary success goals and a weaker cultural commitment to legitimate means exist, and whether this is amplified in contexts of weakened noneconomic social institutions.

A small handful of studies have assessed more directly the cultural arguments implied in IAT. Liqun Cao, Gary Jensen, and Chamlin and Cochran evaluate whether America exhibits the type of exceptional cultural features suggested by IAT. Although there is some debate about the utility of the principal source used in these studies to capture cross-national differences in cultural values, the results of such investigations raise questions about claims that Americans are exceptional in their commitment to monetary success or in their willingness to justify deviant means of pursuing such success.

Two recent studies have attempted to model more directly the causal mechanisms implied in IAT. Baumer and Regan Gustafson integrate aggregate-level survey data on value commitments from the General Social Survey with data on crime rates and other measures for counties and county groups in the United States. Consistent with some of the key predictions of the theory, this study reveals that rates of instrumental crime are higher in places with a relatively strong commitment to monetary success and weak commitment to legitimate means, and they tend to be particularly high in such areas when accompanied by relatively low levels of welfare support and weakened family institutions. Stults and Baumer expand on this analysis by including homicide rates in the empirical analysis and showing that rates of homicide are significantly higher in areas with high levels of commitment to monetary success goals and low levels of commitment to legitimate means, largely because such areas tend to exhibit elevated levels of property crime and drug market activity, which in turn yield higher rates of homicide.

Conclusion

Institutional-anomie theory has emerged as an influential theoretical perspective for explaining aggregate-level variation in serious crime rate and has stimulated a large body of research since initially outlined fully in the first edition of *Crime and the American Dream*. As Messner and Rosenfeld (2006) noted in a recent commentary on the current status of IAT, this signals that the theory has provided some provocative research "puzzles" to the criminological community of scholars. In taking stock of the scholarship that has emerged on IAT, however, they also highlighted some issues, or puzzles, that warrant additional attention in future inquiry, including elaboration on how the social stratification system interacts with other social institutions in producing high rates of crime in advanced industrial societies and a greater focus on illuminating the ways in which the American

cultural structure may be different from or similar to those found in other nations and the implications this may have for observed differences across societies in crime rates. Perhaps not surprisingly given the framework within which they have couched their theory, Messner and Rosenfeld encourage these scholarly pursuits while also emphasizing the importance of doing so through legitimate methodological means. Perhaps future theoretical and empirical developments relevant to IAT will follow both the prescriptions and proscriptions suggested by Messner and Rosenfeld.

Eric P. Baumer

See also Agnew, Robert: General Strain Theory; Cloward, Richard A.: The Theory of Illegitimate Means; Cloward, Richard A., and Lloyd E. Ohlin: Delinquency and Opportunity; Cohen, Albert K.: Delinquent Boys; Currie, Elliott: The Market Society and Crime; Durkheim, Émile: Anomie and Suicide; Merton Robert K.: Social Structure and Anomie

References and Further Readings

Baumer, E. P., & Gustafson, R. (2007). Social organization and instrumental crime: Assessing the empirical validity of classic and contemporary anomie theories. *Criminology, 45,* 617–663.

Beeghley, L. (2003). *Homicide: A sociological explanation.* Lanham, MD: Rowman & Littlefield.

Bernburg, J. G. (2002). Anomie, social change and crime: A theoretical examination of Institutional-Anomie Theory. *British Journal of Criminology, 42,* 729–742.

Cao, L. (2004). Is American society more anomic? A test of Merton's theory with cross-national data. *International Journal of Comparative and Applied Criminal Justice, 28,* 17–31.

Chamlin, M. B., & Cochran, J. K. (1995). Assessing Messner and Rosenfeld's Institutional-Anomie Theory: A partial test. *Criminology, 33,* 411–429.

Chamlin, M. B., & Cochran, J. K. (2007). An evaluation of the assumptions that underlie Institutional Anomie Theory. *Theoretical Criminology, 11,* 39–61.

Cullen, F. T. (1984). *Rethinking crime and deviance theory: The emergence of a structuring tradition.* Totowa, NJ: Rowman and Allenhend.

Cullen, J. B., Parboteeah, K. P., & Hoegl, M. (2004). Crossnational differences in managers' willingness to justify ethically suspect behaviors: A test of Institutional Anomie Theory. *Academy of Management Journal, 47,* 411–421.

Jensen, G. (2002). Institutional anomie and societal variations in crime: A critical appraisal. *International Journal of Sociology and Social Policy, 22*, 45–74.

Maume, M. O., & Lee, M. R. (2003). Social institutions and violence: A sub-national test of Institutional Anomie Theory. *Criminology, 41*, 1137–1172.

Merton, R. K. (1938). Social structure and anomie. *American Sociological Review, 3*, 672–682.

Messner, S. F., & Rosenfeld, R. (1994). *Crime and the American dream*. Belmont, CA: Wadsworth.

Messner, S. F., & Rosenfeld, R. (1997). Political restraint of the market and levels of homicide: A cross-national application of Institutional Anomie Theory. *Social Forces, 75*, 1393–1416.

Messner, S. F., & Rosenfeld, R. (2006). The present and future of institutional-anomie theory. In F. T. Cullen, J. P. Wright, & K. R. Blevins (Eds.), *Taking stock: The status of criminological theory* (Advances in Criminological Theory: Vol. 15, pp. 127–148). New Brunswick, NJ: Transaction.

Messner, S. F., & Rosenfeld, R. (2007). *Crime and the American dream* (4th ed.). Belmont, CA: Wadsworth.

Pratt, T. C., & Godsey, T. W. (2003). Social support, inequality, and homicide: A cross-national test of an integrated theoretical model. *Criminology, 41*, 101–133.

Savolainen, J. (2000). Inequality, welfare state, and homicide: Further support for the Institutional Anomie Theory. *Criminology, 38*, 1021–1042.

Stucky, T. D. (2003). Local politics and violent crime in U.S. cities. *Criminology, 41*, 1101–1135.

Stults, B. J., & Baumer, E. P. (2008). Assessing the relevance of anomie theory for explaining spatial variation in lethal criminal violence: An aggregate-level analysis of homicide within the United States. *International Journal of Conflict and Violence, 2*, 215–247.

MICHALOWSKI, RAYMOND J., AND RONALD C. KRAMER: STATE-CORPORATE CRIME

Raymond J. Michalowski and Ronald C. Kramer's concept of state-corporate crime recognizes that socially injurious actions can be facilitated at the intersection of the political and economic orders, regardless of the existence of criminal codes officially recognizing the malevolence of those actions. Grounded in both the critical criminological discourse of the 1970s and the existing literature on organizational deviance, the concept represents an advance over existing explanations that did not account for the interdependent nature of relationships between public and private institutions. The following discussion chronicles some of the theoretical developments that led to the formulation of the concept of state-corporate crime and articulates the explanatory framework of state-corporate crime. An attempt is also made to highlight some of the case studies examined within its context.

The Concept

Michalowski and Kramer (2006) note that the concept of state-corporate crime was formulated amidst the suite of investigations that followed the 1986 explosion of the NASA space shuttle *Challenger*. However, the episteme of the time did not recognize the functional interdependencies between corporate and government entities, evident in the fact that those two institutions have traditionally been studied separately within the literature on organizational deviance. The concept of state-corporate crime represents an advance over previous studies of corporate or governmental malfeasance in that it recognizes the instrumental role that those relationships play in facilitating socially injurious outcomes.

State-corporate crime involves at least two entities (public and private) and is described by Michalowski and Kramer as "illegal or socially injurious actions that result from a mutually-reinforcing interaction between 1) policies and/or practices in pursuit of the goals of one or more institutions of political governance, and 2) policies and/or practices in pursuit of the goals of one or more institutions of economic production and distribution" (p. 20). Furthermore, Judy Aulette and Michalowski identify two types of state-corporate crime: *state-initiated* and *state-facilitated*. State-initiated corporate crime refers to socially injurious actions that result from corporate entities working at the behest of (or with the tacit approval of) governmental organizations. State-facilitated corporate crime refers to the failure of governmental authorities to create meaningful regulatory or enforcement mechanisms concerning organizational malfeasance. Incorporating insights from a number of differing theoretical perspectives on organizational deviance, the researchers have identified three "catalysts for action" that impact deviant organizational outcomes. These catalysts include the degree of emphasis on goal attainment within organizations, the balance between institutional and noninstitutional means for achieving those goals, and the functional availability of effective sources of social control.

The theoretical rationale for state-corporate crime is found amidst the wave of critical discourse that was one of the hallmarks of criminological theorizing of the 1970s. Richard Quinney's refinement of Edwin Sutherland's original definition of white-collar crime differentiated between occupational and corporate crimes, but did not extend that analysis by linking crime in the workplace with the institutional relationships that exist between corporate and governmental entities. Building upon Quinney's work, itself grounded in Marxian analyses, the theory of state-corporate crime recognizes the importance of power differentials in determining how crime is legally demarcated. In doing so, state-corporate crime recognizes the role that the interests of elites play in structuring both legal codification and enforcement practices with respect to formally addressing socially injurious behavior. Consequently, many of the socially injurious actions addressed within the context of state-corporate crime are neither recognized officially nor form the corpus of behaviors central to conventional criminological discourse (namely street crimes), according to Michalowski and Kramer.

Michalowski and Kramer admit that their framework of state-corporate crime may be less a theory (in the formal sense) and more of an explanatory scheme aimed at identifying, understanding, and giving context to relationships between public and private entities. Despite this self-criticism, the theory (as it has often been referred to) does provide insight into the machinations behind some of the most socially injurious actions perpetrated by man. Consequently, state-corporate crime has at least three useful characteristics.

First, the concept directs attention toward deviant organizational outcomes that can be intensely socially injurious, yet have traditionally been ignored by legal scholars, institutions of formal social control, and criminologists. Second, the concept of state-corporate crime does not treat corporate and governmental institutions atomistically, instead recognizing the importance

and power of relationships between those institutions that are central to their effective functioning. This represents an advance over existing theories and explanations of corporate and governmental wrongdoing that ignore those relationships or that explain such malfeasance in terms of individual agency. Third, state-corporate crime considers how relationships are impacted by differing levels of organizational action at the individual, institutional, and macro (political-economy) levels.

Case Studies

As previously noted, the concept of state-corporate crime was developed subsequent to the explosion of the space shuttle *Challenger*. Kramer's analysis of that tragedy revealed that it was not simply the result of an accident, as so many at the time had presumed, but instead was the result of faulty decision making on the part of government safety experts at NASA and technical advisors and engineers at Morton Thiokol (MTI), the private company that designed and manufactured the doomed solid rocket boosters. Political and economic pressures resulted in an ethos focused on launching shuttles in a timely (hence, profitable) fashion, inhibiting those in authority from responding to the legitimate safety concerns of engineers at both NASA and MTI. The lack of effective oversight and communication between internal divisions at NASA manifested itself in the decision to launch the shuttle in weather deemed too cold for the effective functioning of the O-rings, critical for operation of the solid rocket boosters.

Another case study of state-corporate crime involves the tragic 1991 fire at the Imperial Foods' chicken processing plant in Hamlet, North Carolina, which resulted in the deaths of twenty-five employees. In their analysis of the event, Aulette and Michalowski determined the tragedy was set in motion through a confluence of historical forces and organizational practices coupled with an atmosphere devoid of effective regulatory oversight. The fire resulted when a hydraulic line containing flammable fluid ruptured near an industrial deep-fat fryer, resulting in a fireball and a significant amount of smoke that suffocated workers trapped behind fire escape doors that had previously been barricaded by managers of the facility.

A nuanced analysis of the event revealed that the tragedy was not solely the result of faulty individual decision making on the part of Imperial Foods' management, but had been set in motion years prior due to a number of economically motivated state policies. The state of North Carolina forfeited federal OSH (Occupational Safety and Health) money ostensibly because the state did not envision the protection of worker safety as complementary to its interest of promoting a robust business environment. To make matters worse, the owners of financially troubled Imperial Foods consciously ignored workers' complaints of safety violations concerning the barricading of fire-escape doors, rationalizing those decisions as either related to the prevention of trivial amount of employee theft or to keep insects from contaminating foodstuffs. Both state and local safety inspectors (as well as federal food inspectors) ignored those violations, tacitly allowing the fire-escape doors to entrap workers who could turn to no one for effective protection.

The defense industry was examined by David Kauzlarich and Kramer with respect to its contribution to significant environmental harms. In the rush to develop the first atomic weapons in the midst of World War II, the Atomic Energy Commission (subsequently replaced by the Department of Energy [DOE]) was more concerned with hasty development and testing of weapons than it was with implementing appropriate disposal methods for the volumes of toxic and radioactive waste produced in manufacturing. The secrecy surrounding the Manhattan Project also inhibited effective regulatory oversight, a condition that did not change during the cold war era, when United States weapons production accelerated to keep pace with a rapidly developing Soviet arsenal.

Despite the enactment of environmental legislation in the 1970s, the DOE continued its policy of dumping billions of gallons of toxic waste into the environment. The DOE's self-aggrandized task of national security was emphasized to the extent that noncompliance with existing environmental regulations became departmental ethos; private contractors were given the responsibility of self-regulation by a department reluctant to acknowledge either Environmental Protection Agency oversight or the applicability of environmental regulations. To make

matters worse, the U.S. Department of Justice had a policy of not intervening where one government agency was acting out of compliance with environmental regulations. The end of the cold war and the discovery of massive levels of contamination surrounding weapons production led to the closure of facilities around the country, but not before significant environmental crimes had been perpetrated for more than 50 years.

Finally, the crash of ValuJet flight 592 has been examined within the context of state-corporate crime, which uncovered the patently dangerous conditions that can result from the convergence of a public ideology committed to deregulation coupled with an intense private drive for profit maximization. ValuJet flight 592 plummeted nose first into the Florida Everglades only 10 minutes after takeoff, killing all 110 aboard—the result of a fire that rapidly spread from the plane's cargo hold. Flight 592 contained packages of unused oxygen generators that had been previously removed from older planes in the ValuJet fleet by private maintenance contractors, yet were improperly packaged and shipped in the ill-equipped cargo hold of the doomed flight.

In their analysis of the tragedy, Rick Matthews and Kauzlarich found that the Federal Aviation Administration (FAA) operated with two contradictory organizational directives: the regulation of the airline industry with respect to passenger safety and the promotion of the airline industry's general economic success. The airline industry had been beset by massive consolidation in the wake of passage of the 1978 Airline Deregulation Act. Consequently, the FAA was reluctant to stringently enforce the safety violations of the highly profitable and rapidly expanding ValuJet airline. The lack of effective formal oversight was coupled with a drive for profit maximization by corporate officials at ValuJet, who sacrificed safety in the interest of contracting critical maintenance work to the lowest bidder. The employees of SabreTech, ValuJet's maintenance contractor, were found criminally responsible (in terms of individual agency) for the inappropriate packaging and shipping of the hazardous cargo. However, it was the series of corporate decisions to sacrifice safety in the interests of profit that served as motivation to initially employ relatively inexperienced maintenance contractors, coupled with the knowledge of an institutional climate that indicated federal regulators would do little to intervene in decisions that might challenge the economic longevity of any individual airline.

Douglas J. Dallier

See also Capitalism and White-Collar Crime; Quinney, Richard: Social Transformation and Peacemaking Criminology; Spitzer, Steven: Capitalism and Crime; Sutherland, Edwin H.: White-Collar Crime

References and Further Readings

Aulette, J., & Michalowski, R. J. (2006). The fire in Hamlet. In R. J. Michalowski & R. C. Kramer (Eds.), *State-corporate crime: Wrongdoing at the intersection of business and government* (pp. 45–66). New Brunswick, NJ: Rutgers University Press.

Kauzlarich, D., & Kramer, R. C. (1998). *Crimes of the nuclear state: At home and abroad*. Boston: Northeastern University Press.

Kauzlarich, D., & Kramer, R. C. (2006). Nuclear weapons production. In R. J. Michalowski & R. C. Kramer (Eds.), *State-corporate crime: Wrongdoing at the intersection of business and government* (pp. 67–81). New Brunswick, NJ: Rutgers University Press.

Kramer, R. C. (2006). The space shuttle Challenger explosion. In R. J. Michalowski & R. C. Kramer (Eds.), *State-corporate crime: Wrongdoing at the intersection of business and government* (pp. 27–44). New Brunswick, NJ: Rutgers University Press.

Kramer, R. C., Michalowski, R. J., & Kauzlarich, D. (2002). The origins and development of the concept and theory of state-corporate crime. *Crime and Delinquency, 48,* 263–282.

Matthews, R. A., & Kauzlarich, D. (2006). The crash of ValuJet flight 592. In R. J. Michalowski & R. C. Kramer (Eds.), *State-corporate crime: Wrongdoing at the intersection of business and government* (pp. 82–97). New Brunswick, NJ: Rutgers University Press.

Michalowski, R. J., & Kramer, R. C. (Eds.). (2006). *State-corporate crime: Wrongdoing at the intersection of business and government*. New Brunswick, NJ: Rutgers University Press.

Quinney, R. (1964). The study of white-collar crime: Toward a reorientation in theory and research. *Journal of Criminal Law, Criminology, and Police Science, 55,* 208–214.

Sutherland, E. H. (1949). *White collar crime.* New York: Dryden Press.

MIETHE, TERANCE D., AND ROBERT F. MEIER: AN INTEGRATED THEORY OF VICTIMIZATION

Terance D. Miethe and Robert F. Meier's integrated theory of victimization is a sociological theory that attempts to integrate offender-, victim-, and situation-based theories of crime into a single comprehensive theoretical perspective capable of predicting the occurrence of both personal and property criminal acts. The heuristic model of criminal events that emerges from their theory includes (1) sources of offender motivation, (2) victim characteristics that provide criminal opportunities, and (3) characteristics of the social context in which crime take place. These three related factors are assumed to interact with each other, thus influencing the probability of a criminal event occurring.

Theories of Criminality and Theories of Victimization

Miethe and Meier's approach to crime recognizes the importance of both criminals and victims and the facilitating context that brings them together. Their theory is explicated in their 1994 book titled *Crime and Its Social Context: Toward an Integrated Theory of Offenders, Victims and Situations*. Until the publication of their work, the understanding of the conditions that cause or prevent crime was achieved through theories focusing exclusively on criminals *or* on victims. There had been a dearth of attempts to consider theories of criminality and theories of victimization *jointly* in one theoretical framework.

The study of criminals and their motivation for crime has been a primary focus of criminology since its establishment as an academic discipline. A variety of perspectives, ranging from social learning and social control theories to anomie and social disorganization theories, underscore the fact that criminal motivation is shaped by a range of factors that operate inside and outside individuals, on the micro- and macro-levels of analysis. The sole emphasis on the sources and causes of offender motivation, however, fails to consider how the actions and supply of potential targets shapes the physical opportunities for criminal victimization, according to Miethe and David McDowall.

Therefore, starting in the mid-1970s, criminologists began paying more systematic attention to the opportunity structure for crime and especially to the factors associated with the selection of targets for victimization. Lifestyle and routine activity theories highlighted for the first time the symbiotic relationship between conventional and illegal activities and managed to give a realistic explanation as to why particular persons become crime targets. They noticed that routine activities of everyday life provide an opportunity structure for crime by increasing the supply of attractive crime targets, decreasing the level of their protection, and increasing targets' exposure and proximity to motivated offenders. Miethe and McDowall note that those theories failed, however, to take into consideration the social, psychological, and structural forces that produce criminal motivation.

Noticing that neither an offender nor a victim perspective in isolation takes into consideration what the other regards as essential, Miethe and Meier argued that the ability to explain crime may be substantially improved by the *integration* of theories of criminality and theories of victimization. But they had yet another aspect to consider before proceeding to the integration of the two perspectives.

Offenders, Victims, and the Importance of Contextual Factors

Sociologists had long ago observed that offenders' characteristics that reinforce motivation and victims' characteristics that increase vulnerability do not exist in a vacuum. Rather, they operate in a *social context* that brings them together and that enhances (or diminishes) their effects. Thus, Miethe and Meier argued that a social explanation of crime can never be complete without a sense of the context in which criminal acts take place.

According to Miethe and Meier, there are two main procedures through which social forces in the wider environment can affect (increase or decrease) individuals' risk of victimization. The first takes place when aggregate-level measures of theoretical concepts exhibit a significant *net*

impact on individuals' risks of victimization. Such a net impact effect would be observed if, for example, the high levels of residential mobility, ethnic heterogeneity, population density, and poverty of a neighborhood altered a resident's victimization risks regardless of his or her personal characteristics. The second procedure through which social context can affect individuals' risk of victimization involves a *statistical interaction* between aggregate-level and individual-level measures. Such an interaction effect would be observed if, for example, being non-white increased the risks of violent victimization more in ethnically homogeneous neighborhoods than in ethnically heterogeneous neighborhoods.

Integrated Theory of Criminal Events

Miethe and Meier's integrated theory draws together all three necessary elements for crime: a motivated offender, a vulnerable victim or target, and a facilitating social context. The theory recognizes that an *offender's motivation* to engage in law-breaking acts (crime readiness) is a necessary but insufficient condition in the crime process. Miethe and Meier posit that without the availability of a *suitable target* and a *facilitating environment*, the offender would be unable to act on his or her criminal intentions. Figure 1 shows a graphical representation of Miethe and Meier's heuristic model of criminal events. The model depicts all the relationships among sources of offender motivation, victim characteristics, and the social context.

The *sources of offender motivation* include economic disadvantage, weak social bonds, pro-crime values, psychological or biological attributes, generalized needs (e.g., money, sex, status), and noncriminal alternatives. The aforementioned sources of offender motivation are compatible with several macro-level and micro-level theories of criminality, including social disorganization theory, social control theory, social learning theory, and strain theory as well as theories emphasizing the physiological and psychological capacities of individuals. Macro-level theories concentrate primarily on structural characteristics of aggregates, such as the economic disadvantage of a community or the weak social bonds of residents at the neighborhood level.

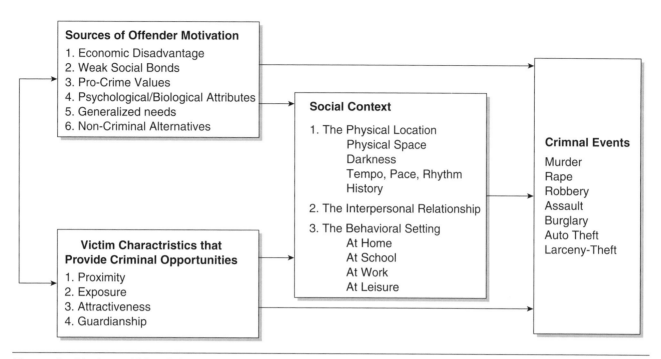

Figure 1   Miethe and Meier's Heuristic Model of Criminal Events

Source: From Miethe, T. D., and Meier, R. F. (1994). *Crime and Its Social Context: Toward an Integrated Theory of Offenders, Victims and Situations*, p. 65. Albany: State University of New York Press. Reprinted with permission.

Micro-level theories, on the other hand, focus on the development of criminality in a single person. Learning theories, for example, emphasize how pro-criminal values are learned by an individual through associations with other criminals, while biological and psychological perspectives focus their attention on heredity, neurological defects, intelligence, personality, and so on.

The list of sources of offender motivation in Miethe and Meier's model is not meant to be exhaustive or rigid. Limitations of existing data-sets and budget constraints in all studies clearly limit the number of sources of offender motivation that a scholar can take into consideration in a single investigation. Therefore, scholars working on a macro or micro perspective should bring into the model the sources of offender motivation that they consider most important. For their own empirical analysis, Miethe and Meier reasoned that an individual's decision to engage in crime is influenced primarily by population mobility, low socioeconomic status, ethnic heterogeneity, and single-parent families since these factors are ultimately indicative of the social forces that trigger criminal motivation.

Turning to *victim characteristics that provide criminal opportunities*, the model includes four fundamental characteristics that have been previously identified by routine activity and life-style theories. These are proximity to potential offenders, exposure to high-crime situations, target attractiveness, and the absence of guardianship. Proximity indicates the physical distance between potential offenders and potential victims, whereas exposure indicates the physical visibility and accessibility of victims or targets to potential offenders. Target attractiveness involves the material or symbolic desirability of persons and targets to potential offenders. Finally, guardianship refers to the effectiveness of individuals or objects in preventing criminal acts. According to Miethe and Meier, all four characteristics are assumed to help define the social context as conducive to crime. At the same time, however, these characteristics are also assumed to have an independent impact on the probability of crime events, regardless of the particular social context.

Moving on to the *social context*, Miethe and Meier have included in their model elements of the physical location, the interpersonal relationship, and the behavioral setting. The social context is where criminal motivations and attractive victim characteristics are translated into action. Thus, according to Miethe and Meier, the amount of physical space in a setting may impede or facilitate the ability of potential victims to run away or the ability of offenders to escape. Poor lighting in a physical setting, on the other hand, may facilitate the commission of a crime by providing greater anonymity and cover for offenders. Furthermore, the periodicity with which events occur (i.e., rhythm) in a physical setting, the number of events per day (i.e., tempo), and the coordination of those events among other different activities (i.e., timing) may bring large numbers of people together causing the physical setting to become a "hot spot" for predatory violations. Finally, Miethe and Meier note that it is not unusual for a physical location to acquire a history of criminal activity that persists over time, and that this pattern may persist even after the composition and structure of the particular area has changed significantly.

The interpersonal relationship between the victim and the offender is brought into the model in order to underscore the different opportunity structure and underlying motivation between a criminal act involving strangers and a criminal act involving victims and offenders known to each other. Thus, according to Miethe and Meier, in the case of domestic violence, for example, it makes little sense to place any great causal significance on the victim's proximity to risky and dangerous physical environments or to emphasize economic marginality as a motivator for crime.

On the other hand, the behavioral setting is brought into the model in order to indicate the activities of the victim at the time of the offense. The four different behavioral settings signified by Miethe and Meier possess particular characteristics that enhance or debase their attractiveness as criminogenic environments. Thus, for example, crimes occurring in or near the home between acquaintances are less likely to draw the attention of third parties (e.g., the police). On the other hand, for crimes occurring between students within schools, it is reasonable to expect that those crimes will draw the attention of school personnel (e.g., teachers, security guards). Moreover, a number of work settings routinely expose employees to motivated offenders (e.g., prisons, convenience stores), and

several leisure settings are especially crime prone because they draw together a large number of different people at nighttime (e.g., bars, taverns).

The last component of Miethe and Meier's heuristic model is the dependent variable of their criminal investigation, the *criminal event*. Their model is expected to be able to explain both personal (e.g., murder, rape, assault) and property victimizations (e.g., burglary, auto theft).

As far as the *causal ordering* between each component is concerned, sources of offender motivation and criminal opportunities provided by victims are related to one another, but the direction of the relationship is unclear (the curved double-headed arrow indicates simply a correlation). The primary impact of both offender motivation and victim characteristics on crime is assumed to be transmitted through the social context (presumed direct causal relationships are represented in the model with a solid arrow). The social context thus becomes the central component for understanding criminal events in Miethe and Meier's model. Nevertheless, the model allows for the occurrence of criminal events even when the nexus of offender motivation, victim characteristics, and the social context is not ideal or optimal. These residual causal relationships are presented in the model with the dashed arrows from offender motivation and victim characteristics to the criminal events.

Conclusion

The publication of Miethe and Meier's integrated approach in 1994 provided scholars with a new way of approaching criminal events. By successfully combining under a unified framework all the ideas and findings from micro-level and macro-level theories, Miethe and Meier were among the first to make a strong case for a multilevel conceptualization of criminal opportunity and crime prevention.

Spyridon Kodellas

See also Brantingham Patricia L., and Paul J.
    Brantingham: Environmental Criminology; Cohen,
    Lawrence E., and Marcus K. Felson: Routine Activity
    Theory; Cornish, Derek B., and Ronald V. Clarke:
    Rational Choice Theory; Hindelang, Michael J.,
    Michael R. Gottfredson, and James Garofalo: Lifestyle
    Theory; Systemic Model of Social Disorganization;
    Wilcox, Pamela, Kenneth C. Land, and Scott A. Hunt:
    Multicontextual Opportunity Theory

References and Further Readings

Miethe, T. D., & McDowall, D. (1993). Contextual effects in models of criminal victimization. *Social Forces, 71,* 741–759.

Miethe, T. D., & Meier, R. F. (1994). *Crime and its social context: Toward an integrated theory of offenders, victims and situations.* Albany: SUNY Press.

MILLER, JODY: GENDERED CRIMINAL OPPORTUNITY

Since the 1980s, an increasing number of social science researchers have begun to reexamine the significance of gender in social processes and interactions. Rather than treating it simply as a secondary variable, many researchers have begun to make the argument that gender is an important component of modern social structure, which helps to shape directly both social beliefs and personal interactions. Thus, individuals behave in a manner that both adheres to and reinforces the broader social stereotypes of masculinity and femininity. Many researchers who subscribe to feminist theories of criminology adopt this ideology in an effort to understand and explain the diverging patterns in men and women's criminal behaviors. With her work, Jody Miller examined the role of gender in street robbery. She found that violent street criminals often accept "traditional" gender roles, which directly influences their criminal behavior. Although men and women may commit similar types of crimes, their methods and goals can vary significantly based on their self-perceived gender role.

Doing Gender

Research has continued to show gender differences in crime rates, with the majority of criminal offenders being male. This phenomenon is especially true for violent street crime, such as murder, rape, robbery, and assault. One argument for the gender gap in criminal involvement is that men and women often behave in a manner that parallels socially prescribed gender roles. According to this ideology, masculinity is often associated with dominant and aggressive behavior, whereas femininity is often associated with subservient and passive behavior. As a result, individuals who adhere to masculine ideals are more likely to commit violent street crime than those that adhere to feminine ideals. In fact, some scholars agree that violent crime is often used as a method of proving one's masculinity in certain situations. Although the concept of committing violent crime to prove one's masculinity helps explain why crime is a male-dominated phenomenon, Miller contends that it fails to account fully for the amount, albeit small, of female violent street crime. However, there is another theory that may help to explain the cause of female violent street crime, while still taking into account the effects of gender. According to some social science scholars, female violent street crime can be explained as situated action.

Crime as Situated Action

Many social science scholars argue that a large portion of criminal activity is merely situated action. First coined by Lucy Suchman in 1987, the term *situated action* refers to any act or behavior that is directly influenced by one's immediate social situation—including social, cultural, economic, and environmental characteristics. According to this concept, individuals may be drawn to crime as a result of their lifestyle and/or personal situation. For example, racially and economically oppressed groups may resort to crime in order to vent their frustration and/or attempt to overcome the oppression, as noted by Sally Simpson. This line of reasoning is frequently used as an explanation for the disproportionately high rates of crime in inner-city areas. These areas are often inhabited by low-income, African American families who have very little opportunity for legitimate means of economic growth. As a result, crime becomes an attractive alternative, leading to high rates of crime by young, African American men.

Although crime is a male-dominated phenomenon, especially violent crime, the influence of situational characteristics on criminality is by no means limited solely to men. The same structural and cultural characteristics that push low-income, inner-city, African American males toward violent street crime have similar influences on their female counterparts (Simpson, 1991). The concept of

636 Miller, Jody: Gendered Criminal Opportunity

crime as situated action helps to explain not only why some women commit seemingly masculine crimes, such as robbery, but also why lower-class, inner-city African American women commit a higher portion of violent street crime than other women. For example, in examining young female offenders, Suzanne Ageton found that lower-income women were more often involved in violent assaultive-type crime, and African American women were involved in personal crimes at much higher proportions than white women. However, it has been often argued that even when women do commit violent crime, gender roles are still rigidly accepted and followed.

Gender and Crime as Situated Action: An Example From the Literature

The effects of structural and cultural characteristics may somewhat offset the influence of gender on crime; it has been found that certain types of women commit "masculine" crimes. Even so, gender effects are not entirely eradicated. In fact, the influence of gender may still remain very significant. Further, some research has shown that it is possible that criminality can be simultaneously influenced by situational characteristics and gender. For example, with her work, Miller found that although both men and women in low-income, inner-city areas were drawn toward street robbery, methods of actual robbery commission varied drastically across gender types.

In her study, Miller interviewed both male and female street robbers from a low-income, inner-city environment. Representative of the population of the area from which her sample was taken, the overwhelming majority of Miller's sample were African American. Miller's intent was to perform a cross-gender comparison of both the motivation for and techniques of street robbery. In doing so, several clear patterns emerged.

Examining why individuals were motivated to commit street robbery, Miller found strong similarities in the motivation for both male and female street robbers. It was found that the desire and/or need for immediate financial or material gain served as the key motivation for both male and female offenders. Thus, robbery could provide the quick and lucrative financial gain that was not available through any other avenue in the area,

such as employment. Miller's discovery provides strong support for the crime as situation action hypothesis, given that both men and women in the area were drawn toward street robbery, a crime which is typically dominated by male offenders.

With her examination of the techniques and methods of street robbery, Miller discovered several clear and repeated differences between male and female street robbers. First, Miller found that men typically selected only male victims whereas women typically selected only female victims. The reasoning behind victim-type selection was based strongly on socially indentified gender roles. Male offenders chose male victims because they felt it was a better declaration of their masculinity, because female victims are "too easy" and rarely have money. Similarly, female offenders typically chose female victims because they were easier to handle; male victims may be more likely to dismiss the offender or fight back. For both the male and female offenders, men were seen as more dominate and aggressive, while women were seen as more submissive and weak.

Further, Miller also found that the methods used by the male and female offenders interviewed were strongly based on gender-role association. For example, the male offenders were more likely to use aggressive, strong-arm tactics when committing robbery, such as using a gun to threaten victims or even assaulting victims. Throughout the crime event, male offenders wanted to portray a sense of domination and masculinity. The female offenders, on the other hand, utilized more finesse in their techniques and rarely used a gun. Often, female offenders would exploit their own femininity to gain the trust of female victims or to sexually entice male victims. On several occasions, female offenders would even initiate sexual interactions, either posing as a prostitute or sexually available stranger. For the majority of the crime events, female offenders wanted to appear weak and/or nonthreatening. It was only during the climax of the crime that they wanted to portray a sense of aggressiveness and physical control.

Finally, Miller continued to find gender-role reinforcement when examining multioffender cooperation. The majority of offenders interviewed chose to commit robbery alone in most instances. However, when they did cooperate, gender stereotypes were strongly upheld. Male offenders typically worked with other male offenders. When male offenders did have female accomplices, the male offender usually performed the robbery, whereas the female offender remained in the car and/or served as a watchman. Likewise, female offenders most often chose male offenders as accomplices, believing that a woman would get in the way or be too weak. Even when a female offender would actually commit the robbery, the male accomplices typically served as dominate aggressors or "muscle" for the group.

Conclusion

Gender-role identification is a phenomenon that is present throughout every social process and inter-action. To that end, it makes sense that crime is also gendered. Crime, and especially violent crime, is often thought of as a masculine activity. However, there are still female offenders in the male-dominated world of crime. A wide-range of situational vari-ables—including social, cultural, economic, and environmental characteristics—may serve to push women into crime, much in the same fashion that they often push men. Still, although women may cross that invisible barrier, the influence of gender is not necessarily removed. Women can be drawn to crime, yet still adhere to socially defined gender stereotypes during the commission of crime. For example, women may base their techniques, target-selection methods, and overall process around gen-der stereotypes, adopting a less-aggressive approach to crime. In doing so, they often serve to reinforce those stereotypes.

Billy Henson

See also Anderson, Elijah: Code of the Street; Bottcher, Jean: Social Practices of Gender; Broidy, Lisa M., and Robert S. Agnew: A General Strain Theory of Gender and Crime; Heimer, Karen, and Stacy De Coster: The Gendering of Violent Delinquency; Klein, Dorie: The Etiology of Female Crime; Miller, Jody: Girls, Gangs, and Gender; Simpson, Sally S.: Gender, Class, and Crime; Steffensmeier, Darrell J.: Organization Properties and Sex Segregation in the Underworld

References and Further Readings

Ageton, S. S. (1983). The dynamics of female delinquency, 1976–1980. *Criminology, 21,* 555.

Anderson, E. (1999). *Code of the street: Decency, violence, and the moral life of the inner city.* New York: W. W. Norton.

Giordano, P. C., Cernkovich, S. A., & Rudolph, J. L. (2002). Gender, crime, and desistance: Toward a theory of cognitive transformation. *American Journal of Sociology, 107*(4), 990–1064.

Jacobs, B. A., & Wright, R. (1999). Stick-up, street culture, and offender motivation. *Criminology, 37,* 149.

Miller, J. (1998). Up it up: Gender and the accomplishment of street robbery. *Criminology, 36,* 37.

Simpson, S. (1989). Feminist theory, crime, and justice. *Criminology, 27,* 605.

Simpson, S. (1991). Caste, class and violent crime: Explaining difference in female offending. *Criminology, 29,* 115.

Simpson, S., & Elis, L. (1995). Doing gender: Sorting out the caste and crime conundrum. *Criminology, 33,* 47.

Steffensmeier, D., & Allan, E. (1996). Gender and crime: Toward a gendered theory of female offending. *Annual Review of Sociology, 22,* 459–487.

Suchman, L. A. (1987). *Plans and situated actions: The problem of human-machine communication.* New York: Cambridge University Press.

West, C., & Zimmerman, D. H. (1987). Doing gender. *Gender and Society, 1,* 125–151.

MILLER, JODY: GENDERED SOCIAL ORGANIZATION THEORY

Jody Miller's work in criminology illuminates how gender shapes crime and victimization. Her work is innovative in its application of the con-cept of gendered social organization to criminol-ogy. Miller's work focuses on how gender shapes experiences of crime and violence for women and girls, as well as men and boys, and on the ways that gender intersects with street environments and offender networks. To understand Miller's theoretical contribution, it is critical to first appre-ciate that in the literature on gendered organiza-tions, gender is more than an individual attribute. It is not something that only individuals possess; it is rather a social, structural, relational, and institutional force. Therefore Miller's theory of gendered social organization in criminology is best understood as the theory of how social, struc-tural, relational, and institutional gender orga-nizes crime and victimization.

This focus has been consistent throughout Miller's work, including, in her research on women and street robbery ("Up It Up"), girls in gangs (*One of the Guys*), sex composition in gangs ("The Impact of Sex Composition on Gangs and Gang Member Delinquency"), neighborhood danger and victimization ("Gender, Neighborhood Danger, and Risk-Avoidance Strategies Among Urban African-American Youths"; *Getting Played*), and human smuggling ("Women's Participation in Chinese Transnational Human Smuggling"). These contributions are discussed as follows.

Gendered Social Organization and Crime

Miller discusses the gendered context of street robbery in "Up It Up: Gender and the Accomplishment of Street Robbery." She concludes that although women and men do not have different motivations for street robbery, the difference in how they reach their goals is related to organizational context—namely, the gender-stratified environment of street robbery. In this study, Miller interviewed active street robbers, 14 women and 23 men. Her findings indicate that women and men enact street robbery in markedly different ways, with women less likely to carry guns and enact direct violence, for example. As in the legitimate economy, their earnings from robbery are also less than men's. In *One of the Guys*, Miller studies the intersection of gang membership and gender using comparative qualitative methods. She details the "patriarchal bargain" struck by girls in gangs in order to balance their experiences of independence, empowerment, and equality while also grappling with the patriarchal hierarchy of gangs and gang activity that so often results in girls' oppression and victimization. Here, Miller's application of gendered social organization theory reveals how the lives of these girls are gendered, how their gangs and gang activities are gendered, and some of the consequences for gang girls and non-gang girls.

Miller's conceptual framework makes visible the ways in which gender structures criminal activities and risks of violence. Miller's work on neighborhood crime, risk, safety, and violence demonstrates this very effectively. In "Gender, Neighborhood Danger, and Risk-Avoidance Strategies Among African-American Urban Youths" by Jennifer Cobbina, Miller, and Rod Brunson, Miller and her coauthors "provide a contextual comparison of how at-risk and delinquent African-American young women and men understand and negotiate neighborhood dangers in distressed urban communities" (p. 675). In past studies of risk and victimization in distressed communities, researchers have paid attention to social and physical proximity to risk factors, often noting the risks connected to structural inequalities. Cobbina et al. find, however, that these structured inequalities are themselves gendered and result in gendered consequences. Young men report feeling at risk in neighborhoods *other than* their own, while young women perceive risk within their own neighborhoods. Both young women and young men fear men's violence.

The gendered structural inequalities in their community mean that the young men in this study are more likely to report feeling safe in their neighborhood. In part, this occurs because the neighborhood is characterized by a gender hierarchy that affords men more control over public space, more freedom of movement, and far more positions of power within street life and social and offender networks. The risks these young men perceive are related to maintaining respect, connections to offender networks, and avoiding threats from law enforcement. Conversely, young women evaluate their risks as related to men's predatory behaviors and their own vulnerabilities as the "weaker" sex; study participants often report that the danger to young women is the threat of sexual violence. For the young women in this study, gendered structural inequalities mean that strategies for safety include avoiding public space in their own neighborhood altogether—a sharp contrast from the young men's strategies. Some of the gendered organizational features of the neighborhood that contribute to these perceptions include "the congregation of male offenders in public spaces and the sexualization of women that results from the drug trade" (p. 692). Gendered social organization theory permits readers of this study to see how gender shapes the neighborhood, its disadvantages, the social and physical space, the risks and strategies for managing risks, and the gendered consequences.

The manner in which gender socially and physically organizes African American girls' experiences of violence in a distressed community is also a focus in Miller's *Getting Played: African American*

Girls, Urban Inequality, and Gendered Violence. In chapter 1 of this book titled "Gender 'n the Hood," Miller discusses how gender shapes urban disadvantage and violence against girls in this setting. As in "Gender, Neighborhood Danger, and Risk-Avoidance Strategies Among African-American Urban Youths," Miller finds that the ways in which gender organizes neighborhood life is highly gendered. Miller notes that the young people in her study viewed risks in gendered terms, whether they believed boys or girls were more at risk. The risks to boys and young men were most often connected to guns and offender behaviors and networks; the risks to girls and young women were connected to men's predatory behaviors, mostly men's sexual violence. Miller's study participants provide information about the physical and social characteristics of their neighborhoods, as well as the risks, including groups of male offenders who congregate in public spaces, public sexual harassment of young women by adult men, the widely held beliefs about women's vulnerability and men's greater strength, public incidents of violence—including domestic violence—against women, and sexual coercion and assault of women.

As in "Gender, Neighborhood Danger, and Risk-Avoidance Strategies Among African-American Urban Youths," the strategies for safety for young women and girls included not only avoiding public space, but also the protection of having known men with them in public space. The young men in Miller's study reported securing safety by being armed, not being alone in public space, and avoiding other neighborhoods and situations that might provoke violence. Miller makes the point that gendered social organization shapes not only what takes place, and who the actors are, but how these youth think about men and women. *Getting Played* demonstrates that social disorganization alone provides an incomplete picture of violence against young women in disadvantaged urban neighborhoods. Instead, gender plays a key role in organizing that violence and the conditions that make it possible.

A final work that illuminates this focus on gendered social organizations is Sheldon Zhang, Ko-Lin Chin, and Miller's study of Chinese transnational human smuggling. Here, Miller and her coauthors demonstrate that human smuggling as an organized criminal enterprise is gendered in

such as way as to "shape the nature of women's involvement" (p. 702). In this study, rather than emphasizing supply and demand as an explanation for women's involvement in an organized criminal venture, Miller and her coauthors examine the internal logic of the organizational structure and activities. They find that women are not excluded or relegated to marginal support work within the operations of human smuggling; rather women often have central positions. However, the strategies used to smuggle are gendered: "Women were more likely than men to facilitate human smuggling by arranging fraudulent marriages and were not involved in maritime operations. Arranged marriages represent the safest method for human smuggling, yield the highest success rate, and garner the highest smuggling fees" (p. 715). In addition, women faced gendered barriers in human smuggling, particularly in relation to the connection between generating and conducting business and interacting with social networks that were dominantly masculine and often corrupt (some government officials, for example). Central to their observations is that human smuggling can be—and often is—framed as a community service, as altruistic. This means that women can be seen as staying within the bounds of feminine caregiver norms while participating in illicit smuggling activities. Examining human smuggling with an eye to how it is structured by gender reveals how the internal logic of Chinese transnational human smuggling reflects unequal gendered patterns in the larger social environments in which the smuggling takes places, and also permits Miller and her coauthors to discover that gendered market demands and niches, gendered migration patterns, and increasing numbers of Chinese women in the workforce all contribute to a gendered labor market in Chinese human smuggling.

Conclusion

Miller's work reveals that crime and victimization are gendered through culture, policy and practice, as well as gendered interactions between individuals and groups. Her work also demonstrates how gender shapes the experiences of women/girls and men/boys who are victims and perpetrators of crime and violence. Her theoretical insights increase our understanding of the influence of organizational context on crime and victimization and on offenders and victims, thus making valuable contributions to the fields of criminology and sociology.

Laura S. Logan

See also Anderson, Elijah: Code of the Street; Moore, Joan W.: Homeboys and Homegirls in the Barrio; Steffensmeier, Darrell J.: Organization Properties and Sex Segregation in the Underworld; Steffensmeier, Darrell J., and Emilie Andersen Allan: A Gendered Theory of Offending

References and Further Readings

Acker, J. (1990). Hierarchies, jobs, bodies: A theory of gendered organizations. *Gender and Society, 4,* 139–158.

Britton, D. M. (2000). The epistemology of the gendered organization. *Gender and Society, 14,* 418–434.

Cobbina, J., Miller, J., & Brunson, R. K. (2008). Gender, neighborhood danger, and risk-avoidance strategies among urban African-American youths. *Criminology, 46,* 673–709.

Miller, J. (1998). Up it up: Gender and the accomplishment of street robbery. *Criminology, 36,* 37–66.

Miller, J. (2001). *One of the guys.* New York: Oxford University Press.

Miller, J. (2008). *Getting played: African American girls, urban inequality, and gendered violence.* New York: New York University Press.

Peterson, D., Miller, J., & Esbensen, F. (2001). The impact of sex composition on gangs and gang member delinquency. *Criminology, 39,* 411–440.

Zhang, S. X., Chin, K., & Miller, J. (2007). Women's participation in Chinese transnational human smuggling: A gendered market perspective. *Criminology, 45,* 699–733.

MILLER, JODY: GIRLS, GANGS, AND GENDER

Jody Miller's work on the gendered nature of gang life is contained mostly in her book *One of the Guys: Girls, Gangs, and Gender.* Miller focuses on two gangs, one in Columbus, Ohio, and another in St. Louis, Missouri, and uses both ethnographic observation and interview techniques to gather data. She also includes an equally sized comparison sample of non-gang-involved girls. Her work challenges many commonly held beliefs regarding the activities and roles of gang-involved girls. Perhaps most importantly, Miller begins by noting that much of the previous work on girl gangs is framed around a dichotomy that explains female gang involvement as either a product of victimization or other social pathology or as a non-normative masculine aberration. In recognizing this, Miller grounds her analysis in the understanding that young women's experiences in gangs are a product of a dynamic interplay between structure and agency, not simply one or the other.

In *One of the Guys* Miller documents a pervasive belief in gender equality among girl gang members. More specifically, the notion of equality for female gang members is one that exists within the unique context of the gang, and not necessarily on the street or society at-large. Here, according to Miller, so-called equality is determined more by girls' beliefs in their ability to fulfill traditional masculine expectations of gang membership and "act like dudes" or "be one of the guys" than any idealistic notion of gender equality (p. 180). Miller observes that gang involvement offers a social location where girls find a measure of gender equality that is not available to similarly situated youth outside the gang. However Miller takes care to illustrate that there is a clear gendered hierarchy within the gangs that privileges masculinity. For example, her respondents note that while female gang members can be one of the guys, an all-girl gang would lack credibility and respect. Further, while many of the respondents in her study maintain a strong belief that females obtain some semblance of gender equality by participating in gangs alongside boys, they espouse the concurrent belief that boys are far better equipped to be gang members than girls. These assertions set up a very clear contradiction and a self-imposed hierarchical structure in girls' and boys' abilities to carry out the work of a gang member.

Miller also critiques the rather simplistic notion that gang involvement offers girls a unique avenue to resist the limiting impositions of traditional gender norms. Miller finds that gender composition of gangs is an important influence on girls' gang behavior, and may help explain the lack of female solidarity within gangs and the friction between non-gang-involved youth. Drawing on Rosabeth Moss Kanter's work on gender in the workplace, Miller finds that the numerical representation of girls in a particular gang shapes group dynamics and also the frequency and type of delinquent behaviors among girls. She finds that girls in predominately male gangs or "tokens" tend to exaggerate masculine, often violent behaviors in an attempt to mask their difference and remain socially invisible. In doing so, girls in male-dominated gang contexts develop an oppositional opinion of girls who do not fit the masculine ideal. Likewise, Miller finds that girls in gangs with a more balanced sex ratio are able to foster a more positive and reciprocal relationship with their female peers. This process, Miller contends, results in situations where gang-involved youths become complicit in the process of gender subordination by reaffirming attitudes and behaviors of male gang members about "other" girls who do not exhibit ideal masculinity. Maintaining status as an accepted or real gang member is thus something girls do at the expense of other girls.

Miller also extends Deniz Kandiyoti's concept of "bargaining with patriarchy" by noting that women and girls must develop different strategies to negotiate varying forms of patriarchal oppression, with gang life being no different. As Miller asserts, "gangs are not uniquely sexist, and do not stand alone in their patterns of gender inequality" (2001, p. 192). Therefore, it stands to reason that young girls will develop a variety of strategies to negotiate the complex, if not contradictory, relations of gang involvement, just as they do away from the gang. Further, many of the youths in Miller's study faced a variety of personal difficulties including sexual assault and familial drug abuse, making the lives of these girls all the more precarious. These facts may make gang membership attractive for some, while others may be lured by the promise of gender equity as one of the guys regardless of how illusory this idea truly is.

Another example of the layered structural inequality of the gang that Miller offers is her discussion of "sexing in," a process by which girls enter a gang by having sex with a member or members, rather than being "beaten" or "jumped in" in the traditional sense. The manner in which girls enter the gang starkly illustrates the gendered hierarchy of gang structures. Girls who choose to be sexed in occupy the lowest rung in the gang in terms of respect as they are seen by all members of the gang as less than girls who were jumped in "like guys." Regardless of this clear distinction, both groups of girls remain subordinate to male gang members who perceive themselves as "harder" than girls, who are less accustomed to the rough, violent duties of the gang. Miller notes that the notion that girls are "softer" than boys often excludes some of them from serious delinquency such as drive-by shootings.

Ultimately, Miller's work on the gendered nature of gang life finds that gangs do not stand apart from the patriarchal oppression that structures everyday life. Contrary to notions of gangs as sites of female solidarity and sisterhood, Miller finds gang life to be highly stratified. The gendered nature of gang life creates an atmosphere where girls compete against and victimize each other to satisfy norms and expectations reflecting a masculine ideal. Miller's description of the false promises of gender equality in gangs is similar to Philippe Bourgois's study of the East Harlem crack market. Like Miller, Bourgois finds that gender, in this case hypermasculinity, plays an important role in the oppression of inner-city residents. Just as Miller's respondents participate in violent, oppressive hierarchies to gain respect as one of the guys, Bourgois's crack dealers commit crimes that often lead to prison or death in the effort to achieve and maintain the respect that is so valued on the streets of East Harlem. In this way, both studies articulate the consequences of the gendered nature of gang and street life that place a premium on respect maintained through hypermasculine hardness. The search for respect as one of the guys encourages marginalized and disadvantaged women and men to participate in their own oppression.

Travis W. Linnemann

See also Campbell, Anne: Girls in the Gang: Miller, Jody: Gendered Social Organization Theory; Moore, Joan W.: Homeboys and Homegirls in the Barrio

References and Further Readings

Bourgois, P. (2003). *In search of respect: Selling crack in el barrio* (2nd ed.). New York: Cambridge University Press.

Kandiyoti, D. (1988). Bargaining with patriarchy. *Gender and Society, 2,* 274–290

Miller, J. (1998). Up it up: Gender and the accomplishment of street robbery. *Criminology, 36,* 37–66.

Miller, J. (2001). *One of the guys: Girls, gangs and gender.* New York: Oxford University Press.

Miller, J. (2002). The strengths and limits of "doing gender" for understanding street crime. *Theoretical Criminology, 6,* 433–460.

Moss Kanter, R. (1977). Some effects of proportion in group life: Skewed sex ratios and responses to token women. *American Journal of Sociology, 82,* 965–990.

MILLER, WALTER B.: LOWER-CLASS CULTURE THEORY OF DELINQUENCY

Subcultural theories of crime and delinquency became very prominent in the late 1950s and early 1960s. Walter B. Miller was an anthropologist who studied youth gangs for many years. Miller's 1958 paper, titled "Lower Class Culture as a Generating Milieu of Gang Delinquency," was one of the most influential publications on subcultural theory. Other prominent criminologists at this time who emphasized the role of subcultures included Albert Cohen and Richard Cloward and Lloyd Ohlin.

The influence of subcultural theories declined significantly in the last few decades of the 20th century. The lack of empirical support for a correlation between social class and crime was a major reason for the declining influence of subcultural theories. However, the role of values as a cause of crime and delinquency remains strongly supported by empirical research, and this may constitute the most enduring contribution of subcultural theorists such as Miller.

Miller described in some detail a set of "focal concerns" or central values that he thought were characteristic of the lower-class culture. In contrast to psychological theories (which may focus on behavioral disorders) or social disorganization perspectives (which may focus on residential instability or high divorce rates), Miller interprets delinquency among street corner groups as—somewhat

ironically—a product of conformity to the standards of lower-class communities. A cultural system of the lower-class community is asserted by Miller to be "a long established, distinctively patterned tradition" that emphasizes values that encourage illegal behavior.

Miller lists six focal concerns roughly in order of their significance in the lower-class culture. First and foremost, *trouble* is described as a focal concern in the lower-class culture. Miller argues that getting into trouble and staying out of trouble with official authorities are major issues or concerns for members of the lower-class culture. Among males, trouble is often expressed through fighting or sexual promiscuity and drinking.

Miller argues that personal status in the lower-class culture is often measured or assessed on a continuum of law-abiding and law-violating behavior. In contrast, middle-class people assess status based on occupational and educational achievement rather than potential trouble or involvement with authorities. Membership in gangs, Miller states, may confer prestige in the subculture; gang membership implies access to power in many neighborhoods. Getting into trouble may satisfy other lower-class culture values or standards, such as the pursuit of excitement and risk, as well as independence from control by authorities.

The second most salient focal concern of the lower-class culture is *toughness*. Toughness is demonstrated by physical prowess (including the ability to fight) and general athletic skill. Adherence to a standard of masculinity is described that shuns sentimental or emotional expression, disdains academic endeavors and skill, and treats women as sexual objects. Miller attributes the focal concern of toughness to the large number of female-headed households in lower-class communities. The lack of male role models is alleged to be problematic in several ways, including the obsessive concern with masculinity in the lower-class culture.

Smartness is the third focal concern of the lower-class culture identified by Miller. This focal concern describes the value placed on the ability to outsmart, con, or take advantage of others (while also being able to avoid being outsmarted or taken advantage of by others). The ability to obtain valued possessions or status by means of mental agility or wit with minimal effort is supposedly a crucial skill in the lower-class culture. While intellectual pursuits are denigrated as effeminate, the mental skills required to outsmart others are highly valued.

There are several settings that allow individuals to display their smartness or mental agility. Gambling, in particular, offers opportunities to outsmart or dupe others. Miller observes that leadership roles in street corner groups are often based on this skill, as well as displays of toughness.

The fourth focal concern described by Miller is termed *excitement*. Individuals in the lower-class culture might be confronted with tedious and boring routines in daily living. People deal with this boredom, according to Miller, by seeking excitement or emotional stimulation.

The focal concern of *fate* is closely linked to the pursuit of excitement or thrills. The lower-class culture is characterized by Miller as emphasizing one's luck and the sense that individuals do not control their fate or destiny. Instead of a sense of mastery, those in the lower-class culture perceive that their lives are determined by forces outside their control.

The fatalistic attitude or value in the lower-class culture generates a disdain for hard work or effort devoted to any long-term goals. Miller states that within the subculture people believe they will be successful (or not) depending on their luck. Thus, this fatalism or absence of a sense of mastery in life leads to the attitude that it is not even worth trying to succeed.

Miller again cites the prevalence of gambling in the lower-class culture as proof of the existence of this focal concern. Although successful involvement in gambling, whether playing poker or betting on horse racing, depends significantly on smartness, the lower-class subculture emphasizes that luck or fate are also crucial factors. Miller observes that certain activities in the lower-class culture, such as gambling, demonstrate several focal concerns simultaneously, including fate, excitement, and smartness.

The sixth and final focal concern emphasized by Miller in the lower-class culture is *autonomy*. Miller describes an inconsistency between what is openly valued in the subculture and what is secretly or covertly desired. People in the lower-class subculture openly discuss their opposition and resentment of authority or external supervision. A frequently expressed sentiment is that "No one is going to push me around." Yet Miller describes the link between "authority" and "nurturance," in that

supervision and firm controls or restraints are also viewed as demonstrations of concern and caring.

The focal concerns of the lower-class culture are often instilled by adolescent male street corner groups or gangs. Miller argues that dysfunctional families in the lower class lead individuals to search for membership in a social group that serves psychological and educational functions. The absence of stable male role models leads to the influence of street corner society, which also provides a sense of belonging. Cohen describes the desire for status and a sense of belonging that may be provided by membership in delinquent gangs.

Miller states that conformity to lower-class standards or values generates crime and delinquency. Gang members who break the law are not afflicted with psychological disorders, but they are in fact viewed as the most capable or fit within the lower-class culture. Ironically, conformity to explicit and implicit values or focal concerns (including toughness, trouble, and excitement) is the principal cause of crime in Miller's subcultural theory.

Ruth Kornhauser provides an emphatic critique of Miller's subcultural perspective. She observes that focal concerns such as trouble express preference for both crime and law-abiding behavior; crime is not unambiguously valued in the subculture. Several studies have shown that offenders and non-offenders from all social class backgrounds tend to evaluate conventional images and behavior more highly than deviant images. Kornhauser concedes that poor children may indeed engage in more violent behavior than do middle-class children, but she attributes this to social disorganization or disordered neighborhoods rather than to values encouraging violence.

Several studies have found that parents of all social classes prefer and try to socialize their children to accept conventional values. Working-class parents are more likely than middle-class parents to value obedience of children, responsibility, and achievement orientation. Kornhauser argues that it is implausible that lower-class parents would attempt to inculcate deviant values; instead, she argues that nearly all parents want the best for their children in terms of conventional accomplishments, and that conformity to both family rules and social rules is highly desired regardless of social class.

Kornhauser states that Miller fails to distinguish social classes as "aggregates" and as "collectivities," as Karl Marx and Max Weber had noted. Only classes that are collectivities with a shared identity and sense of community are capable of transmitting culture. People in the lower or working class of large industrial nations are mere aggregates or a mass that shares only common structural positions (in terms of income or occupational level), but does not generate unique values.

Kornhauser observes that Miller engages in tautological analyses by equating behavior with values; lower-class subcultural values are inferred from behavior (such as aggression, or risk-taking). Such circular reasoning cannot be falsified because those who engage in subcultural behavior are always interpreted as possessing subcultural values.

Charles Valentine argues that most of the focal concerns described in Miller's lower-class subcultural theory are also frequently expressed desires or values in the middle and upper class. Poor people are by no means the only ones who value toughness; higher status individuals openly express admiration for the fiercest competitors, whether in an athletic context or a business setting. Likewise, smartness is just as highly valued among the middle and upper class; individuals who can use their street smarts or wit to outmaneuver others are often admired by people in all social strata. Nor are autonomy and excitement the sole prerogative or pursuit of the lower-class culture; nearly everyone occasionally resents authority figures, and almost everyone enjoys some escape from dull routines.

The issue of the possible existence of a correlation between social class and crime remains an unresolved debate. Concerns remain about the measures of social class, with underclass measures (such as unemployment or welfare status) potentially yielding more substantial differences in crime across strata. Those in the underclass or the "disreputable poor" may be more likely to function as a collectivity than as a mere aggregate; this conception of class could provide support for subcultural theory arguments.

Even more significant for subcultural theory are consistent findings that values (or beliefs in social control theory terms) are strongly linked to crime and delinquency. "Definitions" described by differential association and social learning theorists are among the strongest correlates of delinquent behavior; those who endorse taking advantage of others and breaking the law (if punishment can be avoided)—the sort of trouble identified by Miller—are the most likely to commit criminal and delinquent acts. The characteristics of low self-control, described by Michael Gottfredson and Travis Hirschi in their influential general theory of crime, include risk taking and contempt for diligent and sustained effort; these characteristics are similar to focal concerns of excitement and fatalism in Miller's subcultural theory.

Several recent publications continue to support the subcultural perspective. For example, Derek Kreager argues that instead of race or social class, academic performance is the basis for delinquent subcultural membership. Analyzing data from both cross-sectional and longitudinal studies, Kreager finds that peer acceptance (measured by the number of friendships) is increased by involvement in violent behavior, but only among males who do poorly in school. Consistent with a subcultural theory perspective, violent behavior is positively valued or leads to greater peer acceptance in some contexts.

C. Wesley Younts studied the legitimacy of deviance (in the form of cheating by students on a computer assignment) as affected by status and endorsement of peers. Consistent with subcultural theory, he finds in an experimental design project that endorsement of deviant behavior by peers (regardless of status) increased the likelihood of involvement in deviance. Jeremy Staff and Derek Kreager report that violence can enhance status among peers for males of lower-status families (measured by parental educational attainment). Staff and Kreager conclude that their findings support the subcultural theory interpretation of violence as an alternative means to achieve status for disadvantaged youth.

David Brownfield

See also Anderson, Elijah: Code of the Street; Cloward Richard A., and Lloyd E. Ohlin: Delinquency and Opportunity; Cohen, Albert K.: Delinquent Boys; Kornhauser, Ruth Rosner: Social Sources of Delinquency; Whyte, William Foote: Street Corner Society

References and Further Readings

Brownfield, D. (1986). A reassessment of cultural deviance theory. *Deviant Behavior, 8,* 343–359.

Brownfield, D. (1996). Subcultural theories of crime and delinquency. In J. Hagan, A. R. Gills, & D. Brownfield (Eds.), *Criminological controversies* (pp. 99–123). Boulder, CO: Westview Press.

Cloward, R. A., & Ohlin, L. E. (1960). *Delinquency and opportunity.* New York: Free Press.

Cohen, A. (1955). *Delinquent boys.* Glencoe, IL: Free Press.

Gottfredson, M. R., & Hirschi, T. (1990). *A general theory of crime.* Stanford, CA: Stanford University Press.

Jensen, G., & Rojek, D. (1998). *Delinquency and youth crime* (3rd ed.). Prospect Heights, IL: Waveland Press.

Kornhauser, R. (1978). *Social sources of delinquency.* Chicago: University of Chicago Press.

Kreager, D. (2007). When it's good to be "bad": Violence and adolescent peer acceptance. *Criminology, 45,* 893–923.

Miller, W. B. (1958). Lower class culture as a generating milieu of gang delinquency. *Journal of Social Issues, 14,* 5–19.

Staff, J., & Kreager, D. (2008). Too cool for school? Violence, peer status, and high school dropout. *Social Forces, 87,* 445–471.

Valentine, C. (1968). *Culture and poverty.* Chicago: University of Chicago Press.

Williams, F., & McShane, M. (2004). *Criminological theory.* Upper Saddle River, NJ: Pearson Prentice Hall.

Younts, C. W. (2008). Status endorsement and the legitimacy of deviance. *Social Forces, 87,* 561–590.

MOFFITT, TERRIE E.: A DEVELOPMENTAL MODEL OF LIFE-COURSE-PERSISTENT OFFENDING

The relationship between age and crime presents a wonderful conundrum for criminologists. It is simultaneously one of the most accepted and yet least understood empirical realities of the field. The aggregate age distribution of crime is nearly universal. On average, criminal offending starts in pre-adolescence, increases rapidly during adolescence, peaks around age 17 (for most offenses), and then rapidly declines during the transition to young adulthood. Criminologists are in agreement on this point—and have been for quite some time.

There is considerable disagreement, however, as to what this aggregate age-crime curve represents. Specifically, do individual patterns of criminal offending mimic the aggregate curve? What conclusions about individual patterns of behavior can be reached based on the age-crime curve? One school of thought articulated and embodied by Travis Hirschi and Michael Gottfredson is that the age-crime curve is invariant. That is, it is essentially the same for all individuals. The counterposition is that the age-crime curve conceals heterogeneity of offending patterns, and that there is notable variation in the age-crime curve across individuals. This latter perspective is expressed by David Farrington, among others. This interpretation of the age-crime curve is also the cornerstone of Terrie E. Moffitt's developmental taxonomy of offending.

Theoretical Summary

Moffitt (1993) originally offered her account of antisocial behavior in order to address a persistent reality of criminal behavior: continuity and change. Lee Robins observed in 1978 that while "adult antisocial behavior virtually requires childhood antisocial behavior," it is also true that "most antisocial delinquents do not become antisocial adults" (p. 611). The fundamental implication of this paradox is that criminal behavior is characterized both by stability over time (as in the case of persistent offending) and by marked change. This observation has sparked heated—and as yet unresolved—debates, particularly with respect to the age-crime curve. The core of the debate is the extent of homogeneity that exists among offenders and their involvement in crime over time.

Moffitt offers a theoretical proposition to enlighten the debate. She proposes that the age-crime curve comprises two qualitatively distinct types of offenders, each with their own etiological path into, and out of, delinquent and criminal behavior. Life-course-persistent offenders (LCPs) are characterized by an early onset of problem behavior and marked continuity across much of the life course. Adolescence-limited offenders (ALs) experiment with delinquency during the teen years, but their delinquency is a behavioral anomaly and they will return to prosocial behavior as they age out of adolescence. In detailing the two types of offenders, each with distinct routes to delinquency, Moffitt is able to account for both the continuity and discontinuity of criminal behavior.

Explaining Continuity

The notion that the age-crime curve conceals distinct groups of offenders with different patterns of behavior is not unique to Moffitt's theory. Marvin Wolfgang, Robert Figlio, and Thorsten Sellin were the first to observe that 6 percent of the subjects in a Philadelphia birth cohort were responsible for more than half of the offending among the cohort. The presence of a group of persistent and high-rate offenders was noted in other studies as well, and it serves as the basis for Moffitt's idea of the LCP offender.

LCPs begin offending at an early age and continue offending across most of the lifespan. They comprise about 10 percent of the population, yet they account for about 50 percent of the offenses that are committed. Moffitt locates the causal factors of the LCPs' antisocial behaviors early in childhood. Neuropsychological deficiencies formed before or shortly after birth place a child in a disadvantaged position. The difficult child then has little hope for effective socialization due to the high probability of a detrimental response from caregivers. The original neuropsychological disruptions interact negatively with the environment, which is itself more likely than not to be criminogenic. The result is the early initiation of offending and continuous pathological offending behavior thereafter.

These neuropsychological deficits may be either inherited or acquired. Disrupted neural development during gestation, for example, may be the result of maternal drug abuse, inadequate prenatal nutrition, exposure to toxins, brain insult during delivery, or heritable conditions. Postnatal neurodeficiencies may result from inadequate nutrition, harsh and inconsistent parenting, or lack of stimulation and affection. In addition, child abuse could lead to organic brain damage with neuropsychological implications. A sizable body of research links neuropsychological deficits to antisocial behavior.

Whether inherited or acquired, these neuropsychological deficiencies likely are manifested in the form of undercontrolled or difficult temperament, delayed motor development, low intellectual functioning, poor verbal and execution function, and hyperactivity, as noted by Moffitt and Avshalom Caspi. Outcomes observed among LCPs include weak family bonds, school dropout, alienation and impulsivity, and violent offending, mental health problems, substance use, financial problems, and violence, and adverse physical health outcomes. The high incidence of negative outcomes in domains other than criminal behavior illustrates Moffitt's concept of heterotypic continuity, or behavioral coherence, whereby an underlying trait is expressed across a range of behaviors.

Moffitt is careful to highlight that her approach is neither a pure trait theory nor a pure environmental theory. Continuity of antisocial behavior is one potential product of the interaction between individual traits or characteristics and one's environment; early vulnerabilities may be exacerbated over time to facilitate the continuity of antisocial behavior. Children with cognitive and temperamental disadvantage are more likely born into disadvantaged environments. Parents of difficult children are also less likely to have the resources required to manage their child's disadvantage in a productive or prosocial manner.

Explaining Discontinuity

While LCPs account for the observed continuity of criminal behavior, Moffitt theorizes that a group of ALs is the source of the observed change, or discontinuity, in offending. Adolescence-limited offending is far more common and, in fact, is very nearly normative. For the ALs, delinquency is confined to the period of adolescence. Causal factors must therefore be proximal and able to account for the discontinuity of offending that is the hallmark of ALs.

Given the limited nature of adolescence-limited offending, the theory of causality must be specifically related to the time frame in which they offend—that is, adolescence. Moffitt proposes that a maturity gap has resulted from the earlier occurrence of biological maturity coupled with the lengthening of adolescence. The ALs' offending is the result of their attempts to bridge that gap. As the maturity gap closes with time, inducements for offending behavior disappear and the adolescence-limited offending behavior stops.

ALs do not have a history of antisocial behavior in childhood, which means that they have an established repertoire of conventional, prosocial behavior. Their offending behavior is the result of temporary experimentation with delinquency that emerges alongside puberty. It is ultimately rooted in social processes; ALs mimic the antisocial behavior of their LCP peers. As they reach mature status and acquire the consequent autonomy, the strain of the maturity gap lessens and ultimately disappears, and the ALs return to conventional behavior. Adolescence-limited offenders, by definition, desist as they emerge into young adulthood.

Empirical Status

Life-Course-Persisters

The empirical status of Moffitt's theory can generally be regarded as favorable, with some suggestions in the literature for further specification and refinement of the theory. Much of the empirical research focuses on the life-course-persisters. The existence of a group of LCP-like offenders is empirically supported by a host of studies. Daniel Nagin and Kenneth Land, for example, identified four patterns of offending in a sample of 403 British males studied from ages 8 to 32. These four groups included non-offenders, low-level chronics, adolescence-limiteds, and high-level chronics.

Moffitt's own empirical tests have been conducted on data from the Dunedin Multidisciplinary Health and Development Study, a 33-year longitudinal study of a birth cohort of 1,037 New Zealanders born in 1972 and 1973.

Using data from a birth cohort of several hundred New Zealand males, Moffitt, Donal Lynam, and Phil Silva found that neuropsychological deficits were associated with early onset of delinquency and persistent offending thereafter. Poor verbal ability is particularly predictive of LCP offending. In addition, neuropsychological status did not appear to be significantly related to adolescent-onset delinquency.

In a study of the males and females from the Dunedin data, Moffitt and Caspi found that early onsetters had childhoods marked by inadequate parenting, neurocognitive problems, difficult temperaments, and behavioral problems. Those who experienced adolescent-onset of delinquent behavior did not evince these childhood risk factors.

In an important follow-up of the Dunedin cohort to age 26, Moffitt et al. (2002) tested an essential assertion of the theory: "that childhood-onset, but not adolescent-onset, antisocial behavior is associated in adulthood with antisocial personality, violence, and continued serious antisocial behavior that expands into maladjustment in work life and victimization of partners and children" (p. 180). Their findings support the original tenets of the theory and also demonstrate the presence of heterotypic continuity, or behavioral coherence, whereby antisocial tendencies are expressed across a variety of behavioral domains.

Adolescence-Limiteds

Additional empirical evidence supports Moffitt's hypothesis that adolescence-limited offending is motivated by the co-occurrence of strain resulting from a maturity gap and social mimicry of persistent delinquent peers. From the Dunedin data, Moffitt and Caspi observe that offending among ALs is more strongly correlated with peer delinquency than that of LCPs. In their 2001 analysis of the Youth in Transition data, Alex Piquero and Timothy Brezina found that adolescence-limited offending is motivated, at least in part, by a desire for autonomy. Their findings suggest that the delinquency of the ALs is rebellious but not aggressive, and their research supports Moffitt's hypothesis that the interaction between the onset of puberty with a craving for adult social roles and autonomy is a causal factor in the ALs' delinquency.

David Fergusson, L. John Horwood, and Nagin identified a group of adolescent-onset offenders in their examination of the Christchurch Health and Development study data, which tracks 900 New Zealand children from birth through age 18. They also identified a group that resembled the LCPs, a group of abstainers, and a group they referred to as moderate risk offenders. They used semi-parametric group-based modeling to examine the etiological trajectories of each group. They found that deviant peer affiliations were an important factor in adolescent-onset of offending, but only when such affiliation occurs in the presence of pre-existing moderate risk. These findings suggest that Moffitt's theoretical explanation for ALs' offending behavior may require some consideration of an interaction effect.

Additional Groups

Fergusson and his colleagues are not the only ones who have found evidence of an offending pattern not posited in Moffitt's taxonomy. A third offending prototype emerges across multiple studies and from multiple datasets: the low-level chronics. They offend at low but consistent rates into adulthood, regardless of whether they onset or begin offending in childhood or adolescence. This group was originally given the misnomer "recoveries." Longer term follow-up revealed, however, that what was first thought to be early recovery—that is, a fully realized desistance—was in fact a period of intermittency (Moffitt et al., 2002).

The existence of this group demanded some theoretical revision and extension. According to the original articulation of the theory, those individuals who experience early onset of problem behavior are predicted to continue on to persistent and serious offending, while those who onset during adolescence will experiment only during adolescence and then will desist as they enter young adulthood and take on the attendant adult social roles. The low-level chronics defy these predictions on both counts. The 26-year follow-up data suggest that this group is indistinguishable from the LCPs in childhood but differs in adulthood in that their pathology is internalized. Low-level chronics exhibit depression, anxiety disorders, neuroticism, and social isolation as young adults (Moffitt et al., 2002).

The follow-up study also prompted Moffitt and her colleagues to revisit the parameters of adolescence-limited offending. A nontrivial number of the ALs were still offending at age 26. Moffitt asserts that the explanation for this observation lies in the prolonged maturity gap experienced by later birth cohorts. It is possible that for more contemporary cohorts, true adulthood now begins after age 25. In this case, the continued antisocial behavior at age 26, even among those designated as ALs, is still consistent with the original tenets of the theory. Further bolstering this possibility is the relative success of the ALs compared to the LCPs in the domains of work, education, relationships, health, and mental well-being.

Criticisms and Controversies

John Laub and Robert Sampson have described Moffitt's dual taxonomy as one of the most influential developmental accounts of persistence and desistance in offending. They are also among her most vocal critics. Their concerns with Moffitt's taxonomy take two general forms. Broadly speaking, Sampson and Laub question the assumption that offender typologies are necessary for understanding continuity and change. Specifically, they are concerned that Moffitt overstates the persistence of the LCP, and that prospective identification of offending trajectories is futile, as criminologists are unable do so with any degree of accuracy given the actuarial strategies currently at their disposal.

Laub and Sampson feel that Moffitt overstates the continuity of the LCPs, or put differently, she understates the possibility for change in the LCPs. Based on their follow-up of to age 70 of a sample of boys from Boston initially studied starting in the 1930s by Sheldon and Eleanor Glueck, Sampson and Laub conclude that everyone desists at some point. As such, there is no such thing in the literal sense as the "life-course" persister. The theoretical implication of this observation is that childhood characteristics are not sufficient to accurately predict long-term trajectories of offending. They criticize the post-hoc nature of Moffitt's typology, and they offer data and analysis to suggest that, when tested prospectively, the precepts of Moffitt's taxonomy do not hold. "One fundamental problem is that most typological approaches in criminology are atheoretical and post hoc" (Laub & Sampson, 2003, p. 287). According to Laub and Sampson, Moffitt's theory is defined prospectively but is always tested retrospectively, and this has led to disingenuous support for the theory.

Their analysis of the follow-up Glueck data suggests that early childhood predictors do not prospectively distinguish the various groups of offenders. That is, group membership is not predictable based on individual, childhood, and adolescent risk factors. They interpret this finding as a significant challenge to Moffitt's position that the causal factors of life-course-persistent offending are located in early childhood. All of those goes to echo Sampson and Laub's enduring point that heterogeneity in adult criminal trajectories cannot be explained by childhood differences.

The Meaning of Groups

There are several sources of debate inherent in any use of a typology or offender classification system. A logistic question concerns how many groups are necessary to completely but parsimoniously characterize the population. The debate on this point has both theoretical and methodological facets. Moffitt originally proposed two offending groups, but much research has noted the existence of four, five, or even six groups of empirically identified patterns of offending. Additionally, the reality of intermittency in offending is underdeveloped in most developmental theory (Piquero & Moffitt, 2005). Gaps in offending are widely observed and readily acknowledged, but we know little about the causal pathways in and out of offending in the short term. Moffitt is relatively silent on the topic of intermittency, but the recently identified low-level chronics may be a step in a fruitful direction.

Theoretically, criminologists must ask what these groups actually represent. Are they meaningful groups with clear delineation, or are they an organizing heuristic with applications for theory development but little practical applicability? Barbara Maughan describes debates that have arisen in conjunction with developmental theory exploration, including the differing contributions of categorical versus dimensional approaches to conceptualizing antisocial behavior. She concludes that both approaches have much to offer.

Empirical Concerns

Continued testing and verification of offending patterns remains an empirical priority, but there is also a paucity of empirical work on race and sex differences and the applicability of the theory to females and racial minorities. Persephanie Silverthorn and Paul Frick, for example, question whether the taxonomy applies to girls. They assert that there is no early-starter pathway for girls. Rather, female offending is characterized by a single developmental trajectory and by late onset of offending. Both Fergusson and Horwood (2002) and Moffitt and Caspi (2001) offer evidence to contradict this notion and conclude that Moffitt's theory provides a parsimonious account of the etiology of antisocial behavior for both males and females.

Policy Implications

Moffitt's taxonomy of offending has important implications for prevention and intervention policy,

in terms of both identifying the best subjects for intervention and for the appropriate causal variables to target. Although adolescence-limited offending is near ubiquitous, it is a less troubling form of delinquency. According to Moffitt's theory, it essentially resolves itself within a relatively short period of time. While the ALs are the larger of the offending groups, their delinquent and criminal behavior is not the most harmful. The offending of the LCPs, on the other hand, is more likely to be serious and by definition continues over a much longer period of time. The LCPs, then, represent the most efficacious target for prevention and intervention.

Several of the neuropsychological deficits implicated in the etiology of LCP offending are preventable. Poor prenatal nutrition, prenatal drug and alcohol abuse, and organic damages from injury or exposure to toxic substances, for example, represent ideal venues for intervention to disrupt the causal process toward persistent offending. Recall, though, that the continuity evinced by the LCP is the product of an interaction between their neuropsychological vulnerabilities and their socializing environment. It is possible, then, that increased support for parents and caregivers of children with these challenges could also provide a helpful venue for prevention as well (Farrington & Welsh, 2007).

Sarah Bacon

See also Criminal Career Paradigm; Farrington, David P.: The Integrated Cognitive Antisocial Potential Theory; Giordano, Peggy C., and Stephen A. Cernkovich: Cognitive Transformation and Desistance; Le Blanc, Marc: An Integrated Personal Control Theory of Deviant Behavior; Loeber, Rolf, and Magda Stouthamer-Loeber: Pathways to Crime; Maruna, Shadd: Redemption Scripts and Desistance; Sampson, Robert J., and John H. Laub: Age-Graded Theory of Informal Social Control

References and Further Readings

Farrington, D. P. (1986). Age and crime. In M. Tonry (Ed.), *Crime and justice: A review of research* (Vol. 7, pp. 189–250). Chicago: University of Chicago Press.

Farrington, D. P., & Welsh, B. C. (2007). *Saving children from a life of crime: Early risk factors and effective interventions*. New York: Oxford University Press.

Fergusson, D. M., & Horwood. L. J. (2002). Male and female offending trajectories. *Development and Psychopathology, 14*, 159–177.

Fergusson, D. M., Horwood, L. J., & Nagin, D. S. (2000). Offending trajectories in a New Zealand birth cohort. *Criminology, 38,* 525–552.

Hirschi, T., & Gottfredson, M. R. (1983). Age and the explanation of crime. *The American Journal of Sociology, 89,* 552–584.

Laub, J. H., & Sampson, R. J. (2003). *Shared beginnings, divergent lives: Delinquent boys to age 70.* Cambridge, MA: Harvard University Press.

Maughan, B. (2005). Developmental trajectory modeling: A view from developmental psychopathology. *The Annals of the American Academy of Political and Social Science, 602,* 118–130.

Moffitt, T. E. (1990). The neuropsychology of delinquency: A critical review of theory and research. In N. Morris & M. Tonry (Eds.), *Crime and justice: A review of research* (Vol. 12, pp. 99–169). Chicago: University of Chicago Press.

Moffitt, T. E. (1993). Adolescence-limited and life-course-persistent antisocial behavior: A developmental taxonomy. *Psychological Review, 100,* 674–701.

Moffitt, T. E. (2006). Life-course-persistent versus adolescence-limited antisocial behavior. In D. Cicchetti & D. Cohen (Eds.), *Developmental psychology* (2nd ed., Vol. 3, pp. 570–598). New York: Wiley.

Moffitt, T. E., & Caspi, A. (2001). Childhood predictors differentiate life-course persistent and adolescence-limited antisocial pathways among males and females. *Development and Psychopathology, 13,* 355–375.

Moffitt, T. E., Caspi, A., Harrington, H., & Milne, B. J. (2002). Males on the life-course-persistent and adolescence-limited antisocial pathways: Follow-up at age 26 years. *Development and Psychopathology, 14,* 179–207.

Moffitt, T. E., Caspi, A., Rutter, M., & Silva, P. A. (2001). *Sex differences in antisocial behaviour: Conduct disorder, delinquency, and violence in the Dunedin Longitudinal Study.* Cambridge, UK: Cambridge University Press.

Moffitt, T. E., Lynam, D. R., & Silva, P. A. (1994). Neuropsychological tests predicting persistent male delinquency. *Criminology, 32,* 277–300.

Nagin, D. S., Farrington, D. P., & Moffitt, T. E. (1995). Life-course trajectories of different types of offenders. *Criminology, 33,* 111–139.

Nagin, D. S., & Land, K. C. (1993). Age, criminal careers, and population heterogeneity: Specification and estimation of a nonparametric, mixed poisson model. *Criminology, 31,* 327.

Nagin, D. S., & Tremblay, R. E. (2005). Developmental trajectory groups: Fact or a useful statistical fiction? *Criminology, 43,* 873–904.

Piquero, A. R., & Brezina, T. (2001). Testing Moffitt's account of adolescence-limited delinquency. *Criminology, 39,* 353–370.

Piquero, A. R., Daigle, L. E., Gibson, C., Piquero, N. L., & Tibbetts, S. G. (2007). Research note: Are life-course-persistent offenders at risk for adverse health outcomes? *Journal of Research in Crime and Delinquency, 44,* 185–207.

Piquero, A. R., & Moffitt, T. E. (2005). Explaining the facts of crime: How the developmental taxonomy replies to Farrington's invitation. In D. P. Farrington (Ed.), *Integrated developmental and life course theories of offending* (Advances in Criminological Theory: Vol. 14, pp. 51–72). New Brunswick, NJ: Transaction.

Piquero, A. R., Moffitt, T. E., & Lawton, B. (2005). Race and crime: The contribution of individual, familial, and neighborhood risk factors of life-course-persistent offending. In D. Hawkins & K. Kempf-Leonard (Eds.), *Our children, their children: Race, crime, and the juvenile justice system* (pp. 202–244). Chicago: University of Chicago Press.

Piquero, A. R., & White, N. A. (2003). On the relationship between cognitive abilities and life-course-persistent offending among a sample of African Americans: A longitudinal test of Moffitt's hypothesis. *Journal of Criminal Justice, 31,* 399–409.

Robins, L. N. (1978). Sturdy childhood predictors of adult antisocial behavior: Replications From longitudinal studies. *Psychological Medicine, 8,* 611–622.

Sampson, R. J., & Laub, J. H. (2003). Life-course desisters? Trajectories of crime among delinquent boys followed to age 70. *Criminology, 41,* 555–592.

Silverthorn, P., & Frick, P. J. (1999). Developmental pathways to antisocial behavior: The delayed-onset pathways in girls. *Developmental Psychopathology, 11,* 101–126.

White, H. R., Bates, M. E., & Buyske, S. (2001). Adolescence-limited versus persistent delinquency: Extending Moffitt's hypothesis into adulthood. *Journal of Abnormal Psychology, 110,* 600–609.

Wolfgang, M., Figlio, R., & Sellin, T. (1972). *Delinquency in a birth cohort.* Chicago: University of Chicago Press.

MOORE, JOAN W.: HOMEBOYS AND HOMEGIRLS IN THE BARRIO

The main contributions of Joan W. Moore's research on barrios and gangs in East Los Angeles were her community-focused approach and her unique collaborative methodology. Unlike most studies of gangs by criminologists, Moore's community studies understood gangs, drugs, and prison as integral components of a barrio/ghetto system. Her attention to the role of women in the gang and her collaborative methodology have set a largely unmatched standard in the field. She is one of the few women to do research with gangs, and one of the few social scientists to sustain research in specific neighborhoods over decades.

Moore earned her M.A. from the University of Chicago in 1953 and her Ph.D. in 1959. Everett Hughes's courses on field research would make a lasting impact on her and would lead her to construct her perspective on gangs inductively through empirical research. Her studies at Chicago included courses by Lloyd Warner, Peter Blau, and Louis Wirth. But it was Hughes's methods courses, which sent his mainly white undergraduates out into Chicago's south side to see for themselves how poor black people lived, that would inspire her future Los Angeles research.

Unlike nearly all other researchers on gangs and poor minority communities, Moore did her dissertation on the power elite, exploring the "Stability and Instability in the Metropolitan Upper Class." After she left Chicago, she began research on the Mexican American Study Project at the University of California, Los Angeles. In the midst of the heat of the 1960s social movements, Moore complemented her research on the study of Mexicans in the United States by looking for ways to be involved in the communities she was studying.

She found a home in the Community Concern Corporation that worked with "pintos," or released prisoners who were mostly addicts. As she gave time and expertise to community work, she discovered that the pintos also all belonged to long-standing gangs. Her first book, *Homeboys*, was subtitled *Gangs, Drugs, and Prison in the Barrios of Los Angeles. Homeboys* and her follow-up, *Going Down to the Barrios*, were unique in the literature in (1) understanding of the integral role of gangs in barrios; (2) Moore's unprecedented collaborative research methods that included random sampling of gang *klikas*, or age-graded groups; and (3) laying the groundwork for extensive investigation of the role of women in gangs and drug use.

Gangs and Community

Moore believes her greatest contribution was in situating the study of gangs in the context of their communities. The East Los Angeles Mexican experience, which she had studied in her earlier research, gave her an understanding of how pintos and particularly their gangs fit into barrio life. Unlike the theory-testing approach of James F. Short and Fred Strodtbeck's *Group Process and Gang Delinquency*, or the theoretically driven *Delinquency and Opportunity* of Richard Cloward and Lloyd Ohlin, Moore based her analysis of East Los Angeles gangs on a historical analysis of their barrios: White Fence and Maravilla.

Moore's work stood in sharp distinction to Malcolm Klein's contemporary Los Angeles studies. Klein saw community context as less important than universal characteristics of delinquent peer groups, while Moore looked at how barrio gangs reflected the experience of racism and inequality of Mexicans in the United States. Her perspective and strong community support would earn her the hostility of Klein at the University of Southern California and eventual involuntary termination.

Few scholars after Frederick Thrasher's seminal work would base their analysis of gangs on community dynamics. William F. Whyte described East Boston gangs within a context of the Italian community. But most gang research was concerned mainly with cultural outlook (Walter Miller, Lewis Yablonsky, and Albert Cohen), group processes (Malcolm Klein and James F. Short), or variations in macro-structural features (Richard Cloward and Lloyd Ohlin as well as Irving Spergel). While some attention was paid to race and ethnicity, community context and the Chicago tradition declined throughout the 1940s and 1950s. One reason was that the main proliferation of gangs took place in black, Mexican, and Puerto Rican communities, and there were few minority researchers. Solving the problems of access and valid, reliable, and humane descriptions of minority gangs would become major trademarks of Moore's work.

Moore's *Homeboys* described the persistence of Mexican East Los Angeles gangs over decades as products of Mexican American history. She explained how Chicano gangs differed from the white ethnic gangs of traditional gang research. Rather than the gang being only an adolescent peer group, lasting only a short period before its members matured out of the gang, Moore pointed out that East Los Angeles gangs had persisted for decades. Borrowing from Hughes, she termed these gangs as "quasi-institutionalized" within the barrio. Unlike traditional gang theories, her research saw the gang as both adolescent and adult, firmly tied to heroin and drug addiction, and closely tied to the prison experience.

Moore's description of the ghetto/barrio economic and social system utilized a dual labor market model borrowed from economist Bennett Harrison. Her analysis of the closed worldview of the young barrio males reflected the persistence of a secondary labor market that promised little mobility to barrio youth. Writing in the mid-1970s, Moore was the first researcher to call attention to the sweeping changes in the economy and investigate how those changes might impact gangs.

Collaborative Research

Moore's methodology was derived from her studies under Hughes and Warner, but also was a straightforward way to solve the problem of access and validity in research. For Moore, the problem was obvious:

> Most importantly, unless community participants are actively involved in both the research and its uses, as we have done in this study, both the research and its ultimate uses tend to be highly suspect. While this can be termed politicization, the alternative is not every pleasant either. Unless the community is involved, so-called objective research will almost inevitably be politicized beyond the researcher's control. (Moore, 1978, p. 10)

In order to access the pinto subculture, it was necessary to secure cooperation of pintos. The misuse of research by social scientists was a major issue at the time, with Project Camelot and other examples of research used for elite purposes. For Moore, research needed to be protected from politicization by the powerful, and the only way to safeguard such misuse was to firmly embed research in the community.

Thus, Moore would serve as the Chair of the Board of Directors of the Community Concern Corporation, an organization founded and run completely by pintos: former convicts, drug addicts, and gang members. Her long association with Robert Garcia, former White Fence member, was as important for her research as Doc was for William F. Whyte. But unlike Whyte, Moore's work was embedded in a collaborative effort of dozens of ex-gang members, organized into a research corporation, and dedicated to use the research to aid their community. Moore also testified as an expert witness on behalf of community groups and consultant to a host of community projects. Her involvement continued for many years in East Los Angeles and was not bounded by this or that funded study. Thus she gained credibility within the community that can only be secured with time.

Her collaborative method differed radically from ethnography, Moore wrote in an essay coauthored by Robert Garcia. The research relied on its legitimacy within the community of those being researched and was carried out by trained staff drawn from that same community. For Moore, while this method was ethical, it was also the best means to assure validity. It confronted the tendency, in both ethnography and survey research, for respondents to put on displays and performances for well-meaning researchers. Collaborative research, for Moore, was a way to get to Erving Goffman's "back stage" knowledge, to find out what the actors say to one another, not "perform" to authorities.

This unique research model used random samples of gang members drawn from klikas over the past decades to draw conclusions about gang life. Using the insider knowledge of her pinto collaborators, Moore was able to assemble rosters of gang members in nearly all klikas and randomly sample them for interviews. This produced the first, and in many ways, only truly scientific sample of gang members in the history of gang research. Moore's findings, humanizing gang members and portraying them as real people within a no-exit barrio system, was a direct product of her method.

Women and Gangs

One other way Moore's research stands out is her focus on women. From the beginning of her research, the role of women in community life was obvious, as was the influence of heroin and barrio gangs. She was principal investigator of a "Women and Heroin" study funded by the National Institute on Drug Abuse, and she produced a host of reports and articles about women and drug use. She found that the "cholo" culture of East Los Angeles barrios severely handicapped women as they struggled with drug use and survival. Chicanas, Moore found, were more damaged going into the gangs and were more damaged by their gang experience than males. They were "doubly deviant"—both as gang members and as women, violating conventional gender norms.

Her book *Going Down to the Barrio: Homeboys and Homegirls in Change* returns to Los Angeles to compare gangs active in the 1940s with those active in the 1970s. The study was based on a random sample of male and females and examined how the barrios had changed and not changed over the years. She noted the increasing presence and normalcy of gang members and drug use and sales. She also noted that fully a third of all gang members in East Los Angeles were women, and *Going Down to the Barrio* looked carefully at both males and females. It is difficult to argue with Moore's (1991, p. 136) claim of her examination of women that "such even-handed treatment is virtually unknown in the literature on gangs." Many of Moore's later writings would be devoted to reviews of the literature on females in and around gangs, and what is known of female gangs around the world.

Conclusion

In 1984, Moore was elected president of the Society for the Study of Social Problems, and her work has been pathbreaking. Still, her "outsider" status as a woman doing gang research may have kept her work from the acclaim it deserves. After leaving Los Angeles, she moved to the University of Wisconsin–Milwaukee where she continued her studies of East Los Angeles gangs and then went on to sponsor gang research in Milwaukee and nurture it elsewhere. Among those she mentored in gang research were Diego Vigil, Avelardo Valdez, and John Hagedorn.

In an era when gangs are being increasingly demonized, Moore's research stands out as a model

of how to use social science to humanize the gang member, while pulling no punches on the ugly side of gang life. The bulk of today's federally funded gang studies are concerned with law enforcement questions of control. Moore's research, however, turns attention to the conditions in barrios and ghettos and to how gang members attempt to both survive and make meaning. Her conclusion to *Going Down to the Barrio* might set the research agenda for the next decade. She says that gangs take on increased importance under changing economic circumstances, and have an increased impact on young kids (p. 138). Research in the future will be greatly indebted to the corpus of Moore's work.

John M. Hagedorn

See also Bourgois, Philippe: In Search of Respect; Campbell, Anne: Girls in the Gang; Horowitz, Ruth, and Gary Schwartz: Honor and Gang Delinquency; Jankowski, Martin Sanchez: Islands in the Street; Klein, Malcolm W., and Cheryl L. Maxson: Street Gang Structure and Organization; Maher, Lisa: Sexed Work; Miller, Jody: Girls, Gangs, and Gender

References and Further Readings

Hughes, E. (1971). Bastard institutions. In *The sociological eye: Selected papers* (pp. 98–105). Chicago: Aldine-Atherton.

Klein, M. (1971). *Street gangs and street workers.* Englewood Cliffs, NJ: Prentice Hall.

Moore, J. W. (1978). *Homeboys: Gangs, drugs, and prison in the barrios of Los Angeles.* Philadelphia: Temple University Press.

Moore, J. W. (1991). *Going down to the barrio: Homeboys and homegirls in change.* Philadelphia: Temple University Press.

Moore, J. W., & Garcia, R. (1979). *Research in minority communities: Collaborative and street ethnography models compared.* Milwaukee: Urban Research Center, University of Wisconsin–Milwaukee.

Moore, J. W., & Mata, A. (1981). *Women and heroin in Chicano communities.* Los Angeles: Chicano Pinto Research Project.

Vigil, D. (1988). *Barrio gangs.* Austin: University of Texas Press.

N

NAGIN, DANIEL S., AND RAYMOND PATERNOSTER: INDIVIDUAL DIFFERENCES AND DETERRENCE

This theory, proposed by Daniel Nagin and Raymond Paternoster, combines ideas from several other prominent criminology theories in a unique way. Thus, the *theory of individual differences and deterrence* (IDD) represents an important integration, elaboration, and synthesis of different streams of thought in the field of criminology. Drawing from deterrence theory, IDD places considerable weight on the crime-reducing effects of sanction threats. Although deterrence theory is one of the oldest formal theories of criminal behavior, criminologists have long been dissatisfied with its dominant focus on the effects of sanction threats. To address this concern, economists, social psychologists, and criminologists have proposed a range of so-called rational choice theories that emphasize both the benefits and the costs of criminal behavior.

While most rational choice theories represent an important advance over traditional deterrence-focused theories, many of these perspectives provide limited insight into the problem of how two individuals—faced with the same set of objective costs and benefits—might come to very different decisions about whether and how much to offend. Rational choice theories have long recognized that individuals may simply differ in their tendency to prefer risky or exciting acts or the benefits of immediate gratification. But IDD theory attempts to more completely fill in the picture by specifying a formal theory of why individuals weigh the costs and benefits of offending in different ways.

Deterrence and Rational Choice

The powerful idea that the threat of sanctions can deter individuals from committing crimes traces its roots back to the foundational 18th-century-work of Cesare Beccaria and Jeremy Bentham. This work has become known as the Classical School and its primary argument is that the decision to offend will be sensitive to the certainty, swiftness, and severity of legal sanctions. Rational choice theorists argue that this perspective is too limited since it ignores informal sanction threats and the rewards of criminal behavior. Informal sanction threats and rewards can be easy to measure and quantify, or they can be the result of relatively complex, individual-specific, mental calculation. As Nagin and Paternoster point out, many rational choice theories also allow for a moral dimension in the explanation of offending. Thus, conscience can form a barrier to offending even if the other benefits of offending outweigh the costs. Though the rational choice perspective surely provides a more complete picture of decision-making calculus than deterrence theory, it has been limited by vague and incomplete descriptions of the process by which people approach the actual weighing of costs and benefits.

Key Theoretical Linkages

To more completely specify the process of deterrence and rational choice processes involved in decision making, Nagin and Paternoster draw on several principal theoretical ideas. These ideas flow primarily from the self-control theory of Travis Hirschi and Michael Gottfredson and the biocentric rational-choice perspective of James Q. Wilson and Richard Herrnstein. According to these perspectives, individuals vary in their tendency to think about the long-term implications of their behavior (present-orientation) and the effects of their behavior on other people (self-centeredness). Additionally, these perspectives both maintain that individual differences in present-orientation and self-centeredness are established relatively early in life. Also, once established, these differences are relatively time-stable; individuals who rank high in the population on present-orientation and self-centeredness early in life will tend to rank high in the population on these characteristics later in life.

Additionally, Nagin and Paternoster draw on two key concepts from Travis Hirschi's original theory of social control. According to control theories, people will naturally be inclined to offend because offending is the most expeditious and immediately satisfying solution to many problems. The question, then, is not why people offend but why they do not offend. According to Hirschi, attachment to others, commitments to conformity, involvement in conventional activities, and moral beliefs are barriers to offending activity. Like social control theorists, Nagin and Paternoster argue that attachments to others and commitments to conformity are essential for developing and strengthening relationships and a reputation for dependability.

Finally, the role of chance events and "turning points" discussed in Robert Sampson and John Laub's life-course control theory of criminal behavior allows for a "random component" in the explanation of why some individuals who were previously active offenders are able to turn away from criminality. A caring teacher, persistent relative, or attentive mentor can lead to important life transitions for individuals who might otherwise be doomed to a life of criminal behavior and other serious difficulties. Nagin and Paternoster's theory also allows for the possibility that seemingly random chance occurrences can set the stage for major changes in life direction.

Summary of Individual Differences and Deterrence Theory

Nagin and Paternoster contend that attachments and commitments can be viewed as investments that increase in value with the passage of time. In that sense, attachments and commitments can be viewed as commodities or "personal capital," which can translate into specific benefits (e.g., job security, marital satisfaction, a secure financial position, and comfortable lifestyle). The accumulation of personal capital requires some sacrifice at one point in time in order to reap returns at later points in time. As the assets of relationships and reputations strengthen and mature, people have more to lose by engaging in behaviors that run contrary to those assets. But all individuals are not equally likely to develop reservoirs of personal capital. According to IDD theory, personal capital is most likely to accumulate when people are able to delay gratification and contemplate how their actions affect other people. They do note that the relationship between present orientation and self-centeredness and the development of personal capital is a probabilistic relationship. Chance events, such as those discussed by Sampson and Laub, can intervene to divert people toward and away from the development of personal capital. The theory's key axiom is that individuals with high levels of personal capital have more to lose by engaging in criminal behavior and are, thus, more "deterrable."

Theoretical Implications

Rational choice considerations are predicted to operate for all people, but they are predicted to be more salient for individuals with high levels of personal capital. This elaborated theory of rational choice provides us with concrete, testable hypotheses about why some individuals appear to be more "rational" and sensitive to costs and benefits of offending than others.

Robert Brame

See also Braithwaite, John: Reintegrative Shaming Theory; Gottfredson, Michael R., and Travis Hirschi: Self-Control Theory; Hagan, John, and Bill McCarthy: Social Capital and Crime; Hirschi, Travis: Social Control Theory; Pogarsky, Greg: Behavioral Economics and Crime; Sherman, Lawrence W.: Defiance Theory

References and Further Readings

Gottfredson, M. R., & Hirschi, T. (1990). *A general theory of crime.* Stanford, CA: Stanford University Press.

Hirschi, T. (1969). *Causes of delinquency.* Berkeley: University of California Press.

Nagin, D. S., & Paternoster, R. (1991). The preventive effects of the perceived risk of arrest: Testing an expanded conception of deterrence. *Criminology, 29,* 561–588.

Nagin, D. S., & Paternoster, R. (1993). Enduring individual differences and rational choice theories of crime. *Law and Society Review, 27,* 467–496.

Nagin, D. S., & Paternoster, R. (1994). Personal capital and social control: The deterrence implications of a theory of individual differences in criminal offending. *Criminology, 32,* 581–606.

Sampson, R. J., & Laub, J. H. (1993). *Crime in the making: Pathways and turning points through life.* Cambridge, MA: Harvard University Press.

Wilson, J. Q., & Herrnstein, R. J. (1985). *Crime and human nature.* New York: Simon & Schuster.

NEGOTIATED COEXISTENCE

Christopher Browning, Seth Feinberg, and Robert Dietz's "negotiated coexistence" model of community crime describes the paradoxical process by which intra-neighborhood social ties both contribute to social control orientations within urban neighborhoods and, simultaneously, generate social capital for resident offenders. Neighborhood residents who offend within their own community may draw on social capital to avoid sanction and maintain a presence in the community, complicating the local regulation of crime. The negotiated coexistence model is rooted in, but challenges, the classic social disorganization perspective on crime and John Kasarda and Morris Janowitz's subsequent "systemic" reformulation. Below, the systemic approach and Robert Sampson and colleagues' more recent "collective efficacy" approach to understanding community crime are described; then the entry turns to the core tenets of the negotiated coexistence model. The entry concludes with a brief review of empirical assessments of the negotiated coexistence approach and prospects for future development and testing of the theory.

Social Disorganization and the Systemic Model

In a classic statement of the "social disorganization" perspective, Clifford Shaw and Henry McKay argued that structural disadvantage at the neighborhood level—most notably poverty, residential instability, and racial/ethnic heterogeneity—attenuated the community-level capacity to achieve shared goals, including the local control of crime. In *Juvenile Delinquency in Urban Areas,* Shaw and McKay offered initial empirical support for a link between aspects of neighborhood structural disadvantage and the prevalence of crime. Their insights remain relevant today, as researchers continue to acknowledge the role of neighborhood structural disadvantage in explaining crime rate variations across urban space. Nevertheless, the approach has been criticized for failing to effectively articulate and measure the intervening mechanisms linking disadvantaged macro-level structure with crime.

Kasarda and Janowitz's systemic model of community social dynamics played a key role in the theoretical development of the social disorganization model by highlighting the link between residential stability, local social bonds, and the emergence of locality based solidarities. In their view, the local community could be seen as "a complex system of friendship and kinship networks and formal and informal associational ties rooted in family life and ongoing socialization processes" (1974, p. 329). Accordingly, the prevalence and strength of local networks was posited to be a key intervening social process through which neighborhoods acquired cohesion and identified shared values. Similarly, Ruth Rosner Kornhauser's reformulation of the social disorganization approach emphasized the role of attenuated social ties in linking macro-level structural disadvantage with diminished informal social control capacity. Thus, both approaches placed considerable stock in the capacity of social network ties to foster effective action on behalf of collective goals such as the local control of crime.

Empirical assessment of the regulatory role of social networks, however, has not yielded strong support for the systemic model's assumptions. Research investigating the influence of dense or prevalent neighborhood social networks on local crime rates has not offered consistent evidence that networks contribute to crime control. Empirical support for the contention that networks are a key mediating link in the association between neighborhood structural disadvantage and crime has also been limited. Consequently, the systemic and related approaches have been criticized for lacking an effective explanation of communities with extensive social ties and local attachments that nevertheless maintain relatively high crime rates.

Negotiated Coexistence

The negotiated coexistence model draws on key insights from the systemic and collective efficacy perspectives while positing a more complex and potentially paradoxical relationship between aspects of neighborhood social organization and crime. The negotiated coexistence model incorporates the systemic assumption that local social ties and the solidarities they promote contribute to normative orientations that support the control of crime and criminogenic conditions. Networks, however, are not presumed to function exclusively to limit the prevalence of crime.

The notion that networks may promote crime is certainly not a new one, and can be linked with the long-standing tradition of "sub-cultural" and peer-influence models that focus on the social dissemination of crime-tolerant attitudes. The negotiated coexistence model, however, does not assume that the crime-enhancing impact of neighborhood social networks operates through such a mechanism. Rather, offenders are acknowledged to maintain social ties with both potential offenders as well as "conventional" residents within urban neighborhoods. Ties to mainstream social networks, in turn, provide opportunities for conventional residents to monitor and sanction local offenders but also lead to the accumulation of social capital for the latter. Negotiated coexistence thus describes the process by which local social organization both regulates and protects the presence of potential offenders within urban communities.

Below, the key elements of social organization central to the model of negotiated coexistence—networks and reciprocated exchange, solidarity, trust, and social control—from the standpoint of Alejandro Portes's discussion of the sources of social capital are reviewed. Then insights from the collective efficacy perspective and recent ethnographic research are incorporated to articulate the counter-intuitive process by which local social ties diminish the effectiveness of neighborhood-based informal social control.

The negotiated coexistence model acknowledges the multifaceted nature of social capital and the potential for competition between objectives toward which different social capital types may be deployed. Portes's typology of social capital offers a useful framework for understanding this process. Portes describes three key types of social capital: as applied to neighborhoods, *bounded solidarity* captures locality-based identities and attachments that may foster prosocial activities on behalf of fellow residents (including the control of public space and vulnerability to victimization); *enforceable trust* promotes positive activity on behalf of the neighborhood in exchange for some reward or compensation by the collectivity (e.g., intervention on behalf of a neighbor threatened with victimization in anticipation of praise from the wider community and future unspecified benefits for conformity to shared community values); finally, *reciprocated exchanges* of information, favors, or material assistance contribute to an informal economy of "social chits" between actors, repayment of which is not governed by a clear expectations as to form or timing.

The three forms of social capital identified can be distinguished based on their origin in a common social structure versus direct ties: Bounded solidarity and enforceable trust do not require direct ties between actors but, rather, shared membership in a group; reciprocated exchanges, in contrast, imply interaction. In the context of a neighborhood, the question of whether a particular form of social capital requires a social tie or not has implications for the analysis of two key functions of social capital: social control and network-mediated benefits. Neighborhood-based social control likely arises, principally, out of bounded solidarity and enforceable trust, according to Portes. Sampson and colleagues also link locality-based solidarities and trust with shared expectations for action on behalf of local goals—the combination of which they label "collective efficacy."

The negotiated coexistence model expects that network-mediated exchanges on a large scale will promote community attachment and trust. Network interaction and exchange, however, also results in the accumulation of obligations at a dyad or small group level. Outstanding obligations generated by extensive network exchange (including offenders and potential offenders) may compete with the social control objectives of the collectivity. Network ties that produce social capital for offenders may result in the attenuation of sanctions against them, diminishing the force and effectiveness of neighborhood level social control.

Offenders may accrue benefits both directly and indirectly from more extensive residentially based networks. Offenders who are linked to conventional residents may leverage their potentially rich set of ties and obligations. Intergenerational closure within urban neighborhoods, for instance, may promote social control efforts of local adults directed toward youth who are not their own children. Nevertheless, these efforts are likely to be limited in severity if ties between intergenerationally connected parents are strong. Mary Pattillo captures this countervailing dynamic in an ethnographic analysis of a middle-class African American neighborhood. Although community ties were extensive and identification with the neighborhood was strong, broad-based acquaintance networks and familiarity led to hedging of social control actions. On witnessing a criminal act by a local adolescent, a neighborhood resident stated, "I didn't wanna give this young man's name [to the police] because his mama is such a sweet lady" (Pattillo, 1998, p. 765). The adolescent's social capital (through the network-mediated exchanges of his mother) resulted in a more muted response of the witnessing resident to the offense—specifically, not involving formal authorities. Although potentially benefitting the adolescent in the long run (to the extent that contact with the criminal justice system diminishes long-term prospects), the community is exposed to the continued presence of the adolescent offender.

Offenders may also acquire social capital through direct ties with more conventional neighborhood residents. Scott Decker and Barrik Van Winkle, for instance, found that gang member ties to, and exchanges with, family and extended kin groups were extensive. Other research by Robert MaCoun and Peter Reuter and Mercer Sullivan has documented the level of social (including instrumental) support provided by gang members to within neighborhood-based social networks. Sudhir Alladi

Venkatesh's research suggests that provision of security is also a service frequently provided by local gang members to other community residents. These direct forms of social capital accumulation, though difficult to document, are likely extensive, and may result in conflicts with social control orientations shared at the community level.

As noted, research on the role of network ties in regulating crime has offered mixed evidence on the benefits of networks for the control of local crime. Jeffrey Morenoff, Robert Sampson, and Stephen Raudenbush, for instance, found that while the prevalence of friendship and kinship ties among neighborhood residents positively predicted levels of collective efficacy in Chicago neighborhoods, networks had no direct effect on homicide rates once the level of neighborhood collective efficacy was controlled. Browning and colleagues found that simultaneous estimation of the effect of collective efficacy and social interaction and exchange on crime rates at the community level revealed *positive* effects of social interaction on measures of both violence and property crime. In a direct test of the negotiated coexistence model, social interaction and exchange was found to interact with collective efficacy such that the regulatory effect of the latter was diminished as interaction/exchange increased.

Other research has also offered findings consistent with the expectations of the negotiated coexistence perspective. Examining hypotheses drawn from William Julius Wilson and Douglas Massey and Nancy Denton, Matthew Lee and Graham Ousey found that greater residential exposure of economically disadvantaged to more affluent African Americans does little to reduce violent crime rates. The authors speculated that, consistent with the negotiated coexistence perspective, the protective effects of socioeconomic integration may be offset by the greater likelihood of offender integration into conventional networks when residential exposures are racially homogeneous. Based on in-depth qualitative interviews of a sample of urban youth, Deanna Wilkinson found that social control efforts of local adults were less likely to involve calling the police when social ties between adults and youth were stronger. Thus preliminary tests have offered evidence in support of the basic assumptions of the negotiated coexistence model.

Conclusion

The negotiated coexistence approach acknowledges the ambiguous and complex role played by social network ties in the control of urban neighborhood crime. Urban communities are faced with multiple collective objectives, including the informal control of public space and freedom from predatory crime. Although community social ties may encourage shared values and inclinations to act on behalf of collective goals, they are also sustained by exchange dynamics that may conflict with broader community goals. When outstanding social obligations limit the severity of social control efforts directed against offenders, communities may experience more difficulty in regulating local crime. Future research on the negotiated coexistence model would benefit from more detailed social network data capturing the extent to which potential offenders are integrated into mainstream community networks. Such data, though difficult to collect, would shed more nuanced light on the role of network integration in both fostering and impeding the informal social control of crime.

Chris Browning

See also Bursik, Robert J., Jr., and Harold C. Grasmick: Levels of Control; Krivo, Lauren J., and Ruth D. Peterson: Extreme Disadvantage and Crime; Sampson, Robert J.: Collective Efficacy Theory; Sampson, Robert J., and William Julius Wilson: Contextualized Subculture; Shaw, Clifford R., and Henry D. McKay: Social Disorganization Theory; Systemic Model of Social Disorganization

References and Further Readings

Bellair, P. E. (1997). Social interaction and community crime: Examining the importance of neighbor networks. *Criminology, 35,* 677–704.

Browning, C. R. (2009). Illuminating the downside of social capital: Negotiated coexistence, property crime, and disorder in urban neighborhoods. *American Behavioral Scientist, 52,* 1556–1578.

Browning, C. R., Feinberg, S. L., & Dietz, R. (2004). The paradox of social organization: Networks, collective efficacy, and violent crime in urban neighborhoods. *Social Forces, 83,* 503–534.

Bursik, R. J., & Grasmick, H. G. (1993). *Neighborhoods and crime: The dimensions of effective community control.* New York: Lexington Books.

Clinard, M. B., & Abbott, D. J. (1976). Community organization and property crime. In J. F. Short (Ed.), *Community organization and property crime* (pp. 186–206). Chicago: University of Chicago Press.

Decker, S. H., & Van Winkle, B. (1996). *Life in the gang: Family, friends, and violence.* New York: Cambridge University Press.

Greenberg, S. W., Rohe, W. M., & Williams, J. R. (1982). *Safe and secure neighborhoods: Physical characteristics and informal territorial control in high and low crime neighborhoods.* Washington, DC: U.S. Department of Justice, National Institute of Justice.

Kasarda, J. D., & Janowitz, M. (1974). Community attachment in mass society. *American Sociological Review, 39,* 328–339.

Kornhauser, R. R. (1978). *Social sources of delinquency.* Chicago: University of Chicago Press.

Lee, M. R., & Ousey, G. C. (2007). Counterbalancing disadvantage? Residential integration and urban black homicide. *Social Problems, 54,* 240–262.

Macoby, E. E., Johnson, J. P., & Church, R. M. (1958). Community integration and the social control of juvenile delinquency. *Journal of Social Issues, 14,* 38–51.

MaCoun, R., & Reuter, P. (1991). Are the wages of sin $30 an hour: Economic aspects of street-level drug dealing. *Crime and Delinquency, 38,* 477–491.

Massey, D. S., & Denton, N. A. (1993). *American apartheid: Segregation and the making of the underclass.* Cambridge, MA: Harvard University Press.

Merry, S. (1981). *Urban danger: Life in a neighborhood of strangers.* Philadelphia: Temple University Press.

Morenoff, J. D., Sampson, R. J., & Raudenbush, S. W. (2001). Neighborhood inequality, collective efficacy, and the spatial dynamics of urban violence. *Criminology, 39,* 517–560.

Pattillo, M. E. (1998). Sweet mothers and gangbangers: Managing crime in a black middle-class neighborhood. *Social Forces, 76,* 747–774.

Pattillo-McCoy, M. (1999). *Black picket fences.* Chicago: University of Chicago Press.

Portes, A. (1998). Social capital: Its origins and applications in modern sociology. *Annual Review of Sociology, 24,* 1–24.

Sampson, R. J., Raudenbush, S. W., & Earls, F. (1997). Neighborhoods and violent crime: A multilevel study of collective efficacy. *Science, 227,* 918–923.

Shaw, C. R., & McKay, H. D. (1969). *Juvenile delinquency and urban areas.* Chicago: University of Chicago Press.

Simcha-Fagan, O., & Schwartz, J. E. (1986). Neighborhood and delinquency: An assessment of contextual effects. *Criminology, 24,* 667–703.

Sullivan, M. L. (1989). *Getting paid: Youth, crime, and work in the inner city*. Ithaca, NY: Cornell University Press.

Venkatesh, S. A. (1997). The social organization of street gang activity in an urban ghetto. *American Journal of Sociology, 103*, 82–111.

Warner, B. D., & Wilcox Rountree, P. (1997). Local social ties in a community and crime model: Questioning the systemic nature of informal social control. *Social Problems, 44*, 520–536.

Wilkinson, D. L. (2007). Local social ties and willingness to intervene: Textured views among violent urban youth of neighborhood social control dynamics and situations. *Justice Quarterly, 24*, 185–220.

Wilson, W. J. (1996). *When work disappears*. New York: Knopf.

NEUROLOGY AND CRIME

The beginning of the search for the neurological basis of crime can be traced back to Cesare Lombroso, an Italian criminologist and physician who provided one of the most influential arguments that criminals are born with a nature favorable to crime. Although no direct means exists to examine in vivo the brain anatomy of criminals at the time, Lombroso managed to identify several distinct physical features, which he called "stigmata." This included a slanting forehead, long/no ear lobes, a large jaw with no chin, heavy supraorbital ridges, excessive/absent hair on the body, and an extreme sensitivity/ insensitivity to pain. According to Lombroso, the possession of multiple physical abnormalities indicated that the individual was less developed, a "born criminal," and thus could not adjust to the rules of modern society. Although Lombroso's argument was less than sound, the idea that criminal behavior is influenced by biological predispositions has endured and gained significant interest since then.

With the development of brain imaging, the emphasis has since shifted to establish the connection between disruptions in the neural system and elevated criminal behavior. Criminal behavior, especially aggression, can be observed even in toddlers at the age of 1 to 2 years, when the brain is far from mature to allow full control over behavior. As the neural systems mature, children learn to deal with their aggressive impulses in a socially appropriate manner, and aggressive behavior diminishes as a result. Therefore, it has been predicted that if development of the neural system were interrupted (e.g., prenatal or postnatal damage to the brain), the maldeveloped, immature brain would be unable to function properly in behavior control and moral reasoning and continue to use aggressive behavior as a means to obtain goals.

Several theories have been proposed to further explain the association between neurological deficits and criminal offending. Among them, three major theories have been most widely accepted and intensively tested: Terrie Moffitt's *developmental theory*, Antonio Damasio's *somatic marker hypothesis*, and Jeffrey Gray's *dual biological model*. Below, each hypothesis and the supporting evidence for it is reviewed. The discussion is extended by drawing additional evidence for these hypotheses from individuals with traumatic brain injuries (TBIs) to demonstrate the high prevalence of neuropathology in criminal offenders. This entry concludes by assessing the hypothesized links between neurology and crime and by discussing implications for future studies.

Theories on Neurology and Crime

Moffitt's Developmental Theory of Crime

This theory was developed based on Moffitt's 1993 groundbreaking work indicating that signs of persistent deviant behavior during adolescence can be detected as early as the preschool year and are influenced by the behavior of peer groups. This theory identified two groups of delinquents—the life-course-persistent (LCP) and the adolescent-limited (AL) offenders—based on their ages of onset and trajectories of conduct problems. The AL group may only be engaging in criminal activities as a way of expressing their adolescent rebellion and usually desist from any pathway toward crime. By contrast, the LCP group precociously escalates into serious criminal offenses as a way of expanding the versatility of their antisocial tendencies and usually maintain a lifestyle of repeated criminal offending. According to the theory, the LCP offenders may suffer prenatal and perinatal disruptions in neural development that contribute to their persistent criminal behavior. These neurological deficits, which in most cases were too subtle to require clinical remediation, often manifested as behavioral problems such as inattention, hyperactivity, irritability, and impulsivity. Thus, neurological deficits in the LCP offenders may put them at higher risk for early-onset conduct disorders, which often escalate to persistent delinquent behaviors when interacting with an unsupportive environment.

Moffitt's developmental theory has received strong support from neuropsychological studies confirming that LCP offenders may indeed have neurocognitive impairments that reflect underlying neurological disturbances. For example, one study found that LCP offenders show lower intelligence, impaired spatial memory, and poor performance on tasks targeting frontal functions such as the continuous performance task. Findings from these studies suggest that neuropsychological impairments are especially prominent in LCP offenders. However, the lack of empirical studies assessing the structural and functional integrity in the neural system in these individuals prevent direct testing of the neuropathology in LCP offenders predicted by this hypothesis.

Damasio's Somatic Marker Hypothesis

The somatic marker hypothesis, formulated by Damasio in 1994, argues that emotion could guide or bias the decision-making process through the neural system of the somatic marker mechanism. This theory, although developed based on findings of patients with brain lesions, represents a complementary theory that readily applies to the neurological basis of criminal behavior. Damasio suggested that in real life, decision making involves both cognitive and emotional processing to assess the reward value of the various behavioral options available in any particular situation. When the situations are complex and conflicting, the reward values of the actions are uncertain and ambiguous, which induce physiological affective states (e.g., changes in skin conductance levels) followed by the forming of action-outcome associations (i.e., somatic markers). The somatic markers from all previous experiences are summed to produce a net somatic state to assist future decision making in similar situations by directing the selection of an appropriate action to achieve the most beneficial outcome. This process allows healthy individuals to categorize and learn from negative experiences. Because the ventromedial prefrontal cortex (VMPFC) is the essential component of this somatic marker hypothesis, damage to this structure may disrupt the mechanism and prevent the individual from experiencing the feedback necessary for producing somatic markers to avoid future aversive consequences. Such failure in the process will likely predispose to the inability to learn from punishment thus recidivate during conflict situations.

This hypothesis received a great deal of support from subsequent lesion studies. Patients with bilateral damage to the VMPFC often suffer from behavioral disinhibition, social dysfunction, emotional deficiency, poor decision making, and a lack of insight into their behavioral problem, which may lead to criminal offending. One such case is that of Phineas Gage, a railway foreman who had an iron stake blown through his frontal lobe in an accident involving explosives. Gage survived the injury, recovering his physical and intellectual abilities, but his personality changed dramatically and he became markedly antisocial. In general, the social, emotional, motivational, and behavioral dysfunction of these patients with damage to the VMPFC was often accompanied by a change in personality, which put them at greater risk for criminal offending. Furthermore, it was observed that these patients show aggressive behavior that is exclusively impulsive in nature (Anderson et al., 1999; Grafman et al., 1996), which reflects a limitation of this theory: it cannot account for some types of criminal offending, particularly instrumental aggression (Blair et al., 2005).

Gray's Dual Biological Model

Gray proposed a dual biological model, which at the core are two competing motivational systems: the behavioral inhibition system (BIS) and the behavioral activation system (BAS) (Fowles, 1988; Gray, 1982). The BIS represents an inhibitory system for withholding behavior in ambiguous threatening situations, whereas the BAS is the underlying system for impulsivity. The two systems are located in different parts of the brain. The BIS is in the septo-hippocampal region and the BAS is in the basal ganglia, thalamic nuclei, and the ventral tegmental area (Gray, 1994). This theory has been employed specifically for explaining aggression by Angela Scarpa and Adrian Raine, who suggested that violent behavior is a function of an underactive BIS, an overactive BAS, or a combination of both. This pattern of weak BIS and possibly a strong BAS in this dual biological mechanism has also been referred to when explaining clinical conditions for which criminal recidivism is a core symptom, such as psychopathy (Fowles, 1988). Therefore, it may be predicted that individuals with criminal tendencies would show behavioral features of decreased anxiety, increased impulsivity, and a reward-driven decision-making process due to neurobiological impairments in septo-hippocampal, basal ganglia, thalamic nuclei, and ventral tegmental structures.

Although no study to date has simultaneously examined these behavioral and neurobiological characteristics in criminal offenders, this theory has received considerable support from socio-behavioral and neuroimaging studies separately. For example, significantly high in impulsivity and low in anxiety compared to controls has been found in a group of violent offenders. With regard to neuroimaging literature, studies to date have provided some evidence for deficits in the neural system underlying the BIS system, particularly in the hippocampus, which may contribute to the weakness of this system in antisocial, criminal individuals. For example, it has been demonstrated that violent offenders with APD and type-2 alcoholism show reduced volume in the right hippocampus. In addition, an exaggerated structural hippocampal asymmetry (right > left) has been found in criminal psychopaths. Functional imaging studies also showed reduced blood flow in the hippocampus in violent offenders and murderers However, the integrity of the neural system underlying BAS remains to be examined.

Supporting Evidence From Traumatic Brain Injuries

Although different mechanisms were proposed, all three major theories on neurology and crime predict that neurological deficits in several brain regions, through impairing the processes of attention, decision making, and impulse control, may result in the elevation of criminal behavior. This argument is consistent with findings showing higher rates of traumatic brain injuries in criminal offenders.

Traumatic brain injuries (TBIs), ranging from subclinical to fatal in severity, are one of the leading causes of morbidity and mortality in children and adolescents in the United States. Most TBIs were suffered during a fall, motor vehicle accident, assault, or suicide attempt, and put the individuals at higher risk for developing functional impairments. Evidence has been accumulated suggesting a high correlation between violent crime and neurological brain damage. For example, in a study of 15 death-row inmates, it was found that all violent offenders had a history of severe head injury and 5 had major neurological impairment. Several investigations on delinquent youths also reported similar associations between TBI and antisocial behavior. For example, one study found half of the delinquent youths in their sample had experienced one or more TBIs, and one third of those with TBI histories reported diminished ability in regulating behavior and emotion, sustaining attention, and performing in social and school settings as a result of their TBIs. In a large study of 279 Vietnam veterans, it was found that veterans who suffered penetrating head injuries during their service had higher ratings of violence, aggression, anger, and hostility than those without brain injury. Similarly, one study reported that 27.7 percent of the delinquent youths they studied had suffered significant head injury involving loss of consciousness/amnesia with ongoing cognitive or social impairment.

The severity of antisocial criminal behavior in individuals with TBI not only fails to improve but also becomes greater over time. For example, in a longitudinal study, it was found that the frequency of aggressive behavior and severity of temper bursts in a group of TBI patients increased over time, and the aggressiveness was reported by caregivers as moderate or severe in 31 percent of cases by 2 years post-injury. Similar patterns were documented in a 5-year study following 42 patients with severe TBIs. They exhibited a significant increase in threats of violence at 5 years after the injury (54 percent) compared to 15 percent at 1 year post-injury. They also noted that 7 percent of their sample had been in trouble with the law during the first year post-injury, and that the rate increased to 31 percent at 5 years post-injury. The arrest and conviction rates of individuals with TBIs were especially alarming when compared to the rate of 2 percent of the general population arrested annually. In addition, the increasing arrest and incarceration rates over the years post-injury raise concerns about the long-term effects of traumatic brain injuries.

These findings consistently show that individuals with TBI are more likely to misperceive elements of a situation (e.g., interpret other's sarcasm as a threat), make poor social judgments, overreact to provocative stimuli, and lack the communication skills to verbally dissolve the conflict, especially when the neural damage involves the frontal lobe. As a result, these emotional and behavioral dysfunctions associated with TBIs may increase the likelihood that one would resort to antisocial, criminal behavior when encountering complicated and conflicting situations. The supporting evidence from TBI studies provide strong evidence for a neurological basis of crime and support the theories in connecting deficits in the neural system including the frontal cortex and hippocampus to deviant behavior and violent offending.

Conclusion

The increasing evidence from lesion and brain imaging studies has confirmed the association between neurological deficits and crime, and has prompted the development of several theories including Moffitt's developmental theory, Damasio's somatic marker hypothesis, and Gray's dual biological model. Although supported by a number of empirical studies, these theories fall short in accounting for the wide range of criminal offending. These theories have provided empirically based explanations for impulsive, aggressive types of criminal behavior. However, they are unable to predict the neural mechanisms underlying other types of offending such as instrumental aggression. Future theories incorporating findings from genetic imaging, neuropsychological, and brain imaging methods, while addressing the distinct neurological etiology underlying subgroups of criminal offenders, are needed for the development of a more comprehensive theory on neurology and crime.

Yaling Yang and Adrian Raine

See also Brain Abnormalities and Crime; Ellis, Lee: Evolutionary Neuroandrogenic Theory; Fishbein, Diana H.: Biosocial Theory; Mednick, Sarnoff A.: Autonomic Nervous System (ANS) Theory; Moffitt, Terrie E.: A Developmental Model of Life-Course-Persistent Offending; Psychophysiology and Crime

References and Further Readings

Anderson, S. W., Bechara, A., Damasio, H., Tranel, D., & Damasio, A. R. (1999). Impairment of social and moral behavior related to early damage in human prefrontal cortex. *Nature Neuroscience, 2,* 1031–1037.

Blair, R. J., Mitchell, D, & Blair, K. (2005). *The psychopath: Emotion and the brain.* Hoboken, NJ: Wiley-Blackwell.

Damasio, A. R. (1994). Descartes' error and the future of human life. *Scientific American, 271,* 144.

Damasio, A. R. (1996). The somatic marker hypothesis and the possible functions of the prefrontal cortex. *Philosophical Transactions: Biological Sciences, 351,* 1413–1420.

Fowles, D. C. (1988). Psychophysiology and psychopathology: A motivational approach. *Psychophysiology, 25,* 373–391.

Grafman, J., Schwab, K., Warden, D., Pridgen, A., Brown, H. R., & Salazar, A. M. (1996). Frontal lobe injuries, violence, and aggression: A report of the Vietnam Head Injury Study. *Neurology, 46,* 1231–1238.

Gray, J. A. (1982). *The neuropsychology of anxiety: An enquiry into the functions of the septo-hippocampal system.* Oxford, UK: Oxford University Press.

Gray, J. A. (1994). Nature, nurture, and psychodarwinism. *Nature, 367,* 591.

Lombroso, C. (1876). *L'uomo delinquente.* Milan, Italy: Turin.

Moffitt, T. E. (1993). Adolescence-limited and life-course-persistent antisocial behavior: a developmental taxonomy. *Psychological Review, 100,* 674–701.

Scarpa, A., & Raine, A. (1997). Psychophysiology of anger and violent behavior. *The Psychiatric Clinics of North America, 20,* 375–394.

Yang, Y., Glenn, A. L., & Raine, A. (2008). Brain abnormalities in antisocial individuals: implications for the law. *Behavioral Science and the Law, 26,* 65–83.

NEWMAN, OSCAR: DEFENSIBLE SPACE THEORY

The concept of "defensible space" was first explicated by Oscar Newman in a 1972 book by the same title. The concept, which contains elements of a theory of crime as well as a set of urban design principles, became popular in the 1970s as urban crime problems continued to rise. Defensible space was discussed, utilized, and critiqued widely by criminologists and other social scientists, as well as urban planners, law enforcement officials, and architects. The design concepts have also been implemented in numerous communities in the United States and around the world. Later works by Newman, including *Community of Interest* and *Creating Defensible Space* provide further elaboration of his ideas.

Newman states that defensible space is a model that can inhibit crime in residential environments. These environments might be specific buildings, projects, or entire neighborhoods. His earliest writings focused on urban public housing projects, in particular, the infamous Pruitt-Igoe housing project in St. Louis. Newman was a professor of architecture and city planning at Washington University in St. Louis when he noted that many of the public spaces in the housing project were crime ridden, vandalized and dirty while more private spaces were much better maintained. Newman later extended his ideas to urban residential neighborhoods. He argued that it was possible to design the physical environment of these areas in such a way to decrease crime levels by affecting the behavior of both residents and potential offenders and thus lead to lower levels of crime. More specifically, it was possible to create physical layouts of residential areas that allow residents to better control the areas. It was also possible to create physical layouts that would discourage or deter potential criminals from committing their offenses in these areas.

There are four key concepts in his theory and design principles: territoriality, surveillance, image, and milieu. Newman suggests that physical space can be designed to create areas of territorial influence. Physical elements or markers can be used to define private or semi-private spaces that encourage residents to assume more responsibility for the areas than they would if the areas were fully public spaces. Physical subdivisions that create smaller spaces can encourage occupants to adopt proprietary attitudes which serve as deterrents to crime. Residents will come to see these areas are their own spaces, be more concerned for them, and exert more control over the activities occurring in them. The same elements or markers, whether real (e.g., fences, gates) or symbolic (e.g., signs, plantings) can deter or discourage outsiders from intruding into the areas to commit crime.

Newman also suggests that the physical layout can be designed to improve natural surveillance opportunities for residents. The ability of residents to casually and regularly observe the public areas in one's environment is an important factor in reducing crime in these areas and in lessening residents' fear of crime when they use these public areas. This idea is similar to the argument offered by Jane Jacobs that buildings should be oriented to provide natural surveillance of the street. Specific physical designs that improve surveillance opportunities include the following: the placement of internal public areas such as hallways, lobbies, and elevators in such as way that they can be observed from outside the building; the location of external public areas such as parks and playgrounds so that there are clear sight lines from traffic on surrounding streets; and the provision of adequate lighting to make surveillance possible at night. Newman points out that ensuring opportunities for surveillance does not guarantee that residents will respond to events that they do observe. Here he notes the importance of the interplay between territoriality and surveillance opportunities. Residents will be more likely to intervene when they can observe the area and when they feel some sense of responsibility for what goes on in the area.

Newman's discussion of image and milieu focuses primarily on his analysis of public housing projects. He argues that the image of high-rise public housing projects contributes to a stigmatization of the project and its residents. The large group of high-rise buildings that usually stand out as significantly different from the surrounding community create an image of these areas as "easy hits" for criminality. The image of these areas is also linked to the social characteristics of the residents and to serious design flaws that create the conditions for high crime rates. He suggests that the location of public housing projects within the broader community milieu will have an effect on the level of safety within the project. Specifically, he recommends that these projects should not be built in areas that are already high crime areas; rather, they should be located adjacent to safe activity areas. These areas would include alongside busy public streets and near government offices and institutional areas. Newman reiterates that image and milieu do stand alone in reducing crime but that they must be linked to designs that encourage territoriality and surveillance.

Although aspects of Newman's designs have been implemented in various projects and neighborhoods around the United States and the world, both his theory and his claims about the effectiveness of his design principles in reducing crime have been the subject of much criticism. The broadest challenge to the theory is the claim that it is a form of physical determinism, that is, that the physical environment determines human behavior. While Newman denies that he is making that argument, in his later work he does admit being troubled by his failure to clearly communicate his ideas about both the physical and the social bases of his theory. His writings evolve over time both to revise his original ideas and to incorporate more considerations from other perspectives.

Studies seeking to evaluate the defensible space program would also reveal a number of other conceptual difficulties with Newman's writing. Newman suggests that the theory of defensible space can explain, and that the design principles can reduce, crime. However, he consistently refers to crime in very broad terms. He does not distinguish between very different types of criminal offenses that afflict residential areas. He does not recognize that his theory and design principles might apply more appropriately to some types of crimes than others. Another criticism is that Newman's arguments sometimes appear to be contradictory. For example, in some places, Newman argues that making spaces more private can reduce outsiders' access to these areas and hence improve safety. But he also argues that closing off streets through housing projects can lead to an increase in crime by reducing the natural surveillance that comes with busy thoroughfares.

The results of the many studies of the defensible space designs reveal inconsistent findings. Some of the discrepancies may be due to the varying methodological approaches used to test the theory. Some focus on the building level, while others focus on the block or neighborhood level. Some examine the impact on residents' territoriality and surveillance, while others directly study offender patterns. Some of the studies were conducted in sites where the only difference between communities, or the only change in a community over time, was in the physical design of the area. In other places, the changes in the physical environment were part of a broader, multifaceted plan to reduce crime. In these cases, it is difficult to distinguish the effects of the changes in physical design from the effects of the other elements in the plan.

A number of studies question Newman's assertions about physical design and territoriality. They suggest that there is not a clear, consistent relationship between the physical design of an area and territoriality or informal social control. These studies suggest that the relationship between physical design and territoriality may vary across communities and across different populations. For example, Sally Merry's study in a public housing project found that defensible space designs had very limited influence on the residential social climate. On the other hand, Floyd Fowler and Thomas Mangione's study in one urban neighborhood reported that defensible space features were related to increased territoriality and informal social control, and that in the short term, there was a lower rate of crime in the area. A study by Patrick Donnelly and Charles Kimble examined the effectiveness of a Newman-directed plan that created small, distinct mini-areas in one urban neighborhood by closing off streets that significantly reduced cut-through traffic. Newman argued that these mini-neighborhoods would see less crime since these areas would become more private, neighbors would get to know each other better, and look after their neighbors more closely. Both property crime and violent crime went down dramatically immediately after the plan went into effect. The decline was not due to increased residents' territoriality or surveillance. There was no change in residents' territoriality or informal social control after the plan was implemented. The plan appears to have a direct effect on offenders since the large reductions in crime were due primarily to reductions in crimes committed by persons who lived outside the neighborhood. The street closing plan reduced outsiders' opportunity to become familiar with the area by reducing access to the area. It may also have increased the perceived risks of being caught by reducing potential exit routes from the area after crimes were committed. It also led to a decrease in unpremeditated, opportunistic crimes by reducing routine drive-through traffic.

Many later approaches to criminological theory and crime prevention incorporate ideas and concepts presented by Newman. Over the last three decades, there has been a growing acceptance of the significant role that the physical environment plays in shaping crime. The field of environmental criminology (Brantingham & Brantingham, 1991) emphasizes the importance of place. Routine activity theory focuses on three factors—availability of suitable target, the lack of a suitable guardian to prevent the crime, and the presence of a likely offender—all of which are affected by physical design, territoriality, and surveillance (Felson, 1998). Rational choice theory assumes that offenders weigh the potential benefits and costs of their offenses. They weigh the likelihood of their offense being observed and interrupted and of their being caught. Again, each of these factors are affected by their perception of the physical environment (Cornish & Clark, 1986). Finally, the crime prevention through environmental design and situational crime prevention approaches provide a broader perspective on the physical environment than Newman's original work (Clarke, 1997; Jeffery, 1971).

Patrick G. Donnelly

See also Brantingham, Patricia L., and Paul J. Brantingham: Environmental Criminology; Clarke, Ronald V.: Situational Crime Prevention; Cohen, Lawrence E., and Marcus K. Felson: Routine Activity Theory; Eck, John E.: Places and the Crime Triangle; Felson, Marcus K.: Crime and Everyday Life; Jeffrey, C. Ray: Crime Prevention Through Environmental Design; Physical Environment and Crime

References and Further Readings

Brantingham, P. J., & Brantingham, P. L. (Eds.). (1991). *Environmental criminology*. Prospect Heights, IL: Waveland Press.

Clarke, R. V. (Ed.). (1997). *Situational crime prevention: Successful case studies* (2nd ed.). New York: Harrow and Heston.

Cornish, D., & Clarke, R. V. (1986). Introduction. In D. Cornish & R. V. Clarke (Eds.), *The reasoning criminal* (pp. 1–16). New York: Springer-Verlag.

Donnelly, P. G., & Kimble, C. E. (1997). Community organizing, environmental change, and neighborhood crime. *Crime and Delinquency, 43,* 493–511.

Felson, M. K. (1998). *Crime and everyday life: Insight and implications for society.* Thousands Oaks, CA: Pine Forge Press.

Fowler, F., & Mangione, T. (1986). A three-pronged effort to reduce crime and fear of crime. In

D. P. Rosenbaum (Ed.), *Community crime prevention: Does it work?* (pp. 87–108). Beverly Hills, CA: Sage.

Jacobs, J. (1961). *The death and life of great American cities.* New York: Vintage.

Jeffery, C. R. (1971). *Crime prevention through environmental design.* Beverly Hills, CA: Sage.

Merry, S. E. (1981). *Urban danger: Life in a neighborhood of strangers.* Philadelphia: Temple University Press.

Newman, O. (1972). *Defensible space: Crime prevention through urban design.* New York: Macmillan.

Newman, O. (1980). *Community of interest.* Garden City, NY: Anchor Press/Doubleday.

Newman, O. (1996). *Creating defensible space.* Washington, DC: U.S. Department of Housing and Urban Development.

Reynald, D. M., & Ellfers, H. (2009). The future of Newman's defensible space theory. *European Journal of Criminology, 6,* 25–46.

NUTRITION AND CRIME

In the past, the majority of research on crime tended to focus on social factors, such as socioeconomic status, or home environment. However, as criminologists and other researchers began to recognize the enormously complex nature of the causes of crime, other factors—including biological—became increasingly important to study and explore. Nutrition is one of those factors that fairly recently began to receive attention as a contributing factor to crime and violence. Scientific studies are suggesting an intriguing link between nutrition and antisocial behavior. Early signs of malnutrition correlate with increased antisocial and aggressive behavior, while nutritional interventions have been shown to alleviate antisocial behavior. More in-depth research would especially be helpful for developing new interventions to reduce antisocial behavior and crime.

There are many popular myths—some right, some wrong—about how food can affect one's behavior. One example is the infamous "Twinkie Defense" originated from the trial of Dan White for the murder of San Francisco Mayor George Moscone and Supervisor Harvey Milk in 1978. The alleged rumor was that the defendant's lawyers argued that Dan White committed the murder while on a sugar rush. The controversial verdict drew a lot of attention and debate. Contrary to the popular belief, the lawyers who defended Dan White used a legal defense of diminished capacity, rather than "Twinkie Defense" (Pogash, 2003). However, the term "Twinkie Defense" was not completely groundless. According to a review by David Benton, individual differences in glucose tolerance levels may be relevant to behavioral changes, including irritability and aggression. Although the nutritional factor turned out to be irrelevant in the Dan White case, it nonetheless demonstrates the strong interest in linking nutrition to crime and violence.

The Link to Violence: Observational Studies

Several studies have shown a connection between malnutrition and antisocial behavior. Given the obvious ethical barriers, it is almost impossible to conduct an experimental study that could show causal effects of malnutrition on human subjects. However, a number of observational studies have taken place, and they effectively show a correlation between malnutrition and antisocial behavior. One study by Jianghong Liu and colleagues is especially noteworthy because of its longitudinal nature. This study drew participants from a birth cohort on the island of Mauritius. The participants' signs of malnutrition were assessed at age 3, and they were followed up at ages 8, 11, and 17 to measure the extent of their antisocial and aggressive behavior. Children with signs of malnutrition at age 3 were more aggressive and hyperactive when they were 8-year-olds, had more "externalizing problems" at age 11, and had more conduct disorder and excessive motor activity when aged 17.

Omega-3: A New Area of Increasing Promise

Among numerous nutritional factors, omega-3 has recently been found to show promise as a new field of study. Several studies have examined the possible link between omega-3 deficiency and increased antisocial/aggressive behavior in both humans and animals. Joseph Hibbeln examined the relationship between fish consumption and homicide mortality rate across countries. This cross-national data showed a clear inverse relationship between increasing seafood consumption and decreasing homicide mortality rate. For example, out of the countries examined, Bulgaria had the highest homicide mortality rate of 10.3 per 100,000 and the lowest seafood consumption, while Japan had the lowest homicide mortality rate of 1.8 per 100,000 and the highest seafood consumption.

The link between low levels of omega-3 and increased levels of aggression is also observable in animal studies. Simona Re and colleagues found that canines with low levels of omega-3 were more aggressive. Another study by James DeMar, Jr., and colleagues experimentally placed male rats on either an omega-3-deficient diet, or an omega-3-adequate diet for 15 weeks. At the end of the 15 weeks, the omega-3-deficient group was more aggressive on the isolation-induced resident-intruder test.

Although numerous studies seem to suggest that a lack of omega-3 contributes to increased aggression, it must be recognized that observational studies only establish a relationship. In order to assume a causal relationship, intervention studies need to be conducted.

Treatment Studies: Possible Interventions to Reduce Crime

It is certainly more difficult to conduct controlled experiments than observational studies with nutrition, given the obvious ethical reasons and possible unpredictable side effects that intake of certain nutrition can have on humans. However, several notable intervention studies nonetheless have been conducted, and they help demonstrate a causal relationship between nutrition and aggression and antisocial behavior.

In one intervention study conducted by Adrian Raine and colleagues, 100 children from Mauritius at age 3 were randomly assigned into an experimental enrichment program that provided better nutrition, cognitive stimulation, and more physical exercise. They were matched with a control group who had the normal experience of a Mauritian child at that age, and were followed up at ages 17 and 23 on conduct disorder and crime. The enrichment reduced the crime outcome at age 23 by 34 percent. Of interest, however, was a significant enrichment-by-nutrition interaction for conduct disorder at age 17, showing that conduct disorder was particularly reduced in those who had poor nutritional status prior to the beginning of the intervention. In contrast, there was no significant effect of the intervention in reducing conduct disorder in those with normal nutritional status. This suggests, but does not prove, that nutrition was the active ingredient in the intervention that reduced later conduct disorder. Because children in the intervention had two to three extra meals of fish per week compared to controls, the authors suggested that increased omega-3 may have accounted for the beneficial effects of the enrichment.

C. Bernard Gesch and colleagues conducted a randomized, placebo-controlled trial on 231 young adult prisoners. The subjects were randomly allocated into two groups. One group received vitamin/mineral supplements, while the other received only placebo. The daily supplements consisted of four capsules that contained 1,260 mg linolenic acid, 160 mg gamma leinolenic acid, 80 mg eicosapentaenoic, and 44 mg docosahexaenoic acid, while the placebo simply consisted of vegetable oil. After a minimum of 2 weeks of supplements intake, they found an average of 35.1 percent reduction in offense in the vitamin/mineral supplements group. The authors suggested that even greater behavioral improvements could be achieved with the provision of a formulation that includes more omega-3 fatty acids.

Although this intervention study seems to support a causal link between increased omega-3 and reduced antisocial behavior, as recognized by the authors this study also has limitations. Behaviors in institutions are "untypical," and therefore, there could be possible problems with broadening the experimental result and interpretation to the wider lay population. Furthermore, omega-3 was not the only component of the supplements. Although it is highly likely that the omega-3 intake contributed to the decrease in offenses at least in this study, findings need to be replicated and extended to other populations.

Interestingly, the study by Gesch and colleagues has been recently replicated in the Netherlands. According to "The Links Between Diet and Behaviour: The Influence of Nutrition on Mental Health," published by the Associate Parliamentary Food and Health Forum in January 2008, preliminary results of the Dutch study supported the Gesch study findings. This study conducted randomized, placebo-controlled experiments in eight Dutch correctional institutions. Similar to the Gesch study, 221 young adult offenders were given either the supplements that contained omega-3, omega-6, and other 25 vitamins and minerals, or the placebo for approximately 2.5 months. Strikingly, the supplement group showed a 34 percent drop in the total number of incidents reported. Both the Gesch study and the Dutch replication study are noteworthy because they bolster the potential of nutritional intervention to possibly curb aggression and crime, both in prisons and in the community.

Conclusion

As indicated by the above review, malnutrition is associated with antisocial and aggressive behavior. In addition, nutritional interventions have shown initial promise in reducing antisocial behavior even in prison populations. Although several studies have effectively demonstrated a link between nutrition and antisocial behavior, more studies—especially both prospective longitudinal studies as well as randomized controlled trials—need to be conducted to further explore this field. Some of the possible studies could involve examining the regional differences, long-term effects of nutrition/malnutrition, as well as possible intervention methods to help reduce crimes. Furthermore, with many recent observation and intervention studies demonstrating positive effects of omega-3 on violence and aggression, understanding and exploring of the precise mechanisms by which omega-3 achieves its effects in reducing crime is a particularly important avenue for future research.

Ji Yoon Chung

See also Brain Abnormalities and Crime; Mednick, Sarnoff A.: Autonomic Nervous System (ANS) Theory; Physical Environment and Crime

References and Further Readings

Benton, D. (2007). The impact of diet in anti-social, violent, and criminal behavior. *Neuroscience and Behavioral Reviews, 31,* 752–774.
British Associate Parliamentary Food and Health Forum. (2008). *The links between diet and behavior: The influence of nutrition on mental health.* London: Author.
DeMar, J. C., Jr., Ma, K., Bell, J. M., Igarashi, M., Greestein, D., & Rapoport S. I. (2006). One generation of n-3 polyunsaturated fatty acid deprivation increases depression and aggression test scores in rats. *Journal of Lipid Research, 47,* 172–180.

Gesch, B. C., Hammond, S. M., Hampson, S. E., Eves, A., & Crowder, M. J. (2002). Influence of supplementary vitamins, minerals and essential fatty acids on the antisocial behaviour of young adult prisoners. *British Journal of Psychiatry, 181,* 22–28.

Hibbeln, J. R. (2001). Seafood consumption and homicide mortality. *World Review of Nutrition and Dietetics, 85,* 41–46.

Hibbeln, J. R., Davis, J. M., Steer, C., Emmett, P., Rogers, I., Williams, C., et al. (2007). Maternal seafood consumption in pregnancy and neurodevelopmental outcomes in childhood (ALSPAC study): An observational cohort study. *The Lancet, 369,* 578–585.

Liu, J., Raine, A., Venables, P. H., & Mednick, S. A. (2004). Malnutrition at age 3 years and externalizing behavior problems at ages 8, 11, and 17 years. *American Journal of Psychiatry, 161,* 2005–2013.

Pogash, C. (2003, November 23). Myth of the "Twinkie defense": The verdict in the Dan White case wasn't based on his ingestion of junk food. *San Francisco Chronicle.* Retrieved May 6, 2009, from http://www .sfgate.com/cgi-bin/article.cgi?f=/c/a/2003/11/23/ INGRE343501.DTL

Raine, A., Mellingen K., Liu, J., Venables, P., & Mednick, S. A. (2003). Effects of environmental enrichment at ages 3–5 years on schizotypal personality and antisocial behavior at ages 17 and 23 years. *American Journal of Psychiatry, 160,* 1627–1635.

Re, S., Zanoletti, M., & Emanuele, E. (2008). Aggressive dogs are characterized by low omega-3 polyunsaturated fatty acid status. *Veterinary Research Communications, 32,* 225–230.

NYE, F. IVAN: FAMILY CONTROLS AND DELINQUENCY

In 1958, F. Ivan Nye published *Family Relationships and Delinquent Behavior,* a study of how family structures and parent-child relationships influence the occurrence of juvenile delinquency. Based on a cross-sectional survey of high school students in three small cities in Washington and relying on simple cross-tabular analyses, the study might seem ordinary and limited by modern multivariate standards. However, the book made several important contributions to theory and research on delinquent behavior and still counts as an important milestone of modern criminology.

One contribution was its innovative use of self-report measurement of delinquency in a general survey of ordinary high school students when most delinquency research in 1958 relied on samples of adjudicated delinquents and used police records to measure their illegal behaviors. These "official delinquency" data reported on serious criminal acts committed by mostly lower-class, socially marginal youths from dysfunctional families in poor neighborhoods. Although self-report delinquency measures had been introduced in the 1940s, Nye's work (with James F. Short) provided the first systematic use of this procedure for theoretically meaningful research and showed that self-report measures would yield reliable and valid assessments of illegal behavior. Even though the Nye-Short delinquency scale was noticeably weighted toward minor property crimes and "status offenses," it established a foundation for later uses of self-reports to measure more serious forms of criminal behaviors.

A second contribution was to modify the available received wisdom about juvenile delinquency based on studies of official delinquents. Nye's self-report data showed that acts of juvenile delinquency were frequent and common occurrences; and these involved mostly ordinary and minor forms of misbehavior committed by a larger, diverse collection of adolescents at all social levels. Such behaviors did not seem to involve any special forms of social learning or pathological motivations, but rather were common actions carried out by most adolescents for ordinary reasons of convenience or fun. While inconsistent with traditional accounts of delinquency as seriously antisocial behaviors, these findings were subsequently confirmed in numerous surveys after Nye.

A third contribution of Nye's book was to criminological theory—namely, its explication of *social control theory.* Although some elemental ideas had been identified by other delinquency researchers—for example, Albert Reiss and Jackson Toby—Nye's book provided the first full description of social control theory as a systematic theoretical framework for explaining delinquency and crime. In the introductory chapter, Nye provided a brief (barely five pages) but explicit description of the essential concepts and premises of a social control theory, and indicated how this approach differs from the then-dominant theoretical frameworks of social disorganization, subcultural deviance, strain, culture conflict, and personality maladjustment.

In Nye's formulation, most delinquent behavior involves ordinary acts that do not require unusual forms of specialized learned behaviors or psychotic states. A small amount of delinquency may represent abnormally learned behaviors or express pathological motives, but these are comparatively rare. Most delinquent acts involve behaviors learned from parents, siblings, and peers through the same socialization process by which conforming behaviors are learned. They also are oriented to the satisfaction of common adolescent needs—for example, excitement, fun, recognition, esteem, acceptance, approval, accomplishment. In this view, most delinquency occurs not when adolescents develop abnormal motivations or habits, but when ordinary social controls are weak and fail to inhibit adolescents from seeking their ordinary goals through socially disapproved activities. Nye observed that delinquent behaviors often provide a quicker and easier means to satisfy common adolescent needs than strict adherence to the rules does.

Nye identified four distinctive forms of social control for insuring law-abiding behavior. These included (1) *direct control*, or behavioral compliance gained by punishments, rewards, threats, and bribes—what might also be termed *coercive control*; (2) *indirect control*, or behavioral conformity due to concern about what others think or by adherence to the expectations of valued social memberships— what might also be termed *control by identification*; (3) *internalized control*, or conformity that has been incorporated into a person's own values, attitudes, and habits through education, conditioning, or indoctrination—what might be termed *control by socialization*; (4) *availability of need satisfaction*, or behavior controlled by shaping the behavioral options or alternatives available to people to achieve their personal needs and goals—what today would be called *opportunity control*.

Arguably the most familiar contribution of Nye's 1958 study was its empirical analysis of the impact of family conditions and relationships on juvenile delinquency. Although Nye's description of social control was quite general in scope, his analysis of the high school delinquency data was a much more limited application of the theory; it singularly focused on the family as the primary institution of adolescent social control. Other

relationships, contexts and experiences outside the family (such as schools, peers, jobs, neighborhoods) were not explicitly included in this analysis or in the data collection, although Nye acknowledged that many other non-family factors could be important sources of all forms of social control.

Nye's analysis first examined the impact of family structure on delinquent behaviors, confirming that family locations and configurations do matter but not as much as earlier research on official delinquents has suggested. In Nye's data, family socioeconomic level was not consistently and significantly related to adolescent self-reports of delinquent behavior (in contrast to the strong social class differentials appearing in official delinquency). Also contrary to studies of official delinquents, Nye reported that "broken homes" (i.e., families where a parent is missing due to divorce or loss) were not strongly associated with self-reported delinquent behaviors. For self-reported delinquency, parental absence proved only weakly correlated with children's involvement in delinquency and primarily in "ungovernability" or "acting out" behaviors rather than serious criminal acts. Distinguishing between "legally broken" families (by physical absence of one parent through divorce or death) and "psychologically broken" families (by conflict and animosity between parents), Nye found that delinquent behaviors were significantly more frequent in psychologically broken (but intact) families than in legally broken families. The latter had slightly higher rates of delinquency than intact families (due to some loss of direct control).

Nye's data analyses confirmed that delinquent behaviors were slightly higher in larger families, among later-born children, in urban families, and in families that moved frequently (as measured by the number of different schools children attended). The effects of mother's employment on children's delinquency were more complex, showing a slight overall correlation with delinquent behaviors. By itself, mother's employment led to a slight loss of direct and indirect control, but this correlation was modified by a number of other factors such as the nature of the mother's job, the reasons for mother's employment, size of the family, rural-urban location, and the socio-economic status of the family. According to these results, the correlation between working mothers and children's delinquency was small and non-significant when other social factors were held constant.

The remainder of Nye's analysis focused on interactional, rather than structural, characteristics of families. In contrast to prior studies of parental control, Nye's analysis notably emphasized the two-way nature of the relationships between parents and children, showing that how children perceived and felt about their parents was just as important as parental feelings (i.e., of rejection or approval) toward children. Specifically, children's feelings of respect, attachment, or rejection toward their parents operated as strong moderators of the impact of all forms of parental control efforts. For example, the effectiveness of parents' direct control efforts was contingent on their children's perceptions of fairness and their feelings about their parents' disciplinary efforts. Nye found that social control efforts were most effective (and delinquency rates lowest) when parent-child respect and attachment were mutual.

Noting that prior studies of juvenile delinquency had heavily emphasized strong parental discipline for controlling delinquent behaviors, Nye reported that the relationship was more complicated. When parental efforts at discipline were viewed as excessive, unfair, selective, or rejecting, the impact of discipline were attenuated or reversed. Also, rather than inverse or linear, strictness of parental discipline showed a J-shaped or U-shaped correlation with delinquency, where moderate levels of supervision and punishment exerted the greatest control over delinquent behavior. This also applied to the obverse process of relinquishing control—that is, degree of freedom, autonomy, and responsibility allowed to adolescent children—which also had a J-shaped or U-shaped association with delinquent behavior. Thus, across a variety of different indicators of direct control, moderate ("middle way") levels of discipline and freedom consistently correlated with the least delinquent behavior.

Beyond the traditional focus on direct control through discipline, Nye's analysis strongly emphasized the various forms of indirect and internalized controls for reducing delinquency. The data confirmed the importance of parents and children doing things together in mutually meaningful activities, including regular church attendance as a family, as well as a variety of recreational activities such as sports, amusements, trips, and picnics. The analysis also considered how a variety of less obvious aspects

in parent-child relationships might be correlated with control of juvenile delinquency, such as children's perceptions of how their parents' looked, dressed, or acted in public, and the accompanying feelings of adolescent embarrassment. Perceptions of parents' general social dispositions (e.g., cheerfulness, nervousness, irritability, fussiness) and their ethical habits (e.g., truthfulness, honesty) were consistently correlated with adolescents' delinquent behaviors, especially for boys. Value agreement between children and parents on a variety of social issues was also consistently and significantly correlated with lower levels of delinquent behavior. Nye noted that such interpersonal connections were much more important for indirect and internalized controls, while their effects on direct control of delinquency by parents were weaker and less consistent.

The final part of the data analysis focused on the importance of parents as practical resources to their children. Generosity with money and allowances to children did not have a consistent linear effect on their delinquent behaviors, but rather was U-shaped or J-shaped. Children who viewed their parents as stingier than most had higher rates of delinquent behavior; at the same time, however, children who received more money than most other adolescents (through higher allowances or jobs) also were more delinquent. In contrast, parents as social and informational resources were consistently and strongly (and linearly) related to delinquent behavior. Children who frequently sought advice, information, or help from parents (including schoolwork, jobs, dating, religion, future plans, or sex) were less likely to commit delinquent behaviors. According to Nye, parental resources influenced children's behavior mostly through indirect and internalized controls, rather than direct or disciplinary controls.

In all, Nye's study of family-based controls over children's delinquent behavior examined 313 different cross-tabular comparisons of a variety of family variables with self-reported delinquent behaviors, each selected to evaluate some predictable pattern of social control theory. Nye reported that all except seven comparisons were consistent with social control theory. Such a "shotgun" methodology did not provide a rigorous test of definitive or comparative hypotheses of social control theory; however, Nye's results did provide a very plausible empirical demonstration of the overall ability of a social control framework in its ability to make researchable predictions. Later advances in statistical procedures enabled much more sophisticated and multivariate forms of analysis than the simple cross-tabulations used by Nye. Nonetheless, the conclusions from *Family Relations and Delinquent Behaviors* have proven quite durable and, on the whole, have been substantially replicated by numerous survey studies over the ensuing decades.

Edward L. Wells

See also Gottfredson, Michael R., and Travis Hirschi: Self-Control Theory; Hirschi, Travis: Social Control Theory; Reiss, Albert J., Jr.: Personal and Social Controls and Delinquency; Toby, Jackson: Stake in Conformity; Wells, Edward L., and Joseph H. Rankin: Direct Controls and Delinquency

References and Further Readings

Britt, C. L., & Gottfredson, M. R. (Eds.). (2003). *Control theories of crime and delinquency*. New Brunswick, NJ: Transaction.

Hirschi, T. (1969). *Causes of delinquency*. Berkeley: University of California Press.

Nye, F. I. (1958). *Family relationships and delinquent behavior*. New York: Wiley.

Vold, G. B., Bernard, T. J., & Snipes, J. B. (2002). *Theoretical criminology* (5th ed.). New York: Oxford University Press.

Osgood, D. Wayne, Janet K. Wilson, Jerald G. Bachman, Patrick M. O'Malley, and Lloyd D. Johnston: Routine Activities and Individual Deviant Behavior

In their 1996 article, "Routine Activities and Individual Deviant Behavior," D. Wayne Osgood, Janet K. Wilson, Jerald G. Bachman, Patrick M. O'Malley, and Lloyd D. Johnston extended the routine activity explanation of crime, first developed by Lawrence Cohen and Marcus Felson and by Michael Hindelang and colleagues, to account for individual-level crime and deviance. They theorized that people will commit more deviant and illegal behaviors if they spend more of their time engaged in unstructured socializing with peers in the absence of authority figures. Following the logic of routine activity theory, such activities present many opportunities for offending because the presence of peers makes deviance easier and more rewarding, the absence of authority figures reduces the chances of getting into trouble, and the lack of structure leaves time available.

Osgood and colleagues' viewpoint was built from insights provided by previous studies of time use and deviance, and their theoretical logic combines routine activity theory with several key concepts from previous theoretical work on delinquency, such as Scott Briar and Irving Piliavin's situational

motivation, David Matza and Gresham Sykes's subterranean values, Martin Gold's delinquency as a pickup game, and Michael Gottfredson and Travis Hirschi's situational inducements to crime. The many studies that have investigated offending and time use provide strong support for Osgood and colleagues' position. The routine activity perspective also views the ordinary activities of everyday life as an explanatory bridge between individuals' positions in the larger social structure and important outcomes such as crime. Research also has proved Osgood and colleagues' individual-level version of the approach to be useful for accounting for the connection between individuals' positions in the social structure (e.g., age, sex, class, and neighborhood or school) and deviance (Osgood et al., 1996; Osgood & Anderson, 2004).

The situational explanation of crime found in routine activity theory (sometimes also referred to as lifestyle theory) draws attention to the ways that ordinary, everyday activities can contribute to crime by enhancing opportunities for crime. For instance, Cohen and Felson pointed out that women's growing participation in the labor force after World War II may have contributed to a rise in daytime burglaries by increasing the number of homes that were unoccupied during the day. Prior to Osgood and colleagues' article, applications of the theory had largely been limited to explaining aggregate crime rates and victimization patterns. Their version applied the routine activity perspective both to individual-level offending and to a broader range of deviant behaviors. Felson had often discussed the implications of the routine activity perspective for individual offending, and Osgood and colleagues followed this lead by altering and broadening the theory so that it would not presume a strictly internal motivation for crime and would not be limited to predatory offenses.

An Individual Level Routine Activity Theory

Osgood and colleagues considered two previous theoretical views of the relationship of individuals' time use with crime and deviance and found them wanting. Travis Hirschi's social control theory hypothesized that delinquency would be reduced by the social bond of involvement, which entails spending time in conventional, non-deviant, activities. He reasoned that the more time youths spent in this way, the less time they would have available for delinquent activities, as in the old saying "idle hands are the devil's workshop." Unfortunately, research fails to support this broad prediction, finding instead that, while some non-deviant activities are associated with less delinquency, at least as many others are unrelated or coincide with more delinquency, rather than less. Osgood and colleagues also concluded that it was not useful to focus on how much time people spend in activities that are part of a deviant subculture. Any connection of such activities to deviance presents a problem of theoretical indeterminacy because it can be readily explained by a variety of theories, such as social learning or social control, rather than as consequences of spending time in that fashion.

Revising the Three Elements of Crime

Osgood and colleagues turned to routine activity theory for its emphasis on opportunities for crime arising in the course of ordinary, everyday activities. Cohen and Felson's routine activity theory is built on their conception of crime as comprised of three elements: a motivated offender, a suitable target, and the absence of capable guardians. Osgood and colleagues revised each of these elements to better suit their goal of extending the theory.

Cohen and Felson merely presumed, rather than explained, the existence of motivated offenders. Though that view was consistent with the typical routine activity focus on the contribution of situational factors to crime rates and victimization,

it meant that this version of the theory was not well suited to explaining why some people offend more than others. Osgood and colleagues solved this problem by substituting Briar and Piliavin's proposition that the motivation for delinquency typically stemmed from the opportunities presented by the situation, rather than from deep-seated motives deriving from experiences deep in the person's past. Though Briar and Piliavin had presented this concept of situational motivation as the basis for a social control explanation of delinquency, Osgood and colleagues observed that it was well suited to a routine activity explanation as well. If some types of time use present more situational inducements to deviance than others, then the way people spend their time could account for whether and how often they offend.

In placing the motivation for offending in the situation rather than the person, Osgood and colleagues assumed that most people are susceptible to at least some of the temptations they encounter. They noted that this position was consistent with several prominent threads of delinquency theory. Matza's theory of drift holds that delinquents do not reject conventional values, but rather that they temporarily suspend those values in favor of values supportive of delinquency. Subterranean values—such as values for excitement, conspicuous consumption, and toughness—are also part of the general culture, implying that almost anyone would violate the law in the right circumstance. Emphasizing the situational contribution to motivation for deviance also fits Gold's analogy of delinquency to a pickup game of basketball or baseball, which portrays deviance as typically casual and spontaneous. Like pickup games, in order to take part in delinquency one only needs "to be there when the opportunity arises and when others are willing" (1970, p. 94). Similarly, though Gottfredson and Hirschi emphasize the stable trait of self-control, their theory is founded on a situational conception of motivation in which the immediate gains provided by a crime serve as motivation for that act. Finally, Osgood and colleagues noted that the idea of situational motivation is also a good match to emphasis on gains versus costs at the heart of the rational-choice perspective.

Osgood and colleagues felt that the second of Cohen and Felson's three elements, a suitable target, unnecessarily limited the scope of the theory to predatory offenses that involve tangible objects to steal or damage and specific victims who suffer loss or injury. In order to expand the scope of routine activity theory to encompass a broader range of deviance, Osgood and colleagues substituted the more general notion of situations in which a deviant act is possible and rewarding. Building on the conception of motivation stemming from the situation, they argue that the inducement to deviance would be a function of the ease of the deviant act and the extent of the symbolic and tangible rewards it provides. The relevant situational inducements will depend to some degree on the particular offense. Attending a party where others are smoking pot would be a situational inducement to doing so yourself, while receiving income that is not reported to the government would be a strong opportunity for tax fraud. Osgood and colleagues' focus, however, was activities likely to present situational inducements for a broader range of deviance.

Cohen and Felson's last element, guardianship, is the notion that predatory crime is unlikely when someone is present who would intervene or call the authorities. To extend this idea to other deviant acts, such as substance use or disorderly conduct, Osgood and colleagues substituted the proposition that there is more inducement to deviance in situations where no authority figure is present. They do not limit the term *authority figure* to people such as parents or teachers, but rather apply it to anyone whose role in the situation would require them to take action if trouble arose. For instance, this includes sales people or ticket takers whose work roles would obligate them to respond to fights, theft, or pot smoking. In this theory, the social control function for these authority figures rests on their position in the situation, not on the potential offenders' social bonds. They illustrated this idea by stating, "Whether you like or dislike your father, it will be more convenient to smoke marijuana when he isn't around" (Osgood et al., 1996, p. 640).

What Activities Present Situations Conducive to Deviance?

Osgood and colleagues focused on a pattern of activities that previous research had indicated was most strongly associated with a variety of deviant or problem behaviors. These activities shared three features: socializing with peers, a lack of structure or organization, and an absence of authority figures or supervision. They proceeded to argue that situations conducive to deviance would be especially prevalent during such activities.

The presence of peers can make deviance easier in concrete and tangible ways and make it more rewarding in symbolic ways. As examples of how peers make deviance easier, Osgood and colleagues pointed to friends as a common source of illicit drugs, the company of friends reducing the danger of entering a fight, and the presence of a partner to serve as a lookout being an aid to theft. They felt that the presence of friends was even more important for making deviance appealing as a potential route to gaining status and reputation, noting that peers can provide an appreciative audience for deviant exploits.

Whether activities take place in the presence of authority figures directly reflects one of the three elements of situations conducive to deviance. This element was also one reason that Osgood and colleagues focused on *socializing* with peers, which they contrasted with settings like work, school, and family, where young people are subordinate to supervisors, teachers, and parents. In this vein, routine activity scholars had always emphasized that the risk of crime would be lower during time at home versus elsewhere and (for adolescents) with parents versus apart from them (Felson, 2002; Felson & Gottfredson, 1984).

Activities that lack structure are more likely to present situations conducive to deviance for two reasons. First, Osgood and colleagues note that organized activities typically include individuals in positions of authority, such as coaches at athletic events, officers of organized clubs, and employees at restaurants and theaters. Second, the logic of routine activity theory is that the likelihood of deviance is a function of *how much time* one is exposed to opportunities. The less flexible agendas of structured activities mean that time will be spent in specific ways, leaving relatively little time available for deviance. Though Hirschi's notion of involvement in social control theory predicts that spending time in organized activities will reduce delinquency, from a routine activity perspective that reduction depends on the organized activities leading to a decline in time spent in activities conducive to delinquency, and as Felson had noted, the opposite may well occur. For instance, participation in varsity sports may bring more chances to hang out with team friends after practice and more invitations to unsupervised parties.

Empirical Support

Findings from a broad range of studies provide empirical support for individual-level routine activity theory's central prediction that, when people spend more time in unstructured socializing with peers away from authority figures, they will engage in more deviant behavior. This pattern has been found in studies of samples ranging in age from childhood to the late twenties, for both males and females, for multiple race/ethnicity groups, and for many nations and cultures. Evidence of this relationship extends to a broad range of deviant behaviors including property offenses, violence, illicit drug use, alcohol consumption, and dangerous driving. In addition, the theory is also a good fit to several other well-established findings in criminology, such as the partying lifestyle of serious offenders that Richard Wright and Scott Decker have written about, the huge amount of time that gang members spend hanging around together in unsupervised public places, as noted by Malcolm Klein, and the wide-ranging wandering characteristic of seriously delinquent youths, which Sheldon and Eleanor Glueck pointed out. Furthermore, the connection between deviance and this type of time use is not readily explained by other factors because it holds even when controlling for many other prominent correlates of crime and deviance, and for within-individual comparisons over time that control for all stable differences between people. Finally, Dana Haynie and Osgood demonstrated that delinquency goes with unstructured socializing, regardless of how deviant one's friends are, indicating that this association is not an indirect result of social learning or differential association.

A central theme of the routine activity perspective is that individuals' everyday activities can help explain the connection between positions in the social structure and important outcomes like crime and deviance. Accordingly, Osgood and colleagues showed that unstructured socializing can account for a substantial share of the associations of age, sex, and social class with deviance. The developmental trends are especially strong, with unstructured socializing rising dramatically from childhood through adolescence, and declining thereafter, closely matching the age-crime curve (see Osgood et al., 2005). Osgood and Amy Anderson also showed that unstructured socializing accounts for much of the variation in delinquency across schools, partly from the basic individual-level relationship and partly from an additional context effect.

Conclusion

Osgood and colleagues' application of routine activity theory to individual deviance has had considerable influence, as evidenced by over 200 citations to date, and unstructured socializing with peers is now widely recognized as a likely contributor to delinquency and other problem behaviors. Though evidence supporting the theory is stronger than for most criminological theories, important questions still remain. An experimental test of the causal influence of unstructured socializing would be especially valuable. Also, it would be useful to test the specific opportunity processes hypothesized by the theory through a fine-grained examination of time use surrounding specific offenses. Finally, a good topic for future work would be to develop and test policy implications of the theory for designing crime prevention policies and programs that target time use.

D. Wayne Osgood

See also Briar, Scott, and Irving Piliavin: Delinquency, Commitment, and Stake in Conformity; Cohen, Lawrence E., and Marcus K. Felson: Routine Activity Theory; Felson, Marcus K.: Crime and Everyday Life; Gottfredson, Michael R., and Travis Hirschi: Self-Control Theory; Hindelang Michael J., Michael R. Gottfredson, and James Garofalo: Lifestyle Theory; Hirschi, Travis: Social Control Theory; Matza, David: Delinquency and Drift

References and Further Readings

Briar, S., & Piliavin, I. (1965). Delinquency, situational inducements, and commitment to conformity. *Social Problems, 13,* 35–45.

Cohen, L. E., & Felson, M. (1979). Social change and crime rate trends: A routine activity approach. *American Sociological Review, 44,* 588–608.

Felson, M. (2002). *Crime and everyday life* (3rd ed.). Thousand Oaks, CA: Pine Forge Press.

Felson, M., & Gottfredson, M. (1984). Social indicators of adolescent activities near peers and parents. *Journal of Marriage and the Family, 46,* 709–714.

Glueck, S., & Glueck, E. (1950). *Unraveling juvenile delinquency.* New York: Commonwealth Fund.

Gold, M. (1970). *Delinquent behavior in an American city.* Belmont, CA: Brooks/Cole.

Haynie, D. L., & Osgood, D. W. (2005). Reconsidering peers and delinquency: How do peers matter? *Social Forces, 84,* 1109–1130.

Hindelang, M. J., Gottfredson, M. R., & Garofalo, J. (1978). *Victims of personal crime: An empirical foundation for a theory of personal victimization.* Cambridge, MA: Ballinger.

Klein, M. W. (1995). *The American street gang: Its nature, prevalence, and control.* New York: Oxford University Press.

Matza, D. (1964). *Delinquency and drift.* New York: Wiley.

Matza, D., & Sykes, G. M. (1961). Juvenile delinquency and subterranean values. *American Sociological Review, 26,* 712–719.

Osgood, D. W., & Anderson, A. L. (2004). Unstructured socializing and rates of delinquency. *Criminology, 42,* 519–549.

Osgood, D. W., Anderson, A. L., & Shaffer, J. N. (2005). Unstructured leisure in the after-school hours. In J. L. Mahoney, R. W. Larson, & J. S. Eccles (Eds.), *Organized activities as contexts of development: Extracurricular activities, after-school and community programs* (pp. 45–64). Mahwah, NJ: Lawrence Erlbaum.

Osgood, D. W., Wilson, J. K., Bachman, J. G., O'Malley, P. M., & Johnston, L. D. (1996). Routine activities and individual deviant behavior. *American Sociological Review, 61,* 635–655.

Wright, R. T., & Decker, S. H. (1997). *Armed robbers in action: Stickups and street culture.* Boston: Northeastern University Press.

P

PARMELEE, MAURICE

Maurice Parmelee was one of the early pioneers in American criminology. He was trained as a sociologist, and throughout his career he held a number of positions in the academia and the government. He received his Ph.D. from Columbia University in 1909 and began his teaching career in University of Kansas before moving to University of Missouri. He left academia for the government in 1918, when he was appointed at the War Trade Board in London. He also worked for the Departments of State, Agriculture, Treasury, and Interior. He was appointed to the Bureau of Economic Warfare in 1941 but was forced to resign after being investigated for alleged socialist leanings. Throughout his long career, Parmelee wrote several books on a wide range of sociological topics including monographs on poverty, alcoholism, and human behavior. He also wrote some of the first texts in American criminology: *The Principles of Anthropology and Sociology in Their Relations to Criminal Procedure* and *Criminology*.

Parmelee believed that in order to understand criminal behavior, it was necessary to synthesize discoveries of both natural sciences and social sciences. He asserted that lawyers, jurists, and philosophers had hitherto dominated discussions on crime and there was little scientific understanding of this social phenomenon. Parmelee praised the Classical School in criminology as exemplified by the works of Cesare Beccaria and Jeremy Bentham in its effort to devise a penal system in preserving the fundamental rights and liberties of the individual along with the social need of deterrence of crime. However, Parmelee was skeptical of the theoretical and practical relevance of the doctrine of moral responsibility, and he thought that the fundamental weakness of this perspective is that it fails to see the abnormal and pathological nature of criminal behavior. In his opinion, rather than making a priori assumptions about "free will," criminologists need to study the individual and social pathologies inherent in a criminal person and need to assume a holistic perspective that encompasses the psychological, physical, and sociological aspects of acts of crime. However, acknowledging the variation that exists between the various perspectives, he asserted in *The Principles of Anthropology and Sociology in Their Relations to Criminal Procedure* that criminologists should consider some of the essential elements of criminal acts, such as defiance of prevailing morality, social and individual harm as well as the penal reaction from the society without trying to formulate a single definition that may fail to acknowledge the complexity of these various elements.

Parmelee was influenced by the works of Cesare Lombroso and the Positivist School. While Parmelee acknowledged some of the criticisms leveled against the inherent biological determinism of Lombroso's theory, he praised Lombroso's effort to establish a science of criminology. Parmelee was particularly influenced by the works of Lombroso's follower Enrico Ferri, who called for an integration of different branches of knowledge including anthropology, psychology, statistics, and penology in the new science of "criminal sociology." Parmelee asserted that the sociological and biological perspectives are very similar in their pursuit of scientific explanations for the "natural causes" of criminal behavior and should be effectively combined in the criminological discourse. The search for these so-called natural causes is manifested in Parmelee's propensity to essentialize criminal behavior as inherently deviant, and his belief that psychopathic and demented individuals dominate the ranks of criminals. Some of his statements regarding the innate inferiority of female criminals are viewed as reflecting contemporary prejudices, and may come across as seriously misinformed in our time.

Parmelee was interested in the practical and policy implications of criminology as well. Indeed, he claimed that it is necessary to reorganize the institutions and practices of law enforcement on the basis of scientific knowledge. He asserted that the most crucial task of the criminal justice system is to balance the need for safeguarding individual liberty and defending the society from the harm of crime, which could be achieved through the aid of modern science. He was particularly appreciative of certain institutional innovations in Europe in this regard, including efforts by the Italian government to propagate training in scientific policing methods, the Bertillon method of anthropometric criminal identification in France, and dactyloscopy or the fingerprint identification system used by the British police. He argued that, while the contemporary American criminal justice system strongly emphasizes a humanitarian instinct of reforming the prisoner by an "individualized" penal regime through the use of indeterminate sentences and parole, there is a need to incorporate the advances of modern scientific expertise in the judicial and penal process in order to effectively control crime and rehabilitate the criminal.

Saran Ghatak

See also Beccaria, Cesare: Classical School; Bentham, Jeremy: Classical School; Ferri, Enrico: Positivist School; Lombroso, Cesare: The Criminal Man

References and Further Readings

Craig C. (Ed.). (2007). *Sociology in America: A history.* Chicago: University of Chicago Press.
Gibbon, D. C. (1974). Say, whatever became of Maurice Parmelee anyway? *Sociological Quarterly, 15,* 405–416.
Parmelee, M. (1908). *The principles of anthropology and sociology in their relations to criminal procedure.* New York: Macmillan.
Parmelee, M. (1909). *Inebriety in Boston.* New York: Eagle Press.
Parmelee, M. (1913). *The science of human behavior.* New York: Macmillan.
Parmelee, M. (1918). *Criminology.* New York: Macmillan.
Turner, S. (2007). A life in the first-half century of sociology: Charles Ellwood and the division of sociology. In C. Calhoun (Ed.), *Sociology in America: A history* (pp. 115–154). Chicago: University of Chicago Press.

PARSONS, TALCOTT: AGGRESSION IN THE WESTERN WORLD

The first half of the 20th century may have been one of the bloodiest and most influential in the history of organized human civilization. Short-sighted despots and courageous heads of state vied for control of a world that was becoming increasingly unpredictable and violent. The nationalistic behavior exhibited by some citizens fostered a great deal of unity amongst like-minded (and similarly situated) individuals. Conversely, the latent fear and insecurity created by the tenuous grasp on freedom often manifested itself as aggression toward groups of individuals that were outside the norm or fundamentally different in some arbitrarily defined manner.

As a trained sociologist and a professor of sociology at Harvard University, Talcott Parsons was likely aware of this phenomenon. He had traveled extensively in Nazi Germany prior to the genesis of World War II and had observed first-hand the fervent nationalism being generated by the National Socialist Party. Not long after the war had ended, Parsons penned one of his most important and most frequently overlooked pieces of scholarly work. The substance of this article, titled "Certain Primary Sources of and Patterns of Aggression in the Social Structure of the Western World," was influenced by Parsons's experience as a scholar objectively observing the behavior of individuals involved in large-scale conflicts. As a result of spending time in the 1920s translating *The*

Protestant Ethic and the Spirit of Capitalism, his later work was heavily influenced by Max Weber's concept of "rationalization."

Sparked by a curiosity about the putative origins of aggressive behavior, Parsons endeavored to develop a grand theory about the manifestation of that aggression in the Western world. His theory not only was relevant for the times but also resonated with some of his more notable contemporaries in criminology. Scholars such as Albert Cohen and David Matza expanded upon and applied Parsons's paradigm to the concept of delinquency and the organization of youth gangs. Nevertheless, the ideas espoused by Parsons have received scant attention in the subsequent criminological literature. Francis Cullen argues that this is an egregious oversight because "Parsons's work showed much more awareness of the socially structured character of deviant behavior than many other deviance theorists" (p. 90).

Regardless of the position taken by criminologists about the relative importance of his paradigm for understanding deviant behavior, the theory warrants a more meticulous explanation than has previously been provided in the literature. This entry outlines the particulars of Parsons's theory and explores its relevance for modern criminological theory and practice. Also, bear in mind that when Parsons refers to aggressive behavior, he is not exclusively concerned with the dispositions of youthful offenders. This interpretation has contributed to the tendency for some criminologists to ignore the theory.

Structured Aggression

Any discussion of Parsons's theory has to begin with the unique paradigm through which he examined human behavior. First, his primary concern was with the dynamics of "power relationships." He envisaged aggression as occurring within the context of vast institutional change. According to Parsons's logic, deviant behavior must have a socially structured character. This is because aggression is prevalent throughout society. The proliferation of this potentially "negative" tendency is inversely related to the ability of a society to maintain effective control over its citizenry (Cullen, 1984). Furthermore, behavior cannot be understood apart from the context in which it occurs and the motivations of the individual involved. In other words, it is difficult to appreciate behavior without taking into account the kinds of goals and objects that may be attached to a particular individual in a particular situation. The form that aggression takes will likely be determined by factors that are unique to the situation of the involved parties.

Parsons considered this kind of within-group variation to be much more pervasive (and relevant) than any putative differences between ethnic groups. He goes on to say that "aggression grows more out of weakness and handicap than biological strength" (p. 168). This purported weakness leads to a decrease in the "security" associated with vital human relationships. This is especially true for children, for whom the stability and the relative quality of maternal warmth are quite significant. Ostensibly, children are expected (by their parents) to behave in a manner that reflects positively upon the family unit. While these values may be arbitrarily defined by each individual family, there are some relatively common societal goals that are ubiquitous enough to be considered desirable norms by a preponderance of families. However, because each child is different, there is variation in terms of his or her ability to live up to these goals.

According to Parsons, significant problems arise when children fail to meet expectations or conform to common behavioral standards. Such failures have the potential to create a sense of inadequacy or perhaps even an overwhelming feeling that life is unfair. The former is more likely to occur when one is expected to perform a task that he or she is incapable of performing. The sense of inadequacy is generally exacerbated when others in the group with whom one is in competition succeed in similar endeavors. The latter component becomes more ensconced as the individual becomes increasingly convinced that he or she is being persecuted unjustly or not being given his or her "just due." Once again, this "condition" is often seen as the result of competition between similarly situated individuals, according to Parsons.

The Direction of Aggressive Impulses

Parsons assumes that aggression is the inevitable result of the strain and frustration associated with various stages of human development. The kinds of social and psychological processes experienced during these "stages" serve to direct deviant impulses (Cullen, 1984, p. 90). On the other hand, the stressors, however powerful, engendered in particular moments cannot account for the form that the deviation takes. Viewed through this lens, aggression can be seen as a "master stress" that can manifest itself in various ways (delinquency being just one). Without an adequate enhancement of one's personal sense of security, defensive patterns developed to combat personal attacks, perceived or not, may become entrenched.

Another possibility is that aggressive impulses are stifled because they come into conflict with the moral norms of family and society. This latent aggression may be repressed until a proper outlet is discovered. According to Parsons, this often occurs in symbolic form as displacement on a scapegoat. In this instance, a symbolically appropriate proxy is targeted and the impulse is indirectly gratified. For the perpetrator to avoid being shamed by the rest of the group, the proxy target must come from outside the circle of people who are required to be loved (i.e., mother, father, etc.). In the Western world, which is the primary focus of Parsons's narrative, the dominant feature is the "relatively isolated conjugal family that is primarily dependent upon the income and status of one member, the husband and father" (p. 170). The unique character of this entity comes from the fact that the status achieved by the household is almost entirely contingent upon the achievements of one individual. Though this idea does not necessarily resonate with the modern world where women are regularly employed outside of the home, the suggestion that a mother's love may be contingent upon the child's objective performance is still a uniquely Western quality. Aggression is much more likely to be repressed because this affection is necessary in order to ensure that the child is properly socialized.

Parsons makes it clear that the immediate family is not the only factor influencing a child's aggressive tendencies. In fact, there are a variety of external stressors that produce high levels of insecurity that are structured in reasonably explicit and standardized ways. Whether a stressor is internal or external, because of the father's absence, the mother remains the primary agent of socialization for both girls and boys. Not surprisingly, in the early stages of life, both boys and girls tend to emulate the behaviors exhibited by the mother.

According to Parsons, the "father is not immediately available and his contributions (i.e., work) are intangible and difficult for the child to comprehend" (p. 171). As a result, boys develop early feminine identification. As they grow older and come into contact with outside influences, they experience tangible role confusion. Good behavior comes to be seen as a feminine trait and thus not worthy of reverence. In order to counteract the aforementioned feminine identification problem, boys often overcompensate with hyper-masculine behavior, which Parsons refers to as reaction formation. As the reaction becomes more normalized, the behavior may become a sort of family tradition or identifying character trait.

Women face a different kind of problem when they come to realize that males are considered superior in the adult world, which is in direct contrast to what they saw as a child where the mother was the proverbial center of their world. Their sense of having been deceived by both men and women also leads to direct and indirect expressions of aggressive behavior. Despite being subjected to a different kind of role ambivalence, the general rules about the expression of aggressive behavior being hindered by the need to conform to both youthful and adult social norms also apply to women.

The Emergence of Repressed Aggression

Regardless of gender, these antisocial tendencies are often spawned by intra-familial conflict. However, because the child is hesitant to upset the family structure and be denied affection, these impulses are often repressed or expressed indirectly toward an out-group. Since moral norms preclude most forms of direct expression of aggressive behavior in youths, the bulk of the potential hostile impulses remain bottled. This repression fosters what Parsons refers to as free-floating aggression, which is often taken out on scapegoats that are outside of the immediate kinship group. Ostensibly, aggressive responses are much more likely to be expressed when an individual is either hypersensitive to suggestions of inferiority or vulnerable to distorted beliefs about their own superiority. The latter state of mind is useful in the sense that it tends to allay a hypersensitive individual's anxiety about their own inadequacy. Conversely, such distorted views of reality tend to increase disillusionment and repressed aggression. This makes an individual much more likely to exhibit aggressive behavior during inherently non-hostile situations, according to Parsons. In a social sense, the indirect expression of aggressive behavior onto a group outside of the circle of comfortable insiders is much less dangerous.

As the child matures, their participation in the occupational structure (i.e., the adult world) will produce different stressors. For example, since the most important feature of the Western occupational structure is the concept of functional achievement, a hyper-competitive work environment flourishes. The fact that the "system" is relatively new and ever changing suggests that adherence to traditional norms and values is often impractical. This hypothesis still makes sense today when one considers how quickly technology, especially electronics, evolves and becomes obsolete. The ever-shifting workplace forces employees to constantly adapt to new "moral" standards. Refusing to conform and adapt will likely lead to workplace dissatisfaction, which almost certainly will produce resentment (i.e., aggression). Similar to the situation associated with the family unit, few direct outlets for aggressive impulses are permitted in the "adult" world. As employees are forced to continuously adapt they develop an ever-increasing quantity of stifled aggression. According to Parsons, "the kinship and occupational spheres represent a mutually reinforcing system of forces operating on the individual to generate large quantities of aggressive impulses." This repressed aggression is eventually expressed through processes like the aforementioned displacement on a scapegoat (p. 177).

The bottom line is that the situation often dictates whether aggression will be overtly destructive or more subtly manipulative. This paradigm helps to explain the tendency for people to become unusually nationalistic in certain contexts. For example, Parsons asserts that the inevitable process of change that takes place within cultural units disrupts established social norms and symbolic systems. An easy-to-understand example of how this process plays out can be seen by examining the rise of Nazism in Germany after World War I. The National Socialist Party, and Adolf Hitler more specifically, exploited the lingering resentment felt by Germans after the loss in the aforementioned conflict in order to induce citizens to act on behalf of the nation. However, because of sanctions placed on Germany by the Allied powers in the Treaty of Versailles, they were limited in their ability to act overtly. Such postwar oppression is the kind of situation that is ripe for exploitation by a charismatic leader. Hitler targeted "outside" ethnic groups (mostly Jews) in order to foster the kind of nationalism it would require to galvanize the nation to go to war.

This is an extreme example of what Parsons called displacement on a scapegoat. This kind of rationalization tends to structure the direction of both the actual and potential expression of hostile behavior. In more traditional societies, this process is most disruptive to the social order where social norms are thoroughly entrenched and people are highly resistant to change. Conversely, a fundamentalist reaction to such an infringement is difficult to defend against because the elements that constitute such a position tend to be inextricably linked to the informal solidarity of the group. Knowing this, it is not difficult to envisage why a "foreigner" is an easy target for enterprising nationalistic groups to exploit.

Conclusion

For criminologists, Parsons's main contribution is the postulation that "not only is aggression socially structured, but so also are all other forms of deviant behavior" (Cullen, 1984, p. 94). Deviance can thus be viewed as a hyper-masculine coping mechanism designed to counterbalance mixed role messages received during childhood. That being said, this paradigm is not lacking in practical shortcomings. First, it is often considered highly abstract and only applies to the Western world at one particular point in time. Additionally, since the system is malleable, Parsons could not possibly capture each and every variation within subunits of the population. Finally, the analysis applies unequally to different segments of the population. More specifically, Parsons is mostly evaluating the plight of the urban middle class. Despite these issues, this paradigm is useful for criminological scholars looking for a creative way to interpret social situations and the origins of deviant impulses. The theory should not, however, be viewed as either deterministic or as a paradigm that is only useful for examining juvenile delinquency.

Taylor Trimboli

See also Cloward, Richard A., and Lloyd E. Ohlin:
Delinquency and Opportunity; Cohen, Albert K.:
Delinquent Boys; Cohen, Albert K.: Deviance and
Control; England, Ralph W.: A Theory of Middle-
Class Delinquency; Matza, David: Becoming Deviant;
Sykes, Gresham M., and David Matza: Techniques of
Neutralization

References and Further Readings

Cohen, A. (1955). *Delinquent boys: The culture of the
gang.* New York: Free Press.

Cullen, F. T. (1984). *Rethinking crime and deviance
theory: The emergence of a structuring tradition.*
Totowa, NJ: Rowman and Allenheld.

Gerhardt, U. (2002). *Talcott Parsons: An intellectual
biography.* Cambridge, UK: Cambridge University
Press.

Manfred, F. B., Feldman, G. D., & Glaser, E. (Eds.).
(1998). *The treaty of Versailles: A reassessment after
75 years.* Cambridge, UK: Cambridge University Press.

Parsons, T. (1947). Certain primary sources and patterns
of aggression in the social structure of the western
world. *Psychiatry, 10,* 167–181.

Weber, M. (1905). *The protestant ethic and the spirit of
capitalism.* New York: Scribner's.

PATTERSON, GERALD R.: SOCIAL LEARNING, THE FAMILY, AND CRIME

Gerald R. Patterson is known for his ground-breaking work formulating both a theory of anti-social development in children—*coercion theory*—and practical family interventions and parent training techniques for reducing child and adolescent aggression. His research has resulted in the publication of more than 225 articles, book chapters, and books dating back to 1953, and has had an immeasurable influence on explaining the etiology of juvenile delinquency from a social psychological perspective. In 1977, he co-founded the Oregon Social Learning Center (OSLC) in Eugene, Oregon, where he continues to research and publish as a Senior Scientist.

Patterson's coercion theory assigns a primary etiological role to inadequate parental skills in explaining juvenile delinquency. Coercion theory is a social learning perspective, though it is considered a second-generation extension of Albert Bandura's social learning theory. To clarify, Bandura emphasized the role of the initial learning of aggression through imitation, reinforcement, and punishment contingencies, each assumed to be mediated by cognitive processes. In comparison, coercion theory focuses on the *maintenance of the behavioral performance* (rather than the learning) of aggressive behavior. Further, constructs in the coercion model are observed in real-time, real-world settings, using multiple sources (e.g., parents, siblings, peers, teachers) and methods, which contrasts with the laboratory settings and methods used to formulate Bandura's social learning theory (Larzelere & Patterson, 1990).

The Oregon Model and Coercion Theory

In the early 1960s, Patterson was among a group of researchers at the University of Oregon's Psychology Department interested in developing methods to alter a variety of child behaviors, including aggression. In the early years of his research, Patterson and his colleagues began to discover the critical role operant conditioning played in shaping children's behavior, including reinforcement and behavioral contingency procedures. The research team also realized that their initial research strategy of using rigid laboratory settings created too many methodological limitations, and subsequently began conducting meticulous moment-to-moment, microsocial natural observations in children's family environments as they were happening in real time. The rigorous, detailed observation methods developed by Patterson and his team fostered the discovery of the specific mechanisms by which global risk factors (e.g., poor parental discipline) function to facilitate developmental pathways of antisocial behavior.

The collection of hundreds of home observations of parent and child interactions formed the basis of coercion theory, formally outlined by Patterson in his book, *Coercive Family Process,* published in 1982. Coercion theory provides a model of behavioral contingencies that explains the mutually reinforcing process that occurs between parents and children that fosters childhood aggression. Parents and children essentially "train" or "coerce" each other to behave in ways that increase the likelihood that (1) children will develop antisocial behavior and (2) parents will decrease control over these behaviors. Consider the following behavioral exchange that characterizes the coercive interactions among families of antisocial children frequently observed by Patterson and his fellow scientists: A mother demands behavioral compliance of the child. The child refuses, and responds coercively (e.g., with whining). The mother continues to demand compliance, which escalates the child's coercive behavior (e.g., with temper tantrums). After a short time, the child's coercion becomes exceedingly frustrating to the mother, at which point she surrenders control and allows the child to escape behavioral compliance. For the time being, the child's aversive behavior ceases.

Coercion is referred to as "the contingent use of aversive behaviors of another person" (Patterson, 2002, p. 25). At the heart of coercion theory is the concept of *contingency*, which implies that one event is determined by a preceding event. In the common behavioral exchange described above, the theory focuses on the connection between the child's behavior and the mother's reaction, as well as on the subsequent reaction of the child to the mother's capitulation. In operant conditioning terms, because the child's defiant behavior is negatively reinforced (by escaping behavioral compliance and punishment), the probability of the child engaging in coercive behavior again in the long run increases. Moreover, the mother is reinforced by receiving some momentary peace from the tantrum, which increases the chance of withdrawing control during future aversive encounters with her child. The dyadic reactions demonstrate that behavior is partially influenced by immediate contingent events. These mutually contingent microsocial exchanges between parent and child form the foundational elements for developing early childhood aggression.

One particularly pivotal work by James Snyder and Patterson answered the critical question "How well does coercion work during family conflict episodes compared to everything else the child does during the family conflict episode?" In other words, what is the relative rate of reinforcement for child coercive behavior during family conflict episodes? Snyder and Patterson demonstrated that deviant behavior could be reliably explained by knowing how often child coercive behavior was

reinforced among family conflicts. Relative reinforcement for coercion and density of family conflict have also significantly predicted juvenile arrests after 2 years (Snyder et al., 1997).

Coercion theory is embedded within a social interactionist view that emphasizes that "the child is an active participant whose behavior is a reaction to the behavior of the other family members" (Patterson, 1982, p. 196). "If we are to change aggressive childhood behavior, we must change the environment in which the child lives. . . . The problem lies in the social environment" (Patterson et al., 2002, p. 21). Because the child is reacting to stimuli in his or her environment (e.g., parental demands of compliance), it is the environmental stimuli that must be altered rather than the child's internal attributes or personality. In the mid-1970s, this belief was fundamentally at odds with current trends in the psychological sciences, namely the progression toward cognitive psychology. At the time, the psychology department at the University of Oregon was interested in refocusing their mission on developing the new cognitive sciences. Because the behavioral work of Patterson's team was becoming less valued in the academic setting, the team chose to abandon the psychology department in favor of the Oregon Research Institute, a non-profit research corporation. It proved to be a beneficial move and eventually facilitated the founding of their own non-profit research center as the Oregon Social Learning Center in 1977.

A Developmental Model of Antisocial Behavior

In the early 1980s, it became apparent to Patterson's team that future funding of their research hinged on their ability to intercede and explain delinquent behavior. In 1983, the team was awarded a National Institute of Mental Health (NIMH) 2-year pilot study with fourth-grade boys and their families in Eugene, Oregon. This was the beginning of what was to become the longitudinal Oregon Youth Study (OYS). Data from the OYS were used to test their developmental model of antisocial behavior and various parenting interventions detailed in *Antisocial Boys* written by Patterson, John Reid, and Thomas Dishion in 1992.

Using early stimulus control studies and the OYS, Patterson demonstrated empirically that, over time, microsocial coercive family interactions become the fundamental building blocks through which aggression emerges and is maintained throughout child and adolescent development. Empirical evidence supported the hypothesis that chronic delinquency could be reliably predicted by a series of behavioral deficiencies across the developmental stages between early childhood through early adolescence.

During early childhood, ineffective parenting skills and techniques (poor parental monitoring, harsh and inconsistent discipline, excessive nagging, limited positive reinforcement for prosocial behavior) are seen as determining factors for childhood conduct disorders. This, according to Patterson, is the so-called training ground where children (and unskilled parents and siblings) learn the short-term functionality of their coercive behavior, gradually progressing the severity of coercive tactics from noncompliance, to temper tantrums, and finally to physical aggression. While learning the repertoire of antisocial behaviors, the child also fails to learn appropriate prosocial problem solving skills. Together, these deficiencies put the child at a significant social disadvantage when entering the school years.

Rejection from prosocial peers and academic struggle are common outcomes experienced by conduct-disordered children during middle childhood. Patterson's model demonstrated the importance of peer rejection and academic failure as precursors to both deviant peer group membership and delinquency. As a model of reinforcement, Patterson and colleagues argued that an aggressive child's selection of friends depends on the immediate payoffs of the relationship. Peers who reinforce the child for his or her antisocial behavior are much more likely to be chosen as friends than those who reject such behavior. Patterson characterized this behavior as "shopping" for friends based on the maximum amount of social reinforcement received using the least amount of social energy.

Patterson's developmental model was formally introduced to the criminological community in an article that appeared in *Criminology* co-authored with Dishion. Here, the authors revealed the direct and indirect contributions of both families and peers on delinquency. The model revealed that a lack of parental monitoring and social skills deficits directly increased the likelihood of the child's association with deviant peers. Further, poor parental monitoring, deviant peers, and academic struggles directly increased the chances of engaging in self-reported and officially documented delinquency.

Two Paths to Juvenile Delinquency: Early and Late Starters

As Patterson and his fellow scientists continued to expand their developmental model of juvenile delinquency, they began to realize that two distinct trajectories were necessary to explain delinquent behavior. The first trajectory characterized "early starters" who began with antisocial behavior during the preschool years, arrest at an early age (prior to age 14), chronic juvenile delinquency, followed by adult career offending. The second trajectory reflected "late starters" who did not have the early childhood training of antisocial behavior, whose first arrest was in mid- to late adolescence (age 14 or older), whose delinquency patterns were transient rather than chronic, and who were no more likely to engage in adult criminal behavior than juvenile nonoffenders. An early age onset of delinquency has consistently been shown to be a predictor of adult criminal behavior, beginning with Sheldon and Eleanor Glueck's research. Additionally, other researchers studying developmental models of delinquency have similarly concluded that there may be several paths to juvenile delinquency with varying criminal outcomes as adults.

The early-onset trajectory assumes a systematic progression of child behaviors as a result of a breakdown in parenting skills. This process begins with high rates of overt antisocial behavior as a toddler, advancing to more covert aggression during middle childhood. Later stages progress to include early arrest, chronic juvenile offending, young adult arrest, and adult chronic offending. Such a trajectory has been supported by data from the OYS (Patterson et al., 1998), where boys with early childhood antisocial behavior were 13.6 times more likely to be arrested at an early age compared to boys with little to no early antisocial history. Moreover, with an early arrest, the boys' chances of engaging in chronic juvenile delinquency (three or more juvenile arrests) was nearly 40 times greater than for boys not identified as having an early onset. Lastly, the likelihood of an adult arrest for early starters was significantly greater in comparison to late-starters (.65 vs. .29), and 71 percent of the late-starter boys desisted by having no adult arrest through the age of 23 (Patterson & Yoerger, 2002).

Three qualitative distinctions are made between the two trajectories. The first, and perhaps most important, is the developmental timing in the demonstration of antisocial behavior. Patterson's delinquency model asserts that the early-onset path begins during the preschool years whereas the late-onset path begins during mid-adolescence.

Second, disruptive parenting and peer processes are assumed to occur at much higher levels with early-onset children. The family dynamic of early-starters is typically characterized by ineffective discipline techniques by parents who are oftentimes antisocial themselves. This is much less frequently the case with late starters. Additionally, there is cursory evidence among the OYS sample that early-onset boys tend to be of low socioeconomic status (SES). However, according to Robert Larzelere and Patterson, the role of SES appears to have an indirect influence on delinquency through ineffective parental management processes. The role of deviant peers is manifested distinctly across the trajectories as well. The deviant peer group is much more of a critical factor in the development of antisocial behavior for late-onset adolescents, whereas deviant associates become an important maintenance mechanism for early-onset adolescents who already exhibit firmly established antisocial tendencies.

Third, early-onset boys are characterized as having more significant social deficits than late-onset boys. An inability to accurately detect and interpret social cues from others (i.e., social referencing) is one of the critical deficits observed among early starters. The social competencies of late-onset delinquents are assumed to be stronger than that of early-onset delinquents but weaker than nondelinquents.

Although the two trajectories are distinct, the model assumes the same underlying process toward antisocial behavior, namely the operant coercive and reinforcement process. Timing, level of disadvantage and disruption among contextual variables (e.g., SES, parental divorce), and level of social deficits are the distinguishing factors across the two trajectories. However, aggression and antisocial behavior for both groups are determined by the relative amount of reinforcement received from the social environment for engaging in such antisocial acts. Thus, Patterson's coercion theory assumes a single model can explain how the delinquency process begins, what maintains it, and what determines progression from one developmental stage to the next.

From a criminological context, coercion theory, as with all social learning theories, has fundamentally contrasting assumptions with other criminological perspectives, particularly control theories. Control theories assume that individuals are naturally inclined to engage in antisocial behavior; control mechanisms (e.g., social bonds, self-control, informal social control) must be in place to reduce antisocial behavior and crime. Social learning perspectives, on the other hand, maintain that antisocial behavior is learned over time, similar to any other behavior. Therefore, interventions must disrupt the antisocial learning process and replace them with alternative prosocial skills. Accordingly, poor parenting techniques and harsh discipline are primary treatment targets in the Oregon delinquency model. In fact, Patterson developed time-out, a now widely used punishment intervention strategy, specifically to disrupt child coercive behavior. Conversely, the poor parental skills described in Patterson's coercive theoretical model are viewed by control theorists as poor controls over children's behavior which reduce the child's social bonds and self-control.

Conclusion

The work of Patterson and his colleagues from the OSLC in explicating a developmental model of antisocial behavior continues to be supported by independent criminologists, and has served as a critical foundation to the development of highly effective delinquency prevention interventions, including Scott Henggeler's Multisystemic Therapy and the OSLC's Multidimensional Treatment Foster Care. Perhaps Patterson's most important contribution is the identification of the micro-level processes through which aggression and antisocial behavior is shaped and maintained through daily interactions with parents, peers, teachers, and siblings. The coercive, reinforcement process provides the missing link that longitudinal, risk-factor research cannot: It is one thing to know that poor parental discipline and association with deviant peers are predictive factors for delinquency, and quite another to know exactly how these risk factors function in the day-to-day interactions of children and adolescents.

Patterson's most recent work with Isabela Granic significantly advances his theory by placing it within a dynamic systems perspective. Doing so provides a more thorough and complex explanation, merging two separate, yet interacting, time scales: the micro-level, real-time interactions and the macro-level, global, risk factors that develop over longer time periods. Indeed, his theoretical contributions will continue to have a significant impact on both causal explanations of delinquency and crime and practical applications for preventing and reducing antisocial behavior.

Emily J. Salisbury

See also Bandura, Albert: Social Learning Theory; Farrington, David P.: The Integrated Cognitive Antisocial Potential Theory; Harris, Judith Rich: Why Parents Do Not Matter; Loeber, Rolf, and Magda Stouthamer-Loeber: Pathways to Crime; Moffit, Terrie E.: A Developmental Model of Life-Course-Persistent Offending

References and Further Readings

Bandura, A. (1977). *Social learning theory.* Englewood Cliffs, NJ: Prentice Hall.

Gottfredson, M. R., & Hirschi, T. (1990). *A general theory of crime.* Stanford, CA: Stanford University Press.

Granic, I., & Patterson, G. R. (2006). Toward a comprehensive model of antisocial development: A dynamic systems approach. *Psychological Review, 113,* 101–131.

Hirschi, T. (1969). *Causes of delinquency.* Berkeley: University of California Press.

Larzelere, R. E., & Patterson, G. R. (1990). Parental management: Mediator of the effect of socioeconomic status on early delinquency. *Criminology, 28,* 301–323.

Patterson, G. R. (1982). *Coercive family process.* Eugene, OR: Castalia.

Patterson, G. R. (1992). Developmental stages in antisocial behavior. In R. D. Peters, R. J. McMahon, & V. L. Quinsey (Eds.), *Aggression and violence throughout the life span* (pp. 52–82). Newbury Park, CA: Sage.

Patterson, G. R. (1993). Orderly change in a stable world: The antisocial trait as a chimera. *Journal of Consulting and Clinical Psychology, 61,* 911–919.

Patterson, G. R. (2002). The early development of coercive family process. In J. B. Reid, G. R. Patterson, & J. Snyder (Eds.), *Antisocial behavior in children and adolescents: A developmental analysis and model for intervention* (pp. 25–44). Washington, DC: American Psychological Association.

Patterson, G. R., DeBaryshe, B. D., & Ramsey, E. (1989). A developmental perspective on antisocial behavior. *American Psychologist, 44,* 329–335.

Patterson, G. R., & Dishion, T. J. (1985). Contributions of families and peers to delinquency. *Criminology, 23,* 63–79.

Patterson, G. R., Forgatch, M. S., Yoerger, K., & Stoolmiller, M. (1998). Variables that initiate and maintain an early-onset trajectory for juvenile offending. *Development and Psychopathology, 10,* 541–547.

Patterson, G. R., Reid, J. B., & Dishion, T. J. (1992). *Antisocial boys.* Eugene, OR: Castalia.

Patterson, G. R., Reid, J. B., & Eddy, J. M. (2002). A brief history of the Oregon model. In J. B. Reid, G. R. Patterson, & J. Snyder (Eds.), *Antisocial behavior in children and adolescents: A developmental analysis and model for intervention* (pp. 3–21). Washington, DC: American Psychological Association.

Patterson, G. R., & Yoerger, K. (2002). A developmental model for early- and late-onset delinquency. In J. B. Reid, G. R. Patterson, & J. Snyder (Eds.), *Antisocial behavior in children and adolescents: A developmental analysis and model for intervention* (pp. 147–172). Washington, DC: American Psychological Association.

Reid, J. B., Patterson, G. R., & Snyder, J. (2002). *Antisocial behavior in children and adolescents: A developmental analysis and model for intervention.* Washington, DC: American Psychological Association.

Snyder, J. J., & Patterson, G. R. (1995). Individual differences in social aggression: A test of a reinforcement model of socialization in the natural environment. *Child Development, 57,* 1257–1268.

Snyder, J. J., Schrepferman, L., & St. Peter, C. (1997). Origins of antisocial behavior: Negative reinforcement and affect dysregulation of behavior as socialization in family interaction. *Behavior Modification, 21,* 187–215.

PEACEMAKING CRIMINOLOGY

Peacemaking criminology is a relatively recent and novel approach to understanding both crime and, perhaps more importantly, public and personal reactions to crime. In fact, criminology as peacemaking can be understood as a response to criminal justice policies that were first enacted during the 1960s such as President Johnson's Commission on Law Enforcement and the Administration of Justice and the Omnibus Crime Control and Safe Streets Act. These broad executive and legislative proposals heralded the War on Crime, a law-and-order, get-tough, and war-making response to criminal and delinquent behavior. As Jonathan Simon observes, the "war on crime" has even transformed American democracy and created a culture of fear by which politicians now govern. Peacemaking criminology was born out of disenchantment with the repressive and socially conservative agenda that gave rise to the war-on-crime political movement. According to Ronald Akers and Christine Sellers, peacemaking criminology advances a utopian, crime-free society with a justice system that focuses on peaceful conflict resolution, the restoration of offenders within the community, and the absence of corporal and capital punishments (p. 262).

Origins

Richard Quinney, a Marxist criminologist who rose to acclaim for his conflict theory contained in *The Social Reality of Crime* and his *Critique of Legal Order*, is considered to be the father of peacemaking criminology. Much of the development of peacemaking criminology is wrapped up in the evolution of Quinney's thought from Marxist theory to Buddhist philosophy. Indeed, religious teachings (e.g., peace is the way, turn the other cheek, love thy neighbor, let those without sin cast the first stone) are core principles of peacemaking criminology. In addition to Quinney, other scholars have greatly contributed to peacemaking criminology; included among them is Harold E. Pepinsky. Pepinsky's early scholarship was influenced by the anarchist tradition, but his later work incorporated concepts from peace studies, feminism, and even chaos theory (McEvoy, 2003). Together, Quinney and Pepinsky co-edited *Criminology as Peacemaking*; this single volume is probably the most recognizable collection of essays devoted to fleshing out peacemaking criminology as a bona fide theoretical orientation in the disciplines of criminology and criminal justice.

In defining crime, Quinney, in "The Way of Peace," noted, "Human existence is characterized by suffering; crime is suffering" (p. 4). However, he seemed to eschew further elaborations on the nature of crime, maintaining, "The path to the ending of suffering is through compassion rather than through the theories of science and the calculations of conditioned thought" (p. 9). Instead, Quinney emphasized the relationship between peacemaking and social justice, and he also suggested that nonviolence is the primary guiding philosophy of peacemaking criminology. Quinney critiqued the criminal justice system in the United States by pointing out that violence is the foundation of the domestic legal system. Many crime-control policies, such as corporal and capital punishment, are based on ideas of retribution and violence. Peacemaking criminology rejects any criminal justice policy that inflicts suffering on the victims or the perpetrators of crime.

As mentioned, peacemaking criminology has origins in religion and critical theory, which might seem to make odd bedfellows. In addition to religion and Marxism, Pepinsky suggested that feminism and women's experiences are also integral to peacemaking criminology. The relationship seems to be reciprocal; that is, feminism and peacemaking reinforce one another. According to Pepinsky, peacemaking criminology must embrace womanhood because "people whose men have honored and respected rather than subdued womanhood have been relatively nonpunitive, peaceful societies" (p. 309). He goes on to say, "In a world free of repression, there isn't much need for manhood at all" (p. 309). Gender is important to peacemaking criminology because it can represent an obstacle to social justice when women as a social class are disenfranchised and denied the power to make decisions for themselves. John Fuller and John Wozniak summarize the three major intellectual traditions of peacemaking criminology as religion/humanism, feminism, and critical theory (i.e., Marxism).

Core Themes

Fuller and Wozniak demarcate six grand themes that inform peacemaking criminology: nonviolence, social justice, inclusion, correct means, ascertainable criteria, and the categorical imperative. Nonviolence is the apex principle in peacemaking criminology. Social justice maintains that "only by promoting the welfare of all, including those without power, can a society develop a long-term atmosphere of cooperation and commitment" (Fuller & Wozniak, 2006, p. 261). With inclusion, both the victim and the perpetrator are involved in the criminal justice process (e.g., trial and sentencing). Inclusion promotes forgiveness, conciliation, and restoration. In regard to correct means, Fuller and Wozniak note that the criminal justice system must arrive at solutions to crime in "an ethical and moral way" (p. 262). The theme of ascertainable criteria involves the notion of transparency and education of laypersons in the "language" of the criminal justice system. Lastly, the categorical imperative is the Kantian philosophy of determining the morality of an action based on its applicability to future scenarios, and they advocate a socially just application of this categorical imperative, regardless of class, race, and gender. Taken together, Fuller and Wozniak claim that these six concepts form a cohesive "peacemaking pyramid" with intrapersonal, interpersonal, institutional/societal, and global international implications.

In addition to the peacemaking pyramid advanced by Fuller and Wozniak, Michael Braswell and Jeffrey Gold identify three metatheoretical themes that guide peacemaking criminology. These are mindfulness, connectedness, and caring. Mindfulness means "to move from the passion of single-minded self-interest to a growing sense of compassion that includes others and their needs"; connectedness involves a social context where humans realize that their actions have consequences for others; and lastly caring is akin to the love that a parent has for her/his child (p. 34). These themes went largely unspecified for some time, until John Whitehead, Wayne Gillespie, and Braswell mapped them onto three analytic levels with the ethic of care occupying a cultural level, connectedness signifying a social structural or institutional level, and then mindfulness representing the micro, individual, inter- or intra-personal level of analysis.

Fuller and Wozniak have also sought to further develop their theoretical model of peacemaking criminology by first conceptualizing the theory as a Venn diagram comprising four interlocking circles representing social structure, crimes, social harms, the criminal justice system, and peacemaking alternatives. They also enumerate a number of core peacemaking criminology variables at three empirical levels: personal justice, criminal justice, and social justice. Personal justice variables include crime, positive peace, social harms, peacemaking, responsiveness, dignity, needs, mindfulness, connectedness, right understanding, and peacemaking teaching. Criminal justice variables include mainstream criminology, peacemaking criminology, theoretical perspectives, and peacemaking alternatives. Social justice variables are safe community, social inequality, power relations, social structures, and social transformation.

Applications

Peacemaking criminology continues to be applied to different aspects of the criminal justice system, including policing, courts, and corrections. For instance, Paul Jesilow and Deborah Parsons link the practice of community policing with peacemaking criminology as a method of introducing peacemaking to a traditional policing culture. Another example of peacemaking principles applied to criminal justice practice is Pono Kaulike, a Hawaii criminal court that provides restorative justice practice for healing relationships (Walker & Hayashi, 2007). Yet, perhaps the best known advocacy of applying peacemaking criminology to the criminal justice system is Braswell, Fuller, and Bo Lozoff's integration of restorative justice into the correctional subsystem. They illuminate a variety of peacemaking alternatives to incarceration, including community corrections and faith-based correctional practices. As Braswell et al. conclude, "A bridge of compassion recognizes the harms and fear shared by offenders and victims, but also offers a way back into the community for each as well. Community justice is a context where much restoration can take place" (p. 152).

In addition to the application of peacemaking criminology in the criminal justice system, Kieran McEvoy explores the global relevance of peacemaking, particularly to paramilitary violence in Northern Ireland. She outlines several criteria for a "new" peacemaking criminology. First, McEvoy suggests that "the predominant focus of peacemaking criminology should be upon areas where actual political or ethnic conflict are occurring" (p. 334). Her next point is guided by praxis where "peacemaking criminology should be about a better understanding of the criminological object of study and its relationship to the conflict in order to try to *make a difference*" (p. 334, emphasis in the original). Third, peacemaking criminology must be parallel to human rights speech; moreover, peacemaking criminology should be engaged in advancing human rights on a global level. Lastly, McEvoy raises the possibility of expanding measures of assessment to transcend the technocratic methods of evaluation that are currently popular in the criminal justice field. Taken together, these suggestions from McEvoy are designed to reconfigure the focus of peacemaking criminology from the domestic to the global; by doing so, it reconstitutes peacemaking as a viable method of conflict transformation.

Conclusion

Peacemaking criminology, while a newer perspective on the theoretical landscape, has not been greeted without criticism. Akers and Sellers point out several inconsistencies in advocating peacemaking as criminology, including its ties to religion, feminism, and Marxism. For instance, peacemaking criminology draws heavily from religious teachings, but many religious edicts are violent or they have violent repercussions. Furthermore, consider feminism, which offers an idea of a liberated, independent woman who is not forced to conform to traditional roles of motherhood and nurturer. The peacemaking variant of feminism looks to the "natural" care that mothers display toward their children as a general model for caring. Motherhood, from many feminist perspectives, is a social construction that has been used in the past to subjugate the interests of women to the interests of men. Lastly, Marx advocated violence as a means to emancipate the working class from the shackles of bourgeois hegemony. Peacemaking never advocates violence as an alternative to solve social structural problems. The disconnection between peacemaking criminology and its proposed counterpart theoretical positions (e.g., religion, feminism, and Marxism) thus raises questions about the logical consistency of the peacemaking perspective. Akers and Sellers also criticize peacemaking criminology for being tautological; that is, the cause of crime and its definition (i.e., suffering) are one and the same. They went on to say, "It may be possible to construct a testable, parsimonious, and valid theory

from peacemaking criminology, but at this point it remains a philosophy rather than a theory" (p. 262).

Wayne Gillespie

See also Abolitionism; Anarchist Criminology; Colvin, Mark: Coercion Theory; Colvin, Mark, Francis T. Cullen, and Thomas Vander Ven: Coercion, Social Support, and Crime; Cullen, Francis T.: Social Support and Crime; Cultural Criminology; Drennon-Gala, Don: Social Support and Delinquency; Left Realism Criminology; Postmodern Theory; Quinney, Richard: Social Transformation and Peacemaking Criminology; Regoli, Robert M., and John D. Hewitt: Differential Oppression Theory

References and Further Readings

Akers, R. L., & Sellers, C. S. (2009). *Criminological theories: Introduction, evaluation, and application* (5th ed.). New York: Oxford University Press.

Braswell, M., Fuller, J., & Lozoff, B. (2001). *Corrections, peacemaking, and restorative justice: Transforming individuals and institutions*. Cincinnati, OH: Anderson.

Braswell, M. C., & Gold, J. (1998). Peacemaking, justice and ethics. In *Justice, crime and ethics* (3rd ed., pp. 23–40). Cincinnati, OH: Anderson.

Fuller, J. R., & Wozniak, J. F. (2006). Peacemaking criminology: Past, present, and future. In F. T. Cullen, J. P. Wright, & K. R. Blevins (Eds.), *Taking stock: The status of criminological theory* (Vol. 15, pp. 251–273). New Brunswick, NJ: Transaction.

Jesilow, P., & Parsons, D. (2000). Community policing as peacemaking. *Policing and Society, 10,* 163–182.

McEvoy, K. (2003). Beyond the metaphor: Political violence, human rights and "new" peacemaking criminology. *Theoretical Criminology, 7,* 319–346.

Pepinsky, H. E. (1991). Peacemaking in criminology and criminal justice. In H. E. Pepinski & R. Quinney (Eds.), *Criminology as peacemaking* (pp. 229–327). Bloomington: Indiana University Press.

Pepinsky, H. E., & Quinney, R. (1991). *Criminology as peacemaking*. Bloomington: Indiana University Press.

Quinney, R. (1991). The way of peace: On crime, suffering, and service. In H. E. Pepinsky & R. Quinney (Eds.), *Criminology as peacemaking* (pp. 3–13). Bloomington: Indiana University Press.

Simon, J. (2007). *Governing through crime: How the War on Crime transformed American democracy and created a culture of fear*. New York: Oxford University Press.

Walker, L., & Hayashi, L. A. (2007). Pono Kaulike: A Hawaii criminal court provides restorative justice practices for healing relationships. *Federal Probation, 71*, 18–24.

Whitehead, J. T., Gillespie, W., & Braswell, M. (2008). The future of the peacemaking perspective. In J. F. Wozniak, M. C. Braswell, R. E. Vogel, & K. R. Blevins (Eds.), *Transformative justice: Critical and peacemaking themes influenced by Richard Quinney* (pp. 231–250). Lanham, MD: Lexington Books.

Wozniak, J. F., Braswell, M. C., Vogel, R. E., & Blevins, K. R. (Eds.). (2008). *Transformative justice: Critical and peacemaking themes influenced by Richard Quinney*. Lanham, MD: Lexington Books.

PEERS AND DELINQUENCY

Most Americans are probably familiar with the concept of a delinquent "gang." Most would probably picture a collection of young males who share a common territory, have some organizational structure (e.g., ranks like "warlord" or "lieutenant"), conduct initiation rites, and display common signs of membership (e.g., colors, "tats," or "inks"). Most might also realize that gangs are responsible for only a small (though not trivial) fraction of crime in the United States.

What many Americans might not realize, however, is that gangs exemplify one of the most consistently documented features of delinquent behavior. Most delinquent offenses are not committed by a lone offender but rather by a *group* of youths. To be sure, these groups are usually a far cry from large, organized gangs. Most are small, disorganized, and spontaneous groups that resemble childhood play groups. But they are groups nonetheless, and that means that all of the social processes that occur in human social groups—status competition, loyalty and disloyalty, factionalization, ingratiation, and so on—take place in delinquent groups as well.

Some criminologists see little theoretical significance in the group nature of delinquency. Others, however, see the "groupiness" of delinquency as a potential key to unlocking its causes. This entry reviews the history of research on the group nature of delinquency and the role of peer influence in explaining delinquent behavior.

History

As early as 1931, two famous sociologists at the University of Chicago, Clifford Shaw and Henry McKay, discovered that more than 80 percent of juveniles appearing before the Chicago Juvenile Court had accomplices. Similar findings drawn from police data were routinely reported by scholars from the 1920s through the 1960s. As self-report methods gained acceptance in the 1960s and 1970s, evidence for the group nature of delinquency swelled. Martin Gold, for example, reported that 75 percent of the 2,490 chargeable delinquent offenses reported by his sample of Flint youths were committed in the company of others, and less than 20 percent of respondents in Lyle Shannon's survey of Racine youths said that they had acted alone. Today, the group nature of delinquency is widely accepted as fact by criminologists, and it appears to hold even in countries outside the United States.

As the group nature of delinquency became increasingly apparent during the 20th century, so too did the features of these groups. Nearly all studies show the typical size of delinquent groups to be small—usually two to four members. It appears that group size diminishes with age; groups of four or more are common in late childhood and early adolescence but gradually give way to triads and dyads in middle and late adolescence. Apart from their size, it is also well established that delinquent groups are predominantly unisexual (although males are more common in female groups than vice versa), and they appear to be relatively age homogeneous as well. It is important to bear in mind, however, that small differences in age can hold great significance to adolescents—older adolescents have significantly more privileges than younger ones—and the "instigator" in delinquent groups is often older (and almost never younger) than other group members.

It appears that the small groups that commit most delinquent acts are often subsets of a larger group or clique, which may include a gang. Delinquent groups are neither highly stable nor highly organized. Offenders do not ordinarily stay with the same accomplices over long periods of time, and they often belong to multiple offending groups or cliques at the same time. Within delinquent groups, role definitions and role assignments appear to be unclear and unstable, and shifting membership makes these groups intrinsically unstable. Albert Reiss has argued that the membership of delinquent groups is continually subject to change as a consequence of residential mobility, the incarceration of members, and shifts to conventional careers. The sociologist Lewis Yablonsky once described delinquent groups as "near groups" to capture their fleeting and disorganized character, and his assessment appears to be accurate.

Delinquent Friends

As evidence of the group nature of delinquency accumulated during the 20th century, a parallel pattern was emerging in other research. As early as the 1950s, criminologists noticed that delinquent youths tended to have friends who were delinquent too. In fact, one of the strongest predictors of delinquent behavior known to criminologists today is the number of delinquent friends an adolescent has. The correlation between delinquent behavior and delinquent friends has been documented in scores of studies from the 1950s up to the present day, using alternative kinds of criminological data (self-reports, official records, perceptual data) on subjects and friends, alternative research designs, and data on a wide variety of criminal offenses. Few, if any, empirical regularities in criminology have been documented as often or over as long a period of time as the association between delinquency and delinquent friends.

Delinquent friends are distinctive in certain ways from "straight" friends. They tend, for example, to be "secret" friends, meaning that parents usually know little or nothing about these friends because their children conceal them and their relationships. Mark Warr has also described delinquent friends as "sticky friends"; once acquired, they are not quickly lost. This may be true because hanging out with the "wrong" crowd, once it becomes known, tends to limit opportunities for friendships with non-delinquent youth.

As a rule, delinquent friends share a dislike of school and have low educational aspirations. In fact, this disdain for school appears to be one of the unifying characteristics that draw delinquent youths together at school and elsewhere. Another common characteristic that seems to unite delinquent youths and their friends is conflict with and low attachment to parents. For some youths, this weak attachment is probably a result of their parents' awareness and disapproval of their friends.

Peers and the Origins of Delinquency

Faced with compelling evidence of the social nature of delinquency, some social scientists have turned to this fact when attempting to explain the origins of delinquent behavior. To many modern criminologists, the very idea of peer influence is synonymous with Edwin Sutherland and his famous theory of *differential association*. The first explicit statement of Sutherland's theory appeared in 1939 in the third edition of his *Principles of Criminology*, a popular textbook of the time. A revised and final version appeared in the fourth edition in 1947, 3 years before Sutherland's death. The latter statement of the theory took the form of nine propositions, each followed by brief elaborations or clarifications. The nine propositions were as follows:

1. Criminal behavior is learned.

2. Criminal behavior is learned in interaction with other persons in a process of communication.

3. The principal part of the learning of criminal behavior occurs within intimate personal groups.

4. When criminal behavior is learned, the learning includes (a) techniques of committing the crime, which are sometimes very complicated, sometimes very simple; and (b) the specific direction of motives, drives, rationalizations, and attitudes.

5. The specific direction of motives and drives is learned from definitions of the legal codes as favorable or unfavorable.

6. A person becomes delinquent because of an excess of definitions favorable to violation of law over definitions unfavorable to violation of law.

7. Differential association may vary in frequency, duration, priority, and intensity.

8. The process of learning criminal behavior by association with criminal and anti-criminal patterns involves all of the mechanisms that are involved in any other learning.

9. While criminal behavior is an expression of general needs and values, it is not explained by those general needs and values since non-criminal behavior is an expression of the same needs and values.

Sutherland's theory was in its time a radical theory of criminal behavior. It eschewed popular biological theories of crime, for example, and by situating the origins of crime in the everyday interaction of ordinary people, it favored a strongly sociological and naturalistic explanation of crime. Perhaps its most radical feature was that it treated criminal behavior like any other form of human behavior (sexual behavior, language, food customs), that is, as behavior *learned* from others.

Research on differential association theory has been generally supportive, although some specific precepts of the theory have been called into question. For example, Warr examined the effects of priority and duration on self-reported delinquency at age 17 using data from the National Youth Survey. His analysis indicated that these two dimensions of friendship are not entirely independent. Why? Because adolescents who acquire delinquent friends tend to retain them (remember the "sticky friends" phenomenon), and thus those who acquire such friends at younger ages (greater priority) tend to have longer histories of delinquent friendships (greater duration). Hence, the two elements cannot be regarded as entirely independent components of differential association. Further analysis by Warr indicated that duration has a substantial and statistically significant effect on delinquency. The effect of priority was also significant for three of the four offenses he examined, but in all four cases the effect was *negative*, with *recent* rather than early exposure having the greatest effect on delinquency. That is, one's *current* friends appear to be more influential than one's friends at earlier ages. This is exactly the opposite of Sutherland's prediction, although it is quite consistent with social learning theory.

There is another aspect of Sutherland's theory that has consistently failed to receive support from research. Sutherland argued that individuals become delinquent because they acquire "definitions" (or attitudes) favorable to the violation of law through differential association. In essence, Sutherland was arguing that delinquency is the result of attitude transference, whereby the attitudes of one individual are adopted or absorbed by another. A number of studies over the last three decades, however, have consistently indicated that attitude transference is *not* the process by which differential association operates. For example,

after noting that behavior and attitudes are not always consistent, Mark Warr and Mark Stafford reported that the effect of friends' attitudes on adolescents is small in comparison to that of friends' *behavior*, and the effect of friends' behavior is largely direct, meaning that it does not operate through changing attitudes. Consequently, it seems that adolescents are much more sensitive to the behavior of their friends than their attitudes.

Social Learning Theory

In 1966, Robert Burgess and Ronald Akers published an important paper in which they restated Sutherland's theory of differential association in the terminology of operant conditioning, a rapidly developing branch of behavioral psychology associated with B.F. Skinner that emphasized the relation between behavior and reinforcement. In the intervening years, Akers has devoted his career to developing and testing a social learning approach to the explanation of crime, an approach that, like operant conditioning, emphasizes the role of reinforcement (both positive and negative) in criminal behavior:

> Whether individuals will refrain from or initiate, continue committing, or desist from criminal and deviant acts depends on the relative frequency, amount, and probability of past, present, and anticipated rewards and punishments perceived to be attached to the behavior. (Akers, 1998, p. 66)

Social learning theory benefits from and builds upon the enormous theoretical and empirical development that took place in behavioral psychology during the second half of the 20th century. As its name implies, what most distinguishes social learning theory from other learning theories is its sensitivity to the *social* sources of reinforcement in everyday life. Capitalizing on the work of Albert Bandura, Akers, and others, social learning theory emphasizes interpersonal mechanisms of learning such as imitation (modeling or mimicking the behavior of others) and vicarious reinforcement (observing how other people's behavior is rewarded), as well as direct reinforcement, in the acquisition of behaviors. Thus, adolescents may adopt the delinquent behavior of their friends (e.g., smoking, theft, drug sales) through imitation, because they observe the adult status it confers on them in the eyes of others their age (vicarious reinforcement), because it brings rewards like sexual attractiveness and money (direct reinforcement), and because participating in those activities gains them the admiration and respect of their friends (direct reinforcement). This example is a bit of an oversimplification, because social learning theory focuses on the precise schedules, quantities, and probabilities of both reward and punishment, which can act in complex ways. But it suffices to illustrate the theory.

The empirical evidence supporting social learning theory is extensive and impressive. However, it is disproportionately concentrated on tobacco, alcohol, and other drug use, and on relatively minor forms of deviance (e.g., cheating). The evidence for the theory, consequently, can best be described as positive and promising but somewhat limited in scope.

Companions in Crime

In a recent book titled *Companions in Crime*, Warr identified a number of possible mechanisms of peer influence. What follows is a brief description of some of those mechanisms.

Fear of Ridicule

Ridicule is an expression of contempt or derision for the actions, beliefs, or features of another. Although it is often expressed verbally, ridicule may be conveyed through facial expressions, gestures, laughter, or writing. Often, to ridicule another is to call into question the person's fitness for membership in a group (a family, a club, a gang, a clique of friends).

Fear of ridicule can lead adolescents (and sometimes adults) to join others in behavior that they would never engage in if they were alone, behavior they might find morally repugnant and even dangerous. Ruth Beyth-Marom and colleagues, for example, asked adult and adolescent subjects to list possible consequences of either accepting or declining to engage in risky behaviors (e.g., smoking marijuana, drinking and driving). The reaction of peers was the most frequently cited consequence (mentioned by 80 to 100 percent of respondents across situations) of *rejecting* a risky behavior (e.g., "They'll laugh at me"), but was much less salient as a reason for *performing* the behavior ("They'll like me"). Avoiding ridicule, it seems, is a stronger motivation for deviance than a desire to ingratiate.

For adolescents, the sting of ridicule is heightened by the fear of rejection that plagues many youths, and the enormous importance that adolescents place on peer acceptance. It is through peers that young persons first establish an identity independent of their family of origin, an identity whose very existence ultimately rests in the hands of *other* people. By risking ridicule, adolescents are in effect risking their very identity, a prospect that few would wish to entertain. If maintaining that identity entails an occasional foray onto the other side of the law to avoid peer rejection, it may seem a small price to pay to maintain such a valuable possession.

In the modern world, ridicule is often transmitted by adolescents via text messaging, e-mail, cell phones, and other electronic media, and these communications sometime have the added feature of being anonymous, hiding not only the source of the messages but the number of people transmitting them. Such messages can be especially disturbing to recipients because they imply organized and widespread disapproval by others. The shift of peer relations onto the Internet and other electronic media (e.g., massive online gaming) is part of what Warr has dubbed the "virtual peer group."

Loyalty

Loyalty is a virtue and an element of friendship that is readily appreciated by most people. To remain steadfast to a friend when there are strong pressures to defect is a cultural motif as old as the Last Supper. There is reason to believe that loyalty plays a particularly important role in interpersonal relations among adolescents. Adolescent friendships are *formative* friendships, the first tentative efforts to define an identity outside the family, an identity that may be of enormous importance to a youngster emerging into a new phase of life and a new social world, and an identity whose very newness makes it fragile. When asked to define friendship, adolescents typically cite loyalty—along with intimacy—as the principal features of genuine friendship.

When it comes to delinquency, loyalty means more than simply not "ratting" on one's friends.

It often means engaging in risky or illegal behavior in which one would not otherwise participate in order to preserve or solidify a friendship. Loyalty can be a potent means of demonstrating friendship, and sharing risky behavior provides an excellent opportunity to prove one's loyalty and seal a friendship. In a study using national survey data from young people, Warr found that adolescents were more likely than other age groups to say that they would lie to the police to protect their friends.

Loyalty also provides a form of *moral cover* for illegal conduct. It invokes a moral imperative that supersedes or nullifies the moral gravity of the criminal offense. "Yes, I took part in the robbery, but I did so out of loyalty to Sonny, who would have done the same for me." As a universally recognized virtue, loyalty imparts legitimacy to otherwise illegitimate acts and confers honor on the dishonorable.

Status

The term *status* denotes prestige or respect within a group. Like other primates, human beings generally enjoy and seek status. Richard Savin-Williams, for example, found that young males randomly assigned to a summer camp cabin formed a stable dominance hierarchy within hours after meeting, and that contests over status declined rapidly once that hierarchy was established. Other research corroborates the claim that status hierarchies form rapidly in human groups, and it appears that one of the primary objectives of people when participating in groups is to avoid status loss.

In one of the earliest and most influential efforts to understand gang delinquency, James Short and Fred Strodtbeck provided numerous accounts of how gang members in Chicago sought to acquire status in the gang or fend off threats to their existing status. For example, a gang leader who had been away in detention for some time reestablished his status upon returning to the gang by intentionally provoking a fight with members of a rival gang. In another instance, an influential gang member, after losing a prestigious pool tournament to another clique of the gang, robbed and assaulted a stranger along with some of his team members. The offense seemed to defy any economic or other explanation at the time, but because robbery was a source of status within the gang, Short and Strodtbeck concluded that the action was an attempt to reassert status in the gang.

The importance of status in explaining delinquency can only be appreciated by realizing how precious and fragile a commodity status is among adolescents. Industrial societies deny adult status and its perquisites to adolescents until long after physical maturation has occurred, creating what Terrie Moffitt has called a "maturity gap" that persists for years. For many adolescents, the only potential source of status in their lives lies in the world of their age-peers, and the use of violence or other forms of delinquency to attain or maintain that status may appear well worth the potential costs.

If adolescence carries with it a general problem of status deficiency, imagine what it means to be an adolescent *and* a member of a minority group *and* to live in an economically depressed area. That is the social world described so eloquently and chillingly by Elijah Anderson in his book *Code of the Street*, an account of the social rules of the ghetto. In the inner city world he describes, where status is virtually the only possession that many young persons can claim, there is no greater affront than "dissing" (disrespecting) another, especially in front of others, and the penalty for doing so is often immediate injury or death. Even the most subtle signs of disrespect (e.g., staring) can produce savage results. This helps to explain why homicides and assaults are so often provoked by seemingly trivial matters (e.g., an argument over a small amount of money, or cutting into a line).

Other Mechanisms of Peer Influence

In addition to the foregoing, Warr identified several other mechanisms of peer influence. These include the relief from *boredom* that peers often supply for adolescents, the role of *drugs* in encouraging youth to hang together and engage in deviance, a reliance on peers for *protection* in environments that are dangerous (e.g., schools or neighborhoods where violence is ubiquitous), the sense of *anonymity* that groups afford, and the *moral codes* that groups often establish.

Some of Warr's mechanisms can be logically subsumed under social learning theory. For example, status is a nearly universal reinforcer for humans, just as ridicule is a negative reinforcer (or punishment). Viewed this way, much of Warr's work can be seen as adding greater specificity or detail to the general principles of social learning theory.

Conclusion

Delinquent behavior is predominantly social behavior. Most youthful offenders have accomplices when they violate the law, and most also have delinquent friends who may or may not be among those accomplices during any given delinquent event.

The social character of delinquency, as we have seen, forms the foundation for several etiological theories of delinquency. To critics and proponents of other theories, this evidence is not persuasive. Yes, they argue, delinquent youths have accomplices in delinquency, but they have "accomplices" in almost everything they do—dating, sports, driving, or just hanging out. Yes, delinquent youths have delinquent friends, but this is merely homophily (i.e., the tendency of people to make friends with people like themselves), not evidence of peer influence. Some critics even doubt the companionate nature of delinquency itself, arguing that it is merely an artifact of the way criminologists measure crime.

All of these arguments have been countered with empirical evidence by proponents of peer influence, but the search for answers about the social aspects of delinquency remains one of the most vital areas of research in contemporary criminology.

Mark Warr

See also Akers, Ronald L.: Social Learning Theory; Anderson, Elijah: Code of the Street; Shaw, Clifford R.: The Jack-Roller; Shaw, Clifford R., and Henry D. McKay: Social Disorganization Theory; Short, James F., Jr.: Gangs and Group Processes; Sutherland, Edwin H.: Differential Association Theory and Differential Social Organization; Thrasher, Frederick M.: The Gang

References and Further Readings

Akers, R. L. (1998). *Social learning and social structure: A general theory of crime and deviance.* Boston: Northeastern University Press.

Matsueda, R. L., & Anderson, K. (1998). The dynamics of delinquent peers and delinquent behavior. *Criminology, 36,* 269–308.

Reiss, A. J., Jr. (1986). Co-offender influences on criminal careers. In A. Blumstein, J. Cohen, J. Roth, & C. Visher (Eds.), *Criminal careers and "career criminals"* (pp. 121–160). Washington, DC: National Academy Press.

Warr, M. (2002). *Companions in crime.* New York: Cambridge University Press.

PERCEPTUAL DETERRENCE

Deterrence is a process in which threatened or actual sanctions discourage criminal acts. There are official sanctions, such as incarceration or probation. There are also non-legal punishments; for example, people may refrain from offending to avoid disapproval from others. Three dimensions of punishment are believed to affect crime. In the aggregate, crime rates should diminish as the certainty, severity, and celerity (swiftness) of punishments increase. And, the likelihood that an individual will commit a given crime should relate negatively to that individual's perceptions of the certainty, severity, and celerity of punishment for that crime.

Various approaches have been taken to estimate the existence and size of deterrent effects. Research has investigated the association between crime rates in a place and the authorized punishments in that place. Authorized punishments are the behavioral restrictions authorities are empowered to enforce. They consist of criminal statutes and other behavioral regulations. For example, Radha Iyengar found that mandatory arrest laws for domestic violence increased intimate partner homicide, but decreased "other family" homicides. And David McDowall, Colin Loftin, and Brian Wiersema have investigated the impact of both mandatory sentencing laws and concealed firearms laws on crime rates. Studies have also related crime rates to indicators of actual police activity or enforced punishments. The most prominent examples of this approach model crime rates as a function of the arrest clearance ratio; this ratio consists of the number of arrests divided by the number of crimes known to the police.

While highly informative, these approaches do not directly address *perceptual deterrence*, the subject of this entry. Authorized or actual punishments are expected to reduce criminal activity through their impact on individual perceptions. Thus, perceptual deterrence entails two linkages: threatened or actual punishments must affect perceptions of sanction risk, and in turn, these perceptions must affect decisions to commit or refrain from crime. As for the first linkage, perceptions must be predictably malleable. That is, a deterrence initiative must logically elevate at least one of the three deterrence perceptions (certainty, severity, or celerity); and the net impact of the deterrence initiative on perceptions must be that the targeted individuals are less crime prone.

Sanctions and Perceptions

There is little evidence that sanctioning effects changes in perceptions of informal sanctions or changes in perceptions of the severity or celerity of legal sanctions. However, research has tested how sanctioning affects the perceived certainty of legal punishments. Such research has taken one of two approaches. One approach has been to relate an individual's perception of the certainty of punishment to any consequences that individual has experienced from past offending. Mark Stafford and Mark Warr theorized that being punished for a crime should increase and avoiding punishment for a crime should reduce an individual's estimate of the certainty of punishment for that crime. Another approach to studying deterrence perceptions has been to test the relationship between indicators of sanctioning in a place (typically a county) and residents' perceptions of sanctioning in that place. In testing these expectations, Gary Kleck, Brion Sever, Spencer Li, and Marc Gertz found that individuals' estimates of total arrests per 100 offenses known to the police for homicide, robbery, aggravated assault, and burglary for 1988–1998 in their county of residence were uncorrelated with the actual clearance rate for their counties. Lance Lochner produced similar null results. However, in the most recent application of this approach, using a national sample of school students, Robert Apel, Greg Pogarsky, and Leigh Bates reported a positive association between the objective and perceived risk of being disciplined in school for transgression. All told, some evidence suggests that individuals indeed update their perceptions of sanction certainty based on past punishment experiences, as the perceptual deterrence framework predicts.

Perceptions and Offending

Research has also addressed the second linkage in perceptual deterrence; that perceptions of the certainty, severity, and celerity of legal punishments should relate negatively to the probability of offending. This is an inherently individual-level proposition. Investigating it requires data on individuals' perceptions about the risks of criminal justice punishments and indications of their offending propensity and/or behaviors. There have been two basic approaches to this general question.

One involves scenario or vignette studies. Individuals read fairly detailed scenarios outlining potential crime opportunities and then answer questions based on the scenario. Among the information respondents provide are their perceptions about the risk of punishment and projections of the likelihood they would offend. This approach tends to show that the perceived certainty of legal punishment is a more potent deterrent of criminal activity than the perceived severity or celerity of legal punishment is. Among the advantages of this approach are that respondents give context-specific information, as offending decisions are believed to be unique and dependent on situational features. Another advantage of the scenario approach is that both perceptions and projections of offending probability are elicited contemporaneously (rather than at distinct points in time). This is important because perceptual deterrence is viewed as a contemporaneous process (Grasmick & Bursik, 1990), meaning that behavior is a function of perceptions existing at the time such behavior is contemplated and imminent. There are, however, weaknesses in the scenario approach. One is that the outcome measure is an individual's projection of his or her future, hypothetical behavior, rather than actual offending behavior. Also, the approach most often uses college student and other non-criminally experienced samples.

Another approach to studying the second linkage in perceptual deterrence—offending as a function of perceived sanction risk—uses longitudinal data on perceptions of sanction risk and offending behavior from a sample of individuals at repeated points in time. Thus, assume that data are gathered at n points in time $(t_1, t_2, \ldots t_n)$. Offending between t_1 and t_2 is modeled as a function of risk perceptions at t_1, offending between t_2 and t_3 is modeled as a function of risk perceptions at t_2, and so on. Recent applications of this approach have produced strong evidence that offending relates negatively to perceptions of the certainty of punishment. Unlike the scenario approach, the outcome variable in longitudinal perceptual deterrence research is actual offending behavior. However, this approach does not estimate the contemporaneous relationship between perceptions and behavior; it measures, rather, the relationship between perceptions at the outset of a time period and criminal behavior occurring during that time period.

Perceptual deterrence research identifies individual perceptions of sanction risk as the key intervening variables that determine the impact of deterrence initiatives on the behavior of citizens. Even studies that find empirical relationships consistent with the perceptual deterrence perspective (e.g., individuals who experience punishment elevate their perceptions of sanction certainty) do not explain a large amount of variation in perceived sanction certainty. Beyond this, there are significant unaddressed research questions on perceptual deterrence. These involve the formation and updating of severity and celerity perceptions. As well, perceptual deterrence research has yet to fully explore the potential applicability of heuristics and biases from the judgment and decision making literature and the role of emotion in contemplative criminal behavior (Nagin, 2007).

Greg Pogarsky

See also General Deterrence Theory; Gibbs, Jack P.: Deterrence Theory; Incarceration and Recidivism; Nagin, Daniel S., and Raymond Paternoster: Individual Differences and Deterrence; Pogarsky, Greg: Behavioral Economics and Crime; Pogarsky, Greg, and Alex R. Piquero: The Resetting Effect; Sherman, Lawrence W.: Defiance Theory; Stafford, Mark C., and Mark Warr: Deterrence Theory; Williams, Kirk R., and Richard Hawkins: Deterrence Theory and Non-Legal Sanctions

References and Further Readings

Apel, R., Pogarsky, G., & Bates, L. (2009). The sanctions-perceptions link in a model of school-based deterrence. *Journal of Quantitative Criminology, 25,* 201–226.

Blumstein, A., Cohen, J., & Nagin, D. (1978). *Deterrence and incapacitation: Estimating the effects of criminal sanctions on crime rates.* Panel on Research on Deterrent and Incapacitative Effects, National Research Council. Washington, DC: National Academy of Sciences.

Bridges, G. S., & Stone, J. A. (1986). Effects of criminal punishment on perceived threat of punishment: Toward an understanding of specific deterrence. *Journal of Research in Crime and Delinquency, 23,* 207–239.

Dugan, L., Nagin, D. S., & Rosenfeld, R. (2003). Exposure reduction or retaliation? The effects of domestic violence resources on intimate partner homicide. *Law and Society Review, 27,* 169–198.

Grasmick, H. G., & Bursik, R. J., Jr. (1990). Conscience, significant others, and rational choice: Extending the deterrence model. *Law and Society Review, 24,* 837–861.

Horney, J., & Marshall, I. H. (1992). Risk perceptions among serious offenders: The Role of crime and punishment. *Criminology, 30,* 575–594.

Iyengar, R. (2007). *Does the certainty of arrest reduce domestic violence? Evidence from mandatory and recommended arrest laws* (NBER Working Paper No. 13186). National Bureau of Economic Research, Cambridge, MA.

Kleck, G., Sever, B., Li, S., & Gertz, M. (2005). The missing link in general deterrence research. *Criminology, 43,* 623–659.

Lochner, L. (2007). Individual perceptions of the criminal justice system. *American Economic Review, 97,* 444–460.

Matsueda, R. L., Kreager, D. A., & Huizinga, D. (2006). Deterring delinquents: A rational choice model of theft and violence. *American Sociological Review, 71,* 95–122.

McDowall, D., Loftin, C., & Wiersema, B. (1992). A comparative study of the preventative effects of mandatory sentencing laws for gun crimes. *Journal of Criminal Law and Criminology, 83,* 378–394.

McDowall, D., Loftin, C., & Wiersema, B. (1995). Easing concealed firearms laws: Effects on homicide in three states. *Journal of Criminal Law and Criminology, 86,* 193–206.

Nagin, D. S. (2007). Moving choice to center stage in Criminological research and theory: The American Society of Criminology 2006 Sutherland Address. *Criminology, 45,* 259–272.

Nagin, D. S., & Paternoster, R. (1993). Enduring individual differences and rational choice theories of crime. *Law and Society Review, 27,* 467–496.

Nagin, D. S., & Paternoster, R. (1994). Personal capital and social control: The deterrence implications of a theory of individual differences in criminal offending. *Criminology, 32,* 581–604.

Nagin, D. S., & Pogarsky, G. (2001). Integrating celerity, impulsivity, and extralegal sanction threats into a model of general deterrence: Theory and evidence. *Criminology, 39,* 404–430.

Piliavin, I., Thornton, C., Gartner, R., & Matsueda, R. L. (1986). Crime, deterrence and rational choice. *American Sociological Review, 51,* 101–119.

Pogarsky, G. (2007). Deterrence and individual differences among convicted offenders. *Journal of Quantitative Criminology, 23,* 59–74.

Pogarsky, G. (in press). Deterrence and decision-making: Research questions and theoretical refinements. In M. D. Krohn, A. J. Lizotte, & G. P. Hall (Eds.), *Handbook on crime and deviance.* New York: Springer.

Stafford, M. C., & Warr, M. (1993). A reconceptualization of general and specific deterrence. *Journal of Research in Crime and Delinquency, 30,* 123–135.

Wright, B. R. E., Caspi, A., Moffitt, T. E., & Paternoster, R. (2004). Does the perceived risk of punishment deter criminally prone individuals? *Journal of Research in Crime and Delinquency, 41,* 180–213.

Zimmerman, G. M. (2008). Beyond legal sanctions: The correlates of self-imposed and socially imposed extralegal risk perceptions. *Deviant Behavior, 29,* 157–190.

PERCEPTUALLY CONTEMPORANEOUS OFFENSES

Studies of the fear of crime have consistently shown women to be more afraid of crime, although men are more likely to be victims of crime. Similarly, some measures of fear reveal that the elderly also have fear levels that are disproportionate with their low victimization risk. To explain these discrepancies, in 1984, Mark Warr introduced the theoretical concept "perceptually contemporaneous offenses." A perceptually contemporaneous offense is a crime that is linked to another crime because of a perceived belief that one crime may lead to another more serious crime. Fear of a specific crime is a trigger for fear of several other crimes. For example, the elderly may fear crimes like begging more than younger individuals because of the perceptually contemporaneous offense of assault. Another example given by Warr is that women may fear assault, burglary, or homicide more than men because of the tendency to link these crimes to the additionally fear-producing possibility of rape.

Although perceptually contemporaneous offenses may apply to many different groups in society—including men, women, and the elderly—the majority of the work in this area has focused on how the term applies to women. Warr (1984, p. 700) reasoned that rape is a "master offense" and that for women "fear of crime is fear of rape." Theoretically, the notion of perceptually contemporaneous offenses is consistent with feminist work on fear of crime. Scholars such as Esther Madriz, and Margaret Gordon and Stephanie Riger explained that women's socialization includes education on the threat of rape and on related dangerous spaces and people. In the United States and throughout the world, women's lives tend to be more structured by fear than their male counterparts because of this threat of rape. The irony of this perceived vulnerability and danger is that women tend to fear strangers and places outside their homes and the homes of their friends, while most sexually related crimes occur in familiar places and are not perpetrated by strangers.

In 1995, Kenneth Ferraro added to the literature on perceptually contemporaneous offenses by describing a "shadow of sexual assault" that was produced by women's tendency to associate all crimes with sexual assaults. Ferraro used the shadow hypothesis to predict that the fear of rape would be more influential to fear of crimes such as assault and murder and less influential to fear of crimes like car theft and financial cons, because of the likelihood that women would associate crimes in each group with the "contingency of rape." More recently, in the context of studying fear of gang crime, Jodi Lane and James Meeker have argued that fear of physical harm is a perceptually contemporaneous offense that shadows over many other crimes for both men and women.

Empirical Support

Studies of fear of crime have discovered and corrected numerous measurement issues that can muddy the water in terms of interpreting the results of fear of crime studies and understanding perceptually contemporaneous offenses. First, global, single-item measures of fear of crime (such as the General Social Survey question: How safe do you feel walking alone at night?) present respondents with unrealistic hypothetical situations that may themselves be fear producing and lump quite divergent crimes together into a single question. More refined sets of multiple fear of crime questions, which can later be used to create a fear of crime index, do not include hypothetical situations, and allow the respondent to differentiate between fear levels for different crimes. Similarly, perceived risk or the perceived likelihood that a respondent will be a victim of specific given crimes is a conceptual distinct predictor of fear of crime. Including perceived risk allows researchers to separate cognitive estimations of victimization from more emotional responses to crime such as fear or terror. In order to adequately test the hypothesis that perceptually contemporaneous offenses explain differences between men and women, it is necessary to control for perceived risk and measure both fear of a master offense such as rape and fear of crime, more generally. Theoretically, perceptually contemporaneous offenses suggest that an individual will emotionally reference a more serious crime (e.g., rape) when contemplating being the victim of a less serious crime (e.g., mugging), which will in turn elevate the perceived seriousness of the less serious crime and result in higher levels of fear of crime. Controlling for measures of perceived risk and fear of a master offense should theoretically eliminate group differences. Several of the seminal studies testing the validity of the notion of perceptually contemporaneous offenses are reviewed below.

Warr conducted the first empirical tests of perceptually contemporaneous offenses. Using mail survey data from Seattle residents in 1981, Warr (1984) found that both women and the elderly differed from men and younger individuals in terms of the perceived seriousness of several crimes. Controlling for fear of several other crimes and using an omnibus measure of fear significantly reduced group differences between men and women and between the elderly and younger respondents for several individual measures of fear of crime. This study showed indirect support for the notion of perceptually contemporaneous offenses, particularly

for women where rape was predicted to be a master offense. Later, using the same Seattle survey data, Warr (1985) directly tested rape as a perceptually contemporaneous offense for women. In this study, Warr regressed fear of rape on fear of several other types of crime. The results demonstrated that the shadow of the fear of rape was cast over numerous other circumstances and crimes.

In the book *Fear of Crime: Interpreting Victimization Risk*, Ferraro uses 1990 data from the Fear of Crime in America Survey, which surveyed more than 1,000 respondents by telephone, to investigate the effect of fear of rape on fear of non-sexual crimes. Supporting Ferraro's shadow hypothesis, sex was not a significant predictor of fear of crime when fear of rape was included as a control. Furthermore, a sex-disaggregated analysis found that for women, fear of rape was the strongest predictor of fear of non-sexual crimes. Ironically, the study also reported that changing one's behavior (taking protective measures) because of fear of rape increases fear of crime.

In 1996, Ferraro again analyzed the Fear of Crime in America Survey to test the shadow of sexual assault hypothesis on crime specific measures and found similar results. Fear of rape was a significant predictor of personal crimes—including murder, robbery, assault, and burglary while at home—and its inclusion in regression models either significantly reduced or eliminated the effect of gender on fear. Although fear of rape was a significant predictor of the nonviolent crimes of car theft, burglary, cheat/con, vandalism, and panhandling, the effect was much weaker than the violent crime models and did not have a major effect on gender differences in the model. It appears that women are much more likely to associate the master offense of rape with the threat of face-to-face victimization than with nonviolent crimes.

Using 1997 data from the Mississippi High School Youth Survey, David May extended past tests of the shadow of victimization hypothesis by analyzing a sample of 725 juveniles. The findings of this study were consistent with past studies and supported the notion of perceptually contemporaneous offenses. The fear of sexual assault was the strongest predictor of nonsexual crimes among adolescents. This effect was found in both male and female samples but was stronger for females. May suggests that both adolescent males and females feel a "shadow of powerlessness," which is a function of both gender and age and contributes to juveniles associating sexual assault with nonsexual assault.

Finally, in a study of fear of gang crimes, Lane and Meeker test the "shadow of powerlessness" hypothesis on both men and women using a 1997 survey of 1,000 Orange County, California, residents. Specifically, they control for the master offense of rape that is suggested by feminist theory and the master offense of assault that Warr and others have suggested may also be an important perceptually contemporaneous offense. Regression results indicate that the fear of rape is a significant predictor of fear of graffiti, gang harassment, carjacking, home-invasion robbery, and drive-by shooting for both women and men, but the effect is significantly stronger for women than men. Fear of assault was also a significant predictor of fear of all the above listed crimes. When both measures, fear of rape and fear of assault, were included in the same equation, fear of assault had stronger effects for both men and women, although fear of rape remained a significant predictor of fear of crime in all specific crime models. This study established that, at least for fear of gang-related crime, assault is the primary perceptually contemporaneous offense, and fear of rape is the secondary perceptually contemporaneous offense.

As the aforementioned studies show, there is consistent support for the shadow hypothesis and the existence of perceptually contemporaneous offenses. Consistent with feminist theory, rape operates as a master offense for women. For many women it leads to their taking precautionary behaviors such as restricting travel, work, and socializing to avoid being out in the evenings or alone, to their avoiding places commonly associated with sexual assault such as dark alleys, bars, parks, and large cities, and to their staying clear of strangers. While these behaviors may provide some degree of protection from stranger rape, it does little to protect women from more common forms of sexual assault committed by intimates or acquaintances. Ironically, as Ferraro's 1995 study found, precautionary behaviors tend to increase fear of crime rather than decrease it because these behaviors require additional time and effort spent focusing on violent crime.

A review of the perceptually contemporaneous offense literature also reveals that fear of rape is not exclusive to females. Men, particularly juveniles, also fear rape and associate this threat with numerous other crimes. Furthermore, rape is not the only master offense; assault also casts a "shadow of powerlessness" on several other crimes and similarly affects both men and women.

Sarah Britto

See also Ferraro, Kenneth F.: Risk Interpretation Model; Rape Myths and Violence Against Women; Stanko, Elizabeth A.: Gender, Fear, and Risk

References and Further Readings

Ferraro, K. (1995). *Fear of crime: Interpreting victimization risk*. New York: State University of New York Press.

Ferraro, K. (1996). Women's fear of victimization: Shadow of sexual assault. *Social Forces, 75*, 667–690.

Gordon, M. T., & Riger, S. (1989). *The female fear: The social cost of rape*. Urbana: University of Illinois Press.

Lane, J., & Meeker, J. (2003). Women's and men's fear of gang crimes: Sexual and nonsexual assault as perceptually contemporaneous offenses. *Justice Quarterly, 20*, 337–371.

Madriz, E. (1997). *Nothing bad happens to good girls: Fear of crime in women's lives*. Berkeley: University of California Press.

May, D. (2001). The effect of fear of sexual victimization on adolescent fear of crime. *Sociological Spectrum, 21*, 141–174.

Warr, M. (1984). Fear of victimization: Why are women and the elderly more afraid? *Social Science Quarterly, 65*, 681–702.

Warr, M. (1985). Fear of rape among urban women. *Social Problems, 32*, 238–250.

PHILADELPHIA BIRTH COHORTS, THE

Criminology is a field rich with explanatory theories and sophisticated empirical tests of research hypotheses drawn from these theories. In this deductive process of theory testing, theory precedes the observations of data. Equally important to understanding crime and criminal justice is the inductive analytical process, which begins with observations of data and concludes with theory as the outcome of the research. This is an iterative process that benefits from replication. The goal of inductive research is being able to make inferences about the data that can be generalized beyond the immediate subjects. In the inductive process of theory development in criminology, the Philadelphia Birth Cohorts have been among the most important bodies of data. These data have provided the foundation for understanding many key relationships of frequent or chronic offending and for understanding the transitions between adolescence and adulthood that involve crime and criminal justice interventions, such as the age at onset of offending, crime specialization, escalation in severity, desistance to law-abiding behavior, and the effects of arrests, probation, and incarceration. Research findings from the Philadelphia cohorts also contributed to the development of theories of crime, including the subculture of violence and the life-course theory or developmental perspective.

The impetus for the Philadelphia Birth Cohorts came from Thorsten Sellin, an early criminologist well known for a long career devoted to measuring crime, helping to establish the Uniform Crime Reports, developing culture conflict theory of crime, and research on sentencing and the death penalty. During Sellin's extensive travels, he became familiar with Nils Christie's 1960 dissertation research on a birth cohort in Sweden and appreciative of the opportunities to observe temporal sequencing of events that such longitudinal data allow. He and his former student, Marvin Wolfgang, advocated with several federal agencies to support a birth cohort study in the United States. With initial funding in 1963, researchers at the University of Pennsylvania began retrospective data collection for the 1945 Philadelphia Birth Cohort. For the next 25 years and with considerable support from the National Institute of Health, the National Institute of Mental Health, the Office of Juvenile Justice and Delinquency Prevention, and the Insurance Company of North America, data were collected for cohorts of 9,946 men born in 1945 and 27,160 men and women born in 1958.

Research Designs and Methodology

The 1945 cohort was defined as the population of boys who resided in Philadelphia at least from their 10th to their 18th birthdays. They were born during the final year of World War II and were eligible for, or at risk of, delinquency involvement from 1955 through 1962. Subjects and information about them were identified in an extensive investigation of student files maintained by all public, private, and parochial schools in Philadelphia, juvenile records of both formal arrests and informal remedial referrals from the Philadelphia Police Department, and the roster of names in the Selective Service Systems for males born in 1945. Of the original 14,313 boys, 4,368 subjects were excluded because they had not been Philadelphia residents for the entire period. The considerable effort required to secure agreements with agencies and to coordinate data collection, coding, and analyses, made this the largest study in criminology at the time.

The longitudinal design covering 8 years in the life of the 9,945 cohort members enabled the researchers to examine the association between some demographic characteristics and delinquency, the prevalence and incidence of juvenile crime, as well as transitions over time including the age of the first arrest, escalation of seriousness and specialization of offending, frequency and pace of offending, and desistance. The research adapted the measurement index of offense seriousness developed by Sellin and Wolfgang in 1964 and Markov stochastic modeling techniques that were popular at the time in other scientific fields for analyzing event transitions to view specialization or escalation of offending. The chief product of this research was publication of *Delinquency in a Birth Cohort* by Wolfgang, Figlio, and Sellin.

Like most research, the results of the initial study helped to inspire new and additional questions. Many of the questions arose from the study findings because of the time and data limitations of the original design. First, concluding data collection when subjects reached age 18 provided rich information about the nature and extent of their juvenile offending, but also stimulated curiosity about what sort of adults they became, and particularly those with adult criminality. Second, reliance on official records of crime and delinquency meant that "the dark figure of crime" unknown to police was also unknown to investigators, and this missing dimension was an issue of significant debate generally in criminology during the 1970s.

The school and police data also did not tap other dimensions of the lives of the subjects.

To overcome these difficulties, data collection of the 1945 Philadelphia Birth Cohort ultimately extended to age 30 for a 10 percent sample of 975 subjects. (Note that the 10 percent random sample was originally selected from a 1973 dissertation on middle-class delinquency by Albert Cardarelli. But when a university fire destroyed files of the original cohort population, identifying information remained only for Cardarelli's sample.) Official records of adult crime were collected from the Philadelphia Police Department and the Federal Bureau of Investigation. Most of the adult arrests, approximately 93 percent, were identified by the Philadelphia police records. Face-to-face structured interviews were conducted at age 26 for 567 subjects, a completion rate of 58.2 percent with attrition problems due primarily to inability to locate other men in the sample rather than unwillingness to participate. With the follow-up data, the 1945 Philadelphia Birth Cohort became the first study to have official police contact and arrest records, self-report offense, and victimization information for the same subjects. Moreover, these data were all longitudinally based to enable the experiences of subjects to be tracked over time. Findings from the follow-up efforts are reported chiefly in Wolfgang et al.'s *From Boy to Man, From Delinquency to Crime*. In addition to results from the principal investigators, this volume includes University of Pennsylvania dissertation findings from George S. Bridges, James J. Collins, Edna Erez, Alicia Rand, S. Bernard Raskin, Simon I. Singer, and Paul E. Tracy, Jr.

The 1958 Philadelphia Birth Cohort was a replication of the original design extended to include females. Both of these elements make the 1958 cohort very important to the field of criminology. First, criminology is quite young as a social science and researchers often neglect replication in favor of testing something new. Fortunately, the principal investigators of the 1958 cohort recognized the value of replication in building theory and extending knowledge about crime; they wrote, "When a methodology, like the birth cohort approach, is demonstrated to be important both to theory development and empirical application, and when this method produces a new set of important findings, it should be reiterated in order

to determine whether it is possible to buttress consistency and to affirm the observed findings with other data and with different study populations" (Tracy et al., 1990, pp. 1–2). Born 13 years later, the second Philadelphia cohort was at risk for delinquency from 1968 through 1975. Very different than the at-risk period of the 1945 cohort, the adolescence of the 1958 cohort was a time of conflict and social change in the United States that included civil unrest, escalating involvement of young people with illicit drug use, and the Vietnam conflict. Otherwise, there was considerable consistency in the statutory codes, policies, and procedures followed by the Philadelphia criminal justice agencies, all of which helpto affirm the same research setting for both cohorts and thereby facilitate the replication efforts. Results of the comparisons between the 1945 and 1958 Philadelphia Birth Cohort males are published in Tracy et al.'s *Delinquency Careers in Two Birth Cohorts*.

The inclusion of 14,000 females in the 1958 cohort, approximately half of the total 27,160 subjects, signaled a major step forward in measuring criminality and criminal justice experiences of girls and women, who until this time were virtually ignored by research in criminology. Several dissertations chronicled the experiences of females in the 1958 birth cohort, including their delinquency (Facella, 1983), violence compared to males (Piper, 1983), and juvenile offending compared to the males (Otten, 1985).

Finally, there also was a follow-up data collection effort for the 1958 cohort through age 26. Official records were retrieved from case files maintained by the Municipal and Court of Common Pleas of Philadelphia, which contained both police reports and the criminal history of interventions. A survey was administered to a sample chosen via a stratified quota design based on race, ethnicity, sex, and delinquency status. In 1986, adult offending of the men were examined by P. Tontodonato, and delinquency and crime patterns including stability and changes between the transitions from juvenile and adulthood among both women and men were examined by Kimberly Kempf. The primary publication of findings from follow-up of the 1958 Philadelphia Birth Cohort is Tracy and Kempf-Leonard's *Continuity and Discontinuity in Criminal Career*. All data sets also have been used in secondary analyses by many researchers, and most are accessible through the Interuniversity Consortium for Political and Social Research (ICPSR) collections.

Major Research Findings

The most significant findings of the 1945 Philadelphia Birth Cohort Study came from being able to observe both prevalence and incidence of offending among the subjects. Of the 9,945 subjects, one third had some contact with police as juveniles. Those 3,475 boys accumulated 10,214 police contacts and arrests. Among them, 46 percent (1,613) had only one encounter with police, but 54 percent (1,862) had multiple arrests. Of those recidivists, 627 boys had been arrested five or more times. These chronic recidivists, who accounted for only 18 percent of the delinquents in the cohort and only 6 percent of the entire cohort, were responsible for 52 percent of all the known offenses. Findings of chronic offenders were similar for the 1958 cohort, with 7.5 percent of cohort, or 23 percent of the delinquents, responsible for 61 percent of all offenses and police contacts. The finding that a small proportion of the population became chronic offenders who committed the majority of all crime, including serious violence has been replicated widely and found to be robust.

Offenders in the 1958 cohort were both more active and more serious, overall. Compared to the 10,214 offenses committed by the first cohort, the second cohort had 15,248 recorded delinquent acts, with the rates being 1,159 per 1,000 subjects compared to 1,027 for the boys born in 1945. The differences are even larger for serious crimes. The rate of UCR index offenses for the 1958 cohort (455 per 1,000 subjects) was 1.6 times higher than the 1945 cohort rate (274). For only violent index crimes, the ratio escalated over 3 to 1.

Although the 1958 cohort was responsible for more crime, the age at which the offending began was similar in both studies. The proportions of youths who had their first contact with police by age 9 was about 6 percent in both cohorts; between ages 10 to 14 it was 56 percent in the 1945 cohort and 46 percent in the 1958 cohort; and 47 percent of both cohorts were late starters with first offenses at ages 15, 16, or 17.

Race and socioeconomic status were measured in both of the cohort studies, although the precision of the indicators was not ideal. Race distinguished white and nonwhite subjects, the majority of whom were black. Socioeconomic status assigned each subject a value based on a composite index score of various economic indicators for the census tract in which he or she resided. Race was more evenly distributed in the 1958 cohort with 53 percent nonwhite subjects, compared to only 29 percent nonwhite boys in the 1945 cohort. Both cohorts had slightly less than half of the subjects classified as low socioeconomic status. The racial distribution of socioeconomic status was similar in both cohorts too; low socioeconomic status was classified for 30 percent of white and 84 percent of nonwhite subjects in the 1945 cohort and 31 percent of the white and 73 percent of the nonwhite subjects in the 1958 cohort.

A significant race disparity in delinquency was shown in the 1945 cohort, but declined in the second cohort. In the 1945 cohort, police contacts were identified for 50 percent of the nonwhite boys and 29 percent of the white boys, for a difference of 21 percent. In the 1958 cohort, the race difference in prevalence of offending was 19 percent, with a decline to 42 percent among nonwhite youths and an increase to 23 percent among white youths. The incidence disparity in the first cohort was also pronounced. White delinquents were more likely to have only one offense (55 percent compared to 35 percent for nonwhites) and less apt to be chronic offenders (10 percent, compared to 29 percent). The difference was less pronounced in the second cohort, with white and nonwhite percentages of 52 and 37 for one-time offenders and 15 and 27 for chronic offenders. Thus, chronic delinquency increased for white offenders but declined for nonwhite offenders between the two cohort studies.

The prevalence of delinquency among females was very different than that of males in the 1958 cohort. Of the 14,000 girls, only 1,972 or 14 percent had at least one police encounter before age 18. The boys were two and one-half times more likely to be delinquent, and three times more likely to be chronic offenders than the girls. Despite gender differences in prevalence of offending, the correlates of offending were similar for girls and boys. Nonwhite youths and those classified with lower socioeconomic status were nearly twice as likely as other youths to become delinquent, and one and a half times as likely to offend repeatedly.

Several techniques have been applied to identify cohort subjects who may have specialized in a type of offending or increased in the severity of crimes they committed as they progressed as offenders, and to determine when and who were more likely to quit or desist from crime. Similar findings for these offense patterns were observed in both cohort studies. The most important result regarding offense transition patterns is that the next most likely state for all subjects was to be a nonoffender. No offense was the most likely transition in all types of "criminal careers," and "life-course trajectories." This surprising finding was true even for chronic offenders and those who committed the most heinous crimes. There is some evidence of offense specialization in both cohorts, and it was even more evident among offenders with many arrests. Findings also suggest escalation in offense severity. Both specialization and escalation patterns differed by gender and race. Finally, subjects who specialized or escalated in the severity of their offending while they were juveniles were more likely to continue offending as adults.

The ways in which the criminal justice system responded to youths following their initial police contact, called dispositions, were also examined in the two cohort studies. The disposition system allowed for graduated levels of sanctions along with treatment for juveniles, extending from the lowest remedial warning, to arrest, informal disposition, formal probation, institutionalization, and waiver into the adult system. Findings show that interventions were largely based on appropriate legal criteria, including the youths' offender status and nature of the offenses, but that also due to extra-legal criteria some youths were treated more formally. In the 1945 cohort, results showed both race and socioeconomic effects on police decisions to arrest. Differential processing was less evident in the 1958 cohort, although dispositions for the females rarely extended to formal court interventions. The most important finding was the relationship identified between type of disposition and subsequent offending, which was counter to that desired by an effective criminal justice system. The higher the level of disposition—including both

probation and incarceration—the more likely the youths were to reoffend.

Legacy of the Studies

Although many implications can and have been drawn from the Philadelphia Birth Cohort studies, two are the most noteworthy. First, the most significant discovery of the research was the chronic offender. The amount of crime attributed to the highest rate offenders, led the principal investigators to advise the appropriate direction for formal crime control in their executive summary to the U.S. Department of Justice as follows:

> A juvenile and criminal justice policy that focuses on the few at the most propitious time has the greatest likelihood of effecting change. Social intervention applied to those few need not be merely restrictive and depriving of liberty; it can also be healthful for, and helpful to, those who are under control. (Tracy et al., 1990, p. 26)

The impact of the chronic offender discovery is very evident in the National Academy of Sciences' 1986 volumes on *Criminal Careers and "Career Criminals."* For over two decades, policy makers have focused the most restrictive punishments on the most dangerous offenders. Most recently, the legacy of these studies, particularly the second recommendation of the researchers, can be seen in prevention efforts across the country to improve the situations for at-risk youth and at-risk neighborhoods.

The second legacy of the Philadelphia Birth Cohort studies is widespread acceptance, indeed the prominence, now attributed to longitudinal investigations of crime and criminality. There has been such an exponential growth in the number of longitudinal studies that they are now called life-course studies, most of which adhere to various developmental perspectives of crime. Although the principal investigators of the Philadelphia cohort studies collaborated on a 1970 birth cohort in Puerto Rico (Nevares et al., 1990) and compared findings with contemporary longitudinal research projects in Stockholm, London, Copenhagen, and Racine, Wisconsin, they also had to withstand considerable criticism from naysayers about the time, expense, and even the potential yield of longitudinal research in studying crime. The prominence attributed to longitudinal study among criminologists today is due in large part to the success achieved by the Philadelphia Birth Cohort studies.

Kimberly Kempf-Leonard

See also Criminal Career Paradigm; Glueck, Sheldon, and Eleanor Glueck: The Origins of Crime

References and Further Readings

Cohen, J., Roth, J. A., Visher, C. A., & Blumstein, A. (Eds.). (1986). *Criminal careers and "career criminals"* (Vols. 1–2). Washington, DC: National Academy Press.

Facella, C. S. (1983). *Female delinquency is a birth cohort.* Unpublished doctoral dissertation, University of Pennsylvania.

Gottfredson, M. R., & Hirschi, T. (1986) The true value of lambda would appear to be zero: An essay on career criminals, criminal careers, selective incapacitation, cohort studies, and related topics. *Criminology, 24,* 213–234.

Kempf, K. (1986). *Constancy and change in the criminal career.* Unpublished doctoral dissertation, University of Pennsylvania.

Nevares, D., Wolfgang, M. E., & Tracy, P. E. (1990). *Delinquency in Puerto Rico: The 1970 birth cohort study.* Westport, CT: Greenwood.

Otten, L. (1985). *A comparison of male and female criminality in a birth cohort.* Unpublished doctoral dissertation, University of Pennsylvania.

Piper, E. (1983). *Patterns of violent recidivism.* Unpublished doctoral dissertation, University of Pennsylvania.

Sampson, R. J., & Laub, J. H. (1993). *Crime in the making: Pathways and turning points through life.* Cambridge, MA: Harvard University Press.

Sellin, T., & Wolfgang, M. E. (1964). *The measurement of delinquency.* New York: Wiley.

Tontodonato, P. (1986). *Criminal career patterns on a cohort of young adult males.* Unpublished doctoral dissertation, University of Pennsylvania.

Tracy, P. E., & Kempf-Leonard, K. (1996). *Continuity and discontinuity in criminal careers.* New York: Plenum.

Tracy, P. E., Wolfgang, M. E., & Figlio, R. M. (1990). *Delinquency careers in two birth cohorts.* New York: Plenum.

Wolfgang, M. E., Figlio, R. M., & Sellin, T. (1972). *Delinquency in a birth cohort.* Chicago: University of Chicago Press.

Wolfgang, M. E., Thornberry, T. P., & Figlio, R. M. (1987). *From boy to man, from delinquency to crime.* Chicago: University of Chicago Press.

PHRENOLOGY

Developed in the late 1700s and popularized throughout the early to mid-19th century, phrenology is the study of analyzing and predicting certain psychological traits based on the physical features of the skull. According to Franz Joseph Gall's original work, the basic tenets of phrenology are as follows: First, the brain is an organ of the mind. Second, the brain is composed of 27 distinct organs which function independently. Third, the size of the brain is formed by the various organs. Fourth, the more active or powerful the organ, the greater the size. Fifth, the surface of the skull can be examined to gain the relative size of each organ. Sixth, this provides a description and prediction of physiological functioning and disposition.

Development

The study of phrenology was the result of two major contributions of 18th-century psychology. Physiognomy, founded by Johan Kaspar Lavater, was the assessment of an individual's character through the individual's outer appearance, specifically through the face. Another major contributor was the concept of moral insanity, which was used to explain uncontrollable criminality. This concept was discussed by American psychiatrist Benjamin Rush who proposed that the mind is composed of independent facilities, and that crime is the result of partial insanity in which one facility of the brain stops working. These concepts, along with physiological research, led Gall, a Viennese physician, to develop the early concepts of phrenology.

Gall's interest stemmed from his childhood observations of differences in verbal memory relating to prominent features. He received his medical doctorate from Vienna in 1785. In the 1790s, he began developing a system of organology and brain anatomy. Along with his assistant and later collaborator, the physician Johann Gaspar

Spurzheim, Gall palpated the heads of psychiatric patients, artists, and criminals whenever he could obtain their skulls. Many of Gall and Spurzheim's subjects were suspected of being obtained through an association with local deputy of police, Graf Saurau. They performed hundreds of dissections on the brains of various animals and human cadavers to link the internal anatomy of the brain to the external features of the skull (Gall, 1835).

In Gall's original work, *The Functions of the Brain and of Each of Its Parts*, he proposes that the brain is an organ of the mind that is composed of 27 distinct organs that function independently. He believed that the brain and shape of the skull were formed by the size of these organs, so by analyzing the contours of the skull one could make predictable assumptions of physiological traits and attitudes of the individual. With 27 organs stipulated in the beginning, 19 of which were shared with animals, additional researchers elaborated by adding others. In 1815 Spurzheim added 5 to reach 32; in 1834, George Combe added 3 more totaling 35; and in 1844, H. Lundie added 4 more for a total of 39 organs. The size, or power, of these organs were believed to define abilities in a variety of behavioral characteristics—parental love, benevolence, and self-esteem. Although originally conceived as a deterministic approach, most phrenologists argued that the brain is malleable and plastic; therefore conditions could be managed or resolved with the help of outside influence, specifically psychological or environmental interventions.

Popularizing Phrenology

Phrenology is thought to have two different stages: a scientific phase dating from 1800 to 1830 and a fashionable stage dating from 1820 to 1850. From the early developments by Gall, other researchers took interest and began to lecture and write heavily on the subject. The relationship between Spurzheim and Gall ended by 1813. Gall settled in France and continued to develop his system and write until his death in 1828. Spurzheim settled in England where he wrote *Physiognomical System of Drs. Gall and Spurzheim*, which gained more popularity than Gall's original book. He continued to lecture and demonstrate the Gall system until his unexpected death in Boston in 1832. Other fervent supporters include George and Andrew Combe in the Scottish

city of Edinburgh, where the first phrenology society was created in 1820, and the Fowler brothers in the United States. Many of these researchers, mainly psychiatrists and physicians, were attempting to replace the older metaphysical and theological explanations, ideas that criminals were evil or insane, with a more systematic approach which emphasized the scientific method.

Overlapping with the development of phrenology as a science, a second stage occurred where the study was seen as a fad. Social clubs and traveling marketers appeared throughout several regions in the world with appeal to various social classes. Some practiced phrenology out of interest, while others for financial gain. There was also speculation that many became involved in phrenology to gain social status and authority, not purely for scientific pursuit or reform. By the mid-19th century, heavy debates were being waged in regard to the validity and accuracy of the science. By the 1850s, phrenology was largely defunct and had been discredited, although the Phrenological Association was not disbanded until 1967.

Historical Perspective: Enlightenment and Reform

The development and popularizing of phrenology occurred simultaneously with the Age of Enlightenment, which emphasized reason and logic as the primary source of authority and legitimacy. Through its use of empirical observation, induction, and deduction, phrenology offered many practitioners and members of society a way to look at behaviors, specifically criminality, more scientifically. During this time, the rational choice philosophy, which emphasized crime as a result of free will, was often argued. However, there was growing debate due to the lack of meaningful results stemming from the alleged deterrent effects of punishment. Other sources were being questioned as the cause of criminal behavior. Adolphe Quetelet's statistical analysis on crime seemed to suggest that deviance resulted from societal and economic conditions.

Phrenologist became active in this debate, arguing that crime was the result not of free will but of abnormal brain organization, originating from issues such as poor health, environment, or disease. They argued that according to the philosophy of punishment, which emphasized the ideas that no harm should come to the individual and that proportionate punishment should be allotted, many criminals should not be held responsible because their lack of facilities was no fault of their own. Also coinciding with the penitentiary movement in the United States, many phrenologists argued that criminals should be held from society for the immediate purpose of safety but should also be reformed and balance should be restored to their brains. Phrenologists were common visitors to prisons, working with administrators to develop policies. The debate had an impact on many prison practices through both the addition of treatment during incarceration as well as the use of rewards systems to assist in the reformation of prisoners. Many suggest, in a widely argued debate not discussed here, that the main contribution of phrenology was the reform policies developed from the findings that individuals should not be held responsible for crimes due to damage of their brains.

Phrenology's Contribution

As discussed, prior to the development of phrenology and other similar studies, those who displayed behaviors defined as criminal were thought to be evil or insane. Punishment was often swift and severe. Phrenology brought a new way to look at behaviors through biology that had important implications for treatment and punishment. Although looked on contemporarily as a pseudoscience, phrenology had lasting effects on many fields. The Gall and Spurzheim method of dissection is still considered an excellent teaching aid in the field of neuroscience. In addition, neurologists have a better understanding of how grey matter relates to nerve fibers and increased knowledge into visual field defects thanks to phrenologists (Simpson, 2005).

Specific to the study of crime, evolutionary psychology borrows on the ideas that criminal behaviors can be traced to evolutionary causes, such as brain deficiencies inherited or evolved from certain regions. Biosocial criminology contends that genes interact with the environment, which in turn predisposes some individuals to criminogenic attitudes and behaviors. Specific to policy, phrenologists propagated the idea of punishment away from deterrence and retribution to one of rehabilitation. They were one of the first to recommend indeterminate

sentencing and the separation of criminals into treatment groups according to specific characteristics for more effective treatment purposes. These advancements in our understanding stem from ideas developed through the study of phrenology and other biological theories of the 19th century.

Conclusion

Our knowledge has grown immensely from the unconventional ideas and approaches of the phrenological pioneers. Contemporary biological theories of crime, deemed the *new phrenology*, attempt to explain criminal behavior through brain imaging and genetics. As with any science, early ideas often seem asinine. But these early ideas are the foundation of science as we know it today. The notion that the Earth was flat was once embraced as a fact. The tenets of phrenology are no different. At a time when society was stepping away from religious and supernatural explanations of the world, phrenology was a solid attempt to understand human behavior by using science. Perhaps phrenology is a forgotten and obsolete science, but its impact on criminology and other fields can still be seen today.

Bobbie Ticknor

See also Brain Abnormalities and Crime; Garofalo, Raffaele: Positivist School; Goring, Charles: The English Convict; Kretschmer, Ernst: Physique and Character; Lombroso, Cesare: The Criminal Man; Neurology and Crime; Quetelet, Adolphe: Explaining Crime Through Statistical and Cartographic Techniques

References and Further Readings

Gall, F. J. (1835). *On the functions of the brain and of each of its parts* (W. Lewis, Jr., Trans.). Boston: Marsh, Capen, and Lynn.

Rafter, N. (2005). The murderous Dutch fiddler: Criminology, history and the problem of phrenology. *Theoretical Criminology, 9,* 65.

Rafter, N. (2008). *The criminal brain: Understanding biological theories of crime.* New York: New York University Press.

Rosset, N. (2007). Popular philosophy in early nineteenth-century Scotland. *Journal of Scottish Historical Studies, 27*(2), 150–169.

Simpson, D. (2005). Phrenology and neurosciences: Contributions of F. J. Gall and J. G. Spurzheim. *ANZ Journal of Surgery, 75,* 475–482.

Van Wyhe, J. (2002–2009). *The history of phrenology on the Web.* Retrieved March 13, 2009, from http://www.historyofphrenology.org.uk

Van Wyhe, J. (2004). *Phrenology and the origins of Victorian scientific naturalism.* Aldershot, UK: Ashgate.

Van Wyhe, J. (2004). Was phrenology a reform science? Towards a new generalization for phrenology. *History of Science, 42,* 313–331.

PHYSICAL ENVIRONMENT AND CRIME

Connecting physical environment, crime, and crime prevention is a huge topic. Broader literature reviews appear in the Annotated Further Readings of this volume. This entry narrows the focus by concentrating on the question of causal impacts at the neighborhood or streetblock level, as well as contextual impacts on individuals or households. Further, this entry notes problems with inferring causal impacts of physical environment features. It also highlights difficulties in clearly demonstrating ecological connections between features of physical environment—or other features of neighborhood fabric, for that matter—and hypothesized mediating social, behavioral, or psychological processes taking place at the small group or community level.

The focus of the current entry is a response to questions raised by Robert Sampson, Per-Olof Wikström, and others about whether, despite the many recent statistical and methodological advances in communities and crime research, criminologists are actually any closer to demonstrating neighborhood effects on crime which are causal in nature. A case can be made that conclusive demonstrations of causal neighborhood effects involving physical environment features affecting crime, delinquency, or victimization have not yet appeared *and are extremely unlikely to ever appear.*

At least since the mid-1800s, hopes have run high that changes in the physical environment of a neighborhood or a street would reduce social problems, including delinquency, offending, and victimization rates. Tearing down a neighborhood

of slum housing in the early 20th century, or destroying blocks of alley housing as part of mid-20th-century urban renewal, or dynamiting high-rise public housing communities at the end of the 20th and beginning of the 21st centuries, have clearly had effects on the social problems, offending, delinquency, and victimization rates in *those* locations. The location-based rates have shifted in part because the original households were no longer there, and the replacement households often had different household structures, held different positions in the broader structure of society, and were more spread out spatially. Although the drastic changes in the physical environment were clearly a precondition for the other structural changes, parsing out how much of the social problem rate reductions in those places arose from physical environment changes per se, as compared to the other changes including population shifts, is extraordinarily difficult if not impossible. Estimating physical environment impacts when physical environment changes are less dramatic, or are ongoing, are similarly difficult. The sections below explain in more detail why.

These controversies were highlighted in a trio of articles authored by Jens Ludwig, Susan Clampet-Lundquist and Doug Massey, and Robert Sampson in the July 2008 issue of the *American Journal of Sociology.* The authors debated whether a recent randomized experiment involving the relocation of households eligible for subsidized housing had or had not demonstrated an impact on delinquency, victimization, and related outcomes. No consensus emerged.

Meta-Theoretical Issues

When thinking about physical environment and crime, the interest may be in ecological outcomes, such as neighborhood delinquency rates, or on individual-level outcomes, such as individual levels of delinquent involvement. Regardless of whether the interest is in individual-level or ecological outcomes, a host of challenges get in the way of concluding that the physical environment impacts are causal in nature. Challenges include, among others, controlling for adjacency effects; controlling for compositional effects; the need to analyze predictors, mediating processes, and outcomes using a lagged longitudinal framework operationalizing

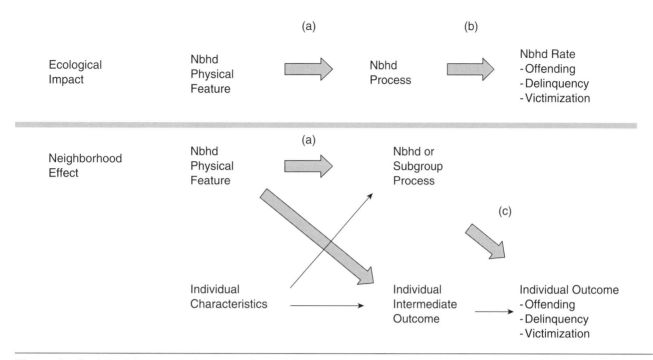

Figure I   Ecological Impacts and Neighborhood Effects

Note: Nbhd = neighborhood effects.

changes; and lack of information about the time horizon for changes of key individual or ecological mediating processes.

If the focus is on ecological outcomes, the research is open to alternative interpretations unless the researcher empirically establishes the superior strength for his or her posited theory compared to plausible competing theories of the following: the contextual impacts making the macro-to-micro link where macro represents context and micro represents individuals; the micro-to-macro link whereby individuals contribute to ecological changes; and the relevant micro-to-micro level mediating dynamics.

If the focus is on individual-level outcomes, the research is open to alternative interpretations unless the researcher establishes that the macro-to-micro links are stronger for his or her theory than they are for competing theories; and that the micro-to-micro links capturing mediating processes are similarly stronger.

Researchers very rarely establish these points. Indeed, those interested in ecological outcomes rarely investigate the macro-to-micro and micro-to-macro links for their own theories, let alone for alternative competing theories. Those interested in individual-level outcomes rarely examine alternative

dynamics and explanations for contextual impacts in the macro-to-micro level link.

Which Neighborhood or Streetblock Level Physical Features?

Which neighborhood or streetblock level physical features are linked to crime, victimization or delinquent acts depends on which broad framework is adopted. Four relevant perspectives include the rational offender perspective, a behavioral geographic crime pattern orientation, human territorial functioning, or the incivilities thesis. The rational offender perspective considers how design, siting, and land use mix all might shape entrance and exit speeds; offender salience or detectability; presence, density, or visibility of attractive targets; or surveillability by others of potential targets or offense locations. A crime pattern orientation highlights how design features like non-residential land use uses, route structures and mix, and images of regions shape potential offender travel patterns, activity spaces, and search spaces. These in turn alter offending, delinquency, and victimization probabilities. Territorial functioning concentrates on resident- and user-generated signs of investment, potential involvement, and oversight, whose presence and patterning depend on and contribute to physical features of locale. Part of the incivilities thesis focuses on physical aspects of the environment that reflect either a lack of resident-based supervision over local spaces (e.g., graffiti which is not painted over or removed) or a lack of local leader or agency effectiveness (e.g., burned out cars which are not towed), or general disinvestment in the locale (e.g., abandoned houses). Any of these might suggest to potential offenders that if they should engage in specific crime or delinquent acts others will not interfere with them. More recently, however, some scholars have highlighted the situational and subcultural dependency of how incivilities are interpreted.

Which Processes Mediate Physical Crime Impacts?

The same specific physical environment features may be of interest to multiple frameworks for multiple reasons involving different dynamics. For example, the presence of specific non-residential land uses, such as bars or check cashing outlets, may be relevant to models based on the rational offending perspective, the incivilities perspective, the crime pattern perspective, and the territorial perspective.

If researchers seek to promote one theoretical framework over another they need to empirically demonstrate several points.

1. Mediating process indicators for the preferred perspective must correlate strongly with one another and also be discriminable from indicators relevant to other perspectives at the level of aggregation where the dynamics are posited.

2. The connections between the relevant physical environment features and the preferred mediating process should be stronger than the corresponding link for non-preferred mediating processes.

3. The preferred mediating processes should connect more strongly with the outcome than do other potential mediators.

Regrettably, there is little research investigating links between the physical environment and crime that meets these criteria. Consequently, little is known about the *relative* relevance of different sociological, social psychological, or psychological mediating processes that can be shaped by physical environment features, or how relative relevance may depend on context or outcome. To put the point more strongly, when thinking about physical environment and crime, the middle of the model is a muddle.

Challenges in Demonstrating Causal Neighborhood Effects

Traditionally, several challenges must be overcome to demonstrate causal neighborhood effects.

1. Compositional characteristics of residents or households must be removed. Usually this is done through partialling on key individual or household demographic factors.

2. Ecological-level fundamental demographic structure also should be taken into account.

3. Spatial adjacency effects should be explored and, if significant patterns of spatial autocorrelation appear, a spatially lagged outcome variable should be constructed and entered as a predictor.

4. The predictors must not be endogenous—that is, predictor scores cannot correlate with the error component of the outcome. This can happen when simultaneous relationships (e.g., offending rates increase abandoned housing rates, abandoned housing rates increase offending rates) are not modeled properly, or when a third, unobserved variable not included in the model influences both a predictor and an outcome (e.g., recent changes in the local political economy affect both abandoned housing rates and local offending rates). This concern can sometimes be handled with individual or indexed (2SLS) instrumental variables, but recent econometric work raises concerns about these approaches.

5. Most troubling are biases arising from non-random selection of individuals or households into neighborhoods. Much work on neighborhood effects recognizes the difficulty of taking selection effects into account but either puts it aside, calls for capitalizing on experimental and quasi-experimental data availability where causality questions may be less clouded, or accepts it as part of ongoing processes of neighborhood differentiation. Another approach suggested is to document specific theoretically relevant processes taking place subsequent to an individual or household entering a neighborhood, but the resources needed for obtaining such indicators may be beyond most study resources.

Consider a longitudinal study that finds impacts of changes in neighborhood physical factors—perhaps only perceived—on changes in heavy drinking, as Terrence Hill and Ronald Angel did in 2005. Consider further, building on Alison Sherley's 2005 article, that changes in the heavy drinking are likely to lead to changes in chances of being victimized. The concern with non-random neighborhood selection suggests that some pre-existing features of individuals or households, not identified in the current causal model, led those individuals or households to take up residence in neighborhoods where physical deterioration would later be increasing. For example, individuals who moved into a neighborhood where physical deterioration later increased may have been men who recently became unemployed, or women who recently became divorced or separated. The problems that result are twofold. Statistical estimates of parameters will not reflect the broader population, since the groups in the neighborhoods are non-random samples. In addition, neighborhood features, or even changing neighborhood features, are treated as having exogenous impact when it would be more accurate to model them as endogenous—reflecting in part the processes of individuals or households selecting neighborhoods.

Conclusion

In the United States, there never will be, nor should there ever be, research studies in which large numbers of non-poor individuals or households from many different types of locations are randomly assigned to live in physically different neighborhoods or streetblocks, with individual or areal offending or victimization or delinquency rates assessed before and after. Nor will there ever be sufficient resources to empirically track delinquency, victimization, and self-reported offending among large numbers of individuals and households over time in many different types of locations as they move through changing neighborhood contexts.

Therefore, given the challenges described above, criminologists will never conclusively demonstrate causal ecological impacts of neighborhood or streetblock physical environment features on individual or collective crime, delinquency, or victimization outcomes. Further, the important ways that physical environment causal impacts might be moderated by important features of context will never be comprehensively understood. So criminologists do not, and probably will not, know enough about the independent causal impacts of physical environment features at the neighborhood or streetblock levels to propose clear, acontextual prevention principles; nor do they or will they know enough to develop systematic guidelines for physical environment and prevention in different types of contexts.

Physical and social features of the residential environment intertwine; are embedded in and shaped by particular social, economic, cultural, and political contexts; are interpreted differently by different groups and individuals; and change over time in complex ways. Therefore, the most to which researchers, prevention and policy advocates, and resource personnel for community constituencies can aspire is to collaborate with key stakeholders in a specific locale at a specific point in time to develop a contextualized problem-oriented approach, and include in this approach clear ideas about how physical environment features in that instance *might* be contributing independently to offending, delinquency, or victimization.

Ralph B. Taylor

See also Brantingham, Patricia L., and Paul J. Brantingham: Environmental Criminology; Clarke, Ronald V.: Situational Crime Prevention; Eck, John E.: Places and the Crime Triangle; Newman, Oscar: Defensible Space Theory; Wikström, Per-Olof H.: Situational Action Theory; Wilcox, Pamela, Kenneth C. Land, and Scott A. Hunt: Multicontextual Opportunity Theory

References and Further Readings

Clarke, R. V. (1983). Situational crime prevention: Its theoretical basis and practical scope. In M. Tonry & N. Morris (Eds.), *Crime and justice: An annual review of research* (Vol. 4, pp. 225–256). Chicago: University of Chicago Press.

Clarke, R. V. (1992). *Situational crime prevention.* Albany, NY: Harrow and Heston.

Crowe, T. D. (1991). *Crime prevention through environmental design: Applications of architectural design and space management concepts.* London: Butterworth-Heinemann.

Fowler, E. P. (1992). *Building cities that work*. Montreal, Canada: McGill-Queens University Press.

Hill, T. D., & Angel, R. J. (2005). Neighborhood disorder, psychological distress, and heavy drinking. *Social Science & Medicine, 61*(5), 965–975.

Innes, M. (2004). Signal crimes and signal disorders: notes on deviance as communicative action. *British Journal of Sociology, 55*, 335–355.

Sampson, R. J. (2006). How does community context matter? Social mechanisms and the explanation of crime rates. In P.-O. Wikström & R. J. Sampson (Eds.), *The explanation of crime: Context, mechanisms, and development* (pp. 31–60). Cambridge, UK: Cambridge University Press.

Sherley, A. J. (2005). Contextualizing the sexual assault event: Images from police files. *Deviant Behavior, 26*(2), 87–108.

St. Jean, P. K. B. (2007). *Pockets of crime: Broken windows, collective efficacy, and the criminal point of view*. Chicago: University of Chicago Press.

Taylor, R. B. (1987). Toward an environmental psychology of disorder. In D. Stokols & I. Altman (Eds.), *Handbook of environmental psychology* (pp. 951–986). New York: Wiley.

Taylor, R. B. (1988). *Human territorial functioning*. Cambridge, UK: Cambridge University Press.

Taylor, R. B. (1998). Crime in small scale places: What we know, what we can do about it. In *Research and evaluation conference 1997* (pp. 1–20). Washington, DC: National Institute of Justice.

Taylor, R. B. (2001). *Breaking away from broken windows: Evidence from Baltimore Neighborhoods and the nationwide fight against crime, grime, fear and decline*. New York: Westview Press.

Taylor, R. B. (2002). Physical environment, crime, fear, and resident-based control. In J. Q. Wilson (Ed.), *Crime: Public policies for crime control* (pp. 413–434). Oakland, CA: Institute for Contemporary Studies.

Taylor, R. B. (2005). Crime prevention through environmental design: Yes, no, maybe, unknowable, and all of the above. In R. Bechtel & A. Churchman (Eds.), *Handbook of environmental psychology* (pp. 413–426). New York: Wiley.

Taylor, R. B., & Gottfredson, S. D. (1986). Environmental design, crime and prevention: An examination of community dynamics. In A. J. Reiss & M. Tonry (Eds.), *Communities and crime* (pp. 387–416). Chicago: University of Chicago Press.

Taylor, R. B., & Harrell, A. V. (1996). *Physical environment and crime*. Washington, DC: National Institute of Justice.

POGARSKY, GREG: BEHAVIORAL ECONOMICS AND CRIME

In 1968, Nobel Prize–winning economist Gary S. Becker laid out an economics-based theory of crime in an article titled "Crime and Punishment: An Economic Approach." To Becker, the theory "simply extend[ed] the economist's usual analysis of choice," which involves a calculated weighing of the costs and benefits of alternative courses of action, to criminal decision making (p. 170). He also went on to argue with the economics-based theory of crime in hand, it was now possible to "dispense with special theories of anomie, psychological inadequacies or inheritance of special traits" (p. 170). Thus, to Becker the economic approach to crime that he pioneered could stand alone without appeal to any sociological or psychological constructs.

Becker's neoclassical economic model of crime argued that people calculate the expected utility of criminal and non-criminal actions and choose the one with the greatest value. Components of expected utility included the costs of crime such as the probability of getting caught and punished, the severity of the punishment, and the gains from criminal and noncriminal actions (e.g., expected income from these two respective sources). The framework can be extended to include social costs such as loss of the good opinion of one's friends if one is apprehended, and the intangible benefits of crime and non-crime such as prestige among fellow offenders and the good opinion of conventional people, respectively. However, in practice, the focus of the economic model is the tangible costs and benefits of the crime and non-crime alternatives.

One of the important features of the neoclassical economic expected utility model is that decision makers are assumed to be immune to epiphenomena such as psychological or emotional states (Loewenstein & Lerner, 2003). In short *Homo economicus* is a calculating, unemotional being motivated only by self-interest, whose interests or preferences are assumed rather than examined as to their source. The economic model also assumes that human beings have an unbounded capacity for calculation and rationality and are not motivated by altruism. There is an enormous body of evidence that individuals do not make choices in a way that conforms with the assumptions of the neoclassical economic model. Thus, human decision makers do not always carefully collect and accurately weigh information before making decisions, they frequently are influenced by shortcuts and biases, and they are more loss averse than the theory can explain. Real human beings also depart from *Homo economicus* in that they frequently fail to make the "best" choice because they have problems with self-control: they spend too much money, drink too much alcohol, and engage in other actions that are immediately pleasurable but have long-term costs. Finally, although the neoclassical economic model assumes that the primary motive for behavior is self-interest, humans frequently behave in the real world as if fairness and morality matter. For example, people will turn down free money if they think they are not getting their fair share, they tip in restaurants they will never visit again, and they refuse to do some behaviors even though it would be personally beneficial and they could "get away with it." Behavioral economics emerged to provide the neoclassical economic model with a more realistic psychological and to a much lesser extent sociological foundation to improve it as a descriptive theory about how people actually make decisions (Camerer et al., 2004).

Over the past 20 years a great deal of empirical research has accumulated that has applied the principles of behavioral economics to specific areas of inquiry such as finance, public economics, wage determination, and organizational economics. Greg Pogarsky and his collaborators have been pioneers in bringing the insights of behavioral economics to the study of criminal decision making.

The Complexity of Decision Making

One of Pogarsky's most important contributions involves how contact with the criminal justice system affects offender perceptions of sanction risks. Rational decision makers are supposed to systematically and rationally update their prior beliefs based on information provided by current experience. For example, if there is a massive recall of Toyota automobiles, a rational decision maker should incorporate that information by lowering their prior estimate as to how reliable a car a Toyota is. Analogously, criminal offenders who commit a

crime and are caught and punished should update their perceptions of the risk of criminal activity by increasing the perceived certainty of punishment and perhaps the perceived severity. There is some evidence that such Bayesian updating of perceptions takes place (Lochner, 2007).

However, in 2003, Pogarsky and Alex Piquero found that offenders do not update according to the economic model and, indeed, do just the opposite of what it predicts. They found that some people decrease the perceived certainty of punishment after getting caught. They call this perceptual distortion *resetting*. Similar to a gambler who may think that the probability that a roulette ball will fall on red is higher after falling on black several consecutive times, Pogarsky and Piquero argue that offenders who have just been caught decrease their perception that they will get caught in the future because they mistakenly think that it would be uncharacteristically unlucky to be caught again. In other words, much like a gambler's fallacy, they think that they suffered bad luck by just getting caught in crime and are "due" to have a streak of good luck. The resetting effect, if correct, represents an important departure from the economic model of updating perceptions based on experience.

Another decision-making bias uncovered by behavioral economists is called *self-serving bias*. Just as all the children in Garrison Keillor's Lake Wobegon are above average, survey evidence shows that individuals overestimate their abilities and contributions. The vast majority of people rate themselves in the top 50 percent of drivers (Svenson, 1981), ethics (Baumhart, 1968), productivity (Cross, 1977), health (Weinstein, 1980), and a variety of other desirable skills. Another interesting example of self-serving bias comes from surveys of married couples in which each married partner is asked what percentage of the housework he or she does. The percentages routinely sum to more than 100 percent (Ross & Sicoly, 1979).

In an application of the self-serving bias to criminology, Daniel Nagin and Pogarsky (2003) conducted an experiment in which student-subjects were given an opportunity to score better on a class quiz by cheating. Experimental conditions manipulated the certainty and severity of possible sanctions for cheating. They found that those with a strong self-serving bias (measured as a tendency to see situations in a light favorable to themselves) were more inclined to cheat than others. In part this was because they believed themselves less likely than others to get caught for cheating.

Another assumption of the neoclassical economic model is that persons consciously weigh the costs and benefits of each possible line of action and choose the alternative that maximizes utility. This model does not, however, take into consideration what has been described as the "self-control" problem. Although the economic model assumes that people choose what is best for themselves, the reality is that we sometimes are unable to resist immediate temptations, with the result that we make decisions that we know are harmful for our long-term self-interest even as we are making them. For example, in deciding whether to buy a high-definition television (HDTV), *Homo economicus* is assumed to weigh the immediate and longer term advantages of having an HDTV against the cost which often includes long-term credit card debt and associated interest and penalty charges. The self-control problem arises when the immediate benefit of having an HDTV, for example watching the Super Bowl on a large HD screen, overwhelms all the other relevant criteria such as how often one will actually use the TV over the long term and, perhaps most importantly, the financial challenge of having to pay for the HDTV in credit card installment payments. Behavioral economists have demonstrated that some people resist an immediate impulse to spend money because they are "tightwads" who experience a strong and immediate "pain of paying" (sharp guilt in spending money) that allows them to defeat the immediate appeal of the HDTV. Others who experience less or no pain of paying are more tempted by the immediate pleasures and act like "spendthrifts" (Prelec & Lowenstein, 1998).

Based on this line of reasoning, Pogarsky (2002) argues that the threat of criminal sanctions will depend on self-control because the benefits of offending are generally immediate and the costs of sanctions are generally delayed. Hence, some people fail to solve the self-control problem because they are relatively unaffected by the long-term costs of committing crimes, while others who have stronger self-control are predicted to be more affected by the long-term costs of their behavior. Consistent with this prediction, Pogarsky found that both the certainty and severity of punishment acted as an effective deterrent for those with a

moderate strength of self-control. He labeled these individuals the "deterrables." However, sanction threats were ineffective for those who had not solved the self-control problem and thereby were overwhelmed by immediate pleasures of crime. This finding was replicated with a different antisocial act in Nagin and Pogarsky (2003) and in a sample of serious offenders in Pogarsky (2007). Pogarsky's theory of the interaction of self-control and deterrence implies that the effectiveness of crime prevention based on the deterrent "bite" of formal sanctions will depend upon the self-control of the targeted population. For example, his theory suggests that enhanced penalties directed at repeat offenders, such as those targeted by "three-strikes"–type laws, will have a negligible impact because repeat offenders likely have very low self-control.

Fairness and Morality

In positing the primacy of self-interest, the neoclassical economic model pays insufficient attention to considerations of fairness or morality in decision-making processes. For example, results from experiments based on "ultimatum games" consistently demonstrate that persons are concerned about fairness at least as much as clear economic gain. The ultimate game involves two parties dividing a fixed amount of money between themselves. One party, the proposer, proposes a division of the sum and the other party, the responder, either accepts the proposed division or rejects it. If the proposal is rejected neither party gets anything. For the responder, the sum offered by the proposer is pure gain. Accordingly, a purely self-interested actor in the tradition of the neoclassical economic model should accept any share greater than zero. In fact, however, in numerous experimental studies responders are unwilling to accept an amount below what they think is fair.

The finding from behavioral economics that considerations of fairness and morality can trump instrumental concerns accord with a substantial body of research showing that perceptions of morality are not only a robust predictor of a wide range of antisocial behaviors but also that perceptions about what is "morally right" are independent of perceived utility. Consistent with the influential role of morality in crime decision making, Pogarsky et al. (2005) found that an actor's updating of perceptions based on his or her personal experiences with offending were nullified in the presence of strong moral feelings.

The failure to consider the role of fairness or morality in decision making reflects a more general limitation of the neoclassical economic model that focuses only on tangible risks and rewards—its neglect of the role of emotions in decision making, which in the view of some criminologists is a critical omission in crime decision making. Behavioral economics has brought the study of persons' emotions back into the neoclassical economic model to explain some important departures from the predictions of that model. (The word *back* is used because early economists were keenly interested in emotions as evidenced by Adam Smith's work, *The Theory of Moral Sentiments*.)

One example is the standard neoclassical economic model's prediction that people will put off dreaded outcomes as long as possible and attempt to enjoy pleasurable outcomes as soon as possible. George Loewenstein, however, found that experiencing a feeling of dread motivated people to get the bad experience over as quickly as possible while feelings of savoring motivated them to delay a good outcome. Consistent with Lowenstein's arguments, Nagin and Pogarsky (2001) found that individuals with a desire to get unpleasant events over with sooner rather than later were the most deterrable. More generally, emotions of dread may lead criminal offenders to "cop a plea" as quickly as possible or to sell a stolen "hot" item too quickly, even when such a bargain might not be in their long-term interest.

Conclusion

Behavioral economics emerged as a separate sub-discipline in order to provide the neoclassic economic model with a more realistic understanding of economic behavior. Armed with the empirical and theoretical insights provided by behavioral economists, Pogarsky and colleagues have begun to modify the rational choice tradition in criminology to include the insights of behavioral economists. The areas where a possible integration of behavioral economics and criminology can be fruitful are too numerous to discuss in this short essay, but additional areas not mentioned above include the consideration of prospect theory–based

utility models, hyperbolic time discounting, as well as an elaboration of such issues as the role of emotional states and heuristics and biases in decision making. As Pogarsky's work demonstrates, criminologists can learn much from a careful study of the behavioral economics literature. Its many intriguing insights can greatly enrich our understanding of criminal decision making.

Daniel S. Nagin and Raymond Paternoster

See also Becker, Gary S.: Punishment, Human Capital, and Crime General Deterrence Theory; Gibbs, Jack P.: Deterrence Theory; Incarceration and Recidivism; Nagin, Daniel S., and Raymond Paternoster: Individual Differences and Deterrence; Perceptual Deterrence; Pogarsky, Greg, and Alex R. Piquero: The Resetting Effect; Sherman, Lawrence W.: Defiance Theory; Stafford, Mark C., and Mark Warr: Deterrence Theory; Williams, Kirk R., and Richard Hawkins: Deterrence Theory and Non-Legal Sanctions

References and Further Readings

Baumhart, R. (1968). *An honest profit*. New York: Prentice Hall.

Becker, G. S. (1968). Crime and punishment: An economic approach. *Journal of Political Economy, 76,* 169–217.

Camerer, C. F., Loewenstein, G., & Rabin, M. (2004). *Advances in behavioral economics*. New York: Russell Sage Foundation.

Cross, P. (1977). Not can, but will college teaching be improved? *New Directions for Higher Education, 17,* 1–15.

Lochner, L. (2007). Individual perceptions of the criminal justice system. *American Economic Review, 97,* 444–460.

Loewenstein, G., & Lerner, J. (2003). The role of affect in decision making. In R. J. Dawson, K. R. Scherer, & H. H. Goldsmith (Eds.), *Handbook of affective science* (pp. 619–642). Oxford, UK: Oxford University Press.

Nagin, D. S. (2007). Moving choice to center stage in criminological research and theory: The American Society of Criminology 2006 Sutherland Address. *Criminology, 45,* 259–272.

Nagin, D. S., & Pogarsky, G. (2001). Integrating celerity, impulsivity, and extralegal sanction threats into a model of general deterrence: Theory and evidence. *Criminology, 39,* 865–892.

Nagin, D. S., & Pogarsky, G. (2003). An experimental investigation of deterrence: Cheating, self-serving bias, and impulsivity. *Criminology, 41,* 167–193.

Paternoster, R., & Simpson, S. (1996). Sanction threats and appeals to morality: Testing a rational choice model of corporate crime. *Law and Society Review, 30,* 549–583.

Pogarsky, G. (2002). Identifying "deterrable" offenders: Implications for research on deterrence. *Justice Quarterly, 19,* 431–450.

Pogarsky, G. (2007). Deterrence and individual differences among convicted offenders. *Journal of Quantitative Criminology, 23,* 59–74.

Pogarsky, G. (in press). Deterrence and decision-making: Research questions and theoretical refinements. In M. D. Krohn, A. J. Lizotte, G. P. Hall (Eds.), *Handbook on crime and deviance.* New York: Springer.

Pogarsky, G., Kim, K., & Paternoster, R. (2005). Perceptual change in the National Youth Survey: Lessons for deterrence theory and offender decision making. *Justice Quarterly, 22,* 1–29.

Pogarsky, G., & Piquero, A. R. (2003). Can punishment encourage offending? Investigating the "resetting" effect. *Journal of Research in Crime and Delinquency, 40,* 95–120.

Prelec, D., & Loewenstein, G. (1998). The red and the black: Mental accounting of savings and debt. *Marketing Science, 17,* 4–28.

Rick, S., & Lowenstein, G. (2008). The role of emotion in economic behavior. In M. J. M. Lewis, J. M. Haviland-Jones, & L. Feldman Barrett (Eds.), *Handbook of emotions* (3rd ed., pp. 138–156). New York: Guilford Press.

Ross, M., & Fiore, S. (1979). Egocentric biases in availability and attribution. *Journal of Personality and Social Psychology, 37,* 322–336.

Svenson, O. (1981). Are we all less risky and more skillful than our fellow drivers? *Acta Psychologica, 9,* 143–148.

Weinstein, N. D. (1980). Unrealistic optimism about future life events. *Journal of Personality and Social Psychology, 39,* 806–820.

POGARSKY, GREG, AND ALEX R. PIQUERO: THE RESETTING EFFECT

Individual or specific deterrence rests on the assumption that punished individuals will refrain from engaging in subsequent criminal behavior out of fear or the upward revision of sanction threat perceptions. However, a number of studies have found that individuals may actually be more likely to lower their perceptions of detection and apprehension and therefore continue to offend following punishment. Two competing explanations emerge for this "positive punishment effect." Under one explanation, individuals with the lowest expectations for punishment are also the most committed offenders who have increased exposure to and experiences with punishment. Greg Pogarsky and Alex R. Piquero provide an alternative explanation—which they call *resetting*—that draws on a judgment and decision-making bias called the gambler's fallacy. Under resetting, offenders decrease or "reset" their perceptions of apprehension following punishment, believing they would have to be extremely unlucky to be apprehended again (p. 96). Resetting provides a causal explanation for the seemingly counterintuitive positive punishment effect.

The Gambler's Fallacy

The resetting effect is based on a psychological decision-making bias called the gambler's fallacy, or the Monte Carlo fallacy. The gambler's fallacy, as described by Amos Tversky and Daniel Kahneman, is the unfounded belief that variations from the expected in one direction are likely to be evened out by future variations in the other direction. This is commonly referred to as being "due." For example, card players may increase their wages following a loss believing they are due to win; baseball players may believe they are due for a hit following a slump; and lottery players may play specific numbers that have not been selected, or avoid numbers that have been selected, in previous draws.

The gambler's fallacy stems from the belief that things should "even out" (a psychological heuristic called the representative heuristic). That is, individuals incorrectly project long-term expectations to short-term random events, falsely interpreting independent events as interdependent. Consider flipping a (fair) coin. Since flips of a coin are independent, the probability of obtaining a head (or tail) on any single flip is 0.5. Further, the probability of obtaining 1 tail after 10 consecutive heads and the probability of obtaining another head following 10 heads are equally rare: $P = 0.5^{11} = 1$ in 2,048. Thus, one is equally likely to obtain a head after 10 previous heads as one is to obtain a tail. There is no reason to think that things must even out. The gambler's fallacy describes the situation in which an individual's belief in consistency results in a disproportionate propensity to pick tails in the preceding scenario. It is the false belief that the extremely rare event of obtaining 10 heads in a row is unlikely to be followed by another flip of heads.

Resetting and Offending

Resetting applies the gambler's fallacy to perceptual deterrence. According to deterrence theory, individuals are more likely to offend when they perceive the risks of punishment to be low. Pogarsky and Piquero note that offenders may also believe, like gamblers and lottery players, that extremely rare events (e.g., punishment) are unlikely to reoccur. This is consistent with Frank P. McKenna's finding that individuals have a tendency to think that bad things are relatively unlikely to happen to them. Jack Gibbs noted that it is also consistent with the "law of averages," under which previously punished individuals may believe that their luck will even out and subsequent violations of the law will not result in punishment. As a result, individuals may "reset" or reduce their sanction threat perceptions following punishment, which in turn, makes them more likely to engage in criminal behaviors in the future, according to Bruce Jacobs.

To test the resetting hypothesis, Pogarsky and Piquero identified individuals prone to the gambler's fallacy by asking them to indicate the likely outcome (heads, tails, or equally likely) of a coin flip after four previous, consecutive flips resulted in heads. Individuals identifying the next coin flip as "tails" were considered to have even-out reasoning consistent with the gambler's fallacy. Using this probabilistic proxy for the interdependence of random events, Pogarsky and Piquero found partial evidence for the resetting effect. After dichotomizing their sample into high-risk (committed) and low-risk (naïve) offenders, analyses showed that perceptions of punishment certainty were significantly lower for low-risk offenders who had previously been punished. Further, lower perceptions of punishment certainty were highly correlated with the gambler's bias (as measured above). There was no evidence of resetting, however, for high-risk offenders. According to Pogarsky and Piquero, high-risk offenders may be less likely to consider potential deterrents to punishment (Pogarsky, 2002),

or resetting may simply be confined to low-risk offenders. Still, without more empirical research on resetting, its application to deterrence theory remains largely theoretical.

Conclusion

Pogarsky and Piquero proposed resetting, an application of the gambler's fallacy to deterrence theory, as a possible explanation for the positive punishment effect. Under resetting, when relatively rare events occur (e.g., being arrested or pulled over while driving), individuals consider it unlikely that they will reoccur, at least in the short run. Individuals may therefore reduce their perceptions of apprehension, rather than increase them, following a rare occurrence like punishment. Resetting provides a credible explanation for a somewhat counterintuitive finding, yet needs a more substantial base of empirical support to be considered viable. Pogarsky and Piquero found partial support for the hypothesis, but researchers have failed to replicate and develop new tests of resetting. Thus, there is a general lack of empirical support for the hypothesis.

Still, by extending a judgment and decision-making bias in probabilistic reasoning to criminal decision making, the resetting effect represents an extension of the theoretical boundaries of deterrence theory. Much like the flexibility of deterrence theory to incorporate extralegal sanctions, perceptions, visceral influences, and enduring individual differences in the propensity to offend, resetting symbolizes the willingness of deterrence researchers to integrate ideas from various domains of research and criminological theories.

Gregory M. Zimmerman

See also Gibbs, Jack P.: Deterrence Theory; Nagin, Daniel S., and Raymond Paternoster: Individual Differences and Deterrence; Pogarsky, Greg: Behavioral Economics and Crime; Stafford, Mark C., and Mark Warr: Deterrence Theory; Williams, Kirk R., and Richard Hawkins: Deterrence Theory and Non-Legal Sanctions

References and Further Readings

Andenaes, J. (1974). *Punishment and deterrence*. Ann Arbor: University of Michigan Press.

Clotfelter, C. T., & Cook, P. J. (1993). The "gambler's fallacy" in lottery play. *Management Science, 39,* 1521–1525.

Gibbs, J. P. (1975). *Crime, punishment, and deterrence.* Amsterdam: Elsevier.

Gilovich, T. (1983). Biased evaluation and persistence in gambling. *Journal of Personality and Social Psychology, 44,* 1110–1126.

Jacobs, B. A. (1996). Crack dealers and restrictive deterrence: Identifying narcs. *Criminology, 34,* 409–431.

McKenna, F. P. (1993). It won't happen to me: Unrealistic optimism or illusion of control? *British Journal of Psychology, 84,* 39–50.

Paternoster, R., & Piquero, A. R. (1995). Reconceptualizing deterrence: An empirical test of personal and vicarious experiences. *Journal of Research in Crime and Delinquency, 32,* 251–286.

Piquero, A. R., & Paternoster, R. (1998). An application of Stafford and Warr's reconceptualization of deterrence to drinking and driving. *Journal of Research in Crime and Delinquency, 35,* 3–39.

Piquero, A. R., & Pogarsky, G. (2002). Beyond Stafford and Warr's reconceptualization of deterrence: Personal and vicarious experiences, impulsivity, and offending behavior. *Journal of Research in Crime and Delinquency, 39,* 153–186.

Pogarsky, G. (2002). Identifying "deterrable" offenders: Implications for research in deterrence. *Justice Quarterly, 19,* 431–452.

Pogarsky, G., & Piquero, A. R. (2003). Can punishment encourage offending? Investigating the "resetting" effect. *Journal of Research in Crime and Delinquency, 40,* 95–120.

Sherman, L. W. (1993). Defiance, deterrence, and irrelevance: A theory of the criminal sanction. *Journal of Research in Crime and Delinquency, 30,* 445–473.

Tversky, A., & Kahneman, D. (1974). Judgment under uncertainty: Heuristics and biases. *Science, 185,* 1124–1131.

Zimring, F. E., & Hawkins, G. J. (1973). *Deterrence: The legal threat in crime control.* Chicago: University of Chicago Press.

POLLAK, OTTO: THE HIDDEN FEMALE OFFENDER

The majority of criminologists throughout the 19th and 20th centuries were primarily focused on explaining male offending patterns. The exclusion of the examination of female offending is not unique to criminology. Other academic disciplines (e.g., medicine) have historically excluded females from research investigations. Criminologists of these eras attributed criminal behavior to biological or social factors that were beyond the control of an individual. However, the focus was on explaining male criminality. The failure to explore female criminality may be attributed to the fact that those putting forth theories of offending were male criminologists or that, since male criminality was more prevalent, criminologists focused their attention on these offenders.

In 1950, Otto Pollak asserted that the criminality of women is a neglected field of research and proposed his own explanations for female offending. This entry devotes discussion to theoretical precursors to Pollak's explanations for female offending, his theory, empirical support for his propositions, and criticisms levied against it.

Theoretical Precursors

The early examinations of female offending were conducted at the end of the 19th century into the mid-20th century. Those prominent researchers offering explanations of female criminality include Cesare Lombroso and William Ferrero, W. I. Thomas, Sigmund Freud, and Otto Pollak. These early theorists' ideas about female offending were consistent with the Positivist School of criminology, which held that crime was due to some individual difference (i.e., biologically determined) as opposed to a rational choice. Lombroso and Ferrero stated that the explanation for both male and female offending is due to atavistic traits or the denigration in evolutionary human development. Essentially, involvement in criminality was due to their biology—that is, these criminals were born this way. The researchers posited that females who committed crimes were masculine and exhibited an excess of male characteristics (e.g., excess body hair, moles, broad shoulders). In a departure from a biological explanation for female offending, Thomas claimed that females committed crime for the thrill or excitement and the yearning for new experiences. According to Thomas, due to societal expectations of monogamy, females have pent-up sexual energy and this sexual tension is released in the commission of criminal acts. Freud, like Thomas, viewed female offending as being linked to female sexuality. He asserted that females have a masculinity complex due to penis envy. Those females who cannot resolve their penis envy overidentify with the male identity and will commit crimes. In sum, theorists prior to Pollak attributed female criminality to biology or their sexuality. Additionally, there were relatively few theories that provided any explanation for female offending prior to the publication of Pollak's work.

The Hidden Female Offender

In 1950, Pollak published *The Criminality of Women* in which he summarized previous research on women and crime, challenged the extent of involvement in crime by females, discussed the types of crimes committed by females, and explained female offending as being attributed to a mix of biological, psychological, and sociological factors.

Pollak begins his discussion of female offending by asserting that the true nature of female crime is masked. He points to the use of official statistics, which are misleading and do not account for the true extent of female criminality. Pollak suggests that many of the crimes that females commit are underreported, and that when females offend, they often are detected less than when males commit similar crimes. Additionally, he notes that when apprehended, females are treated more leniently in the criminal justice system. After all, Pollack states that law enforcement officials tend to be men who are brought up to be chivalrous. Thus, law enforcement officials are more lenient toward female criminals (i.e., less likely to arrest), which results in fewer females being captured in criminal statistics.

Pollak notes that there are differences in the methods of crime commissions and asserts that there are two characteristics of female crime: (1) female offenders are deceitful, and (2) females victimize those that they have personal ties to such as children, family members, and friends. In regard to the first characteristic, Pollak claims that women are adept at hiding crimes they commit due to their biology. He asserts that women have become accustomed to deceiving men (e.g., hiding discomfort from menstruation and faking orgasms). Thus, the ability to deceive comes almost naturally for women. Pollak states that females choose victims that they know, because of social customs which

dictate that females should not initiate contact with strangers. In other words, females are socialized not to fraternize with strangers, which propels them to target acquaintances, family, and friends for victimization.

Pollak discusses the many crimes that women commit against the person including homicide, baby farming, infanticide, aggravated assault, false accusations, and sex offenses against children. He states that when females commit homicide, they are more likely to use poison. As homemakers, preparer of meals, and nurturers to the sick, females are in the perfect social role to utilize poison to carry out their crimes. Pollak admits that the true number of aggravated assaults committed by females is unknown; however, when women do commit the crime, the victim is someone they know. Since females are deceitful according to Pollak, they are more prone than men to resort to false accusations. Females who make false accusations tend to be young, and the accusations may take place in the atmosphere of race antagonism. That is, a Caucasian female may make a false rape accusation against an African American man to avoid social ostracism if it is discovered that she is having a romantic relationship with this individual or to avoid any consequences of an illicit sexual encounter. As for the commission of sexual offenses against children, Pollak asserts that many of these crimes that females commit never reach the attention of the law. After all, females' social roles as teachers or governesses allow them to commit the crime with relatively little detection (i.e., unless the offender passes a sexually transmitted disease to the victim).

Pollak describes the many crimes that women commit against property, including robbery, burglary, larceny, blackmail, and fraud. He argues that their participation in these crimes is underreported in official criminal statistics. For the crimes of robbery and burglary, Pollak explains that females use their sex roles not only to "bait" the victim but also to avoid detection. For example, females may work with a male accomplice to carry out these crimes by distracting the victim with her sexuality and allowing the male accomplice to commit the criminal act. This technique allows females to commit these crimes more effectively and to avoid detection more easily. The sex mores of society, Pollak argues, provide females with many opportunities to commit blackmail. For instance, a female may pretend to be pregnant in order to elicit monies from her male victim. For the married male victim, payment to the female is necessary so that his wife does not discover his adulterous ways.

According to Pollak, the emancipation of women in society that has allowed them to pursue occupations and assume greater roles in society has resulted in more opportunities for females to commit crime. Thus, he claims that female crime has increased. In sum, Pollak posits that females are committing a wide range of crimes against persons and property and are using their sex roles and social roles not only to carry out their crimes but also to remain undetected.

Empirical Support

Although Pollak makes several assertions about female offending, there has not been one direct empirical test of his theory. Rather, researchers have explored several aspects of his propositions. One of his propositions that has been examined most frequently has been termed the *leniency theory*. This refers to Pollak's assertion that female offenders are treated more leniently in the criminal justice system due to the chivalrous attitudes held by law enforcement and court officials. The research on the leniency proposition has been mixed. Some researchers assert that the notion that a chivalrous criminal justice system exists is a myth. On the other hand, several researchers have found that females are indeed more likely to be treated leniently in the criminal justice system (e.g., less likely to be arrested and convicted). In 2004, Lisa Stolzenberg and Stewart D'Alessio found that females had a lower probability of being arrested for a variety of crimes, including kidnapping, forcible fondling, simple assault, and intimidation compared to their male counterparts. There is some debate in the field as to whether females receive shorter sentences than male offenders when similar crimes are committed and when prior arrests and convictions are controlled. In a 2007 study where sentencing data from the U.S. Sentencing Commission were examined, researchers found that females were indeed sentenced more leniently. The average sentence that females received was two years less than the sentences that males received for similar offenses. Other researchers disagree with such findings. They contend that, while many

studies have found that females may be treated more leniently (e.g., less likely to be convicted), when sentenced, female offenders actually receiver harsher punishments than their male counterparts. After all, females are expected to conform to societal roles (i.e., nurturers, caregivers), and when they deviate from these socially prescribed roles, they are treated more harshly when sentenced. Meda Chesney-Lind states that females have disproportionately received harsher sentences for drug offenses than males. More research is needed to ascertain the full extent of sentencing disparity.

Critique

Several researchers have critiqued Pollak's explanation for female criminality. Frances Heidensohn states that Pollak does not explain why some female deviance and criminality surfaces and is processed in the criminal justice system. Instead, Pollak focuses on the discussion of female criminality being a hidden phenomenon. Heidensohn also criticizes Pollak for his failure to explain what functional needs of society are being fulfilled by allowing females to engage in criminality. That is, if female crime is being ignored, how is this assisting in the functioning of society at large?

Carol Smart critiques Pollak for his failure to recognize that a double standard exists for females within the criminal justice system. While it may be true that female offenders might be treated more leniently by police or in the court system, he ignores the fact that many female offenders (e.g., prostitutes) are negatively discriminated against (i.e., more likely to be arrested and charged) by the criminal justice system. Smart also criticizes Pollak's interpretation of state and federal statistics. She asserts that the statistical data and the comparisons he used to make his points about the involvement of females in various criminal acts are inaccurate and misleading. Finally, Smart contends that Pollak's claim that female criminality is influenced by biological and sociological factors is a perpetuation of stereotypes of female offenders first promulgated by Lombroso and Ferrero.

Since the publication of Pollak's book, many criminologists have explored the factors of why females commit crime, and modern criminologists have further refined the understanding of female criminality. Criminologists today assert that prior sexual abuse is a predominant factor as to why females begin a pathway into criminality. It is proposed that for females, early sexual abuse explains both onset into and persistence in criminality.

Elaine Gunnison

See also Adler, Freda: Sisters in Crime; Chesney-Lind, Meda: Feminist Model of Female Delinquency; Freud, Sigmund: The Deviant Woman; Klein, Dorie: The Etiology of Female Crime; Lombroso, Cesare: The Female Offender; Smart, Carol: Women, Crime, and Criminology; Thomas, W. I.: The Unadjusted Girl

References and Further Readings

Anderson, E. A. (1976). The "chivalrous" treatment of the female offender in the arms of the criminal justice system: A review of the literature. *Social Problems, 23,* 350–357.

Chesney-Lind, M. (1997). *The female offender: Girls, women, and crime.* Thousand Oaks, CA: Sage.

Freud, S. (1933). *New introductory lectures on psychoanalysis.* New York: W. W. Norton.

Heidensohn, F. M. (1968). The deviance of women: A critique and an enquiry. *British Journal of Sociology, 19,* 160–173.

Lombroso, C., & Ferrero, W. (1895). *The female offender.* London: Fisher Unwin.

Pollak, O. (1950). *The criminality of women.* Philadelphia: University of Pennsylvania Press.

Smart, C. (1976). *Women, crime, and criminology: A feminist critique.* London: Routledge and Kegan Paul.

Thomas, W. I. (1923). *The unadjusted girl.* Boston: Little, Brown.

PONTELL, HENRY N., AND KITTY CALAVITA: EXPLAINING THE SAVINGS AND LOAN SCANDAL

When the extent of the savings and loan crisis came to light in the late 1980s, most economic and financial experts claimed that economic forces and poor business decisions brought down the industry. Skeptical, Henry N. Pontell, an experienced white-collar crime researcher, and Kitty Calavita, a sociology of law scholar, obtained funding from the Academic Senate at the University of California,

Irvine and later, a grant from the National Institute of Justice (NIJ) to study the crisis. Over 3 years they interviewed 105 government policymakers, prosecutors, enforcement officials, and regulators from a wide variety of agencies including the Resolution Trust Corporation, the FBI, the Secret Service, and the Office of Thrift Supervision in Washington, D.C., and its in-field offices. In Washington, D.C., they interviewed individuals from the General Accounting Office (GAO, now the Government Accountability Office), the Office of the Comptroller of the Currency, and the congressional staff of the House and Senate Banking Committees. They also reviewed published reports and congressional hearing and analyzed data from the Resolution Trust Corporation, the Office of Thrift Supervision, and the Executive Office of the U.S. Attorney. Using these data, Pontell and Calavita meticulously documented the role of savings and loan insiders, who deliberately defrauded depositors, stole from their own institutions, and gambled on risky ventures with government-insured funds, and documented the vast network of outsiders who made these "crimes possible, delayed their prosecution, and multiplied their costs" (Calavita, Pontell, & Tillman, 1998, p. 170). Systematic political collusion, they concluded, was essential for the continuous perpetration of the frauds.

Calavita and Pontell examined the role of the insurance industry, regulators, prosecutors and the state in the crisis, issues of organizational and organized crime, and the impact of system capacity. They also addressed critics by testing alternate hypotheses. In all, they produced 13 articles and a book: *Big Money Crime.* Robert Tillman of St. Johns University shared authorship of the book and of four of the articles. William K. Black, a former savings and loan regulator and now on the Economics and Law faculty of the University of Missouri, Kansas City, coauthored an article with Pontell and Calavita.

History

In the wake of the stock market crash of 1929 and the subsequent run on banks, the federal government created the Federal Home Loan Bank Board (FHLBB) in 1932 to encourage savings and home ownership. The FHLBB had responsibility for promulgating and enforcing regulations and for examining and supervising savings and loan associations. The National Housing Act of 1934 created the Federal Savings and Loan Insurance Corporation (FSLIC) to insure savings and loan deposits. In return for deposit insurance, the federal government restricted savings and loans to providing fixed-rate home loans, limited the interest savings and loan associations could pay depositors and charge lenders, and prevented them from having branch offices. Despite these restrictions, savings and loan associations generated consistent profits by paying 3 percent interest on savings accounts and issuing home mortgages at 6 percent until the 1970s when the economy entered a period of high interest rates (reaching 13.3 percent in 1979) and low economic growth. Making matters worse, middle-income savings and loan depositors, who now had access to high-interest-bearing financial instruments such as money market accounts, withdrew their funds from low-interest-bearing savings and loan accounts. With Regulation Q prohibiting them from paying more than 5.5 percent interest on deposits, savings and loan associations could not compete because their money was tied up in long-term low-interest fixed mortgages. By 1980, 85 percent of the country's savings and loan associations were losing money (Calavita & Pontell, 1990).

The deregulatory policies initiated after Ronald Reagan's presidential inauguration appeared to address the savings and loan associations' problems. Congress passed two major laws, the Depository Institutions Deregulation and Monetary Control Act of 1980 and Garn-St Germain Depository Institutions Act in 1982. The laws phased out limits on interest rates and permitted savings and loan associations to deemphasize their historic mission of granting home mortgages for the working class by allowing them to engage in unsecured commercial lending, issue consumer loans and credit cards, invest in a wide range of high-risk/high-yield ventures, and make direct investments in their own property. Congress increased federal deposit insurance from $40,000 to $100,000 per account. This, together with changes in accounting practices and a new rule that allowed a single stockholder to own a federally insured savings and loan, provided opportunities for speculative and fraudulent activities without perpetrators having to risk their own money.

Contrary to being a panacea, deregulation created new problems. Calavita and Pontell (1990) called deregulation the "cure that killed," and it played a central role in the crimes that were the hallmarks of the savings and loan crisis. Deregulatory laws that permitted savings and loan associations to offer higher interest rates created frenzied competition for deposits. Still burdened with low-interest long-term mortgages, deregulation of interest rates led to even more debt as the spread between what savings and loan associations took in and paid out increased.

Deregulation also decreased the number of regulators to safeguard the industry and limited their role. Under the principles of laissez-faire capitalism, regulators should be unnecessary because businesses would suffer the consequences of imprudent or self-destructive acts. Unfortunately, the $100,000 federal insurance on deposits provided a safety net that allowed savings and loan operators to take undue risks without concern, because they were gambling with other people's money.

The number of insolvent savings and loan associations grew during the 1980s. By 1986, FSLIC was insolvent. Lacking the funds to cover the growing number of insolvent savings and loan associations, it was slow to react and allowed insolvent savings and loan associations to continue to operate. In 1988, industry losses totaled $7.5 billion. FSLIC closed or sold 220 savings and loans that year; however, it left another 300 insolvent institutions operating.

Over 2,900 banks and savings and loan associations failed or needed government assistance between 1980 and 1994 (FDIC, 1998, p. 4). The failures cost taxpayers $150 to $175 billion dollars, which made it the costliest white-collar crime scandal up to that time (Calavita, Pontell, & Tillman 1998, p. 1). If one includes interest payments on government bonds over 30 years, the cost approaches $500 billion. A GAO study of the 26 most costly savings and loan failures found that every one of these institutions was a victim of insider fraud and abuse. Furthermore, a 1989 GAO report indicates that criminal activity was a primary factor in 70 to 80 percent of the savings and loan failures. In 1987, the FHLBB referred over 6,000 cases to the Justice Department for prosecution and another 5,000 cases in 1988 (Pontell, Calavita, & Tillman, 1994). By October

1988, FSLIC sued the officers of 51 failed savings and loan associations for misconduct.

The Crimes

Pontell and Calavita found savings and loan fraud generally involved a complicated network of industry insiders and outsiders who worked together. They classified directors, officers, shareholders, and employees of the savings and loan associations as insiders. Account holders, borrowers, and hired guns—brokers, agents, and appraisers—were considered outsiders. Interested in lucrative contracts, appraisers, accountants, and lawyers frequently became co-conspirators that made savings and loan scams possible.

Calavita and Pontell identified three main categories of savings and loan crimes that often overlap: collective embezzlement or looting, hot deals, and covering up. The category "hot deals," used in *Big Money Crime,* was called "desperation dealing" or "unlawful risk-taking" in many of their articles.

Hot deals provided the cash that was siphoned from savings and loans and the transactions that disguised the crimes. The four types of insider dealings within the hot deals category—land flips, nominee loans, reciprocal lending, and linked financing—ignore underwriting practices and generally need the assistance of outsiders, such as accountants and appraisers. While deregulation made it permissible for savings and loan associations to engage in non-traditional high-risk activities, hot deals dealing went beyond allowable limits. Land flips are real estate transactions in which land is transferred back and forth among parties with the intention of fraudulently inflating its value. The land is then used as collateral for loans. Nominee lending involves the use of a straw borrower to represent the real borrower inside the thrift who did not want to be identified. This tactic is used to circumvent restrictions on insider borrowing and loan-to-one borrower regulations. Reciprocal lending also evades insider lending restrictions. Insiders at two or more institutions agree to make loans to each other contingent upon receiving a comparable loan in return. An institution making a loan to an insider of another institution is not illegal. Making these loans on a reciprocal basis without underwriting

is fraud. Reciprocal loans involving multiple participants and institutions become a daisy chain. Linked financing or loans occur when there is an explicit understanding that deposits, generally large brokered deposits, are made so the depositor/borrower with credit problems will receive a loan. It is illegal to offer a loan contingent upon receipt of a deposit.

Collective embezzlement is analogous to "robbing one's own bank." It is the looting of an institution for personal gain at the expense of the institution with either the implicit or explicit consent of its management. This is believed to be the most costly category of savings and loan crimes.

Covering up is used to paint a misleading picture of the institution's health and disguise illegal activity, which is generally accomplished through manipulation of savings and loan books and creation of fictitious entities. All 26 failed savings and loan associations studied by the GAO were cited for accounting deficiencies.

Criminal Justice Response

Despite the unprecedented scale of the financial crisis, the government's response was limited by resource constraints, interagency coordination difficulties, and the complexity of the frauds. As a result, the government focused on containing the crisis rather than on punishing offenders. In the end, a relatively high proportion of those charged were convicted and a significant number received prison sentences, unusual for white-collar offenders. Pontell and Calavita argue that the reason these individuals received prison sentences while most white-collar offenders do not is because of the threat they posed to the economy.

Conclusion

Pontell and Calavita contribute their unique talents and perspectives as they unravel the complexity of the scandal. Their work is well respected and many of their articles appear in anthologies. However, NIJ, which funded their research, never published their final report.

Using theories of state, Calavita and Pontell provide an understanding of the role of government in the events. The instrumentalist perspective expects those with economic power to use that power to gain political currency. Clearly, political leaders, dependent upon campaign contributions, intervened on behalf of several savings and loan operators. Notably the Keating Five—Senators Alan Cranston, Dennis DeConcini, John Glenn, John McCain, Donald Riegle—received $1.3 million in campaign contributions from Charles Keating and met with regulators on his behalf. According to the structural perspective, while the state often finds it in its own interest to assist business, it has a vested interest in protecting the nation from threats to its economy and therefore should work to contain collective embezzlement.

Calavita and Pontell coined the term *collective embezzlement* to describe a previously unobserved phenomenon in which an institution, in this case a savings and loan association, is both the weapon used to perpetrate the crime and is the victim of the crime. Collective embezzlement is now part of white-collar-corporate crime vernacular.

Pontell and Calavita drew four fundamental conclusions from the scandal:

1. The primary cause of the savings and loan crisis was deliberate insider fraud that was facilitated by systematic political collusion.

2. Deregulation, increased federal insurance, and lenient treatment of offenders created a criminogenic environment that facilitated, if not encouraged, these crimes.

3. The typical corporate crimes perpetrated in the industrial sector are committed on behalf of the corporation with the intent of increasing profits. Financial crimes perpetrated during the savings and loan crisis, however, were against the institution itself and almost destroyed the American financial system.

4. Financial capitalism and the casino economy, where profits are increasingly made from manipulating money, create new opportunities for white-collar crime because the amount of money that can be garnered from financial fraud is virtually endless.

Susan Will

See also Capitalism and White-Collar Crime; Geis, Gilbert: Perspectives on White-Collar Crime Scandals; Michalowski, Raymond J., and Ronald C. Kramer: State-Corporate Crime; Ross, E. A.: Sin and Society; Sutherland, Edwin H.: White-Collar Crime

References and Further Readings

Black, W. K. (2005). *The best way to rob a bank is to own one.* Austin: University of Texas Press.

Calavita, K., & Pontell, H. N. (1990). "Heads I win, tails you lose": Deregulation, crime and crisis in the savings and loan industry. *Crime and Delinquency, 36,* 309–341.

Calavita, K., Pontell, H. N., & Tillman, R. (1997). *Big money crime: Fraud and politics in the S&L crisis.* Berkeley: University of California Press.

Federal Deposit Insurance Corporation. (1998). *Managing the crisis: The FDIC and RTC experience 1980–1994.* Washington, DC: U.S. Government Printing Office.

Pontell, H. N., Calavita, K., & Tillman, R. (1994). Corporate crime and criminal justice system capacity. *Justice Quarterly, 11,* 383–410.

POSTMODERN THEORY

In the 1980s, postmodern theory gained prominence in the field of criminology. Prior to this time, understanding about criminal phenomena was exclusively informed by empirical inquiry. Methods developed and advanced in order to make sense of the physical world were utilized in an attempt to comprehend human conduct but from within the realm of the social world. This orientation, known as the modern, is based on the assumptions that human behavior is rational and predictable and that truth is discernable and absolute. Thus, the conditions, causes, and control of crime are capable of being explained. Postmodern theory rejects these contentions and challenges the positivist notions underlying much of contemporary society.

Drawing primarily upon the work of French scholars, postmodernism as applied to criminology asserts that conventional understanding about truth and knowledge fails to adequately account for the inconsistencies and contradictions of human behavior and social life. For the postmodernist, there is no finite truth or privileged knowledge. Indeed, it is in this way that everyone is considered an expert. Although this perspective has garnered criticism, its influence on how we make sense of crime and the society in which it occurs continues to grow.

It is first worth noting that postmodernism, as a theory of dissent, resists comprehensive and convenient delineation. In other words, while most criminological theories offer something approximating a cohesive framework, postmodernism consists of a diverse and, as some claim, infinite number of positions. Although each position articulates the theory in distinct and perhaps somewhat conflicting ways, they share a commonality in their criticism of the modern.

Modernity is a term used to describe the period following the Middle or Dark Ages. However, during what is commonly known as the Enlightenment or the Age of Reason, a philosophical shift occurred. Prior to this time, social life was understood within the context of theologically based concepts. That is, the belief was that human nature and behavior were guided by a higher power, and an external struggle between good and evil persisted. Following the Enlightenment, reason triumphed over the divine. Rather than behavior influenced by the sacred and prophetic, humans were considered to be rational beings capable of assuming responsibility, employing free choice, and pursuing hedonistic desires (Best & Kellner, 1991).

This turn to reason combined with ever-advancing scientific methods provided the foundation for the modern era and, correspondingly, a number of criminological theories. For example, rational choice theory and social bond/self-control theory both presume that the criminal is rational and engages in self-satisfying behavior. With rational choice theory, the criminal decides whether or not to commit a crime based on a calculation of the benefits and costs. With social control theory, the youthful offender fails to appropriately socialize (bond) or engages in delinquent social learning yielding a lack of self-control that, in adulthood, makes the person prone to criminal behavior. The justice system's reliance upon deterrence, punishment, and rehabilitation can be traced to these and many other modernist ideas.

As the prefix *post* suggests, postmodernism follows modernity. The theory developed in two phases. Among those comprising the first and second stages, Jean Baudrillard, Michel Foucault, Jacques Derrida, Gilles Deleuze and Felix Guattari, Jean-Francois Lyotard, and Julia Kristeva each played a distinct and significant role in cultivating and advancing postmodern thought. Some, such as

Foucault, did not label themselves as postmodernists. Nevertheless, their collective work is widely credited with helping to establish the theory's leading principles.

The positions taken by most first and second wave postmodernists can be linked directly to the work of French psychoanalyst, Jacques Lacan. Drawing upon the concept that describes people as desiring and unfulfilled human subjects rather than as unitary and self-contained individuals, Lacan proposed how discourse analysis could help to account for this. For Lacan, subjects and their sense of reality are shaped by and through communication and the specialized meaning (desire) attached to and embedded within the language they employ when interacting or conversing. This meaning is often referred to by postmodernists as a *regime of signs*. Thus, a regime of signs such as the law (or legalese) conveys circumscribed meaning (desire) leaving outside the scope of consideration alternative ways of speaking. When replacement forms of conveying meaning integral to the identity of a person are declared "irrelevant," "immaterial," or "prejudicial," then the subject's true self (being) is similarly dismissed, according to Stuart Henry and Dragan Milovanovic.

These Lacanian assertions are discernable in poststructuralist theory, the science of semiotics, and deconstructive methodology. Each notion has served as a foundation for a number of postmodernist principles. Poststructuralists argue that the meaning of "texts," which includes written and spoken communication, can never be deciphered in such a way that absolute truth is discernible. Semioticians examine words, phrases, and gestures as signs that represent something more or other than what is purposely communicated. As a discursive method of analysis, deconstructionism maintains that human interactions and social phenomena are interconnected. As such, they can be disassembled and reassembled to ensure that minority and alienated "voices" are included, according to Bruce Arrigo.

Based on these shared concepts, postmodernists challenge the modernist idea that humans possess categorical knowledge; rather, they embody certain types of knowledge or levels of certainty. According to Milovanovic, claims of knowing a particular truth revealed through seemingly objective scientific methods are typically understood as establishing or maintaining oppressive power relations. As such, postmodern theorists dismiss the idea of absolute or categorical knowledge and truth. Instead, truth is conditional, positional, and relational. It exists for individuals or groups based on specific and often unique circumstances. Postmodernists allege that, because truth is not absolute, scientific inquiry fails to fully reveal reality. In other words, positivist science offers a way of understanding, but it does not provide the sole method for comprehending human behavior and social phenomena.

Postmodern Applications in Criminology

Since its emergence, the logic of postmodern theory has increasingly been applied to a number of crime and justice problems. One example is the way in which the courts consistently seek to determine an offender's competency. A system of psycholegal discourse exists that specifies what mental health or wellness is. If the individual communicates in a manner consistent with the established rhetoric, he or she will be deemed fit for trial, incarceration, or even execution. However, if the individual deviates in any way from the system-supporting language, normalization follows through disciplinary control within correctional or other related regulatory institutions. Thus *depathologization*—cleansing or sanitizing a subject's psychiatric status by utilizing system-maintaining language—may ultimately hinder individuals from experiencing their own linguistic reality, their own recovery or healing. In response, postmodernists endeavor to deterritorialize desire (privileged standpoints) within and throughout (criminal justice) control apparatuses.

From the modern perspective, individuals are expected to assume socially responsible roles and exist as stable beings. However, postmodernism asserts that these activities merely serve to create identities based on "either/or" categories. In other words, people are characterized as "deviants or conformists; law violators or law abiders; villains or heroes" (Arrigo, 1995, p. 454). Rather than linguistically proscribing static identities, postmodernists maintain that a more complete (and honest) portrayal of the human subject would include diverse opportunities for role negotiation; multiple standpoints or epistemologies; and fluid renditions of truth, reason, progress, and identity.

Deleuze and Guattari refer to this subject as a "body without organs" or "BwO." "The full BwO is that person who escapes repetition ... and mobilizes [a] greater range of potentialities" (Arrigo et al., 2005, p. 47).

For example, postmodern feminist scholars raise concerns regarding role formation and what they term the "gendered" subject. From their perspective, the extant grammar utilized to describe women and minorities is exclusively "malestream" and misogynous. In other words, the status of the feminine in society is defined in masculine terms. As such, the identities of women and minorities are reduced and repressed, particularly through criminal, legal, and correctional practices.

To illustrate, some postmodernists question the education and employment opportunities available to females serving time in prison. Skills such as "mothercraft" along with sewing, cooking, and cleaning are commonly taught or offered for pay. From these "regimes of femininity," the traditional identity of a white, middle-class heterosexual woman is forced upon those incarcerated. However, through these expressions of "identity politics," the insistence on such a traditional feminine image inadvertently creates possibilities for resistance and agency. Indeed, within these spaces women can reject the correctional powers that attempt to proscribe (name) female identity. As a response, some incarcerates may assume roles that challenge the traditional image of a woman, including the pursuit of lesbian relationships.

Another example of postmodernism's application to criminology can be found in the increasing number of "jailhouse lawyers." These are individuals who, while serving time in a correctional institution, educate themselves about the law and practice it within the confines of the facility. As Jim Thomas and Milovanovic described them, jailhouse lawyers are like "primitive rebels" who are more concerned with doing rather than pursuing a chosen political agenda. While they may be perceived as revolutionaries representing the downtrodden and demoralized, their resistance may be attributed to the realization that they must seek an identity that enables them to survive within the conditions of their confinement. In other words, as Arrigo and Milovanovic argue, the incarcerated subject self-creates an identity while also raising opposition to the power exercised by the correctional system.

Postmodern theory and its application to criminology incite debate among scholars in the field. Those who challenge the postmodern perspective typically raise three prominent criticisms. Critics comprising the first camp argue that if society accepts that absolute truth or knowledge cannot be established, then ultimately nothing can be determined about the human condition or society itself. Critics comprising the second group argue that postmodernism seeks only to deconstruct social phenomena rather than offering novel ways to effectively improve society. Those within the third cluster argue that postmodern analyses are often dense and that this opaqueness may disguise an underlying political agenda.

Collectively, naysayers conclude that postmodern theory fails to adequately inform and advance our understanding of the issues presented with crime and punishment. In other words, opponents charge that postmodern theory is of limited utility when addressing the distinct needs of criminals, victims, and the justice system. For example, some detractors maintain that discourse analysis lacks an adequate theoretical foundation. As such, it does not grow our knowledge or serve as a means to explain such matters as crime causality and how it can be controlled. Other critics, such as Martin Schwartz and David O. Friedrichs, argue that the postmodern approach is fundamentally extraneous to crime and justice studies; thus, it should not be considered within the realm of criminological thought.

Future Directions

Despite these criticisms, postmodern advocates maintain that its theoretical variants and its assemblage of principles are not only worthwhile, but also critical to realizing social change. However, there are a number of challenges that must be overcome. Those who endorse a postmodern approach to justice propose an alternative set of questions when considering the crime problems present in society. In the past, criminological scholars have pondered such questions as What is crime? Under what conditions do crimes occur? Who creates the law? On what conditions is the law created? As noted previously, these and other rational-based inquiries have for years guided empirical investigation that have informed numerous modern criminological theories. For the postmodernist, these theories constitute the unwitting foundation for a criminal justice system that exacts power and ultimately, harm, over the human subject.

According to postmodernists, future inquiry must first seek to determine what the political, economic, cultural, or other conditions are that facilitate the formation of these (rather than other) questions. In this way, scholars, practitioners, and students within the criminological field will have the opportunity to undertake probing and deliberate introspection. This sort of critical engagement is necessary if the goal is to discern and to prevent (unknowing) contributions to the oppression of others through the prevailing discourse in use.

Equipped with a new line of questioning, postmodernists assert that crime must be reconceived as the power to harm others through reduction and repression. As Henry and Milovanovic explained, "This is not necessarily an evil individual or the passive product of social forces. Rather, the criminal and potential purveyor of harm is found to be a believer in the omnipotence of reality, truth, and certainty; an excessive investor in the representation of reality; and an investor in the power to frame others' realities in ways that mangle their creative souls" (p. 241). Therein is the principal challenge to postmodernism and to those who advocate its inclusion within criminology.

Beyond this barrier, postmodernism continues to face criticism regarding its efficacy in responding to practical matters such as predicting and controlling crime. Proponents of the theory interpret this overly deterministic and reductionistic desire to specify and "correct" deviancy as a struggle for power over the subject's increasingly territorialized body. Indeed, as Deleuze and Guattari demonstrated, the subject's body within contemporary society is typically static and imprisoned by a discourse that demands status quo role taking. From a postmodern perspective, this is a person whose voice is silenced and who is harmed by unspoken but felt forces of reduction and repression.

Further, in recent years, several alternative approaches to justice have emerged that challenge conventional retributive responses to crime. For example, restorative justice programs now exist that aim to foster healing and understanding by engaging the victim, the offender, and often members of the community in dialogue. Critics of restorative justice programs charge that the discourse employed is still within the linguistic framework of reduction and repression. Thus, postmodernists argue for "replacement discourses." These are methods of communicating and interacting that potentially are transformative. How and to what extent replacement discourses can be provisional, positional, and relational in diverse sites of meaning-making contestation is the source of future postmodern exploration.

Conclusion

Although challenges lie ahead, postmodernists continue to advocate transformation within the criminological field and society at large. To be successful, the social change that this orientation seeks must hurdle the modernist perspective as operating within contemporary social systems and institutions. For those who advance a postmodern society, the belief is that change will only come when these linear, static systems of thought and action embrace the nonlinear and the unpredictable dimensions of human social existence. Thus, what must be resisted are constructions of "new and different" hierarchical conceptions of truth, justice, law, or crime that subsequently function in rigid and totalizing ways. Instead, postmodernism seeks ongoing change; one that emancipates both the human subject and the social order to which such subjects are intimately bound through the medium of evolving discourse.

Under conditions such as these, human actors and agents within the criminal justice field (e.g., offenders, victims, police officers, judges, attorneys, and correctional institution administrators) and those outside of it (the general public) will increasingly experience their freedom, their humanity. This is a freedom that extols rather than dismisses irony, contingency, discontinuity, incompleteness, and disorder as dimensions of social life. This is the ever-changing path to reassembling a more compassionate society constructed in languages of possibility. These are methods of communicating and strategies for interacting in which all human subjects are more fully emancipated from harms of repression and reduction.

Bruce A. Arrigo and Heather Y. Bersot

See also Chambliss, William J.: Power, Conflict, and Crime; Peacemaking Criminology; Quinney, Richard:

Social Transformation and Peacemaking Criminology; Spector, Malcolm, and John I. Kitsuse: Constructing Social Problems

References and Further Readings

Arrigo, B. A. (1995). The peripheral core of law and criminology: On postmodern social theory and conceptual integration. *Justice Quarterly, 12,* 448–472.

Arrigo, B. A., & Milovanovic, D. (2009). *Revolution in penology: Rethinking the society of captives.* Lanham, MD: Rowman & Littlefield.

Arrigo, B. A., & Milovanovic, D. (Eds.). (2010). *Postmodernist and post-structuralist theories of crime.* Surrey, UK: Ashgate.

Arrigo, B. A., Milovanovic, D., & Schehr, R. C. (2005). *The French connection in criminology: Rediscovering crime, law, and social change.* Albany: SUNY Press.

Arrigo, B. A., & Williams, C. R. (Eds.). (2006). *Philosophy, crime and criminology.* Urbana: University of Illinois Press.

Best, S., & Kellner, D. (1991). *Postmodern theory: Critical interrogation.* New York: Guilford Press.

Bosworth, M. (1999). *Engendering resistance: Agency and power in women's prisons.* Sydney, Australia: Ashgate.

Deleuze, G., & Guattari, F. (1987). *A thousand plateaus.* Minneapolis: University of Minnesota Press.

Henry, S., & Milovanovic, D. (1996). *Constitutive criminology: Beyond postmodernism.* London: Sage.

Milovanovic, D. (2002). *Critical criminology at the edge: Postmodern perspectives, applications, and integrations.* Westport, CT: Praeger.

Schwartz, M., & Friedrichs, D. O. (1994). Postmodern thought and criminological discontent: New metaphors for understanding violence. *Criminology, 32,* 221–246.

Thomas, J., & Milovanovic, D. (1999). In S. Henry & D. Milovanovic (Eds.), *Constitutive criminology at work: Applications to crime and justice* (pp. 227–248). Albany: SUNY Press.

PRENATAL INFLUENCES AND CRIME

Over the past 20 years, researchers have made considerable progress in uncovering various social, psychological, and biological risk factors that predispose to criminal behavior. One area in particular that has received increasing attention has been the role of early health risk factors in contributing to antisocial behavior. A large body of research has now convincingly demonstrated that several prenatal risk factors—including malnutrition, birth complications, and prenatal nicotine and alcohol exposure—significantly increase risk for antisocial and criminal behavior across the lifespan. Research has increasingly revealed that childhood externalizing behavior, such as conduct disorder, aggression and hyperactivity, represents a major predisposition to adult crime and violence. Thus, insight into the etiology of childhood antisocial behavior is critical to attempts to understand, and possibly prevent, adult criminality. Research on prenatal influences on crime has generally focused on four main domains: minor physical abnormalities, prenatal nicotine and alcohol exposure, birth complications, and malnutrition.

Minor Physical Abnormalities

Minor physical abnormalities (MPAs) have been associated with pregnancy disorders and are considered to be indicators of fetal neural maldevelopment near the end of the first trimester (Firestone & Peters, 1983). Since the epidermis and the central nervous system (CNS) have shared embryological origins, MPAs are seen as indirect markers of atypical CNS and brain development. MPAs consist of fairly minor physical abnormalities such as low-seated ears, adherent ear lobes, and a furrowed tongue. Although there may be a genetic component to MPAs, they may also be caused by environmental factors that affect the fetus, such as anoxia, bleeding, and infection (Guy et al., 1983).

Several studies have found a relationship between elevated numbers of MPAs and increased antisocial behavior in children, adolescents, and adults. In particular, MPAs have been linked to violent as opposed to nonviolent offending. For instance, Arseneault, Tremblay, Boulerice, Seguin, and Saucier showed that MPAs measured at age 14 in 170 males predicted violent but not nonviolent delinquency at age 17. The authors reported that these effects were independent of childhood physical aggression or family adversity. In another study by Kandel, Brennan, Mednick, and Michelson, an increased level of MPAs was

associated with recidivistic violent criminal behavior. The authors assessed MPAs in 265 11- to 13-year-old Danish children, and found that recidivistic violent offenders had a greater number of MPAs compared with subjects with one or no violent offenses, according to police records of criminal behavior when the subjects were 20 to 22 years of age. These studies suggest that prenatal insults toward the end of the first 3 months of pregnancy may increase risk for violent behavior as a result of abnormal brain development.

A number of studies have also reported that MPAs interact with social factors in predisposing to violent and antisocial behavior. A 1988 study by Mednick and Kandel measured MPAs in 129 boys during visits to a pediatrician at age 12. The authors found that MPAs were associated with violent crime, but not nonviolent property offenses, when the subjects were 21 years old. Interestingly, however, when the authors divided subjects into those from unstable, nonintact families and those from stable families, they found that MPAs only predicted later criminal involvement for those reared in unstable, nonintact homes. A similar finding was reported by Brennan, Mednick, and Raine, who evaluated adult violent offenses in a sample of 72 male offspring of parents with psychiatric diagnoses. The authors found particularly high rates of adult violent crime in individuals who had both family adversity and MPAs compared to those who had only one of these risk factors. In another study, Pine, Shaffer, Schonfeld, and Davies investigated the interaction of MPAs and environmental risk factors, such as low socioeconomic status, spousal conflict, and marital disruption, in predicting later disruptive behavior disorders. The authors found a significant interaction between MPAs and environmental risk, such that individuals with both increased MPAs and environmental risk, assessed at age 7, were at greater risk for disruptive behavior in general and for conduct disorder, in particular, at age 17. These three studies suggest that MPAs interact with adverse environmental experiences such that psychosocial factors lead to antisocial and violent behavior more strongly, and sometimes only, among individuals with high biological risk. Neurological abnormalities such as MPAs thus appear to increase susceptibility to psychosocial risk factors for antisocial and violent behavior.

Prenatal Nicotine and Alcohol Exposure

Extensive evidence has now established beyond a reasonable doubt that children who are exposed to maternal smoking during pregnancy are at increased risk for later antisocial behavior that extends over the life course. Maternal prenatal smoking has been shown to predict conduct disorder, delinquency, and adult criminal and violent offending. Several studies have also reported a dose-response relationship between the extent of maternal smoking during pregnancy and the extent of later antisocial behavior in offspring.

In addition to nicotine exposure, it has long been established that fetal alcohol exposure significantly increases risk for antisocial behavior in adolescents and adults. Heavy alcohol consumption while pregnant can result in fetal alcohol syndrome (FAS), which is characterized by a host of cognitive, behavioral, social, and physical deficits. However, Schonfeld, Mattson, and Riley have observed deficits even in those who have been prenatally exposed to alcohol who do not meet diagnostic criteria for FAS. For instance, research has found high rates of delinquency in children and adolescents with heavy fetal alcohol exposure, even if they do not have FAS. In addition, studies have shown that adolescents who were prenatally exposed to alcohol are overrepresented in the juvenile justice system. One study by Fast, Conry, and Loock revealed that 3 percent of adolescents in a juvenile inpatient forensic psychiatry unit were diagnosed with FAS, and 22 percent were diagnosed with fetal alcohol effects. Another study by Streissguth et al. reported that 61 percent of adolescents, 58 percent of adults, and 14 percent of children between the ages of 6 and 11 with fetal alcohol exposure had a history of trouble with the law.

Several studies have documented interactions between maternal prenatal smoking and psychosocial risks in the prediction of later violence. These studies are notable for their large sample sizes, assessment of long-term outcomes, prospective data collection, and control for potential confounds such as parental antisocial behavior, drug use, and low socioeconomic status. For instance, Brennan, Grekin, and Mednick examined the number of cigarettes smoked daily during pregnancy by the mothers of 4,169 males born between

1959 and 1961 in Copenhagen, Denmark. The authors found a dose-response relationship between the extent of prenatal maternal smoking and the extent of nonviolent and violent crime when the subjects were 34 years of age. Moreover, these effects were specific to persistent criminal behavior, rather than that confined to adolescence. Among subjects whose mothers smoked 20 cigarettes a day while pregnant, there was a twofold increase in adult violent offending, according to arrest records. However, the authors found that when maternal prenatal smoking was combined with delivery complications, there was a fivefold increase in adult violent offending; in contrast, prenatal nicotine exposure without delivery complications did not lead to increased violence in offspring. In another study, Rasanan et al. reported that the offspring of women who smoked during pregnancy had a twofold increase in violent crime at age 26, and that, when prenatal nicotine exposure was combined with being raised in a single-parent family, there was an 11.9-fold increase in recidivistic violent offending. Moreover, prenatal nicotine exposure led to a 14.2-fold increase in recidivistic violence when combined with four psychosocial risk factors: teenage pregnancy, single-parent family, unwanted pregnancy, and developmental motor delays. In this study, as in the one above, risk was particularly increased for persistent violent offending, rather than violence in general or property crime. Finally, a 2000 study by Gibson and Tibbetts documented an interaction between prenatal nicotine exposure and parental absence in predisposing to early onset of antisocial behavior and offending.

Birth Complications

In addition to MPAs and prenatal nicotine and alcohol exposure, research has also focused on birth complications, such as premature birth, low birth weight, placement in a neonatal intensive care unit, forceps delivery, Cesarean section, anoxia, resuscitation needed after delivery, preeclampsia in the mother, and low Apgar score. A number of well-designed studies have demonstrated that obstetric complications interact with psychosocial risk factors in predicting conduct disorder, delinquency, and impulsive crime and violence in adulthood. For example, Werner found that birth complications combined with a disruptive family environment (which included such experiences as maternal separation, illegitimacy, marital discord, parental mental health problems and paternal absence), predisposed to delinquency over and above either biological or psychosocial risk factor independently.

Two prospective longitudinal studies by Raine, Brennan, and Mednick in 1994 and 1997 also provide evidence of the importance of biosocial interactions in predicting violent crime. In the first of these studies, Raine et al. evaluated whether the early experience of extreme maternal rejection (e.g., unwanted pregnancy, attempts to abort the fetus, and institutional care of the infant during the first year of life) interacted with birth complications in predisposing to adult violent crime in a sample of 4,269 males born in Copenhagen, Denmark, between 1959 and 1961. The authors found that birth complications significantly interacted with maternal rejection in predisposing to violent crime at 18 years of age. The importance of this finding is highlighted by the fact that while only 4 percent of the sample experienced both birth complications and maternal rejection, this group was responsible for 18 percent of the violent offenses perpetrated by the whole sample. In a subsequent study, the same authors followed up this sample to age 34 to reassess criminal violence. The authors replicated the biosocial interaction for violent but not nonviolent crime. In addition, they found that the results applied specifically to serious violence, rather than violent threats, and to early-onset as opposed to late-onset violence. Similar biosocial interactions between obstetric complications and various psychosocial risk factors (e.g., parental mental illness, poor parenting, familial adversity) have been reported in studies using large samples from around the world.

In contrast to this, two studies failed to find an interaction between birth complications and environmental risk factors: a 2002 study by Cannon et al. and a 2000 study by Laucht et al. However, there are several notable differences between these studies and those cited above. In the first of these studies, the sample consisted of 601 individuals with schizophrenia spectrum disorders; thus, there may have been other differences in brain functioning in this population that obscured findings related to violence. In the second of these studies,

follow-up of a small sample of 322 children was limited to age 8. Some authors have suggested that CNS insults resulting from perinatal complications may be especially related to life-course-persistent antisocial behavior rather than to child antisocial behavior. Thus, the vast majority of the evidence suggests that birth complications combined with psychosocial risk factors predispose to violent crime.

While not a birth complication per se, evidence from Ikaheimo et al. also suggests that a high body mass index (BMI) and small head circumference at age 12 months are associated with a substantially increased risk of violent but not non-violent offending in adulthood. Interestingly, the authors found that measures of BMI at age 1 were stronger predictors of violent behavior than measures of BMI at age 14, which they argue implicates genetic and early environmental factors, rather than social learning, in accounting for the relationship between BMI and violence.

Malnutrition

There is growing recognition that along with other early health risk factors, malnutrition represents an important risk factor for the development of antisocial behavior in children and adults. Research on malnutrition has focused on both macromalnutrition, such as protein-energy malnutrition, and malnutrition caused by micronutrient deficiencies, such as iron and zinc micromalnutrition. Epidemiological studies have documented associations between increased aggressive behavior and vitamin and mineral deficiency (Werbach, 1992). Further support for the link between malnutrition and antisocial behavior comes from a study by Neugebauer, Hoek, and Susser. They demonstrated that the male offspring of nutritionally deprived pregnant women had 2.5 times the normal rate of antisocial personality disorder in adulthood when malnutrition occurred during the first and second trimesters of pregnancy—the period of time when brain growth is most rapid.

While the links described above are intriguing, they do not provide conclusive evidence of a relationship between malnutrition and antisocial behavior. More compelling evidence that malnutrition leads to antisocial behavior comes from a number of experimental studies in both children and adults. Although not focused specifically on the prenatal period, a recent longitudinal prospective study by Liu et al. presents a particularly powerful illustration of how early childhood malnutrition may predispose to antisocial behavior later in life. In this study, Liu et al. demonstrated that children with iron, zinc or protein deficiencies at age 3 had greater externalizing behavior problems at ages 8, 11, and 17. In comparison to control subjects, malnourished children at age 3 were more aggressive or hyperactive at age 8, had more externalizing behavior at age 11, and had greater conduct disorder and excessive motor activity at age 17. Behavior problems were measured with three different instruments at each age, suggesting that findings were largely invariant to the nature of measurement. Findings were also independent of psychosocial adversity and not moderated by gender. Moreover, Liu et al. found a dose-response relationship between the extent of malnutrition at age 3 and the extent of behavior problems at ages 8 and 17, suggesting that malnutrition was an important factor in predisposing to antisocial behavior.

Effects of early nutritional interventions on later behavior have also been found. Although not specific to nutritional enrichment, one highly successful early intervention for criminal and antisocial behavior consisted of home visits by nurses to mothers in which nutritional guidance was a major component. A randomized controlled trial by Raine et al. in 2003 also demonstrated that an enrichment program consisting of nutrition, education, and physical exercise from ages 3 to 5 significantly reduced antisocial behavior at age 17 and criminal behavior at age 23. Moreover, the authors found that the beneficial effects of the intervention were greater for children who exhibited signs of malnutrition at age 3, suggesting that the nutritional components of the intervention were the active elements in the enrichment program. Prevention, intervention, and treatment studies focused on malnutrition thus represent a promising direction for future research.

Conclusion

A substantial body of evidence suggests that several prenatal risk factors predispose to adult antisocial behavior and violence. Research has specifically linked minor physical anomalies, in utero nicotine and alcohol exposure, birth complications and malnutrition to later aggression and crime. Supporting evidence comes from a range of studies using diverse methodologies, including intervention approaches, early childhood enrichments, and prospective longitudinal designs. This methodological diversity, in addition to the experimental nature of some studies, lends further support to the relationship between health risk factors and antisocial behavior. The studies detailed above suggest that prevention efforts aimed at increasing maternal prenatal health and childhood nutrition and interventions designed to reduce birth complications and other causes of brain dysfunction may represent viable approaches for reducing violent crime.

Melissa Peskin and Adrian Raine

See also Brain Abnormalities and Crime; Environmental Toxins Theory; Lahey, Benjamin B., and Irwin D. Waldman: Developmental Propensity Model; Mednick, Sarnoff A.: Autonomic Nervous System (ANS) Theory; Moffitt, Terrie E.: A Developmental Model of Life-Course-Persistent Offending; Nutrition and Crime; Raine, Adrian: Crime as a Disorder

References and Further Readings

Arseneault, L., Tremblay, R. E., Boulerice, B., Seguin, J. R., & Saucier, J. F. (2000). Minor physical anomalies and family adversity as risk factors for violent delinquency in adolescence. *American Journal of Psychiatry, 157,* 917–923.

Brennan, P. A., Grekin, E. R., & Mednick, S. A. (1999). Maternal smoking during pregnancy and adult male criminal outcomes. *Archives of General Psychiatry, 56,* 215–219.

Brennan, P. A., Mednick, S. A., & Raine, A. (1997). Biosocial interactions and violence: A focus on perinatal factors. In A. Raine, P. A. Brennan, D. Farrington, & S. A. Mednick (Eds.), *Biosocial bases of violence* (pp. 163–174). New York: Plenum.

Cannon, M., Huttenen, M. O., Tanskanen, A. J., Arseneault, L., Jones, P. B., & Murray, R. M. (2002). Perinatal and childhood risk factors for later criminality and violence in schizophrenia. *British Journal of Psychiatry, 180,* 496–501.

Fast, D. K., Conry, J., & Loock, C. A. (1999). Identifying Fetal Alcohol Syndrome among youth in the criminal justice system. *Journal of Developmental and Behavioral Pediatrics, 20,* 370–372.

Firestone, P., & Peters, S. (1983). Minor physical anomalies and behavior in children: A review. *Journal of Autism and Developmental Disorders, 13,* 411–425.

Galler, J. R., & Ramsey, F. (1989). A follow-up study of the influence of early malnutrition on development. *Journal of the American Academy of Child and Adolescent Psychiatry, 26,* 23–27.

Gibson, C. L., Piquero, A. R., & Tibbetts, S. G. (2000). Assessing the relationship between maternal cigarette smoking during pregnancy and age at first police contact. *Justice Quarterly, 17,* 519–542.

Guy, J. D., Majorski, L. V., Wallace, C. J., & Guy, M. P. (1983). The incidence of minor physical anomalies in adult male schizophrenics. *Schizophrenia Bulletin, 9,* 571–582.

Ikaheimo, P., Rasanen, P., Hakko, H., Hartikainen, A., Laitinen, J., Hodgins, S., et al. (2007). Body size and violent offending among males in the Northern Finland 1966 birth cohort. *Social Psychiatry and Psychiatric Epidemiology, 42,* 845–850.

Kandel, E., Brennan, P. A., Mednick, S. A., & Michelson, N. M. (1989). Minor physical anomalies and recidivistic adult criminal behavior. *Acta Psychiatrica Scandinavica, 79,* 103–107.

Laucht, M., Esser, G., Baving, L., Gerhold, M., Hoesch, I., Ihle, W., et al. (2000). Behavioral sequelae of perinatal insults and early family adversity at 8 years of age. *Journal of the American Academy of Child and Adolescent Psychiatry, 39,* 1229–1237.

Liu, J., Raine, A., Venables, P., & Mednick, S. A. (2004). Malnutrition at age 3 years predisposes to externalizing behavior problems at ages 8, 11 and 17 years. *American Journal of Psychiatry, 161,* 2005–2013.

Mednick, S. A., & Kandel, E. S. (1988). Congenital determinants of violence. *Bulletin of the American Academy of Psychiatry and the Law, 16,* 101–109.

Neugebauer, R., Hoek, H. W., & Susser, E. (1999). Prenatal exposure to wartime famine and development of antisocial personality disorder in early adulthood. *Journal of the American Medical Association, 4,* 479–481.

Pine, D. S., Shaffer, D., Schonfeld, I. S., & Davies, M. (1997). Minor physical anomalies: Modifiers of environmental risks for psychiatric impairment? *Journal of the American Academy of Child and Adolescent Psychiatry, 36,* 395–403.

Raine, A. (2002). Biosocial studies of antisocial and violent behavior in children and adults: A review. *Journal of Abnormal Child Psychology, 30,* 311–326.

Raine, A., Brennan, P., & Mednick, S. A. (1994). Birth complications combined with early maternal rejection at age 1 year predispose to violent crime at age 18 years. *Archives of General Psychiatry, 51,* 984–988.

Raine, A., Brennan, P., & Mednick, S. A. (1997). Interaction between birth complications and early maternal rejection in predisposing individuals to adult violence: Specificity to serious, early-onset violence. *American Journal of Psychiatry, 154,* 1265–1271.

Raine, A., Mellingen, K., Liu, J. H., Venables, P. H., & Mednick, S. A. (2003). Effects of environmental enrichment at 3–5 years on schizotypal personality and antisocial behavior at ages 17 and 23 years. *American Journal of Psychiatry, 160,* 1627–1635.

Rantakallio, P., Laara, E., Isohanni, M., & Moilanen, I. (1992). Maternal smoking during pregnancy and delinquency of the offspring: An association without causation? *International Journal of Epidemiology, 21,* 1106–1113.

Rasanen, P., Hakko, H., Isohanni, M., Hodgins, S., Jarvelin, M. R., & Tiihonen, J. (1999). Maternal smoking during pregnancy and risk of criminal behavior among adult male offspring in the northern Finland 1996 birth cohort. *American Journal of Psychiatry, 156,* 857–862.

Scarpa, A., & Raine, A. (2007). Biosocial bases of violence. In D. J. Flannery, A. T. Vazsonyi, & I. D. Waldman (Eds.), *The Cambridge handbook of violent behavior and aggression* (pp. 151–169). Cambridge, UK: Cambridge University Press.

Schonfeld, A. M., Mattson, S. N., & Riley, E. P. (2005). Moral maturity and delinquency after prenatal alcohol exposure. *Journal of Studies on Alcohol, 66,* 545–554.

Streissguth, A. P., Barr, H. M., Kogan, J., & Bookstein, F. L. (1996). *Understanding the occurrence of secondary disabilities in clients with fetal alcohol syndrome (FAS) and fetal alcohol effects (FAE).* Washington, DC: Centers for Disease Control and Prevention.

Wakschlag, L. S., Pickett, K. E., Cook, E. C., Benowitz, N. L., & Leventhal, B. L. (2002). Maternal smoking during pregnancy and severe antisocial behavior in offspring: A review. *American Journal of Public Health, 92,* 966–974.

Werbach, M. R. (1992). Nutritional influences on aggressive behavior. *Journal of Orthomolecular Medicine, 7,* 45–51.

Werner, E. E. (1987). Vulnerability and resiliency in children at risk for delinquency: A longitudinal study from birth to young adulthood. In J. D. Burchard & S. N. Burchard (Eds.), *Primary prevention of psychopathology* (pp. 16–43). Newbury Park, CA: Sage.

PRISON INSURGENCY THEORY

It is commonly expected that prisons are violent places, given the nature of the individuals housed within them. Some prison violence takes place at the individual level, which consists of violence between inmates or between inmates and correctional staff. Besides interpersonal violence, prisons across the United States and the world have also experienced collective violence (i.e., group violence) or riots. There are estimates of over 1,000 prison riots having occurred in the United States in the 20th century. From just 1950 to 1960 more than 100 riots transpired in American prisons. However, some of the most infamous riots, readily known to the public because of their extreme amounts of violence, took place from 1970 through 1993. Among these were the uprisings at Attica in New York, Joliet in Illinois, the New Mexico State Penitentiary in Santa Fe, and Southern Ohio Correctional Facility in Lucasville, Ohio.

Penologists have examined many of these events and provided multiple theoretical explanations for their occurrence. One such explanation is the prison insurgency theory. This theory views the prison riot as being similar to an action of civil disobedience or unrest (i.e., a collective uprising against the state or civil authority). This theoretical explanation of prison riots blends elements of authoritative action/inaction and breakdown/disorganization of prison conditions with tenets of social revolution theories.

Penologists who study prison riots agree that no two riots are exactly alike. In fact, prison riots can take on many different forms and have multiple lasting effects upon a correctional institution. Because the conditions that produce prison riots are present in some prisons but not in others, the best way to investigate the underlying causes of prison riots is to look for commonalities or similarities between these unique events. It was in that light, that prison insurgency theory sought to explain the etiology of prison riots.

The Beginning Stages

The earliest articulation of prison insurgency theory began with Bert Useem and Peter Kimball's landmark book titled *States of Siege: U.S. Prison Riots, 1971 to 1986*. To begin, the authors adopted a unique definition of a prison riot. They put forth the notion that "a prison riot occurs when authorities lose control of a significant number of prisoners, in a significant area of the prison, for a significant amount of time" (p. 4). Using this definition, they suggested that riots do not take place in all prisons rather in prisons with a particular "pathology" (p. 218).

To explore this idea, they used archival data from nine prison riots as well as interviews with inmates, prison staff, and prison administrators to develop the first underpinnings of prison insurgency theory. From their analysis, Useem and Kimball concluded that the "key factor has not been the organization of the inmates but the disorganization of the state. The riot-prone system is characterized by certain ailments which, on one hand, sap the ability of the state to contain disturbances and, on the other hand, convince inmates that imprisoning conditions are unjust" (p. 218). These two important elements served as precursors to riotous behavior and were typically found in prisons that experienced "a breakdown in administrative control and operation of the prison" (p. 218). Some specific examples of this breakdown included scandals, escapes, inconsistent rules for inmates and guards, weak administrators, public dissent among correctional officers, disruption of everyday routines for eating, work, and recreation (p. 219). In total, Useem and Kimball saw prison riots as a result of the disorganization of the state, rather than the organization and mobilization of resources by inmates.

When administrative control broke down, Useem and Kimball suggested the occurrence of two profound effects. First, inmates experienced an increase in their feelings of deprivation. This increase in deprivation usually followed a worsening of prison conditions, when compared to previous standards as subscribed to by prison officials or outside members of society. Essentially, inmates felt they were living in substandard conditions as compared to earlier conditions. An example of this was found in the New Mexico riot of 1980. Just prior to the riot, a new warden took over the facility, inmates lost educational and recreational programs, there was an increase in inmate-on-inmate violence, and prison officials initiated a "snitch" system where inmates reported other inmate behavior to correctional personnel (Useem, 1985). All of these conditions were perceived as more deprived than the conditions inmates faced in the years prior, thus serving to increase their contempt for prison administrators.

In conjunction with the sense of increased deprivation was the perceived legitimacy of prison administrators and guards. Useem and Kimball (1989) suggested that when administrators and staff appeared more powerful, the inmates perceived the prison conditions as more legitimate. So, the combination of increased deprivation and a weak administrative staff fostered the likelihood of riotous behavior. Just because prison conditions were bad did not guarantee a riot: there had to be interplay between worsening conditions and staff legitimacy.

Useem and Kimball found that a second negative effect of administrative breakdown was a lapse in prison security. They pointed to several occasions of security failures in prisons just prior to riotous behavior. For example, at Attica, steel gates broke and there were no radios; at New Mexico State Penitentiary, guards left the doors open and "unbreakable" glass was not. These glaring security problems increased the likelihood that inmates would take legitimate collective action because they saw the compound as vulnerable.

The combination of deprivation and breakdown theories by Useem and Kimball was seen as a great contribution to the explanation of prison riots. However, they never really provided an adequate definition of administrative breakdown. They thoroughly discussed its precursors and effects, but failed to provide an actual conceptualization of the term.

A New Twist

Several years after the aforementioned work, Useem polished his theory of administrative breakdown into a theory of social revolution/social protest to explain prison riots. This state-centered theory of administrative breakdown as the cause of prison riots directly parallels theories of revolution that have overturned governments and monarchies. The work of Jack Goldstone and Useem saw prison riots as "rebellions against power" (p. 987). They teased out several similarities between prison riots and revolutions: frequency of the event, the occurrence of these events in waves, variability in form and function of riots and revolutions, and that both

of these types of unrest lead to substantial social change.

Goldstone and Useem used archival data from 13 major prison riots, from 1952 to 1993, to assess their state-centered theory of prison riots. All of the prisons in their sample were either medium-security or high-security facilities. Again, the authors suggested that "prison riots are not random events," but rather "there appears to be a syndrome or set of circumstances that typically prefigures a prison riot" (p. 999). They contend five specific conditions serve as precursors to prison riots, all of which are borrowed from state-centered theory of revolutions. Those five circumstances are

1) fiscal stress or other conditions that undermine the balance between a prison administrations resources and capacities and its administrative burdens, eroding the effective administration and implementation of prison policies; 2) dissention between the warden and corrections officers or internal conflicts among the corrections officers, which prevent the prison staff from supporting and advancing warden's policies; 3) grievances among the prison inmates about the warden's or staff's actions, or about their inaction or inability to ameliorate material conditions, that depict the warden or staff as ineffective or unjust, providing a motivation for protest against the prison administration; 4) the spread of ideologies of protest or rebellion, indicating that grievances and a desire for change are widely shared among prison inmates; and 5) warden or staff actions, taken in response to expressions of grievances, that are seen as excessive, arbitrary, unjust, ineffective or precluding peaceful reform, therefore turning efforts by aggrieved parties to seek remedy into attempts to create a prison riot. (pp. 1002–1003)

The authors contended that these conditions often combine together to create institutional breakdown, thus increasing the probability of a riot.

Goldstone and Useem provided specific examples of their five predictors of riot behavior, which were drawn from interviews and records gathered during their research. In addition to qualitative proof, the authors also presented statistical analysis to support their theory of prison insurgency. Only 8 of the 13 prison riots had all of the conditions present. Three of the sample prisons had four conditions present and two prisons had three of the conditions present. Overall, riots happened most often when all five conditions were present and *could* happen if only three or four conditions were present. Most important was the fact that when the five revolutionary conditions were absent, so too were riots in the majority of cases. If even three of the conditions were absent, riots were less likely to occur.

Goldstone and Useem also specified which of the five factors were most prevalent prior to the occurrence of a riot. Fiscal stress (factor 1) and the spread of ideologies of protest and rebellion (factor 4) were present in all 13 riots. The dissention between wardens and correctional officers (factor 2) and grievances among inmates about warden or staff actions (factor 3) were present in 11 of the riots. Factor 5, warden or staff actions taken in response to grievances by inmates, was present in 11 of the riots. Thus, it appeared that, while some of these conditions stood alone as important determinants of collective behavior, when taken in combination with one another they had an even stronger impact on riot potential.

Conclusion

Prison insurgency theory (i.e., the state-centered approach) is still being examined as an explanation for prison riots. Overall, this theory seeks to explain collective violence from the perspective of administrative and institutional breakdown rather than focusing on the temperament of inmates themselves. There have been several challengers to this perspective including the inmate-balance theory, administrative control theory, threshold theory, and deprivation theory. All of these theories explain certain elements of prison riots, but prison insurgency theory seems to provide the most robust explanation for the majority of riotous behavior. Prison insurgency theory is successful because it places its focus on maintaining social order in prisons, rather than on just monitoring "bad" inmates. Given this, it is certainly possible that new fiscal constraints on state and federal governments combined with a plethora of institutional problems (e.g., crowding, loss of programs, lack of staff) could create a situation of more collective violence via institutional and administrative breakdown. The extreme cost of prison riots, in the form of structural damage, loss of life, and so on, will fuel the continued examination of prison insurgency theory as the preeminent explanation of collective violence behind bars.

Karen F. Lahm

See also Colvin, Mark: Social Sources of the New Mexico Prison Riot; DiIulio, John J., Jr.: Prison Management and Prison Order; Sykes, Gresham M.: Deprivation Theory; Toch, Hans: Coping in Prison

References and Further Readings

Goldstone, J. A., & Useem, B. (1999). Prison riots as microrevolutions: An extension of state-centered theories of revolution. *American Journal of Sociology, 104*, 985–1029.

Skopcol, T. (1979). *States and social revolutions.* Cambridge, UK: Cambridge University Press.

Useem, B. (1985). Disorganization and the New Mexico prison riot of 1980. *American Sociological Review, 50*, 677–688.

Useem, B., & Goldstone, J. A. (2002). Forging social order and its breakdown: Riot and reform in U.S. prisons. *American Sociological Review, 67*, 499–524.

Useem, B., Graham-Camp, C., & Camp, G. M. (1996). *Resolution of prison riots: Strategies and policies.* New York: Oxford University Press.

Useem, B., & Kimball, P. A. (1987). A theory of prison riots. *Theory and Society, 16*, 87–122.

Useem, B., & Kimball, P. A. (1989). *States of siege: U.S. prison riots, 1971–1986.* New York: Oxford University Press.

Useem, B., & Reisig, M. D. (1999). Collective action in prisons: Protests, disturbances, and riots. *Criminology, 37*, 735–759.

PSYCHOPHYSIOLOGY AND CRIME

Psychophysiological research has contributed to a significant empirical understanding of the biological mechanisms underlying crime. There is now little scientific doubt that genes play a significant role in antisocial behavior. With the advantages of ease of data collection (especially heart rate) and their noninvasive features, psychophysiological measures have proved to be valuable in filling the gap between genetic risk for crime and the brain abnormalities that give rise to antisocial, violent, and psychopathic behavior in some people.

Most psychophysiological research has assessed autonomic and central nervous system functioning at a baseline level or in response to external stimuli using measures such as skin conductance activity, heart rate, startle blink, electroencephalography (EEG), and event-related potentials (ERPs). The psychophysiological correlates of criminality are summarized in the following sections: autonomic arousal, orienting, fear conditioning, emotion modulation, and EEG/ERPs. In each section, empirical findings are first summarized and followed by theoretical interpretations. Finally, important issues including biosocial interactions, protective factors, and crime prevention/intervention are briefly described.

Autonomic Arousal

Empirical Findings

Skin conductance is measured from electrodes placed on the fingers or palm of the hand and is controlled exclusively by the sympathetic nervous system. Skin conductance activity captures small fluctuations in the electrical activity of the skin, with enhanced conductivity (i.e., activity) elicited by increased sweating. It reflects both arousal (levels and number of non-specific skin conductance responses) and responsivity (e.g., reactivity to neutral or emotional stimuli). Heart rate measures the number of heart beats per minute. It includes resting levels and phasic activity (reactivity to external stimuli) and reflects the complex interactions between sympathetic and parasympathetic nervous system activity.

Studies on both criminal and community populations have generally indicated that antisocial individuals are characterized by autonomic underarousal as indicated by low skin conductance activity and low resting heart rate. Fewer nonspecific skin conductance responses and reduced skin conductance levels have been found in nonpsychopathic antisocial individuals in comparison to the normal controls. In 1993, Adrian Raine conducted a review of arousal studies conducted since 1978 and reported that 4 of 10 studies conducted found significant effects for lower skin conductance levels and/or fewer non-specific

responses among antisocials. Specifically, a 1992 prospective study by Kruesi et al. has also shown that in a sample of behavior disordered children, low skin conductance levels measured at age 11 years predict institutionalization at age 13 years. In sum, although not all studies reveal skin conductance underarousal in antisocials, there is some evidence associating low skin conductance activity with general antisocial behavior.

Of all psychophysiological research on antisocial behavior, the best replicated finding appears to be that of lower resting heart rate in noninstitutionalized antisocial populations (Ortiz & Raine, 2004), particularly in children and adolescents. This low heart rate–antisociality association is found to be unique and robust. No other psychiatric condition—such as alcoholism, depression, schizophrenia, and anxiety—is characterized by reduced heart rate. In addition, studies have generally indicated that this association is not confounded by factors such as physical size, exercise and sports activity level, excess motor activity and inattention, substance abuse, intellect and academic achievement, and various forms of psychosocial adversity. This low heart rate–antisocial behavior relationship has also been found across countries and cultural contexts. Finally, longitudinal studies have suggested that lower resting heart rate as early as age 3 years may be an early risk factor for the later development of aggressive and antisocial behavior (Raine et al., 1997).

Theoretical Interpretation

Stimulation seeking and fearlessness theories have been proposed to interpret autonomic underarousal in antisocials. The stimulation seeking theory assumes that there are individual differences in arousal levels and that arousal levels are consistently lower in criminals than in non-criminals. These antisocials bring their arousal to an optimal level by engaging in pathological stimulation-seeking behaviors, including aggressive and antisocial behavior.

Alternatively, fearlessness theory proposes that higher heart rate and skin conductance levels indicate fearfulness and higher anxiety. Fearlessness or lack of anxiety is argued to be a prerequisite for engaging in disruptive behavior because fearless individuals are less concerned about negative outcomes from their actions. In this framework, lack of fear or anxiety, indicated by autonomic underarousal, may reduce the effectiveness of punishment, impede socialization processes, and eventually predispose individuals to antisocial behavior.

Orienting

Empirical Findings

Orienting responses deficits have also been implicated in antisocial individuals. When presented with a novel stimulus in one's environment, an individual normally shows an orienting response (a "what is it" response) together with increased autonomic activity (e.g., enhanced skin conductance levels). This skin conductance orienting response has been considered to indicate the degree of information processing in that larger skin conductance reactivity is associated with better attention allocation and information processing—and thus with better functioning of the nervous system in response to an external stimuli.

Evidence has linked orienting response deficits with antisocial behavior, especially in psychopathic, antisocial, and criminal subjects who also exhibit schizotypal features, such as paranoia, reduced emotionality, and inability to make close friends. The cognitive deficits indexed by reduced orienting responses may contribute to fear conditioning deficits discussed later. Lack of attentional processing to initially neutral stimuli that warn of impending punishment would be expected to result in poorer conditioning. Similarly, lack of orienting may also partly account for underarousal, since arousal reflects tonic levels of activity, which may in part be a function of moment-to-moment responsivity to events in the environment.

Theoretical Interpretation

Prefrontal deficits may contribute to both reduced skin conductance orienting responses and antisocial behavior. Brain imaging studies have revealed decreased skin conductance orienting responses in relation to reduced prefrontal cortex volume and function. Together with evidence of prefrontal deficits in antisocial and schizophrenic individuals as uncovered by brain imaging and neuropsychological research (Raine & Yang, 2006), this prefrontal abnormality may give rise to both autonomic orienting deficits and antisocial behavior, especially in the violent individuals with schizotypal features.

Fear Conditioning

Empirical Findings

Fear conditioning is a form of Pavlovian conditioning through which individuals learn the social significance of previously neutral stimuli through a process of association. In a typical classical conditioning paradigm, the neutral stimulus initially elicits no emotional reaction. However, after repeated pairings with the unconditioned stimulus (UCS), the neutral stimulus becomes a conditioned stimulus (CS) and obtains the potential to elicit a conditioned response (CR). Normally, after a number of trials, the CS signals the UCS onset and induces emotions associated with the anticipation of the aversive UCS. For example, stealing cookies (CS) or even the thought of stealing cookies will eventually elicit distress (UCR) after repeatedly paired with punishment (UCS) in children and this distress or fear is thought to deter them from stealing. In this context, conditioning deficits may result in the failure to associate punishment and disruptive behavior and predispose individuals to antisocial behavior.

Fear conditioning in humans has been most frequently studied using skin conductance measures. When classical conditioning is assessed using skin conductance, a neutral, non-aversive tone (CS) is presented to the subject, followed a few seconds later by either a loud tone or an electric shock (UCS). The key measure is the size of the skin conductance response elicited by the CS after a number of CS-UCS pairings. The larger the response to the CS after pairing with the UCS, the better the conditioning.

Empirical studies have consistently shown that poor skin conductance fear conditioning is associated with aggressive and antisocial behavior in children and adult populations. Specifically, one longitudinal study by Yu Gao et al. has also revealed that poor skin conductance conditioning at age 3 years is linked to more aggressive behavior at age 8 years and also predispose individuals to criminal behavior at age 23 years. In sum, poor conditioning may play a significant role in the development of antisocial behavior.

Theoretical Interpretation

Reduced classical fear conditioning has been a key concept in theories of aggressive/antisocial behavior and crime. Hans Eysenck conceptualized a conscience as a set of classically conditioned emotional responses that is developed relatively early in life, and that there are individual differences in the degree to which individuals develop a conscience. Individuals with good fear conditioning develop a conscience that deters them from antisocial and aggressive behavior. In probabilistic terms, the greater the individual's capability to develop conditioned fear responses, the greater the conscience development and the lower will be the probability of becoming aggressive and antisocial.

The somatic marker hypothesis was initially proposed by Antonio Damasio in 1994 to account for the poor social decision making observed in antisocial, sociopathic individuals. Based on this theory, the individual's ability to generate emotions is manifested as alterations in physiological state and registered in the brain as changes in somatosensory region activation. Damasio posited that conditioned emotional responses facilitate enhanced decision making by reducing the number of options from which to choose. The reduction occurs when an individual experiences uneasy feelings conditioned during prior negative experiences with that option, resulting in their intuitively or deliberately deciding to eliminate it from further consideration. As a result, inappropriate decisions are generally excluded, and cognitive resources—particularly frontal functions such as planning flexibility and working memory—are freed up to evaluate only those options that are viable to that individual. The risk for antisocial behavior is elevated when an individual cannot generate or does not appreciate the significance of somatic markers. The findings of deficient skin conductance conditioning in aggressive individuals, and the enhanced autonomic functioning observed in at-risk individuals who avoid crime, fit particularly well within this model. Low resting heart rate in antisocial individuals may similarly reflect disruption in the somatic marker network and consequently increase risk-related behavior.

Emotion Modulation

Emotion modulation deficits have been mainly examined using startle blink measures. Startle blink activity measures the automatic eye-blink response that occurs to a startling probe stimulus such as a loud noise or a puff of air to the eye. The magnitude of the startle blink response varies with the valence of an ongoing emotional state; presentation of pleasant stimuli is typically found to attenuate and unpleasant stimuli to potentiate the startle response compared with presentation of neutral stimuli. Moreover, because the startle response is a reflex, it is thought to index emotional reactions at a very basic and primitive level. Startle potentiation (i.e., increased startle magnitude) is thought to reflect defensive reactivity, negative affect, and temperamental differences in negative emotionality.

Startle potentiation deficits have been found in criminal and non-criminal male psychopathic samples as well as in women with psychopathy. For example, in 1993 Patrick, Bradley, and Lang conducted a study of criminals who were classified according to their level of antisocial behavior and emotional detachment; in this study criminals with high emotional detachment (including psychopaths) exhibited reduced startle potentiation while anticipating an aversive stimulus, whereas criminals with low emotional detachment exhibited robust startle potentiation. These findings suggest that psychopaths display a core emotional deficit in fear potentiation and defensive response modulation. This has been interpreted as suggesting that the core personality traits of psychopathy are associated with the temperamental predisposition of reduced responsivity to emotional cues, especially if they are aversive or threatening.

EEG and ERPs

EEG and ERP are two frequently used psychophysiological measures in studies of central nervous system functioning in antisocial individuals.

Slow-Wave EEG and Underarousal

EEG data are collected by putting a standardized array of surface electrodes on an individual's scalp, and reflect regional electrical activity of the brain. The different power bands—delta, theta, alpha, beta—are associated with increasing degrees of consciousness or arousal. For example, individuals with high levels of cortical activity show a predominance of fast alpha and beta wave whereas in individuals with low cortical activity, theta and delta waves are predominant.

A large number of studies have implicated EEG abnormalities in criminal individuals. The most commonly reported findings are more slow-wave (i.e., theta and delta) EEG—reflecting underarousal—especially in frontal and temporal regions of the brain. Specifically, evidence has emerged that increased slow-wave EEG activity in adolescence predicts official criminal convictions later in life (Raine et al., 1990). This excessive slow-wave EEG may indicate cortical immaturity resulting in impaired inhibitory control, or cortical underarousal that predisposes toward compensatory stimulation seeking, which eventually gives rise to emotional and behavioral dysregulation in those prone to criminal behavior.

Frontal Asymmetry

Another line of research concerns frontal EEG asymmetry in antisocial individuals. Frontal asymmetry has been widely used as a measure of underlying approach-related or withdrawal-related behavioral tendencies and affective style in children and adults. In general, relatively greater left frontal activity (i.e., relatively reduced left alpha power) is suggested to be associated with positive affect and/or approach motivation and behavior, whereas relatively greater right frontal activity (i.e., relatively reduced right alpha power) is related to negative affect and/or withdrawal motivation and behavioral patterns.

Some studies, such as Santesso et al., have associated atypical frontal asymmetry with externalizing behavior in children and with anger proneness and aggressive traits in adults. These associations, however, may vary based on gender and social factors. In general, atypical frontal EEG asymmetry may indicate abnormal emotional reactivity and affective style that give rise to the disruptive behavior seen in antisocials and criminals.

ERPs

The ERP refers to averaged changes in the electrical activity of the brain in response to external stimuli. The most consistent association has been found for abnormal P300. This is a positive-going waveform occurring approximately 300 milliseconds after a stimulus, which is thought to represent deployment of neural resources to task-relevant or novel information. Reduced P300 amplitude and longer P300 latency are characteristics of non-psychopathic antisocials. In contrast, the findings on P300 and psychopathy have been inconsistent. In fact, P300 deficits have also been associated with other externalizing behavior problem, including drug abuse, child conduct disorder, and attention deficit hyperactivity disorder (Patrick, 2008). Therefore, it is possible that the P300 abnormality may be a psychophysiological indicator of the broad externalizing behavior characterized by impulse control problems.

Important Issues

Biosocial Interaction

Although psychophysiological research has enabled scientists to uncover various biological underpinnings of antisocial and violent behavior, it is critical to bear in mind that it is the complex interplay among a variety of factors—including biological, environmental, and social influences—that predispose some individuals to engage in antisocial behavior. For example, it has been reported that boys with a low resting heart rate are more likely to be rated as aggressive by their teachers if their mother was pregnant as teenager, if they were from a low social class family, or if they were separated from a parent before age 10. They are also more likely to become adult violent criminals if they also have a poor relationship with their parents and come from a large family, according to David Farrington.

Alternatively, a number of studies have found that psychophysiological factors, particularly measures of skin conductance and heart rate, reveal stronger relationships to antisocial behavior in those from benign social backgrounds that lack the classic psychosocial risk factors for crime (Raine, 2002). For example, studies have shown that poor skin conductance conditioning is a characteristic for antisocial individuals from relatively good social backgrounds (Hemming, 1981; Raine & Venables, 1981). Specifically, low heart rate at age 3 years has been found to predict aggression at age 11 years in children from high but not low social classes (Raine et al., 1997). These findings, as argued by the "social push" hypothesis, suggest that psychophysiological risk factors may assume greater importance when social predispositions to crime are minimized. In contrast, social causes may be more important explanations of antisocial behavior in those exposed to adverse early home conditions (Raine, 2002).

Protective Factors

Some studies have focused on psychophysiological correlates as protective factors against antisocial and criminal behavior. For example, in a prospective longitudinal study, 15-year-old antisocial adolescents who did not become criminals by age 29 showed higher resting heart rate levels, higher skin conductance arousal, and better skin conductance conditioning when compared to their antisocial counterparts who became adult criminals (Raine et al., 1995, 1996). In Brennan et al.'s study on adolescents who had criminal fathers and thus were at higher risk for antisocial outcomes, those who desisted from crime had higher skin conductance and heart rate orienting reactivity in comparison with those who eventually became criminals. Therefore, enhanced autonomic nervous system functioning, as indexed by higher levels of arousal, better conditioning, and higher orienting responses, may serve as biological protective factors that reduce the likelihood that an individual will become an adult criminal.

Crime Prevention and Intervention

Efforts have been made to integrate biological findings into prevention and intervention programs. One line of research concerns directly altering one's psychophysiological functioning. For example, in one longitudinal study, better nutrition, more physical exercise, and cognitive stimulation from ages 3 to 5 years was shown to produce long-term psychophysiological changes 6 years later at age 11 years, including increased skin conductance level, more orienting, and a more aroused EEG profile. This environmental enrichment was also found to reduce criminal offending at age 23 years (Raine et al., 2003; Raine et al., 2001).

Future prevention and intervention programs could be improved by acknowledging the importance of biological moderators and differentiating subgroups based on their psychophysiological characteristics. For example, Stadler et al. found that a cognitive-behavioral intervention program for children with disruptive behavior problems (aggression, delinquency, and attention problems) was of greater benefit to children with high heart rate levels compared to those with low heart rate levels. Similarly, in a pilot study on adolescents at high risk for drug abuse, conducted by Fishbein et al., individuals who are unresponsive to interventions demonstrated fewer skin conductance responses to two boring and tedious tasks (continuous performance test and delay of gratification) and higher skin conductance responses to the risky choices in a more stimulating task, relative to those who had better responses to the intervention program.

Conclusion

In general, antisocial individuals are characterized by (1) autonomic underarousal as indicated by reduced skin conductance non-specific responses, lower skin conductance levels, and lower resting heart rate; (2) poor skin conductance fear conditioning; (3) more slow-wave EEG and atypical frontal EEG asymmetry; and (4) abnormal P300 patterns as reflected by reduced P300 amplitude and longer P300 latency. Skin conductance orienting deficits in antisocials may be more specific to those who also have schizotypal features, whereas the emotion modulation deficits as indicated by impaired startle potentiation are associated with psychopathic traits, especially the emotional detachment feature. Psychophysiological risk factors interact with psychosocial variables in predisposing certain individuals to antisocial and criminal behavior. Meanwhile, evidence of psychophysiological protective factors against the development of antisocial behavior has emerged. Finally, prevention and intervention programs aimed at reducing antisocial behavior would benefit enormously by targeting their efforts on selected individuals based on their psychophysiological characteristics or by directly improving their psychophysiological functioning. Certain psychophysiological measures, including heart rate activity, can be recorded relatively easily (e.g., using portable equipment or taking a pulse), and as such they are especially valuable to the criminologists who are attempting to explore the biological etiology of crime.

Yu Gao and Adrian Raine

See also Brain Abnormalities and Crime; Fishbein, Diana H.: Biosocial Theory; Hare, Robert D.: Psychopathy and Crime; Lahey, Benjamin B., and Irwin D. Waldman: Developmental Propensity Model; Mednick, Sarnoff A.: Autonomic Nervous System (ANS) Theory; Neurology and Crime; Raine, Adrian: Crime as a Disorder

References and Further Readings

Brennan, P. A., Raine, A., Schulsinger, F., Kirkegaard-Sorensen, L., Knop, J., Hutchings, B., et al. (1997). Psychophysiological protective factors for male subjects at high risk for criminal behavior. *American Journal of Psychiatry, 154,* 853–855.

Damasio, A. R. (1994). *Descartes' error: Emotion, reason, and the human brain.* New York: Grosset/Putnam.

Farrington, D. P. (1997). The relationship between low resting heart rate and violence. In A. Raine, P. A. Brennan, D. P. Farrington, & S. A. Mednick (Eds.), *Biosocial bases of violence* (pp. 89–106). New York: Plenum Press.

Fishbein, D., Hyde, C., Coe, B., & Paschall, M. J. (2004). Neurocognitive and physiological prerequisites for prevention of adolescent drug abuse. *Journal of Primary Prevention, 24,* 471–495.

Gao, Y., Raine, A., Venables, P. H., Dawson, M. E., & Mednick, S. A. (2010). Association of poor childhood fear conditioning and adult crime. *American Journal of Psychiatry, 167,* 56–60.

Gao, Y., Raine, A., Venables, P. H., Dawson, M. E., & Mednick, S. A. (in press). Reduced electrodermal fear conditioning from ages 3 to 8 years is associated with aggressive behavior at age 8 years. *Journal of Child Psychology and Psychiatry.*

Harmon-Jones, E. (2003). Clarifying the emotive functions of asymmetrical frontal cortical activity. *Psychophysiology, 40,* 838–848.

Hemming, J. H. (1981). Electrodermal indices in a selected prison sample and students. *Personality and Individual Differences, 2,* 37–46.

Kruesi, M. J. P., Hibbs, E. D., Zahn, T. P., Keysor, C. S., Hamburger, S. D., Bartko, J. J., et al. (1992). A 2-year prospective follow-up study of children and adolescents with disruptive behavior disorders. *Archives of General Psychiatry, 49,* 429–435.

Lorber, M. F. (2004). Psychophysiology of aggression, psychopathy, and conduct problems: A meta-analysis. *Psychological Bulletin, 130,* 531–552.

Ortiz, J., & Raine, A. (2004). Heart rate level and antisocial behavior in children and adolescents: A meta-analysis. *Journal of American Academy of Child and Adolescent Psychiatry, 43,* 154–162.

Patrick, C. J. (1994). Emotion and psychopathy: Startling new insights. *Psychophysiology, 31,* 319–330.

Patrick, C. J. (2008). Psychophysiological correlates of aggression and violence: An integrative review. *Philosophical Transactions of the Royal Society, 363,* 2543–2555.

Patrick, C. J., Bradley, M. M., & Lang, P. J. (1993). Emotion in the criminal psychopath: Startle reflex modulation. *Journal of Abnormal Psychology, 102,* 82–92.

Raine, A. (1993). *The psychopathology of crime.* London: Academic Press.

Raine, A. (1996). Autonomic nervous system activity and violence. In D. M. Stoff & R. B. Cairns (Eds.), *Aggression and violence: Genetic, neurobiological, and biosocial perspective* (pp. 145–168). Mahwah, NJ: Lawrence Erlbaum.

Raine, A. (2002). Biosocial studies of antisocial and violent behavior in children and adults: A review. *Journal of Abnormal Child Psychology, 30,* 311–326.

Raine, A., Brennan, P. A., Farrington, D. P., & Mednick, S. A. (1996). *Biosocial bases of violence.* New York: Plenum Press.

Raine, A., Mellingen, K., Liu, J., Venables, P. H., & Mednick, S. A. (2003). Effects of environmental enrichment at ages 3–5 years on schizotypal personality and antisocial behavior at ages 17 and 23 years. *American Journal of Psychiatry, 160,* 1627–1635.

Raine, A., & Venables, P. H. (1981). Classical conditioning and socialization—A biosocial interaction. *Personality and Individual Differences, 2,* 273–283.

Raine, A., Venables, P. H., Dalais, C., Mellingen, K., Reynolds, C., & Mendrek, A. (2001). Early educational and health enrichment at age 3–5 years is associated with increased autonomic and central nervous system arousal and orienting at age 11 years: Evidence from the Mauritius Child Health Project. *Psychophysiology, 38,* 254–266.

Raine, A., Venables, P. H., & Mednick, S. A. (1997). Low resting heart rate age 3 years predisposes to aggression at age 11 years: Evidence from the Mauritius Child Health Project. *Journal of American Academy of Child and Adolescent Psychiatry, 36,* 1457–1464.

Raine, A., Venables, P. H., & Williams, M. (1990). Relationships between CNS and ANS measures of arousal at age 15 and criminality at age 24. *Archives of General Psychiatry, 47,* 1003–1007.

Raine, A., Venables, P. H., & Williams, M. (1995). High autonomic arousal and electrodermal orienting at age 15 years as protective factors against criminal behavior at age 29 years. *American Journal of Psychiatry, 152,* 1595–1600.

Raine, A., Venables, P. H., & Williams, M. (1996). Better autonomic conditioning and faster electrodermal half-recovery time at age 15 years as possible protective factors against crime at age 29 years. *Developmental Psychology, 32,* 624–630.

Raine, A., & Yang, Y. (2006). Neural foundations to moral reasoning and antisocial behavior. *Social, Cognitive, and Affective Neuroscience, 1,* 203–213.

Santesso, D. L., Reker, D. L., Schmidt, L. A., & Segalowitz, S. J. (2006). Frontal electroencephalogram activation asymmetry, emotional intelligence, and externalizing behaviors in 10-year-old children. *Child Psychiatry and Human Development, 36,* 311–328.

Stadler, C., Grasmann, D., Fegert, J. M., Holtmann, M., Poustka, F., & Schmeck, K. (2008). Heart rate and treatment effect in children with disruptive behavior disorders. *Child Psychiatry and Human Development, 39,* 299–309.

QUETELET, ADOLPHE: EXPLAINING CRIME THROUGH STATISTICAL AND CARTOGRAPHIC TECHNIQUES

Adolphe Quetelet was one of the first to explore official data on populations and crime. He is best known in criminology for his application of statistics and maps to describe crime patterns and trends in locations and the characteristics of offenders (using the term *social mechanics*). His important findings regarding the spatiotemporal distribution of crime provide the foundation for criminologist's interest in crime and place. Finally, as Terence Morris notes, his shift in emphasis from criminal motivation to crime as primarily a socioeconomic phenomenon with individual behavior as one element set the stage for the development of opportunity-based theories of crime such as routine activity theory and environmental criminology.

Quetelet in Context

Quetelet made his contributions to criminology before the discipline officially existed. He was born in Belgium and worked in 1820s France/Belgium during a period of social unrest that culminated in the French Revolution. When he began his career, information on social phenomena was almost non-existent. Paul Lazarsfeld notes that two major barriers to coordinated, state-sponsored data collection existed: a populace who viewed attempts to conduct a census as precursors to increased taxes, and governments who treated any data about their population as a military secret. The French Revolution served as a turning point for these concerns. As some of the revolutionary governments came into power, the public was given access to census data. The application of statistics to social data was in its infancy in the social sciences, and research on criminal behavior was conducted via description rather than measurement. This was the context in which Quetelet's ideas were formed.

As a young man, Quetelet was interested in the arts and literature. At approximately 20, his interests took an abrupt turn when he met a mathematician who influenced him to study mathematics. After receiving his doctorate, Quetelet began to teach mathematics and became interested in starting an astronomical observatory in Brussels. In 1923, he was sent to Paris to learn what equipment would be needed for the observatory. While in Paris, he met Joseph Fourier and Pierre-Simon Laplace, two French mathematicians, and learned of their work with probability theory. Both these mentors had previously worked with social data in addition to astronomical data. Quetelet immediately began to think about how he could apply statistics to the measurement of the human body. From these efforts, he developed the body mass index (BMI) for measuring obesity which is still used today. The finding of a regularity measure across individuals set the stage for his application of statistics to social data.

Applying Statistics to Social Phenomena

Quetelet believed that general causes could be identified for human behavior just as they were used to identify laws for physical behavior. His involvement in the planning of the Belgian population census provided the basis for his explorations of population and crime statistics. In the course of investigating social data from the census, he began to notice patterns in both the rates and the distribution of characteristics across a population. The distribution closely resembled the error distributions that he had learned about from Fourier and Laplace. He began to apply the law of error being used to measure physical phenomena in astronomy to social characteristics. In doing so, he became the first to apply probability theory to social phenomena. As a result of this application he also recognized the power of using the normal curve to understand empirical distributions rather than as only an error law.

Based on his findings he created a new field of analysis, social mechanics, which focused on mapping and analyzing physical and social characteristics of people. George B. Vold and colleagues note this term most likely was drawn from celestial mechanics, which studies regularities in data describing the physical environment. To inform his investigations he collected and analyzed a variety of characteristics from several countries. At first, he concentrated on describing the physical characteristics of the population. He "calculated the average weight and height of his subjects, cross-tabulated these with sex, age, occupation, and geographical region and then submitted these correlations to the perturbational influence" of social class and other factors (Beirne, 1987, p. 1151). In doing so, he demonstrated the regularities found in the physical world also existed in the physical characteristics of humans and in the social world when large numbers of empirical observations were used. The more observations used, the greater the accuracy of the average in describing the population.

These findings led him to believe that, given enough data, he could develop representative portraits of the typical "average man" for each country and for all humans. In his classic work *Research on the Propensity for Crime at Different Ages*, Quetelet states, "If the *average man* were ascertained for one nation, he would present the type of that nation. If he could be ascertained according to the mass of men, he would present the type of the human species altogether" (p. 3, emphasis in the original). Piers Beirne says Quetelet saw this portrait of the average man across all nations as analogous to the center of gravity in the physical sciences. At the same time, Quetelet was careful to point out general laws which hold true for large groups cannot be applied to individuals. This was an important distinction later empirically demonstrated by William Robinson. While Quetelet began social mechanics with physical characteristics, he soon branched out to include social phenomena such as suicide, marriage, and crime. These social phenomena, termed *moral statistics*, were already being studied by other Franco-Belgian statisticians most notably André-Michel Guerry.

Quetelet on Crime

In 1827, the first statistical information on crime was published in the *Comte général de administration de la justice criminelle en France* (*General Administration of Criminal Justice in France*). When data about crime became available, Quetelet was able to analyze it and conclude that crime followed the same type of patterned behavior as physical phenomena. Quetelet also discovered relative constancy across time in "the ratios of the number of accused to convicted and of accused to inhabitants, and of crime against persons to crimes against property" among others (Beirne, 1987, p. 1153). This finding was not in agreement with what the classical and neoclassical traditions of crime causation. They held that people possess free will and their decisions are rationally based. However, if crime was a result of free will there should have been far more variability in crime rates. In this way, Quetelet's research findings began to place him in the center of a heated, long-term debate between those who subscribed to free will and those who subscribed to social determinism.

Quetelet on Criminal Propensity and the Correlates of Crime

Having established the stability of crime rates across time, Quetelet began to examine the characteristics of offenders. He found individuals who were young, male, poor, uneducated, or unemployed were the most likely to be arrested and convicted of a crime. At the same time, some of the lowest crime areas were those with the highest concentrations of poverty and unemployment. In combination, these findings led him to conclude the residents of these areas were traveling to wealthier areas to commit their crimes. His integration of opportunity into the discussion of crime presaged the later appearance of opportunity-based theories of the late 20th century.

Characteristics such as education and poverty were less important to causing crime because their effects were contingent on other factors. For example, Quetelet believed that it was not poverty that drove criminal behavior but inequality. More specifically, it was situations in which great wealth and great inequality existed in the same place that produced more crime. Where all were poor but still able to survive, crime remained low. He also found that increased education did not uniformly decrease crime. More highly educated individuals tended to commit violent crime while less educated individuals committed property crime.

Quetelet identified the two most important factors in the propensity toward crime as sex and age. Males were four times as likely to be involved in crime. Digging deeper, he noted that the difference in the ratio of women to men for crimes against persons was much greater than for property crimes. Further investigation of the ages of criminals revealed an early version of Darrell Steffensmeier and colleagues' now-familiar age-crime curve. Criminal propensity was highest between ages 21 and 25 and then dropped off slowly at first and more rapidly with increasing age. Again the significance of these patterns was in identifying stable characteristics associated with criminal behavior.

These findings led him to make his most famous and controversial statement. Given the stability of crime types and the characteristics of individual's committing them, Quetelet saw crime as a relatively constant outcome of social conditions and thus society in general. "The crimes which are annually committed seem to be a necessary result of our social organization. . . . *Society prepares crime, and the guilty are only the instruments by which it is executed*" (Quetelet, 1831/1984, p. 108, as quoted in Beirne, 1987, p. 1158, emphasis in the original). With this statement Quetelet was only expressing his acknowledgment of the influence of both individual and social factors on criminal behavior. However, free-will adherents were outraged. They interpreted his statement as a rejection of individual decision making. Quetelet frequently tried to explain his position—that

individuals make decisions that are influenced by individual and social conditions—so as to quell these complaints. But he enjoyed little success.

In his later work, Quetelet increasingly relied on the normal distribution. Based on the normal distribution, he inferred "every man, therefore has a certain propensity to break the laws" (Quetelet, 1831/1984, p. 94) but that these propensities were rarely acted on. He moved beyond averages and began using the normal distribution to calculate the upper and lower bounds of "normal" changes in the values. Values within these limits were considered to be normal while those outside were classified as deviant. This led him to see the average man as law-abiding with a particular moral disposition that included moderate alcohol consumption, investments, and saving regularly. Those outside the statistical limits for the average man were the opposite (e.g., drunkards, gamblers, unemployed). Beirne notes that since Quetelet saw low moral values as one of the causes of crime his policy recommendations were to continue the implementation of Cesare Beccaria's suggestions for reform but also to improve education related to morals and address social ills. Later in his career, Quetelet increasingly mentioned biological origins of the individual and social facts that were correlated with criminal behavior. In this way, his research (along with others) became the basis for Cesare Lombroso's later work on biological causes.

Quetelet also discussed the twin roles of temptation and opportunity in determining whether an individual will commit a crime. The number of crimes committed is related to the number of individuals who are exposed to favorable circumstances "whether through the existence of objects suitable to excite *temptation* or through the *ease* of committing crime. It is not sufficient, in fact, that man had the intention to do evil. It is necessary, besides, that he have the opportunity and the means for it" (Quetelet, 1831/1984, p. 16, emphasis in the original). These factors would form the basis for the rational choice perspective and more general opportunity theories of crime.

Contributions to Theoretical Development of Place-Based Criminology

In addition to his contributions to the development of sociology, Quetelet's mapping of crime data, along with that of Guerry and others, is widely acknowledged to have set the stage examining the place-based aspects of crime. Quetelet was instrumental in originating what Kevin Courtright and Robert Mutchinick have identified as the cartographic school of criminology and David Weisburd and colleagues have called place-based criminology.

The making of maps was a key development because it allowed the exploration of the spatial pattern of crime. Specifically, maps enabled researchers to ask questions such as Is crime spread evenly throughout France or is it concentrated in only a few areas? If some places have more crime than others, what might explain those differences? Maps also allowed Quetelet to make associations between major water transportation routes and criminal activity. Additionally, Quetelet examined the influence of climate on the propensity for criminal activity. By using the total number and rate of crime in "departments" (roughly the size of counties in the United States), he created maps of the distribution of crime across France. Darker shading on the map represented places where the number of crimes committed was above the average for France. Lighter shading represented places which were below the average rate of crime. By mapping the data, he was able to deduce general patterns in the geographical variation in the number of both crimes against persons and crimes against property. Crimes against persons were highest in the south of France and in Corsica. Crimes against property were highest in the northern part of France.

As Paul and Patricia Brantingham note, the mapping of the early 19th century provided a set of consistent findings which formed the foundation for place-based criminology. First among these was that crime is concentrated in a few areas rather than uniformly distributed. Second as evidenced by the distribution of property and person crime, different crimes have different spatial patterns. Third, the concentrations of crime are related to social characteristics. Fourth, spatial patterns of crime were relatively stable over time.

Quetelet may be surprised at the progression of criminological theory since his time. David Weisburd and Tom McEwen observe that difficulties in collecting additional data and challenges in map making proved to be significant technical obstacles to further development of cartographic criminology. At the same time, a general movement toward positivism shifted the focus to individual and biological causes of crime. Until the Chicago School of the 1920s, there was very little development in the analysis of the spatial/place-based elements of crime. In the 1920s and 1930s, members of the Chicago School began studying the ecology of juvenile delinquency but at a much smaller level of analysis, the neighborhood. Like Quetelet, they examined both temporal stability and spatial distributions. Unlike Quetelet, they focused on the distribution of juvenile delinquents' home addresses across the neighborhood of a single city.

Chicago School theorists such as Ernest Burgess and Robert Park resurrected the study of place and crime and extended it to show how the morphology of the growth cities was related to the patterns of crime that occurred. Because of the emphasis on similarities between growth and change in organisms and growth and change in cities, this line of inquiry became known as ecological criminology. In addition to showing a link between social characteristics of neighborhoods and juvenile delinquency, Clifford Shaw and Henry McKay also found that delinquency was concentrated in relatively few neighborhoods rather than spread throughout the city. Also similar to Quetelet, their data showed that levels of juvenile delinquency in neighborhoods tended to be relatively stable over time. However, their work added the knowledge that the stability of crime patterns persisted even if the people living within those neighborhoods changed. Although they were studying different countries, at different scales and in different centuries, Shaw and McKay's findings reinforced the major findings of Quetelet from 100 years prior. Despite these revolutionary findings, ecological influences on criminal behavior fell out of favor, and the discipline of criminology returned to a focus on individuals rather than places. It was not until the 1950s and 1960s when researchers such as Terence Morris, Calvin Schmid, and Sarah Boggs began to look once again at ecology and the spatial patterns of crimes and criminals.

Perhaps the final contribution of Quetelet that remains to be recognized (although it was alluded to earlier) is as a foundation for the development of opportunity theories of crime. In the early 1970s, Paul and Patricia Brantingham began to examine the role of human behavior patterns as they related to crime. At the same time, C. Ray

Jeffrey and Oscar Newman began studying how changes in the physical design could prevent crime. Ronald Clarke's situational crime prevention grew out of these efforts. All of these perspectives are based upon the assumption that opportunity is the foundation for crime patterns. Thus, they draw directly from Quetelet's earlier observations about the roles of opportunity and temptation in fostering crime events. It was the theoretical, methodological, and empirical contributions of Quetelet which provided the basis for the development of place-based criminology in the late 21st century.

Elizabeth R. Groff

See also Brantingham, Patricia L., and Paul J. Brantingham: Environmental Criminology; Clarke, Ronald V.: Situational Crime Prevention; Cohen, Lawrence E., and Marcus K. Felson: Routine Activity Theory; Cornish, Derek B., and Ronald V. Clarke: Rational Choice Theory; Eck, John E.: Places and the Crime Triangle; Lombroso, Cesare: The Criminal Man

References and Further Readings

Beirne, P. (1987). Adolphe Quetelet and the origins of positivist criminology. *American Journal of Sociology, 92*(5), 1140–1169.

Brantingham, P. J., & Brantingham, P. L. (1991). *Environmental criminology.* Prospect Heights, IL: Waveland Press. (Original work published 1981)

Courtright, K. E., & Mutchnick, R. J. (2002). Cartographic school of criminology. In D. Levinson (Ed.), *Encyclopedia of crime and punishment* (pp. 175–177). Thousand Oaks, CA: Sage.

Lazarsfeld, P. F. (1961). Notes on the history of quantification in sociology—trends, sources and problems. *Isis, 52,* 277–333.

Morris, T. (1957). *The criminal area.* New York: Routledge and Kegan Paul.

O'Connor, J. J., & Robertson, E. F. (2009). Lambert Adolphe Jacques Quetelet [Electronic version]. Retrieved April 1, 2009, from http://www-groups.dcs .st-and.ac.uk/~history/Biographies/Quetelet.html

Quetelet, A. J. (1842). *A treatise on man and the development of his faculties* (T. Smibert, Trans.). New York: Burt Franklin.

Quetelet, A. J. (1969). *A treatise of man.* Gainesville, FL: Scholar's Facsimiles and Reprints. (Original work published 1842)

Quetelet, A. J. (1984). *Research on the propensity for crime at different ages* (S. F. Test Sylvester, Trans.).

Cincinnati, OH: Anderson. (Original work published 1831)

Vold, G. B., Bernard, T.J., & Snipes, J. B. (2002). *Theoretical criminology.* Oxford, UK: Oxford University Press.

Weisburd, D. L., Bruinsma, G., & Bernasco, W. (2008). Units of analysis in geographic criminology: Historical development, critical issues and open questions. In D. Weisburd, W. Bernasco, & G. Bruinsma (Eds.), *Putting crime in its place: Units of analysis in spatial crime research* (pp. 3–31). New York: Springer-Verlag.

Weisburd, D. L., & McEwen, T. (1997). Introduction: Crime mapping and crime prevention. In D. L. Weisburd & T. McEwen (Eds.), *Crime mapping and crime prevention: Crime prevention studies* (Vol. 8, pp. 1–26). Monsey, NY: Criminal Justice Press.

QUINNEY, RICHARD: SOCIAL TRANSFORMATION AND PEACEMAKING CRIMINOLOGY

Richard Quinney is a sociologist who gained international renown as a radical criminologist. In various writings, he drew attention to the relationship between capitalism and crime and also analyzed crime and its control from a number of perspectives. Quinney's notoriety and progression as a criminologist can be discerned through an examination of five standpoints including his (1) characterization by scholarly peers, (2) biography and career stages, (3) movement of writings from perspective to perspective to perspective, (4) focus on social transformation and peacemaking criminology, and (5) legacy of work for the field of criminology. A key theme of this entry is that, during the major stages of his intellectual career, Quinney laid the foundation for his articulation of a peacemaking criminology. Thus, this perspective represents a growth in his way of thinking rather than a rejection of his earlier criminologies.

Characterization by Scholarly Peers

Quinney is known as one of the 15 pioneers in criminology (Martin et al., 1990). Quinney's criminological writings began in the 1960s and spanned each decade into the 1990s. He retired as a professor emeritus in 1998. His work continues to be discussed in prominent introductory sociology and criminology textbooks as an example of how a conflict theory approach can be applied to the study of crime. Recent crime theory textbooks also have attributed the origins and development of Marxist criminology and peacemaking criminology to his writings. Further illustrative of his impact, Quinney ranked in 2000 among the top 10 most-cited scholars in criminology (Wright, 2000, p. 119). In 1984, he received the Edwin H. Sutherland Award from the American Society of Criminology. This annual award recognized his outstanding contributions to criminological theory. Also, from the American Society of Criminology, he was presented the Major Achievement Award by the Critical Criminology Division in 1998. In 1986, he earned the Fulbright Lecture and Research Award from the Department of Political Science and Sociology at University College in Galway, Ireland. In 1992, he obtained the President's Award from the Western Society of Criminology. In 2009, he attained the Sullivan Tifft Vanguard Award from the Justice Studies Association for his "outstanding service to the academic discipline of criminology for the past 40 years."

The next part of this entry discusses Quinney's biography and career stages. After that, his movement from perspective to perspective to perspective is delineated in relation to his career stages.

Biography and Career Stages

Several writings have provided reflections and accounts about the life of Quinney (Wozniak, in press). When such writings are examined as a whole, basic tendencies become apparent in the biography and career stages of this prominent criminologist. First, these accounts of his life emphasized the importance of his growing up during the Great Depression on his family farm in Walworth County, which is 5 miles from Delavan, Wisconsin (near the state capital, Madison). Second, his childhood experiences were typical for the times such that he performed farm chores and helped in the breeding of pigs; played trombone in the high school band; and wrote and took pictures for the school newspaper. Third, during Quinney's grade school and high school years, a quality of his personal character began that persisted for the rest of his life. This quality is that he tended to emerge among his peers as a leader. For example, during the eighth grade, he

agreed to give the commencement speech; during high school, he formed a musical band to play at school dances; and he was elected as the president of the student body at Carroll College.

As an undergraduate student at Carroll College, Quinney again took some typical paths. For instance, he joined a fraternity and worked during the summer months as a hospital orderly. This latter job was pursued to gain firsthand work experience in keeping with his plan to become a hospital administrator. In fact, he majored both in biology and sociology to blend his educational interests toward a future hospital administration career path. However, during another summer employment as a hospital bill collector in Chicago, he disliked calling patients to pay their bills. As a result, upon graduating with a bachelor of science degree from Carroll College in 1956, Quinney decided to pursue graduate sociology studies at Northwestern University. He was greatly encouraged by the sociology department chair, Kimball Young, to study sociology at an advanced level. There, he assisted in the teaching of a criminology course, which was his initial exposure to the sociological study of crime (Trevino, 1984). Again, emerging as a leader among his peers, Quinney received his master's degree in sociology in 9 months. This took place upon his completion of his master's thesis, which was a study of the growth of a city and the complexity of its human relations titled *Urbanization and the Scale of Society*.

After completing his master's degree, Quinney embarked on doctoral studies in sociology. In 1957, he was awarded a research assistantship in the rural sociology program at the University of Wisconsin–Madison. Providing insight into directions his academic career would take over the next three decades, Quinney commented in his *Autobiographical Reflections* about his times as a sociology doctoral student. He wrote about himself in the third person and referred to himself as "Earl," which is his first name; he changed his name to "Richard" in the 1960s:

In those graduate school days, students were encouraged to dabble in fields of study outside sociology. Earl took courses in the philosophy of science, physical and cultural anthropology, American history, social and intellectual history, and archaeology, as well as the full range of courses in sociology. He spent days of complete abandonment in a carrel in the university library and in the State Historical Society library. Gradually he began to focus on the relation of social institutions, especially religious and legal institutions, to the larger social and economic order. At a time in the 1950s when most graduate students were not exposed to Marxist ideas, it began to occur to him that the world was dominated by those with money and power. (p. 47)

As a sociology doctoral student, Quinney shifted his main interests from rural sociology to social theory and chose to complete one of his comprehensive exams on criminology. Notably, he was planning to conduct his dissertation research on religion with Howard Becker as his supervisor, who died unexpectedly at the beginning of this dissertation project (Martin et al., 1990).

In 1960, Quinney took a temporary Instructor of Sociology position at St. Lawrence University in Canton, New York. There, he began again to undertake a dissertation project about crime and asked Marshall Clinard to serve as his supervisor. Under Clinard's direction, he completed his dissertation, *Retail Pharmacy as a Marginal Occupation: A Study of Prescription Violation*. He received a Ph.D. in sociology in 1962. Quinney's dissertation was conventional and mainstream in nature. According to Martin et al., Quinney's dissertation "was based on a functionalist perspective" (p. 386).

After completing his doctorate, Quinney served as a sociology professor at nine other universities in the United States. First, he worked as an assistant professor at the University of Kentucky from 1962 to 1965. Second, he was employed as an associate professor at New York University from 1965 to 1970 and as a professor from 1970 to 1973. Third, in the years between those latter two appointments, he had a sabbatical and research and writing leaves from New York University from 1971 to 1974. He spent his sabbatical and these leaves at the Department of Sociology at the University of North Carolina at Chapel Hill.

Fourth, he was a visiting professor at the City University of New York (Brooklyn College and the Graduate Center) from 1974 to 1975. Fifth, he was a visiting professor at Boston University during the fall of 1975. Sixth, he was a visiting professor at Brown University from 1975 to 1978 and an

adjunct professor from 1978 to 1983. Seventh, he was a distinguished visiting professor at Boston College from 1978 to 1979 and an adjunct professor from 1980 to 1983. Eighth, he was a professor at the University of Wisconsin–Milwaukee during spring 1980. Ninth, he was a professor of sociology at Northern Illinois University from 1983 until his retirement in 1998.

Movement of Writings From Perspective to Perspective to Perspective

As noted, Quinney's doctoral dissertation involved a mainstream sociological analysis of prescription violation in the retail pharmacy occupation. He published various journal articles from his dissertation research. His working relationship with his dissertation supervisor, Marshall Clinard, also embellished his early academic career. They coauthored a well-received book that formulated an expansive typology of criminal behavior systems.

So, what happened in Quinney's academic life and research work that led him to be known as a key American spokesperson for radical criminology and as a sharp critic of the relationship of capitalism to crime? Before addressing this question in terms of his specific career stages, some related observations can be made.

First, as mentioned earlier, Quinney, during his youth, displayed an ability to be a leader among peers. Thus, he adopted more of a stance of an innovator in criminology rather than a follower in this field. Second, Quinney's upbringing tended to influence his analysis of how crime comes to be experienced by people in contemporary society and his notions of populism (i.e., a focus upon the interests of the common people). Third, according to Anderson (2008), Quinney's journey in criminology was "to, through, and beyond Marxism" and involved work that entailed a sense of empathy with individual suffering and the oppressed (p. 3).

Fourth, as discussed earlier, Quinney was encouraged as a sociology doctoral student to "dabble in fields outside sociology." Not only did he take courses at the University of Wisconsin at Madison in anthropology, in archaeology, in American, social, and intellectual history, and in the philosophy of science, but he also widely read in other disciplines throughout his academic career in the 1960s to 1990s. He was trained as a sociologist who focused upon criminology, but his writings commonly extended beyond the borders of the disciplines of sociology and criminology.

In contrast, there have been thoughts among criminologists that Quinney's continued shift from perspective to perspective to perspective in criminology was generally a jumbled, incoherent collection of writings that were somewhat out-of-step with the ongoing theories and research of mainstream criminology. In fact, after Quinney delivered his acceptance speech for his 1984 Edwin H. Sutherland Award, a discussion arose among those in the audience about whether "Quinney was saying goodbye to criminology" because he had a new focus on a prophetic, religious orientation in his analysis of society (Martin et al., 1990, p. 398).

However, a different interpretation of Quinney's career work in criminology can be offered. When his career stages were examined with his criminology writings as a whole, there was much more of a pattern, rather than a discontinuity, in his intellectual enterprise. Importantly, as discussed below, his intellectual stages were highly cohesive, deeply humane in orientation, and socially progressive in many respects.

Thus, the remainder of this section first lays out when and where Quinney produced his varying perspectives in criminology. Second, the discussion also indicates how his experiences with social activism and socially progressive groups played an important role in his development of crime analysis from perspective to perspective to perspective. Third, this section identifies each of the theoretical perspectives that he applied to crime and his core writings linked to each of these perspectives. Fourth, this section shows that each perspective and set of writings were consistent with Quinney's call for the development of peacemaking criminology.

Furthermore, it is instructive to note that Quinney authored *Bearing Witness to Crime and Social Justice* in which he commented upon and provided illustrations of his writings from the 1960s through the 1900s. In the preface of this book, he made three sets of observations, which presented an inter-connected rationale about why he moved from perspective to perspective to perspective in his writings in keeping with ever-changing developments of the United States in the latter 1900s.

First, Quinney wrote the following about his initial years as a sociology professor:

When I began graduate school in 1956, the dominant stance in the social sciences—in sociology in particular—was the acceptance of existing social conditions. Perhaps because of my background, on the edge of two worlds, town and country, I became an observer and critic of the status quo. . . . Enough to say here that as I studied sociology I became greatly interested in the social problems endemic to the country. Asking, of course, Why? And how could things be different? (p. x)

Second, in regard to the political unrest of the 1960s and 1970s and how it was linked to the development of Marxist and radical criminology, Quinney stated,

Clearly, what was defined as crime was a product of the economic and political life of the country. Criminal laws were constructed to protect special interests and to maintain a specific social and moral order. This understanding of law and order was evident in the turmoils of the time: the civil rights movement for radical equality, the protests against the war in Vietnam, and the revolts within the universities. At the same time, there was emerging a legal apparatus, called the criminal justice system, to control threatening behavior and to preserve the established order. Critical criminology developed with an awareness of these events and conditions. By many names—radical, Marxist, progressive—a critical criminology was created to understand and to change the direction of the country. (p. x)

Third, Quinney stipulated that his writings from perspective to perspective to perspective were commonly linked as follows:

My own travels through the 1960s, the 1970s, the 1980s, and the 1990s were marked by a progression of ways of thinking and acting: from the social constructionist perspective to phenomenology, from phenomenology to Marxist and critical philosophy, from Marxist and critical philosophy to liberation theology, from liberation theology to Buddhism and existentialism. And then to a more ethnographic and personal mode of thinking and being. It is necessary to note that in all of these travels nothing was rejected or deleted from the previous stages; rather, each new stage of development incorporated what had preceded it. Each change was motivated by the need to understand crime in another or more complex way, in a way excluded from a former understanding. Each stage incorporated the changes that were taking place in my personal life. There was to be no separation between life and theory, between witnessing and writing. (pp. x–xi)

In this light, Quinney's criminological writings over the course of his career can be visualized (as he also tended to view it) as "artifacts of one social theorist who is trying to make sense of the world, who is bearing witness to the sufferings in the world, and who is hoping at the same time for a better world" (p. x).

Another lens to distinguish the genesis of Quinney's writings is to view his academic career as falling into five periods:

1960–1965. Canton, New York, and Lexington, Kentucky—first teaching jobs. Civil rights movement begins. *Criminal Behavior Systems*, empirical research, first articles.

1965–1971. New York City. Antiwar protests. Counter-culture, *The Problem of Crime, The Social Reality of Crime*, radical sociology, photography.

1971–1974. Chapel Hill, North Carolina. Sabbatical leaves from NYU. Resigns from full professor position. Socialist community, *Critique of Legal Order.* Beginning of *Class, State, and Crime.*

1974–1983. Providence, Rhode Island. Part-time teaching positions. Marxism, theology, spiritual search, revision of *The Problem of Crime*, writing of *Providence*, Buddhism.

1983–2000. Return to the Midwest. DeKalb, Illinois. Ethnography of everyday life, keeping of journals, photography, teaching environmental sociology, teaching peace and social justice, personal essays, *Criminology as Peacemaking, For the Time Being, Borderland.*

During each of these periods, Quinney's academic work was coupled with an active and direct involvement in various political (civil rights movement, antiwar protests, socialist community meetings) and interpersonal growth (spiritual search, study of Buddhism, ethnographic writings, photography) interests and activities. Relatedly, at the height of development of Marxist and radical theories and research of the Department of Criminology at the University of California, Berkeley, he traveled there to become acquainted firsthand with socially progressive ideas emerging about crime, evolving from criminology professors and students at the Berkeley campus and community.

Again, in Quinney's way of thinking, each of his criminological writings was done to "make sense of the world" in hope "for a better world." For example, in his coauthored book *Criminal Behavior Systems*, he played a key role in applying a functionalist analysis of crime that was unprecedented in its comprehensiveness and scope. That is, no other criminology book or research during that period of time examined nine types of criminal behavior (violent personal, occasional property, public order, conventional, political, occupational, corporate, organized, professional) in terms of five categories (legal aspects, criminal career, group support, legitimate behavior, societal reaction, and legal processing). It was also during his New York City stage of the 1960s that he spent long periods of time examining crime statistics on 23rd Street at the National Council on Crime and Delinquency Library.

Hence, during his employment as a sociology professor in New York City, Quinney authored two books, both published in 1970. One was titled *The Problem of Crime*, which was essentially a textbook of five chapters covering the meaning of crime (e.g., nature, types, and sources of criminal law); the development of criminology (e.g., before the 1800s, the 1800s, the 1900s), contemporary study of crime (e.g., criminal statistics, causal and philosophical assumptions in crime data); crime in American society (e.g., urban crimes, public morality crimes, business crimes, political crimes); and the future of crime. Similar to his earlier book, *The Problem of Crime* provided a broad treatment of salient themes addressed in each chapter. In this work, he pinpointed the need to pay closer attention to the "politicality of crime" given that much of the behavior that society labels as criminal had a political character.

In *The Social Reality of Crime*, Quinney's intent was to shift attention away from searching for the causes of crime and toward a reorientation of the study of crime about how the justice system affects criminal behavior. Here, according to Martin et al., he was concerned with how definitions of criminals were constructed and how they were applied. Adapting emphases of conflict theory and phenomenology in his analysis, he posited in the *Social Reality of Crime* that the relationship between crime and the social order could be understood in terms of six propositions:

1. Crime is a definition of human conduct created by authorized agents in a politically organized society.

2. Criminal definitions describe behaviors that conflict with the interests of segments of society that have power to shape public policy.

3. Criminal definitions are applied by segments of society that have power to shape the enforcement and administration of criminal law.

4. Behavior patterns are structured in segmentally organized society in relation to criminal definitions, and within this context persons engage in actions that have relative probabilities of being defined as criminal.

5. Conceptions of crime are constructed and diffused in the segments of society by various means of communication.

6. The social reality of crime is constructed by the formulation and application of criminal definitions, the development of behavior patterns related to criminal definitions, and the construction of criminal conceptions. (pp. 15–23)

Similar to *The Problem of Crime* and the *Social Reality of Crime*, both of Quinney's books, published while he was living in Chapel Hill, North Carolina, were conceived to address "how one becomes labeled a criminal" rather than to answer why an individual commits crime. That is, *Critique of Legal Order: Control in Capitalist Society* and *Class, State, and Crime* were designed to move beyond the basic tenets of conflict theory and phenomenology and toward a theoretical approach grounded more in Marxist theory.

In *Bearing Witness to Crime and Social Justice*, Quinney stated that he began *Critique of Legal Order* with "a call for a critical understanding of crime and the legal system. With a critical Marxian philosophy, I suggested, we could demystify the existing social order and, at the same time, create a world that moves us beyond the exploitation and oppression of capitalism" (p. xii).

To build his arguments in *Critique of Legal Order*, Quinney reviewed how positivist, social constructionist, and phenomenological modes of thinking were inadequate to accomplish an understanding of the American legal order. Instead, a critical Marxist approach provided better insight about "how the capitalist ruling class establishes its control over those it must oppress" (Quinney, p. 36). Moreover, Martin et al. maintained that this book illustrated that a class analysis could be applied to criminal law and crime control.

In essence, to revamp the social order, according to Quinney, it would require a transition from capitalism to socialism, which is further proposed in *Class, State, and Crime*. He used a structural Marxist approach to explain legal order in this latter book, which discussed crime and the development of capitalism. It is here that the often used depiction of Quinney's work appeared, which is that a capitalist economy produced crimes of domination and repression (committed by owners and the state to maintain the economic status quo); crimes of accommodation and adaptation (offenses committed by the workers and the poor to deal with class position deprivations); and crimes of resistance (committed by workers and the poor who have developed a class consciousness). According to Quinney, "only by going beyond capitalism to socialism, could the contradictions that produce the crime problem be confronted. Crime will continue to be 'inevitable' as long as capitalist society exists" (1977, p. 126).

Additionally, *Class, State, and Crime* was concerned with "the prophetic meaning of social justice" which involved "the urge toward justice in human affairs. This urge becomes the will of divine origin operating in history, providing the source of inspiration to all prophets and revolutionaries" (p. 29). Quinney further maintained,

Our prophetic heritage perceives the driving force of history as being the struggle between justice and injustice. We the people—in a covenant with God—are responsible for the character of our lives and our society, for the pursuit of righteousness, justice, and mercy. The social and moral order is consequently rooted in the divine commandments; morality rests on divine command and concern rather than on the relativity of reasonableness. (pp. 29–30)

This assertion in *Class, State, and Crime* of a need to apply themes of religion and spirituality into analyses of crime stemmed from Quinney's Marxist view that capitalist justice has an emphasis on human manipulation and control (i.e., workers are enslaved, that all things and human beings are transformed into objects, and that a demotion of our world into a mere environment; a demonic quality to our political state). Hence, Quinney expanded his application of notions of religion and spirituality into his discussion of *Providence: The Reconstruction of Social and Moral Order*. Quinney described his personal impetus for *Providence*: "More than ever before, I began to combine the spiritual and the material. . . . After twenty-five years of excluding religious questions from my life, I was returning to questions that were essentially religious" (2001, p. 38).

Providence turned attention toward the religious response to capitalism and included a chapter on "a religious socialist order." In keeping with his previous analysis, in *Providence* he pointed out that a prophetic imagination "reflects the presence of the divine in history. Things of the world have their meaning not so in themselves as in the spiritual, in the word of God revealed in the world" (p. 113). Quinney ended *Providence* with these imageries: "Our historical struggle is thus for the creation of a social and moral order that prepares us for the ultimate of divine grace—the Kingdom of God fulfilled. Peace and justice through the Kingdom of God" (p. 114).

Social Transformation and Peacemaking Criminology

So far, this entry has examined Quinney as a criminologist through three standpoints. These are his characterization by scholarly peers, his biography and career stages, and his movement from perspective to perspective to perspective. This analysis revealed his tendencies to act as a leader among his peers; promote ideas reflecting his experiences with populism ideals; and link his sociological interests with concerns in other related fields of study. However, only some key books of Quinney were addressed in this entry. Space limitations do not permit further analysis of over 30 books and nearly 80 journal articles that he produced during his lifetime. Nonetheless, Quinney's

work has an ongoing concern to promote the development of social transformation in our contemporary society. This concern for social transformation closely coincided with his call and support for a peacemaking approach to emerge in criminology.

A first example of Quinney's concern with social transformation is in *Critique of Legal Order*. In the first chapter of this book, he posited that there are types of philosophical approaches that could be used to understand the legal order: positivistic, social constructionist, phenomenological, and critical. He suggested that in his work, he passed through each of the first three phases and was in the fourth (i.e., critical) approach (Martin et al., 1990, p. 394). Upon demonstrating shortcomings of the first three approaches, he endorsed adopting a critical philosophy of the legal order so that a critical-Marxian analysis of crime control in capitalist society could be developed. According to Quinney,

> In critically understanding (and demystifying) our current historical reality, we are in a position to act in a way that will remove our oppression and create a new existence. Though we are subject to the objective conditions of our age, as human beings we are also collectively involved in transforming our social reality. Our praxis is one of critical thought and action—reflecting upon the world and acting to transform it. . . . We can free ourselves from the oppression of the age only as we combine our thoughts and our actions, turning each back upon the other. (1974, p. 197)

A second example of Quinney's concern with social transformation is seen in *Class, State, and Crime*. He elaborated on the relationship between crime and capitalism and illustrated how the prophetic meaning of justice (as described earlier) affected the thinking of people in our society today. He spoke very positively about the latter:

> Through the prophetic tradition, a tradition that is present also in the prophetic voice of Marxism . . . , a meaning of justice that can transform the world and open the future is once again emerging. Marxism and theology are confronting each other in ways that allow us to understand our existence and consider our essential nature. (1977, p. 33)

A third example of social transformation in Quinney's work is apparent in the third edition of his *Problem of Crime*, which included as its subtitle *A Peace and Social Justice Perspective*. In a chapter titled "Peace and Social Justice," Quinney and John Wildeman observed,

> The peace and social justice perspective continues to develop in criminology. There are proposals and programs on mediation, conflict resolution, and reconciliation; there is the movement to abolish the death penalty; and there are humanist programs of rehabilitation and community organization. These are the practices of a criminology of peacemaking, a criminology that seeks to alleviate suffering and thereby reduce crime. . . . This is a criminology that is based necessarily on human transformation in the achievement of peace and justice. Human transformation takes place as we change our social, economic, and political structure. And the message is clear: Without peace within us and in our actions, there can be no peace and justice in our results. Peace is the way. (p. 110)

Moreover, Quinney and Wildeman recognized that changing the social structure needed to coincide with social transformation at the personal level. Thereby, they emphasized,

> Without *inner* peace in each of us, without peace of mind and heart, there can be no *social* peace between people and no peace in societies, nations, and in the world. To be explicitly engaged in this process, of bringing about peace on all levels, of joining ends and means, is to be engaged in *peacemaking*. . . . The radical nature of peacemaking is clear: No less is involved than the transformation of our human being. Indeed, we will be engaged in action, but action will come out of our transformed being. Rather than attempting to create a good society first and then trying to make ourselves better human beings, we have to work on the two simultaneously. The inner and the outer are the same. . . . The transformation of ourselves and the world becomes our constant practice, here and now. (1991, p. 117)

Further, on social transformation, Quinney and Wildeman concluded,

All of this is to say, to us as criminologists, that crime is suffering and that the ending of crime is possible only with the ending of suffering. And the ending both of suffering and of crime—the establishing of justice—can come only out of peace, out of a peace that is spiritually grounded in our very being. . . . To eliminate crime—to end the construction and perpetuation of an existence that makes crime possible—requires a transformation of our human being. We as human beings must *be* peace if we are to live in a world free of crime, in a world of peace. (pp. 118–119, emphasis in the original)

These latter three examples of Quinney's analyses of social transformation generally linked with his views of peacemaking criminology (Wozniak, 2008). Overall, there are six peacemaking criminology writings by Quinney as follows:

1. "The Theory and Practice of Peacemaking in the Development of Radical Criminology"
2. *The Problem of Crime: A Peace and Social Justice Perspective*, Third Edition
3. "The Way of Peace: On Crime, Suffering, and Service"
4. "A Life of Crime: Criminology and Public Policy as Peacemaking"
5. "Criminology as Moral Philosophy, Criminologist as Witness"
6. "Socialist Humanism and the Problem of Crime: Thinking About Erich Fromm in the Development of Critical/Peacemaking Criminology"

His second peacemaking criminology writing was addressed above in terms of its visions of social transformation. His first peacemaking criminology writing on the "The Theory and Practice of Peacemaking in the Development of Radical Criminology" specified that peacemaking is a "criminology that seeks to alleviate suffering and thereby reduce crime" (p. 5). He added that crime is one form of suffering all around us along with other forms such as poverty, hunger, violence, homelessness and destruction of the environment. Moreover, our criminal justice system is founded on violence, according to Quinney, and is a system that assumes violence can be overcome by violence. In this social context, he suggested the need for both social transformation (i.e., changing our social, economic, and political structure) and personal transformation (i.e., care given to the inner life of us). In Quinney's view, no peace can result without peace within us and in our actions.

In his "Way of Peace" chapter, Quinney identified a list of assumptions supporting a rationale for the development of peacemaking criminology. He again contended that inner and social peace must come together at the same time and social transformation pertained to "the transformation of our human being. Political and economic solutions without this transformation inevitably fail" (p. 4).

Quinney's fourth peacemaking criminology writing "A Life of Crime: Criminology and Public Policy as Peacemaking" challenged criminologists to re-examine their personal and professional agenda. Thereby, he suggested that criminologists would do well to support peacemaking criminology as a "compassionate criminology" that "recognizes the interrelatedness of everything; that everyone is connected to each other and to their environment"— while also recognizing that crime rates still remain high and that our justice system has limited success in its correctional settings (p. 3). In this article, he encouraged personal transformation. On social transformation, Quinney similarly recommended that the "objective is quite simple: to be kind to one another, to break down barriers that separate us from one another, to live moment-to-moment our connection to all that is . . . our oneness" (p. 6).

Quinney dealt with social transformation in one other peacemaking article, "Socialist Humanism and the Problem of Crime: Thinking About Erich Fromm in the Development of Critical/Peacemaking Criminology." Quinney noted that Fromm, as a lifelong activist for peace, posited that the establishment of peace is a central task of humanity. In regard to social transformation, Quinney stated, like he had done in his "A Life of Crime" article, in peacemaking criminology, "the objective is clear: be kind to one another, to transcend the barriers that separate us from one another and to live everyday life with a sense of independence" (p. 26). He concluded: "Positive peace exists when the sources of crime— poverty, inequality, racism, and alienation—are not present" (p. 28). Hence, punishment (negative peace) is not the way of peace; positive peace (i.e., striving to eliminate the structure of violence and crime) is the objective of peacemaking criminology.

Legacy of Work for the Field of Criminology

This entry has demonstrated that the paths that Quinney had taken in becoming a peacemaking criminologist involved more patterns than discontinuities. Quinney's upbringing as a young boy living with his family on a small Wisconsin farm induced him to have a focus on the interests of common people throughout his career as a sociology professor and criminologist. Although he was best known for applying conflict theory into the field of criminology, Quinney took many controversial stands in his criminological writings as a way to "make better sense of the world" in hope "for a better world." Through his involvement in criminological perspectives ranging from functionalism to Marxist theory and critical philosophy to peacemaking criminology, he commonly brought socially progressive ideas into criminological discourse.

Quinney produced his varied writings addressing perspective to perspective to perspective of criminology upon ongoing connection with people actively and directly involved in political and community movements and interpersonal growth interests and activities. Hence, his call for the development of a combined personal and social transformation was far from being an academic lip service. Indeed, he put his urging to develop this combined type of transformation into actual practice in his daily life.

Quinney's travels from his life on a Wisconsin farm to becoming a peacemaking criminologist enabled his academic writings to contribute a host of themes to be part of the teaching and research literature of criminology in the latter 1900s. His legacy for criminology was multiple and predicated upon compassion and sensitivity for those experiencing social harms and personal indignities. It seems reasonable to further suggest that no one in the field of criminology has addressed the study of crime in the constantly evolving, personally engaging, and socially uplifting ways that Quinney had done over the course of four decades.

In illustration of this point, the following is a list of concerns that Quinney's criminology writings brought into focus for past and current times:

- How justice systems affect criminal behavior.
- How definitions of criminals are constructed and applied.

- It is important to demystify the existing social order.
- There is a need to create a world that moves us beyond the exploitation and oppression of capitalism.
- Instead of attempting to resocialize the individual offender, we need to revamp the legal order.
- Concern should be directed toward the prophetic meaning of social justice.
- Views of crime need to combine the spiritual and material.
- It is useful to adopt a critical philosophy of the legal order.
- There is a need to reflect upon the world and act to transform it.
- Peacemaking is a criminology that seeks to alleviate suffering and thereby reduce crime.
- Social transformation involves inner peace and outer peace.
- Criminologists would do well to support peacemaking criminology as a "passionate criminology."
- The objective is quite simple—to be kind to one another, to break down barriers that separate us, and to link moment-to-moment our connection to all.

In sum, these and other compelling themes in Quinney's work have resulted from his travels to peacemaking criminology. Criminologists, with all in society, would do well to continue to address such themes now and in the future. In *The Problem of Crime*, Quinney and Wildeman state, "Without peace within us and in our actions, there can be no peace and justice in our results. Peace is the way" (p. 10).

John F. Wozniak

See also Abolitionism; Anarchist Criminology; Chambliss, William J.: Power, Conflict, and Crime; Colvin, Mark: Coercion Theory; Peacemaking Criminology

References and Further Readings

Anderson, K. B. (2008). Richard Quinney's journey: The Marxist dimension. In J. F. Wozniak, M. C. Braswell, R. E. Vogel, & K. R. Blevins (Eds.), *Transformative justice: Critical and peacemaking themes influenced by Richard Quinney* (pp. 33–41). Lanham, MD: Lexington.

Clinard, M. B., & Quinney, R. (1967). *Criminal behavior systems: A typology.* New York: Holt, Rinehart and Winston.

Martin, R., Mutchnick, R. J., & Austin, W. T. (1990). *Criminological thought: Pioneers past and present.* New York: Macmillan.

Pepinsky, H. E., & Quinney, R. (Eds.). (1991). *Criminology as peacemaking.* Bloomington: Indiana University Press.

Quinney, R. (1963). Occupational structure and criminal behavior: Prescription violation by retail pharmacists. *Social Problems, 11,* 179–185.

Quinney, R. (1970). *The problem of crime.* New York: Dodd, Mead.

Quinney, R. (1970). *The social reality of crime.* Boston: Little, Brown.

Quinney, R. (1974). *Critique of legal order: Crime control in capitalist society.* Boston: Little, Brown.

Quinney, R. (1977). *Class, state, and crime: On the theory and practice of criminal justice.* New York: Longman.

Quinney, R. (1980). *Providence: Reconstruction of social and moral order.* New York: Longman.

Quinney, R. (1982). Leaving the country: A Midwest education in sociology in the 1950s. *Wisconsin Sociologist, 19,* 54–66.

Quinney, R. (1984). Journey to a far place: The way of autobiographical reflection. *Humanity and Society, 8,* 182–198.

Quinney, R. (1989, Winter). The theory and practice of peacemaking in the development of radical criminology. *The Critical Criminologist, 1,* 5.

Quinney, R. (1991). *Journey to a far place: Autobiographical reflections.* Philadelphia: Temple University Press.

Quinney, R. (1991). The way of peace: On crime, suffering, and service. In H. E. Pepinsky & R. Quinney (Eds.), *Criminology as peacemaking* (pp. 3–13). Bloomington: Indiana University Press.

Quinney, R. (1993). A life of crime: Criminology and public policy as peacemaking. *Journal of Crime and Justice, 16*(2), 3–9.

Quinney, R. (1998). *For the time being: Ethnography of everyday life.* Albany: SUNY Press.

Quinney, R. (2000). *Bearing witness to crime and social justice.* Albany: SUNY Press.

Quinney, R. (2000). Criminology as moral philosophy, criminologist as witness. In R. Quinney (Ed.), *Bearing witness to crime and social justice* (pp. 193–213). Albany: SUNY Press.

Quinney, R. (2000). Socialist humanism and the problem of crime: Thinking about Erich Fromm in the development of critical/peacemaking criminology. In

K. Anderson & R. Quinney (Eds.), *Erich Fromm and critical criminology: Beyond the punitive society* (pp. 21–30). Urbana: University of Illinois Press.

Quinney, R. (2001). *Borderland: A Midwest journal.* Madison: University of Wisconsin Press.

Quinney, R., & Wildeman, J. (1991). *The problem of crime: A Peace and social justice perspective* (3rd ed.). Mountain View, CA: Mayfield.

Trevino, J. (1984). *Richard Quinney: A biography.* Paper presented at the Annual Meeting of the American Society of Criminology, Cincinnati, OH.

Wozniak, J. F. (2008). The relevance of Richard Quinney's writings on peacemaking criminology: Toward personal and social transformation. In J. F. Wozniak, M. C. Braswell, R. E. Vogel, & K. R. Blevins (Eds.), *Transformative justice: Critical and peacemaking themes influenced by Richard Quinney* (pp. 167–190). Lanham, MD: Lexington.

Wozniak, J. F. (2008). Toward a theoretical model of peacemaking criminology: An essay in honor of Richard Quinney. In J. F. Wozniak, M. C. Braswell, R. E. Vogel, & K. R. Blevins (Eds.), *Transformative justice: Critical and peacemaking themes influenced by Richard Quinney* (pp. 141–166). Lanham, MD: Lexington.

Wozniak, J. F. (in press). Becoming a peacemaking criminologist: The travels of Richard Quinney. In F. T. Cullen, C. L. Johnson, A. J. Meyer, & F. Adler (Eds.), *The origins of American criminology* (Advances in Criminological Theory: Vol. 16). New Brunswick, NJ: Transaction.

Wozniak, J. F., Braswell, M. C. Vogel, R. E., & Blevins, K. R. (Eds.). (2008). *Transformative justice: Critical and peacemaking themes influenced by Richard Quinney.* Lanham, MD: Lexington.

Wright, R. A. (2000). Recent changes in the most-cited scholars in criminology: A comparison of textbooks and journals. *Journal of Criminal Justice, 28,* 117–128.

R

Racial Threat and Social Control

Racial threat refers to the real or perceived threat that minorities may pose to a dominant racial or ethnic group's political power, economic well-being, or sense of personal safety. Theorists presume racial threat, sometimes termed *minority threat*, *social threat*, *racial group threat*, or simply *group threat*, to be the basis for the mobilization of various forms of social control by those who have the power to do so. As applied by researchers, racial threat in its economic, political, or personal safety aspect has helped account for such diverse forms of social control as laws supporting racial segregation, felon disenfranchisement, opposition to affirmative action, public lynching, and a range of measures related to the administration of justice. The latter is the context in which racial threat is particularly relevant for criminology. Criminologists have hypothesized that racial threat is consequential for such justice-related outcomes as the size and funding of police departments, rates of arrest, killings by police, civil rights complaints against the police, correctional expenditures, rates of incarceration, individual chances of imprisonment, the establishment of death sentences, and executions.

In general, scholars have conceptualized racial threat at the aggregate or macro-level and have used the size or concentration of racial and ethnic minority groups as the principal indicators. In its theoretical origins and for most research to date, the relative proportion of African Americans in a given population or geographic unit has been taken as the measure of racial threat. However, researchers have also measured the economic dimension of racial threat at the aggregate level with the ratio of black to white unemployment rates and black to white income inequality. Studies have assessed the political component of racial threat using the ratio of black to white voters.

In recent years, macro-level formulations of racial/ethnic threat have included the relative size of Latino populations. Researchers using this theoretical perspective have increasingly made reference to ethnic or minority threat as opposed to the concept of racial threat, because the Latino population has grown much faster than other minority groups in the United States. Some who have studied minority threat in an international context have applied the concept to the size and distribution of immigrants in a given country or region. Empirical examinations of the response to illegal immigrants in the United States have made a similar application.

Several researchers have suggested that *perceived* threat from racial or ethnic minorities may be as important as aggregate concentrations of populations in relation to the mobilization of social controls. Tests of this perspective have approached threat in terms of the perceived racial or ethnic composition of place or by means of a direct assessment of criminal threat presumably posed by racial or ethnic minorities. Studies have measured perceived economic threat by asking respondents to estimate the chances that a white person will not get a job or promotion while an equally or less qualified black person would.

Some research into criminal justice decision making, especially as it relates to criminal sentencing, has conceptualized racial threat at the individual level. These examinations have tested the hypothesis that justice officials may perceive minority defendants, because of their race or ethnicity, to be more dangerous to the community and, on that account, to sentence them more harshly than whites.

Development of the Perspective

The racial threat and social control perspective originated with conflict theory which characterizes society in terms of different groups competing for resources, position, and power. Herbert Blumer was one of the first to formally describe the conflict between racial groups in the context of threat from the minority group to the dominant group. He observed that, over time, dominant group members develop the view that certain resources are the exclusive privilege of their group. Blumer argued that one way in which dominant group members react to perceived challenges to those exclusive privileges is with racial prejudice. It is the "fear or apprehension that the subordinate racial group is threatening, or will threaten, the position of the dominant group" that provides one important impetus to racial prejudice (p. 4). He presumed such threats to include economic competition as well as challenges to the dominant group's status, power, and other privileges.

In his seminal work, *Toward a Theory of Minority-Group Relations*, Hubert Blalock took racial threat theory a step further and hypothesized ways in which minority threat would be related to actions by the majority group that would have social control consequences. Blalock's argument was that a growing or more mobilized black minority will lead to discrimination by the white majority because of the economic or political power threats posed to the latter. In Blalock's formulation, the perception of threat on the part of the white majority was expected to increase as the size of the black minority grew. However, he predicted that whites' discriminatory responses to perceived threats would vary depending on whether the threat was to their economic well-being or political power.

Blalock expected activities designed to suppress economic threat and maintain economic dominance to expand in volume as that threat was perceived to grow. However, he hypothesized this expansion would occur at a decelerating rate. This non-linear pattern presumed that initial activities designed to hinder the economic achievements of the black minority would be successful, making further controlling activities by the white majority less necessary. Blalock also predicted a non-linear relationship between perceived political threat and discriminatory controls on the part of majority whites, but here the anticipated pattern was one of accelerating discrimination. In short, it was hypothesized that in order to successfully maintain political power, white majority "mobilization" would have to increase at a faster pace than that of the increase in size of the black minority.

Blalock discussed three types of discrimination that could develop in response to threat. The first of these was *political discrimination*, which could take a variety of forms. Historically, poll taxes, grandfather clauses, illiteracy tests, and white-only primaries were obvious attempts to circumvent the 15th Amendment to the Constitution, passed shortly after the Civil War, which prohibited denial of suffrage on account of race, color, or previous conditions of servitude. In addition, there is substantial evidence that the potential threat of newly enfranchised African Americans played a significant role in the enactment of felon disenfranchisement laws in many states.

Symbolic segregation was a second form of discrimination described by Blalock as a white response to racial threat. He listed as an example of symbolic segregation the enactment of various Jim Crow laws, which had the symbolic purpose of drawing lines between the dominant white majority and the threatening black minority. This took many forms, including the legally enforced separation of drinking fountains, restrooms, waiting rooms, and restaurants. While such measures had no direct economic or political consequence, they were seen as having symbolic value, especially for those whites "whose status claims are otherwise negligible" (p. 165).

Finally, Blalock depicted a third form of discrimination involving the development of what he characterized as *threat-oriented ideologies*. These ideologies comprised "certain exaggerated beliefs concerning the threatening aspects of the Negro personality," which in his view functioned "to rally white sentiment and justify violent or extreme forms of social control" (p. 167). In the United States, the belief that young black men are predisposed to crime and violence has been a prominent threat-oriented ideology for some time. As discussed in the next section, the iconic representation of black criminal threat has become a salient and enduring feature of popular discourse and has been a clear focus of much recent research making use of the racial threat framework.

Criminal Threat and Social Control

For the purpose of criminological inquiry, theorists have gradually expanded the presumed threat posed by blacks and other minorities from the political and economic dimensions emphasized by Blalock to include the threat or perceived threat of crime. Most criminological research dealing with the concept of racial or minority threat makes use of aggregate indicators of threat and social control (e.g., percent black and arrest rates). However, as Allen Liska and Mitchell Chamlin observed some time ago, the implicit and generally unmeasured predicate of such macro level relationships is the perceived threat of crime. Specifically, "the threat hypothesis . . . suggests that a high percentage of nonwhites produces an emergent property, 'perceived threat of crime,' which increases arrest rates by increasing pressure on police to control crime" (pp. 384–385).

While the presumed association of crime with black men is well established in American culture, there is some evidence that it has grown substantially more conspicuous since the end of civil rights activism in the 1960s. Among the identified factors contributing to the growth of this conflation of race and crime are political strategies intended to mobilize electoral support by playing on white fear and media stereotypes that reinforce the putative connection between race and criminal threat. Scholars suggest that the connection between race and crime has become so well established in popular culture that, for some people, talking about crime and crime control is seen as a code for talking about race. Moreover, they argue that such coded language has become a staple of what Robert Entman termed *modern racism*. In the past 10 years, however, media and political discourse has noticeably shifted to encompass what is characterized as a growing threat of crime from Latino males, particularly that involving drugs and violence. So the iconography of perceived criminal threat now clearly includes both a racial and ethnic dimension.

Conclusion

Racial and minority threat theory has proven to be an increasingly visible stimulus for criminological research. For example, threat research has established that cities with higher minority percentages have larger police departments, higher arrest rates, and police who are more likely to use deadly force. States with larger concentrations of African Americans were the earliest to establish felon disenfranchisement laws and the slowest to abandon those measures. Studies have shown that such states have higher rates of incarceration, are more likely to have the death penalty, and are also more likely to carry out executions. Empirical examinations have linked both fear of crime and popular support for the death penalty to the racial composition of place. Evidence has also demonstrated that the perceived risk of criminal victimization rises with the proportion of the population that is either Latino or black. Finally, researchers have found that the more crime is associated with African Americans, the stronger the public support for harsh criminal justice punishments. It is clear that the range and diversity of research grounded in this perspective continues to grow as does the relevance of the threat perspective to the field.

Justin Pickett and Ted Chiricos

See also Chambliss, William J.: Power, Conflict, and Crime; Chiricos, Ted: Racial Threat and Fear; Turk, Austin T.: The Criminalization Process; Vold, George B.: Group Conflict Theory

References and Further Readings

Blalock, H. M. (1967). *Toward a theory of minority-group relations.* New York: Wiley.

Blumer, H. (1958). Race prejudice as a sense of group position. *Pacific Sociological Review, 1*, 3–7.

Chiricos, T., Welch, K., & Gertz, M. (2004). Racial typification of crime and support for punitive measures. *Criminology, 42*, 359–390.

Entman, R. M. (1990). Modern racism and the images of blacks in local television news. *Critical Studies in Mass Communication, 7*, 332–345.

Liska, A. E. (1992). *Social threat and social control.* Albany: SUNY Press.

Liska, A. E., & Chamlin, M. B. (1984). Social structure and crime control among macrosocial units. *American Journal of Sociology, 90,* 383–395.

Quinney, R. (1970). *The social reality of crime.* Boston: Little, Brown.

Vold, G. B. (1958). *Theoretical criminology.* New York: Oxford University Press.

RAINE, ADRIAN: CRIME AS A DISORDER

Adrian Raine is one of the more prominent criminologists in modern times to examine the potential for psychological or psychiatric disorders to serve as the basis of criminal behavior. According to Raine, crime is linked with diagnoses found in the *Diagnostic and Statistical Manual of Mental Disorders*, text revision (*DSM-IV-TR*) and/or neurophysiological deficits that are identifiable by medical science. While crime, in and of itself, is not considered a disorder, the possession of antecedent disorders are thought to be contributory factors associated with crime. In other words, crime may be symptomatic of a psychologically disordered state. Like many theorists who study crime from a mental health and/or psychological perspective, Raine often refers to crime as being antisocial behavior. Such a term encapsulates a variety of behaviors, including those that are not criminal but are problematic and/or perceived as odd within a given society.

One key feature of Raine's early research is his tendency to use psychometric measures and research that seems more consistent with the field of psychology than criminology. Indeed, this approach is reflected in a study conducted in 1985 in which Raine sought to find a connection between psychopathy and schizophrenia as well as borderline personality disorder. Raine utilized Hare's Psychopathy Checklist as well as scales derived from the various *DSM-IV* criteria for schizophrenic and borderline personality disorders. Research prior to Raine's 1985 study indicated connections between these disorders and criminal behavior. However, Raine found no support for such connections. This finding is important because, in many cases, Raine tended to refute the research of other authors based on his own findings.

Raine has conducted other studies that have also attempted to validate the findings of well known researchers such as Hans Eysenck. In a 1981 study, Raine and Peter Venables tested Eysenck's theory of socialization as a means of explaining antisocial conduct. Specifically, Eysenck's theory contended that criminal behavior and the seriousness of that behavior had its roots in individual differences in susceptibility to classical conditioning experiences. Ultimately, Raine and Venables found only weak (if any) support for Eysenck's work. The purpose to bringing these early studies into this portrayal of Raine and his theory on "Crime as a Disorder" is to demonstrate the skeptical eye that he maintained while conducting research. It is clear that, during the early stages of his career, he went to great lengths to ensure that his research was rigorous and sound.

In 2004, Raine wrote an exclusive article for BBC News where he provided a very candid, clear, and focused discussion of his views regarding criminality and pathology. In doing so, Raine pointed toward theories that focus on social factors such as poverty and unemployment, noting that the evidence implicating pathology and brain impairments is much more compelling. According to Raine (2004), it is the existence of brain impairments that play a key role in criminality, particularly repetitive criminality. Raine notes that research on genetic and biological factors have played an equal or greater role in explaining criminal behavior. He has referred to his particular area of interest as *biocriminology*, which consists of scientific studies that are traditional akin more to psychiatric and/or neuropsychological research than that of the typical sociological tradition. Consistent with a biological approach, Raine notes the various forms of brain imaging, such as functional magnetic resonance (f-MRI) and positron emission tomography (PET) scans.

Raine further points to a plethora of research studies that have determined that poor functioning in the prefrontal cortex—an area of the brain that engages in higher order reasoning—is a key causal factor related to life persistent criminality. Deficits in the cerebral cortex have been associated with murderers, psychopaths, persons with aggressive characteristics, schizotypal, and antisocial personality characteristics. Other researchers such as

Terrie Moffit have produced a variety of studies that are consistent with Raine's contentions.

Raine (1993) points toward the use of electro-encephalograms (EEGs) with various subjects from the criminal, delinquent, psychopathic, and violent population. A large number of these studies, such as those conducted by J. Volavka in 1987 and V. Milstein in 1988, have found that a variety of abnormal EEG readings in certain specific criminal populations, especially those who engage in repetitive offending (Bartol & Bartol, 2007). With such empirical evidence, one may wonder why it is that this type of research is not accepted in a more matter-of-fact manner by mainstream criminologists. The answer to this lies in the flaws that exist in the methodologies of many of these studies. Raine (1993) has acknowledged that many of these studies do have obvious limitations, both due to the procedure used and in regard to their general use among broader criminal populations.

Nevertheless, it is equally true that as many (and perhaps more) limitations exist with studies from the fields of sociology and/or "soft" psychology. The term *soft psychology* is meant to refer to those psychological experiments that lack the use of hard science approaches as is found with medical-based and neurophysiological research. In such cases, the rigor of these experiments, being based on standardized surveys and psychometric scales, is not considered as great as those that also have some sort of physiological measure that is triangulated with the use of the survey or psychometric tool. Though this is not to discount the research conducted through the use of standardized psychological instruments, particularly those that have been found to be valid and reliable in their psychometric properties, this is to say that the inclusion of physiological measures from f-MRIs, PET scans, and EEGs helps provide an additional scientific measure that augments data obtained from standardized instruments and also counterbalances many of the weaknesses in their administration (Bufkin & Lutrell, 2005). It is with this in mind that biocriminality utilizes physiological measures to find associations among the criminal population, particularly those who are recidivists.

As with populations of children with attention deficit hyperactivity disorder, many offenders who are repetitively persistent in their criminal behavior possess cerebral imbalances in stimulation and/or

learning ability (Bennett et al., 2004). This research dovetails with longitudinal research by Terrie Moffitt and Anthony Walsh that showed that continued criminal activity among life-course-persistent offenders is associated with physiological factors. A child's propensity toward antisocial—and later criminal—behavior emerges from inherited or acquired neurophysiological deficits. These deficits are usually first manifested as subtle cognitive deficiencies, a difficult temperament, and/or hyperactive behavior. These deficits are consistent with research on stimulation, sensation seeking, learning, and the tendency to engage in high-risk and/or aggressive behaviors (Bartol & Bartol, 2007). This research provides an interesting landscape against which Raine notes that the brains of criminal offenders tend to be physically different from non-criminals and, according to Raine, results show "an 11 percent reduction in the volume of grey matter (neurons) in the prefrontal cortex" (2004, p. 2). Neuropsychological research has clearly demonstrated that a lack of neurons in any area of the brain means less brain activity, and this is particularly true of the prefrontal cortex region of the brain, according to Neil Carlson.

Raine has pointed out that, similar to other researchers, findings demonstrate that neurological deficits can explain recidivist offending across an offender's entire life course. Spanning from childhood to later adulthood, the recidivist tends to have a number of corollary characteristics and experiences that dovetail with his or her continued criminality. Quite often, antecedent variables that are common among these offenders are neurophysiological abnormalities and deficits that either occur at birth or are the result of injury, head trauma, or illness during the offender's early years. Compared to other offenders, these offenders tend to be more aggressive and also tend to have histories of poor judgment and impulse control. According to Raine, the "bad brains" of these offenders literally leads to bad behavior, to put it in simple terms.

Raine (2004) has also noted that numerous studies of sibling twins and adoptive siblings provide evidence that genetic processes have a casual contribution for nearly half of all antisocial and criminal behavior. Raine's deference to twin studies came after he had conducted a careful review of the research literature on twin studies. From this review, Raine concluded that "summary statistics from

13 twin analyses show that 51.5 percent of MZ twins are concordant for crime compared to 20.6 percent for DZ twins, indicating substantial evidence for genetic influences on crime" (1993, p. 289).

Aside from genetics, Raine (2004) notes that for half of the causal factors that are environmental, biology is still intertwined as an explanatory factor. As an example, one might consider children who are victims of child abuse. If the child suffers some sort of head trauma or similar injury, brain damage can follow, which in turn often leads to future antisocial and aggressive behavior. Raine has also pointed to research revealing that childhood malnutrition has been linked to low IQs and conduct disorder. He notes research that shows that when 3-year-olds are given better nutrition and appropriate physical exercise for a period of 2 years or more, they have better brain functioning (EEG measures) by age 11 when compared with control groups. Further, longitudinal research shows a 35 percent reduction in criminal behavior when subjects turn 23, as compared with control groups.

Raine's contentions are supported by other well-known criminological researchers, such as Terrie Moffit as well as Jana Bufkin and Vickie Lutrell. When this research is considered in conjunction with twin-based studies, very convincing evidence emerges in support of biopsychological and/or biosociological approaches to explaining criminal behavior. Thus, it would appear that Raine is not alone in his belief that neurophysiological factors serve as primary causal variables for a large proportion of the criminal behavior that occurs.

Raine has concluded that given the current state of research, the biological and genetic findings are irrefutable. He has also noted that these findings provide some implications from a crime prevention standpoint. In fact, Raine has noted that one reason for the failure to stop much of the crime that occurs is due to a persistent tendency for social activists and policy makers to ignore the biological and genetic contributions to the causation of crime. In response to this oversight, Raine has noted a need to place resources on new interventions that improve human brain structure and functioning among persons at risk of becoming repeat offenders.

It is with this knowledge that Raine has concluded that for crime to be significantly reduced, society must make an active effort to provide interventions that begin in early childhood. He notes the need for improved prenatal and perinatal health care, improved nutrition for the child that carries over beyond early childhood, and the use of medications for severely aggressive children. Raine points to the possibility of new drugs that might correct faulty neurotransmitters and brain abnormalities that cause violence. Further, it may be that corrective brain surgery may prove helpful with criminals who display violent behavior. All of these possibilities have been noted by Raine (1997, 2004).

While such interventions are yet to be seen, the potential contributions of biological and biopsychological explanations of crime have been clearly established by Raine. He clearly notes that biological factors cannot and do not explain all of criminal behavior by themselves. Rather, it is Raine's (1997) contention that many (but not all) instances of repeated criminal behavior may represent some type of disorder or psychopathology in a manner similar to depression, schizophrenia, or other conditions that are recognized as bona fide clinical disorders. He points toward criteria used to determine psychopathology as an overall gestalt from which criminal behavior can be compared. In doing this, he provides a compelling argument that biopsychological factors are intimately involved in the origins of criminal behavior. It is also clear that through his research and writings, Raine has helped reshape the development of criminology as a discipline.

Robert D. Hanser

See also Brain Abnormalities and Crime; Neurology and Crime; Prenatal Influences and Crime; Psychophysiology and Crime; Schizophrenia and Crime

References and Further Readings

Arseneault, L., Tremblay, R. E., Boulerice, B., Seguin, J. R., & Saucier, J. (2000). Minor physical anomalies and family adversity as risk factors for adolescent violent delinquency. *American Journal of Psychiatry, 157,* 917–923.

Bartol, C., & Bartol, A. (2007). *Criminal behavior: A psychosocial approach.* Upper Saddle River, NJ: Prentice Hall.

Bennett, D., Pitale, M., Vora, V., & Rheingold, A. (2004). Reactive vs. Proactive antisocial behavior: Differential correlates of child ADHD symptoms. *Journal of Attention Disorders, 7,* 197–204.

Bufkin, J. L., & Luttrell, V. R. (2005). Neuroimaging studies of aggressive and violent behavior: Current findings and implications for criminology and criminal justice. *Trauma, Violence, and Abuse, 6*, 176–191.

Carlson, N. (2004). *Physiology of behavior* (8th ed.). Boston: Allyn & Bacon.

Eysenck, H. J. (1973). *The inequality of man.* San Diego, CA: EDITS.

Moffitt, T. E. (1993). Adolescence-limited and life-course-persistent antisocial behavior: A developmental taxonomy. *Psychological Review, 100*, 674–701.

Moffitt, T. E., & Walsh, A. (2003). The adolescence-limited/life-course-persistent theory of antisocial behavior: What have we learned? In A. Walsh & L. Ellis (Eds.), *Biosocial criminology: Challenging environmentalism's supremacy* (pp. 125–144). Hauppage, NY: Nova Science.

Raine, A. (1993). *The psychopathology of crime: Criminal behavior as a clinical disorder.* New York: Academic Press.

Raine, A. (2004). Biological key to unlocking crime. *BBC News.* Retrieved from http://news.bbc.co.uk/1/hi/programmes/if/4102371.stm

Raine, A. (2006). *Crime and schizophrenia: Causes and cures.* New York: Nova Science.

Raine, A., Brennan, P., Farrington, D. P., & Mednick, S. A. (Eds.). (1997). *Biosocial bases of violence.* New York: Plenum.

Raine, A., Lencz, T., & Mednick, S. A. (Eds.). (1995). *Schizotypal personality disorder.* Cambridge, UK: Cambridge University Press.

Raine, A., & Sanmartin, J. (Eds.). (2007). *Violence and psychopathy.* New York: Springer.

Raine, A., & Venables, P. H. (1981). Classical conditioning and socialization—a biosocial interaction? *Personality and Individual Differences, 2*, 273–283.

RAPE MYTHS AND VIOLENCE AGAINST WOMEN

Rape is defined by the Federal Bureau of Investigation in the *Uniform Crime Reports* as "the carnal knowledge of a female forcibly and against her will." Rape is one of the least reported violent crimes in the United States. Thus, according to the Bureau of Justice Statistics, between 1992 and 2000, on average 63 percent of completed rapes, 65 percent of attempted rapes, and 74 percent of completed and attempted sexual assaults against females were not reported to the police. Many rape and sexual assault survivors often do not come forward to report their crimes because they fear they would not be believed by their support system or because they do not define themselves as rape victims. In many cases, rape victims are reluctant to acknowledge being raped due to prevailing social and cultural biases related to rape. Statistics and research also show that it is difficult to charge and convict perpetrators of rape. A key source of victim reluctance to report victimization and of difficulties in convicting offenders are stereotypical attitudes and pervasive false beliefs about rape, its victims, and perpetrators. These beliefs and prevailing attitudes have been coined as "rape myths."

Rape myths revolve around the definition of rape victim (the "real" victim), the circumstances in which forced sex is defined or perceived as rape, the nature of victim-offender relationship that lead to or "justify" rape, and proper victim reactions to rape. Below, prevailing rape myths about women, the theories that explain their origin or persistence, and the impact of these myths on violence against women are described. Finally, measures to prevent or attenuate the impact of myths on violence against women are discussed.

Common Rape Myths About Women

Several studies indicate a wider range of common myths about female rape victims. Nine prominent rape myths are described.

1. *Women dressed "indecently" or "inappropriately" ask for it (rape).* It is evident in research that rape can happen to anyone. Women cannot be blamed for being raped due to their appearance. Rape is not about sex but rather power and control by the rapist over the victim.

2. *She wanted to be raped.* Female rape victims presumably act sexy or tease men because they want to get raped. If a woman encourages a man or reaches a certain point in their intimacy short of sexual intercourse and then gets raped, then she has agreed to have sex with her partner. There is also a belief that women fantasize about being raped or want to be raped by men they do not know.

3. *It wasn't really rape.* If the female victim does not have any visible bruises or injuries or has not fought back against the perpetrator, it is not rape. If the female victim did not clearly say "no" to the rapist, it means she wanted to have sex and therefore cannot argue that the forced sex is not rape.

4. *He didn't mean to rape her; a wife cannot be raped.* In certain instances, the man may have gotten sexually carried away and never meant to rape her; it just happened, because men cannot control themselves. Another variant of this myth pertains to married couples. A husband forcing his wife to have sex without her consent is not committing rape. They are married and sex is assumed to be part of the marriage contract and should be expected.

5. *She may have lied that she has been raped or women may hype the impact of rape in their lives.* One of the prevalent myths indicates that women who report being raped may have enjoyed the sex with their perpetrator and then changed their mind later. Hence, these so-called victims may be lying about their victimization. Another existing stereotype about female victims is that they can just forget the horrible experience and move on. Research shows that nearly one third of all rape victims develop symptoms of posttraumatic stress disorders related to rape and that 11 percent or more suffer from it for a prolonged period of time.

6. *Most rapists are either black or Hispanic.* This myth suggests that rape is perpetrated only or mostly by racial minorities and is often minority perpetrators prey on white women. Research shows that the majority of violent crimes against women (80 to 90 percent) are intra-racial—that is, are committed by someone of the same racial background as the victim.

7. *Most rapists wait in a dark alley waiting to attack a (female) stranger or rapes happen only in "bad" neighborhoods.* Studies show that the majority of the rapes take place at the home of the victim or the offender. Nearly 60 percent of rape and sexual assault incidents are reported by victims as occurring in their own home or at the home of a friend, a relative, or a neighbor.

8. *Victims who are drunk or on drugs are responsible for their rape.* There is a correlation between alcohol usage and becoming a rape victim, and some rapes are perpetrated after the offender has caused the victim to consume substances. Legally, however, sexual intercourse without the victim's consent, or when the victim is incapacitated due to substance usage, is considered rape.

9. *Rape victims come mainly from minority or marginal communities or are not "good women"; rape victims deserve to be raped as they have bad reputations or much sexual experience.* Research shows that rape occurs at all communities and at all levels of socio-economic status. Also, having prior sexual experiences does not make it legal to force sex on women. All women have the right to select their partners regardless of prior or extent of their experience. Furthermore, even prior sexual relationship with a specific man cannot be a justification for rape at a later point.

It should be noted that there are also rape myths about male victims, mostly those who are raped by other men. They include the following: (1) *Being raped by a male attacker is tantamount to or results in loss of masculinity.* (2) *Only gay men are sexually assaulted by men.* (3) *Men are incapable of functioning sexually unless they are sexually aroused.* (4) *Men cannot be forced to have sex against their will.* (5) *Men are less affected by sexual assault than women.* (6) *Men are always ready to accept any sexual opportunity.* (7) *A man is expected to be able to defend himself against sexual assault.* These myths also portray men as incapable of controlling their behavior under certain circumstances, and blame the victim if rape occurs. The theories explaining rape myths about women, listed in the next section, explain rape myths about male victims as well.

Theories Explaining the Origins or Persistence of Rape Myths

Theories explaining rape myths address cultural and societal factors responsible for the emergence and persistence of rape myths about women as victims.

Feminist Theories

Feminist theories emphasize the role of patriarchy (or male hegemony) as the cultural basis underlying gender roles and power differentials between the sexes. Stereotyping of gender roles is widely practiced in most cultures: girls are expected to be passive and behave in a "feminine" manner; boys are expected to be "masculine" and are positively reinforced for being aggressive. Feminist theories emphasize inequality, dominance, or other sources of women's oppression as being at the root of rape myths about women. They argue that rape myths reflect or contribute to men's ability to control and dominate women.

Just World Theory

According to this theory, individuals believe that the world is a just and orderly place; therefore, those who are harmed get what they "truly deserve." The desire to blame a woman for becoming a rape victim is a way to maintain intact our beliefs in a just world and reduce fear of victimization. Thus, a woman deserves to be raped if she has dressed that way or she drank with her date.

It should be noted that these theories can also explain rape myths about men as victims, portraying them as not masculine, as responsible for their victimization, and for deserving the rape.

Impact of Rape Myths and Measures to Reduce Its Impact

The impact of rape myths vary across ages, ethnicities, and gender. Studies have found that older women are more likely to support rape myths than younger women. Significant differences are found across race/ethnicity and class. Rape myths also cause women not to consider themselves as victims, and to blame themselves for the rape and for failing to report the incident to authorities. Research shows further that rape myths are related to the prospects that women from certain communities or with certain attributes will be victimized or how the police and judicial system would respond to them.

Despite legal reforms that addressed various rape myths, or passage of laws that challenge prevailing beliefs about the "real" victim or condition that "justify" rape, there are many individuals who subscribe to the myths and blame victims for their victimization. Educating the citizenry, beginning at the public school and continuing at college level, is a starting point to bring about awareness concerning rape. Media could be another prime tool to undermine the stereotypes embodied in rape myths and for providing accurate portrayals of victims and their victimization. Continued education, as well as sensitivity and cultural competence training are also necessary to ensure that agents of the criminal justice system (police, prosecutors, judges) and members of the health care and medical systems are aware of the many subtle ways in which rape myths affect how victims feel or behave, and how law enforcement and medical systems respond to the victimization.

Edna Erez and Meghna Bhat

See also Koss, Mary P.: The Prevalence and Sources of Rape; Russell, Diana E. H.: The Politics of Rape; Schwartz, Martin D., and Victoria L. Pitts: A Feminist Routine Activity Theory; Stanko, Elizabeth A.: Gender, Fear, and Risk

References and Further Readings

Andre, C., & Velasquez, M. (1990). The just world theory [Electronic version]. *Issues in Ethics, 3*(2). Retrieved September 15, 2008, from http://www.scu.edu/ethics/publications/iie/v3n2/justworld.html

Chapleau, K. M., Oswald, D. L., & Russell, B. L. (2008). Male rape myths: Role of gender, violence and sexism. *Journal of Interpersonal Violence, 23,* 600–615.

Federal Bureau of Investigation. (2006). *Uniform crime reports: Crime in the United States, 2006.* Washington, DC: U.S. Department of Justice.

Lonsway, K. A., & Fitzgerald, L. F. (1994). Rape myths: In review. *Psychology of Women Quarterly, 18,* 133–164.

Lonsway, K. A., & Fitzgerald, L. F. (1995). Attitudinal antecedents of rape myth acceptance: A theoretical and empirical reexamination. *Journal of Personality and Social Psychology, 68,* 704–711.

Rennison, C. M. (2002). *Rape and sexual assault: Reporting to police and medical attention, 1992–2000.* Washington, DC: Bureau of Justice Statistics, U.S. Department of Justice.

Tjaden, P., & Thoennes, N. (2006). *Extent, nature and consequences of rape victimization: Findings from the National Violence against Women Survey.* Washington, DC: National Institute of Justice, U.S. Department of Justice.

Wilson, P. (1978). *The other side of rape.* Queensland, Australia: University of Queensland Press.

Winkler, C. (2002). *One night: Realities of rape.* New York: AltaMira Press.

RATIONAL CHOICE AND WHITE-COLLAR CRIME

Rational choice theory serves to explain why and under what conditions any particular white-collar offender opts to commit a criminal offense. Criminal justice theorists readily understand that such factors incorporate a consideration of deterrence and overall situational factors leading to criminal behavior. This entry focuses on the nature of rational choice theory and institutional factors that help to explain the connection between rational choice and white-collar crime. Special attention is given to Raymond Paternoster and Sally Simpson's rational choice theory of corporate crime.

General Considerations

The concept of rational choice theory is derived from the notion that individuals consciously and deliberately choose criminal behavior of their own free will. For example, an individual choosing to undertake a white-collar act assesses the nature of the immediate action and the chances of successfully completing the action without facing systematic criminal justice sanctions.

The components of criminal behavior forming rational choice considerations are the immediate background or social situation (e.g., an urban setting for violent crime or office setting for white-collar criminals), justification for the physical attack on individuals or the financial property of individuals and/or corporations, and the prospects of "getting away" with the criminal action. The immediate situation dictates whether criminal activity is rational through self-justification of the specific action and an understanding that individuals can continually violate such laws with impunity. Repeated criminal behavior without detection leads individuals or financial entities to assume that white-collar crime (e.g., embezzlement or corporate fraud practices) is normative and acceptable for immediate and long-term gain.

Rational choice is also closely connected with the conception of routine activity theory. The notion of routine activities assumes a particular pattern of behavior associated with a person (or group) and a given setting. In the case of street crime, a particular mall or bar may be a facilitator of collective activity.

Such activity might be considered deviant if there are illicit actions, such as violent assaults or the exchange of illegal drugs within the setting. A systematized pattern of such behaviors leads to a lifestyle defined as deviant in its basic nature.

White-collar crime can take a similar direction. Corporations or individual employees embrace criminal activity "because they can." Upper-echelon managerial ranks within corporate organizations at times engage in corruptive practices. Such practices as embezzlement, junk bond trading, manufacture of defective products, and environmental damage result from this process. For example, Bill Moyers and others in the now-famous PBS documentary *Chemical Wars* document how Union Carbide plants in Baton Rouge (otherwise known as "Cancer Alley") allegedly served to undermine the health of their workers. Long-time workers were systematically dying of cancer-related illnesses. It was not until much later that investigators discovered notations in worker files. These documents indicate implicit knowledge of the chemical compounds and the dangers of contamination or exposure.

Enron is another such example of how corporations shield illegal practices through layers of bureaucratic information management. Kenneth Lay and Jeffrey Skilling were cognizant of the fact that the financial reports falsely reflected an ongoing profit margin. In reality, the company was drowning in debt while leveraging their cash flow through American and offshore financial institutions. Used computers and other corporate property were routinely certified higher than their asset value.

In addition, as noted in the documentary *The Smartest Guys in the Room*, Enron artificially manipulated energy prices in the state of California. In the interim, employees could not withdraw their pension funds, and investment houses funneling retirement funds into Enron were misled into believing that the firm was solvent. Kenneth Lay also forged a tight alliance with former President George W. Bush and former Vice President Dick Cheney. This alliance enabled Lay to influence energy regulation. For example, several energy regulation bills Lay drafted were submitted into the system and eventually passed into law by the United States Congress. In the end, billions of dollars in corporate and individual investor funds were systematically defrauded by Kenneth Lay, Jeffrey Skilling, and other corporate officials.

Finally, white-collar crime as a rational choice potentially flourishes in an atmosphere of lax regulation. Lack of general deterrence or a failure of governmental regulatory bodies to follow through on corporate malfeasance can have harmful results. Deterrence must come from active investigations by federal prosecutors or governmental officials within the Federal Trade Commission, Securities and Exchange Commission, or the Food and Drug Administration. Lack of diligence can lead to overpricing and product safety issues with a direct impact on unsuspecting consumers.

The circumstances of Bernard Madoff's $65 billion Ponzi scheme typify the regulatory problem. Federal officials expend limited resources in the investigation and prosecution of white-collar crime. Past scandals involving savings and loan institutions and junk bond securities fraud were revealed long after major economic theft was perpetrated. Federal agencies looked the other way in expressing indifference until the full state of the damage was revealed. In the case of Madoff, media reporting on *60 Minutes* revealed that investigators were alerted to the unlikely legitimacy of the Madoff investment yields of 10 to 12 percent. However the Securities and Exchange Commission took no action at the time. As a result, more victims were swindled and the Ponzi scheme reached historic proportions.

What can we learn from the Madoff example? The obvious point is that failure to hold white-collar criminals culpable in the early stages of an inquiry produces reinforced behavioral actions. Lack of certain deterrence from within the system reinforces the rational choice behavior. Further, the failure to apply serious punishment in most white-collar crime cases gives the impression that the criminal justice system is lenient on these transgressions.

Rational Choice and Corporate Crime

Paternoster and Simpson (1993) developed the most systematic work in this area, proposing a *rational choice theory of corporate crime*. Corporate crimes are illegal offenses that employees commit on behalf of the company for which they work (e.g., fix prices). Paternoster and Simpson call their approach a *subjective utility theory* because it links corporate offending to the perceived, rather than to the objective, costs and benefits of breaking the law.

Paternoster and Simpson include three types of perceived costs in their theory. First, there is the extent to which employees contemplating crimes on behalf of the corporation believe that they might personally be formally sanctioned for their lawbreaking, such as being prosecuted by the criminal justice system. Second, these employees might fear informal sanctions, such as damaging the reputation of the company or being ostracized by family and friends in the community. Third, there is the possibility of losing self-respect. This could be a matter of feeling shame or guilt. In general, those perceiving fewer formal, informal, and self-imposed costs would be more likely to decide to engage in a corporate crime.

Paternoster and Simpson also focus on the perceived costs of trying to comply with regulatory rules (e.g., obey environmental pollution laws or workplace safety laws). Trying to follow the law may result in inefficient business practices that depress company profits and hurt an employee's career. They also assert that corporate decision makers perceive benefits of not complying with legal standards. Thus, noncompliance might allow the company to be more profitable than competitors who follow the rules. In turn, this might increase the value of company stock and induce more investments from financial institutions.

Paternoster and Simpson argue further that morality matters in the decision to offend. This occurs in two ways. First, moral inhibitions refer to the belief that it is "wrong" to violate safety, environmental, financial, and similar rules. Such morality thus might overrule any simple cost-benefit calculation an employee might have. The failure to consider morality is thus an important omission in crass rational choice theories. Second, employees also perceive the legitimacy or fairness of the rules the company is being asked to follow. If they believe that regulations are unreasonable or being applied capriciously, this might remove their moral inhibitions and free them to consider the sheer rationality of breaking the law.

Paternoster and Simpson conclude their model by specifying two additional factors. First, because corporate crimes are committed within an organizational setting, situational and contextual factors might determine whether any specific offense is committed. Thus, some corporate organizations might place employees under inordinate pressure to make profits or might have business dealings that present many opportunities to offend (e.g., financial companies). Second, they caution that past behavior also matters: employees who have broken the law in the past are likely to do it again.

Complexities of Corporate Decision Making

Paternoster and Simpson present a nuanced rational choice theory, emphasizing different types of costs (formal, informal, and self-imposed sanctions), how complying with rules can involve sets of costs and benefits, how personal morality and the morality of those imposing rules on employees make the decision to offend seem wrong or right, how organizational pressures and opportunities matter, and how past behavior can make future behavior more likely. In their view, the rationality of the decision to engage in corporate crime is complex and contingent on a host of factors intersecting in time and space.

In later work, Paternoster and Simpson (1996; see also Simpson et al., 2002) have argued that the nature of corporate decision making is more complex than can be accounted for by a rational choice theory. Although they assert that rational choice remains an integral component of the decision to engage in a corporate crime, they also observe that a broad array of other factors is involved in such offending. For example, some laws are broken not purposefully but because corporate employees make risky decisions with unforeseen consequences. Thus, products can be marketed that prove to be dangerous to consumers. Employees might have been negligent in failing to appreciate the flaws in the product but may not have made a "rational" choice to trade off harm to consumers for corporate profits. It also is possible that some corporate decisions, including illegal ones, are made not after careful calculations but out of mere habit. Finally, employees might decide to break the law to benefit their unit's performance, even though the illegality might impose costs on the corporation (e.g., fines, public embarrassment) that the illegal act cannot justify.

Conclusion

White-collar and corporate crime seem to be ideal for analysis through rational choice theory because they involve decisions made within business environments where rationality—the pursuit of profits

and the minimizing of costs—is presumably valued. This insight is important and should be considered carefully in developing any coherent theory of white-collar offending. Nonetheless, the decision to offend—whether by offenders in city streets or in corporate suites—is complex and bounded by a host of moral, legal, and situational factors. A complete explanation of white-collar criminality thus must be based on a rich and nuanced theory of decision making that studies how criminal choices reflect both rational calculation and contextual constraints.

Lloyd Klein

See also Benson, Michael L.: The Collateral Consequences of White-Collar Offending; Cressey, Donald R.: Embezzlement and White-Collar Crime; Geis, Gilbert: Perspectives on White-Collar Crime Scandals; Vaughan, Diane: The Normalization of Deviance

References and Further Readings

Benson, M. L., & Simpson, S. S. (2009). *White-collar crime: An opportunity perspective.* New York: Routledge.

Paternoster, R., & Simpson, S. (1993). A rational choice theory of corporate crime. In R. V. Clarke & M. Felson (Eds.), *Routine activity and rational choice* (Advances in Criminological Theory: Vol. 5, pp. 37–58). New Brunswick, NJ: Transaction.

Paternoster, R., & Simpson, S. (1996). Sanction threats and appeals to morality: Testing a rational choice model of corporate crime. *Law and Society Review, 30*, 549–583.

Shover, N., & Hochstedler, A. (2006). *Choosing white-collar crime.* New York: Cambridge University Press.

Simpson, S. S., & Piquero, N. L. (2002). Low self-control, organizational theory, and corporate crime. *Law and Society Review, 36*, 509–548.

Simpson, S. S., Piquero, N. L., & Paternoster, R. (2002). Rationality and corporate offending decisions. In A. R. Piquero & S. G. Tibbetts (Eds.), *Rational choice and criminal behavior: Recent research and future challenges* (pp. 3–24). New York: Routledge.

RECKLESS, WALTER C.: CONTAINMENT THEORY

Walter C. Reckless is one of the most recognized criminologists of the past century, though this nearly was not the case for this three-time president of the American Society of Criminology (1964, 1965, and 1966). According to Randy Martin, Robert Mutchnick, and W. Timothy Austin, it was not until an auto accident resulting in permanent injuries ended Reckless's quest for a musical career that he would pursue social science studies at the University of Chicago. While there, Reckless found himself under the tutelage of renowned sociologists Robert Park and Ernest Burgess and, after receiving his bachelor's degree, was offered a graduate assistantship in sociology to study vice in the surrounding area (Martin et al., 1990, p. 180). This exposure to the shadier side of life helped foster an interest and birthed a career. As observed by the scholars, Reckless's association with Park led to his involvement in participant observation research at local Chicago roadhouses and resulted in his dissertation turned book *Vice in Chicago* in 1931.

As Martin and his colleagues note, while serving in his first academic position at Vanderbilt University, Reckless wrote extensively, including the first text ever published on *Juvenile Delinquency* with Mapheus Smith and the second text in *Social Psychology* with Ernest T. Krueger. In 1940, he would continue his distinguished career at Ohio State University where Reckless would eventually retire from in 1969 (Martin et al., 1990, p. 181). Among his accomplishments, such as the often-cited building of the Criminology-Corrections program, Reckless wrote several influential texts, including his famous work, *The Crime Problem*. The volume published in 1950 was to be the first of seven editions.

According to Randy Martin and his colleagues, Reckless's research while at Ohio State University, with Simon Dinitz and others, would set the stage for containment theory, Reckless's explanation for delinquency and crime. Reckless's research would center on the insulating role that self-concept plays against delinquency, and it was this essential concern about insulating qualities of various personal and social features that became the foundation of containment theory. Containment theory was not formally expressed by Reckless until the third edition of his book *The Crime Problem* and in abbreviated form in the article "The New Theory of Delinquency and Crime," which appeared in the journal *Federal Probation* in 1961.

Containment Theory

Though interdisciplinary in nature, containment theory is considered one of the earliest control theories because it is focused on what stops people from engaging in crime—or rather, what "contains" people (contains or containment essentially being used in place of the term *controls*). As noted by Richard Dodder and Janet Long, containment theory enjoyed much of its popularity in the 1950s and 1960s and has become a staple in the field of criminological theory. While, according to some scholars, the theory has gone out of vogue in recent years, containment theory has kept its foundational place in criminological theory.

The first conceptions of the theory were birthed when Reckless was exploring the shortcomings of other approaches meant to explain delinquency and crime. Early criminological theories were understood in terms of "pushing" and/or "pulling" individuals toward deviance (e.g., differential association theory was recognized as a pull theory; Albert Cohen's subcultural theory represents a combination push and pull theory). According to Reckless, the problem with these approaches was that they failed to account for those youths that did not engage in delinquency in spite of being confronted with pushes and/or pulls toward delinquent ways. This also was the case with the approach promoted by Reckless's mentors, social disorganization theory.

Reckless acknowledged that social disorganization approaches to the study of delinquency and crime enjoyed popularity for a generation. He believed, however, that there was a fundamental oversight with this approach. Although he did believe there was merit to social disorganization theory, Reckless claimed that social disorganization alone was insufficient to completely address the issue of delinquency and crime. He asserted that the largest proportion of people in disorganized or instable areas do not turn out to be delinquent or criminal at all. In fact, most of these people lead lives of relative conformity. This meant that social disorganization approaches, as well as other theories relying on push and/or pull orientations, needed something more if they were to add further to explanations of crime and delinquency.

It was this understanding that brought Reckless to the fundamental questions that gave rise to containment theory: "Why do some persons break through the tottering (social) controls and others do not? Why do rare cases in well-integrated society break through the lines of strong controls?" (1961a, p. 339).

Reckless believed that it was the interplay between inner self-controls and outer social controls that was in part responsible for whether or not an individual would engage in delinquency and criminality. Further, contrary to some other theorists, Reckless thought social disorganization was not about the stress related to social and economic pressures directly. Instead, he believed that where social disorganization played a causal role in delinquency and crime was when social disorganization led specifically to a breakdown in social controls. Important to his line of reasoning was Reckless's prior observations of religious sects. Reckless's observations of these closed and highly controlled groups also contributed to and solidified his beliefs that the community served the express function of external social control.

The Foundation for Containment Theory

As stated above, Reckless relied upon a collection of earlier observations from his solo and collaborative research in formulating containment theory. Some of this research focused upon the notion of self-concept wherein it was observed that a good self-concept provided a youth with a protective shield and/or insulation against delinquency. A poor self-concept had the opposite effect, rendering an individual susceptible to delinquency. This observation apparently held over time, leading Reckless to assume that good and poor self-concept is a reflection of the internalization of favorable and unfavorable socialization and in that way an important internal buffer against delinquency.

Similar to many theorists, Reckless also looked to the observations of others when formulating his new explanation of delinquency and, in doing so, weaved together the central tenets of containment theory. Reckless expressly mentioned the work of researchers Albert J. Reiss, F. Ivan Nye, and Fritz Redl when walking readers through the logic of containment theory.

Reiss discussed the predictive value of personal and social controls on delinquent behavior in his influential work with Chicago juveniles. Reiss's

observation and assessment of the different dimensions of control were not lost on Reckless. Reckless would incorporate this understanding into his own work, particularly the observation that personal controls were more influential than social controls on recidivism. Also, Reiss's notion of personal controls, such as self-control, would essentially mirror what Reckless would call inner containment.

Nye's research further illuminated the ways in which controls are important to regulating personal behavior. Nye's research specifically highlighted four types of control factors that were discussed by Reckless: direct control, internalized control, indirect control, and the availability of alternative means to goals. All had a place in restraining delinquent behavior. Reckless states that, according to Nye, punishment and discipline are among the features of direct control. Inner control is essentially self-control, and indirect control is a result of not wanting to disappoint meaningful others by deviant behavior. Of course, individuals must have an alternative to deviant behavior, which explains the fourth aspect of control identified by Nye. Hence, Reckless's and Nye's explanations share similar features. Both are similar in scope in that they are only meant to explain general deviance. Also, Nye's notion of direct control can be likened to Reckless's outer containment concept. Internalized control can be seen as mirroring Reckless's concept of inner containment.

Redl and Wineman's formulation of the "behavior control system" was also relied on by Reckless as offering support for containment theory. Redl's work considered inner psychological processes thought to be involved in whether or not an individual would engage in delinquency and crime. Specifically, the concepts identified by Redl were the ego (and its accompanying 22 ego functions) and the superego, which were thought to be central to inner control. The ego functions were seen by Redl as important in managing life situations and included things such as frustration tolerance, temptation resistance, learning from experience, and taking care of possessions. The superego is seen as one's conscience and the incorporation of parental values that serve to regulate behavior. Reckless ultimately included the ego and a well-developed superego as potentially important elements to his concept of inner containment. Reckless's inclusion of these concepts, however, seemed to be as much about a concern over attracting scholars in other disciplines to use and possibly specify containment theory. According to Reckless, "It is important to incorporate Redl's thinking on the ego and super-ego as the behavior control system within the person, so as to indicate that the components of containment theory can be specified by psychiatrists, psychologists, and psychoanalysts just as readily by sociologists" (1961a, p. 354).

Inner and Outer Containment

As is the tradition of control theories, containment theory assumes that people are very prone to getting in trouble. The idea is that individuals must be controlled or contained from committing delinquent and criminal acts. The core of the theory is *containment*—that is, personal and social safeguards that shield the individual from committing deviancy. Containment rests on the principles of control. According to Reckless, containment theory "seeks to feret [ferret] out more specifically the inner and outer controls over normative behavior" (1961b, p. 44). To do this, Reckless consolidated the particular characteristics identified in his and others' research into exclusive themes of inner and outer containment. Containment theory, in essence, is Reckless's attempt to ascertain what controls work best at which level to regulate conduct and therefore delinquency and crime.

The principal social control concepts of containment theory are inner and outer containment. Inner containment involves the personal, social controls over behavior. Reckless believed that these included self-control, a good self-concept, ego strength, and so on. In essence, these are the qualities that serve as inner regulators against delinquent behavior. According to Reckless, outer containment dealt with the structural buffers in the youth's proximal, social environment that served to restrain them. These immediate social constraints included such things as "a consistent moral front to the person, institutional reinforcement of his norms, goals, expectations, the existence of a reasonable set of social expectations, effective supervision and discipline (social controls), provision for reasonable scope of activity (including limits and responsibilities) as well as alternatives and safety valves, opportunity for acceptance, belongingness" (1961b, p. 45). To Reckless, these structural factors around the individual served to "contain" the youth against delinquency and crime.

To Err Is Human: "Pulls" and "Pushes" Toward Delinquency

According to Reckless, environmental pressures can exact influence over people to the extent that they are not contained and/or protected. In that regard, inner and outer containment serve as a buffer from these external conditions. Environmental conditions that may steer individuals toward deviancy may take various forms, such as poverty or deprivations, conflict and discord, external restraint, minority group status, and limited access to success in an opportunity structure. Reckless further elaborated upon these environmental pressures in describing them as environmental "pulls." Pulls represent the features of the environment that may serve to attract some individuals toward deviancy. According to Reckless, pulls might be environmental distractions, attractions, temptations, carriers of delinquent and criminal patterns, and subcultures.

Reckless also observed what he considered to be "ordinary" pushes. Pushes are based in individual psychology and are considered to be internal motivators toward deviancy. Pushes may include internal drives and frustrations, feelings of restlessness, disappointments, hostility, inferiority, and rebellion. Reckless acknowledged that there are some extreme internal motivations (pushes) that cannot be contained such as those derived from mental illness (i.e., compulsions). According to Reckless, such pathological compulsions were beyond the abilities of normal, ordinary containment.

Again, containment theory posits that normative behavior is brought about by "resisting" deviancy and directing youth toward legitimate social expectations. According to Reckless, both inner and outer containment are core between the pressures and pulls of the external environment and inner drives and pushes.

Scope of Containment Theory

As stated earlier, Reckless argues that containment theory is a general theory of crime, explaining the wide range of behaviors between the extremes of deviancy. According to Reckless, at one end of the continuum is individual pathology. This group includes behaviors caused by mental illness, among other things (e.g., compulsions; behavior as the result of organic brain damage). The opposite extreme of behaviors, though deviant, would essentially be considered "normal" given the circumstances and fall beyond those behaviors that containment theory means to explain. Individuals at this extreme, explains Reckless, have been socialized by family or some affiliate and/or marginalized group to behave as societal deviants (e.g., criminal tribes of India, gypsies).

The Recognized Limitations and Validity of Containment Theory

To Reckless, one of the strengths of containment theory was the ability to tailor the theory to the different disciplines that engage in the study of deviancy. Arguably, containment theory can be used by psychiatrists, psychologists, sociologists, and practitioners equally, as the theory reportedly explains delinquency from an interdisciplinary perspective. According to Reckless, "All of these experts look for dimensions of inner and outer strength and can specify these strengths in their terms" (1961b, p. 46). However, there are problems with containment theory specifically and control theories generally.

Richard Dodder and Janet Long have observed that there is a general lack of testable statements in relation to containment and the proposed relationship with deviant behavior. Ironically, one could argue that this in part was intended by Reckless when making his statement of the theory. Reckless offered that research would have to identify the "one or two" essential elements of inner and outer containment that act as the regulators of normative behavior. He further states that research, ultimately, would have to sort out which of the inner and outer regulatory systems operated together. Problematically, a theory written in this way may lead to more speculation than answers.

Dodder and Long further scrutinize the limited ability of containment theory to explain female deviance, considering socialization processes arguably differ between the sexes in respect to self-concept. Recall that, according to containment theory, a good self-concept is supposed to insulate individuals from deviancy. If the processes are different depending on sex, one would expect that containment theory might not apply to females. This criticism is reasonable, particularly since Reckless relied on observations of boys for his theory. Another criticism of containment theory is recognized by Thomas Kelley and rests in the idea that many of the inner motivations and environmental conditions identified by Reckless tend to be highly transient even over short time periods. Given that many of these conditions are evanescent, it is difficult to isolate the mechanisms identified by containment theory leading to deviancy.

Reckless and Dinitz tested elements of containment theory with little success. As noted by Randy Martin and his colleagues, these studies have been referred to collectively as "the Good Boy–Bad Boy" series and ran from circa 1956 to 1972. Although failing to initially support containment theory, others, such as Don Gibbons and Marvin Krohn, have noted methodological flaws that would give pause to these initial results. It also has been observed by these scholars that later empirical assessments found more varied results beyond what could be accounted for by the theory. There is still contention as to whether containment theory, whether original, revised, or specified, can be revived.

Conclusion

Containment theory is considered one of the earliest control theories of crime. With its "personality-oriented" slant, the theory is credited by some with laying the foundation of contemporary theoretical approaches to explaining delinquency and crime (Martin et al., 1990, p. 198). Randy Martin, Robert Mutchnick, and W. Timothy Austin (and others) are explicit in their claim that Reckless's containment theory is the "cornerstone in the foundation of contemporary control theory" and "that the work of Travis Hirschi, which has become synonymous with control theory, constitutes an extension of Reckless' ideas into broader social contexts" (p. 198).

However, there are some detractors of this position that have noted that containment theory, as well as other theories of its time, are nothing more than extensions or reformulations of previous works. For instance, Don Gibbons and Marvin Krohn assert that containment theory consists of "old wine in a new bottle" (1991, p. 107). Although one can see the merit in both positions on containment theory, it is undeniable that Reckless's approach has had an impact and has served as a foundation from which others' work was formed.

Jamie L. Flexon

See also Durkheim, Émile: Anomie and Suicide; Gottfredson, Michael R., and Travis Hirschi: Self-Control Theory; Hirschi, Travis: Social Control Theory; Nye, F. Ivan: Family Controls and Delinquency; Reiss, Albert J., Jr.: Personal and Social Controls and Delinquency; Sampson, Robert J., and John H. Laub: Age-Graded Theory of Informal Social Control; Shaw, Clifford R., and Henry D. McKay: Social Disorganization Theory

References and Further Readings

Dodder, R. A., & Long, J. R. (1980). Containment theory reevaluated: An empirical explication. *Criminal Justice Review, 5,* 74–84.

Gibbons, D. C., & Krohn, M. D. (1991). *Delinquent behavior* (5th ed.). Englewood Cliffs, NJ: Prentice Hall.

Hirschi, T. (1969). *Causes of delinquency.* Berkeley: University of California Press.

Kelley, T. M. (1996). A critique of social bonding and control theory of delinquency using the principles of psychology of mind [Electronic version]. *Adolescence, 31*(122). Retrieved November 18, 2008, from http://findarticles.com/p/articles/mi_m2248/is_n122_v31/ai_18435715/pg_1?tag=artBody;c011

Martin, R., Mutchnick, R. J., & Austin, W. T. (1990). *Criminological thought: Pioneers past and present.* New York: Macmillan.

Nye, F. I. (1958). *Family relationships and delinquent behavior.* New York: Wiley.

Quinney, R., & Wildeman, J. (1977). *The problem of crime: A critical introduction to criminology* (2nd ed.). New York: Harper and Row.

Reckless, W. C. (1961a). *The crime problem* (3rd ed.). New York: Appleton Century Crofts.

Reckless, W. C. (1961b). A new theory of delinquency and crime. *Federal Probation, 25,* 42–46.

Redl, F., & Wineman, D. (1951). *Children who hate.* Glencoe, IL: Free Press.

Reiss, A. J., Jr. (1951). Delinquency as the failure of personal and social controls. *American Sociological Review, 16,* 196–206.

REGOLI, ROBERT M., AND JOHN D. HEWITT: DIFFERENTIAL OPPRESSION THEORY

Differential oppression theory, originally published by Robert M. Regoli and John D. Hewitt in *Delinquency in Society* in 1991, contends that children have little power to influence their social world. They have almost no choice regarding with whom they associate and, have limited resources available to influence others or to support themselves independently of adults. In comparison to adults, children are relatively powerless and are expected to submit to the power and authority of adults. When this power is used to deny children self-determination and impede them from developing a sense of competence and self-efficacy, it becomes oppression (Finkelhor, 2008).

All children are oppressed. The oppression of children falls on a continuum, ranging from simple demands for obedience to rules designed for the convenience of adults to physical, sexual, and emotional abuse. Differential oppression theory states that the involvement of children in crime is best understood as adaptive reaction to oppressive social situations created by adults. Differential oppression theory is organized around four principles:

1. Because children lack power due to their age, size, and lack of resources, they are easy targets for adult oppression.

2. Adult oppression of children occurs in multiple social contexts and falls on a continuum ranging from benign neglect to malignant abuse.

3. Oppression leads to adaptive reactions by children.

4. Children's adaptations to oppression create and reinforce adults' views of children as inferior, subordinate, and being troublemakers. This view enables adults to justify their role as oppressor and further reinforces children's powerlessness.

Forms of Oppression

The term *oppression* is a summation of the abusive, neglectful, and disrespectful relations children confront. Oppression occurs in different settings and falls on a continuum ranging from benign neglect to malignant abuse. Oppression takes place whenever adults act in ways that belittle children as being something less than authentic and feeling human beings. While there are occasions when adults exercise power over children out of sincere concern for the child's welfare, other times adults' use of power over children is about the needs and interests of the adult rather than the child. Oppressive structural forces, such as poverty and residing in a disadvantaged neighborhood, also negatively influence parenting practices. However, the underlying source of this oppression is found in the mistreatment adults received as children and continue to experience as adults. Therefore, the oppression adults inflict on children is part of a chain of coercion that is transmitted from one generation to the next.

Healthy development requires that social contexts provide opportunities for children to fulfill their physical, intellectual, psychological, and social developmental needs. Unfortunately, for many children, the social contexts they find themselves in are oppressive and damaging. Using a developmental-ecological perspective can provide a means for understanding how the oppression of children occurs within multiple social contexts that may interact to produce harmful outcomes. These contexts include both micro-level relationships with family and friends and macro-level structural elements, such as age, class, neighborhood, and race, which expose people to different types of oppression.

Micro-Level Oppression

The most severe oppression adults inflict upon children is maltreatment. The major forms of child maltreatment include physical abuse, sexual abuse, neglect, and emotional abuse. Certain parenting styles are more likely to oppress children. Some parents oppress children when they impose and maintain adult conceptions of social order. These parents see children as extensions of themselves rather than as individuals. The children are required to obey rules designed to reinforce adult notions of right and wrong behavior. To exert greater control over their children, parents and other adults sometimes use coercion or force. Coercion may become excessive, lead to physical harm and long-term psychological damage, and is

a mechanism for transmitting an ageist ideology that diminishes the value of children in relation to adults across society.

Other parents oppress children through neglectful parenting that fails to meet their children's physical, emotional, and educational needs. Examples of physical neglect include abandonment and inadequate supervision. Emotional neglect includes inattention to the child's needs for affection and spouse abuse in the child's presence. The allowance of chronic truancy and failure to attend to special educational needs are examples of educational neglect. Neglect occurs any time a caretaker fails to provide one of the basic ingredients essential for developing a child into a physically, intellectually, emotionally, and psychologically healthy person. Although single incidents of neglect may have no noticeable harmful effects, in some cases, they result in death. Chronic patterns of neglect also may result in developmental delays or emotional disabilities.

Macro-Level Oppression

Macro-level social forces such as poverty also oppress children. Children living in poverty are most likely to experience oppression. This oppression can be viewed developmentally, and is cumulative as children continue to grow and develop in destitute conditions. During the early years, poverty oppresses children by impairing their physical health status at birth and providing less access to resources that may moderate the negative consequences of those problems. For healthy development, young children need exposure to stimulating materials or experiences. Children living in poverty are less likely to have access to these materials or experiences. Often their homes are unsafe, lacking heat and adequate plumbing. In addition, they have increased exposure to chemical toxins, such as lead, which are associated with cognitive deficits, lower school achievement, and long-term impairment of neurological function (Needleman, Schell, Bellinger, Leviton, & Allred, 1990). Rather than receiving cognitively stimulating experiences, young children living in poverty may rarely leave their home. Environmental and work-related conditions limit their access to the outdoors. Poor children are more likely to live in housing located in commercial and industrial areas, which often lack safe outdoor places for them to play and limit opportunities for social interaction and cognitive development (Macleod, 2008).

Poverty also has oppressive influences on school-age and adolescent children. During middle childhood and adolescence, children increasingly come into direct contact with their neighborhoods through involvement in school and informal neighborhood groups. For young people, the physical features of their neighborhood establish the boundaries of their social universe. Some neighborhoods offer youth a variety of supervised instruction and structured activities, while others send the majority of the children out on the street. Due to the restricted tax base in poor distressed neighborhoods, limited public resources are available to support the education, recreation, and health needs of youth and their families. In contrast, youth living in wealthy neighborhoods have opportunities that poor children are not offered, like summer camp and music lessons. Instead, adolescents growing up in poverty have higher exposure to physical danger and criminal activity (Wilson, 2009).

Because successful adaptation at each stage of youth development is influenced by earlier developmental histories, long-term exposure to oppressive living conditions likely results in worse developmental outcomes (McNulty, 2001). High-risk contexts such as poverty and child maltreatment may have lasting effects when they damage crucial adaptive systems such as adult-child attachment, intelligence, and self-regulation of emotions and behavior. Persistent poverty is consistently found to have more adverse effects than transitory poverty on children's cognitive development and school achievement. Children living in poverty for long periods experience more negative life events and adverse conditions that may place demands on their coping resources well beyond what they can handle. This may trigger a cycle of lifelong deficiencies encompassing many contexts of their lives.

Adaptations to Oppression

Most children adapt to oppression through *passive acceptance* and subsequent obedience, an obedience built upon fear, which derives from implied threats and intimidation. Children learn that obedience is expected. Such adaptations among children are similar to the passive acceptance of adaptations of prison inmates and immersion in the cycle of violence for battered women. These children outwardly accept their inferior positions, but develop a repressed hatred for their oppressors, adapting to the structures of domination in which they are immersed. Once a situation of violence and oppression has been established, it engenders an entire way of life and behavior for those caught up in it, oppressors and oppressed alike. The oppressed are likely to believe they have no purpose in life except what the oppressor prescribes for them.

Passive children do not fully explore personal autonomy; they never become the "author of their own life." Repression results in negative self-perceptions that manifest themselves in different problem behaviors including crime, delinquency, alcoholism, drug addiction, eating disorders, and psychiatric disorders.

A second adaptation to oppression is the *exercise of illegitimate coercive power*. Some adolescents are attracted to delinquency because it helps them establish a sense of autonomy and control (Katz, 1988). Delinquent acts can immediately make things happen and provide the child with a sense of restored potency denied him or her by adults. Sexual misbehavior and violations of the criminal law, for example, derive greater symbolic importance for the child to the extent they demonstrate resistance to adult attempts to exert control over his or her behavior.

A third adaptation is the *manipulation of one's peers*. Through the manipulation of others within the peer group, a child who has experienced oppression may acquire a sense of strength and control not otherwise felt (Marwell, 1966). The school bully is an example. Unfortunately, the mere involvement of a child with his or her peers leads many adults to view the involvement as problematic in itself. Adults may then react by exercising even greater control over the child's interaction with others.

The fourth adaptation is *retaliation*, which may include criminal acts ranging from property crimes to violent offenses. It is the most severe and least common of the adaptations. Children may engage in retaliation to get back at the people or the institutions they see as being the source of their oppression. School vandalism can occur because a student is angry with a teacher. Some children will strike directly at their peers by assaulting or killing them. Others try to hurt their parents by turning inward by becoming chronically depressed and possibly committing suicide (Ianni, 1989).

Conclusion

Confronted by oppressive forces, children adapt. Adults individually or collectively affect children and children react. While children *as a group* are oppressed, the impact is most significantly experienced at the individual level. Oppression is differentially experienced, both in its application and impact. Children adapt differentially and the individual reasons for how particular children adapt are unknown. Even children growing up in the same family, in the same neighborhood, and experiencing similar oppressive situations will exhibit different adaptations.

Current research has established a good, strong examination of the connection between oppression and adolescent problem behaviors. While many research studies have tested elements of differential oppression theory, some of the most promising research assessing the theory is by Carolyn Smith and David Farrington. They explored the extent to which antisocial behavior in parents predicted antisocial behavior in children in two successive generations. They also examined the degree to which a man's childhood antisocial behavior predicted antisocial behavior in his own children, the ways that parenting problems were related to delinquency in two successive generations, and the extent to which intergenerational continuities in antisocial behavior were mediated by parenting. They found that between generations, antisocial parents in the first generation predicted conduct problems among children in the next two generations. Within generations, second-generation child conduct problems predicted adult antisocial behavior and antisocial partnerships, which in turn predicted conduct problems among their children (the third generation). Parental conflict and authoritarian parenting led to early childhood conduct problems in two successive generations. Second-generation boys who were poorly supervised by their parents were themselves poor supervisors as fathers. Both first and second generations displayed assortative mating, which means that antisocial males tended to marry antisocial females. In this way, parents

specifically, and adults generally, cultivate delinquency, violence, and other maladaptive behaviors directly as a consequence of the way they treat children (Smith & Farrington, 2004).

Future research must examine why one child adapts to abuse by passively accepting the situation and developing an eating disorder while another child experiencing similar abuse adapts by bullying others and still yet another child retaliates by murdering the offending adult. Continued research on differential oppression theory is underway.

Robert M. Regoli

See also Anderson, Elijah: Code of the Street; Colvin, Mark: Coercion Theory; Katz, Jack: Seductions of Crimes; Prenatal Influences and Crime

References and Further Readings

Colvin, M. (2002). *Crime and coercion*. New York: St. Martin's Press.
Finkelhor, D. (2008). *Childhood victimization*. New York: Oxford University Press.
Hewitt, J. D., & Regoli, B. (2003). Differential oppression theory and female delinquency. *Free Inquiry in Creative Sociology, 31*, 165–174.
Ianni, F. (1989). *The search for structure*. New York: Free Press.
Katz, J. (1988). *Seductions of crime*. New York: Basic Books.
Kingston, B., Regoli, B., & Hewitt, J. (2003). The theory of differential oppression: A developmental-ecological explanation of adolescent problem behavior. *Critical Criminology, 11*, 237–260.
Macleod, J. (2008). *Ain't no makin' it*. Boulder, CO: Westview Press.
Marwell, G. (1966). Adolescent powerlessness and delinquent behavior. *Social Problems, 14*, 35–47.
McNulty, T. (2001). Assessing the race-violence relationship at the macro level. *Criminology, 39*, 467–490.
Miller, A. (1990). *For your own good*. New York: Farrar, Straus & Giroux.
Needleman, H., Schell, A., Bellinger, D., Leviton, A., & Allred, E. (1990). The long term effects of low doses of lead in childhood. *New England Journal of Medicine, 322*, 83–88.
Regoli, R. M., & Hewitt, J. D. (1991). *Delinquency in society*. New York: McGraw-Hill.

Regoli, R. M., Hewitt, J. D., & DeLisi, M. (2010). *Delinquency in society* (8th ed.). Boston: Jones & Bartlett.

Smith, C., & Farrington, D. (2004). Continuities in antisocial behavior and parenting across three generations. *Journal of Child Psychology and Psychiatry, 45*, 230–247.

Wilson, W. J. (2009). *More than just race.* New York: W. W. Norton.

REISS, ALBERT J., JR.: PERSONAL AND SOCIAL CONTROLS AND DELINQUENCY

Albert J. Reiss, Jr., was one of the pioneers in the areas of crime and criminology. Although Reiss may be best known for his contribution to social control theory, he also wrote important works in a number of areas such as policing, self-report surveys, male prostitution, and corporate crime. Nevertheless, his most important contribution to the field of criminology may have been his work in the area of social control theory. In 1951, in his article "Delinquency as the Failure of Personal and Social Controls" in the *American Sociological Review*, he introduced the ideas of personal and social controls and the important roles they played in reducing delinquency. He expanded on those ideas in another article the following year in the same journal. These concepts became important precursors for what later became known as social control theory and remain relevant to the field of theoretical criminology more than half a century after he introduced them.

At the time Reiss published his seminal work, the field of criminology was largely driven by ideas from the Chicago School of thought, which is also where Reiss received his academic training. These theorists focused primarily on the negative effects of deviant peers and disorganized neighborhoods. Although the Chicago School is definitely recognizable in the work of Reiss, particularly around his social control concept, his concept of personal control was a much more individualistic concept. Reiss defined a personal control as "the ability of the individual to refrain from meeting needs in ways that conflict with the norms and rules of the community" and a social control as "the ability of social groups or institutions to make norms or rules effective" (1951, p. 196). The core of Reiss's argument was that youths were drawn to delinquency and only personal and social controls kept youths from engaging in delinquency.

According to Reiss, "delinquency results when there is a relative absence of internalized norms and rules governing behavior in conformity with the norms of the social system to which legal penalties are attached, a breakdown in previously established controls, and/or a relative absence of conflict in social rules or techniques for enforcing such behavior in the social groups or institutions of which the person is a member" (1951, p. 196). In other words, Reiss proposed that delinquency resulted from a lack of personal or social controls. Reiss also suggested that these personal and social controls would be more effective in preventing delinquency among those youths who have not committed delinquency than those recidivists who have previously engaged in delinquent activity and are now attempting to refrain from further delinquency.

Reiss observed that individuals develop personal controls from their primary groups (e.g., family, school, church) and that these primary groups are important in exerting social controls over an individual's behavior. According to Reiss, these primary groups exercise social control over youths by providing roles and discipline techniques that encourage conformity. Reiss contended that delinquency occurs when the techniques of these primary groups that are designed to reduce delinquency fail.

Reiss suggested that the family plays several important roles in developing personal and social controls. These roles include (1) meeting the economic and material needs of its members; (2) providing models for conformity by establishing non-delinquent norms; (3) maintaining unity (both structurally and psychologically), thus allowing the child to grow up in a two-parent home with two conformist role models; and (4) establishing and maintaining conformist rules and expectations for behavior among family members.

Reiss also explained the role of the community and the institutions within the community in developing personal controls. Many of his ideas regarding institutional control are directly linked to the social disorganization perspective that was commonly found among those trained at the University of Chicago during that time period. Reiss suggested that youths gain personal controls by submitting to the authority and conformist values of conformist institutions found in their community. As social disorganization theorists assert, these conformist institutions are more likely to be found in communities that are less congested and physically overcrowded and in communities with fewer permanent residents. Reiss also argued that the school played an important part in developing personal controls among youths. Because schools generally provide settings where conformist norms are used to control behaviors and its personnel "represent acceptable models of authority and provide rational guides for behavior" (Reiss, 1952, p. 711), those youths who accept those norms enjoy the school experience, attend school regularly, and do not present behavior problems for the schools are thus more likely to have strong personal controls.

Reiss defines a youth with strong personal controls as one who "is characterized by a) mature ego ideals or non-delinquent social roles, i.e. internalized controls of social groups governing behavior in conformity with non-delinquent group expectations, and b) appropriate and flexible rational controls over behavior which permits conscious guidance of action in accord with non-delinquent group expectations" (p. 203). These youths can delay satisfaction of their needs until they obtain that satisfaction through conformist means. According to Reiss, a youth with strong personal controls has a well-developed superego and an appropriate level of self-esteem. These personal controls thus assist the youth in refraining from delinquency.

In his 1951 article, Reiss used official juvenile court records from white male juvenile probationers in Cook County, Illinois, to determine whether youths with strong personal and social controls were less likely to recidivate. He suggested that those juveniles with higher degrees of personal and social controls would be less likely to recidivate than their counterparts with fewer of these controls. In his assessment of these data, he found that, in general, his ideas were supported. Using largely demographic and contextual measures rather than purely theoretical measures developed later, Reiss's analysis revealed that those with greater personal controls (e.g., delinquents whose parents were together, whose natural parents were married, whose parents had higher monthly incomes) and

greater social controls (e.g., delinquents where were not frequently truant, who had lived in the same home for over 10 years) had lower levels of recidivism. His theoretical perspective laid the foundation for both Travis Hirschi's social bond perspective and, to a lesser extent, Michael Gottfredson and Hirschi's self-control theory.

Elements of personal and social controls articulated by Reiss are found in numerous versions of both social control and self-control theories. Hirschi's social bond theory has received wide empirical support (although a number of criticisms of the theory exist as well). Reiss, along with Walter Reckless, F. Ivan Nye, and David Matza, are often viewed as the "grandfathers" of the social bond theory articulated by Hirschi a decade later and thus remain influential members of the theoretical community of criminology.

David C. May

See also Gottfredson, Michael R., and Travis Hirschi: Self-Control Theory; Hirschi, Travis: Social Control Theory; Kornhauser, Ruth Rosner: Social Sources of Delinquency; Le Blanc, Marc: An Integrated Personal Control Theory of Deviant Behavior; Matza, David: Delinquency and Drift; Nye, F. Ivan: Family Controls and Delinquency; Reckless, Walter C.: Containment Theory; Sykes, Gresham M., and David Matza: Techniques of Neutralization; Toby, Jackson: Stake in Conformity

References and Further Readings

Farrington, D. P. (Ed.). (2008). *Integrated developmental and life course theories of offending* (Advances in Criminological Theory, Vol. 14). New Brunswick, NJ: Transaction.

Gottfredson, M., & Hirschi, T. (1990). *A general theory of crime.* Stanford, CA: Stanford University Press.

Hirschi, T. (1969). *Causes of delinquency.* Berkeley: University of California Press.

McCord, J. (Ed.). (1995). *Coercion and punishment in long-term perspectives.* New York: Cambridge University Press.

Reiss, A. J., Jr. (1951). Delinquency as the failure of personal and social controls. *American Sociological Review, 16,* 196–207.

Reiss, A. J., Jr. (1952). Social correlates of psychological types of delinquency. *American Sociological Review, 17,* 710–718.

ROSE, DINA R., AND TODD R. CLEAR: COERCED MOBILITY THEORY

Responding to rising violent crime rates during the 1980s, criminal justice policies transferred to a "get tough" approach characterized by harsh sentencing guidelines that imprisoned individuals at a much higher rate and for longer sentences. This shift has resulted in a rapid growth of the incarcerated population, influencing minorities and the poor disproportionately. Throughout their lifetime, black men are seven times more likely to experience incarceration than their white counterparts, and black women are eight times more likely to experience incarceration than white women (Bonzcar & Beck, 1997). These "get tough" policies have resulted in large proportions of residents from select impoverished neighborhoods being removed from their neighborhoods due to incarceration. Although, it may seem commonsensical that incarcerating offenders increases public safety—thus improving the quality of life for the other residents—Dina R. Rose and Todd R. Clear propose that this strong reliance on incarceration presents negative unintended consequences for the vitality of these neighborhoods. The following section discusses the theoretical foundation and conceptual framework for Rose and Clear's proposition, which has become known as *coerced mobility theory*.

Theoretical Foundation

Considering incarceration as a formal control of the state, coerced mobility theory posits that an excessive dependence on formal control impedes communities' ability to self-regulate, further attenuating informal social control. In essence, communities that are overreliant on formal control are characterized by more social disorganization.

As an extension of social disorganization theory, coerced mobility is also concerned with the effects of residents moving in and out of the community—that is, the residential instability of the neighborhood. However, unlike social disorganization theory that has primarily focused on voluntary mobility, coerced mobility focuses on mobility due to formal control through the mechanism of incarceration. Traditional social disorganization theory asserts that neighborhoods characterized by poverty, racial/ethnic heterogeneity, and high residential mobility will experience social disorganization, resulting in higher crime rates. Coerced mobility focuses primarily on the influence of mobility through the means of incarceration. Neighborhoods with residential instability—whether it be voluntary or coerced—impedes social integration and cohesion (Crutchfield, 1989; Sampson, 1991), increases anonymity (Warner & Pierce, 1993), and thus weakens informal social control (Sampson & Groves, 1989).

Research has also focused on the different levels of control necessary for a community to function. Robert Bursik and Harold Grasmick identify three different levels of control. Private control exists between family members and close friends. Parochial control exists between those individuals and community institutions that people interact with on a regular basis, such as schools and churches. Public controls involve relationships outside of the community, such as the criminal justice system. Private and parochial controls are considered to be forms of informal social control, while public control is considered formal social control. These three levels of control are interrelated and are essential for a community to achieve self-regulation. For example, as a community's informal control decreases, the community's reliance on formal control increases. This may further attenuate informal social control. Coerced mobility theory proposes that concentrated incarceration has implications for these different levels of control.

A Nonrecursive Model

Social disorganization has traditionally been modeled as a recursive theory. For example, Bursik and Grasmick's *basic systemic model of crime* proposes that the social condition variables of poverty, high residential mobility, and racial/ethnic heterogeneity attenuate private and parochial controls. The weakened informal social control leads to the community relying more heavily on formal control. Those communities that do not achieve sufficient informal and formal control are characterized by social disorganization which, in turn, leads to higher crime. However, this recursive model implies that removing offenders only improves neighborhood life—that is, it ignores the possible feedback effects of incarceration on community structure, informal social control, and crime. To the extent that this reciprocal relationship weakens the community structure, unintended consequences of incarceration would exist. Thus, incarceration is not purely beneficial for neighborhoods but rather further diminishes a community's ability to self-regulate, leading to higher crime (Rose & Clear, 1998).

Coerced mobility theory is an extension of Bursik and Grasmick's basic systemic model of crime in that it introduces a feedback loop. Rose and Clear propose that public controls, specifically crime control through the mechanism of incarceration, further influence the exogenous variables of the model (poverty, residential mobility, and racial/ ethnic heterogeneity).

How does incarceration influence the community structure? First, incarceration impacts the socioeconomic composition of the community by affecting the labor and marriage markets. Second, incarceration increases residential mobility in a community because each time an offender is incarcerated, he or she is removed from the community. Relying on formal control—that is, mass incarceration specifically—there is a constant influx of offenders exiting and reentering the community. Third, incarceration affects the heterogeneity of a community. Traditionally, social disorganization theory was primarily concerned with racial/ethnic heterogeneity because it was presumed that this heterogeneity was characterized by different norms and values. However, today most poor communities are not racially or ethnically heterogeneous but the heterogeneity in values and norms persist. Removing individuals from a community allows for new individuals to enter the community who may possess different norms or values. Also, when offenders return to the community after incarceration, they bring more criminalistic values and norms back into the community.

Social and Human Capital

Rose and Clear refer to the private and parochial controls of Bursik and Grasmick's model as elements of social capital. For Rose and Clear, social capital consists of the social skills and resources

necessary for a community to make positive change. The use of organized groups enhances the community's ability to achieve the shared goals of the community. By promoting community residents to interact, social capital builds trust and cohesion among community members. This facilitates the enforcement of the norms of the community, which in turn strengthens informal social control.

According to Rose and Clear, human capital consists of the human skills and resources necessary for individuals to function such as, reading and writing. Social capital and human capital are interrelated. For example, communities that are rich in social capital foster the development of human capital. These communities are able to exert more control over the residents of the community, producing better educated and more employable individuals who possess human capital. Further, it requires human capital to obtain social capital. Consequently, those communities rich in social capital are also rich in human capital and those communities lacking social capital also lack human capital.

Most of the social disorganization research has examined the role of social ties or integration, focusing on their importance in relation to crime prevention. Rose and Clear pose the opposite question. They ask, "How much disruption can networks sustain before they fail to function?" (p. 456). A disruption of these networks reduces the social capital of a community leading to weaker informal social control and limiting a community's ability to self-regulate. Previous research has proposed that the relationship between social networks and social disorganization is linear. Rose and Clear proposes a potential threshold, claiming that there is a minimum amount of healthy social networks necessary for the community to self-regulate. In regards to incarceration, a community may be able to withstand the removal of a small proportion of males from the community. But when a large proportion of families are affected by incarceration, the social networks may be so disrupted that informal social control breaks down and a community is no longer able to self-regulate. This leads to an overreliance on formal control which, in turn, further weakens informal social control. Because these neighborhoods that experience concentrated incarceration are deficient in social and human capital to begin with, the effects of incarceration on the neighborhood are even more detrimental.

Influences of Incarceration on Neighborhood Order

Rose and Clear approach the possible unintended consequences of incarceration with a "systems" model. From this model, "criminals are seen as embedded in various interpersonal, family, economic, and political systems" (p. 457). Rose and Clear propose that these legitimate and illegitimate systems have a direct effect on a neighborhood's ability to exert informal social control. Rose and Clear use existing empirical evidence to demonstrate these influences.

Familial Systems

Families have been dramatically affected by incarceration policies; and as previously mentioned, these policies have impacted poor and minority families disproportionately. For example, about three in five African American high school dropouts will be incarcerated at some point in their life. This is at a rate of five times greater than their white counterparts (Pettit & Western, 2004). Forty percent of those males are fathers who had lived with their children (Western et al., 2004). The removal of a parent has several consequences. For example, when a father is incarcerated, many families have to relocate. This often means moving into crowded accommodations and potentially changing school districts. Sometimes, a new male enters the family to replace the incarcerated father, causing family disruption. Often, mothers acquire secondary employment to make up for the lost income, resulting in less parental supervision for the children. These circumstances may attenuate family cohesiveness, potentially leading to delinquency. Research also reveals that children of incarcerated parents are more likely to experience problems in school, depression, anxiety, aggression, and low self-esteem.

At the very least, mass incarceration of males from a community reduces the number of adults available to provide supervision to the children in the community. Research by Sudhir Alladi Venkatesh has shown that even offenders provide

supervision and have positive influences on neighborhoods. They may act as protectors, encourage school attendance, or provide renovation to a neighborhood park or recreation area.

Removing a large proportion of parent-age males affects the marriage market of the community by limiting the number of available male partners for females. The surplus of females may result in females remaining in unhealthy relationships, as well as in males having less incentive to remain faithful and in a committed relationship. All of these studies demonstrate that families have been disrupted by incarceration and that much of this disruption has been concentrated in poor and minority communities. Because families serve as the primary socialization unit for children, these family disruptions contribute to a slow erosion of the social capital of a community, according to Rose and Clear.

Economic Systems

Rose and Clear note that communities where a large proportion of residents engage in both legal and illegal work often experience local economic devastation by the incarceration of its residents. By removing large numbers from the job market within the community, human capital is diminished.

Incarceration affects offenders' and their families' economic situation by decreasing income from the household or family. Research has demonstrated that mothers rely on other individuals within their network to help sustain their family. The mothers left behind frequently resort to public assistance for survival. These communities that experience a high rate of welfare do not promote healthy private labor markets (Clear, 2007).

Research has also demonstrated that economic difficulty is a strong predictor of aggregate crime rates. Some research has even suggested that the unemployment rate of the community may be even more influential to people's criminality than their individual employment status.

Incarceration directly reduces an individual's human capital. During incarceration, offenders rarely receive job training that is transferrable to the community. Typically, offenders do not return to their community any more prepared for employment than prior to incarceration, except for now they carry the added stigma of being incarcerated.

There is also evidence that incarceration leads to economic marginality. Being incarcerated limits individuals to unstable, low-wage jobs that provide little opportunity for advancement (Uggen et al., 2005). This type of employment may reduce the individual's stake in conformity potentially leading to future criminal involvement (Crutchfield & Pitchford, 1997).

At the community level, incarceration policies destroy communities by shifting government funding from the community toward building and managing correctional institutions. Funds are removed from schools and other programs that provide social services and transferred to the criminal justice system. To the extent that these social programs promoted informal social control and facilitated the creation and maintenance of social networks, the elimination of these programs further weakens informal social control within the community.

Political Systems

Social capital is produced through the interrelationship between community institutions, organizations, and outside agencies, according to Rose and Clear. Neighborhoods deficient in social capital may not be able to organize and take collective action when problems occur within the community. They also may not be able to obtain external resources because they lack the necessary network. Concentrated incarceration may disrupt networks that facilitate the functioning of community programs that promote social networks and informal social control. Rose and Clear contend that "we need not make the argument that offenders are active participants in local political efforts. Rather, we need only make the argument that their removal disrupts the networks of other individuals who otherwise might participate" (p. 463).

Rose and Clear also contend that residents are less likely to participate in local politics if they do not believe that they are legitimate or effective. Many of the communities hit the hardest by incarceration policies do not think that the government and/or the criminal justice system works on their behalf. According to Tom Tyler, in these communities the state is most likely to be viewed as coercive rather than fair. When individuals view the law as illegitimate, they are less likely to conform to the law.

Within these communities that experience concentrated incarceration, going to prison is "normal," it is part of life, and in some cases a rite of passage. Because incarceration is ubiquitous in these communities, the experience of incarceration loses the uncertainty and mystery that surrounds it, according to Rose and Clear. This may weaken the deterrent power of incarceration. Rose and Clear also suggest potential brutalization effects, such as those that have been found with the death penalty. Rose and Clear contend that "the politics of imprisonment may be a combination of increasing resentment and decreasing marginal gain" (p. 465).

Illegitimate Systems

Concentrated incarceration also influences illegitimate activity within the community. The vast majority of crime occurs locally, rooted in interpersonal relationships and group relations. According to Rose and Clear, it is these relations that may be seen as illegitimate systems. Because most crime occurs within groups, it is important to understand the effect of removing a member of the criminal group. It is likely that the group sustains the disruption and continues to engage in criminal activity. Sometimes, the group recruits a new member to replace the member who was incarcerated. The recruitment of new members may lead individuals who otherwise would have stayed on the periphery of criminal activity to become more deeply involved in criminal behavior.

In sum, this discussion illustrates that concentrated incarceration weakens informal social control through the familial, economic, political, and illegitimate systems of offenders. In turn the neighborhood becomes highly disorganized community, resulting in higher crime rates.

A Preliminary Examination of Coerced Mobility

Clear, Rose, Elin Waring, and Kristen Scully provided the first partial empirical test of Rose and Clear's coerced mobility theory. They explored the effects of incarceration on crime rates in 80 Tallahassee, Florida, neighborhoods. At that time the data needed to test the nonrecursive model, as proposed in Rose and Clear, were unavailable. However, remaining consistent with Rose and

Clear, Clear et al. examined the affect of a neighborhood's incarceration rate of 1 year on the crime rate of the neighborhood on the next year. They hypothesized a curvilinear relationship between admissions and crime. First, with low levels of admissions, they hypothesized that crime rates will be reduced; however, when admissions reach a certain level, they hypothesized that the relationship between admissions and crime becomes positive and high levels of admissions increases the crime rate. This relationship was proposed by Rose and Clear in 1998.

Clear et al. used admissions and releases from prison in 1996 to measure the magnitude of coerced mobility and the crime rate for each neighborhood for the dependent variable. As hypothesized by Rose and Clear, the analysis provided some support that the relationship between admissions to prison and crime is nonlinear. They found that a moderate level of incarceration is associated with a reduction in the crime rate of the neighborhood. However, when the level of incarceration reaches a certain point, incarceration is associated with an increase in the crime rate. While Clear et al. is only a partial test of coerced mobility theory, the results furnish preliminary support for the theory.

Community Justice: The Policy Implications of Coerced Mobility

In his book *Imprisoning Communities: How Mass Incarceration Makes Disadvantaged Neighborhoods Worse*, Clear not only further expands coerced mobility theory, but he also provides a more fully developed response to the problem of coerced mobility and mass incarceration. Clear proposes that if the problems of mass incarceration are to be addressed it is necessary to reform the sentencing policies in the United States and to adopt a new philosophy of penal justice. Before the criminal justice system can seriously think about reducing the corrections population, sentencing reform is necessary. Because the prison population is determined by how many enter prison and how long they stay, the criminal justice system needs to send fewer individuals to prison and for shorter amounts of time. This will require rethinking policies such as mandatory sentencing, especially for drug offenders.

Clear proposes that the United States should embrace community justice. Community justice refers to all crime prevention strategies that explicitly include the community. The emphasis is placed on the quality of life of the residents of the community. The emphasis shifts from individual-level outcomes and individual good to community-level outcomes and the common good of the neighborhood (Clear & Karp, 1999). Community justice strategies should target the neighborhoods plagued by mass incarceration, the norms and values of these communities, and their schools, jobs, and housing institutions. It is through the coordinated efforts of private, parochial, and public controls that community justice functions. By strengthening the private and parochial controls of the neighborhood, this should in turn strengthen the informal social control of the neighborhood—in time leading to lower crime rates.

Conclusion

As an extension of social disorganization theory, coerced mobility theory proposes that concentrated incarceration—similar to the voluntary mobility included in most social disorganization models—weakens informal social control within the community and its ability to self-regulate. Informal social control is weakened through the various systems that the offenders are embedded. The inability to self-regulate, the deficiencies in human and social capital, and the overreliance on formal control foster social disorganization, which ultimately leads to higher crime rates. While traditionally removing offenders from a community has been viewed as purely beneficial for the community, Rose and Clear propose that unintended consequences of concentrated incarceration exist, and they demonstrate how criminal justice policies may exacerbate the exact problem the policy attempts to alleviate.

Kristin Swartz

See also Bursik, Robert J., Jr., and Harold C. Grasmick: Levels of Control; Shaw, Clifford R., and Henry D. McKay: Social Disorganization Theory; Systemic Model of Social Disorganization; Wilson, William Julius: The Truly Disadvantaged

References and Further Readings

Anderson, E. (1990). *Streetwise: Race, class, and change in an urban community*. Chicago: University of Chicago Press.

Bonczar, T. P., & Beck, A. J. (1997). Lifetime likelihood of going to state or federal prison. Washington, DC: Bureau of Justice Statistics.

Bursik, R. J., Jr., & Grasmick, H. G. (1993). *Neighborhoods and crime: The dimensions of effective community control.* New York: Lexington Books.

Clear, T. R. (2007). *Imprisoning communities: How mass incarceration makes disadvantaged neighborhoods worse.* New York: Oxford University Press.

Clear, T. R., & Karp, D. R. (1999). *The community justice ideal: Preventing crime and achieving justice.* Boulder, CO: Westview.

Clear, T. R., Rose, D. R., Waring, E., & Scully, K. (2003). Coercive mobility and crime: A preliminary examination of concentrated incarceration and social disorganization. *Justice Quarterly, 20,* 33–64.

Cochran, J. K., Chamlin, M. B., & Seth, M. (1994). Deterrence or brutalization? An impact assessment of Oklahoma's return to capital punishment. *Criminology, 32,* 107–134.

Crutchfield, R. D. (1989). Labor stratification and violent crime. *Social Forces, 68,* 489–512.

Crutchfield, R. D., & Pitchford, S. R. (1997). Work and crime: The effects of labor stratification. *Social Forces, 76,* 93–118.

Edin, K., & Lein, L. (1997). Work, welfare, and single mothers' economic survival strategies. *American Sociological Review, 62,* 253–266.

Hagan, J. (1993). The social embeddedness of crime and unemployment. *Criminology, 31,* 465–492.

Hagan, J., & Dinovitzer, R. (2000). Collateral consequences of imprisonment for children, communities, and prisoners. In M. Tonry & J. Petersilia (Eds.), *Crime and justice: A review of research—Prisons* (Vol. 26, pp. 121–162). Chicago: University of Chicago Press.

Pettit, B., & Western, B. (2004). Mass imprisonment and the life course: Race and class inequality in U.S. incarceration. *American Sociological Review, 69,* 151–169.

Rose, D. R., & Clear, T. R. (1998). Incarceration, social capital, and crime: Implications for social disorganization theory. *Criminology, 36,* 441–479.

Sampson, R. J. (1991). Linking the micro- and macro-level dimensions of community social organization. *Social Forces, 70,* 43–64.

Sampson, R. J., & Groves, W. B. (1989). Community structure and crime: Testing social disorganization theory. *American Journal of Sociology, 94,* 774–802.

Tyler, T. (1990). *Why people obey the law.* New Haven, CT: Yale University Press.

Uggen, C., Wakefield, S., & Western, B. (2005). Work and family perspectives on reentry. In J. Travis &

C. Visher (Eds.), *Prisoner reentry and crime in America* (pp. 209–243). New York: Cambridge University Press.

Venkatesh, S. A. (1997). The social organization of street gang activity in an urban ghetto. *American Journal of Sociology, 103,* 82–111.

Warner, B. D., & Pierce, G. L. (1993). Reexamining social disorganization theory using calls to the police as a measure of crime. *Criminology, 31,* 493–517.

Western, B., Patillo, M., Weiman, D. (2004). Introduction. In M. Patillo, D. Weiman, & B. Western (Eds.), *Imprisoning America: The social effects of mass incarceration* (pp. 1–18). New York: Russell Sage.

Wilson, W. J. (1987). *The truly disadvantaged: The inner city, the under-class, and public policy.* Chicago: University of Chicago Press.

ROSS, E. A.: SIN AND SOCIETY

On September 14, 1901, President William McKinley died from wounds inflicted by unemployed factory worker and anarchist Leon Czolgosz. McKinley's successor, 42-year-old Theodore Roosevelt, was and remains the youngest man ever to hold the office of president. With his comparative youth and considerable energy, and with interests ranging from history to hunting, Roosevelt was the ideal leader for a Progressive era that marked the beginning of the modern age in America.

Progressivism was a broad-based reform movement that included politicians, feminists, intellectuals, artists, and writers. Key targets for the largely middle-class Progressives were large corporations and trusts, together with the small number of wealthy industrialists and financiers who controlled them. Progressive intellectuals sought solutions to problems generated by the rapid pace of industrialization, urbanization, and population change across the United States. Crusading Progressive journalists—given the name "muckrakers" by an ambivalent Roosevelt—devoted their energies to exposing wrongdoing and corruption in public life and corporate America (Mowry, 1962).

Social Control and Public Opinion

In the same year that Roosevelt took office, Edward Alsworth Ross—known as E. A. Ross—published his book *Social Control*. Ross was one of a group of pioneering American sociologists who rejected the evolutionary model of human progress propounded by the British philosopher and sociologist Herbert Spencer. For Ross and his contemporaries, social progress was not circumscribed by the laws of nature, but could be directed and enhanced by reform-minded social scientists working in tandem with government. Ross dismissed as a "common delusion" the idea that people's innate capacity for goodness is sufficient to maintain social order. Rather, social stability depends on a core of values that brings together diverse individuals under communal ideals. These communal ideals operate as a collective mind that regulates behavior and encourages desired conduct.

President Roosevelt evidently read and approved of *Social Control* (Ross, 1965, p. ix). Like much of Ross's early work, the book addresses the problem of order in a newly modernized America. At the center of Ross's sociological vision is social control: the internalization of behavioral, moral, and ideological standards. In the book, Ross outlines the formal and informal forces that sustain social order in highly differentiated societies.

The formal force that directly maintains social order is *law*, described by Ross (1959, p. 57) as "the cornerstone of the edifice of order." Legal sanctions are certain, corporal (in the main), irresistible, and detached; but in complex societies, law is perceived as inflexible, even clumsy.

The informal force of social order is *public opinion*; that is, the psychological pressure exerted by society in order to encourage or discourage conduct. Public opinion has many advantages over the more mechanical force of law: it is nuanced, flexible, immediate, and cheap. The transgressions that public opinion polices are moral, not legal, enabling it to apply pressure in anticipation of wrongful conduct. As Ross (1959, p. 43) notes, "Its premonitory growl is more preventive than the silent menace of justice." Yet public opinion also has myriad faults. It lacks clarity, both in terms of the behavior it requires and the sanctions it imposes; it is instinctive, impulsive, and passionate; it is crude in technique and indefinite in purpose.

Despite its faults, Ross regarded public opinion as the locus of social control; the "germ" from which all the instruments of social order develop. For this reason, it was crucial that public opinion

be directed by the wise: influential men who constituted the "nerve centers . . . of society" and "rallying points of public opinion" (1959, p. 47). Both Ross the pioneering sociologist and Roosevelt the Progressive politician were positioning themselves for roles as nerve centers in a reformed, refocused America.

Following his re-election in 1904, Roosevelt initiated a package of reforms designed to curtail the detrimental effects of industrialization. Roosevelt's "square deal" aimed to balance the claims of producers and consumers, managers and workers, and to regulate powerful trusts and corporations. Ross meanwhile worked on a series of essays that drew attention to the same harmful behaviors that the "square deal" sought to eliminate. When the essays were brought together in a short book intended for a lay audience, Ross wrote to Roosevelt, inviting him to contribute a short preface. The president accepted.

Sin and Society

The essays that became *Sin and Society* were published between 1905 and 1907 in the *Atlantic Monthly*, a journal devoted to literature, politics, science, and the arts. Ross's theme was "social sins"—a range of corrupt and exploitative practices that had emerged in modern industrial America. The use of the word *sin* was deliberate and intended to appeal to a Progressive audience who no longer regarded religion as the primary source of moral standards. As social problems, corporate greed and corruption could be assuaged by a collective response, but only one underpinned by a system of social control sturdy enough to stand up to the new forms of misconduct that industrialization had inadvertently unleashed.

In his preface to *Sin and Society*, Ross distances the book from his work in the field of social psychology. His method, he explains, is to speak to the intellect rather than to touch the heart; his target is public opinion, not individual conduct. At present, Ross argues, public opinion is simply not keeping pace with contemporary wrongdoing: "It never occurs to the public that sin evolves along with society. . . . In today's warfare on sin, the reactions of the public are about as serviceable as gongs and stink-pots in a modern battle." In order to counter contemporary sin, Ross claims that public opinion needs a new code of ethical behavior (Ross, 1965, p. vii–viii).

Ross identifies the interdependence of the time as the source of new sins. In complex societies, we entrust others with responsibility for our food, work, education, and health, thus creating endless opportunities for wrong-doing and breaches of faith. At the same time, what Ross refers to as "the older sin" (p. 5)—crimes of violence, cruelty and lust—are, he asserts, in decline. The frantic pace of modern life drains away the energy that was formerly expended in violent behavior. Meanwhile, the new sins—and the new sinners—are on the rise.

Ross explains the success of modern sin in three ways. First, he says, it lacks the repulsive quality of "primitive sin" (p. 7), at least on the surface. Blood is rarely shed, and even when it is, there is no personal contact between victim and slayer. Modern homicide comes courtesy of those who fail to fence off dangerous machinery or send passengers out to sea with defective life preservers. By the same token, property crime is no longer furtive or disagreeable; rather, they are more indirect and refined.

In the second place, modern sin is not accompanied by the melodrama and signs of guilt that are traditionally associated with crime. It is not committed down dark alleys by slouching, scowling villains dressed like Dickens's Bill Sykes, but by serene, cigar-smoking gentlemen in immaculate linen and silk hats (p. 10). Neither can its proponents be incorporated within the criminological frameworks of the 19th century; they are not Cesare Lombroso's "born criminals," whose depravity is biologically determined and irresistible, but simply "the creatures of Crooked Thinking and Opportunity" (p. 28). As a consequence, these quasi-criminals or "criminaloids" remain in good odor with public opinion and with themselves; unrecognized, they lack the "spiritual attitude" of the old-fashioned offender (p. 48).

Finally, the crimes these serene, cigar-smoking gentlemen commit are impersonal. They do not strike at selected individuals but at anonymous members of the public; some do not even have victims at all. If no one falls into the dangerous machinery or relies on the defective life preservers, the sinner is merely "chancing it" or "augmenting risk" (p. 12). Even more impersonal are the sins

that damage democratic institutions (and thereby the American people as a whole): the corrupt editor who undermines the freedom of the press; the corrupt bosses who "murder" representative government.

It is the sins of corporations in particular that Ross views as requiring expert intervention. In the modern business environment, corporations have become distant and impersonal. They "sin by syndicate," unmoved by the limitations placed on individual businessmen by conscience and public opinion. Here Ross returns to a theme that he introduced in *Social Control*: the inability of public opinion to sustain its power in the face of wrong-doing that is traced back to a group rather than a single individual. It is this inability, Ross claims, that fuels the disregard of public opinion within the realm of business management (1959, p. 44).

In *Sin and Society*, though, Ross is less dismissive of public opinion. In an ideal world, company directors would be held legally accountable for misconduct and abuses, but in the meantime, American citizens need to channel their anger. Rather than allowing itself "to be kept guessing which shell the pea is under," public opinion needs to curb corporate abuses by aiming wrath directly toward the top—the sinning directors (pp. 125–126).

The appeal of Ross's critique for Progressive politicians like Theodore Roosevelt (as well as for academics like Ross himself) lay in the solution he proposed for the elimination of what he termed "latter-day iniquity." As a broad national trend, Progressivism reflected a modernist belief in the ability of men and women to act on and change their world. Ross shared this belief but feared that left to themselves, the American people were incapable of adjusting their conception of wrongdoing to incorporate the "fresh parasites" who had emerged in post-industrial America. A collective response to change was clearly required, but so was expert supervision. As long as public opinion continued to categorize sinners according to "the old righteousness," it would be necessary for professionals—politicians and professors—to maintain control of social defense.

Conclusion

Sin and Society was the response of a leading Progressive sociologist to the unintended consequences of rapid industrialization. For Ross and his political counterparts, there was nothing unalterably sinful in basic human nature. The origins of evil could be traced back to society and exorcised from it through the combined forces of professional experts and enlightened public opinion.

Ross was very much aware of his status as a pioneer in sociology, and he accepted that in time his theories and ideas would be superseded. *Social Control* is credited with establishing a paradigm for the discipline and is generally regarded as his best work. Today, however, it is little read and largely forgotten. Even in his own lifetime, Ross acknowledged that subsequent scholarship had rendered large parts of it "junk" (Hertzler, 1951). *Sin and Society*, his only foray into criminological theory, seems to have fared even worse. In an extensive account of Ross's life and work published in the *American Sociological Review*, the book receives short shrift as one of a series of "semi-popular" books that showcased Ross's analyses (Hertzler, 1951, p. 607).

Sin and Society indisputably contains its share of the rhetorical flourishes and overgeneralizations that characterize much of Ross's work on the salient public issues of his day. Ross produced no quantitative analyses in support of his thesis, but this did not stop him from dismissing statistical evidence pointing to an upsurge in the "bloody crime" that he asserted was in decline. Unfortunately, time has shown his conviction that the older sins of "brutality, lust and cruelty are on the wane" (1965, p. 5) to be—as Ross himself might have put it—junk.

That said, there is a lot to value in this analysis of modern sins and sinners. Ross's account of "new varieties of sin" and the "criminaloids" who commit them is the largely unacknowledged forefather of Edwin Sutherland's theory of white-collar crime (Sutherland, 1940, 1949; see, however, Cullen et al., 2006). Moreover, a new generation of scholars have suggested that Sutherland's focus on the individual, high-status offender (an emphasis that is absent from Ross's analysis), created an "imprisoning framework" that neglects the structural and organizational dimensions of white-collar crime (Braithwaite, 1985; Shapiro, 1987, 1990). A key insight of recent scholarship—namely, that the social organization of trust in complex societies provides endless opportunities

for abuse—appears on the first pages of *Sin and Society*:

> Modern sin takes its character from the mutualism of our time. Under our present manner of living, how many of my vital interests I must entrust to others! . . . Most sin is preying, and every new social relation begets its cannibalism. . . . Every new fiduciary relation is a fresh opportunity for breach of trust. (Ross, 1965, p. 3)

In its way, Ross's theory of "social sins" has been as enduring as the Progressive ideals he championed a century ago (Clift, 2009).

Amanda Matravers

See also Clinard, Marshall B.: The Black Market; Michalowski, Raymond J., and Ronald C. Kramer: State-Corporate Crime; Sutherland, Edwin H.: White-Collar Crime

References and Further Readings

Borgatta, E. F., & Meyer, H. J. (Eds.). (1959). *Social control and the foundations of sociology: Pioneer contributions of Edward Alsworth Ross to the study of society*. Boston: Beacon Press.

Braithwaite, J. (1985). White-collar crime. In R. H. Turner & J. F. Short (Eds.), *Annual review of sociology* (Vol. 11, pp. 1–25). Palo Alto, CA: Annual Reviews.

Clift, E. (2009, March 13). A progressive moment. *Newsweek*. Retrieved April 20, 2010, from http://www.newsweek.com/id/189122

Cullen, F. T., Cavender, G., Maakestad, W. J., & Benson, M. L. (2006). *Corporate crime under attack: The fight to criminalize business violence* (2nd ed.). Cincinnati, OH: Anderson.

Hertzler, J. O. (1951). Edward Alsworth Ross: Sociological pioneer and interpreter. *American Sociological Review, 16*, 609–613.

McMahon, S. H. (1999). *Social control and public intellect: The legacy of Edward A. Ross*. New Brunswick, NJ: Transaction.

Mowry, G. E. (1962). *The era of Theodore Roosevelt and the birth of modern America*. New York: Harper and Row.

Ross, E. A. (1959). Social control: A survey of the foundations of order. In E. F. Borgatta & H. J. Meyer (Eds.), *Social control and the foundations of sociology: Pioneer contributions of Edward Alsworth Ross to the study of society*. Boston: Beacon Press.

Ross, E. A. (1965). *Sin and society: An analysis of latter-day iniquity*. Boston: Houghton Mifflin.

Ross, E. A. (1977). *Seventy years of it: An autobiography*. New York: Arno Press.

Shapiro, H. (1987). The social control of impersonal trust. *American Journal of Sociology, 93,* 623–658.

Shapiro, H. (1990). Collaring the crime, not the criminal: Liberating the concept of white-collar crime. *Annual Sociological Review, 55,* 346–365.

Sutherland, E. H. (1940). White-collar criminality. *American Sociological Review, 5,* 1–12.

Sutherland, E. H. (1949). *White collar crime.* New York: Dryden.

RUSSELL, DIANA E. H.: THE POLITICS OF RAPE

In *The Politics of Rape,* first published in 1975, Diana E. H. Russell considered the consequences of rape, an extreme form of aggressive male behavior toward women. Russell attempted to determine what leads men to act aggressively toward women and why, as well as what the consequences and repercussions for the victim are as a result. Further, she explores the ways that society regards the crime, the victims, and the perpetrators of rape. She conducted and analyzed 22 in-depth interviews with rape victims. These narratives served as the vehicle for exploring the underlying social assumptions, views, and beliefs about rape. Included in the accounts are examples of the different forms the crime can take (rape by strangers, marital and date rape, gang rape, incest), as well as examples of reactions to the crime by the victims themselves and by their friends and family members. Russell also includes a chapter with interviews of four male rapists, which she uses to underline her main argument that rape is a sexist crime and that its sexist nature has severe and lasting consequences for victims. Finally, Russell offers suggestions about how to prevent the occurrence of rape at both the institutional and individual levels.

Social Conceptions of Rape

Written before laws banned domestic abuse and marital rape, Russell explored a topic that, at the time, was not considered to be as prevalent as it actually was and had not yet been systematically explored in the social sciences. Rape was not regarded as a social crisis that demanded attention, largely because the crime was underreported by victims to the police, leading to lower statistical evidence that rape was occurring. Since rape was not an issue being publicly discussed, its absence in public discourse supported falsely held beliefs that rape was not a serious issue of concern for most Americans. Russell points out that the proclivity of women to not report instances of rape, even violent cases, was largely due to the victims' fear of how they would be treated by authorities and members of their own social circles.

At the time of Russell's research, victims' charges of rape were often not believed by police or not taken seriously, prosecution of rapists rare, and conviction rarer still. Victims were socially stigmatized. Common understandings of rape were either that it was impossible for a woman to be raped and a victim must have "wanted it," or that the victim must have provoked the attack in some way and "had it coming." Because of the prevalence of these views, many victims feared social stigmatization if others found out they had been raped. The extent to which these views affected treatment of victims is highlighted by the allowance of a woman's sexual past to be admitted as evidence in rape prosecutions in order to show that the would-be rapist had good cause for thinking any protest on behalf of the victim was disingenuous and part of the "game."

Race, Class, and Rape

Russell argues that rape is a crime of misogynistic aggression, not passion. The victim interviews illustrate this conception of rape, as they point to explanations for the crimes that lie outside of a need or desire for sex. Building off the evidence of the victim's testimonies, Russell considers the effects of race and class relations in an attempt to uncover what attitudes lead men to perpetrate rape and how these attitudes and beliefs shape society's views about and the treatment of rape.

Black and white interracial and intraracial rapes stem from somewhat different attitudes, both of which have their roots in the legacy of American slavery. Historically, interracial rape in the United

States was most often perpetrated by white males against black females. Seemingly, this view of white superiority and the male right to use black women carried over into contemporary times, as some of the black victims of rape reported the need of the attacker to put them down or keep them in their place. Conversely, white victims of black attackers reported that the attacker either wanted to conquer a white woman or to use them as a way to get back at the men their aggression was really aimed at. Feeling that they had been raped in order to get back at the males she "belonged" to was not an uncommon theme in the interviews, as raping a woman was considered the ultimate insult either to the individual man or to the class of men charged with her protection. Women who were victimized by rape were then seen as "unclean" or "damaged." In turn, sullying the reputation of a woman then sullied the reputation of the men with whom she was associated.

Intraracial rape, the most common form the crime takes, resulted from men feeling the need to show their superiority over women they equal in other respects. Date and marital rape most often fall under this category, with the male needing to keep the power dynamic in his favor in the relationship.

Class considerations also appear in Russell's analysis, though the pattern of perpetrators is different from that of victims. While there is no evidence that perpetrators are limited to one class background, the majority have low socioeconomic status. Russell sees a parallel between the effects of class background on perpetrators to that of the effect of race; both are a way to show one's masculine power over others when the perpetrator may feel their power or masculine identity is threatened. Conversely, victimization is distributed relatively equally across classes, especially when the rape was perpetrated by a stranger.

Russell argues that while attitudes about class and race can shed some light on the issue of rape, the most important beliefs to be scrutinized are those regarding gender. Social attitudes about what men and women are expected to do and how they are supposed to act go furthest in helping to understand rape. Beliefs surrounding expected behavior are so engrained in individuals that efforts to fulfill gender roles can have the ultimate consequence—rape.

The Role of Gender

Through analysis of the victims' interviews, Russell examines how ideas and beliefs about rape are largely based on gender roles. It is these roles that inform expectations about how men and women are to relate to each other. They are also the mechanism to determine what is considered acceptable behavior and the response of one sex toward the other.

Describing male and female roles as the "masculine mystique" and "feminine mystique," Russell concludes that at its core rape is a sexist crime that is a direct reflection of these beliefs. Males are expected to be strong and dominant. They are the heads of the families, the authorities over women. "Macho" attitudes, grounded in power and superiority, are also part of the male mystique. In addition, men have sexual expectations placed on them. They are assumed to be virile, to have sexual appetites, and to take pride in fulfilling sexual desires. As a complement to the power-driven identities of their male counterparts, women are expected to be passive and submissive in their relations with men. They are to be dependent on men for their well-being, with their identities largely based in the perceptions males have toward them. Sexual expectations for women are vastly different from men; as they are to focus on male pleasure and it is shameful for them to focus on their own sexual desires.

Due to the way these gender roles inform the course of relationships and communication between men and women, Russell argues that rape is a sexist crime and that it occurs more frequently than is acknowledged by the media or society. Underacknowledgment of rape as a crime by victims and perpetrators is one of the results of the definitions and assumptions perpetuated by gender roles.

Because of gender roles, men feel a sense of superiority over women that both consider the normal dynamic in relations between sexes. This superior feeling leads to a sense of male entitlement to female bodies and to sexual gratification. Women, believing that they are to be submissive to men, may also accept that they are supposed to be at the mercy of male sexual desires. This belief can lead to women submitting to sexual demands unwillingly.

Another consequence of gender roles is the idea that rape is not possible, because all protests against sexual advances are hiding the true desires of the woman—that is, she indeed approves of the sexual advance made toward her. Women are supposed to want attention from men, and thus they do what it takes in order to receive that attention. This includes conforming to the male's ideal of "beauty," a standard commonly achieved through cosmetics and clothing. This effort works to garner the attention of men, but at the same time women must maintain their pure identity by distancing themselves from impure acts. This simultaneous attraction and rejection leads to the belief that women will say "no" to sexual advances when they actually mean "yes" in order to avoid the man thinking she is "easy." Women are expected to want and to give into sexual relations with men, while acting to the contrary. This view of women leads to the belief that a woman must protest against sexual advances, but will, and want, to give in when pressed. Since women are thought to be allowing and wanting the act to take place, despite any protest made, it cannot be rape.

Men also face the expectation that they are to prove their worth relative to others through success and achievement, specifically by showing power and capability to overcome any obstacle. This success or worth can be achieved in many different realms of life: financial, familial, and romantic. When men have failed or feel that their worth is not recognized or diminished in some way, they may act in a way that reestablishes their position. Some manifestations of this are benign, but when a man feels he cannot achieve romantically he may resort to rape. Several women Russell interviewed reported that they were raped by men whose prior sexual advances toward them had been dismissed. Their frustration at not being able to overcome this romantic obstacle ultimately led the men to rape. The feeling that women are in the category of problems to be conquered, and that in the end they could be conquered, illustrates an aspect of the misogynistic nature of rape.

Conclusion: Rape Prevention

As a conclusion, Russell offers suggestions for rape prevention. A central problem in rape prevention is that receiving institutional protection often deprives independent women of their personal freedoms. Among her recommendations for institutional changes are altering the way hospitals deal with rape victims, increased research into the causes of rape, and changes in the penal system to better treat and rehabilitate rapists. Acknowledging that institutional reforms like those suggested are often slow to happen, especially when they are regarding a problem not yet identified as such, Russell focuses on ways individuals may help prevent rape. These suggestions include forming victim support groups, learning self-defense and resistance techniques, and forming neighborhood alert organizations.

April Dawn Henning

See also Inequality and Crime; Koss, Mary P.: The Prevalence and Sources of Rape; Messerschmidt, James W.: Masculinities and Crime; Patterson, Gerald R.: Social Learning, the Family, and Crime; Rape Myths and Violence Against Women

References and Further Readings

Henderson, H. (2007). Feminism, Foucault, and rape: A theory and politics of rape prevention. *Berkeley Journal of Gender, Law and Justice, 22,* 225–253.
Russell, D. E. H. (1975). *The politics of rape: The victim's perspective.* New York: Stein and Day.
Russell, D. E. H. (1998). *Dangerous relationships: Pornography, misogyny and rape.* Thousand Oaks, CA: Sage.

S

SACCO, VINCENT F., AND LESLIE W. KENNEDY: THE CRIMINAL EVENT PERSPECTIVE

The criminal event perspective (CEP) is not a traditional theory of why people commit crime; instead it offers a way of identifying and organizing information to understand criminal activity. In other words, it is not a theory of criminality but a road map to understanding crime. The CEP is an explanation of crime that is firmly rooted in the philosophy of environmental criminology, and shares similarities with routine activity theory. Building from this foundation, the CEP directs focus to the factors necessary for commission of a crime.

Introduced by Vincent F. Sacco and Leslie W. Kennedy in 1996, the criminal event perspective is defined by three characteristics. First, the CEP focuses on studying crime, not criminality, which is consistent with the philosophy of environmental criminology. Second, the CEP identifies and encourages the exploration of multiple factors that contribute to the occurrence of crime. In other words, understanding crime requires exploration of a broad, inclusive list of variables. Finally, the CEP examines crime as an event, not an act. From this perspective, crime is not an isolated act but an event with different stages that coalesce to form a criminal event. These three characteristics underpin the CEP and define its contribution to the field. This discussion explores each characteristic in detail and describes how they unite to form the foundation of the criminal event perspective's approach to crime.

Crime, Not Criminality

Criminological theories often focus on explaining criminality or the reason why people commit crime. In addressing this goal, traditional theories frequently study crime by attempting to explain the motivation of the offender. In other words, the offender and their motivation to commit crime is the primary focus of the theory. For example, social learning theory offers an explanation for the action of offenders based on human learning processes. Social bond theory suggests that offenders do not learn to commit crime; rather, they are born ready to commit crime and it is only through effective social bonds that crime be averted. Both theories emphasize offenders and the reason(s) why they commit crime while offering different explanations for offender motivation.

More recently, theories have begun focusing on the importance of opportunity in understanding criminal activity. Opportunity is argued to be a key ingredient in crime and a crucial component of study for developing effective crime prevention policy. More broadly, opportunity theories focus on explaining crime rather than criminality. Routine activity theory is arguably the best known of these approaches. Its core explanation for crime is represented in the statement that crime occurs when a motivated offender and a suitable target interact in time and space without guardianship (Cohen and Felson, 1979). Thus, while a motivated offender is necessary, it is not sufficient. In other words, opportunity (i.e., suitable targets without guardianship) is also a necessary condition for the commission of a criminal offense. Much of the research within this tradition has focused on the role of targets and guardians leading to its categorization as an opportunity theory.

The CEP continues in this vein by acknowledging that both offenders and victims (i.e., targets) are crucial to the criminal event. Specifically, the CEP mirrors the approach of routine activity theory by identifying specific necessary components for crime to occur. In addition, the CEP re-emphasizes the role of offenders in crime, which reflects earlier criminological theorizing focused on the motivation of the offender. Thus, the CEP acknowledges the importance of offenders (and their motivation), but also embraces the role of opportunity in understanding crime.

Components of the Criminal Event Perspective

A second characteristic of the CEP is its emphasis on studying multiple variables necessary for the commission of a crime. The CEP groups these factors into two dimensions. Understanding crime requires consideration of offenders, victims, and the social context within which the activity occurs. In addition, the precursors of the crime, the transaction itself, and the aftermath of the crime are all central to understanding crime. In other words, the proximate and distal factors surrounding crime offer crucial information regarding the criminal event.

The first dimension, comprising offenders, victims, and social context, reflects core elements that must be present for crime to occur. The CEP argues for study of offender decision making based on the principles of rational choice theory. This approach posits that individuals base their decisions on a cost-benefit analysis. Victims also play a pivotal role in crime, not as a direct cause of crime, but as a necessary component of the event. Finally, the social context of the event is also crucial to understanding crime. The social context refers to factors including, but not limited to, the geographic location, the time of the event, or a combination of environmental influences that combine to create the social world. In short, the

social context refers to the environment and its role in encouraging or inhibiting crime.

The second dimension of the CEP involves study of the precursors, the specific transaction (i.e., the crime), and the aftermath of the criminal event. Exploration of this dimension is a key characteristic defining the study of crime as an event, and not as an act. Emphasizing a broader examination of crime to include factors occurring before, during, and after the actual crime is arguably the key contribution of the CEP and is a primary defining characteristic of the approach.

Sacco and Kennedy suggest that precursors to the crime include situational and geographic factors that influence interactions between individuals that may lead to crime. For example, such factors may include the relationship between the offender and victim or the rules that define particular behaviors as acceptable (e.g., the law). At the time of the crime, the interactions between the participants also assist in defining the nature of the crime. For example, studying transactions may involve exploring how the offenders or victims define their role in the crime or in understanding the offender or victim's perceptions of how economic or political pressures affected the commission of the crime. Finally, the aftermath of the crime offers insight through exploration of factors occurring once the crime is complete. For example, the role of the police, the degree of harm caused by the crime, and the long-term impact of the specific crime on the broader society are all factors to consider in the study of crime.

The CEP emphasizes specific, necessary components of crime (i.e., offenders, victims, and the social context) and its temporal considerations, including the precursors, the transaction, and the aftermath of the crime. Collectively, each of these components requires study to fully understand crime.

Crime as an Event, Not an Act

As described by Sacco and Kennedy, the CEP also suggests that criminal activity should be viewed as an event, not simply an act. When crime is viewed as simply an isolated act, the role of social context in crime may not receive the proper attention and/or the processes defining or contributing to the act may be ignored. As previously mentioned, crime requires offenders and victims, but defining crime as an event encompasses other crucial elements not often identified in criminological theories. For example, key considerations include, but are not limited to, the physical time and location of the crime, the role of law in defining what activities constitute crime, the personal histories between the parties, and the environmental context of the crime.

These factors are not exhaustive but identify primary factors necessary to understanding criminal activity. The CEP could theoretically include additional factors and future research may in fact supply new important vectors to the CEP. Exploring crime as an event, not an act, requires the acknowledgement that multiple factors collectively influence the commission of crime.

By defining crime as an act, previous criminological theories may have missed the explanatory power of key components that converge to create a criminal event. Sacco and Kennedy suggest that while studying offenders and their motivation is important, a holistic approach that emphasizes multiple facets of crime offers a fuller explanation for crime. As succinctly stated by Meier, Kennedy, and Sacco, "We are, in other words, getting a more complete picture of the factors that promote and curtail crime and that attempt to address its consequences" (2001, p. 4). Thus, the CEP emphasizes the importance of viewing crime as an event in which multiple factors coalesce, rather than simply an act by a single individual.

Conclusion

Due to common assumptions, the CEP is frequently associated with routine activity theory. There are, however, differences that define each approach's contribution. Routine activity theory essentially claims that crime occurs as a result of offenders interacting with victims without adequate guardianship and these instances are often a product of normal activity patterns of everyday life (Cohen & Felson, 1979). The most common criticism of this explanation is the lack of importance placed on the motivation of the offender.

The CEP differs from routine activity theory by encouraging study of offenders and their motivation. In addition, the CEP also emphasizes exploration of the broader social, economic, and legal structures and their role in influencing criminal events. In the language of the CEP, the study of victims and the social context of crime needs to be

coupled with an examination of the offender and an exploration of the precursors to the crime, the crime itself, and the aftermath of the crime (i.e., the criminal event). Thus, the CEP encourages attention not only to the crime but also to the dynamic and contextual nature of the event. In this manner, the CEP offers a systematic approach to understanding crime.

The CEP offers a road map for understanding crime that moves beyond the exploration of crime as a compartmentalized act (i.e., only the combination of offender motivation and opportunity) to analyzing criminal activity as an event with multiple causal factors. The CEP focuses primarily on crime, but its inclusive nature allows existing criminological theories of offender motivation to fit within this framework. In this manner, the CEP offers a holistic and comprehensive guide to studying and understanding crime.

Rob Tillyer

See also Clarke, Ronald V.: Situational Crime Prevention; Cohen, Lawrence E., and Marcus K. Felson: Routine Activity Theory; Eck, John E.: Places and the Crime Triangle; Felson, Marcus K.: Crime and Everyday Life; Miethe, Terance D., and Robert F. Meier: An Integrated Theory of Victimization

References and Further Readings

Anderson, A. L., & Meier, R. F. (2004). Interaction and the criminal event perspective. *Journal of Contemporary Criminal Justice, 20,* 416–440.

Cohen, L. E., & Felson, M. (1979). Social change and crime rate trends: A routine activity approach. *American Sociological Review, 44,* 588–608.

Meier, R. F., Kennedy, L. W., & Sacco, V. F. (2001). Crime and the criminal event perspective. In R. F. Meier, L. W. Kennedy, & V. F. Sacco (Eds.), *The process and structure of crime: Criminal events and crime analysis* (pp. 1–28). New Brunswick, NJ: Transaction.

Pino, N. W. (2005). Serial offending and the criminal events perspective. *Homicide Studies, 9,* 109–148.

Sacco, V. F., & Kennedy, L. W. (1996). *The criminal event: An introduction to criminology.* Belmont, CA: Wadsworth.

Weaver, G. S., Wittekind, J. E., Huff-Corzine, L., Corzine, J., Petee, T. A., & Jarvis, J. P. (2004). Violent encounters: A criminal event analysis of lethal and nonlethal outcomes. *Journal of Contemporary Criminal Justice, 20,* 348–368.

SAMPSON, ROBERT J.: COLLECTIVE EFFICACY THEORY

Collective efficacy is defined as the process of activating or converting social ties among neighborhood residents in order to achieve collective goals, such as public order or the control of crime (Sampson, 2006a; Sampson, Raudenbush, & Earls, 1997). Empirically, collective efficacy has been represented as a combined measure of shared expectations for social control and social cohesion and trust among neighborhood residents. The theory of collective efficacy helps explain one of the most robust findings in criminological research, that crime is nonrandomly distributed across geographic space. Collective efficacy also explains why neighborhood characteristics such as concentrated poverty and high levels of residential turnover are positively related to crime. Neighborhoods vary in their capacity for efficacious action, and Robert J. Sampson, Stephen W. Raudenbush, and Felton Earls argue that this variation explains differences across neighborhoods in levels of crime and violence.

In order to understand the theoretical utility of the concept of collective efficacy, it is vital to comprehend the intellectual foundation of the theory. Collective efficacy theory is rooted in the social disorganization tradition in sociology and criminology, yet augments the disorganization model in important ways. In the social disorganization model, neighborhood organization is facilitated by the density of neighborhood social networks; however, empirical research has demonstrated that strong social ties among neighbors do not always lead to the social control of crime and may even foster criminal behavior. Moreover, research by Mark Granovetter has demonstrated that weak social ties may be a more important resource for individuals than strong, cohesive ties. The theory of collective efficacy resolves these apparent inconsistencies related to the importance of social networks by arguing that the social control of crime may be *facilitated* by strong neighborhood ties and associations, but does not necessarily require cohesive ties.

This entry proceeds by first describing early conceptions of social disorganization and then more recent formulations of the theory. Next, the entry turns to a description of how the theory of collective efficacy explicitly addresses criticisms of social disorganization and therefore serves as a more valid model of the utility of neighborly social networks for the social control of crime. The essay concludes with a discussion of future directions in the development of the theory of collective efficacy.

Social Disorganization

Clifford Shaw and Henry McKay's conceptualization of social disorganization was influenced by the ecological perspective of their Chicago School of Sociology predecessors Robert Park and Ernest Burgess and the social psychological perspective of W. I. Thomas and Florian Znaniecki. Shaw and McKay's social disorganization thesis can be conceived as describing the macro-level processes that lead to variation in rates of delinquency across neighborhoods, and the micro-level (i.e., social psychological) processes underlying these macro-level factors. Shaw and McKay suggest that urban growth processes characterizing Chicago and other United States cities at the end of the 19th and beginning of the 20th century produced neighborhoods marked by drastic differences in physical and economic conditions. Furthermore, they found vast differences in systems of values across these neighborhoods, although they did argue that conventional values were still dominant in all areas.

Shaw and McKay sought to understand why rates of delinquency varied across localities, and why delinquents were concentrated in certain localities. Shaw and McKay mapped the home addresses for over 100,000 delinquents processed by the Cook County (Illinois) Juvenile Court from 1900 to the mid-1930s and found that delinquents were concentrated in four areas of Chicago—Italian delinquents on the near west side, Italians to the near north, black youth on the south side, and Polish delinquents in South Chicago. Shaw and McKay concluded that variation in delinquency across areas was a function of the extent of social disorganization across these areas, where social disorganization refers to the breakdown in the social institutions of a community (e.g., family, schools, churches, and political groups). In other words, these institutions were ineffective at maintaining social order and control. The implication is that to prevent or reduce crime and delinquency, it is necessary to alter conditions of neighborhoods and not simply focus on the individuals within those neighborhoods.

Chapter 7 of Shaw and McKay's book *Juvenile Delinquency and Urban Areas* details the main theoretical points of their argument by describing exactly why variations in community structures and organization lead to variation in delinquency. Central to this discussion is their emphasis on "differential systems of values." Shaw and McKay note that in both high and low socioeconomic status neighborhoods, the dominant value system is conventional, but in low socioeconomic status areas there is a competing system of values that residents (particularly youths) must contend with. This is not to say that the more affluent and less delinquent areas do not have unconventional values and behavior, but rather that there is greater uniformity and consensus on values in those areas which insulates youth from the criminal element. In contrast, in high delinquency areas youths are routinely brought into contact with unconventional attitudes and behaviors that conflict with the dominant (conventional) value systems. These unconventional attitudes still emphasize the achievement of status and economic gain, but different means to achieve these ends are formulated and transmitted. In other words, these unconventional values support delinquent behavior.

Related to the arguments of Thomas and Znaniecki, Shaw and McKay argue that the weakening of social institutions in disorganized areas hinders efforts to reinforce conventional value systems. Furthermore, they contend that low rate delinquency areas are more often characterized by a community consensus on how to deal with social problems and how to collectively regulate unconventional behavior like delinquency, but high delinquency areas lack such consensus. Central to this point is that in certain neighborhoods, traditional forms of social control are weakened and ineffective at countering the advance of these unconventional value systems and the resulting criminal behavior.

Extensions and Revisions of Social Disorganization Theory

Recent formulations of social disorganization theory have focused more on the social control and collective action aspects of the theory, and have come to define social disorganization as the inability

of a community structure to realize the common values of its residents and maintain effective social controls (Bursik, 1988; Kornhauser, 1978; Sampson & Groves, 1989). With an emphasis on the importance of relational networks to facilitate social control, current formulations of the social disorganization thesis have utilized the *systemic model*, which identifies the social organization of communities by focusing on the local community networks. In the systemic model, local community is viewed as a complex system of friendship and kinship networks and of formal and informal associational ties rooted in family life and socialization processes that are fashioned by societal institutions. These social ties facilitate the creation and maintenance of social capital, where social capital refers to a resource that arises from social relations. Social capital, in turn, facilitates social control. Thus, the systemic model of social disorganization posits that the structure and characteristics of these social networks determines the capacity with which a neighborhood can engage in the control of various behaviors, including crime.

A Critique of Social Disorganization Theory

One central challenge to Shaw and McKay's social disorganization theory are findings of the simultaneous occurrence of internally organized local communities and high crime rates in those areas. If dense neighborhood social networks are supposed to advance the social control of crime, then how do we explain the observation that some neighborhoods characterized by strong social ties are nevertheless overrun with crime? There are numerous examples of research that have found that high rates of crime occur in socially organized neighborhoods. Some of the most vivid evidence of this can be seen in the work of William F. Whyte.

In the opening statements of *Street Corner Society*, William F. Whyte describes the common perception of the "Cornerville" neighborhood of Boston ("Eastern City") as a crime-ridden and disorganized local community. This perception, he claims, was constructed through secondhand information and sensationalized newspaper accounts. These sources may describe some of the realities of Cornerville, such as the presence of rackets and corruption, but Whyte's work demonstrates that the strength and density of social relations were much different than commonly perceived by outsiders. Cornerville was not an area in chaos and disorganization, but rather a neighborhood with sure signs of organization. However, in the course of finding a strong, dense network of social ties in Cornerville, he also uncovered an extensive criminal network and an organized gang life. Thus, what appears to be disorganized from outside the local community is actually quite different when viewed from the street corner, even if there is a high incidence and prevalence of crime.

The theory of collective efficacy helps explain why Whyte found high crime in the presence of an internally organized neighborhood. One lesson learned from Whyte's study is that dense social ties among neighborhood residents, and the social capital derived from these relations, are certainly resources available to control crime and misbehavior, but they must be used or activated toward a specific purpose, like stopping neighborhood crime. Sampson asserts that collective efficacy is "the activation of social ties to achieve shared expectations for action" (2006b, p. 39). Whyte's Cornerville was characterized by dense social ties, yet those ties were not activated to reduce crime.

Collective Efficacy

Sampson argues that social networks and the strength of social ties alone cannot explain the social control of crime, given that strong ties are not always conducive to action. While the systemic model of social disorganization assumes that relational networks are related to, and even facilitate, the exercise of control, they are not sufficient for explaining social control because nonconforming behavior may be tolerated by network members as long as it does not interfere with the attainment of common goals. Again we know from the research of Whyte that dense social networks do not always translate into low crime.

Jeffrey Morenoff, Sampson, and Raudenbush argue that researchers must move beyond a reliance on social capital and density of ties when examining the determinants of crime. They describe social capital as a "resource potential," but one that must be activated and utilized. To move beyond social capital and strong ties and associations, Sampson, Raudenbush, and Earls conceptualize collective efficacy as a mechanism through

which social capital confers benefits on neighborhoods. Collective efficacy is the process of activating or converting social ties among neighborhood residents in order to achieve collective goals, such as public order or the control of crime. This formulation relies on trust and a shared willingness to actively engage in social control as key dimensions explaining crime. As Sampson asserts, "social networks foster the conditions under which collective efficacy may flourish, but they are not sufficient for the exercise of control" (2006b, p. 39). In other words, when neighbors have mutual trust for each other, this facilitates social control but does not guarantee it. Similarly, Barry Wellman argues that social scientists have become preoccupied with local solidarity, "rather than a search for functioning primary ties" (p. 1202). The point is that strong ties and a union of interests are secondary in importance to a consideration of whether the structure of ties provides some function or benefit irrespective of strength or sentiment. So the emphasis should not be put upon whether social ties are strong, but whether ties (among neighbors, institutions, and also extralocal entities) provide resources, information, or social control.

The Mechanism of Collective Efficacy

It is vital to ask what exactly is the causal mechanism underlying collective efficacy? Is collective efficacy simply a form of group intervention to stop a criminal event from occurring, or does collective efficacy more broadly involve the collective socialization of youths toward prosocial behavior? Sampson (2006a) characterizes these dilemmas as one of distinguishing between the *situational* and *enduring* effects of collective efficacy. With the former, collective efficacy inhibits crime in a given neighborhood regardless of where the would-be criminal resides, while in the latter collective efficacy in an individual's neighborhood of residence influences her behavior even when she leaves the confines of the neighborhood (Kirk, 2009). Theoretically, the answers to these questions lie in Sampson and colleagues' (1997) conception of social control. While many studies in criminology conceive of social control as the direct supervision of behavior—whether by parents, teachers, or neighbors—Sampson and colleagues define social control more broadly.

Drawing on the definition employed by Morris Janowitz, Sampson, Raudenbush, and Earls define social control as "the capacity of a group to regulate its members according to desired principles" (p. 918). The precise means to achieve these desired principles are many and may include group intervention *and* collective socialization.

Empirically, research to date convincingly demonstrates a situational effect of collective efficacy on neighborhood crime rates, yet research by David Kirk as well as Sampson, Morenoff, and Raudenbush has also shown that neighborhood collective efficacy does not significantly predict individual levels of delinquency. This may result because collective efficacy is situational (as opposed to enduring), with little staying power once residents are outside the boundaries of the given neighborhood (Sampson, 2006a). A necessary next stage in the theoretical development of collective efficacy is to sort out if collective efficacy has an enduring influence on crime in addition to a situational influence.

David S. Kirk

See also Kornhauser, Ruth Rosner: Social Sources of Delinquency; Shaw, Clifford R., and Henry D. McKay: Social Disorganization Theory; Systemic Model of Social Disorganization; Whyte, William Foote: Street Corner Society

References and Further Readings

Burgess, E. W. (1967). The growth of the city: An introduction to a research project. In R. E. Park, E. W. Burgess, & R. D. McKenzie (Eds.), *The city* (pp. 47–62). Chicago: University Chicago of Press. (Original work published 1925)

Bursik, R. J., Jr. (1988). Social disorganization and theories of crime and delinquency: Problems and prospects. *Criminology, 26,* 519–551.

Granovetter, M. S. (1973). The strength of weak ties. *American Journal of Sociology, 78,* 1360–1380.

Janowitz, M. (1975). Social theory and social control. *American Journal of Sociology, 81,* 82–107.

Kirk, D. S. (2008). The neighborhood context of racial and ethnic disparities in arrest. *Demography, 45,* 55–77.

Kirk, D. S. (2009). Unraveling the contextual effects on student suspension and juvenile arrest: The independent and interdependent influences of school,

neighborhood, and family social controls. *Criminology, 47,* 479–520.

Kornhauser, R. (1978). *Social sources of delinquency.* Chicago: University of Chicago Press.

Morenoff, J. D., Sampson, R. J., & Raudenbush, S. W. (2001). Neighborhood inequality, collective efficacy, and the spatial dynamics of homicide. *Criminology, 39,* 517–560.

Park, R. E. (1967). The city: Suggestions for investigation of human behavior in the city. In R. E. Park, E. W. Burgess, & R. D. McKenzie (Eds.), *The city* (pp. 1–46). Chicago: University of Chicago Press. (Original work published 1925)

Pratt, T. C., & Cullen, F. T. (2005). Assessing macro-level predictors and theories of crime: A meta-analysis. In M. Tonry (Ed.), *Crime and justice: A review of research* (Vol. 32, pp. 373–450). Chicago: University of Chicago Press.

Sampson, R. J. (2006a). Collective efficacy theory: Lessons learned and directions for future inquiry. In F. T. Cullen, J. P. Wright, & K. R. Blevins (Eds.), *Taking stock: The status of criminological theory* (Advances in Criminological Theory: Vol. 15, pp. 149–167). New Brunswick, NJ: Transaction.

Sampson, R. J. (2006b). How does community context matter? Social mechanisms and the explanation of crime. In P.-O. Wikström & R. J. Sampson (Eds.), *The explanation of crime: Context, mechanisms, and development* (pp. 31–60). Cambridge, UK: Cambridge University Press.

Sampson, R. J., & Groves, W. B. (1989). Community structure and crime: Testing social disorganization theory. *American Journal of Sociology, 94,* 744–802.

Sampson, R. J., Morenoff, J. D., & Raudenbush, S. W. (2005). Social anatomy of racial and ethnic disparities in violence. *American Journal of Public Health, 95,* 224–232.

Sampson, R. J., Raudenbush, S. W., & Earls, F. (1997). Neighborhoods and violent crime: A multilevel study of collective efficacy. *Science, 227,* 918–924.

Shaw, C. R., & McKay, H. D. (1942). *Juvenile delinquency and urban areas.* Chicago: University of Chicago Press.

Thomas, W. I., & Znaniecki, F. (1918). *The Polish peasant in Europe and America* (Vols. 1–2). Chicago: University of Chicago Press.

Wellman, B. (1979). The community question: The intimate networks of East Yorkers. *American Journal of Sociology, 84,* 1201–1231.

Whyte, W. F. (1993). *Street corner society* (4th ed.). Chicago: University of Chicago Press. (Original work published 1943)

Sampson, Robert J., and John H. Laub: Age-Graded Theory of Informal Social Control

A debate over the significance of criminal careers dominated theoretical criminology, beginning in the mid-1980s. On one side, Alfred Blumstein et al. (1986, 1988a, 1988b) promoted a criminal career model to describe the volume of crime committed over an individual lifespan, including age of onset, frequency of offending, age of termination (desistance), and career length. The criminal careers paradigm suggested that each of these parameters warranted investigation and, possibly, distinct theoretical explanations. In opposition, Michael Gottfredson and Travis Hirschi argued that these supposed distinct parameters were not necessary for understanding the causes of crime; stable individual differences in self-control accounted for crime committed over an individual criminal career. Furthermore, because of the stability of these differences, there was no need to measure criminal career lengths, or even to conduct longitudinal research. This debate fueled many theoretical and quantitative advances in criminology throughout the 1990s, and continues to impact research today.

In 1993, Robert J. Sampson and John H. Laub joined the fray by introducing a compelling new age-graded theory of informal social control in their book *Crime in the Making: Pathways and Turning Points Through Life*. This theory has become the leading life-course theory of crime. The theory does not side with either Blumstein's criminal career model or Gottfredson and Hirschi's self-control theory; rather, it attempts to walk a middle ground, drawing useful elements from both perspectives. Sampson and Laub side with Blumstein in terms of embracing the value of longitudinal research and explanations of crime that takes into account not just the beginning of a criminal career but persistence and desistance as well. They reject the stable individual differences hypothesis of Gottfredson and Hirschi, claiming instead that individual propensity to offend may vary over the life course due to a number of factors, primarily informal social controls. Their recent theoretical reformulation, presented in *Shared Beginnings, Divergent Lives*, identifies a number of factors in addition to informal social control that explain crime across the life course, the most important of which are routine activities and human agency. According to the theory, social control, routine activities, and human agency, both directly and in interaction, affect trajectories of crime across the entire life course.

The Unraveling Juvenile Delinquency Study

Sampson and Laub's life-course theory is drawn from their analysis of a groundbreaking data set. The data for a multiple-wave prospective study of juvenile and adult criminal behavior were originally collected by Sheldon and Eleanor Glueck and presented in their book *Unraveling Juvenile Delinquency*. The research design involved a sample of 500 male delinquents ages 10 to 17 and 500 male nondelinquents ages 10 to 17 matched case-by-case on age, race/ethnicity, IQ, and low-income residence in Boston. The two groups grew up in similar high-risk environments of poverty and exposure to antisocial conduct. Because of this environmental similarity and the matching design, differences in offending between the two groups cannot be attributed to sex, age, ethnicity, IQ, or residence in slum areas.

The initial period of data collection lasted from 1940 to 1948. The average age in this first time period was 14. This sample of 1,000 boys was followed up twice—at age 25 and again at age 32. As a result, extensive data are available for nearly 90 percent of the original sample at all three age periods. The Gluecks collected a wide range of data for analysis relating to criminal career histories, criminal justice interventions, family life, school and employment history, and recreational activities for the subjects in childhood, adolescence, and young adulthood.

Despite the richness of this study, the original case files were left nearly forgotten in the basement of the Harvard Law School Library until they were discovered by John Laub in 1987. Following the discovery of the original files for this study, Sampson and Laub spent 6 years (1987–1993) reconstructing, augmenting, and analyzing the full longitudinal data set. Sampson and Laub's analysis of this reconstructed data, presented in *Crime in the Making*, was driven by the challenge to develop and test a theoretical model that would account for crime and deviance in childhood, adolescence, *and* adulthood. Their age-graded theory integrates the life-course perspective with social control theory to meet this challenge.

The Life-Course Perspective

The life-course perspective provides a broad framework for studying lives over time. Sociologists, criminologists, and psychologists all use life-course methods to help explain and predict major life changes and decisions. It has been applied to numerous domains of human behavior, including crime. According to Glen H. Elder, Jr., the life course is a pathway through an individual's life that follows a sequence of culturally defined, age-graded roles and social transitions. For example, entering the workforce is a culturally defined event that would be part of most people's pathways.

Elder maintains that two central concepts underlie the analysis of life-course dynamics: trajectories and transitions. *Trajectories* may be described as pathways or lines of development throughout life. These long-term patterns of behavior may include work life, marriage, parenthood, and criminal behavior. *Transitions*, on the other hand, are short-term events embedded in trajectories, which may include starting a new job, getting married, having a child, or being sentenced to prison. Because transitions and trajectories are so closely connected, transitionary events may lead to *turning points*, or changes in an individual's life course. For example, getting married may have a great influence on one's life and behavior, from changing where a person lives or works to changing the number and type of friends with whom one associates. Turning points are closely linked to role transitions and are helpful in understanding change in human behavior over the life course. Turning points in adulthood modify life trajectories, creating life paths that cannot be predicted from childhood characteristics or events. Contrary to Gottfredson and Hirschi's position, life-course theory holds that people continue to be strongly influenced by society throughout adulthood.

Age-Graded Theory of Informal Social Control

Sampson and Laub developed a theory of age-graded informal social control in an attempt to explain childhood antisocial behavior, adolescent delinquency, and adult crime. The key component of this theory is that delinquency and crime have an inverse relationship with an individual's bond to society. The theory is organized around three major themes. First, informal family and school social controls are the fundamental social structures that influence behavior and explain delinquency in childhood and adolescence. Second, antisocial behavior in childhood has a strong likelihood of continuing through adulthood across a variety of life domains. Finally, informal social control in adulthood explains changes in criminal behavior over the life span, independent of prior individual differences in criminal propensity.

Structure and Process in Adolescent Delinquency

Sampson and Laub believed that the separation of structural and process-oriented explanations for the onset of delinquency was a mistake. This theory joins structural and process variables, along with individual characteristics, into a single theoretical model. It explains onset with both structural factors, such as poverty or broken homes, and process variables, such as attachment to family and school. Structural context thus influences informal social controls, which in turn explain variations in delinquency.

In *Crime in the Making* Sampson and Laub point to three components of informal social control in the family context: consistent discipline, monitoring, and attachment to the family. To the extent that these three link the child to the family (and ultimately, to society), they inhibit delinquency. These three components of informal control can reduce delinquency through emotional bonds, or through direct control (monitoring and punishment). The school context is another important socializing institution in the prevention of delinquency. Attachment to school and school performance are inversely related to delinquency.

The age-graded theory of informal social control also suggests that social structural factors, such as family disruption, unemployment, residential mobility, and socioeconomic status, indirectly affect delinquency through social bonds. These factors are considered to be structural because they indicate a person's structural position in society. Sampson and Laub claim that previous research has failed to account for the influence of the social structural context on delinquency through family life and social bonds. Some authors argue that socioeconomic disadvantage has potentially adverse effects on parents, such that parental difficulties are more likely to develop and good parenting is impeded. Similarly, factors related to socioeconomic disadvantage, such as poverty and household crowding, may disrupt bonds of attachment between the child and school and may lead to educational deficiencies. If true, one would expect poverty and disadvantage to have indirect effects on delinquency via the influence of parenting and education. Therefore, Sampson and Laub predict that family and social bonding will mediate the effects of structural background factors on delinquency.

Continuity Between Adolescent Delinquency and Adult Offending

Sampson and Laub point to weak social bonds to explain continuity in antisocial behavior across adolescence and adulthood. That is, early antisocial behavior, such as delinquency, conduct disorder, and violent temper tantrums, predicts adult antisocial behavior, such as crime and substance abuse. In addition, adolescent antisocial behavior predicts weak adult social bonds. These weak bonds become evident in erratic labor force participation, low educational attainment, and poor quality of marital attachment. These outcomes occur independently of the sociological and psychological variables that are traditionally used to predict delinquency, such as social class background, ethnicity, and IQ.

Sampson and Laub emphasize a developmental model of cumulative continuity to explain the correlation between adolescent delinquency and adult crime. Their "cumulative disadvantage" concept, presented in 1997, suggests that delinquency continues into adulthood because of its negative consequences for future life chances. For example, arrest, official labeling, incarceration, and other negative life events associated with delinquency may lead to decreased opportunities, including school failure and unemployment. Delinquent activities are also likely to sever informal social bonds to school, friends, and family and to jeopardize the development of adult social bonds. In this way, childhood delinquency has an indirect effect on adult criminal behavior through the weakening of social bonds. Thus, the theory proposes that crime, deviance, and informal social control are intimately linked over the full life course.

Changes in Offending Across the Life Course

Despite the considerable continuity between adolescent offending and adult crime, Sampson and Laub (1993) hold that salient life events and socialization experiences in adulthood can, to some extent, counteract the influence of early life experiences. They recognize that the concepts of continuity and change are not mutually exclusive, and their theory attempts to explain both. Using the imagery of the life-course perspective, they identify certain turning points in the life course, such as marriage, work, and the military, which can alter life trajectories. The social ties that are an inevitable component of most adult transitions (e.g., marital attachment, job stability) provide social capital and can change an individual's path from a delinquent trajectory to a nondelinquent one or vice versa. In other words, pathways to both crime and social conformity are modified by key institutions of social control in the transition to adulthood, regardless of past indicators of an individual's criminal propensity.

Contrary to the emphasis of many life-course researchers, Sampson and Laub argue that the mere occurrence of an event (e.g., getting married or getting a job) or the timing of that event are not the determining factors in their effects on life-course trajectories. Rather, the changes in social bonds and social capital that occur in conjunction with a transition may divert life trajectories. Similarly, the mere presence of a relationship between adults is not sufficient to produce social capital. Instead, adult social ties are important insofar as they create interdependent systems of obligation and restraint that impose significant costs for translating criminal propensities into action. For example, being married will not increase social control if the relationship is not strong. However, close emotional ties and mutual investment between spouses increase the social bond between individuals and, all else being equal, should lead to a reduction in criminal behavior. Sampson and Laub hold that adults, regardless of delinquent background, are inhibited from committing crime in proportion to the amount of social capital invested in work and family relationships. On the other hand, those subject to weak informal social control as adults—that is, those without strong family obligations or steady work—are freer to engage in deviant behavior, even if they were nondelinquent in adolescence.

While this focus on change may appear inconsistent with the earlier discussion of the stability of antisocial behavior over time, evidence suggests that continuity is far from perfect. In fact, most antisocial adolescents do not become antisocial adults (Robins, 1978). Additionally, lives are often unpredictable, and change is ever present. Sampson and Laub propose a dynamic theory of social capital and informal social control that incorporates explanations of stability and change in criminal behavior. Adult social ties can modify childhood trajectories of crime despite general stability. Specifically, they suggest that adult social bonds have a direct negative effect on adult criminal behavior, controlling for childhood delinquency. A person whose youthful life course seems to predict a criminal adulthood may, in fact, experience a well-defined turning point that leads to social stability and engagement instead.

Age-graded theory brings together the concepts of continuity and change. This theoretical framework proposes a dynamic process whereby transitions within trajectories generate turning points in the life course. Sampson and Laub identify three kinds of positive turning points for adult offending trajectories: a cohesive marriage, meaningful work, and serving in the military. They also identify prolonged incarceration and subsequent job instability during the transition to young adulthood as a negative turning point that prevents the formation of social capital and conformity.

Revised Theory

While Sampson and Laub made considerable headway in explaining criminal behavior across the life course with their theory, lingering questions remained, so they followed up on the Glueck men one more time, searching out records and interviewing subjects who were then about age 70. In particular, Sampson and Laub wished to further explore the relationship between age and crime, especially in later years, and to better integrate qualitative and quantitative data. They presented their findings in their 2003 book *Shared Beginnings, Divergent Lives*. Their study involved three sources of new data collection: criminal record checks, death record checks, and personal interviews with a sample of 52 of the original Glueck men, stratified to ensure variability in patterns of persistence and

desistance in crime. These combined data represent a roughly 50-year window on "criminal careers," allowing them to update the Glueck men's lives at the close of the 20th century and connect them to life experiences as far back as early childhood.

Analysis of these quantitative and qualitative data led Laub and Sampson to significantly modify their age-graded theory of informal social control. While they maintain that social bonds help to explain persistence and desistance throughout the life course independent of pre-existing factors, they invoke a number of other causal factors as well. They suggest that criminal behavior, or lack thereof, is a result of individual actions (choice) in conjunction with social situations and influences linked to key institutions. More plainly, they identify social controls, structured routine activities, and purposeful human agency as causal elements in explaining crime throughout the life course. The lack of these factors helps explain late onset of criminal behavior, or persistence in criminal behavior. The presence of all three of these factors helps explain desistance in adulthood independent of a history of antisocial behavior.

The core proposition of Laub and Sampson's theory remains intact in its newest version: levels of offending are reciprocally related to social bonds throughout the life course. In the revised theory, they seek to expand the understanding of informal social control across the entire life course by highlighting how social bonds interact with individual choice and situational context. They note that social bonds may interact with age and life experiences. That is, the inhibiting effect of the increased costs of offending due to potential loss of social capital may increase with age (Shover, 1996).

Structured routine activities, such as going to work every day, tend to limit the variety of situations an individual finds himself or herself in, thus reducing the array of behavioral choices available (Birkbeck & LaFree, 1993). Laub and Sampson (2003) contend that structured routine activities enhance the effect of social controls on offending. Persistent offenders are notable in their lack of structured routine activities across the life course. On the other hand, increased routine activities facilitate desistance from crime regardless of prior offending trajectories.

The third factor proposed to shape offending trajectories across the life course is human agency, a core principle of the life-course perspective. At first glance, the concept of human agency might seem inconsistent with the social control perspective, since a key distinction of control theories is their assumption of universal motivation to offend. Laub and Sampson offer a less stringent version of control theory, assuming that human nature, and thus the motivation to offend, is changeable. In addition, their concept of human agency cannot be understood simply as a proxy for motivation. Rather, their concept of agency has the element of projective, or transformative action within structural constraints. Laub and Sampson refer to agentic moves within structural context as "situated choice."

Beyond these three causal factors, Laub and Sampson's expanded theory of age-graded informal social control gives theoretical expression to "random developmental noise." They conceive of development as the constant interaction between individuals and their environment, coupled with the factor of chance (Lewontin, 2000). This implies that there will always be considerable heterogeneity in criminal offending no matter how many factors are taken into account. In addition, prospective identification of meaningful long-term patterns of offending is not possible. That is, while distinct trajectories of criminal offending may be evident in post-hoc analyses, these trajectories cannot be reliably predicted prospectively (Eggleston et al., 2004; Laub & Sampson, 2003).

In addition to identifying three core causal factors which explain crime throughout the life course, Laub and Sampson draw heavily from their life-history interviews to describe in detail the mechanisms of desistance. The major self-described turning points that they found important in the process of desistance from crime include marriage, the military, reform school, work, and neighborhood change. They maintain that there are multiple pathways to desistance, not limited to these particular institutions. Rather, they identify general mechanisms whereby these institutions facilitate desistance. These institutional or structural turning points all involve, to varying degrees, new situations that (1) knife off the past from the present, (2) provide both supervision and new opportunities for social support and growth, (3) change and structure routine activities, and/or (4) provide the opportunity for identity transformation. While

cognitive transformation is implicated in some desisting offenders, Sampson and Laub believe that most offenders choose to desist in response to structurally induced turning points that serve as a catalyst for long-term behavioral change. In the short term, these institutions interrupt and replace previous social and situational motivations to commit crime, while in the long term they enhance commitments to conformity.

Conclusion

Raymond Paternoster and his colleagues (1997) suggested that Sampson and Laub's theory of informal social control could be classified as a general theory of crime, because age-graded social control explains both continuity and change in offending throughout the life course. Although one may be skeptical of this classification due to fundamental disagreements with the other prominent general theories, particularly Gottfredson and Hirschi's, Laub and Sampson (2003) agreed that theirs is a general theory. While they sharply disagree with Gottfredson and Hirschi over the static versus dynamic nature of crime-producing processes across the life course, Laub and Sampson's theoretical statements signal allegiance with Gottfredson and Hirschi on a number of other contemporary debates in criminology. They agree, for example, that the search for separate explanations for the processes of onset, persistence, frequency of offending, career length and desistance, promoted by the criminal careers perspective, is unnecessary. Likewise, they agree that typological theories of crime, which promote distinct etiologies of crime for different groups, are also mistaken. Their agreement on these matters simply stems from their adherence to a general theory of crime, albeit very different general theories. The revised version of age-graded theory more clearly specifies Laub and Sampson's position relative to both sides of the criminal careers debate of the late 1980s.

In summary, Laub and Sampson's revised age-graded theory of informal social control was developed in response to questions arising from new data on the Glueck men that their original theory had difficulty answering. Their original theory, which was developed in an attempt to explain crime and deviance in childhood, adolescence, and adulthood, was not fully able to account for offending patterns across the entire life course. Laub and Sampson identify three causal factors that affect offending patterns for all people both directly and in interaction: social controls, routine activities, and human agency. They suggest that development is best conceived of as the constant interaction between individuals, their environment, social interactions, and random processes. Together, these factors result in considerable heterogeneity in trajectories of offending, and make it difficult to predict adult offending trajectories based on youth or adolescent risk factors. This unpredictability drives Laub and Sampson's interest in adult-onset offending, desistance, and "zigzag criminal careers." Age-graded theory, although a general theory of crime, like Gottfredson and Hirschi's, embraces the notion of change. It is at root a hopeful theory that describes the ways in which supposed career criminals, life-course-persistent offenders, or those with low self-control may exit a life of crime.

Gary Sweeten

See also Criminal Career Paradigm; Glueck, Sheldon, and Eleanor Glueck: The Origins of Crime; Gottfredson, Michael R., and Travis Hirschi: Self-Control Theory; Hirschi, Travis: Social Control Theory; Moffitt, Terrie E.: A Developmental Model of Life-Course-Persistent Offending

References and Further Readings

Birbeck, C., & LaFree, G. (1993). The situational analysis of crime and deviance. *Annual Review of Sociology, 19,* 113–137.

Blumstein, A., Cohen, J., & Farrington, D. P. (1988a). Criminal career research: Its value for criminology. *Criminology, 26,* 1–35.

Blumstein, A., Cohen, J., & Farrington, D. P. (1988b). Longitudinal and criminal career research: Further clarifications. *Criminology, 26,* 57–74.

Blumstein, A., Cohen, J., Roth, J., & Visher, C. (Eds.). (1986). *Criminal careers and career criminals.* Washington, DC: National Academy Press.

Eggleston, E. P., & Laub, J. H. (2002). The onset of adult offending: A neglected dimension of the criminal career. *Journal of Criminal Justice, 30,* 603–622.

Eggleston, E. P., Laub, J. H., & Sampson, R. J. (2004). Methodological sensitivities to latent class analysis of long-term criminal trajectories. *Journal of Quantitative Criminology, 20,* 1–26.

Elder, G. H., Jr. (1994). Time, human agency, and social change: Perspectives on the life course. *Social Psychological Quarterly, 57,* 4–15.

Glueck, S., & Glueck, E. (1950). *Unraveling juvenile delinquency.* New York: Commonwealth Fund.

Gottfredson, M., & Hirschi, T. (1986). The true value of lambda would appear to be zero: An essay on career criminals, criminal careers, selective incapacitation, cohort studies, and related topics. *Criminology, 24,* 213–234.

Gottfredson, M., & Hirschi, T. (1987). The methodological adequacy of longitudinal research on crime. *Criminology, 25,* 581–614.

Gottfredson, M., & Hirschi, T. (1988). Science, public policy, and the career paradigm. *Criminology, 26,* 37–55.

Gottfredson, M., & Hirschi, T. (1990). *A general theory of crime.* Stanford, CA: Stanford University Press.

Hirschi, T. (1969). *Causes of delinquency.* Berkeley: University of California Press.

Laub, J. H., Nagin, D. S., & Sampson, R. J. (1998). Trajectories of change in criminal offending: Good marriages and the desistance process. *American Sociological Review, 63,* 225–238.

Laub, J. H., & Sampson, R. J. (2001). Understanding desistance from crime. In M. H. Tonry (Ed.), *Crime and justice: A review of research* (Vol. 28, pp. 1–69). Chicago: University of Chicago Press.

Laub, J. H., & Sampson, R. J. (2003). *Shared beginnings, divergent lives: Delinquent boys to age 70.* Cambridge, MA: Harvard University Press.

Lewontin, R. (2000). *The triple helix: Gene, organism, and environment.* Cambridge, MA: Harvard University Press.

Moffitt, T. E. (1993). Adolescence-limited and life-course-persistent adolescent behavior: A developmental taxonomy. *Psychological Review, 100,* 674–701.

Moffitt, T. E. (1994). Natural histories of delinquency. In E. G. M. Weitekamp & H. Kerner (Eds.), *Cross-national longitudinal research on human development and criminal behavior* (pp. 3–64). Dordrecht, Netherlands: Kluwer Academic.

Paternoster, R., Dean, C. W., Piquero, A., Mazzerolle, P., & Brame, R. (1997). Generality, continuity, and change in offending. *Journal of Quantitative Criminology, 13,* 231–266.

Patterson, G. R., & Yoerger, K. (1993). Developmental models for delinquent behavior. In S. Hodgins (Ed.), *Mental disorder and crime* (pp. 140–172). Newbury Park, CA: Sage.

Robins, L. N. (1978). Sturdy childhood predictors of adult antisocial behavior: Replications from longitudinal studies. *Psychological Medicine, 8,* 611–622.

Sampson, R. J., & Laub, J. H. (1993). *Crime in the making: Pathways and turning points through life.* Cambridge, MA: Harvard University Press.

Sampson, R. J., & Laub, J. H. (1994). Urban poverty and the family context of delinquency: A new look at structure and process in a classic study. *Child Development, 65,* 523–540.

Sampson, R. J., & Laub, J. H. (1997). A life-course theory of cumulative disadvantage and the stability of delinquency. In T. P. Thornberry (Ed.), *Developmental theories of crime and delinquency* (pp. 133–162). New Brunswick, NJ: Transaction.

Sampson, R. J., & Laub, J. H. (Eds.). (2005). *Developmental criminology and its discontents: Trajectories of crime from childhood to old age* (The Annals of the American Academic of Political Science No. 602). Thousand Oaks, CA: Sage.

Sampson, R. J., Laub, J. H., & Wimer, C. (2006). Does marriage reduce crime? A counterfactual approach to within-individual causal effects. *Criminology, 44,* 465–508.

Shaw, C. R., & McKay, H. (1942). *Juvenile delinquency and urban areas.* Chicago: University of Chicago Press.

Shover, N. (1996). *Great pretenders: Pursuits and careers of persistent thieves.* Boulder, CO: Westview Press.

SAMPSON, ROBERT J., AND WILLIAM JULIUS WILSON: CONTEXTUALIZED SUBCULTURE

In 1995, Robert J. Sampson and William Julius Wilson developed a theory of race and crime that explains racial differences in violent crime in terms of the community contexts in which people live. This theory draws heavily on Sampson's earlier criminological research grounded in social disorganization theory, and Wilson's earlier sociological research on the causes and consequences of urban inequality. Though Sampson and Wilson do not use the term *contextualized subculture,* this concept is a key part of their *theory of race, crime, and urban inequality.* This theory is one of the most prominent contemporary sociological explanations of the relationship between race and crime, and it has generated much empirical research, which has tested and supported the theory. Rather than trying to distinguish between offenders and nonoffenders, macrosocial theories such as this examine how both structural and cultural characteristics of communities are related to variation in crime rates across communities.

Sampson and Wilson begin by noting that African Americans are disproportionately involved in and victimized by violent crime. To explain racial differences in crime, Sampson and Wilson describe the importance of community context, and begin with the observation that blacks and whites in America tend to live in very different "ecological contexts." As Wilson demonstrated in *The Truly Disadvantaged,* blacks are much more likely than whites to live in areas of concentrated poverty. For example, in 1980, 38 percent of poor blacks lived in areas of extreme poverty, while only 7 percent of poor whites lived in such areas (Sampson & Wilson, 1995, p. 41). In addition, most poor blacks live in areas with high rates of family disruption. This is not the case for poor whites, who tend to live in areas of greater family stability. Sampson and Wilson write, "In not one city over 100,000 in the United States do blacks live in ecological equality with whites when it comes to these basic features of economic and family organization" (p. 42). Why do poor blacks and whites live in profoundly different contexts?

Structural Component of the Theory

Sampson and Wilson describe various historical and contemporary structural factors that have contributed to this concentration of poor blacks in areas of extreme poverty and family disruption. These factors include deindustrialization and job loss in central cities; migration of middle- and upper-income black families out of inner-city neighborhoods, which weakens the social institutions of the community; urban renewal projects that produced population and housing loss in the inner city; housing policies deliberately intended to discriminate against minorities and concentrate the poor in public housing in particular neighborhoods; and other political and institutional policies that have contributed to neighborhood deterioration, such as redlining, lax municipal code enforcement, and withdrawal of municipal services from poor neighborhoods.

Given the very different community contexts in which poor blacks and poor whites reside, perhaps the relationship between race and violent crime is confounded with racial differences in community context. Indeed, Sampson and Wilson note that variation among blacks in crime rates corresponds to the various contexts in which blacks live. They argue that the sources of violent crime are similar across race. For both blacks and whites, violent crime is linked to structural variation in economic and family organization across communities.

Cultural Component of the Theory

In addition to this structural dimension, Sampson and Wilson's theory also includes a strong cultural component—the idea of "contextualized subculture." The concentration of poverty, family disruption, and residential instability in particular communities produces social disorganization, social isolation, and cultural adaptations. Sampson and Wilson conceptualize *structural social disorganization* in terms of the prevalence of social networks in the community (e.g., density of friendship and kinship networks, organizational participation, institutional stability) and the ability of the community to informally address local problems and exert social control (e.g., willingness of residents to respond to problems caused by unsupervised groups of teenagers).

Communities characterized by concentrated poverty, family disruption, and residential instability are not only more socially disorganized (in terms of social networks and informal social control) but also more culturally disorganized. In areas of concentrated disadvantage and instability, mutual trust and communication among neighbors are difficult to achieve, and the search for common values is undermined. In addition, where structural forces like those described above have separated disadvantaged communities from the larger society, the cultural values of the larger society become attenuated. In their place emerges a value system that seems to legitimize, or at least tolerate, crime and deviance. Sampson and Wilson describe the *social isolation* of communities of concentrated disadvantage that "deprives residents not only of resources and conventional role models, but also of cultural learning from mainstream social networks that facilitate social and economic advancement in modern industrial

society" (p. 51). In other words, residents of these extremely impoverished communities are cut off from the institutions and individuals of mainstream society. This isolation then leads to *cultural adaptations,* as residents adjust to the conditions of life in areas of concentrated disadvantage.

Sampson and Wilson are careful to distinguish their ideas about social isolation and cultural adaptations from subcultural perspectives such as the culture of poverty and the subculture of violence. The latter perspectives view behaviors (e.g., violence) as resulting from the internalization of norms and values that are at odds with the values of conventional society, and that condone, rationalize, and call for particular behaviors, such as violence. This view implies that these internalized, alternative values influence behaviors, regardless of the context. But Sampson and Wilson's theory views behaviors as "cultural adaptations to constraints and opportunities"—adaptations that do not require the internalization of values conducive to violence (p. 51). Those who live in areas of extreme poverty do not accept an alternative value system that approves of violence and crime. Yet they come to expect crime and deviance as an unavoidable part of the "cognitive landscape" of everyday life, and they adapt by developing "ecologically structured norms" about expected standards and behaviors (p. 50). These norms, in turn, influence the likelihood of crime and deviance. According to this perspective, mainstream cultural values simply become irrelevant in certain structural contexts. This view implies that norms and behaviors change with the context in which they occur.

In summary, Sampson and Wilson's theory argues that structural forces create communities of concentrated disadvantage that are socially isolated from mainstream society, where cultural adaptations undermine social organization and the control of crime. The disproportionate involvement of blacks in violent crime is not linked to race per se, but rather to the fact that poor blacks and whites live in distinct ecological contexts.

Research Evidence

A great deal of empirical research has tested Sampson and Wilson's general assertion that neighborhood context, rather than individual-level factors, can explain variation in crime and delinquency rates. This research has shown how neighborhood disadvantage shapes structural social disorganization and, ultimately, crime rates. Numerous studies have shown that neighborhood context (e.g., concentrated poverty, residential mobility, family structure, immigrant concentration) influences crime rates (e.g., delinquency, gang fights, robbery, homicide) primarily through its effects on neighborhood social organization, measured in terms of informal social control (e.g., confronting those who cause neighborhood disturbances), kinship and friendship ties, participation in neighborhood organizations, and collective efficacy (a combination of cohesion among neighbors and a willingness to exert informal social control). For example, in 1997, Sampson and his colleagues found that collective efficacy (a neighborhood-level variable) influenced multiple measures of violence, and it mediated a large portion of the effects of neighborhood context (concentrated disadvantage and residential stability) on violence.

A 1998 study by Sampson and Dawn Jeglum Bartusch provides evidence regarding the cultural component of Sampson and Wilson's theory. They examined how structural characteristics of neighborhoods explain racial and ethnic differences in normative orientations about law, police, and deviance. Sampson and Bartusch analyzed survey data regarding tolerance of deviance (including violence), satisfaction with police, and "legal cynicism," which represents views about the legitimacy of laws. They found that, compared to white respondents, blacks and Latinos were less tolerant of deviance and violence, less satisfied with policing in their neighborhoods, and more cynical about the legitimacy of law. This contradicts the subculture of violence perspective, which hypothesizes a cultural tolerance of violence among blacks. Yet, when Sampson and Bartusch examined these issues at the neighborhood level, they found that areas of concentrated economic disadvantage and residential instability showed high levels of tolerance of deviance, dissatisfaction with police, and legal cynicism. In addition, once neighborhood-level differences in concentrated disadvantage were taken into account, race no longer significantly affected satisfaction with policing and legal cynicism. This means that it is neighborhood context, rather than race-specific attitudes, that explains normative orientations about police and

law. In other words, blacks appear to be more cynical about the legitimacy of law and less satisfied with policing because they are disproportionately likely to live in areas of concentrated disadvantage. As Sampson and Bartusch conclude,

In support of contextual accounts of subculture, it thus appears that there is an ecological structuring to normative orientations—"cognitive landscapes" where crime and deviance are more or less expected and institutions of criminal justice are mistrusted. . . . Normative orientations toward law and deviance are rooted more in experiential differences associated with neighborhood context than in a racially induced subcultural system. (pp. 800–801)

Extension of the Theory

Robert Sampson and Lydia Bean recently proposed new directions for research on communities, race, and crime. Their proposal calls for (1) an expanded view of neighborhood context that considers how characteristics of surrounding communities and citywide dynamics may influence what happens in a particular neighborhood, (2) a consideration of increases in the Latino American population, and of how Sampson and Wilson's theory of race and crime might be extended to ethnicity and crime and used to explain lower levels of violence in Latino immigrant communities, and (3) a more dynamic, relational perspective on culture and structure that views culture as both shaping and shaped by social structure.

Dawn Jeglum Bartusch

See also Inequality and Crime; Kobrin, Solomon: Neighborhoods and Crime; Krivo, Lauren J., and Ruth D. Peterson: Extreme Disadvantage and Crime; Sampson, Robert J.: Collective Efficacy Theory; Shaw, Clifford R., and Henry D. McKay: Social Disorganization Theory; Wilson, William Julius: The Truly Disadvantaged

References and Further Readings

Morenoff, J. D., Sampson, R. J., & Raudenbush, S. W. (2001). Neighborhood inequality, collective efficacy, and the spatial dynamics of urban violence. *Criminology, 39,* 517–559.

Sampson, R. J., & Bean, L. (2006). Cultural mechanisms and killing fields: A revised theory of community-level racial inequality. In R. Peterson, L. Krivo, & J. Hagan (Eds.), *The many colors of crime: Inequalities of race, ethnicity, and crime in America* (pp. 8–36). New York: New York University Press.

Sampson, R. J., & Jeglum Bartusch, D. (1998). Legal cynicism and (subcultural?) tolerance of deviance: The neighborhood context of racial differences. *Law and Society Review, 32,* 777–804.

Sampson, R. J., Morenoff, J. D., & Gannon-Rowley, T. (2002). Assessing "neighborhood effects": Social processes and new directions in research. *Annual Review of Sociology, 28,* 443–478.

Sampson, R. J., Raudenbush, S., & Earls, F. (1997). Neighborhoods and violent crime: A multilevel study of collective efficacy. *Science, 277,* 918–924.

Sampson, R. J., & Wilson, W. J. (1995). Toward a theory of race, crime, and urban inequality. In J. Hagan & R. D. Peterson (Eds.), *Crime and inequality* (pp. 37–54). Stanford, CA: Stanford University Press.

Wilson, W. J. (1987). *The truly disadvantaged: The inner city, the underclass, and public policy.* Chicago: University of Chicago Press.

SCHIZOPHRENIA AND CRIME

Schizophrenia is a devastating mental illness, and one of a larger class of psychotic disorders defined by the presence of delusions (false beliefs) and/or hallucinations (sensory perceptions without external sensory input). Schizophrenia may also be characterized by disorganized speech and behavior and by negative symptoms such as social, cognitive, and emotional withdrawal. Sensationalized accounts of dangerous, violent, and criminal behavior committed by schizophrenic persons have proliferated through the popular media; and the assumption of schizophrenia-associated crime and violence has contributed to public fear, stigma, social rejection, and even the denial of services and programmatic funding to schizophrenic individuals (Raine, 2006). In reality, most schizophrenic persons are not criminal or violent. Given this common misperception, a review of the empirical schizophrenia-crime/violence literature—along with proposed explanations for the relationship based in psychological, neurobiological, and social theory—appears timely.

Two converging lines of evidence continue to support a relationship between schizophrenia and crime: First, higher rates of psychosis and schizophrenia are found in criminal or delinquent populations; and second, schizophrenia patients are much more criminal and violent than the general population. In most cases, family or close network members are the victims of severe violent crimes, and most offending is found among young males in early illness stages. Examination of the schizophrenia-crime link began over a century ago with early psychoanalytic proposals and published case histories. This inquiry has progressed through research in different areas, including studies of violence within psychiatric hospital settings, of criminal behavioral histories of mentally ill individuals, and of national registry case linkages.

Schizophrenia and Specific Crime Types

Violent Crimes

Violent schizophrenic crime research has examined a broad range of violence indicators, from assaults in psychiatric hospitals to criminal record violent convictions. Much of what is currently known about schizophrenic violence is based upon studies of newly admitted schizophrenia inpatients, who often experience emotional turmoil along with intense psychotic symptoms (Krakowski, 2005). Forensic inpatient samples indicate that, violent psychotic offenders are often first-time offenders who committed severe physical assaults against intimates. Non-hospitalized schizophrenic persons may engage in the spectrum of violent behaviors observed in the general population, from minor assaults to brutal murders. And limited evidence suggests some schizophrenic and mentally ill murderers may be characterized by specific motivational, behavioral, and emotional characteristics (Häkkänen & Laajasalo, 2006; Nijman et al., 2003).

Property and Drug Crimes

To date, nonviolent or property offending among schizophrenic persons has not been systematically studied, though incidental data indicate that schizophrenic offenders may commit vagrancy crimes and minor thefts for motives other than material gain. Substance use rates among schizophrenic persons are high, possibly representing efforts to use legal and illegal substances to ameliorate psychotic symptoms. Individuals with schizophrenia are more likely than others to abuse substances and be criminal and violent (Douglas & Skeem, 2005).

Sexual Crimes

Sexual crimes appear comparatively rare among schizophrenic persons. Individuals with schizophrenia and other psychotic disorders comprise only small percentages (i.e., 2 to 5 percent) of sexual offender populations (Alish et al., 2007), and they demonstrate reduced proportional rates of sexual offense convictions in comparison to non-mentally ill individuals in case linkage studies. Rare descriptive reports suggest a complex relationship between schizophrenia and sexual offending.

Psychological Factors: Schizophrenia Symptoms

Individual psychological symptoms may explain schizophrenic crime and violence, and research on delusions and hallucinations in the mentally ill (including schizophrenia but also mood and substance use disorder patients) have provided some evidence for this explanation.

Delusions

Previous research indicates a general association between delusions and violence among mentally ill persons; and a substantial minority of violence committed by psychotic persons appears to be delusionally driven (Taylor, 2006). Specific delusions (i.e., persecutory) may contribute more to violence risk (Bjorkly, 2002a); and symptoms such as threat (i.e., perceptions of threat or harm from others) and control-override (i.e., mind control or thought insertion) have been shown to be separately associated with violent behaviors (Link et al., 1998). Additionally, several rare delusions of misidentification appear related to violence. These include Capgras syndrome (the belief that familiar persons have been replaced by physically identical imposters), subjective doubles or Doppleganger syndrome (the belief that oneself has a double or impersonator), Fregoli syndrome (the belief that

another person has changed his or her physical identity while his or her psychological identity remains the same), and intermetamorphosis (the belief others have undergone radical physical and psychological changes to become persecutors (Malloy et al., 1992). Hostility and suspiciousness toward the misidentified person may lead to extreme violence. For example, in one reported case, a Capgras patient decapitated his father—whom he thought to be a robot imposter—in order to find the "batteries in his head." Though many schizophrenic patients will not act on their delusions, the risk for doing so may increase with accompanying emotional distress (Bjorkly, 2002a), challenge to the delusion by others (Taylor, 2006), or the absence of protective social support networks and professional supervision (Douglas & Skeem, 2005).

Hallucinations

The literature on command hallucinations (i.e., voices ordering action) is disparate—with some studies examining the relationship between command hallucinations and compliance, some the factors associated with acting on command hallucinations, and some the relationship between command hallucinations and dangerous behavior. Despite methodological problems, evidence indicates that some individuals who hear violent commands will act on them. However, violent command hallucinations do not produce action in isolation. Other factors mediate the process, such as beliefs about voices (malevolence/benevolence, power, voice recognition or familiarity, trust, voice quality such as pressure or persistence, content of instruction, emotion), general reasoning processes leading to action (including beliefs about disobedience), hospital environment, and presence of concurrent delusions (Bjorkly, 2002b).

Neurobiological Factors

Antisocial schizophrenic individuals may represent a biologically distinct subgroup of schizophrenic persons. For example, brain imaging studies indicate structural and functional differences in frontal and temporal regions among aggressive, violent, and antisocial schizophrenia patients in comparison to those who are not. EEG anomalies have characterized violent but not nonviolent schizophrenia patients and controls, and electrodermal deficits appear to distinguish individuals with both antisociality and a mild form of schizophrenia from those having either condition alone. Molecular genetic studies report that specific genotypes related to neurotransmitter functioning differentiate antisocial from non-antisocial schizophrenia patients, and specific neuropsychological deficits appear to distinguish antisocial schizophrenics from their non-antisocial and non-schizophrenic counterparts (Schug & Raine, 2009).

Social and Biosocial Factors

Theory of Mind

Theory of Mind (ToM) is the ability to represent the mental states of one's self and others. Deficits in ToM functioning might explain the social withdrawal, poverty of speech, and repetitive behaviors seen in schizophrenia. Thought insertion and delusions of control may reflect impairments in the ability to represent one's own intentions to act, whereas reference and persecutory delusions may reflect difficulties in representing the mental states of others. Research in forensic populations has shown that unique ToM deficits differentiate schizophrenia from non-schizophrenia patients, violent from nonviolent schizophrenia patients, and differentiate among symptom-specific subtypes of schizophrenia patients (Abu-Akel & Abushua'leh, 2004; Murphy, 2006).

Treatment Issues

Issues related to standard biosocial treatment and management approaches (i.e., pharmacological and psychosocial therapies) may directly influence schizophrenic violence and criminality. Violence in schizophrenic outpatients has been associated with difficulties in basic social areas, including psychosocial treatment adherence, medication compliance, and treatment alliance (Douglas & Skeem, 2005). Additionally, new biosocial research into the prevention and treatment of schizophrenia indicates that early environmental enrichment (i.e., nutritional, educational, and physical exercise) at ages 3 to 5 years reduced a mild form of schizophrenia and antisocial behavior 14 to 20 years later (Raine et al., 2006).

Risk Factors

Biosocial risk factors have been examined in longitudinal studies of crime and schizophrenia. Though violence largely post-dates schizophrenia in violent schizophrenic persons, violence may be part of the preschizophrenia phase of young criminals, and there may exist a distinct subgroup of "early start" schizophrenic offenders characterized by pre-schizophrenia criminality (Hodgins, 2004). Finally, poor educational attainment, poor grades for attention at school, higher birth weight, and larger head circumference have been linked to adult criminality in schizophrenia patients in registry linkage studies (Cannon et al., 2002).

Conclusion

Empirical evidence continues to suggest a solid schizophrenia-crime relationship. There is a need for a second generation of crime-schizophrenia research—that focuses on risk factors for both disorders in an attempt to elucidate common psychological, biological, and social etiological mechanisms. Such research may lead to a better understanding of schizophrenic individuals who become criminal and help reduce the negative stigma unjustly attached to those who do not.

Robert A. Schug and Adrian Raine

See also Brain Abnormalities and Crime; Mednick, Sarnoff A.: Autonomic Nervous System (ANS) Theory; Mental Illness and Crime; Psychophysiology and Crime; Raine, Adrian: Crime as a Disorder

References and Further Readings

Abu-Akel, A., & Abushua'leh, K. (2004). "Theory of mind" in violent and nonviolent patients with paranoid schizophrenia. *Schizophrenia Research, 69,* 45–53.

Alish, Y., Birger, M., Manor, N., Kertzman, S., Zerzion, M., Kotler, M., et al. (2007). Schizophrenia sex offenders: A clinical and epidemiological comparison. *International Journal of Law and Psychiatry, 30,* 459–466.

Bjorkly, S. (2002a). Psychotic symptoms and violence toward others—a literature review of some preliminary findings. Part 1. Delusions. *Aggression and Violent Behavior, 7,* 617–631.

Bjorkly, S. (2002b). Psychotic symptoms and violence toward others—a literature review of some preliminary findings. Part 2. Hallucinations. *Aggression and Violent Behavior, 7,* 605–615.

Cannon, M., Huttunen, M. O., Tanskanen, A. J., Arseneault, L., Jones, P. B., & Murray, R. M. (2002). Perinatal and childhood risk factors for later criminality and violence in schizophrenia. *British Journal of Psychiatry, 180,* 496–501.

Douglas, K. S., & Skeem, J. L. (2005). Violence risk assessment: Getting specific about being dynamic. *Psychology, Public Policy, and Law, 11*(3), 347–383.

Häkkänen, H., & Laajasalo, T. (2006). Homicide crime scene behaviors in a Finnish sample of mentally ill offenders. *Homicide Studies, 10,* 33–54.

Hodgins, S. (2004). Criminal and antisocial behaviours and schizophrenia: A neglected topic. In W. F. Gattaz & H. Häfner (Eds.), *Search for the causes of schizophrenia* (Vol. 5, pp. 315–341). Darmstadt, Germany: Steinkopff Verlag.

Krakowski, M. (2005). Schizophrenia with aggressive and violent behaviors. *Psychiatric Annals, 35,* 45–49.

Link, B. G., Stueve, A., & Phelan, J. (1998). Psychotic symptoms and violent behaviors: Probing the components of "threat/control-override" symptoms. *Social Psychiatry and Psychiatric Epidemiology, 33,* S55–S60.

Malloy, P., Cimino, C., & Westlake, R. (1992). Differential diagnosis of primary and secondary Capgras delusions. *Neuropsychiatry, Neuropsychology, and Behavioral Neurology, 5*(2), 83–96.

Murphy, D. (2006). Theory of mind in Asperger's syndrome, schizophrenia and personality disordered forensic patients. *Cognitive Neuropsychiatry, 11*(2), 99–111.

Nijman, H., Cima, M., & Merckelbach, H. (2003). Nature and antecedents of psychotic patients' crimes. *Journal of Forensic Psychiatry and Psychology, 14*(3), 542–553.

Raine, A. (2006). Pursuing a second generation of research on crime and schizophrenia. In A. Raine (Ed.), *Crime and schizophrenia: Causes and cures* (pp. 3–12). New York: Nova Science.

Raine, A., Liu, J., Venables, P., & Mednick, S. A. (2006). Preventing crime and schizophrenia using early environmental enrichment. In A. Raine (Ed.), *Crime and schizophrenia: Causes and cures* (pp. 249–265). New York: Nova Science.

Schug, R. A., & Raine, A. (2009). Comparative meta-analyses of neuropsychological functioning in antisocial schizophrenic persons. *Clinical Psychology Review, 29,* 230–242.

Taylor, P. J. (2006). Delusional disorder and delusions: Is there a risk of violence in social interactions about the core symptom? *Behavioral Sciences and the Law, 24,* 313–331.

SCHUR, EDWIN, M.: RADICAL NON-INTERVENTION AND DELINQUENCY

Radical non-intervention was developed by Edwin M. Schur as an alternative way of dealing with juvenile delinquency. The theory holds that juvenile delinquency is common among all socioeconomic classes. The theory further proposes that "delinquents" are no different from "non-delinquents," except that "delinquents" have been processed through the court system. Radical non-intervention maintains that the juvenile court's authority in children's lives is too broad and that laws illegal only for children (e.g., running away, incorrigibility, tobacco use) should be abolished. Additionally, radical non-intervention theory proposes that the "delinquent" label given to juveniles processed by the court system can increase their delinquency. When children are labeled as "bad" or "delinquent," they are often viewed as such in their community (e.g., by parents, teachers), which may increase their sense of alienation and risk of further delinquency. Radical non-intervention theory argues that juveniles should be left alone as much as possible for minor "delinquency" violations. Finally, to form a better juvenile justice system, radical non-intervention proposed five priorities for reform.

The Delinquency Label

Adverse consequences result from being processed through the court system. Specifically, court processing labels the juvenile as a delinquent. Once that occurs, juveniles adopt that identity and often perform in accordance with the label and associate with similar youths. For example, in school, teachers may treat delinquent children differently than "regular" children. The "bad" youths then associate themselves with other "delinquents," increasing their proclivity toward delinquency. Some courts attempt to identify "at-risk" youth and place them in programs aimed at correcting pre-delinquent behaviors, effectively labeling the youths as "pre-delinquent." Radical non-intervention theory suggests that children placed in treatment programs for "pre-delinquency" may feel like they are being punished for a behavior that is not illegal. This sense of injustice by the court system may cause youths to distrust the system and lead them to rebel against it, thus increasing the probability of further, more serious delinquency.

The Juvenile Court System

Radical non-intervention theory holds that courts intervene too often into the lives of juveniles. The theory argues that although the court claims to know what is best for children, in fact, children are the only ones who know what is best for their unique situations. As a result, the theory proposes that voluntary treatment programs (as opposed to compulsory programs) should be included in juvenile justice policies. Additionally, the theory proposes removing all status offenses from the juvenile court's jurisdiction. Minor violations should be handled outside of the juvenile court to avoid negative labels caused by system interaction.

Priorities for a Better Juvenile Justice System

Radical non-intervention theory suggested that the policies of the juvenile justice system should be modified to better suit the needs of youths who enter it. Five key priorities are proposed to accomplish this.

• *First, reassess the ways of thinking about juvenile problems.* Juvenile misconduct is inevitable; therefore, society must abandon the idea that juvenile delinquency is limited to certain individuals. Children act the way they do, whether it be "delinquent" or not, because of social norms and customs. To change the negative behaviors of children, society must consider these influences and attempt to rectify them.

• *Policies that indirectly influence delinquency may be more important than those that directly influence delinquency.* According to radical non-intervention, juvenile behavior reflects the norms and values of greater society; therefore, adults

should not be surprised that juveniles commit delinquent acts. The theory proposed that policies aimed at combating juvenile delinquency will not change children's behavior because they do not address the underlying issues leading to delinquency. Widespread social change regarding how society views and reacts to children's behavior must occur if we are to reduce "delinquent" behavior.

• *To eliminate injustice toward juveniles, society must take them more seriously.* The bonds a child has to society can be an effective deterrent to juvenile delinquency; therefore, more focus should be placed on strengthening those bonds. This begins by creating a legal system that respects children and, in turn, can be respected *by* children. The juvenile justice system must take into account that delinquents are not "bad," "sick," or "malicious" children; they are simply the products of a society that has little respect for its youth.

• *The juvenile justice system should focus less on "treating" those deemed delinquent, and more with dispensing justice.* Radical non-intervention theory proposed that courts should focus less on "treating" broad juvenile problems that may lead to delinquency, such as incorrigibility and idleness. In turn, the court should concern itself with defining specific penalties for law violations, which apply equally to all youths who commit the violation. As a result, discretion and discrimination within the juvenile court would be reduced, and the court could then be respected by youths.

• *Juvenile justice professionals must utilize a variety of approaches to the delinquency "problem."* According to the theory, delinquency prevention programs should be conducted in the youths' community and should employ "indigenous" personnel—persons who live in the community and have experience dealing with delinquent children—as opposed to outside professionals. Additionally, since juveniles may view treatment programs that are held in correctional facilities as punishment, treatment programs should be non-institutional and voluntary. According to the theory, voluntary programs have two significant benefits: (1) since youths can choose whether or not they enter a program, they may feel that the court respects their decisions more, and (2) discretion and discrimination in the adjudication process may be reduced. As Schur stated, "Our young people deserve something better than being 'processed.' Hopefully, we are beginning to realize this" (p. 171).

Stacy C. Moak and Shaun M. Gann

See also Becker, Howard S.: Labeling and Deviant Careers; Hirschi, Travis: Social Control Theory; Matza, David: Delinquency and Drift; Sutherland, Edwin H.: Differential Association Theory and Differential Social Organization; Sykes, Gresham M., and David Matza: Techniques of Neutralization

References and Further Readings

Becker, H. S. (1963). *Outsiders: Study in the sociology of deviance*. New York: Free Press.

Platt, A. (1969). *The child savers: The invention of delinquency*. Chicago: University of Chicago Press.

Schur, E. M. (1973). *Radical non-intervention: Rethinking the delinquency problem*. Englewood Cliffs, NJ: Prentice Hall.

Shelden, R. G. (n.d.). *Resurrecting radical non-intervention: Stop the war on kids*. San Francisco: The Center on Juvenile and Criminal Justice. Retrieved January 5, 2009, from http://www.cjcj.org/files/radical.pdf

Schwartz, Martin D., and Victoria L. Pitts: A Feminist Routine Activity Theory

Violence, particularly sexual assault, has been a frequent topic of research for several decades, especially for feminist researchers. Generally, feminist research suggests that there are high levels of sexual assault against women due to a patriarchal, rape-supportive culture. However, not all women have the same heightened risk for sexual assault victimization. What the feminist perspective does not adequately account for are the variations in rape victimization rates across the female population. This is where the importance of theory focusing on individual statuses and lifestyles becomes important.

Routine activity theory is one perspective that addresses the differential risks for victimization among individuals by examining lifestyle. The strength of this theory is that it focuses on the idea that crime is not a random occurrence in society but follows regular patterns regarding situation and place—and how these interact with individual characteristics and behaviors. This theory can be used as an enhancement to a theory, such as feminism, to discuss why, although all women may be at greater risk for sexual assault, some women have higher risks than others.

Martin D. Schwartz and Victoria L. Pitts greatly enhanced the discussion of the sexual assault of college women by utilizing an approach that combined feminism and routine activity theory into a discussion that explores the idea that while women are the more likely victims of sexual assault there are lifestyles college women have that may work to increase their victimization risks. These lifestyles are those that frequently put them into contact with men when they are in vulnerable situations (such as drinking alcohol). Routine activity theory can explain, in the context of feminism, why some women have higher risks than others. Alternatively, feminism can aid a routine activity theory by placing the analysis of lifestyle into the context of cultural and societal norms and values about violence, especially violence against women.

Routine Activity Theory

To elaborate, research inspired by routine activity theory has consistently shown that criminal victimizations are not randomly distributed in society (see Cohen & Felson, 1979). Instead, victimization is associated with lifestyles and daily routines of individuals, which in turn may be linked to demographics. These routines influence the amount of exposure one has with potential offenders, how valuable or vulnerable they or their property is as a target, and how well guarded they or their property are. When potential offenders, suitable targets, and incapable (or absent) guardians converge, victimization is likely to occur.

Routine activity theory specifically suggests that the social context of criminal victimization is a central issue in understanding victimization risks. Certainly, a person may be willing to commit crime given an opportunity, but if that opportunity never arrives, the crime will not occur. Opportunities may not come for several reasons. It may be that the potential offender does not find any target of sufficient vulnerability or any property of sufficient value to merit attempting an offense. It is also possible that a suitable target may be perceived as too well guarded to merit an attempt.

Routines in activities are products and consequences of lifestyles; it is the lifestyle of individuals that carry them through settings, contexts, and interactions, which may either increase or decrease the possibility of their victimization. Movement through time and space exposes individuals to varying numbers and varieties of potentially motivated offenders as well as provides for differing perceptions of people's vulnerability/suitability as a target. Additionally, as individuals move between and among settings, their activities alter their possibilities (and self-identified needs) to have access to guardianship measures. Clearly, some lifestyles and activities enhance victimization likelihood by involving individuals with "dangerous" others or those who are disposed to perceive persons with certain characteristics as more or less vulnerable or acceptable as targets. It is the identification of the specific lifestyle factors, activities, and statuses that increase or decrease victimization risks that is the goal of routine activity theory.

Even so, individuals' behaviors and routines take place within the context of society and cultural norms and values. Individuals typically behave in ways that the culture or subculture in which they live support. Individuals' perceptions and interactions with others are based, in part, on the attitudes and thoughts of those around them (e.g., their primary group members). As such, interpreting the behaviors of individuals must take into account the larger context in which these behaviors occur. This is where a theory explaining the cultural orientations of one group of people toward other groups of people can help account for the variations in victimization risks across not just individuals but also larger groups of people.

Feminism and Sexual Assault

At the core of a feminist view on sexual assault is the belief that men assault women (both sexually and physically) in an effort to maintain a position of dominance over women. Men are first of all seeking to individually maintain power and control over specific other women (those they directly victimize). The actions of individual men toward individual women also, however, have important effects throughout society. Sexual assault, then, is seen as a way for one class of people (men) to instill fear in—and therefore impose restrictions on the activities of—a second class of people (women).

Additionally, men form or become members in social or peer groups that work to encourage or buffer any guilt or shame associated with the sexual assault of women. Thus, the odds of sexual assault continuing to occur are increased.

Feminist views on sexual assault are supported by a large body of empirical research. What is most telling about this research is that rapists themselves frequently explain their actions using the words of feminist theory. Rather clearly, then, feminist theories offer important insights about the nature, general causes, and societal role of sexual assault. However, what the feminist perspective does not adequately account for are the variations in rape victimization rates (i.e., victimization risks) across subgroups of the female population. This is where the importance of theory focusing on individual behavioral routines becomes important.

A combination of feminism and routine activity theory to understanding sexual assault victimization risks for female college students thus focuses on identifying activities and lifestyle factors that are associated with increased exposure to motivated offenders or male social peer groups, heightened perceptions of the woman as a suitable/vulnerable victim, and a minimization of effective guardianship. Therefore, it is necessary to identify the behaviors and lifestyle factors that have been shown in previous research to be related to female college students' sexual victimization risk. In this regard, it is important to identify not only why women are at increased risk of victimization, but also what factors are associated with the increased risk of some women as compared with women in general.

Schwartz and Pitts

As mentioned, Schwartz and Pitts conduct one of the few studies on female sexual assault that incorporates both feminist and routine activities perspectives. They discuss that women are the more likely targets for sexual assault victimization, but they also note—through an analysis of lifestyle—which women have relatively higher risks for such victimization than others. They accomplish this theoretical intermingling with great success. Their discussion focuses on the idea that feminism can enhance our understandings of the three core concepts of routine activity theory: potential offenders, suitable targets, and absent or incapable targets.

Specifically, while routine activity researchers typically take the concept of potential offenders for granted, assuming there are plenty of such individuals "out there," feminism can enhance this explanation by noting that men may be more motivated to sexually assault females because of a rape-supportive culture in the United States that works to normalize and downplay violence against women. In such a climate, it is no wonder that women are frequently assaulted violently by men. In this type of culture, then, the number of potential sexual assault offenders is going to be high. This can clearly be seen in the case of college campuses.

Relatedly, in a culture with values and beliefs that allow men to assault women without feeling guilt or shame, it is also likely that there will be few, if any, willing or capable guardians who would stop a progressing or possible sexual assault against a woman. This would be particularly likely to happen in a male social peer group with pro-violence-against-women attitudes. Further, given the lower penalties that men experience for sexually assaulting women, any guardianship or deterrence that the criminal justice system would provide is diminished significantly.

Finally, women are the obvious suitable targets in an atmosphere such as this. Since women are viewed as being the acceptable targets of male aggression, they are vulnerable and accessible. This effect is compounded in a locational hot spot like a college campus. In this location, men are more likely to be members in social peer groups that promote violence against women. Further, women are typically in close proximity to these male social groups, increasing their vulnerability and suitability as targets.

In their research, Schwartz and Pitts note that a closer examination of the concept of suitable targets would highlight the types of factors (alcohol use and friendships with men who sexually abuse women) that would enhance the targeting of women by potential offenders. They find support for their contentions: women who drank more often and women who had male friends who got women drunk for the purposes of sexually assaulting them were more likely to be sexually assaulted themselves.

While these findings are highly informative and move beyond (1) the pure feminist contention that all women are suitable targets for sexual assault due to their gender and society's view of it as an acceptable choice for sexual assault and (2) the routine activity theory assertion that individuals have higher risks for sexual assault victimization when they are engaging in behaviors that place them into greater proximity to potential offenders, they are also limited. For example, this approach does not examine whether there may be other lifestyle factors that increase a woman's proximity to potential (and perhaps highly motivated) offenders or a woman's vulnerability or suitability as a target to males who are culturally supported in their desire to assault women sexually. Numerous questions, therefore, remain. Are there ways that women can reduce their risks for sexual assault by, for example, utilizing more personal forms of self-protection, rather than relying on men to act as guardians? Are there other routines related to the use of alcohol that influence a woman's risks for sexual assault? Does drug use elevate a woman's suitability as a target or increase her proximity to potential offenders? Are there other forms of leisure activities that heighten the risks for sexual assault? Given that college campuses are hot spots for sexual assault, are there particular campus activities that increase or decrease a woman's risks for victimization? Finally, are there lifestyles relating to a woman's youth that can aid in an understanding of her suitability to men as a target for sexual assault?

In the end, Schwartz and Pitts provide an excellent step forward in several areas of academic exploration: they enhance our understanding of routine activity theory by incorporating feminist assertions (and visa versa). They also aid in our understanding of the heightened sexual assault victimization risks for college women. Finally, they conduct a first-rate empirical analysis of a theoretical synthesis that can aid scholars in their interpretations of criminal victimization, particularly sexual assault.

Elizabeth Ehrhardt Mustaine

See also Cohen, Lawrence E., and Marcus K. Felson: Routine Activity Theory; Felson, Marcus K.: Crime and Everyday Life; Hindelang, Michael J., Michael R. Gottfredson, and James Garofalo: Lifestyle Theory; Rape Myths and Violence Against Women; Stanko, Elizabeth A.: Gender, Fear, and Risk

References and Further Readings

Cohen, L. E., & Felson, M. (1979). Social change and crime rate trends: A routine activity approach. *American Sociological Review, 44,* 588–608.

Mustaine, E. E., & Tewksbury, R. A. (2002). Sexual assault of college women: A feminist routine activities analysis. *Criminal Justice Review, 27,* 89–123.

Schwartz, M. D., & DeKeseredy, W. (1997). *Sexual assault on the college campus: The role of male peer support.* Thousand Oaks, CA: Sage.

Schwartz, M. D., & Pitts, V. L. (1995). Exploring a feminist routine activities approach to explaining sexual assault. *Justice Quarterly, 12,* 9–31.

SELLIN, THORSTEN: CULTURE CONFLICT AND CRIME

During the late 1920s and early 1930s, the large number of individuals immigrating to the United States led some Americans to raise questions about the norms and cultural values of the newly arrived groups. In particular, concerns were raised about possible conflicts between the norms and cultural values of the society from which they had come and those in existence within the United States. Some argued that these differences would lead to high rates of criminal behavior among immigrants as a result of the cultural conflict. Concerns were also raised about the possibility of a weakening of American society.

Two potential types of criminal behavior stemming from conflict between the different norms and values were identified. The first possible conflict was seen as arising from the cultural values immigrants themselves had brought with them and the differing norms and values that already existed in the United States. The second conflict was viewed as developing during the period of time after immigrants had arrived and were being assimilated but were starting to follow behavioral patterns that were in conflict with the normative standards of American society.

Some sociologists began to study immigrants after they had arrived in the United States and settled in "disorganized" areas where the existing norms and values oftentimes were thought to be opposed to those of the dominant society. As a result, the issue of culture conflict was prominent among those who studied crime. For example, the ecological studies so popular in that era, particularly in the research conducted in the city of Chicago (Shaw et al., 1929) with their studies about "delinquency areas," had led them to focus much of their attention upon the social pathology of various aspects of the "zone of transition."

In order to better understand the issue of culture conflict and criminal behavior, in 1935 the Social Science Research Council selected a sociologist from the University of Pennsylvania, Thorsten Sellin, and a criminologist, Edwin H. Sutherland of the University of Chicago, to be the two members of a Subcommittee on Delinquency. The subcommittee on delinquency chose the issue of culture conflict and its role in the causation of crime, since at the time the idea of culture was a source of both social and academic interest.

Both men brought with them differing types of expertise that were considered essential to the project. Sutherland was starting to develop his theory of differential association which, while primarily utilizing a social psychological approach to the study of criminal behavior, was also concerned about structural factors and so left room in his theory for the inclusion of the idea of culture conflict. Sellin had also been working in the criminology area, but he was more involved in activities that focused on the development of criminology as a science (Laub, 1983). When the final report was published, Sellin was identified as the sole author as he had developed and subsequently written the bulk of the manuscript.

The completed manuscript, *Crime and Culture Conflict,* was published by the Social Science Research Council in late 1938. Due in large part to the publication of this manuscript, the relationship between culture, subculture, and crime continued in American criminology throughout the next few decades. So pervasive was this approach that it led J. Pinatel to comment that "as a consequence of its general nature, the theory of culture conflict has permeated many modern developments in American sociological criminology" (p. 5).

Culture Conflict and Conduct Norms

The central idea behind culture conflict as a source of crime, as developed by Sellin, was that different groups learned different conduct norms and that these norms would violate the dominant norms of American society, in particular the criminal law. Conduct norms were viewed by Sellin as rules based on the social attitudes of groups toward the various ways in which a person might act under certain circumstances. When a person's actions and reactions are governed by rules or norms, they are conduct norms. Accordingly, conduct, by definition, could occur only in situations that are defined by some social group and governed by a rule of some sort.

In his monograph, Sellin reaffirmed the idea that the criminal law is a body of norms that binds all those who live within the political boundaries of a state and are enforced through the coercive force of the state. Furthermore, he stated that the specific character of these legal rules depends upon the character and interests of those groups that influence legislation. He emphasized the idea that such groups are not necessarily in the majority, a notion that was becoming popular at the time. Instead, his focus was upon the lack of congruence between criminal laws promulgated by a dominant majority group and the moral ideas of different social groups subjected to the criminal laws of the state. Since the norms embodied in the criminal law change as the values of the dominant groups change, what is defined as crime varies from time to time and also from place to place. The view of culture conflict as a source of crime maintained that different groups learned different conduct norms and that these conduct norms would become a fixture of the criminal law. According to Sellin, the "conduct which the state denotes as criminal is, of course, that deemed injurious to society or, in the last analysis, to those who wield political power within that society and therefore control the legislative, judicial, and executive functions which are the external manifestations of authority" (p. 3).

When developing his conception of conduct norms, Sellin combined two ideas: (1) the notion that members of a society are not equally committed to the norms contained in the criminal law, and (2) that members of a society are not equally committed to other conduct norms. The result of these variations in degree of commitments, he observed, is conflict. According to Sellin, a conflict of norms occurs when more or less differing rules of conduct govern the specific situations in which a person may find himself or herself. The conduct norm of one group of which a person is a member may permit one response to this situation while the norm of another group may possibly permit the very opposite response.

Sellin then proceeded to examine the concept of culture conflict, pointing out that a number of studies had studied this issue and its relationship to delinquency (Shaw et al., 1929). Importantly, these studies assumed the existence of legal and nonlegal conduct norms that were in conflict with each other. He noted that the concept had been used in two ways: sometimes culture conflict was regarded as the result if the migration of conduct norms from one culture complex to another, sometimes as a by-product of a cultural growth process.

The primary and most commonly used of these two definitions focused on the crime and delinquency rates of immigrants who had recently arrived in the United States, particularly those who lived in those areas identified as the zone of transition in large American cities. The research conducted in Chicago led to the interpretation of the differing crime and delinquency rates within the various areas of the city as the result of different cultural values. The areas with low delinquent behavior were characterized by uniformity, consistency, and universality of conventional cultural values, while the zone of transition, with the highest rates of delinquency, experienced the greatest amount of competing and conflicting cultural values (Shaw & McKay, 1969).

Sellin also used the concept of culture conflict in a secondary way. He demonstrated that as a modern industrial and mercantile society developed, the process of social differentiation produced a conflict of conduct norms. As a result, a vast extension of impersonal control agencies has emerged. These agencies were designed to "enforce rules which increasingly lack the moral force which rules receive only when they grow out of emotionally felt community needs." One by-product of the development of complex societies, then, is certain life situations "governed by such conflicting norms that no matter what the response of the person in such a situation will be, it will violate the norms of some social group concerned" (p. 48).

Conduct Norms and the Causes of Crime

Sellin started his investigation of conduct norms by discussing the need for criminologists to actively search for the causes of crime. Up until that time, criminologists had used the legalistic definition of crime, an approach he found problematic in terms of differentiating criminals from noncriminals. He was critical of the legalistic definition of crime that had been used most commonly by criminologists because he felt "that the categories set up by the criminal law do not meet the needs of scientists because they are of 'a fortuitous nature' and do not 'arise intrinsically' from the nature of the subject matter" (p. 19).

In Sellin's view, if the study of crime was to attain an objective and scientific status, it could not allow itself to be restricted to the terms and boundaries of inquiry established by law makers. In particular, he felt that the concept of crime should be extended beyond violations of legal codes to include violations of moral and social codes. He believed that while all societies have standards of behavior or conduct norms, not all these standards are necessarily reflected in law. In this context, terms such as *deviance, nonconformity,* and *antisocial conduct* were preferred to that of *crime,* because the latter is unable to include all criminal acts. An important feature of this approach is that it does not require any reference to the criminal law at all.

In order to move the field of criminology away from this problem, Sellin supported a different conception to the approach to etiological questions in criminology. As such, he proposed the concept of conduct norms be used instead. Conduct norms stemmed from those life situations that are repetitious and socially defined and that require definite responses from people. Attached to these responses are norms that define the reaction or response "which in a given person is approved or disapproved by the normative group" (Sellin, 1938, p. 28). A normative group was any group held together by common interests, sufficient to bring forth group attitudes toward any inquiry of these interests. All groups were considered by Sellin to be, in a sense, normative. As societies grow, the more complex the culture becomes, and the more likely it is that the values within these groups will fail to agree.

Conduct norms were viewed by Sellin as the result of the values of the group that had formulated it. There is, for every person in a society, in each life situation in which he or she finds himself or herself, a right (or normal) and a wrong (or abnormal) way of reacting, with the norm being dependent upon the values that has formulated it. Social groups place restrictions on the actions of their members in the attempt to secure protection of social values that have been injured by unrestricted conduct. All reactions or activity in situations governed by them could be called conduct.

Conclusion

The insights made by Sellin about culture conflict and conduct norms became popular at the time, but its appeal diminished due largely to cultural homogenization in the United States, a process that has been attributed to the rise of the various forms of the mass media (Tittle & Paternoster, 2000). Perhaps its most enduring contribution to criminology was its influence upon Edwin Sutherland, who viewed the second usage of culture conflict as developed by Sellin to be basic to the explanation of crime. The concept in this sense later became the principle of differential association. Accordingly, the history of the culture conflict concept is tightly entwined with the development of Sutherland's differential association theory, which ultimately became the most prominent theory in American criminology during the 1940s and 1950s. A number of years later, when he was discussing the history of his own theory, Sutherland reported that he inadvertently stated the principles of differential association before he realized he had a theory. Significantly, his statement included the concept of conflict of cultures.

Colin H. Goff

See also Anderson, Elijah: Code of the Street; Miller, Walter B.: Lower-Class Culture Theory of Delinquency; Shaw, Clifford R., and Henry D. McKay: Social Disorganization Theory; Sutherland, Edwin H.: Differential Association Theory and Differential Social Organization; Wolfgang, Marvin E., and Franco Ferracuti: Subculture of Violence Theory

References and Further Readings

Laub, J. (1983). Interview with Thorsten Sellin. In J. Laub (Ed.), *Crime in the making* (pp. 166–181). Boston: Northeastern University Press.

Lejins, P. P. (1987). Review essay. *Criminology, 25,* 975–988.

Lilly, J. R., Cullen, F. T., & Ball, R. A. (2007). *Criminological theory: Context and consequences* (4th ed.). Thousand Oaks, CA: Sage.

Pinatel, J. (1968). Thorsten Sellin and the principal trends in modern criminology. In M. E. Wolfgang (Ed.), *Crime and culture: Essays in honor of Thorsten Sellin* (pp. 3–10). New York: Wiley.

Sellin, T. (1938). *Culture, conflict, and crime.* New York: Social Science Research Council.

Shaw, C., Forgaugh, F. M., McKay, H. D., & Cottreel, L. S. (1929). *Delinquency areas.* Chicago: University of Chicago Press.

Shaw, C., & McKay, H. D. (1969). *Juvenile delinquency and urban areas: A study of rates of delinquency in relation to differential characteristics of local communities in American cities.* Chicago: University of Chicago Press.

Sutherland, E. H. (1956). Development of the theory. In A. Cohen, A. Lindesmith, & K. Schuessler (Eds.), *The Sutherland papers* (pp. 13–29). Bloomington: Indiana University Press.

Tittle, C. R., & Paternoster, R. (2000). *Social deviance and crime: An organizational and theoretical approach.* Los Angeles: Roxbury.

Wolfgang, M. E. (Ed.). (1968). *Crime and culture: Essays in honor of Thorsten Sellin.* New York: Wiley.

SHAW, CLIFFORD R.: THE JACK-ROLLER

First published in 1930 and reissued in 1966, *The Jack-Roller* is the life history of "Stanley," a 23-year-old Chicago man who had compiled by the time of its initial publication an extensive record of delinquency, crime, and incarceration both as a juvenile and a young adult. This entry describes the book, highlights aspects of Stanley's background and personality that contributed to his delinquency, comments briefly on the intellectual context of early-20th-century Chicago in which *The Jack-Roller* was compiled and published, and concludes with observations on the potential value and limitations of offender autobiographies as sources of data about crime.

Stanley

Stanley was the product of a large blended family with an employed but alcoholic father and an emotionally indifferent, if not abusive, stepmother. The family's residence was in low income and high delinquency areas of Chicago. Stanley's conflict with and antipathy for his stepmother figure prominently in his early life, and she is singled out repeatedly by him as a major source of his problems. She also condoned or encouraged his stealing.

Stanley began running away from home and living on the streets well before adolescence. He found close at hand both cultural conditions and delinquent companions that offered little resistance, if they did not facilitate, his drift into low-level crime. *Jack-rolling* is a dated name for strong-arm robbery, typically committed by yoking from behind victims who are adjudged unlikely to offer effective resistance. *Mugging* is the more contemporary name for it.

Perhaps the most noteworthy aspect of Stanley's personality was his lifelong interpersonal abrasiveness. He was quick to take offense and retaliate at perceived signs of interpersonal disrespect or unfair treatment from others. Whether this was rooted in part in his family's precarious material circumstances and the inevitable disrepute that accompanies it is unclear, but Stanley was unmistakably a product of the working class and its culture. The significance of this and the possibility that his prickly personality had origins at least in part in repeated disrespectful treatment by authority figures and others are not considered in *The Jack-Roller*.

Shaw

Clifford R. Shaw, who encouraged Stanley to write his autobiography, provided topical categories for and edited it and was instrumental in seeing it through to publication. At the time, Shaw was on the staff of the Institute for Juvenile Research, an innovative Chicago-based state agency created to study and develop promising responses to juvenile delinquency. Shaw was educated at the University of Chicago, where sociologists viewed crime and other forms of social pathology as products of socially disorganized urban conditions.

One chapter of *The Jack-Roller* describes the social and cultural aspects of the neighborhoods in which Stanley's family resided during his formative years. Shaw and his colleagues believed that life histories could lay bare the interaction of individual characteristics, family dynamics, and adverse neighborhoods. The "boy's story" could show

how these various factors were understood and responded to by him, and the part they played in the development and sequencing of delinquency. Truancy, for example, generally preceded onset of minor delinquency and gave way in turn to more serious infractions.

Just as Shaw believed that disadvantaged and poorly integrated urban areas spawned delinquency, he also believed that the key to turning offenders away from these pursuits was placing them in more conventional and socially integrated environments. He employed this approach with Stanley, which may have contributed to his successful avoidance of prolonged criminal participation. *The Jack-Roller* was followed in later years by publication of additional life histories of delinquents, coauthored by Shaw and his colleague, Henry D. McKay.

Conclusion

The Jack-Roller, its compiler, and its subject have been examined critically from a variety of intellectual perspectives and also in light of changing theoretical approaches to criminal offenders. It is a case study. Case studies can serve as the source of theoretical and conceptual stimulation, but their utility for rigorous testing of theoretical explanations is extremely limited. What is clear is that there is little about Stanley and his background that distinguish him from a high proportion of street-level thieves and hustlers. They can suggest shortcomings of or needed modifications to general explanations. Given these limitations of case studies, the value of *The Jack-Roller* may lie in the extent to which its contents and descriptions are consistent with similar autobiographical statements. On this count, the book reveals Stanley, his childhood and delinquency, and his subsequent desistance from crime to be remarkably similar to the lives of a high proportion of street thieves and hustlers. This is clear from the work of subsequent investigators who mined multiple life histories for analytic generalizations.

A half-century after *The Jack-Roller* was published, a sequel appeared that brought readers up to date on how Stanley's life unfolded in later years (Snodgrass, 1982). His life was not free of difficulties, including a short involuntary stay in a state mental hospital following conflict with his first wife. Eventually, however, Stanley terminated

criminal participation, relocated to California, and maintained legitimate employment in sales. Retired for several years, he passed away on April 25, 1982.

Neal Shover

See also Cullen, Francis T.: Social Support and Crime; Giordano, Peggy C., and Stephen A. Cernkovich: Cognitive Transformation and Desistance; Life-Course Interdependence; Peers and Delinquency; Sampson, Robert J.: Collective Efficacy Theory; Sampson, Robert J., and John H. Laub: Age-Graded Theory of Informal Social Control; Shaw, Clifford R., and Henry D. McKay: Social Disorganization Theory; Shover, Neal: Great Pretenders

References and Further Readings

Becker, H. S. (1966). Introduction. In C. R. Shaw, *The jack-roller: A delinquent boy's own story* (pp. v–xviii). Chicago: University of Chicago Press.

Maruna, S., & Matravers, A. (2008). N = 1: Criminology and the person. *Theoretical Criminology, 11*, 427–442.

Shaw, C. R. (1930). *The jack-roller, a delinquent boy's own story*. Chicago: University of Chicago Press.

Shover, N. (1996). *Great pretenders: Pursuits and careers of persistent thieves*. Boulder, CO: Westview Press.

Snodgrass, J. (1976). Clifford R. Shaw and Henry D. McKay: Chicago criminologists. *British Journal of Criminology, 16*, 1–19.

Snodgrass, J. (Ed.). (1982). *The jack-roller at seventy: A fifty year follow-up*. Lexington, MA: D. C. Heath.

SHAW, CLIFFORD R., AND HENRY D. MCKAY: SOCIAL DISORGANIZATION THEORY

Originally developed by Clifford R. Shaw and Henry D. McKay, two researchers from the University of Chicago, social disorganization is one of the most popular criminological theories today. Unlike most other theories, it is concerned with understanding why crime rates are higher in some communities than others. Thus, it focuses on the macro-level distribution of crime rates across areas, not on why any one individual may be more or less likely to engage in criminal acts than another.

As the name implies, the theory posits that communities can be classified on a continuum of disorganization, from low to high. According to the theory, some communities are highly disorganized and experience more crime compared to other communities that are less disorganized and experience less crime. The key to combating crime, then, is to reduce levels of social disorganization. Just how that can be accomplished is explained shortly but first it is necessary to understand the intellectual history of social disorganization theory and its ascendancy in criminological thought during the 20th century.

Social Disorganization Theory's Intellectual Roots

Often considered the original architects of social disorganization theory, Shaw and McKay were among the first in the United States to investigate the spatial distribution of crime and delinquency across urban areas. Their research built on work done by other Chicago School researchers, in particular Robert E. Park and Ernest W. Burgess, whose concentric zone theory examined how critical changes of the time (e.g., industrialization, urbanization, and immigration) affected the nature of social life in Chicago communities. Park and Burgess's theory characterized zones within the city, some marked by disorganizing characteristics and attributes. It was not until years later, however, with the work of Shaw and McKay, that crime became part of the equation.

In their work, *Juvenile Delinquency and Urban Areas*, Shaw and McKay applied the concentric zone model developed by Park and Burgess to the study of juvenile delinquency. Shaw and McKay's primary interest was to study the relationship between community and delinquency and determine the extent to which differences in characteristics of local areas paralleled variation in rates of delinquency. They sought to address questions such as, To what extent do variations in rates of delinquency correspond to demonstrable differences in economic, social, and cultural characteristics of local communities? How are delinquency rates affected over time by successive changes in the nativity and nationality composition of the population?

To answer these questions, Shaw and McKay examined the distribution of delinquency in Chicago communities based on juvenile court cases and commitments for three time periods: 1900 to 1906, 1917 to 1923, and 1927 to 1933. One of their key findings was that delinquency was not randomly distributed throughout the city; rather, it tended to cluster in certain areas. Stated alternatively, rates of juvenile delinquency were consistent with an ordered spatial pattern. The highest rates were found in the inner-city areas and declined with distance from the city center. Using maps and other visuals, Shaw and McKay demonstrated that its distribution was closely related to the location of industrial and commercial areas and to the composition of the population in the area (e.g., rates of poverty and families on relief), in line with the concentric zone model. Because they had data over time, Shaw and McKay were also able to demonstrate a consistency in the general processes regarding the distribution of delinquency across neighborhoods. They found that high delinquency communities in Chicago remained high delinquency communities over several decades, regardless of which racial or ethnic group inhabited the area.

A key "social fact" about crime that is central to social disorganization theory can be gleaned from the early Chicago School studies: crime and delinquency co-occur with other social problems in communities, including poverty, dilapidated housing, and residential instability, among others. For the Chicagoans, this implied a connection between broader social and economic conditions of areas and crime. This discovery was important because until then biological determinism, which assumes that all or virtually all human behavior, including criminal behavior, is innate and cannot be changed or altered, had served as the primary explanation for understanding crime. Early Chicago School studies were thus important for pointing out that crime is present in certain areas of the city where there is social, economic, and cultural deprivation. Researchers emphasized that residents in these areas were not biologically abnormal or personally disoriented; rather, they were viewed as responding naturally to disorganized environmental conditions. The implication of this finding for the field of criminology is clear: just as "kinds of people" explanations are needed to understand crime, "kinds of places" explanations are also needed to account for the ecological concentration of crime and delinquency.

In sum, the findings from Shaw and McKay and other Chicago School studies formed the basis of social disorganization theory, a theory chiefly concerned with understanding the relationship between community characteristics and crime.

Theoretical Overview

According to social disorganization theory, some neighborhoods are socially disorganized and have high crime rates while others are less disorganized and have lower crime rates. Social disorganization can be defined as the inability of a community to realize the common values of its residents and maintain effective social controls (Bursik, 1988). Thus, socially disorganized communities are ineffective in combating crime, a common value or goal among residents. Alternatively, crime is more successfully prevented in socially organized communities.

Socially organized and disorganized communities are quite different, according to the theory. Characteristics of socially organized communities include (1) solidarity, or an internal consensus on important norms and values (e.g., residents want and value the same things, such as a crime-free community); (2) cohesion, or a strong bond among neighbors (e.g., residents know and like one another); and (3) integration or social ties, with social interaction occurring on a regular basis (e.g., residents spend time with one another) (Kubrin et al., 2008, p. 87). Socially disorganized communities, in contrast, typically lack solidarity, cohesion, and integration among residents.

According to the theory, these characteristics are critical because they help to foster informal social control, a key factor for preventing crime within communities. Informal social control is the scope of collective intervention that the community directs toward local problems, including crime (Kornhauser, 1978). It is the informal, nonofficial actions taken by residents to combat crime in their communities. Consider, for instance, a group of neighbors who patrol the streets at night to fight crime. Or consider residents who watch each other's homes when a family is on vacation to prevent burglaries. Or consider residents who scold neighborhood youth when they act out of line or cause trouble. These individuals represent the eyes and ears of the community and their presence is often enough to deter others from committing crime.

Solidarity, cohesion, and integration or social ties generate informal social control, which ultimately prevents crime. This is why socially organized communities have lower crime rates than socially disorganized communities—they have greater levels of informal social control.

In recent years, theorists have added another dimension to this explanation. Robert Sampson, Stephen Raudenbush, and Felton Earls argue that social cohesion and networks may be necessary, but not sufficient, for social control and that what is missing is the key factor of purposive action (i.e., how social ties are activated and resources mobilized to enhance social control). For the latter to occur, they argue, residents must be willing to take action and intervene, which depends in large part on conditions of mutual trust and solidarity among neighbors. Sampson et al. therefore propose a new construct—collective efficacy—which captures this linkage of trust and intervention for the common good. They argue high levels of collective efficacy within communities should lead to lower crime rates, similar to the effect of social ties and informal social control. In sum, socially organized communities marked by social integration, cohesion and ties, informal social control, and collective efficacy should have comparatively lower crime rates compared to socially disorganized communities which lack these characteristics. This is often found to be the case in studies of neighborhood crime.

But social disorganization theory does not stop here in its explanation of crime. The theory also specifies the larger structural characteristics of communities that contribute to levels of disorganization, or conversely, organization. Early Chicago School researchers focused on three neighborhood characteristics they believed distinguished disorganized communities: poverty, residential instability, and racial/ethnic heterogeneity. They were able to demonstrate, to some degree, that Chicago communities marked by these characteristics had higher crime rates than those without such characteristics. They theorized this was primarily due to lower levels of social integration and informal social control, in line with the theory. But they were never able to empirically test this theoretical assertion.

It is important to note that the neighborhood characteristics just described are not direct causes of crime within communities. Rather they indirectly affect crime through their influence on social integration and informal social control. Thus, high poverty neighborhoods typically have higher crime rates than low poverty neighborhoods not because poverty in and of itself causes crime but because poorer neighborhoods, according to the theory, have fewer ties and less informal social control, leading to higher crime rates. The same can be argued for the other neighborhood characteristics. Along these lines, the neighborhood characteristics of communities are commonly referred to as exogenous sources of social disorganization while solidarity, cohesion, integration, informal social control, and collective efficacy constitute the intervening dimensions of social disorganization.

Over the decades, research on social disorganization theory has taken numerous directions. In one direction, researchers have examined additional structural characteristics of communities theorized to cause disorganization including family disruption (e.g., divorce and single-parent households), education levels (e.g., residents with a high-school diploma), population density (e.g., population per square mile), and population composition (e.g., number of young males). Researchers have also been concerned with empirically testing the full social disorganization model by showing that neighborhood characteristics affect levels of social integration, informal social control, and collective efficacy, which in turn affect crime rates. Progress aside, there have been and continue to be some noteworthy criticisms of Shaw and McKay's early work as well as the theory more generally.

Earlier Critiques

As noted earlier, at the time, the work of Shaw and McKay and other Chicago School researchers had a profound impact on the study of crime. However, interest in the relationship between community characteristics and crime began to recede in the 1950s when the field of criminology moved toward more micro-level or individual theories of crime causation, including social learning, social control, and labeling theories (Kubrin et al., 2008, p. 90). Concurrent with this shift, several early criticisms of the theory emerged. One key criticism centered on the theory's central concept of social disorganization. Shaw and McKay at times did not clearly differentiate the presumed outcome of social disorganization (i.e., increased rates of crime and

delinquency) from disorganization itself. In early writings, the delinquency rate of an area was often both an example of disorganization and something caused by disorganization. As one example, in his study, Calvin Schmid used houses of prostitution and homicides as indices of social disorganization yet disorganization is theorized to cause these very things. Eventually, this problem was resolved when theorists attempted to clarify the unique conceptual status of social disorganization by defining it in terms of the capacity of a neighborhood to regulate itself through formal and informal processes of social control (recall the formal definition of social disorganization discussed earlier).

Another early criticism centered on what some referred to as the theory's inherent biases about lower-class communities and disorganization, biases generated from the relatively homogeneous, middle-class backgrounds of the theorists themselves. Critics questioned: Is it true that physical, economic, and population characteristics are objective indicators of social disorganization, or does the term reflect a value judgment by the theorists about lower-class lifestyle and living conditions? Several theorists believe the latter. For instance, Edwin Sutherland preferred to use the term *differential social organization* because of his belief that "the organization of the delinquent group, which is often very complex, is social disorganization only from an ethical or some other particularistic point of view" (p. 21). According to this line of reasoning, some urban neighborhoods may not be so much disorganized as simply organized around different values and concerns. Although it is impossible to completely remove such biases from social disorganization or any theory for that matter, researchers today are much more aware of this bias and prefer a more nuanced explanation of what generates social disorganization within neighborhoods.

Perhaps the most damaging early criticism had to do with researchers' ability to empirically test the social disorganization model. Although Shaw and McKay collected data on characteristics of areas and delinquency rates for Chicago communities and were able to visually demonstrate a relationship between the two using maps and other visuals, theirs did not constitute a test, in the strict sense, of social disorganization theory. Nor did future studies for decades to come. The norm for quite a long time was to use Census data to characterize neighborhoods in terms of poverty, residential mobility, racial and ethnic heterogeneity, and other factors along with official crime data to show the two were related, and then to theorize that this was due to intervening levels of social ties and informal social control. The criticism was that without empirically verifying the true proposed theoretical path—neighborhood characteristics lead to crime indirectly through social ties and informal control—the theory had not been properly tested.

It was not until 1989 that researchers were able to formally test social disorganization theory, including specifying the true nature of the relationships among ecological characteristics of communities, levels of social disorganization, and crime. Robert J. Sampson and W. Byron Groves used data from a large national survey of Great Britain to empirically test the theory. They constructed community-level measures of neighborhoods (specifically, poverty, residential mobility, and racial/ethnic heterogeneity) and the mediating dimensions of social disorganization, and they then determined how both sets of factors influenced neighborhood crime rates. Their findings were largely supportive of social disorganization theory: communities characterized by strong social ties and informal control had lower rates of crime, and, more importantly, these dimensions of social disorganization were found to explain, in large part, the effects of community structural characteristics (e.g., poverty) on crime rates. Apart from Sampson and Groves, today only a handful of studies successfully empirically examine all the theoretical processes laid out by social disorganization theory. Far more research is needed before we are able to confidently understand why some communities produce higher crime rates than others.

A final early criticism relates to the theory's reliance on official data, especially in terms of measuring crime. All but a handful of studies use official data to document crime patterns across neighborhoods when testing social disorganization theory. Even Shaw and McKay relied on official court records to determine the distribution of juvenile court cases and commitments. Yet few scholars have considered the extent to which neighborhoods themselves are a consideration in police and court decisions and there is a significant degree of

community-specific bias that may exist within police departments (Bursik, 1988). In other words, some neighborhoods are more likely to be "over-policed" than others. Thus, the assumption that policing practices do not vary across neighborhoods is unfounded. The question remains: Given variation, how might policing practices influence official data collection? Whatever the answer, it is clear that official rates represent a mixture of differentials in neighborhood behavior patterns, neighborhood propensities to report behavior, and neighborhood-specific police orientations. Thus, a more ideal situation involves collecting alternative indicators of neighborhood crime and delinquency based on self-report or victimization data to be used in conjunction with official records. Such data collection efforts are occurring more and more through the use of large-scale surveys in cities throughout the United States (e.g., the Project on Human Development in Chicago Neighborhoods, the Seattle Neighborhood and Crime Project, and the Neighborhood Project in Denver, Chicago, and Philadelphia).

There are several additional earlier criticisms of social disorganization theory, many of which are detailed in Robert Bursik's classic 1988 piece, "Social Disorganization Theory: Problems and Prospects." A more recent analysis of the theory, highlighting on-going challenges to social disorganization theory, was completed decades later by Charis Kubrin and Ronald Weitzer in "New Directions in Social Disorganization Theory." Below some of the more vexing on-going challenges confronting the theory are described.

On-Going Challenges

Today, disorganization theorists continue to document how community characteristics and crime go hand in hand. The theory is very much alive and kicking. But as with any theory, there remain several challenges confronting social disorganization theory. One of the most critical on-going issues surrounds the definition of what constitutes a neighborhood. The concept "neighborhood" is central to the theory yet researchers have not arrived at a consensus, either conceptually or operationally, on the definition of a neighborhood. This is due, in part, to variability in people's perceptions of neighborhood boundaries. For some residents, their neighborhood constitutes the street they live on; for others, it constitutes the few blocks surrounding their home; and still for others, it is a much larger section of the city in which they live. This variability is often not captured in social disorganization research due to an overreliance on official data. Because studies use official data as their source, researchers most commonly operationalize neighborhoods in terms of census tracts—an official designation of the U.S. Census Bureau. Jointly defined by the Census Bureau and local groups, census tracts are small, permanent subdivisions of a county with homogeneous population characteristics, status, and living conditions. Most census tracts in the United States have between 2,500 and 8,000 residents. In the majority of disorganization studies, researchers measure neighborhood characteristics using census tracts as a proxy.

But this may be problematic. Census tract boundaries are invisible to residents, so they represent, in many cases, meaningless, unidentifiable units. It is unlikely that residents, even those who have lived in an area for a long period of time, can identify the particular census tract in which they reside. The point here is that the extent to which researchers believe they are capturing *neighborhood* measures of social disorganization and crime remains unclear. Of course, this problem is minimized with the use of other forms of data. In the rare case when researchers collect their own data through surveys, they are able to more accurately specify the concept of "neighborhood." In survey questions, researchers often define what constitutes a neighborhood using common, unofficial designations that are more consistent with residents' perceptions. One example comes from a large-scale survey of Seattle neighborhoods where participants were told the following at the start of the survey: "We would like to start off by asking you some questions about your home and your neighborhood. While people might define their neighborhood in different ways, we would like you to think about it roughly in terms of the area within 3 blocks on any side of your current home. Your block will refer to the area between the cross-streets on either side of your home." Although this may not constitute the ideal definition of neighborhood for all residents, it is clear this designation is preferred to the the census tract. As fewer and fewer studies rely on official data to test the basic

assumptions of social disorganization theory, more refined definitions and accurate measurements of the central concept of "neighborhood" will result. No doubt this will increase our understanding of why crime rates are higher in some communities than others.

A second on-going challenge involves testing the true nature of the social disorganization model. As you may recall from the earlier discussion on the work of Shaw and McKay and other Chicago School scholars, social disorganization theory, at its heart, is a dynamic theory. It is dynamic because it is primarily interested in processes of change within communities and their effect on crime rates over time. Chicago School researchers were keenly interested in the adaptation of social groups to processes of urbanization and changing forms of social organization, which is why they collected data that spanned several decades.

Even today, a key assumption is that neighborhood levels of informal social control and collective efficacy are influenced by changes in neighborhood ecological structures, such as change in the racial composition of the population. Despite this assumption, nearly all studies testing social disorganization do not directly examine processes of change. According to Charis Kubrin and Ronald Weitzer, "The full set of dynamics that may lead to disorganization can only be discerned when long-term processes of urban development are considered, yet the majority of studies that test social disorganization theory are cross-sectional" (p. 387). In other words, most empirical tests of the theory do not use longitudinal data that allow one to directly examine dynamic processes at work. Instead, researchers use cross-sectional data, which provide a snapshot at one point in time, to assess relationships among neighborhood characteristics, social disorganization, and crime. Although informative, these studies are unable to examine the effects of processes such as gentrification and segregation on the distribution of crime and delinquency, issues that go to the heart of the theory. Apart from recognizing the need to collect data that span several years or even decades, Kubrin and Weitzer suggest that researchers develop more sophisticated models for assessing change. They provide one example, the growth-curve model, and illustrate how its use in neighborhood crime studies could benefit social disorganization theory.

A final ongoing challenge relates to what many consider to be social disorganization's narrow focus on intra-neighborhood influences on crime, or those influences that occur exclusively *within* communities. But communities are not islands unto themselves; they are shaped and influenced by the larger urban political and economic context within which they are embedded. According to critics, then, social disorganization theory as traditionally conceptualized is hampered by a restricted view of community that fails to account for the larger political and structural forces that shape communities, including governmental policies at local, state, and federal levels as well as private investment practices within communities. As Kubrin and Weitzer note, political and economic decisions may have direct effects on community crime rates (e.g., when a halfway house is introduced into a neighborhood and its members commit crime) as well as indirect criminological effects such as by increasing the level of joblessness (through deindustrialization or disinvestment), residential instability (through housing, construction, or demolition policies), and population density (through public housing or zoning policies).

One particularly relevant example of extra-community influences is related to a community's access to capital, particularly home mortgage lending. Redlining and disinvestment by banks, fueled by regulatory initiatives (or lack thereof) may contribute to crime within a community through neighborhood deterioration, forced migration via gentrification, and instability. Alternatively, access to mortgage loan dollars and effective regulation of bank practices (e.g., enforcement of fair lending and community reinvestment requirements) may reduce crime within a neighborhood directly by introducing capital into the community or indirectly by promoting homeownership and reducing residential instability in the long run.

Whatever the precise mechanism at work, at issue for the theory is a general disregard for extra-community forces that shape neighborhood dynamics, with implications for social disorganization and crime. As Sampson asserts, "neglecting the vertical connections (or lack thereof) that residents have to extra-communal resources and sources of power obscures the structural backdrop to community social organization" (p. 102). A more complete social disorganization framework would thus

incorporate the role of extra-community institutions and the wider political environment in which local communities are embedded.

Several additional on-going challenges facing the theory, both substantive and methodological, are discussed by Kubrin and Weitzer. No doubt as the theory continues to evolve and transform in the 21st century, new challenges will emerge, even as old ones become resolved. Regardless of old and new challenges, social disorganization theory holds an important place in criminological history and will continue to do so as long as researchers remain interested in understanding why crime rates are higher in some communities than others.

Charis E. Kubrin

See also Bursik, Robert J., Jr., and Harold C. Grasmick: Levels of Control; Crime Hot Spots; Kobrin, Solomon: Neighborhoods and Crime; Krivo, Lauren J., and Ruth D. Peterson: Extreme Disadvantage and Crime; Sampson, Robert J.: Collective Efficacy Theory; Shaw, Clifford R.: The Jack-Roller; Spergel, Irving A.: Neighborhoods and Delinquent Subcultures; Stark, Rodney: Deviant Places; Systemic Model of Social Disorganization

References and Further Readings

Bursik, R. J. (1988). Social disorganization: Problems and prospects. *Criminology, 26,* 519–551.

Elliott, D. S., Wilson, W. J., Huizinga, D., Sampson, R. J., Elliott, A., & Rankin, B. (1996). The effects of neighborhood disadvantage on adolescent development. *Journal of Research in Crime and Delinquency, 33,* 389–426.

Kornhauser, R. R. (1978). *Social sources of delinquency.* Chicago: University of Chicago Press.

Kubrin, C. E., Stucky, T. D., & Krohn, M. D. (2008). *Researching theories of crime and deviance.* New York: Oxford University Press.

Kubrin, C. E., & Weitzer, R. (2003). New directions in social disorganization theory. *Journal of Research in Crime and Delinquency, 40,* 374–402.

Sampson, R. J. (2001). Crime and public safety: Insights from community-level perspectives on social capital. In S. Saegert, P. J. Thompson, & M. R. Warren (Eds.), *Social capital and poor communities* (pp. 89–114). New York: Russell Sage.

Sampson, R. J., & Groves, W. B. (1989). Community structure and crime: Testing social-disorganization theory. *American Journal of Sociology, 94,* 774–802.

Sampson, R. J., Raudenbush, S. W., & Earls, F. (1997). Neighborhoods and violent crime: A multilevel study of collective efficacy. *Science, 277,* 918–924.

Schmid, C. (1928). *Suicides in Seattle, 1914 to 1928.* Seattle: University of Washington Press.

Shaw, C. R., & McKay, H. D. (1942). *Juvenile delinquency and urban areas.* Chicago: University of Chicago Press.

Stark, R. (1987). Deviant places: A theory of the ecology of crime. *Criminology, 25,* 893–909.

Sutherland, E. H. (1973). Development of the theory. In K. Schuessler (Ed.), *Edwin H. Sutherland on Analyzing Crime* (pp. 13–29). Chicago: University of Chicago Press. (Original work published 1942)

Warner, B. D., & Wilcox Rountree, P. (1997). Local social ties in a community and crime model: Questioning the systemic nature of informal social control. *Social Problems, 44,* 520–536.

SHELDON, WILLIAM H.: SOMATOTYPES AND DELINQUENCY

Some of the earliest criminological theories equated crime to the biological makeup of humans. Because some of the earlier biological studies either overstated the causal nature of biological variables or were completely disproved due to methodological shortcomings or antiquated statistical techniques, a majority of criminologists today dismiss the biological research on criminality without a second thought. James Q. Wilson and Richard J. Herrnstein suggest that many criminologists are not attuned to biological and psychological concepts involved with the causes of criminality due to their sociological training; "physical correlates of crime are often dismissed by most criminologists, for whom these are at best historical stages in the development of their subject" (p. 72). Because of this lack of understanding of the biological approach or the inherent bias of most sociological theories of criminality, the debate of whether or not criminals are characterized by a certain type of body-build has long been debated in the field of criminology. Hans Eysenck and Gisli Gudjonsson argued that the study of physique is a complex subject, due primarily to many different typologies and methods of measurement.

In the 1940s, William H. Sheldon attempted to study the relationship between human physique and criminality. Sheldon graduated from the University of Chicago with a Ph.D. in psychology in 1926 and with an M.D. in 1933. He held positions as a professor at the University of Oregon Medical School, where he was also the director of the constitution clinic, and the director of the Biological Humanics Foundation in Cambridge, Massachusetts. His work led him to the belief that the psychological foundation of humans was predominantly supported by biological underpinnings.

In this search to link physique and behavior, Sheldon developed the idea of the somatotype; this is a personal score that is determined by different measurements taken from a human body. Sheldon posited three types of extreme somatotype: mesomorphs who are athletically built, endomorphs who are overweight, and ectomorphs who are underweight. Sheldon suggested that these somatotypes corresponded directly to psychological states. That is, mesomorphs are active, dynamic, assertive, and aggressive; endomorphs are relaxed, comfortable, and extroverted; and ectomorphs are introverted, thoughtful, inhibited, and sensitive.

Here, Sheldon's body of work and the research linking somatotypes to criminality is examined. First, Sheldon's classification system and the research that resulted from initial studies on somatotypes are explored. Second, somatotypic classification methods produced to advance the work of Sheldon are discussed. Finally, the decline of somatotyping as both a function of measurement constraints and theoretical shortcomings is reviewed.

William Sheldon and Somatotypes

Dating back to the times of Cesare Lombroso, there have been numerous attempts to study the links between physique and criminality that have yielded different methods of measuring physique. Some of these measurements have been simplistic while others have been complex. For instance, Earnest Hooton separated height and weight into a 3×3 matrix, or nine subgroups, to see if there was a relationship between physique and crime; height was identified as short, medium, and tall, and weight was identified as slender, medium, and heavy. This example outlines a simple method of determining physique.

A more complex method of determining physique can be found in the work of Ernst Kretschmer.

While a host of physique studies were completed in Europe in the 1800s, one of the preeminent studies of physique was completed by Kretschmer. Originally published in 1931, Kretschmer's study, *Physique and Character,* comprised 400 patients of every age and occupation in a hospital in an effort to link physique and character. Kretschmer's key contribution to physical determination was the three types of physique he established: the asthenic, athletic, and pyknic forms. A person could contain characteristics from each of Kretschmer's types, making for a blended physical type. According to Kretschmer, the extreme asthenic type of physique has a "deficiency in thickness combined with an average unlessened length" (p. 22); this type is characterized as weak and frail. The extreme athletic type of physique is "recognized by the strong development of the skeleton, the musculature and also the skin" (p. 25). The extreme pyknic type of physique "is characterized by the pronounced peripheral development of the body cavities, and a tendency to a distribution of fat about the trunk, with a more graceful construction of the motor apparatus" (p. 30).

Drawing directly from the work of Kretschmer, Sheldon outlined the study of physique and the measurement of somatotypes in *The Varieties of Human Physique.* His theory was founded on the assumption that it is possible to determine physical differences among human beings. Sheldon focused on three extreme physical types, adapted from embryology, which correspond approximately to Kretschmer's physical typology: endomorphs (pycknic), mesomorphs (athletic), and ectomorphs (asthenic). These three types were selected because they illustrated the most extreme cases of physique. Sheldon and colleagues defined endomorphy as the "relative predominance of soft roundness throughout the various regions of the body" (1940, p. 5). Mesomorphy means the "relative predominance of muscle, bone, and connective tissue" (p. 5). Ectomorphy means the "relative predominance of linearity and fragility" (p. 5); Sheldon noted that this form had the largest brain and central nervous system.

To refine his measurement, Sheldon examined 400 male undergraduate students at the University of Chicago. In an effort of standardization, subjects were photographed naked from three angles: a front view, a side view, and a back view. The subject stood on a pedestal a certain distance away from the camera. From the 400 subjects, 4,000 photographs were amassed and examined. From these photographs, 17 measurements (dependent on the height to convert into ratio form) were taken from a body. From this, a three-number scale was derived to conclude a person's somatotype. The first number in the score reflects the amount of endomorphy in an individual, the second number represents the amount of mesomorphy in an individual, and the third number represents the amount of ectomorphy present in an individual. Thus, an extreme endomorph would receive a score of 7-1-1, an extreme mesomorph would receive a score of 1-7-1, and an extreme ectomorph would receive a score of 1-1-7. There are potentially 343 different identifiable somatotypes when using Sheldon's classification procedure.

In 1949, Sheldon put his method of somatotyping to the test in studying crime for the first time. Sheldon followed the lives of a sample of 200 young men from the Hayden Goodwill Inn. Because it was a social service agency, the sample consisted of youth with antisocial personalities as well as delinquent histories. This gave Sheldon's study a comparison group of non-criminals on which to base his results. Although Sheldon examined many different sociological variables as well as biological variables, Sheldon's chief finding among the criminal sample, in terms of somatotypes, was that mesomorphy was the most common somatotype. In essence, Sheldon concluded that delinquents were more inclined to being mesomorphically built. With the exception of a 30-year follow-up study, this would also mark the last time that Sheldon's method of somatotyping would be used in the study of the link between physique and crime.

In the 30-year follow up of Sheldon's research, Emil Hartl et al. reexamined the 200 men whose biographies were presented by Sheldon in 1949. Hartl et al.'s major finding was that future adult criminals differed from non-criminal subjects in the sample in terms of mesomorphy. As in Sheldon's original study, criminals were more likely to have a mesomorphic build. In their discriminant function analysis on all of the data, Hartl et al. found mesomorphy to be the strongest discriminating variable. When conducting a multiple regression on criminal behavior, however, Hartl et al. indicated that none of the variables relating to morphology, mesomorphy, endomorphy, or ectomorphy were statistically significant. In other words, the somatotype did a poor job in predicting future criminality.

Extended Somatotype Classifications

Sheldon's somatotyping approach was inevitably eclipsed by the work of Richard Parnell in 1958. Parnell's method of somatotyping was considered to be more objective than Sheldon's. This method of somatotyping emphasized the phenotype, not the somatotype. The phenotype is the body as it appears at a particular point in time (Parnell, 1958, p. 4). Because of this, Parnell indicated that his method for somatotyping was not a good variable for prediction purposes. Unlike Sheldon, Parnell labeled his physical types on the chart as Fat, Muscularity, and Linearity, which correspond to the endomorph, mesomorph, and ectomorph, respectively.

Inspired by the somatotyping work of Sheldon and Parnell, Sheldon and Eleanor Glueck conducted an analysis on the relationship between physique and crime. The Gluecks (1951) compared the physiques between a sample of delinquents and a sample of non-delinquents. The Gluecks relied on a physical anthropologist to measure the somatotypes of their subjects. It was Parnell's method of somatotyping that was used to study the physique of individuals in the Gluecks' sample; the Gluecks merely interpreted the results. The Gluecks concluded that mesomorphy was more predominant among the delinquents, while the control group of non-delinquents contained no predominance of any single somatotype.

The Gluecks (1956) examined this data source further by examining the physique of criminals in relation to other sociological variables and traits they had found. The Gluecks looked at the relationship between physique and several categories of variables that included neurological traits, intelligence, character, family, environment, and personality. While some of the variables in each category were found to be correlated with the different body types, the Gluecks concluded that there is no combination of physical traits and sociological traits that could predict delinquency in an individual. This is true even for the mesomorphs, who comprised the majority of the criminal sample.

Besides the Gluecks' study, two other studies utilized Parnell's somatotyping procedure. Juan

Cortes and Florence Gatti examined the relationship between a person's physique and the need for achievement, or motivation. They examined 100 delinquent youths and a comparison group of 100 non-delinquents in a high school. In both groups, a significant and positive relationship was found between mesomorphy and motivation; they also found that a significant, but negative, relationship existed between ectomorphy and motivation. Cortes and Gatti concluded that a relationship existed between mesomorphs and the desire to achieve (p. 412).

Boyd McCandless, W. Scott Persons, and Albert Roberts examined perceived criminal opportunity and body build among delinquent youth. McCandless et al. examined 500 adjudicated delinquent youth by both somatotyping the youth and administering a questionnaire to measure opportunity. McCandless et al. hypothesized that mesomorphs would be more likely to have committed more delinquent acts than either ectomorphs or endomorphs. However, their regression analysis lent no credence to this. Race was the only variable to have a significant relationship with perceived criminal opportunity.

After the McCandless et al. study in 1972, research utilizing somatotypes was discontinued predicated on many of the issues discussed in the next section. It was not until 2008 that a new method of somatotyping emerged. In an effort to utilize a newer, more refined method of somatotyping, Sean Maddan, Jeffery Walker, and J. Mitchell Miller utilized the body mass index (BMI) as a measure of an individual's somatotype.

The body mass index, often referred to as the Quetelet Index, utilizes a person's height and weight to gauge the total body fat in adults. It is an indicator of optimal weight for health and different from lean mass or percent body fat calculations because it only considers height and weight (National Heart, Lung, and Blood Institute, 1998). This measure correlates primarily to body fat and can be used on either males or females. The BMI is a "heterogeneous phenotype" (Feitosa et al., 2002, p. 72) or how the person's physique is at a given point in time. In this sense it is a measure of somatotyping more similar to Parsons's method, which was based on physical phenotype as well.

A person's BMI is calculated by dividing weight (in kilograms) by height (in meters) squared. The

BMI equation relies heavily on the subject's height. The relationship between the physique and height of an individual was mentioned frequently in the literature. Even Sheldon foreshadowed the importance of height and weight in measuring somatotypes noting that with height-weight norms, it will be possible to create a scale of height-weight measures for each different somatotype. BMI values can range from one and up, making it a continuous, interval level variable. According to the BMI, a person who is an endomorph receives a BMI score of 26 and above, a person who is a mesomorph will receive a BMI score of between 19 and 25, and a person who is an ectomorph will receive a score of less than 19.

To test the reliability of the BMI measure, Maddan and colleagues took Sheldon's original sample data from *Varieties of Delinquent Youth* and compared the results of his somatotyping technique with the same sample using the BMI scale to determine the individual's somatotype. The bivariate correlation analyses that were completed to measure the relationship between the two types of somatotype measures showed a strong relationship between Sheldon's method of somatotyping and the BMI measure. These analyses indicate that the BMI is a reliable measure of somatotyping.

The most important finding of the Maddan et al. research was that somatotypes still accounted for some of the variation in violent and non-violent prison sentences in a sample of male prisoners (N = 5,000) taken in Arkansas from 1975 to 2000. While the somatotype showed effects, the impact was minor across the somatotype measures. The logistic regression analysis illustrated that the somatotypes had a statistically significant effect, albeit weak, and added to the overall model. More importantly, the direction of the effects was in line with previous research on physique and criminality. Mesomorphic offenders were more likely to be in prison for a violent offense than their endomorphic counterparts. The direction was the same for ectomorphs, but this variable failed to gain statistical significance.

Issues With Somatotype Studies

The biological approach to studying criminality has been much maligned. These studies have suffered from methodological issues, ranging from measurement to sampling, and conceptual issues, ranging from untestability to logic. One of the key problems with biological studies has been with regards to the types of variables included in analyses. Most of the biological research, not including the work in this area today, has focused primarily on strictly biological variables. The other major problem for biological studies has been with regards to control groups. Most of the biological research has focused only on a single group, which has greatly decreased the worth of much of the biological research. Somatotyping has its own set of problems and shortcomings.

There are several limitations to the research on delinquency and somatotypes. First, Sheldon's method of somatotyping was very time consuming and expensive. It took 3 to 4 months to compare the data gathered from the three different pictures of each subject. This time did not include the time it would take to analyze the data with other data in the study, in the case of criminology, delinquency, social, and other structural variables. Second, and due to the time period in criminological development, little data were collected on females. Third, the study on the link between crime and biology, in general, and somatotyping, specifically, is that the results are either mixed or weak.

The final, and maybe most important, limitation of the somatotyping research before 2008, was the technique that had to be used to measure somatotypes. Sheldon's procedure (and reformulations of his method) required not only that subjects be naked, but also that several pictures were taken of the naked subjects. Today, a researcher would have difficulty finding subjects and securing approval by an institutional review board to conduct the study.

Conclusion

Adrian Raine asserted that "no factor linked to crime should be viewed in the anachronistic terms of genetics versus environment" (p. 204). To do this is both divisive and overly simplistic. Criminologists should move toward an integration of genetic and social factors for crime in an effort to examine how these two factors relate to one another. This entry has focused on a biological approach that has largely fallen to the wayside of criminological history: somatotypes.

While several studies have been conducted on somatotyping and criminality over the last 50 years, overall interest in the subject has waned. This is due primarily to the stigma that has been associated with conducting research on the link between biological causes of crime in the past, the methodological shortcomings of some of the work in this area, and some of the causation overstatements made in relation to findings. Even though this is the case, it is hard to discard some of the findings from the somatotype literature in spite of some of the methodological shortcomings. Research has consistently shown that mesomorphic physiques are more associated with criminal groups than with non-criminal control groups. This makes it difficult to simply dismiss the relevance of somatotypes as correlates to criminal behavior.

Physique is not the cause of crime. This much is known from all of the studies related to somatotyping. However, the majority of criminal subjects represented in research do have a mesomorphic body type. The remaining challenge for criminologists is to determine what it is about mesomorphy that is related to criminality and why this is so.

Sean Maddan

See also Glueck, Sheldon, and Eleanor Glueck: The Origins of Crime; Hooton, Earnest A.: The American Criminal; Kretschmer, Ernest: Physique and Character; Wilson, James Q., and Richard J. Herrnstein: Crime and Human Nature

References and Further Readings

Cortes, J. B., & Gatti, F. M. (1966). Physique and motivation. *Journal of Consulting Psychology, 30,* 408–414.

Eysenck, H. J., & Gudjonsson, G. H. (1989). *The causes and cures of criminality.* New York: Plenum.

Feitosa, M. F., Borecki, I. B., Rich, S. S., Arnett, D. K., Sholinsky, P., Myers, R. H., et al. (2002). Quantitative-trait loci influencing body-mass index reside on chromosomes 7 and 13: The National Heart, Lung, and Blood Institute family heart study. *American Journal of Human Genetics, 70,* 72–82.

Glueck, S., & Glueck, E. (1951). *Unraveling juvenile delinquency.* Cambridge, MA: Harvard University Press.

Glueck, S., & Glueck, E. (1956). *Physique and delinquency.* New York: Harper & Brothers.

Hartl, E. M., Monnelly, E. P., & Elderkin, R. D. (1982). *Physique and delinquent behavior: A thirty-year follow-up of William H. Sheldon's varieties of delinquent youth.* New York: Academic Press.

Hooton, E. A. (1968). *Crime and the man.* New York: Greenwood.

Kretschmer, E. (1970). *Physique and character: An investigation of the nature of constitution and of the theory of temperament.* New York: Cooper Square.

Maddan, S., Walker, J. T., & Miller, J. M. (2008). Does size really matter? A reexamination of Sheldon's somatotypes and criminal behavior. *Social Science Journal, 45,* 330–344.

McCandless, B. R., Persons, W. S., III, & Roberts, A. (1972). Perceived opportunity, delinquency, race, and body build among delinquent youth. *Journal of Consulting and Clinical Psychology, 38,* 281–287.

National Heart, Lung, and Blood Institute. (1998). *Clinical guidelines on the identification, evaluation, and treatment of overweight, and obesity in adults: The evidence report.* Washington, DC: National Institute of Health.

Parnell, R. W. (1958). *Behavior and physique: An introduction to practical and applied somatometry.* London: Edward Arnold.

Rafter, N. (2007). Somatotyping, antimodernism, and the production of criminological knowledge. *Criminology, 45,* 805–834.

Raine, A. (1993). *The psychopathology of crime: Criminal behavior as a clinical disorder.* New York: Academic Press.

Sheldon, W., Hartl, W. M., & McDermott, E. (1949). *Varieties of delinquent youth: An introduction to constitutional psychiatry.* New York: Harper & Brothers.

Sheldon, W., Stevens, S. S., & Tucker, W. B. (1940). *The varieties of human physique: An introduction to constitutional psychology.* New York: Harper & Brothers.

Wilson, J. Q., & Herrnstein, R. J. (1985). *Crime and human nature.* New York: Simon & Schuster.

SHERMAN, LAWRENCE W.: DEFIANCE THEORY

Criminological theory and criminal justice policy have long focused on the relationship between sanctions and criminal behavior. Deterrence and labeling are two major theoretical traditions that emphasize sanctions as a key explanatory factor, providing contradictory predictions of the impact of those sanctions on behavior. Deterrence theorists predict that sanctions, especially those which are swift, certain, and proportionally severe, will deter or reduce further criminal behavior. Additionally, criminal justice policy is often predicated on the assumption that sanctions deter offenders. Labeling theory, on the other hand, predicts that sanctions will stigmatize the offender, producing increased offending (i.e., secondary deviance) in the future. The empirical evidence supporting either deterrence or labeling has been mixed. Recognizing this diversity in the effects of sanctions, Lawrence W. Sherman has argued that the apparent pattern of sanction effects observed in existing research exhibits two themes. First, the impact of sanctions appears to depend on perceptions of fairness, in that sanctions viewed as unfair are more likely to increase offending. Second, sanctions appear to increase crime among out-groups while deterring crime among in-groups. Suggesting that existing theory is incapable of accounting for these patterns, Sherman proposed *defiance theory* to explain the conditions under which sanctions will increase criminal activity versus deterring offending.

Defiance Theory

The starting point in Sherman's defiance theory is the differential effects of sanctions. Research suggests that, in varying instances, sanctions may either deter or increase future offending. In an effort to explain the conditions under which sanctions increase criminal behavior, Sherman developed the concept of defiance, which is defined as "the net increase in the prevalence, incidence, or seriousness of future offending against a sanctioning community caused by a proud, shameless reaction to the administration of a criminal sanction" (p. 459).

Defiance may take several forms. Similar to deterrence, defiance may be either specific (i.e., the reaction of an individual to his or her own punishment) or general (i.e., the reaction of a group to the punishment of a group member). Additionally, individuals may exhibit either direct defiance, reacting against the sanctioning agent, or indirect defiance, reacting against another individual who vicariously represents the sanctioning agent. Sherman provides examples of the different types of defiance. For example, an individual who assaults a police officer during an arrest is exhibiting specific, direct defiance. An individual who assaults his or her spouse following a domestic violence arrest is exhibiting specific, indirect defiance. General, direct defiance is illustrated by the South African ambush killings of police officers, who were viewed as the tools of oppression during the apartheid era, a perception that has lingered. The 1992 Los Angeles riots following the acquittal of the four police officers who beat Rodney King during a traffic stop provide an example of general, indirect defiance.

Conditions for Defiance

Sherman argues that defiance is likely to occur when the sanctioned individual views his or her punishment as unfair or illegitimate, is poorly bonded, and denies the shame of the punishment. In contrast, sanctions are expected to produce deterrence when the sanctioned individual is well bonded, views the sanction as legitimate, and accepts the shame he or she feels, remaining proud of his or her connection to the community, recognizing the harm that his or her actions have caused, and attempting to repair that bond. Sanctions are irrelevant to future offending when these factors are evenly balanced. For example, when a well-bonded offender denies the shame associated with the unfair sanction, the expected outcome will likely be irrelevance, not deterrence. In this instance, the perceived unfairness of the sanction and the failure to accept the shame that accompanies the sanction will nullify any deterrent effect produced by the strong social bond. With this discussion, Sherman is able to theoretically account for the mixed effects of sanctions.

Defiance theory focuses on explaining the defiant reaction to a sanction. Specifically, there are four necessary conditions for defiance to occur: (1) the sanction must be defined by the offender as unfair, (2) the offender must be poorly bonded to society, (3) the sanction must be viewed by the offender as stigmatizing, and (4) the offender must refuse to acknowledge the shame produced by the sanction. In proposing his theory and identifying these four conditions, Sherman has borrowed from John Braithwaite's theory of reintegrative shaming, Tom Tyler's concept of procedural justice, and Thomas Scheff and Suzanne Retzinger's discussion of the role of shame and rage in destructive conflicts.

Perceptions of Fairness

According to Sherman, one key theme in understanding whether a sanction produces defiance or deterrence is the perceived fairness or legitimacy of the sanction or sanctioning agent. Unfairness may be related to disrespect by the sanctioning agent or a perception that the punishment is arbitrary or discriminatory. Whether the unfairness of a punishment is substantive or perceptual, unfair or unjust sanctions may not have their intended deterrent effect. According to Tyler's procedural justice perspective, sanctions that are perceived as unfair reduce the legitimacy of law enforcement or the criminal justice system, which reduces the likelihood of compliance. If an individual perceives a punishment as unjust, he or she may begin to question the law itself and feel justified in disregarding it. Scheff and Retzinger contend that societal disapproval, when expressed disrespectfully or to a person with weak social bonds, may evoke anger. Reintegrative shaming theory likewise argues that sanctions that stigmatize and label the offender may weaken existing social bonds and produce increased offending. Thus, perceptions of the fairness of a sanction and the experience of being stigmatized by a sanction may interact with an individual's social bonds to produce defiance.

Social Bonding

Procedural justice argues that when the legitimacy of formal sanctions breaks down, social sanctions are expected to take their place. Thus, social bonding also plays a large role in defiance theory. In particular, Sherman relies on some elements of reintegrative shaming theory to explain the connection between unfair or stigmatizing sanctions and social bonds. For Braithwaite, individuals who have strong social bonds (i.e., interdependency) may be more likely to experience reintegrative sanctions, which are rejecting of the act but avoid applying a label to the individual. Thus, reintegrative sanctions are likely to be viewed as fair and to produce deterrence. Disintegrative sanctions, however, are rejecting of both the act and actor, stigmatizing the sanctioned individual. These sanctions are more likely to be viewed as unfair and disrespectful. Sherman likewise recognizes the potential criminogenic effect of stigmatizing sanctions, especially among individuals with weak social bonds. He argues that individuals with strong social bonds will not react defiantly to a punishment perceived as unfair so as not to jeopardize those bonds. On the other hand, individuals with weak social bonds are more likely to deny the shame of being sanctioned and respond with indignation and anger. This angry, prideful reaction sets the stage for defiance and increased offending.

Experiencing Shame

An individual's reaction to the shame of a sanction is the final link in the explanation of defiance. Sherman highlights the role of shame, pointing both to reintegrative shaming theory and to Scheff and Retzinger's work on the master emotions of shame and pride. Both Braithwaite and Scheff and Retzinger argue that individual reactions to the shame of a sanction will vary depending on an individual's level of social bonding. Similarly, labeling theory suggests that secondary deviance (i.e., defiance for Sherman) occurs as a reaction to the experience of being sanctioned, in that individuals may perceive their punishment as an attack and may act defiantly as a defense to society's disapproval.

Scheff and Retzinger criticize early versions of labeling theory for failing to take emotions, especially shame, into account. For these authors, societal disapproval is described as a threat to the sanctioned individual's social bonds. If the individual accepts the shame that he or she feels and recognizes the harm he or she has caused, the individual may seek to avoid that behavior in the future (i.e., deterrence). Braithwaite's theory of reintegrative shaming presents a similar argument. On the other hand, if the person refuses to acknowledge or rejects that shame, he or she may respond with self-righteous anger. Scheff and Retzinger describe a shame/rage spiral, in which rage is a protective measure against shame, a way of rejecting the shame, and a defense against a perceived attack. Thus, this shame/rage spiral occurs when a person's bond is threatened, the shame is not acknowledged, and behavior is interpreted as an attack. This produces violence, hatred, and resentment which may lead to defiance. For Sherman, shame, or the refusal to acknowledge shame, is the primary causal mechanism in explaining defiance.

Empirical Evidence for Defiance Theory

Sherman concludes his theoretical formulation by noting that "until recently, the science of sanction effects has been short on facts and even shorter on theory. Now, it seems, the available theory has gotten ahead of the facts" (p. 468). Despite the promise of defiance in explaining variation in sanction effects, there have been no complete tests of the theory since its development. Most of the evidence that can be marshaled in support of the theory is derived from studies not originally designed to examine its propositions.

Some research supports the notion that perceptions of unfairness, either to the law being imposed or to the sanction itself, are likely to lead to more criminal offending (i.e., defiance). Sherman highlights research suggesting that previously sanctioned individuals are less likely to be deterred. It may be that, because few people are formally sanctioned for offending, those who do receive a punishment perceive their treatment as comparatively unfair and respond defiantly by engaging in further delinquency. Additional research examining police-citizen encounters indirectly tests some of the propositions articulated by defiance theory. These studies primarily focus on the offender's (or citizen's) perceptions of fair treatment by police officers in their encounters. Raymond Paternoster, Robert Brame, Ronet Bachman, and Sherman examined the effect of arrest on the likelihood of engaging in subsequent domestic assaults and found that the offender's perceptions of fair treatment by police were important determinants of future offending. Other studies of police-citizen interactions support the premise that individuals who feel that they are unfairly treated by police are more likely to be resistant. In other words, the perceived legitimacy of a police officer's action is an important predictor of citizen compliance or resistance. When the police are perceived to be respectful to citizens, compliance is more likely. Confrontational and physical actions on the part of police, on the other hand, are more likely to produce resistance, possibly because the actions are interpreted as unfair and stigmatizing. This body of research supports Sherman's argument that defiance is more likely to occur when sanctions are perceived as unfair. While these results are suggestive, they do not address the key to defiance theory, which is an individual's perception of the sanction.

A more recent study examined the perceptual nature of defiance theory and the impact of those perceptions on future offending more closely and has provided the most complete test of the theory to date. Leana Bouffard and Nicole Leeper Piquero found that individuals who perceived a sanction as unfair and were poorly bonded had higher rates of offending in the future. While much existing research demonstrates that perceptions of unfairness and social bonding have a strong connection to offending, the role of shame in producing defiance remained unclear in this study. Other research, however, has supported the role of shame in offending. Unfortunately, the existing research generally provides only piecemeal support for defiance theory. Studies specifically designed to link the theory's propositions together are necessary.

Future Directions for Defiance Theory

Other researchers have highlighted the links between Sherman's defiance theory and other explanatory mechanisms. For example, within psychology, the personality construct of grandiosity (i.e., exaggerated perceptions of self-worth) may inform the path to defiance, in that grandiose or self-centered individuals may be more likely to reject the sanctioning agent and the shame associated with being sanctioned, resulting in a defiant response. In criminology, research also suggests that individuals with low levels of self-control are more likely to perceive sanctions as unfair and to respond with anger. Though not specifically addressed by Sherman or necessarily intended, one advantage of defiance theory is that in linking concepts, like emotion and social bonding, it offers an integrative perspective that accounts for either defiance or deterrence.

From the life-course and criminal career perspective, defiance may also be seen as an explanation of continuity in and desistance from offending. The theory can explain desistance by arguing that if an individual defines a sanction as unfair and stigmatizing but has strong social bonds, that person may accept the shame that he or she feels or be unwilling to jeopardize his or her bonds through a defiant reaction. According to Sherman, these individuals will be deterred from future offending (i.e., they will desist). This theory also provides an explanation for continuity, which is the defiant response of a poorly bonded offender who defines his or her sanction as unfair and stigmatizing and refuses to acknowledge the shame he or she feels. These individuals may continue or escalate their offending, becoming involved in secondary deviance. Thus, exploring defiance theory from a longitudinal, life-course perspective is another promising avenue for research.

Conclusion

It is difficult to truly assess the value of Sherman's defiance theory with the paucity of studies that directly test its propositions. Rather, the existing research provides suggestive evidence supporting some elements of the theory, particularly perceptions of fairness and social bonding. What remains is to explicitly design studies that link these elements together as proposed by the theory and to explore the connections between this and other theories. At this point, the theory is relevant to understanding the importance of the interplay between perceptions of fairness, social bonding, and the experience of shame, but future research is necessary to fully explore these relationships.

Leana Bouffard

See also Becker, Howard S.: Labeling and Deviant Careers; Braithwaite, John: Reintegrative Shaming Theory; Gibbs, Jack P.: Deterrence Theory; Hirschi, Travis: Social Control Theory; Lemert, Edwin M.: Primary and Secondary Deviance; Perceptual Deterrence; Tyler, Tom R.: Sanctions and Procedural Justice Theory

References and Further Readings

Bouffard, L. A., & Piquero, N. L. (2010). Defiance theory and life course explanations of persistent offending. *Crime and Delinquency, 56,* 227–252.
Braithwaite, J. (1989). *Crime, shame, and reintegration.* Cambridge, UK: Cambridge University Press.
Paternoster, R., Brame, R., Bachman, R., & Sherman, L. W. (1997). Do fair procedures matter? The effects of procedural justice on spouse assault. *Law and Society Review, 31,* 163–204.
Scheff, T. J., & Retzinger, S. M. (1991). *Emotions and violence: Shame and rage in destructive conflicts.* Lexington, MA: Lexington Books.
Sherman, L. W. (1993). Defiance, deterrence, and irrelevance: A theory of the criminal sanction. *Journal of Research in Crime and Delinquency, 30,* 445–473.
Tyler, T. R. (1990). *Why people obey the law.* New Haven, CT: Yale University Press.

SHORT, JAMES F., JR.: GANGS AND GROUP PROCESSES

The city of Chicago remains a bastion for sociological research. Known as the Chicago School, observation and ethnographic research stemming from the University of Chicago essentially birthed the ecological study of crime and criminals. An integral part of Chicago School research was the identification of delinquent and criminal groups operating in neighborhoods, especially gangs. Frederick Thrasher's 1927 study of 1,313 gangs commenced this line of gang research and his work is still influential to this day. Roughly four generations of scholars produced extensive gang-relevant research at the individual and neighborhood level that shaped how law enforcement, policymakers, and the public came to view gangs.

The Chicago way of analyzing ecological problems paved the way for more elaborate techniques of research methods. James F. Short, Jr., a University of Chicago graduate and student of Clifford Shaw, and a working group of colleagues (Desmond Cartwright, Robert Gordon, Kenneth Howard, and Fred Strodtbeck) came together to conduct a major study of gang activity in Chicago. They sought to examine the breadth of existing gang and lower class-specific macro-level theories of delinquency. Although data were collected across a variety of fronts, the working group relied heavily on the field work conducted by the detached workers assigned to the 16 gangs included in the study. The research culminated in Short and Strodtbeck's seminal work *Group Process and Gang Delinquency.* The authors recognized that the phenomena of gangs and the delinquency tied to these groups could not be studied solely at a structural level, nor could they be analyzed merely at an individual level.

Emerging from Short and Strodtbeck's research was the finding that the group itself was decidedly responsible for a considerable amount of the behavior perpetrated by its members. This led Short to critique an especially important problem not only for the study of gangs but also for criminology in general—the level of explanation problem. Individual-level, micro-level or meso-level, and macro-level research explain different problems. This was the central thesis to Short and Strodtbeck's book, and something that Short has continued to emphasize over the last four decades. Short and Strodtbeck concluded that their results indicated that for theoretical explanations of delinquency, the group processes within the gang were crucial in facilitating delinquency.

Group Processes Within the Context of the Level of Explanation Problem

As mentioned above, over the course of Short's career, he has insisted that criminology suffered from a level of explanation problem. In his 1997 presidential address to the American Society of Criminology, Short commented that research examining differing units of analysis often lay victim to "talk[ing] past each other" (1998, p. 3). Short's Chicago research demonstrated this point; macro-level and individual-level undertakings could not fully explain the social challenges that delinquent gangs posed. In other words, the core levels of explanation (individual and macro) were missing a nucleus—a microsocial unit of explanation. Short highlighted this in his presidential address and argued that an emphasis on microsocial contexts can bridge the gap between individual and macro approaches to explain crime.

Traditionally, especially during the time of Short's research, the field of sociology focused on structural or macro-level theories of delinquency and crime. Macro-level approaches focus on larger environmental and social forces beyond the immediate control of the individual that interact to produce crime. Key concepts include the community, societal goals, opportunities for success, social support, race, and economic deprivation. Influential macro-level theories include Clifford Shaw and Henry McKay's social disorganization theory; Albert Cohen's subcultural theory; Francis Cullen's social support, Robert Sampson, Stephen Raudenbush, and Felton Earls's collective efficacy, and Richard Cloward and Lloyd Ohlin's and Robert Merton's strain/anomie. Short and Strodtbeck recognized the importance of these factors but were critical of the lack of individual-level variables. "Personality variables, for example, for all practical purposes are ignored" (p. 18). Partly in response to the rejection of individualism, individual-level approaches (e.g., the Gluecks' research) to crime explanation were not acknowledged until the advent of survey research (Lilly et al., 2007). These types of approaches focus on individual deficits and control-based concepts—of which Short recognized the limitation in research at the time—and are now far more prevalent in the literature.

Short ultimately found that the micro-level of explanation, or a group process perspective, best characterized the delinquency patterns of youth gang members. In Short's words, "much of the behavior we were observing was influenced by the immediate situations of actions on the street, especially the interaction of gang members with one another" (1997, p. 46). Short explained that this was at odds with existing explanations of gang delinquency but imposed on the working group that context and group processes were central to explaining this behavior. What research failed to produce prior to Short and colleagues' investigation was conceptualizing the importance of living *group lives*. People did not function only among themselves or as just another individual in the city. People functioned within a network of family, coworkers, and peers with whom they lived, worked, and played (Short, 1998). Within these networks operated particular and intimate norms in which informal social controls essentially created specific types of order.

The question that Short addressed was, What is it about the gang that facilitates this behavior? The answer to this question lies in the heart of Short's research. "Group norms create risks for group members which would not exist for non-members" (Short & Strodtbeck, 1965, p. 45). In other words, participation in this group may spark money-making opportunities and companionship, but the very existence of the group sparks conflict both within the group and with other groups enclosed in the confines of urban America. Short and Strodtbeck described some of this delinquency as a response to status threats that are situationally determined. These threats—especially within the company of gang peers—to status, leadership, territory, and ego must result in a response. Short and Strodtbeck remarked that "[t]o the extent that a child acquires the lower class, culturally patterned bias against planful behavior, he will be drawn to situations where the 'action' is likely to involve choices which crucially affect his ability to stay out of trouble" (pp. 282–283). These behaviors and responses manifest in the presence of the gang. For the purposes of understanding gang behavior, Short uncovered what has been a topic of interest for a host of researchers over the last four decades.

The microsocial processes operating within the group are compatible with existing theories (e.g., social learning/process-based theory: differential association, differential reinforcement, modeling) that contend that individual/personality traits and environmental settings are either too imprecise or too impersonal to explain group behavior. This is why learning or process theory is so applicable to Short's contentions. In addition, this is also why existing learning or process theories hold up so well empirically in explaining deviant peer group and gang involvement.

Why Group Processes Trump the Individual-Level and Macro-Level

Explanations of Delinquent Behavior

While observation and ethnography may have dominated the early days of criminological research, the survey design restructured the way criminologists conducted research and devised theory thereafter. As J. Robert Lilly, Francis Cullen, and Richard Ball pointed out, Travis Hirschi's 1969 study "was perhaps most instrumental in demonstrating the power of the self-report study to assess competing delinquency theories" (p. 308). This line of methodology then translated into the longitudinal design, where subjects were followed over a period of time and systematically surveyed. While the Gluecks and Marvin Wolfgang, Robert Figlio, and Thorsten Sellin had been conducting this research for some time, the longitudinal design really accelerated in the 1980s. These research ventures provided a unique opportunity to test many of the influential theories and concepts relevant to gang delinquency research. For example, longitudinal studies coordinated by the Office of Juvenile Justice and Delinquency Prevention in Denver, Pittsburgh, and Rochester (New York), were able to measure delinquent involvement before, during, and after gang involvement, especially pertinent to understanding Short's key conceptual claims.

According to Short, the group is where individual and macro variables intersect to produce behavior. Gangs typically germinate in economically deprived areas (macro-level), and gang member attributes (individual-level) amenable to the gang are then exploited in group interaction. In other words, these larger perspectives are contingent upon group interaction to produce behavior. Because longitudinal designs have the ability to test delinquent involvement prior to and subsequent to gang involvement, quasi-experimentally, they can test what sort of effect the gang had on an individual's behavior. The longitudinal studies mentioned above have produced a wealth of information for gang researchers. The results from Denver, Pittsburgh, and Rochester found that during periods of gang membership, an individual's involvement in delinquency was elevated. This was consistent across cities in the United States, and evidence has been found abroad suggesting that the gang has an impact on behavior that goes beyond typical individual and environmental processes.

A key theoretical argument guided the above research. In 1993, Terence Thornberry and colleagues first articulated this argument from their findings in Rochester. Three models could be posited to explain gang behavior: (1) a selection or "types of persons" model, (2) a facilitation or "types of groups" model, and finally (3) an enhancement model that is a blend of the two models. It followed that selection models emphasize the criminal characteristics or traits of the individual. Thornberry et al. argued that this model is consistent with propensity, opportunity, and control-type theories. The facilitation models emphasize the group characteristics that facilitate the behavior of the individual, with the authors placing this in line with learning and process-type theories.

These theoretical assumptions stipulated by Thornberry and colleagues provided an appropriate platform for the propensity/process debate while using the gang to test each theory's core assumptions. In summarizing the studies mentioned above that examine these models, Marvin Krohn and Terence Thornberry concluded that "perhaps the safest conclusion to draw is that there is a minor selection effect, [and] a major facilitation effect" (p. 147), thus lending credence to the learning or process-based theory. Gottfredson and

Hirschi may respond to Krohn and Thornberry's conclusion by arguing that the gang provides better "masks" and "shields," thus facilitating opportunities to commit crime (p. 209). No matter whether one subscribes to the opportunity/propensity or learning/process explanations of crime, what should be taken from these empirical examinations is that the group or the gang is responsible for producing delinquent and criminal behavior.

Conclusion

Short's group process perspective has had a large impact on gang delinquency theory over the past four decades. His main piece with Strodtbeck, *Group Process and Gang Delinquency*, has been cited nearly 500 times (Google Scholar) and is a must-read for researchers and practitioners interested in better understanding gang behavior and gang member delinquency.

The problem, however, is that Short's message of studying group processes has been largely undermined by the emphasis placed on conducting individual-level research. Short stated that "[f]orty years later . . . the group process perspective remains undeveloped. The research that we did has been cited frequently and appreciatively, but later gang research by sociologists and anthropologists has focused less on group processes than on correlates of individual self-reports" (2005, pp. 4–5). This dilemma arises because most studies are not designed to have the capacity to analyze a representative sample of gang members from multiple gangs. This goes to the heart of the level of explanation problem that Short has addressed over the years and something that Malcolm Klein addressed in his call for more comparative gang research.

Short's contention that group processes are instrumental in facilitating gang member behavior has been validated by both longitudinal and qualitative research over the years. As more elaborate statistical techniques and methodological advances emerge (e.g., network analysis) and are used to study gang and gang member behavior, Short's work will be used as the anchor to that research.

David C. Pyrooz and Scott H. Decker

See also Cloward, Richard A., and Lloyd E. Ohlin: Delinquency and Opportunity; Cohen, Albert K.: Delinquent Boys; Klein, Malcolm W., and Cheryl L.

Maxson: Street Gang Structure and Organization; Thornberry, Terence P.: Interactional Theory; Thrasher, Frederick M.: The Gang; Vigil, James Diego: Multiple Marginality Theory

References and Further Readings

Akers, R. L. (1998). *Social learning and social structure: A general theory of crime and deviance*. Boston: Northeastern University Press.

Cloward, R. A., & Ohlin, L. E. (1960). *Delinquency and opportunity: A theory of delinquent gangs*. New York: Free Press.

Cohen, A. K. (1955). *Delinquent boys: The culture of the gang*. New York: Free Press.

Decker, S. H. (1996). Collective and normative features of gang violence. *Justice Quarterly, 13*, 243–264.

Decker, S. H., & Van Winkle, B. (1996). *Life in the gang: Family, friends, and violence*. Cambridge, UK: Cambridge University Press.

Esbensen, F.-A., Winfree L. T., Jr., & He, N. (2001). Youth gangs and definitional issues: When is a gang a gang, and why does it matter? *Crime and Delinquency, 47*, 105–130.

Gottfredson, M. R., & Hirschi, T. (1990). *A general theory of crime*. Stanford, CA: Stanford University Press.

Hirschi, T. (1969). *Causes of delinquency*. Berkeley: University of California Press.

Krohn, M. D., & Thornberry, T. P. (2008). Longitudinal perspectives on adolescent street gangs. In A. M. Liberman (Ed.), *The long view of crime: A synthesis of longitudinal research* (pp. 128–160). Washington, DC: National Institute of Justice.

Lilly, J. R., Cullen, F. T., & Ball, R. A. (2007). *Criminological theory: Context and consequences*. Thousand Oaks, CA: Sage.

McGloin, J. M., & Decker, S. H. (2009). Theories of gang behavior and public policy. In H. D. Barlow & S. H. Decker (Eds.), *Criminology and public policy: Putting theory to work* (pp. 212–225). Philadelphia: Temple University Press.

Short, J. F., Jr. (1997). *Poverty, ethnicity, and violent crime*. Boulder, CO: Westview.

Short, J. F., Jr. (1998). The level of explanation problem revisited: The American Society of Criminology 1997 presidential address. *Criminology, 36*, 3–36.

Short, J. F., Jr., (2005). Why study gangs? An intellectual journey. In J. F. Short & L. A. Hughes (Eds.), *Studying youth gangs* (pp. 1–14). Lanham, MD: AltaMira.

Short, J. F., & Strodtbeck, F. L. (1965). *Group process and gang delinquency*. Chicago: University of Chicago Press.

Sutherland, E. H. (1939). *Principles of criminology* (3rd ed.). Philadelphia: Lippincott.

Thornberry, T. P. (1987). Toward an interactional theory of delinquency. *Criminology, 25,* 863–891.

Thornberry, T. P., Krohn, M. D., & Lizotte, A. J. (1993). The role of juvenile gangs in facilitating delinquent behavior. *Journal of Research in Crime and Delinquency, 30,* 55–87.

Thrasher, F. M. (1963). *The gang: A study of 1,313 gangs in Chicago* (Abridged). Chicago: University of Chicago Press. (Original work published 1927)

SHOVER, NEAL: GREAT PRETENDERS

Neal Shover's *Great Pretenders* synthesizes conclusions from a scholarly career spanning four decades and devoted largely to the study of persistent street offenders. It is relevant as an empirical work and analysis for all who would develop theory for this type of offender. The male recidivists examined compose much of the crime problem and drain tremendous criminal justice resources. They are the primary source of concern in the ongoing public conversation of the crime problem and policies to address it. Interpretations from the book are aimed at a small segment of those who offend, but this persistent minority represents a population that cannot be ignored.

Shover focuses on the pursuits and careers of street offenders who return to criminal activity following a period of incarceration for earlier crime. The project draws on diverse data that include results of research on street offenders by other investigators, offenders' published autobiographies, interviews collected in three ethnographic studies of persistent thieves, and secondary analysis of inmate surveys.

Shover's primary goal is not theoretical development or testing; rather, his aim is to present the decisions and consequential contingencies of offenders' lives through their eyes. While a view of *crime as choice* frames the discussion, it is clear early on that those who wish to view crime purely as economic choice or who hope to reduce rates of offending exclusively by increasing punishment will find disappointment in these pages. This use of choice can accommodate sophisticated cultural analysis as well as simple costs and benefits of crime, as is seen in the six stories of difficult lives and prolonged participation in crime that initiate the analysis.

Before focusing precisely on the world as seen by thieves, Shover describes the historical context of criminal opportunity. Dramatic technological changes that have opened and constrained opportunities for crime over the last century are documented. There have been, for example, technological improvements to make large sums of money inaccessible to thieves that rely on the handy skills of tradesmen; peeling or punching holes in safes full of cash can no longer be accomplished by ordinary men with ordinary tools. Brazen large-scale heists of trains or banks, always high-risk prospects, will almost inevitably end badly for malefactors who cannot outrun the communication technology of their age or easily leave criminal notoriety behind. The all-too-prevalent dream of big scores and outlaw careers uninterrupted by punishment is far out of reach for most would-be street offenders. Nevertheless, some opportunities expand. Drug dealing and fraud offer lucrative potential. And there are goods and money in houses, stores, and pockets accessible to any with the inclination to steal fairly small sums at the risk of what would be off-putting penalties for most.

The implication in the discussion of historical developments is that currently there is something akin to a dual labor market for offenders. Lucrative illicit opportunities are available for those with patience and ability to manage personnel and plans or who develop sophisticated strategies for committing discrete crimes. There is some promise in crime for those who can devote forethought and resources to designing offenses that insulate from law enforcement and who can avoid mistakes and the worst damage from living life as party. The bulk of robbery and burglary are committed by men with no such resources, inclinations, or abilities.

Disadvantage and disrepute not only constrain opportunities but also affect what is pursued. Most lower-class men will choose hard work befitting their social and occupational training, but there are multiple identities that can conduce in crime available to them as well. Some offenders, drawn mainly from the lower rungs of their class, also embrace a lifestyle centered not on the commitments of work and family but on concern with immediate social settings and appearances in them. Drugs and alcohol are the typical organizing activities in these settings. Shover calls related pursuits and the mind-set that potentially make regular intoxication, unstructured days, and theft attractive *life as party*.

Within the broad pursuit of it, there are several prevailing identities that mark stylistically distinctive accomplishment of the criminal lifestyle, and that define how thieves categorize themselves and their peers. They vary on forms of drug use, abilities to manage crime and drugs, and the degree of commitment to crime relative to conventional pursuits. One prevalent category, the noncriminal identity, does not derive from direct pursuit of a criminal course or character project, but from fatalistic and alienated worldviews of poor men who have spent long periods of life down on their luck. These know that in their ranks hard times and criminal mistakes eventuating in heavy costs are mundane eventualities. Prison is a misfortune, but is not a completely unexpected shock. Other culturally reproduced lifestyles that are prominent in the lower classes are more closely linked to crime and related pursuits. These include the thief, hustler, dope fiend, and screw-up. Alongside diminished chances of acquiring the financial security and stability that are rewards in respectable and licit occupational pursuits, the attractions of crime are especially likely to draw those ensconced in crime commensurate outlooks.

The second half of *Great Pretenders* is devoted to understanding what criminal careers, from first to last crime, look like in the population of persistent thieves and why this is the case. It is established firmly, for example, that many young males engage in serious delinquency and that few do so frequently or over long periods of time. Even among those who engage in serious delinquency frequently and who continue to do so past their teenage years, many will stop committing crimes by their early to mid-20s. Those who persist in crime even after they are punished as adults may be peculiar statistically and qualitatively.

Through practice, seasoned offenders begin to see environments and opportunities from the perspective of thieves who know how to do it. Few opportunities for theft may be taken as experience teaches that they are plentiful, but they also will not escape the notice of those who have learned to look. Most persons pay little attention to jars of coins on mantles, storeroom windows left ajar, vehicles in driveways that indicate gun collections in houses, cigar boxes under registers, or illegal gambling machines in country convenience stores. Those who have larceny sense cannot help but notice. Many must actively suppress thoughts of committing crime when apparent opportunity knocks. Therefore, it can take herculean commitment for those who see criminal opportunity everywhere to change thinking and desist from crime. Rewarding relationships and jobs help offenders to abide.

For those who spend long periods of time committing crime and paying the price for it, crime-reducing commitments can remain elusive contingencies, however. Nevertheless, neglect of family and work has consequences for aging thieves that may get through to many eventually and that can lead to dramatic shifts in outlook. Those with extensive past troubles often come to see the rewards to be found in familial relationships and the types of pursuits associated with them. These awakenings to the pleasure of stability and associated rewards are one way in which persistent offenders come to recognize their past mistakes, to view crime as self-defeating, and to develop the resolve which is almost necessary for them to change. Fortunately, middle age is not too late for such realizations.

Those who are to make a late transition out of crime often confront and acknowledge eventually that offending has paid paltry returns and done tremendous damage when all is considered. Years are a limited resource. Potential to undo harm to loved ones and self-respect diminishes. Therefore, prison time is more costly with age and occurs in ever longer stints. Stubborn continuance in crime and its associated pursuits and any tendency to proudly or lackadaisically shirk the costs diminishes with maturity. Aging offenders develop a more complex understanding of criminal folly, and it saddens them to know that another generation is at the trailhead representing onset of lengthy criminal careers. They tend to accept, however, that the young will not listen to what they have to say, perhaps indicating recognition of the thickness of blinders that accompany a criminal lifestyle and outlook.

The closing pages of *Great Pretenders* address attempts by the state to make crime less attractive by threats and confinement. When policy is measured against conclusions of this study, the prospects for crime control based on philosophies that emphasize reducing crime with near exclusive use of aggressive and tough criminal justice policies seem gloomy. A central reason may be that policy-makers have devoted almost no attention to imagining how their initiatives and the resultant conditions are experienced by the economically marginalized and troublesome citizens of low repute. At a time when political moods in the country ardently questioned the prospects of government to intervene, plan for, and correct problems, so great was faith in aggressive crime control that few questioned whether it could deter the persistent and potentially dangerous offenders at which it was aimed. Even less attention was given to potential unexpected and collateral costs. The irony of this penal policy is that it strips options and visits the heaviest penalties on already vulnerable offenders "just as they are beginning to contemplate the possibility of going straight" (Wright, 1997).

Overoptimistic assessments of deterrent potential of punishment result in part from the fact that academics and policy makers are ill-positioned to understand the chaotic contexts and inattention to preparation for lucrative careers in the ranks that produce persistent offenders. To those accustomed to the careful metrics—organization and planning common among economists and business professors—it is a mystery why countless bakeries, laundries, construction ventures, and neighborhood bars open without business plans and fail soon after. Continued participation in crime remains a mystery as well.

Many thieves are not moved by attempts to scare them with harsh penalties because at the moment of crime they do not care about the consequences. They have learned that stealing requires the ability to set aside fear of the unknown, and may have been surrounded by offending and offenders for much of life. If punishment is unduly tough, it might anger some and further entrench them in alienated and angry attitudes. For others, it will present a chance to show that they can take whatever is given without acquiescing to pressures to change personal pursuits or identities. If offenders were ill-suited for dealing with their shortcomings and consequences of their choices before long periods of incarceration, some will be less so upon release. There are always the inefficient and morally unattractive options of incarcerating tremendous numbers of persons cheaply and repeatedly or keeping them until they

are old and tired. Intelligent and efficient sanctioning requires acknowledging that even persistent thieves are redeemable, helping them to escape their own histories and taking reasonable chances.

Insights from *Great Pretenders* have had their greatest academic influence on those intrigued by offenders' thinking and reasoning. It is pronounced in contemporary qualitative research, where Shover has exercised considerable tutelage, and which is almost necessarily influenced by the book (Maruna, 2006). Research that allows offenders to provide straightforward insight into their lives, views of the world, and what they are trying to accomplish often draws heavily from this work. Among other things, the book accompanies a renewed theoretical and empirical attention to the temporal level between background and situational factors and also accompanies a cultural and symbolic interactionist turn in criminology (Ulmer, 2003). Here, storylines that pull together individual characteristics, interactions, and/or settings for interaction in ways that increase chances of crime are revealed (Agnew, 2006). *Great Pretenders* also foretells the recently invigorated interest, especially in developmental and life-course perspectives, in the changing meanings of offending associated with age and experience. However, it is not only qualitative researchers who are influenced. Any who deign to understand street offenders encounter the unusual metrics described in this and other foundational accounts of contemporary theft and street-life. The knowledge imparted by these explorations now is incorporated into all forms of inquiry into experienced offenders' decision making (Nee, 2003).

Andy Hochstetler

See also Anderson, Elijah: Code of the Street; Economic Theory and Crime; Perceptual Deterrence; Shaw, Clifford R.: The Jack-Roller; Steffensmeier, Darrell J., and Jeffery T. Ulmer: The Professional Fence; Sutherland, Edwin H.: The Professional Thief

References and Further Readings

Agnew, R. (2006). Storylines as a neglected cause of crime. *Journal of Research in Crime and Delinquency, 43*, 119–147.

Maruna, S. (2006). Review of "In Their Own Words": Criminals on crime. *Australian and New Zealand Journal of Criminology, 39*, 268–283.

Nee, C. (2003). Research on burglary at the end of the millennium: A grounded approach to understanding crime. *Security Journal, 16,* 37–44.

Shover, N. (1985). *Aging criminals.* Newbury Park, CA: Sage.

Shover, N. (1996). *Great pretenders: Pursuits and careers of persistent thieves.* Boulder, CO: Westview Press.

Ulmer, J. T. (2003). Demarginalizing symbolic interactionism: A comment on interactionism's place. *Symbolic Interaction, 26,* 19–31.

Wright, R. T. (1997). Review of "Great Pretenders: Pursuits and careers of persistent thieves." *Contemporary Sociology, 26,* 360–361.

Wright, R. T., & Decker, S. H. (1996). *Burglars on the job: Streetlife and residential break-ins.* Boston: Northeastern University Press.

Wright, R. T., & Decker, S. H. (1997). *Armed robbers in action: Stick-ups and street culture.* Boston: Northeastern University Press.

SIMON, RITA J.: WOMEN AND CRIME

In 1975, Rita J. Simon authored a pioneering book called *Women and Crime.* It was one of the first publications to examine women and their criminality from a sociological/gendered perspective. Prior to its publication, female criminality was often attributed to mental, emotional, and biological weaknesses embedded in the nature of women. Even the mainstream theories of criminology (i.e., strain, bonding, differential association) provided very little explanation of how and why women engaged in crime. Most of the "traditional" theories of crime simply applied the theoretical explanations of male criminality to those of women criminals.

With the Feminist Movement of the 1970s in full swing, Simon's work delved into the sociological forces surrounding women's opportunity to engage in crime. She investigated crime statistics in the United States from the early 1950s to the early 1970s and concluded that increased labor force participation, via the women's liberation movement, led to increased crime rates for women during that 20-year period. To further support her point, she also cited a similar increase in female crime rates across several other industrialized countries. In addition, Simon looked at how women were treated in the criminal justice system by examining convictions and sentencing patterns in federal and state courts. Lastly, she described the issues and concerns of women in prison in the United States during that time period. She focused on such topics as programming opportunities, separation from children and families, and the conditions inside of women's prisons. This entry provides an overview of Simon's liberation hypothesis, describes the treatment of women in the criminal justice system with an emphasis on the chivalry hypothesis, and presents some points of view in opposition to Simon's work.

Liberation/Opportunity Thesis

One of the major ideas put forth by Simon in *Women and Crime* was that women's criminality was linked to the opportunities, social skills, and networks available to women in American society. This idea ran counter to the existing notion that women offenders had mental and genetic deficiencies that caused their criminality. From a sociological perspective, Simon suggested that prior to the Feminist Movement, women's criminal options were limited because most women were relegated to the home. Before the changes of the 1970s, the role of women consisted of being a good wife, mother, and homemaker. All of these functions required women to spend most of their time in the home, leaving very little discretionary time for other activities, especially crime. As a result of the Feminist Movement, these roles shifted, and women became "liberated" or "emancipated" from the home. They were able to find paid employment outside the home, which allowed them greater opportunity to involve themselves in crime. In essence, Simon disputed the long-standing idea that women were more moral than men and were, therefore, less criminal. She suggested that if women had the same opportunities to commit crimes as men, they would take advantage of those opportunities. Increased participation in the labor force during the 1970s provided women with criminal options they had not had in the past.

In addition, Simon also purported that the position women occupied in the labor force was related to the *types* of crimes they had the chance to commit. Her opportunity/liberation thesis hypothesized that, over time, women's crime rates would rise sharply for property and white-collar crimes, such as larceny/theft, embezzlement, fraud, and forgery. The increased opportunity of working outside the home would provide women with more chances to engage in job-related and property offenses. In fact, Simon saw a future where the rates of white-collar offenses for men and women would be similar as women continued to increase their status outside the home. As a corollary, Simon contended that liberation from the home would not make women more violent, but actually reduce their aggressive behavior. As women became more involved in the labor force, and as their education increased, they would feel happier and less likely to alleviate their frustration by acting out violently.

Simon also believed that labor force participation would decrease the victimization of women. As women's labor force participation increased, women became more confident and on guard for potentially violent situations. Women would also gain more financial independence and establish social networks to escape from abusive relationships.

In the original version of Women and Crime, Simon demonstrated support for the liberation/opportunity thesis by citing arrest statistics from the Uniform Crime Reports. The Uniform Crime Reports is compiled annually by the Federal Bureau of Investigation (FBI) and is based on arrest statistics reported from local police agencies across the United States. In particular, Simon focused on two categories of arrests from 1953 to 1972. The first, Index Crimes, included homicide, robbery, aggravated assault, burglary, larceny/theft, and auto theft. Forcible rape was excluded. The second category, Type II offenses, included offenses such as other assaults, arson, vandalism, weapons, prostitution, drugs, gambling, liquor laws, and so on. Simon's data showed that, over the period of her study, women's arrests increased over 20 percent for all crimes and over 50 percent for serious crimes. Of great importance is that most of the serious crime arrests were for property offenses (i.e., more than 60 percent). Her analysis was bolstered by a slew of other statistics, including arrests from other industrialized countries.

Simon's analysis showed that over the 20-year span of the study, the greatest increases in female arrests were reported for larceny/theft, embezzlement and fraud, forgery, and counterfeiting rather than other serious types of crimes. These figures supported

her opportunity theory. During the same time frame, women's arrest rates for violent crimes remained steady, supporting Simon's contention that employment in the community would work to stabilize or reduce women's violent behavior.

Women and the Criminal Justice System

In addition to presenting arrest statistics, Simon also examined the courtroom treatment of women versus that of males who committed similar crimes. Simon offered a two-pronged perspective to describe the treatment of women. On the one hand, Simon suggested that women were treated more leniently and received "softer" treatment by judges. She labeled this approach paternalism or chivalry. In a courtroom operating from this mind-set, when a man and a woman were charged with the same offense, the woman would receive preferential treatment. The female offender would be less likely to be convicted and formally sentenced. If she was convicted, she would most likely serve less time than her male counterpart. Simon suggested that when prosecutors and judges had to punish a female they often equated her with their mother or sister and were, therefore, less likely to move forward with official punishment. The fact that many women had children also swayed the judgment of court officials, who did not want to separate families. In other words, the chivalrous judicial system could not see women as criminals and acted in a paternalistic manner toward female offenders.

To prove her point, Simon examined the treatment of male and female offenders in assault and larceny cases. Specifically, women were more likely to be released on bail, have their case dismissed, or receive probation as compared to men who had committed the same offenses. Overall, Simon discovered that the idea of paternalism or chivalry toward women criminals holds moderately true for both assault and larceny. Also of interest is that Simon actually interviewed judges and state attorneys in the Midwest asking them about paternalism or chivalry toward female criminals. More often than not, these officials admitted that they were not as punitive toward women criminals as men.

In opposition to the chivalry hypothesis, Simon suggested that some court personnel treat women criminals with much more disdain than men. In fact, she suggested that some judges were likely to punish women more severely when compared to men who had committed similar offenses. In this scenario, Simon believed that women criminals were perceived as acting so far out of their sex or gender roles that judges punished them for not only being criminals but also for violating the standards of femininity. Thus, the punishments meted out in these courts were more punitive for women because they were breaching societal expectations as well as the law. Again, Simon presents a litany of data from state and federal courts regarding outcomes and convictions disaggregated by gender and offense. Her federal data for the period 1964 to 1971 revealed that women were more likely than men to be convicted for certain crimes: fraud, embezzlement, and forgery. Her state conviction data from Ohio and California courts supported these findings as well.

Besides the courtroom, Simon also included a short section in *Women and Crime* about women in prison, whom she labels "the forgotten offenders." Simon suggested that with the liberation afforded to women during the era of women's rights, the number of women entering state and federal prisons should have also increased along with arrest rates. However, the statistical data she presented actually showed, that from 1950 to 1970, there was not a spectacular increase in the number of women entering federal institutions. State data from New York yielded similar results, suggesting that the women's movement did not directly affect women's prison populations.

Moreover, Simon examined the availability of educational and vocational programming for women inmates across the United States in comparison to those programs offered to males. In general, she found that women were offered fewer programs, and the programs that they were offered, especially vocational programs, did not prepare women for successful reentry into the community. At the time, women inmates were typically offered vocational training that was gender stereotyped, such as sewing, horticulture, cosmetology, and housekeeping. More importantly, these programs had less earning potential than the training offered to male inmates. Therefore, a woman who left prison would find it difficult to make ends meet on such low wages. Her problem was compounded if she had a family to support. Thus, she was more likely to return to crime and find herself back in

prison. Simon's work exposed important disparities between programs offered to male and female inmates. These issues are still being examined by today's criminologists.

Opponents of Simon

Since the publication of *Women and Crime* in 1975, many criminologists have challenged Simon's theoretical explanations of why women commit crime. Several concerns about her data from the Uniform Crime Reports have been raised. As mentioned above, Simon used arrest rate data compiled between 1953 and 1972. Since 1953 was the first year that women's arrests were gathered by the FBI, its accuracy is suspect. Much of the data could be inaccurate or flawed. Second, Simon used arrests as a representation of actual crime rates. The Uniform Crime Reports gives the number of arrests, not the number of persons arrested. Thus, one individual who committed multiple offenses might be overrepresented in these data. A third underlying problem with the data is that the FBI does not collect data from every police precinct in the United States. Local jurisdictions report their information voluntarily and typically count only crimes "known" to the police. This means that some crime is potentially missed. There are only a few ways in which crimes can be known by the police: A victim or a witness can report the crime to the police, or a police office can witness a crime as it takes place. Since not all crime is reported to the police, and officers rarely witness a crime actually taking place, it becomes obvious that the Uniform Crime Reports is undercounting criminal activity. Compounding this reporting problem is the capability of law enforcement personnel to use discretion in deciding whether to arrest. In light of these filters, criminologists estimate that less than half of all crimes are reported. Therefore, the data from the Uniform Crime Reports may be an underestimate of the true nature and amount of women's criminality.

Besides problems with the Uniform Crime Reports, methodological errors have been noted in the way Simon operationalized or measured her key dependent variable of white-collar crime. She showed increases in embezzlement and fraud, as well as forgery and counterfeiting, but many criminologists believe these crimes are poor indicators of white-collar crime. Some recent criminological research has found that the majority of women's white-collar crime is "petty" in nature when compared to the white-collar activities of men. They found that the most common white-collar crimes committed by women were welfare and benefit fraud. Their forgery often involved writing bad checks for lesser amounts than men. Also, women who embezzle were usually not CEOs or bank presidents. More often than not, they were lower level workers, like the bank teller or clerical worker, who sneaked out a dollar a day in change rather than bilking customers out of billions with elaborate schemes. Women in these financial occupations held relatively low paid positions when compared to men. Thus, their opportunity to commit the costliest white-collar crimes was very limited.

Simon did not address any of those issues. These findings actually contradict her work, largely because she predicted that women's liberation would uplift women to higher occupational statuses. In reality, that neither was nor is necessarily happening. Even today, most bank presidents and top Wall Street executives are men. Men still reside at the top of the labor force hierarchy and maintain a greater opportunity to commit the costliest white-collar crimes than women. So although women's arrest rates did increase during Simon's study period, labor force participation and opportunity were not the sole predictors of that.

One last point needs to be made about Simon's methodology. She presented a vast amount of arrest data for women but never actually reported the real number of arrests. She presented all of her data as percentages and/or a percent change in offending. She often showed a huge percentage increase in arrests for a specific crime, but in actual numbers the increase was not that great. For example, from 1965 to 1975, the number of women arrested for murder increased by 500 percent. If one looks at the actual numbers of arrests, murders rose only from one to five instances. This absence of raw arrests distorts the true picture of women's criminality, which is that women still make up a very small percentage of criminal activity compared to men.

Not all criticism of Simon's work is based on her methodology. Her strongest opponents target her opportunity or liberation thesis. As mentioned previously, Simon linked the women's movement, in the form of increased labor force participation, to increased crime rates for women. While women's crime rates did increase during the time period examined by Simon, many criminologist believe that the women's movement had very little to do with that. Rather, some of her critics suggest that economic necessity was and still is the major impetus behind women's criminality. Advocates of this position agree that more women are working than in years past, but the majority of them are still relegated to jobs at the lower end of the economic spectrum, both in prestige and pay. This contradicts the liberation hypothesis in that women, in large numbers, have not gained the occupational status that Simon espoused. Thus, women are committing crimes not because they have access to high-powered, high-paying jobs but rather out of financial need or desperation. Current data show that most of the women represented in today's criminal justice system are often poor, undereducated, and involved with alcohol and/or drugs. This image is quite opposite of the picture put forth by Simon's liberation hypothesis.

The Future of Women and Crime

Simon has revised *Women and Crime* twice since its initial publication in 1975. In her 1991 and 2005 editions, she continued to provide updated arrest data as well as information on women in the criminal justice system today. She highlighted the enormous changes that have taken place since her first edition. Moreover, Simon also included current discussions on the sexual abuse of women prisoners and women on death row. Her current data provided continued support for the opportunity thesis. But, in the end, Simon suggested that her opportunity theory should not stand alone as the sole explanation for women's criminality. Rather, she proposed a multifaceted approach containing elements of liberation and economic marginalization as the most fitting explanation for the increase in women's criminality.

Despite her detractors, Simon is a pioneer in the study of women and crime. She brought to light many of the critical issues faced by women offenders and continues to examine the changing issues of women in the criminal justice system both in the United States and abroad.

Karen F. Lahm

See also Adler, Freda: Sisters in Crime; Chesney-Lind, Meda: Feminist Model of Female Delinquency; Smart, Carol: Women, Crime, and Criminology; Steffensmeier, Darrell J., and Emilie Andersen Allan: A Gendered Theory of Offending

References and Further Readings

Adler, F. (1975). *Sisters in crime: The rise of the new female criminal.* New York: McGraw-Hill.

Messerschmidt, J. (1986). *Capitalism, patriarchy, and crime: Toward a socialist feminist criminology.* Totowa, NJ: Rowman & Littlefield.

Pollack-Byrne, J. (1990). *Women, prison, and crime.* Pacific Grove, CA: Brooks/Cole.

Simon, R. J. (1975). *Women and crime.* Lexington, MA: Lexington Books.

Simon, R. J., & Ahn-Redding, H. (2005). *The crimes women commit, the punishments they receive* (3rd ed.). Lexington, MA: Lexington Books.

SIMPSON, SALLY S.: GENDER, CLASS, AND CRIME

Sally S. Simpson is well known for her research and contributions related to intersections between gender, class, race, and crime. Throughout her research, Simpson's examination of gender and crime is juxtaposed against the effects of race, ethnicity, and social class of both the offender and the victim. Further, Simpson provides quantitative research on these intersections, something that is not common in much of the mainstream literature. Most other research on this topic has been qualitative in nature. Although these qualitative approaches have added to the discipline's understanding of such intersections, particularly in regard to showing how race and class influence perceptions of structure and opportunities for crime, qualitative approaches alone leave many questions unanswered.

Though Simpson has written many pieces on feminist criminology and is well-versed on women and criminal behavior, it is apparent that her research is multifaceted when examining the female offender. Feminist criminologists have often utilized qualitative approaches due to the claim that it is difficult to make categorical distinctions necessary for quantitative analyses. This is particularly true in those cases where the sample of female offenders is small, such as with studies that use snowball sampling. However, Simpson and Carole Gibbs have noted that qualitative methods may also be preferred by feminist criminologists because they comport better with the epistemology of feminist criminology.

Simpson and Gibbs (2004) examined the gender, race, and class patterns of offending using data from the National Longitudinal Survey of Youth. The analysis concentrated on the responses provided by the 2,716 males and females aged 15 to 16 years who responded to wave 1 and wave 2 interviews. When conducting this research they used a number of control variables, such as age, urban area, and prior delinquency. Simpson and Gibbs used these data because of their suitability to examining intersectional groups; minority youth had been oversampled and the survey contained numerous indicators of social class. Specifically, this study examined whether constructs developed from four neutral or, according to Karen Heimer and Candace Kruttschnitt, male-oriented theories, explained juvenile offending better than intersectional models that accounted for the effects of gender, race, and class on delinquency. The results of this study demonstrated significant differences in delinquency based on the gender, race, and class of the participant.

In particular, Simpson and Gibbs (2004) found that intersectional analyses by class, gender, and race provided a better data fit than did the four male-centered theories. As an example, it was noted that multiple sex partners among female offenders was a better predictor of delinquency than social class among delinquent youth. Just as interesting, a mother's social control was found to have a stronger impact on reducing delinquency for African Americans than for Caucasian Americans, but this was also better explained by intersectional models than by control theory (one of the four male-centered theories). These examples and other findings in the 2004 research by Simpson and Gibbs indicate that intersectional analyses by class, gender, and race can produce better explanations for delinquent behavior than do other more prominent male-centered theories.

The findings from this research essentially suggest that quantitative analysis is an effective means for finding intersectional differences that result from gender, class, and race. Equally important, these findings also demonstrate how quantitative approaches can lend additional support to feminist assertions that general (or male-oriented) theories of delinquency are less universal than their proponents claim. This research is important because often feminist criminology has been viewed as a "soft" approach to explaining criminality due to the lack of quantitative empiricism.

When looking back at research and/or publications produced by Simpson throughout her career, there is a clear tendency for her work to point out the need for a more sophisticated examination of female crime. This is particularly true in regard to intersections between gender and race. In 1995, Simpson and Lori Elis noted that while many researchers up to that time had examined the relationship between inequality and criminal behavior (including class, gender, and racial oppression), few researchers had considered how gender and racial oppression are associated with causal factors related to delinquency. In reviewing the state of the literature, at that time, Simpson and Elis generated several hypotheses related to masculinity, femininity, and social institutions such as work, family, peer groups, and schools. They found that both gender and race modify the effect of independent variables on both property and violent delinquency. This study was important because it laid the groundwork for continued examination of race, gender, and social class as causal factors that work in tandem yet have their own distinct and unique contributions. Further, this study examined delinquency as well as adult criminality, providing an added dimension to the study of female criminal behavior. Going back even further into Simpson's research career, it can be seen that Simpson (1991) exhibits a passion for examining gender issues within the context of race and class. Indeed, Simpson noted that in years prior to 1991, criminological research had targeted gender as a key variable in examining participation and persistence in criminal behavior. Even at this time, Simpson had led the charge to examine male and female crime within a race, class, and gender context. In this work, Simpson demonstrates how race and class combine to produce female populations who are socially situated in a unique set of circumstances that produce unique patterns of criminality. This examination of race and class focused

largely on underclass African American females. Simpson also examined violent crime committed by African American females and compared this with violent crime committed by white females and provided plausible explanations for variance in violent crimes between these two groups.

Further, Simpson examined three specific theoretical perspectives—neo-Marxist, power-control, and socialist-feminist theories—and evaluated each for intragender and racial inclusivity. Simpson concluded that class-oppressed men, regardless of whether they are Caucasian or African American, tend to have privileges extended to them due to their role as men in a sexist and patriarchal society. She also notes that class-oppressed Caucasians—whether male or female—have privileges that are extended to them as whites in a Caucasian dominated and racist society. More to the point, Simpson concludes that those persons who are African American, female, and poor have a tripled amount of discrimination against them emanating from classism, racism, and sexism that bears down upon them, keeping them trapped in a world of injustice and discrimination.

From her earliest of years, it can be seen that Simpson has followed and examined race-gender-class interactions in criminal behaviors. One of her earlier works makes this clear. In Simpson's 1989 article titled "Feminist Theory, Crime, and Justice," Simpson provides a perceptive overview of the research on female offending and on the progress that feminist criminology had made within the field. However, even at this early stage of her career, she provides an interesting subsection discussion on race and crime amidst the article's broader scope on women and crime. In this work, Simpson contends that poorly conceived offender self-report surveys had given criminologists a convenient rationale for ignoring the race-crime relationship. In this regard, Simpson notes that this apparent research oversight worked well within the prevailing political climate of the time but also points out that such negligent forms of research leads to a prevailing set of problems since less critical (and thereby less productive) perspectives are examined. This is important because this also meant that until the time that race and class were considered, crime prevention and crime intervention approaches overlooked key aspects of crime that would better address the issue. Simpson urged feminist criminologists to undertake research focusing on the gender-race-class connection in criminal etiology. She also noted that the data were sparse at this time, problematic, and with very few analytic contributions being made. Simpson also observed that research often relied on quantitative analyses that simply dichotomize race into being either Caucasian or African American. In other cases, an additional category may be included, but more often than not, this was typically classified as simply being a non-white category that included all other groups aside from African Americans and Caucasians.

Simpson's early piece pointed to the need to examine minority women in feminist research, noting that much of the data indicated that significant differences existed between African American and Caucasian crime rates. She further pointed toward unique structural and cultural contexts for African American women. These cultural and structural pushes and pulls often do not exist for Caucasian women. Simpson notes that the ethnography of lower-class deviant networks can describe how male and female criminality may differ among the underclass and lower classes and how instrumental crimes (e.g., hustling, pimping, gambling) are often interdependent in minority communities (Simpson, 1989). Although there may be some degree of interdependence among the criminal community of minority offenders, patriarchy still exists within these communities.

Simpson notes that even within the criminal element, women still play a subservient role in most cases. This is especially true among minority groups. Male dominance and control continue to be reproduced within interpersonal relationships between men and women, and this sense of dominance is also reinforced in informal organizations such as street gangs. While some of the crimes committed by women can be viewed as establishing autonomy, most of it is seen as stemming from abusive relationships between men and women and/or frustrations associated with racial discrimination and oppression based on social class. Due to the cultural differences between African Americans and Caucasians and because the overwhelming majority of female criminologists in the early nineties were Caucasian, Simpson speculated that perhaps most theories—including feminist theories—were centered on the Caucasian experience. Since that time, of course, the field of criminology has made great strides in acknowledging this deficit in the research and the need to address racial issues for both male and female offending.

In discussing the criminal justice system's response when contending with the race and gender intersection, Simpson observes that some research has found that the interaction between race and gender is a key factor that influences arrest decisions. Indeed, she notes that the chivalry hypothesis—the notion that the criminal justice system is less harsh of females due to their status as women—exists only for Caucasian female offenders. She contends that minority women are treated more harshly than Caucasian counterparts because they are not as likely to exhibit expected gender-stereotyped behaviors. Simpson has also noted that race and gender have been found to intersect through victim characteristics, leading her to conclude that although chivalry may exist for Caucasian women, it does not appear to exist for African American women. Adding to this, similar to many feminist scholars, Simpson contends that in sentencing, variation may be related to what are referred to as counter-type offenses. Here, women are treated more harshly when they commit nontraditional female crimes such as assault or murder, because their offenses violate female sexual norms.

At present, Simpson tends to conduct the majority of her research on corporate and white-collar crime, which seemingly represents a shift in her career interests. Likewise, she serves as the Chair of the Department of Criminology and Criminal Justice at the University of Maryland, reflecting her position as a leader among colleagues and scholars in the field of criminology. Still, Simpson occasionally returns to the study of gender, race, and class (Simpson, 2008). Regardless, her many contributions are well regarded among her peers as evidenced by her receipt of the 2008 Distinguished Scholar Award from the Division on Women and Crime within the American Society of Criminology. Thus, it is clear that Simpson has left a permanent mark upon the research landscape of feminist criminology, demonstrating the need for researchers to consider the cumulative effects that tend to occur in our society through multiple routes of marginalization, particularly those that occur at the intersection of the race, gender, and social class of the offender population.

Robert D. Hanser

See also Daly, Kathleen: Women's Pathways to Felony Court; Heimer, Karen, and Stacy De Coster: The Gendering of Violent Delinquency; Messerschmidt, James W.: Masculinities and Crime; Miller, Jody: Girls, Gangs, and Gender

References and Further Readings

Simpson, S. (1989). Feminist theory, crime, and justice. *Criminology, 27,* 605–631.

Simpson, S. (1991). Caste, class and violent crime: Explaining differences in female offending. *Criminology, 29,*115–135.

Simpson, S. (2002). *Corporate crime, law and social control.* Cambridge, UK: Cambridge University Press.

Simpson, S. (2008). Introduction to special issues on historical and contemporary views of social control, race, crime, and justice. *Crime, Law, and Social Change, 49,* 241–244.

Simpson, S., & Elis, L. (1994). Is gender subordinate to class? An empirical assessment of Colvin and Pauly's Structural Marxist theory of crime. *Journal of Criminal Law and Criminology, 82,* 453–480.

Simpson, S., & Elis, L. (1995). Doing gender: Sorting out the caste and crime conundrum. *Criminology, 33,* 47–81.

Simpson, S., & Gibbs, C. (2004). *Making sense of intersections: Does quantitative analysis enlighten or obfuscate?* Presentation at the American Society of Criminology, 56th Annual Meeting.

Simpson, S., & Gibbs, C. (2005). Intersectionalities: Gender, race, poverty, and crime. In K. Heimer & C. Kruttschnitt (Eds.), *Gender and crime* (pp. 269–302). New York: New York University Press.

SKOGAN, WESLEY G.: DISORDER AND DECLINE

Wesley G. Skogan's *Disorder and Decline: Crime and the Spiral of Decay in American Neighborhoods* is a classic study in the fields of sociology and criminal justice. In *Disorder and Decline,* Skogan examines the concept of disorder, which refers to minor offenses and other disreputable behaviors and conditions that can potentially impact the quality of life in neighborhoods. Specifically, Skogan investigates how minor disorders relate to serious criminal activity, citizen fear of crime, and neighborhood destabilization.

Skogan draws extensively on survey data from nearly 13,000 respondents to study disorder and its impact. The respondents were residents of 40 neighborhoods in six U.S. cities: Newark (New Jersey), Philadelphia, Atlanta, Chicago, Houston, and San Francisco. The surveys were originally administered as part of five separate studies conducted between 1977 and 1983. All of the surveys asked residents to answer questions on a variety of topics pertaining to neighborhood life, including disorder, personal victimization, community satisfaction, and fear of crime. Skogan also supplements the survey data with information collected from field observations and interviews with residents in Chicago, Philadelphia, and San Francisco.

The results of Skogan's analyses offer important insights concerning the relationship between disorder and neighborhood life. For example, although an individual act of disorder may be relatively minor in severity, citizens often take notice of the accumulation of disorder and report it as a serious concern. Many survey respondents rated activities and conditions such as public drinking, harassment by youth, noisy neighbors, vandalism, trash and litter, and dilapidated buildings as serious problems in their communities. The results also suggest that minor offenses can have a negative impact on residents' quality of life. Thus, disorder was associated with fear, anger, demoralization, residential dissatisfaction, and the desire to move out of neighborhoods. Perhaps the most frequently discussed result of the study, however, concerns the relationship of disorder to criminal offending. Even after controlling for neighborhood demographic characteristics, such as poverty and neighborhood instability, Skogan discovered that disorder was significantly related to serious crime. Places that experienced greater problems with disorder were also more likely to experience problems involving serious criminal activity.

After establishing the link to neighborhood decline and serious crime, Skogan examined methods to manage disorder and its related problems.

In doing so, he discussed a variety of proactive police tactics tied to the community policing philosophy, as well as efforts designed to organize and mobilize citizens around common problems in their communities.

The Concept of Disorder

The term *disorder* is often identified with, or used synonymously with, terms such as *incivilities*, *nuisance offenses*, *quality-of-life offenses*, or simply *minor offenses*. As described in *Disorder and Decline*, disorder refers to a wide range of conditions and activities that are considered less severe than felony crimes but are nonetheless regarded as serious problems in communities. Disorders can be, but are not necessarily, violations of criminal or civil codes. Nevertheless, disorderly conditions and conduct are considered problematic because they violate communal values and social norms held by neighborhood residents.

Skogan distinguishes between two types of disorder: social and physical. Human activities, such as aggressive panhandlers who intimidate passersby, individuals who engage in street prostitution, people who use drugs and alcohol in public, or rowdy teenagers who harass pedestrians, are examples of social disorders. Persistent conditions, such as abandoned cars on the street, litter along sidewalks, broken windows in buildings, or discarded drug paraphernalia in alleyways, are examples of physical disorders. Since the publication of *Disorder and Decline*, it has become common for scholars studying communities and crime to utilize Skogan's distinction between physical and social disorders when constructing research designs and reporting findings.

The concept of disorder continues to be the subject of considerable discussion and debate in academic circles. Because disorder refers to such a broad array of activities, researchers cannot always agree on consistent definitions of just what is, and what is not, disorder. Several other factors complicate discussions over disorder. As Skogan notes, disorders do not always result in a "victim" in the traditional sense; rather, entire neighborhoods can be the victims of ongoing disorderly acts and conditions. Additionally, the type and amount of disorder that communities can absorb may vary from place to place. A busy entertainment district, for instance, may have the capacity to tolerate a certain level of public intoxication, public urination, and aggressive panhandling without great consequence to the well-being of that neighborhood. The same amount of those activities in an otherwise quiet retirement community, however, could cause that neighborhood to quickly deteriorate.

It is important to note that the conceptualization of disorder in *Disorder and Decline* has become the familiar use of the term within the criminological research literature. This conceptualization differs from a less common use of the term, which refers to acts of rioting and/or civil disobedience that are displayed by crowds during periods of civil unrest.

Impact on Theory and Public Policy

Skogan's research in *Disorder and Decline* is closely associated with the *broken windows hypothesis*—a theory proposed by James Q. Wilson and George L. Kelling. According to the broken windows hypothesis, minor offenses, if left untended, can lead to a breakdown in community social control. In places where residents are unable to manage minor offenses, criminals will feel more at ease to operate, believing that no one cares about the community. Serious criminal offenses, therefore, will be more likely in places where there is unchecked disorder. *Disorder and Decline* was the first major piece of research to provide empirical support for the broken windows hypothesis. Taken together, the conclusions from *Disorder and Decline*, along with the theory of broken windows, suggest a major policy implication: if communities can manage problems of disorder, they may well be able to prevent problems related to serious felonies and violence.

Since the publications of *Disorder and Decline* and the broken windows essay, efforts to manage disorder (i.e., order maintenance strategies) have become popular in many communities. These strategies have become most closely associated with the activities of public police, primarily because officers often possess discretion regarding the enforcement of disorder. One of the first large-scale applications of the order maintenance principle occurred in the New York City subways during the early 1990s, where a reduction in serious crime was associated with the police management of disorderly offenses such as turnstile jumping (Kelling

& Coles, 1996). Many other police agencies have adopted order maintenance practices, and these strategies have been empirically linked to crime reduction in places such as Jersey City, New Jersey (Braga et al., 1999); Lowell, Massachusetts (Braga & Bond, 2008); New York City (Corman & Mocan, 2002; Kelling & Sousa, 2001; Messner et al., 2007; Rosenfeld et al., 2007); and counties in California (Worrall, 2006).

Critical Analysis of *Disorder and Decline*

Practitioners, policy makers, and many members of the research community who are familiar with *Disorder and Decline* are generally supportive of its findings. Several within the academic community have been more critical, however, citing both methodological and theoretical concerns. Bernard Harcourt, and Robert Sampson and Stephen Raudenbush, for example, suggest that the relationship between disorder and serious crime is not as strong as Skogan's analysis would indicate, except perhaps for the crime of robbery. Similarly, Ralph Taylor finds some support for the idea that disorder leads to serious crime, but he suggests that other characteristics of neighborhoods are more reliable predictors of later criminal activity.

Although scholars continue to debate the strength of the disorder-crime link, some have argued that managing disorder is nevertheless an important task when maintaining the quality of life in neighborhoods. David Thacher, for example, suggests that minor disorders alone may be intrinsically harmful to communities. Efforts to reduce disorderly behaviors and conditions, therefore, may have value regardless of whether they also reduce more serious crime.

Other academics have voiced concerns over the moral complexities of enforcing order in neighborhoods. Because the definition of disorder is varied and inconsistent, that which is considered disorderly to some people may be considered acceptable behavior to others. Skogan himself is concerned with this aspect of disorder, and he cautions that the communal desire for order maintenance could potentially reflect an intolerance of the values and rights of individuals.

Balancing communal interests with individual rights remains a significant issue when enforcing disorder in communities. As Skogan's research demonstrates, however, minor offenses can have a dramatic impact on neighborhood life. As such, citizens should consider the control of disorderly activities and conditions to be an important goal in community management.

William H. Sousa

See also Sampson, Robert J.: Collective Efficacy Theory; Skogan, Wesley G., and Michael G. Maxfield: Coping With Crime; Wilson, James Q., and George L. Kelling: Broken Windows Theory

References and Further Readings

Braga, A. A., & Bond, B. J. (2008). Policing crime and disorder hot spots: A randomized controlled trial. *Criminology, 46,* 577–607.

Braga, A. A., Weisburd, D. L., Waring, E. J., Mazerolle, L. G., Spelman, W., & Gajewski, F. (1999). Problem-oriented policing in violent crime places: A randomized controlled experiment. *Criminology, 37,* 541–580.

Corman, H., & Mocan, N. (2002). *Carrots, sticks and broken windows* (NBER Working Paper No. 9061). Cambridge, MA: National Bureau of Economic Research.

Harcourt, B. (1998). Reflecting on the subject: A critique of the social influence conception of deterrence, the broken windows theory, and order-maintenance policing. *Michigan Law Review, 97,* 291–389.

Kelling, G. L., & Coles, C. M. (1996). *Fixing broken windows: Restoring order and reducing crime in our communities.* New York: Free Press.

Kelling, G. L., & Sousa, W. H. (2001). *Do police matter? An analysis of the impact of New York City's police reforms* (Civic Report No. 22). New York: Manhattan Institute.

Messner, S. F., Galea, S., Tardiff, K. J., Tracy, M., Bucciarelli, A., Piper, T. M., et al. (2007). Policing, drugs, and the homicide decline in New York City in the 1990s. *Criminology, 45,* 385–414.

Rosenfeld, R., Fornango, R., & Rengifo, A. F. (2007). The impact of order-maintenance policing on New York City homicide and robbery rates: 1988–2001. *Criminology, 45,* 355–384.

Sampson, R. J., & Raudenbush, S. W. (1999). Systematic social observation of public spaces: A new look at disorder in urban neighborhoods. *American Journal of Sociology, 105,* 603–651.

Skogan, W. G. (1990). *Disorder and decline: Crime and the spiral of decay in American neighborhoods.* New York: Free Press.

Taylor, R. B. (2001). *Breaking away from broken windows.* Boulder, CO: Westview Press.

Thacher, D. (2004). Order maintenance reconsidered: Moving beyond strong causal reasoning. *Journal of Criminal Law and Criminology, 94,* 101–133.

Wilson, J. Q., & Kelling, G. L. (1982, March). Broken windows: The police and neighborhood safety. *The Atlantic Monthly,* 29–38.

Worrall, J. L. (2006). Does targeting minor offenses reduce serious crime? A provisional, affirmative answer based on an analysis of county-level data. *Police Quarterly, 9,* 47–72.

SKOGAN, WESLEY G., AND MICHAEL G. MAXFIELD: COPING WITH CRIME

In the Omnibus Crime Control and Safe Streets Act of 1968, Congress authorized the Law Enforcement Assistance Administration (LEAA) to administer federal monies to assist state and local law enforcement agencies to fight crime through better training and equipment, and support criminological and criminal justice research. In the mid-1970s, the LEAA funded and published a series of national evaluations of individual and collective responses to crimes (e.g., citizen patrols, Operation Identification) and inaugurated the Community Anti-Crime Program to assist community organizations to respond to crime. The now-defunct LEAA, which was abolished in 1982, funded *The Reactions to Crime Project* (RTC) at the Center for Urban Affairs and Policy Research at Northwestern University. The RTC was a 5-year (1975–1980) interdisciplinary, multimethod project lead by Fred DuBow to inquire into how crime shaped the attitudes of city residents toward crime and how they individually and collectively responded to crime. Wesley Skogan and Michael Maxfield's book, *Coping With Crime: Individual and Neighborhood Reactions,* was among the three major volumes produced that presented the RTC's major results (see also Lewis & Salem, 1981; Podolefsky & DuBow, 1981).

In *Coping With Crime,* Skogan and Maxfield primarily are "concerned with how city dwellers cope with the problems of crime and fear of crime" (p. 11). The authors examine the apparent paradoxes in the relationships between crime, fear, and reactions to crime. Specifically, they investigate why "more people are fearful of crime than report being victimized," and why "people who are least likely to be victimized are among the most likely to report being fearful" (p. 11). They also observe yet another crime- and fear-related paradox: urban dwellers' risks of victimization and their fears heightened at a time when a large sum of federal dollars was flowing to state and local budgets to encourage urban residents to adopt personal precautionary measures and participate in collective strategies.

Skogan and Maxfield developed, at the time, a new victimization perspective to examine more fully these paradoxes. Their model proposes a guide to explaining two fundamental relationships that underline these crime-fear-reaction paradoxes: the relationship between crime and fear of crime, and how and why they respond to both. Their model of the antecedents to reactions to crime links the theoretical underpinnings of individuals' personal and household qualities (e.g., sex, age, family income, race) and neighborhood conditions (e.g., disorder problems, neighborhood integration) to their victimization experiences and learning about crime (e.g., media exposure, personal communication networks). These factors in turn are linked to the relationship between individuals' fear of crime and their reactions to protect themselves and their property from victimization. These reactions include personal precaution, household protection, community involvement, and flight to the suburbs.

Adhering to a strong quantitative approach, Skogan and Maxfield use a triangulation of data collection strategies to strengthen their methodology and results. They relied primarily on survey data from more than 1,300 telephone interviews conducted in 1997 in 10 residential neighborhoods in three large cities: Chicago, Philadelphia, and San Francisco. They also incorporated content analysis of daily newspapers serving these cities, on field observation reports of selected neighborhoods and interviews with community leaders and local officials, and supplementary data from the

Census Bureau victimization surveys conducted in 1971 and 1974 for those three cities.

Explaining the Crime-Fear Paradoxes

In *Coping With Crime,* Skogan and Maxfield unpack the relationship among the individual-level and neighborhood-level correlates of fear and develop plausible explanations for the crime-fear paradoxes. Few people were personally victimized, but many reported high levels of fear; and those most likely to experience a personal victimization, namely young males, were among the least fearful. Clearly, personal victimization cannot directly explain high levels of fear that plague cites.

One explanation Skogan and Maxfield offer to this apparent paradox is that low-victimization groups, such as women and the elderly, report high levels of fear and are more vulnerable on two dimensions. First, women and the elderly are physically vulnerable to attack; they are less able to defend against attack and are more likely to experience long-term negative mental and physical health care issues if attacked. Second, others, such as low-income individuals, are socially vulnerable because they live primarily in high-risk neighborhoods and, once victimized, they are not able to recover from the financial consequences of victimization. While both dimensions of vulnerability contribute to understanding the crime-fear paradox, Skogan and Maxfield find that these two dimensions of vulnerability are independent of each other. This discovery suggests that each has its own unique impact on fear.

Skogan and Maxfield also examine several features of residential neighborhood conditions and integration that seem to produce perceptions of problems with crime and heighten fear. They find that residents' perceptions of neighborhood disorders, such as abandoned buildings, teenagers hanging out, and vandalism, and their perceptions of crime are clearly interconnected; both factors are related to fear of crime levels. Residents' fear of crime tends to be higher in communities where they perceive "big problems" with neighborhood disorder and crime. Two aspects of neighborhood integration, residential ties and social ties, are linked to the degree of perceived disorders. They report that there is a weak-to-moderate tendency

for individuals who have strong social and residential ties to report being less fearful. Interestingly, neighborhood crime and disorder problems, residential and social integration, and personal vulnerability are related to each other; yet, when they are considered simultaneously, *each* significantly predicts fear.

Beyond the importance of personal and neighborhoods characteristics to explaining fear, Skogan and Maxfield find that indirect experiences with crime, particularly talking with neighbors about local crime, affect fear differently depending on the community context. Residents in high-crime and low-crime neighborhoods talk to one another about local crime. But in low-crime areas, residents, especially those who are well-integrated, talk more often about what little crime there is in their neighborhoods. This communication tends to elevate their fear levels. Individuals who are integrated into their communities usually live in low-crime areas. Ironically, then, the very social and residential structure that keeps crime low encourages the communication about local criminal incidents and results in heightened fear. As Skogan and Maxfield note, the analysis of the communication about crime helps to explain why relatively high fear levels are often found in low-crime communities—yet another paradox about fear of crime.

Why People React as They Do in Response to Crime

Understanding the crime-fear paradox and the relationship among its individual- and neighborhood-level factors provides an insightful working model for Skogan and Maxfield to further probe the fear-and-participation nexus. People engage in a variety of crime prevention precautions to reduce the risk of being personally victimized. Skogan and Maxfield find that the frequency by which they engage in precautionary behaviors is related to their fear, personal vulnerability, and neighborhood conditions.

Households also engage in measures to prevent burglary and property theft. Turning to how and why people react to property crimes, contrary to their expectations Skogan and Maxfield find (1) that vulnerability measures are related to fear but mostly in the "wrong direction" and (2) that perceptions of crime conditions are not related to fear. The less vulnerable households—homeowners, whites, higher-income residents and single-family dwellers—did the most to protect their property. But being either a direct or vicarious burglary victim and perceiving burglary as a problem were not related to household protection. One explanation that they offer to this seemingly paradoxical result is that those who have an economic investment in the community and have strong ties to the neighborhood's social network are more likely to protect their home and property.

Skogan and Maxfield's exploration of the correlates of participation in organized community response to crime are both supportive and contradictory of arguments suggesting that crime discourages involvement in organized community responses while it also stimulates fear. On one hand, participation in collective anti-crime efforts was higher among residents who had experienced a burglary and who believed their neighborhoods were getting worse. On the other hand, participation was lowest among those residents who felt unsafe in the neighborhoods. As the authors note, the relationships among these variables are confounded, however: "with the exception of Blacks, those who are the most involved in these activities are those who personally seem the least affected by crime problems" (p. 240).

One option for urban residents is flight to the suburbs to escape the perceived risks of crime. According to Skogan and Maxfield, in the Chicago metropolitan area, both push and pull factors—but more so pull factors—influence residential relocation to the suburbs. Their findings suggest that "the problem of flight to the suburbs is a white flight problem"; "[b]lack families are more likely to remain in the center city" (p. 245). Whites' relocation decision was based on pull factors such as changes in the household composition or life-cycle considerations. Whites were not pushed by perceived crime problems in their neighborhood, but crime and safety were among the pull factors shaping their suburban relocation decision.

Influence on Fear of Crime and Community Crime Prevention Research

Skogan and Maxfield's book is a seminal work that influenced at least two lines of research. First,

their work was influential to better understanding the measurement of fear of crime and its correlates. Building from Skogan and Maxfield's fear of crime measures, Mark Warr and Mark Stafford, and Randy LaGrange and Kenneth Ferraro made contributions to conceptually refining fear and developing offense-specific measures of fear. Second, their work influenced the next generation of neighborhood-centered studies that further examined various sociological and political aspects of the relationships between crime, fear, and disorders, and rigorously evaluated the effectiveness of collective community action to reduce crime and fear. In this vein, the main crime-fear-reaction findings reported in *Coping With Crime* have continued to define Skogan's community-focused research agenda for nearly three decades.

Bonnie S. Fisher

See also Altruistic Fear; Ferraro, Kenneth F.: Risk Interpretation Model; Fisher, Bonnie S., and Jack L. Nasar: Fear Spots; Lewis, Dan A., and Greta W. Salem: Incivilities and Fear; Stanko, Elizabeth A.: Gender, Fear, and Risk

References and Further Readings

Lewis, D. A. (Ed.). (1981). *Reactions to crime: Individual and institutional responses.* Beverly Hills, CA: Sage.
Lewis, D. A., & Salem, G. W. (1981). *Crime and urban community: Toward a theory of neighborhood security.* Washington, DC: National Crime Justice Reference Service.
Ferraro, K. F., & LaGrange, R. (1987). The measurement of fear of crime. *Sociological Inquiry, 57,* 70–101.
Podolefsky, A., & DuBow, F. (1981). *Strategies for community crime prevention: Collective responses to crime in urban America.* Springfield, IL: Charles C Thomas.
Skogan, W. G. (2009). Wesley G. Skogan homepage. Retrieved June 1, 2010, from http://www.skogan.org
Skogan, W. G., & Maxfield, M. G. (1981). *Coping with crime: Individual and neighborhood reactions.* Beverly Hills, CA: Sage.
Rosenbaum, D. P (Ed.). (1986). *Community crime prevention: Does it work?* Beverly Hills, CA: Sage.
Warr, M., & Stafford, M. C. (1983). Fear of victimization: A look at the proximate causes. *Social Forces, 61,* 1033–1043.

SMART, CAROL: WOMEN, CRIME AND CRIMINOLOGY

Carol Smart's book *Women, Crime and Criminology* focuses on female offenders and criminality. Smart summarizes the nature of female criminality, presents classical and contemporary studies of female criminality, and provides a feminist critique of prostitution/rape, the treatment of female offenders, and the myths surrounding female offenders and mental illness.

The Nature of Female Criminality

Smart postulates that criminology conceals women in the same manner that they are concealed in other aspects of life. She argues that as a direct result of the low status of women in society, academics, criminologists, and policy makers evidence disinterest in female criminality. Circumstances that contribute to this disinterest include the statistical bias of criminal reporting (e.g., there are sex-specific offenses—categorization and legal definitions such as prostitution and infanticide only define it as a crime for one particular sex—and sex-related offenses can be committed by either sex but are predominately committed by a particular sex), and problems in statistical analysis. These circumstances lead to the illusion that female criminality is subordinate to male criminality and, as a result, little attention is paid to the nature and needs of female offenders.

Studies of Female Criminality

Smart presents a summary of classical and contemporary studies of female criminality. The classical studies include what she deems to be the pioneering studies of female criminality. They are as follows: Cesare Lombroso and Guglielmo Ferrero's biological abnormality explanations that include atavism and social Darwinism, W. I. Thomas's focus on socially induced pathology, and Otto Pollak's combination of biological and psychological factors in association with social factors. Smart argues that these three theories were based upon common misperceptions of the character and nature of women and therefore are unable to correctly capture the nature of female criminality.

Contemporary theories presented were John Cowie, Valerie Cowie, and Eliot Slater's focus on biological determinism, abnormal chromosomal structure, and personality deficiencies and Gisela Konopka's focus on sociological and psychological factors such as maladjustment, poverty, and differential social structure. Smart demonstrates how these theories add to the development and understanding of female criminality. Even so, she argues that studies of female criminality remain biased because they lack the inclusion and understanding of gender roles, distinctions between sex and gender, social structure and status, cultural contexts and expectations specific to females, and the positioning of women within society.

The Feminist Critique

Smart presents a feminist critique of the factors, perceptions, and myths surrounding gender and crime. She focuses on prostitution/rape, the treatment of female offenders, and mental illness.

Prostitution/Rape

Smart's critique argues that studies of prostitution/rape are too biologically/psychologically oriented, and that they do not focus on the subordinate social position of women or the sexual double standard for males and females. Classical and contemporary theorists view female prostitutes as primitive, degenerate, uncivilized, mentally defective, unnatural, problematic, sexually confused, and pathological. Smart calls for an examination of the social structure, financial necessity, and limited opportunities afforded to women prior to establishing prostitution as a moral crime. She points out that while the women are viewed as morally repugnant offenders that are to be punished harshly, those that use their services are not viewed as immoral, inferior, or criminal.

Smart also believed a double standard applies to rape victims and perpetrators of rape. Instead of being viewed as a crime of hatred toward women, rape is viewed as the result of a male's violent sexual desire with a biological basis and desire to procreate. The belief that women enjoy masochistic activities and precipitate rape by not forcefully rejecting their advances has led to a social and cultural belief surrounding rape, the treatment of rape victims, and punishment for perpetrators that is inferior.

Treatment of Female Offenders

Smart argues that the cultural double standard, use of the biological determinism model, and lack of consideration of social status has influenced general viewpoints of female offenders and policy decisions regarding their treatment. The wording of rape and prostitution legislation reflects condemnation and voluntary involvement of women. Discretion among police and court officials leads to discriminatory treatment, such as a female being arrested or sentenced harshly for a sexually deviant crime whereas a male is not brought into the system at all. The social expendability of females produce high arrests for gender-specific crimes, heavy sanctioning in the court system, and institutionalization into correctional facilities that perpetuate dependency on their subordinate position and offer stereotypical, if any, programs.

Mental Illness

Smart also argues that the pathological basis of female criminality assumes females to be irrational, illogical, and sick or ill. This assumption denies the existing socioeconomic structure and the intention or choice of the offender. The cultural stereotype of females as less rational, less intelligent, and more dependent than males, allows for female offenders to fit better in a pathological model and its forms of treatment than male offenders. She proposes this viewpoint is dangerous for the following reasons: criminal behavior is seen as an equivalent to mental illness, treatment should "cure" this mental illness, criminal behavior may be excused, and women who report victimization are viewed as neurotic or mentally ill. These misperceptions have led to inappropriate diagnosis, inapplicable policy, a lack of appropriate correctional programs, and the treatment of female criminality as an outcome of mental instability.

Conclusion

Smart states that although women have not been entirely ignored in the studies of crime and deviance, studies are inadequate in their understanding of social, cultural, and characteristics and nature of women and have relied on a biologically deterministic model. To advance studies of female criminality and societal understanding of female offenders,

she warns against proceeding in a manner that will continue to render women invisible within crime and criminology. She concludes that research is necessary in the following areas: types of offenses committed by women and girls and the form that their involvement in criminality and delinquency takes; the attitudes of police, probation officers, and social workers toward delinquent girls and criminal women; the treatment of women and girls in the court system and corrections; and the structure and purposes of criminal laws. As one of the first female authors to call attention to the neglect of women within criminology and as an advocate for the use of a feminist approach, Smart helped inspire the movement to focus on women and crime.

Alana Van Gundy-Yoder

See also Freud, Sigmund: The Deviant Woman; Klein, Dorie: The Etiology of Female Crime; Lombroso, Cesare: The Female Offender; Pollak, Otto: The Hidden Female Offender; Rape Myths and Violence Against Women; Thomas, W. I.: The Unadjusted Girl

References and Further Readings

Cowie, J., Cowie, V., & Slater, E. (1968). *Delinquency in girls.* London: Heinemann.

Konopka, G. (1966). *The adolescent girl in conflict.* Englewood Cliffs, NJ: Prentice Hall.

Lombroso, C., & Ferrero, W. (1895). *The female offender.* London: Fisher Unwin.

Pollak, O. (1961). *The criminality of women.* New York: A. S. Barnes.

Smart, C. (1976). *Women, crime, and criminology: A feminist critique.* London: Routledge.

Thomas, W. I. (1923). *The unadjusted girl. With cases and standpoint for behavior analysis.* Boston: Little, Brown.

SOUTHERN SUBCULTURE OF VIOLENCE THEORY

Criminologists have long observed and debated the causes of high rates of violence in the American South, particularly the Appalachian region. Researchers have identified social structural, environmental, and cultural sources in numerous theoretical statements that have alternatively emphasized ecological and cultural forces. Southern subculture of violence theory (SSV) is more of a perspective (similar to, for example, conflict theory) than a single testable theory (such as routine activities or social control theories, which feature more easily measureable predictors of crime). While several variables have been shown to covary with violence in the South, cultural elements such as ideas, values, and beliefs supportive of aggression have captured research focus increasingly in recent years as evidenced by important contemporary contributions to theoretical criminology that extend the SSV tradition.

A southern subculture of violence has been debated for several decades in both social science and historical contexts. These statements have oriented around retaliatory violence, generally, and homicide, specifically. While early statements generalized the southern culture and violence relationship to the entire region, the SSV perspective has evolved to focus rather specifically on white-on-white homicide in the southern highlands—the only theoretical lineage addressing this United States population segment. The perspective has been influential to the development, survival, and recent resurgence of *cultural transmission* as a major, empirically confirmed cause of crime and is thus significant to the advancement of criminological thought. This entry surveys the conceptual framework and evolution of the SSV perspective mindful of the history and axioms of subculture theory, generally. A review of the empirical evidence supporting the southern subculture argument, essentially social-psychological reinforcement of defense of honor through violent expression as normative, is followed by consideration of SSV theory's further development.

Conceptual Framework

SSV extends the subculture theoretical school that enjoyed a dominant position in criminology during the 1950s and 1960s due to major seminal statements from leading criminologists such as Albert Cohen, Lloyd Ohlin, and Walter B. Miller that were developed around heterogeneous, inner-city and gang delinquency contexts rather than the more homogeneous rural South. Marvin Wolfgang and Franco Ferracuti offered the seminal theory of subcultural violence, which generalized the scope

of the perspective to explain violence as a function of value conflict between the dominant or mainstream culture and criminal subculture. The dominant culture places high value on human life and typically frowns on violence, for example, while devalued life and quick resort to violence are normative in subcultural settings. Consistently emphasizing the criminogenic nature of ideas, values, and beliefs, these early subculture theories established that (1) criminal values are derived from various social conditions (e.g., poverty, social disorganization, familial instability) and (2) crime is considered more normal behavior within the environment of the subculture.

The rise of conflict and learning theories of crime during the 1970s negatively impacted and thus slowed the development of subculture theory. Conflict theory viewed much of subcultural crime as political resistance against a classist and racist society whose surplus labor control relegated subculture to exogenous status in favor of focus on inequality-based socialization processes encouraging delinquency and crime. The rise of positivistic criminology during the 1970s and 1980s, largely practiced through multivariate analysis of combinations of social ecological and social interaction factors, also moved theoretical attention to other social sources of crime and delinquency than cultural factors. Because subculture was presented as inherently criminal, it was deemed tautological and thus unscientific. The subculture lineage was extended during these times of hard academic scrutiny largely due to focus on violent crime in the American South.

Southern Subculture of Violence Thesis

In regard to accounting for disproportionately high rates of southern violence, the social ecological approach to crime—explanations incorporating demographic, socioeconomic, and environmental variables—has entailed extensive consideration of various causes. Rurality, gun ownership, the historical effects of slavery, poverty, religion, and temperature have been identified as factors that heighten violence in the southern environment (Erlanger, 1976). High temperatures, for example, purportedly lessen patience, elevate frustration, and ultimately accentuate hostility—especially in overcrowded homes in impoverished areas. Readily available guns common in hunting cultures typical to the rural South, coupled with an eye-for-an-eye religious outlook, made violence a frequent regional reality. These covariates of violence, however, have been either falsified or shown to be spurious. The temperature argument, for example, has been refuted recently by a social isolation argument that posits that very hot weather forces people indoors and retards both movement and the rate of social interaction. Limited interaction, in turn, decreases the chances for arguments and physical altercations in the first place. Race is strongly correlated with violence in all regions and is thus not a factor in SSV inquiry. The causal significance of the other frequently hypothesized sources for southern violence have similarly been limited, not because they are statistically insignificant but because they do not account for why crime is higher in the South than in the West, Midwest, and other rural areas with approximate social ecological conditions.

Accordingly, criminologists turned attention to culture in attempt to realize a more explanative theory. Focus on culture as the basis of regional violence, particularly homicide, is rooted in southern history. The notion of honor among southern gentlemen requiring "satisfaction" for insults through violence (e.g., feuds and duels), coercion related to maintaining slavery, and collective social resentment lingering from the War Between the States and subsequent economic exploitation during Reconstruction all reinforced normative lawlessness and violence. These values became culturally embedded and, although the factors that led to their development have faded into history, pass from generation to generation as normal behavior. Most importantly, an ethos honor came to the forefront of the southern subculture of violence thesis. This ethos distinguishes between typically random acts of violence and southern violence.

Southern violence, as characterized in the SSV tradition, is instrumental and intimately related to the defense of honor/reputation of self and family. After controlling for race and other cofounders, homicide in the South is as much as four times higher than in other regions of the United States. Only homicides involving insults and personal attacks, however, are more frequent in the South as southerners typically disapprove of violence generally. Vested in the driving force of collective conscious, an honor-based line of inquiry has emerged as the dominant theme in SSV research.

Culture of Honor

While several theorists have emphasized honor, a *culture of honor* hypothesis framed by Richard Nisbett and Dov Cohen is the most comprehensive. After providing figures documenting homicide rate differences between the North and South, Nisbett and Cohen present multifaceted empirical evidence supporting attitudes toward violence that centers on the concept of defense of honor. Through experimental ethnography, southerners are shown to define and react to insults with greater anger and aggression than non-southerners. Laboratory studies have demonstrated that southerners experience far greater physical (cortisol and testosterone level fluctuation), psychological (dominance projection, anger), and cognitive (attitudinal endorsement of violence in dispute resolution) distress in argumentative and conflictual situations when compared to non-southerners.

The culture of honor theory posits that a regional collective conscious not only endorses but mandates conditional use of violence. Social policy and law concerning marital affairs and child-rearing, for example, reflect a higher value on state non-intervention and a continuation of a states rights legacy derived from the necessity of local and vigilante social control during the 18th and 19th centuries when most of the South was a frontier area with limited legal authority. Southern legal codes, especially those pertaining to violence for protective purposes and defense of honor, also support the Nisbett and Cohen hypothesis. Gun control laws reinforce the frontier mentality of self-reliance for protection and provision (i.e., hunting) as indicated by U.S. senators and representatives voting patterns on gun restriction issues. Similarly, laws pertaining to self-defense (e.g., degree of citizen entitlement to utilize force in defense of home and property and obligation to retreat by innocent persons in lieu of fighting back against an assailant) provide southerners a "right to fight" that would be unlawful in most states. The "true man law," for example, conveys the moral and social premium placed on standing one's ground to the point of killing another person if necessary when attacked. Failure to do so is often equated with cowardice and dishonor, while "showing fight" enhances reputation and respect in the community. Southern legal perspectives on capital punishment, domestic violence, corporal punishment, and national defense policy also reinforce the use of violence.

The foremost contribution of the culture of honor theory, however, is the integration of cultural transmission and ethnic perspectives. While southern history and current laws provide a context facilitative of violence, much of the violent crime in the South can be accounted for by other than cultural factors. Minority representation and poverty, which are both relatively higher in the South than other regions, account for much of the violence in the region as elsewhere in the country. When these factors are controlled for, however, southern violence—particularly homicide—is noticeably pronounced in the Appalachian region. Scrutiny of violence in the southern highlands provides unique opportunities for criminological analysis. Whereas southern violence, generally, is considered a function of high levels of social disorganization associated with high minority populations and low levels of socioeconomic status, the southern highlands have low minority population representation and comparatively low levels of in and out migration. Thus, a highly homogenous population enables examination of violence in a context of social stability in a white-on-white context. Because the honor ethos is pervasive throughout the region, all social classes internalize the conditional use of violence as socially acceptable if not required and are ostensibly affected. Moreover, the temperature argument is also naturally controlled due to the milder temperatures in Appalachia compared to the rest of the region.

Nisbett and Cohen also observe that the dominant ethnic group in the South is the Scots-Irish. It is argued that the herding culture developed by these people in the British Isles emphasized violence in small group/extended clan context so as to protect livestock from rival clans (i.e., economic survival) and as political resistance against a suppressive English state. Projection of fierceness and willingness to engage literal acts of aggression were traits that transferred across continents with the Scots-Irish migration to the United States and became culturally embedded in mountainous regions where they settled. Quick reaction to personal affronts to one's family necessarily was met with suppressive violence, so as to deter both predation on weak targets and the need for further violence itself. In a

very real sense, this is a "best defense is a good offense" type of logic as portrayed in *Born Fighting: How the Scots-Irish Shaped America*, James Webb's account of the Scots-Irish in the United States. Indeed, through topographical comparison of lowland, foothills, and mountain counties, Nisbett and Cohen demonstrate that violence and elevation are positively correlated—a reality that is empirically observed throughout Appalachia and attributed to Scots-Irish culture. The backwards, violence, and almost always southern hillbilly stereotype has been consistently projected in popular culture over several decades as indicated by a sequence of films and television programs (e.g., *The Beverly Hillbillies*, *The Dukes of Hazzard*, and *Deliverance*), evidencing violence and family pride as core characteristics of Southern mountain people.

Critique

The most obvious problem with the SSV perspective, generally, and the culture of honor proposition, specifically, is that southern culture itself is not adequately addressed in either measurement or historical development. While Nisbett and Cohen present an interdisciplinary and multifaceted hypothesis, they fail to account for why homicide is substantially higher in southern Appalachia than in northern Appalachia, even though both are predominantly occupied by the Scots-Irish who subscribe to an honor ethos. Additionally, analyses have relied on behavior measurement at the individual level—perhaps an ecological fallacy for a theory emphasizing a collective (i.e., macro) level focus.

While economic factors are vital to the perspective, attention to historical and sociocultural realities specific to the region offers perhaps the best chances for furthering SSV theory. Lingering effects of Confederate nationalism, for example, clearly continue to shape southern culture and may well facilitate further specification of the honor-violence relationship. Whereas Cohen and Nisbett submit that herding culture values have transferred across continents and over several centuries, the Appalachians today, while still highly homogenous, have more ethnic diversity and much less of a herding economy. The Confederate experience is considered by most native southern Appalachians as a second war for southern American independence that was unsolicited, defensive, and necessary. It served to solidify a we-versus-them outlook that is an innate attribute of virtually all subcultures. The necessity of defensive violence that derived from the war continues to have contemporary relevance through states rights doctrines and politics that gives currency to the honor premise. In that slavery was never economically viable in Appalachia and thus never widespread, focus on Confederate nationalism (measureable through Confederate social heritage organization affiliation and participation) offers further focus on white-on-white violence while logically isolating Southern highland culture. To date, the extant SSV literature minimizes the significance of the war and its aftereffects to slavery that was not consequential in Appalachian context anyway.

Another advancement opportunity lies in examination of migration patterns. While the mountain South is becoming more diverse, the fundamental subculture characteristic of culture conflict provides naturally competing hypotheses regarding demographic change. On one hand, consistent with the subculture perspective, outside pressure will only strengthen cultural values—a sort of solidifying the core. Alternatively, there may well be a cultural tipping point that offsets cultural endorsement of violence.

J. Mitchell Miller

See also Anderson, Elijah: Code of the Street; Cohen, Albert K.: Delinquent Boys; Miller, Walter B.: Lower-Class Culture Theory of Delinquency; Wolfgang, Marvin E., and Franco Ferracuti: Subculture of Violence Theory

References and Further Readings

Anderson, E. (1999). *Code of the street: Decency, violence, and the moral life of the inner city*. New York: W. W. Norton.

Borg, M. J. (1997). The Southern subculture of punitiveness? Regional variation in support for capital punishment. *Journal of Research in Crime and Delinquency, 34*, 25–45.

Brearley, H. C. (1932). *Homicide in the United States*. Chapel Hill: University of North Carolina Press.

Chu, R., Rivera, C., & Loftin, C. (2000). Herding and homicide: An examination of the Nisbett-Reaves hypothesis. *Social Forces, 78*, 971–987.

Cohen, D. (1996). Law, social policy, and violence: The impact of regional cultures. *Journal of Personality and Social Psychology, 70*, 961–968.

Cohen, D., & Nisbett, R. E. (1994). Self-protection and the culture of honor: Explaining southern homicide. *Personality and Social Psychology Bulletin, 20*, 551–567.

Ellison, C. G., Burr, J. A., & McCall, P. L. (2003). The enduring puzzle of southern homicide. *Homicide Studies, 7*, 326–352.

Erlanger, H. S. (1976). Is there a subculture of violence in the South? *Journal of Criminal Law and Criminology, 66*, 483–490.

Faust, D. G. (1988). *Confederate nationalism: Ideology and identity in the Civil War South*. Baton Rouge: Louisiana State University Press.

Gastil, R. D. (1971). Homicide and a regional culture of violence. *American Sociological Review, 36*, 412–427.

Hackney, S. (1969). Southern violence. *American Historical Review, 74*, 906–925.

Hawley, F. F., & Messner, S. F. (1989). The Southern violence construct: A review of arguments, evidence, and the normative context. *Justice Quarterly, 6*, 481–511.

Hayes, T. C., & Lee, M. R. (2005). The Southern culture of honor and violent attitudes. *Sociological Spectrum, 25*, 593–617.

Nisbett, R. E., & Cohen, D. (1996). *Culture of honor: The psychology of violence in the South*. Boulder, CO: Westview Press.

Odum, H. W. (1947). *The way of the South: Toward a regional balance of America*. New York: Macmillan.

Webb, J. (2004). *Born fighting: How the Scots-Irish shaped America*. New York: Broadway Books.

Wyatt-Brown, B. (1984). *Southern honor: Ethics and behavior in the Old South*. New York: Oxford University Press.

SPECTOR, MALCOLM, AND JOHN I. KITSUSE: CONSTRUCTING SOCIAL PROBLEMS

Malcolm Spector and John I. Kitsuse published *Constructing Social Problems* in 1977. This short book became the key statement for a new sociological approach to studying social problems: *social constructionism*. In recent decades, constructionist theory has guided a large number of empirical studies of different social problems, even as the theory has evolved.

American sociologists began teaching courses with the title "Social Problems" early in the 20th century. These courses were usually taught to first-year or second-year undergraduates. A typical class summarized sociological knowledge about crime, race relations, and a series of other troubling social conditions. These topics were presumably related, in that each was a condition that somehow harmed society—a social problem.

Spector and Kitsuse noted that, even as the social problems course became a standard part of the sociology curriculum, the concept of social problems had attracted critics. These critics argued that the various conditions classified as social problems had little in common: some involved troubled individuals (such as suicide or mental illness); some involved much larger entities, even the entire globe (such as world population). What definition could encompass such different phenomena? Moreover, the critics noted that harmful conditions were not necessarily regarded as social problems. People might disagree about whether a particular condition was harmful, or whether it should be seen as a social problem. What was considered a social problem at one time might be seen as perfectly acceptable at another time, and it was easy to point to conditions that were considered social problems in some societies but not others.

This explains the dramatic first sentence in *Constructing Social Problems*: "There is no adequate definition of social problems within sociology, and there is not and never has been a sociology of social problems" (p. 1). Any definition that characterized social problems as particular types of conditions would be unsatisfactory. Therefore, Spector and Kitsuse sought to redirect sociological thinking about social problems. Instead of defining social problem in terms of some presumably objective quality of social conditions (such as harmfulness to society), they defined it in terms of subjective reactions—people characterizing social conditions as social problems. Thus, they defined social problems as "the activities of individuals or groups making assertions of grievances and claims with respect to some putative conditions" (p. 75).

Social Construction

In this view, social problems are seen not as conditions but as a process. There is only one quality that suicide, world population, and all other social problems have in common: People define them as social problems. Through definitional processes, people create—or *construct*—social problems. (At the time Spector and Kitsuse were writing, many sociologists were adopting the term *social construction* [Berger & Luckmann, 1966].) Consider an example from Kathleen Lowney and Joel Best: the crime of stalking. During the late 1980s, public attention began to focus on celebrities who were being harassed or attacked by fans; this was sometimes termed *starstalking*. By the early 1990s, the meaning of *stalking* had shifted. Instead of being thought of as something that happened to celebrities, it was now understood to be relatively common, typically involving women being stalked by ex-husbands or ex-boyfriends, and potentially ending in serious violence. While such behaviors were not new, within just a few years, those behaviors were defined as constituting a social problem and assigned a new name, and virtually all states passed laws making stalking a crime. In other words, through claims by victims, journalists, battered women's advocates, and others, stalking was constructed as a social problem.

Studies of social problems construction frequently adopt terminology that Spector and Kitsuse originated. For instance, analysts describe advocates making *claims* that particular conditions should be considered social problems, and they call those advocates *claimsmakers*. Constructionist analysts may examine how a particular claimsmaking campaign attracted public attention, or they may compare campaigns at different times (e.g., tracing how different definitions of sexual abuse emerged during different historical periods [Jenkins, 1998]) or in different places (e.g., examining how different cities or different countries developed distinct conceptions of homelessness and devised different policies to deal with the problem [Bogard, 2003]).

Criminologists examine a related process—*criminalization*. Criminalization occurs when laws are passed designating new crimes (such as the anti-stalking laws passed in the early 1990s). This is a topic that concerns criminologists from various theoretical schools: functionalists tend to interpret criminalization as evidence of an evolving societal consensus; conflict theorists tend to view it as a means by which elites seek to maintain their positions of power; and labeling theorists see it as a product of moral crusades. Constructionists may adopt any of these interpretations, but they always understand criminalization as one possible outcome of constructionist processes. That is, constructionists never forget that, in order to pass laws that create new crimes, advocates must construct the issue so as to convince lawmakers that an offense is a serious problem, worthy of being criminalized.

Similarly, sociologists study the parallel process of *medicalization*, whereby social conditions are understood to be medical problems, diseases requiring treatment (Conrad, 2007). As the influence of medical authorities has grown over the past century, a medical vocabulary (i.e., words such as symptom, syndrome, and treatment) has been applied to a wide range of social problems, including many crimes. There are often competing claims about particular social problems. Thus, some claimsmakers argue that drug abuse is best understood as a crime that merits punishment; others insist that addiction is a disease that should be treated; while still others call for decriminalization, redefining drug use as a legitimate choice, analogous to drinking. Over time, the accepted construction of some condition may shift, so that what has been considered a crime comes to be understood as a disease, and so on.

Social constructions can be heavily publicized and presented in dramatic terms. Criminologists are generally suspicious of media warnings about crime waves, which often reflect little more than waves in press coverage of crimes. Similarly, constructions of drug problems often take the form of drug scares, claims that some drug suddenly poses a particularly grave threat to society. Sociologists sometimes use the term *moral panic* to describe alarming dangers posed by deviants. Because claimsmakers must compete to gain the attention of the public, the press, and policymakers, dramatic rhetoric is often chosen to make the advocate's cause seem especially important (Hilgartner & Bosk, 1988). As a consequence, attention is continually shifting to different problems as new claims arise.

Theoretical Issues

The constructionist approach is sometimes misunderstood by those who think that socially

constructed means false. Thus, a critic, in referring to the moral panic over satanic ritual abuse (claims that in retrospect seem to have had no factual basis), might argue that "satanic ritual abuse was a social construction." Certainly this is true, but constructionists understand that all social problems—both those that are well documented, as well as those that may seem fanciful—are socially constructed. In both sorts of cases, claimsmakers seek to draw attention to some condition they consider troubling.

Another critique, which led to debate among constructionists, concerned what Steve Woolgar and Dorothy Pawluch termed *ontological gerrymandering*. Here, critics argued that social constructionists must not exempt themselves from their own analyses. That is, social constructionists routinely view claims as social constructions and, in doing so, contrast those claims with other knowledge which the analyst does not question. But of course whatever knowledge constructionists accept also has been socially constructed. Doesn't this pose a logical problem? Some constructionists responded to this critique by adopting a *strict constructionist* approach and by trying to avoid incorporating any socially constructed assumptions into their analyses—an approach that seemed to require abstract analysis, because empirical research inevitably required taking some knowledge for granted. Most constructionists, however, adopted a stance of *contextual constructionism* that, while acknowledging that all knowledge is socially constructed, understands that, as a practical matter, analysts need to be able to focus their attention on particular issues. (On this debate, see the essays in Holstein and Miller [2003].)

Spector and Kitsuse suggested the case study as an appropriate method for conducting sociological research, and there have been hundreds of studies that trace the social problems process. Often, these address particular stages in that process, and link constructionism to other sociological specialties. Many case studies focus on claimsmakers and their campaigns; here, constructionist analyses often overlap with sociological research on social movements (in cases where activists are prominent claimsmakers) or science and medicine (in cases where experts are the leading claimsmakers). Other studies focus on particular aspects of the social problems process. For instance, analyses of the media's role in constructing social problems incorporate insights from mass media research, while studies that focus on the public's reactions to claims draw on research on public opinion.

Most claimsmakers hope to inspire policy—such as the passage of a new law. Still other construction-ist analyses explore how the process of creating social policies incorporates particular understandings of what is at issue; this research reflects work in political sociology and political science. And social policies have to be implemented; police officers, pub-lic defenders, and others carry out social problems work and, in the process, devise their own construc-tions of the problem and how, in practice, it should be addressed. The social problems process never ends: People assess how policies actually work (activ-ity that links constructionism to evaluation research), and the flaws they identify often become the basis for new claims, which start the cycle yet again.

While most analysts concentrate on the construc-tion of social problems in the contemporary United States, a growing number of studies examine his-torical cases of the social problems process or look at social problems construction in other countries. Some of this work is explicitly comparative in that it contrasts two or more cases across time or space. But all case studies are implicitly comparative in that they show how particular issues have been con-structed under particular circumstances and invite comparisons with other researcher's findings. Often it is possible to see how claimsmaking campaigns influence one another, how claims originate in one country but then spread to others, or how claims devised to construct one problem are adapted and applied to other problems.

The constructionist orientation—thinking criti-cally about how people define, not just social prob-lems, but all aspects of their world—has spread widely beyond sociology (Holstein & Gubrium, 2008). It is used by other social scientists, especially political scientists, psychologists, historians, and, of course, criminologists, so that people writing from many different perspectives are able to interpret the social construction of crime and criminal justice.

Joel Best

See also Becker, Howard S.: Labeling and Deviant Careers; Katz, Jack: Seductions of Crime; Postmodern Theory; Sudnow, David: Normal Crimes; Turk, Austin T.: Criminalization Process

References and Further Readings

Berger, P. L., & Luckmann, T. (1966). *The social construction of reality*. New York: Doubleday.

Best, J. (2008). *Social problems*. New York: Norton.

Bogard, C. J. (2003). *Seasons such as these*. Hawthorne, NY: Aldine de Gruyter.

Conrad, P. (2007). *The medicalization of society*. Baltimore: Johns Hopkins University Press.

Hilgartner, S., & Bosk, C. (1988). The rise and fall of social problems. *American Journal of Sociology, 94*, 53–78.

Holstein, J. A., & Gubrium, J. F. (Eds.). (2008). *Handbook of constructionist research*. New York: Guilford.

Holstein, J. A., & Miller, G. (Eds.). (2003). *Challenges and choices*. Hawthorne, NY: Aldine de Gruyter.

Jenkins, P. (1998). *Moral panic*. New Haven, CT: Yale University Press.

Jenness, V., & Grattet, R. (2001). *Making hate a crime: From social movement to law enforcement*. New York: Russell Sage Foundation.

Lowney, K. S., & Best, J. (1995). Stalking strangers and lovers. In J. Best (Ed.), *Images of issues* (2nd ed., pp. 33–57). Hawthorne, NY: Aldine de Gruyter.

Spector, M., & Kitsuse, J. I. (1977). *Constructing social problems*. Menlo Park, CA: Cummings.

Woolgar, S., & Pawluch, D. (1985). Ontological gerrymandering. *Social Problems, 32*, 214–227.

SPERGEL, IRVING: NEIGHBORHOODS AND DELINQUENT SUBCULTURES

Following in the tradition of Richard Cloward and Lloyd Ohlin's *Delinquency and Opportunity*, Irving Spergel's examination of three different neighbor-hoods in a large city seeks to explain the connec-tion between delinquent norms and neighborhoods. In *Racketville, Slumtown, Haulburg*, Spergel's focus is specifically on the content and location of these delinquent norms, which are not necessarily the cause for delinquent acts. Spergel conducted firsthand observation and interviews with delin-quent youths, non-delinquent youths, drug users, and social workers who provided services to three neighborhoods in an unidentified Eastern United States city. Spergel finds that the criminal subcul-ture in each neighborhood is distinct from the others. He identifies these subcultures as the racket, conflict, and theft. The formation of one subculture versus another in a neighborhood is dependent on the conventional and criminal means available to the youths in the neighborhood.

Theoretical Underpinnings

Spergel's work is grounded ultimately in strain theory. Robert Merton's strain theory suggests that crime is the result of a cultural definition of success as monetary wealth. Opportunities for success are not equally distributed, however. The gap between success aspirations and reality causes persons to adapt to the strain; one such adaptation is crime. In addition to Merton's idea that legitimate means for attaining success are not equally distributed, Richard Cloward contended that illegitimate means are unequally distributed as well. A year later, Cloward and Ohlin expanded this theory to include an explanation of why different types of deviant subcultures form. Spergel situates his work within this framework, focusing on the illegitimate means available to delinquents in three neighborhoods: "The fundamental assumption of this study is that in lower-class urban communities certain distinct types of delinquent subcultures are created and thrive under the impetus of socially unacceptable opportunities available to youths for achieving acceptable, culturally induced success goals" (p. xv).

Methods

Spergel's data were collected in a large, unidentified Eastern U.S. city during the summer of 1959 and 1960. A mix of participant observation and formal interviews were used in each of the three neighborhoods, with most data coming from a total of 90 core interviewees. Ten delinquents, 10 non-delinquents, and 10 drug-using youths were interviewed from each of the three neighborhoods. Selection of the respondents was non-random, and Spergel cautions that there were "no systematic checks on validity or reliability" (p. xx). A key limitation was that Spergel focused exclusively on anomie and means for achieving success goals—other variables were not explored. Spergel's goal was explaining the delinquent youth subculture, not the origins of adult criminal behavior, so the narrow focus is less limiting than it appears at first blush.

Racketville, Slumtown, and Haulburg

Spergel named the neighborhoods under study according to their dominant delinquent subculture. In each neighborhood, Spergel found a dominant culture of the criminal racket, conflict, or thievery. This dominant culture did not preclude other acts—there was conflict in the neighborhood characterized by rackets, for example—but each neighborhood had a prevailing cultural connection to a particular type of delinquent behavior.

Racketville was characterized by the racket—that is, by organized criminal activity. Numbers games, off-track betting, loan sharking, narcotics selling, and organized prostitution were common crimes organized by the rackets. In Racketville, illegitimate opportunities were abundant, while legitimate opportunities were limited. These two types of opportunities were closely integrated, with crime having a business-like structure. Youths were under direct pressure to succeed. Opportunities to learn criminal values and techniques for carrying out crime were common. While upper-echelon positions in the rackets were not filled by juveniles, youngsters were groomed for the racket from a young age. Weak basic conventional norms tended not to encourage the use of the limited conventional means available to achieve success. Youths in Racketville had a value orientation that was the most criminal of the three neighborhoods, yet delinquent youth often were not directly involved in the rackets as juveniles. They were expected to be involved in the rackets as adults.

Slumtown was the most disorganized neighborhood studied. Gang fights—defined as group-based ritualized, systematic violence—were common. Such fighting was a preoccupation in Slumtown—a way of life. There were few means for obtaining monetary success of any kind, legitimate or illegitimate. Youths in Slumtown had high aspirations and created their own definitions of success in gang fighting. Specifically, in Slumtown, a youth's success goals revolved around reputation (or "rep")—attaining and maintaining one's reputation was paramount. These reputations were built and lost as the result of "heart," or toughness, displayed during fights. Crises and disputes with rival gangs were artificially created to maintain a level of violence required to attain status for gang members. While violence existed in Racketville and Haulburg, the delinquent subculture in Slumtown was organized around these conflicts. Conflict was a way to acquire prestige but was not a way to prepare for a criminal career. Violence was practiced not as a pathway to a criminal career but to attain immediate status, which was fleeting. Delinquents in Slumtown aspired to conventional careers but did not expect to attain them.

Haulburg was characterized by theft. Haulburg was, in many ways, a midpoint between Racketville and Slumtown. In Haulburg, there were partially limited conventional and criminal opportunities. The general orientation of Haulburg youths was more legitimate than in Racketville, which prevented systematic rackets from taking hold in Haulburg. Access to partial material success eliminated the need for a new avenue to gain success, such as gang conflict (as was seen in Slumtown). In Haulburg, criminal activity was only semi-organized but was stable. Material goods were valued in Haulburg. Reputations were made by thievery but not by violence. Haulburg youths with inadequate preparation for conventional careers could gain success through somewhat sophisticated criminal activity in the form of burglary, forgery, auto theft, and shoplifting. These theft-related activities were more organized and systematic in Haulburg than in Racketville and Slumtown, though the latter two neighborhoods also experienced theft. While theft was a way of life, violence was generally not permitted by neighborhood residents. Youths joined gangs in Haulburg primarily for short-term financial gain.

Unlike Cloward and Ohlin, Spergel does not consider drug users separately. Instead, Spergel considers drug users—retreatists, to use Cloward and Ohlin's term—as a subtype of each culture. Drug use can help youths ease the transition from delinquent to adult. Drug users need money to purchase drugs, and they may obtain funds through criminal or legitimate means. In all three neighborhoods, drug addiction led to low status among delinquents.

Gang Formation and Membership

In each neighborhood, the groups of youths (loosely termed "gangs") predated the membership of Spergel's interview subjects. The genesis of the gangs varied by neighborhood. In Racketville, groups

formed as a defense against other gangs. The formation of these gangs was (at least tacitly) supported by local adults, and the gangs were largely aimed at keeping undesirable groups out of the neighborhood. At the time of Spergel's research, there was little friction between groups within Racketville.

In Slumtown, groups were created to earn status and maintain neighborhood integrity. If Racketville gangs were defensive, Slumtown gangs were offensive in nature. Because conflict was required to maintain reputation in Slumtown, gangs were often engaged in violence with other gangs in Slumtown. The alliances and conflicts between groups were complex, with groups often moving into and out of conflict with one another.

In Haulburg, the reason for gang formation was rooted not in conflict but rather in a shared neighborhood experience: The original members had grown up together on the same street. The gangs in Haulburg were less organized than in the other two areas, but members did occasionally get into unorganized brawls with other groups. Most of these brawls were non-gang-related disputes and were limited to fist-fighting.

Gang membership was fluid in each of the neighborhoods, with a less-than-clear understanding of exactly who was in a gang and who was not. In Spergel's data, membership in a gang was not necessarily stable, and was not a once-and-for-all social fact. Furthermore, though success goals varied by neighborhood, youths joined gangs in each neighborhood to obtain success goals. Youths joined the gang in Racketville out of friendship or social interaction. Stable, long-term affiliations were forged with other members. These relationships could be leveraged later in life through the criminal rackets. In Slumtown, youths joined the gang out of a desire for reputation or prestige, not for friendship. Slumtown youths even changed gangs when the reputation of a gang changed. In Haulburg, gangs formed for the purpose of short-term financial gain and were characterized by limited but friendly interaction.

The Gap Between Success Goals and Opportunities

Spergel found that delinquents in all three areas had higher goals for their weekly wages than non-delinquents. That is, aspirations of delinquents were higher than non-delinquents. Delinquents in Racketville had the highest wage goals of any group in the study. In all three areas, delinquents had internalized both conventional and criminal success goals. There was little doubt among Racketville youths that they could obtain a fairly decent job. Even so, these youths felt they could get more money and prestige from the racket. In Slumtown, youths perceived no chance of having a decent job and were generally pessimistic about the future. Slumtown youths placed a greater value on lucky breaks than did youths in other areas. Haulburg youths generally expected to gain semi-skilled jobs with medium pay.

In general, there were large gaps between aspirations and expectations among Spergel's delinquent respondents as compared to non-delinquent respondents. Racketville had the smallest gap between aspirations and expectations, due largely to illegitimate means available. Racketville delinquents were not technically "deviant," since they were subjected to a normative process of induction and socialization into the rackets. In Slumtown, delinquents were deviant in that they were involved in violence. Slumtown youths perceived very few opportunities for obtaining monetary success. Slumtown and Haulburg youths were nearly equal in terms of the gap between aspirations and expectations. Haulburg youths perceived slightly more access to means for obtaining success, placing them between Slumtown and Racketville youths.

Conclusion

Spergel found numerous differences between the groups of delinquents in each of the neighborhoods he studied. These differences suggest that the dominant type of delinquent behavior within a neighborhood is sensitive to the neighborhood context. Spergel concluded his study by offering policy implications for this theory that included suggestions for improving access to livable housing, quality education, employment, and services in neighborhoods.

Troy Payne

See also Cloward, Richard A.: The Theory of Illegitimate Means; Cloward, Richard A., and Lloyd E. Ohlin: Delinquency and Opportunity; Cohen, Albert K.: Delinquent Boys; Kobrin, Solomon: Neighborhoods and Crime; Merton, Robert K.: Social Structure and Anomie

References and Further Readings

Agnew, R. (2006). *Pressured into crime: An overview of general strain theory.* Los Angeles: Roxbury.
Cloward, R. A. (1959). Illegitimate means, anomie, and deviant behavior. *American Sociological Review, 24,* 164–176.
Cloward, R. A., & Ohlin, L. E. (1960). *Delinquency and opportunity: A theory of delinquent gangs.* New York: Free Press.
Cullen, F. T. (1988). Were Cloward and Ohlin strain theorists? Delinquency and opportunity revisited. *Journal of Research in Crime and Delinquency, 25,* 214–241.
Merton, R. K. (1938). Social structure and anomie. *American Sociological Review, 3,* 672–682.
Spergel, I. (1964). *Racketville, Slumtown, Haulburg.* Chicago: University of Chicago Press.

SPITZER, STEVEN: CAPITALISM AND CRIME

According to Marxist criminologists such as Steven Spitzer, crime in capitalist societies cannot be fully understood unless criminologists comprehend the nature of the capitalist economic system, the class relations upon which that system rests, and the ways in which those class relations in turn reproduce the economic system. These relations determine to a large extent how crime is defined, who gets labeled and processed as "criminals," and the social response to crime.

Spitzer argues that understanding crime and deviance requires criminologists to reflect on who and what are considered to be deviant (1975, p. 638). Why, for example, is so little attention paid to corporate crime compared to street crime? How do we account for changing definitions of crime and deviance? Why are certain groups disproportionately singled out for processing by the criminal justice system? For Spitzer, the answers to such questions require criminologists to appreciate that crime and other forms of deviance are aspects of broader social conflict between the working and ruling classes in capitalist society.

Spitzer's perspective on the relationships between capitalism and crime draws upon the classical Marxist argument that the ruling class controls capitalist societies because they own and control the means of production, such as factories, businesses, and banks. This kind of ownership allows the ruling class to exploit the labor power of the working class in the sense that workers, while paid a wage for the value they create through their labor, also produce surplus value (or profit) which is appropriated by owners of the means of production. However, maintaining this exploitative relationship requires that the ruling class find ways to maintain social harmony. If the economic system is to be reproduced, the working class must believe in the legitimacy of a system that is inherently unjust. Following Marx, Spitzer argues that such legitimacy is maintained and reproduced through the "superstructure": institutions like the family, religion, media, and schooling that provide psychological and cultural resources to justify the economic system.

However, a central predicament of capitalism is that it creates "problem" populations, consisting of people who represent a threat to the functioning and growth of the economic system, and a corresponding need to protect the "assets, profits and all concrete forms of capital itself" (Spitzer, 1979, p. 187). Specifically, Spitzer argues that over time, capitalists increasingly rely upon technological developments and innovations to increase rates of profit. This process also causes workers to be displaced as machines, technology, and new production methods gradually replace the need for human labor. Thus, over the history of capitalism, more and more workers have become expendable and therefore problematic. For example, the unemployed, the poor, student radicals, and those who are marginalized pose a threat to the legitimacy of the system because their existence challenges the doctrine that capitalism is an economic arrangement based on equality of opportunity and condition. Spitzer argues that there are two general categories of such problem populations. First, *social junk* consists of individuals who have refused, are unable, or have failed to take part in the capitalist system, such as the aged, handicapped, drug addicts, or the mentally ill. As such, social junk do not represent a direct threat to the capitalism because they generally do not question it. Thus, they require regulation and containment, rather than more aggressive forms of control.

The second category, which he calls *social dynamite*, is more problematic in that these individuals directly challenge the legitimacy of capitalist relations of production and the coercion and dominance associated with those relations. Spitzer argues that such social dynamite is generally more youthful, alienated, and politically volatile than social junk and therefore subject to more formal control as represented by the criminal justice system (1975, p. 646).

Having laid the groundwork for a theory of the linkages between capitalism and crime, Spitzer discusses the methods by which social life is regulated to secure public order and a disciplined working class (Spitzer, 1979). Thus, the earlier capitalist state had been responsible not only for political governance but also for the development of highly bureaucratized regulatory systems such as the police, the courts, and the correctional systems that in turn are responsible for "processing" criminality. More recently, however, Spitzer maintains that such institutions have increasingly been subject to privatization and the logics of profit-making as evidenced by the growth, for example, of private policing (Spitzer & Scull, 1977).

While Spitzer's ideas are regarded as influential, they have been subject to two main criticisms. First, his emphasis on crime as a by-product of the class conflict inherent to capitalism does not address the reality that most crimes are intra-class. Second, the perspective does not address important questions of differences in criminal behavior and victimization between groups on the basis of race/ethnicity and gender, nor the ways in which these identities condition and shape criminal behavior and the social reaction to it.

Shahid Alvi

See also Bonger, Willem: Capitalism and Crime; Chambliss, William J.: Power, Conflict, and Crime; Colvin, Mark, and John Pauly: A Structural Marxist Theory of Delinquency; Marx, Karl, and Frederick Engels: Capitalism and Crime

References and Further Readings

Spitzer, S. (1975). Toward a Marxian theory of deviance. *Social Problems, 22*, 638–651.

Spitzer, S. (1979). The rationalization of crime control in capitalist society. *Contemporary Crises, 3*, 187–206.

Spitzer, S., & Scull, A. (1977). Privatization and capitalist development: The case of the private police. *Social Problems, 21*, 18–29.

STAFFORD, MARK C., AND MARK WARR: DETERRENCE THEORY

The deterrence doctrine has been a mainstay in criminological theory and criminal justice policy since the early writings of Jeremy Bentham and Cesare Beccaria in the 18th century. The doctrine entails the basic assumption that people refrain from crime or reduce their criminal involvement because they fear punishment (Gibbs, 1975). Two types of deterrence have been posited: (1) *specific deterrence*, meaning the reduction of criminal offending among those directly experiencing punishment, and (2) *general deterrence*, meaning the omission or reduction of crime among people in the general population indirectly experiencing punishment, that is, perceiving it as threatening.

The Reconceptualization

In 1993, Mark Stafford and Mark Warr reconceptualized the deterrence doctrine, arguing that these two types are not solely contingent on the direct or indirect experience of punishment. Punishment avoidance may also yield deterrence. Specifically, punishments imposed or avoided may be felt directly through personal experience or indirectly through the experiences of others. The direct (individual is punished) and indirect (individual perceives others being punished) experience of punishment presumably decreases an individual's inclination to offend by increasing the perception of punishment risk. Conversely, punishment avoidance presumably increases the likelihood of criminal offending by decreasing a potential offender's perception of punishment risk, regardless of whether avoidance is direct (individual avoids punishment) or indirect (individual perceives others avoiding punishment).

Implications for General and Specific Deterrence

According to Stafford and Warr's reconceptualization, general deterrence is influenced by knowledge of others who have been punished or avoided punishment. Specific deterrence is the result of personal experience with punishment or punishment avoidance. Two types of general deterrence are therefore possible, indirect experience of punishment and indirect experience of punishment avoidance; and two types of specific deterrence are possible, direct experience with punishment and direct experience with punishment avoidance (Paternoster & Piquero, 1995, p. 252). The influence of punishment on criminal involvement for all types is mediated by the perception of punishment risk: Experiencing punishment increases perceived risk, thus promoting general or specific deterrence, and avoiding punishment decreases perceived risk, thus undermining the possibility of general or specific deterrence.

Stafford and Warr claim that empirically estimating the influence of punishment on behavior via perceived risk is complex because people experience a mixture of punishment processes. An individual may have direct and indirect experience with punishment imposition and avoidance when contemplating crime. This mixture produces several possible outcomes, thus prompting the theorists to advocate for research that includes direct and indirect punishment imposition and avoidance because "punishment avoidance may do more to encourage crime than punishment does to discourage it" (p. 125).

Additionally, Stafford and Warr assert that specific and general deterrence are not likely to be equally important across populations (p. 128). They contend that criminal involvement among those with little direct experience of punishment imposition and avoidance is likely to involve general deterrence processes, while criminal involvement for those with direct experience of punishment imposition and avoidance is likely to involve specific deterrence processes. All types of punishment experiences should be included in research to disentangle the mixture of influences punishment may have on behavior. Those studies would require measuring an individual's perceptions of certainty and severity of punishments, perceptions of the certainty and severity of punishment for others within their immediate social network, self-reported criminal behavior that includes punishment imposition and avoidance, and estimates of others' criminal behavior, including reports of punishment imposition and avoidance (p. 133).

The Theoretical Contribution

Stafford and Warr extended deterrence theory by challenging two assumptions guiding research on deterrence. First, deterrence theorists had long assumed the direct experience or indirect threat of punishment was the only ingredient in the deterrence process. Thus, research neglected to inquire about punishment avoidance experiences. Stafford and Warr's revision incorporated punishment avoidance and treated it as analytically distinct from direct or indirect punishment imposition.

Second, general and specific deterrence presumably operated on two different populations. Law-abiding citizens were subject to general deterrence whereas criminal offenders were affected by specific deterrence. However, any person or population experiences a mixture of general and specific deterrence processes, rendering it necessary to study specific and general deterrence in combination rather than separately.

Besides challenging these two assumptions, a major contribution of the theory is that it integrated the deterrence doctrine into the larger framework of social learning theory. Stafford and Warr used the principles of vicarious learning and experiential learning to inform their reformulation of general and specific deterrence.

Empirical Support

Three studies tested the main tenets of Stafford and Warr's theory: Alex Piquero and Greg Pogarsky's 2002 study; Alex Piquero and Raymond Paternoster's 1998 study; and Paternoster and Piquero's 1995 study. The former two studies looked at the deterrent effect of various punishments on estimated intentions to drive after drinking, whereas the latter study investigated underage drinking and marijuana use. The study on alcohol and marijuana use involved a survey, distributed among 10th grade students (N = 1,422) in southeastern United States. It was completed twice, with the second questionnaire being administered 1 year later. The first study on drunken driving used a 62-item telephone survey of licensed drivers aged 16 or older (N = 1,686). Participants were selected by random digit dialing with samples stratified by population. The most recent drunken driving study included 250 students from a southwestern U.S. university who completed a questionnaire. The respondents included those who responded to an e-mail invitation to participate in a study about driving while intoxicated.

The drunken driving studies included various direct punishment experiences as independent variables: Piquero and Pogarsky used being stopped by police, whereas Piquero and Paternoster used being arrested by police and being pulled over at a roadside checkpoint. Indirect or vicarious punishment experiences were measured by friends' arrest in Piquero and Pogarsky's study, and by license suspension or jail time in Piquero and Paternoster's study. Piquero and Pogarsky calculated punishment avoidance as the percentage of people known by the respondent who had escaped detection while driving drunk, whereas Piquero and Paternoster calculated punishment avoidance as the respondent's estimate of how often those convicted of drunk driving get the prescribed punishment.

For the Paternoster and Piquero's study that focused on alcohol and marijuana use, direct punishment experience included being caught by police, being taken to the police station, being arrested, or taken to juvenile court. Punishment avoidance was measured by the frequency with which the respondent had avoided detection. Vicarious punishment and avoidance was not directly measured, but the frequency of friends' substance use was used as a proxy. Each of these studies included measurements of respondents' perceived certainty of punishment, with perceived severity of punishment included in the drunk-driving studies.

Besides punishment variables, these studies also considered factors that may influence behavioral outcomes through deterrence and non-deterrence mechanisms. For example, moral evaluations of illegal behavior were incorporated on the assumption that those who disapprove of drinking and driving are more likely to perceive that formal sanctions will be imposed, thus promoting deterrence. Thus, in addition to asking about one's own moral attitudes toward drinking and driving, Piquero and Paternoster asked about friends' moral attitudes as a way to ascertain a vicarious analog of one's own moral beliefs. Similarly, informal surveillance and closeness of emotional bonds with conventional others were used as indicators of likely informal sanctions. More specifically, Paternoster and Piquero posited that conventional others would reinforce the risky nature of alcohol and marijuana use, thus monitoring the respondent's behavior. As a final example, Piquero and Pogarsky included impulsivity since research had shown that it influences how individuals weigh future outcomes and thus may interfere with the perceptual processes associated with deterrence.

The findings reported in these studies were mixed in terms of their support of Stafford and Warr's theory. For example, Paternoster and Piquero found that personal and vicarious punishment imposition and avoidance increased perceived punishment risk, that general and specific deterrence work concurrently, but that a person's prior experience will influence which type of deterrence has a stronger effect. Such findings are consistent with the theory, but they also found that the direct experience of punishment led to additional offending, which contradicts the theory. Consider Piquero and Paternoster's findings, which also provide mixed support for the theory. They found that personal experience with punishment avoidance reduced the perceived risk of punishment; but vicarious punishment avoidance decreased drunken driving intentions, whereas the vicarious imposition of punishment increased those intentions. Moreover, personal experience with punishment had no influence on drunken driving intentions. Finally, Piquero and Pogarsky found that direct and indirect punishment avoidance experiences decrease perceptions of punishment risk and relate positively to offending, in support of Stafford and Warr's theory, but prior punishment and vicarious punishment experiences encouraged future intentions to drive after drinking.

Critiques of the Reconceptualization

Tests of Stafford and Warr's theory are inconclusive, but this may be due to the limitations of each study. Piquero and Pogarsky as well as Piquero and Paternoster relied on secondary data, resulting in potential measurement issues. For example, Paternoster and Piquero were unable to analyze vicarious punishment and punishment avoidance experiences. Of concern in the second study is the operationalization of a respondent's personal experience with punishment; being stopped at a roadside checkpoint may not suffice for a punishment experience, unless it is followed by arrest or conviction. Although Paternoster and Piquero used original data, they also measured personal experience with punishment in a potentially problematic way—being pulled over by a police officer. Further, only Paternoster and Piquero used self-reports of actual behavior. The other two studies used behavioral intentions measured in the context of hypothetical scenarios. The issue here is that intentions in such scenarios may not necessarily correspond to actual behavior in real-world circumstances.

These studies found that experiences with punishment, or the avoidance thereof, have some, although mixed influence on the likelihood of actual or projected offending. However, punishment may not be the main determinant of the perceived certainty of punishment. Other researchers posit that perceptions may also be influenced by extralegal sanctions, low self-control, and beliefs favorable to crime, and association with delinquent peers (Cullen & Agnew, 2006). For this reason, some argue that the theory should be incorporated into an integrated theory of crime. Certainly, future studies should use original longitudinal data, investigate the influence of alternative punishment criteria, and extend data collection to other populations. Until such research is done, the empirical status of Stafford and Warr's reconceptualization of deterrence remains an open question.

Stephanie D'Auria and Kirk Williams

See also General Deterrence Theory; Gibbs, Jack P.: Deterrence Theory; Nagin, Daniel S., and Raymond Paternoster: Individual Differences and Deterrence; Perceptual Deterrence; Williams, Kirk R., and Richard Hawkins: Deterrence Theory and Non-Legal Sanctions

References and Further Readings

Cullen, F. T., & Agnew, R. (2006). Reviving classical theory: Deterrence and rational choice theories. In F. Cullen & R. Agnew (Eds.), *Criminological theory: Past to present* (pp. 404–414). New York: Oxford University Press.

Gibbs, J. P. (1975). *Crime, punishment, and deterrence.* New York: Elsevier.

Paternoster, R., & Piquero, A. (1995). Reconceptualizing deterrence: An empirical test of personal and vicarious experiences. *Journal of Research in Crime and Delinquency, 32,* 251–286.

Piquero, A., & Paternoster, R. (1998). An application of Stafford and Warr's reconceptualization of deterrence to drinking and driving. *Journal of Research in Crime and Delinquency, 35,* 3–39.

Piquero, A., & Pogarsky, G. (2002). Beyond Stafford and Warr's reconceptualization of deterrence: Personal and vicarious experiences, impulsivity, and offending behavior. *Journal of Research in Crime and Delinquency. 39,* 153–186.

Pogarsky, G., & Piquero, A. (2003). Can punishment encourage offending? Investigating the "resetting" effect. *Journal of Research in Crime and Delinquency, 40,* 95–120.

Stafford, M., & Warr, M. (1993). A reconceptualization of general and specific deterrence. *Journal of Research in Crime and Delinquency, 30,* 123–135.

STANKO, ELIZABETH A.: GENDER, FEAR, AND RISK

Elizabeth A. (Betsy) Stanko is one of the key researchers who has focused on the causes and consequences of women's risk and fear of crime over the last two decades. She is a self-described "radical feminist criminologist" (Stanko, 1998b, p. 57), who believes that she sometimes cares "too passionately about the issue of violence against women" (Stanko, 1998a, p. 35). In 1997, she earned her Ph.D. at the City University of New York (Stanko, 2004). Interestingly, she did not start out her career steeped in feminism but rather came to it after spending time researching criminal justice system actors (e.g., prosecutors and police), setting up a shelter for battered women, and teaching a course on women and crime in the 1970s—finding that there was not much research on women's experiences committing or being victimized by crime. In addition, her personal experience with sexual harassment contributed to her desire to do research and policy-related work that was relevant to women's experience of powerlessness and invisibility (Stanko, 1998a, 2007).

Since 2003, Stanko has worked for the London Metropolitan Police, currently as the head of research and analysis. But she spent much of her career as a sociologist working in academe both in the United States and in Britain. She went into her new role in the practitioner world in hopes of using her extensive knowledge on women's experiences with crime and fear to help shape police practices in the field—to practically bridge the divide between academe and the real world (Stanko,

2004, 2007). She has authored many scholarly articles and chapters and two books focusing on how gender affects perceived risk and fear of crime. Much of her work has focused on qualitative interviews with women, and some men, about their personal safety. This entry discusses her influential arguments regarding these issues.

One of the most consistent findings in fear of crime research for decades has been that women are more afraid than men. Indeed, much scholarly research has focused on trying to explain women's greater fear in light of the fact that men are much more likely to be victimized by violent street crime. Stanko has argued that the structural, cultural, and physical context women experience in a male-dominated society easily explains their heightened fear of crime. Specifically, she argues that women's "ordinary experiences" (Stanko, 1985, p. 2) lead them to believe and worry every day that they are at risk of being victimized by men in many situations. She believes that violence is an "ordinary part of life," and that people regularly adjust their lives to manage the risk and danger they face both inside and outside the home (Stanko, 1990, p. 5). In fact, many of these adjustments are so routine that they are considered common sense (e.g., locking doors and avoiding unsafe areas of the community). She first made this argument about the ordinariness of violent experiences for women in her influential book *Intimate Intrusions*, where she noted, "To be a woman—in most societies, in most eras—is to experience physical and/or sexual terrorism at the hands of men" (p. 9).

She continually has argued that women, in particular, are more at risk because of their powerless position in society. For example, she believes that male violence is an important component in the social control of women generally, and so women face unique experiences with danger that are not an issue for men. Specifically, she has noted that "the reality of sexual violence is a core component of 'being' female" in male-dominated societies, and she argues that women's fear recognizes this condition (Stanko, 1994b, p. 122). In essence, although women are not always victimized, fear of victimization by men is a constant for women throughout their lives, because they are always at risk of being victimized especially by intimates and acquaintances, although women are not *always* afraid. Women's experiences, of course, vary based on their environmental, economic, and familial contexts, and so their level of fear and the amount and type of protective measures vary as well. Nevertheless, women's fear and the precautions they take are legitimately based in their life contexts rather than irrational, as many scholars who focus on "stranger danger" have argued.

According to Stanko (1985, 1992, 1994a, 1994b), most criminologists ask the wrong questions in their effort to understand female fear of crime, leading them to believe that women should not be as afraid as they often are. She argued that focusing on public crimes as measures of victimization (like those reported in official crime and victimization statistics) points to males being hurt more by violence but ignores the important and probably more frequent private experiences that women have with problematic male behavior, much of which can be categorized as violent by women. Women are more likely to be victimized by people close to them, and these experiences do not always become known to the police. These "hidden" experiences include male behaviors that clearly would be classified as crime if the police were aware of them (e.g., rape, battering, and incest) and those that might not be crimes but are nevertheless threatening to women (e.g., whistles, sexual comments, and unwanted touching). The latter experiences, she has termed "little rapes," pointing to the continuum of male violence that women experience in their daily lives, as opposed to the stereotypical street violence that some believe is the cause of women's fear (Stanko, 2000, p. 154).

Importantly, Stanko also has argued that when women are victimized, academics and practitioners ask why *they* are victimized rather than asking why *men* hurt them, thereby putting the focus and blame on the woman (Stanko, 1985, 2002). This approach to the problem, then, puts the personal and societal responsibility for women's victimization on the women rather than men. People ask questions like why was she out at night by herself, why was she wearing those skimpy clothes, why did she choose to stay with her abusive husband, and why did she keep the victimization a secret? For example, Stanko (1998b) has noted that police advise women regarding ways to keep themselves safe, assuming that women have the power and ability to prevent crimes by men, rather than focusing police efforts on finding ways to keep men from hurting women.

This concentration on women's responsibility for men's behavior then leads women to *feel* that they are accountable for protecting themselves from men and they then try to predict which men that they encounter in their daily lives will be violent, including not just strangers but more often acquaintances, friends, and intimates. This heightened awareness leads women to see every man as a potential victimizer and makes women feel vulnerable and more afraid. It also leads them to take more precautions to protect themselves, although they may more easily control their risk of victimization by strangers than by intimates (e.g., by avoiding certain geographical areas, staying inside at night, listening for footsteps, or examining bushes when they walk by).

Notably, she has argued that when women feel threatened by men, they often keep it to themselves and question their own feelings (and sometimes feel shame) because society considers it normal for men to act unruly toward them (e.g., make sexual comments and tease them). Women wonder whether something is wrong with them rather than with the men who are doing the behaviors that make them feel uncomfortable. Stanko has argued that men who commit violent crimes against women are assumed to be abnormal; yet, such crimes are just the extreme end of typical male behavior, and many men who commit these crimes are "ordinary" guys (Stanko, 1985, 1990, 1994a, 1994b, 2002). According to Stanko (1985, 2002), when women are victimized, criminologists and others tend to separate them into a category different from other women, as if victimization was not a condition of being a woman. Again, this points to the general problem that she believes plagues society and scholarly research—the focus on male street crime as atypical rather than as one piece of a larger continuum of negative behaviors that can have a hurtful impact on women and therefore lead to heightened fear of crime.

In her current role, working with practitioners who struggle with how best to respond to people impacted by crime, Stanko is able to marry the academic world of scientific information with the practical reality of policing and work to improve system responses to women's experiences with men's violence. It is a strong possibility that her influential impact in the academic criminological field will now be expanded into the practical world and make a major mark there as well. Her efforts may eventually lead to a reduction in women's fear of crime by increasing societal and practitioner understanding of the causes. This increased understanding may then affect how these entities respond to women's negative experiences with men. By changing careers, Stanko is among the few scholars who have taken their influential ideas into the "real world" in hopes of prompting positive changes in the criminal justice system.

Jodi Lane

See also Rape Myths and Violence Against Women; Russell, Diana E. H.: The Politics of Rape

References and Further Readings

Rand, M., & Catalano, S. (2007). *Criminal victimization, 2006.* Washington, DC: U.S. Department of Justice.

Stanko, B. (2004). A tribute to 10 years of knowledge. *Violence Against Women, 10,* 1395–1400.

Stanko, B. (2007). From academia to policy making: Changing police responses to violence against women. *Theoretical Criminology, 11,* 209–219.

Stanko, E. A. (1985). *Intimate intrusions: Women's experience of male violence.* London: Routledge & Kegan Paul.

Stanko, E. A. (1990). *Everyday violence: How women and men experience sexual and physical danger.* London: Pandora.

Stanko, E. A. (1992). The case of fearful women: Gender, personal safety, and fear of crime. *Women & Criminal Justice, 4,* 117–135.

Stanko, E. A. (1993). Everyday violence and experience of crime. In P. J. Taylor (Ed.), *Violence in society* (pp. 169–180). London: Royal College of Physicians of London.

Stanko, E. A. (1994a). The case of fearful women: Gender, personal safety, and fear of crime. *Women & Criminal Justice, 4,* 117–135.

Stanko, E. A. (1994b). Challenging the problem of men's individual violence. In T. Newburn & E. A. Stanko (Eds.), *Just boys doing business? Men, masculinities and crime* (pp. 32–45). London: Routledge.

Stanko, E. A. (1996). Women, crime, and fear. *The Annals of the American Academy of Political and Social Science, 539,* 46–58.

Stanko, E. A. (1998a). Making the invisible visible in criminology: A personal journey. In S. Holdaway & P. Rock (Eds.), *Thinking about criminology* (pp. 35–54). Toronto, ON: University of Toronto Press.

Stanko, E. A. (1998b). Warnings to women: Police advice and women's safety in Britain. In S. L. Miller (Ed.), *Crime control and women: Feminist implications of criminal justice policy* (pp. 52–71). Thousand Oaks, CA: Sage.

Stanko, E. A. (2000). Naturalising danger: Women, fear and personal safety. In M. Brown & J. Pratt (Eds.), *Dangerous offenders: Punishment and social order* (pp. 147–163). London: Routledge.

Stanko, E. A. (2002). Ordinary experiences. In Y. Jewkes & G. Letherby (Eds.), *Criminology: A reader* (pp. 251–261). London: Sage.

STARK, RODNEY: DEVIANT PLACES

Rodney Stark contributed greatly to the field of criminal justice and to the theory of deviant places versus deviant people with his work titled "Deviant Places: A Theory of the Ecology of Crime." Before this work is discussed, it is necessary first to look back at the history of studies on crime and place, starting with social disorganization theory.

Previous Research

Despite the original theory being over 50 years old, social disorganization theory remains one of the most influential contextual theories of crime and delinquency. Clifford Shaw and Henry McKay developed social disorganization theory. They first built their idea on Burgess's concentric zone theory. Burgess outlines the growth of the city of Chicago by describing five concentric zones. Zone I is the central business district and the industrial district; this is the center of the city. Zone II is the zone of transition, also known as the slum area. This zone is in transition from being a residential area to a business and industry area. Zone III is a residential area known as the zone of working men's homes. This zone consists of working-class families. Zone IV is known as the residential zone. This zone is residential, but it is nicer than zone III. Zone V is known as the commuters' zone. This zone is also residential. It is generally located outside the city limits and is considered to be the suburb. Shaw and McKay used this information in conjunction with the data they collected to develop social disorganization theory.

Shaw and McKay collected data from juvenile court records. They plotted the addresses of the juvenile delinquents they obtained through court records on a map of the city of Chicago. They found that the highest rates of delinquency were in the zones closest to the center of the city and declined as one moved further out from the center of the city. They also discovered that rates of delinquency were highest in these areas despite different racial and ethnic groups inhabiting the areas over time. They found as these racial/ethic groups departed the center of the city and moved to zones farther from the center of the city, their rates of delinquency fell. This suggests that it is the area that people live in and not the individuals themselves, that is the cause of crime.

In the areas with high rates of delinquency, juveniles were left to do what they wanted with little supervision or support. This occurred because in these areas there was a breakdown in conventional institutions such as families, churches, and schools. As a result, there was little or no informal social control. The lack of control can all be attributed to certain common characteristics in these areas, including rapid urban growth, a high population turnover, ethnic heterogeneity, and poverty/low socioeconomic status (Lilly et al., 2007). It is because of these conditions that there is a breakdown in conventional institutions that lead to a lack of social control, which in turn leads to a higher rate of delinquency. Because of rapid urban growth, ethnic heterogeneity, a high population turnover, and poverty, residents of these areas are not able to come together and have common values to maintain effective control of their neighborhood (Kornhauser, 1978).

Although Shaw and McKay's work has remained very important, during the 1970s and 1980s the study of crime tended to become more individually focused in that criminologists were more concerned about individual causes of crime rather than looking at contextual theories to explain crime. However, in the late 1980s contextual theories of crime—that is, theories that emphasized that kinds of places mattered—began to re-emerge as viable explanations of crime. Stark's work contributed to this resurgence in the study of contextual theories.

Deviant Places

The unique aspect of Stark's perspective is that he combines past criminological works that support contextual theory and creates 30 propositions producing a theory of ecology of crime. He incorporates not only past contextual works but also works centered on individuals. In so doing, he shows that different types of approaches can be intertwined to support contextual theories. In his 30 propositions, he included such theories as differential association, collective efficacy, social disorganization, concentric zone, deterrence, and social bond.

Although Stark has 30 separate propositions, they build off of each other. The first nine propositions discuss dense and crowded neighborhoods. He discusses how the more dense a neighborhood is, the more social interactions there will be. With an increase in social interactions, non-criminal kids in the neighborhood will have more interactions with deviant kids, compared with a less dense neighborhood. His second proposition discusses moral cynicism. Stark theorizes that when people live in a dense neighborhood, they cannot keep up appearances as well as people in a less dense neighborhood. Because appearances are not kept up, these people are more exposed to conduct that would normally be kept behind closed doors. As a result, there is a greater likelihood that people are not credible as positive role models in dense neighborhoods. These first two propositions are unique in the contextual theory literature. In this article, Stark is able to combine social interactions of individuals with the result it will have on the deviance of an area. He was also able to combine the concept of a dense neighborhood with the concept of moral cynicism.

In these first nine propositions, Stark also discussed crowding of homes in a neighborhood and how that would affect the deviance level of the neighborhood. He states that crowding in homes leads to people spending more time outside; spending more time outside leads to less supervision of children. When children are unsupervised, they will potentially have poor school achievement and, as a result, less of a stake in conformity. Crowding within the home can also lead to more conflict with family members, which can result in weak attachments to family and less of a stake in conformity.

Stark also discusses neighborhoods with mixed land use in his propositions. In his 10th and 11th propositions, he states that neighborhoods with mixed land use foster opportunity for deviance due to the displacement of more retail outlets. He also theorizes that with mixed land use, there are more places for people to congregate outside.

In his 13th proposition, Stark points out that neighborhoods with mixed land use have a high rate of transience. With more transience, there are fewer attachments among residents in the neighborhood. Transience also weakens neighborhood organizations and institutions since people who are transient are less likely to form ties to neighborhood organizations. When there are fewer attachments among residents and weakened organizations, there will be less formal and informal social control. Also in neighborhoods where people are more transient, it is more difficult to determine who does not belong in the area, again reducing social control.

In his 16th and 17th propositions, Stark points out that neighborhoods that are poor, have mixed land use, and have a higher rate of transience tend to be dilapidated as well. Stark then notes that dilapidation leads to social stigma. In proposition 18, Stark observes that, not only does dilapidation cause social stigma for a neighborhood, but high rates of deviance in a neighborhood create social stigma as well.

According to Stark, people who live in a stigmatized neighborhood have less of a stake in conformity. This occurs because they have less to lose if they are caught being deviant. Another problem with stigmatized neighborhoods is that people who are successful and positive role models tend to move out as soon as possible. Additionally, people who could potentially be positive role models do not move *into* stigmatized neighborhoods. Therefore, the neighborhood as a whole is stigmatized and has less successful people to serve as positive role models.

Proposition 22 through proposition 24 are concerned with demoralized people living in stigmatized neighborhoods. When Stark discusses the demoralized, he defines them as people who are not able to function properly in society. Such people include the mentally ill, chronic alcoholics, and the mentally handicapped. According to proposition 23, the more demoralized people there are in a neighborhood, the more victims there will be. This occurs because there will be more opportunity to victimize. Further, the more demoralized people there are in a neighborhood, the less chance there is for people to succeed; therefore, they have a lower stake in conformity.

In his 25th proposition, Stark asserts that stigmatized neighborhoods will have more lenient law enforcement. With more lenient law enforcement in a neighborhood, there will be an increase in moral cynicism. This occurs because people see crime taking place with no consequences, and thus they lose respect for conventional moral standards.

In propositions 27 through 30, Stark explains the progression of what occurs when there is lenient law enforcement in a neighborhood. In short, lenient law enforcement leads to more crime and deviance—a reality explained by applying deterrence theory and opportunity-based theories. When there is less of a likelihood of being caught for a crime, more crimes will transpire. Also, lenient law enforcement draws deviant people to that neighborhood. When there are large numbers of deviant people in a neighborhood, there will be a higher visibility of crimes and more opportunity to engage in criminal activity. The more visible crime and deviance is in a neighborhood, the more rewarding and safe it will appear for offending purposes.

Conclusion

The 30 propositions described above make up Stark's theory of the ecology of crime. Not one of these propositions stands alone. Rather, they flow together to make a progression of what occurs in deviant places. In his article, he emphasizes the importance of studying not only individual explanations of crime but contextual explanations of crime as well.

Since Stark has published his insights, research has assessed his theory. Steven Barkan tested the household crowding effect on area crime rates. This corresponds with the first eight propositions in Stark's article. Barkan found support for this part of Stark's theory. His analysis revealed that household crowding is positively related to crime. In other words, neighborhoods with more household crowding have more crime than neighborhoods with less household crowding. Findings such as this support the conclusion that continued attention should be paid to contextual theories of crime—theories showing that place matters as far as an explanation of crime.

Beth Ellefson

See also Brantingham, Patricia L., and Paul J. Brantingham: Environmental Criminology; Crime Hot Spots; Eck, John E.: Places and the Crime Triangle; Physical Environment and Crime; Shaw, Clifford R., and Henry D. McKay: Social Disorganization Theory; Wilcox, Pamela, Kenneth C. Land, and Scott A. Hunt: Multicontextual Opportunity Theory

References and Further Readings

Barkan, S. E. (2000). Household crowding and aggregate crime rates. *Journal of Crime and Justice, 23,* 47–64.

Kornhauser, R. (1978). *Social sources of delinquency: An appraisal of analytic models.* Chicago: University of Chicago Press.

Lilly, R. J., Cullen, F. T., & Ball, R. A. (2007). *Criminological theory: Context and consequences* (4th ed.). Thousand Oaks, CA: Sage.

Sampson, R. J., & Groves, W. B. (1989). Community structure and crime: Testing social disorganization theory. *American Journal of Sociology, 94,* 774–802.

Shaw, C. R., & McKay, H. D. (1969). *Juvenile delinquency and urban areas* (2nd ed.). Chicago: University of Chicago Press.

Stark, R. (1987). Deviant places: A theory of the ecology of crime. *Criminology, 25,* 893–909.

STEFFENSMEIER, DARRELL J.: ORGANIZATION PROPERTIES AND SEX SEGREGATION IN THE UNDERWORLD

Darrell J. Steffensmeier's "Organization Properties and Sex Segregation in the Underworld" is one of the first criminological theories to hypothesize that organizational properties of offender groups can account for the roles, activities, and offending behaviors of women. A seemingly ubiquitous finding in criminological research on offending is the gender gap in serious crime, combined with what Steffensmeier calls "institutionalized sexism in the underworld." However, Steffensmeier posits that this is a variable to be explained, and "offer[s] a series of propositions and hypotheses linking female access to crime groups to their structure and methods of operation" (p. 1010).

To do so, Steffensmeier draws from both criminological opportunity theories and sociological theories of labor market stratification. His goals are to explain the following:

> 1) The *existence* of sex-segregation in organized criminal enterprise, resulting in a) the exclusion or underrepresentation of women in organized crime and b) their allocation to less-valued roles within crime groups when they are allowed to participate; and 2) the *variability* of sex-segregation across the spectrum of organized crime activities. (p. 1010, emphasis in the original)

While the former goal has received the most attention from scholars in the intervening years since publication, the latter is perhaps equally or more significant in its import.

Steffensmeier's explicit concern is with crime that is organized for joint economic gain, rather than individual crime and/or that which is based on noneconomic motives. He begins by specifying the *typical* nature of women's offending. First, he notes, it tends to be either individualistic in nature rather than organized, or in peripheral or supportive roles to male partners. Second, female crime groups are characterized as less stable, more obscure, and less serious and lucrative than male crime groups. Moreover, Steffensmeier documents the consistent finding that gender segregation is prevalent in such organized crime groups.

Comparable to sociological explanations of gendered labor market segmentation—which reject human capital accounts for organizational explanations for such patterns—Steffensmeier seeks explanation for sex segregation in the organizational practices of crime groups. Specifically, he argues, "The fact that crime in its more organized and lucrative dimensions is a virtual male phenomenon is in large part attributable to three related factors: homosocial reproduction, sex-typing, and the task environment of the crime" (p. 1012). Homosocial reproduction refers to the tendency within groups for in-group preferences and out-group antipathy to affect decision making, resulting in exclusionary practices. As crime groups tend to be dominated numerically by men, women are denied access altogether or are relegated to less lucrative and more peripheral roles.

Similarly, sex-typing is used to define women as less capable of participating in certain activities within criminal enterprises. For example, as Steffensmeier explains, "male offenders see much criminal work as too *hard* or too heavy, or too dangerous for women . . . [and] also see women as not as *capable* or not as skilled, or not as *stable*" (p. 1013, emphasis in the original). Likewise, "women are viewed as gossip-prone, emotional, and untrustworthy" (p. 1014). The cumulative effect is that women are blocked from opportunities to build sustained criminal connections. Finally, Steffensmeier argues that the task environment of such crime is one that is shaped by the threat of both criminal justice intervention and the use of violence. As a consequence, "a premium is placed on attributes such as trust and reliability and on physical characteristics such as strength and 'muscle'" (p. 1014)—all attributes that women are defined as lacking. As a consequence, women are either excluded entirely from such criminal enterprises, or their roles and activities are either limited or sexualized.

Numerous studies support Steffensmeier's account of how and why women are excluded from or marginalized in criminal enterprises. However, an important but often overlooked facet of Steffensmeier's theory is his account of the "*variability* of sex segregation across the spectrum of organized crime activities" (p. 1010, emphasis in the original). Like scholars who examine the impact of gender within the formal labor market, Steffensmeier argues that the organizational context of criminal groups affects the extent that homosocial reproduction and sex-typing take place, and thus the degree and nature of women's exclusion and marginalization.

Specifically, he argues that women's roles will vary "along five dimensions or organizational properties":

1) The *uncertainty* of the environment facing crime organizations; 2) the *modus operandi* of criminal enterprise, i.e., whether crime organizations accomplish by fraud or stealth rather than force or fear;

3) the *rationality* of crime organizations in achieving illegal profits; 4) the *complexity* or extent which crime organizations are organized; and 5) the degree of *professionalization* of crime organizations. (p. 1017, emphasis in the original)

Steffensmeier argues that sex segregation will be more marked in illicit groups that require physical strength or violence, as these are defined as prototypically male characteristics. In addition, when such groups face competition or threat from other groups, have exclusively economic goals (rather than in combination with social and/or political goals), or exhibit greater organizational complexity and professionalization, women's marginalization will be heightened.

For example, increased uncertainty and greater rationality in goals will lead to more in-group preferences and out-group antipathy to increase a sense of security in operations; likewise, a "rational" focus may result in the utilization of women in sex-typed ways deemed most effective to the enterprise; and increased structural complexity and professionalization will result in greater hierarchical differentiation in the division of labor, which again will be shaped by homosocial reproduction and sex-typing. Steffensmeier proposes that the factors outlined in his propositions will be both additive and interdependent in their effects.

To date, few studies have applied these propositions to examine the variability in the extent and nature of gender stratification in illicit networks. Such organizational level analyses offer great promise for enriching our understanding of the processes that create, sustain, and undermine the exclusion and marginalization of women in criminal networks and organized crime groups.

Jody Miller

See also Adler, Freda: Sisters in Crime; Miller, Jody: Gendered Social Organization Theory; Simon, Rita J.: Women and Crime; Simpson, Sally: Gender, Class, and Crime; Steffensmeier, Darrell J., and Emilie Andersen Allan: A Gendered Theory of Offending

References and Further Readings

Acker, J. (1990). Hierarchies, jobs, bodies: A theory of gendered organizations. *Gender and Society, 4,* 139–158.

Britton, D. M. (2000). The epistemology of the gendered organization. *Gender and Society, 14*, 418–434.

Maher, L. (1997). *Sexed work: Gender, race, and resistance in a Brooklyn drug market.* New York: Clarendon Press.

Miller, J. (2001). *One of the guys: Girls, gangs, and gender.* New York: Oxford University Press.

Mullins, C. W., & Wright, R. (2003). Gender, social networks, and residential burglary. *Criminology, 42,* 911–940.

Peterson, D., Miller, J., & Esbensen, F.-A. (2001). The impact of sex composition on gangs and gang member delinquency. *Criminology, 39,* 411–439.

Reskin, B. F. (2000). Getting it right: Sex and race inequality in work organizations. *Annual Review of Sociology, 26,* 707–709.

Steffensmeier, D. J. (1983). Organizational properties and sex segregation in the underworld. *Social Forces, 61,* 1010–1032.

Steffensmeier, D. J., & Terry, R. (1986). Institutional sexism in the underworld: A view from the inside. *Sociological Inquiry, 56,* 304–323.

Zhang, S., Chin, K.-O., & Miller, J. (2007). Women's participation in Chinese transnational human smuggling: A gendered market perspective. *Criminology, 45,* 699–733.

STEFFENSMEIER, DARRELL J., AND EMILIE ANDERSEN ALLAN: A GENDERED THEORY OF OFFENDING

The 1960s cultural revolution, including the women's movement, focused attention and created a spate of research on female offending. Although it had long been known that male offending surpassed female offending in frequency and seriousness, theory testing in criminology rarely involved female samples and theories of female offending were not yet well developed. Due to the changing social context, however, questions about the origins of female offending and whether they differ from those of males became central to sociological criminology in the 1970s. Scholars debated and empirically tested whether gender-neutral traditional theories of criminology or gender-specific theories could better explain female offending.

To develop a middle-range theory of gender and offending, Darrell J. Steffensmeier and Emilie Andersen Allan exhaustively reviewed theory and empirical research relating to female and male offending. *Middle-range theory* integrates general theories of behavior with empirical findings on group differences so as to better understand their origin and nature (Merton, 1957). Middle-range theory aims to integrate empirical observations and established social facts to drive theory building that generates propositions to be further tested. Middle-range theories converge into grander theoretical explanations as the subfield develops. Steffensmeier and Allan's gendered paradigm draws on causal forces identified by traditional crime theories but also integrates theory and research on gender, pointing to the importance of the *organization of gender* and biological sex differences as a starting point for future inquiry.

Steffensmeier and Allan's gendered paradigm draws on traditional crime theories (e.g., social learning, control, rational choice), feminist theories, and extant research to explain gender differences in the frequency and nature of crime—that is, the greater offending rates of males, particularly for more serious violent crimes and lucrative property crimes. Gendered approaches are most needed to understand serious offending where gender differences and gendered influences are greatest. The paradigm also addresses contextual differences in female and male offending, such as women's greater victimization of intimates and family; their tendency to work alone or, if in organized crime groups, to play secondary or sexual roles; and female motivations and pathways that involve victimization by men, romantic involvements with men, and protection of children and relationships.

Steffensmeier and Allan's approach encompasses both general as well as gendered influences in elucidating the complexities of criminal behavior. This perspective takes the approach that the broad contours of traditional criminological theories can explain variation in both female and male offending, but that gendered concerns mediate how criminogenic factors shape the form and frequency of offending. The organization of gender mediates some of the effects of broad social forces on offending.

The gendered paradigm explains differences in the form and frequency of women's and men's offending as derived from the organization of gender, as well as physical and sexual differences. The organization of gender refers to gender differentiated identities, roles, and commitments and the institutions and social arrangements that construct gender and, consequently, shape motives and opportunities for offending.

Steffensmeier and Allan identify five key elements of the organization of gender that increase the probability of prosocial responses by females and antisocial responses by males and condition gender differences in motives and opportunities for offending. They are (1) gender norms and focal concerns, (2) moral development and affiliative concerns, (3) social control, (4) physical strength and aggression, and (5) sexuality. These factors impact the willingness (motives) and ability (opportunities) of women and men to commit various crimes. After briefly describing the five areas, their applicability to understanding patterns of female and male offending are highlighted.

The Organization of Gender and Criminal Involvement

Gender Norms and Focal Concerns

Gender norms are unwritten, though commonly understood, guidelines defining appropriate behavior, beliefs, and attitudes for females and males. Gender norms are enforced socially and through internalized gender role socialization. Two powerful focal concerns orient femininity norms and impose greater taboos against female crime: nurturant role obligations, and female beauty and sexual virtue. These focal concerns shape criminal opportunities, motivations, and risk-taking preferences and strategies both in general and by type of deviant response.

Women are socialized to be responsive to the needs of others and attentive to the physical and emotional well-being of people they care about (Haynie et al., 2007). Enactment of nurturing roles and obligations offers informal rewards and reinforces gender-related identities. Women are expected to establish and maintain kin and neighborly relationships, accept familial obligations such as child or elder care, act in a submissive, accommodating manner, and attend to their physical appearance while protecting their sexual virtue. These relational concerns tend to constrain

and shape opportunities for illicit activity. In contrast, males are rewarded for acting independently and being adventurous, competitive, and unemotional. Men are expected to be brave, strong, aggressive, rational, independent, adventurous, and dominating.

Stereotypes of women as caring, submissive, and domestic are incompatible with crime, whereas definitions of masculinity—being ingenuitive, aggressive, or a risk taker—are more consonant with what is criminal. Expectations that women should be more guarded of their sexuality and concerned about physical appearances contrast with expectations that men should be sexually adventurous or even aggressive and concerned with displaying symbols of success or status. These differing gendered expectations regarding sexuality shape the availability and acceptability of deviant roles. Women's criminal roles tend to capitalize on female sexuality (e.g., prostitution, decoy) whereas men's criminal roles are more varied.

Moral Development and Affiliative Concerns

Closely related to gender norms, gender differences in moral development restrain women from violence and criminal behavior harmful to others. Women are socialized to an "ethic of care" that encourages women to be more responsive to the needs of others and to fear separation from loved ones. Men, however, are exposed to an "ethic of independence," conditioning men toward status-seeking, even at the expense of others. Gendered affiliative concerns are such that women act as health sentries, especially for their sons and husbands/boyfriends, and they produce or transmit moral culture.

Affiliative concerns not only inhibit women from undertaking harmful criminal activities but also shape women's motives, such as violence to protect a loved one or criminal activity to preserve a relationship. Examples include buying drugs for a partner going through withdrawal, a physical altercation with a rival love interest of her partner, or murder/assault to protect a child from abuse (Schwartz, 2007). In contrast, men's ethic of independence encourages competitiveness, aggression, and status seeking. At the extremes of the seriousness spectrum, men predominate instrumental violent offenses such as profit-motivated kidnapping, extortion, bank robbery, dog fighting, and the trafficking/smuggling arms, drugs, human body parts, or endangered species (Schwartz et al., 2009). The male code of the streets is based on intense masculinity norms, and violence often results from challenges to one's reputation (Anderson, 1999).

Social Control

Females' behaviors are often more closely monitored and informally sanctioned, restricting female freedoms, associations with deviant others, and opportunities for illicit activities. Moreover, stricter supervision may also decrease women's willingness to commit crime by reducing their appetite for risk (or channeling it toward sustaining valued relationships) and increasing attachment to family or other authority figures and prosocial peers. Males, however, are not as closely supervised and spend more unstructured time with peers, increasing their ability and willingness to engage in risky behaviors, particularly those oriented toward status or competitive advantage.

Physical Strength and Aggression

On average, men are larger than women, have greater endurance, and possess more upper body strength. More controversial are sex differences in aggression and in the capacity for violence derived from hormonal or other physical features of men versus women. These physical differences may influence the frequency and nature of female and male offending because involvement in lucrative, violent, or organized crime often requires physical prowess for committing crimes, protection, enforcing contracts or agreements, and recruiting and managing criminal associates.

Equally important as actual physical differences, however, are social and cultural *perceptions* of women as less powerful, lacking the potential for violence, and more vulnerable to victimization. These social and cultural interpretations of average sex differences may limit women's willingness to engage in serious crime or hamper men's willingness to involve female partners in crime. Real or perceived physical differences may help to account for women's solo or secondary roles in crime, their disproportionate involvement in minor property offenses, and their defensive use of violence against partners and aggressive use of violence against smaller children.

Sexuality

Females may utilize their sexuality for criminal gain such as in prostitution or as a tool to gain entry into criminal groups. Female offenders may also use gender stereotypes by playing up their sexuality to dupe males, such as by appearing sexually available in order to set up a male robbery victim (Miller, 1998). Traditional notions of femininity and sexuality offer criminal opportunities for some and place limitations on others. For example, females are typically supervised more closely (e.g., by parents, partners) to guard against sexual exploitation or victimization but this monitoring may lessen girls' opportunities for deviance. Sexual and strength differences also increase the likelihood that females will align themselves with males for protection (e.g., as co-offenders).

The Context of Offending

Gender norms, biological differences, and gendered risk-taking preferences influence the *context of offending*—the circumstances and nature of the crime including the setting, victim, purpose of offense, and injury/loss. Therefore, females who commit violent crimes are more likely than males to target people they know and less likely to use weapons or cause severe injury. Female property offenders are less likely to confront their victims (e.g., embezzling versus robbery), and to steal lesser amounts and are more likely to justify their theft as for their family or spouse.

Research highlights how social arrangements related to gender and gendered inequalities shape motives and opportunities and, consequently, patterns of offending. First, gendered social relations and dominant gender norms disadvantage females in terms of recruitment into crime groups and upward mobility within crime groups (Steffensmeier, 1983). Within crime groups, women tend to function in one of two roles: sexual roles that use or exploit female sexuality as a resource (e.g., prostitution, to gain entry into a crime group by aligning with a male) or "cover" roles in which women conceal criminal activity because they are viewed less suspiciously and as less threatening or dangerous or can take advantage of males by playing on gender stereotypes (e.g., appearing sexually available to set up a robbery victim).

Crime groups tend to be male-dominated and controlled. The principle of homosocial reproduction suggests the powerful tend to reproduce themselves, particularly in highly stratified settings (Steffensmeier, 1983). Males, who control the underworld (as well as the upperworld), tend to choose other males with whom to work, associate, and do business. Existing gender norms and stereotypes further limit female opportunities for involvement in lucrative and more organized crime because male offenders typically view criminal work as too difficult or dangerous for women or as too degrading for them. Males are also reluctant to work with women because they are viewed as less skilled, more emotional and less trustworthy, and less capable of deploying violence (Steffensmeier, 1983; Steffensmeier & Terry, 1986). Existing gender stratification and gender norms often preclude women from developing skills and criminal social networks necessary for lucrative property crimes (Steffensmeier, 1986; Steffensmeier & Ulmer, 2005). Rather women are placed in stereotypical gender roles within crime groups, which do not often lead to career advancement.

Lisa Maher and Kathleen Daly's research on women's roles in the crack cocaine drug market provides an excellent illustration of how gender norms and cultural perceptions of physical strength and aggression limit and shape patterns of female offending. Based on ethnographic fieldwork conducted over 3 years, they conclude that the drug trade is highly gender stratified, with women sometimes playing lesser roles such as "advertising" the drug, copping for others, or selling drug accessories; infrequently acting as street-level drug dealers; and almost never occupying high-level owner/manager positions.

Gender stereotypes of women as less threatening provided opportunities tangential to the drug trade for women as service providers to male patrons from outside the community. Less often, women were used temporarily as street dealers in high-risk situations because it was believed that they could operate under less suspicion from authorities. In this way, managers hoped to play on the "gendered blindspots" of law enforcement. Generally, though, women were perceived to lack the toughness and capacity for violence required for success in the drug trade. Females could not often develop criminal social networks or enhance

their skills, maintaining the skewed sex ratio in the underworld. Although a few women became dealers through their roles as wives/girlfriends of distributors, more often males were selected into higher level positions by other males, sometimes their kin—a process of homosocial reproduction.

Female opportunities are somewhat more numerous in less organized, more amateur minor property crime operations (Steffensmeier & Terry, 1986). In their roles as girlfriends or wives, women are provided criminal opportunities for supportive roles as drivers, lookouts, and holders of stolen property, drugs, or weapons. Women also have unique advantages in cashing stolen or forged checks, welfare fraud, shoplifting, and other offenses that take place in the course of female-typical activities such as shopping or banking. This accounts for the narrower gender gap for minor property crime.

Conclusion

Steffensmeier and Allan's gendered paradigm values contributions of traditional theories but also takes seriously gendered aspects of social life and social change to advance the field's understanding of both male and female offending patterns. Steffensmeier and Allan systematized the proliferation of research on female crime and integrated it with existing scholarship on gender and on crime to develop a model that better explains females' relatively greater involvement in minor property and violent crimes compared to males' much greater involvement in serious violence and lucrative property crime. This theory has significantly enhanced understanding of the gender-crime relationship, one of the strongest identified by criminologists.

Future research calls for empirical tests that operationlize and test variables from Steffensmeier and Allan's gendered approaches. Intersectionalities between gender and race, ethnicity, and disadvantage also should be articulated and explored. There is much value as well in qualitative work focused on local contexts of female and male offending that reveal how gender and gender-related arrangements and conditions continue to powerfully influence offending patterns.

Jennifer Schwartz

See also Messerschmidt, James W.: Masculinities and
Crime; Miller, Jody: Gendered Social Organization
Theory; Simpson, Sally S.: Gender, Class, and Crime;
Steffensmeier, Darrell J.: Organization Properties and
Sex-Segregation in the Underworld; Steffensmeier,
Darrell J., and Jeffery T. Ulmer: The Professional Fence

References and Further Readings

Anderson, E. (1999). *Code of the Streets: Decency,
violence and the moral life of inner cities.* New York:
W. W. Norton.

Haynie, D., Steffensmeier, D. J., & Bell, K. (2007).
Gender and serious violence: Untangling the role of
friendship sex composition and peer violence. *Youth
Violence and Juvenile Justice, 5,* 235–253.

Maher, L., & Daly, K. (1996). Women in the street-level
economy: Continuity or change? *Criminology, 34,*
465–491.

Merton, R. K. (1957). *Social theory and social structure*
(Rev. ed.). New York: Free Press of Glencoe.

Miller, E. M. (1986). *Street woman.* Philadelphia: Temple
University Press.

Miller, J. (1998). Up it up: Gender and accomplishment
of street robbery. *Criminology, 36,* 37–66.

Schwartz, J. (2007). Comparing women and men who
kill: Gender differences in homicide offending. In
M. DeLisi & P. Conis (Eds.), *Violent offenders:
Theory, research, public policy, and practice*
(pp. 119–140). Boston: Jones and Bartlett.

Schwartz, J., Steffensmeier, D. J., & Feldmeyer, B.
(2009). Assessing trends in women's violence via data
triangulation: Arrests, convictions, incarcerations, and
victim reports. *Social Problems, 56,* 494–525.

Steffensmeier, D. J. (1983). Sex-segregation in the
underworld: Building a sociological explanation of sex
differences in crime. *Social Forces, 61,* 1010–1032.

Steffensmeier, D. J. (1986). *The fence: In the shadow of
two worlds.* Totowa, NJ: Rowman & Littlefield.

Steffensmeier, D. J., & Allan, E. (1996). Gender and
crime: Toward a gendered theory of female offending.
American Review of Sociology, 22, 459–487.

Steffensmeier, D. J., & Terry, R. (1986). Institutional
sexism in the underworld: A view from the inside.
Sociological Inquiry, 56, 304–323.

Steffensmeier, D. J., & Ulmer, J. T. (2005). *Confessions of
a dying thief: Understanding criminal careers and illegal
enterprise.* New Brunswick, NJ: Aldine Transaction.

Zhang, S., Ko-Lin, C., & Miller, J. (2007). Women's
participation in Chinese transnational human
smuggling: A gendered market perspective.
Criminology, 45, 699–733.

STEFFENSMEIER, DARRELL J., AND JEFFERY T. ULMER: THE PROFESSIONAL FENCE

Following in the tradition of Edwin Sutherland's *The Professional Thief* and William Chambliss's *Box Man,* Darrell J. Steffensmeier's *The Fence: In the Shadow of Two Worlds* and Steffensmeier and Jeffery T. Ulmer's *Confessions of a Dying Thief: Understanding Criminal Careers and Criminal Enterprise* provide a close-up view into the dynamics of criminal careers and the social organization of criminal enterprise, as experienced by a veteran thief and fence (stolen-good dealer) and his network of key associates. Sam Goodman, the key informant for the research, was a longtime thief, fence, and quasi-legitimate businessman. He had a criminal career that spanned 50 years, beginning in his mid-teens and ending with his death when he was in his 60s. The study is based on continuous close contact with Sam over several decades, multiple interviews with his network of associates in crime and business, and an intense series of interviews with him shortly before he died.

These two works together—*The Fence* and *Confessions*—represent the most significant treatments of "fencing stolen goods" in criminological literature. But equally important, they also represent two of the most significant works in criminology over the past quarter century for their substantial contributions to research and theory on crime and criminal careers and for their detailed accounts of underworld criminal operations and enterprise and how the criminal underworld has changed since Sutherland's classic treatment in *The Professional Thief.*

Before addressing the "fencing" side of *The Fence* and *Confessions,* it is important to first recognize some unique contributions and the broader significance of these works. First, beyond their descriptions of fencing, these two works offer detailed and vibrant accounts of the ins and outs of running burglary crews, the rewards and pitfalls of crime, the importance of networking and developing "spider webs" of contacts for success in criminal enterprise, the ways that people seek out and create crime opportunities (rather than simply assuming that people passively respond to opportunities), and the many intersections and blurred boundaries between legitimate and illegitimate activity that often exist in criminal enterprise. Second, they provide a rich depiction of the criminal underworld, including its stratification or pecking order, elements of racism and sexism in its organization, and its changes throughout the 20th century. Third, *Confessions* spells out four basic categories of thieves and burglars, along with the stages of career development they typically go through: *greenies* or *rookies* (stage 1), *in-between* or *roughhouse* burglars (stage 2), a small subset of *decent* or *good* thieves (stage 3), and *semiretired* or *moonlighters* (stage 4).

Fourth, these works provide one of the most intimate and detailed descriptions of the criminal career of a persistent and active offender, accounting for more than 50 years of his life and criminal career up to his death. Through these accounts, *The Fence* and *Confessions* make a fifth contribution by offering keen insight into the sources and complexities of criminal persistence/desistance, commitment, turning-points and transitions, specialization, displacement, and other life-course processes in criminal careers. At the same time, they also challenge mainstream perceptions about criminal careers and methodological approaches for studying them. For example, Steffensmeier and Ulmer illustrate that offenders often do not completely desist from crime but instead "moonlight" or drift in the gray areas between conventionality and deviance. However, they also argue that even the most persistent career criminals are rarely deviant in all areas of their lives. Furthermore, *Confessions* returns several times to the issue of whether offenders generally specialize or exhibit versatility in crime, arguing that specialization varies by age/career stage, criminal skill level, and place in the underworld.

Methodologically, Steffensmeier and Ulmer also send a clear message to students and scholars illustrating the usefulness of long-term, in-depth qualitative interviews (compared to one-shot surveys) for obtaining more nuanced and richer pictures of criminal offending and criminal careers, particularly in light of the fact that some of the most noteworthy elements of Sam's criminal career remained hidden from the interviewers for decades until a final series of intense deathbed interviews.

Last, *Confessions* provides an integrated learning-opportunity-commitment life-course framework that incorporates elements of key criminological theories and that is illustrated in a reader-friendly way for both students and scholars through captivating real-life examples offered in Sam's personal accounts and then tied back to criminological theory more explicitly through the authors' commentary on Sam's narratives. This framework extends and elaborates Richard Cloward and Lloyd Ohlin's opportunity theory in particular, treating the concept of opportunity in a more agency/choice–centered way by emphasizing how skilled, committed offenders often actively seek out or create opportunities for learning and performing criminal skills. *Confessions* also delineates in a meaningful way the key dimensions of what constitutes access to learning (civil, preparatory, technical) and performance (tools, targets, contacts) opportunities for pursuing crime and how these opportunities may vary by age, gender, race/ethnicity, and place in society.

Fencing

Perhaps the most substantial and most specific contribution of *The Fence* and *Confessions* is in the information these works provide about the trade in stolen goods and fences who are at the heart of it. Fencing—the crime of buying and reselling stolen merchandise—is one of the links that binds theft to the larger social system. Without receivers and dealers to dispose of stolen property, thieves would have to rely on their own connections, and both the costs and the risks of crime would increase substantially. The fence in turn provides opportunities for interested people to buy goods at less than market prices.

Steffensmeier and Ulmer explain that fencing remains a rather poorly researched area in criminology, for several reasons. First, it often wears the cloak of legitimate business and is carried out in a rational, businesslike manner, so that it has few of the qualities traditionally associated with crime. Second, because fencing is a crime with low visibility and is conducted in secrecy, researchers have directed their attention to more visible crimes such as theft, or to violent crimes against persons for which statistics are available. Third, the cloak of secrecy and fences' typical practice of maintaining a legitimate "front" (i.e., a legitimate business as a cover for illegal activity) make detailed investigation difficult.

The Business of Fencing

The Fence and *Confessions* describe fencing as an enterprise requiring resourcefulness, charisma, ingenuity, and a good grasp of market practices and economic competition. Along with prevailing market conditions, pricing norms are determined by what is fair, and a sense of justice is developed based on the risks borne both by the thief and by the fence. Fences must pay a fair price so that thieves will come back to them again with stolen goods. However, because of their greater experience and knowledge, fences tend to dominate thieves in the pricing of stolen goods. The thieves often need money quickly, have few options other than to agree to the fence's offer, and are under pressure to get rid of the stolen merchandise. Fences also often use chicanery to pad their profits by duping thieves (especially small-time thieves) about quality, quantity, and price.

These studies document that "wheelin and dealin" fences (i.e., professional dealers) rely on extensive networks, developed through word-of-mouth, referrals, and sponsorship by underworld figures. Major fences also play an active role in coaching thieves on techniques of theft and product identification, and in developing long-term relationships with buyers. Rewards of fencing include money, reputation in the criminal community, excitement, a sense of mastery over one's life, and pride in being a sharp businessman. Sam, and dealers like him, justify their fencing involvement by claiming that the fence is not the same as a thief, does little harm to the victims of theft, does not differ much from legitimate businesspeople, is able to operate only with the support of legitimate people (including the police), breaks no more rules than most people, and does a lot of good for others.

All fences are by definition businesspeople: they are middlemen in illegitimate commerce, providing goods and services to others, regardless of whether they operate from a legitimate business or rely solely on individual resources. Although a few operate independent of any business front, most fences are simultaneously proprietors or operators of a legitimate business, which provides a cover or front for the fencing. Businesses most often favored are those having a large cash flow (e.g., coin and gem shop, secondhand store, auction house, pawn shop, restaurant) and the flexibility to set one's own hours (salvage yard, bail-bonding). For some fences, the trade in stolen goods is the major source of income and the central activity of their business portfolio. For others, fencing is either a profitable sideline to their legitimate entrepreneurship or one of a number of illicit enterprises they are involved in.

Contrary to some accounts, the typical fence is hardly a "respectable businessman." Instead, according to Steffensmeier and Ulmer (2005), the typical fence is characterized by one or more of the following: (1) prior criminal contact or background in criminal or quasi-legal activities, such as theft, hustling, or the rackets in general; (2) operation of a quasi-legitimate business such as a secondhand discount store, salvage yard, an auction house, a foundry, or a bail-bonding business; (3) affinity with the underworld, such as ongoing business interactions and leisure activities (e.g., poker games, drinking beer) with established members of the underworld to acquire the skills and contacts necessary to run a fencing business; and (4) business interactions that may require force or the threat of "getting rough" to enforce prior agreements and keep others from taking advantage of the fence in business deals.

The Professional Fence and Other Types of Stolen Goods Handlers

By the late 18th and early 19th century, with the growth of fencing operations accompanying industrialization, it was commonplace for students of fencing to distinguish among receivers according to their criminal intent and scale of operations (Colquhoun, 1800; Crapsey, 1872). Jerome Hall subsequently distinguished professional dealers from other "occasional" or "lay" criminal receivers based on whether they intend to resell the stolen property or plan to use it for personal consumption and based on the regularity or frequency with which they purchase stolen goods. Paul Cromwell and colleagues added that receivers could be further differentiated by the scale or volume of purchases of stolen property and by the level of commitment to purchasing stolen goods. Subsequently, Steffensmeier and Ulmer (2005) proposed that criminal receivers and other buyers of stolen goods may be differentiated by (1) whether they deal directly with thieves, (2) the frequency with which they purchase stolen property, (3) the scale or volume of purchases of stolen property, (4) the purpose of purchase (for personal consumption or resale), and (5) the level of commitment to purchasing stolen property.

Steffensmeier and Ulmer delineate four major groupings of criminal receivers or handlers of stolen goods, including the late-20th-century emergence of online or cybercrime fences involved in dealing stolen goods on the Internet. The four major groupings include the following:

1. The *amateur or "Joe Citizen" buyer* refers mainly to the "ordinary Joe Blow" who once in a while buys stolen goods to use himself or to peddle to one of his friends or close acquaintances. Amateur buyers tend to exhibit the lowest level of commitment and experience in buying stolen goods.

2. The *occasional or part-time dealer* is an in-between dealer, the guy who buys off-and-on and then peddles it out of his store or maybe on the street or at an auction, and may include drug dealer fences and neighborhood hustlers who occasionally dabble in low-level fencing as a sideline activity within his primary occupation or business.

3. The *professional fence* refers to the "regular" or "bigger" dealer whose buying and selling stolen goods is more frequent and lucrative than low-level fencing and is "a main part of what he does" (e.g., Sam Goodman throughout the height of his criminal career in fencing). Professional fences also include so-called master fences, which are characterized in *Confessions of a Dying Thief* as referral fences or as the fence's fence, who do not deal directly with thieves but instead stay behind the scenes and deal only with other fences and underworld contacts.

4. The *online buyer and seller* fences stolen goods through websites. This type has accompanied the rise in popularity of online auctions (like eBay.com) and is a fast-growing distribution path that emerged in the late 1990s. The online trade in stolen goods overlaps the other forms of criminal receiving and is also a major avenue for self-fencing stolen goods today.

In *The Fence*, Steffensmeier further elaborates that fences or dealers can also be distinguished along other dimensions. One dimension is their vulnerability to law enforcement based on how much they are able to conceal their fencing trade by their legitimate business identity—that is, whether the trade in stolen goods is *fully covered, partly covered,* or *uncovered* by their legitimate business front. The second dimension is their product specialization based on the kinds and variety of stolen goods they handle. At one pole is the *specialist,* who handles only certain kinds of goods such as auto parts, jewelry, or antiques; at the other pole is the *generalist,* who will buy and sell virtually anything a thief offers.

Fence's Relationship to Theft

The fence does play a primary role in the marketing of stolen property, but *The Fence* and *Confessions* explain that this role is often exaggerated by commentators and law enforcement officials. The old saying "if no fences, no thieves" assumes that thieves are not autonomous in their stealing behaviors and that theft is largely attributable to the existence of fences. However, this also ignores the involvement of a variety of other participants in an illegal trade. Instead, as these books delineate, other participants that support the exchange of stolen goods include merchants who are tempted to purchase stolen goods at cheap prices in order that they may sell at a higher profit; budget-conscious consumers who are often willing to buy stolen goods "no questions asked" with little encouragement; victims of theft who are willing to forego prosecution once their stolen goods have been restored to them or they have received compensation; insurance companies and private detective agencies that protect the fence from public or legal reaction to the theft, either by diluting the rightful owner's desire to pursue those responsible by providing compensation, or by cooperating with him for the return of stolen property; and, notably, cooperating authorities who, in exchange for muted investigation, are receptive to good deals on merchandise or are willing to accept information offered by fences to help recover particularly important merchandise and to arrest thieves. Official complicity of some kind is often a requisite for lengthy career involvement in fencing stolen goods, without which professional fences would be unable to "deal" regularly and over a period of time.

Conclusion

Both *The Fence* and *Confessions* are part of a long and rich tradition in criminology of studying people who approach crime as their work or as a business. As in conventional lines of entrepreneurship, access is facilitated by having a background and skills conducive to the trade or line of criminal work. These skills, in turn, are taught and transferred by way of tutelage and sponsorship. *The Fence* and *Confessions* also show (1) how conventional career concepts such as apprenticeship, work satisfaction, and networking are applicable to crime as work and (2) the parallels between legitimate and illegal enterprise. Planned theft, racketeering, running a bookmaking operation, and fencing stolen goods involve many of the same laws of supply and demand and the same fundamental assumptions that govern entrepreneurs in the legitimate marketplace. Indeed, the similarities appear sufficiently strong, as *Confessions* documents, that it is common for seasoned thieves, racketeers, and illicit entrepreneurs like Sam Goodman to view themselves as businessmen and to perceive little difference between their actions and the behaviors of legitimate entrepreneurs.

Both *The Fence* and *Confessions* contribute to a real-life understanding of crime and the underworld, including the meaning and elaboration of crime skills, how contacts are made, how older career offenders may moonlight at crime while mainly engaging in conventional work, and how offenders justify their criminality. Additionally, *Confessions* discusses the underworld as a "field" in Pierre Bourdieu's sense and elaborates how career property offenders and criminal entrepreneurs may be located in and committed to the underworld as a field of status, striving, and achievement. Finally, although criminologists know quite a bit about the "careers" of low-level and ordinary offenders who have typically slowed or exited crime by age 30 or 40, *The Fence* and *Confessions* provide a rare glimpse into the criminal career of a persistent active offender and into the inner workings and practices of theft (including the trade in stolen goods) and the underground economy. Both works make substantial scholarly contributions to criminology, while also being very reader friendly.

Ben Feldmeyer

See also Convict Criminology; Shaw, Clifford R.: The Jack-Roller; Criminal Career Paradigm; Shover, Neal: Great Pretenders; Sutherland, Edwin H.: The Professional Thief

References and Further Readings

Bradley-Engen, M. S. (2009). *Naked lives: Inside the worlds of exotic dance.* Albany: SUNY Press.
Bourdieu, P. (1977). *Outline of a theory of practice.* London: Cambridge University Press.
Cloward, R. A., & Ohlin, L. E. (1960). *Delinquency and opportunity: A theory of delinquent gangs.* New York: Free Press.
Colquhoun, P. (1800). *A treatise on the commerce and police of the River Thames.* London: Printed for Joseph Mawman.
Crapsey, E. (1972). *The nether side of New York.* New York: Sheldon and Co.
Cromwell, P., Olson, J., & Avary, D. (1996). Who buys stolen property? A new look at criminal receiving. In P. Cromwell (Ed.), *In their own words: Criminal on crime* (pp. 47–56). Los Angeles: Roxbury.
Hall, J. (1952). *Theft, law, and society* (2nd ed.). Indianapolis, IN: Bobbs-Merrill.
Klockars, C. (1974). *The professional fence.* New York: Free Press.
Matsueda, R. L., Piliavin, I., Gartner, R., & Polakowski, M. (1992). The prestige of criminal and conventional occupations: A subcultural model of criminal activity. *American Sociological Review, 57,* 752–770.
Steffensmeier, D. J. (1986). *The fence: In the shadow of two worlds.* Totowa, NJ: Rowman & Littlefield.
Steffensmeier, D. J., & Ulmer, J. T. (2005). *Confessions of a dying thief: Understanding criminal careers and criminal enterprise.* New Brunswick, NJ: Aldine Transaction.
Steffensmeier, D. J., & Ulmer, J. T. (2006). Black and white control of numbers banking in black communities, 1970–2000. *American Sociological Review, 71,* 123–156.
Ulmer, J. T. (2000). Commitment, deviance, and social control. *Sociological Quarterly, 41,* 315–336.

STINCHCOMBE, ARTHUR L.: REBELLION IN A HIGH SCHOOL

In the classic study *Rebellion in a High School,* Arthur L. Stinchcombe presents his theory of expressive alienation, which he defines as the psychological attitude that underlies rebellious behavior. The work has helped criminologists understand deviance and rebellious behavior among adolescents in high school. Strain theorists Robert Merton and Albert Cohen influenced Stinchcombe, whose work contributes to an understanding of youth delinquency, particularly in schools. Stinchcombe describes in detail the main tenets of expressive alienation, and he highlights the structural, cultural, and psychological underpinnings of this attitude.

Study and Method

Rebellion in a High School presents the results of a study that was completed in a California high school with approximately 1,600 students. The school was located in a logging and sawmill town. Stinchcombe completed 6 months of anthropological observation followed by a survey of the student population. Seventy questions measured attitudes toward the school and toward future careers and also assessed levels of deviance and rebelliousness.

Rebellion and Expressive Alienation

Stinchcombe defines rebellion as a form of deviance. As such, it cannot occur without the prior existence of a norm. School authorities determine school norms pertaining to processes such as attendance, participation, and assignments. Stinchcombe measures rebellion with an index of three indicators: skipping school with a gang of kids, receiving a flunk notice in a non-college-prepatory class, and/or being sent out of class by a teacher (p. 12).

Stinchcombe highlights three main sources of expressive alienation. The first of these is social structural. Rebels perceive a low degree of articulation between future status and the present activity in the school. In other words, from the perspective of the student, school activities do not seem to prepare them for future jobs. For example, future manual workers are alienated by school because it does not teach them the skills that they will need in the labor market.

The second source of expressive alienation is cultural. Rebels do not identify with the system of symbols that are used by adults to describe adolescents; they identify with adult symbols related to

their class perspective. For example, for students who are bound for the bureaucratic and professional labor market, good grades and respect from teachers are self-affirming. Alternatively, future working-class laborers and housewives look to dating, smoking, and car ownership to evaluate both current and future status.

The third source is psychological. Rebels have internalized the system of success—the rewards and privileges that govern both the school and the professional labor market. However, they do not possess the means to achieve middle-class jobs, and so they reject the social world that evaluates them in terms of middle-class success. As a result, expressive alienation replaces the success orientation.

Attitudinal Manifestations

The psychological state of expressive alienation has four attitudinal manifestations. The first state is short-run hedonism. For hedonists, "the world is interpreted as a place in which it does not pay to sacrifice existing pleasures for uncertain goals. . . . [It is] indicated by an inclination not to see the connection between work and future rewards" (pp. 17–19). A primary indicator of short-run hedonism was boredom in class.

The second state is negativism. Negativism is an attitude that rejects all conforming behavior and all moral attachment to legitimate institutions. Conformists and people with attachments to legitimate institutions are rejected and disrespected. This attitude was most common in rebels who reported a combination of the indicators of rebellion (i.e., skipping and flunking, being sent out and skipping).

The third state is alienation from the status system. Inherent in any formal organization is a status system established by authorities. A status system involves (1) a group of judges, (2) a set of standards, (3) a recognized process according to which people present themselves for judgment, (4) a set of arrangements by which the judges receive information on which to base judgment, and (5) a set of status rewards allocated by judges (pp. 26–27). A rebel is alienated from the status system when any or several of these elements are, or appear to be, unfair or illegitimate. In addition to the status system that the authorities impose is the one that students use to rank among themselves. Rebels are more alienated from both the authoritative status system of the school and the status system of the student community.

The fourth state is autonomy. Rebels deny the morality of the school. The status system in the school is considered to be illegitimate and a demand for autonomy is a positive moral claim against the school. In many cases, autonomy can be found in a delinquent clique or subculture which defines itself in opposition to the school and its systems of meaning. This solidarity can be used to garner rights in the adult community with which rebels identify. "The delinquent subculture, then, claims for adolescents the personal autonomy ordinarily associated with adulthood" (p. 41).

Conclusion

Stinchcombe's distinctive contribution is the "expressive alienation" concept. Expressive alienation results from the structure of the school and explains adolescent rebellion in terms of alienation from adult authorities. Importantly, it is the *anticipated* social class of students—as opposed to the social class of parents—that explains rebellious behavior and the underlying expressive alienation attitude. Expressive alienation is a response to what many criminologists call "strain" and anticipated Robert Agnew's contribution to strain theory, where crime and deviance are not necessarily tied to class or culture, but are responses to self-generated norms based on perceived failure, actual or anticipated.

Cathy Borck

See also Agnew, Robert: General Strain Theory; Cloward, Richard A., and Lloyd E. Ohlin: Delinquency and Opportunity; Cohen, Albert K.: Delinquent Boys; Merton, Robert K.: Social Structure and Anomie; Sutherland, Edwin H.: The Professional Thief

References and Further Readings

Agnew, R. (1992). Foundation for a General Strain Theory of crime and delinquency. *Criminology, 30,* 47–87.

Cohen, A. K. (1955). *Delinquent boys: The culture of the gang.* New York: Free Press.

Merton, R. K. (1938). Social structure and anomie. *American Sociological Review, 3,* 672–682.

Stinchcombe, A. L. (1964). *Rebellion in a high school.* Chicago: Quadrangle Books.

SUDNOW, DAVID: NORMAL CRIMES

A normal crime is a crime in which the features of the criminal and the features of the crime align in such a way to fit preconceived notions about who commits what crimes and how. As opposed to stereotypes of crimes and criminals, the system of normal crimes is organized around the penal codes and formal classifications of crimes, as well as around the routine experiences of those who use the codes to organize their everyday work—namely those involved in the criminal justice system. This system of conceptions of crimes and schemas of criminal behavior then organize the behavior of those in the judicial system. The concept of the normal crime, as first described by David Sudnow in his classic 1965 article in *Social Problems,* "Normal Crimes: Sociological Features of the Penal Code in a Public Defender Office," has been adopted into a wide variety of criminological and sociological understandings of routine court activity and other arenas where a "typical" expectation is taken among many, sometimes competing, actors.

Normal Crimes in the Public Defender Office

In this study of meaning and practice in a public defender's office, Sudnow demonstrates how crimes and criminals become "normal" and how the designation of normal affects the way in which the various constituents of the court community act toward a given case. In this analysis, he engages in dialogue with two groups of criminologists and sociologists who critique the ways in which penal codes are analyzed in research. The first group, which he terms the revisionist perspective, seeks to create categories of crimes that are enriched by information about motive and background on the criminal. The second group, with which he initially aligns himself, seeks to understand penal codes as the way in which the workers of the criminal justice environment orient themselves toward their work. Critiquing this second perspective as "more promissory than productive," Sudnow wants to expand on John Kitsuse and Aaron Cicourel's position regarding how to use official statistics and understand how legal officials use criminal codes in their daily work.

To understand the everyday meanings of the penal code, Sudnow analyzes the practices of the public defender's office. In his county of analysis, over 80 percent of cases are pled out, whereby defenders settled the case by pleading guilty instead of going to trial. The defenders usually plead guilty to charges that are lesser than the charges with which they were originally charged, lesser here implying a shorter or more lenient sentence. Often, however, these lesser charges are neither "necessarily included lesser offense" nor explicitly "situationally included lesser offense." Necessarily included charges are those that are implicit in the greater charge; assault with a deadly weapon, for example, necessarily includes the lesser charges of weapons possession and simple assault. Situationally included charges are those that are committed by the way in which the greater charge occurred; Sudnow uses the example of a child molestation situationally being associated with an adult loitering in a school yard. It is not necessary to the crime of child molestation that an adult loiter in a school yard, but instead it is a common way in which child molesters find their victims.

In this example of the child molestation charge and the lesser charge of loitering in a school yard, Sudnow found that many cases of molestation were pled down to the loitering charge regardless of the mode of the molestation. The defendant may or may not have been in or around a schoolyard before, during, or after the crime occurred, but because loitering is a typical feature of such a crime, it became an expected lesser charge when pleading down molestation charges. While loitering might be a situationally included lesser charge of child molestation, it might be a part of the plea despite the actual facts of the crime, that is, whether or not the offender did loiter in a school yard. Sometimes, however, the lesser charges are merely potentially related to the crime, and could be a lesser charge related to a necessarily included charge. Burglary does not always necessarily include theft, though petty theft is often the lesser charge for burglary; child molestation does not always situationally derive from loitering, though loitering is often a lesser charge for molestation. Sudnow seeks to answer why some situationally included, or potentially necessarily included, but factually inaccurate charges, become the lesser plea.

The first part of this answer is that the actors involved in the criminal court, specifically public defenders, have mutually come to a schema of who commits certain crimes. The background of a person—including race, class, gender, education level, and criminal record—combines with the kind of crime and patterns in the ways those crimes are typically committed to produce an expected template of criminal and crime. As Sudnow states, "I shall call *normal crimes* those occurrences whose typical features . . . are known and attended to by the [public defender's office] for any of a series of offense types the [public defender's office] can provide some form of proverbial characterization" (1965, p. 260, emphasis in the original). There are six components of this concept: (1) a focus on characterizations of offense types, (2) the features attributed to offenders and offenses are not important for the type of charge but factor into the plea arrangements, (3) those features are specific to the community in which the public defender operates, (4) routine offenses constitute the normal type of crime, (5) geographic and socio-economic variables play into the status of normal crime, and (6) mastery of what is considered a normal crime is an important part of the socialization of the public defender.

The second part of Sudnow's answer as to why factually inaccurate charges end up being the charge to which an offender pleads guilty focuses on the practices of the public defenders and their relationship to other members of the criminal court community. Public defenders have a series of goals, usually in line with the goals of the prosecutors, judges, police, and so on. Their goal is not to prove the innocence of their clients, nor even to provide good defense at trial. Instead, the mutual goals of public defenders and prosecutors are to avoid trial and get a guilty plea out of the offender, all while making sure the offender is somehow held accountable for his or her actions while not making punishment so onerous as to cause the offender to reject the plea deal. The scheme for normal crimes thus guides what is an acceptable offer of a plea bargain, as each crime has a typical lesser charge depending on whether or not the offender fits a given profile of a typical criminal. Sudnow shows how a public defender might delineate between a regular criminal and a crime of opportunity in deciding which type of normal crime was committed, and thus for which lesser charge to bargain.

Beyond the schemas for normal crimes, then, the practices of the public defenders show how normal crimes are socially constructed and deployed in interactions. Sudnow analyzes the routine of the public defender regarding each case. First, the defender meets with the accused in the jail. Each defender might meet with any number of clients on a given day. During this brief encounter, the defender asks the client for his or her version of the events. Based on the kinds of questions asked by the defender, it is clear to Sudnow that the defender presumes guilt on the part of the client. The goal of the defender is to determine the facts of the case only to determine the kind of normal crime that occurred; the defender is uninterested in pursuing a plea of innocence. Sudnow cites an example of a defender asking a man accused of child molestation as to the mode of the crime, despite the man's denial that he had abused the child. His goal is to determine whether a plea for loitering is appropriate or not, as Sudnow describes two types of normal child moles- tation (familial and stranger) and the defender's goal of determining which kind of normal molestation the crime fits. Typically, however, most of those clues are in the original charges filed by the district attorney and supporting police evidence.

After the first interview, the defender will primarily deal with the defendant in court, with very little con- tact outside of court. In the courtroom, the defender is a routine actor, to the extent that the defense table becomes the defender's own desk. In Sudnow's court of study, the public defender's office assigned different defenders to different situations: some attended to the first interview, while others handled the pleas, and still others handled sentencing. Typically, a defendant would see at least two different defenders, and the preparation for the case for each defender would come from the sometimes paltry case file. The impor- tance of having a shared conception of what to expect from a given situation is, therefore, important, because it helps to align the actions of the different defenders across the same case as well as the same defender across what are seen to be similar cases.

The plea bargaining process is quite routinized, based upon the shared goals of the defender and the prosecutors and the shared conceptions of nor- mal crimes. Typically, the defender and the prose- cutor will meet informally to discuss the plea bargain, but in normal situations, this is very brief. The prosecutor and defender are thus a kind of team, working backstage to coordinate their actions in an efficient manner with the front-stage appear- ance of justice served.

Since most of the cases that are dealt with by public defenders are pled out, the cases that do go to trial are considered exceptional. Sudnow identi- fies two cases in which this happens: the case is not a normal crime or the defendant is "stubborn." The first situation is quite rare; because public defenders are only dealing with indigent clients, many of whom have criminal records already, the atypical criminal or crime rarely appears on their docket. Atypical crimes are crimes where the typi- cal features do not align in some way. This could be because of the particular kind of crime, in its scale or heinousness, or the attention of the public on the outcome of the case. A guilty plea, in this case, would undermine the morality of the district attorney's office and the overall judicial system; to avoid this, a trial is held.

In contrast, most of the trials encountered by the public defender are cases of the stubborn defendant, one who refuses to plead guilty to a lesser charge and maintains his or her innocence. In this instance, a defender is obligated to go to trial in order to continue to cover for the backstage nature of the plea bargain. Were a defender to go directly to a prosecutor with a plea that the defendant later rejected in open court, the entire system of plea bar- gaining might be revealed to public scrutiny. While a public defender tries to convince the client to plea to a lesser charge, this does not always work.

In either trial situation, however, the public defender must change position regarding the pros- ecutor and perform the duties of a defense attor- ney. The public defender's behavior in each trial, however, can be very different. For the normal crime with a stubborn defendant, the defender plays the part of a dutiful but compliant attorney. While the defender may object when called for and cross-examine witnesses, the defender does not introduce evidence or witnesses himself or herself, nor does he or she take great pains to attend to the client's version of events. Instead, the defender does just enough defense work to avoid a mistrial or grounds for appeal. The defender is still complying with the system of shared conception of normal crimes and the presumed guilt of the defendant. In the case of an exceptional, non-normal crime, how- ever, the public defender must drastically change the performance and, due to greater public scrutiny of his or her behavior, act as if in opposition to the prosecutor's stance. This is not done because the underlying assumptions about the crime or criminal have changed, but because of the nature of the backstage operation between the defenders and prosecutors that keep the routine judicial system running that might be exposed through deviations from that routine.

Kate Jenkins

See also Becker, Howard S.: Labeling and Deviant Careers; Spector, Malcolm, and John I. Kitsuse: Constructing Social Problems; Vaughn, Diane: The Normalization of Deviance

References and Further Readings

Kitsuse, J. I., & Cicourel, A. V. (1963). A note on the official use of statistics. *Social Problems, 11*, 131–139.

Sudnow, D. (1965). Normal crimes: Sociological features of the penal code in a public defender office. *Social Problems, 12*, 255–276.

Sudnow, D. (1967). *Passing on: The social organization of dying*. New York: Prentice Hall.

SUTHERLAND, EDWIN H.: DIFFERENTIAL ASSOCIATION THEORY AND DIFFERENTIAL SOCIAL ORGANIZATION

Edwin Sutherland's development of differential association theory in 1947 marked a watershed in criminology. The theory, which dominated the discipline for decades, brought Chicago-style sociology to the forefront of criminology. It is well known that differential association explains individual criminality with a social psychological process of learning crime within interaction with social groups. Less well known is Sutherland's attempt to explain aggregate crime rates across groups and societies. Here, he specified the theory of differential social organization to explain rates of crime with an organizational process that implies group dynamics. This entry reviews Sutherland's theory of differential association, discusses attempts at revision, and assesses the empirical status of the theory. It also examines recent attempts to revisit and elaborate the concept of

differential social organization as well as current areas of research in which it is being used.

Differential Association Theory

Sutherland stated differential association theory as a set of nine propositions, which introduced three concepts—normative conflict, differential association, and differential group organization—that explain crime at the levels of the society, the individual, and the group. This section discusses relationships among these concepts, drawing from Ross L. Matsueda's "The Current State of Differential Association Theory."

Normative Conflict: The Root Cause of Crime in Society

At the societal level, crime is rooted in normative conflict. For Sutherland, primitive, undifferentiated societies are characterized by harmony, solidarity, and consensus over basic values and beliefs. Such societies have little conflict over appropriate behaviors and, consequently, little crime. With the industrial revolution, however, societies developed advanced divisions of labor, market economies, and a breakdown in consensus. Such societies become segmented into groups that conflict over interests, values, and behavior patterns. These societies are characterized by specialization rather than similarity, coercion rather than harmony, conflict rather than consensus. They tend to have high rates of crime. Sutherland hypothesized that high crime rates are associated with normative conflict, which he defined as a society segmented into groups that conflict over the appropriateness of the law: some groups define the law as a set of rules to be followed under all circumstances, while others define the law as a set of rules to be violated under certain circumstances. Therefore, when normative conflict is absent in a society, crime rates will be low; when normative conflict is high, societal crime rates will be high. In this way, crime is ultimately rooted in normative conflict, according to Sutherland and Donald Cressey.

Differential Association Process: Explanation of Individual Criminal Acts

At the level of the individual, the process of differential association provides a social psychological explanation of how normative conflict in society translates into individual criminal acts. Accordingly, criminal behavior is learned in a process of communication in intimate groups. The content of learning includes two important elements. First are the requisite skills and techniques for committing crime, which can range from complicated, specialized skills of computer fraud, insider trading, and confidence games, to the simple, readily available skills of assault, purse snatching, and drunk driving. Such techniques are necessary but insufficient to produce crime. Second are definitions favorable and unfavorable to crime, which consist of motives, verbalizations, or rationalizations that make crime justified or unjustified, and include Gresham Sykes and David Matza's *techniques of neutralization.* For example, definitions favorable to income tax fraud include "Everyone cheats on their taxes" and "The government has no right to tax its citizens." Definitions favorable to drunk driving include "I can drive fine after a few beers" and "I only have a couple of miles to drive home." Definitions favorable to violence include "If your manhood is threatened, you have to fight back" and "To maintain respect, you can never back down from a fight."

These definitions favorable to crime help organize and justify a criminal line of action in a particular situation. They are offset by definitions unfavorable to crime, such as "Tax fraud deprives Americans of important programs that benefit the commonwealth," "All fraud and theft is immoral," "If insulted, turn the other cheek," "Friends don't let friends drink and drive," and "Any violation of the law is wrong." These examples illustrate several points about definitions of crime. First, some definitions pertain to specific offenses only, such as "Friends don't let friends drink and drive," whereas others refer to a class of offenses, such as "All fraud and theft is immoral," and others refer to virtually all law violation, such as "Any violation of the law is wrong." Second, each definition serves to justify or motivate either committing criminal acts or refraining from criminal acts. Third, these definitions are not merely ex-post facto rationalizations of crime but rather operate to cause criminal behavior.

Sutherland recognized that definitions favorable to crime can be offset by definitions unfavorable to crime and, therefore, hypothesized that criminal behavior is determined by the ratio of definitions favorable to crime versus unfavorable to crime. Furthermore, he recognized that definitions are not all equal. Definitions that are presented more frequently, for a longer duration, earlier in one's life, and in more intense relationships receive more weight in the process producing crime.

The individual-level hypothesis of differential association theory can now be stated. According to Matsueda, a person will engage in criminal behavior if the following three conditions are met:

1. The person has learned the requisite skills and techniques for committing crime.

2. The person has learned an excess of definitions favorable to crime over unfavorable to crime.

3. The person has the objective opportunity to carry out the crime.

According to Sutherland, if all three conditions are present and crime does not occur, or a crime occurs in the absence of all three conditions, the theory would be wrong and in need of revision. Thus, in principle, the theory is falsifiable.

The process of differential association with definitions favorable and unfavorable to crime is structured by the broader social organization in which individuals are embedded. This includes the structures and organization of families, neighborhoods, schools, and labor markets. This organization is captured by the concept of differential social organization.

Differential Social Organization Explanation of Group Rates of Crime

At the level of the group, differential social organization provides an organizational explanation of how normative conflict in society translates into specific group rates of crime. According to differential social organization, the crime rate of a group is determined by the extent to which that group is organized against crime versus organized in favor of crime. In industrialized societies, the two forms of organization exist side by side—and indeed are sometimes interwoven in complex ways, such as when police take bribes and participate in organized extortion, or baseball players take steroids in full view of teammates. Sutherland hypothesized that the relative strength of organization in favor of crime versus organization against crime explains the crime rate of any group or society. Thus, compared to suburban neighborhoods, inner-city neighborhoods are weakly organized against street crimes and strongly organized in favor of such crimes. Compared to other groups, the Mafia is strongly organized in favor of crime and weakly organized against crime. Compared to the United States, Japan is strongly organized against crime and weakly organized in favor of crime.

Moreover, the group-level process of differential social organization is linked to the individual-level process of differential association. Groups that are strongly organized in favor of crime display numerous and intense definitions favorable to crime. Conversely, groups that are strongly organized against crime display numerous and intense definitions unfavorable to crime. Matsueda suggests that it follows that differential social organization explains group crimes rate by influencing the availability of definitions favorable and unfavorable to crime within the group. When groups are strongly organized in favor of crime and weakly organized against crime, they will present an abundance of definitions favorable to crime and few definitions unfavorable to crime. Individuals in such groups have a high probability of learning an excess of definitions of crime. Whether they do, depends on their actual learning. Even in high crime communities, some residents are isolated from the abundant criminal definitions and exposed to the few anti-criminal definitions in the community. Those residents will refrain from crime because of an excess of definitions unfavorable to crime. The opposite also holds. In low-crime communities, some residents are exposed to the few criminal definitions in the community, and isolated from the abundant anti-criminal definitions. Given the opportunity and skills, they will engage in crime because of an excess of definitions favorable to crime.

Extensions and Empirical Tests of Differential Association

Extensions

Although the core features of differential association theory have persisted to the present, the theory has undergone several modifications and extensions. Early attempts to modify the theory specified hypotheses of differential identification,

in which individuals identify with either criminals or non-criminals, and differential anticipation, in which individuals anticipate the consequences of delinquent or non-delinquent behavior.

Perhaps the most elaborate revision is associated with Ronald Akers, who incorporated social learning principles into the theory, which posits that crime is initially learned through direct imitation or modeling. Then, the probability of continuing criminal behavior is determined by differential reinforcement, the relative rewards and punishments following the act. Reinforcement can be direct or vicarious, whereby simply observing another's criminal behavior being reinforced will reinforce one's own criminal behavior. Definitions of crime are learned through this process and affect behavior directly, as well as indirectly by serving as cues (discriminative stimuli) for law violation.

A more recent extension of differential association theory, proposed by Karen Heimer and Matsueda in 1994, incorporates the symbolic interactionist concept of taking the role of the other as a link between group control, cognition, and behavior. Here, taking the role of significant others and considering delinquency from the standpoint of others is a cognitive process by which anticipated reactions of others, reflected appraisals of self from the standpoint of others (the looking-glass self), and delinquent peer associations (along with habits) lead to future delinquency. Such processes produce group social control of both delinquent and non-delinquent acts; delinquency is a result of *differential social control*, the relative strength of conventional versus delinquent group controls. Differential social control specifies specific mechanisms by which groups control the behavior of members, while retaining Sutherland's emphasis on the learning of delinquency and the importance of definitions of law violation.

Empirical Tests

Empirical studies of differential association generally use self-report surveys of adolescents and young adults. A key issue is how to measure an excess of definitions favorable to crime, a prerequisite for testing the theory. Long ago, Matsueda argued that if definitions of law violation can be viewed as a single continuum, they can be treated as a latent variable with operational implications for fallible survey measures of definitions. This strategy found that definitions of delinquency mediated effects of parent and peer attachment on delinquent behavior, and therefore that differential association is supported over social control theories for non-black (Matsueda, 1982) and black youths (Matsueda & Heimer, 1987). Panel studies have also supported the hypothesis that definitions are causally linked to delinquency and violence for males and females (Heimer & DeCoster, 1999) and that techniques for monetary crimes are important (McCarthy, 1996).

Empirical research has also found some support for the hypothesis that differential reinforcement adds explanatory power in models of delinquency. The concepts of imitation and anticipated social rewards from crime appear to add to the explanation of delinquency. Finally, recent research suggests that delinquent peer association has a smaller effect on delinquency when estimated longitudinally, when disentangling peer selection from peer effects, and when measuring delinquent peers from the peers themselves. Dana Haynie has linked differential association to social network theory and found that network density and centrality of delinquent peer groups are key predictors of delinquency. In sum, most empirical research finds general support for differential association and social learning theories.

Specifying Theoretical Mechanisms for Differential Social Organization

Sutherland spent considerable time refining his individual-level theory of differential association, but devoted less time to his more sociological theory of differential social organization, which consequently never progressed beyond its original rudimentary form. In 2006, Matsueda tried to resurrect the concept of differential social organization, pointing to a little-known chapter Sutherland wrote on wartime crime—in which he identifies a number of mechanisms by which social organization may affect crime rates during war—and developing the dynamic collective action implications of the theory. This discussion draws from that work.

The concept of differential social organization, like social organization more generally, can be separated into two analytically distinct forms. From the standpoint of a snapshot or cross-section, social organization consists of structures, including social network ties, norms and sanctions, consensus versus

conflict, and access to resources. Here, the extent to which those structures are used for crime versus used to combat crime determines the instantaneous distribution of crime. From the standpoint of a dynamic process over time, social organization consists of collective action, social change, and the process by which consensus and conflict are built up. The latter process has been largely ignored in the criminology literature on social organization and crime. Nevertheless, the role of collective action can be inferred from Sutherland's own words, when he wrote that organization against crime and in favor of crime consist of two principal elements: "consensus in regard to objectives and in implementation for the realization of objectives" ([1943]1973, p. 126). In other words, such organization is the result of collective action, and it entails building consensus over a problematic situation and then translating that consensus into action.

The Structure of Social Network Ties

If we first consider differential social organization cross-sectionally, a key element is the structure of network ties. James Coleman argued that closed network structures enable greater social capital and social control. Imagine a diagram of a triangle, with points A, B, and C at each corner. In this diagram of an open structure, points A and B are linked by a line (or side) to C, but not connected to each other. This would be like a triangle in which two sides are connected but not the third. In this situation, A and B can independently and additively influence C by using individual sanctions, developing trust, establishing norms, using moral persuasion, and the like. But they cannot engage in joint behavior because they lack social ties. Now imagine another figure in which all sides of a triangle are connected. In this diagram of a closed structure, points A and B are linked not only to C but also to each other. As a result, they not only can influence C independently, but—because they interact with each other—can jointly (multiplicatively) influence C by developing coordinated strategies, simultaneous sanctions, similar rhetorical arguments, and the like.

Coleman gives a second example of parents and children. In an open structure, the two children are friends but their parents do not know one another. In a closed structure, not only do the children know one another but the parents are also friends. In the open structure, the parent can only influence their own child's behavior. But in the closed structure, because the parents know one another, they can now work collectively to control or influence all the children. Thus, they can monitor each others' children, call each other, and coordinate their punitive strategies, rhetorical arguments, and so on. Robert Sampson, Stephen Raudenbush, and Felton Earls find support for the hypothesis that intergenerational closure, as an element of neighborhood collective efficacy, is negatively associated with neighborhood rates of violence.

The Strength of Weak Ties

Closed structures tend to form dense networks of like-minded actors because assortative matching is typically based on homophily, which creates close relationships among similar individuals. Strong ties within a homogenous group not only encourage conformity but also lead to the circulation and recirculation of similar ideas. Such groups will tend to be stable and have strong internal social control—through shared information, consensus over goals, and strong norms and sanctions. On the down side, the group's homogeneity and closed structure will cause it to be rigid, lack cognitive flexibility, and have difficulty adjusting to changes in the environment.

In contrast, groups that are not entirely closed, but have weak ties to other groups, will benefit from information flows between groups through bridging ties. The information flowing across the bridge will expose members of each group to novel ideas, since it is coming from a set of comparatively dissimilar individuals. Mark Granovetter argues that weak ties provide group members with information on the latest ideas, fashions, and job openings, as well as increasing the likelihood of members being organized into social movements. Conversely, the absence of weak ties not only isolates members but also presents obstacles to building a critical mass necessary to produce a political movement or goal-oriented social organization.

Such structures provide a basis for theorizing about organization for and against crime. For residents of affluent neighborhoods, who enjoy regular employment, good incomes, and sufficient time and resources to address local problems

(e.g., delinquency), a mix of strong and weak ties is empowering. Strong ties enable such residents to reach consensus about shared problems, agree on promising solutions, and work collectively to try out such solutions. Weak ties to outsiders enable them to introduce innovative solutions by providing fresh ideas and information, and to draw directly on ties to outside social agencies. For residents of disadvantaged neighborhoods, high rates of residential mobility, poverty, and lack of time and resources undermine their ability to reach consensus about crime control beyond the kinship network, identify novel ways of controlling crime, link to other agencies, and act collectively. Moreover, in such neighborhoods, disadvantaged youths, who have high rates of school failure and bleak labor market trajectories, have a strong incentive to develop alternate ways of gaining status, perhaps in illicit ways. Such innovation may be more likely when the group of disadvantaged youths have weak ties to other disadvantaged groups who share the same objective situation. To link these structures to instrumental action, we turn to theories of collective action.

Collective Action Frames

Structures of network ties, political opportunities, and institutional support help explain opportunity structures for collective action but have little to say about the moment-to-moment dynamics of emerging collective action and, in particular, about how the framing of grievances may foster social movements. David Snow and Robert Benford argue that individuals actively produce, maintain, and fight for meanings about issues they hold dear by using *collective action frames*, which are emergent beliefs and meanings that foster social movements by framing a problematic situation as calling for an action-oriented collective solution. The process of frame alignment—linking the interpretive frameworks of individuals and social movement organizations—is the key task for social movement organizers. Moreover, collective action frames are more effective when they define the problem and its solution collectively rather than individually, define the opposition as them versus us, and define an injustice that can be corrected through collective action.

Collective action frames can help us understand the dynamics of differential social organization.

Effective collective action frames can be instrumental for concerned residents to mobilize their neighbors to create neighborhood watches, assist in supervising children, and contact law enforcement to create a safer neighborhood. This form of organization against crime, of course, requires the existence of social network ties—including strong and weak ties. In the case of neighborhood collective efficacy, residents use a neighborhood frame, in which they draw upon values of a safe and clean neighborhood, appeal to neighborhood pride, and create collective identities as neighbors, and an anti-crime frame, which emphasizes the evils of delinquency, drugs, and misbehavior.

Collective action frames may also contribute to organization in favor of crime. One can speak of a street frame that is used to make sense of situations on the streets of inner-city impoverished neighborhoods. Like other frames, street frames contain vocabularies of motive, rules, and tacit sanctions for violating rules. Elijah Anderson has identified the dimensions of rules or norms within the street frame. The most fundamental norm is "never back down from a fight." Violations of this rule will result in a loss of street credibility, social standing, and self-esteem, and an increase in the likelihood of being preyed upon in the future. Status on the street is achieved by demonstrating "nerve"—a willingness to express disrespect for other males by getting in their face, throwing the first punch, pulling the trigger, messing with their women—which builds a reputation for "being a man." Moreover, the phrase, "I got your back," implies that street youths will protect friends and loved ones from insult, disrespect, or attack from others. Indeed, an insult or assault on one's "crew" calls for revenge or payback. Finally, decent youths, not just street youths, have an incentive to learn the tenets of the code of the street. Ignorance of the code may provoke a violent confrontation by staring too long at a street youth, stepping on someone's toe, or failing to project a look of someone not to be messed with.

The street frame is available on the streets to use instrumentally to incite collective action, maintain a sense of honor, and gain respect and status. For example, knowing the tenets of the frame, youths in search of a reputation seek to increase their status by "campaigning for respect"—by challenging, humiliating, or assaulting others, and disrespecting them by stealing their material possessions or

girlfriends. When a member of a group is disrespected or assaulted, other members need only invoke the street frame, with its attendant rules, motives, and sanctions, to mobilize the group to exact payback.

Social Efficacy: The Intersection of Structural Networks and Collective Action

Individuals will vary not only in the value they place on safety or criminality but, more importantly, in their own ability to persuade others to pursue an objective. In this context, *social efficacy* is defined as an individual's ability to create consensus over group objectives and procedures and to translate the procedures into action. Such individuals use higher stages of moral reasoning to consider not merely the parochial issues that affect their own self-interest but also the community as a whole, including the way in which various roles operate within the neighborhood and between the neighborhood and relevant institutions. They would likely be capable of code-switching. Social efficacy is a more specific application of Albert Bandura's concept of self-efficacy, which refers to "people's beliefs about their capabilities to produce designated levels of performance that exercise influence over events that affect their lives" (p. 71). Social efficacy refers to an objective ability to organize social groups to realize a common goal, rather than a perceived belief about one's capability to produce general effects important to one's life (Matsueda, 2006).

The way in which an efficacious individual is embedded in a neighborhood's social relationships may be critical for collective efficacy. For example, in a network highly centralized around a well-connected hub (a node with high degree centrality and between-ness centrality), if the hub is occupied by a socially efficacious individual (who values the neighborhood), the neighborhood's structure is conducive to collective efficacy. With social ties to nearly all residents, the socially efficacious hub is in a position to mobilize residents to improve the neighborhood. In contrast, in an identical neighborhood network structure, but with an inefficacious hub, the presence of efficacious residents on the network's periphery is unable to compensate for the inefficacious hub. This is because their structural location limits their ability to mobilize their neighbors. Social efficacy can also be crucial to organization in favor of crime: gang leaders may be particularly effective, structurally and personally, in mobilizing street youths into gang membership and violence. It may also be crucial for genocide, to which we now turn.

Differential Social Organization and Genocide in Darfur

John Hagan and Wenona Rymond-Richmond's provocative theory of genocide draws on differential social organization viewed dynamically, in which access to resources, collective action frames, and social efficacy play key roles (Matsueda, 2006). The authors focus on organization in favor of crime and specify a multilevel model, in which a macro-level relationship is explained by a micro-level causal process. They argue that, at the macro-level, the Sudanese genocidal state is a function of two intersecting events: competition for land and resources between Arabs and black Africans and a state-led pro-Arab ideology emphasizing the supremacy of Arab Muslims over African Muslims. The macro-level constructs, competition and ideology, produce two conflicting, meso-level, locally organized interest groups—Arabs and black Africans. According to Hagan and Rymond-Richmond, individual members of the Arab groups, having internalized the racist ideology, engage in violent acts accompanied by dehumanizing racial epithets—micro-level purposive action consistent with their interests in the competition for land and resources. The authors show that the racial epithets derived from the collective action frames dehumanize Africans in stark and disturbing terms. Moreover, such individual actions coalesce into collective action, including collective violence, rape, and other atrocities, justified by a collectivized racial intent, culminating into a "fanatical fury." This collective action, which occurs not only with the tacit knowledge, but also active participation of the Sudanese state, creates widespread genocidal victimization.

Hagan and Rymond-Richmond creatively use the concept of social efficacy to explain the crucial role of Janjaweed militia leaders in fostering collective acts of genocide. These military leaders, particularly Musa Hilal, are already in positions of authority, well-networked, and skilled leaders. The term *social*

efficacy refers to a person whose social skills and location in the social structure—a network node—make the individual particularly adroit at mobilizing others into action (Matsueda, 2006). The military leaders prove instrumental in mobilizing Arab militia and, in particular, in promoting a racist collective action frame to justify mass killings, rapes, and other atrocities. Hagan and Rymond-Richmond analyze survey data on Darfur, finding strong support for their multilevel theory of genocide.

Differential Neighborhood Organization

Recent research has applied differential social organization to neighborhood social control. Robert Sampson and Corina Graif analyze survey data for Chicago and cluster analyze community-level indicators of collective efficacy, local networks, organizational involvement, and conduct norms, and leadership-based social capital—the latter, which identifies positional leaders, taps into the concept of social efficacy (although they do not use the term). They then apply multidimensional scaling to cluster communities based on indices of differential social organization into distinct clusters of communities (urban village, cosmopolitan efficacy, conduct norms, and institutional alienation), and then regress the clusters on neighborhood structure. They find that neighborhood disadvantage is negatively associated with collective efficacy and organizational involvement and positively associated with leadership capital, and that residential stability is positively associated with local networks conduct norms, organizational involvement, and leadership-based capital.

Elsewhere, Matsueda has specified a multilevel model of differential social organization, in which individual investments in social capital (e.g., reciprocated exchange) follow a rational choice process (Matsueda, in press). Social capital, in turn, results in positive externalities for the community, such as providing social capital that translates into collective efficacy, a form of organization against crime, and negative externalities, such as providing social capital that translates into a social system governed by the code of the street, a form of organization in favor of crime. This framework raises additional questions, such as coordination problems (e.g., the free-rider problem), the origin of norms and sanctions, and solutions based on game theory.

Conclusion

Differential association theory remains an important theoretical perspective in criminology, continuing to stimulate empirical research and attempts at revision. Although historically most research has focused on the individual differential association process, the last few years has seen a resurgence of interest in the sociological counterpart, differential social organization. The latter has opened new puzzles and provided a framework for incorporating sociological mechanisms governing social structure and social organization.

Ross L. Matsueda

See also Akers, Ronald L.: Social Learning Theory; Burgess, Robert L., and Ronald L. Akers: Differential Association-Reinforcement Theory; De Fleur, Melvin L., and Richard Quinney: A Reformulation of Sutherland's Differential Association Theory; Heimer, Karen, and Ross L. Matsueda: A Theory of Differential Social Control; Peers and Delinquency; Sampson, Robert J.: Collective Efficacy Theory; Sellin, Thorsten: Culture Conflict and Crime; Shaw, Clifford R., and Henry D. McKay: Social Disorganization Theory; Sutherland, Edwin H.: The Professional Thief; Sutherland, Edwin H.: White-Collar Crime

References and Further Readings

Akers, R. L. (1998). *Social learning and social structure: A general theory of crime and deviance*. Boston: Northeastern University Press.

Anderson, E. (1999). *Code of the street: Decency, violence and the moral life of the inner city*. New York: W. W. Norton.

Bandura, A. (1994). Self efficacy. In V. S. Ramachaudran (Ed.), *Encyclopedia of human behavior* (Vol. 4, pp. 71–81). New York: Academic Press.

Benford, R. D., & Snow, D. A. (2000). Framing processes and social movements: An overview and assessment. *Annual Review of Sociology, 26*, 611–639.

Coleman, J. S. (1990). *Foundations of social theory*. Cambridge, MA: Harvard University Press.

Glaser, D. (1956). Criminality theories and behavioral images. *American Journal of Sociology, 61*, 433–444.

Granovetter, M. (1973). The strength of weak ties. *American Journal of Sociology, 78*, 1360–1380.

Hagan, J., & Rymond-Richmond, W. (2009). *Darfur and the crime of genocide*. Cambridge, UK: Cambridge University Press.

Haynie, D. (2001). Delinquent peers revisited: Does network structure matter? *American Journal of Sociology, 106*, 1013–1057.

Heimer, K., & De Coster, S. (1999). The gendering of violent delinquency. *Criminology, 37*, 277–318.

Heimer, K., & Matsueda, R. L. (1994). Role-taking, role-commitment, and delinquency: A theory of differential social control. *American Sociological Review, 59*, 365–390.

Kubrin, C. E., Stucky, T. D., & Krohn, M. D. (2009). *Researching theories of crime and deviance*. New York: Oxford University Press.

Matsueda, R. L. (1982). Testing control theory and differential association: A causal modeling approach. *American Sociological Review, 47*, 489–504.

Matsueda, R. L. (1988). The current state of differential association theory. *Crime and Delinquency, 34*, 277–306.

Matsueda, R. L. (2006). Differential social organization, collective action, and crime. *Crime, Law, and Social Change, 46*, 3–33.

Matsueda, R. L. (in press). Rational choice research in criminology: A multi-level approach. In R. Wittek, T. Snijders, & V. Nee (Eds.), *Handbook of rational choice social research*. New York: Russell Sage.

Matsueda, R. L., & Heimer, K. (1987). Race, family structure, and delinquency: A test of differential association and social control theories. *American Sociological Review, 52*, 826–840.

McCarthy, B. (1996). The attitudes and actions of others: Tutelage and Sutherland's theory of differential association. *British Journal of Criminology, 36*, 135–151.

Sampson, R. J., & Graif, C. (2009). Neighborhood social capital as differential social organization: Resident and leadership dimensions. *American Behavioral Scientist, 52*, 1579–1605.

Sampson, R. J., Raudenbush, S., & Earls, F. (1997). Neighborhoods and violent crime: A multilevel study of collective efficacy. *Science, 277*, 918–924.

Small, M. L. (2002). Culture, cohorts, and social organization theory: Understanding local participation in a Latino housing project. *American Journal of Sociology, 108*, 1–54.

Snow, D. A., & Benford, R. D. (1992). Master frames and cycles of protest. In A. D. Morris & C. M. Mueller (Eds.), *Frontiers in social movement theory* (pp. 133–155). New Haven, CT: Yale University Press.

Sutherland, E. H. (1947). *Principles of criminology* (4th ed.). Philadelphia: Lippincott.

Sutherland, E. H. (1973). Wartime crime. In K. Schuessler (Ed.), *Edwin H. Sutherland on analyzing crime* (pp. 120–128). Chicago: University of Chicago Press. (Original work published 1943)

Sutherland, E. H., & Cressey, D. R. (1978). *Criminology.* Philadelphia: Lippincott.

Sutherland, E. H., Cressey, D. R., & Luckenbill, D. F. (1992). *Principles of criminology* (11th ed.). Lanham, MD: AltaMira Press.

Sykes, G. M., & Matza, D. (1957). Techniques of neutralization: A theory of delinquency. *American Sociological Review, 22,* 664–670.

SUTHERLAND, EDWIN H.: THE PROFESSIONAL THIEF

Much of what is known about professional criminals comes from journals, diaries, autobiographies, and first-person accounts given to writers and criminologists. The best-known account of professional theft is Edwin Sutherland's classic book *The Professional Thief.* A fascinating glimpse into the underworld of professional thieves and con men, the account is based on the recollections of Broadway Jones, alias Chic Conwell—a thief, ex-drug addict, and ex-con who worked for 20 years as a pickpocket, shoplifter, and confidence man. Conwell's recollections include details about the roles of members of the *mob* (a criminal group), their criminal *argot* (slang) and *code* (unwritten norms and rules of the thief subculture), the *fix* (ways of avoiding conviction and/or doing time in prison), and thieves' images of the police, the law, and society at large.

Sutherland's Professional Thief

Much of the book was actually written by Conwell, but Sutherland edited it for publication and wrote two interpretive chapters. His analysis concluded that professional thievery has five basic features: technical skill, status, consensus, differential association, and organization.

- *Technical Skill.* Professional thieves (like bricklayers, lawyers, and physicians) possess a set of talents and skills. Some combination of wits, speaking ability, manual dexterity, specialization, and contacts is needed to plan and execute crimes, dispose of stolen goods, and manipulate the criminal justice system in those cases involving arrests.

- *Status.* Like other professionals, the professional thief holds a certain status based on ability, character, lifestyle, wealth, and power. Professional thieves often show contempt for amateur, small-time, and snatch-and-grab thieves.

- *Consensus.* Professional thieves share similar values and develop a philosophy or rationale regarding their activities and criminal specialty that aids them in their criminal careers.

- *Differential Association.* Professional thieves tend to associate chiefly with other professional thieves and to maintain barriers between themselves and members of "straight" society.

- *Organization.* Professional theft is organized in the sense that technical skills, status, consensus, and differential association entail both a core of knowledge informally shared by thieves and a network of cooperation.

Sutherland further concludes that the professional thief is a graduate of a developmental process that includes the acquisition of specialized attitudes, knowledge, skills, and experience; makes a regular business of stealing—it is his occupation or a principal means of livelihood; and identifies with the world of crime. The recruitment of persons into professional thievery involves a process of recognition, selection, and tutelage. Recognition by other professional thieves, according to Sutherland, is a necessary and definitive characteristic of the professional thief. Without such recognition, no amount of knowledge and experience can provide the criminal with the opportunities and contacts for a successful career in profit-seeking crime. In turn, after acquiring at least some recognition, *selection* (e.g., being recruited, vouched for) and *tutelage* (learning of skills, techniques, and attitudes favorable to theft through informal means) are interrelated and continuous processes in the course of more crime opportunities and advances to greater recognition and commitment to crime as "work" or a "business." Sutherland and

Conwell view professional theft as an occupation or business with much of the same internal organization and socialization processes as that characterizing legitimate professions like law, medicine, or carpentry. They write,

> A person can be a professional thief only if he is recognized and received as such by other professional thieves. Professional theft is a way of life. One can get into the group and remain in it only by consent of those previously in the group. Recognition as a professional thief by other professional thieves is the absolutely necessary, universal and definitive characteristic of the professional thief. (Sutherland, 1937, p. 212)

However, some contemporary criminologists have criticized Sutherland's depiction of professional thieves (circa 1900–1925). Some critics note that in sociology, the concept of "profession" refers to occupations that entail esoteric, useful knowledge after lengthy training, a code of ethics, and a claimed service orientation for which they are granted autonomy of operation and various concomitants such as high prestige and remuneration (Hagan, 1998, p. 294). In this light the term *professional* may be inappropriately applied to criminal activities and criminals, even very skilled ones.

A second criticism is that Sutherland's treatment restricts professional crime to thieves or hustlers who rely on wit and nonviolent techniques (Steffensmeier & Ulmer, 2005). It excluded criminals involved in "heavy" theft such as truck hijackers, stickup men, arsonists, and "hit" men. Excluded, too, are those practitioners of crime and vice who are involved in the "rackets" and illicit businesses such as bookmakers, dealers in stolen goods, drug traffickers, sex merchants, mafioso, and racketeers and background operators more generally. Many of those involved in these activities fit the elements of "professionalism" enumerated by Sutherland as much or likely more so than did Conwell.

Third, it is arguable that many "skilled" criminals are only slightly better than other crooks at lying, cheating, and stealing; labeling them "professionals" should be done carefully. Some criminologists who have studied career criminals suggest alternate terms for those who

commit more sophisticated crimes and face a lesser chance of arrest or conviction; for example John Mack suggests *able criminal*, Neal Shover suggests *good thief*, and Darrell Steffensmeier suggests *seasoned offenders*. Still others, such as Frank Hagan, suggest the term *semi-professional*.

Fourth, although many writers (including Sutherland) insert the wording into their reports on crime, the category "professional criminal" is seldom, if ever, applied by criminals themselves. Even seasoned thieves and hustlers do not use the word *professional* or *nonprofessional*. Instead, they refer to themselves (or others) as thieves or hustlers; as good thieves, good hustlers, or good people; as aces-in-the-hole, first-class or decent thieves, wise-guys, and so forth. Nevertheless, thieves are aware of the word's meaning in the larger society, and may use it as a shorthand way of communicating with members of straight society.

Significance and Contributions of *The Professional Thief*

The Professional Thief was a foundational work that shaped the early theoretical and empirical development of the field of criminology. In addition to conceptualizing and detailing core aspects of the professionalism of theft and the process of becoming (and continuing to be) a seasoned thief or con artist, *The Professional Thief* makes numerous contributions to theory and research in criminology. First, along with *White Collar Crime* (the first large-scale sociological analysis of upperworld criminality), *The Professional Thief* was instrumental in Sutherland's efforts to develop differential association as a general theory of criminal behavior. Thieves and white-collar criminals overlap in many ways, according to Sutherland. Both sets of activities require tutelage and specialized skill, and prestige among colleagues was enhanced, not diminished, because of criminal activity. But they also differ, apparently because they identify with different social worlds. As Sutherland saw it, "Professional thieves, when they speak honestly, admit that they are thieves," while white-collar criminals "think of themselves as honest men," defining what they've done as nothing more malevolent than "shrewd business practice" (1937, pp. 95–96). Since criminality is learned, it can be and is learned at all social levels. Furthermore, differential association is very much a process-oriented, life-course perspective, although Sutherland did not use the terminology that life-course criminology does today.

Second, although the concept "criminal opportunity" is not spelled out in *Professional Thief*, it is strongly implicit and was subsequently rendered explicit by Richard Cloward who drew heavily from the work. Cloward observed that criminal opportunities, like conventional opportunities, are not evenly distributed throughout society. They consist of opportunities to both learn and perform skills and lines of activity, and are differentially available according to one's social statuses (e.g., race, gender, ethnicity, age, social class) and the groups or networks in which one's life is embedded. Steffensmeier (1983) and Steffensmeier and Jeffrey Ulmer (2005), in turn, extended Cloward's and, by extension, Sutherland's notions about criminal opportunity. They further spell out the operational meaning of learning and performance opportunities for crime as involving (1) different types of criminal knowledge: *civil* (conventional knowledge that can be easily transferred to criminal activity), *preparatory* (orientations and techniques/skills that are obtained by simply being around groups or settings where crime takes place), and *technical knowledge* (knowledge and skills that are mainly or only acquired by access to tutelage from experienced criminals); and (2) the means for performing or "conducting" the crime itself, which include physical, and perhaps mental, capabilities. It also can entail access to requisite tools *or* hardware, to suitable places and targets, and to contacts or support networks (which may include "criminal" as well as "respectable" persons).

A third contribution involves Sutherland's ranking or status hierarchy of criminal specialties. Sutherland set forth a five-level status hierarchy (pecking order) that existed across criminal specialties in the early 20th century, as shown in Table 1 (left side).

As already noted, however, Sutherland dealt only with the theft subculture while ignoring racketeers and syndicate figures who—on the basis of money,

power, and prestige—both then and now constitute the highest-status criminal roles. Also, recent changes in the underworld, especially the expanding drug market, have contributed to some shifts in the money, power, and prestige of criminal roles. Thus, the underworld stratification system as set forth in *The Professional Thief* differs somewhat from Steffensmeier and Ulmer's contemporary update of the pecking order of criminal specialties in the late 20th/early 21st century, as displayed in the right side of Table 1.

A fourth contribution is Sutherland's application of an occupational perspective in *The Professional Theft*, which helped establish a long and rich tradition in criminology of studying people who approach crime as their work. A number of criminologists and sociologists after Sutherland have analyzed crime as work, and *The Professional Thief* at least implicitly inspired their work. David Maurer, a linguistic scholar, focused on con men and pickpockets in *The American Confidence Man* and *The Wiz Mob*. Ned Polsky later wrote about pool hustlers and their work situation, Shover studied the skills and contacts of "good burglars," the careers of aging property offenders, and lifestyles and worldviews of ordinary thieves. Peter Letkemann examined the work methods of robbers and safemen in *Crime as Work*, and Robert Prus and C. R. D. Sharper concentrated on the careers of professional card and dice hustlers in *Road Hustler*. Malin Akerstrom, in *Crooks and Squares*, described the work methods of types of thieves and drug addicts. Steffensmeier in *The Fence* and Steffensmeier and Ulmer in *Confessions of a Dying Thief* further extended this type of analysis by examining the skills and work habits of burglars and professional fences or large-scale dealers in stolen goods. These works also show (1) how conventional career concepts such as apprenticeship, work satisfaction, and networking are applicable to crime as work and (2) the continuities between the socialization patterns of those criminals for whom crime is an occupation or business and conventional workers and business people. These are only a few of many other worthy examples could be cited.

All these studies emphasize the lifestyle and work habits of criminals as much or more than analyzing the reasons or motivations for their criminal activities. They address questions such as

Table I   Status Hierarchy of Criminal Offenders

Sutherland's Professional Thief	*Steffensmeier and Ulmer (2005)*
1. Big con operators and bank burglars	Illicit businesses: racketeers, mafiosi, background operators
2. Forgers and counterfeiters, safe burglars	Big-time fences, major bookmakers (who "bank" or control their own pool of betting money), upper-level drug dealers, black market specialists
3. Short-con operators, "penny-weighters," house and store burglars, armed robbers or "stick-up men"	Big con operators, safecracker burglars, truck hijackers
4. Shakedown workers, hotel and sneak thieves	House and commercial burglars, armed robbers, forgers and counterfeiters, cartage thieves, auto thieves
5. Pickpockets and shoplifters	Short-con operators, small time fences, bookmakers, midlevel drug dealers
	Shoplifting and other varieties of small time theft, check kiting, pimping
	Street level hustlers, snatch and grab thieves, low-level drug dealers
	Drug addict thieves

Source: Steffensmeier, D. J., & Ulmer, J. (2005). *Confessions of a dying thief: Understanding criminal careers and criminal enterprise* (pp. 215–219, 231–235). New Brunswick, NJ: Aldine Transaction.

the following: What problems are faced by criminals, and what strategies do they use to solve them? What are the pros and cons of a criminal lifestyle in comparison with a more conventional one? What skills are involved in a criminal lifestyle? How are contacts made? What is the mix of rewards and motivations? How does aging affect crime skills and rewards?

These works (and others) also confirm that many aspects of Sutherland's characterization of the processes involved in becoming a professional thief, the thief's relationship to the general society, and the larger subculture of theft are largely applicable today. As was true when Sutherland sketched it, one becomes an established thief (racketeer) today through stealing with, and tutelage by, other seasoned thieves. From them, one learns criminal techniques (physical, interpersonal, perceptual, and definitional) and how to manipulate the criminal justice system; and, in the process of learning all this, the offender becomes connected into a network of criminal and quasi-criminal actors with whom the person can establish mutually advantageous working relationships. More so than

the ordinary thief, professional or good thieves can be characterized as having a lot of *criminal capital*—including physical capital (tools like guns and wire cutters, physical strength or threat), human or personal capital (resourcefulness, criminal insight, violence, conning ability), social capital (reputation, networks of useful people, kinship ties), and perhaps even cultural capital (e.g., knowledge of underworld culture, argot, meanings). Having a lot of criminal capital both reduces the risks of crime and increases the prospects for safer and more profitable crime opportunities, for example, by increasing the offender's attractiveness to co-offenders and crime networks (Morselli et al., 2006; Steffensmeier, 1983, 1986).

Last, Sutherland observed that professional thieves tend to specialize on a relatively small number of crimes that are related to one another, although they may transfer for longer or shorter periods of time from one specialty to another. Years later, some criminologists argued that self-report survey data, primarily from juvenile or young adult samples, show that offenders typically did not specialize but instead exhibited diversity in offending. They argued that this was evidence against differential association and social learning theory. Steffensmeier and Ulmer helped to clarify this issue by noting that Sutherland's differential association theory (and *The Professional Thief*) did not imply specialization as a general principle of offending, and they presented evidence that specialization varies by offender age/career stage, criminal capital and skill level, crime type/category, and niche in the underworld. In reality Sutherland's differential association theory leaves specialization as an empirical question—different learning processes, messages, and settings can produce diversity in offending or specialization.

Darrell Steffensmeier and Jeffrey Ulmer

See also Cloward, Richard A.: The Theory of Illegitimate Means; Shaw, Clifford R.: The Jack-Roller; Steffensmeier, Darrell J., and Jeffery T. Ulmer: The Professional Fence; Sutherland, Edwin H.: Differential Association Theory and Differential Social Organization

References and Further Readings

Akerstrom, M. (1985). *Crooks and squares: Lifestyles of thieves and addicts in comparison to conventional people*. New Brunswick, NJ: Transaction.

Cloward, R. A. (1959). Illegitimate means, anomie, and deviant behaviour. American *Sociological Review, 24*, 164–176.

Hagan, F. (1998). *Introduction to criminology* (4th ed.). Chicago: Nelson-Hall.

Letkemann, P. (1973). *Crime as work*. Englewood Cliffs, NJ: Prentice Hall.

Mack, J. (1975). *The crime industry*. London: Saxon House.

Maurer, D. (1964). *The whiz mob: A correlation of the technical argot of pickpockets with their behavior pattern*. New Haven, CT: Yale University Press.

Maurer, D. (1974). *The American confidence man*. Springfield, IL: Charles C Thomas.

Morselli, C., Tremblay, P., & McCarthy, B. (2006). Mentors and criminal achievement. *Criminology, 44*, 17–44.

Polsky, N. (1967). *Hustlers, beats, and others*. Chicago: Aldine de Gruyter.

Prus, R., & Sharper, C. R. D. (1977). *Road hustler: The career contingencies of professional card and dice hustlers*. Lexington, MA: D. C. Heath.

Shover, N. (1972). Structures and careers in burglary. *Journal of Criminal Law, Criminology, and Police Science, 63*, 540–549.

Steffensmeier, D. J. (1983). Organization properties and sex-segregation in the underworld: Building a sociological theory of sex differences in crime. *Social Forces, 6*, 1010–1032.

Steffensmeier, D. J. (1986). *The fence: In the shadow of two worlds*. Totowa, NJ: Rowman & Littlefield.

Steffensmeier, D. J., & Ulmer, J. (2005). *Confessions of a dying thief: Understanding criminal careers and criminal enterprise*. New Brunswick, NJ: Aldine Transaction.

Sutherland, E. (1937). *The professional thief*. Chicago: University of Chicago Press.

Sutherland, E. (1949). *White collar crime*. New York: Holt, Rinehart and Winston.

SUTHERLAND, EDWIN H.: WHITE-COLLAR CRIME

The concept of white-collar crime, introduced by Edwin H. Sutherland in his presidential address to the 34th annual meeting of the American Sociological Society in 1939, had two fundamental themes. First, it called attention to serious occupational law-breaking by upper-level persons in business, politics, and the professions. Second, it tied the portrait of such criminal activity to a theoretical construct that Sutherland, in his presidential address (published in 1940 as "White-Collar Criminality") had labeled "differential association."

Sutherland's presidential address and a decade later his classic monograph *White Collar Crime* embedded the words *white-collar crime* in our language. The term appears constantly in and on the mass media, statutes employ it as a catch-all designation for certain illegal behaviors, and judges refer to it in decisions and sentencing justifications in ways that indicate a common public understanding of what is meant.

In his presidential address, Sutherland referred to notorious swindlers, many of whom, in Matthew Josephson's colorful term, were labeled "robber barons"—business tycoons who bought legislatures, robbed investors, and ran roughshod over competitors. But these wrongdoers could not be grouped and examined in a manner that would yield scientifically useful theoretical generalizations. At best, they were case histories—war stories—that had among them only some similarities that might be molded into a superficial explanatory scheme.

The title of Sutherland's presidential address printed in the program was "The White-Collar Criminal," but the published version was called "White-Collar Criminality" and the subsequent monograph bore the title *White Collar Crime.* The shift in emphasis is significant. By the time he published the book, Sutherland largely had abandoned his focus on human malefactors and had resorted to the only approach reasonably available to him at the time by presenting case histories of violations by corporate entities. Sutherland had been employing graduate students since 1928 to locate and codify reports of corporate wrongdoing (Sutherland, 1956). But as Donald Cressey, Sutherland's intellectual acolyte, would point out, Sutherland had to anthropomorphize the corporations, that is, to treat them as if they were individuals whose actions could best be interpreted by the social psychological theory that Sutherland advocated. For Cressey, this was a feckless enterprise: only people could think and act; organizations were mindless entities.

In promulgating his material on white-collar crime, Sutherland belittled, indeed ridiculed, ideas that served as then-current explanations of crime, including feeblemindedness, poverty, immigrant status, broken homes, and Oedipal complexes. In what would become a much-quoted observation, Sutherland wrote, "We have no reason to think that General Motors has an inferiority complex or that the Aluminum Corporation of American has a frustration-aggression complex" (1956, p. 96). This polemic, however, was more a reflection of Sutherland's antipathy toward psychiatric theory that a strong debating point. To truly carry his argument, he would have had to demonstrate (or at least argue) that such pathologies could not be located in those running the corporations rather than in the businesses themselves.

White-collar crime was Sutherland's polemical trump card in debates regarding criminological theory. If elite offenders, such as violators of antitrust laws, did not manifest personal or social characteristics tied to criminal activity, then those conditions could not be presumed to account for all crime.

Sutherland's differential association theory presumed to explain every form of crime. It maintained that criminal behavior is learned from social interactions. Considerations such as tutelage in regard to illegal tactics and the inculcation on the job of values and attitudes that deemed law breaking as the preferred course of action were asserted to underlay white-collar crime. It did not appear to occur to Sutherland that there might not be any satisfactory theory, then or thereafter, that could provide an acceptable interpretation of all crime and that white-collar crime might better be understood by theoretical constructs that did not explain domestic violence, rape, or other offenses.

The Impetus for *White Collar Crime*

There are hints in Sutherland's life story and academic career that indicate why he would turn for the first time and so forcefully to the subject of white-collar crime when he was in his mid-fifties. By all accounts, Sutherland was a cautious man but also a well-meaning one. He favored the capitalist system, but he deplored its excesses and its insensitivity to the public welfare. He had the courage to criticize his government as "racist" during World War II for its interment of 120,000 Japanese, more than half of them U.S. citizens, who obviously posed no threat to the United States. But he was reluctant to offer an assistantship to a black graduate student in the Indiana University sociology department, which he chaired, not because he was prejudiced against the student or his race but because to do so would go against the prevailing sentiment of the times (Snodgrass, 1972).

In his academic life, Sutherland had been indoctrinated into the ethos that muckraking was propaganda and that the true social scientist should adopt a neutral pose toward his or her study material. At the same time, he rebelled against what he saw as the sterility of much of the criminological and sociological enterprise—his devotion was to research and writing that advanced the common good, not work that drew scholarly plaudits from a handful of other specialists. His crusade against white-collar crime meshed with his reformist inclinations.

A one point, shortly before the publication of *White Collar Crime,* Sutherland wrote in his criminology textbook that the definition of white-collar crime should embrace behaviors which "are not even a violation of the spirit of the law, for the parties concerned have been able by bribery and other means to prevent the enactment of laws to prevent wrongful and injurious behavior" (1947, p. 37). It is difficult to imagine a more radical (and, in some regards sensible) criminological concept. Sutherland retreated from that position in *White Collar Crime*, but that he enunciated it at all indicates his strong moral revulsion against what he labeled white-collar crime.

Family Background

Sutherland was born in Gibbon, Nebraska, on August 13, 1893, the third of seven children. His father, a Baptist minister, soon moved the family to Ottawa, Kansas, where he taught history for 9 years. He then relocated to Grand Island in Nebraska to assume the presidency for 20 years of Grand Island College, a Baptist school from which Sutherland graduated in 1904.

The populist fervor that permeated the Midwest during Sutherland's youth undoubtedly played a leading role in forming his ideological mindset. Typical was the platform of the *Alliance-Independence*, a populist Nebraska newspaper, that argued that "corporations, which have so long dominated and corrupted our politics and robbed our people through extortionist charges, [should be] retired from power" and inveighed against office holders who were "selfish men who ignore the law and violate their official oaths that they may enrich themselves at the expense of the taxpayers" (Cherney, 1981, p. 41).

Sutherland largely abandoned churchgoing in later life, and one of his jabs at organized religion appears in *White Collar Crime* where he writes that "in the earlier years the religious journals were notorious as accessory to misrepresentation in advertising" (p. 126). Nonetheless, the powerful Christian precepts regarding moral behavior in human transactions clearly influenced Sutherland's repugnance for exploitative business practices, even though he sought to camouflage these views as neutral social science inquiry. As sociologist Jon Snodgrass observed, Sutherland veered away from religious orthodoxy, but he remained "a man of compulsive virtue and integrity. . . . While he may have given up the orthodoxy of his Baptist upbringing, he never lost its scruples" (p. 223).

Academic Career

Sutherland began teaching at Sioux Falls College in South Dakota in 1906 and soon thereafter enrolled in the sociology department at the University of Chicago, staffed by a group of preeminent scholars. Sutherland received his Ph.D. in 1913, with majors in both sociology and political economy. He taught for 6 years (1913–1919) at William Jewell College in Liberty, Kansas, before joining the University of Illinois faculty (1919–1926), then moving to Minnesota (1926–1929), followed by a year of overseas research on prisons for the Bureau of Social Hygiene. He joined the Chicago faculty from 1930 to 1935 and then became founding chair of the Indiana University department, a position he held until his death on October 11, 1950.

The Presidential Address

Sutherland, then 56 years old, introduced the term *white-collar crime* in his presidential address in Philadelphia at a joint meeting of the American Sociological Society and the American Economic Association. He reviewed major instances of financial fraud by business magnates such as the railroad entrepreneurs and monopolists. He also catalogued legal actions taken by the criminal courts and the regulatory agencies against most of the prominent corporations in the United States. The offenses that drew his attention included antitrust violations, false advertising, theft of trade secrets, and bribery.

Sutherland opened his address with the observation that economists, while they were acquainted with the methods of business, rarely examined these methods in terms of crime, while sociologists, though often students of criminal behavior, rarely considered it as an ingredient of business. One of his tasks, Sutherland maintained, was to raise the consciousness within both disciplines with regard to white-collar crime which, in this the first of his many vexing and varying definitions, Sutherland characterized as "crimes in the upper or white-collar class, composed of respectable or at least respected business and professional men" (1940, p. 1).

To illustrate his theme, Sutherland listed a roster of crimes by physicians who he presumed were more honest than most professional persons. The list included abortions (illegal at the time); sale of prohibited narcotics; services to underworld figures, such as cosmetic surgery to help them avoid capture; fraudulent reports of accident cases; and unnecessary treatments. He declared that many persons who were supposed to oversee business activities were partial to the violators and that they had been recruited from and would return to the companies they failed to regulate.

Sutherland noted that newspapers tended to ignore or to bury on the back pages reports of business crimes. This was, he suggested, because they were beholden to corporate advertisers they dared not offend and because they themselves committed white-collar crimes, such as skirting the child labor laws by hiring underage boys and girls and labeling them as "independent contractors" rather than as employees.

Sutherland also documented the wrongdoing of notorious business magnates and maintained that what he deemed to be the inconsequential penalties meted out to them resulted from the fact that judges shared the same background as the offenders, having grown up in the same neighborhoods, gone to the same schools, and been members of the same clubs and churches.

White Collar Crime

It took another decade after the presidential address before Sutherland completed and Dryden Press issued his classic *White Collar Crime*. The Dryden monograph omitted several chapters that the publishers had asked to be excised on the ground that they feared lawsuits for defamation because Sutherland called certain corporations "criminal" although their violations had not been dealt with by a criminal court. It would be more than 30 years before an "uncut version" of *White Collar Crime* would be published (Sutherland, 1983).

Sutherland declared that his only aim was to invigorate criminological theory, a statement that some view as disingenuous. He maintained that his concern was with "the purpose of developing the theories of criminal behavior, not for the purpose of muckraking or reforming anything except criminology" (1940, p. 1). Some question the sincerity of this disclaimer given, for instance, Sutherland's characterization of utility companies:

[T]he utility corporations for two generations or more have engaged in organized propaganda to develop favorable sentiments. They devoted much attention to the public schools in an effort to mold the opinion of children. Perhaps no group except the Nazis have paid so much attention to indoctrinating the youth of the land with ideas favorable to a special interest, and it is doubtful whether even the Nazis were less bound by considerations of honesty in their propaganda. (1949, p. 210)

Sutherland insisted that the white-collar offenses he studied were truly criminal acts, however the legal system might (or might not) deal with them. His position here provoked strong criticism from some sociologists, particularly some who also had legal training. They argued that Sutherland was pinning a "criminal" label on persons who had been dealt with civilly or administratively. Paul Tappan lashed out at what he saw as the disregard for legal definitions in Sutherland's writing on white-collar crime. "One seeks in vain for criteria to determine the white-collar criminality," Tappan wrote. "Is it the conduct of one who wears a white collar and who indulges in occupational behavior to which some particular criminologist takes exception? It may easily be a term of propaganda" (Tappan, 1947, p. 99). Tappan was correct in that white-collar crime can be considered a term of propaganda directed against specified illegal activity with the intent to control such behavior, just as the term *crime* can be seen as implicit propaganda directed at law-breakers with the intent to deter and to capture and punish them.

Sutherland's defense relied on an analogy to medicine. No matter what treatment a patient receives—be it the poultices and bloodletting of earlier times or the streptomycin of Sutherland's time—a person who has tuberculosis is a tubercular person. Someone who commits a white-collar crime, Sutherland insisted analogously, remains a criminal whether or not the offense is discovered or how it is dealt with.

Sutherland compared the "rap sheets" of businesses to those of robbers and professional criminals, such as con men, and maintained that the companies were professional crooks since they had more law violations charged against them. Given the plentitude of laws regulating businesses and the number of persons who might violate them, some sociologists and criminologists consider this comparison far-fetched.

Sutherland believed that white-collar crime is more likely than street offenses to tear at the heart of a social system and to render its citizens cynical and selfish: "White-collar crimes violate trust and therefore create distrust," he wrote. "This lowers social morale and produces social disorganization. . . . Ordinary crimes, on the other hand, produce little effect on social institutions or social organization" (Sutherland, 1949, p. 13).

Conclusion

The subject of white-collar crime today serves much the same function that Sutherland assigned to it more than 60 years ago. First, it identifies and highlights a particular form of law-breaking that persistently has been viewed as distinct from the general problem of crime. At the beginning of 2009, a columnist in *The New York Times* bemoaned the fact that government investigators had determined that 50 billion American dollars allocated to rebuilding the Iraq infrastructure had been stolen by corrupt forces. What bothered the writer most of all was what had vexed Sutherland: The American public seemed indifferent to news of this gigantic swindle.

Second, white-collar crime has continued to haunt and befuddle theorists seeking all-embracing explanations of crime. The most popular current theoretical construct, promulgated by Michael Gottfredson and Travis Hirsch, maintains that an absence of self-control underlies all criminal behavior. But this formulation seems to collapse when attempts are made to apply it to the notorious spate of white-collar offenses that erupted after the turn into the current century. The crimes of upper echelon law-breakers at Enron, WorldCom, Adelphia, Arthur Andersen, and similar corporations and partnerships did not contain the characteristics that Gottfredson and Hirschi argued mark all criminal behavior, including such things as short-term goals and impulsive conduct (Benson & Moore, 1992; Steffensmeier, 1989).

Gilbert Geis

See also Clinard, Marshall B.: The Black Market; Cressey, Donald R.: Embezzlement and White-Collar Crime; Geis, Gilbert: Perspectives on White-Collar Crime Scandals; Ross, E. A.: Sin and Society; Sutherland, Edwin H.: Differential Association Theory and Differential Social Organization

References and Further Readings

Benson, M., & Moore, E. (1992). Are white-collar and common criminals the same? An empirical and theoretical critique of a recently proposed general theory of crime. *Journal of Research in Crime and Delinquency, 29,* 251–272.

Caldwell, R. G. (1958, March). A re-examination of the concept of white-collar crime. *Federal Probation, 22,* 30–36.

Cherney, R. W. (1981). *Populism, progressivism and the transformation of Nebraska politics, 1885–1915.* Lincoln: University of Nebraska Press.

Coffee, J. C., Jr. (1981). "No soul to damn, no body to kick": An unscandalized inquiry into the problem of corporate punishment. *Michigan Law Review, 79,* 396–459.

Cressey, D. R. (1988). Poverty of theory in corporate crime research. *Advances in criminological theory* (Vol. 1, pp. 31–56). New Brunswick, NJ: Transaction.

Geis, G. (2007). *White-collar and corporate crime.* Upper Saddle River, NJ: Prentice Hall.

Geis, G., & DiMento, J. F. C. (2002). Empirical evidence and the legal doctrine of corporate criminal liability. *American Journal of Criminal Law, 29,* 341–375.

Geis, G., & Goff, C. (1988). Introduction. In E. H. Sutherland, *White collar crime: The uncut version* (pp. ix–xxxiii). New Haven, CT: Yale University Press.

Gottfredson, M. R., & Hirschi, T. (1990). *A general theory of crime.* Stanford, CA: Stanford University Press.

Josephson, M. (1934). *The robber barons.* New York: Harcourt Brace.

Snodgrass, J. (1972). *The American criminological tradition: Portraits of men and ideology in a discipline.* Unpublished doctoral dissertation, University of Pennsylvania, Philadelphia.

Steffensmeier, D. J. (1989). On the causes of "white-collar" crime: An assessment of Hirschi and Gottfredson's claims. *Criminology, 27,* 345–358.

Sutherland, E. H. (1940). White-collar criminality. *American Sociological Review, 5,* 1–12.

Sutherland, E. H. (1947). *Principles of criminology* (4th ed.). Philadelphia: Lippincott.

Sutherland, E. H. (1949). *White collar crime.* New York: Dryden Press.

Sutherland, E. H. (1956). Crimes of corporations. In A. Cohen, A. Lindesmith, & K. Schuessler (Eds.), *The Sutherland papers* (pp. 78–96). Bloomington: Indiana University Press.

Sutherland, E. H. (1983). *White collar crime: The uncut version.* New Haven, CT: Yale University Press.

Tappan, P. W. (1947). Who is the criminal? *American Sociological Review, 12,* 96–102.

Sykes, Gresham M.: Deprivation Theory

A topic of great interest to penologists involves how subcultures are created and perpetuated by prison inmates. A culture reflects the various aspects of a society that enable its members to co-exist in the same geographic area in relative harmony. The defining aspects of any culture that separate one from another include a society's economy and means of sustenance, means of communication, value system, and stratification system. Inmate cultures are not completely distinct from outside cultures and so are often referred to as subcultures that exist within a broader society. Nonetheless, inmates develop some of their own values and norms to facilitate their adaptation to prison, to reduce conflict with each other, and to insulate themselves from correctional officers and prison administrators. Their language also includes some rather unique terms that reflect the deprivations of their environment. The rarity of currency also leads inmates to rely on a barter economy in order to trade goods with one another. Finally, a stratification system where inmates occupy various niches also develops in order to meet certain needs within the inmate population.

Overview

Gresham M. Sykes sought to understand *why* inmates develop their own subcultures during incarceration. While an assistant professor at Princeton University, Sykes was encouraged by the warden of the New Jersey State Penitentiary to conduct prison research at his facility. Sykes accepted this invitation and examined the social psychological aspects of prison life and the inherent frustrations faced by prison inmates. He argued

that the prison subculture was a reflection of these frustrations or "pains of imprisonment." With Sykes's classic work, *The Society of Captives*, the *deprivation* model of inmate adaptation emerged.

Sykes collected data from the New Jersey State Penitentiary during the mid-1950s. The maximum-security prison, built in the late 18th century, held 1,200 inmates and employed approximately 300 staff members. Data were compiled from official prison records, prison policies and regulations, inmate files, inmate interviews, staff interviews, and personal observations. Sykes was interested in examining differences in how inmates adjusted to the prison environment. His original intent was to formally test hypotheses related to inmate adjustment, but he changed his objective upon realizing that the current knowledge base on inmate roles was insufficient. He opted instead for an exploratory study of the prison social system.

From a sociological perspective, a prison can be understood as a social system that centers on efforts to establish and maintain absolute authority over inmates. This perspective is most applicable to maximum-security prisons where most every aspect of the prison environment is geared toward security and control. Security is the responsibility of the guards who exercise authority over inmates. Control is exerted through the use of rewards and punishment. According to Sykes, however, the ability of an institution to maintain complete control over inmates is more of an illusion than reality.

This was apparent in the numerous crimes and rule violations committed by inmates during incarceration. Sykes derived this information from prison disciplinary records, but both inmates and guards agreed that authorities only discovered a fraction of the actual number of violations. Sykes believed that the custodial staff was "engaged in a continuous struggle to maintain order" (1958, p. 42) but was largely unsuccessful in their efforts. In this maximum-security prison, conflict permeated the relationship between guards and inmates. Guards may have been granted legitimate authority to exercise control over the inmates, by virtue of their position, but inmates did not acknowledge this authority. Guards had to rely on persuasion and bribery to make sure inmates complied with their orders. The use of physical force was viewed as "inefficient" given that the inmates outnumbered the guards by a ratio of nearly 10 to 1.

Sykes found the prison's use of rewards and punishments to be an ineffective way to control inmates. The formal means of punishment—solitary confinement, loss of privileges, and altered work assignments—were typically not viewed as punitive by the inmates. Inmates were already confined, had few privileges, and had little say over their work assignments. Even the use of such rewards as mail, visitation, and "good time" were flawed because they were things given to all inmates upon their incarceration. Inmates viewed these rewards as rights, not privileges to be earned for their good behavior. They instead determined their own rewards, which were acknowledged by the guards. In exchange for compliance, a guard might "look the other way" for rule violations or warn inmates of an impending cell search.

The Pains of Imprisonment

Sykes observed that incarceration inflicted a different type of suffering on an inmate relative to the more physical punishments inflicted on criminals before the 19th century. Inmates were placed in a deprived environment where the living conditions were significantly different from those on the outside. He recognized that while the incarceration experience might differ for inmates, most inmates in his study perceived the prison environment as "depriving or frustrating in the extreme." Sykes called these deprivations the pains of imprisonment and described the five most common types.

Deprivation of Liberty

The most obvious deprivation involves banishing inmates to an institution and having their movements restricted within that institution. Incarceration removes inmates from their social network of family and friends. Inmates are permitted to communicate with those on the outside through correspondence and visits but most find their social ties diminished while incarcerated. Sykes reviewed the visiting records for a sample of the inmates and discovered that 41 percent had received no visits within the past year.

Deprivation of Goods and Services

At the time of Sykes's study, prison officials provided inmates with only basic necessities including clothes, food, shelter, and medical care. While many inmates may not have had all of these things prior to incarceration, there was no comparison between the quality of life inside versus outside of prison. An inmate's clothing consisted of a uniform with their number stenciled on it. There was little variety in the food, and medical care only had to be adequate. Inmates sought special amenities. Cigarettes, alcohol, more food (or at least a greater variety of food), and extra furnishings for their cells were among the more desired items. The emphasis placed on the importance of acquiring material goods in the American culture contributed further to this deprivation during incarceration.

Deprivation of Heterosexual Relationships

Sykes observed the sexual frustration experienced by inmates to be significant. Some inmates engaged in homosexual behavior as a means of alleviating that frustration, but the absence of heterosexual relationships still diminished inmates' perceptions of their own masculinity. Outside of prison, a heterosexual male's self identity is shaped, in part, by his interactions with women. Incarcerated men were denied those interactions in the prison under study.

Deprivation of Autonomy

Inmates lose their ability to make their own decisions while incarcerated. Prison rules and regulations control virtually every aspect of an inmate's life. Inmates are told when to get up, eat, sleep, shower, and work. Even "free" time is scheduled and regulated. Inmates perceive many of these rules to be unnecessary and used by guards only to exert their authority.

Deprivation of Security

Prisons are intended to protect society from criminals, but there is little protection of inmates from each other. Prisons bring offenders with extensive histories of violence into close proximity with less violent offenders, and inmates must remain alert for potential attacks by others. Those who would not otherwise be violent but who want to appear tough might also become aggressive simply to avoid being victimized.

Inmate Adaptations

Sykes argued that incarceration was punishment by nature of the above deprivations of imprisonment. These pains were not just felt by inmates, they threatened the inmates' self-identity. While the pains were an unavoidable part of being sent to prison, the inmate social networks found in prison could lessen the effects. Inmates who became part of an inmate social group (subculture) took on a new collective identity. They found adaptation to the prison environment easier when they were part of a group of inmates who experienced the same pains. Belonging to the group also provided opportunities for inmates to acquire goods and services beyond those supplied by the prison.

Sykes identified several "argot roles" occupied by the inmates in their social networks. Inmates displayed certain characteristic behaviors that were acknowledged by other inmates as well as the prison staff. The inmates themselves defined the roles. Prison "rats" or "squealers" were inmates who reported illegal or prohibited activities to prison officials. Inmates either snitched on other inmates as a way to win favor amongst the guards, to eliminate competition in an illegal enterprise, or in retaliation. Regardless of the motive, ratting out fellow inmates was perceived to be the absolute worst thing a prisoner could do because it was an offense against all inmates. Most inmates also disliked the "center men." Center men identified more with the guards than the other inmates and often went out of their way to accommodate the guards.

Inmates acquired goods and services beyond those provided by the prison either legitimately by shopping at the prison store or through illegitimate channels. Inmates participated in a barter system where they traded items amongst themselves. Not all inmates were willing to participate, and those who used force to take things from others were called "gorillas." "Merchants," on the other hand, sold items for profit. Inmates disliked both the gorillas and merchants because their activities disrupted their traditional barter system.

Despite the fact that the prison prohibited homosexual activities, and the vast majority of inmates who engaged in these activities were not considered homosexual, inmates categorized the homosexuals into three groups. "Wolves" were aggressors who forced themselves upon other inmates as a way to confirm their masculinity. These inmates resorted to homosexual sex as a means of adaptation. Upon their release, they would resume heterosexual relationships. "Punks" and "fags" were passive participants. Punks were forced into having sex with another inmate, while fags enjoyed having sex with other men (those who were homosexual before coming to prison). Because of their passive participation in homosexual sex, other inmates perceived them as feminine.

Some of the other roles were shaped by inmates' interactions with guards. Inmates who were openly defiant and antagonistic toward the guards were called "ball busters." Inmates were never expected to cooperate with the guards, but the ball busters were viewed as troublemakers. Their behavior often had negative consequences for all inmates. "Real men" displayed self-respect by appearing neither compliant nor hostile toward the guards. Other inmates admired them for their independence and self-restraint. Some inmates also used violence as a means of displaying their masculinity. The "toughs" were quick tempered and always willing to fight. Inmates admired them, but were also afraid of them. The "hipsters" were inmates who pretended to be tough but were perceived as cowards because they selectively picked fights with weaker inmates. These inmates would try to gain acceptance into any social group that would have them.

Significance and Subsequent Research

Sykes acknowledged that his study of inmate social systems as exploratory since he did not test specific hypotheses. Subsequent researchers set out to do what Sykes did not: establish relationships between prison deprivations and inmate attitudes and behaviors. Charles Tittle and Drollene Tittle interviewed a sample of imprisoned narcotic addicts. They measured the addicts' adherence to the prison code, time spent in the facility, their perceptions of difficulty adjusting to the environment, levels of alienation, participation in therapy, and the difference between the addicts' aspirations and expectations for success outside of the institution. Their findings offered support for several of the ideas put forth by Sykes. Time spent in the institution was associated with the addicts' adherence to the prison code. The pains of imprisonment were also lessened for addicts who adopted the inmate code.

Charles Wellford surveyed a sample of inmates from a Washington, D.C., prison about various aspects of their socialization into a subculture, time spent in prison, phase of their incarceration (beginning, middle, end), and criminal social type. Wellford presented these inmates with a series of hypothetical scenarios and asked them to rate their level of approval or disapproval with the behavior of the inmate in each scenario. He found no relationship between time spent in prison and adoption of the inmate code. By contrast, phase of incarceration and criminal social type were both related to adoption of the code. He concluded that prisonization depended more on the characteristics of inmates *prior to* their incarceration as opposed to the prison environment. Adoption of the inmate code was stronger for inmates who belonged to a criminal subculture on the outside.

In 1971, Barry Schwartz conducted a test using a sample of delinquents from the Glen Mills School for boys. His research also showed that several factors derived from an inmate's environment were significant predictors of their attitudes and behaviors, but pre-institutional factors were also important (similar to Wellford).

In 1974, Ronald Akers, Norman Hayner, and Werner Gruninger compiled data from seven prisons across the United States in order to determine if the *type* of prison was important for understanding the influences of deprivation. Prisons were classified along a treatment-custody continuum. Three prisons were classified as "treatment," three as "custodial," and one prison as "intermediate." A sample of inmates from each facility was administered questionnaires to assess their affiliation with an inmate social system, participation in prison programs, and their drug use and homosexual activities while incarcerated. They found that institutions with considerable amounts of drug use also had high amounts of homosexual activity, both of which were more frequent in custody-oriented prisons. This finding offered support for the deprivation model. In 1977, these same researchers conducted a study of prisonization with inmates from five different countries (including the United States) and also found that measures of deprivation were better predictors of inmate attitudes. Related to this theme, Michael Reisig and Yoon Ho Lee verified the applicability of Sykes's deprivation model to prisons in Korea.

In his study of a medium security prison, Charles Thomas administered inmate surveys tapping an inmate's degree of alienation and length of confinement (deprivation variables) as well as the inmate's pre-prison characteristics and their expectations for success after release. Three outcome measures were examined: the degree to which an inmate subscribed to subculture values, an inmate's level of opposition to the prison organization, and the degree to which an inmate perceived himself to be criminal. Thomas found that deprivation measures were better predictors of the first two outcomes.

Consistent with Sykes's observation that guards relied upon bribery to get inmates to comply with prison rules because inmates did not acknowledge the guards' authority, Richard Cloward found a similar theme in a northeast army prison. He observed that some inmates refused to accept their subordinate status. By adopting one of the argot roles described by Sykes, inmates secured positions within the prison's "illegitimate opportunity structure" that afforded them status. For example, the merchant gained status by controlling access to goods and services. Guards decided how much illicit activity would be tolerated through their control over the accessibility of these desirable positions.

In 1972, Schwartz identified one other deprivation, aside from those identified by Sykes, after reviewing several inmate autobiographical accounts of prison life. He argued that inmates also had to adapt to the *loss of privacy*. Virtually all of an inmates' time was spent in the presence of others. Activities that were once done in private, such as dressing or showering, took place in the company of other inmates and guards. Visits with family members were supervised and personal letters opened by officials. Inmates were subjected to routine strip and cell searches. Assimilation into an inmate subculture appeared to be a contradictory way of adapting to the loss of privacy; however, Schwartz believed that this particular deprivation helped explain two conflicting tenets of the inmate code. Inmates were expected to remain loyal to their group but at the same time to "do their own time."

Hans Toch provided a slightly different slant to Sykes's line of inquiry when he identified several needs of inmates that were consistent with Sykes's deprivations. Toch interviewed a sample of male inmates from five New York maximum-security prisons. He found that inmates consistently expressed concerns over privacy, safety, structure, support, emotional feedback, social stimulation, activity, and freedom. Toch developed the Prison Preference Inventory, an assessment tool used to measure the extent to which inmates express these needs.

Forty-three years after its publication, Sykes' *Society of Captives* was judged to be the most influential book ever written on prison (Reisig, 2001). Sykes's analysis of the prison environment has generated a considerable amount of research over the past 50 years.

John Wooldredge

See also DiIulio, John J., Jr.: Prison Management and Prison Order; Giallombardo, Rose: Women in Prison; Irwin, John, and Donald R. Cressey: Importation Theory; Toch, Hans: Coping in Prison

References and Further Readings

Akers, R., Hayner, N., & Gruninger, W. (1974). Homosexual and drug behavior in prison: A test of the functional and importation models of the inmate system. *Social Problems, 21,* 410–422.

Akers, R., Hayner, N., & Gruninger, W. (1977). Prisonization in five countries: Type of prison and inmate characteristics. *Criminology, 14,* 527–554.

Cloward, R. (Ed.). (1960). *Theoretical studies in social organization of the prison.* New York: Social Science Research Council.

Giallombardo, R. (1966). *Society of women: A study of a women's prison.* New York: Wiley.

Hagan, J. (1995). The "imprisoned society": Time turns a classic on its head. *Sociological Forum, 10,* 519–525.

Irwin, J., & Cressey, D. (1962). Thieves, convicts, and the inmate culture. *Social Problems, 10,* 142–155.

Reisig, M. (2001). The champion, contender, and challenger: Top-ranked books in prison studies. *Prison Journal, 81,* 389–407.

Reisig, M., & Lee, Y. (2000). Prisonization in the Republic of Korea. *Journal of Criminal Justice, 28,* 23-31.

Schwartz, B. (1971). Pre-institutional vs. situational influence in a correctional community. *Journal of Criminal Law, Criminology and Police Science, 62,* 532–542.

Schwartz, B. (1972). Deprivation of privacy as a "functional prerequisite": The case of the prison. *Journal of Criminal Law, Criminology and Police Science, 63,* 229–239.

Sykes, G. (1958). *The society of captives: A study of a maximum security prison.* Princeton, NJ: Princeton University Press.

Thomas, C. (1977). Theoretical perspectives on prisonization: A comparison of the importation and deprivation models. *Journal of Criminal Law and Criminology, 68,* 135–145.

Tittle, C., & Tittle, D. (1964). Social organization of prisoners: An empirical test. *Social Forces, 43,* 216–221.

Toch, H. (1977). *Living in prison.* New York: Free Press.

Wellford, C. (1967). Factors associated with adoption of the inmate code: A study of normative socialization. *Journal of Criminal Law, Criminology, and Police Science, 58,* 197–203.

Sykes, Gresham M., and David Matza: Techniques of Neutralization

Many theories of crime suggest that one of the most important elements in the process of criminal engagement is the psychological process of sanitizing the conscience so that it can be accomplished without suffering guilt. For this reason, much has been written about the ways that offenders make sense of or account for their criminal acts and related behaviors. Perhaps the most well-known explanation of this process was proposed by Gresham M. Sykes and David Matza with what is now referred to as *neutralization theory*. According to Sykes and Matza, when offenders contemplate committing criminal acts, they use linguistic devices to neutralize the guilt of committing crime. By doing so, they can commit crime without serious damage to their self-concept. This simple explanation of crime has had a tremendous impact on criminological theory. This essay describes the theoretical foundation of the theory and its place in the history of criminology. It then discusses several of the lingering issues about neutralization theory and how the theory has withstood empirical evaluations. It concludes with a discussion about how the theory has been applied in criminal justice policy.

Theoretical Foundation

Sykes and Matza's influential article began with a critique of subcultural theorists of the time. Subcultural theorists argued that delinquent boys rebelled against the dominant social order by rejecting middle-class standards and replacing them with a new, often delinquent, set of values. Sykes and Matza disagree, contending that subcultural theorists overstated the extent to which delinquents rejected conventional values. They argue that everyone, even lower-class delinquent gang members, retains some commitment to the dominant value system of society.

They base their argument on four key points. First, if delinquent subcultures do exist, then delinquents should view their criminal behavior as morally correct. Therefore, they should not experience guilt or shame for engaging in the act or for being caught doing so. Second, delinquents should value the opinions and lifestyles of those promoting similar delinquent lifestyles and dismiss the opinions of conventional others. Third, if offenders unconditionally accept crime, then it would be expected that they would treat all victims equally. Fourth, offenders should be immune to the demands of conformity. Critiquing each of these claims, Sykes and Matza argue that delinquents do often feel guilt and shame for participating in illegal behaviors; show respect and admiration for honest, law-abiding others; make clear distinctions about who can and cannot be victimized; and still participate in the same social functions that law-abiding citizens do (including church, school, and family activities). Together, these factors suggest that delinquents are able to distinguish between right and wrong and are subject to influences of both conventional and delinquent subcultures. That is, young offenders are well aware of the wrongfulness of their actions.

Yet, if delinquents maintain at least minimal commitments to the dominant social order, then how are they then able to violate its norms? If people are committed to the social order, they typically experience guilt or shame for violating, or even contemplating violating, social norms. This guilt, and its potential for producing a negative self-image, helps to dissuade most people from engaging in criminal or deviant acts. Therefore, in order to participate in deviant behavior under such conditions, people must find ways to rationalize their actions or to neutralize the guilt associated with them. People do this by relying on linguistic devices that when invoked, blunt the moral force of the law and neutralize the guilt of criminal participation. Through the use of these techniques

social and internal controls that serve to check or inhibit deviant motivational patterns are blocked, allowing individuals to engage freely in delinquency without serious damage to their self-image. In this way, offenders can remain committed to the dominant normative system and interpret their deviant actions as acceptable or proper.

All of these neutralization techniques emerge from thoughts and beliefs that are widely prevalent in society and not something created anew. In fact, delinquent neutralizations are legitimated by the juvenile justice system itself. For example, when agents of convention, from social workers to judges, argue that delinquents are the helpless products of their environment, they unwittingly contribute to the internalization of neutralizing excuses. What delinquents hear in these cases confirms their viewpoints that their behaviors are acceptable and beyond their control. The mitigation procedures built into the legal machinery itself lends credence and support to adolescent interpretations of delinquency being excusable.

Sykes and Matza outline five techniques of neutralization that allow offenders to engage in wrongdoing (i.e., denial of responsibility, denial of injury, denial of the victim, condemnation of condemners, and the appeal to higher loyalties). First, offenders can rid themselves of negative self-images through the *denial of responsibility*. Offenders deny responsibility by claiming that their behaviors are accidental or due to forces beyond their control. They see themselves as victims of circumstance or as products of their environment. A second technique is the *denial of injury*. Here, the wrongfulness of one's behavior is determined by whether anyone was hurt and by whether the actor intended to do any harm. Offenders can excuse their behaviors if they believe that no one was truly harmed. Offenders who use these techniques may claim that their behavior is inappropriate in general but in this particular instance it is acceptable because no real harm was caused by their actions. Sometimes offenders admit that their actions cause harm but neutralize moral indignation by *denying the victim*. This can be done in one of two ways. First, they may contend that some victims act improperly and thus deserve everything that happens to them. Offenders define their own actions as a form of rightful retaliation or punishment, thereby claiming the victim does not deserve victim status. Denial of the victim also occurs if the victim is absent, unknown, or abstract. In these situations, the offender can ignore easily the rights of victims because the victims are not around to stimulate the offender's conscience. A fourth technique is the *condemnation of the condemner*. Instead of focusing on their own actions, delinquents focus on the motivations or behaviors of the people who disapprove of them. Offenders claim that their condemners are hypocrites or "deviants in disguise." The importance of this technique is that the offenders shift the focus to the actions of others while making their behavior seem less important. The final technique described by Sykes and Matza is the *appeal to higher loyalties*. Offenders shield themselves from internal and external controls by claiming that their behavior is consistent with the moral obligations of a specific group to which they belong. Here the offender acknowledges the conventional norms of society, and may agree with them, but chooses to violate the law because other norms are thought to be more pressing.

Sykes and Matza's original list of five offender justifications is not the last word on offender accounts. Their theory has subsequently been expanded to different types of offenders and offenses, and new techniques appear to emerge with each new exploration into a deviant group. For instance, qualitative studies of white-collar offenders have produced several new techniques including the defense of necessity, the claim of normality, and the claim of entitlement. Studies of property offenders have introduced the techniques of the metaphor of the ledger, justification by comparison, and postponement. It is almost certain that this list of additional neutralizations will grow as research in the area continues.

Neutralization Theory's Place in Criminology

The influence of neutralization theory is unquestionable. Sykes and Matza's short article is one of the most frequently cited and influential explanations of criminal behavior through the first part of the 21st century. According to the Social Science Citation Index, the article has been cited over 900 times between the time it was published and the end of 2009. Perhaps the greatest testament to the importance of neutralization theory is the fact that it is no longer confined to the study of juvenile

delinquents, or even adult offenders. Neutralization techniques are used universally in response to inconsistencies between one's actions and one's beliefs. Not only has neutralization theory been used to help understand issues as serious as rape, murder, and genocide, but also it has been used to explain participation in less serious deviant behaviors such as playing bingo, Sunday shopping among Mormons, and entering pre-teen daughters into beauty pageants. Neutralization theory has also been used to explain how survivors of domestic violence cope with their victimization. Finally, neutralization theory has found a receptive audience in studies of organizational and white-collar crime.

Neutralization theory is usually understood as a single component of a larger theory. Alone, the theory provides insufficient explanation for differences in crime across cultures, groups, genders, or the like. As such, the theory's value is rightly understood as enhancing or developing existing theoretical frameworks for understanding offending. Indeed, neutralization theory has been linked to almost so many different wider traditions of criminological thought over the years that it is difficult to know how to classify it in the criminological canon. Introductory textbooks consider it variously as a part of control theory, psychological theories, learning theory, and subcultural theory. In addition, neutralization techniques have been incorporated into reintegrative shaming theory, rational choice theory, and even as a small component of life-course theory, leaving very few areas of contemporary criminological theory untouched by its reach.

As initially proposed, neutralizations were an extension and refinement of Edwin Sutherland's differential association theory. Sutherland argued that, through interacting with others, offenders learned not just the techniques of crime, but also the definitions (i.e., motives and rationalizations) favorable to crime. Sykes and Matza argued that up until that time researchers had ignored the content of what was learned, preferring instead to focus on the process by which delinquency was learned. Thus, techniques of neutralization were thought to make up a crucial component of Sutherland's definitions favorable to violation of law. Eventually, neutralization theory began to be viewed as more than a refinement of differential association theory and became an independent theory of crime and deviance. Matza's drift theory was instrumental in this process as neutralization took a primary role in the theory.

The incorporation of neutralizations into Matza's theory of delinquency and drift led others to classify neutralization theory as a component of control theory. For instance, neutralization theory can be considered as one component of containment theory. Containment theory argues that refraining from criminal behavior requires a blend of self factors (inner containment) and social factors (outer containment). Strong inner and outer containments insulate individuals from becoming involved in crime. In addition, norm erosion—ignoring the moral significance of norms, the neutralization of what ought to be done, and emancipation from internalized norms—is an important factor in the breakdown of inner containments.

To a lesser degree, neutralization theory has been incorporated into the writings of rational choice theorists. Contemporary rational choice theorists have moved away from early economic models, preferring models of behavior that recognize bounded decision-making processes. Rational choice theorists now devote much of their time to modeling the various stages of criminal decision making, including initiation, continuance, and desistance. Neutralization is thought to play a significant part in the decision-making process at each of these stages, and therefore investigators frequently take them into account when modeling criminal decision making and devising crime prevention programs.

The theory is also firmly established within the canon of work dealing with account-making in sociology. The sociology of accounts borrowed heavily from neutralization theory. Accounts can also be seen as an important refinement of the original neutralization formulation, although it is not always incorporated into contemporary discussions of neutralization theory. Similar to the techniques of neutralization, accounts are meant to verbally bridge the gap between action and expectation when an individual behaves in a way that is inconsistent with normative expectations. Accounts can be justifications or excuses. Justifications are accounts where actors accept responsibility for their actions, but deny the pejorative quality associated with it. Excuses, on the other hand, are accounts where the actor admits that the act in question is bad, wrong, or inappropriate but denies full responsibility.

The techniques of neutralization make up a large part of justifications. For instance, denial of injury, denial of victims, condemnation of condemners, and appeal to higher loyalties can be viewed as a tentative list of types of justifications. The remaining (and probably most central) technique, denial of responsibility, is incorporated into the appeal to defensibility as one of many excuses. Subsequent research suggests that actors use justifications and excuses depending on the deviant act they are engaging in. For example, actors tend to provide justifications for violent offenses, but excuses for property crimes. Violent crimes are often the product of a dispute between two parties, and offenders frequently interpret their role as one of self-defense or a reasonable reaction to hostile provocation. Property crimes, on the other hand, can rarely be interpreted in this way, and so are more frequently excused.

Theoretical Issues

In their original formulation of theory Sykes and Matza state that techniques of neutralization must precede deviant behavior in order to make such behavior possible. This statement makes two crucial claims about the techniques of neutralization that are often overlooked in empirical work using neutralization theory. First, there is a specific chronological sequence of neutralizations and delinquent behavior. Neutralizations are not just a posteriori rationalizations as they precede delinquency. Without them, guilt and negative self-images would prevent people from engaging in crime. It is this aspect of the theory that is the most significant stumbling point for neutralization theory. Sykes and Matza are clear in their contention that neutralizations precede delinquency; otherwise, delinquents could not free themselves of the potential harm to their self-concept. Critics argue that neutralizations are simply after-the-fact rationalizations meant to justify wrongdoing. This debate has continued essentially unabated ever since.

Second, and just as important, Sykes and Matza emphasize that this order is not meant to imply a deterministic or causal relationship. Neutralization techniques enable crime but do not require it. Matza develops this argument much more explicitly with his concept of "drift," which is defined as a temporary period of irresponsibility or an episodic relief from moral constraint. Neutralization enables drift by freeing the individual from the moral bind of law and order. Once set in a state of drift, a young person is likely to willfully choose to commit a crime under circumstances of preparation (or familiarity with the particular offense type) or desperation. Matza's concept of desperation is linked to the delinquent's central neutralization technique, the denial of responsibility, or what is referred to as a "mood of fatalism." In the mood of fatalism, common to the experience of drift, delinquents believe that they have been uncontrollably thrust into new situations like a billiard ball. This feeling of helplessness simultaneously relieves the individual from the binds of morality and also encourages the delinquent to want to take control of his or her situation and prove that he or she can make something happen. Considering the limited options available to adolescents, this frequently means committing a new type of offense in order to regain a sense of being in control of their environment.

Another issue with the theory involves who will and will not use neutralizations. Sykes and Matza made explicit that only those actors who are committed to conventional norms rely on neutralization techniques to protect their self-concept when committing crime or delinquency. It is because of their commitments that they experience guilt or shame for engaging in deviant behaviors. Recent research suggests that the assertion that all people are committed to the dominant culture is overstated. For example, many offenders are committed to their misdeeds and need not take effort to justify them. A small proportion of people becomes highly committed to delinquent values. Since these individuals are relatively unattached to mainstream values, there may be nothing for them to neutralize. For instance, persistent street offenders do not experience guilt about engaging in serious forms of crime and thus often do not neutralize their criminal actions. They do, however, need to neutralize when they violate subcultural norms that oppose doing "the right thing" in their social world, like snitching or failing to retaliate when wronged.

There is also evidence that those who have a strong commitment to conventional norms do not employ neutralizations. Youths who have strong attachments to family are less likely to accept neutralizations than those with weaker familial attachments. The high levels of moral commitment are thought to create too much guilt to be overcome by simple neutralization techniques. Therefore, only less committed individuals would have the need and ability to use them effectively.

Research suggests that there is a curvilinear relationship between use of neutralizations and commitment to conventional norms. Neutralization use is most commonly associated with individuals who either identify as members of mainstream society or who are in a state of drift: partially committed to conventional values and to a certain lifestyle or set of behaviors that is labeled as deviant. An absence of neutralization is associated with people and groups who are either hypercommitted to dominant moral values or else strongly committed to a subcultural frame of reference. For those who are strongly attached or who exaggerate conventional morals (e.g., adult virgins), neutralizations are simply ineffective. For those who are weakly committed (e.g., persistent offenders), neutralizations are simply not needed because these individuals are strongly committed to a subcultural lifestyle. Thus, it is only those whose commitments fall somewhere in the middle who both accept and rely on neutralizations to excuse their behaviors.

Critiques and Evaluations

Empirical assessments of the theory typically use cross-sectional survey designs to test the core assumptions of the theory by locating a sample of known offenders and a control group sample of "innocents," then asking respondents in both groups to agree or disagree with a list of neutralizations (often in relation to hypothesized scenarios). One research strategy is to compare a sample of known delinquents with a sample of non-delinquents to determine if the delinquents are more accepting of neutralizations than are non-delinquents, as predicted by neutralization theory. The second way this question has been addressed is by using measures of neutralization acceptance to predict self-reported delinquency in a single sample. Both designs have been used to examine the correlation of neutralization scores and relatively minor deviant acts such as college cheating, workplace deviance, drinking behaviors, shoplifting, and minor delinquency. Overall, this research has found positive but weak effects of neutralizations on deviance. Unfortunately, the bulk of this research has utilized cross-sectional designs, which are unable to disentangle the sequential relationship of neutralizations and deviance. Without the benefit of longitudinal designs, there is no way to determine if neutralizations precede criminal behavior or if they are merely after-the-fact rationalizations. For the most part, findings show that excuse acceptance is related to future participation in minor deviance. Even the few longitudinal designs produce weak, mixed support for the theory.

Despite this mostly underwhelming empirical support for neutralization theory, criminologists have not given up hope on the theory. Researchers have offered a variety of explanations for the mixed findings, and they argue that most studies have been limited in their ability to support or disprove the theory with certainty. In general, although survey research has provided a great deal of information regarding the use of neutralizations, this line of research suffers from several seemingly insurmountable methodological limitations.

First, Sykes and Matza's seemingly uncomplicated theory is often misrepresented in this evaluation research. For instance, except for the few longitudinal designs, survey research has been unable to accurately determine if neutralizations precede criminal behavior. Many tests of neutralization theory are actually testing whether people who have been convicted of a crime tend to score higher on neutralization-like measures than young people who have not. This, of course, is not a test of the rationalization process.

Likewise, neutralization research often fails to distinguish between beliefs that serve to neutralize conventional bonds and beliefs that simply show unconventional commitment. In typical neutralization measurements, respondents are asked if they agree with statements such as, "People should not blame Marcus for stealing if this was the normal thing to do where Marcus lived" or "Suckers deserve to be taken advantage of." Acceptance of these statements is subject to multiple interpretations. They could mean that respondents thought this was a good excuse or else they could have thought stealing or taking advantage of others was morally acceptable regardless of whether an excuse was used or not. Thus, they can be interpreted as acceptance of unconventional values rather than neutralizations.

Fundamental flaws in most research on neutralization may be responsible for the mixed results showing links between neutralization use and criminal behavior. Most tests presume a causal relationship between neutralizations and offending that misrepresents the contention that neutralizations only allow for delinquency. Therefore, neutralizations are only likely to lead to delinquency among those who are in situations in which the neutralizations are applicable; encounter opportunities for delinquency; and have a strong need or desire to commit the offense. For example, college students who think it is acceptable to cheat on exams if other people around them are cheating must believe that people around them are actually cheating. This same explanation can be used to explain the findings that females accept the same number of, if not more, neutralizations than males, but commit far less crime and delinquency. This reformulation of neutralization theory may explain the contradictory findings of other researchers.

Researchers also frequently rely on inappropriate samples. For instance, several of the most frequently cited tests of neutralization theory utilize all-too-convenient samples of university students enrolled in criminology or sociology courses. Generalizing from such samples to the population of typical interest to criminologists (e.g., street offenders) is problematic. Using non-criminal samples means that findings must be questioned, regardless of whether they offer support or not for the theory.

Neutralization research relies heavily on incarcerated samples, where a person's incarcerated status is used as evidence of deviance. The many problems with using incarcerated samples are magnified in cognitive research, where familiar findings of low self-efficacy, weak locus of control, and overall levels of frustration and hostility are quite obviously magnified or distorted by the deprivations of liberty associated with incarceration. Such prison-based cognitions may have no relevance to the same person's thinking patterns outside of such a total institution. Furthermore, there are countless situational demands inherent in the prison setting that can magnify the possibility of response bias.

The conflicting results of previous research may be due to several methodological problems. First, there has been an over-reliance on quantitative techniques. Typical tests of the theory rely on survey measures that were not originally designed to measure neutralization concepts. There are few empirical tests of the theory that have used qualitative methods. When qualitative methods are used, investigators typically describe the neutralizations used by offenders to neutralize a specific form of deviance without testing or expanding the theory. Researchers use the theory only as a conceptual tool to understand participation in crime or deviance.

Finally and most importantly, survey research on neutralizations suffers from a fundamental artificiality problem. As opposed to the exploratory studies that have uncovered neutralizations in spontaneous explanations of deviant behavior, survey-based studies measure neutralizations almost exclusively in the abstract. Typical neutralization items on a survey include questions like, "It's alright to physically beat up people who call you names." Questioning a respondent's approval or disapproval of criminal behavior—even in select, hypothetical situations like this—treats neutralizations as generalized beliefs rather than personal reconstructions of events from a person's own life.

Yet Sykes and Matza argued that neutralizations matter because these cognitive beliefs protect an offender from serious damage to his or her self-image. They are techniques for preserving a non-criminal self-concept, despite the commission of criminal acts. If an act has never been committed, and is therefore not a threat to the person's identity, it requires no neutralization in the formal sense. This logical argument has in fact been empirically demonstrated in several studies that indicate that offenders tend to subscribe primarily to neutralizations relating to offenses they had personally committed.

Pencil-and-paper questionnaires regarding abstract neutralizations may be missing the real cognitive insight of neutralization theory: the way people reconstruct and schematize their *own* past lives can have an important impact on their future behavior. Causal schemata like explanations and accounts are highly personalized phenomena based in salient episodes in a person's own life experience. Moreover, cognitive psychologists argue that our causal beliefs are storied; that is, they take the form of narratives and depend upon a person's lived context and perspective. People use rationalizations to provide their often chaotic lives with a sense of meaning, control, and predictability. Abstract questionnaire items may not be able to tap into this aspect of a person's identity in a meaningful way.

Implications of Neutralization Theory on Criminal Justice Policy

Neutralization theory is intended to help explain the occurrence of certain kinds of deviant and criminal behavior; as such, it is perhaps natural that its adherents would see implications in the theory for criminal justice or correctional policy. For instance, neutralization theory has been used in developing crime prevention programs. The idea here is that by learning the linguistic devices that offenders use to make their crimes palatable, program designers can actively attack these belief systems. By neutralizing the neutralizations, potential offenders would not be able to define their actions as non-criminal and thus would refrain from criminal behavior. True to situational crime prevention's roots, "removing excuses" in this way does not entail making long-term changes in the disposition of the offender. Instead, situational crime prevention theorists argue that programs geared toward removing excuses should still focus on highly specific forms of crime and should be presented at the time criminal decisions are being made. For instance, organizational managers are encouraged to openly discuss the neutralizations that wayward employees use. Bringing these neutralizations into the open is thought to force employees to consciously consider their actions when stealing from the company.

Likewise, restorative justice interventions, such as family group conferencing—where offenders sit down with family members, community elders, and their victims in a reintegrative shaming process—are largely premised on social-cognitive principles, with the explicit aim of undermining offender neutralizations. In fact, nearly every form of offender treatment—from the 12 Steps model of Alcoholics Anonymous to the confrontational techniques of therapeutic communities—involves some strategies for overcoming denial and challenging offender rationalizations. In fact, the ascendancy of cognitive-based treatment programs in correctional settings has triggered a new generation of research into the role of offender excuses and justifications in criminal behavior. After all, the premise behind much of this cognitive programming owes a considerable debt to the neutralization idea: Offending is partially facilitated by a cognitive mind-set that justifies and rationalizes criminal behavior.

Finally, around the same time that criminologists were exploring how offenders made sense of their crimes, law enforcement personnel began developing interrogation techniques involving offering justifications to suspects to obtain confessions. This interrogation technique, known as the Reid Technique of Interviewing and Interrogation, made use of similar concepts that criminologists were discovering, specifically that offenders relieve their feelings of guilt about their criminal behavior by utilizing specific linguistic techniques (i.e., neutralizations). The Reid Technique consists of a series of behavior-provoking questions that assist interrogators in determining a suspect's truthfulness. Once an interrogator has enough information to believe that the suspect committed a crime, the interrogator verbalizes moral justifications to the suspect to explain why the interrogator thinks the suspect committed the crime. Law enforcement practitioners can improve their interrogation techniques by understanding the mind-set and justifications offenders use both prior to their involvement in crime and following the event.

It should be pointed out, however, that these various applications are a long way from the origins of neutralization theory in criminology. Sykes and Matza hoped that rather than pathologizing offenders, neutralization theory would do the opposite: demonstrating how similar juvenile delinquents really were to the rest of us. Indeed, the wider research on excuse-making in social psychology suggests that they were probably right in this regards. Psychologists argue that not only is it perfectly normal to offer up excuses and justifications for one's shortcomings, that doing so is socially expected and rewarded.

Heith Copes and Shadd Maruna

See also Benson, Michael L.: Fall From Grace: The Collateral Consequences of White-Collar Offending; Braithwaite, John: Reintegrative Shaming Theory; Cognitive Theories of Crime; Matza, David: Delinquency and Drift; Sutherland, Edwin H.: Differential Association Theory and Differential Social Organization

References and Further Readings

Agnew, R. (1994). The techniques of neutralization and violence. *Criminology, 32,* 555–580.

Maruna, S., & Copes, H. (2005). What have we learned from fifty years of neutralization research? In M. Tonry (Ed.), *Crime and justice: A review of research* (Vol. 32, pp. 221–320). Chicago: University of Chicago Press.

Maruna, S., & Mann, R. (2006). Fundamental attribution errors? Re-thinking cognitive distortions. *Legal and Criminological Psychology, 11,* 155–177.

Matza, D. (1964). *Delinquency and drift.* New York: Wiley.

Sykes, G. M., & Matza, D. (1957). Techniques of neutralization: A theory of delinquency. *American Sociological Review, 22,* 664–670.

Topalli, V. (2005). When being good is bad: An expansion of neutralization theory. *Criminology, 43,* 797–835.

Systemic Model of Social Disorganization

After falling into disregard for several decades, social disorganization theory re-emerged in the last part of the 20th century in the form of the systemic model of social disorganization theory. This version of social disorganization theory clarified and specified the key concepts of social disorganization theory in ways that Clifford Shaw and Henry McKay, the original developers of the theory, had not done. Specifically, the systemic version of social disorganization theory further clarified levels of neighborhood informal social control as the key factor responsible for variations in crime rates and further specified that informal social control was predicated on the levels of social ties within communities.

This reformulation of social disorganization theory became very popular, and received much attention in terms of research and policy. As the 20th century turned to the 21st however, another slightly different version, the collective efficacy version, of social disorganization also appeared. Both versions, however, emphasize the importance of neighborhood levels of informal social control. Most contemporary research done within a social disorganization framework will be identified as either examining the systemic or collective efficacy model. This entry discusses the development of the systemic version of social disorganization theory from the original theory, some of the critical findings from examinations of the systemic version, and some of the questions this version of social disorganization theory has generated.

Social Disorganization Theory and the Theoretical Development of the Systemic Version

Social disorganization theory was developed by Shaw and McKay in the early 1900s. They presented the central ideas of their theory in their book, *Juvenile Delinquency and Urban Areas.* The theory was an attempt to explain their findings about the patterns of delinquency across neighborhoods. Specifically, they found that neighborhoods with high levels of delinquency tended to remain high in delinquency across time, even after many of the original residents had moved to other neighborhoods, and the ethnicity of the neighborhood had completely changed. They also found that high rates of delinquency were associated with neighborhood characteristics of low socioeconomic status, residential instability, and ethnic heterogeneity. Their theory explained the relationship between these structural features of neighborhoods and rates of crime and delinquency in terms of neighborhood variation in levels of social disorganization.

Based largely on William Thomas and Florian Znaniecki's work, Shaw and McKay define social organization in terms of "the presence of social opinion with regard to problems of common interest, identical or at least consistent attitudes with reference to these problems, the ability to reach approximate unanimity on the question of how a problem should be dealt with, and the ability to carry this solution into action through harmonious co-operation" (p. 184). Ruth Rosner Kornhauser later re-articulated this in the definition of social disorganization most commonly used today: "social disorganization is the inability to realize common values" (p. 120). More specifically, in relation to the structural components of social disorganization, Kornhauser states, "social disorganization means the lack of articulation of social structure with common values. Structural disorganization is manifested in institutional inability to provide routes to valued goals, and in discontinuities in socialization and control, which further hinder the quest for and achievement of common values" (p. 120). Thus, social disorganization became viewed largely as a neighborhood's inability to

provide *informal social control* of behavior inconsistent with values commonly held among residents. Informal social control has been predominantly conceptualized in two ways: as informal surveillance and direct intervention. Informal surveillance refers to keeping an eye on what's going on in the neighborhood; watching for, and being able to recognize, strangers in the neighborhood; and watching neighbors' homes and property when they are away. Direct intervention refers to anything that residents themselves do to stop inappropriate behaviors. This can include socialization techniques, such as encouraging or rewarding appropriate behaviors or pointing out inappropriate behavior and reminding residents of neighborhood standards. But it also includes many other behaviors, such as questioning strangers, chastising children for misbehaving, gossiping among residents about inappropriate behavior, reporting to children's parents about their misbehavior, or administering other informal sanctions (or threats of informal sanctions) for inappropriate behavior.

With this newly clarified definition of social disorganization, along with the availability of new data sources (such as the National Crime Victimization Survey), the 1980s brought a renewed interest in addressing some of the earlier problems related to examining the theory, and social disorganization theory once again was viewed as worthy and capable of empirical research. This newly re-emerged social disorganization theory viewed a community's inability to socialize and informally control behaviors that occurred within the neighborhood as the seminal concept mediating the neighborhood structural effects of poverty, residential instability, and racial/ethnic heterogeneity on crime and delinquency.

Such a view of social disorganization came to rely on a "systemic" definition of community, and was thus referred to as the *systemic model of social disorganization.* The systemic view of community developed in contrast to earlier characterizations that viewed modern urban life as comprising mostly highly segmented, impersonal, and superficial relationships. For example, Louis Wirth, like other sociologists before him, argued that due to the density and heterogeneity of modern urban populations, social life in these areas was much different from social life in rural areas. In particular, he noted that "the bonds of kinship, of neighborliness, and the sentiments arising out of living together for generations under a common folk tradition are likely to be absent or, at best, relatively weak" (p. 11). Mutual acquaintanceship between neighbors was viewed as lacking, allowing "a certain degree of emancipation or freedom from the personal and emotional controls of intimate groups" (p. 13).

John Kasarda and Morris Janowitz referred to the above model of urban social life as the linear development model "because linear increases in the population size and density of human communities are assumed to be the primary exogenous factors influencing patterns of social behavior" (p. 328). In contrast to this view, Kasarda and Janowitz present the systemic model. In this model, "the local community is viewed as a complex system of friendship and kinship networks and formal and informal associational ties rooted in family life and on-going socialization processes" (p. 329). The systemic view of community viewed the social fabric of communities as made up of friendship and relational ties. This view focused on residential stability as the most important exogenous variable affecting community behaviors, as it affected the "friendship and kinship bonds and formal and informal associational ties within the local community" (p. 330).

It is within the framework of this systemic view of community that social disorganization theory re-emerged with great excitement in the late 20th century. This model of social disorganization argued that the capacity of a neighborhood to provide informal social control develops out of the friendship networks and associational ties of its residents (Bursik & Grasmick, 1993). Friendship networks and associational ties are often referred to simply as social ties. Friendship networks generally refer to the number of friends and relatives one has in the neighborhood and/or the level of neighboring behaviors engaged in with neighbors, such as borrowing tools or food, helping neighbors with problems, or engaging in activities together. Associational ties generally refer to the number of neighborhood-based organizations—such as churches, ethnic organizations, parent-teacher associations, and neighborhood associations—in which residents participate.

These social ties are argued to be largely determined by community structural factors of poverty, residential instability, and racial/ethnic heterogeneity. Specifically, communities with high rates of poverty, residential mobility, and racial or ethnic heterogeneity are hypothesized to be less able to support lasting, wide-ranging friendship networks. Neighborhoods with high mobility rates are neighborhoods in which fewer residents are likely to know each other, simply because it takes time to develop relationships. Heterogeneity also diminishes community ties, as racial and ethnic differences among residents may impose barriers to friendships and broad-based organizational ties, thereby limiting the breadth of neighborhood networks. Poverty constrains the choices people have regarding where, and among whom, they can live. Poverty, according to William Julius Wilson, may directly decrease social ties due to the demanding and "negative" nature of social ties in an impoverished community. Because of these issues, poverty may lead to withdrawing from social networks.

While social ties are influenced by these structural characteristics of communities, social ties in turn affect the level of informal social control of inappropriate behavior and crime. Social ties are viewed as the foundation for informal social control because they provide the mechanism through which the articulation of shared values occurs and support for enforcing those values is generated within communities. When neighbors interact with one another, they come to mutually shape a shared expectation for the standards of behavior that are acceptable within the community. With this shared understanding of what is and is not appropriate in the neighborhoods, residents can then expect that others will support them when they enforce those shared expectations for appropriate behavior. In communities where residents know many or most of their neighbors and have a shared understanding of behaviors that are inappropriate, they will be more likely to define inappropriate behavior as such and intervene in some way to stop it. Further, when residents know one another, the use of informal social control is more likely to be effective. Residents are going to be more concerned with what others think if they are friends or participate in the same organization or have mutual acquaintances that may spread gossip about them. On the other hand, residents that do not know each other, rarely interact, and are not part of a shared network, are unlikely to care what others think of them.

In this model, then, communities with wider friendship and associational ties are viewed as having the ability to work together to solve neighborhood problems, especially through their ability to supervise and informally control neighborhood youths. The level of crime and delinquency is, in turn, viewed as being decreased due to the supervision and control of youths as well as other residents and non-residents in the neighborhood.

This basic systemic model was expanded by Robert Bursik and Harold Grasmick in their book *Neighborhoods and Crime* in which they further specified the types of relationships that are important in neighborhood social control. Building on Albert Hunter's three-tiered approach to social control, they provide an understanding of how different types of social relationships can be associated with variation in neighborhood informal social control. Hunter identified social control as existing at the private, parochial, and public levels. Bursik and Grasmick expound upon the importance of social relationships at each of these levels.

Private social control is that which is "grounded in the intimate informal primary groups that exist in the area" (Bursik & Grasmick, 1993, p. 16). These intimate, primary relations include family members and friends. Because there is some emotional or affective tie among these members, they are able to provide socialization and/or control through both caring support and threatened withdrawal of support or respect. Parochial social control is based in "broader local interpersonal networks and the interlocking of local institutions, such as stores, schools, churches, and voluntary organizations" (p. 17). Parochial ties are thus "relationships among neighbors that do not have the same sentimental attachment" (p. 17). Nonetheless, people are often affected by how other residents or members of neighborhood organizations view them and therefore are sensitive to their reactions to their behavior. Finally, the level of public social control is concerned with the community's ability to procure services from external agencies. Central here are relationships between neighborhood residents and others outside the neighborhood, particularly relationships between the community and representatives of agencies that effect control within the neighborhood, such as the police and municipal service agencies.

These conceptualizations of social ties fit well with ideas of social capital that were also being re-popularized. Social capital refers to the human resources that can be drawn upon to accomplish goals. For example, Robert Putnam discusses social relationships in terms of "bonding" and "bridging" social capital. Bonding social capital refers to social networks among small groups of people that bring them closer together. It develops through informal interactions in the everyday lives of families and individuals living in communities. Alternatively, Putnam refers to bridging social capital as social ties between neighborhood residents and organizations and individuals outside of the neighborhood. This form of social capital refers to more loosely connected networks of large numbers of individuals typically linked through indirect ties. Bridging social capital connects neighborhoods and people to others, across diverse social groups and/or localities. Bridging social capital includes connections to institutions and organizations that may facilitate access to needed resources for community-initiated solutions to problems.

While not often explicitly stated, this multi-tiered conceptualization of social ties also widened the types of intervening subsumed within social disorganization models to include indirect intervention. That is, the inclusion of public social control and public (or bridging) social ties now further broadened the systemic model to consider how relationships between the community and external agencies affected the regulation of criminal or delinquent behavior. To the extent that residents had strong ties to external agencies, such as the police, they may be more likely to negotiate effective and judicious responses from them. In such neighborhoods, residents are more likely to feel that external agencies can be trusted to help address inappropriate or criminal behavior.

Empirical Examinations of the Systemic Model

While Shaw and McKay's social disorganization theory had generated much research relating neighborhood structural characteristics of poverty, residential mobility, and ethnic heterogeneity to measures of crime and/or delinquency, the reformulation of social disorganization theory into the systemic model made it clear that the key variables of the theory were not captured in this previous research. Empirical examination of the systemic model of social disorganization would also require measures on the extent of social networks within neighborhoods and between neighborhoods and external agencies, as well as measures of informal social control. While measures of poverty, mobility, and ethnic heterogeneity are available from census data and measures of crime can be generated from police reports, the key measures of the theory—social ties and informal social control—require data collection through interviews, surveys, or fieldwork. Further, to statistically examine this model, data from many neighborhoods would be required.

At the time that the systemic model was theoretically emerging, few large data sets were available that contained these central variables. Thus, the earliest studies were often limited to data collected in only a small number of neighborhoods. One of the first empirical examinations of this model with a sufficiently large number of neighborhoods to allow for elaborate statistical analyses was presented by Robert Sampson and W. Byron Groves in 1989. Their study was based on the British Crime Survey, which included data from 238 electoral wards in England and Wales.

In this study, Sampson and Groves conceptualize social disorganization as the capacity to bring about informal social control based on informal (kinship and friendship networks) and formal (organizational) associational ties. Friendship and kinship networks were measured by asking respondents "how many of their friends (on a five-point scale ranging from none to all) resided in the local community, which was defined as the area within a 15 minute walk of the respondent's home" (pp. 783–784). Organizational participation was measured in terms of the percentage of residents who participated in committee and club meetings. Their indicator of informal social control was based on residents' levels of supervision of youths within the neighborhood. Specifically, they asked respondents "how common it was . . . for groups of teenagers to hang out in public in the neighborhood and make nuisances of themselves" (p. 784). They avoid the potential problem of police bias in the measure of crime by using unofficial measures of crime rates—specifically, victimization rates and self-reports of crime.

While not all of the findings were consistent with the systemic model, many of them were. Some of the critical significant findings from this study that were consistent with the systemic model

were that socioeconomic status increased organizational participation and decreased unsupervised peer groups; ethnic heterogeneity increased unsupervised peer groups, and residential stability increased local social networks. Further, the results showed that friendship networks and organizational participation significantly reduced rates of victimization and that unsupervised youth peer groups significantly increased rates of victimization. It was also found that these intervening measures of social disorganization accounted for at least some of the effect of the community structural characteristics (socioeconomic status, residential mobility, ethnic heterogeneity and family disruption) on crime victimization rates.

Other studies also began to examine the role of social ties in relation to both informal social control and crime. Bursik (1999) found that measures of friendship networks and associational ties were significantly related to a measure of social control, specifically the perception of a loss of respect from others if one was arrested for assault.

Similarly, using the 1977 Police Services Study data on 60 neighborhoods, Paul Bellair examined the effect of frequency of neighbor social interactions on crime victimization data. He reported that measures of cumulative social interactions that include both frequent and infrequent interactions among neighbors significantly decrease victimization rates.

However, the role of social ties in providing the necessary building material for social control also began to be called into questioned. Some studies suggested that social ties may not be necessary for informal social control, other studies suggested that social ties may actually diminish the effectiveness of informal social control, and still other studies found that the effects of social ties depend on the type of social ties.

For example, two ethnographic studies specifically questioned the role of social ties in bringing about informal social control. Mary Pattillo's ethnographic study of Groveland, a neighborhood on the South side of Chicago, suggests that social networks within neighborhoods may have both positive and negative effects for social control. Pattillo argues that neighborhood networks are important in keeping residents in line with neighborhood norms and allowing residents to successfully intervene in inappropriate behavior. For example,

Pattillo describes a situation in which an older resident who had lived in Groveland for nearly 20 years, reprimanded a young teenager for carrying a beeper (which she associated with drug dealing) and successfully had the girl return the beeper to her father. But Pattillo also argues that dense neighborhood ties mean that residents are often tied to illegitimate as well as legitimate networks. Because of these dense neighborhood ties, Pattillo observes that residents may be less likely to provide social control by mobilizing the police. Referring to a resident's unwillingness to call the police and get a young man in trouble because "his mama is such a sweet lady," Pattillo states, "This comment illustrates that while dense neighborhood networks and the resulting familiarity can improve some informal efforts at social control, it can thwart the use of public or formal means of control" (pp. 763–764).

Similarly, in an ethnographic study of a low-crime neighborhood on the edge of Chicago, Patrick Carr found that residents there did not have dense social ties and were often fearful and reluctant to intervene directly with youths. However, the neighborhood was rich in neighborhood organizations and was home to many municipal workers, including police and firemen. Therefore, many residents used these resources to address problems. In this neighborhood, 90 percent of respondents to in-depth interviews were more likely to call the police rather than intervene with a group of misbehaving teens. Carr concludes that strong ties are not "the keys to the process of informal social control" (p. 1279). Rather, "neighborhoods that are not characterized by dense social ties may be capable of exercising effective control over crime and disorder because of the ease with which they can avail themselves of political and institutional resources outside the neighborhood" (p. 1280).

Indeed, finding a lack of importance of social ties in determining levels of informal social control in their study of Chicago neighborhoods led Robert Sampson, Stephen Raudenbush, and Felton Earls to develop a slightly different model of social disorganization theory known as the *collective efficacy model*. Sampson et al. found that their indicator of collective efficacy, which combines measures of social cohesion and trust with measures of perceived willingness of neighbors to intervene, was a better predictor of violent crime

rates than were measures of social ties. While measures of social ties and social interaction were both positively related to collective efficacy, they do not include these measures in their final model. They conclude, therefore, that their results suggest that "dense personal ties, organizations, and local services by themselves are not sufficient; reductions in violence appear to be more directly attributable to informal social control and cohesion among residents" (p. 923).

While the above studies raise important questions about the role of social ties, the research assessing these questions is frequently muddied by both the scarcity of research specifically examining the relationship between social ties and informal social control and the lack of precision in the measurement of the type of informal social control used by residents. Most of the research examining the role of social ties in providing informal social control does not distinguish between control carried out by community members themselves (private or parochial control, bonding social capital) versus control carried out through community members invoking the police or other formal agents of control (public control, bridging social capital).

Most empirical examinations of social disorganization theory have used very ambiguous terms with regard to what residents perceive their neighbors are likely to do. Measures of informal social control have generally been based on questions asking the likelihood of neighbors intervening, or doing something to stop, a number of inappropriate behaviors. Even though much of the social disorganization literature has assumed that these are measures of direct intervention, neighbors can attempt to stop untoward conduct not only directly but indirectly by engaging formal social control agents, such as the police and other authorities.

But there are qualitative differences between these approaches to intervening that have been asserted to be relevant to examining the systemic model of social disorganization theory. It can be argued that from a systemic model of social disorganization theory, social ties within the community are only likely to facilitate the likelihood of direct intervention. That is, to the extent that neighbors know one another and have broad ranging ties, they are more likely to both feel comfortable intervening in inappropriate behavior and be successful in their intervention. The resident who knows neighborhood children and who knows their parents is more likely to feel capable of intervening in the children's misbehavior, as well as socializing children to prevent misbehavior. Further, because the children know that the resident knows their parents and may well report back to them, the intervention has a higher likelihood of getting long-term positive results.

On the other hand, when residents do not have strong relationships with neighbors, they may be more likely to use indirect intervention by reporting the behavior to the police or other local authorities, such as apartment managers or neighborhood associations. While both forms of intervention can be viewed as informal social control, in that they are initiated by residents, the specific *type* of social ties (among neighbors versus between neighborhood and outside agencies) is likely to be relevant for determining which form of intervening (direct or indirect) will be used. This issue has not been well examined. Do ties within the neighborhood encourage the use of direct informal social control and do ties between neighborhoods and outside organizations (such as the police) encourage the use of indirect informal social control? With few exceptions, social ties have not been specifically examined in terms of private, parochial, and public, and informal social control has not been examined in terms of direct and indirect control.

A 2007 study by Barbara Warner specifically examined the relationship between social ties within the neighborhood and direct and indirect informal social control. Findings from this study suggest that social ties among residents significantly increase direct informal social control but are not significantly related to indirect informal social control.

Social Ties and the Role of Subcultural Values

Findings questioning the role of social ties have also led researchers to think more about the context of social ties. These researchers have pointed out that not all social ties are likely to increase prosocial norms and conventional behavior. For example, social ties among gang members may provide informal social control within their group, but they may not decrease what most neighbors might consider inappropriate neighborhood behavior.

The context in which the social ties develop is clearly relevant. For example, in neighborhoods in

which some residents do not share conventional law abiding values, the number of social ties may not be important for creating informal social control. Indeed, in such communities, social ties may be supportive of non-normative values. This, then, raises the question, "Under what neighborhood conditions do social ties decrease crime?"

Warner and Pamela Wilcox Rountree examined this question with neighborhood data from Seattle, Washington. While they did not examine residents' values or neighborhood subculture, they did find that social ties significantly decreased assault only in neighborhoods that were predominantly white. In neighborhoods that were predominantly minority and predominantly racially mixed, social ties did not have a significant deterrent effect on assault. They suggest that, in part, the lack of effectiveness of social ties in minority or racially mixed neighborhoods may be due to the emergence of oppositional cultures in these neighborhoods.

Alternatively, it has been argued that it may not be the presence of an oppositional culture that diminishes the effects of social ties but, simply weak conventional values. While residents of even the poorest neighborhoods may believe in the conventional value system, due to the constraints of everyday life, they may not be able to fully embrace and live out those values. A broad understanding among residents of how the stresses of everyday life may lead neighbors to act in less than normatively defined ways may decrease the likelihood of informal social control even when ties are strong. Although residents may view behaviors as inappropriate, they may also acknowledge few realistic alternatives, particularly if there are broad ties within the neighborhood that might communicate a shared plight. In this case, conventional values are weakened and informal social control may not occur.

Future Areas of Research

The systemic model of social disorganization theory has emphasized the role of social ties as they pertain to the development and provision of informal social control and consequently, crime reduction. While the model was responsible for breathing new life into social disorganization theory and turning attention to neighborhood-wide solutions to crime problems, there is still a limited amount of research that includes all aspects of the model.

Future research in this area is likely to focus on the measurement of social ties at all three levels (private, parochial, and public), different forms of informal social control (direct and indirect), and the various cultural contexts in which ties exist.

Barbara D. Warner

See also Bursik, Robert J., Jr., and Harold C. Grasmick: Levels of Control; Kobrin, Solomon: Neighborhoods and Crime; Kornhauser, Ruth Rosner: Social Sources of Delinquency; Negotiated Coexistence; Shaw, Clifford R., and Henry D. McKay: Social Disorganization Theory; Sampson, Robert J.: Collective Efficacy Theory

References and Further Readings

Bellair, P. E. (1997). Social interaction and community crime: Examining the importance of neighbor networks. *Criminology, 35,* 677–703.

Bursik, R. J., Jr. (1988). Social disorganization and theories of crime and delinquency: Problems and prospects. *Criminology, 26,* 519–551.

Bursik, R. J., Jr. (1999). The informal control of crime through neighborhood networks. *Sociological Focus, 32,* 85–97.

Bursik, R. J., Jr., & Grasmick, H. G. (1993). *Neighborhoods and crime: The dimensions of effective community control.* New York: Lexington Books.

Carr, P. J. (2003). The new parochialism: The implications of the beltway case for arguments concerning informal social control. *American Journal of Sociology, 108,* 1249–1291.

Kasarda, J. D., & Janowitz, M. (1974). Community attachment in mass society. *American Sociological Review, 39,* 328–339.

Kornhauser, R. R. (1978). *Social sources of delinquency: An appraisal of analytic models.* Chicago: University of Chicago Press.

Pattillo, M. E. (1998). Sweet mothers and gangbangers: Managing crime in a black middle-class neighborhood. *Social Forces, 76,* 747–774.

Putnam, R. (2000). *Bowling alone: The collapse and revival of American community.* New York: Simon & Schuster.

Sampson, R. J., & Groves, W. B. (1989). Community structure and crime: Testing social-disorganization theory. *American Journal of Sociology, 94,* 774–802.

Sampson, R J., Raudenbush, S. W., & Earls, F. (1997). Neighborhoods and violent crime: A multilevel study of collective efficacy. *Science, 277,* 918–924.

Shaw, C. R., & McKay, H. D. (1942/1969). *Juvenile delinquency and urban areas.* Chicago: University of Chicago Press.

Thomas, W. I., & Znaniecki, F. (1927). *The Polish peasant in Europe and America.* New York: Alfred A. Knopf.

Warner, B. D. (2003). The role of attenuated culture in social disorganization theory. *Criminology, 41,* 73–97.

Warner, B. D. (2007). Directly intervene or call the authorities? A study of forms of neighborhood social control within a social disorganization framework. *Criminology, 45,* 99–129.

Warner, B. D., & Wilcox Rountree, P. (1997). Local social ties in a community and crime model: Questioning the systemic nature of informal social control. *Social Problems, 44,* 520–546.

Wilson, W. J. (1996). *When work disappears: The world of the new urban poor.* New York: Vintage.

Wirth, L. (1938). Urbanism as a way of life. *American Journal of Sociology, 44,* 1–24.

T

TANNENBAUM, FRANK: THE DRAMATIZATION OF EVIL

When Frank Tannenbaum's book *Crime and Community* was published in 1938, it helped to lay the foundation for the labeling perspective through the introduction of the concept of the "dramatization of evil." At the time of his writing, Tannenbaum's perspective was unique because it acknowledged the important influence that groups have on criminal activity. By contrast, the prominent criminological theories of the period focused almost exclusively on the individual characteristics that influenced participation in crime. Instead of attributing criminal involvement to individual traits, Tannenbaum viewed crime as the product of a labeling process where interactions between groups and society play a crucial role in the defining of behaviors as criminal and the subsequent application of a label on an individual. For Tannenbaum, understanding the dynamics of group behavior and the need of society to define people as good or evil are central to understanding how criminals are created.

According to Tannenbaum, the labeling process begins when a conflict occurs between a group and the community that results in a maladjusted act being defined as evil or criminal. To illustrate this stage of the process, he provides an example of a group of young males playing ball too loudly outside of a movie theater. In turn, the patrons and owner become irritated by the noise and call the police to stop the group and arrest the youths. For Tannenbaum, the involvement of the criminal justice system and the creation of a criminal record for the young males would never have been necessary if their interests were considered in the same degree as the interests of the owner and movie patrons. He contends that by defining the playing of ball as evil, a process has begun that is difficult to reverse and can unintentionally increase the likelihood that the youths will partake in criminal behavior in the future.

Tannenbaum asserts that central to the conflict that exists between the group and the greater community is that each of the parties perceives the behavior differently. For the young males, certain acts such as climbing trees and throwing rocks are viewed as simply a way of having fun, while the community views it in a different manner and considers it troublesome behavior that requires the intervention of the criminal justice system. According to Tannenbaum, this conflict of values results in the second major stage of the labeling process that occurs when there is a shift in the definition of an act as evil to the definition of the individual who is committing the act. He contends that this shift in perception has a significant impact on both the community and the individual. From the community's point of view, the youth is now viewed as a troublemaker and a person who is inherently bad. However, as Tannenbaum asserts, a similar transformation has also taken place in the individual that results in the youth identifying himself as a delinquent as well. Once the label is applied and has taken hold, all parties unconsciously work to preserve it.

According to Tannenbaum, the third stage in the labeling process occurs when the individual has fully internalized the label and has identified himself or herself as a delinquent. He asserts that a consequence of the label is that the youth begins to feel isolated from society which leads him or her to further adopt the values of the gang and continue committing maladjusted acts. Tannenbaum contends that the greatest consequence of the labeling process is that only a handful of the youths are arrested for committing a particular act while it is likely that all of the members of the gang are guilty of the behavior. For Tannenbaum, the separation of a young male from his group is problematic because it results in the youth being treated differently from his peers and causes him to be thrown into an environment where he is regarded as a criminal and unlike the rest of the community. He asserts that this process further aids the individual's self-identification with the delinquent label.

For Tannenbaum, the first dramatization of evil occurs when the youth is singled out from his or her group and treated differently for partaking in the same types of behavior as other members of the gang. He argues that this act, or what he calls the first "tag," has a substantial influence on the future criminal behavior of an individual (p. 19). Tannenbaum contends that the initial application of a label on a youth works to provoke the continuance of the same kinds of behaviors that resulted in his or her original involvement with the criminal justice system. Although the first label is the most influential from Tannenbaum's perspective, he asserts that future tagging and the reinforcement of the delinquent label plays an important role in making the label attach to the individual. Tannenbaum contends that the more the label is reinforced by the community, the greater the likelihood that the youth will continue to commit crime and adopt values that are contradictory to those of greater society.

A key aspect of Tannenbaum's position is that the application of a label has detrimental effects regardless of whether it is given by individuals who aim to punish the youth or by those with good intentions. He contends that even in the case of reformers, the constant focus on an individual's negative behavior further solidifies the person's self-identification as a delinquent and perpetuates further criminal behavior. For Tannenbaum, the only way to resolve this problem is to refuse to

initiate the process and dramatize evil. He asserts, "The less said about it the better. The more said about something else, still better" (p. 20). From Tannenbaum's perspective, the refusal to begin the labeling process and define individuals as evil is the only promising solution for preventing individuals from entering a criminal career.

Heidi Scherer

See also Becker, Howard S.: Labeling and Deviant Careers; Chambliss, William J.: The Saints and the Roughnecks; Lemert, Edwin M.: Primary and Secondary Deviance; Matza, David: Becoming Deviant

References and Further Readings

Becker, H. S. (1963). *Outsiders: Studies in the sociology of deviance*. New York: Free Press.
Chambliss, W. J. (1997). The saints and the roughnecks. In J. M. Henslin (Ed.), *Down to earth sociology: Introductory readings* (pp. 246–280). New York: Free Press.
Tannenbaum, F. (1938). *Crime and community*. New York: Ginn.

TAYLOR, IAN, PAUL WALTON, AND JOCK YOUNG: THE NEW CRIMINOLOGY

The New Criminology is the magical *Alice in Wonderland* rabbit hole through which most contemporary critical and radical criminologists fell on their way to whatever approach to studying crime and society they now pursue. It is also one of criminology's contemporary classics, as well as a dependable fountain of ideas for new theoretical paths and methodological challenges. Assessing its long-term impact on criminology—more than 36 years since its publication—can be accomplished by starting with how it was received at birth and ending with an overview of what it has spawned. This plan necessitates a summary of what its authors—Ian Taylor, Paul Walton, and Jock Young—claimed they wanted to do.

After 2.5 years of writing that expanded the American social reaction theorists' emphasis on the activities of rule-creators and rule-enforcers in the criminal process, they concluded that much of criminological theory had become insulated and isolated from sociological theory—so much so that the study of criminals' central relationships to structures of power, domination, and authority had all but disappeared. Instead, over time, criminology had been aligned with the classical utilitarian approach to the protection of individuals from excessive punishment and various varieties of biological, psychological, and social positivism. What was needed—Taylor, Walton, and Young argued—was a theoretical approach that examined crimes, deviance, and dissent as confrontations with social structures and the social arrangements within which the criminal process is played out.

Taylor et al. attempted to "open out the criminological debate" by providing both formal and substantive guidelines for the development of a "fully social theory of deviance [and] social control" (p. 269). With a focus on developed societies dominated by a capitalist mode of production and division of labor, their seven-point requirement for a critical criminological theory stressed constructing a perspective that analyzed a wide view of the political economy of deviant acts and state reactions to them. They also emphasized the need for a social psychology of crime, one that recognized that individuals may consciously choose "the deviant road . . . as the one solution to the problems posed in a contradictory society" (p. 271). This social psychology would also study the contingencies and conditions that are crucial to the decisions to take action against deviants.

Early Reactions

In a highly complimentary foreword by the noted American Marxist, Alvin Gouldner, *The New Criminology* was described as so powerful in its critique of traditional criminology that "it redirects the total structure of technical discourse concerning 'crime' and 'deviance'" (p. ix). One year later, Elliott Currie praised it as an important document in the "effort to build a more humane criminology" and "probably the most comprehensive critical review of 'the field' that has been produced so far" (p. 133). In a few short years, the title of the book became the moniker for a new school of criminology. The new radical perspective was more intellectually sophisticated and

well-grounded in criminological literature and continental philosophy than that found in its counterpart in the United States. And unlike the minority position of radical criminology in the United States, it grew to share equal partnership with conventional criminology.

This was accomplished in no small part by its clear articulation of its objections to the assumption that the social order was based on a public consensus and traditional criminology's overly deterministic treatment of crime. To overturn these assumptions, the new criminology stressed that conventional studies of crime were too narrowly entrenched in theories and paradigms that assumed that they had a monopoly on the "correct," "scientific," and "deterministic" understanding of human nature and social order.

Another major persuasive argument in the opened debate was to make crime the central focus of concern for social scientists rather than the peripheral topic it had become by traditional positivism with its notions about objectivity. For the new criminology, the latter concept had been created by "positivism . . . in its pursuit of a mistaken scientificity" (Young, 1988, p. 161). By shifting the focus on crime from traditional positivism to a perspective that emphasized the political nature of crime, the new criminology made crime the central plank for social scientists wishing to illuminate both order and social disorder.

The New Criminology generated sound and thoughtful criticism. Whereas some of it diminished the book's early praise, it did not deliver a death knell to its critiques of traditional positivism or its call for developing a political economy of crime. Three major problems were identified.

In addition to being just plain wrong in some of their discussion of conventional criminology, Taylor et al. gave misleading impressions that criticism of biological explanations of crime (as understood in the early 1970s) applied equally to psychological and sociological determinism. The writing style of *The New Criminology*, according to Currie, was too closely akin to the finely tuned interests in the field of criminology, and thus a barrier to creating a meaningful exchange with criminals and deviants. Lastly, an approach that integrated biological and psychological explanations of crime would have been more useful.

Left Realism

One of the most lasting strengths of the new criminology perspective is that its supporters have for so long continued to respond to their critics and changing social context with new critical thinking. One of the first examples of this intellectual virtue came in Britain as its "New" Right with Margaret Thatcher succeeded in a 1979 Conservative/Tory Party victory. It was committed to making ideological and political breaks with the assumptions and rules governing the social democracy that developed in Britain during the 1940s. The Conservatives ushered in a new ideology, with an agenda committed to privatizing for-profit government industries and imposing restrictions on welfare, national health, and educational support.

As the New Right's policies were being formulated and implemented, radical criminology recognized that although the tide had turned, it was not a tsunami as much as dramatic ideological shift that provided a background against which *The New Criminology* was re-evaluated. British critical criminologist Stan Cohen wrote that it had not changed the institutional foundations of the country's criminology; they were intact and unchanged—a conclusion that was not seriously disputed.

One of the major weaknesses of the new criminology, according to Roger Matthew and Jock Young, was that it had improperly concentrated on the impact of the state on the criminal at the expense of neglecting the effect of crime upon the victim. For radical criminology, the basic and proper subject matter would have been the social relations among the offender, the state and the victim. As a partial remedy to this oversight and the claim that radical criminology was in a state of crisis, radical criminologists moved away from the new criminology and developed an approach to studying crime that they called *left realism*. It placed less emphasis on the state and focused more on the causes of crime and its victims. This was a significant shift in British radical criminology. It was not so much a move away *from* theoretical issues as *toward* research and statistical analyses of crime causation and its consequences.

Left realism was explicitly concerned with the origins, nature, and impact of crime in the working class. But this was not just an emphasis on victims. It was also concerned with "risk rate of vulnerability" of certain sections of the community. The complexity of this point is illuminated by thinking of the working class as victims of crime from all directions. Young notes that the more people are economically and socially marginalized, the more likely it is that *both* working-class and white-collar crime will occur against them. This perspective also placed great emphasis on studying crime as people experienced it whether it was sexism, racism, policy, police brutality, and any number of everyday crimes.

The uniqueness of this perspective was—and still is—its strong interest in the class and power dimensions of crime causation and what can be done about it. It, too, represents an effort at synthesizing several theories, including labeling, strain, subcultural, radical Marxism, and some feminist perspectives. Left realism has now been in criminology's market place of theories for more than a quarter century, and its appeal, contributors, and criticisms have come from a number of countries, including Australia, Britain, Canada, and the United States. One issue is whether it has strayed too far from its roots in radical thought, especially Marxism. Another concern is its emphasis on realistic approaches to the causes of crime come far too close to advocating punitive control strategies popular with conservative ideology.

Extended Influence

The early contributions by the new criminology and realist criminology were part of the emergence of the "new left" in North America and Britain during the late 1960s and early 1970s. Its scope of creative criticism focused not only on the issues discussed here with positivism of traditional criminology but also on what became known as the anti-psychiatry movement, prison support groups, campus sit-ins, and community action efforts. Both perspectives have also contributed to a long list of concepts that are now staples of criminological culture, whatever its political persuasion (Young, 1988, p. 164). These include a powerful critique of the mechanical determination associated with some biological explanations of crime, the social construction of statistics, emphasis on the endemic rather than a solely class-based conception of crime, and the largely invisible victimization of domestic violence against women, the abuse of children, and racism.

During the late 1990s, two events occurred that provided an opportunity to reevaluate the impact of the new criminology and at the same time provide a vicarious evaluation of left realism. The first was at first glance a historic shift in Britain's politics that held the promise of a new and different political policy. The second was the publication of *The New Criminology Revisited*.

In May 1997, Tony Blair was elected as the youngest prime minister since 1812 to the most popular new government in British history, ending two decades of Conservative rule. As the New Labor Party it promised a transition to a "New Britain" that would support community inclusiveness, modernized health care, a reduction of runaway welfare, globalization, poverty reduction, a more cooperative relationship with the European Union, and the devolution of Scotland and Wales.

Skeptics, however, were soon questioning whether Blair and New Labor were any less conservative than their predecessors. This perspective was given considerable credence post-9/11 because of Blair's support for President George W. Bush, the Iraq war, and legislative initiatives that he supported that were strongly criticized as violations of human rights, invasions of privacy, illegal, and unjust (Lea, 2005). To some critics, while initially influenced by left realism, New Labor's approach was soon equally as authoritarian, punitive, and conservative as that of the Tories. New policies included more private prisons, curfews on young people, enhanced use of electronic monitoring, harassing beggars, zero tolerance, and automatic sentences for persistent petty offenders. In addition, privatizing for profit various public services—including health, education, and criminal justice agencies—increasingly became Blair's touchstone. Incarceration increased to the point that England had the highest per capita rate in Western Europe. It is against these changes that the impact of *The New Criminology* of 1973, and its critical heir apparent, left realism, were reevaluated.

In retrospect, the editors and contributors largely reaffirmed most, if not all, of the major points advanced in 1973. They are as follows: (1) Crime and the processes of criminalization are embedded in the core structures of society, whether they are in class relations, its patriarchal form, or its inherent authoritarianism. (2) The sole and precise aim of the new criminology is improving the human condition. The new criminology has a utopian commitment. (3) The new criminology was and still is not committed to corrections as supported establishment criminology a là administrative criminology. Human behavior does not need "correcting." (4) The new criminology is wedded to social change. Its adherents wish to do more than make professional contributions to human knowledge. (5) The new criminology aims to deconstruct criminological theories in an attempt to construct a social theory of crime and deviance.

Current Impact

Today, there are scant publications that have new criminology or left realism in the title. Nonetheless, some of the ideas from these perspectives remain potent influences for examining working-class crime problems as well as important forerunners to much that now captures the imagination of scholars examining late modernity and crime. Most prominent here is the major work of Young between 1999 and 2007.

In *The Exclusive Society*, the first of two completed works in a promised trilogy on late modernity and crime, Young traced the ways in which he calls the "relentless forces of production" propelled society into late modernity. It was the movement from "the golden age" of stability of the post–World War II to the crisis years of the late 1960s onward. In essence, it was a movement that replaced relative stability in work, family and community, material certainty, and uncontested values with risk, uncertainty, individual choice, and pluralism layered with deep-seated economic and ontological precariousness not uncharacteristic of the worldwide problems associated with the banking and housing crisis of 2008–2009 and beyond. According to Young, it was a structural transition from modernity to late modernity that witnessed the socio-economic, political, spatial, and cultural marginalization of the underclass.

The Vertigo of Late Modernity, the second volume in the trilogy, expanded the arguments contained in *The Exclusive Society*. Among its plethora of ideas about late modernity, turbo-capitalism and insecurities are pivotal. The former, Young argues, shifted manufacturing abroad, downsized, deskilled, and automated to such extent that it undermined the social embeddedness of jobs, community, and at times the family. One result was the creation of a high level of instability and what he calls a pervasive sense of unfairness and disembeddedness. These experiences are both generated and reinforced by what Young terms the shock of plural values that come from mass migration and from what those viewing global media have experienced on the street and on the screen. These further destabilized any firm sense of identity and security.

According to Young, this resulted in a sense of resentment from those looking up as well as down the social structure. For those looking down, there is a sense of vertigo, a sense of fear of falling as swathes of jobs, from bank clerks to car workers, are eliminated and downgraded. The middle class at the same time is pressured by lengthened working hours, dual careers, and commutes from the suburbs. By comparison, the lower class is limited by low pay, unstable jobs, and sporadic unemployment. However, they are not an underclass that is separate and apart from the middle class. Although they share the cultural values of the wider society and are structurally bound to it by low wages, they nonetheless are excluded from structured security or economic advancement.

The impact of *The New Criminology* on Young's most recent work on late modernity and crime is self-admittedly clear. Just as C. Wright Mills's *The Sociological Imagination* inspired Walton, Taylor, and Young to develop a theory of deviance and crime that linked private problems (crime) with public issues (crime policies), so did it serve as an injunction to connect crime to the "bustling hyperpluralism of the 21st century" (Young, 2008, p. 524). Other contemporary explorations into crime in late modernity have also been inspired and benefited from the critical insights and admonitions contained in the 1973 classic. These include cultural criminology and to a lesser extent convict criminology, and the new "consumer criminology" by Steve Hall, Simon Winlow, and Craig Ancrum. The impact of *The New Criminology* is deep and wide.

J. Robert Lilly

See also Bonger, Willem: Capitalism and Crime; Chambliss, William J.: Power, Conflict, and Crime; Cultural Criminology; Currie, Elliott: The Market Society and Crime; Left Realism Criminology; Marx, Karl, and Frederick Engels: Capitalism and Crime

References and Further Readings

Alvi, S. (2005). Left realism. In R. A. Wright & J. M. Miller (Eds.), *Encyclopedia of criminology* (Vol. 2, pp. 931–933). New York: Routledge.

Cohen, S. (1981). Footprints in the sand. In M. Fitzgerald, G. McLenna, & K. Pease (Eds.), *Crime and society: Readings in history and theory* (pp. 220–276). London: Routledge and Kegan Paul.

Currie, E. (1974). Reviews of *The New Criminology*. *Issues in Criminology, 9*, 123–142.

Ferrell, J., Hayward, K., & Young, J. (2008). *Cultural criminology*. London: Sage.

Gouldner, A. (1973). Foreword. In I. Taylor, P. Walton, & J. Young, *The new criminology: For a social theory of deviance* (pp. ix–xiv). London: Routledge & Kegan Paul.

Hall, S., Winlow, S., & Ancrum, C. (2008). *Criminal identities and consumer culture*. Cullompton, Devon, UK: Willan.

Incaridi, J. (Ed.). (1980). *Radical criminology: The coming crisis*. Beverly Hills, CA: Sage.

Lea, J. (2005). *Terrorism, crime and the collapse of civil liberties*. Lecture presented to the Criminology Society, Middlesex University in April. Retrieved June 20, 2006, from http://www.bunker8.pwp.blueyonder.co.uk/misc/terror.htm

Matthews, R., & Young, J. (Eds.). (1992). *Issues in realist criminology*. London: Sage.

Reiner, R. (2007). *Law and order: An honest citizen's guide to crime and control*. Cambridge, UK: Polity Press.

Taylor, I., Walton, P., & Young, J. (1973). *The new criminology: For a social theory of deviance*. London: Routledge and Kegan Paul.

Walton, P., & Young, J. (Eds.). (1998). *The new criminology revisited*. New York: St. Martin's.

Young, J. (1986). The failure of criminology: The need for a radical realism. In J. Young & R. Matthews (Eds.), *Confronting crime* (pp. 4–30). London: Sage.

Young, J. (1988). Radical criminology in Britain. *British Journal of Criminology, 28*, 159–183.

Young, J. (2008). Vertigo and the global Merton. *Theoretical Criminology, 4*, 523–527.

Young, J., & Matthews, R. (Eds.). (1992). *Rethinking criminology: The realist debate*. London: Sage.

THIO, ALEX: RELATIVE DEPRIVATION AND DEVIANCE

In "Social Structure and Anomie," Robert Merton presented both a macro-level anomie theory and micro-level strain theory. At the macro-level, Merton argued there were two structures in society: the cultural structure and the social structure. The cultural structure consists of the culturally defined goals and the norms or culturally proscribed means that should be utilized to achieve the goals. The social structure consists of an individual's location in society and determines the means available to the person. When there is a disjunction between the culturally defined goals and the means that people have available to them, strain is placed on the norms, which results in a state of anomie or normlessness. When anomie ensues, people are free to use whatever means necessary to achieve their goals and thus often results in high crime rates.

Although Merton's anomie theory has been widely used in the disciplines of criminology and sociology, Alex Thio disagrees with Merton's argument that members of the lower class have a higher disconnection between their aspirations and their opportunities resulting in higher crime rates. Thio suggests that Merton does not see the important relationship between social class and relative deprivation. In addition, Thio explains that there is a difference between relative and absolute deprivation, a component of power theory. Therefore, Thio believes that many criminologists overlook the participation in deviant behaviors by higher-class members of society. In fact, he suggests that the advantaged are more likely to participate in deviant activities for a variety of reasons, especially because of relative deprivation.

Two Types of Deprivation

In "A critical look at Merton's anomie theory," Thio argues that there are two different types of deprivation: (1) absolute deprivation and (2) relative deprivation. Absolute deprivation, which is considered to be objective deprivation, occurs when there is a real deficiency in a particular resource or necessity, such as income (Stiles et al., 2000). For example, if an individual has an income level below the poverty line, he or she is considered to be poor or experiencing absolute deprivation. Thus, Thio argues that although individuals that experience absolute deprivation do set high goals, they realize that these goals are too unrealistic and unlikely to be achieved given their current situation, such as living in poverty.

Relative deprivation, on the other hand, is considered by Thio to be more subjective. Relative deprivation is a feeling of being unable to achieve relatively high aspirations compared to other people or being jealous of the material objects or income level another person possesses. For instance, although individuals may have an annual salary of $100,000, they may feel as if they are poor compared to their colleagues, friends, neighbors, or family members that have an annual salary of more than $100,000. Therefore, relative deprivation can be seen as a social comparison. People in society are always comparing themselves to what others have and "try to keep up with the Joneses." This social comparison can lead individuals to believe that they need more money and thus push them to participate in deviant acts to acquire more money. Hence, the more people experience relative deprivation, the more likely they are to commit deviant acts, according to Thio.

For example, higher-class members of society are more likely to have very high goals, sometimes so high that they suffer from relative deprivation. Therefore, higher-class members are more likely to commit white-collar crimes or profitable deviance, such as tax evasion, embezzlement, and corporate price-fixing in order to attain their extremely high goals. On the other hand, lower-class members are more likely to have lower goals (compared to higher-class members) and experience absolute deprivation, thus, pressuring them to commit more street crimes or less profitable crimes, such as robbery, burglary, and assault (Thio, 1975, pp. 152–153).

The Relationship Between Relative Deprivation and Power Theory

Relative deprivation is a small part of a larger theory called power theory, which explains why the powerful members of society are more likely to commit profitable deviance. Specifically, power theory proposed three reasons why it is easier for higher-class than lower-class members of society to commit crimes: (1) "the powerful have a stronger deviant motivation," (2) "the powerful enjoy greater deviant opportunity," and (3) "the powerful are subjected to weaker social control" (Thio, 2010, pp. 46–47).

According to Thio, the first premise of power theory is associated with relative deprivation. The powerless or those living in poverty are assumed to have lower aspirations. Therefore, they do not expect much out of life and do not set high goals. In contrast, the powerful or higher-class members of society have higher aspirations, usually aspirations that are so high that the goals are unattainable. The strong desire to achieve these high goals leads higher-class members of society to participate in deviant activities in order to attempt to attain their aspirations.

The second premise of power theory argues that the powerful are more likely to participate in deviant activities because they are less likely to be arrested due to their occupational positions as CEOs and bankers. These positions enable them to have greater access to large amounts of funds where few people would suspect their involvement in deviant behaviors. Therefore, these individuals are less likely to be caught and sanctioned.

The third premise of power theory suggests powerful and wealthier individuals have a greater influence in creating and enforcing the laws, therefore experiencing a reduced amount of social control. For example, wealthier individuals and those caught committing white-collar crimes are usually given more lenient sentences whereas lower-class criminals are more likely to receive stricter sentences. As a result, wealthier individuals may believe that they have a smaller likelihood of getting arrested, and, if they are arrested, that they will more than likely receive a fine or more lenient sentence.

In conclusion, criminologists may be overlooking higher-class members' participation in deviant activities and focusing on lower-class members' deviancy. Thio argues there is a strong association between relative deprivation (a component of power theory) and deviant behaviors, particularly among higher-class members of society. In light of today's recent scandals involving powerful individuals (e.g., Enron, Bernard Madoff), Thio's ideas regarding relative deprivation and deviance may provide valuable insight into understanding the crime committed by higher-class individuals.

Wendi Elizabeth Goodlin

See also Anomie and White-Collar Crime; Blau, Judith R., and Peter M. Blau: Inequality and Crime; Integrated Theories of White-Collar Crime; Merton, Robert K.: Social Structure and Anomie; Sutherland, Edwin H.: White-Collar Crime

References and Further Readings

Merton, R. K. (1938). Social structure and anomie. *American Sociological Review, 3*, 672–682.

Merton, R. K. (1968). *Social theory and social structure.* New York: Free Press.

Rushing, W. A. (1972). *Class, culture, and alienation.* Lexington, MA: D. C. Heath.

Stiles, B. L., Liu, X., & Kaplan, H. B. (2000). Relative deprivation and deviant adaptations: The mediating effects of negative self-feelings. *Journal of Research in Crime and Delinquency, 37*, 64–90.

Thio, A. (1973). Class bias in the sociology of deviance. *The American Sociologist, 8*, 1–12.

Thio, A. (1975). A critical look at Merton's anomie theory. *Pacific Sociological Review, 18*, 139–158.

Thio, A. (2010). *Deviant behavior* (10th ed.). Boston: Allyn & Bacon

THOMAS, W. I.: THE UNADJUSTED GIRL

Is the unadjusted girl really that unadjusted, deviant, delinquent, or criminal? For W. I. Thomas the answer to this question depends on the situation, and it is not just one situation that should be taken into account. After all, there are the situations of the family, school, and the larger society. In each of these situations, there is the possibility that individuals will think and act differently. Rather than to think in one singularly directed mind, Thomas wrote that those living in the early-20th-century industrialized American city confronted a multitude of situational definitions. In his book *The Unadjusted Girl,* he was able to illustrate the conflict between old and new world definitions of a situation. He was also able to show that there were certain universal desires that conflicted with societal definitions of the situation leading to the "demoralization" of girls. Thomas concluded that the unadjusted girl's desires and definitions of the situation are not in synch with the social and legal definitions in society.

Thomas published *The Unadjusted Girl* in 1924 at a time when female deviance and criminality were generally described as pathological. They were often described as biologically or psychologically pathological when criminality was defined in terms of female sexuality. But by today's standards the unadjusted girl may seem quite normal. Still, there is a pattern that Thomas relates, and it is one where universal desires are officially condemned leading to more serious delinquent and criminal conduct. Modern society can make a bad situation of impoverishment even worse when it fails to recognize its subject's unique desires. As is often the case today, even sociologically oriented criminologists at the time tended to focus on the more visible delinquency of impoverished inner-city boys and their delinquent gang. Less focus was on the less visible activities of girls whose sexuality was considered too embarrassing for even criminologists.

Thomas was able to show that female criminality is not only a consequence of how officials see their sexuality, but also of how society's definitions of the situation conflict with basic human desires. He illustrated how the unadjusted becomes a maladjusted girl. In retrospect, this is because acts that would be considered as acceptable today were then treated as serious offenses. Serious consequences emerge if you define an act in a certain way as Robert Merton's fulfilling prophecy theory draws largely on Thomas's definition of the situation. Thus, we have a significant scholar in Thomas who can be credited for inspiring subsequent generations of social reaction theorists.

The social reaction theorist views crime and its reaction as inextricably related to one another. There is no attempt to take pathology or gender for granted. Pathology is considered a social construction, and is often framed as making a bad situation even worse. The poverty of immigrants is a bad situation that can lead to an even worse situation when officials label those who are impoverished as deviant, delinquent, or criminal. The social reaction perspective sees deviance rather than criminality as the cause of the delinquent or criminal identity.

Thomas's analysis of unadjusted girls is initially based on earlier studies of Polish immigrants in America (Thomas et al., 1958). In those studies, he collected the letters of immigrants and analyzed their experiences living in America. In the *Unadjusted Girl,* he focused on young girls and their letters to relatives as well as letters in newspaper advice columns. The editors of these advice columns served as an inexpensive form of counseling. The letters repeated immigrants' stories of culture conflict in old-world and new-world desires. Thomas's approach was clearly inductive, and it was not based on a tightly controlled representative population of girls. Rather, the stories of impoverished immigrant girls are grounded in a selective set of documents loosely organized around a general theory of deviance. To begin Thomas derives a universal set of human desires. They are referred to as wishes and are classified into the desire for "security," "adventure," "response," and "recognition." Each of these desires either singularly or in combination are related to the documented immigrant letters and cases. The recognition of these desires leads to definitions of the situation. For instance, one may desire money and define his or her work situation as the place for obtaining money. Similarly, the immigrant girls that Thomas studied desired love, and they defined the situation within the context of their desires for love, and at times of solicitation money. Critical to understanding the unadjusted girl is understanding her definitions of the situation and how they are in conflict with that of her family's and society's definition of appropriate sexuality.

While the first concept introduced in Thomas's book on human desires is largely ignored, the second concept relating definitions of the situation has had a long-lasting impact in criminology. The straightforward principles of differential association by Edwin Sutherland draw on Thomas's definitional situation. Criminality is possible when there is an excess of definitions favorable to violating the law. Similarly, Marvin Wolfgang found support for a subculture of violence among young black males by a definition of the situation as one requiring their quick resort to violence. The qualitative aspects of sociological criminology have been enriched by contemporary ethnographers like

Elijah Anderson who observed a code of the streets that is not conceptually different from Thomas's definitions of the situation.

To appreciate Thomas, it is important to first consider the way he framed human desires and definitions of the situation. This is a four-part framing as is the framing of the walls of a squared house. Thomas suggests one could not exist without the other. Moreover, the framing of human desires leads to definitions of the situation that takes on a form that is specific to place. The second point to Thomas's analysis is the regulation of human desires and how they have produced conflicting definitions of the situation. The complexity of legal definitions confronting social definitions is a familiar sociological story that should be revisited based on Thomas's analysis. It is one that is grounded in the idea that for society to regulate, it has created its social institutions to replace the tightly knit village like communities. This entry first considers desires and definitions of the situation, and then how society regulates those desires and definitions.

Desires and Definitional Situations

Few criminologists today are willing to grapple with the depth of conscious and unconscious emotions that motivate offenders. Motivation is generally avoided in most theories of social control; it is always assumed to be there. But it is considered more the business of detectives and psychoanalysts than that of criminological sociologists. Instead, they prefer to assume that people are either naturally good or bad depending on the version of socialization theory that they advocate. Thomas proposed a set of conscious and unconscious desires. He framed them as "wishes," and he organized his analysis of deviance around the desire for security, adventure, response, and recognition.

First, the desire for *security* may be associated with the desire for money and may clearly fit in with Merton's version of anomie theory and the American Dream. But the wish for security could include more than just money. Distinguished psychologists like Erick Erickson spoke of ontological security, and Abraham Maslow related the desire for security as the base for any hierarchal view of human needs. To be without food and shelter is to be without the security of knowing that you will

be able to live into the next day. This would surely be the case for the impoverished immigrants that Thomas observed, and consequently their desire for money made sense not as a way of social status but as a way of staying alive. Moreover, the desire to leave the immigrant's country of origin for America may be viewed simply as the wish to live in a more secure place. The cases that Thomas studied were overwhelmingly representative of Eastern European Jewish immigrants. He quoted liberally from the advice letter columns in the Yiddish-American newspaper *The Forward*. The name of that newspaper exemplifies the impoverished Jewish immigrants' hope to live in a more secure place where they might look forward to a life free of discrimination and old-world racial and ethnic superstitions.

The second desire that Thomas identifies is the wish for *adventure*. The desire for adventure might be considered the reverse of the wish for security, but not if one considers that moving on can lead to a more secure place. The immigrant is a bohemian who is willing to leave the familiarity of his old-world place for the adventure of going off into the new world. But the wish for adventure may be considered a basic desire that transcends the mundane world of school and work in a modern industrial world. Surely the desire for adventure is relevant in a range of criminological theories, such as Jack Katz's adolescent sneaky thrills thesis and David Matza's idea of drift as a response to the desire to make things happen. Early-20th-century sociologists, such as Frederick Thrasher who observed Chicago youth gangs, also noted the impoverished inner-city kids' pursuit of play; the more affluent youths had their organized recreational activities available to them.

The remaining two wishes are the desires for *response* and *recognition*, which can be broadly defined as representing the emotional side of life or, for that matter, love. Few would deny the significance of love and the need to feel needed, and to be able to be recognized and to recognize. Surely, Thomas could have spoken of love, but preferred the term *response* and suggested that this is the most social of all desires. Once in America, the arranged immigrant marriages of the past seemed less than satisfying, and indeed marriage itself, Thomas observed in the letters, seemed to be under attack. This is because they repressed the basic drive for love in a way that could no longer be successfully applied in the industrial world of early-20th-century America. The desire for recognition is to be recognized by others and is most often associated with status and prestige.

Of course, the desires that Thomas identified are not mutually exclusive or exhaustive of a wider range of emotions, impulses, and needs. The wish for security, adventure, response, and recognition are overlapping desires. They are overlapping in the letters that Thomas relates. Surely, the desire for recognition can overlap with the desire for response, and each of these desires is placed within the context of definitions of the situation. It is definitions from the standpoint of the individual first, and then from the person's point of view as it may be structured by family, neighborhood, and school situations.

But why is it necessary to consider all these definitions of the situation? Because they account for the complexity of a society's continuous attempt to regulate individual desires and prevent its girls from becoming unadjusted girls.

Thomas was certainly ahead of his time in observing the complexity of human desires and definitions of the situation. His was a theory of cognition that resisted the more dominating Chicago School paradigm that emphasized the significance of place based on concentric zones of the city. Concentric zones suggested that an area's residents thought alike and were equally disorganized. For Thomas, the singular definition of a situation as a disorganized place could not exist in the modern world. It was more likely to exist in the Eastern European Jewish Shtetl (village) where place and community were homogenously defined. But the story of modernity is one where new and old world definitions confront one another. There is a pluralistic set of competing beliefs to consider making definitions of the situation increasingly reflexive. According to Thomas, definitions of the situation are "a stage of examination and deliberation" (p. 42). The reflexivity of human action is critical to the analysis of contemporary society as advocated by contemporary social theorists, such as Anthony Giddens. Indeed, social structures are temporary structures for individuals who continuously reframe their social systems based on a life-long series of situational definitions. It is these definitions that are the means through which

wishes produce actions and actions create newly derived definitional situations.

Regulating Desires

If one moves beyond a singular view of a community, one can see the difficulty that impoverished immigrant girls faced in adjusting to industrialized 20th century America. Their familial old-world community could not be duplicated in the industrial modern world of the city. Immigrants often lacked extended family relationships to assist them in their struggle to adjust to American society. Thomas based his observations on immigrant letters, and it is in those letters that he was able to identify the complex sources of regulation. Modern-day complexity in competing definitions of a situation was most directly observable in the cases of impoverished Jewish immigrant girls. In the Eastern European village, life was tightly regulated, and religiosity closely maintained a precisely limited set of definitions. There was little opportunity to deviate because life in the shtetl was highly regulated. Moreover, there was the struggle for the basics like staying alive so the desires for response and recognition were less important in the pre-modern village than in the densely populated heterogeneously organized spaces of the city. The freedom of space was the freedom for desires that moved beyond that of security and reflected the age-old pursuit of love and recognition.

There was not only the complexity of old-world and new-world ideas as associated with place, but also the complexity of regulating by means of patriarchy. The patriarchy of the village was replaced with the patriarchy of the juvenile court, and the idea that women's sexuality must be regulated more than that of men's. Just as impoverished immigrants were repressed in their countries of origin, so too were women repressed in America by their less than equal position in modern society. Remember that Thomas was writing at the beginning of the 20th century at a time when women still did not have the right to vote, and feminism referred to a few radicals. The promise of American freedom was largely limited to freedom of religion and freedom to own property. It was not the freedom to pursue sex outside of marriage, especially for those girls late into adolescence.

The failure to regulate appropriately individual desires Thomas attributed to the weakness of social institutions. He saw delinquency less a product of individual failings or a lack of self-control, and more a consequence of the inability of social institutions to reproduce the communities of the past. Thomas was not the first to note that society had to make up for its lost community. But he may have been the first sociologist to redefine community based less on a physical place and more on definitions of the situation. Thomas quotes a Polish immigrant as stating that community reaches "as far as the report of a man reaches—as far as a man is talked about" (p. 44). Surely, the way individuals can be talked about in the modern world is not directly linked to an individual's physical place of residence. The norms and values of a complex society are less a product of face-to-face interaction, and more a product of an evolving image of self. Definitions of the situation naturally extended that image, which is reflected in more of an imaginary community than one that is physically grounded in a geographically identifiable place.

The concluding chapters of *The Unadjusted Girl* relate how legal definitions produce court appearances, institutionalization, and parole. Legal definitions are clearly in conflict with social definitions. They extend into the offices of probation officers who in their reports describe the unadjusted girl as a girl with multiple offenses. But the unadjusted girl is a disadvantaged girl, and it is the cumulative disadvantages of being an impoverished immigrant Jewish girl that produced the fascinating detailed case of Esther. The case of Esther in Thomas's next to the last chapter relates how a trivial act of shoplifting, coupled with her sexuality, leads to repeated institutionalization. Esther is caught in between several worlds. She is an impoverished Jewish immigrant without family to support her. She dreams of the old country and of an imaginary lover that is still there. She is repeatedly institutionalized for minor violations of parole. She might be considered a serious life-course offender, except for the fact that the parole reports Thomas liberally quotes draw on little that would suggest serious offending.

The story that Thomas tells in his case studies is loosely grounded in the concept of social class. He states that the "well-organized family, with property and standing, is in a position both to regulate and gratify the wishes of its members" (p. 151). As is the case today, the affluent have the resources to

prevent their troubled youths from moving on to become serious offenders. Similarly, Thomas's answer to preventing the unadjusted girl is to first gratify their wishes. This would require society to recognize the sexual desires of girls so that they are on par with that which is permitted for boys. Second, he would redefine the seriousness of the initial offense and advocate methods for diverting and decriminalizing. He quoted liberally juvenile justice reformers who advocated a juvenile court, and obviously wished to see it thrive in the wake of its alternative in form of a stigmatizing criminal court. Sophisticated labeling theorists, such as Edwin Lemert, undoubtedly would agree that society needed to adjust its institutions so that its less serious offenders receive treatment and not stigmatizing forms of punishment via the criminal court.

Today, many of the acts that Thomas reports would be considered trivial. Nowadays people are allowed to express their sexuality outside of marriage. But at the time, most experts thought that sex outside of marriage could lead to moral degeneration, delinquency, and crime. On this point, Thomas relates the opinion of an expert panel of physicians and psychologists who mostly state that premarital sex is to be avoided. This would seem absurd today when "hooking up" is considered the norm for many middle-class youths. Even the term *demoralization* in a loosely configured world would hardly be used. Surely, times have changed, although there still is inconsistency among experts as to the appropriateness of adolescent sexuality. When sexuality is combined with money, such as through an act of shoplifting or for that matter solicitation, it is still considered a serious offense; and it is not clear if its seriousness is related to the complexities of troubles that adolescents face routinely in today's uncertain times.

Thomas recognized that the impoverished immigrants' family was too disorganized to provide the regulative definitions that would stick in the minds of adolescents. Impoverished families could not provide the regulative force of control that was observable in affluent families. He saw hope in the school system, but not one that standardized its method of educating and failed to recognize the unique desires of its students. The story that Thomas tells is one of complexity, marginalization, conflict, and poverty in a patriarchal world.

Methodological Note

Thomas's books have been criticized because of their lack of methodological rigor. This is a common complaint generated by more quantitatively oriented social scientists who may question the representativeness of case analysis. Thomas fails to provide the details that today's academic reviewers would demand with regards to sample representativeness. We know little about the selection of the letters that Thomas cites, and the larger population from which they were obtained.

Critics might also accuse Thomas of selecting his letters to fit the story of immigrant desires that he wished to tell. But the theory of desires and conflicting definitions seemed to have emerged inductively after Thomas spent several years studying and translating immigrant letters. We can also assume that the letters were written by people who were literate. We know little about those immigrants who were illiterate. Thomas could not possibly have been able to relate their stories. In this sense, the immigrant poor that Thomas analyzed are not the most seriously disadvantaged.

The distinguished symbolic interactionist Herbert Blumer has also been critical of Thomas's larger sets of writings. He has concluded that there are many missing details. Blumer would have liked more detail on the background of the cases Thomas examined. We know little about the families from where they came other than the facts revealed in the letters. Still, Blumer was undoubtedly greatly influenced by Thomas along with numerous qualitatively as well as quantitatively oriented sociologists and criminologists.

Conclusion

Thomas was the first scholar of significance to provide a vision of female criminality that departed from the dominating perspective of biological and psychological pathologies. Thomas's unadjusted girl was not pathologically delinquent or criminal. She was unadjusted to society's patriarchal definitions to regulate her desires. These desires were largely a function of immigrant wishes. They included dreams that go beyond the wish for money. Thomas's focus on immigrant girls reflected their old-world and new-world repressions. They were repressed in their country of origin, and they were repressed in America for their gender at birth.

The freedom that American society provided was largely for those who were members of the dominant white-male-Protestant culture. Thomas wrote at a time when women were just given the right to vote. They were second class citizens despite the promise of American freedom.

For the impoverished, Thomas told a familiar story of culture conflict in his definitions of the situation. The immigrant poor confronted a legal system that would be quick to label its girls as deviant, delinquent, and even criminal simply because they expressed their sexuality. Although the cases that Thomas cited might seem quite dated, there is still much that we can learn from a close reading of Thomas. There is a theory and method to his writings. Society must be attuned to its members' wishes, and it must be able to regulate their wishes in systems that are sensitive to them as individuals and to their culturally inspired situational definitions.

Simon I. Singer

See also Anderson, Elijah: Code of the Street; Becker, Howard S.: Labeling and Deviant Careers; Lemert, Edwin M.: Primary and Secondary Deviance; Shaw, Clifford R., and Henry D. McKay: Social Disorganization Theory; Tannenbaum, Frank: The Dramatization of Evil; Thrasher, Frederick M.: The Gang; Whyte, William Foote: Street Corner Society

References and Further Readings

Blumer, H. (1979). *Critiques of research in the social sciences: An appraisal of Thomas and Znaniecki's* The Polish Peasant in Europe and America. New York: Transaction.

Bressler, M. (1952). Selected family patterns in W. I. Thomas' unfinished study of the Bintl Brief. *American Sociological Review, 71,* 563–571.

Erickson, E. (1963). *Childhood and society.* New York: W. W. Norton.

Giddens, A. (1990). *The consequences of modernity.* Stanford, CA: Stanford University Press.

Katz, J. (1988). *Seductions of crime: Moral and sensual attractions in doing evil.* New York: Basic Books.

Lemert, E. M. (Ed.). (1951). *Social pathology: A systematic approach to the theory of sociopathic behavior.* New York: McGraw-Hill.

Maslow, A. (1970). *Motivation and personality.* New York: Harper & Row.

Matza, D. (1964). *Delinquency and drift*. New York: Wiley.

Merton, R. K. (1995). The Thomas theorem and the Matthew effect. *Social Forces, 74*, 379–422.

Shaw, C. R., & McKay, H. D. (1942). *Juvenile delinquency in urban areas*. Chicago: University of Chicago Press.

Thomas, W. I. (1923). *The unadjusted girl: With cases and standpoint for behavior analysis*. Boston: Harper Torchbooks.

Thomas, W. I., Znaniecki, F., & Zaretsky, E. (1958). *The Polish peasant in Europe and America*. Boston: Dover.

Thrasher, F. M. (1963). *The gang: A study of 1,313 gangs in Chicago*. Chicago: University of Chicago Press.

Tönnies, F. (1957). *Gemeinschaft und Gesellschaft* [Community and society]. East Lansing: Michigan State University Press.

THORNBERRY, TERENCE P.: INTERACTIONAL THEORY

Terence P. Thornberry called his theory "interactional" because it was developed based on the premise that crime and delinquency is a behavioral outcome of social *interactions* between a person and his or her environment. Guided by a strategy he called "theoretical elaboration," Thornberry combined two major social psychological perspectives of delinquency, control theory and social learning theory, into an initial version of interactional theory designed to explain delinquent behavior better than when each theory is used separately. The significance of interactional theory, however, goes beyond its proposed merging of these two individual theories. The theory's unique contribution has been to offer a dynamic model of bidirectional causality and developmental changes across three stages of adolescence (ages 11–20): early, middle, and late adolescence. Up until this time, criminologists had only sporadically discussed and explored changes in the influence of delinquency predictors during adolescence as well as bidirectional (or reciprocal) causal relationships between these predictors and delinquency. However, Thornberry's interactional theory was the first fully developed model of bidirectional causality and life-course dynamics in criminology.

The initial version of interactional theory was later extended by Thornberry and Marvin Krohn to allow for a life-course explanation of continuity and change in offending not only in adolescence but also in preschool years, childhood, and late adolescence/emerging adulthood. As a result, the extension broadened the definition of deviant behavior, from delinquent to antisocial behavior, and the scope of theoretical explanation by incorporating strain as well as control and social learning concepts into its model. The extended version also emphasizes the importance of studying continuity and change in prosocial as well as antisocial, behaviors for a full understanding of the life-course patterns of human behavior. Finally, it proposes a model of intergenerational continuity in behavior over time. These extensions as well as the initial model have made unique contributions to the field, and any discussion of criminological theory neglecting Thornberry's interactional theory would be incomplete.

Foundation for an Interactional Theory

Thornberry began with Travis Hirschi's version of control theory, which he elaborated upon by using propositions and empirical findings of Ronald Akers's social learning theory, in order to construct a more accurate model of delinquency causation. In this sense, the intellectual origin of interactional theory is the Durkheimian tradition of social control. That is, Thornberry agrees with Hirschi that we are all born with deviant motivation—a natural tendency or impulse to violate social norms for easy and immediate personal gains. If social constraints are absent or ineffective, we come to naturally engage in deviant acts, as our inborn tendency is free to be expressed.

However, Thornberry departs from Hirschi, arguing that the lack or weakening of social control would not automatically result in delinquency, though it would make delinquency possible along with other forms of behaviors, prosocial as well as antisocial. Delinquency remains a possibility until an interactive setting in which delinquency is learned, performed, and reinforced as Akers suggests. In other words, according to Thornberry, the absence or weakening of social control is a necessary but not a sufficient condition for delinquent involvement. Thus, Hirschi's social control theory needed to be extended to include concepts and propositions of Akers's social learning theory.

Core Concepts

Based on empirical findings from previous research, Thornberry selected three concepts from Hirschi's theory (attachment to parents, commitment to school, and belief in conventional values) and two from Akers's theory (association with delinquent peers and delinquent values). These five concepts are used to explain delinquent behavior, which refers to all types of "acts that place the youth at risk for adjudication" (1987, p. 867), including both minor (e.g., status offenses) and serious or violent activities. Given this broad scope of the behavioral outcome concept, interactional theory is a general theory intended to account for a variety of delinquent acts. Similarly, to fully develop implications of the two constituent theories, the five explanatory concepts are also broadly defined (p. 866). Using these six concepts, Thornberry first built a baseline model of early adolescence (ages 11–13) by describing interrelationships among the concepts. In doing so, he constructed a model that addresses two main limitations of the previous research on delinquency: unidirectional causality and the lack of developmental perspective.

Bidirectional Causality

The basic premise of interactional theory is "human behavior occurs in social interaction and can therefore best be explained by models that focus on interactive processes" (Thornberry, 1987, p. 864). Being consistent with this premise, the interactional model specifies relationships among the six concepts as bidirectional rather than unidirectional based on empirical findings from previous research. For example, Hirschi's social control theory proposes an adolescent's attachment to parents reduces the chance of engaging in delinquent behavior. Thornberry elaborated on this unidirectional (or recursive) proposition by adding the reversed causality to the original relationship based on empirical evidence that an adolescent's involvement in delinquency reduces the chance of his or her feeling attached to parents (Liska & Reed, 1985). Similarly, he specified mutually increasing, bidirectional relationships between an adolescent's association with delinquent peers and delinquent behavior, to which Akers's social learning theory alluded but previous researchers paid little attention.

In this way, the bidirectional perspective was applied to relationships among the six core concepts, while the strengths of those relationships are not necessarily expected to be of equal strength. For instance, the baseline model of early adolescence includes reciprocal relationships, one of which is stronger than the other, like the relationships between attachment to parents and association with delinquent peers. On the other hand, not all relationships were specified as bidirectional based on existing theories and research. For example, in the early adolescent model, one relationship was described as unidirectional (e.g., attachment to parents a belief in conventional values, but not the other way around), whereas three pairs of the six variables were specified to have no relationship, neither unidirectional nor bidirectional: attachment to parents—delinquent values; belief in conventional values—delinquent behavior,; and belief in conventional values—delinquent values. In these specifications, belief in conventional values is expected to have limited influence on other variables because conventional beliefs tend to be widely shared among adolescents in this developmental stage (i.e., ages 11–13).

Developmental Extension

To address the problem of the nondevelopmental nature of most theories in criminology, Thornberry extended the basic model of early adolescence to explain interrelationships among core concepts at middle (ages 15–16) and late adolescence (ages 18–20). While the models for the early and middle adolescence share essentially the same causal structure, some changes in relationships are expected as adolescents make a transition from one developmental stage to the next. For example, the overall influence of attachment to parents is weaker during middle than early adolescence as the locus of interaction and control moves from the family and parents to school and peers. As a result, the influence of peers, especially delinquent peers, is expected to increase. Another developmental change concerns the increased casual significance of delinquent values as a result of these values becoming more fully articulated and having stronger effects on other variables. Thus, during middle adolescence the family and parents decline in relative importance, while school and peers increase in causal significance.

Thornberry then added two new variables to the preceding model to reflect types of developmental changes expected during later adolescence: commitment to one's own family and commitment to conventional activities (e.g., employment, attending college, and military service). These new sources of bonds to conventional society largely replace attachment to parents and commitment to school, even though they still have limited roles in explaining delinquency. Though belief in conventional values has strong relationships with the new variables, it has no relationship with other variables except association with delinquent peers, with which it has weak bidirectional relationships.

On the other hand, association with delinquent peers and delinquent values both have strong reciprocal relationships with delinquent behavior. This would increase the chance of sustained delinquency unless the amplifying causal loop involving the three delinquent variables gets interrupted by changes taking place in this developmental stage. Thornberry proposes that two new variables are key sources of such change, offering an explanation for the empirically observed pattern of discontinuity in offending (desistance). That is, commitment to conventional activity and to one's own family would create new prosocial roles (e.g., employee or parent) and networks of attachments (e.g., social relationships with employer and other coworkers; or building relationship with spouse and/or nurturing own child). In turn, there one might reduce delinquent involvement and even break the cycle toward criminal careers.

Social Structure

Another premise of interactional theory is that behavioral trajectories are embedded in the social structure. Thus, a person's location in the structure of social roles and statuses (i.e., race, class, sex, and community of residence), especially a position in early stage of life, is important to consider since it sets the basic path of the behavioral trajectories from the beginning. To illustrate, Thornberry focused on social class of origin. Based on empirical findings about class differences in family disruption, poverty, and residential community, he suggested that children from lower-class families are "*initially* less bonded to conventional society and more exposed to delinquent values, friends, and behaviors" (1987, p. 885, emphasis in the original) than those from middle-class families. This class difference in the initial values of interactional variables would place those children on different paths of the initial values' development over time, including bidirectional relationships among the variables.

Extensions of an Interactional Theory

Almost 15 years later, Thornberry and Krohn proposed an extended version of interactional theory to broaden the scope of its initial model in three major ways. First, the life span of interest was expanded from adolescence (ages 11–20) to "the full life course, from infancy through adulthood" (2001, p. 301), thereby broadly defining the primary outcome behavior as antisocial rather than delinquent. Second, the extended model includes a discussion of prosocial as well as antisocial behaviors to enhance the explanation of antisocial careers, which still remain the theory's main focus. Third, while not explicit, the initial version of interactional theory was further elaborated upon, using a strain perspective.

Antisocial Careers

Positing that the initiation of antisocial careers occurs throughout the life course, Thornberry and Krohn proposed four ideal types of continuity and change in antisocial behavior: precocious offenders, early onset offenders, later onset offenders, and late bloomers. They constructed a 2 × 2 table of the four types by dividing the life course into two stages—"early" and "later"—and asking whether antisocial behavior was present or absent in each stage. While using the ideal types for a heuristic purpose, they posited there is an unlimited variance in the timing of antisocial careers' onset and termination and the length of their duration over the continuum of the life course rather than suggesting that there is a certain number of antisocial career types as others had done.

While disproportionately small in the population, *precocious offenders* are characterized by very early onset and long-term duration of antisocial careers. Specifically, they start to engage in antisocial behavior prior to about age 6, during toddlerhood and the preschool years, and continue their antisocial behavior through childhood to adulthood. Their precocious onset can be explained by an intense combination of individual traits (e.g., negative temperamental qualities and neuropsychological deficits), ineffective parenting (e.g., inconsistent rule setting and explosive physical discipline), and a severely disadvantaged position in the social structure (e.g., chronic poverty and welfare dependence). Structural adversity generates emotional distress (e.g., anger and depression) for both parents and their children, increasing the chance of very-early-onset-offending. This sets the stage for cumulative disadvantage of precocious offending and subsequent maladjustment in family, school, peer relations, and beliefs interacting over the life course, making patterns of persistent and serious antisocial behaviors likely.

Early onset offenders share many of the precocious offenders' risk factors for antisocial behaviors, which contribute to their initiation of offending during the elementary school years (about ages 6–12). However, they are unlikely to experience the intense coupling of those factors like precocious offenders, and environmental factors—parental and social structural—tend to contribute more to the onset than individual deficits. Thus, their initiation of antisocial behaviors is likely to occur after toddlerhood and the preschool years. As they begin to attend school and broaden social networks, their risk factors (which were dormant due to familial protection and/or limited antisocial opportunity) increasingly become the source of antisocial behaviors as those factors interact with the external social environment. For example, difficult temperament (which was restrained by parental control) begins to interact with the new environment of school and new relations with peers and teachers, resulting in their rejection and negatively affecting performance at school. These types of stressors and resultant stress weaken social bonds and increase access to deviant opportunity structures, such as delinquent peers and gangs in the community. Although they are expected to show a substantial degree of continuity in offending, their antisocial careers are more likely to come to an end (i.e., to desist) due to improved social environments (e.g., family's upward mobility), loosely coupled causal factors, and effective treatments received (e.g., delinquency prevention program).

Thornberry and Krohn's (2001, p. 299) *later onset offenders* "begin offending during the early adolescent years and, for most, terminate their involvement in delinquency before the end of adolescence." After being largely prosocial throughout the elementary school years, these adolescents, who are mostly without individual deficits, begin to get exposed to environmental risk factors, from which they were protected by their conventional bonds and close control by parents and teachers. While trying to establish age-appropriate autonomy, adolescents experience increasing tension in their relationships with parents and teachers and feel anger toward them. As a result, adolescents gravitate toward each other because their experiences are similar, at the same time distancing themselves from parents and teachers. One of the consequences is to engage in deviant lifestyles, experimental use of drugs, and minor forms of delinquency. But they begin to disengage from these activities as the need for autonomy is met and they prepare for transition to adulthood. Some of the actions, however, can have profound, long-term consequences (e.g., teenage parenthood).

Thornberry and Krohn later added a fourth type, *late bloomers*, who initiate antisocial behaviors during late adolescence and early adulthood. These individuals are likely to have a number of individual deficits (e.g., low intelligence), which becomes an obstacle to building human capital, but those deficits' causal influence is kept in check, being buffered by supportive family and school environment and social structural advantages. However, as they leave such protective environments to seek employment and independence, a lack of human capital becomes a major disadvantage entering into adulthood. The loss of buffering factors, coupled with increasing life stressors and deviant peer influence, leads to problem behaviors, including excessive drinking and drug use and addiction.

Continuity and Change in Antisocial Behavior

Precocious, early onset, and later onset offenders, and late bloomers are *not discrete* categories, into which all offenders are supposed to be classified. They are presented as exemplary scenarios describing an infinite number of cases on a continuum of antisocial careers, defined by the onset and desistance of antisocial behaviors over the life course. For example, while the age of onset of precocious offenders will be definitely younger than that of early onset offenders, interactional theory is little interested in offering a cutoff age distinguishing the two. Instead, the theory focuses on explaining how the age of onset is determined by "the *combination* and *interaction* of structural, individual, and parental influences" (Thornberry & Krohn, 2001, p. 295, emphasis in the original). Like initiation, termination of antisocial behaviors is a product of the combination and interaction of the three continuous variables, which also explains why the earlier the onset, the more delayed the desistance.

Prosocial Careers

Similar to precocious offenders, individuals whose behaviors remain prosocial throughout the life course constitute a relatively small proportion of the population. The absence or control of negative temperamental qualities, strong bonds to the family, and effective parenting set the stage for the continuity of prosocial behavior early in the life course, providing a foundation for conventional life styles and prosocial relations with others, such as teachers and peers. These individuals are less likely to face structural adversity than their antisocial counterparts as their families tend to be economically secure and structurally stable, thus reducing strain and stress. As a result, from the early years through adolescence, they are likely to develop human and social capital necessary for smooth, on-time transitions to adulthood.

Intergenerational Extensions

Exploring the intergenerational implications of his theory, Thornberry proposed another extended model of behavioral continuity across three generations. The model includes variables of grandparents' as well as parents' characteristics and behaviors to explain their children's antisocial and prosocial behaviors. While the model contains the same theoretical variables—social bonds, effective parenting, antisocial peers, stressors, and structural adversity—Thornberry elaborated his theory, using empirical findings about behavioral continuity across generations and suggesting alternative, non-social explanations of intergenerational transmission of antisocial behaviors, such as genetic factors.

Sung Joon Jang

See also Agnew, Robert: General Strain Theory; Akers, Ronald L.: Social Learning Theory; Hirschi, Travis: Social Control Theory; Moffitt, Terrie E.: A Developmental Model of Life-Course-Persistent Offending; Sutherland, Edwin H.: Differential Association Theory and Differential Social Organization

References and Further Readings

Agnew, R. (1992). Foundation for a general strain theory of crime and delinquency. *Criminology, 30*, 47–87.

Akers, R. L. (1977). *Deviant behavior: A social learning perspective*. Belmont, CA: Wadsworth.

Burkett, S. R., & Warren, B. O. (1987). Religiosity, peer influence, and adolescent marijuana use: A panel study of underlying causal structures. *Criminology, 25*, 109–131.

Hirschi, T. (1969). *Causes of delinquency*. Berkeley: University of California Press.

Jang, S. J. (2002). The effects of family, school, peers, and attitudes on adolescents' drug use: Do they vary with age? *Justice Quarterly, 19*, 97–126.

Krohn, M. D., Lizotte, A. J., Thornberry, T. P., Smith, C., & McDowall, D. (1996). Reciprocal causal relationships among drug use, peers, and beliefs: A five-wave panel model. *Journal of Drug Issues, 26*, 405–428.

LeGrange, R. L., & White, H. R. (1985). Age differences in delinquency: A test of theory. *Criminology, 23*, 19–46.

Liska, A. E., & Reed, M. D. (1985). Ties to conventional institutions and delinquency. *American Sociological Review, 50*, 547–560.

Moffitt, T. E. (1997). Adolescence-limited and life-course-persistent offending: A complementary pair of developmental theories. In T. P. Thornberry (Ed.), *Developmental theories of crime and delinquency* (Advances in Criminological Theory: Vol. 7, pp. 11–54). New Brunswick, NJ: Transaction.

Thornberry, T. P. (1987). Toward an interactional theory of delinquency. *Criminology, 25*, 863–891.

Thornberry, T. P. (1989). Reflections on the advantages and disadvantages of theoretical integration. In S. F. Messner, M. D. Krohn, & A. E. Liska (Eds.), *Theoretical integration in the study of deviance and crime: Problems and prospects* (pp. 51–60). Albany: SUNY Press.

Thornberry, T. P. (1996). Empirical support for interactional theory: A review of the literature. In J. D. Hawkins (Ed.), *Delinquency and crime: Current theories* (pp. 198–235). New York: Cambridge University Press.

Thornberry, T. P. (2005). Explaining multiple patterns of offending across the life course and across generations. *Annals of the American Academy of Political and Social Science, 602*, 156–195.

Thornberry, T. P., & Krohn, M. D. (2001). The development of delinquency An interactional perspective. In S. O. White (Ed.), *Handbook of youth and justice* (pp. 289–305). New York: Plenum.

Thornberry, T. P., & Krohn, M. D. (2005). Applying interactional theory to the explanation of continuity and change in antisocial behavior. In D. P. Farrington (Ed.), *Integrated developmental and life-course theories of offending* (Advances in Criminological Theory: Vol. 14, pp. 183–209). New Brunswick, NJ: Transaction.

THRASHER, FREDERICK M.: THE GANG

Frederick M. Thrasher was one of Robert Park and Ernest Burgess's students in the 1920s Sociology Department of the University of Chicago. His dissertation, *The Gang: A Study of 1313 Gangs in Chicago,* became the seminal work on the topic and theoretically his group process perspective remains influential today. Other University of Chicago dissertations in those years include studies on *The Hobo* by Nels Anderson, *The Gold Coast and the Slum* by Harvey Zorbaugh, and *The Black Family* by E. Franklin Frazier. With other studies and dissertations, these works formed the distinctive style and perspective that composed the Chicago School of Sociology.

Thrasher's work exemplifies three linked strengths and weaknesses of the Chicago School: (1) an ecological but ethnically neutral theory; (2) a lack of analysis of girls' lives; and (3) an understanding of male gang and delinquent behavior based in spontaneity, social disorganization, and group process.

Ecology: The Problem of Space and Race

Thrasher cast his study of gangs within the concentric circle model of cities authored by Burgess. Gangs formed, Thrasher argued, in the interstitial areas, or neighborhoods in between the slums of "first settlement" and the residential zones of an upwardly and outwardly mobile working class. Gangs were fundamentally the product of the lack of controls over second-generation immigrant youth. As the customs and traditions of the old world weakened, schools and other local institutions proved incapable of supervising rebellious youth. Thrasher's theory, as Ruth Kornhauser pointed out, is a pure control model: Delinquency is the result of lack of institutional supervision or parental control over the actions of youth.

Gangs were conceived as one component of an urban ecological system. Thrasher called gangs a phenomenon of human ecology. To Park, Burgess, and Thrasher, social systems in Chicago, and by implication other industrial cities, resembled a living organism, or the natural process of the evolution of all life. Thrasher and others of the Chicago School often described their study topics as natural histories. The universal laws of science, the Chicago School asserted, could be applied to social phenomena that were the unplanned, natural product of the city's growth.

What was needed, said Park, was the hard work of going out and observing these natural processes first hand through the actions of people who inhabited "hobohemia" or "gangland" and writing down what was seen like a journalist. Thrasher, like others of the Chicago School, practiced field research learned from anthropological studies in colonial societies. Chicago students worked from field stations in the neighborhoods where gangs formed, not cloistered behind the library walls of ivory towers. The field study method is one of the lasting contributions of the Chicago School. Park's empiricism has always been a corrective to the abstract theorizing that came to later dominate American sociology with Harvard's Talcott Parsons.

Thrasher and the Chicago School's field research studied deviants in "natural areas" of the city, but their ethnographic method gave little attention to the role of institutions, such as the real estate industry and banks. Institutional policies—like the placement of streets, railroads, or conditions for home loans—were often seen as "natural" and not as deliberate decisions advancing certain interests. To the Chicagoans, the concept of the natural areas of the city, like gangland, was the product of ecological processes, not political or economic choices.

Related to the concept of natural areas was ethnic succession. Thrasher and the Chicago School were optimistic about the progress of modernity and promise of the industrial age. As immigrant groups settled in Chicago, similar to new plants, they had to struggle for survival in the least satisfactory soil, the slums. As time went on and immigrants obtained work in Chicago's booming industries, they were able to move out toward more fertile soil, the second zone of Burgess's schema, placed "naturally" in the areas just outside the slums. Conflict characterized this process as new immigrant groups invaded the slums, displacing the previous tenants who headed toward the suburbs where they displaced a prior ethnic group.

Consistent with notions of the inevitability of progress, immigrants climbed a ladder of ethnic succession, traversing Burgess's concentric circles. This model, the Chicagoans argued, defined the social and spatial mobility of people in cities. Gangs were merely the by-product of this modernizing process and were fated to fade away as their ethnic group improved their economic and spatial position. Most adolescent gang members "naturally" and inevitably matured out of the gang and got married, got a job, and settled down. Thrasher's application of the Chicago School concepts of natural areas and ethnic succession would have serious consequences for his treatment of race.

For Thrasher, African Americans were just another ethnic group that fit into the overall model. The Gang spends very little time describing black gangs. The Chicago School, led by Park, a long-time secretary to Booker T. Washington, was firmly opposed to racism and discrimination, seeing them as residual prejudices of the past. Their insistence that crime and delinquency were the product of social conditions, not the characteristics of specific ethnic groups, fiercely combated nativist and racist opinion. But their characterization of the black community as subject to the same ecological laws as other immigrants does not appear to have substantial empirical support. Thrasher and the Chicagoans continued to see "the ghetto" as only Jewish and failed to apply it to the African American "black belt." What Kenneth Clark described as the dark ghetto could hardly be conceptualized as a natural phenomena, and its invisible walls blocked African Americans from the spatial and economic mobility enjoyed by white ethnics. The black ghetto, though its implications were evident at the time to W. E. B. Du Bois

and others, did not fit into the Chicago School ecological perspective.

Even in Burgess's classic diagram, the orderly concentric zones superimposed on Chicago were marred by a deep black line running from the central business district of the Loop nearly to Hyde Park. This black belt, the segregated African American Bronzeville, did not fit the neat, "natural" pattern of ethnic succession of other groups. Segregation—enforced by laws, real estate practices, and white gang violence—violated the "natural" ecological processes that governed the spatial and economic mobility of white ethnic immigrants. Black gangs, contrary to Thrasher's views, would be subject to deliberate and harmful social processes very different than their Italian, Irish, or Polish brothers.

Thrasher thus underestimated the significance of the 1919 race riots that for Du Bois and others decisively demonstrated a non-equivalence of the black/white ethnic experience. Thrasher made scant reference to those traumatic race riots, treating them as just one more example of ethnic and gang conflict, not as a sign of difference in social processes. Today's black gangs, which have persisted now for more than half a century, are difficult to account for with Thrasher's ethnically neutral theory.

While more contemporary Chicago School figures such as William Julius Wilson have investigated the significance of race—declining or not—Thrasher's focus on ecology, social disorganization, and natural histories of groups, has generally informed gang research today. Thrasher's legacy, like that of the Chicago School, is that space, not race, is the essential defining characteristic of gangs.

Gender: Masculinity and the Problem of the Invisibility of the Female Experience

Thrasher was not alone in the Chicago School in essentially ignoring female experience. For Thrasher, the gang was fundamentally a male phenomenon, a product of the strivings and "quest for new experience" of second-generation immigrant boys. Thrasher found only 5 or 6 female gangs among his 1,313 gangs in Chicago.

Thus, for Thrasher, the boy gang is the paradigmatic group, so exciting that "no healthy boy could hold himself aloof from it" (p. 26). He wrote admiringly: "Gangs represent the spontaneous effort of boys to create a society for themselves where none adequate to their needs exists" (p. 37). Thrasher's analysis of masculinity centered on a sociological rejection of any gang instinct. For Thrasher, like others in the Chicago School, understanding deviant behavior was best accomplished through an analysis of the social conditions that boys faced growing up. According to Thrasher, human nature is plastic and "his habits may be infinitely varied in varied circumstances" (p. 43). To say gangs are instinctually male, according to Thrasher, "is not acceptable in the light of modern knowledge" (p. 246). The process of male gang formation for Thrasher, and the Chicago School, was fundamentally social, not psychological.

According to Thrasher, girls followed more traditional social patterns of behavior that was more conformist than that of rebellious boys. Girls were also more closely supervised and thus had fewer opportunities to hang out on street corners and form gangs. While girls form cliques or clubs, these are generally not conflict groups, Thrasher said. He wrote that fighting female peer groups are almost never found in immigrant communities where girls were more closely supervised.

Later research on female peer groups questioned Thrasher's views, but at that time no empirical studies of female gangs were made in Chicago or anywhere else. Peggy Giordano in the 1970s challenged Thrasher's basic assumption of the non-conflictual nature of female peer groups. Giordano discovered that delinquency for girls was strongly related to peer friendships and was not merely the product of personal adjustment. The peer group was extremely salient for the delinquent girls in Giordano's study, a conclusion generally accepted today.

Some, like Freda Adler, claimed that contemporary girls' aggression was the result of women's liberation and a changed view by girls of their female role. But Thrasher and the Chicago School carried out few studies on girls' lives, a legacy that continues to plague criminologists today. Jane Addams was among the few Chicago School era figures to take an active interest in females, but her work was marginal to the male scholars of Hyde Park. For Thrasher, the white ethnic male experience was universal and this assumption has influenced research on gangs from the 1920s onward.

Group Process: The Problem of Spontaneity and Social Disorganization

The most influential concept of Thrasher's theory of gangs has been his description of the group process of gang formation under conditions of social disorganization. This conceptualization remains the dominant paradigm for the study of gangs today, especially through the important studies of both James F. Short, Jr., and Malcolm Klein.

Thrasher argued that the gang was an extension of the childish play group in the crowded areas of the city. Such groups naturally formed leaders, and a variety of other roles for members. The processes of group formation, applicable to all groups, can be applied to gangs. Thrasher's definition is an extended description of this process:

> The gang is an interstitial group originally formed spontaneously, then integrated through conflict. It is characterized by the following types of behavior: milling, movement through space as a unit, conflict, and planning. The result of this collective behavior is the development of tradition, unreflective internal structure, *esprit de corps*, solidarity, morale, group awareness, and attachment to a local territory. (p. 57)

Thrasher's book was a definitive sociological answer to the popular notion that delinquency and gangs exhibited a criminal mind. Theoretically, Thrasher's definition does not mention crime, a definitional issue that has continued to divide gang researchers today. Some, like Malcolm Klein, insist that criminal acts define gangs. But others, like James Short, more consistent with Thrasher, argue that crime is what needs to be explained and so to include it in the definition would be circular reasoning. Thrasher's original definition was an aspect of the Chicago School's efforts to turn the attention of scholars, government officials, and the public away from the psychology of crime to conditions in poor communities. Thrasher and his fellow students and teachers were in the forefront of social reform in the 1920s.

Thrasher starts *The Gang* with a description of gangland, the areas of Chicago which are home to his 1,313 gangs, carefully plotted on a map that was a pull-out in the first edition. For Thrasher, it was the conditions of social disorganization that spawned the formation of gangs as a boyish response to lack of supervision and an arena for exciting activities. Playgroups formed in such areas spontaneously and then came into conflict with other groups and authorities, like police and teachers. This conflict integrated the group, causing it to develop an identity and unreflective structure within a specific neighborhood.

Thrasher claimed his definition had universal significance, citing studies in London, New York, Boston, and other cities. His famous statement that "no two gangs are alike," was meant to reflect variation of group processes within a standard male adolescent response to common, socially disorganized, conditions. A chart displaying the different types of gangs—from a casual crowd and playgroups to the gang and then on to criminal gangs, secret societies, political machine, and other diffuse, solidified, or conventionalized groups—was meant to provide a universal blueprint to the natural history of gangs.

Though often not noted, Thrasher's study of gangs took place during Prohibition in 1920s Chicago, when the Capone-run Italian gangs battled the Irish and others for supremacy in the control of illegal alcohol. Homicide rates were by far the highest in Chicago's history, not exceeded until the end of the 1960s. Rather than describe these 1920s "beer wars," The Gang was fundamentally devoted to describing delinquency and adolescents and their roots in the playgroup. Thrasher's concerns with the lack of supervision of young boys was intended, in part, to deflect public attention from the young adult gang violence of the time, and argue for progressive social reform for children and families.

Thrasher's model did provide for organized crime as one possible outcome of the youthful gang. He briefly describes the liquor syndicates that were dominated by the master gangs of the city. He also describes the Social Athletic Clubs that were organized by politicians and pulled young gang members into recreation and licit and illicit electoral work. Thrasher also criticized the media attention to "spectacular" crimes and crime waves. He argued that the public needed to pay more attention to "the roots of the problem," which included "inadequate family life; poverty; deteriorating neighborhoods; and ineffective religion, education, and recreation" (p. 491). He believed this

matrix needed to be tackled all at once if the gang problem was to be solved.

Thrasher described the extensive influence of adult gangs in Chicago, but did not foresee their persisting significance in the crime syndicates and politics. In The Gang, Thrasher had found that 243 of the 1,313 were adult or mixed adult gangs. He also claimed there were over 500 Social Athletic Clubs "of the gang type" formed in part by the encouragement of politicians, saloon-keepers, and/or social welfare agencies. Capone's mob, based in Social Athletic clubs and crews in Italian neighborhoods, later formed the "Outfit" and persists to this day. It still dominates many illegal markets and is closely linked to Chicago's Democratic Party machine.

The Irish Social Athletic Clubs were crucial in the violence that enforced the segregated barriers to mobility for the African American population. The violence continued over decades and segregation, not mobility, remains a characteristic of the African American experience. Segregation, extreme concentrations of African Americans in high-rise housing, and continuing high levels of poverty were among the conditions that gave rise to institutionalized black gangs that have dominated neighborhoods in Chicago for decades. Thrasher, like his Chicago School colleagues, failed to understand the non-equivalence of the African American and white ethnic experience. His belief in progress, ethnic succession, and other "natural" processes failed to sufficiently account for a very different experience of black Chicagoans.

The role of adult gangs in the formation, support, and incorporation of adolescents into master gangs was not emphasized by Thrasher. Thrasher noted the role of the prison in supporting gang members who were machine supporters, but, as with other institutions, he spent little time analyzing the influence of prison. Internationally, as well as in Chicago, prison has been found to be one way gangs form and exercise their power back to the streets. Thrasher's universal group process definition excludes such gangs. Contemporary researchers, following in Thrasher's method, often exclude prison gangs and drug crews as not true street gangs since they fail to conform to the process of neighborhood-based gang formation. Thrasher's book may have blinded research toward some paths to understanding, even as it illuminated others.

Conclusion

Thrasher moved on to New York University in 1928 but produced no more notable writings. His attempts to discover and study gangs in New York similar to those he found in Chicago were unsuccessful. He wrote an introduction to James C. Farrell's *Young Lonigan*, one in the classic trilogy describing the Irish youngster Studs Lonigan on Chicago's south side. In this 1932 essay, Thrasher praises Studs as a "real boy" in an "unequalled" book of adolescent life. Thrasher does not note the participation of the fictional Lonigan in the 1919 race riots, a very important topic for Farrell. For Thrasher, the youthful experience of Studs Lonigan was an example of the universal processes of poor adolescents, not differences in race.

The vividness of Thrasher's descriptions of the process of gang formation has maintained the status of *The Gang* as the most influential study of gangs in history. But the narrowness of his focus on male, white ethnics, within a modernist paradigm of social mobility, has influenced research today in ways that minimize the salience of both gender and race.

John M. Hagedorn

See also Gangs and the Underclass; Kobrin, Solomon: Neighborhoods and Crime; Shaw, Clifford R., and Henry D. McKay: Social Disorganization Theory; Short, James F., Jr.: Gangs and Group Processes; Spergel, Irving A.: Neighborhoods and Delinquent Subcultures

References and Further Readings

Clark, K. B. (1965). *Dark ghetto: Dilemmas of social power*. New York: Harper & Row.

Farrell, J. T. (1978). *Studs Lonigan*. New York: The Vanguard Press. (Original work published 1932)

Giordano, P. C. (1978). Girls, guys and gangs: The changing social context of female delinquency. *Journal of Criminal Law and Criminology, 69*, 126–132.

Kornhauser, R. (1978). *Social sources of delinquency: An appraisal of analytic models*. Chicago: University of Chicago Press.

Short, J. F., & Strodtbeck, F. L. (1965). *Group process and gang delinquency*. Chicago: University of Chicago Press.

Simpson, D. W. (2001). *Rogues, rebels, and rubber stamps: The politics of the Chicago City Council from 1863 to the present*. Boulder, CO: Westview Press.

Thrasher, F. (1927). *The gang: A study of 1,313 gangs in Chicago*. Chicago: University of Chicago Press.

TITTLE, CHARLES R.: CONTROL BALANCE THEORY

After reviewing and critiquing extant criminological theories, Charles R. Tittle concluded that most fail as general theories of crime and deviance because they do not offer breadth, comprehensiveness, precision, or depth. These limitations do not mean that these theories are inadequate explanations of crime phenomena. In fact, each adds to the understanding of deviant and criminal behavior by focusing on a particular causal factor, and more importantly, each has generated at least modest support. This sentiment, however, does imply that existing theories are both restricted and incomplete. Tittle proposed an integrated criminological theory drawing from learning, anomie, conflict, social control, labeling, utilitarian, and routine activities theories. As such, control balance theory is a general theory that not only is designed to explain all forms of deviant behavior but also to account for conforming behaviors.

Original Theory

In the original formulation of control balance theory, deviance is defined as "any behavior that the majority of a given group regards as unacceptable or that typically evokes a collective response of a negative type" (Tittle, 1995, p. 124). Deviance can be divided into six different categories: predation, exploitation, defiance, plunder, decadence, and submission. Predation involves direct acts of physical violence, manipulation, or property theft, which benefit the perpetrator and have no regard for the well-being of the victim. Exploitation is indirect predation where others or the situational context is used to coerce, manipulate, or steal from a victim for the benefit of the exploiter. Defiance refers to the indifference of individuals toward an individual, a group, or norms and values of a designated individual or group. Plunder is the pursuit of one's own goals with little regard for the effects of one's own actions on others and is considered especially heinous. Decadence deals with unpredictable and impulsive acts that have no rational motivation but instead deal with the whims of the moment. Submission is passive obedience toward others.

Control balance theory centers on the concept of control, or more specifically a control balance ratio, which is the ratio of the amount of control exercised relative to the amount of control experienced. Much like other social control theories, control balance theory contends that controls operate in some individuals by inducing conforming behavior; however, the theory also suggests that controls can serve as the motivating factor for deviant behavior in others. Thus, everybody is assumed to have both a global and a situational control ratio. The general control ratio reflects one's typical ability to exercise control relative to being the object of control, while the situational control ratio represents an individual's ability in a specific situation or circumstance to exercise control relative to being controlled. As such, "an individual's control ratio is not fixed; it varies from place to place, from time to time, and from situation to situation" (Tittle, 2001, p. 317).

Control imbalances become the most important concept in the theory not only by motivating an individual toward deviance generally but also by relating it to the specific type of deviance that an individual will engage in. Control imbalances can manifest as either surpluses or deficits. Control surpluses result when an individual exercises more control than he or she is subject to, while control deficits emerge when an individual is subject to more control than he or she exercises. Deviance becomes one possible avenue for individuals to balance the control in their lives. When control is balanced, individuals exercise an equal amount of control to the amount to which they are subjected. Therefore, the central causal process focuses on the cognitive balancing of control in an individual's life.

Tittle originally argued that control imbalances are related to specific forms of deviance. Control surpluses, it was argued, are most related to autonomous forms of behavior, while control deficits relate to repressive acts. Autonomous forms of deviance are utilized when actors wish to expand their reach of control and involve more indirect actions on the part of the actor. These actions "do not require direct confrontation with victims or other objects of deviant action nor does it require the perpetrators to openly associate with actions or the behaviors" (Tittle, 2004, p. 399). The theory suggested that

minimal surpluses would relate to acts of exploitation, moderate surpluses would lead to acts of plunder, and large surpluses would be expressed by acts of decadence. Repressive forms of deviance are employed when an individual seeks to gain more control and involve "directly confrontational actions that are openly associated with the person doing them" (Tittle, 2004, p. 399). The theory suggested that minimal deficits would lead to acts of predation, moderate deficits would relate to acts of defiance, and large deficits would be expressed through acts of submission. As such, the theory proposes a curvilinear or U-shaped relationship between one's control balance ratio and deviance. In other words, those wielding the most control and those who have the least control are proposed to be the ones most likely to engage in deviant acts.

The control balance ratio is one part of the deviance-generating process which Tittle (2001, p. 323) describes as "complicated and highly conditional." As a general theory, it is believed that the process will be the same for all individuals, but because everyone has different sets of contingencies or conditions, the outcomes involved—conformity or different varieties of deviance—will vary across persons. Overall, there are a number of necessary elements involved in the control balancing process that must come together for deviance to result.

First, there must be some motivation or a predisposition toward deviance. This is where the control balance ratio and its related control imbalances come into play. As has been noted, control imbalances provide the needed push for corrective action or rebalancing of one's cognitive control. However, there are additional elements also at work under motivation for deviance. Most notably, the theory assumes that there is a desire for autonomy for all persons. According to Tittle (1995, p. 145), the desire for autonomy or "escaping control over oneself and exercising more control over the social and physical world than one experiences" is almost universal among humans.

Second, the theory assumes that most people become intermittently aware of their control circumstances so there must be a provocation or a situational stimulus that makes the individual aware of the control imbalance. It is this provocation that signals to the individual that a corrective action, such as deviance, must occur to rebalance his or her control ratio. However, for the provocation to illicit a deviant response, the event must make the individual experience some sort of feelings of discomfort, such as debasement or humiliation. Thus, much like theories of anomie and strain, it is the feelings of negative emotion generated by some stimulus that promote the necessary action to correct the control balance to which in the individual is now aware.

Motivation alone is not enough for deviance to occur. Next, the individual must have the opportunity to commit an act of deviance. Opportunity is defined as "a circumstance where that behavior is possible" (Tittle, 1995, p. 169). Thus, the concept of opportunity is very much in line with other criminological theories, especially those that argue that opportunities for deviance are plentiful and readily available, such as routine activity theory. Finally, given the presence of motivation and the plethora of opportunities available, who turns to deviance and what types? This depends on the number of contingencies or constraints present for any one individual. Contingencies refer to any aspect of an individual, social relationship, organizational structure, or the physical environment that may influence how the control balancing process operates (Tittle, 1995, p. 201).

Control balance theory, much like deterrence or rational choice theories, suggests that constraints will factor into the choice of behavior. Constraints are defined as "the probability, or perceived probability, that potential control will actually be exercised" (Tittle, 1995, p. 167). For example, situational constraints will influence how individuals will chose which behavior is best suited to restore their control balance by considering the counter controls that will likely be used against them. Since more serious forms of deviance are more likely to generate a counter control more often than not, these types of deviance will not be utilized by most people to restore the balance. Instead, most individuals will turn to less serious forms of deviance that will re-establish their balance without jeopardizing other aspects of their life. Who then engages in serious deviance? According to the theory, serious deviance is reserved for those who can overcome or negate the counter controls—namely those with small control deficits or those with the greatest control surpluses.

In sum, the original version of control balance theory suggests a contingent balancing process that (1) takes into account an individual's motivations toward deviance, or control imbalances, (2) suggests when these motivations may be acted upon such as when they are made cognizant to an individual by means of a situational provocation and that when coupled with negative emotions (such as debasement or humiliation), and (3) contends with numerous different contingencies that must be managed by the individual that either promote or prohibit deviance.

Control Balance Theory Revised

Since control balance theory was first introduced in 1995, the theory has been both criticized and subjected to empirical testing. Some have criticized the theory for being overwhelming or hard to understand because of the level of complexity employed, for proffering vague if not confusing concepts and definitions, and for unduly limiting categories of behaviors. Empirical tests of the theory have primarily been conducted with student samples and have found support for the theory's major premises as well as evidence contrary to the theoretical arguments. For example, empirical tests have found that both types of control imbalances, deficits and surpluses, predict both repressive and autonomous forms of deviant behavior. In "Refining Control Balance" Tittle responded to the criticisms as well as addressed some of the unexpected findings by revising the theory. In the refined version of the theory, he addresses the inconsistencies and conceptual ambiguities that emerged as well as proposes a new categorization of deviant acts.

One of the primary issues Tittle addressed was the inconsistent conceptualizing of seriousness. In this regard, there are two points of clarification needed. First, he notes that throughout the original version of the theory, statements about the concept of seriousness were unclear and created difficulty in distinguishing between it, deviance, and constraint. This was particularly the case when seriousness was presented as a constraint. Constraint and seriousness were never intended to be the same thing and, in fact, are separate concepts. He clarifies seriousness as "a feature of deviant acts implying their potential for arousing counter control; it is not simply a collective cognitive judgment about the wrongness of particular acts or the damage they might cause" (Tittle, 2004, p. 403). Second, the qualitative distinctions of seriousness (i.e., minimal, moderate, or large surplus or deficits) originally used were based on speculation and not actual data, and thus they have been abandoned in the revised theory.

Tittle also calls for the discontinuation of the use of predictions regarding repressive and autonomous categories of deviant behavior. Since empirical findings suggest that there is significant overlap in these two concepts, control imbalances are now predicted to explain all forms of deviant behaviors, such that those experiencing control surpluses may engage in either repressive or autonomous forms of deviant behavior and not just autonomous forms of deviance as previously predicted. In addition to doing away with categories of deviance, the revised theory reconceptualizes submissive acts. While no longer classifying submissive behavior as a deviant act, it is also not considered conforming behavior; rather, submissive acts are in a category of their own. The refined theory now "attempts to explain conformity and deviance as products of control balancing and it attempts to explain submission as a failure of control balancing" (Tittle, 2004, p. 404).

Finally, Tittle (2004, p. 405) departs from the original presentation of a deviance typology in favor of a single continuum of deviance, which he refers to as control balance desirability and defines as "a quality possessed in different degrees by various potential deviant acts." Control balance desirability is viewed as a composite variable with two indicators: (1) the long-term effectiveness of the deviant act for altering a control imbalance and (2) the impersonality of the act. The latter refers to the "extent to which a given form of misbehavior requires the perpetrator to be directly and personally involved with a victim or object that is affected by the deviance" (Tittle, 2004, p. 405). Therefore, the type of deviance that will be used by individuals to rebalance their control will be based on their perceptions of the control balance desirability. Acts that are deemed high on the desirability continuum most likely will be employed because they will provide long-term relief from the control imbalance and because the selected acts are impersonal, and thus offer a lower likelihood of counter control.

For the most part, control balance theory still operates as originally proposed. That is, a situational provocation brings to an individual's attention his or her control imbalance that, coupled with debasement or humiliation, requires some sort of corrective or rebalancing behavior, normally a deviant act. However, now the theory proposes that the type of deviance employed will depend on the control balance desirability of the act. The actual selection will be influenced by a person's control ratio, the opportunity to commit the deviant act, constraints that are in place, and a person's level of self-control. A person's control ratio is important, as before, for providing the motivation toward deviance—that is, the imbalance creates the need for a corrective action. Opportunity is also carried over from the original formulation in that there must be an opportunity to engage in a behavior for an individual to carry it out. Constraint reflects the possible magnitude of the counter controlling consequences or the seriousness of the act as well as the situational risk present or the actual chances of experiences counter controls. Finally, newly added into the decision-making process is the individual's level of self-control. The original theory implied that control balancing is a rational process, whereas the revised theory recognizes that not everyone is rational. Therefore, "the outcomes expected from the theory will vary with the self-control of a person" (Tittle, 2004, p. 416).

Nicole Leeper Piquero

See also Braithwaite, John: Reintegrative Shaming Theory; Colvin, Mark: Coercion Theory; Gottfredson, Michael R., and Travis Hirschi: Self-Control Theory; Hirschi, Travis: Social Control Theory; Regoli, Robert M., and John D. Hewitt: Differential Oppression Theory; Sherman, Lawrence W.: Defiance Theory

References and Further Readings

Braithwaite, J. (1997). Charles Tittle's control balance and criminological theory. *Theoretical Criminology, 1,* 77–97.
Hickman, M., & Piquero, A. R. (2001). Exploring the relationship between gender, control balance and deviance. *Deviant Behavior, 22,* 323–351.
Leeper Piquero, N., & Piquero, A. R. (2006). Control balance and exploitative corporate crime. *Criminology, 44,* 397–430.
Tittle, C. R. (1995). *Control balance: Toward a general theory of deviance.* Boulder: CO: Westview.
Tittle, C. R. (2001). Control balance. In R. Paternoster & R. Bachman (Eds.), *Explaining criminals and crime* (pp. 315–334). Thousand Oaks, CA: Sage.
Tittle, C. R. (2004). Refining control balance. *Theoretical Criminology, 8,* 395–428.

TITTLE, CHARLES R., DAVID A. WARD, AND HAROLD G. GRASMICK: THE CAPACITY AND DESIRE FOR SELF-CONTROL

Michael Gottfredson and Travis Hirschi's general theory of crime, or self-control theory, has been one of the most debated and empirically tested theories of the last half century. Charles R. Tittle, David A. Ward, and Harold G. Grasmick, however, argue that self-control theory has not succeeded as "the ultimate general theory" because it has not been modified to address the critiques levied against it (2004, p. 145). Tittle et al. suggest that self-control theory can be improved upon theoretically and thus empirically predict more crime if self-control theory would differentiate between the capacity for self-control and the desire to exercise it.

Gottfredson and Hirschi's self-control theory argues that the root cause of crime and analogous behaviors is whether individuals can restrain themselves from committing acts that have long-term consequences greater than the short-term benefits. Since all individuals are equally motivated to commit crime, according to control theories, whether individuals have adequate levels of self-control to withstand the temptations of crime, which are normally short-term, is the essential key to understanding why more people do not commit crime. Gottfredson and Hirschi argue that the relationship between traditional criminological variables, such as doing poorly in school or being unemployed, and crime is spurious because they are all caused by inadequate self-control. Thus, they believe that low self-control is "*the* individual-level cause of crime" (p. 232, emphasis in the original), aside from age which they do not feel can be addressed by sociological theories. Since its introduction, Gottfredson and Hirschi's version of self-control theory has been tested extensively and has been shown to be a consistent and significant predictor of a wide variety of crimes (e.g., Pratt & Cullen, 2000).

Even with its strong empirical support, Tittle et al. contend that a major issue with self-control theory is its lack of conceptual clarity for its most important concept—self-control. Tittle et al. illustrate that Gottfredson and Hirschi's discussion of self-control primarily focuses on differences in behavioral preferences (e.g., being adventuresome, active, and physical), rather than traits or characteristics. When the statements do not focus on behavioral preferences, they refer to the "lack of *capability* for controlling behavior" (p. 147, emphasis in the original).

Tittle et al. argue, however, that Gottfredson and Hirschi also allude to the desire to exercise self-restraint in four passages in their original work, such as in the phrase "ability and willingness to delay gratification" (p. 96). Tittle and colleagues propose that the desire to self-regulate is a common theme that runs throughout many criminological theories (e.g., self-theories, social learning theory, social bond theory, and rational choice theory), albeit for different reasons. Compared with capability, which is internally focused, the desire to exercise self-control has strong connections to external factors, since individuals are aware of the consequences of their actions in their immediate environment.

Tittle and colleagues argue that knowing an individual's desire to exercise self-control is as important as his or her capability to do so. For example, some individuals might have the capability to exercise self-control, but they choose not to do so. On the other hand, other individuals might have inadequate levels of self-control, but they do not commit crime because they so "fervently want to control themselves that they refrain from criminal acts" (p. 147). In addition, the two concepts should interact. Individuals with little capability to self-control, and little interest in even trying, are more at risk for criminal offending. Similarly, individuals with a high capability and a strong desire to restrain themselves are less likely to offend.

Empirical research has found support for the importance of "desire to exercise self-control" in understanding deviance (Cochran et al., 2006; Tittle et al., 2004). "Desire to exercise self-control" scales—consisting of items based on other criminological theories, such as pride, losing respect of others, praise, legal ramifications, guilt, and morality—are statistically different from self-control capability measures, indicating that desire to self-control is distinct from self-control ability. Furthermore, self-control desire has significantly predicted the commission of crime, as measured by crime indexes and specific crime types (e.g., assault, theft, illegal gambling, tax cheating, and DWI)

(Tittle et al., 2004), and academic dishonesty (Cochran et al., 2004), even when controlling for the influence of self-control ability. Additionally, the strength of self-control ability decreases as self-control desire increases.

Further examination of interaction effects, however, have contradicted some of Tittle et al.'s original hypotheses (Cochran et al., 2006; Tittle et al., 2004). Self-control ability is a fairly strong predictor of crime even when the person's desire to exercise it is weak. "Being able to restrain oneself apparently helps people actually restrain themselves, as self-control theory suggests" (Tittle et al., 2004, p. 164). Self-control ability, however, is not as strong a predictor for those with higher levels of self-control desire. Thus, when individuals do not have strong desire to exercise self-control, their self-control abilities have a much larger influence on whether they commit crime. When they want to control their behavior, however, their ability to actually do so is less relevant.

Although the interaction effects of self-control ability and self-control desire are contrary to self-control theory and Tittle et al.'s hypotheses, Tittle et al. found that the cumulative effects of self-control ability and self-control desire are as predicted. They divided respondents into four groups: (1) high levels of ability and desire, (2) low levels of ability and desire, (3) high levels of ability but low levels of desire, and (4) high levels of desire but low levels of ability. They discovered that individuals who rank high on both ability and desire were the least likely to commit crime, while those who scored low on both were the most likely to commit crime. Even though individuals in the other two categories fall somewhere in the middle, it appears that those with high levels of desire but low levels of ability commit less crime than those with high levels of ability but low levels of desire. When Cochran et al. divided their sample into the same four groups, however, they found that the lowest levels of cheating were found within the two groups that contained the high self-control capacity respondents.

Gottfredson and Hirschi assert, "In our view, lack of self-control does not require crime and can be counteracted by situational conditions or other properties of the individual. At the same time, we suggest that high self-control effectively reduces the possibility of crime—that is, those possessing it will be substantially less likely at all periods of life to engage in criminal acts" (p. 89). Tittle et al. modify self-control theory by arguing and empirically demonstrating that more can be understood about the commission of crime if both ability to self-control and desire to self-control are examined. Thus, Tittle et al. have discovered an important individual property that is closely tied to situational contexts that can explain which individuals with low levels of self-control will be more likely to act on temptations.

Adam M. Bossler

See also Gottfredson, Michael R., and Travis Hirschi: Self-Control Theory; Hirschi, Travis: Social Control Theory; Nye, F. Ivan: Family Controls and Delinquency; Reckless, Walter C.: Containment Theory

References and Further Readings

Cochran, J. K., Aleksa, V., & Chamlin, M. B. (2006). Self-restraint: A study on the capacity and desire for self-control. *Western Criminology Review, 7,* 27–40.

Gottfredson, M. R., & Hirschi, T. (1990). *A general theory of crime.* Palo Alto, CA: Stanford University Press.

Hirschi, T. (2004). Self-control and crime. In R. F. Baumester & K. D. Vohs (Eds.), *Handbook of self-regulation: Research, theory, and applications* (pp. 537–552). New York: Guilford Press.

Pratt, T. C., & Cullen, F. T. (2000). The empirical status of Gottfredson and Hirschi's general theory of crime: A meta-analysis. *Criminology, 38,* 931–964.

Reckless, W. C. (1967). *The crime problem* (4th ed.). New York: Appleton-Century Crofts.

Tittle, C. R. (1995). *Control balance: Toward a general theory of deviance.* Boulder, CO: Westview Press.

Tittle, C. R., Ward, D. A., & Grasmick, H. G. (2004). Capacity for self-control and individuals' interest in exercising self-control. *Journal of Quantitative Criminology, 20,* 143–172.

TOBY, JACKSON: STAKE IN CONFORMITY

Social control theorists attempt to explain conformity to the rules and norms of society, not delinquency. Delinquent behavior is treated as a given; thus it is conformity that must be explained.

Many different variations of social control theory exist, yet they all focus on the social influences that work to restrain individuals to keep them from engaging in illegal behavior.

Jackson Toby, a sociology professor at Rutgers University, first introduced the concept of stake in conformity in 1957 with his published article titled "Social Disorganization and Stake in Conformity: Complementary Factors in the Predatory Behavior of Hoodlums." Toby wanted to explain why property delinquency rates were high in the United States despite the economic prosperity enjoyed by most Americans. Toby referred to the offenders who typically committed the acts of burglary, robbery, and auto theft as "hoodlum type thieves" who were usually young and resided in lower-class neighborhoods. Delinquents had little or nothing to lose by their illegal behavior and were therefore less likely to resist the temptations of delinquency. Families exercise control over their children; however, parental controls start to lose their effectiveness as children become adolescents. Communities could also be an important source of informal social control, provided there is widespread disapproval of crime. Toby found this not to be the case in lower-class communities where he observed delinquency to be more common compared to the suburbs.

Toby's stake in conformity theory was put forth in response to claims made by social disorganization theorists Clifford Shaw and Henry McKay that structural factors such as high rates of poverty, transiency, and heterogeneity explained the variation in rates of delinquency across neighborhoods. Toby believed these structural characteristics to be insufficient because they did not explain why many juveniles (particularly females) residing in socially disorganized areas did not become delinquent. In an earlier study of delinquency rates across cities in New Jersey, Toby found that the rates of officially recorded delinquency were higher in areas with high rates of *family disorganization* (larger proportion of single-family households). Toby argued in his article "The Differential Impact of Family Disorganization" that "well-integrated" families helped insulate juveniles from the criminogenic influences of a neighborhood and/or peer group. The influence of family disorganization was different for boys and girls as well as for juveniles of

different ages. Family disorganization appeared to be more relevant for understanding the delinquency of girls and juveniles between the ages of 7 and 15. While previous research had downplayed the significance of broken homes in explaining delinquency (e.g., Shaw and McKay), Toby demonstrated the importance of including such intervening variables in delinquency research.

Toby's concept of stake in conformity emulates control theory with the idea that individuals who have a stake in conformity are insulated from the enticements of illegal behavior. Further, Toby asserted that communities comprising large proportions of individuals with low stakes in conformity (unemployed, poor, less educated) will have higher rates of delinquency than communities with low proportions. Toby's theory offers not only an explanation of an individual's involvement in delinquency but of rates of delinquency as well. Toby's theory was influenced by the work of one of the most prominent sociologists of the 20th century, Talcott Parsons. Parsons was Toby's professor and mentor at Harvard University where Toby earned his Ph.D. in 1951.

Toby's stake in conformity theory was used by researchers to explain inconsistent findings across study sites in the deterrent effect of arrest for domestic violence. Results from the Minneapolis Domestic Violence Experiment revealed that suspects arrested for misdemeanor domestic violence had lower rates of recidivism compared to suspects who were counseled or separated (Sherman & Berk, 1984). Replications of the experiment, however, found that arrest only "worked" as a deterrent for suspects who were married and/or employed at the time of their arrest (Sherman et al., 1992). Individuals without a stake in conformity are less able to resist the temptations of illegal behavior and therefore less likely to be deterred with criminal justice sanctions. Toby believed it was possible to deter individuals without relying on formal punishment. The threat of social stigma could be enough to deter individuals, provided there is widespread disapproval of the behavior (Toby, 1981).

Toby also applied his stake in conformity theory to school violence and published several articles on the topic. He argued that criminologists were quick to attribute violence in the schools to a breakdown in school discipline without providing an explanation for *why* schools had lost their control over disruptive youth. Toby believed that beginning in the 1960s and 1970s, many schools experienced an increase in the number of disruptive students "who lacked a stake in behavioral conformity to school rules" (Toby, 1998, p. 70). Compulsory education laws that increased the minimum age at which juveniles were permitted to drop out of school, along with programs designed to encourage youths to stay in school, only increased the number of youths who did not want to be there and had no interest in maintaining an environment conducive to learning. Toby (1998) called these youths "internal dropouts"—youngsters who fail to see the relevance of what is being taught or who are academically unprepared. Youths without a "stake in behavior conformity" are found in both inner-city and suburban schools, but the social stigma associated with dropping out tends to be greater in the suburbs (Toby, 1999). Juveniles who are required to stay in school may eventually feel "trapped" and resort to extreme forms of violence (Toby, 2002). While many criminologists proposed such strategies as better screening for weapons to provide a safe school environment, Toby advocates an educational system based on voluntary attendance, an idea that many criminologists believe would lead to increased dropout rates, limited career opportunities for these youths, and subsequently more crime. It is important to point out that Toby also encouraged school systems to allow dropouts to return at any time (and any age) they desired to do so.

Amy B. Thistlethwaite

See also Briar, Scott, and Irving Piliavin: Delinquency, Commitment, and Stake in Conformity; Gibbs, Jack P.: Deterrence Theory; Hirschi, Travis: Social Control Theory; Reckless, Walter C.: Containment Theory; Shaw, Clifford R., and Henry D. McKay: Social Disorganization Theory; Sherman, Lawrence W.: Defiance Theory

References and Further Readings

Shaw, C., & McKay, H. (1942). *Juvenile delinquency and urban areas.* Chicago: University of Chicago Press.
Sherman, L., & Berk, R. (1984). The specific deterrent effects of arrest for domestic assault. *American Sociological Review, 49,* 261–272.
Sherman, L., Smith, D., Schmidt, J., & Rogan, D. (1992). Crime, punishment and stake in conformity: Legal and informal control of domestic violence. *American Sociological Review, 57,* 680–690.
Toby, J. (1957). The differential impact of family disorganization. *American Sociological Review, 22,* 505–512.
Toby, J. (1957). Social disorganization and stake in conformity: Complementary factors in the predatory behavior of hoodlums. *The Journal of Criminal Law, Criminology, and Police Science, 48,* 12–17.
Toby, J. (1971). *Contemporary society: An introduction to sociology* (2nd ed.). New York: Wiley.
Toby, J. (1974). The socialization and control of deviant motivation. In D. Glaser (Ed.), *Handbook of criminology* (pp. 85–100). Chicago: Rand McNally.
Toby, J. (1979). Societal evolution and criminality: A Parsonian view. *Social Problems, 26,* 386–391.
Toby, J. (1981). Deterrence without punishment. *Criminology, 19,* 195–209.
Toby, J. (1998). Getting serious about school discipline. *Public Interest, 133,* 68–83.
Toby, J. (1999, June). Obsessive compulsion: The folly of mandatory high-school attendance. *National Review,* pp. 30–34.
Toby, J. (2001). Let them drop out: A response to the killings in suburban high schools. *Weekly Standard, 6*(29), 18–23.
Toby, J. (2002). Is a weapons-screening strategy for public schools good public policy? *Journal of Health Politics, Policy and Law, 27,* 261–265.
Wooldredge, J., & Thistlethwaite, A. (2002). Reconsidering domestic violence recidivism: Conditioned effects of legal controls by individual and aggregate levels of stake in conformity. *Journal of Quantitative Criminology, 18,* 45–70.

TOCH, HANS: COPING IN PRISON

Hans Toch's perspective on coping in prison can briefly be stated as the efforts of inmates to adjust to their environment by negotiating stressors induced by the institutional setting. Although Toch made numerous contributions to penology and criminology more broadly, his perspective on coping in prison may be his most notable. Toch's perspective is perhaps best represented by his books *Living in Prison: The Ecology of Survival* and *Coping: Maladaption in Prisons,* coauthored with Kenneth Adams and J. Douglas Grant. The books resulted from two large-scale studies of inmates confined in prisons operated by the state of New York that Toch directed while he was serving as a professor in the School of Criminal Justice at the State University of New York at Albany. This entry reviews each of these scholarly works, followed by a discussion of Toch's theoretical contributions and impact on correctional practice.

Living in Prison: The Ecology of Survival

Living in Prison was based primarily on findings from in-depth interviews with inmates housed within five maximum-security prisons operated by the State of New York. Toch framed the study within a psychological perspective on transactions, which assumes human uniqueness and recognizes that individuals' needs may vary within the same context. Toch recognized differences among inmates in how they prioritized their needs, which contributed to how they perceived aspects of prison environments. Therefore, the same aspects of a prison environment may influence inmates differently based on whether that feature of the environment frustrated or facilitated satisfaction of their needs.

Toch identified seven environmental concerns that were salient for inmates in prisons: privacy, activity, safety, structure, support, emotional feedback, and freedom. Privacy refers to a preference for isolation, peace, and quiet and to the absence of environmental irritants (e.g., noise, crowding). Satisfaction of the need for privacy involves reducing external stimuli to streamline experience and ease adjustment. Activity reflects a concern about understimulation. Activity may be important to inmates who need their time to be filled with distraction, entertainment, or action. Safety refers to a concern for one's physical well-being and a preference for social and physical settings that provide protection and minimize the chance of being victimized. Structure is a preference for predictability, orderly routines, clear-cut rules, and consistent enforcement. Support reflects a concern for reliable, tangible assistance from persons and settings, and for services that facilitate self-advancement and self-improvement. Emotional feedback is a concern about being loved and appreciated and refers to a desire for relationships that provide emotional sustenance and empathy. Freedom is a concern about maintaining autonomy and a desire for minimal restrictions on space and activity. In addition to the seven environmental concerns revealed by the interviews, Toch also identified social stimulation as a potential concern. Social stimulation is a concern with congeniality and a preference for settings that provide an opportunity for social interaction and companionship.

Toch observed that the importance of environmental requirements varied across inmates due to their personal experiences and motives. For example, Toch found that different environmental preferences corresponded with different background characteristics of inmates (e.g., race, criminal history). Differences between inmates influenced the needs required to facilitate coping and ultimately adjustment to the prison environment.

Toch's findings led him to develop the Prison Preference Inventory (PPI), which is an instrument designed to measure the specific environmental preferences of inmates. The questionnaire portion of the PPI presents inmates with a set of paired comparisons, each of which taps one dimension of the environment, and asks them to choose between the two. Using data collected from samples of inmates from the federal prison system, New York, Pennsylvania, Connecticut, and California, Toch found support for the reliability of the eight dimensions of the PPI and also evidence suggesting the instrument was valid. Toch viewed the PPI as a prison classification instrument that could determine the environmental concerns of inmates permitting staff to match them to the appropriate environment (e.g., institutional programs, staffing patterns, inmate groupings). According to Toch, matching inmates to the environment that corresponded to their needs could make coping easier and facilitate adjustment.

Given the relevance of safety concerns for the prison environment, Toch conducted a more in-depth examination of inmates' concern for safety. He revealed that inmates' concerns were related to the prospect of victimization. He observed that violent victimization (particularly homosexual rape) was extremely rare in most prisons. The threat of victimization, however, was a constant reality that contributed to stress for many inmates. Toch found that inmates coped with the threat of victimization by compartmentalizing the prison environment into safe and unsafe places. Cataloging the social and physical environment of prisons in this way facilitated environmental adaptation for many inmates.

He also observed that inmates defined subenvironments or "niches" that met their individual environmental concerns and facilitated adaptation. Niches are functional subsettings that contain desired objects, space, resources, and people. Inmates perceived niches as ameliorative; they were viewed as a potential instrument for the relaxation of stress and the achievement of psychological equilibrium. Niches could also provide inmates with an increased sense of control and autonomy within their environment. Further, niches allowed inmates to find common cultural interests with fellow niche members and reduced the unpredictability of prisons by permitting inmates to control the amount of stimulation they were exposed to. According to Toch, niches could be supplied by the prison (e.g., special housing units, programming) or created by inmates.

Coping: Maladaptation in Prisons

The book *Coping* resulted from a study of the patterns of disruptive and disturbing behaviors of inmates released from facilities operated by the State of New York during 1982 and 1983. Toch and colleagues applied the criminal career paradigm to studying inmates. They introduced the notion of a prison career—the period of incarceration between admission and release characterized by a sequence of natural events and transitions. Examining prison careers permitted the comparison of the behavior of inmates confined in the same institution at one point in time to their behavior at another.

Toch and colleagues described coping as an effort at problem solving. Maladaptive behavior, by contrast, included the failure to cope, as well as unsuccessful coping attempts. Thus, maladaptive coping behaviors were problem-solving behaviors that were attempts by inmates to negotiate the threats and opportunity structures of prison environments. For their study, maladaptive behaviors were operationalized as prison rule infractions and use of prison mental health services.

Toch and colleagues revealed that infractions were more common in the early part of inmates' prison careers, but steadily declined after peaking around 6 to 9 months' imprisonment. They also found that younger inmates were more disruptive, but that disruptive behaviors decreased with age. They discovered that the vast majority of inmates were nondisruptive (i.e., successful in coping), while less than 10 percent of inmates were chronic disciplinary problems.

Toch and colleagues found that mental health problems were also more common in the early part of inmate careers. Longer-term inmates, however, often displayed increases in mental health problems when they neared release. They also revealed that most inmates tend to specialize in either disruptive or disturbed behaviors. For those inmates that did exhibit both behaviors, they typically manifested both types of behavior at the same time. Overall, Toch and colleagues concluded that admission to the prison environment is an intense and difficult process, but that for most inmates adaptation and coping will occur over time.

Using a subsample of inmates whose prison careers were characterized by extreme maladaptiveness, Toch and colleagues revealed taxonomies of coping motivations that manifest themselves in institutional disruption. These five behaviorally driven categories represented goals that were to be achieved by inmates and included gratifying impulses, enhancing esteem, pursuing autonomy, seeking refuge, and maintaining sanity. With the exception of seeking refuge and maintaining sanity, aggressive behavior was instrumental in achieving each of these goals. Inmates who engaged in maladaptive coping used violence, defiance, and rage to fulfill their desires, feel better about themselves, express their independence, and/or cope with psychological strain. In contrast, retreat and withdrawal were maladaptive behaviors that accomplished the goal of seeking safety and sanctuary from those who use aggression. Finally, inmates attempted to maintain their sanity by escaping reality or exploding in episodes of bizarre behavior and/or violent conduct inspired by stress, paranoia, or delusions.

Toch and colleagues also discussed factors that contributed to improved behavior (i.e., coping) among maladaptive inmates. These factors included involvement in activity, support from staff, attachment to prosocial others, detachment from negative environmental stimuli, placement in environments that offer respite from noxious stimuli, placement in environments that offer sanctuary or reassurance of safety, placement in asylums, insight through reassessment of self, deterrence, relaxation, and maturation.

Theoretical Contributions

Toch offered a number of important insights regarding inmate behavior. Toch, a Princeton University–trained psychologist, brought a fresh perspective to penology, which had been dominated by sociologists prior to the publication of *Living in Prison*. Although scholars (e.g., Gresham Sykes) had underscored the relevance of prison environments (e.g., environmental deprivations) for shaping inmate behavior, these perspectives had become less relevant because the environmental "deprivations" that these scholars described were reduced considerably as a result of the inmate rights movement and the evolution of prisons from closed to more open systems (Jacobs, 1977). However, Toch recognized the influence of environments on need satisfaction. According to Toch, the environments of prisons could interact with differences between inmates by facilitating or inhibiting need satisfaction. Differences between inmates in how they perceived prison environments could, therefore, influence their adjustment to prison.

Toch's observation regarding prison careers also cast doubts on prevailing perspectives on prisonization, the process by which inmates gradually adopt the values and conform to the norms of the inmate culture. Researchers, such as Donald Clemmer, had described this process as a function of time served or as an inverted U shape. In the U-shape process, upon admission to prison, inmates retained their commitment to conventional society. However, as their exposure and integration into the inmate value system increased, they conformed to the inmate code of behavior and conduct; inmates thus manifested the greatest amount of disruptive behaviors during the middle of their sentence. As their release date approached, inmates once again became committed to mainstream values. In contrast, Toch observed a coping process where the concentration of oppositional behaviors occurred after admission. As inmates progressed through their prison careers, they learned to cope with the prison environment, facilitating adjustment and decreasing disruptive behaviors.

Impact on Correctional Practice

Toch's most notable contribution may have been his influence on correctional practice. As a result of the way in which he conducted much of his research, Toch was one of the first scholars to give a voice to inmates and emphasize the inmate perspective. As such, he was influential in motivating a greater concern for the humane treatment of inmates.

Toch was also one of the first scholars to underscore the importance of person-environment fit. In doing so, he placed the focus not only on inmates but also on how prisons were managed. He argued for using information to match inmates to environments (e.g., people, services, settings) in order to facilitate adaptation. These insights offered substantive recommendations that correctional administrators could put into practice.

Toch's observations also initiated the development of classification instruments that aided in the placement and treatment of inmates. Although many prisons used classification tools, most were system-oriented instruments based on static criteria such as inmates' criminal history. Toch recognized the need for system oriented assessment tools, but he also argued for consideration of inmates needs. Toch's PPI was one of the first classification tools that were person oriented. Even though subsequent studies have determined that the predictive validity of the PPI is relatively weak, Toch's development of the tool still contributed to the construction of other, more predictive, assessment tools that consider both inmates' risks and needs. In a number of jurisdictions, the information derived from classification tools has been used to manage inmates more effectively and more humanely.

Benjamin Meade and Benjamin Steiner

See also Colvin, Mark: Social Sources of the New Mexico Prison Riot; Criminal Career Paradigm; DiIulio, John J., Jr.: Prison Management and Prison Order; Gendreau, Paul, D. A. Andrews, and James Bonta: The Theory of Effective Correctional Intervention; Irwin, John, and Donald R. Cressey: Importation Theory; Sykes, Gresham M.: Deprivation Theory

References and Further Readings

Clemmer, D. (1940). *The prison community*. New York: Rinehart.

DiIulio, J., Jr. (1991). Review: Understanding prisons: The new old penology. *Law and Social Inquiry, 16,* 65–99.

Jacobs, J. B. (1977). *Stateville: The penitentiary in mass society*. Chicago: University of Chicago Press.

Summers, R., & Dear, G. E. (2003). The prison preference inventory: An examination of substantive validity in an Australian prison sample. *Criminal Justice and Behavior, 30*, 459–482.

Sykes, G. M. (1958). *The society of captives*. Princeton, NJ: Princeton University Press.

Toch, H. (1977). *Living in prison: The ecology of survival*. New York: Free Press.

Toch, H. (1981). Inmate classification as a transaction. *Criminal Justice and Behavior, 8*, 3–14.

Toch, H., Adams, K., & Grant, J. D. (1989). *Coping: Maladaptation in prisons*. New Brunswick, NJ: Transaction.

Wheeler, S. (1961). Socialization in correctional communities. *American Sociological Review, 26*, 697–712.

Wright, K. (1988). The relationship of risk, needs, and personality classification systems and prison adjustment. *Criminal Justice and Behavior, 15*, 454–471.

TURK, AUSTIN T.: THE CRIMINALIZATION PROCESS

Austin T. Turk has been referred to as "the deviance theorist who has persisted longest in an effort to develop a non-Marxist framework for the analysis of conflict processes" (Orcutt, 1983, p. 321). Approximately 40 years ago, in the book *Criminality and Legal Order*, Turk presented his theory of criminalization and normative-legal conflict. He described the conditions under which differences between authorities and subjects will result in overt conflict. Authorities are decision makers (e.g., police, judges, lawyers, prosecutors) and subjects are individuals affected by those decisions. Subjects are distinguished from authorities by their inability to manipulate the legal processes. Turk was influenced by the work of Ralf Dahrendorf, who introduced the terms *domination* and *subjection* in *Class and Class Conflict in Industrial Society*.

According to Turk, the potential for authority-subject conflict is always present. However, not all authorities have equal opportunity to influence the law. Turk claims "first-line enforcers," such as the police, have the greatest impact on subject criminalization. While norms of deference usually maintain the balance of the authority-subject relationship, in certain situations, police must rely upon coercion to gain compliance; Turk refers to this as "nightstick law."

Similar to Thorston Sellin, Turk claims that criminality is the result of cultural distinctions. Subjects may be unaware of or may not accept specific legal rules. Turk (1966, p. 285) discusses variation in cultural norms:

> The greater the cultural differences between the evaluator and violator, the less likely are psychological sanctions which assume a capacity and readiness to subtle cues to get through to the violator, and therefore sanctioning will have to be more physically coercive in order to enforce the norm.

Nonviolent forms of persuasion by authorities, such as verbal announcements or body language, may be insufficient to achieve the compliance of people who harbor conflicting views or values. For example, when officers encounter citizens from a different culture, race, or ethnicity, the odds of conflict increase.

The Role of Cultural and Social Norms

In certain situations, according to Turk, cultural (i.e., written laws, procedures, and written policies) and social (i.e., actual behavior or the law as it is enforced) norms determine when conflict is more or less likely to occur. The odds of conflict are greatest when there is consistency between cultural and social norms, as conflict is fundamental in the composition of the authority-subject relationship. If authorities and subjects harbor contrasting beliefs and act accordingly with these beliefs, there is little room left for compromise. However, conflict is less likely if cultural and social norms are disparate. While cultural beliefs may clash, both authorities and subjects fail to practice what they preach. Turk argues, "neither party is very prone to fight over an essentially meaningless set of symbols" (1969, p. 56).

In *Criminality and Legal Order*, Turk presents four basic situations affecting the odds of authority-subject conflict; each one has a different potential for conflict. These situations are the (1) congruence of norms for both authorities and subjects (high-high), (2) congruence of norms for subjects but not authorities (high-low), (3) congruence of norms for authorities but not subjects (high-low), and (4) congruence of norms for neither authorities or subjects (low-low). In situations 2 and 3, the likelihood of overt conflict falls in the middle range. However, conflict is more likely if it is the authorities' cultural and social norms that are congruent since authorities are less tolerant than subjects are in accommodating any differences. "Flagrant, persistent disregard for the law will, nevertheless, force authorities to act to demonstrate that they are still in charge, that they are still able to assert their will against resistance in showdown" (Turk, 1969, p. 64).

In the event that cultural norms do clash, authorities and subjects will appeal to their own distinct values. While authorities are inclined to appeal to legal rules or written policies, subjects tend to appeal to extralegal norms, such as their right to privacy or natural law.

Conflict Tied to Organization and Sophistication

Conflict between authorities and subjects is also associated with levels of *organization* and *sophistication*. Organization is determined by both the social complexity of a relationship and by social support. When a characteristic has been integrated into a system of relationships (implying that it is a critical part of some role which the individual performs), then it can be projected that a sizable degree of coercion would be required to put a stop to the behavioral pattern (Turk, 1969, p. 58).

Authorities are organized by definition, as the authority structure itself implies an extensive degree of organization by controlling members of a society. Subjects, however, may or may not be highly organized. The more social support subjects have for their behavior, the less inclined they will be to compromise. Turk also discusses the simplicity and complexity of the behavior. Activities that are more complex (i.e., activated into a system of relationships or some important role the individual performs) are more *organized* and are more challenging to break.

Turk describes *sophistication* as the knowledge used in order to manipulate the opposition. The odds of conflict are greater when authorities and subjects are unsophisticated. Unsophisticated subjects are less skilled in assessing the strengths and weaknesses of their position relative to authorities and, consequently are less able to avoid open warfare with authorities. Less sophisticated authorities are unable to achieve their goals without the need for coercive force. Sophistication is apparently a prerequisite for enduring authority; therefore, it may be reasoned that just as authority implies organization, it also entails sophistication. However, social control agents, such as the police, vary a great deal to the extent to which their practices are affected by the appreciation for knowledge. The various combinations of organization and sophistication result in differing probabilities of conflict within the respective congruent and incongruent conditions. The result is a matrix with 32 possibilities. The likelihood for conflict is greatest when subjects are organized and authorities and subjects lack sophistication.

Turk (1969, p. 63) cautions that the cells in the matrix do not represent any empirical observations but only relative odds of conflict:

[W]e do not know just how unlikely is conflict in this minimum chance situation. . . . All that can be postulated is that this will be the lowest value of the 32 possibilities and that the value will be somewhere above .00, because the authorities are, after all, on public record against an attribute actually found in some part of the population.

Critiques of Turk's Theory

Turk's theory has been criticized by both conflict and consensus criminologists. His attempt to generate a non-ideological conflict theory has been called submissive, abstract, and tautological. In their critique of Turk's theory, Ian Taylor and colleagues call it "one of permanent adjustment of the subordinate to the powerful under present social arrangements" (p. 251). They suggest that criminologists focus instead on the origin of conflict, which they view as social and economic inequality. However, Turk is less troubled with the sources of conflict than with the conditions in which it is manifested.

Consensus theorists have also criticized Turk for dismissing a significant body of knowledge which has shown that consensus rather than conflict characterizes American society (Akers, 1979). Turk maintains, however, that consensus is just an illusion. He claims "whether they realize it or not, people are inevitably involved in intergroup struggles over who shall have what resources in a finite world" (1982, p. 35).

Turk's level of abstraction has raised some concerns about tautology. For example, the contention that systems of social control serve the need of authorities seems true by definition (Orcutt, 1983). So does the allegation that "lawbreaking is taken to be an indicator of failure or lack of authority; it is a measure of the extent to which rulers and ruled, decision-makers and decision-acceptors, are not bound together in a stable authority relationship" (Turk, 1969, p. 48). Taylor et al. have claimed that Turk's overall abstraction exaggerates what are actually modest theoretical contributions.

Research on Turk's Theory

Given the wide-ranging recognition of Turk's theory, there have been only a few empirical studies published on it since its inception. The challenge is to pinpoint measureable indicators of sophistication, organization, and cultural and social norms. Examining domestic violence police reports in Charleston, South Carolina, Richard Greenleaf and Lonn Lanza-Kaduce identified markers for sophistication and organization. They found that greater organization (e.g., if the disputants were married, more than one individual was arrested, and whether there were witnesses to the assault) and a lack of sophistication (the extent of police experience, the sobriety of the subject, and if the call was in progress) predicted police-citizen conflict.

Informed by Turk and guided by Greenleaf and Lanza-Kaduce, Robert Weidner and William Terrill examined observational data and concluded that police-citizen conflict was related to organization and sophistication. This connection remained strong despite the introduction of several control variables. Weidner and Terrill concluded that "like Greenleaf and Lanza-Kaduce . . . we found support for the idea that the likelihood of police-suspect conflict is negatively related to the level of officer's and subject's ability to manipulate situations or sophistication" (p. 100).

Most recently, Brian Kowalski and Richard Lundman examined Turk's theory at police traffic stops. They found mixed results claiming, "Net of control measures, including the legal reason for the stop, and extralegal measures, such as driver gender, the data provide modest to strong support for parts of Turk's (1969) theory and absolutely no support for others" (p. 814).

Conclusion

According to Robert Bohm, Turk's conflict theory is not considered a radical theory since he does not emphasize the root causes of authority, power, or the economic structures of society. For Turk, what is critical is the balance between coercion and consensus and the authority-subject relationship. Turk views lawbreaking as an indicator of the failure of authority. "Therefore, any political community, whether called *democratic* or *totalitarian,* will be maintained in part by coercion; no social order can ever depend fully upon the consent of the governed" (Turk, 1969, p. 48, emphasis in the original).

Richard G. Greenleaf

See also Bonger, Willem: Capitalism and Crime; Chambliss, William J.: Power, Conflict, and Crime; Sellin, Thorsten: Culture Conflict and Crime; Vold, George B.: Group Conflict Theory

References and Further Readings

Akers, R. A. (1979). Further critical thoughts on Marxist criminology: Comments on Turk, Quinney, Toby, and Klockars. *Criminology, 16,* 527–543.

Bohm, R. M. (1997). *A primer on crime and delinquency.* Belmont, CA: Wadsworth.

Dahrendorf, R. (1959). *Class and class conflict in industrial society.* Stanford, CA: Stanford University Press.

Gibbons, D. (1979). *The criminological enterprise: Theories and perspectives.* Englewood Cliffs, NJ: Prentice Hall.

Greenleaf, R. G., & Lanza-Kaduce, L. (1995). Sophistication, organization, and authority-subject conflict: Rediscovering and unraveling Turk's theory or norm resistance. *Criminology, 33,* 565–586.

Kowalski, B. R., & Lundman, R. J. (2008). Sociologist Austin Turk and policing: Structural reinforcers and reversals of the positional authority of police. *Sociological Forum, 23,* 814–844.

Lanza-Kaduce, L., & Greenleaf, R. G. (1994). Police-citizen encounters: Turk on norm resistance. *Justice Quarterly, 11,* 605–623.

Lanza-Kaduce, L., & Greenleaf, R. G. (2000). Age and race deference reversals: Extending Turk on police-citizen conflict. *Journal of Research in Crime & Delinquency, 37,* 221–236.

Orcutt, J. (1983). *Analyzing deviance.* Chicago: Dorsey.

Sellin, T. (1938). *Culture conflict and crime.* New York: Social Science Council.

Taylor, I., Walton, P., & Young, J. (1973). *The new criminology.* New York: Harper & Row.

Turk, A. T. (1966). Conflict and criminality. *American Sociological Review, 31,* 338–352.

Turk, A. T. (1969). *Criminality and legal order.* Chicago: Rand McNally.

Turk, A. T. (1982). *Political criminality: The defiance and defense of authority.* Newbury Park, CA: Sage.

Weidner, R., & Terrill, W. (2005). A test of Turk's theory on norm resistance using observational data on police-suspect encounters. *Journal of Research in Crime and Delinquency, 42,* 84–109.

TURNER, RALPH H.: DEVIANT ROLES AND THE SOCIAL CONSTRUCTION OF BEHAVIOR

Ralph H. Turner served as president of the American Sociological Association in 1969 and is a founding faculty member of the Department of Sociology at UCLA. While Turner's academic contributions range across many subfields in sociology, including social movements, occupational stratification, and social psychology, his research on moral judgment, labeling, and role theory is most relevant to criminologists. Turner draws upon symbolic interactionism and structural-functionalism to explain the production and allocation of social roles, as well as the agency of individuals in continuously defining, redefining, accepting, and rejecting role assignments or labels. In doing so, Turner bridges micro- and macro-levels by linking the structural functional differentiation of roles and collective behaviors (e.g., rioting) with flexible labels produced and negotiated through symbolic communication in social interactions.

Moral Judgment

Turner's (1952, 1954) research on moral judgment focuses on how role-specific ideologies are associated with responses to norm violation. In particular, he studies the social control responses of friends in two hypothetical scenarios: theft of $500 and premarital sexual activity. Turner finds that disapproving actors react to a norm-violating friend by assuming one of six roles: rejective, responsible, responsible assisting, moral passive, amoral passive, and amoral assisting. Moreover, the role relationship between the norm violator and the social control agent influences the response to social control (e.g., self-punishment, rectification). Thus, behavioral patterns are created, maintained, and modified in interaction with others and are dependent on the role relationships between actors.

The Social Construction of Violent Collective Behavior

Complementing his research on individual reactions to norm violation, Turner shows that the definition of "insiders" and "outsiders" contributes to community reactions to, and the symbolic meanings of, violent collective behavior. Using the 1965 Watts Riot as a case in point, Turner and colleagues (Jeffries et al., 1971; Turner, 1969) demonstrate that the interpretation of collective disturbances as either "protest" or "crime" is dependent on the predisposing experience and ideology of the definers. To the extent that community members view the riot as a credible symbolic communication of injustice and an attempt to work within the system for accommodation, it will be defined as a legitimate protest. When disturbances are viewed as unlawful violent actions or rebellions, however, they are defined as criminal acts.

In their study of the 1943 Zoot-Suit Riot in Los Angeles, Turner and Samuel Surace (1956) find that community reactions to groups symbolically identified as outsiders can be violent. Collective violence toward "Zooters" (bleeding into the indiscriminate use of violence toward all Mexicans) is recognized as the "social control without due process" of a group who had been symbolically branded in the media as outsiders. As a result, the crowd displayed a uniform reaction to shared negative symbols that neutralized norms prohibiting violence.

Turner (1972a) observed a different reaction to violence (shootings and bombings) at the campuses of UCLA, Claremont Colleges, and the University of California, Santa Barbara in 1969. In each case, the collegiate communities could not be certain that the offenders were outsiders. Rather than escalating conflict, the social bonds developed through shared experience and identity fostered group solidarity in response to serious intragroup threat. Turner (1967) argues that solidarity is similarly important for explaining community reactions to other types of crises, such as natural disasters. During intragroup threats or crises, there is a natural reversion to the mechanical solidarity characteristic of small-scale societies described by Émile Durkheim and an escalation of in-group altruism.

Role Theory

Labeling theorists see deviance as a label that is applied to an individual by the public or other officials, after which the "deviant" identity assumes the master status. In transferring the agency associated with role definition from the deviant to the definers, labeling theory treats individuals as little more than passive recipients of labels rather than as active agents who accept, reject, or negotiate the label (Turner, 1972b). Turner describes three circumstances under which individuals willingly assume the deviant role: when confronted with conflicting group loyalties, when attempting to neutralize social pressures, and when modifying or transforming their own conventional value system. His theorizing about the creation of deviant role identities through social interaction is embedded in role theory. This interactional approach assumes that roles are not fixed but emerge in the context of negotiation with "alter roles" and "legitimate definers" to create meaning for behavior. At the same time, Turner (2002) recognizes that the functional differentiation of social roles creates a network that structures groups, organizations, and societies.

Elizabeth Griffiths

See also Becker, Howard S.: Labeling and Deviant Careers; Lemert, Edwin M.: Primary and Secondary Deviance; Spector, Malcolm, and John I. Kitsuse: Constructing Social Problems

References and Further Readings

Jeffries, V., Turner, R. H., & Morris, R. T. (1971). The public perception of the Watts Riot as social protest. *American Sociological Review, 36,* 443–451.
Turner, R. H. (1952). Moral judgment: A study in roles. *American Sociological Review, 17,* 70–77.
Turner, R. H. (1954). Self and other in moral judgment. *American Sociological Review, 19,* 249–259.
Turner, R. H. (1969). The public perception of protest. *American Sociological Review, 34,* 815–831.
Turner, R. H. (1967). Types of solidarity in the reconstituting of groups. *The Pacific Sociological Review, 10,* 60–68.
Turner, R. H. (1972a). Deviance avowal as neutralization of commitment. *Social Problems, 19,* 308–321.
Turner, R. H. (1972b). Integrative beliefs in group crises. *The Journal of Conflict Resolution, 16,* 25–40.
Turner, R. H. (2002). Role theory. In J. H. Turner (Ed.), *Handbook of sociological theory* (pp. 233–254). New York: Kluwer Academic/Plenum.
Turner, R. H., & Surace, S. J. (1956). Zoot-Suiters and Mexicans: Symbols in crowd behavior. *American Journal of Sociology, 62,* 14–20.

TYLER, TOM R.: SANCTIONS AND PROCEDURAL JUSTICE THEORY

Focusing on personal experiences with authorities including legal authorities (i.e., police officers and judges), Tom R. Tyler's theory of procedural justice explains the effects of the fairness of procedures used by authorities. In criminology and criminal justice, the theory seeks to answer such important questions as why people obey the law, why people cooperate with legal authorities, and why people have trust and confidence in legal authorities. According to the theory, people's evaluations of and reactions to legal authorities are shaped by their judgments about the fairness of the procedures through which authorities exercise their discretion. Specifically, people are more likely to accept the constraints imposed by the law and legal authorities if they believe legal authorities use fair procedures in their decision making and treatment of members of the public. Furthermore, the effects of procedural justice judgments are often found to be stronger than those of the judgments about outcome fairness and outcome favorableness. Tyler's theory of procedural justice has facilitated the development of a process-based model of regulation including process-based policing. This process-based model is different from the traditional coercive approach that is based on the deterrent effects of sanctions.

The Implications of Fair Procedures

Procedural justice refers to the fairness of procedures by which punishments and rewards are distributed. There are different perspectives explaining why people are concerned with procedural justice. For example, the instrumental perspective views fair procedures as an instrument leading to fair outcomes. If the procedures are perceived as fair, the final decision outcome is more likely to be accepted as fair. In contrast, Tyler's theory of procedural justice contends that the fairness of procedures is important because of its psychological implications, independent of the favorableness or fairness of outcomes. This approach is based on the assumption that one's membership in a social group as a basis for self-identity is a powerful aspect of social life. Specifically, Tyler's theory argues that procedures are evaluated in terms of their psychological implications for one's membership within the social group and relationship with the group authority using the procedures. A fair procedure indicates a positive relationship with the group, while an unfair procedure implies a negative or low-status position within the group. In other words, fair procedures by the group authority suggest that the group is worth identifying with and being involved in, while unfair procedures suggest that the group does not respect or care about the group member that the authority is dealing with. Because of these implications about one's social importance to the social group, one's attitudes and reactions toward the group or group authorities are strongly affected by his or her judgments about the fairness of the procedures.

Judgments of Procedural Justice

According to the theory, there are two key procedural elements affecting people's judgments of procedural justice: the quality of authorities' decision making and the quality of interpersonal treatment. In the evaluations of the quality of decision

making, people are concerned with the accuracy, neutrality, and consistency of the decision and their representation or voice in the decision-making process. In empirical research on procedural justice during police-citizen encounters, for example, the quality of decision making is usually measured with survey items asking whether the police accurately understand and apply the law, make their decisions based on facts instead of their personal biases or opinions, consider people's opinions when deciding what to do, try to get the facts in a situation before deciding how to act, give honest explanations for their actions to the people they deal with, apply the rules consistently to different people, and treat people the same as anyone else would be in the same situation.

The quality of interpersonal treatment also affects people's judgments of procedural justice. People care about how they are treated by the authorities, and if they are treated with dignity and respect, they are more likely to view the procedure as a fair procedure. In empirical research on procedural justice during police-citizen encounters, for example, the quality of interpersonal treatment is usually measured with such survey items as whether the police treat people with dignity and respect, treat people politely, respect people's rights, show concern for people's rights, really want to help, and take the situation seriously. Taken together, the quality of decision making and the quality of interpersonal treatment determine whether a procedure is perceived as fair or not. And according to the theory, the judgments of procedural justice affect people's voluntary acceptance of the decisions made by the authorities.

The Process-Based Model of Regulation

Tyler's theory of procedural justice has important implications for establishing a law-abiding society in which legal authorities have the capacity for securing citizens' immediate voluntary compliance with their decisions and long-term compliance with the law. Based on the findings of procedural justice effects, a process-based model of regulation has been developed. This model of regulation recognizes the limited effectiveness of criminal sanctions in securing citizen compliance and cooperation. Though legal authorities may deter crime and citizen defiance through the use of sanctions and threats, effective social regulation depends on citizens' voluntary self-regulatory behavior. To manage undesirable behavior and encourage general compliance, this model of regulation emphasizes the procedural justice of legal authorities rather than the deterrence of sanctions.

According to the theory, there are three reasons for immediate voluntary deference to the decisions of legal authorities, including the favorableness of the decisions, the fairness of the decisions, and the fairness of the procedures by which legal authorities exercise their discretion. Compared with the other two reasons, the fairness of the procedures usually has the major influence on people's willingness to accept the decisions. For example, during the encounters with police officers and judges, people are more likely to consent and cooperate if they feel that the decision-making process and the treatment they have received are fair.

In the analysis of long-term compliance and everyday law-related behavior, the theory argues that the effects of procedural justice during interactions with legal authorities can continue over time and eventually lead to voluntary cooperation of and support for legal authorities in one's daily life. Specifically, the judgments of procedural justice during interactions shape one's evaluations about the legitimacy of legal authorities. When the procedures used by legal authorities are viewed as fair, people are more likely to have trust and confidence in the motives of legal authorities and believe that legal authorities are legitimate. The legitimacy of legal authorities, in turn, leads to feelings of obligation to obey the law. In other words, people will take the responsibility to obey the law and cooperate with legal authorities in their daily lives if they believe legal authorities are legitimate and entitled to be obeyed.

In sum, the process-based model of regulation emphasizes the key role of procedural justice in shaping citizens' immediate and long-term compliance. Use of fair procedures by legal authorities both leads to citizens' voluntary compliance during encounters and increases the legitimacy of legal authorities which has long-term impacts on citizens' everyday cooperation and support. Furthermore, there is a spiraling effect; that is, the fairness of procedures have greater impacts if legal authorities are perceived more legitimate during encounters. Taken together, these findings in the research on procedural justice suggest that the process-based model of regulation is a proactive strategy in which legal authorities act in a procedurally fair manner to build and maintain legitimacy. Research has also found that people in different racial and ethnic groups are concerned with procedural justice issues and evaluate legal authorities in basically the same way, suggesting that the process-based model of regulation is an effective strategy in different communities.

Process-Based Policing

Process-based policing is a major development in the process-based model of regulation. According to this model, citizens are concerned with the quality of police decision making and the quality of the treatment by police officers during encounters in their evaluations of the fairness of police procedures. When they believe that they are treated in a procedurally fair manner, citizens are more likely to feel that they are valued members of society. As a result, citizens are more willing to cooperate with police officers during encounters and defer to their decisions. This model also suggests that the effects of procedural justice occur even when the police decision conflicts with one's immediate self-interest. Procedural justice judgments, furthermore, facilitate the development of the perception that the police are legitimate and moral. Once the police are viewed as trustworthy and having a good relationship with the public, citizens' obligation to comply is formed and support for the police is enhanced.

Process-based policing recognizes the importance of procedural justice during police-citizen encounters and emphasizes the function of legitimacy-building in officers' daily interactions with citizens. This process-based approach to policing differs from the traditional view in the police subculture that emphasizes the use of coercive force such as physical force and verbal threats to obtain citizen compliance. Because its focus on the manner of policing (i.e., the quality of police decision making and the quality of interpersonal treatment), process-based policing is suggested as compatible with most of the strategies implemented in community policing and restorative policing.

Empirical research has evaluated the effects of procedural justice in policing. Judgments of procedural justice have been consistently found to have strong psychological effects on people's subjective perceptions, such as their perceptions about the legitimacy of the police, overall trust and confidence in the police, specific views about racial profiling, willingness to comply with the law, willingness to cooperate with the police, and willingness to accept decisions made by police officers. However, only limited research has examined effects of procedural justice judgments on future objective behavior of citizens (e.g., reoffending and crime reporting), and the findings are mixed. There are also a very limited number of social observational studies investigating the effects of fair procedures in police decision making and interpersonal treatment on citizen cooperative behavior (e.g., citizen compliance and demeanor) during encounters. In general, police behavior related to procedural justice has been found to have strong effects on citizen behavior, but the importance of procedural justice varies across different situations.

Mengyan Dai

See also Braithwaite, John: Reintegrative Shaming Theory; Economic Theory and Crime; Lafree, Gary D.: Legitimacy and Crime; Sherman, Lawrence W.: Defiance Theory; Williams, Kirk R., and Richard Hawkins: Deterrence Theory and Non-Legal Sanctions

References and Further Readings

Tyler, T. R. (1990). *Why people obey the law*. New Haven, CT: Yale University Press.

Tyler, T. R. (2003). Procedural justice, legitimacy, and the effective rule of law. In M. Tonry (Ed.), *Crime and justice: A review of research* (Vol. 30, pp. 283–357). Chicago: University of Chicago Press.

Tyler, T. R., & Huo, Y. J. (2002). *Trust in the law*. New York: Russell Sage.

VAUGHAN, DIANE: THE NORMALIZATION OF DEVIANCE

Sociologist Diane Vaughan has developed an empirically grounded theoretical argument that many unlawful or deviant organizational actions can best be understood as the result of a social process she calls *the normalization of deviance*. The normalization of deviance occurs when actors in an organizational setting, such as a corporation or a government agency, come to define their deviant acts as normal and acceptable because they fit with and conform to the cultural norms of the organization within which they work. Even though their actions may violate some outside legal or social standard and be labeled as criminal or deviant by people outside the organization, organizational offenders do not see these actions as wrong because they are conforming to the cultural mandates that exist within the workgroup culture and environment where they carry out their occupational roles.

Vaughan's concept of the normalization of deviance makes several important contributions to criminological theory. First, it offers a useful corrective to the tendency to see all crimes, including organizational crimes, as the result of individual rational choices; that is, calculated decisions where the costs and benefits of wrongdoing are weighed by the actors before acting. Second, it advances our sociological understanding of how organizational cultures narrow choices and shape social definitions of what is rational and acceptable at any given moment, and how these choices and definitions can lead to unlawful or deviant behavior on behalf of the organization.

The *Challenger* Launch Decision and Theory Elaboration

Vaughan developed the concept of the normalization of deviance in her landmark study, *The Challenger Launch Decision: Risky Technology, Culture, and Deviance at NASA* in 1996. The Space Shuttle *Challenger* exploded on January 28, 1986, killing the seven astronauts on board. The immediate cause of the disaster was a technical failure: the failure of the rubber-like O-rings in the joints of the Solid Rocket Boosters to properly seal out hot propellant gases. The presidential commission created to investigate the explosion (known as the Rogers Commission) identified production pressures and a flawed decision-making process at NASA and documented a history of problems with the O-rings. A number of narratives emerged that depicted the NASA managers responsible for the launch as *amoral calculators* who had engaged in a variety of safety rule violations (see Vaughan, 1998, p. 23). But Vaughan's exhaustive research contradicted the conventional explanation of calculated managerial wrongdoing. As she pointed out, "No fundamental decision was made at NASA to do evil; rather, a series of seemingly harmless decisions were made that incrementally moved the space agency toward a catastrophic outcome" (1996, p. 410). According to Vaughan, it was not deviance per se, but conformity that was responsible for the *Challenger* disaster.

To understand Vaughan's analysis of the normalization of deviance at NASA, it is important to first spell out her theoretical strategy. Vaughan calls the overall strategy *theory elaboration*, by which she means "inductive strategies for more fully developing existing theories that explain particular research findings by merging different theoretical perspectives in a more general way" (2007, p. 3). Her particular strategy in this case is to combine different levels of analysis to elaborate theory. Sociologists generally tend to focus on two levels of analysis: macro and micro. The macro-level concerns large-scale social structures and institutions and the micro-level deals with human agency in the form of face-to-face interaction and the process of acting toward things based on social meanings created and modified through interpretive work. While there is theoretical consensus among sociologists about attempting to bridge the gap between structure and agency, Vaughan points out that "making the macro-micro connection is an unresolved empirical problem" (2007, p. 4).

Her position is that research on white-collar crime can make an important contribution to making this theory-elaborative connection across macro- and micro-levels of analysis by including a middle- or meso-level: formal and complex organizations. Criminologists who study white-collar crime often focus on organizations and occupations such as business corporations, industries, states, and government agencies. Vaughan believes that this research shows how structure and agency can be brought together to enhance our understanding of *situated action*; that is, behavior that takes place in socially organized settings. As she notes (2007, p. 4),

> Organizational settings make visible the ways that macro-institutional forces outside of organizations and occupations are joined with micro-processes, thus affecting individual decisions and actions. Organizations provide a window into culture, showing how culture mediates between institutional forces, organizational goals and processes, and individual illegality so that deviance becomes normalized in organizational settings.

The Normalization of Deviance at NASA

Vaughan's revisionist history and sociological explanation of the *Challenger* launch decision

provides an important illustration of this theory-elaborative strategy. Her primarily archival and specialized interview data show that over time the work group culture at NASA, in the context of institutional pressures and aerospace industry norms, began to normalize signals of danger and technical deviations in its official risk assessments. Since the space shuttle was an experimental technology it was normal to have technical problems at the agency. Small changes that were slight deviations from the normal work process gradually became the norm and provided the basis for further deviations over time. According to Vaughan, there was an incremental descent into poor judgment at NASA. Routine judgments within the agency were made to move forward despite the technical problems that came to be defined as normal and acceptable. The result was the development of a cultural belief that it was safe to fly the shuttle, even though ultimately it was not and disaster ensued. This organizational worldview, the NASA managers' interpretation of technical information with regard to the risky technology of the shuttle, was shaped by larger social forces and environmental contingencies such as the production pressures the agency experienced. Thus, macro-, meso-, and micro-factors linked together in combination to produce the fatal outcome for the *Challenger*.

A growing body of research offers support for Vaughan's theoretical argument that, when corporate managers or government officials make decisions that appear to outsiders as clearly deviant, they are, in fact, often conforming to cultural mandates that have developed inside the organization. As she concludes, "Thus, in some social settings deviance becomes normal and acceptable; it is not a calculated decision where the costs and benefits of doing wrong are weighed because the definitions of what is deviant and what is normative have been redefined within that setting" (2007, p. 11).

Implications for Social Control

Vaughan's strategy of theoretical elaboration through the inclusion of the meso-level of analysis and her development of the concept of the normalization of deviance within organizational settings have important implications for the social control of white-collar, corporate, and state crimes. If sociologists and criminologists restrict their explanations of crime to only one level of analysis, they will produce only partial understandings of the phenomenon. A partial explanation of crime can only produce a partial strategy for crime prevention and control. A more complete explanation of criminal or deviant acts, one that combines the different levels of analysis, would provide a firmer basis on which to construct more appropriate and successful social control strategies.

Theories that portray white-collar offenders as amoral calculators or which focus only on individual failings in decision making often leave out the broader structural and cultural conditions that lead to the normalization of deviance. As with traditional forms of crime, this leads to the creation of control policies that target individual criminals, not the larger criminogenic social forces. Such policies will be as ineffective in dealing with white-collar crime as they have been with regard to street crime. As Vaughan has pointed out, the failure to address the cultural and structural conditions that led to the normalization of deviance at NASA and the *Challenger* explosion resulted in another space shuttle disaster 17 years later with the loss of the *Columbia* and her crew. The *Columbia* Accident Investigation Board discovered that NASA had once again normalized a technical anomaly with catastrophic consequences. If control policies are only directed at replacing or punishing individual corporate managers or state officials and do not address the larger structural, cultural, and organizational forces that shape decisions in the workplace, they will be ineffective. As Vaughan's analysis shows, only by addressing the macro-level influences, the meso-level forces and the micro-processes that shape the normalization of deviance can successful strategies be developed to prevent and control organizational crime and deviance.

Ronald C. Kramer

See also Anomie and White-Collar Crime; Integrated Theories of White-Collar Crime; Michalowski, Raymond J., and Ronald C. Kramer: State-Corporate Crime; Rational Choice and White-Collar Crime

References and Further Readings

Calavita, K., Pontell, H. N., & Tillman, R. (1997). *Big money crime: Fraud and politics in the savings and loan crisis*. Berkeley: University of California Press.

Clinard, M. B., & Yeager, P. C. (1980). *Corporate crime*. New York: Free Press.

Columbia Accident Investigation Board. (2003). *Report*. Washington, DC: Government Printing Office.

Goldhagen, D. (1996). *Hitler's willing executioners*. Cambridge, MA: Harvard University Press.

Green, P., & Ward, T. (2004). *State crime: Governments, violence and corruption*. London: Pluto Press.

Kelman, H. C., & Hamilton, V. L. (1989). *Crimes of obedience*. New Haven, CT: Yale University Press.

Kramer, R. (2010). From Guernica to Hiroshima to Baghdad: The normalization of the terror bombing of civilian populations. In W. J. Chambliss, R. J. Michalowski, & R. C. Kramer (Eds.), *State crime in the global age* (pp. 118–133). Devon, UK: Willan.

Michalowski, R. J., & Kramer, R. C. (2006). *State-Corporate crime: Wrongdoing at the intersection of business and government*. New Brunswick, NJ: Rutgers University Press.

Pontell, H. N., & Geis, G. (Eds.). (2007). *International handbook of white-collar and corporate crime*. New York: Springer.

Powell, W. W., & DiMaggio, P. J. (Eds.). (1991). *The New institutionalism in organizational analysis*. Chicago: University of Chicago Press.

Presidential Commission on the Space Shuttle *Challenger* Accident. (1986). *Report to the President by the Presidential Commission on the Space Shuttle* Challenger *Accident* (5 vols.). Washington, DC: U.S. Government Printing Office.

Vaughan, D. (1996). *The* Challenger *launch decision: Risky technology, culture, and deviance at NASA*. Chicago: University of Chicago Press.

Vaughan, D. (1998). Rational choice, situated action, and the social control of organizations. *Law & Society Review, 32*, 23–61.

Vaughan, D. (2007). Beyond macro- and micro-levels of analysis, organizations, and the cultural fix. In H. N. Pontell & G. Geis (Eds.), *International handbook of white-collar and corporate crime* (pp. 3–24). New York: Springer.

VIGIL, JAMES DIEGO: MULTIPLE MARGINALITY THEORY

Throughout the history of gang research, many theories have been proposed to explain gang membership. Most of these explanations have been applied broadly in describing gang membership among homogenous racial/ethnic groups such as African American or Hispanic gangs, but ignore the specific role that race/ethnicity plays in gang formation. One notable exception is James Diego Vigil's multiple marginality theory, which focused on explaining the specific mechanisms by which individuals from various racial/ethnic populations become gang members. In his seminal work, *Barrio Gangs*, Vigil concentrated on how multiple marginality results in gang involvement among Chicano youth. In his later work, *A Rainbow of Gangs*, he extended this model to African American, Vietnamese, and Salvadoran groups. The main purpose of the multiple marginality framework was to describe the development of gangs and explain why individuals become members. In *Barrio Gangs*, Vigil argued that it was important to understand the origins of the gang in order to address the problems associated with gang behavior.

The premise of the multiple marginality framework is that racial/ethnic minority individuals are exposed to multiple stresses including ecological, economic, social-cultural, and psychological factors that ultimately result in the development of gangs. The more risks and stresses individuals accrue, the more likely they are to experience marginalization. Marginalization essentially "is the relegation of certain persons or groups to the fringes of society, where social and economic conditions result in powerlessness" (Vigil, 2002, p. 7). It occurs when individuals are exposed to a combination of factors that put them in a position of disadvantage and results in "low socio-economic status, street socialization and enculturation, and problematic development of a self-identity" (Vigil, 1988, p. 9). This marginalization process begins with macro-historical and macro-structural factors, such as discrimination and immigration, which negatively impact ecological/economic factors. As individuals experience ecological/economic stress, this affects the ability of social institutions—such as the family, school, and law enforcement—to direct socialization and exert social control. Social control is integral to the socialization process because it is "the ability to control, manage, restrain, or direct human behavior" in a positive manner (Siegel, 2007, p. 509). As a consequence of this lack of social control, posits Vigil, gangs develop

as an adaptation to marginalization and enable coping with the pressures of urban street life.

Based on the premise of his multiple marginality theory, the solution to the gang problem, according to Vigil, was to address the social and economic inequalities that are inherent in our society and experienced primarily by racial/ethnic minorities. Since that would characterize a significant undertaking, Vigil argued that, at the very least, increasing the ability of the various social control institutions to influence the behavior of youths in a positive manner should be sufficient in decreasing gang membership among racial/ethnic minority group members.

Multiple Marginality Theory

Vigil's multiple marginality theory presents a developmental process that considers multiple factors (e.g., ecological, economic, social-cultural, and psychological) that contribute to gang membership for racial/ethnic minority youths. While this framework incorporates elements from previous theories to explain gang membership, it provides a unique framework in which the historical and cultural backgrounds of racial/ethnic minority groups are considered in describing gang formation. Vigil originally developed his theory to explain the incidence of gang membership among Chicanos. As he applied his theory to other minority groups, it became a comprehensive theory of gang membership that considered how the specific experiences of individual racial/ethnic minority groups in the United States has resulted in youth joining gangs.

According to Vigil, the marginalization process occurs in a developmental sequence in which exposure to marginalizing factors further impacts marginalization related to other factors. For example, as people experience discrimination, this determines their economic status in society, which can influence the stability of the home resulting in low supervision of children, ultimately leading to street socialization and gang membership for youths. Additionally, some individuals are more influenced than others, with those that are the most marginalized ultimately becoming gang members.

The marginalization process begins with the impact of macro-historical elements (i.e., racism, social and cultural repression, and fragmented institutions) and macro-structural elements (i.e., immigration/migration and enclave settlement).

These macro-historical and macro-structural factors to which individuals are exposed influence their ecological/economic situation in life, which is often characterized by poverty, lack of suitable housing, and decreased employment. Due to discrimination, racism, and economic status, racial/ethnic minorities have been relegated to the poorest and most substandard areas of housing. As a consequence, these groups have been largely segregated based on their economic status and racial/ethnic minority group membership, making acculturation and participating in mainstream society difficult, thus further impacting their economic marginalization. Eventually, these ecological/economic stressors influence the effectiveness that social control institutions such as the family, school, and law enforcement have in positively affecting the behavior of the community's youths.

Since family, school, and law enforcement provide much of the socialization regarding acceptable behaviors for youths, a breakdown in these social control institutions can result in a pattern of socialization toward the norms of the street (street socialization) instead of toward law-abiding behavior. Many racial/ethnic minority families are affected by ecological/economic stress resulting from discrimination, cultural conflict, and disruption. As families struggle to make ends meet or to find steady employment, their ability to provide social control for their children decreases, resulting in neglect as well as in decreased attachment and supervision. Furthermore, family stress and instability are often passed down generation to generation, leading to continuing problems including the institutionalization of gangs in a community.

Marginalization that begins in the family context is acerbated by "segregated, underfunded, inferior school[s], where [minority students] encounter cultural insensitivity and an ethnocentric curriculum" (Vigil, 2002, p. 9). School marginalization leads to further economic stresses as racial/ethnic minority individuals experiencing marginalization in the school context often drop out, thus influencing their future opportunities for legitimate employment. Those that are not positively socialized in the context of the family and school (informal social controls), eventually come to the attention of law enforcement, which becomes the last option of social control (formal social control) and socialization. Additionally, for many minority groups,

negative experiences characterize the interactions with these institutions, decreasing their ability to exert social control. For example, due to discrimination, language barriers, and culturally irrelevant curriculum, many individuals elect to stop going to school, which negates its ability to have a positive influence on the socialization process. As marginalized youths experience a degradation of social control institutions, they turn to the gang for the socialization experience that allows them to "participate in public life, albeit a street one" (Vigil, 1988, p. 64).

In addition to the agents of social control that assist with the early socialization of individuals, Vigil (2002) outlines four stages of the socialization process: connections, engagement, involvement, and belief. Individuals who navigate this process successfully join the ranks of dominant, conforming society, while those that do not often participate in deviant behavior, including gang membership. Connections represent one stage of the socialization process. These are bonds that individuals develop with others, including family, peers, schools, and law enforcement. For a positive socialization process to occur, it is important for individuals to develop these bonds with conforming individuals versus their gang peers. Engagement, another element of socialization, is "the expression of well defined goals and the striving for higher status" (Vigil, 2002, p. 24). For marginalized youths, who are often not involved in schools or the job force and thus cannot envision realizing their dreams, engagement becomes difficult. Involvement in conventional activities (e.g., after-school activities, jobs, church) is also integral to the socialization process, as youths who are occupied in conforming behaviors have little time to participate in delinquent behavior. Finally, a belief in conventional norms hinders much deviance as those who believe in the rules and laws are less likely to violate them. This socialization process allows for the development of positive social bonds, without which street socialization occurs.

When positive social bonds are not created, a street socialization process is initiated and serves as an adaptation to marginalization for racial/ethnic minority youths. Individuals are socialized to the norms of the street instead of to the conventional beliefs of mainstream society. As social control decreases, individuals have more time to spend with their peers on the streets. Through street socialization, gangs develop to fill the void left by the defunct social control institutions for the most marginalized youth. The gang then becomes the mechanism by which socialization and enculturation of youth occurs.

Conclusion

Vigil's (1988, p. 173) multiple marginality framework provides an "integrative interpretation" of how racial/ethnic minority individuals, who may be marginalized due to a variety of factors, find themselves as gang members. While his theory offers a broad framework in which to understand gang membership, it is also unique in that it stresses understanding gang formation within the context of the historical situation of each racial/ethnic minority group in the United States. While this important contribution begins to expand our knowledge of the reasons why gang membership tends to be concentrated among racial/ethnic minority youths, there are a number of issues that research needs to address in order to appreciate the contribution of this theory to our overall understanding of gang membership. First, in his application of the framework, Vigil neglects to operationalize many of his concepts or test the nature of his theory beyond qualitative analysis. Second, to date, there is only one known empirical test (by Adrienne Freng and Finn-Aage Esbensen) of the applicability of the multiple marginality framework to explaining gang membership beyond Vigil's own work.

In their research, Freng and Esbensen begin to examine these shortcomings. Additionally, they also include white youths, a group that Vigil does not consider in his conversations. This research did find overall support for multiple marginality as an explanation for current gang membership. When the theory was applied separately to various racial/ethnic groups, differences did appear depending on whether "current" (individuals reported currently being a gang member) or "ever" (individuals reported being a gang member at some point) gang membership was being examined. For "current" gang members, ecological/economic factors were more important in explaining gang membership for whites, while social control/street socialization

elements were significant for African Americans and Hispanics. These differences disappeared when examining "ever" gang membership, as social control/street socialization variables predicted gang membership for all groups. These findings and the lack of other research utilizing this theory point to the need for further examination of the multiple marginalization framework in order to more fully understand its contribution to the larger discussion of gang theory.

Adrienne Freng

See also Gangs and the Underclass; Hirschi, Travis: Social Control Theory; Moore, Joan W.: Homeboys and Homegirls in the Barrio; Peers and Delinquency; Wilson, William Julius: The Truly Disadvantaged

References and Further Readings

Freng, A., & Esbensen, F. A. (2007). Race and gang affiliation: An examination of multiple marginality. *Justice Quarterly, 24*, 600–628.

Siegel, L. (2007). *Criminology: Theories, patterns, and typologies*. Belmont, CA: Thomson/Wadsworth.

Vigil, J. D. (1988). *Barrio gangs: Street life and identity in southern California*. Austin: University of Texas Press.

Vigil, J. D. (2002). *A rainbow of gangs: Street cultures in the mega-city*. Austin: University of Texas Press.

Vigil, J. D. (2004). Gangs and group membership: Implications for schooling. In M. A. Gibson, P. Gandara, & J. P. Koyama (Eds.), *School connections: U.S. Mexican youth, peers, and school achievement* (pp. 87–106). New York: Teachers College Press.

Vigil, J. D., & Long, J. M. (1990). Emic and etic perspectives on gang culture: The Chicano case. In C. R. Huff (Ed.), *Gangs in America* (1st ed., pp. 55–68). Newbury Park, CA: Sage.

VILA, BRIAN J., LAWRENCE E. COHEN, AND RICHARD S. MACHALEK: EVOLUTIONARY EXPROPRIATIVE THEORY

Originally developed by Lawrence E. Cohen and Richard S. Machalek and published in the

American Journal of Sociology in 1988, a general theory of expropriative crime has been tested by Bryan Vila and Cohen in 1993 and revised and extended by Vila in 1994. Currently referred to as evolutionary expropriative theory (EET), this perspective is more aptly termed a paradigm in that it presents a conceptual blueprint that purports to organize a range of phenomena and generate more specific theories about the causes and nature of crime. The aim of this paradigm is to provide a comprehensive explanation of crime that encompasses the individual and ecology in a dynamic, interactive, and evolving set of processes.

Conceptual Framework

According to the original formulation, the scope of EET pertained to expropriative crime or crime that is directed toward obtaining a material resource (e.g., property) from another person. Although broad in scope, EET draws heavily from the field of evolutionary ecology. Cohen and Machalek were explicitly interested in the behavioral strategies individuals employ within a range of interdependent ecological conditions to obtain the thing they desire. As such, concepts related to pathological states as determinates of crime are not the primary mechanisms involved in understanding expropriative crime. Thus, expropriative crime is seen as normal. Cohen and Machalek also believed that sociological theories of crime needed to take into account evolutionary principles into their theorizing. Therefore, how behavioral strategies evolve in a given population is of utmost concern. One way, according to these theorists, is to invoke culturally mediated processes over time or cultural evolution. Behavioral strategies are therefore embedded in the ongoing cultural evolution of a population. Cultural evolution can be thought of as the transmission of ideas, values, attitudes, and practical methods to extract needs and desires from a given habitat or ecology across or within generations. Cultural evolution is analogous to biological evolution and is thought to be a neglected mechanism for situating the study of crime. It is important to point out that behavioral strategies vary across individuals because of the conditioning ecological effects that provide a range of differential options. In other words, the behavioral options available to persons are not necessarily evenly distributed and therefore the

strategies will themselves potentially vary from person to person. The primary unit of analysis in the study of expropriative crime is the behavioral strategies themselves. Although a unique departure from traditional criminological theories, Cohen and Machalek offered no empirical tests derived from this conceptual framework.

If we accept that expropriative crime be viewed as a normal or steady state in a system, under what ecological conditions will expropriative crime increase? Cohen and Machalek (1988, p. 497) advance several predictions with regard to this question: "1) more opportunities for expropriation exist because of productive innovation, 2) expropriative strategies are transmitted with greater facility, 3) the execution costs of employing expropriation are lower, and 4) competition among expropriators is less intense or the yield of expropriative strategies is greater." From this, one can see that increases in expropriative crime are directly tied to greater opportunities when conditions of greater production exist, learning of these behavioral strategies increases, cost benefits are favorable, and there are less expropriators around and therefore less competition. One can deduce the rational economic underpinnings of this theory as well as its learning or cultural transmission component.

Empirical Support

In a 1993 article, Vila and Cohen offered an empirical test of the original Cohen and Machalek formulation. Acknowledging the difficulty of a direct test of the original theoretical perspective, Vila and Cohen developed a game-theoretic analysis that assessed the logical structure of the conceptual framework and performed a series of computer-based simulations on the model in an effort to evaluate potential real world effects in relation to its major deductions. Game-theoretic models attempt to assess the dynamic behavior of a complex system by using a simplified model to understand the general behavior of the complex system. One example of a game-theoretic analysis is the prisoner's dilemma. The prisoner's dilemma is comprising two persons who are separated from one another by law enforcement and have been involved in a crime. Each prisoner has the option of telling the authorities the other prisoner was guilty or maintain silence. If both prisoners are silent, then they will each receive a moderate sentence. If both prisoners talk, then each prisoner will receive a long sentence. If one talks and the other does not, the one that speaks goes free and the other receives a long sentence. Since both prisoners are separated neither knows what the other will do. Multiple iterations can be played out to examine the short-term and long-term outcome of such a simple scenario. Results of game-theoretic analysis and computer simulations generally supported the logical basis of EET and the primary hypotheses generated under this paradigm. However, as Vila and Machalek report, results also suggest that several revisions are necessary to advance this perspective.

Reformulation

In 1994, Vila reformulated the original Cohen and Machalek theory into a broader paradigm with the aim to explain all types of crime such as expressive (e.g., sexual assault), economic (e.g., illicit drug distribution), and political (e.g., terrorism). This general paradigm synthesized findings from multiple fields that have studied crime and antisocial behavior and also encompasses macro and micro explanations. Compared with other theoretical criminological perspectives that are partial explanations of crime, the revised EET boldly organizes biological factors (which were largely absent from the original formulation), developmental or life-course principles, and micro-ecological and macro-ecological factors into a evolutionary viewpoint on all forms of crime. Vila rightly critiques many criminological theories for their disciplinary parochialism. What this means is that most theorists construct theories that are congruent with their disciplinary training (i.e., sociologically trained criminologists developing sociological theories of crime). In addition to broadening EET to include the interaction from multiple levels of analysis and research findings from multiple disciplines, the revised EET retains the crime as strategy contained in the original formulation. Vila argues that this does not simply mean that humans are rational cost-benefit calculators only, but that individuals think and behave strategically "without any conscious awareness" due to socialization and learning effects. These "strategic styles" exhibited by persons can be aggregated into subpopulation and population styles, and that is how individual and

society is seamlessly integrated. In terms of etiology, biological factors are reciprocally influenced by sociocultural factors and developmental factors that provide the propensity for the motivation for crime. Motivation to crime is expressed and influenced by differential ecological opportunities that are conditioned at the macro level. Based on this reasoning, Vila suggests several crime control strategies. These include protection and avoidance to reduce opportunities, deterrence to reduce motivation, and nurturance to reduce the individual developmental pathways to antisocial behavior.

Critique

Developing a general paradigm of crime is needed and commendable. EET in its revised version provides a unique synthesis of broad scope and potential utility. Strength is its transdiciplinarity and sensitivity to evolutionary principles (the theory of evolution is probably the most successful paradigm ever). Further, the crime control strategies suggested are plausible and internally consistent with the overall paradigm. Despite these strengths, EET has not been very successful in drawing in converts. Few criminologists have worked within this paradigm and explicit empirical tests of theories developed under its auspices are rare, even though the revised EET has captured many of the salient explanatory features necessary to explain crime in broad evolutionary terms. As such, EET is consistent with recent biosocial criminology which has ascended as one of the preeminent theoretical perspectives for contemporary and future criminology.

There are several reasons why EET is not popular. First, EET is complicated and abstract and thus invokes concepts from fields in which criminologists have little training or are perhaps antagonistic toward (criminologist have been notoriously averse to biological approaches). Criminological scholars are typically highly invested in specific theoretical strains (sociological derived theories have been hegemonic in modern criminology). EET may be so broad that it is clumsy and difficult to apply. Second, as a paradigm EET cannot be directly tested—although theories explicitly generated from the paradigm can. Third, few datasets have all the variables necessary to execute statistical modeling of specified constructs and thus as a practical matter only partial tests can proceed.

Alternative tests such as game-theoretic analysis, non-linear dynamics, and computer simulations are highly mathematical and typically not part of criminological training; this is perhaps another reason why other researchers have not worked in this theoretical vein. Although EET has not fully realized its potential as a general theory of crime, it does offer a "big picture" interdisciplinary perspective worthy of reading and serious consideration.

Michael G. Vaughn

See also Cornish, Derek B., and Ronald V. Clarke: Rational Choice Theory; Felson, Marcus K.: Crime and Nature; Wilcox, Pamela, Kenneth C. Land, and Scott A. Hunt: Multicontextual Opportunity Theory; Wilson, James Q., and Richard J. Herrnstein: Crime and Human Nature

References and Further Readings

Cohen, L. E., & Machalek, R. (1988). A general theory of expropriative crime: An evolutionary ecological approach. *American Journal of Sociology, 94*, 465–501.

Vila, B. J. (1994). A general paradigm for understanding criminal behavior: Extending evolutionary ecological theory. *Criminology, 32*, 311–359.

Vila, B. J., & Cohen, L. E. (1993). Crime as strategy: Testing an evolutionary ecological theory of expropriative crime. *American Journal of Sociology, 98*, 873–912.

VOLD, GEORGE B: GROUP CONFLICT THEORY

George B. Vold is widely considered to be one of the most influential contributors to early American criminology. He was born in 1895 to Norwegian immigrants and grew up on a farm in South Dakota, where he subsequently graduated from South Dakota State College. He earned graduate degrees at University of Chicago (M.S.) and University of Minnesota (Ph.D.). His entire career as a professor and researcher was spent at the University of Minnesota. He wrote several books and had many research contributions, including studies of the Massachusetts prison system, revisions to the psychopathic personality laws of Minnesota, and a consultancy with the Minnesota Crime Commission. He retired from the University of Minnesota in 1964, was awarded the prestigious Edwin Sutherland Award by the American Society of Criminology in 1966, and died in 1967.

It is in his last book, *Theoretical Criminology*, that he proferred a group conflict theory of crime. While this book was widely hailed as one of the best, if not the best, summaries and critical assessments of theories of crime, his original contribution of a group conflict theory (GCT) made it all the more special. Additional authors updated and expanded upon Vold's classic work in five subsequent editions (from 1967 to 2010). The following section summarizes Vold's group conflict theory and then places it in the context of other conflict theories of crime. Any quotations will cite page numbers from Vold's original *Theoretical Criminology*.

Group Conflict Theory

Vold's introduction to GCT begins with its basic considerations. Humans cannot be divorced from their group associations. Society in essence is an aggregate of groups that interact in dynamic sequences. Groups gain and lose status over time in an ongoing struggle toward increasing their status relative to other groups. Progress in society is based on this conflict between groups, because if it were not for the struggle of different groups to gain power and status over each other, there would be no incentive for advancement. Groups are formed by individuals with common interests and needs that cannot be satisfied on their own: they need a collectivity for optimal potential. However, the relationship between individual and group interests change over time: "New groups are therefore continuously being formed as new interests arise, and existing groups weaken and disappear when they no longer have a purpose to serve" (p. 205).

Groups conflict with each other when their interests overlap, and competition naturally arises. Some groups exist without conflict if their territories do not overlap, but others rub shoulders and defend themselves against each other. The most dangerous threat to a group is not a simple overlap of interests but the possibility that another group may replace it. The more dangerous the threat, the more group members become loyal to their group;

and complete identification with other group members is the penultimate stage of a truly homogenous and harmonic group. Group conflict can result in a number of differing scenarios depending on the relative imbalances in group strength, ranging from utter defeat of one group over another to some sort of compromise that may favor the slightly stronger group. In developing this notion of conflict as group-oriented, Vold relied heavily on Simmel's sociology of conflict (Simmel & Wolff, 1950).

Vold next illustrates an application of GCT to alcohol regulation in America, a fundamental chronic battle in which the groups involved range from prohibitionists to those who believe there should be minimal regulation. At the height of the prohibitionists' power, alcohol was outlawed altogether. Under the modern system, alcohol is regulated from state to state and to some extent from community to community, through taxes, licenses, inspections, policies, crimes involving alcohol (such as driving under the influence), and so forth, all of which are results of compromises reached after groups attempt to gain the backing of the organized state. The extent of their lobbying success determines the nature of the compromises. More generally, and with respect to crimes, groups that

> produce legislative majorities win control over the police power and dominate the policies that decide who is likely to be involved in violation of the law. . . . The principle of compromise from positions of strength operate at every stage of this conflict process. Hence, there is bargaining in the legislature between prosecution and defense in connection with the trial; between prison officials and inmates; and between parole agents and parolee. (p. 209)

The next step Vold takes is to relate crime to the behavior engaged in by minority groups. He first cites studies that demonstrate that offenders usually have associates and companions and essentially work in collective action that can be seen as oriented toward defense against the interests of organized society. An example of such a collective entity is the juvenile gang, which "cannot achieve its objectives through regular channels, making use of, and relying for protection on, the police power of

the state" (p. 210). It operates at odds with the majority, which is "the established world of adult values and power" (p. 211). Another example Vold points to is conscientious war objectors (those who are convicted of the federal offense of refusing to participate in war activities due to personal moral beliefs and ideology). This example highlights the reality that minority group members often cannot be easily coerced to align their behavior with that proscribed by the majority. Conscientious war objectors usually maintain such strong beliefs in the rightfulness of what they are doing that they are impervious to sanctions by the organized state. Similarly, criminals that are members in other types of minority groups and have a strong group identification are not readily amenable to attempts by the majority to alter their behavior. In fact, their group may not even believe its behavior is criminal, since criminality is a constructed term to them, one that is defined and enforced by more powerful and more societally integrated majority groups.

It should be reinforced that group power dynamics can change over time, and therefore a group's behavior that was once criminalized may become legitimate. For example, after the United States began a "war on terror" in Iraq (in 2003), many citizens who previously had supported most military actions began to question the legitimacy of the U.S. presence and behavior in Iraq. Conversely, sometimes behaviors that are not criminalized can become criminal due to a shift in power between groups. For example, much corporate behavior—such as harming the environment or decisions to not recall defective products because lawsuit expenses are outweighed by recall costs—that was essentially ignored by the government has increasingly become criminalized or enforced more severely due to outrage by public interest groups and the public-at-large.

The last of Vold's arguments is that many crimes whose offense labels seem ordinary (although perhaps serious) stem not so much from the desire to engage in crime but are instead committed toward the purpose of maintaining or enhancing a group's power control position. He provides several examples. One of the most extreme is political revolution by groups seeking major reform. Revolutionary conflict can spawn all types of offenses, such as murder, property theft and damage, assault, and treason. Yet these offenses are enforced against only the unsuccessful group (either the rebel protesters or the governing establishment). Often, group power dynamics can shift rather rapidly, and this time the crimes are enforced against the previously successful group. Frequently, these sorts of conflicts will occur after an election. As an example, in 2009, Iran broke out in a massive conflict between two groups: the administration, headed by Mahmoud Ahmadinejad (an incumbent president who officially won the election), and those, in significant numbers, who believed the election was encumbered by fraud and that Mir Hossein Mousavi was the true winner. The former group consisted of hard-line traditionalists who are antagonistic toward the western world, whereas the latter represent typically younger Iranians who wish to align more with countries like the United States and believe in improving democracy in Iran. The government has moved to deem almost all actions by protesters unlawful and has enforced these declarations primarily by street-level justice (e.g., shooting or beating protesters) and censorship (limiting communication between Iranians and the world outside Iran). If perchance Ahmadinejad's opponents were to gain power, it is likely that some members of the former regime would be held criminally liable for their actions during this conflict.

Other examples include violence and property damage stemming from labor union–management disputes during which compromise and settlement can often take months to reach, and civil rights movements, such as the struggle for black equality in America. In all these instances, enormous amounts of criminal offenses are generated but are enforced in a manner aligned with the interests of the dominant group. Crime in these situations thus can be seen as committed for group interests rather than for individual interests (except to the extent that group identification merges the two).

Conclusion

Vold's group conflict theory, one should note, is only one of many conflict theories, others include the works of Thorsten Sellin, Austin Turk, Richard Quinney, William J. Chambliss and Robert B. Seidman, and Donald Black. Vold's operates solely at the group level, whereas some conflict theories, such as Black's, operate at the individual level. Of all these, Vold's is the oldest, with one exception: Sellin presented a theory based on cultural conflict in 1938. Today Vold's work is still viewed as having made a huge impact on criminological theory.

Jeffrey Brian Snipes

See also Chambliss, William J.: Power, Conflict, and Crime; Quinney, Richard: Social Transformation and Peacemaking Criminology; Sellin, Thorsten: Culture Conflict and Crime; Turk, Austin T.: The Criminalization Process

References and Further Readings

Bernard, T. J., Snipes, J. B., & Gerould, A. L. (2010). *Vold's theoretical criminology* (6th ed.). New York: Oxford University Press.

Black, D. (1976). *The behavior of law.* New York: Academic Press.

Chambliss, W. J., & Seidman, R. B. (1971). *Law, order, and power.* Reading, MA: Addison-Wesley.

Quinney, R. (1970). *The social reality of crime.* Boston: Little, Brown.

Sellin, T. (1938). *Culture, conflict and crime.* New York: Social Science Research Council.

Simmel, G., & Wolff, K. H. (1950). *The sociology of Georg Simmel.* Glencoe, IL: Free Press.

Turk, A. T. (1969). *Criminality and legal order.* Chicago: Rand McNally.

Vold, G. B. (1958). *Theoretical criminology.* New York: Oxford University Press.

WALTERS, GLENN D.: LIFESTYLE THEORY

The intellectual curiosity for delinquent and/or criminal offending groups has been a dominant feature of the American criminological landscape for well over 100 years. While theoretical models and frameworks abound, critical concepts such as peer groups, social disorganization (e.g., collective efficacy), strain, social learning, differential association, self-control, rational choice, "career criminals" versus "criminal careers," and criminal propensity, to name a few, have come to define certain theoretical epochs in American criminology. Yet despite these advancements, the criminological debate continues. There persists an enduring interest in understanding and explaining the human (criminogenic) decision-making processes within developmental and/or integrative theories—an approach which seems to be consistent with the level of empirical evidence that has been amassed in this time period. Glenn D. Walters's *lifestyle theory* can be considered an early variant of a developmental-integrative theory of criminality, although his most recent work calls for an integrative-interactive theory of lifestyles. The following entry focuses on the foundational elements of lifestyle theory and its contribution to explicating criminality.

Lifestyle Theory

Walters, a clinical psychologist who has worked extensively with incarcerated criminal offender populations since the mid-1980s, offers a unique theory of human development grounded in basic philosophical fundamentals concerning the nature of humans, *normal* development, the nature and cause of deviancy, and change. At best, lifestyle theory offers a conceptual scheme for understanding criminality and proposes a clinically based model of intervention; countervailing the "nothing works" attitude toward prison-based rehabilitative efforts. Its theoretical heritage is rooted in early developmental theories of crime, social learning, personality theory, differential association theory, social control theory, general strain theory, the general theory of crime, the rational choice perspective, "the meaning of crime" theories, and cognitive treatment-behavioral models. Lifestyle theory's theoretical heritage is clearly evidenced in its 10 guiding postulates, which conceive of crime as a lifestyle of personal irresponsibility and social victimization.

Lifestyle theory is predicated on understanding the human (criminogenic) decision-making process as evolving over three primary yet interrelated areas, commonly referred to as the three Cs: (1) *conditions*, (2) *choices*, and (3) *cognitions*. Lifestyle theory holds that crime is a consequence of (external/internal) conditions to which a person is exposed, the choices he or she makes in life, and the cognitions he/she invokes in support of an evolving criminal lifestyle. Contemporary theoretical explanations of criminality must take into account an offender's belief system and resultant choices. It is only by focusing on the root cause of crime—that is, the criminogenic belief system of the "average" offender—that it is possible to understand how a person structures his or her experiences into specific cognitive patterns; belief systems that are supportive of a criminal lifestyle which promotes irresponsibility, self-indulgence, interpersonal intrusion, and chronic rule breaking. For lifestyle theorists, these behavioral characteristics are manifestations arising from earlier predispositions (conditions) leading to subsequent choices that are supportive of a particular belief system.

Conditions

Lifestyle criminality is the outcome of a sequence of early life events shaped by certain protective and risk factors operating simultaneously with one's social, physical, and psychological environment. How a person reconciles earlier developmental tasks (e.g., social attachment, self-image, and sensation-seeking behavior) and life events in these respective environments "determines" whether the individual adopts a frame of reference supportive of criminogenic options and concomitant lifestyles. Lifestyle theory is not deterministic but is defined by its emphasis on task theories of human development; the choices one makes relative to such early developmental tasks becomes critical in understanding adult criminality. Specifically, historical developmental conditions, vis-à-vis (1) *individual* variables (e.g., age, heredity, autonomic response, personality, language acquisition, and self image) and (2) *situation* variables (e.g., social environment, class, gender, culture, and peer relations), coupled with current-contextual conditions vis-à-vis (3) *person-centered* variables (e.g., a negative affect state) and (4) *situation* variables (e.g., environmental cues, interpersonal conflict, social influence, criminal companions), either expand or contract one's range of options. For Walters, this combination of factors inevitably delimits corresponding choices.

Choices

Lifestyle theory's emphasis is on understanding juvenile delinquency and adult criminality as being indicative of highly interrelated developmental points along the same continuum. At the foreground of this behavioral continuum are the choices a person enacts in support of such options. While *conditions*, both historical and contextual, function to

create certain criminogenic pathways and/or barriers to them, how respective informational cues are processed by an individual is dependent on the individual's input, processing, and output of information. First, risk and protective factors, exacerbating and mitigating factors, opportunity, and target selection are four primary informational sources that define the input stage. Second, how that information is processed is highly circumscribed by a person's cognitive maturation, limited time horizon, and motivation. Third, the decision (output) to engage or pursue a criminal option is a direct result of an individual's informational assessment of the prior two stages. However, according to Walters, the process is nonlinear, and there is a high degree of informational overlap in the process). For lifestyle theorists, the decision-making process and subsequent choices humans make are based on emotions, self-centeredness, and a delimited sense of time. This involves a highly emotive decision-making process defined by specific cognitive patterns or belief systems supportive of a criminal lifestyle.

Cognitions

Criminal lifestyles are a reflection of both structure and function leading to an identity process reified by a belief system that is behaviorally, cognitively, socially, and emotionally interactive, reciprocal, and integrative. A belief system or a series of criminal belief systems are comprising different *styles* of thinking (e.g., mollification, "cutoff," entitlement, power orientation, sentimentality, superoptimism, cognitive indolence, and discontinuity) that promote and substantiate a *criminal style* thinking and subsequent pattern of action. Subsequently, criminal belief systems reflect unrealistic, self-justifying, fragmented, and short-term thinking. The overall cognitive patterning in lifestyle theory is non-static; primacy is assigned to an individual's sense of affiliation, status, control, opportunity, and self-efficacy. While common cognitive traits; criminal belief systems adopt those that are facilitative and supportive of a criminal lifestyle.

Change

In terms of rehabilitative or correctional intervention, lifestyle theory proposes a fourth C—*change*—which is rooted in altering the aforementioned antisocial/criminal cognitive patterns. According to lifestyle theory, the criminal offender will not change unless there is a reason to do so largely because the criminal lifestyle is simply too rewarding and past correctional efforts (e.g., selective incapacitation), have only served to minimize accountability, remove personal responsibility, and, to some degree, reinforce an offender's "way of life." Under a lifestyle theory approach, the criminal offender, not society, should ultimately be held responsible for his or her actions. Therefore, contemporary rehabilitative or correctional efforts must provide incentives for criminal offenders to change—although the ultimate motivation for any change does rest with the criminal offender. The therapeutic tenets of personal accountability, self-competence, confidence building, and community support define the core elements of change under a lifestyle theory approach. While informed by research in desistance theory and "unassisted" change, a lifestyle theory of therapeutic change is, according to Walters, a model for clinical intervention.

Conclusion

Lifestyle theory is based on a condition-choice-cognition-change developmental continuum. Its central tenet is that crime is a lifestyle defined by supportive belief systems that are rooted in early developmental tasks, which produce specific thinking styles that lead to criminogenic options/choices. Lifestyle theory is not based on traditional notions of correctional intervention and/or crime control. Rather, its correctional programmatic philosophy is based on elements of desistance theory and natural recovery or "unassisted" change, fundamental concepts that have been underdeveloped in traditional criminological research. Lifestyle theory evolved from traditional inductive research since its inception based on clinical observations of incarcerated criminal offender groups. New study populations, such as non-incarcerated offenders, and traditional methods of theory testing should be employed in order to assess its empirical veracity. Lifestyle theory offers a contemporary conceptual model for understanding criminality, ideally primed for empirical testing and further refinement by the next generation of criminological scholars.

Wilson R. Palacios

See also Athens, Lonnie: Interaction and Violence; Lahey, Benjamin B., and Irwin D. Waldman: Developmental Propensity Model; Matza, David: Delinquency and Drift; Moffitt, Terrie E.: A Developmental Model of Life-Course-Persistent Offending; Wilson, James Q., and Richard J. Herrnstein: Crime and Human Nature

References and Further Readings

Agnew, R. (1985). A revised strain theory of delinquency. *Social Forces, 64,* 151–167.
Akers, R. L. (1998). *Social learning and social structure: A general theory of crime and deviance.* Boston: Northeastern University Press.
Cornish, D. B., & Clarke, R. V. (1985). *The reasoning crime: Rational choice perspectives on offending.* New York: Springer-Verlag.
Glueck, S., & Glueck, E. (1968). *Delinquents and non-delinquents in perspective.* Cambridge, MA: Harvard University Press.
Gottfredson, M. R., & Hirschi, T. (1990). *A general theory of crime.* Stanford, CA: Stanford University Press.
Hirschi, T. (1969). *Causes of Delinquency.* Berkeley: University of California Press.
Katz, J. (1988). *Seductions of crime: Moral and sensual attraction of doing evil.* New York: Perseus Books.
Mead, G. H. (1934). *Mind, self, and society.* Chicago: University of Chicago Press.
Sampson, R. J., & Laub, J. H. (1993). *Crime in the making: Pathways and turning points through life.* Cambridge, MA: Harvard University Press.
Walters, G. D. (2000). *Beyond behavior: Construction of an overarching psychological theory of lifestyles.* Westport, CT: Praeger.
Walters, G. D. (2000). *The self-altering process: Exploring the dynamic nature of lifestyle development and change.* Westport, CT: Praeger.
Walters, G. D. (2002). *Criminal belief systems: An integrated-interactive theory of lifestyles.* Westport, CT: Praeger.

WELLS, EDWARD L., AND JOSEPH H. RANKIN: DIRECT CONTROLS AND DELINQUENCY

Prior to Edward Wells and Joseph Rankin's 1988 article that focused on parental control and delinquency (see also Rankin & Wells, 1990), the relationship between *direct parental control* and involvement in delinquency had not been extensively studied by theorists. Although examined by F. Ivan Nye in 1958, direct control had decreased in theoretical importance in large part due to the prominence of Travis Hirschi's social bond theory. Hirschi argued that the key bond between parents and children was attachment. Youngsters who were emotionally attached to their parents cared about what their parents thought and, as a result, refrained from conduct—including delinquent acts—of which their parents disapproved. Even when not with them, parents had a psychological presence in their children's lives and thus exerted *indirect control* over their behavior.

Although not discounting the impact of the social bond of attachment, Wells and Rankin argued that the exclusive focus on indirect control diverted attention away from the systematic investigation of how direct parental control affected delinquent involvement. Building on Nye's work, they noted that direct control involved parents specifying their behavioral expectations (normative regulation), monitoring their children's conduct, and then disciplining or punishing children when misbehavior occurred. This control is direct because it largely involves parents having contact with their children and specifically attempting to regulate their behavior.

In their work, Wells and Rankin addressed these issues and reconceptualized the relationship between direct parental controls and delinquency. They revisited and included tenets of previous control theories such as Nye's direct control theory and Hirschi's social bond theory. They also examined the existing research on direct controls that focused on structural variables as well as recent research that had tested measures of parental supervision and the impact of various family elements on delinquency. The aim of their research was to see if direct controls are theoretically and empirically irrelevant and, if so, whether this relationship is more complex than had been previously measured.

Initial Study

Wells and Rankin tested their re-conceptualization on the Youth in Transition data, a longitudinal data set administered to a national sample of males. The initial analysis included data gathering at Waves I and II. The independent variables, which measured direct control, included (1) regulation/restriction—parents control over friends and activities, (2) strictness—perceived parental strictness as reported by participant, (3) punishment—parents ignoring or punishing wrongdoing, and (4) punitiveness—vigorousness and frequency of punishment.

The dependent variable utilized was a juvenile delinquency scale that measured levels of school delinquency, theft-vandalism, assault-threat, trouble with parents, trouble with police, and total delinquency.

Wells and Rankin's key findings were that (1) moderate levels of parental strictness show the lowest association with delinquency but low and high levels of strictness result in higher levels of delinquency, (2) frequent and severe punishment (punitiveness) was associated with higher levels of delinquency, and (3) trouble with police evidenced the least consistent relationship with delinquency. Thus, they found that the relationship between parental controls and juvenile delinquency is not simple, direct, or linear but complicated. It may be linear or non-linear and may be positive or negative. The study showed that direct parental controls are related to juvenile delinquency, but that the effect and statistical strengths of the relationships are dependent on the type of control examined and the form of testing utilized.

Second Study

This study set the stage for Wells and Rankin to continue testing and reconceptualizing direct parental controls. In 1990, they built upon their initial study and used previous research from social control theory, social learning theory, and child developmental perspectives to revisit their model. Their specific hypotheses were (1) that strong punishment by parents will effectively reduce delinquency only when there is a clear contingent relation between misbehaving and being punished and (2) that the impact of direct controls on delinquency is conditional upon the level of attachment between parents and children.

Although they again used the Youth in Transition Study, the variables differed from the original study. They included a scale for indirect control (attachment, identification, and positive communication with parents), a scale for direct control (supervision, strictness, contingency of punishment, and strength of punishment), and a scale for juvenile delinquency (school delinquency, family delinquency, theft-vandalism, assault-threat, trouble with police, and total delinquency). The key extension in their second study was the addition of the family process and attachment variables.

The second study confirmed their initial findings; parental controls did evidence a relationship with juvenile delinquency. Attachment also proved to be a key risk factor or predictor for juvenile delinquency. The effects of the variables were consistent throughout the measures of delinquency. The interactions that Rankin and Wells had proposed were statistically significant, but showed less strength then they originally predicted. They suggested that these limitations might be because the test of the hypothesis was inappropriate, the data set measurements may not have been measured accurately, the inability to control for additional causal variables, or the theories utilized may have needed qualification and further development.

Conclusion

Wells and Rankin have spotlighted the relationship between direct parental controls and delinquency in numerous venues. They brought attention to a relationship that was deemed as linear and/or nonexistent, reconceptualized the variables and the models, and found that appropriate measures and testing will evidence a stronger relationship between direct parental controls and juvenile delinquency than what theorists had previously claimed. In each study, they also called for the need to examine this relationship further, clarify the interactions between variables (in particular delinquency, contingency of punishment, and attachment), and to examine additional theoretical frameworks. Last, they discuss the implications that follow from their findings. They propose that implications for policy and prevention include developing effective childrearing processes, providing early parental intervention programs, and continuing examination of whether parental controls, either direct or indirect, are predictive of juvenile delinquency.

Alana Van Gundy-Yoder

See also Briar, Scott, and Irving Piliavin: Delinquency, Commitment, and Stake in Conformity; Hirschi, Travis: Social Control Theory; Nye, F. Ivan: Family Controls and Delinquency; Patterson, Gerald R.: Social Learning, the Family, and Crime; Reiss, Albert J., Jr.: Personal and Social Controls and Delinquency

References and Further Readings

Hirschi, T. (1969). *Causes of delinquency*. Berkeley: University of California Press.

Nye, F. I. (1958). *Family relationship and delinquent behavior*. New York: Wiley.

Rankin, J. H., & Wells, L. E. (1990). The effect of parental attachments and direct controls on delinquency. *Journal of Research in Crime and Delinquency, 27,* 140–165.

Rankin, J. H., & Wells, L. E. (2006). Social control theory and direct parental controls. In S. Henry & M. M. Lanier (Eds.), *Essential criminology reader* (pp. 119–128). Boulder, CO: Westview Press.

Seydlitz, R. (1993). Complexity in the relationships among direct and indirect parental controls and delinquency. *Youth and Society, 24,* 243–275.

Wells L. E., & Rankin, J. H. (1988). Direct parental controls and delinquency. *Criminology, 26,* 263–285.

WHYTE, WILLIAM FOOTE: STREET CORNER SOCIETY

Street Corner Society, by William Foote Whyte, is a neighborhood study recording the complex relationships among gangs, police, racketeers, and politicians in "Cornerville," now revealed as Boston's North End. This pioneering work in gang studies, participant observation and ethnic studies, published in 1943, has become a classic of sociological research and a model of urban ethnography.

Cornerville

In this participant observation study, Whyte studied two groups of second-generation Italians. Doc and his gang, the Nortons, were labeled the "corner boys" for their claim to the public space in their working-class neighborhood. The street corner was their turf, in contrast to Chick and his fellow club members, the "college boys," who were focused on getting a college education, and social mobility. Whyte also looked at the social structure of racketeering and politics in the community, diagramming the complex workings of the organizations within the community. He describes the political machine, with its voting patterns and numbers games in detail. Whyte discovered the interconnections between these street gangs, the politicians, and the racketeers, showing that the community was indeed organized and not a chaotic and problematic "slum." His work offered scholars a theoretical framework and methodological approach to exploring the dynamics and structures of small groups, leadership patterns, organizations, institutions, and communities.

Whyte first researched and wrote *Street Corner Society* on a fellowship from Harvard University prior to beginning his Ph.D. studies at the University of Chicago, where he revised the manuscript for his doctoral thesis. While Whyte was influenced by the Chicago School of Sociology and his advisors Lewis Worth and Herbert Blumer, he resisted framing his argument into the social disorganization framework of lower-class neighborhoods being dangerous problem areas characterized by high incidences of poverty, crime, and delinquency, then popular at Chicago and elsewhere. Through diagrams and written analysis, he shows how a disadvantaged ethnic group is highly organized, with many cohesive groupings. He concludes that "Cornerville's problem is not a lack of organization, as there are numerous patterns of interactions between individuals and groups, but the failure of its own social organization to mesh with the structure of society around it. The Italians are looked upon by upper class people as among the least desirable of the immigrant peoples" (Whyte, 1993b, p. 273).

Thus, this book offers insight into urban ethnicity and provides a basis for contemporary comparative research. It paints a portrait of a specific group, examining the Italian American community and the tension faced by those with ambition. Loyalty to the group is rewarded by the ethnic community, but it may lead to stigmatized status in the rest of society. Similarly, this dispute can be found today in the United States and in other industrialized nations with large numbers of immigrants, as the question of assimilation and cultural pluralism continues to stir debate. There are parallels between Italian Americans and Mexican Americans, as well as among other first- and second-generation immigrant groups, who often have long-term attachments to their neighborhoods or barrios.

Methods

Regarding methodology, Whyte used participant observation. Living in Cornerville for the 3 years of the study enabled him to closely observe, interact with, and develop a rapport with members of the community on an intimate and casual basis. This allowed him to get "insider" information to be able to see discrepancies between what people said and what they did. With the 1955 edition of the book, Whyte added a methodological appendix to the book, detailing his frank and detailed accounts of the research process, including his mistakes and ethical violations, such as intervening in an argument to improve relations with a racketeer and voting four times in a congressional election. We learn how his lack of research focus and research design allowed him ultimately to secure a clearer picture of the group he was studying. This disclosure encouraged other social scientists to write up their own accounts, creating more readily available methodological material (Whyte, 1993a). Additionally, Whyte included some key "informants," or individuals in the community, to help him with the research. Doing this allowed Whyte to gain access to certain venues, as well as to cultivate a trust among those in the community. Whyte has pointed out that he guided his involvement with Doc and "Sam Franco," or Angelo Orlandella, two leaders in the community, in terms of the principle of interpersonal reciprocity, where he tried to be helpful to them in ways he could, and they in turn seemed satisfied with the relationship. Whyte has described this process of collaboration as participatory action research, and he demonstrates how to build a reciprocal and beneficial relationship between key informants and the researcher. As Orlandella stated in an interview:

Whyte had identified me as a leader . . . for the first time there was some recognition in my life that even I had something to contribute to society. We observed and analyzed together our observations to determine whether or not the data being collected made sociological sense.

Further, getting feedback from Whyte was most important to me as his assistant and collaborator. It was so different, someone was interested. (Joe, 1993, p. 49)

While gangs of the present are different from gangs of the 1930s, the commonality is that gangs have informal leaders. As Whyte advocates, one needs to be able to identify the informal leader because he or she is the person that proposes action for the group. Additionally, for intervention and change to take place, one needs to work with the leader. In order to see what is going on in complex organizations, it is crucial to focus on the organized social structure of the community and the individuals in that community to most effectively see what is happening.

This methodology has left a legacy for gang research. A few gang researchers have based their studies on this type of collaborative approach (e.g., Brotherton & Barrios, Hagedorn, Venkatesh), providing insight into contemporary gang issues. This participant observation approach is vital to understanding today's gangs in a way that differs from social surveys. While statistical analyses can reveal certain aspects of social life, they cannot get at the lived everyday experiences of individuals. There is a subjective, selective process involved in participant observation (Boelen, 1992) since the researcher cannot observe and document all social action. Whyte argues, however, that the researcher must take a stand and describe what she or he believes to be going on in order for it to be useful for policy and program planning.

Conclusion

Whyte's *Street Corner Society* is a classic ethnographic study documenting the social cleavages and class structure in American society. It has influenced many researchers due to its methodology and attention to social interaction and has had an enduring legacy on contemporary research of ethnic groups and gangs.

Leslie A. Martino-Velez

See also Cloward, Richard A., and Lloyd E. Ohlin: Delinquency and Opportunity; Cohen, Albert K.: Delinquent Boys; Sampson, Robert J.: Collective Efficacy Theory; Shaw, Clifford R., and Henry D.

McKay: Social Disorganization Theory; Spergel, Irving: Neighborhoods and Delinquent Subcultures

References and Further Readings

Adler, P. A., Adler, P., & Johnson, J. M. (Eds.). (1992). Street corner revisited [Special issue]. *Journal of Contemporary Ethnography, 21.*

Boelen, W. A. M. (1992). Street corner society: Cornerville revisited. *Journal of Contemporary Ethnography, 21,* 11–51.

Brotherton, D., & Barrios, L. (2004). *The almighty Latin king and queen nation: Street politics and the transformation of a New York City street gang.* New York: Columbia University Press.

Hagedorn, J. (1998). *People and folks: Gangs, crime and the underclass in a rustbelt city* (2nd ed.). Chicago: Lakeview Press.

Joe, K. (1993). The legacy of *Street Corner Society* and gang research in the 1990s: An Interview with William F. Foote. *The Gang Journal, 1,* 45–51.

Orlandella, A. (1993). *A more effective strategy for dealing with inner city street corner gangs.* Unpublished manuscript.

Venkatesh, S. (2000). *American project: The rise and fall of a modern ghetto.* Cambridge, UK: Cambridge University Press.

Whyte, W. (1992). *Participatory action research.* Newbury Park, CA: Sage.

Whyte, W. (1993a). Revisiting *Street Corner Society. Sociological Forum, 8,* 285–298.

Whyte, W. (1993b). *Street corner society* (4th ed.). Chicago: University of Chicago Press.

WIDOM, CATHY SPATZ: THE CYCLE OF VIOLENCE

The cycle of violence is the process in which individuals who are victims of child abuse become more likely to engage in violent and criminal behavior as adults. Cathy Spatz Widom has been a leading scholar on the cycle of violence and has published research that (1) shows support for the cycle of violence, (2) attempts to explain the cycle of violence, (3) examines how females in particular respond to child abuse and neglect, and (4) attempts to explain resilience to abuse and neglect. Her primary research was the building block that established support for the relationship between abuse and neglect. Subsequent follow-ups and extensions have been conducted that elaborated on the relationship between childhood victimization and crime.

The Primary Research

In 1992, sponsored by the National Institute of Justice, Widom sought to examine whether violence begets violence. That is, Widom looked to answer the question "How likely is it that today's abused and neglected children will become tomorrow's violent offenders?" (1992, p. 1). Widom refers to the cycle of violence as the idea that individuals who are exposed to violence through abuse in childhood will be predisposed to violence as adults.

Widom's research technique, the prospective cohorts design, provided a major advance to literature examining the link between child abuse and criminal behavior. This is because it identified a sample of abused and neglected children and longitudinally followed them to adulthood. It was considered prospective (as opposed to retrospective) because it began with the independent variable of interest (in this case child abuse) and followed subjects in order to examine long-term consequences (in this case criminal behavior). Doing so allowed Widom to use child abuse to predict the likelihood of engaging in criminal behavior as a juvenile and adult.

Widom's technique is also considered rigorous for two other reasons. First, she used a large "treatment" sample of youth who were abused and neglected as well as a comparison or "control" group of youths who were not abused and neglected. Widom was thus able to examine differences in criminal behavior between a large group of 908 youths who were abused and neglected to a group of 667 youths who were not. Second, Widom's method of selecting the comparison group worked to control for other measures that would likely produce a spurious relationship. That is, Widom selected youths for the comparison group who were similar in terms of race, gender, socioeconomic status, and jurisdiction. Doing this ensured that one of these factors did not artificially cause the appearance of a relationship between child abuse and criminal behavior.

The sample of abused subjects was taken from official court records of youths in a Midwestern jurisdiction whose parental figures were charged with abuse and neglect before the youths were age 11 (for a review of the methods, see Widom, 1992). The comparison sample consisted of youths taken from the same jurisdiction who were of similar age, sex, race, and socioeconomic status. The court documents of the abused and neglected sample were reviewed, and each incident of abuse and neglect was categorized into either physical abuse, sexual abuse, or neglect. The outcome variable for the analysis was arrest for criminal behavior. Local, state, and federal background checks were used to gather information regarding the number and types of arrests for the treatment and comparison subjects. Widom also conducted a second phase of the study in which the subjects were located and interviewed as adults. This was used to provide insight into other social consequences of abuse.

Descriptive analyses of the court records indicate that who perpetrated the abuse varied by abuse type. For example, mothers and fathers accounted for almost all incidents of neglect, but only accounted for about a quarter of incidents of sexual abuse. Unknown and known unrelated adults accounted for the majority of incidents of sexual abuse. Although physical abuse was committed by the mother and father in over 55 percent of the cases, stepfathers also accounted for almost a quarter of these incidents.

Widom found that being a victim of abuse or neglect increased the likelihood of arrest as a juvenile and as an adult. While only 17 percent of the comparison group experienced a juvenile arrest, 28 percent of the abused and neglected group did. This means that being abused and neglected increased the odds of a juvenile arrest occurring by 54 percent. As an adult, 29 percent of the abused sample was arrested compared to only 21 percent of the comparison group, equating to a 38 percent increase in the likelihood of an adult arrest for the treatment group. Further, the abused and neglected group was at an increased risk for being arrested for violence. Eight percent of the comparison group was arrested for a violent crime whereas 11 percent of the abused group was arrested. This indicates that being abused or neglected increased the odds of a violent arrest by 39 percent. Also of interest, Widom's findings indicate that being neglected and being physically abused were the two types of abuse that were most strongly associated with being arrested for violence. She also located 500 of the original treatment subjects 20 years later and conducted 2-hour interviews regarding the participants' social and mental issues. Preliminary findings suggest that abuse may also encourage poor emotional health, substance abuse, and failure in the educational and occupational realms.

These results show support for the cycle of violence hypothesis, indicating that being physically abused was associated with increased odds of being arrested for violence. Further, being neglected also increased the likelihood of a violent arrest occurring, suggesting that the neglect of children also has criminogenic consequences. Finally, the results reveal that childhood victimization increases the likelihood of all criminal behavior, not just violent acts.

In 2001, Widom and Michael Maxfield provided a 6-year follow-up on the official arrest records of the participants in Widom's 1992 study. The 6-year follow-up is significant because it increases the average age at the follow-up from 26 to 32, thus gathering more valid and reliable information from the participants when they were firmly situated in adulthood. Generally speaking, Widom and Maxfield's results are consistent with Widom's earlier findings. They found that 27 percent of the abused and neglected group experienced a juvenile arrest, compared to only 17 percent of the comparison group. This means that the odds of a juvenile arrest were 59 percent higher in the abused and neglected group. For adult arrests, 42 percent of the abused and neglected group, versus 33 percent of the comparison group, was arrested as adults, equating to an increase in the odds of being arrested by 28 percent for the abused and neglected group. Finally, the abused and neglected group was 30 percent more likely to be arrested, with 18 percent of the abused and neglected group being arrested versus 14 percent of the comparison group.

Of interest, Widom and Maxfield's findings also indicated that abuse and neglect placed females at an increased risk for arrests, including violent and drug arrests. When examining race, the effects of abuse and neglect were shown to be stronger for African Americans. These findings indicate that gender and race are important factors to consider when assessing the relationship between child abuse and later criminal behavior.

In sum, Widom's primary research on the cycle of violence used a rigorous prospective cohorts design to examine the impact of official records of abuse and neglect on the likelihood of being arrested. This work, coupled with Widom and Maxfield's follow-up, provided four major conclusions. First, they reveal that being abused or neglected in childhood is associated with arrests both as a juvenile and as an adult. Second, physical abuse and neglect, in particular, are associated in increases in violence. This suggests that it is not only violence that begets violence, but also that neglect is an important risk factor for violent arrests. Finally, this research indicates race and gender are important moderators of the relationship between child abuse and arrests.

Explaining the Relationship Between Child Abuse and Criminal Behavior

Although this research demonstrates that abuse and neglect are risk factors for criminal behavior, it fails to illuminate the causal link between abuse and crime. To do this, more information is needed regarding the intermediate outcomes through which abuse influences criminal behavior. Acknowledging this issue, Widom extended her original research by locating the study participants and conducting in-person interviews (see Widom & Maxfield, 2001). These interviews lasted around 2 hours and collected information on potential mediators and moderators of the relationship between child abuse and criminal behavior. This research is presented in a series of articles that attempt to explain the relationship between childhood victimization and later criminal behavior.

When explaining the relationship between two concepts, one major goal is to identify the intermediate outcomes, or the factors that are the reason that the cause is creating the effect. That is, intermediate outcomes are factors that explain why child abuse increases the likelihood of criminal behavior. For example, physical abuse may cause a youth to struggle in school. School failure could then encourage delinquency in adolescence. In this example, school failure is the intermediate outcome because it is the mechanism through which physical abuse impacts criminal behavior. Widom's extensions of her primary research have been instrumental to identifying the intermediate outcomes that explain the relationship between child abuse and criminal behavior.

The Role of Running Away

In 1999, Jeanne Kaufman and Widom examined whether running away was a mechanism through which child abuse affected criminal behavior. To measure running away, the authors used both official records of juvenile arrests for running away as well as self-report measures obtained from the supplemental interviews. Kaufman and Widom first established that the abused and neglected group was more likely to have run away from home. Depending upon the measure, they found that youths in the abused and neglect sample were 2.5 to 3.5 times more likely to report running away from home as a juvenile. Next, Kaufman and Widom examined the relationship between running away and juvenile arrest. Their findings indicate that both running away and being abused and neglected independently predict juvenile arrests. This finding suggests that although childhood victimization encourages criminal behavior through running away from home, this does not explain the entire relationship between childhood victimization and juvenile arrests.

The Role of Aggression and Alcohol Problems

Widom, Amie Schuck, and Helene Raskin White (2006) examined the intermediate outcomes of aggression and alcohol problems in the relationship between childhood victimization and arrests for violence. During the follow-up interviews, the respondents were asked whether, before age 15, they engaged in a series of aggressive behaviors (e.g., hurting animals, using weapons, destroying property, and starting fights). Alcohol problems were assessed at the time of the interview and measured the total number of lifetime alcohol symptoms (e.g., experiencing withdrawal symptoms, marked tolerance, or continuing to use even though the use is causing problems). Using structural equation modeling, Widom et al. showed a pathway from abuse to violent arrests through aggressive symptoms and alcohol problems. That is, abuse and neglect were associated with increases in the measure of aggressive symptoms and aggressive symptoms were associated with increases in alcohol problems. Finally, alcohol symptoms were

associated with increases in the likelihood of arrests for violence. It is worth noting that beyond the impact of childhood victimization, abuse also maintained a direct effect on violent arrests. Thus similar to the relationship between childhood victimization and juvenile arrests, the indirect effects are not able to explain the entire relationship between abuse and criminal behavior.

Females, Childhood Victimization, and Criminal Behavior

Another area that Widom has studied is the extent to which there are gender differences in the cycle of violence. Both Widom's primary study and Widom and Maxfield's follow-up study found that in females, abuse and neglect was associated with criminal behavior. Widom and Joseph Kuhns (1996) examined the relationship between child abuse and promiscuity, teen pregnancy, and prostitution. They found that abused females were almost three times more likely to report engaging in prostitution. Males who were abused were not more likely to engage in prostitution. When examining the impact of different types of abuse, Widom and Kuhns found that sexual abuse and neglect, not physical abuse, predicted engaging in prostitution. Contrary to their predictions, they did not find that sexual abuse (or any other type of abuse) was related to promiscuity or teen pregnancy.

Shuck and Widom attempted to explain the relationship between female child abuse and later alcohol problems using an intermediate measure of emotional health. Their measures of emotional health included depressive symptoms, worthlessness, social isolation, self-esteem, and the use of drugs or alcohol to cope with problems. They found that abused and neglected individuals scored higher on depressive symptoms, worthlessness, self-esteem, and using drugs to cope with problems. Further, these items were found to be correlated with experiencing alcohol problems. Shuck and Widom's multivariate findings suggested that, all else being equal, child abuse affects later alcohol problems through its impact on depression and by encouraging women to adopt a coping strategy that involves using drugs and alcohol.

White and Widom (2008) examined whether measures of females' reports of posttraumatic stress disorder, stressful life events, and delinquent behavior mediated the relationship between childhood victimization and measures of substance abuse as an adult. Self-report measures of the mediators were obtained during young adulthood (around age 29), while measures of illicit drug use and alcohol problems during adulthood (around age 40) were obtained from another supplemental survey of the individuals that were able to be located. They found that all three measures were predicted by childhood victimization and that the measures in turn predicted problems with substance abuse. When examining the relationship between abuse and illicit drug use in adulthood, White and Widom found that again all three factors partially mediated the relationship between child abuse and neglect.

Helen Wilson and Widom elaborated upon White and Wilson by considering four other mediating factors between child abuse and neglect and illicit drug use. Their intermediate measures consisted of prostitution, homelessness, criminal behavior, and school problems. In females, they found that these four measures were highly related and that they were best understood as a combined measure of social problems. Using this combined measure, Wilson and Widom found that females who experienced child abuse and neglect also scored highly on the measure of social problems and that social problems were in turn related to illicit drug use.

To summarize, Widom's research on female offenders has found support for the effects of childhood abuse and neglect on the criminal behavior. This research has shown that childhood sexual abuse and neglect is related to gender specific crimes such as prostitution. Widom has also published research suggesting that childhood victimization has a negative impact on mental and emotional health, stressful life events, delinquency, and more general measures of social disadvantage in early adulthood. Further, these negative outcomes in early adulthood predict drug and alcohol use in later adulthood. Taken as a whole, this suggests that the relationship between childhood victimization and later substance abuse is mediated by social and psychological factors.

Explaining Resilience

Although Widom's research has found substantial support for the negative impact of child abuse on

criminal behavior, it has also consistently noted that criminal behavior is not inevitable. Many individuals are resilient in the face of child abuse, and not surprisingly, there are individual and environmental characteristics that encourage resilience. Widom and Linda Brzustowicz (2006) examined how biological factors inhibit the relationship between childhood victimization and criminal behavior. Specifically, they examined whether genotypes for monoamine oxidase A (MAOA) moderated the relationship between child abuse and criminal behavior. MAOA is a chemical in the brain that helps to regulate levels of neurotransmitters. Low levels of MAOA have been found to be associated with aggression, sensation seeking, and psychopathy. The genotype for MAOA indicated whether the individual was at genetic risk to have low levels of MAOA. Widom and Brzustowicz found that individuals that were abused and neglected and had the genotype for high levels of MAOA did not experience higher levels of criminal behavior. Conversely, those with the genotype for high levels of MAOA did report more criminal behavior. This reveals that biological predispositions may help explain why some individuals do not respond to child abuse and neglect with criminal behavior.

Kimberly DuMont, Widom, and Sally Czaja (2007) attempted to predict resilience using both individual and environmental factors. They measured resilience by examining success in a wide variety of social domains, such as criminal behavior, school, employment, and housing. They found that overall, 48 percent of the youths in their sample that were abused and neglected met their criteria for resilience. They also found that measures of stable placements, stressful events, supportive relationships, and interactions between socioeconomic status and cognitive ability all predicted stability. This suggests that both individual and environmental factors can encourage prosocial growth in children who are abused and neglected.

Conclusion

Widom has shown substantial support for the cycle of violence. This was accomplished using a sophisticated, prospective cohorts design that examined the long-term impact of abuse and neglect on criminal behavior. Further, her research suggests that it is not just the cycle of violence that exists; rather, multiple forms of abuse and neglect are tied to multiple types of criminal behavior, such as prostitution and substance abuse. Also of interest, Widom has attempted to explain the relationship between abuse and criminal behavior. Her research reveals that, especially for females, the relationship between childhood victimization is at least partially explained through measures of emotional health, stressful life events, and other social events during adulthood. Finally, Widom has also shown that individual and social factors, such as levels of MAOA and supportive relationships, are related to resilience in the face of childhood victimization.

Matthew D. Makarios

See also Agnew, Robert S.: General Strain Theory; Alarid, Leanne Fiftal, and Velmer S. Burton, Jr.: Gender and Serious Offending; Chesney-Lind, Meda: Feminist Model of Female Delinquency; Fishbein, Diana H.: Biosocial Theory

References and Further Readings

DuMont, K. A., Widom, C. S., & Czaja, S. J. (2007). Predictors of resilience in abused and neglected children grown-up: The role of individual and neighborhood characteristics. *Child Abuse and Neglect, 31,* 255–274.

Kaufman, J. G., & Widom, C. S. (1999). Childhood victimization, running away, and delinquency. *Journal of Research in Crime and Delinquency, 36,* 347–370.

Shuck, A. M., & Widom, C. S. (2001). Childhood victimization and alcohol symptoms in females: Causal inferences and hypothesized mediators. *Child Abuse and Neglect, 25,* 1069–1092.

Widom, C. S. (1992). *The cycle of violence* (NCJ No. 136607). Washington, DC: National Institute of Justice.

Widom, C. S. (2000). *Childhood victimization: Early adversity, later psychopathology* (NCJ No. 180077). Washington DC: National Institution of Justice.

Widom, C. S. (2000). Childhood victimization and the derailment of girls and women into the criminal justice system. In J. E. Samuels & J. Thomas (Eds.), *Plenary papers of the 1999 Conference on Criminal Justice Research and Evaluation: Enhancing policy and practice through research: Vol. 3. Research on women and girls in the justice system* (pp. 27–36) (NCJ No. 180973). Washington, DC: National Institute of Justice.

Widom, C. S., & Brzustowicz, L. M. (2006). MAOA and the "Cycle of Violence": Child abuse and neglect, MAOA genotype, and risk for violent and antisocial behavior. *Biological Psychiatry, 60,* 684–689.

Widom, C. S., & Kuhns, J. B. (1996). Childhood victimization and subsequent risk for promiscuity, prostitution, and teenage pregnancy: A prospective study. *American Journal of Public Health, 86,* 1607–1612.

Widom, C. S., & Maxfield, M. G. (2001). *An update on the cycle of violence* (NCJ No. 184894). Washington, DC: National Institute of Justice.

Widom, C. S., Schuck, A. M., & White, H. R. (2006). An examination of pathways from childhood victimization to violence: The role of early aggression and problematic alcohol use. *Violence and Victims, 21,* 675–690.

White, H. R., & Widom, C. S. (2008). Three potential mediators of the effects of child abuse and neglect on adulthood substance use among women. *Journal of Drug Problems, 69,* 337–347.

Wilson, H. W., & Widom, C. S. (2009). A prospective examination of the path from child abuse and neglect to illicit drug use in middle adulthood: The potential mediating role of four risk factors. *Journal of Youth Adolescence, 38,* 340–354.

WIKSTRÖM, PER-OLOF H.: SITUATIONAL ACTION THEORY

Why do people engage in acts of crime? Two central ideas in criminological theory are that people's crime involvement is dependent on (1) *who* they are (their characteristics and experiences) and (2) *where* they are (the features of the environments in which they take part). Although many criminological theories have contributed considerably to our understanding of the role of person and environmental differences in crime causation, these two strands of thinking are rarely combined into a developed integrated theoretical framework.

Most criminological theory lacks an expounded theory of action that specifies how putative person and environmental characteristics (and particularly their interaction) impact action (acts of crime). Without knowing how (through what process) suggested person and environmental factors are supposed to influence acts of crime, it is arguably difficult to evaluate their potential role and relative importance in crime causation and thus problematic to properly integrate person and environmental influences (and the role of person and environment change) in the explanation of people's crime involvement (and its changes).

A further problem with many criminological theories is that they are not always fully explicit about what the theory is meant to explain (i.e., what crime is). Since an explanation is always an explanation *of* something, it is difficult to develop an effective account of the causes of crime without a clear definition of what crime is (i.e., of what the theory aims to explain).

Situational Action Theory

Situational action theory (SAT) is a newly developed general theory of moral action and crime that aims to integrate person and environmental explanatory perspectives within the framework of a situational action theory. It seeks to address central problems in mainstream criminological theory; the unclear definition of crime, the poor understanding of causal mechanisms, the poor integration of levels of explanation, and the inadequate understanding of the role of development and change. The theory builds upon insights from various conventional criminological theories and research traditions as well as draws upon social and behavioral sciences theory and research more generally.

The fundamental arguments of situational action theory are that

1. Acts of crime are moral actions (actions guided by what is the right or wrong thing to do or not to do in a particular circumstance) and therefore need to be explained as such.

2. People engage in acts of crime because they (a) come to see such acts as a viable action alternative and (b) choose (habitually or deliberately) to carry them out.

3. The likelihood that a person will come to see an act of crime as an action alternative and choose to carry out such an act ultimately depends on his or her crime propensity (grounded in his or her action-relevant moral values and emotions and capability to exercise self-control) and its interplay with his or her exposure to criminogenic settings (defined by their action-relevant moral rules and the level of their enforcement).

4. The role of broader social conditions and their changes (like social integration and segregation), and the role of individual development and change (life histories), should be analyzed as the causes of the causes.

5. Relevant causes of the causes of crime are only those social conditions and aspects of life-histories that can be demonstrated to influence the development of people's propensity (morality and ability to exercise self-control) and influence the emergence of, and people's differential exposure to, settings with particular criminogenic features (settings whose moral context and deterrent qualities may encourage or discourage acts of crime).

A Realist Approach

Situational action theory intends to provide causal explanations that tell us why and how acts of crime occur. SAT is based on a realist perspective. Two important assumptions of realism are (1) the world exists independent of us and our theorizing about it (e.g., in science we do not invent causes, we discover them); and (2) many important explanatory processes are unobservable, or partly unobservable (i.e., scientific knowledge is not only what is observable).

A realist perspective does not deny that different people may perceive the same reality differently but it insists that such differences can be rationally explained by factors such as differences in people's skills, knowledge, values, and experiences. For example, why some people in a particular setting will see crime as an action alternative and others not has to do with differences in their moral values and moral habits.

In a realist perspective just establishing causation (i.e., demonstrating that if we manipulate x then y will change in predicted ways) is not enough to provide a scientific explanation, we also have to demonstrate through what process the alleged cause/s make/s the effect happen. A proper theory of crime causation provides explanation by suggesting plausible causal processes (mechanisms) that link the putative cause/s and the effect and thus tells us how the outcome is produced. It thereby answers the question of why people engage in acts of crime.

Crime as Moral Action

There is little doubt that when explaining crime we explain human actions. Actions are sequences of bodily movements—or withheld bodily movements—under the guidance of the actor (e.g., speaking or hitting). However, any particular action can, in principle, be defined as a crime and there are variations over historic time and between places (e.g., countries) in what kinds of action are regarded as crime. Moreover, specific actions, like hitting or even shooting another person, may be considered crimes in some circumstances but not in others.

What defines crime is thus not any particular type of action but the fact that carrying out a particular action (or refraining from carrying out an action) in a particular circumstance is regarded as breaching a rule of conduct stated in the law. The question of explaining why some acts are regarded as crime and others are not is an important question. However, a question that is different from the question of why people follow or breach the rules of law. The question of why we have the rules of conduct we have, and why people follow or breach those rules, may be regarded as the two prime questions of criminology. Here we are only concerned with the latter.

Situational action theory argues that crime is best analyzed as moral action. SAT defines *moral action* as action guided by moral rules about what it is right or wrong to do in a particular circumstance. It defines *crimes* as breaches of moral rules defined in law. The *law* is a set of moral rules of conduct, but far from all moral rules are regulated by law. Acts of crime are thus viewed as a special case of moral rule breaking more generally. The advantage of conceptualizing crime as breaches of moral rules defined in law is that it focuses on what all kinds of crime, in all places, at all times, have in common: namely, (moral) rule breaking. What is to be explained by a theory of moral action is thus why people (follow and) breach moral rules, and what is to be explained specifically by a (sub-) theory of crime is why people (follow and) breach moral rules defined in law.

Any action that is guided by rules of what is right or wrong to do in a particular circumstance is a moral action. There is no difference in that respect between, for example, lying to a friend, stealing a CD in a shop, or blowing up a person by a roadside bomb. All are examples of moral actions. Hence, they can all be explained within the same theoretical framework. What may differ in the explanation of different kinds of moral action (acts of crime) is not the process (the perception-choice process) leading up to the action, but the content of the moral context (the action-relevant moral rules) and a person's morality (the action-relevant moral values and emotions) that drive the process and the broader social processes (the causes of the causes) that generate particular moral contexts (contents) in which people develop and act. In all cases (e.g., lying, shoplifting, or roadside bombing), the actor has to perceive the particular action as a viable alternative and choose to carry out the act. However, the specific moral background that guides whether, for example, an act of shoplifting is perceived as an action alternative will differ from that which guides whether an act of roadside bombing is perceived as an action alternative.

The Importance of Rules and Rule Guidance

Situational action theory is based on explicit assumptions about human nature and its relation to social order. Humans are viewed as essentially rule-guide actors and social order as fundamentally based on the adherence to common rules of conduct (the social order is essentially a moral order). Explaining human moral action and crime has to do with understanding the interplay between common moral rules of conduct and a person's moral rules in shaping his or her moral development and providing grounds for his or her moral actions.

Most criminological theory does not have an explicit theory of action. Theories that do generally allude to the importance of choice (as guided by self-interest and rationality) without further detailing its role in the explanation of crime. SAT accepts that rationality and self-interest (at times) play a role in guiding human action, but it reasons that on a more fundamental level humans are rule-guided actors. Human actions (including acts of crime) therefore ultimately have to be explained as rule-guided action.

The Situational Mechanism

Most criminological theory focuses on either the role of the person or the environment in the explanation of crime. Situational action theory is developed to overcome the common (but unfruitful) divide between person and environmental explanations of moral action and crime. It achieves this by proposing a situational mechanism (a perception–choice process), which links the person and his or her environment to his or her actions. It postulates that all action (including acts of crime) is ultimately an outcome of (1) what action alternatives a person perceives and, on that basis, (2) what choices he or she makes. In contrast to most choice-based theories, which focus on how people choose among predetermined alternatives, situational action theory stresses the importance of why people perceive certain action alternatives (and not others) in the first place. Perception of action alternatives thus plays a more fundamental role in explaining action than the process of choice (which is secondary to perception of action alternatives).

SAT provides a clear demarcation criterion for evaluating which person and environment factors (correlates) are potential causes or merely correlates; only those person and environmental factors that can be demonstrated to (directly or indirectly) affect how a person perceives his or her action alternatives and make choices are causally relevant in the explanation of moral action (and acts of crime). "Indirectly" refers to factors that may be considered causes of the causes—for example, factors that affect a person's development of morality and capability to exercise self-control or factors that affect the emergence of criminogenic settings.

Two Kinds of Agency: Deliberation and Habit

One of the most difficult problems in explaining human action is reconciling the role of deterministic and voluntaristic forces in the explanation of action. Most criminological theories appear to operate with (at least) an implicit assumption that human action is deterministic. SAT aims to integrate behavioristic (deterministic) and voluntaristic (free will) approaches to the explanation of moral action and crime. It does so by recognizing that human action (including law abidance and acts of crime) may be (predominantly) caused either by habit or rational deliberation.

Man is the source of his or her actions. To say that people have agency is to say that they have causal powers (powers to make things happen). SAT asserts that people exercise agency within the context of rule-guided choice. Rule guidance can take the form of either deliberation or habit. Habitual action involves automatically applying experienced based moral rules of conduct to a setting, while deliberation involves taking moral rules of conduct into consideration when actively choosing between action alternatives. Habitual action is oriented toward the past, while deliberate action is oriented toward the future. When people act habitually, they routinely apply past experiences to guide current action; when they act deliberately they try to anticipate future consequences of perceived action alternatives and choose the best course of action.

Only in choice processes when people deliberate do they exercise free will and are they subject to the influence of their ability to exercise self-control (internal control) or respond to deterrence cues (external controls). Whether or not a choice of action tends to be an outcome of deliberation or habit depends on the actor's familiarity with the circumstances in which he or she operates. Habits are created by repeated exposure to particular circumstances, which leads to action becoming automated, rather than deliberate, in these and similar circumstances.

The Role of Motivation: A Necessary but Not Sufficient Cause of Moral Action

People commit acts of crime for all sorts of reason (e.g., greed, anger, or boredom). There are no particular motives (e.g., desires, needs, or wants) that make people breach moral rules (commit acts of crime). However, to claim that motivation has no role in crime causation is a mistake. According to SAT, motivation is a necessary but not sufficient cause of moral action. It is part of the process that moves people to action and has a general directional influence on what kinds of acts of moral rule breaking a person may perceive and consider.

The two main classes of motivation in crime causation are temptation and provocation. These motivations come about as an outcome of the person-setting interaction. A temptation occurs (1) when there is a connection between a person's desires (wants, needs) and an opportunity to fulfill a desire or (2) when there is an opportunity for a person to fulfill a commitment he or she has made. A provocation occurs when a friction (an unwanted external interference) causes a person to feel anger or annoyance.

While acknowledging that motivation (temptations, provocations) has a general directional influence on moral action, SAT states that the crucial factor in the explanation of moral action is the interplay between a person's morality (values, emotions) and the moral context in which he or she operates. The outcome of this interaction will serve as a moral filter determining whether or not he or she will act upon temptations or provocations. Many people are, for example, disadvantaged and frustrated for various reasons, without breaking moral rules (or committing acts of crime) to overcome or change conditions perceived to cause their disadvantage or frustration.

Person and Propensity

Propensity may be defined as a person's tendency to see crime (or a particular type of crime) as an action alternative and to act upon such an alternative. The idea that people have different propensities to engage in acts of crime is the idea that if different people encounter the same setting they will respond differently. Some are more likely than others to engage in acts of crime.

Individuals will vary in their propensity to engage in a particular moral action depending on their moral values and emotions. Moral emotions (shame, guilt) attached to violating a particular moral rule may be regarded as a measure of the strength with which a person holds a particular moral rule. For example, while many people may think it is wrong to steal something from another person, some may feel very strongly about this while others may not. Those who feel less strongly about stealing from others may be regarded as having a higher propensity to engage in such action.

An individual's ability to exercise self-control (i.e., to act in accordance with his or her morality in the face of temptations and provocations) can also significantly affect his or her crime propensity. An individual's ability to exercise self-control is influenced both by relatively stable individual characteristics (executive capabilities) and momentary influences, such as high levels of stress and intoxication (see Wikström & Treiber, 2007).

However, the ability to exercise self-control is only important when an individual perceives crime (or moral rule breaking) as an alternative, because self-control exerts its effects through the process of choice. When an individual deliberates over whether or not to commit an act of crime, his or her ability to exercise self-control influences the process of choice and plays a causal role in his or her decision to offend (or not offend).

Environment and Exposure

People do not act in a social vacuum. It is important to bear in mind that propensities always need some environmental inducement to get activated. Individuals will vary in their exposure to moral contexts (external moral rules and their enforcement linked to particular settings). The extent to which moral rule following in a particular context is enforced (supervised and breaches sanctioned) may be regarded as the strength of the moral context. The idea that settings vary in their criminogenic features is the idea that the same person will respond differently to different kinds of settings. A person will be more likely to engage in acts of crime in some settings than in others.

A key assumption of SAT is that human action (and development) is directly influenced only by the settings in which people take part. A *setting* may be defined as the part of the environment that an individual, at a particular moment in time, can access with his or her senses, including any media present. The key environmental factor that determines whether or not a setting is criminogenic is its moral context (the moral rules that apply to the particular setting and their levels of enforcement). The configuration of the settings a person takes part in (during a specific period of time) may be referred to as his or her *activity field* (e.g., daily or weekly activity field). A person's activity field is the environment to which he or she is exposed during a specific period.

In terms of analyzing action, the moral context of settings is significant because it is within such a context that opportunity (which may create temptation if connecting to a person's particular desires and needs or his or her commitments) and friction (which may create provocation if evoking feelings of annoyance or anger in a person) appear. Temptation and provocation are key motivational elements emerging from the person-setting interaction. However, as discussed earlier, it is the moral context of the setting (its moral rules and deterrent qualities), and its interaction with a person's morality and ability to exercise self-control, that, by acting as a moral filter, will determine whether or not a person will act on a particular temptation or provocation.

The Importance of Causal Interaction: Propensity and Exposure

Causes of moral actions (and acts of crime) are the factors which influence the moral perception of action alternatives and influence the process of moral choice. Causes of crime are thus factors which influence a person to see an act of crime (a particular crime) as an action alternative and factors that influence a person's process of choice to carry out such an action alternative.

All human action is a result of the interaction between person and environment. According to situational action theory, all moral actions are an outcome of a person's propensity (to engage in the particular moral action) and his or her exposure to environmental inducements (to engage in the particular moral action):

$$\text{Propensity} \times \text{Exposure} = \text{Action}$$

The situational action theory does not propose a simple additive model of propensity and exposure but that propensity and exposure interact to determine a person's crime involvement (Figure 1). Specific combinations of propensity and exposure are likely to produce specific outcomes in terms of a person's level of crime involvement.

The *action relevant propensity* is those moral values and emotions (supported or undermined by the person's capability to exercise self-control) that are relevant to a particular moral action. For example, if we aim to explain acts of shoplifting, all those moral values and emotions relevant to seeing acts of shoplifting as an action alternative and relevant to choosing such an alternative for action constitute the action relevant propensity.

The *action relevant exposure* is those criminogenic features of the moral context of a setting (the perceived moral rules and their level of enforcement) that are linked to acting on a particular temptation or provocation.

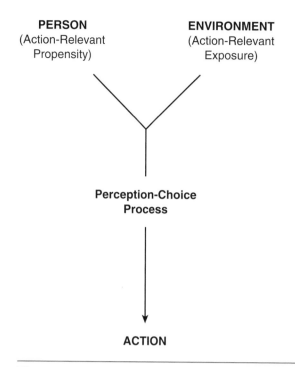

Figure 1 The Basic Situational Model

The *causal process* that links the interplay of propensity and exposure to action is the moral perception–moral choice process earlier detailed. This process can, depending on the familiarity of the circumstances, be predominantly habitual (expressing moral habits) or deliberative (expressing moral judgments) in nature.

To say that propensity and exposure (their interaction) are causes of action (acts of crime) does not deny the role of agency. Propensity and exposure set the context within which people exercise agency (act deliberate or by habit). Agency is exercised through the perception-choice process. Propensity and exposure (their interaction) is the input to this process. To say that propensity and exposure are causal factors means that changes in propensity and exposure will lead to changes in action through their impact on the perception-choice process.

The Principle of Moral Correspondence and the Role of Controls

At the core of the proposed propensity-exposure interaction in SAT is the principle of moral correspondence. The principle states that moral action is guided by the interplay between a person's morality and the moral rules of the setting in which he or she operates. A person's morality (values and emotions) can either encourage or discourage a particular moral action, and the moral rules of the setting in which he or she takes part can either encourage or discourage a particular moral action. The combination of the two gives four ideal type possibilities (as illustrated in Table 1).

In the case where both the person's morality and the moral rules of the setting encourage a particular moral action, this action will be likely (assuming that the person is tempted or provoked to act in this way). By contrast, in the case in which both the person's morality and the moral rules of the setting discourage a particular moral action, this action will be unlikely.

In the case where a person's morality discourages a particular action, but the moral rules of the setting encourage it, his or her capability to exercise self-control (internal control) will play a crucial role in determining whether or not he or she will act. For example, the capability to exercise self-control may come into play in the action choice for a young person who does not think it is right to smoke cannabis but may be tempted to try it out because he or she attends a "coffee shop" (a place where smoking pot is legal) in Amsterdam with a group of friends who all want to and think it is okay to smoke cannabis.

In the case where a person's morality encourages a particular moral action, but the moral rules of the setting discourage it, the level of deterrence (external controls) may play a key role in a person's action choice. For example, if an act is illegal but the person does not have a moral problem with carrying it out, the perceived risk of getting caught (and the perceived consequences thereof)

may come into play as a causally relevant factor in his or her choice process.

Controls will thus come into play only when there is a discrepancy between a person's morality and the moral rules of the setting. This may be referred to as *the principle of the conditional relevance of controls* (because internal and external controls are only causally relevant under certain moral conditions).

All this depends on there being an initial motivation (temptation, provocation) to act in a certain manner. If a person is not tempted or provoked to carry out a certain kind of act, his or her moral values and emotions, and the moral rules of the setting, that apply to this particular kind of action (and the controls) lack relevance for his or her actions.

The Role of Development and Change

According to situational action theory, changes in a person's actions stems from changes in his or her propensity (i.e., changes in his or her morality and ability to exercise self-control) and/or changes in his or her exposure (i.e., changes the time he or she spends in criminogenic settings). Changes in propensity and exposure cause changes in action (e.g., engagement in acts of crime) by bringing about change in the moral perception–moral choice process that guide moral action.

$$(\text{Change}) \text{ Propensity} + (\text{Change}) \text{ Exposure} = (\text{Change}) \text{ Action}$$

Changes in propensity and exposure are not unrelated from a developmental perspective. Changes in exposure may lead to changes in

Table 1 What Makes a Particular Moral Action Likely: The Principle of Moral Correspondence and the Role of Controls Illustrated

		Moral Rules of Setting	
		Encouraging	Discouraging
Morality	Encouraging	Action likely, controls irrelevant	Action dependent on level of deterrence
	Discouraging	Action dependent on capability to exercise self-control	Action unlikely, controls irrelevant

propensity through changes in the processes of socialization and habituation. For example, if a person spends increasing time in moral contexts favoring a certain kind of moral rule breaking, this may (through the processes of moral education and moral habituation) affect his or her propensity to engage in such acts. Changes in propensity may lead to changes in exposure through changes in setting selection. For example, if a person comes to find a certain moral action (e.g., drug use) morally acceptable (and is motivated to commit that action), the person may be more likely to seek out settings that support that action. However, in the explanation of crime causation, it is crucial not to confuse the question of why a person chooses to be in a certain setting and the effect of this setting on the person's actions (acts of crime). Why people are exposed to certain environments (of which self-selection is one cause) and how these environments affect their actions (e.g., acts of crime) are two different questions. The former is a question that belongs to the explanation of the causes of the causes, and the latter to the explanation of the causes of a person's engagement in acts of crime.

The Role of Broader Social Conditions

SAT maintains that to be able to explain the role in crime causation of broader social factors and social change, as well as individual development and life histories, one first has to understand what moves people to action (to engage in acts of crime). Knowing what moves people to engage in acts of crime gives us guidance as to which broader social conditions, and aspects of people's life histories, are important candidates as the causes of the causes (or indirect causes) that move people to action.

People act and develop in settings. According to SAT, the key to understanding the potential role of broader social conditions (like disadvantage, integration, and segregation) in crime causation (as possible causes of the causes) is to understand how these social conditions and their related social processes help create particular kinds of settings (with particular moral contexts and levels of enforcement) in which people develop (form their morality and ability to exercise self-control) and act (express their morality and ability to exercise self-control).

Societies vary in their social integration (cohesion and trust) and moral integration (homogeneity of moral values held by the population and their correspondence to moral rules expressed by the larger society, e.g., in terms of laws). It is reasonable to assume that societies that have higher degrees of social and moral integration will have less moral rule breaking and crime because there will be less room for a discrepancy between individual and collective moral rules.

Changes in the broader social environment in which people's daily lives are embedded (e.g., political, economical, and social changes of relevance to moral actions) may instigate changes in the kinds of moral contexts present in a society and the processes of exposure of different groups of people to particular moral contexts. In turn, this may (in the longer term) affect the moral education of the population, or segments of the population, and (in the short term) affect the moral contexts in which people, or groups of people, act.

Per-Olof H. Wikström

See also Clarke, Ronald V.: Situational Crime Prevention; Cornish, Derek B., and Ronald V. Clarke: Rational Choice Theory; Gottfredson, Michael R., and Travis Hirschi: Self-Control Theory; LaFree, Gary D., and Christopher Birkbeck: Situational Analysis of Crime; Sampson, Robert J., and William Julius Wilson: Contextualized Subculture

References and Further Readings

Bohuana, N., & Wikström, P.-O. (2008). *Theorising terrorism: Terrorism as moral action.* London: Jill Dando Institute, University College of London.
Wikström, P.-O. (2004). Crime as an alternative: Towards a cross-level situational action theory of crime causation. In J. McCord (Ed.), *Beyond empiricism: Institutions and intentions in the study of crime* (Advances in Criminological Theory: Vol. 13, pp. 1–37). New Brunswick, NJ: Transaction.
Wikström, P.-O. (2005). The social origins of pathways in crime. Towards a developmental ecological action theory of crime involvement and its changes. In D. P. Farrington (Ed.), *Integrated developmental and life-course theories of offending* (Advances in Criminological Theory: Vol. 14, pp. 211–245). New Brunswick, NJ: Transaction.
Wikström, P.-O. (2006). Individuals, settings and acts of crime. Situational mechanisms and the explanation of crime. In P.-O. Wikström & R. J. Sampson (Eds.),

The explanation of crime: Context, mechanisms and development (pp. 61–107). Cambridge, UK: Cambridge University Press.

Wikström, P.-O. (2007). Deterrence and deterrence experiences: Preventing crime through the threat of punishment. In S. G. Shoham, O. Beck, & M. Kett (Eds.), *International handbook of penology and criminal justice* (pp. 345–378). London: CRC Press.

Wikström, P.-O. (2007). The social ecology of crime: The role of the environment in crime causation. In H. J. Schneider (Ed.), *Internationales handbuch der kriminologie* (Vol. 1, pp. 333–357). Berlin; New York: de Gruyter.

Wikström, P.-O. (2007c). In search of causes and explanations of crime. In R. D. King & E. Wincup (Eds.), *Doing research on crime and justice* (2nd ed., pp. 117–139). Oxford, UK: Oxford University Press.

Wikström, P.-O., & Sampson, R. J. (2003). Social mechanisms of community influences in crime and pathways in criminality. In B. B. Lahey, T. E. Moffitt, & A. Caspi (Eds.), *The causes of conduct disorder and serious juvenile delinquency* (pp. 118–148). New York: Guilford Press.

Wikström, P.-O., & Trieber, K. (2007). The role of self-control in crime causation. Beyond Gottfredson and Hirschi's general theory of crime. *European Journal of Criminology, 4,* 237–264.

Wikström, P.-O., & Treiber, K. (2009). Violence as situational action. *The International Journal of Conflict and Violence, 3,* 75–96.

Wikström, P.-O., & Treiber, K. (2009). What drives persistent offending. The neglected and unexplored role of the social environment. In J. Savage (Ed.), *The development of persistent criminality* (pp. 389–420). Oxford, UK: Oxford University Press.

WILCOX, PAMELA, KENNETH C. LAND, AND SCOTT A. HUNT: MULTICONTEXTUAL OPPORTUNITY THEORY

Pamela Wilcox, Kenneth C. Land, and Scott A. Hunt's multicontextual criminal opportunity theory explains how individual-level and environmental-level opportunity affect the likelihood of crime events. Many criminologists have acknowledged the role of opportunity in explaining crime and victimization. Lawrence E. Cohen and Marcus

Felson's routine activity theory, in particular, has informed both individual-level and environmental-level opportunity models of crime and victimization, suggesting that routine activities will determine the likelihood that the necessary elements of a crime—a motivated offender and a suitable target in the absence of capable guardians—will converge in time and space. In addition, multilevel opportunity models have been used to explore the ways in which environmental factors might condition, or moderate, the effects of individual-level opportunity on crime and victimization risk. In other words, these models explore whether there are *cross-level interactions* (i.e., the effects of individual-level factors on crime vary depending on the environmental-level context) that contribute to the likelihood of crime.

Despite these empirical inquiries, there has been little theoretical development to explain and predict the presence and direction of cross-level interactive effects in opportunity models of crime and victimization. To this end, Wilcox, Land, and Hunt integrate micro-level and macro-level routine activities theories with control theory to present a dynamic, multicontextual criminal opportunity theory of crime events. In doing so, they specify the main effects of individual-level and environmental-level contexts on criminal opportunity and, in turn, on crime events. Further, they explain how the environmental-level context might interact with the individual-level context, thus moderating its effect on the likelihood of crime. Grounded in a market economy perspective, Wilcox, Land, and Hunt provide specific theoretical predictions regarding the interaction effects across levels of opportunity structures.

The Main Effects of Individual and Environmental Opportunity on Crime

Multicontextual opportunity theory begins with the classical criminological assumption that individuals are driven by the pursuit of pleasure and the avoidance of pain. In doing so, Wilcox, Land, and Hunt assert that the very nature of humans explains the motivation for crime, and thus proceed to explain the conditions which are conducive to crime. Influenced by both the micro-level and macro-level interpretations of routine activity theory, they identify opportunity as their central theoretical construct and suggest that two levels of analysis matter in explaining the role of opportunity in the occurrence of crime. Specifically, they define opportunity as "the convergence in time and space of motivated offenders and suitable targets in the absence of capable guardians in individual- and environmental-level contexts" (p. 60).

Wilcox, Land, and Hunt elaborate on the constructs that comprise their multilevel conception of criminal opportunity. Within the individual-level context, they describe motivated offenders, suitable targets, and capable guardianship in greater detail. In terms of motivated offenders, Wilcox, Land, and Hunt's classical perspective regarding human nature leads them to "assume universal and constant criminal motivation in the human population" (p. 60). Yet they do suggest that individuals may be differentially exposed to motivated offenders depending on the degree to which their activities take them away from the home. The rhythm, tempo, and timing of these activities will also differentially expose individuals to motivated offenders. Individual-level target suitability refers to the degree to which individuals and objects possess qualities of vulnerability, antagonism, and gratifiability. Vulnerability refers to the extent to which the target can be "accessed, damaged, destroyed, duped, transported, and/or transferred with ease and speed" (p. 62); antagonism refers to the degree to which a target elicits hostile or apathetic reactions; and gratifiability reflects the level of pleasure, either physical or monetary, offered by the target. Finally, individual-level capable guardianship refers to the degree to which individuals have social ties, such as their attachments to others, their commitments to social institutions, and their involvement in conventional activities. Further, capable guardianship is also tied to interpersonal control, which restricts criminal acts through formal and informal control, as well as non-human protective devices. In sum, the individual-level context for criminal opportunity is defined by these three constructs—motivated offenders, suitable targets, and capable guardianship—and has a direct effect on crime.

The environmental-level context that creates opportunity for crime is tied to the collective, or aggregate, features of people and objects that reflect the concentration of motivated offenders, attractive targets, and capable guardianship.

Wilcox, Land, and Hunt introduce the term *bounded locales* to describe environments that are situated within a specific space and time. Exposure to motivated offenders at the environmental-level is a function of the concentration of individuals within a bounded locale. This concentration can be residential, in that individuals occupy the space constantly, or ephemeral, in that individuals enter and leave the space. For example, the concentration of motivated offenders within a small town might be more residential, as few people enter or leave the town during the course of their routine activities. Conversely, the concentration of motivated offenders in a large metropolis might be more ephemeral, as routine work and leisure activities draw people in and out of the city's core at different times of the day and days of the week. Within the environmental-level context, aggregate target suitability is the degree to which individuals and objects in a bounded locale collectively possess the traits of vulnerability, antagonism, and gratifiability. Finally, aggregate capable guardianship is the collective degree to which individuals and objects in a bounded locale have social ties and experience social control. Similar to the individual-level context, the environmental-level context defines opportunities for crime and has a direct effect on crime.

In sum, multicontextual opportunity theory suggests that both individual-level and environmental-level contexts directly influence the likelihood of crime events. For example, an individual's risk of burglary victimization is not simply tied to the opportunity provided by his or her own lifestyle and routine activities, but also to the aggregate-level opportunity of the neighborhood in which the individual resides. If the individual fails to lock his doors, this contributes to the opportunity for crime. In addition, living in a neighborhood in which it is the community norm to leave one's doors unlocked also contributes to criminal opportunity independent of whether the individual in fact locks his doors or not.

The Interactive Effects of Environmental- and Individual-Level Opportunity on Crime

Multicontextual opportunity theory suggests that both individual-level and environmental-level opportunity contexts affect the likelihood of criminal acts. As described in the section above, each has a direct effect on crime. In addition, environmental-level opportunity can impact criminal acts by moderating the relationship between individual-level opportunity and criminal acts. In other words, the relationship between individual-level opportunity and crime is not constant, but one that can change depending on the environmental-level context. For example, the degree to which residential burglar alarms reduce the risk of burglary victimization may vary across neighborhoods, as environmental-level opportunity at the neighborhood level influences the relationship between individual-level opportunity and crime.

Though there has been some empirical inquiries regarding the moderating effect of environmental-level opportunity on individual-level opportunity, or cross-level interactions, such analyses lacked a theoretical base from which to derive testable hypotheses. Wilcox, Land, and Hunt's multicontextual opportunity theory fills this void by explicitly specifying the moderating effects of environmental-level opportunity and grounding these predictions in a theoretical rationale. To this end, they rely on economic theory of markets which suggests that human beings seek to maximize utility by seeking pleasure and avoiding pain. Based on this core principle, Wilcox, Land, and Hunt derive three related principles to describe how the supply of motivated offenders affects the market for crime. All else being equal, an increase in the supply of motivated offenders (1) creates a market that has greater exposure to motivated offenders, (2) elevates the market value of targets in that environment, and (3) reduces the market costs of criminal acts. Using similar logic, Wilcox, Land, and Hunt advance principles about the supply of aggregate suitable targets and the supply of aggregate capable guardianship. All else being equal, as the supply of suitable targets increases, the market value of any single target declines. Similarly, as the supply of aggregate guardianship increases, the market costs of criminal acts increase.

Based on the rationale of economic theory of markets, Wilcox, Land, and Hunt specify nine cross-level interactions that describe how environmental-level opportunity might condition the effects of individual-level opportunity on crime. Specifically, they consider how the individual-level effects of exposure to motivated offenders, target suitability, and capable guardianship on crime might change depending on the environmental-level supply of motivated offenders, target suitability, and capable guardianship.

Multicontextual opportunity theory suggests that individual-level exposure to motivated offenders will increase the likelihood of crime. However, this positive relationship between individual-level exposure to motivated offenders and crime may be strengthened or weakened depending on the environmental-level context. All else being equal, an increase in the environmental-level supply of motivated offenders will strengthen this relationship, as a large supply of motivated offenders makes individual-level exposure to motivated offenders even riskier. Similarly, an increase in aggregate target suitability will also strengthen the relationship between individual-level exposure to motivated offenders and crime. When the environment is densely populated with suitable targets, the value of each is reduced, thus making individual-level exposure all the more important in terms of defining risk. Finally, environmental-level capable guardianship serves to weaken the relationship between individual-level exposure to motivated offenders and crime, as the presence of environmental-level guardianship serves as a deterrent for crime.

Like individual-level exposure to motivated offenders, individual-level target suitability also increases the likelihood of crime, though this positive relationship may be strengthened or weakened by the environmental-level context. A large supply of motivated offenders serves to strengthen this relationship because the demand for targets is enhanced. However, a large supply of suitable targets in a bounded locale weakens the relationship between individual-level target suitability and crime, as the value attached to any single target is diminished with the increased supply. Finally, environmental-level guardianship also weakens the positive relationship between individual-level target suitability and crime because of its deterrent effect on crime.

Individual-level capable guardianship is negatively related to crime, but again, this negative relationship can be strengthened or weakened depending on environmental-level opportunity. For example, an increase in the aggregate supply of motivated offenders will weaken the negative relationship between individual-level guardianship and crime, as the demand for targets increases and the costs associated with individual-level targets (i.e., guardianship) become less important to motivated offenders. Conversely, an increase in environmental-level target suitability will strengthen the negative relationship between individual-level guardianship and crime. Because there is high supply of targets available, offenders can more easily avoid costly (i.e., well-guarded) targets. Finally, an increase in environmental-level guardianship will also strengthen the negative relationship between individual-level guardianship and crime, as environmental-level guardianship deters crime and enhances the deterrent effect of individual-level guardianship.

Conclusion

In sum, multicontextual opportunity theory suggests that opportunity at both the individual- and environmental-levels has a direct effect on crime. In addition, multicontextual opportunity theory posits that environmental-level opportunity can moderate the effects of individual-level opportunity on crime. That is, the strength of the relationship between individual-level opportunity factors and crime will vary depending on the environmental context. Grounded in an economic theory of markets, multicontextual opportunity theory provides specific theoretical predictions regarding the presence and direction of cross-level interactions in multilevel opportunity models of crime and victimization.

Marie Skubak Tillyer

See also Brantingham, Patricia L., and Paul J. Brantingham: Environmental Criminology; Cohen, Lawrence E., and Marcus K. Felson: Routine Activity Theory; Cook, Philip J.: Supply and Demand of Criminal Opportunities; Cornish, Derek B., and Ronald V. Clarke: Rational Choice Theory; Felson, Marcus K.: Crime and Everyday Life

References and Further Readings

Cohen, L. E., & Felson, M. (1979). Social change and crime rate trends: A routine activity approach. *American Sociological Review, 44*, 588–608.

Sampson, R. J., & Wooldredge, J. D. (1987). Linking the micro- and macro-level dimensions of lifestyle-routine activity and opportunity models of predatory

victimization. *Journal of Quantitative Criminology, 3*, 371–393.

Wilcox, P., Land, K. C., & Hunt, S. A. (2003). *Criminal circumstance: A dynamic multicontextual criminal opportunity theory.* New York: Aldine de Gruyter.

Wilcox, P., Madensen, T., & Tillyer, M. S. (2007). Guardianship in context: Implications for burglary victimization risk and prevention. *Criminology, 45*, 771–803.

Wilcox Rountree, P., Land, K. C., & Miethe, T. D. (1994). Macro-micro integration in the study of victimization: A hierarchical logistic model analysis across Seattle neighborhoods. *Criminology, 32*, 387–414.

WILLIAMS, KIRK R., AND RICHARD HAWKINS: DETERRENCE THEORY AND NON-LEGAL SANCTIONS

Deterrence theory is one of the oldest criminological theories, dating back hundreds of years to the Classical School and the work of Jeremy Bentham and Cesare Beccaria. However, it was not until the last quarter of the 20th century that criminologists attempted to systematize it (e.g., Gibbs, 1975; Tittle, 1980). This included attempts to identify (1) the process by which legal punishments deter and (2) ways of integrating deterrence theory with other theories of crime causation. Kirk R. Williams and Richard Hawkins have made important contributions to the literature on these issues in a series of articles where they look at the role of legal and non-legal sanctions in the deterrence process.

Criminologists traditionally have interpreted deterrence theory as asserting that people will be deterred from committing crimes to the extent they fear legal sanctions (Gibbs, 1975). However, Williams and Hawkins have argued that this interpretation is too restrictive because it ignores how non-legal sanctions are involved in the deterrence process (see also Carmody & Williams, 1987). The traditional interpretation assumes that deterrence results only from the direct costs of legal sanctions as when a person refrains from committing a crime out of fear of being fined (forfeiture of money) or imprisoned (deprivation of liberty). Williams and Hawkins's argument is that while the direct costs of legal sanctions are integral to the deterrence process, so are non-legal sanctions that can result from legal sanctions, as when a bus driver loses her job for a conviction for driving under the influence or a boy is disciplined by his parents because he has been arrested for shoplifting. According to Williams and Hawkins, such non-legal sanctions represent the indirect costs of legal sanctions, and legal sanctions can deter people from committing crimes by triggering them.

Daniel Nagin reported findings from a study of tax evasion, which illustrates Williams and Hawkins's argument. He found that there was at least some chance that middle-class persons would cheat on their taxes if enforcement was limited to the threat of civil actions involving only fines. However, there was no chance they would cheat if enforcement put their "reputation and community standing at stake" (p. 352). Hence, legal sanctions deterred best when tied to non-legal sanctions.

To the extent that legal sanctions deter by triggering non-legal sanctions, as Williams and Hawkins have argued, people should think of legal sanctions in terms of their deleterious non-legal consequences, and these non-legal consequences should decrease the likelihood that people will commit crime. Williams and Hawkins (1989b, 1992) have examined these issues in two studies of the direct and indirect costs of wife assault. In the first study, the direct costs of legal sanctions were measured by men's perceptions of the (1) perceived likelihood of going to jail for wife assault and (2) perceived severity of arrest (how bad it would be to be arrested for wife assault). The indirect costs of non-legal sanctions were measured by the perceived likelihood that various non-legal sanctions would result from an arrest: loss of self-respect, partner leaving or getting a divorce, disapproval/loss of respect from friends and relatives, and loss of job. Williams and Hawkins (1989b) found that although most of the men believed it was unlikely they would go to jail if arrested for wife assault, they perceived arrest as very severe because of its indirect costs (see also Carmody & Williams, 1987). The most important determinant of perceived arrest severity was loss of self-respect, followed by loss of partner, social disapproval, and loss of job. Williams and Hawkins (1989b, p.175) concluded that "these social ramifications may be

crucial mediating linkages between arrest and involvement in wife assault."

In the second study, Williams and Hawkins (1992) examined the extent to which self-reported wife assault was affected by (1) perceived assault costs and (2) the perceived indirect costs of arrest. Perceived assault costs were measured by men's perceptions of the likelihood of losing (1) a spouse/partner, (2) respect of friends/relatives, and (3) self-respect for committing wife assault. Perceived assault costs were linked only to assault itself, not arrest. The perceived indirect costs of arrest included the same types of losses (e.g., losing a spouse/partner), but they were linked to arrest (e.g., what would be the chances of losing the respect of your friends if you were arrested for hitting your spouse or partner?). A composite measure of the perceived indirect costs of arrest had a significant negative effect on men's self-reported wife assault, but there was no effect for perceived assault costs that were not linked to arrest.

While the thrust of Williams and Hawkins's argument is that legal sanctions can deter by triggering non-legal sanctions, they also have discussed another way that legal and non-legal sanctions can combine in the deterrence process. Non-legal sanctions may condition the deterrent effects of legal sanctions such that legal sanctions deter best when applied to persons who are most likely to suffer non-legal sanctions. To illustrate this logic, Williams and Hawkins (1986, p. 566) have said about the deterrent effects of arrest that "the greater the perceived [indirect] costs of arrest . . . , the greater should be the negative effects of perceptions of certainty [of arrest] on the incidence of crime."

The same kind of logic is useful for interpreting the results of the famous domestic violence experiments conducted by Lawrence Sherman and his colleagues. In one such experiment in Milwaukee, Sherman, Douglas Smith, Janell Schmidt, and Dennis Rogan randomly determined whether 1,200 suspected domestic batterers would be (1) arrested or (2) warned by the police without an arrest. They, then, compared rates of new domestic violence by the two groups. Overall, arrest was no more effective than a police warning in decreasing the likelihood of new violence. However, the overall arrest effect hid a more complex pattern. While arrest decreased the likelihood of new violence by married and employed persons, it increased the likelihood of new violence by unmarried and unemployed persons. These findings suggested to Sherman and his colleagues that "the effectiveness of legal sanctions rests on a foundation of informal control" (p. 688). The Williams-Hawkins interpretation is similar: married and employed people have a lower likelihood of assault after an arrest for it because they fear that non-legal sanctions (e.g., loss of partner or job) could result from another arrest.

In addition to arguing that legal sanctions can deter by triggering non-legal sanctions and discussing how non-legal sanctions may condition the deterrent effects of legal sanctions, Williams and Hawkins (1989a; Williams, 1992, 2005) have attempted to integrate deterrence theory with other theories of crime causation. They first attempted to integrate deterrence theory and social bonding theory by examining how wife assault was affected by fear of legal sanctions and Travis Hirschi's social bonding variables: attachment (affective ties to significant others), commitment (investment in long-term goals), involvement (time and energy given to conventional activities), and moral belief (perceived legitimacy of conventional rules). Treating the perceived risk of arrest for wife assault as a measure of moral beliefs, they found that men were most likely to be non-assaulters if they perceived a high risk of arrest for wife assault, placed importance on socializing with significant others (a measure of attachment), and strongly condemned wife assault, which they took to be a second measure of moral beliefs (Williams & Hawkins, 1989a).

Williams (1992) has included legal and non-legal sanctions in a study of partner assault where he integrated deterrence theory and Richard Gelles's exchange/social bonding theory of family violence. Williams posited that perceived non-legal sanctions for partner assault should be reduced by perceived isolation from the police, perceived power, and perceived approval of partner assault. Reductions in perceived non-legal sanctions, in turn, should increase the likelihood of partner assault. Perceived isolation from the police was measured by the perceived certainty of arrest for wife assault (a perceived legal sanction). To measure perceived non-legal sanctions, men and women first were asked to estimate the likelihood that several non-legal sanctions would result from an arrest for partner assault: partner leaving or

threatening to get a divorce, loss of friends/relatives' support, and loss of self-respect. Then, they were asked to estimate "how bad it would be for them if these arrest costs occurred" in order to measure the perceived severity of the non-legal sanctions (Williams, 1992, p. 624). The cross-product of the responses to the perceived likelihood and perceived severity questions was computed for each type of non-legal sanction, and these cross-products were added to construct a composite measure of perceived non-legal sanctions. Consistent with Williams's expectations, perceived isolation from the police (perceived certainty of arrest for partner assault), perceived power, and approval of partner assault significantly reduced perceived non-legal sanctions, which increased the likelihood of partner assault.

More recently, Williams (2005, p. 673) has attempted to expand deterrence theory by "incorporating mediating and moderating influences of [legal] sanctions" for partner assault. The threat or imposition of legal sanctions for partner violence should reduce its likelihood through deterrence, but also through normative declarations, meaning shared beliefs that partner assault is unacceptable, and procedural justice or the perceived fairness of imposing legal sanctions. Like deterrence, normative declarations and procedural justice result from the threat or imposition of legal sanctions and, hence, should mediate their effects on partner assault. The effects of legal sanctions should also be conditioned by differential sensitivity to legal sanctions, which results from behavioral risk. People at risk for committing partner assault should have a low sensitivity to legal sanctions, and this low sensitivity should reduce the effects of deterrence, normative declarations, and procedural justice on the likelihood of partner assault.

Williams and Hawkins have contributed considerably to our understanding of the deterrence process and how legal sanctions combine with other variables, including non-legal sanctions and variables from other theories of crime causation, to deter people from committing crimes. Given that deterrence continues to be one of the principal justifications for legal punishment in Western societies, the importance of those contributions cannot be underestimated.

Mark C. Stafford

See also General Deterrence Theory; Gibbs, Jack, P.:
Deterrence Theory; Nagin, Daniel S., and Raymond
Paternoster: Individual Differences and Deterrence;
Perceptual Deterrence; Stafford, Mark C., and Mark
Warr: Deterrence Theory

References and Further Readings

Akers, R. L. (1990). Rational choice, deterrence, and
social learning theory in criminology. *Journal of
Criminal Law and Criminology, 81,* 653–676.
Carmody, D. C., & Williams, K. R. (1987). Wife assault
and perceptions of sanctions. *Violence and Victims, 2,*
25–38.
Gelles, R. J. (1983). An exchange/social control theory. In
D. Finkelhor, R. J. Gelles, G. T. Hotaling, & M. A.
Straus (Eds.), *The dark side of families* (pp. 151–165).
Beverly Hills, CA: Sage.
Gibbs, J. P. (1975). *Crime, punishment, and deterrence.*
New York: Elsevier.
Hirschi, T. (1969). *Causes of delinquency.* Berkeley:
University of California Press.
Nagin, D. S. (1998). Deterrence and incapacitation. In
M. Tonry (Ed.), *The handbook of crime and
punishment* (pp. 345–368). New York: Oxford
University Press.
Pratt, T. C., Cullen, F. T., Blevins, K. R., Daigle, L. E., &
Madensen, T. D. (2006). The empirical status of
deterrence theory. In F. T. Cullen, J. P. Wright, &
K. R. Blevins (Eds.), *Taking stock: The status of
criminological theory* (Advances in Criminological
Theory, Vol. 15, pp. 367–395). New Brunswick, NJ:
Transaction.
Sherman, L. W., Smith, D. A., Schmidt, J. D., & Rogan,
D. P. (1992). Crime, punishment, and stake in
conformity. *American Sociological Review, 57,* 680–690.
Stafford, M. C., & Warr, M. (1993). A reconceptualization
of general and specific deterrence. *Journal of Research
in Crime and Delinquency, 30,* 123–135.
Tittle, C. R. (1980). *Sanctions and social deviance.* New
York: Praeger.
Williams, K. R. (1992). Social sources of marital violence
and deterrence. *Journal of Marriage and the Family,
54,* 620–629.
Williams, K. R. (2005). Arrest and intimate partner
violence. *Aggression & Violent Behavior, 10,* 660–669.
Williams, K. R., & Hawkins, R. (1986). Perceptual
research on general deterrence. *Law and Society
Review, 20,* 545–572.
Williams, K. R., & Hawkins, R. (1989a). Controlling
male aggression in intimate relationships. *Law and
Society Review, 23,* 591–612.
Williams, K. R., & Hawkins, R. (1989b). The meaning of
arrest for wife assault. *Criminology, 27,* 163–181.
Williams, K. R., & Hawkins, R. (1992). Wife assault,
costs of arrest, and the deterrence process. *Journal of
Research in Crime and Delinquency, 29,* 292–310.

WILSON, JAMES Q., AND RICHARD J. HERRNSTEIN: CRIME AND HUMAN NATURE

James Q. Wilson and Richard J. Herrnstein's *Crime and Human Nature: The Definitive Study of the Causes of Crime* (hereafter referred to simply as *Crime and Human Nature*) is a major work in criminological theory. When published in 1985, it was viewed as controversial for its insistence on an individual-level unit of analysis to explain crime which was at odds with the prevailing structural approach taken by sociological criminological theory. Nearly 25 years later, *Crime and Human Nature* is hailed as a work that marked a paradigm shift in criminology, one which embraced interdisciplinary perspectives to understand crime, particularly the roles of constructs from biology and neuropsychology that have been shown to underscore human behavior. Today, *Crime and Human Nature* is generally viewed as uncontroversial and, instead, as one of the works that helped usher criminology into the 21st century. This entry is organized into three sections: (1) it provides a general overview of *Crime and Human Nature*, (2) it describes the criminological reaction to it, and (3) it illustrates the contemporary place of *Crime and Human Nature* in criminological theory and criminological research.

Overview

Crime and Human Nature is one of the most influential theoretical works in criminology. With 1,000-plus citations, it is among the most cited books in the fields of criminology and criminal justice (Cohn & Farrington, 1994, 1998). To advance what they purported to be the definitive explanation for crime, Wilson and Herrnstein observed that there was tremendous variation among individuals in terms of their involvement in antisocial behavior.

Thus, whereas most people viewed crime as a course of action that should almost never be taken, others perceived that criminal behavior provided many rewards. Whereas most people had internalized fears and concerns about committing crime and being punished by the criminal justice system, others were behaviorally uninhibited and seemingly prone to commit crime. Whereas many people could defer gratification and thus maintain and complete responsibilities with distant payoffs, others had a short attention span and required almost immediate gratification of their desires. Whereas many people were adequately controlled or deterred from committing crime by the mere threat of criminal prosecution, still others seemed to rarely or even never learn from punishment experiences. Finally, whereas most people successfully abstained from criminal activity—at least to the degree of never acquiring an arrest record—still others accumulated extensive arrest records based on the seriousness, length, and frequency with which they committed crime and other antisocial behaviors. In short, Wilson and Herrnstein wondered which biological, developmental, situational, and adaptive processes gave rise to individual characteristics that predict crime. And the bodies of scholarship that they chose to review centered on studies from an array of disciplines that generally showed individual-level variation in crime and factors that predispose people to commit crime.

To Wilson and Herrnstein, the etiology of crime stemmed from within the individual, and their central theoretical goal was to establish the fact that individuals differ at birth in the degree to which they are at risk for criminality. Although this appears at face value to suggest a genetic or natural propensity to crime, Wilson and Herrnstein overtly rejected such deterministic viewpoints. According to Wilson and Herrnstein, "there *is* a human nature that develops in intimate settings out of a complex interaction of constitutional and social factors, and that nature affects how people choose between the consequences of crime and its alternatives" (p. 508, emphasis in the original). In this sense, Crime and Human Nature literally attempted to describe the complex ways that constitutional and environmental factors—or nature and nurture—blend together to produce human dispositions and behavior.

The publication of Crime and Human Nature was seemingly destined to attract attention based on the scholarly reputations of its authors. Arguably, Crime and Human Nature is known as much for the star power of its authors as its substantive argument. By 1985, both Wilson and Herrnstein were accomplished authors, both were distinguished academics whose research crossed over into the public domain at least in terms of the media coverage of their works, and both were viewed as conservative which in academic circles is controversial (DeLisi, 2003). More than these external circumstances, however, Crime and Human Nature wrestled the study of crime from what Wilson and Herrnstein would suggest was the "stranglehold" of sociology.

Borrowing from economics, they articulated the idea that crime was fundamentally a matter of choice. As such, rational choice theory and the thought processes of individual actors were essential in understanding why some people committed crime and used violence against others. Borrowing from psychology, Wilson and Herrnstein articulated that choosing to commit crime was not simply the outcome of rational calculus but that choice was itself molded and influenced by an array of factors, such as family members, social class, environmental influences, and prior learning. Borrowing from biology, Wilson and Herrnstein suggested "the existence of biological predispositions means that circumstances that activate behavior in one person will not do so in another, that social forces cannot deter criminal behavior in 100 percent of the population, and that the distribution of crime within and across societies may, to some extent, reflect underlying distributions of constitutional factors. Crime cannot be understood without taking into account predispositions and their biological roots" (p. 103). With its insistence on the individual and its friendliness to biology and other academic perspectives, Crime and Human Nature shook the discipline of criminology and the behavioral sciences generally.

The Criminological Reaction to Crime and Human Nature

Unlike most academic books which are received by obscurity or an occasional review, Crime and Human Nature prompted considerable attention from the popular press (e.g., *Time, Newsweek,* and *The New York Times,* among others) and criminological community alike. For instance, in *Scientific American,* Leon Kamin assessed,

> The Wilson and Herrnstein work ought not to be judged in isolation. Their selective use of poor data to support a muddled ideology of biological determinism is not unrepresentative of American social science in the sixth year of the Reagan presidency. The political climate of the times makes it easy to understand why social scientists now rush to locate the causes of social tensions in genes and in deep-rooted biological substrata. (p. 25)

In his review in *The Journal of Criminal Law and Criminology,* Theodore Ferdinand characterized *Crime and Human Nature* as overly simple and a work that advances the understanding of crime little if at all. In the journal *Contemporary Crises* (which is now titled *Crime, Law and Social Change*), Philip Jenkins derided *Crime and Human Nature* as a manifesto for Reagan-era criminal justice. In his review in the journal *Contemporary Sociology,* Lawrence Cohen suggested that "this book replaces the liberal biases of much contemporary criminology with the conservative ideology that has come to be associated with the authors" (p. 202).

By and large, the criminological response to Wilson and Herrnstein's work was to view it as an attack on the very fiber of criminology. This sentiment appears prominently in Jack Gibbs's review of the book in *Criminology,* the official journal of the American Society of Criminology. According to Gibbs (1985, p. 381),

> American sociologists tend to take a proprietary interest in criminology and to think of the leading theories about crime as "sociological." Hence, Wilson and Herrnstein's tome (639 pages but only $22.95) may startle numerous sociologists, and those who suffer from high blood pressure should be cautious in reading it. Sociologists are accustomed to occasional forays by economists into criminology, but many will be unprepared for a flank attack by formidable scholars from political science (Wilson) and psychology (Herrnstein).

Based on the tone of these reviews, it is reasonable to conclude that *Crime and Human Nature* touched a nerve in the criminological community. Two overriding points are worth noting. First, Wilson and Herrnstein's treatise is frequently described as a deterministic theory of criminal behavior that is rooted in biology. However, many view *Crime and Human Nature* as less of a theory per se than a review of research from multiple fields that bear on human behavior and antisocial behavior. Indeed, Wilson and Herrnstein themselves would not even characterize their work as simple, deterministic, or singularly rooted in biology. For example, Herrnstein suggested, "Criminal behavior is behavior. It is not necessary to prove that human behavior is multiply determined, for it is obvious. Nothing we do, not even coughing or sneezing, has just one governing antecedent condition. The more complex the set of antecedent conditions, the less sense it makes to frame questions about behavior in terms of causes" (p. 62). Second, *Crime and Human Nature* is more of a signaling call for criminologists to quit denying that individual-level constitutional variables are meaningful, but not exclusive, explanations for criminal and non-criminal behavior. Equally meaningful are other variables at criminologists' disposal, such as socialization processes, the stratification system, and culture. The consideration of both constitutional and environmental factors will help develop believable rationales for why some persons choose to repeatedly violate the social contract and why most persons behave lawfully (DeLisi, Conis, & Beaver, 2008).

The Contemporary Place of *Crime and Human Nature* in Criminological Theory and Criminological Research

According to Thomas Kuhn, a major indicator of the importance of a piece of scholarship is whether it signaled a paradigm shift in the way that science is conducted in a particular field. This clearly happened with *Crime and Human Nature.* The seriousness and, at times, viciousness with which criminologists received it are evidence that its ideas were at the time foreign to the ways that criminology as an academic discipline conceptualized and explained criminal behavior. In 1985, there was a clear preference for sociological explanations that pointed to structural or societal factors as social forces that molded the thoughts and behaviors of individuals. Moreover, crime was believed to be caused by statuses that individuals occupied at various times, such as employment status or class position. The psychology of individuals, and certainly the inner-workings of their brains were believed to be irrelevant to crime and criminology. *Crime and Human Nature* changed all of that.

Although Wilson and Herrnstein bore the brunt of the criticism of a "new" criminology that embraced psychology and biology, other important works emerged in the years shortly after *Crime and Human Nature* that in essence carried the torch ignited by Wilson and Herrnstein. Thus, the low self-control construct in Michael Gottfredson and Travis Hirschi's *A General Theory of Crime* published in 1990 is similar in its assertion that self-control is the indispensible variable to explain crime. Although Gottfredson and Hirschi were also criticized for their insistence that an individual-level construct was the essential predictor of crime, the criticism lacked the venom of that directed against Wilson and Herrnstein. Moreover, Gottfredson and Hirschi's theory has been repeatedly tested by criminologists who at least viewed its ideas as worthy of empirical scrutiny.

In 1993, another major work appeared which was in the same vein as *Crime and Human Nature* and that work was the developmental taxonomy theory presented by Terrie Moffitt and published in the journal *Psychological Review*. Moffitt's work explicitly incorporates ideas from neuroscience and neuropsychology to explain pathological criminal behavior among a small subgroup of offenders known as life-course-persistent offenders. Interestingly, although Moffitt's work is heavily imbued with biological and psychological concepts, it has been largely immune from the criticism that only sociology has something meaningful to say about the causes of crime. Thus, in just 8 years from 1985 to 1993, the use of biology and psychology (in conjunction with sociology) to explain crime morphed from controversial to accepted. Today this is even more the case, as life-course perspectives on crime routinely span the fields of pediatrics, child and adolescent psychiatry, developmental psychology, behavioral and molecular genetics, neuroscience, such as brain scans and neuro-imaging, public health and medicine, and many others.

Another predominant area of research in 21st-century criminology is the study of serious, violent, and chronic offenders also known as career criminals (Laub & Sampson, 2003; Loeber & Farrington, 1998; Sampson & Laub, 1993). A major scholarly achievement of research in this area is to identify risk factors that are associated with recurrent, pathological criminal involvement and protective factors which can insulate individuals from getting into and leading lives of crime. This area also owes a debt of gratitude to Wilson and Herrnstein whose work zeroed in on the small group of criminals that are most damaging to society and examined the many ways that serious offenders are behaviorally different from non-offenders.

Finally, in the wake of the mapping of the human genome, scientists are each day producing insights on the ways that biological concepts, such as brain functioning and gene expression, interact with the environment to produce human behavior. Today, it is obvious that prosocial and antisocial behaviors, such as crime, are the outcome of a complex interaction between phenomena that are studied in a diverse range of fields of inquiry. Today this realization is obvious and accepted. But not too long ago, such a viewpoint was controversial and Wilson and Herrnstein's *Crime and Human Nature* took a considerable drubbing for steering criminology away from sociology and onto a more inclusive, interdisciplinary course. For that, it is a lasting and important work in the criminological canon.

Matt DeLisi

See also Criminal Career Paradigm; Gottfredson, Michael R., and Travis Hirschi: Self-Control Theory; Herrnstein, Richard J., and Charles Murray: Crime and the Bell Curve; Moffitt, Terrie E. A.: Developmental Model of Life-Course-Persistent Offending; Neurology and Crime

References and Further Readings

Cohen, L. E. (1987). Social control, deviance, and the law: Throwing down the gauntlet: A challenge to the relevance of sociology for the etiology of criminal behavior. *Contemporary Sociology, 16,* 202–205.

Cohn, E. G., & Farrington, D. P. (1994). Who are the most influential criminologists in the English-speaking world? *British Journal of Criminology, 22,* 204–225.

Cohn, E. G., & Farrington, D. P. (1998). Changes in the most-cited scholars in major American criminology and criminal justice journals between 1986–1990 and 1991–1995. *Journal of Criminal Justice, 26,* 99–116.

DeLisi, M. (2003). Conservatism and common sense: The criminological career of James Q. Wilson. *Justice Quarterly, 20,* 661–674.

DeLisi, M., Conis, P. J., & Beaver, K. M. (2008). The importance of violent offenders to criminology. In M. DeLisi & P. J. Conis (Eds.), *Violent offenders: Theory, research, public policy and practice* (pp. 1–14). Sudbury, MA: Jones & Bartlett.

Ferdinand, T. N. (1986). Book review. *The Journal of Criminal Law and Criminology, 77,* 237–243.

Gibbs, J. P. (1985). Review essay. *Criminology 23,* 381–388.

Gottfredson, M. R., & Hirschi, T. (1990). *A general theory of crime.* Stanford, CA: Stanford University Press.

Herrnstein, R. J. (1995). Criminogenic traits. In J. Q. Wilson & J. Petersilia (Eds.), *Crime* (pp. 39–64). San Francisco: Institute for Contemporary Studies Press.

Jenkins, P. (1986). Review essay of Crime and human nature. *Contemporary Crises, 10,* 329–335.

Kamin, L. L. (1985, April). Is crime in the genes? The answer may depend on who chooses the evidence. *Scientific American,* pp. 22–25.

Kuhn, T. S. (1962). *The structure of scientific revolutions.* Chicago: University of Chicago Press.

Laub, J. H., & Sampson, R. J. (2003). *Shared beginnings, divergent lives: Delinquent boys to age 70.* Cambridge, MA: Harvard University Press.

Loeber, R., & Farrington, D. P. (Eds.). (1998). *Serious and violent juvenile offenders: Risk factors and successful interventions.* Thousand Oaks, CA: Sage.

Moffitt, T. E. (1993). Adolescence-limited and life-course-persistent antisocial behavior: A developmental taxonomy. *Psychological Review, 100,* 674–701.

Raine, A. (1993). *The psychopathology of crime: Criminal behavior as a clinical disorder.* San Diego, CA: Academic Press.

Sampson, R. J., & Laub, J. H. (1993). *Crime in the making: Pathways and turning points through life.* Cambridge, MA: Harvard University Press.

Wilson, J. Q., & Herrnstein, R. J. (1985). *Crime and human nature: The definitive study of the causes of crime.* New York: Free Press.

WILSON, JAMES Q., AND GEORGE L. KELLING: BROKEN WINDOWS THEORY

Broken windows theory has had a substantial impact on criminological theory and, in particular, on police policy. James Q. Wilson and George L. Kelling, the theory's creators, predicted that disorder is a precursor of serious crime. They posited that disorderly conditions in a neighborhood or community lead to the development of a serious crime problem in that area if the disorder is not eliminated quickly. Many people were drawn to the theory by its simplicity. It is a to-the-point theory of crime and policing, and this straightforwardness has been very attractive to policymakers, police administrators, and some academic criminologists.

The present entry, which is an overview of the basic premises of broken windows theory and policing, proceeds in four sections. First, core tenets of the theory are defined and the theoretical mechanisms purported to cause crime are detailed. The proposed role of police in the broken windows process is also described. Second, results from empirical examinations of broken windows theory and policing are summarized. Third, the major theoretical critiques of broken windows are discussed. Finally, the entry ends with an outline of the future directions of broken windows theory and policing.

Broken Windows Theory: Disorder and Crime

The basic premise of broken windows theory is fairly straightforward: Disorder causes a breakdown in local social control, and this breakdown allows crime to flourish. The logical converse, so said the theory's creators, was that catching disorder early and eliminating it promptly would prevent this breakdown in control and the consequent spike in crime. Broken windows theory revolves around the concept of "disorder," which is subdivided into "physical disorder" and "social disorder." Physical disorder refers to litter on the sidewalks, abandoned houses or storefronts, evidence of vandalism or graffiti, and other unpleasant structural conditions. Social disorder includes things like aggressive panhandling, prostitution, low-level drug peddling, groups of teens loitering on street corners, and other actions that violate social norms (and, sometimes, the law) and make people uncomfortable or afraid.

According to broken windows theory, physical and social disorder are concentrated in some areas and create neighborhoods or communities characterized by general states of disarray. These areas evince an overall lack of internal control, both at the informal and formal levels. Disorder conveys the impression that local residents are either unable or unwilling to exercise informal social control and that the local police are similarly tolerant of deviant and criminal behavior. This perceived lack of control in the neighborhood or community makes people afraid of serious victimization because they believe that if something even as relatively mundane as disorder cannot be reined in, then certainly there is nothing being done to prevent serious criminals from running amok. Those persons who are not involved in deviant, disorderly, or criminal behaviors thus withdraw from public spaces. They avoid using public areas such as parks and opt, instead, to stay home. The streets are thus devoid of law-abiding people and are wide open to all manner of miscreants.

The flight of prosocial individuals from public spaces and the resultant filling up of those spaces with disorderly persons and conditions set the stage for what Wilson and Kelling termed a "criminal invasion" (p. 32). Within the neighborhood or community itself, those whose offenses have been previously confined to disorderly actions may be emboldened by the lack of social control in the area and may start committing more serious street crimes. Other criminals, already proficient in predation, may be attracted to the neighborhood or community by the apparent lack of informal and formal social control. Soon, the argument goes, the area is rife with serious crime and the streets are unsafe for everyone, law abiding and disorderly alike.

Broken windows theory, as originally formulated by Wilson and Kelling, was not just a theory of crime; it also was a theory of policing. Wilson and Kelling's focus was on the things police could do to prevent and reduce crime; specifically, the authors heavily emphasized the role of police as the primary enforcers of the local order. Police were the ones who needed to detect physical and social disorder and to intervene immediately. The authors claimed, "Though citizens can do a great deal, the police are plainly key to order maintenance" (p. 36). The architects of broken windows theory, then, placed order maintenance (or, conversely, disorder prevention/reduction) squarely in the hands of the police.

Wilson and Kelling also specified a "tipping point." Neighborhoods below this point were good candidates for order maintenance policing, because even though disorder might be a serious problem, the plunge into serious crime had not yet occurred and, therefore, police could intervene and prevent the final outcome of disorder from coming to fruition. Neighborhoods beyond the tipping point, however, had taken that plunge, and police in these areas were too bogged down with serious crime to realistically hope to address disorder. Wilson and Kelling implied that broken windows theory applied in a universal manner to all types of neighborhoods, which made broken windows a generalized approach that, supposedly, could be adopted by communities and neighborhoods of all types.

The Empirical Status of Broken Windows Theory

Tests of Broken Windows Theory

One of the most commonly cited analyses of broken windows theory is that by Wesley G. Skogan, whose statistical models demonstrated a connection between disorder and robbery at the neighborhood level and lent empirical support to broken windows theory. Subsequent reanalyses of the same data by Bernard E. Harcourt showed that disorder did not affect any crimes other than robbery and that this relationship was neighborhood-specific. Ralph Taylor found that the presence of disorder in a given neighborhood at one time point did not predict very well the presence of serious crime in that neighborhood at a later time point. The overall pattern suggested that some types of disorder predicted some types of crime in some neighborhoods.

In 1999, Robert J. Sampson and Stephen W. Raudenbush suggested that rather than disorder being the cause of crime, disorder and crime are both products of the same underlying problem: low collective efficacy. When informal social control and capacity for collective mobilization in a neighborhood are deficient, disorder and crime are both likely outcomes. Other authors have also questioned broken windows' assumption of disorder as an independently-operating causal construct. Disorder, which broken windows theory assumes to have an independent effect on fear and social withdrawal, may actually be one component of an overall state of disadvantage or disorganization within a neighborhood or community.

Tests of Broken Windows Policing

Analyses of broken windows policing have yielded mixed results. The first and most famous implementation of broken windows occurred in New York City in the early 1990s. The advent of this strategy coincided with a large drop in violent crime in New York City and this co-occurrence has been viewed by broken windows supporters as proof of the theory's validity). Several authors, however, have reanalyzed data from the New York City experience and have concluded that there is actually little reason to think that broken windows policing was responsible for much, if any, of the crime drop). Further evaluations of other broken windows policing efforts have produced some results supporting the strategy and others disconfirming it.

Major Criticisms of Broken Windows Theory

Inconsistency in the Definitions and Meanings of Disorder

The most formidable challenge facing broken windows theory is that of defining its key construct: disorder. Nearly every test of broken windows theory that has been conducted has constructed its disorder scales in a way unique from all other tests of the theory. This variation has resulted in between-study employ of disorder scales that can look quite different from one another. Many of the items used in disorder scales—such as prostitution and low-level drug selling—are actually crimes, which further complicates matters. In addition, researchers have uncovered notable disparities between researcher-observed and citizen-perceived measures of disorder. Observed disorder may also predict certain types of crimes while perceived disorder may predict other types). In short, the conceptual definition of disorder is vague and there is no widely accepted method of measuring this construct.

Ignoring the Causes of Disorder

Wilson and Kelling and subsequent broken windows commentators (e.g., Kelling and Coles) have devoted effort to explicating the *consequences* of disorder, but few have confronted the issue of the *causes of* disorder. There are many reasons why neighborhoods and communities fall into disarray. Many of the social and economic problems faced by inner-city areas can be traced to the phenomenon of "middle-class flight," where people with the economic means to do so relocate from the city into nearby suburbs. They take with them tax bases, economic viability, and local businesses. Neighborhoods and communities that have fallen victim to middle-class flight and the ensuing socioeconomic crumble may well be disorderly, but disorder is not the *cause* of the problem. Low collective efficacy as well as high residential turnover and particular types of land use all contribute significantly to disorder and, in many cases, also have a direct link with crime.

The Future of Broken Windows Theory

The brightest future for broken windows theory is one in which the theory is better contextualized. Broken windows theory bears many similarities to the Clifford Shaw and Henry McKay's classic theory of social disorganization, with the important difference that Wilson and Kelling divorced disorder from its broader social and economic environment and imbued it with a meaning and significance all of its own. This move has proved to be a shortcoming in the theory. Disorder does matter, but so do poverty, residential instability, racial segregation, and other systemic socioeconomic factors that marginalize segments of society and disadvantage certain neighborhoods and communities. Police have a vital role to play in community improvement and quality of life for local residents, but true improvement and lasting public safety happen only when multiple agencies and groups collaborate to identify local solutions and develop creative solutions. There is no one single agency—police or otherwise—that can do this alone.

Jacinta M. Gau

See also Brantingham, Patricia L., and Paul J. Brantingham: Environmental Criminology; Lewis, Dan A., and Greta W. Salem: Incivilities and Fear; Sampson, Robert J.: Collective Efficacy Theory; Shaw, Clifford R., and Henry D. McKay: Social Disorganization Theory; Skogan, Wesley G.: Disorder and Decline; Wilson, William Julius: The Truly Disadvantaged

References and Further Readings

Braga, A. A., Weisburd, D. L., Waring, E. J., Mazerolle, L. G., Spelman, W., & Gajewski, F. (1999). Problem-oriented policing in violent crime places: A randomized controlled experiment. *Criminology, 37,* 541–580.

Corman, H., & Mocan, N. (2005). Carrots, sticks, and broken windows. *Journal of Law and Economics, 48,* 235–266.

DiIulio, J., Jr. (1995). Arresting ideas [Electronic version]. *Policy Review, 74,* 12.

Eck, J. E., & Maguire, E. R. (2000). Have changes in policing reduced violent crime? An assessment of the evidence. In A. Blumstein & J. Wallman (Eds.), *The crime drop in America* (pp. 207–265). Cambridge, UK: Cambridge University Press.

Fagan, J., Zimring, F. E., & Kim, J. (1998). Declining homicide in New York City: A tale of two trends. *Journal of Criminal Law and Criminology, 88,* 1277–1323.

Gau, J. M., & Pratt, T. C. (2008). Broken windows or window dressing? Citizens' (in)ability to tell the difference between disorder and crime. *Criminology and Public Policy, 7,* 163–194.

Harcourt, B. E. (2001). *Illusion of order: The false promise of broken windows policing.* Cambridge, MA: Harvard University Press.

Harcourt, B. E., & Ludwig, J. (2006). Broken windows: New evidence from New York City and a five-city social experiment. *University of Chicago Law Review, 73*(1), 271–320.

Katz, C. M., Webb, V. J., & Schaefer, D. R. (2001). An assessment of the impact of quality-of-life policing on crime and disorder. *Justice Quarterly, 18,* 825–876.

Kelling, G. L., & Bratton, W. J. (1998). Declining crime rates: Insiders' views of the New York City story. *Journal of Criminal Law and Criminology, 88,* 1217–1231.

Kelling, G. L., & Coles, C. M. (1996). *Fixing broken windows.* New York: Simon & Schuster.

Kelling, G. L., & Sousa, W. H., Jr. (2001). *Do police matter? An analysis of the impact of New York City's police reforms.* New York: The Manhattan Institute.

Kubrin, C. E. (2008). Making order of disorder: A call for conceptual clarity. *Criminology and Public Policy, 7,* 203–214.

Novak, K. J., Hartman, J. L., Holsinger, A. M., & Turner, M. G. (1999). The effects of aggressive policing of disorder on serious crime. *Policing: An International Journal of Police Strategies and Management, 22,* 171–190.

Piquero, A. (1999). The validity of incivility measures in public housing. *Justice Quarterly, 16,* 793–818.

Ross, C. E., & Mirowsky, J. (1999). Disorder and decay: The concept and measurement of perceived neighborhood disorder. *Urban Affairs Review, 34,* 412–432.

Sampson, R. J. (2006). Collective efficacy theory: Lessons learned and directions for future inquiry. In F. T. Cullen, J. P. Wright, & K. R. Blevins (Eds.), *Taking stock: The status of criminological theory* (Advances in Criminological Theory: Vol. 15, pp. 149–168). New Brunswick, NJ: Transaction.

Sampson, R. J., & Cohen, J. (1988). Deterrent effects of the police on crime: A replication and theoretical extension. *Law and Society Review, 22,* 163–189.

Sampson, R. J., & Raudenbush, S. W. (1999). Systematic social observation of public spaces: A new look at disorder in urban neighborhoods. *American Journal of Sociology, 105,* 603–651.

Sampson, R. J., & Raudenbush, S. W. (2004). Seeing disorder: Neighborhood stigma and the social construction of "broken windows." *Social Psychology Quarterly, 67,* 319–342.

Shaw, C. R., & McKay, H. D. (1942). *Juvenile delinquency in urban areas.* Chicago: University of Chicago Press.

Skogan, W. G. (1990). *Disorder and decline.* Berkeley: University of California Press.

St. Jean, P. K. B. (2007). *Pockets of crime: Broken windows, collective efficacy, and the criminal point of view.* Chicago: University of Chicago Press.

Taylor, R. B. (2001). *Breaking away from broken windows.* Boulder, CO: Westview Press.

Wilcox, P., Quisenberry, N., Cabrera, D. T., & Jones, S. (2004). Busy places and broken windows? Toward defining the role of physical structure and process in community crime models. *Sociological Quarterly, 45,* 185–207.

Wilson, J. W. (1987). *The truly disadvantaged: The inner city, the underclass, and public policy*. Chicago: University of Chicago Press.

Wilson, J. Q., & Kelling, G. L. (1982, March). The police and neighborhood safety: Broken windows. *Atlantic Monthly*, pp. 29–38.

Worrall, J. L. (2006). The discriminant validity of perceptual incivility measures. *Justice Quarterly, 23*, 360–383.

Worrall, J. L. (2006). Does targeting minor offenses reduce serious crime? A provisional, affirmative answer based on an analysis of county-level data. *Police Quarterly, 9*, 47–72.

WILSON, WILLIAM JULIUS: THE TRULY DISADVANTAGED

The Truly Disadvantaged by William Julius Wilson provides criminology the opportunity to discuss the intersection of race, poverty, and crime, which has been a controversial and sensitive topic within the field. Although criminologists are not new to the study of race and crime, interpreting, theorizing, and making policy recommendations have proven more problematic. The numerous works by Wilson, and more specifically *The Truly Disadvantaged*, have furnished criminology with a context to discuss race, class, and crime, so as to further the understanding of these relationships and their implications for social policy.

Biography

Wilson's experiences provide the background for his groundbreaking work on race and poverty. Wilson was born in 1935 in Derry Township, Pennsylvania. After his father's unexpected death, he, his mother, and five siblings used public assistance for a short time. He did well in his primary educational years. He graduated from Wilberforce University in Ohio in 1958, with degrees in sociology and history. He spent the next 4 years in the Army. After he was discharged, he enrolled in Bowling Green State University in Ohio. He graduated with his masters in sociology and history in 1961. He attended Washington State University where he completed his doctorate degrees in sociology and anthropology, in 1966. His first academic position was at the University of Massachusetts, Amherst. Several years later he accepted a position at the University of Chicago, in the Department of Sociology. While there, he also served as director of the Center for the Study of Urban Inequality. In 1996, he accepted a joint appointment at Harvard University in the John F. Kennedy School of Government and the Department of Afro-American Studies.

Throughout his life, he has been recognized and awarded for his exceptional thought and writings. While in the military, he was awarded a Meritorious Service Award. While at the University of Massachusetts, Amherst he was recognized with the 1970 Distinguished Teacher of the Year Award. For 6 years, he served as the Lucy Flower Distinguished Service Professor at the University of Chicago. In 1991, he was elected into the National Academy of Sciences. He has also been elected to the American Academy of Arts and Sciences and the American Philosophical Society. He is the second African American sociologist to serve as president of the American Sociological Association. Today, Wilson is sought by many groups within academia and in the private sector for his insight, knowledge, and expertise in policy issues, especially in relation to urban poverty.

Research

Early in Wilson's academic career, he recognized his interest in race and social problems. As he continued his schooling, he furthered and narrowed his interests in examining race and class (more specifically poverty). His most significant works centered on these interests, sparking much debate and controversy, within numerous disciplines and governmental agencies.

Although Wilson produced numerous works, his books provide an evolution of his research agenda on race and poverty. In 1973, he published his first book, *Power, Racism, and Privilege: Race Relations in Theoretical and Sociohistorical Perspective*. This volume examined empirical evidence to compare race relations between the United States and South Africa.

His next work, titled *The Declining Significance of Race: Blacks and Changing American Institutions*, received widespread attention within the study of race and class. Wilson argued that social class tells more about the plight of poor

African Americans in the United States than race. When comparing poor African Americans to poor White Americans, Blacks still lagged significantly behind in community resources and economic opportunities. He argued that class was more important than race in understanding access to power and privileges in the United States, specifically for African Americans. Wilson does not deny racial discrimination, racial oppression, racial segregation, or any aspect of race, but he believes that changes in the economy and the political order shifted the focus from race to class. This book received significant discussion within academia and among organizational leaders, and won numerous awards within the field of sociology.

His next two books were built on his previous works to focus on the issue of inner city or urban poverty. In 1987, Wilson published *The Truly Disadvantaged: The Inner City, the Underclass, and Public Policy*. This volume, which is discussed more in depth below, focuses on urban Blacks or the underclass within in the United States and on their continual plight into poverty. In 1996, he published *When Work Disappears: The World of the New Urban Poor*, which outlines the loss of jobs for the underclass due to suburbanization and lack of training and educational opportunities for urban Blacks. He supplied policy and program recommendations to advocate opportunities to jobless urban dwellers.

Lastly, Wilson and Taub published *There Goes the Neighborhood: Racial, Ethnic, and Class Tensions in Four Chicago Neighborhoods and Their Meaning for America*. This work investigates examining four different Chicago neighborhoods to explore the timeliness of ethnic change in relation to social class. In March 2009, Wilson published *More Than Just Race: Issues for Our Time* with the intent to focus race and poverty discussions on the integration of social and cultural factors. Although Wilson's major works were not directly focused on criminality, his major thesis of race and poverty are a continual research focus for criminologists in understanding crime and all its dynamics within urban areas.

The Truly Disadvantaged

In *The Truly Disadvantaged* Wilson began his exploration of the plight of the "ghetto underclass" by focusing on societal and historical events since the 1960s, though he acknowledged the sources of inner-city problems are very complex. He argued that the urban areas of today and the problems experienced in these areas stem from significant changes that took place during this time. He provided empirical evidence from census data on Chicago to show specifics on the plight of African Americans in urban settings. Wilson also focused on female-headed households, teenage pregnancy, and births to non-married parents as they have been directly associated with poverty.

Historical and contemporary discrimination are central to understanding the social isolation experienced by the underclass, with Wilson arguing that historical effects were more detrimental than current discriminatory practices. He made this argument by addressing the discrimination experienced by African Americans that migrated from the South to northern cities. He observed that those that migrated tended to be younger in age, which made them less likely to represent higher incomes or professional positions. Younger persons became more vulnerable to a weakened urban labor market susceptible to the economic changes that occurred in the 1970s. This involved the shift from goods-producing to a service-oriented market and the flight of industries from inner-city areas. Although affirmative action policies were in place, urban areas became concentrated with minorities, poverty, single-parent families, and welfare dependency, greatly influenced by the decrease in job opportunities. During this same time period, many middle-class urban dwellers also moved out of the city, to the suburbs, to further their job availability. This left a concentration of impoverished people to comprise the inner city or the ghettos that were now socially isolated from mainstream society. This social isolation contributed to behaviors that were not appropriate in "good" work histories. Wilson argues that this social isolation, not the culture of poverty, is the key concept to understanding the underclass.

Furthering the concept of the "truly disadvantaged," Wilson showed that the experiences of African American families were directly related to male joblessness in urban areas. Since the 1960s, black women have faced a decreasing pool of marriageable or financially secure men, which contributes to the increase in female-headed households. Wilson argued in *The Truly Disadvantaged* that male joblessness, not welfare policies, were paramount to the deterioration of black families.

Ghetto neighborhoods became characterized as unemployed, lacking adequate schools, single-parent households, and dependency on governmental resources. Wilson argued that this transition left urban areas socially isolated from mainstream social networks and conventional role models, perpetuating residents' existence in these inner-city areas, with little to no way out. Wilson discussed how this group of people is truly disadvantaged, though his policy recommendations provide a controversial, but relevant solution to his presented arguments. He proposed the highly debated strategy of limiting policies that tend to be race specific, such as affirmative action, and increasing more universal policies such as obtaining full employment. He advocated for the assurance of child support and child care, and for national policies that focused on economic growth and labor market initiatives. Wilson believes that these policies and the recognition of the underclass as truly disadvantaged can encourage policy makers to refocus their agendas to assist this group.

Contributions to Criminology

In *The Truly Disadvantaged*, Wilson referenced some criminal activity by racial distributions. Crime is another consequence for the underclass due to their social isolation and lack of job opportunities for younger persons in urban areas. Although briefly discussed, Wilson addresses race and violent crime in this book. He discussed empirical evidence from Chicago, but also assumed this occurs in other large inner-city areas. The data revealed that African Americans are more likely to commit murder, but also more likely to be a victim of murder. He discussed the relationship between high rates of violent crime as having a direct relationship with underclass neighborhoods in Chicago. The specific link between race and violent crime was furthered by the work of Robert Sampson and Wilson.

Sampson and Wilson argued that criminologists fear discussions of race due to being labeled a racists or being misunderstood. They believe their work would allow dialogue to occur on race,

crime, and inequality by focusing on the structural patterns that have given rise to the continued social isolation of the truly disadvantaged and that have created the macro-level barriers that contribute to cultural adaptations developed in urban poverty areas. The conversation of race and crime should center within the community.

The focus on communities is not new to criminology. Early works by Clifford Shaw and Henry McKay provided a community focus in their work on structural factors that lead to juvenile delinquency in urban neighborhoods. Shaw and McKay focused on economic status, ethnic heterogeneity, and residential mobility as macro-variables accounting for variations in delinquency. Sampson and Wilson began with these same factors to discuss race and violent crime. They acknowledged that African Americans, similar to any racial or ethnic group, are not homogeneous. They argued that cultural explanations that may exist by racial or ethnic group membership must be placed in the context of structural components within a community. Violent crime then is grounded in the macro differences among communities based on economic and family organization.

Throughout the article, Wilson's key components for the existence of the truly disadvantaged were reinforced. Sampson and Wilson argued that the most significant factors to understanding the relationship between race and crime are the differences in African American communities characterized by social disorganization and social isolation. Research supports the relationship between community social disorganization and crime (Bursik, 1988; Kornhauser, 1978; Sampson & Groves, 1989; Shaw & McKay, 1942). Social disorganization is characterized by segregation, migration, discrimination in housing, and economic transformations. These factors interact with community characteristics of residential instability, concentrated poverty, and family disruptions to hinder social organization. Social isolation—or more specifically cultural social isolation—stems from community barriers that limit communication and common values from the larger society. Sampson and Wilson ultimately argue that to understand race and violent crime, the community context must be the paramount factor. To understand violent crime rates, researchers should examine urban community structures and significant cultural changes that occurred during the 1970s and 1980s to understand the childhood socialization experiences of adults today. Sampson and Wilson limit the importance of race by supporting the focus on structural components of communities, so as to understand violent crimes rates in the United States.

Wilson's work has influenced other topics related to the study of race and crime. For example, Graham Ousey reported continued support for Wilson's work by finding that regardless of race, a decrease in manufacturing jobs had an indirect effect on juvenile homicide rates through economic deprivation and female-headed households. Similarly, Michael Reisig and Roger Parks wanted to examine the role community policing could play in helping the underclass. They found police should make the effort to establish mutual trust among the community members they assist because it improves quality of life for the neighborhood.

Conclusion

Wilson's work continues to be debated and studied in sociology and criminology. He provides scholars a platform to view race as a factor in the study of criminality, though not as the most significant indicator of crime. Criminologists should acknowledge his work in their future research projects examining race and crime by recognizing community characteristics and neighborhood context that include numerous variables extending beyond race.

Jennifer Gossett

See also Anderson, Elijah: Code of the Street; Krivo, Lauren J., and Ruth D. Peterson: Extreme Disadvantage and Crime; Sampson, Robert J.: Collective Efficacy Theory; Sampson, Robert J., and William Julius Wilson: Contextualized Subculture; Shaw, Clifford R., and Henry D. McKay: Social Disorganization Theory

References and Further Readings

Bursik, R. J. (1988). Social disorganization and theories of crime and delinquency: Problems and prospects. *Criminology, 26*, 519–552.
Greene, H. T., & Gabbidon S. L. (2000). *African American criminological thought*. Albany: SUNY Press.
Kornhauser, R. (1978). *Social sources of delinquency*. Chicago: University of Chicago Press.
Ousey, G. C. (2000). Deindustrialization, female-headed families, and black and white juvenile homicide rates, 1970–1990. *Sociological Inquiry, 70*, 319–391.
Reisig, M. D., & Parks, R. B. (2004). Can community policing help the truly disadvantaged? *Crime and Delinquency, 50*, 139–167.
Sampson, R. J., & Groves, W. B. (1989). Community structure and crime: Testing social disorganization theory. *American Journal of Sociology, 94*, 774–802.
Sampson, R. J., & Wilson, W. J. (1998). Toward a theory of race, crime and urban inequality. In D. R. Karp (Ed.), *Community justice: An emerging field* (pp. 97–115). Lanham, MD: Rowman & Littlefield.
Shaw, C., & McKay, H. (1942). *Juvenile delinquency and urban areas*. Chicago: University of Chicago Press.
Wilson, W. J. (1973). *Power, racism, and privilege: Race relations in theoretical and sociohistorical perspective*. New York: Macmillan.
Wilson, W. J. (1978). *The declining significance of race: Blacks and changing American institutions*. Chicago: University of Chicago Press.
Wilson, W. J. (1987). *The truly disadvantaged: The inner city, the underclass, and public policy*. Chicago: University of Chicago Press.
Wilson, W. J. (1991–1992). Another look at the truly disadvantaged. *Political Science Quarterly, 106*, 639–656.
Wilson, W. J. (1996). *When work disappears: The world of the new urban poor*. New York: Alfred A. Knopf.
Wilson, W. J. (2009). *More than just race: Issues for our time*. New York: W. W. Norton.
Wilson, W. J., & Taub, R. P. (2007). *There goes the neighborhood: Racial, ethnic, and class tensions in four Chicago neighborhoods and their meaning for America*. New York: Vintage.

WOLFGANG, MARVIN E., AND FRANCO FERRACUTI: SUBCULTURE OF VIOLENCE THEORY

Marvin E. Wolfgang and Franco Ferracuti have been touted as among the most widely cited criminological scholars in history. Their primary work, titled *The Subculture of Violence*, represents a marvel achievement among interdisciplinary researchers. Wolfgang was a professor of sociology while Ferracuti was an Italian professor of psychology as well as a physician. When considering this combination of disciplines that both authors brought into their research and when considering that these authors provided a cross-cultural (if not multicultural) perspective to their research, it is no wonder that their work has been considered an unparalleled achievement addressing the complexities associated with multidisciplinary and multicultural approaches. As E. E. Sainsbury (p. 63) noted when this thesis was first released, "interdisciplinary research usually results in a disjointed display of separate systems of knowledge," which often limits the means by which a given project can maximally benefit from the multiple perspectives available—perspectives that would typically be considered a strength to a research project.

Sainsbury notes that Wolfgang and Ferracuti's integrated theory synthesized knowledge and provided a new perspective in examining lethal violence among groups. Further, it is believed that criminology was an especially suitable field for interdisciplinary studies. With this in mind, it would seem that their study of subcultures was also particularly appropriate, both because such a study comports well with a comparison of cultural perspectives—in this case, a comparison of subcultural perspectives—and because subcultures lend themselves well to definition and examination. Wolfgang and Ferracuti brought together a variety of propositions about subcultures from various disciplines and used an array of biological, psychological, and sociological approaches to explain how and why violence may become part of a subculture's integral norms and mores.

As presented by Wolfgang and Ferracuti, the *subculture of violence theory* has been used to explain violence (particularly homicide) in a number of contexts and for a variety of different social groups (Cao et al., 1997; Dixon & Lizotte, 1987; Ellison, 1991). Wolfgang and Ferracuti published their seminal work in 1967 with the intent to explain murders that were crimes of passion rather than utility. They made the observation in their work that these crimes of passion tended to be concentrated within specific ecological areas and also were found more frequently among certain socioeconomic groups. In particular, they discovered that homicide rates were the highest among young adult males in lower-class urban environments.

In their effort to explain the reason for this observation, Wolfgang and Ferracuti utilized elements of Edwin Sutherland's differential association theory in their work, contending that the development of favorable attitudes and norms toward violence generally involved some type of learned behavior. In this regard, it was noted that some subcultures socially teach their young to use violent alternatives as their primary repertoire of responses to problems that life presents. Within these subcultures, violence is expected and is often seen as a requirement for slights and conflicts that may seem trivial to persons who are not members of the subculture. According to Wolfgang and Ferracutti, the subculture of violence formulation simply suggests that there is a very clear theme of violence in the lifestyle of subculture members. The socialization process and interpersonal relationships tend to revolve around a constant preoccupation with violence.

As noted earlier, the seminal work by Wolfgang and Ferracuti focused on the crime of homicides, particularly those committed as heat of passion crimes. Further, Wolfgang and Ferracuti were very careful to exclude rare or problematic offenders. Among those who were excluded were those persons who were mentally ill, noting that while this group indeed deserves study, their research focused on those individuals who were not anomalies among offenders who have committed homicide. Further, Wolfgang and Ferracuti were careful to eliminate premeditated homicides, noting their rarity and the fact that many of these criminals may have evaded detection, creating a dark figure of homicide crime in their analysis. Rather, their concern was with the bulk of the homicides that had occurred at the time; crimes of passion and violent slayings. In laying out their thesis, Wolfgang and Ferracuti proposed a series of tenets or key themes to explaining violent subcultures. To provide the reader with a clear understanding of Wolfgang and Ferracuti's work, this entry furnishes an overview of each of these tenets with a brief explanation as to their meaning and importance. Before proceeding to these tenets, it should be pointed out that many theorists since the time of the original work have used this theory to explain why some regions have higher rates of homicide than do others (Borg, 1997; Dixon & Lizotte, 1987). Thus, the utility of this theory has made it one that can be applied in multiple locations and social contexts. As will become clear, Wolgang and Ferracuti provided a set of propositions that define their theory yet, at the same time, allow for sufficient flexibility, for their theory to be adapted to explain homicide in a variety of cultures. These tenets are discussed in the paragraphs that follow.

No subculture can be totally different from, or totally in conflict with, the society from which it has emerged. By this, Wolfgang and Ferracuti noted that a subculture of violence is not merely a message of violence, it also consists of a set of connecting values and mores that are shared by the broader culture that permeates a society and allows the subculture to exist. While some overtones of violence may exist within the broader society, there are typically rules and rituals that are assigned to these sanctioned forms of violence. This is particularly true when it comes to the use of homicide. Further, Wolfgang and Ferracuti note that it is unlikely that a subculture would require formal social organization or even highly structured roles. Rather, it is the values that are shared in rank order and with similar intensity that would seem to be critical elements in the definition of a subculture. These factors are what also tend to normalize the use of violence within a given group.

Just because a subculture of violence may develop, it does not mean that members of that subculture will respond with violence to all confrontations and/or sources of frustration. Essentially, members of this subculture tend to view violence as a response that is used to either gain revenge or "save face" when presented with specific social challenges that are considered demeaning or dishonorable. As an example, a member of this subculture may be presented with a slight that is made toward his biological mother. In such circumstances and in some subcultures, such a slight would require a retaliatory act of violence so that one's own honor (and that of his mother's honor) is maintained and kept intact. A failure to use quick and serious violence—even lethal violence—will tend to be perceived as weakness by other members. On the other hand, consider a scenario where that same subculture member is ridiculed for his misbehavior (even embarrassing misbehavior) while drinking the night before. In such a case, this type of ridicule is

often considered "in fun" or due to the member's being "crazy," essentially being equated to humor and the life of the party. In these cases, it may be expected that members exchange words, but the actual progression to violence may not be required nor expected. In essence, the dynamics are different because the intent behind the ridicule is also different. Wolfgang and Ferracuti make it clear that persons who live in a subculture of violence could not engage constantly in violence, especially homicide (Cullen & Agnew, 2006). In actuality, this simply stands to reason; any subculture that was continuously involved in lethal violence would eventually extinguish itself, either through attacks upon members internally or due to the continuous casualties incurred due to never-ending conflicts with parties external to the subculture. Nevertheless, there is a heightened degree of mortality in these subcultures and the ready access to weapons, particularly firearms, enhances the likelihood of lethality. Further, the brandishing of weapons may be considered a norm that is required, if nothing else due to the need for self-defense from other groups who likewise seek out violence. In these cases, the mere possession of weapons, especially the *known* possession of weapons, can serve as a deterrent for one's enemies. When multiple subcultures of violence exist in the same vicinity (as with competing street gangs), the possession of lethal weapons conveys a willingness to resort to violence—an expectation that violence will at some point occur, and the expectation that retaliation from one's enemies will follow any act of violence that is inflicted (Cullen & Agnew, 2006).

The constant state of vigilance and willingness to engage in violence demonstrates how violence permeates that culture and its sense of identity. In this case, the number of incidents where a member engages in violence and the seriousness of that violence can serve as a social barometer of the member's assimilation within the subculture. In such circumstances, the overt use of violence and the use of serious violence (especially homicide) indicates the level of commitment that a member has to that subculture. This is true in many gangs, especially prison gangs, where members may be required to commit some act of lethal violence as a requirement for membership and/or to gain an elevated status or rank within the gang. Wolfgang and Ferracuti also observe that among members of a given subculture, one would be able to recognize quantitative differences on psychological instruments and psychometric scales between members who are more prone to violence than those who are not as committed to a belief system grounded in violence. These differences would likely include the differential perception and processing of violent stimuli (including perceived aggressive intent where there is none), levels of compassion and/or remorse for violent acts, and/or differences in cognitive problem-solving skills. A number of other characteristics associated with the willingness to use violence and/or an actual history of violence might also provide useful quantitative measures. Note that this aspect of the theory likely reflects Ferracuti's influence. From this and other observations, it will become clear that Ferracuti's background in psychology helped shape the formulation of this subcultural theory.

Subcultures of violence will tend to consist of members from a limited age range, consisting largely of persons who are in late adolescence to middle age. This tenet simply addresses an observation that actually tends to be true with criminal behavior in general; crime is most often a young person's exploit. Indeed, criminals tend to age out of their activities and/or age down in the frequency and seriousness of those activities over time. Thus, this tenet simply comports with the broader criminal population and therefore is simply a logical extension of what was already known about the offending population. Further still, violent crime specifically tends to be committed by younger rather than older offenders. Thus, there is a greater localization, incidence, and frequency of violence among youthful offenders, and this then translates to a heightened affinity among these younger offenders for subcultural groups that emphasize the use of violence.

Nonviolence is considered a counter-norm; peaceful approaches to the resolution of conflict are not respected between and among members. For members who do not act in-kind to situations that require a violent response, their acceptance by others in the subculture will decrease. In fact, if the social circumstances are considered serious enough, these members may even be dismissed from the group. In short, cowardice and weakness are seen to bring dishonor on the group and on the individual member. In cases where the requirement

for violence is considered a particularly strong expectation, members who fail to meet their obligation may themselves be killed by others in the subculture. This is particularly true within some organized crime groups, particularly Italian and/or Sicilian organized crime groups and, on some occasions, the Japanese Yakuza. In cases where the virtual execution of members who fail to live up to the subcultural expectations of lethal violence occurs, these acts are often seen as a means of ensuring loyalty and adherence among other members of the group. Further, these executions provide a sense of group cohesion in affirming the agreed-upon belief that lethal violence is inherent and pivotal to the group's identity and survival. The failure of a member to exact lethal violence when it is required under clearly defined and mandatory circumstances is akin to an act of treason among these groups. This reaction is consistent with what nation-states themselves may do with treasonous individuals during historical points of national crisis and/or large-scale warfare. This observation is important because it demonstrates that the willingness to engage in lethal violence and the actual act of lethal violence when it is required can be considered a survival behavior for the group as a whole; members are interdependent on one another to adhere to the social expectation or the entire group can be jeopardized by the weakness of the sole individual who violates this tenet. Thus, in some cases, there can be more at stake than honor alone. Lethal violence can serve as a feature that vanquishes one's enemy and thereby enhances survival and the quality of that survival within one's own group.

The various mechanisms of learning inherent to differential association theory and social learning theory apply to violent subcultures; violence is a learned behavior that is reinforced through shared identity and associations that favor violent acts. This tenet explains how norms and values are shaped within the group as a whole and also explain how norms may vary from group to group both in the type of lethality of violence as a product of differential associations and differential forms of reinforcement. This aspect alone is worth mentioning since, at the time that Wolfgang and Ferracuti first published their work on the subculture of violence theory, scholars and researchers were critical of theories that could not specifically identify how the learning of criminal behavior occurred. However, this tenet also addresses differences among individuals who are members of the same subcultural group. Indeed, these researchers astutely observe that not all persons exposed to the presence of a subculture's values will internalize and commit to those values in an identical manner. This would be true even if their level of exposure to subcultural influences were identical. Indeed, Wolfgang and Ferracuti note that differential personality variables should be taken into account with any integrated social-psychological theory that explains subcultural influences on violence. Further, it is contended that aggression is a learned response that is facilitated by social influences and mechanisms and ultimately becomes a habitual response that is congruent with the personality characteristics of the person who commits violent acts. As was mentioned earlier, these aspects of this tenet and other tenets reveal Ferracuti's preference for psychological approaches to explaining violent crime. The infusion of psychology, including social psychology, becomes apparent when the authors explain how violence is learned, both individually (as with personality psychology and the psychology of learning) and as a group (both social psychology and the psychology of learning).

Within subcultures, the use of violence may not be perceived as wrong behavior and, as a result, is not likely to generate feelings of guilt or remorse among members. This is a very important aspect of this theory and, in actuality, tends to reflect the emotional framework of psychopaths (Hare & McPherson, 1984; Hare & Quinn, 1971) and/or offenders diagnosed with antisocial personality disorder (American Psychiatric Association, 2000). These groups of offenders tend to have a greater propensity to violence than do other offenders and, in many cases, their autonomic nervous systems do not seem to process anxiety, fear, and even guilt or remorse as do other persons in the general population. While it is not the intent of this entry to digress into the psychological framework of these types of offenders, it is important to note that both biological and social factors are thought to play an etiological role. Thus, the learned attitudes toward violence, particularly lethal violence, is akin to many of the learning experiences of psychopathic and antisocial offenders. As one may recall, this entry previously noted that

these offenders will also tend to have psychological and personality characteristics that are quantifiable through psychometric tests, including such characteristics as levels of compassion or remorse. Thus, the field of psychology potentially provides a number of contributions in specifically addressing the individual characteristics of members of violent subcultures.

Lastly, the lifestyles of members of these subcultures enable them to use violence as a primary method of problem solving when faced with difficult circumstances. Wolfgang and Ferracuti note that in many cases, the acts of violence that these offenders commit tend to be within the subcultural group itself or between other groups who share similar subcultural beliefs. Since their violent acts seldom include members of the broader nonviolent culture, the emergence of guilt and remorse seldom occurs among these offenders.

The subculture of violence theory has enjoyed a wide degree of popularity. Several researchers have extended the theory to include analyses of different subcultures in the United States and elsewhere in the world. This serves as a notable indicator of this theory's utility. The basic tenets of this theory demonstrate how both social forces and individual learning come into play to explain the use of lethal violence, particularly lethal violence among criminal subcultures. Further, this theory provides a clear yet broad explanation for acts of violence among groups. Likewise, the multidisciplinary nature of the theory makes it uniquely pliable to a wide array of circumstances. Finally, the fact that this is one of the most widely cited theories in the field of criminology speaks volumes to its important role in the discipline—a role that continues to be played out even today.

Robert D. Hanser

See also Akers, Ronald L.: Social Learning Theory; Anderson, Elijah: Code of the Street; Sellin, Thorsten: Culture Conflict and Crime; Southern Subculture of Violence Theory

References and Further Readings

American Psychiatric Association. (2000). *Diagnostic and statistical manual of mental disorders: Text revision* (4th ed.). Washington, DC: Author.

Borg, M. J. (1997). The Southern subculture of punitiveness? Regional variation in support for capital punishment. *Journal of Research in Crime and Delinquency, 34,* 25–45.

Cao, L., Adams, A., & Jensen, V. J. (1997). A test of the black subculture of violence thesis: A research note. *Criminology, 35,* 367–379.

Cullen, F. T., & Agnew, R. (Eds.). (2006) *Criminological theory: Past and present.* Los Angeles: Roxbury.

Dixon, J., & Lizotte, A. J. (1987). Gun ownership and the southern subculture of violence. *American Journal of Sociology, 93,* 383–405.

Ellison, C. G. (1991). An eye for an eye? A note on the southern subculture of violence thesis. *Social Forces, 69,* 1223–1239.

Felson, R. B., Liska, A. E., South, S. J., & McNulty, T. L. (1994). The subculture of violence and delinquency: Individual vs. school context effects. *Social Forces, 73,* 155–173.

Hare, R. D., & McPherson, L. M. (1984). Violent and aggressive behavior by criminal psychopaths. *International Journal of Law and Psychiatry, 7,* 35–50.

Hare, R. D., & Quinn, M. (1971). Psychopathy and autonomic conditioning. *Journal of Abnormal Psychology, 77,* 223–239.

Kennedy, L. W., & Baron, S. W. (1993). Routine activities and a subculture of violence: A study of violence on the street. *Journal of Research in Crime and Delinquency, 30,* 88–112.

Sainsbury, E. E. (1968). The subculture of violence. *Probation Journal, 14,* 63–64.

Wolfgang, M. E., & Ferracuti, F. (1967). *The subculture of violence: Towards an integrated theory in criminology.* London: Tavistock.

WORTLEY, RICHARD: A REVISED SITUATIONAL CRIME PREVENTION THEORY

The theory and practice of situational crime prevention has evolved since its earliest version that first appeared nearly 30 years ago. Much of the pioneering work and many of the subsequent developments of the theory are credited to the extensive scholarship of Ronald V. Clarke. However, several other scholars, such as Richard Wortley, have also played a pivotal role in extending situational crime prevention. Specifically, Wortley's work on *situational precipitators* represents a major theoretical and practical extension of situational crime prevention.

A brief discussion of rational choice theory and Clarke's version of situational crime prevention is necessary to provide some theoretical grounding for Wortley's later work on situational precipitators. Broadly, situational crime prevention tries to reduce crime by making highly specific crime opportunities seem unattractive to potential offenders. The idea that some situations are perceived to offer "better" opportunities for committing crime suggests that offenders are active decision makers who rationally weigh the potential gains of crime against its potential costs (Clarke & Cornish, 1985). Therefore, premised upon rational choice theory, the resulting formula for situational crime prevention is markedly straightforward: increase the perceived risks and effort of crime and reduce the promise of rewards to make offending a less attractive option to those looking to break the law.

The version of situational crime prevention described above emphasizes the utility of reducing opportunities to prevent crime. Wortley's central claim, however, is that focusing exclusively on opportunity reduction provides an incomplete picture of the person-situation interaction that underlies crime and its prevention. As he puts it, opportunity reduction is likely only "half of the situational crime prevention story" (2001, p. 63). He means that the interplay between a person and the individual's immediate situation is more complex than the opportunity-reduction approach suggests and cannot be fully articulated by considering opportunity alone.

The opportunity-reduction approach assumes that individuals *already* primed for criminal behavior capitalize on crime opportunities perceived as attractive from a cost-benefit analysis and forego those deemed less attractive from the same calculus. Wortley, however, emphasizes that the quality of criminal opportunity structures *and* the motivation to commit crime are both influenced by the situational features of his or her immediate environment. Put plainly, criminal opportunities and criminal motivation are *both* situationally dependent. Thus, situational features do not only influence whether or not crime is committed by way of a good opportunity; there are also situational factors that precipitate the motivation to commit crime in the first place.

A Revised Theory

Wortley offers a two-stage model to demonstrate how situational precipitators and opportunities are related, but separate, concepts that speak to different parts of a crime event. Situational features that precipitate illegal behavior should first be considered. The idea is that crime events would not occur if situational precipitators were absent or controlled. The logic is simple: if situations do not compel individuals to offend, would-be offenders do not possess the motivation to transform criminal opportunity into criminal action. Next, it is necessary to address what happens when situational precipitators have readied an individual to commit crime. It is at this time that the "already-motivated" offender considers the instrumental or rational aspects of the opportunity structure he is currently facing (i.e., the risks, rewards, and effort of crime) before deciding whether or not offending is a good choice. In all, Wortley's conceptualization suggests that situational precipitators and crime opportunities are temporally linked. That is, once situational precipitators ready an individual for crime, he *then* considers the perceived gains and risks of the present crime opportunity.

The model's two "loops" suggest that crime is most readily prevented when each element (i.e., situational precipitators and crime opportunities) receives balanced attention. For instance, focusing too heavily on controlling situational precipitators minimizes the importance of blocking crime opportunities—effectively facilitating criminal activity. Likewise, relying solely on opportunity reduction ignores the fact that illegal behavior can be situationally precipitated.

Wortley illustrates these dynamics by considering how prisons might control frustration and violence among inmates. Prisons that only focus on reducing opportunities create highly restricted environments that likely precipitate frustration and violence while prisons that are too lax on restrictions are likely riddled with opportunities for inmate misconduct. These examples show that controlling situational precipitators and reducing opportunities both warrant equal attention in crime prevention.

A major contribution of situational precipitators is that they reveal additional ways to prevent crime beyond using opportunity-reduction strategies alone. Since two unique situational forces influence potential offenders (i.e., the perceived costs and benefits of crime and situational precipitators), it makes sense that two classifications of techniques for preventing crime are needed. First, Clarke's situational prevention techniques target the instrumental costs and benefits of crime by targeting opportunity structures. Second, Wortley's techniques are designed to control the situational precipitators that induce offending. Although each set of techniques is distinct, Wortley argues that controlling precipitating factors is a complimentary, not competing, supplement to Clarke's taxonomy.

In all, Wortley discusses four ways in which situational features might precipitate criminal behavior. First, situations supply *prompts* that cue the performance of criminal behavior; exert *pressure* that compel people to offend; *permit* offending by weakening moral codes; and *provoke* criminal responses by arousing negative emotions. Accordingly, Wortley's classification of techniques for controlling situational precipitators of crime is headed by four main strategies: controlling prompts, controlling pressures, reducing permissibility, and reducing provocations. Each category contains four specific techniques resulting in a 16-celled taxonomy. Each of these categories and the corresponding techniques are discussed in more detail as follows.

Situational Precipitation of Criminal Behavior

Controlling Prompts

Certain situations emit cues capable of prompting criminal behavior. Based on social learning theory, the idea is that individuals are sometimes compelled to commit crime because an immediate situational stimulus produces a criminal response. Thus, Wortley stresses the need to control triggers, provide reminders, reduce inappropriate imitation, and set positive expectations to control a range of criminogenic prompts.

Situational features sometimes activate an automatic or impulsive behavioral response. Examples of such behavioral triggers include pornographic materials that stimulate sexual arousal resulting in sexual offending or the sight of armed prison guards inducing correctional frustration and violence. Accordingly, some strategies for *controlling triggers* include restricting pornography or controlling guns.

Providing reminders is another way to counteract environmental triggers that prompt criminal behavior. Strategies like posting warning signs or installing litter bins remind individuals that stealing, not wearing a seatbelt, littering, and a variety of other antisocial behaviors are inappropriate.

Some individuals engage in certain activities after observing the behavior of others. Therefore, *reducing inappropriate imitation* is a way to dissuade individuals from modeling the illegal activities they observe others doing. Some examples of this technique include removing vandalism and graffiti or monitoring the type of television programs a person watches.

Individuals sometimes enter situations carrying certain expectations and will behave according to the environment they anticipate. For example, people expecting a violent setting might enter that situation already primed for aggressive behavior. Therefore, *setting positive expectations*, like providing prisoners with domestic furnishings or repairing urban decay, should let individuals know that law-abiding conduct is required.

Controlling Pressures

Individual behavior can be influenced by various social pressures and standards. People often satisfy these demands by behaving in ways they think others would like. Therefore, situations that exert social pressures and precipitate criminal activity must be controlled. Social pressures can be controlled by reducing inappropriate conformity, reducing inappropriate obedience, encouraging compliance, and reducing anonymity.

Peer pressure is a powerful tool that social groups often use to get other individuals to conform to their viewpoints and behavior. Thus, *reducing inappropriate conformity* is a way to discourage people from following the unfavorable conduct of others. Some tactics for doing so include encouraging independence from delinquent groups or screening the social crowds that youth are allowed to associate with.

Just as individuals sometimes conform to the criminal beliefs of others and offend, people might

also obey the direct orders of others to perform illegal acts. Therefore, *reducing inappropriate obedience* by encouraging whistle-blowers or empowering individuals to stand firm against unlawful demands could curb criminal behavior.

The opposite of reducing inappropriate obedience is utilizing legitimate authority and positive communication to *encourage compliance* with law-abiding behavior. For example, setting rules and posting signs might persuade others to comply with legal expectations.

Group membership provides a "canopy" that can veil individual behavior. Some individuals might use the security and comfort of group anonymity to behave delinquently when they would have otherwise not broken the law on their own. *Reducing anonymity*, like crowd control, is a way to expose individuality among group members and reduce crime that is facilitated by group participation.

Reducing Permissibility

Offenders often use a variety of excuses to justify their involvement in criminal activity. That is, criminals convince themselves that their illegal behavior is permissible by neutralizing their wrongdoing. Some situational features actually permit offenders to commit crime by undercutting their good sense (i.e., moral reasoning). Accordingly, situational prevention techniques like rule setting, clarifying responsibility, clarifying consequences, and personalizing victims can be used to reduce the permissibility of crime.

It is more difficult for individuals to justify their illegal behavior when there are rules instructing them to obey the law. Thus, *rule setting* can disable the types of situational precipitators that would otherwise permit individuals to commit crime. Specifically, posting anti-crime policies or establishing *and* enforcing codes of conduct at places that enable criminal activity could reduce crime.

Committing crime is easier to morally defend when offenders can blame their behavior on other factors. Therefore, offenders should be made personally accountable for their actions by *clarifying responsibility*. For instance, controlling alcohol use removes a person's ability to blame intoxication for his or her misconduct.

Committing crime is also easier to morally defend when offenders can deny the damages caused by their actions. Thus, providing offenders with information about the costs of crime could *clarify consequences* and make them think twice before committing crime.

Criminals can make their offending seem more permissible by perceiving their victims as anonymous outsiders or someone deserving of an attack. Therefore, situational techniques should be designed to humanize otherwise nameless victims. For instance, improving owner-employee relationships and job security is one method to *personalize victims* and reduce internal thefts in stores.

Reducing Provocations

Some situations produce negative emotions (i.e., stress and frustration) that provoke aggressive behavior or other forms of misconduct. There are a variety of stress-inducing environmental factors that generate such antisocial reactions—like crowded places, noise pollution, and inclement weather. There are four ways to reduce these and other provocations: reducing frustration, reducing crowding, respecting territory, and controlling environmental irritants.

Reducing frustration is important because negative emotions produced by frustrating factors can transform into antisocial behavior. Therefore, designing roads to curb road rage, providing better food and entertainment at bars to reduce aggression, or improving playground conditions to prevent school bullying are some ways to control frustration that leads to misbehavior.

People usually do not prefer crowded places—crowds often make people anxious, impatient, and frustrated. *Reducing crowding* by regulating patron density and movement at nightclubs is one way to minimize such emotions that generate misconduct.

Individuals are likely to relax and behave in their own personal space; however, the invasion of this space can result in stress and aggression. For both of these reasons, situational measures should be taken to *respect territory*. For instance, prison violence could be reduced by respecting the privacy of an inmate's cell (i.e., refraining from unnecessary intrusions).

People can be bothered by their environment in a variety of ways. From heat waves to loud noises,

it is important to *control environmental irritants* conducive to crime. Providing smoke-free, climate controlled, or quiet places could prevent frustrations that result in wrongdoing.

Conclusion

In sum, Wortley expanded crime prevention theory and practice by introducing the concept of situational precipitators as well as the techniques to control them. Wortley's taxomony has since been critically assessed by other noted crime prevention scholars (see Cornish & Clarke, 2003). It has been determined that situational precipitators and criminal opportunity are of equal importance for understanding crime events. Accordingly, the techniques to control situational precipitators have been integrated into the most recent framework for situational crime prevention.

Justin A. Heinonen

See also Brantingham, Patricia L., and Paul J. Brantingham: Environmental Criminology; Clarke, Ronald V.: Situational Crime Prevention; Cornish, Derek B., and Ronald V. Clarke: Rational Choice Theory; Eck, John E.: Places and the Crime Triangle; Felson, Marcus K.: Crime and Everyday Life; Sacco, Vincent F., and Leslie W. Kennedy: The Criminal Event Perspective

References and Further Readings

Clarke, R. V. (1980). "Situational" crime prevention: Theory and practice. *British Journal of Criminology, 20,* 136–147.

Clarke, R. V. (1983). Situational crime prevention: Its theoretical basis and practical scope. In M. Tonry & N. Morris (Eds.), *Crime and justice: An annual review of research* (Vol. 4, pp. 225–256). Chicago: University of Chicago Press.

Clarke, R. V. (1995). Situational crime prevention. In M. Tonry & D. Farrington (Eds.), *Crime and justice: A review of research* (Vol. 19, pp. 91–150). Chicago: University of Chicago Press.

Clarke, R. V. (1997). Introduction. In R. Clarke (Ed.), *Situational crime prevention: Successful case studies* (pp. 3–36). Guilderland, NY: Harrow and Heston.

Clarke, R. V., & Cornish, D. B. (1985). Modeling offenders' decisions: A framework for research and policy. In M. Tonry & N. Morris (Eds.), *Crime and justice: An annual review of research* (Vol. 6, pp. 147–185). Chicago: University of Chicago Press.

Cohen, L. E., & Felson, M. (1979). Social change and crime rate trends: A routine activity approach. *American Sociological Review, 44,* 588–608.

Cornish, D. B., & Clarke, R. V. (2003). Opportunities, precipitators, and criminal decisions: A reply to Wortley's critique of situational crime prevention. In M. Smith & D. Cornish (Eds.), *Theory for practice in situational crime prevention* (Vol. 16, pp. 41–96). Monsey, NY: Criminal Justice Press.

Wortley, R. (2001). A classification of techniques for controlling situational precipitators of crime. *Security Journal, 14,* 63–82.

Wortley, R. (2002). *Situational prison control: Crime prevention in correctional institutions.* Cambridge, UK: Cambridge University Press.

XYY AGGRESSION THEORY

It is generally believed that aggressive and violent behavior arises from the combination of hereditary influences and the effects of several environmental risk factors. However, some early researchers argued that criminal and violent behavior was mainly explained by hereditary factors. For instance, Cesare Lombroso, an Italian doctor, theorized that "born criminals" could be distinguished by atavistic stigmata (physical features) such as a large jaw, sloping forehead, or a single palmar crease. Later, in the 1960s, the relationship between heredity factors and criminality was highlighted by the so-called XYY syndrome. This came about because several studies had suggested that affected individuals commit criminal and violent acts more frequently than expected. Given that normal XY males display higher levels of violence and aggression than females, one plausible hypothesis is that having an extra Y chromosome might contribute to even higher levels of crime and violence in XYY males.

The XYY Syndrome or 47,XYY Males

XYY syndrome is a chromosome disorder that only affects males. Males with this disorder have a duplicate Y chromosome. A chromosome is a structure of DNA and protein that is found in the cell nucleus. Humans have 23 pairs of chromosomes, a total of 46. In each set of chromosomes, 2 are known as the sex chromosomes (X and Y),

and the other 22 pairs are referred to as the autosomes. Human females have two X chromosomes, whereas males have one X and one Y chromosome. Each parent contributes one chromosome to each pair; so a child gets half of his or her chromosomes from the mother and the other half from the father. Within each chromosome, there are numerous genes and each gene occupies a specific position on a chromosome. Genes control physical traits such as eye color, hair texture, and height. Genes also influence the predisposition to temperaments and traits, or liability toward a disease or mental disorder. For example, specific genes may account for a predisposition to schizophrenia. In some rare instances, a chromosome anomaly occurs in males. Instead of one Y chromosome being transmitted from the father, two copies of the Y chromosome are transmitted, pairing with one X. Rather than having 46 chromosomes, therefore, a male receives an extra Y chromosome, producing what is called a 47,XYY karyotype. Karyotype is a summary of the chromosome constitution of a person. The 47,XYY karyotype does not result from any genetic factor but instead occurs randomly during meiosis in a single generation. Meiosis is the process whereby sperm or egg cells are produced. Since the 47,XYY karyotype is the result of a random error during meiosis, it does not run in families and therefore is not considered to be heritable.

Sex chromosome anomalies such as XYY are less likely to be spontaneously aborted, compared with chromosome anomalies related to the autosomes. Sex chromosome anomalies also seem to produce less severe clinical manifestations than autosome anomalies.

Epidemiology

The incidence of 47,XYY karyotype is 1 per 1,000 males. In other words, one boy in about 1,000 boys are born with a 47,XYY karyotype. The majority of XYY males go through life without knowing their karyotype. It is estimated that around 10 percent of these males are detected prenatally when the mother undergoes examination to detect other chromosomal anomalies such as Down's syndrome. The usual indications for those being karyotyped postnatally are developmental delay in motor and cognitive milestones and/or behavior problems during childhood.

Physical and Developmental Characteristics

The physical characteristics associated with the XYY syndrome include accelerated growth in childhood, already before the onset of puberty, and a significantly greater height as adults compared with average males. These XYY males have normal body proportions. In general, they have no problems associated with puberty or fertility. Their testosterone levels have been found to be low or normal. Severe acne was earlier reported to be related to XYY, but today dermatologists doubt that there is a relationship.

Regarding developmental characteristics, affected individuals may have an IQ 10 to 15 points below that of 46,XY boys, and they are at higher risk for delayed speech development, as well as more likely to require educational help. An increase in behavioral problems such as temper tantrums, distractibility, and hyperactivity has also been reported. However, aggression has not been frequently found in XYY boys.

Early Findings

The first case of an XYY karyotyped male was published by Sandberg et al. in 1961. A case of a 44-year-old man with average intelligence and without physical defects, despite 47 chromosomes was described. The man's chromosome constitution was determined because one of his children was born with Down's syndrome and another was born without any internal sex organs.

One of the first reports on a possible relationship between sex chromosome anomalies and aggressive and criminal behavior came from a survey conducted in Sweden. In three institutions for criminals or "hard-to-manage" inmates, a total of 760 male subjects were examined. Of these, 2.2 percent were found to be chromatin positive, indicating that males with sex chromosomal anomalies may be overrepresented in prisons.

This led Jacobs et al. to examine the hypothesis that an extra Y chromosome predisposes an individual to unusually aggressive behavior. In other words, as the Y chromosome defines the male, and because males are generally more aggressive than females, it was hypothesized that an extra Y chromosome would produce a particularly aggressive individual. To investigate their hypothesis, a study was carried out in a Scottish maximum security hospital. The subjects were defined as "mentally subnormal male patients with dangerous, violent, or criminal propensities." Of 203 inmates, 197 were screened for chromosome abnormalities. Twelve subjects were found to have some form of chromosome abnormality and seven (3.5 percent of the 197 subjects) had 47,XYY karyotype. They compared their findings to a group of randomly selected newborn males and to a group of randomly selected adult males. In none of the two control groups were an XYY constitution found. The authors concluded that it was not clear whether the increased frequency of XYY males in this institution was related to their aggressive behavior or their mental deficiency, or a combination of both. Regardless, the finding of a higher frequency of XYY males in a criminal mental institution, compared with the general male population, was later replicated in several studies.

During this time, a number of infamous murderers were either diagnosed with XYY syndrome or believed to be affected. One of them was Daniel Hugon, who in 1968 in Paris was charged with the brutal murder of an elderly prostitute. Throughout the trial, his lawyers argued that he was mentally unfit to stand trial because of his chromosomal abnormality. The court appointed a panel of experts to testify on the possible contribution of the chromosomal abnormality to the crime. As a result, Hugon only received 7 years imprisonment, which was a somewhat lesser penalty than usual for this type of crime. Another infamous murderer that was believed to be affected was Richard Speck, who murdered eight student nurses in Chicago in 1966. After his trial, it was established that he was not affected. However, by then, it had already been widely reported in the popular media that Richard Speck suffered from the XYY syndrome, or as it was referred to, the "supermale" syndrome.

Due to these early research studies and the attention in the media, the misconception of XYY males as a unique group of uncontrollably aggressive sociopaths had emerged in society. However, there were several limitations to these early reports that should be kept in mind. Many studies were based on very small samples, with inadequate or mismatched control groups. They were also limited to the study of institutionalized individuals or patient groups, and not the general population. Some were case reports based on a single individual with an extreme antisocial and violent behavior.

More Recent Findings

More recent population-based studies found no evidence that men with sex chromosome anomalies are particularly aggressive. One of the most convincing studies to dispel the myth that XYY males are particularly prone to violence was the one by Witkin, Mednick, and Schulsinger, based on comprehensive data from the Danish draft board on intelligence, criminal convictions, and socioeconomic background in a cohort of 4,000 men. The tallest 16 percent of these men were screened for the 47,XYY karyotype, and a much higher incidence (12 men, or 1 in 345) of the syndrome was found compared to the general population (1 in 1,000). Although a significantly higher number of XYY males (42 percent) were convicted of crimes compared to normal males (9 percent), the crimes were mainly of a nonviolent nature, such as shoplifting and vehicular offenses. There were no differences in violent crime convictions for XYY and normal males. Furthermore, the XYY males had significantly lower intelligence and educational attainment than normal males, suggesting that the higher rate of criminal convictions in XYY males may be due to cognitive dysfunction rather than aggressive tendencies.

Thus, the notion of an association between aggressive behavior and XYY males cannot be substantiated. At the same time, there is some evidence of a higher frequency of XYY males in prison and mental institutions, compared with the general male population. A review concluded that there is a three- to fourfold overrepresentation of XYY males in mental and penal settings. However, there is little or no evidence that aggressive and violent crime is particular related to 47,XYY karyotype. Instead, the vast majority of crimes committed by XYY males seem to be property offenses, rather than violence against the person. A notable example is a recent study conducted by Götz et al. Using a population-based sample of men with sex chromosome anomalies identified by screening 34,380 infants at birth, and also normal controls (XY), the XYY males showed a significantly higher frequency of antisocial behavior in adolescence and adulthood, as well as more and criminal convictions than the controls. The XYY males committed more offenses overall, and particularly in the categories of theft and breach of peace. However, further analyses showed that this was mainly mediated through their lowered intelligence resulting from their chromosome abnormality. This suggests that the increased risk of criminal behavior in XYY males may stem from a combination of hyperactivity, lowered cognitive functioning, and other personality features. Thus, 47,XYY appears to give rise to risk factors for offending, which predispose to an increased rate of property offending, but not violent, aggressive behavior per se.

Conclusion

According to empirical research, there is little or no evidence that aggressive and violent behaviors are elevated in XYY males. There is, however, some evidence that these men may be overrepresented in mental and prison settings. The majority of crimes committed by XYY males seems to be against property rather than violence against person. The increased likelihood of XYY males being in prison populations is most likely a consequence of overactivity, learning difficulties, and lowered cognitive functioning, along with other risk factors that increase in antisocial and criminal behavior, albeit not particularly of an aggressive type.

Catherine Tuvblad, Laura A. Baker,
and Adrian Raine

See also Brain Abnormalities and Crime; Fishbein, Diana H.: Biosocial Theory; Mednick, Sarnoff A.: Autonomic Nervous System (ANS) Theory; Prenatal Influences and Crime; Wilson, James Q., and Richard J. Herrnstein: Crime and Human Nature

References and Further Readings

Abramsky, L., & Chapple, J. (1997). 47,XXY (Klinefelter syndrome) and 47,XYY: Estimated rates of and indication for postnatal diagnosis with implications for prenatal counselling. *Prenatal Diagnosis, 17*(4), 363–368.

Aksglaede, L., Skakkebaek, N. E., & Juul, A. (2008). Abnormal sex chromosome constitution and longitudinal growth: Serum levels of insulin-like growth factor (IGF)-I, IGF binding protein-3, luteinizing hormone, and testosterone in 109 males with 47,XXY, 47,XYY, or sex-determining region of the Y chromosome (SRY)-positive 46,XX karyotypes. *Journal of Clinical Endocrinology and Metabolism, 93*, 169–176.

Cacey, M., Segall, L. J., Street, D. R. K., & Blank, C. E. (1966). Sex chromosome abnormalities in two state hospitals for patients requiring special security. *Nature, 209*, 641.

Götz, M. J., Johnstone, E. C., & Ratcliffe, S. G. (1999). Criminality and antisocial behaviour in unselected men with sex chromosome abnormalities. *Psychological Medicine, 29*, 953–962.

Jacobs, P. A., Brunton, M., Melville, M., Brittain, R. P., & McClemont, W. F. (1965) Aggressive behavior, mental sub-normality and the XYY male. *Nature, 208*, 1351–1352.

Kessler, S., & Moos, R. H. (1970). The XYY karyotype and criminality: A review. *Journal of Psychiatric Research, 7*, 153–170.

Linden, M. G., Bender, B. G., & Robinson, A. (1996). Intrauterine diagnosis of sex chromosome aneuploidy *Obstetrical and Gynaecology, 87*, 468–475.

Plewig, G., & Kligman, A. M. (2000). *Acne and rosacea.* Philadelphia: Springer-Verlag.

Rutter, M. (2006). *Genes and behaviour: Nature-nurture interplay explained.* Oxford, UK: Blackwell.

Rutter, M., Giller, H., & Hagell, A. (1998). *Antisocial behavior by young people.* Cambridge, UK: Cambridge University Press.

Sandberg, A. A., Koepf, G. F., Ishihara, T., & Hauschka, T. S. (1961). An XYY human male. *Lancet, 26*, 488–499.

Schiavi, R. C., Theilgaard, A., Owen, D. R., & White, D. (1984). Sex chromosome anomalies, hormones, and aggressivity. *Archives of General Psychiatry, 41*, 93–99.

Schiavi, R. C., Theilgaard, A., Owen, D. R., & White, D. (1988). Sex chromosome anomalies, hormones, and sexuality. *Archives of General Psychiatry, 45*, 19–24.

Strachan, T., & Read, A. P. (1999). *Human molecular genetics 2.* New York: Wiley.

Walzer, S., Gerald, P. S., & Shah, S. A. (1978). The XYY genotype. *Annual Review of Medicine, 29*, 568–570.

Witkin, H. A., Mednick, S. A., Schulsinger, F., Bakkestrom, E., Christiansen K. O., Goodenough, D. R., et al. (1976). Criminality in XYY and XXY men. *Science, 193*, 547–555.

YOCHELSON, SAMUEL, AND STANTON E. SAMENOW: THE CRIMINAL PERSONALITY

Before formulating their approach to correctional treatment in *The Criminal Personality* in 1974, Samuel Yochelson and Stanton E. Samenow worked with correctional populations for a period of about 15 years. Unfamiliar with treating offenders, but armed with a curiosity about them and a desire to contribute something of value to society, Yochelson abandoned his private practice and focused his attention on treating offenders. After working with criminal patients for about 6 years, he noticed that the results of therapy with criminals were very different from the ones he observed with his non-criminal patients. He decided that criminal individuals were inherently different from non-criminals and sought to find the causes of these differences (Yochelson & Samenow, 1976).

The opportunity to do such a thing was presented in Washington, D.C., at Saint Elizabeth's Hospital, where Samenow, whom he had known for some years, joined him. St. Elizabeth's Hospital offered an excellent opportunity, because at the time in Washington, D.C., crime could be considered a product of mental illness. Furthermore, the hospital offered a multidisciplinary environment, where biological, sociological, and psychological causes of crime could be explored. Correctional facilities could not offer the same opportunities (Yochelson & Samenow, 1976).

The results of their extensive studies and follow-ups with criminals were published in three volumes titled *The Criminal Personality*. The first volume, published in 1976, presented the authors' approach to how criminals think, how they evaluate their surrounding environment, and their action patterns. The second volume, published in 1977, described procedures that should be employed by correctional counselors to produce change in the way criminals think. The third and final volume, published in 1986, extended the approaches to drug-using offenders.

Characteristics of a Criminal Personality

In laying down the foundations of their theory of criminality in the first volume of *The Criminal Personality*, Yochelson and Samenow examined the existing biological, sociological, and psychoanalytic theories of why individuals become criminals. They argued that research on biological causes of criminality yielded conflicting and unconvincing results. For instance, research on offender intelligence produced results that revealed criminals as both of average intelligence, and below normal IQ level. They discredited biological claims on the premise that not enough was known about the inheritance of personality traits to attribute biological factors as causes of criminality (Yochelson & Samenow, 1976).

Sociological explanations were also considered unsatisfactory in explaining criminality. Specifically, Yochelson and Samenow argued that criminals come from a wide range of socio-economic backgrounds. Families were also ruled out, as siblings in one family can take completely different life paths. Furthermore, the authors argued about the possibility that it is the criminals who choose their environment and not the environment that influences their behavior. In this context, the criminal is viewed more as a victimizer instead of as victim of the environment (Yochelson & Samenow, 1976).

Lastly, while psychoanalytical theories identified certain personality traits of criminals as common (e.g., lying), they have failed to explain how the criminal mind operates. This is precisely what the authors set out to do: to describe the way criminals think and ultimately to change it through a series of cognitive-behavioral strategies. In doing so, they acknowledged that their strategies of change are an expansion of the work of William Glasser in reality therapy and Albert Ellis in rational-emotive therapy.

According to Yochelson and Samenow, criminals show signs of delinquent behavior beginning in childhood. They behave differently from non-criminal individuals in every sphere of life, and there is continuity to their behavior. Criminals usually ridicule rules in favor of excitement and seek out other delinquents. They exploit the school or workplace to be successful without working hard or completely give up on their attendance.

At the same time, one of the most interesting things about criminals is that they view themselves as good people. Despite all the injuries that criminal individuals have inflicted onto others, they do not see their behavior as criminal. They absolutely maintain that they are right in any given moment, and what society views as criminal, they view as normal (Yochelson & Samenow, 1977).

In all areas of life, criminals take advantage of others in order to gain the maximum gratification by inflicting financial, emotional, and sometimes physical harm. Most importantly, the authors argued vehemently in the first volume that criminals make choices from early in life about their behavior, and are not victims of the environment. Therefore, changing the environment would not produce results. The criminal has to change.

Thinking Errors

Also in Volume 1 of *The Criminal Personality*, Yochelson and Samenow maintained that criminals think differently from non-criminal individuals. They relied on Ellis's work to explain how criminals view and react to their environment. In accordance with Ellis, the authors did not view criminals as hideous people. Rather, criminals were viewed as ordinary people, who simply try to cope with everyday life but do so in irrational ways. The irrational thoughts that they employ in trying to solve different everyday life situations are called *thinking errors*.

Yochelson and Samenow identified more than 50 thinking errors that make up criminal thinking. These thinking errors can be narcissistic in nature, self-defeating, or blame shifting. Specifically, they suggested that criminals would exhibit behaviors such as blaming the victim, failing to understand the concept of injury to others, refusal to accept responsibility, refusal to accept criticism, and other thinking patterns that would support their delinquent activities. Furthermore, their irrational thoughts lead criminals to experience emotions such as self-pity, depression, and anger. Criminals then tend to isolate or distance themselves from non-criminal individuals, making their recovery more difficult (Ellis, 1965).

Another central element of the approach that Yochelson and Samenow offered is the reasoning and rationality that goes into the commission of a crime. While the authors argued that the causes of criminal behavior lay in the thinking processes that are occurring as the crime occurs, they refuted the idea of a crime committed in the heat of the passion.

In this view, "no crimes have occurred when they were thought of for the first time" (Yochelson & Samenow, 1976, p. 453). Criminals rationally think about their crimes and make choices freely about their behavior. Incorporated in this same view is the concept of deterrence. Every criminal has different levels of internal (e.g., conscience, religious beliefs) and external (e.g., fear of getting caught, shame from relatives) deterrents that he or she struggles with before committing the crime. When the desire to commit the crime becomes stronger than the deterrents, the criminal has reached the "cutoff" point. Because criminals seek thrill and excitement, but they come from different backgrounds, the cutoff points are different for each of them (Yochelson & Samenow, 1976).

Changing Criminal Thinking

The strategies and processes that should be engaged in changing thinking errors and criminal thinking are outlined in the second volume of *The Criminal Personality*. Specifically, the authors delineated the steps and techniques that the correctional counselors should utilize to produce a change in their clients' thinking processes.

According to Yochelson and Samenow, there are three prerequisites to the change process. First, the criminal must be vulnerable and want to change at the time when the new techniques are presented to him or her. Not every criminal is susceptible to change and therefore prepared to undergo the cognitive-restructuring programs. Second, the counselor must be trained and have knowledge of the criminal's thinking processes. Lastly, the new techniques and skills should be presented and taught to the client through a set of cognitive-restructuring strategies.

Thus, according to this model, it is the job of the counselor, the staff, and the inmates to work together to identify and eliminate thinking errors. Staff and inmates are trained to identify the thinking errors and to correct them. Then, the irrational thoughts are replaced with prosocial and responsible ways to respond to everyday life situations. Among such prosocial attitudes are accepting no excuses for irresponsible behaviors, teaching principles of good decision making, teaching the criminals the process of taking the perspective of others, and pointing out instances in which the criminals do not take responsibility for their actions.

The attitude of the counselor toward the clients is also very important because it influences the change process. Thus, the counselor should be firm, yet understanding and open-minded, and not seem judgmental. Both constructive criticism and compassion become part of the counseling strategies (Yochelson & Samenow, 1977).

The Drug-Using Criminal

While the authors maintained that the thinking errors and the techniques to correct them work on drug-abusing offenders, just as well as on non-abusing offenders, they argued that drug users and their crimes have been misunderstood by most of the research and the treatment modules available. Many offenders and even treatment counselors blame the drugs as the source of crime in drug-abusing offenders. In the third volume of *The Criminal Personality*, Yochelson and Samenow argued that this view is incorrect. According to their view, these criminals only use drugs or alcohol to quell their depression, fears, failures, or boredom. Drugs make them optimistic and drive away the depression that many of these individuals are feeling. The authors observed that most drug users are depressed and see themselves as worthless.

In accordance with the cognitive-restructuring strategies that they offer in the first two volumes, the authors argued that thinking errors can be identified to help clients avoid the risky situations in which they are most likely to use drugs. Furthermore, the same techniques can be used to help drug users replace the irrational thoughts with healthy prosocial ones.

Conclusion

Throughout the three volumes of *The Criminal Personality*, Yochelson and Samenow sought to provide an answer to criminal behavior. They believed the answer was within the person and not the surrounding environment. The individual was responsible for the acts undertaken. As such, they ultimately believed that if one changes the way one thinks about the world, the behavior would also change.

Mirlinda Ndrecka

See also Andrews, D. A., and James Bonta: A Personal, Interpersonal, and Community-Reinforcement (PIC-R) Perspective on Criminal Conduct; Cognitive Theories of Crime; Dodge, Kenneth A.: Aggression and a Hostile Attribution Style; Hare, Robert D.: Psychopathy and Crime; Raine, Adrian: Crime as a Disorder; Sykes, Gresham, M., and David Matza: Techniques of Neutralization; Walters, Glenn D.: Lifestyle Theory

References and Further Readings

Elliott, B., & Verdeyen, V. (2002). *Game over! Strategies for redirecting inmate deception*. Lanham, MD: American Correctional Association.

Ellis, A. (1965). *Rational emotive psychotherapy*. New York: Institute for Rational Living.

Glasser, W. (1965). *Reality therapy: A new approach to psychiatry*. New York: Harper & Row.

Samenow, S. (1984). *Inside the criminal mind*. New York: Times Books.

Walters, G. (1990). *The criminal lifestyle: Patterns of serious criminal conduct*. Newbury Park, CA: Sage.

Yochelson, S., & Samenow, S. (1976). *The criminal personality: Vol. 1. A profile for change*. New York: Jason Aronson.

Yochelson, S., & Samenow, S. (1977). *The criminal personality: Vol. 2. The change process*. New York: Jason Aronson.

Yochelson, S., & Samenow, S. (1986). *The criminal personality: Vol. 3. The drug user*. New York: Jason Aronson.

Annotated Further Readings

The author(s) of each entry have furnished a list of works that, if consulted, will further illuminate the topic of interest. Each recommended reading is annotated so that its relevance is clarified. Importantly, the Annotated Further Readings section is organized to correspond with the format used in the Reader's Guide: by the 21 schools of thought and then by topic within each school. In this way, these materials provide an easily accessible and invaluable resource for readers inspired to delve more deeply into any specific theory or broader way of thinking within criminology.

1. The Classical School of Criminology

Beccaria, Cesare: Classical School

Beccaria, C. (1995). *On crimes and punishments and other writings* (R. Bellamy, Ed., & R. Davies, Trans.). New York: Cambridge University Press. (Original work published 1764)

> *The text of* On Crimes and Punishments *plus selections from Beccaria's academic lectures, economic writings, and intellectual correspondence. Includes a useful bibliographical sketch, chronology, bibliographical glossary, and explanatory footnotes. This is the most useful English edition for students reading Beccaria for the first time.*

Beccaria, C. (2008). *On crimes and punishments and other writings* (A. Thomas, Ed., & A. Thomas & J. Parzen, Trans.). Toronto, ON: University of Toronto Press. (Original work published 1764)

> *The text includes* On Crimes and Punishments *plus three significant contemporary scholarly reactions by Ferdinando Facchinei (1765), Pietro and Allessandro Verri (1765), and Voltaire (1766). The book also includes a text related to Beccaria's political work reforming the death penalty in Lombardy and contains an extensive introduction to Beccaria's life and ideas by the prominent Italian scholar Alberto Burgio. This translation has greater literary elegance than the Cambridge edition.*

Davis, D. (1957). The movement to abolish capital punishment in America, 1787–1861. *The American Historical Review, 63,* 23–46.

> *A historical account of capital punishment reform in America that includes an extensive discussion of Beccaria's influence in the United States. This scholarly article also relates Beccaria's ideas to those of political philosopher John Locke and addresses the use of Beccaria's secular arguments by members of American religious communities that advocated the abolition of capital punishment.*

Maestro, M. (1973). *Cesare Beccaria and the origins of penal reform.* Philadelphia: Temple University Press.

> *The only book-length biography of Beccaria published in English. Maestro provides much useful information about Beccaria's life, work, and relations with European intellectuals and statesmen, but his assessment of Beccaria's ideas is unsophisticated and his narrative tends toward hagiography.*

Bentham, Jeremy: Classical School

Becker, G. S. (1968). Crime and punishment: An economic approach. *Journal of Political Economy, 76,* 169–217.

> *This classic article is an excellent example of a modern attempt to provide an economic analysis of crime on the basis of Bentham's theory of deterrence and for the illustration of the logical development of*

Bentham's theories, which recognized the importance of economic factors in explaining crime.

Harrison, R. (1983). *Bentham*. London: Routledge & Kegan Paul.

A useful introduction, focusing on Bentham's semantics and account of meaning, his views on the relation of fact and value, and the sphere of public and private ethics. The account of Bentham's psychology is weak, perhaps because his views have been superseded by subsequent discoveries.

Schofield, P. (2006). *Utility and democracy: The political thought of Jeremy Bentham*. Oxford, UK: Oxford University Press.

Arguing that the key to Bentham's political thought lies in his semantics and in his theory "fictions," Schofield shows its implications for Bentham's moral theory, the account of natural law and natural rights, constitutional law and the problem of codification, and issues related to legal reform.

Schofield, P. (2009). *Bentham: A guide for the perplexed*. London: Continuum.

A short, general introduction to Bentham, with chapters devoted to his moral theory, the Panopticon, and torture. The author shows the relation of these issues to Bentham's account of language and "fallacies."

Semple, J. (1993). *Bentham's prison: A study of the panopticon penitentiary*. Oxford, UK: Clarendon Press.

A sympathetic study of Bentham's plan of the Panopticon, providing an alternative to Foucault's rather foreboding analysis of the institution. Semple generalizes the "inspection principle," suggesting that the Panopticon provides a standard of visibility and transparency that can be applied to public institutions and government.

2. The Positivist School of Criminology

Aschaffenburg, Gustav: German Criminology

Becker, P., & Wetzell, R. F. (Eds.). (2006). *Criminals and their scientists: The history of criminology in international perspective*. New York: Cambridge University Press.

Comprehensive international history of criminology from the 19th to the mid-20th century. Contains several essays on the German and international reception of Lombroso as well the further development of criminology in the 20th century that allow the reader to place Aschaffenburg in a broader context.

Busse, F. (1991). *Gustav Aschaffenburg (1866–1944): Leben und Werk*. Unpublished doctoral dissertation, University of Leipzig, Leipzig, Germany.

A biographical dissertation on Aschaffenburg that provides a fair amount of detail about his life and work.

Galassi, S. (2004). *Kriminologie im deutschen kaiserreich: Geschichte einer gebrochenen Verwissenschaftlichung* [Criminology in Imperial Germany: History of a partial scientization]. Stuttgart, Germany: Steiner.

A history-of-science study of the development of criminology in Imperial Germany (1871–1918) that discusses Aschaffenburg as the most important exponent of a criminological "Vereinigungstheorie"— that is, a theory combining environmental and biological explanations of criminal behavior.

Wetzell, R. F. (2000). *Inventing the criminal: A history of German criminology, 1880–1945*. Chapel Hill: University of North Carolina Press.

Shows that German biomedical research on crime predominated over sociological research and thus contributed to the rise of eugenics and the targeting of criminals for sterilization under the Nazi regime. But Wetzell also argues that German criminology was characterized by a continuing tension between the criminologists' hereditarian inclinations and an increasing methodological sophistication that demonstrated the complexity of the interaction of heredity and milieu. Important study for placing Aschaffenburg in larger context.

Ferri, Enrico: Positivist School

Beck, N. (2005). Enrico Ferri's scientific socialism: A Marxist interpretation of Herbert Spencer's organic analogy. *Journal of the History of Biology, 38,* 301–325.

This article analyzes Ferri's position on Marxian Socialism and discusses Spencer's influence on Ferri. Both Spencer's and Ferri's positions and work are discussed in depth.

Ferri, E. (1900). *Socialism and modern science: Darwin, Spencer, Marx* (R. R. La Monte, Trans.). New York: New York International Library. (Original work published 1894)

This work makes comparisons between socialism and modern science. Ferri believed that Marxian socialism was a product of Darwin's and Spencer's work. According to Ferri, Marxian socialism had the most scientific value.

Garofalo, Raffaele: Positivist School

Allen, F. A. (1960). Raffaele Garofalo. In H. Mannheim (Ed.), *Pioneers of criminology* (pp. 254–276). London: Stevens and Sons.

This essay by Francis A. Allen is one of the few in-depth studies dealing with Garofalo's ideas. Allen's analysis, which was carried out from a juridical point of view, looks at Garofalo's theories, their influence on later juridical thought, and the coexistence of Classical School elements in his ideas.

Gibson, M. (2002). *Born to crime. Cesare Lombroso and the origins of biological criminology.* Westport, CT: Praeger.

Mary Gibson's book provides a useful tool for examining Garofalo's ideas in more depth and, above all, for contextualizing his figure and works within the cultural scene of the second half of the 19th century and the first decade of the 20th century.

Goring, Charles: The English Convict

Driver, E. (1972). Charles Buckman Goring. In H. Mannheim (Ed.), *Pioneers in criminology* (pp. 429–442). Montclair, NJ: Patterson Smith.

This work provides an interesting summary of Goring's work. It is within the academic reach of any student.

Goring, C. (1972). *The English convict: A statistical study.* Montclair, NJ: Patterson Smith. (Original work published 1913)

The original work, available in reprinted form, consists of extensive presentations of the statistical data and the calculations conducted by Goring. It is not an easy book to read without some knowledge of statistics, although it is logically presented.

Jones, D. A. (1986). *History of criminology: A philosophical perspective.* Westport, CT: Greenwood Press.

This work is a valuable presentation of the history of criminology, although it is dated.

Kretschmer, Ernst: Physique and Character

Enke, W. (1968). Ernst Kretschmer. In D. Sills (Ed.), *International encyclopedia of the social sciences* (pp. 450–452). New York: Macmillan/Free Press.

This entry provides a valuable chronology and overview of Kretschmer's life and work. It provides the necessary background to understanding Kretschmer and his ideas.

Kretschmer, E. (1970). *Physique and character.* New York: Cooper Square. (Original work published 1921)

This edition of Kretschmer's work is very readable. Its presentation is clear and, although its conclusions

are out of date, its presentation is easily understood by non-scientists.

Roebuck, J. (1967). *Criminal typology: The legalistic, physical-constitutional-hereditary, psychological-psychiatric, and sociological approaches.* Springfield, IL: Charles C Thomas.

This work provides a thorough comparison of the different ways criminal behavior is generally classified. Although the work is dated, its explanation of the different classifications is still valuable.

Lombroso, Cesare: The Criminal Man

Becker, P., & Wetzell, R. F. (2006). *Criminals and their scientists: The history of criminology in international perspective.* Cambridge, UK: Cambridge University Press.

While exploring the historical developments of criminology, this work provides an account of how scientists from different countries reacted to and were influenced by the publication of Cesare Lombroso's L'uomo delinquente.

Horn, D. G. (2003). *The criminal body. Lombroso and the anatomy of deviance.* New York: Routledge.

This work shows how the construction of the born criminal as an atavistic being was dependent on new practices of measuring and documenting that sought to differentiate deviant bodies from normal bodies.

Lombroso, C. (2006). *Criminal man* (M. Gibson & N. H. Rafter, Eds.). Durham, NC: Duke University Press.

This book makes available key excerpts in English from all five editions of Lombroso's L'uomo delinquente and summarizes some of the main developments of Lombroso's theories within the different editions.

Pick, D. (1989). *Faces of degeneration: A European disorder, c. 1848–c. 1918.* Cambridge, UK: Cambridge University Press.

This is an excellent work on how degeneration theories developed in France, Italy, and England. The second part of the book focuses on Lombroso, and explains the specific Italian historical context of Lombroso's criminal anthropology.

Phrenology

Rafter, N. H. (2008). *The criminal brain: Understanding biological theories of crime.* New York: New York University Press.

Nicole Rafter, a Senior Research Fellow in the College of Criminal Justice at Northeastern University, provides a historical context of how biological theories of crime emerged and implications of those theories on biosocial criminology today.

Van Wyhe, J. (2004). *Phrenology and the origins of Victorian scientific naturalism.* Aldershot, UK: Ashgate.

John van Wyhe of the Department of History and Philosophy of Science at Cambridge University wrote Phrenology and the Origins of Victorian Scientific Naturalism *as an extension of his dissertation work. Van Wyhe provides an in-depth analysis of the roots of British phrenology during the early to mid-1800s in this five-part book.*

Quetelet, Adolphe: Explaining Crime Through Statistical and Cartographic Techniques

Beirne, P. (1987). Adolphe Quetelet and the origins of positivist criminology. *American Journal of Sociology, 92*(5), 1140–1169.

Beirne gives readers an in-depth overview of Quetelet's life within the context of his time. Quetelet's contributions to the development of positivist criminology are clearly outlined as well as those of his contemporaries.

Quetelet, A. J. (1984). *Research on the propensity for crime at different ages* (S. F. Test Sylvester, Trans.). Cincinnati, OH: Anderson. (Original work published 1831)

The introduction to the English translation of Quetelet's classic work offers a nice contextual background on the man. Quetelet outlines his theories here and presents the classic statistical tables and map examples.

Weisburd, D. L., Bruinsma, G., & Bernasco, W. (2008). Units of analysis in geographic criminology: Historical development, critical issues and open questions. In D. Weisburd, W. Bernasco, & G. Bruinsma (Eds.), *Putting crime in its place: Units of analysis in spatial crime research* (pp. 3–31). New York: Springer-Verlag.

The introduction to this book offers a comprehensive history of crime and place research. It will be informative for anyone seeking a good overview of the subject.

3. Early American Theories of Crime

Aichhorn, August: Wayward Youth

Freud, S. (1962). *The ego and the id.* New York: W. W. Norton. (Original work published 1923)

This work provides the reader with an overview of psychoanalytical principles. Although Freud discussed

how delinquency and personality are connected, he did not apply his work in practice.

Wulach, J. S. (1983). August Aichhorn's legacy: The treatment of narcissism in criminals. *International Journal of Offender Therapy and Comparative Criminology, 27,* 226–234

Wulach provides an overview of the instrumental work of Aichhorn in addressing narcissistic youths in an institutional setting. His pioneering work set the stage for future psychoanalysts.

Alexander, Franz, and William Healy: Roots of Crime

Alexander, F., & French, T. M. (1946). *Psychoanalytic therapy: Principles and application.* Lincoln: University of Nebraska Press.

This text provides an overview of the many techniques used in psychoanalytic therapy with particular focus on decreasing the time traditional therapy requires. Traditional psychoanalytic therapy was quite lengthy, and Alexander and French recognized the need to employ brief techniques. These techniques are introduced and explained in the context of proper psychoanalysis.

Healy, W. (1915). *The individual delinquent: A text-book of diagnosis and prognosis for all concerned in understanding offenders.* Boston: Little, Brown.

This textbook focuses on early childhood psychological development in the context of later delinquency. Healy places particular emphasis on temperament development and environmental influences on development.

Dugdale, Richard L.: The Jukes

Carlson, E. A. (2001). *The unfit: A history of a bad idea.* Cold Spring Harbor, NY: Cold Spring Harbor Laboratory Press.

Carlson provides a careful examination of the notion that those deemed "unfit" due to weak minds, weak physical constitutions, or weak moral standards were problems within society. He fits the research in the late 19th century within traditional thinking dating back to biblical times. He then describes the eugenics movement and the role that eugenics played in the Holocaust atrocities.

Degler, C. N. (1991). *In search of human nature: The decline and revival of Darwinism in American social thought.* New York: Oxford University Press.

Degler traces the development of early criminological research that grew from the work of Charles Darwin. The eugenics movement peaked during the period from the late 1800s through the early decades of the 1900s. This author examines the heredity-environment debate, while chronicling the influence of scholars that emphasized the role of the environment and then the later works provided more support for biological/hereditary interpretations of the research findings.

Rafter, N. H. (1988). *White trash: The eugenic family studies, 1877–1919.* Boston: Northeastern University Press.

Rafter reviews 15 studies that fit her conception of "eugenic family studies." She also reprints 11 of the original works in this volume. As such, this is a great source for finding many of these works. Rafter offers an insightful analysis of this body of research.

Eugenics and Crime: Early American Positivism

Bruinius, H. (2006). *Better for all the world: The secret history of forced sterilization and America's quest for racial purity.* New York: Knopf.

This book is an introduction to the eugenics movement and its major actors, presented in a narrative fashion and explaining each individual's personal background as well as probable motives for their involvement. Bruinius traces the movement from its earliest beginnings with Francis Galton to its height in the 1930s.

Pickens, D. (1968). *Eugenics and the progressives.* Nashville, TN: Vanderbilt University Press.

This is a solid introduction to the eugenics movement in the United States, especially for those individuals who are not familiar with it. Each chapter of the book is dedicated to a particular time frame. Within each section, Pickens explains the key actors of the time and the movement's current status of development and power.

Goddard, Henry H.: Feeblemindedness and Delinquency

Black, E. (2003). *The war against the weak: Eugenics and America's campaign to create a master race.* New York: Four Walls Eight Windows.

A historical review of the eugenic movement in the United States.

Smith, J. D. (1985). *Minds made feeble: The myth and the legacy of the Kallikaks.* Rockville, MD: Aspen.

An assessment of the impact of the Kallikak study in the contemporary eugenic movement.

Zenderland, L. (2001). *Measuring minds: Henry Herbert Goddard and the origin of American intelligence testing.* Cambridge, UK: Cambridge University Press.

An account of Goddard's role in the popularization of intelligence testing in the United States.

Hooton, Earnest A.: The American Criminal

Barkan, E. (1993). *The retreat of scientific racism: The changing concept of race in Britain and the United States between the World Wars.* Cambridge, UK: Cambridge University Press.

A study of the debates regarding race in early 20th century American anthropology that includes substantial references to Hooton's work.

Rafter, N. H. (1997). *Creating born criminals.* Urbana: University of Illinois Press.

A historical overview of biological and psychological theories in early American criminology.

Rafter, N. H. (2004). Earnest A. Hooton and the biological tradition in American criminology. *Criminology, 42,* 735–771.

An assessment of Hooton's place in the history of American criminology.

Insanity and Crime: Early American Positivism

Dain, N., & Carlson, E. T. (1962). Moral insanity in the United States 1835–1866. *American Journal of Psychiatry, 118,* 795–801.

Norman Dain and Eric Carlson trace the evolution of the concept of moral insanity during the middle part of the 1800s. Dain and Carlson delineate the arguments of both the psychiatrists who were influenced by the positivist movement, as well as those who favored moralist explanations of insanity.

Rafter, N. H. (2008). *The criminal brain: Understanding biological theories of crime.* New York: New York University Press.

Nicole Rafter thoroughly elucidates the emergence and evolution of biological theories of criminology. From the 19th-century notion of moral derangement to the 21st-century study of neurotransmitters, Rafter offers a fascinating account of the development of criminological theory.

Parmelee, Maurice

Craig, C. (Ed.). (2007). *Sociology in America: A history.* Chicago: University of Chicago Press.

A volume that brings together several articles on the origin and early history of American sociology.

Sheldon, William H.: Somatotypes and Delinquency

Rafter, N. H. (2007). Somatotyping, antimodernism, and the production of criminological knowledge. *Criminology, 45*, 805–834.

Rafter's work examines archival documents to explore Sheldon's personal views on his somatotype research. Couched within this discussion of Sheldon's personal views about his work is an exploration of the ambivalence with which somatotyping is treated in introductory textbooks and classes.

4. Biological and Biosocial Theories of Crime

Alcohol and Violence

Babor, T., Caetano, R., Casswell, S., Edwards, G., Giesbrecht, N., Graham, K., et al. (2003). *Alcohol: No ordinary commodity: Research and public policy.* New York: Oxford University Press.

This is a comprehensive volume to which several leading alcohol epidemiologists and others have contributed. The book first establishes the need for alcohol policy via a discussion of alcohol-related harm, then highlights several different strategies and interventions for reducing these harms, and finally outlines how effective alcohol policy can be formulated. The focus of this book is not on violence, but the topics it covers are essential to those interested in alcohol and violence.

Parker, R. N. (1995). Bringing "booze" back in: The relationship between alcohol and homicide. *Journal of Research in Crime and Delinquency, 32*, 3–38.

This article details one of the first structural-level analyses that helped reintegrate alcohol back into the study of serious interpersonal violence in the United States. The study tests hypotheses derived from several theoretical perspectives as they relate to different types of homicides, revealing that the effects of other common correlates of homicide rates may be dependent upon levels of alcohol consumption.

Parker, R. N., & Rebhun, L.-A. (1995). *Alcohol and homicide: A deadly combination of two American traditions.* Albany: SUNY Press.

This book is unique in several respects. It first outlines historical features associated with alcohol and violence in America. It then discusses several theoretical reasons for why we might expect alcohol to be related to violence. This is accompanied by a description of the authors' own theoretical explanation of the alcohol-violence association, which they label selective disinhibition. Given these

theoretical underpinnings, it then reports the results of two empirical tests, one that examines the impact of alcohol availability on homicide in more than 250 American cities and the other that gauges the effects of increasing the drinking age to 21 on youth homicides in the United States.

Pernanen, K. (1991). *Alcohol in human violence.* New York: Guilford Press.

A classic work in research on alcohol and violence. This comprehensive book employs both official and observational data to describe the role of alcohol in everyday violent events such as barroom encounters and fights. It carefully weaves quantitative and qualitative data into a cohesive story that reveals the importance of social, psychological, and situational factors in explaining the alcohol-violence association.

Pridemore, W. A., & Eckhardt, K. (2008). A comparison of victim, offender, and event characteristics of alcohol- and non-alcohol-related homicides. *Journal of Research in Crime and Delinquency, 45*, 227–255.

One way to illuminate the role of alcohol in violence is to delineate how alcohol-related violent events are different from non-alcohol-related violent events. In this article, the authors reveal several distinguishing victim, offender, and event characteristics of alcohol-related homicides. The authors also provide a new grounded typology of homicide events based upon alcohol use by homicide offenders and victims.

Brain Abnormalities and Crime

Blair, R. J., Mitchell, D., & Blair, K. (2005). *The psychopath: Emotion and the brain.* Hoboken, NJ: Wiley-Blackwell.

James Blair has influenced the field of neurobiology and criminal behavior with his proposed models on aggression and moral development. In this book, Blair provides a summary of neurobiological findings on psychopathic, criminal behavior and a modified Integrated Emotion Systems Model, which further his proposed Violent Inhibition Mechanism Model.

Damasio, A. R. (1996). The somatic marker hypothesis and the possible functions of the prefrontal cortex. *Philosophical Transactions: Biological Sciences, 351*, 1413–1420.

Antonio Damasio provides further discussion on his somatic marker hypothesis and applies it to human reasoning and decision-making processes. Damasio also clarifies in this article the neural system underlying his hypothesis.

Yang, Y., Glenn, A. L., & Raine, A. (2008). Brain abnormalities in antisocial individuals: Implications for the law. *Behavioral Science and the Law, 26,* 65–83.

In this review article, Yaling Yang and her colleagues provide an overview on the up-to-date findings on structural and functional brain abnormalities on violent and criminal offenders. A discussion also is presented on implications of these findings in the legal system.

Ellis, Lee: Evolutionary Neuroandrogenic Theory

Ellis, L. (2000). Theories of criminal/antisocial behavior. In L. Ellis & A. Walsh (Eds.), *Criminology: A global perspective* (Part III). Boston: Allyn & Bacon.

Ellis proposes his evolutionary neuroandrogenic theory in this book chapter. This chapter provides the initial framework underlying the theory by describing the two components to the theory, which are evolution and neuroandrogens.

Ellis, L. (2003). Biosocial theorizing and criminal justice policy. In A. Somit & S. A. Peterson (Eds.), *Human nature and public policy: An evolutionary approach* (pp. 97–120). New York: Palgrave Macmillan.

This book chapter presents a detailed overview of Ellis's evolutionary neuroandrogenic theory and proposes several hypotheses derived from the theory. It also highlights hypotheses that are specifically relevant to the criminal justice system.

Ellis, L. (2003). Genes, criminality, and the evolutionary neuroandrogenic theory. In A. Walsh & L. Ellis (Eds.), *Biosocial criminology: Challenging environmentalism's supremacy* (pp. 13–34). Hauppauge, NY: Nova Science.

This book chapter presents a review of Ellis's evolutionary neuroandrogenic in the context of biosocial criminology.

Ellis, L. (2005). A theory explaining biological correlates of criminality. *European Journal of Criminology, 2,* 287–315.

This journal article provides a detailed description of Ellis's evolutionary neuroandrogenic theory. It also discusses 12 biological correlates of crime that are relevant to evolutionary neuroandrogenic theory.

Ellis, L., Das, S., & Buker, H. (2008). Androgen-promoted physiological traits and criminality: A test of the evolutionary neuroandrogenic theory. *Personality and Individual Differences, 44,* 699–709.

This study is the first empirical test of three hypotheses derived from evolutionary neuroandrogenic theory: (1) do males commit more crimes than females; (2) are physiological traits associated with higher levels of androgens associated with criminal behaviors, especially violent behaviors; and (3) are sex differences in levels of crime explained by androgen-promoted physiological traits. Overall, the findings from this study provide general support for evolutionary neuroandrogenic theory.

Environmental Toxins Theory

Carson, R. (1962). *Silent spring.* Cambridge, MA: Houghton Mifflin.

Silent Spring is a classic work that documents the harm that pesticides can cause and challenges the chemical industry for misleading the public about pesticide production. The book is often credited as the reason that the pesticide DDT was banned. It is also referenced as the turning point in the modern environmental movement and widespread concern about environmental toxins.

Colborn, T., Dumanoski, D., & Myers, J. P. (1997). *Our stolen future: Are we threatening our fertility, intelligence, and survival? A scientific detective story.* New York: Dutton.

Our Stolen Future examines the relationship between synthetic chemicals known as endocrine disrupters and birth defects, sexual abnormalities, and reproductive failures among animals. The book is credited for advancing the public policy debate about the role of endocrine disruptors. This work provides a nice introduction about the potential problematic effects of environmental toxins.

Needleman, H. (1990). The future challenge of lead toxicity. *Environmental Health Perspectives, 89,* 85–89.

This article examines the history and development of understanding of the harmful effects of lead. Needleman uses research on the effects of lead to point out the potential for lead exposure to lead to anti-social behavior and crime.

Zakrewski, S. (2002). *Environmental toxicology.* New York: Oxford University Press.

This is an introductory textbook that provides the reader with a basic understanding of the impact of various toxic chemicals on the human body; details environmental problems such as air and water pollution; and examines how society controls and regulates environmental toxins.

Eysenck, Hans J.: Crime and Personality

Eysenck, H. J. (1996). Personality and crime: Where do we stand. *Psychology, Crime and Law, 2,* 143–152.

This is Eysenck's last work on crime and personality. It provides an up-to-date account of his final thinking on the subject matter. In the article, he argues that personality plays a central role in mediating between genetic and environmental forces in explaining the causes of criminality.

Gudjonsson, G. H. (1997). Crime and personality. In H. Nyborg (Ed.), *The scientific study of human nature. Tribute to Hans J. Eysenck at eighty* (pp. 142–164). Oxford, UK: Elsevier Science.

This paper provides a detailed reivew of Eysenck's theory of crime and personality, reviews the emprical evidence for the therory, and shows how the theory has changed over time. The main conclusion is that Eysenck's work has been more influencial in terms of stimulating resarch into the causes of crime than into its prevention and control.

Fishbein, Diana H.: Biosocial Theory

Beaver, K. M. (2009). *Biosocial criminology: A primer.* Dubuque, IA: Kendall/Hunt.

This book provides an overview of biosocial criminology. It explains the biological concepts and it also provides a detailed overview of the biosocial research bearing on the etiology of crime and delinquency.

Walsh, A. (2002). *Biosocial criminology: Introduction and integration.* Cincinnati, OH: Anderson.

This book introduces the reader to the biosocial perspective. It places particular emphasis on showing how biological concepts can be integrated into existing criminological theories.

Walsh, A., & Beaver, K. M. (Eds.). (2009). *Biosocial criminology: New directions in theory and research.* New York: Routledge.

This edited book contains a series of original essays written by some of the leading biosocial experts, each of which tackles a different issue related to the biosocial perspective.

Wright, J. P., Tibbetts, S. G., & Daigle, L. E. (2008). *Criminals in the making: Criminality across the life course.* Thousand Oaks, CA: Sage.

This book provides an in-depth examination of the causes to criminality. In doing so, it injects biosocial research into the life-course perspective to show how biology and the environment work together in the creation of criminals.

Harris, Judith Rich: Why Parents Do Not Matter

Galton, F. (1973). *Inquiries into human faculty and its development.* New York: AMS Press. (Original work published 1883)

This book provides insight into the early thoughts of Galton on the importance of heredity and human social behavior.

Harris, J. R. (2006). *No two alike: Human nature and human individuality.* New York: W. W. Norton.

Judith Rich Harris provides a coherent review of the literature dealing with twin studies, an elaboration of group socialization theory, and an explanation for personality differences.

Wasserman, D., & Wachbroit, R. (Eds.). (2001). *Genetics and criminal behavior.* Cambridge, UK: Cambridge University Press.

The authors of this edited book provide an excellent review of a literature that substantiates that genetic factors are important to understanding the development of some forms of criminal activity.

Herrnstein, Richard J., and Charles Murray: Crime and the Bell Curve

Ellis, L., & Walsh, A. (2003). Crime, delinquency and intelligence: A review of the worldwide literature. In H. Nyborg (Ed.), *The scientific study of general intelligence: A tribute to Arthur Jensen* (pp. 343–365). Oxford, UK: Elsevier Science.

This book chapter surveyed the worldwide literature on delinquency and crime up to 2001. Data from many countries indicate that low IQ places individuals at risk for a variety of antisocial behaviors. The relationship between IQ and crime/delinquency is always stronger in official statistics than in self-reports due to the fact that very few serious offenders are ever represented in self-report studies.

Flynn, J. (2007). *What is intelligence: Beyond the Flynn effect.* Cambridge, UK: Cambridge University Press.

This book is the culmination of the author's 20-year examination of the so-called Flynn effect, which is the documentation of secular gains in IQ over 70 years. The gain is not in question, but what caused it is. This book is Flynn's efforts to answer the question from a much different point of view than Herrnstein and Murray.

Neisser, U., Boodoo, G., Bouchard, T., Boykin, A., Brody, N., Ceci, S., et al. (1995). *Intelligence: Knowns and unknowns: Report of a task force established by the board of scientific affairs of the American Psychological Association*. Washington, DC: American Psychological Association.

This is the report of the American Psychological Association's task force that was formed specifically to address many of the points made by Herrnstein and Murray. The task force basically supported almost all of the scientific points made by Herrnstein and Murray, such as the lack of class or race bias in IQ tests, the considerable genetic contribution to intelligence, and the fact that IQ predicts so many life outcomes more strongly than any other factor. They also affirmed the large IQ gap between black and whites, but tip-toed around the possibility that this could be partially genetic.

Mednick, Sarnoff A.: Autonomic Nervous System (ANS) Theory

Mednick, S. A. (1977). A biosocial theory of the learning of law-abiding behavior. In S. A. Mednick & K. O. Christiansen (Eds.), *Biosocial bases of criminal behavior* (pp. 1–8). New York: Gardner.

In the unveiling of ANS theory, Mednick becomes one of the first modern biosocial criminology proponents. This theory proposal chapter covers the essentials of the construct, including hypotheses and measurement.

Mednick, S. A., Gabrielli, W. F., Jr., & Hutchings, B. (1987). Genetic factors in the etiology of criminal behavior. In S. A. Mednick, T. E. Moffitt, & S. A. Stack (Eds.), *The causes of crime: New biological approaches* (pp. 74–91). New York: Cambridge University Press.

Following up an article in the journal Science *several years earlier, this adoption study finds that the delinquency of adopted children is very similar to their biological parent's criminality. This finding is especially strong in terms of chronic recidivism.*

Mednick, S. A., Kirkegaard-Sorensen, L., Hutchings, B., Knop, J., Rosenberg, R., & Schulsinger, F. (1977). An example of biosocial interaction research: The interplay of socioenvironmental and individual factors in the etiology of criminal behavior. In S. A. Mednick & K. O. Christiansen (Eds.), *Biosocial bases of criminal behavior* (pp. 9–23). New York: Gardner.

In the initial test of ANS theory, Mednick and his colleagues find that EDRec is only related to criminal behavior in the lower-middle and middle classes. This study serves as a pilot study for the larger, nationally representative sample in Denmark.

Neurology and Crime

Damasio, A. R. (1996). The somatic marker hypothesis and the possible functions of the prefrontal cortex. *Philosophical Transactions: Biological Sciences, 351,* 1413–1420.

Antonio Damasio provides further discussion on his somatic marker hypothesis and applies it to human reasoning and decision-making processes. Damasio also clarifies in this article the neural system underlying his hypothesis.

Yang, Y., Glenn, A. L., & Raine, A. (2008). Brain abnormalities in antisocial individuals: Implications for the law. *Behavioral Science and the Law, 26,* 65–83.

In this review article, Yaling Yang and her colleagues provide an overview on the up-to-date findings on structural and functional brain abnormalities on violent and criminal offenders. A discussion is also provided on the implications of these findings in the legal system.

Nutrition and Crime

Benton, D. (2007). The impact of diet in anti-social, violent, and criminal behavior. *Neuroscience and Behavioral Reviews, 31,* 752–774.

David Benton is a psychology professor at University of Wales, Swansea. He provides a general, extensive overview of nutrition and its possible link to antisocial and criminal behavior.

Hibbeln, J. R., Davis, J. M., Steer, C., Emmett, P., Rogers, I., Williams, C., et al. (2007). Maternal seafood consumption in pregnancy and neurodevelopmental outcomes in childhood (ALSPAC study): An observational cohort study. *The Lancet, 369,* 578–585.

This study explores the possible effects lack of omega-3 consumption by pregnant mothers on children's later neurodevelopment and behavior.

Prenatal Influences and Crime

Raine, A. (2002). Biosocial studies of antisocial and violent behavior in children and adults: A review. *Journal of Abnormal Child Psychology, 30,* 311–326.

In this article, Adrian Raine provides an overview of the data linking prenatal risk factors to antisocial behavior, focusing in particular on biosocial interactions. He also summarizes research on biosocial interactions within a host of other domains related to violence.

Raine, A., Brennan, P., & Mednick, S. A. (1997). Interaction between birth complications and early maternal rejection in predisposing individuals to adult violence: Specificity to serious, early-onset violence. *American Journal of Psychiatry, 154,* 1265–1271.

The authors follow up on data from a previous study they conducted to report on the interaction between birth complications and maternal rejection in predisposing to violent behavior.

Raine, A., Mellingen, K, Liu, J. H., Venables, P. H., & Mednick, S. A. (2003). Effects of environmental enrichment at 3–5 years on schizotypal personality and antisocial behavior at ages 17 and 23 years. *American Journal of Psychiatry, 160,* 1627–1635.

This study offers an example of the type of intervention that may prove beneficial in future efforts to prevent antisocial behavior.

Wakschlag, L. S., Pickett, K. E., Cook, E. C., Benowitz, N. L., & Leventhal, B. L. (2002). Maternal smoking during pregnancy and severe antisocial behavior in offspring: A review. *American Journal of Public Health, 92,* 966–974.

The authors review the evidence linking prenatal nicotine exposure to later antisocial behavior.

Psychophysiology and Crime

Lorber, M. F. (2004). Psychophysiology of aggression, psychopathy, and conduct problems: A meta-analysis. *Psychological Bulletin, 130,* 531–552.

In this meta-analysis of 95 studies the relationships between three measures of heart rate and skin conductance activity—resting, task, and reactivity—and three types of antisocial spectrum behavior—aggression, psychopathy, and conduct problems— were examined. Results provide important empirical and clinical implications and suggest that age and stimulus valence may moderate the psychophysiology–behavior relationships.

Raine, A., Brennan, P. A., Farrington, D. P., & Mednick, S. A. (1996). *Biosocial bases of violence.* New York: Plenum Press.

This book provides an overview of research that integrates biological and psychosocial processes in attempts to explain violence. Biosocial theories of aggression and violence in children and adults are discussed, and directions for future studies are provided.

Schizophrenia and Crime

Raine, A. (2006). Pursuing a second generation of research on crime and schizophrenia. In A. Raine (Ed.), *Crime and schizophrenia: Causes and cures* (pp. 3–12). New York: Nova Science.

This chapter discusses the co-occurrence of schizophrenia and crime, the issue of stigmatization, applications of schizophrenia-crime research, and the need for a second generation of research that breaks into new territory.

Schug, R. A., & Raine, A. (2009). Comparative meta-analyses of neuropsychological functioning in antisocial schizophrenic persons. *Clinical Psychology Review, 29,* 230–242.

In this article, evidence for a biologically distinct subgroup of antisocial individuals with schizophrenia is reviewed, and results from preliminary meta-analyses of studies of cognitive performance in antisocial schizophrenic persons compared to their non-schizophrenic and non-antisocial counterparts, which suggest specific patterns of brain dysfunction, are reported.

Vila, Brian J., Lawrence E. Cohen, and Richard S. Machalek: Evolutionary Expropriative Theory

Cohen, L. E., & Machalek, R. (1988). A general theory of expropriative crime: An evolutionary ecological approach. *American Journal of Sociology, 94,* 465–501.

This article presents the original version of the ecological expropriative theory. One of the major foci is on behavioral strategies that are propagated throughout the population and are related to forms of expropriative crime. These behavioral strategies are learned via cultural transmission.

Vila, B. J. (1994). A general paradigm for understanding criminal behavior: Extending evolutionary ecological theory. *Criminology, 32,* 311–359.

This article argues for a revision of the original theory and extension to all forms of crime. One of the major refinements is the inclusion of biological evolutionary content to augment cultural evolutionary content described in the original theory. A wide variety of interdisciplinary concepts are interwoven in order to derive this general paradigm of crime.

Wilson, James Q., and Richard J. Herrnstein: Crime and Human Nature

Gottfredson, M. R., & Hirschi, T. (1990). *A general theory of crime.* Stanford, CA: Stanford University Press.

Moffitt, T. E. (1993). Adolescence-limited and life-course-persistent antisocial behavior: A developmental taxonomy. *Psychological Review, 100,* 674–701.

In the wake of James Q. Wilson and Richard J. Herrnstein's Crime and Human Nature, *a series of works appeared that embraced the use of individual-level constructs from a range of academic disciplines, including sociology, psychology, biology, genetics, and neuroscience, to explain involvement in antisocial behaviors. Two of these works, Gottfredson and Hirschi's self-control theory and Moffitt's developmental taxonomy, are even more influential than Wilson and Herrnstein's work based on the number of citations and empirical tests of these theories. More broadly, these works show that the use of individual-level variables from across disciplines is now commonplace, and contemporary research that does so is well received and not criticized as with Wilson and Herrnstein.*

Raine, A. (1993). *The psychopathology of crime: Criminal behavior as a clinical disorder.* San Diego, CA: Academic Press.

Another important work by Adrian Raine explores the biopsychological correlates and bases of antisocial behavior from a more clinical perspective. Raine's work summarizes scholarship from fields removed from mainstream criminology and can be seen as an update of Wilson and Herrnstein.

XYY Aggression Theory

Rutter, M. (2006). *Genes and behaviour: Nature-nurture interplay explained.* Oxford, UK: Blackwell.

This book summarizes genetics in relation to mental disorders and normal psychological characteristics, as well as environmental determinants. It covers causes and risks, nature and nurture, heritability of different mental disorders and traits, patterns of inheritance including XYY, environmentally mediated risks, and gene-environment interaction.

Rutter, M., Giller, H., & Hagell, A. (1998). *Antisocial behavior by young people.* Cambridge, UK: Cambridge University Press.

This is a comprehensive review of international research evidence on antisocial behavior. The book covers many different aspects of the field, including different types of delinquent behavior, time trends, heritable and environmental risk factors, and theories, including XYY.

Witkin, H. A., Mednick, S. A., Schulsinger F., Bakkestrom, E., Christiansen, K. O., Goodenough, D. R., et al. (1976). Criminality in XYY and XXY men. *Science, 193,* 547–555.

This is an important paper in the field. Based on a large Danish sample, the authors showed that the association between XYY and violent behavior was confounded by cognitive dysfunction.

5. Psychological Theories of Crime

Andrews, D. A., and James Bonta: A Personal, Interpersonal, and Community-Reinforcement (PIC-R) Perspective on Criminal Conduct

Andrews, D. A., Bonta, J., & Hoge, R. D. (1990). Classification for effective rehabilitation: Rediscovering psychology. *Criminal Justice and Behavior, 17,* 19–52.

This article outlines the importance of assessment tools in guiding treatment delivery. It provides a good grounding for Andrews and Bonta's arguments regarding their theory's clinical relevance.

Gendreau, P. T., Little, T., & Goggin, C. (1996). A meta-analysis of the predictors of adult offender recidivism: What works! *Criminology, 34,* 575–607.

This article examines the research on factors associated with criminal behavior. The factors identified mirror those discussed by Andrews and Bonta and provide a meaningful framework for the principles of effective intervention.

Lowenkamp, C. T., Latessa, E. J., & Holsinger, A. M. (2006). The risk principle in action: What we have learned from 13,676 offenders and 97 correctional programs? *Crime and Delinquency, 52,* 77–93.

This article reviews the risk principle and the importance of reserving intensive services for higher risk clients. In particular, the study reviews programs providing services for offenders. Those programs that provided intensive services for lower risk clients had higher recidivism rates.

Pratt, T. C., & Cullen, F. T. (2000). The empirical status of Gottfredson and Hirschi's general theory of crime: A meta-analysis. *Criminology, 38,* 931–964.

This article discusses Gottfredson and Hirschi's self-control theory. However, Pratt and Cullen also note that while self-control theory is predictive of crime, it is the addition of other risk factors, such as attitudes and peers, that provide a fuller understanding of criminal behavior.

Bandura, Albert: Social Learning Theory

Bandura, A. (1977). *Social learning theory.* Englewood Cliffs, NJ: Prentice Hall.

Bandura formally presents social learning theory in this work. It is a must-read to gain a comprehensive understanding of the theory. Specifically, he presents how behavior begins and how the anticipation of consequences and actual consequences of behavior moderates further similar behavior. He clarifies the idea of the reciprocal relationship between the person, the environment, and the behavior.

Bandura, A. (1979). The social learning perspective: Mechanisms of aggression. In H. Toch (Ed.), *Psychology of crime and criminal justice* (pp. 198–236). New York: Holt, Reinhart, and Winston.

Social learning theory is formally applied to aggressive behavior by Bandura in this work. While still theoretical, the systematic and detailed application of the theory to aggression provides a useful look at the practical application of the theory to criminal behavior.

Bandura, A. (2007). Albert Bandura. In G. Lindzey & W. M. Runyan (Eds.), *A history of psychology in autobiography* (Vol. 9, pp. 43–75). Washington, DC: American Psychological Association.

This work provides the reader an entertaining memoir of Albert Bandura. In his own words, Bandura describes his early life in rural Alberta to his eventual appointment at Stanford University. He narrates a story that engagingly contextualizes his academic pursuits over half a century.

Cognitive Theories of Crime

Berkowitz, L. (1989). Frustration-aggression hypothesis: Examination and reformulation. *Psychological Bulletin, 106*(1), 59–73.

This work describes Berkowitz's extension and reformulation of Dollard et al.'s original frustration-aggression hypothesis.

Dodge, K. A., & Coie, J. D. (1987). Social information processing factors in reactive and proactive aggression in children's peer groups. *Journal of Personality and Social Psychology, 53,* 1146–1158.

This work explains Dodge's hostile attribution model in relation to aggression among children.

Dollard, J., Doob, L. W., Miller, N. E., Mowrer, O. H., & Sears, R. R. (1970). Frustration and aggression. In E. Megargee & J. Hokanson (Eds.), *The dynamics of aggression* (pp. 22–32). New York: Harper & Row.

This work explains the frustration-aggression hypothesis as it relates to criminal and delinquent behavior.

Gilligan, C. (1982). *In a different voice: Psychological theory and women's development.* Cambridge, MA: Harvard University Press.

This work elaborates upon Kohlberg's moral development theory, and identifies the moral development of women.

Huesmann, L. R., & Eron, L. D. (1984). Cognitive processes and the persistence of aggressive behavior. *Aggressive Behavior, 10*(3), 243–251.

This work outlines Huesmann and Eron's cognitive scripts model.

Kohlberg, L. (1976). Moral stages and moralization: The cognitive developmental approach. In T. Lickona (Ed.), *Moral development and behavior: Theory, research and social issues* (pp. 31–52). New York: Holt, Rinehart, and Winston.

This work provides an overview of moral development theory, summarizes the state of the research, and elaborates on its applicability to juvenile offending.

Piaget, J., & Inhelder, B. (1958). *The growth of logical thinking from childhood to adolescence.* New York: Basic.

This work includes the first statements of Piaget's cognitive development theory among children and adolescents.

Samenow, S. E. (2004). *Inside the criminal mind.* New York: Crown.

This work describes Yochelson and Samenow's updated theory on criminal thinking errors.

Yochelson, S., & Samenow, S. E. (1976). *The criminal personality: Vol. 1. A profile for change.* New York: Jason Aronson.

This work describes Yochelson and Samenow's original theory on criminal thinking errors.

Dodge, Kenneth A.: Aggression and a Hostile Attribution Style

Dodge, K. A., & Somberg, D. R. (1987). Hostile attributional biases among aggressive boys are exacerbated under conditions of threats to the self. *Child Development, 58,* 213–224.

> *In this essay, Dodge and Somberg detail more specific situations that highlight the differences between aggressive and nonaggressive boys. They report that under conditions of threat, aggressive boys are more likely to make hostile attributions in ambiguous circumstances.*

Unnever, J. D. (2005). Bullies, aggressive victims, and victims: Are they distinct groups? *Aggressive Behavior, 3,* 153–171.

> *In this essay, Unnever examines whether there are three distinct types of behaviors that are associated with bullies, aggressive victims (those who bullied but are themselves bullied), and victims and whether proactive and reactive aggression predict their bullying behaviors.*

Freudian Theory

Eysenck, H. (1987). *The rise and fall of the Freudian empire.* New York: Plenum.

> *The criticisms of Freudian theory are many. This text provides excellent insights into the weakness of this most influential yet consistently controversial, theoretical perspective.*

Freud, S. (1953). *A general introduction to psychoanalysis.* New York: Permabooks.

> *There is no better route to understanding the Freudian perspective on criminal behavior than from the theorist himself. His writings are highly accessible to the reader and intuitively applicable to the understanding of deviance and criminality.*

Glueck, S., & Glueck, E. (1950). *Unraveling juvenile delinquency.* Cambridge, MA: Harvard University Press.

> *A classic study in the field of criminology, Glueck and Glueck root many of their theoretical assumptions in psychoanalytic thought. Their empirical evaluation of their theoretical propositions is an excellent example of cross-sectional research and data interpretation.*

Glueck, Sheldon, and Eleanor Glueck: The Origins of Crime

Blokland, A. (2005). *Crime over the life span: Trajectories of criminal behaviour in Dutch offenders.* Leiden, Netherlands: NSCR.

> *This study exemplifies the benefits of a large sample followed over a long span of years facilitating the study of hitherto neglected latecomers to crime and older offenders. The results point to the existence of a group of very persistent offenders to a late age who tend to specialize in property offenses, different from the commoner trajectory of recidivists who desist earlier. There are policy implications for the use of incapacitating sentences that are apt to be applied at a point when criminal careers are anyway commencing desistence or to offenders who are not dangerously violent. Given a large sample, it becomes possible to study subgroups, for example to differentiate the careers of female offenders who appear half as numerous as men, have more intermittent offending careers, and may respond differently to marriage and the arrival of children.*

Farrington, D. P., & Welsh, B. C. (2007). *Saving children from a life of crime: Early risk factors and effective intervention.* Oxford, UK: Oxford University Press.

> *Theories of causation of delinquency derived from longitudinal studies of offending have had much influence on the design of delinquency prevention projects targeting young children and their families. Some of these—like the well-known Perry Project of pre-school intellectual enrichment, outstanding for its control group and long follow-up—have been shown to produce significant reduction of delinquency potential, both short and long term. Family-based interventions, particularly schemes of education in parenting, have also proved beneficial. These successes go some way to validate and justify longitudinal career analysis. The authors believe that a government-based national strategy is needed to promote community projects baaed on methods that have been shown to work.*

Hawkins, J. D., & Herrenkohl, T. I. (2007). Prevention in the school years. In D. P. Farrington & J. W. Coid (Eds.), *Early prevention of adult antisocial behaviour* (pp. 265–291). Cambridge, UK: Cambridge University Press.

> *The enormous contrasts in the delinquency potential of leavers or dropouts from different schools have been shown to be largely due to differences at intake. This might seem to indicate, as early studies such as the Gluecks suggested, that delinquency potential is irrevocably fixed in the pre-school years. This review points to a more optimistic conclusion. Techniques of classroom management, the application of consistent carrot-and-stick measures to the control of aggression and bullying, the inclusion of social skills training in*

the curriculum, the enlistment of pupils in cooperative tasks, attention to individual pupils' problems of comprehension, and the application of appropriate cognitive behavior modification methods have all been found to have some effect. This is important because longitudinal studies show that school leaving age can be a critical turning point in delinquency careers, when those lacking the practical or social skills needed in the job market encounter special stress. Unfortunately, small demonstration projects in schools are indicators of what is possible, but in a less-than-ideal world, implementation on a national scale is problematic.

Thornberry, T. P., & Krohn, M. D. (Eds.). (2003). *Taking stock of delinquency: An overview of findings from contemporary longitudinal studies.* New York: Kluwer Academic/Plenum.

As criminal career data from diverse samples have accumulated, it is instructive to note how the same basic patterns re-emerge, notably the link between early onset of offending and the likelihood of continuing recidivism and the close association among adverse features of family backgrounds, poor parenting, poor performance and behavior at school, and subsequent delinquency. As data for later years of the life span have become available, it has become increasingly evident that static models of career progression do not explain the measurable delinquency-inhibiting effects of events such as marriage or the exacerbating effects of, for example, maltreatment during adolescence or substance abuse. The serious collateral damage of delinquency in its impact on chances of establishing stable relationships, preserving a family, or achieving economic security has also become clearer.

Hare, Robert D.: Psychopathy and Crime

Blair, J., Mitchell, D., & Blair, K. (2005). *The psychopath: Emotion and brain.* Malden, MA: Blackwell.

Blair et al. provide one of the most current theoretical perspectives on the etiology of psychopathy. They also discuss key empirical findings that have been advanced in recent years. The book is written to appeal to experts, graduate students, and advanced undergraduate students.

Hare, R. D. (1993). *Without conscience: The disturbing world of the psychopaths among us.* New York: Pocket.

This book is a very readable explanation that is accessible to students and laypersons alike. Hare

discusses some of the possible causes of psychopathy, and provides clear descriptions of the disorder. The existence and nature of white-collar psychopaths is discussed as well.

Millon, T., Simonsen, E., Birket-Smith, M., & Davis, R. D. (Eds.). (1998). *Psychopathy: Antisocial, criminal, and violent behavior.* New York: Guilford.

Patrick, C. J. (Ed.). (2006). *Handbook of psychopathy.* New York: Guilford.

Both of these edited volumes provide comprehensive overviews of psychopathy. The leading experts in the field cover such topics as the etiology of this disorder; the biological, psychological, and social correlates of psychopathy; clinical and practical implications; and current directions and dilemmas facing the field.

Kohlberg, Lawrence: Moral Development Theory

Gilligan, C. (1986). *In a different voice: Psychological theory and women's development.* Cambridge, MA: Harvard University Press.

Carol Gilligan challenges Kohlberg's theory of moral development for its lack of attention to the moral development of girls. It affords a feminist perspective on identity development in girls and is considered a classic work in feminist thought. Gilligan's reformulation of the stages of moral development for women is based on interviews with college women around their views toward abortion.

Killen, M., & Smetana, J. (Eds.). (2006). *Handbook of moral development.* Hillsdale, NJ: Psychology Press.

A more recent edited volume, the 26 chapters discuss reformulations of Kohlberg's perspective and provide a number of chapters on culture and diversity. Descriptions of new educational approaches to moral and character development are also presented. One section of five chapters addresses moral development and aggressive behavior in children.

Laufer, J., & Day, M. (Ed.). (1983). *Personality theory, moral development and criminal behavior.* Lexington, MA: Lexington Books.

This is an edited volume that provides several chapters on moral development, including a thorough review of the theory's applicability to offenders by Jennings, Kilkenny, and Kohlberg. The chapter also discusses early Just Community interventions. Additional chapters assess the theories relevance to psychopathy and offenders court-ordered to restitution.

Lahey, Benjamin B., and Irwin D. Waldman: Developmental Propensity Model

Eisenberg, N., & Mussen, P. H. (1991). *The roots of prosocial behavior in children.* New York: Cambridge University Press.

> *This book discusses the biological, psychological, and environmental factors that contribute to healthy child development. The authors also introduce the concept of dispositional sympathy, which is a protective factor against conduct problems.*

Farrington, D. P., & West, D. J. (1993). Criminal, penal and life histories of chronic offenders: Risk and protective factors and early identification. *Criminal Behaviour and Mental Health, 3,* 492–523.

> *This article discusses the protective and risk factors for antisocial behaviors. The authors identify four important risk factors for chronic offending: troublesomeness, delinquent sibling, convicted parent, and—important to Lahey and Waldman's model— daring.*

Kagan, J., Reznick, J. S., & Snidman, N. (1988). Biological bases of childhood shyness. *Science, 240,* 167–171.

> *This journal article assesses variation in shyness in children from a biological perspective. The authors discuss how behaviorally disinhibition children would spontaneously react in novel situations. These children grew up to become more talkative and interactive with unfamiliar children and adults.*

Lahey, B. B., & Waldman, I. D. (2003). A developmental propensity model of the origins of conduct problems during childhood and adolescence. In B. B. Lahey, T. E. Moffitt, & A. Caspi (Eds.), *Causes of conduct disorder and juvenile delinquency* (pp. 76–117). New York: Guilford Press.

> *Lahey and Waldman propose their developmental propensity model of the origins of conduct problems in this book chapter. This chapter provides a detailed account of the development and components of their model.*

Lahey, B. B., & Waldman, I. D. (2005). A developmental model of the propensity to offend during childhood and adolescence. In D. P. Farrington (Ed.), *Integrated developmental and life-course theories of offending* (Advances in Criminological Theory: Vol. 14, pp. 15–50). New Brunswick, NJ: Transaction.

> *Lahey and Waldman describe their developmental propensity model of the origins of conduct problems*

> *in this book chapter. They place a particular emphasis on applying their model to the developmental trajectories of juvenile delinquency.*

Moffitt, T. E. (1993). Adolescent-limited and life-course-persistent antisocial behavior: A developmental taxonomy. *Psychological Review, 100,* 674–701.

> *Moffitt presents her dual taxonomy theory in this journal article by discussing two distinct groups of offenders (i.e., adolescent-limited and life-course-persistent). She also describes the unique causal processes underlying each trajectory.*

Media Violence Effects

Freedman, J. L. (2002). *Media violence and its effect on aggression: Assessing the scientific evidence.* Toronto, ON: University of Toronto Press.

> *In this book, University of Toronto psychology professor Jonathan Freedman argued that the available scientific evidence suggests that there is no causal link between exposure to violence in media and aggressive or criminal behavior. He presented explanations concerning why, in his view, the alleged link between media violence and aggression has become so widely accepted in the absence of credible evidence establishing such a link. He also provided reasons why media violence may not have impacts on aggression.*

Grossman, D., & DeGaetano, G. (1999). *Stop teaching our kids to kill: A call to action against TV, movie, and video game violence.* New York: Crown.

> *West Point psychology and military science professor Dave Grossman and media violence expert Gloria DeGaetano argue in their book that there is incontrovertible evidence of a causal link between violent media content and criminal aggression. Additionally, they issue a call to action and provide recommendations to address youth violence.*

Potter, W. J. (2003). *The 11 myths of media violence.* Thousand Oaks, CA: Sage.

> *In this book, University of California, Santa Barbara communications professor W. James Potter identifies 11 different media violence myths that, in his view, facilitated the creation of violent media productions. Among other things, he challenges the notion that media violence primarily only impacts children and that the First Amendment provides protection to those who produce violent media content. He also advances a public health approach to regulating media content.*

Mental Illness and Crime

Hails, J., & Borum, R. (2003). Police training and specialized approaches to respond to people with mental illness. *Crime and Delinquency, 49,* 52–61.

This article examines some of the various approaches that police forces have begun to use to deal with mentally ill offenders. It explores how mentally ill offenders affect the police force and various techniques that police officers can use to manage mentally ill offenders in a more effective manner.

James, D. J., & Glaze, L. E. (2006). *Mental health problems of prison and jail inmates.* Washington, DC: Bureau of Justice Statistics, U.S. Department of Justice.

This report examines the percentages of individuals who are mentally ill in prison and jail populations. It provides statistics for the various backgrounds of these individuals and how they differ from non-mentally ill individuals.

Moore, M. E., & Hiday, V. A. (2006). Mental health court outcomes: A comparison of re-arrest and re-arrest severity between mental health court and traditional court participants. *Law and Human Behavior, 30,* 659–674.

This article is one of the first studies to examine the effectiveness of mental health courts. Because mental health courts are relatively new in their inception, there have been very few studies that have examined the effectiveness of these courts in terms of recidivism.

Silver, E. (2006). Understanding the relationship between mental disorder and violence: The need for a criminological perspective. *Law and Human Behavior, 30,* 685–706.

This article examines the potential theoretical relationships between mental illness and crime. Silver articulates that this relationship may be able to be explained through current criminological theories. He then elaborates on how social learning theory, general strain theory, social bond theory, the age-graded theory of crime, rational choice theory, and social disorganization theory may apply to mental illness.

Patterson, Gerald R.: Social Learning, the Family, and Crime

Granic, I., & Patterson, G. R. (2006). Toward a comprehensive model of antisocial development: A dynamic systems approach. *Psychological Review, 113,* 101–131.

This article attempts to merge Patterson's coercion theory with a dynamic systems approach, providing a more nuanced and advanced model of the theory.

This is recommended to readers who are interested in following the latest development of coercion theory.

Reid, J. B., Patterson, G. R., & Snyder, J. (Eds.). (2002). *Antisocial behavior in children and adolescents: A developmental analysis and model for intervention.* Washington, DC: American Psychological Association.

This edited book is a compilation of Patterson and colleagues' research spanning the last 30 years. It provides a historical perspective on the development of the Oregon delinquency model, chapter summaries of research testing various constructs of coercion theory, and intervention strategies for preventing and disrupting child and adolescent antisocial behavior.

Raine, Adrian: Crime as a Disorder

Raine, A. (1997). *The psychopathology of crime: Criminal behavior as a clinical disorder.* New York: Academic Press.

This is the premier text for anyone interested in research by Adrian Raine. This text is grounded in experimental research and empirical approaches to explaining potential causes of criminality. Raine provides a very good argument for biological causes as well as environmental factors related to criminal behavior.

Raine, A. (2006). *Crime and schizophrenia: Causes and cures.* New York: Nova Science.

This is a very unique book that squarely addresses an issue that is often avoided: the crime and schizophrenia association. In most of the contemporary criminological literature, there is a tendency to dismiss this association and/or to resist its possibility. Raine provides a scientific demonstration of the association as a means of generating new research on the crime-schizophrenia relationship to benefit offenders who are so afflicted, the victims of their crimes, and society as a whole.

Raine, A., & Sanmartin, J. (Eds.). (2007). *Violence and psychopathy.* New York: Springer.

This book presents some of the key contributions made at the Fourth International Meeting on the Biology and Sociology of Violence held in November 1999. One primary point throughout this book is the notion that violence and psychopathy simply cannot be understood solely in terms of social and environmental forces and influences.

Walters, Glenn D.: Lifestyle Theory

Katz, J. (1988). *Seductions of crime: Moral and sensual attraction of doing evil.* New York: Perseus.

Katz employs a comprehensive qualitative theoretical framework for exploring the common-sense attitude violent criminal offenders adopt in their accounts of past criminal acts. Through a qualitative lens, Katz provides a conceptual scheme for coming to terms with the mundane as well as the horrific aspects of violent crime.

Walters, G. D. (2000). *Beyond behavior: Construction of an overarching psychological theory of lifestyles.* Westport, CT: Praeger.

This is one of two volumes reflecting Walters's most current research. This first volume offers a contemporary assessment of lifestyle theory by focusing on an integrative-interaction approach to understanding and explaining criminality. It presents an expansive yet readable theoretical treatise on lifestyle theory.

Walters, G. D. (2000). *The self-altering process: Exploring the dynamic nature of lifestyle development and change.* Westport, CT: Praeger.

Walters, in this second volume, outlines the change process that retains its developmental characteristics as those found in criminal belief system(s). Its coverage of desistance theory and "natural" recovery, as fundamental principles in understanding the change process via a lifestyle theory framework is comprehensive and provides a "blueprint" for those wishing to continue the work.

Yochelson, Samuel, and Stanton E. Samenow: The Criminal Personality

Elliott, B., & Verdeyen, V. (2002). *Game over! Strategies for redirecting inmate deception.* Lanham, MD: American Correctional Association.

Elliott and Verdeyen modified the model proposed by Walters in order to make it easier to use by correctional counselors. They transformed the criminal "thinking patterns," into what they called "cognitive distortions." By working on changing these distortions, the counselors seek to change how criminals think.

Walters, G. (1990). *The criminal lifestyle: Patterns of serious criminal conduct.* Newbury Park, CA: Sage.

The work of Yochelson and Samenow and the principles of cognitive-behavioral strategies that they developed have been widely used in the treatment of offenders in correctional facilities. Their strategies in correcting the 52 "thinking errors" that criminals employ to justify their actions have gained popularity among many correctional counselors. Their work was further expanded and modified by Walters, who

consolidated these thinking errors into eight criminal thinking patterns.

6. The Chicago School of Criminology

Burgess, Robert L., and Ronald L. Akers: Differential Association-Reinforcement Theory

Akers, R. L. (1973). *Deviant behavior: A social learning approach.* Belmont, CA: Wadsworth.

This book provides a summary of his social learning theory, which constitutes the most current and complete presentation of a social learning theory of criminal behavior. Importantly, Akers's book is written in a style that is easily grasped by most readers.

Burgess, R. L., & Akers, R. L. (1966). A differential association-reinforcement theory of criminal behavior. *Social Problems, 14,* 128–147.

This article is Burgess and Akers's response to Sutherland's theory of differential association.

Sutherland, E. H. (1947). *Principles of criminology* (4th ed.). Philadelphia: Lippincott.

This book contains the most complete statement of his theory of differential association and is the version of differential association theory to which Burgess and Akers are responding.

De Fleur, Melvin L., and Richard Quinney: A Reformulation of Sutherland's Differential Association Theory

Burgess, R. L., & Akers, R. L. (1966). A differential association-reinforcement theory of criminal behavior, *Social Problems, 14,* 128–147.

Here, Burgess and Akers develop social learning theory, which adapted Sutherland's original theory of differential association theory in an attempt to account for a wider variety of criminal behavior.

Gaylord, M., & Galliher, J. (1988). *The criminology of Edwin Sutherland.* New Brunswick, NJ: Transaction.

This book is a very thorough and detailed resource on the life and work of Sutherland. Gaylord and Galliher examine the development of differential association theory as well as Sutherland's other important contributions to criminology.

Kobrin, Solomon: Neighborhoods and Crime

Kobrin, S. (1951). The conflict of values in delinquency areas. *American Sociological Review, 16,* 653–661.

This article lays out Kobrin's major theoretical contributions to social disorganization theory, describing continuums between delinquents and non-delinquents and differential neighborhood organization.

Kobrin, S. (1959). The Chicago Area Project: A 25-year assessment. *Annals of the American Academy of Political and Social Science, 322,* 19–29.

Here, Kobrin summarizes the theory and practice of the Chicago Area Project under his direction.

Kornhauser, Ruth Rosner: Social Sources of Delinquency

Hirschi, T. (1969). *Causes of delinquency.* Berkeley: University of California Press.

The first chapter of this classic book contains the classification (strain, social control, cultural deviance) still used by many theorists. Kornhauser's then-unpublished manuscript is cited heavily, suggesting that her writing influenced Hirschi's theoretical organization.

Messner, S. F., & Rosenfeld, R. (2007). *Crime and the American dream* (4th ed.). Belmont, CA: Thomson.

Messner and Rosenfeld update Merton's theory of anomie at the macro level. Although the authors do not agree completely with Kornhauser's insights and theoretical critiques, the fact that they explicitly address her criticisms indicates the important place that Social Sources of Delinquency maintains in criminology.

Sampson, Robert J.: Collective Efficacy Theory

Kirk, D. S. (2009). Unraveling the contextual effects on student suspension and juvenile arrest: The independent and interdependent influences of school, neighborhood, and family social controls. *Criminology, 47,* 479–520.

David Kirk was Robert Sampson's doctoral student at the University of Chicago. In this article, Kirk extends the conception of collective efficacy to understand school environments. Just as neighborhood collective efficacy reveals how social ties in the neighborhood community can be activated in order to promote social control, collective efficacy within the domain of schools is a mechanism that activates the communal organization within a school in order to control student behavior.

Pratt, T. C., & Cullen, F. T. (2005). Assessing macro-level predictors and theories of crime: a meta-analysis. In M. Tonry (Ed.), *Crime and justice: A review of research* (Vol. 32, pp. 373–450). Chicago: University of Chicago Press.

Pratt and Cullen provide a comprehensive meta-analysis of the empirical literature on the ecological predictors of crime, including collective efficacy.

Sampson, R. J. (2006). Collective efficacy theory: Lessons learned and directions for future inquiry. In F. T. Cullen, J. P. Wright, & K. R. Blevins (Eds.), *Taking stock: The status of criminological theory* (Advances in Criminological Theory: Vol. 15, pp. 149–167). New Brunswick, NJ: Transaction.

Sampson, R. J. (2006). How does community context matter? Social mechanisms and the explanation of crime. In P.-O. Wikström & R. J. Sampson (Eds.), *The explanation of crime: Context, mechanisms, and development* (pp. 31–60). Cambridge, UK: Cambridge University Press.

These two chapters by Robert Sampson provide discussions of the intellectual legacy of collective efficacy theory, a description of empirical evidence in support of the theory, and an overview of future directions in the theoretical development of collective efficacy.

Shaw, Clifford R.: The Jack-Roller

Becker, H. S. (1966). Introduction. In C. R. Shaw, *The jack-roller: A delinquent boy's own story* (pp. v–xviii). Chicago: University of Chicago Press.

This introduction to the 1966 reissue of The Jack-Roller *makes the case for the value of life histories of delinquents.*

Maruna, S., & Matravers, A. (2008). N = 1: Criminology and the person. *Theoretical Criminology, 11,* 427–442.

This paper examines the uses, advantages, and shortcomings of life histories for understanding and answering larger questions about crime, punishment, and criminal careers.

Shover, N. (1996). *Great pretenders: Pursuits and careers of persistent thieves.* Boulder, CO: Westview.

This study of the lives and careers of street-level thieves draws heavily from dozens of life histories and shows their value as sources of generalizations about offenders.

Snodgrass, J. (1976). Clifford R. Shaw and Henry D. McKay: Chicago criminologists. *British Journal of Criminology, 16,* 1–19.

This article describes and interprets the social, intellectual and personal context in which Clifford R. Shaw and his colleagues worked.

Snodgrass, J. (Ed.). (1982). *The jack-roller at seventy: A fifty year follow-up*. Lexington, MA: D. C. Heath.

> *This sequel to* The Jack-Roller *makes clear that in later life, as in his early years, there was much about Stanley that is typical of street-level thieves.*

Shaw, Clifford R., and Henry D. McKay: Social Disorganization Theory

Kubrin, C. E., & Weitzer, R. (2003). New directions in social disorganization theory. *Journal of Research in Crime and Delinquency, 40*, 374–402.

> *This article addresses current problems, both substantive and methodological, and charts some promising new directions in social disorganization theory.*

Sampson, R. J., & Groves, W. B. (1989). Community structure and crime: Testing social-disorganization theory. *American Journal of Sociology, 94*, 774–802.

> *This study constitutes the first empirical analysis of the mediating factors of social disorganization theory using survey data from communities in Britain.*

Shaw, C. R., & McKay, H. D. (1942). *Juvenile delinquency and urban areas*. Chicago: University of Chicago Press.

> *A classic text that provides the foundation of social disorganization theory. Shaw and McKay convincingly demonstrate the spatial relationship between social conditions of neighborhoods and rates of delinquency in Chicago communities over time.*

Stark, R. (1987). Deviant places: A theory of the ecology of crime. *Criminology, 25*, 893–909.

> *In this article, Stark calls for the resurrection of social disorganization theory reminding readers that along with "kinds of persons" theories of crime, we also need "kinds of places" theories. Using basic assumptions of social disorganization theory, Stark creates a set of propositions to be tested by disorganization theorists.*

Spergel, Irving: Neighborhoods and Delinquent Subcultures

Agnew, R. (2006). *Pressured into crime: An overview of general strain theory*. Los Angeles: Roxbury.

> *In this book, Agnew provides a contemporary summary and updating of strain theory. As such, Agnew revitalized the work of Robert Merton, Albert Cohen, Richard Cloward and Lloyd Ohlin, and Irving Spergel.*

Cullen, F. T. (1988). Were Cloward and Ohlin strain theorists? Delinquency and opportunity revisited. *Journal of Research in Crime and Delinquency, 25*, 214–241.

> *In this essay, Francis Cullen highlights Cloward and Ohlin's emphasis on the role of illegitimate means in channeling motivated offenders into one criminal role rather than another.*

Steffensmeier, Darrell J., and Jeffery T. Ulmer: The Professional Fence

Bradley-Engen, M. S. (2009). *Naked lives: Inside the worlds of exotic dance*. Albany: SUNY Press.

> *This work applies and expands key ideas from* The Fence *and* Confessions *to describe the skills, challenges, pitfalls, rewards, and rationales that shape the lives and careers of exotic dancers.*

Matsueda, R. L., Piliavin, I., Gartner, R., & Polakowski, M. (1992). The prestige of criminal and conventional occupations: A subcultural model of criminal activity. *American Sociological Review, 57*, 752–770.

> *A key theme of this article concerns stratification in the underworld and the prestige ranking of criminal specialties and roles within it. It draws from* The Fence *and was drawn upon in turn by* Confessions.

Steffensmeier, D. J., & Ulmer, J. T. (2006). Black and white control of numbers banking in black communities, 1970–2000. *American Sociological Review, 71*, 123–156.

> *Steffensmeier and Ulmer draw heavily from ideas in* Confessions *to highlight the importance of cultural and social capital in shaping success in a criminal enterprise like numbers gambling; how "criminal capital" and opportunities for success in the underground economy are shaped by upperworld and underworld racial and ethnic stratification; and how the underground economy is affected by changes in the legitimate market economy.*

Ulmer, J. T. (2000). Commitment, deviance, and social control. *Sociological Quarterly, 41*, 315–336.

> *The author describes continuity and change in criminal careers in terms of changes in structural, personal, and moral commitments, and also describes commitment to crime and to conventional life as two sides of the same coin. This commitment framework is featured prominently in* Confessions' *discussions of the careers of skilled property offenders and criminal entrepreneurs.*

Sutherland, Edwin H.: Differential Association Theory and Differential Social Organization

Akers, R. L. (1998). *Social learning and social structure: A general theory of crime and deviance*. Boston: Northeastern University Press.

This book summarizes over 30 years of theoretical and empirical work specifying and respecifying a revision of differential association theory using principles of social learning theory.

Matsueda, R. L. (1988). The current state of differential association theory. *Crime and Delinquency, 34,* 277–306.

Matsueda was a doctoral student of Donald Cressey who, in turn, was a doctoral student of Edwin Sutherland. This article summarizes differential association theory, finds the highly influential critique of differential association by Ruth Kornhauser to be misguided by creating a caricature of the theory, and updates revisions and research on Sutherland's theory.

Matsueda, R. L. (2006). Differential social organization, collective action, and crime. *Crime, Law, and Social Change, 46,* 3–33.

This article attempts to revitalize the concept of differential social organization by drawing out the dynamic collective action implications of the theory, and by specifying causal mechanisms from sociological theory, including social networks and social capital, weak ties, collective action frames, collective action thresholds, symbolic interaction, and stages of moral reasoning.

Sutherland, E. H. (1947). *Principles of criminology* (4th ed.). Philadelphia: Lippincott.

The fourth edition of Sutherland's classic textbook dominated the field for over half a century and presents the final version of his theory of differential association.

Sutherland, E. H. (1973). Wartime crime. In K. Schuessler (Ed.), *Edwin H. Sutherland on analyzing crime* (pp. 120–128). Chicago: University of Chicago Press.

This volume brings together a number of unpublished papers by Sutherland, including his account of the development of differential association, his critique of his own theory, and his overlooked essay on differential group organization and wartime crime.

Sutherland, E. H., Cressey, D. R., & Luckenbill, D. F. (1992). *Principles of criminology* (11th ed.). Lanham, MD: AltaMira Press.

The final edition of Sutherland's textbook, which spanned over 60 years, with Cressey and Luckenbill as co-authors.

Sutherland, Edwin H.: The Professional Thief

Letkemann, P. (1973). *Crime as work*. Englewood Cliffs, NJ: Prentice Hall.

In this book, Peter Letkemann draws heavily on the writings of Sutherland and Everett Hughes's sociology of occupations to present an occupational perspective on crime as "work," with special focus on the practices and skill of burglars and robbers.

Prus, R., & Sharper, C. R. D. (1977). *Road hustler: The career contingencies of professional card and dice hustlers*. Lexington, MA: D. C. Heath.

This work applies Sutherland's notion of "professional thief" to card and dice hustlers (via "C.R.D. Sharper" and hustlers he knew). Prus expands on Sutherland's theory of differential association by incorporating key ideas from symbolic interactionism to better explain the processes by which criminal careers stabilize.

Steffensmeier, D. J., & Ulmer, J. (2005). *Confessions of a dying thief: Understanding criminal careers and criminal enterprise*. New Brunswick, NJ: Aldine Transaction.

Along with the companion work The Fence *(authored by Steffensmeier),* Confessions *applies and expands key ideas of Sutherland to theft and fencing specifically as well as to theories of crime and deviance generally. In so doing, both works elucidate the how, when, and why of criminal involvements (including how they stabilize); the organization of crime and criminal enterprise; the role of opportunities in shaping criminal involvement, including their range and variability across individuals and groups; and how these opportunities have changed in recent decades.*

Thrasher, Frederick M.: The Gang

Clark, K. B. (1965). *Dark ghetto: Dilemmas of social power*. New York: Harper & Row.

The classic work on the "invisible walls" that shape the ghetto. Unlike the Chicago School, Clark applies the historical concept of the ghetto to the African American experience.

Giordano, P. C. (1978). Girls, guys and gangs: The changing social context of female delinquency. *Journal of Criminal Law and Criminology, 69,* 126–132.

A sound scientific work establishing the female peer groups as a major influence in the lives of girls. Thrasher failed to give adequate attention to the realities of girls' lives.

Kornhauser, R. (1978). *Social sources of delinquency: An appraisal of analytic models.* Chicago: University of Chicago Press.

This essential work examines the adequacy of theoretical explanations for delinquency.

Short, J. F., Jr., & Strodtbeck, F. L. (1965). *Group process and gang delinquency.* Chicago: University of Chicago Press.

This work is a thorough comparison of the adequacy of completing sociological perspectives on gangs, based on careful empirical research in Chicago in the 1950s and early 1960s.

Turner, Ralph H.: Deviant Roles and the Social Construction of Behavior

Turner, R. H. (1954). Self and other in moral judgment. *American Sociological Review, 19,* 249–259.

This article describes the interrelationship between role-specific expectations for one's own behavior and expectations for the behavior or reactions of others when judging morally questionable activities.

Turner, R. H. (1969). The public perception of protest. *American Sociological Review, 34,* 815–831.

This article describes the social construction of deviance by exploring the how violent collective disturbances are defined as either protest or crime.

Turner, R. H. (1972). Deviance avowal as neutralization of commitment. *Social Problems, 19,* 308–321.

This article builds on labeling theory to understand when and under what conditions individuals accept a deviant label.

Turner, R. H. (2002). Role theory. In J. H. Turner (Ed.), *Handbook of sociological theory* (pp. 233–254). New York: Kluwer Academic/Plenum.

This chapter summarizes Turner's role theory with particular attention to the interactive nature of role-making and the resolution of role conflict.

Whyte, William Foote: Street Corner Society

Adler, P. A., Adler, P., & Johnson, J. M. (Eds.). (1992). Street corner revisited [Special issue]. *Journal of Contemporary Ethnography, 21.*

Commemorating the 50th anniversary of the publication of Street Corner Society, *the* Journal of Contemporary Ethnography *dedicated a special issue to contemporary issues surrounding the book, particularly the debate surrounding the postmodernist critique of probing into the implicit authority of ethnographic analysis and writing.*

Brotherton, D., & Barrios, L. (2004). *The almighty Latin king and queen nation: Street politics and the transformation of a New York City street gang.* New York: Columbia University Press.

Brotherton and Barrios provide a detailed analysis of the rise and fall of the Almighty Latin King and Queen Nation's reform process. It pays attention to history, social context, and patterns of social change within gangs over time.

Hagedorn, J. (1998). *People and folks: Gangs, crime and the underclass in a rustbelt city* (2nd ed.). Chicago: Lakeview Press.

Hagedorn interviewed gang members in Milwaukee about their participation in drug trafficking. The results show a wide range in duration and consistency among drug-selling gang members. Hagedorn attributes the inconsistent pattern of gang drug trafficking to the effects of economic restructuring in inner-city America.

7. Cultural and Learning Theories of Crime

Akers, Ronald L.: Social Learning Theory

Akers, R. L. (1985). *Deviant behavior: A social learning approach* (3rd ed.). Belmont, CA: Wadsworth.

Ronald Akers demonstrates how social learning theory can be applied to the explanation of a wide variety of deviant behaviors.

Akers, R. L. (2009). *Social learning and social structure: A general theory of crime and deviance.* New Brunswick, NJ: Transaction.

In this reissued version of the 1998 book of the same title, Ronald Akers details social learning theory's origins and theoretical statement, reviews the empirical research he has conducted to test the theory, and adds a social structural component to the theoretical model to enhance the theory's ability to account for crime and deviance. This book contains a new introduction by Akers that updates the theory's status.

Anderson, Elijah: Code of the Street

Anderson, E. (1990). *Streetwise: Race, class, and change in an urban community.* Chicago: University of Chicago Press.

In this ethnographic work, Anderson addresses the issue of how a black and impoverished community and a racially mixed middle-class and upper-class community are able to co-exist in the same public spaces. The work in Code of the Street *developed from this book.*

Wilson, W. J. (1987). *The truly disadvantaged: The inner city, the underclass, and public policy.* Chicago: University of Chicago Press.

William Julius Wilson provides an in-depth discussion of the social pathologies of inner-city communities and an explanation for these social ills. Similar to Anderson (1999), Wilson identifies the devastating implication isolation from mainstream society has on communities.

Bennett, William J., John J. DiIulio, Jr., and John P. Walters: Moral Poverty Theory

Bennett, W. J., DiIulio, J. J., Jr., & Walters, J. P. (1996). *Body count: Moral poverty . . . and how to win America's war against crime and drugs.* New York: Simon & Schuster.

In this book, William Bennett, John DiIulio, and John Walters introduce their moral poverty theory. The authors define moral poverty, discuss its influence on violent crime and drugs in America, and offer solutions to the problem of moral poverty.

Gottfredson, M. R., & Hirschi, T. (1990). *A general theory of crime.* Stanford, CA: Stanford University Press.

Gottfredson and Hirschi offer a theory about self-control and crime. This theory includes the characteristics that Bennett et al. attribute to moral poverty but offers a different way to view their connection to crime.

Matza, David, and Gresham M. Sykes: Subterranean Values and Delinquency

Inglehart, R., Basanez, M., Dietz-Medrano, J., Halman, L., & Luijkz, R. (2004). *Human beliefs and values: A cross cultural sourcebook on the 1999–2002 value surveys.* Buenos Aires, Argentina: Siglo XXI Editores.

This work demonstrates support for the cognitive process intuited by Sykes and Matza.

Rokeach, M. (1973). *The nature of human values.* New York: Free Press.

Provides a summary of the developments of the social psychology of values that took place after Sykes and Matza published the idea of subterranean values.

Schwartz, S. H. (2006). A theory of cultural value orientations: Explication and applications. *Comparative Sociology, 5,* 137–182.

While, Schwartz (2006) does not use the term "subterranean," this work conceives of values—similar to Sykes and Matza—as existing in a hierarchical cognitive system that directs behavior through our preferences and attitudes.

Miller, Walter B.: Lower-Class Culture Theory of Delinquency

Brownfield, D. (1986). A reassessment of cultural deviance theory. *Deviant Behavior, 8,* 343–359.

In this article, the contributions of subcultural theories of crime and delinquency are re-examined. If social class is measured in terms of unemployment status and receipt of welfare benefits, then there is more support for the subcultural theory (regarding predictions such as the positive correlations between class and measures of subcultural values and between class and crime itself).

Brownfield, D. (1996). Subcultural theories of crime and delinquency. In J. Hagan, A. R. Gills, & D. Brownfield (Eds.), *Criminological controversies* (pp. 99–123). Boulder, CO: Westview.

In this chapter, the emphasis on culture and on structure in criminological theories is reviewed. An innovative way to conceive of "subcultures" in terms of gender differences in criminal behavior is considered.

Jensen, G., & Rojek, D. (1998). *Delinquency and youth crime* (3rd ed.). Prospect Heights, IL: Waveland Press.

In this text, the authors provide a very useful comparison of the three major theories in criminology (social control, subcultural or cultural deviance, and anomie perspectives). Jensen and Rojek discuss central assumptions of all three theories. For example, what do subcultural theorists assume about human nature and conflict or consensus about social rules, in comparison to the assumptions made by social control theorists regarding human nature and social rules?

Peers and Delinquency

Akers, R. L. (1998). *Social learning and social structure: A general theory of crime and deviance.* Boston: Northeastern University Press.

In this important work, Ronald Akers carefully delineates the principles of social learning theory, reviews the state of evidence and applies the theory to specific behaviors such as rape and drug abuse.

Matsueda, R. L., & Anderson, K. (1998). The dynamics of delinquent peers and delinquent behavior. *Criminology, 36*, 269–308.

> *This article offers a useful survey of the literature on delinquent peers and a thoughtful treatment of issues surrounding their measurement and effects.*

Reiss, A. J., Jr. (1986). Co-offender influences on criminal careers. In A. Blumstein, J. Cohen, J. Roth, & C. Visher (Eds.), *Criminal careers and "career criminals"* (pp. 121–160). Washington, DC: National Academy Press.

> *Perhaps the best treatment of co-offending ever published, this report helped revitalize research on the topic.*

Warr, M. (2002). *Companions in crime.* New York: Cambridge University Press.

> *This book summarizes decades of research on co-offending and peer influence and sets forth a variety of possible mechanisms of peer influence.*

Sellin, Thorsten: Culture Conflict and Crime

Lejins, P. P. (1987). Review essay. *Criminology, 25*, 975–988.

> *In this essay, Peter Lejins gives an excellent overview of the biography of Thorsten Sellin as well as his intellectual career. Of particular importance is the coverage of the diversity of the career of Sellin.*

Lilly, J. R., Cullen, F. T., & Ball, R. A. (2007). *Criminological theory: Context and consequences* (4th ed.). Thousand Oaks, CA: Sage.

> *Lilly, Cullen, and Ball present a number of informative chapters where they overview the type of work being conducted by sociologists during the era in which Sellin was writing Culture Conflict and Crime.*

Wolfgang, M. E. (Ed.). (1968). *Crime and culture: Essays in honor of Thorsten Sellin.* New York: Wiley.

> *This volume contains 21 articles focusing upon various aspects of the academic career of Sellin. The articles are written by former students, colleagues, and academics who knew Sellin during various stages of his career.*

Southern Subculture of Violence Theory

Anderson, E. (1999). *Code of the street: Decency, violence, and the moral life of the inner city.* New York: W. W. Norton.

> *Though not about southern violence per se, this award-winning urban ethnographic essay is the most*

widely acknowledged, contemporary theoretical treatment of subcultural deviance and crime. The book details the reality and life challenges specific to inner-city life (e.g., fear of crime and violence, teen pregnancy, drug use, and gangs) and how the urban underclass has developed a "streetcode" as a means of survival and interaction. Inner-city residents are dichotomized as "decent" or "street," with the latter category displaying and intergenerationally transferring a criminal subculture.

Nisbett, R. E., & Cohen, D. (1996). *Culture of honor: The psychology of violence in the South.* Boulder, CO: Westview.

> *The disproportionate amount of violence in the American South is thoroughly examined in this brief book that makes a strong case indicting the South's distinctive regional attitudes, beliefs, and behaviors concerning honor. Situating southern values in the historical context of immigrant Scots-Irish herding economies to the southern highlands, this social-psychological/subcultural theory makes a compelling case for a southern subculture of violence based on geographical, historical, and social scientific evidence. In so doing, a thorough review and critical critique of alternative explanations for southern violence are provided.*

Webb, J. (2004). *Born fighting: How the Scots-Irish shaped America.* New York: Broadway Books.

> *In as much as the Scots-Irish have been identified as the primary offending and victimization group in the extant southern subculture of violence literature, this part historical and part descriptive book traces the migration of the Scots-Irish to the United States and illustrates a tough and independent-minded Celtic people whose historical struggles against Rome and Britain have resulted in generational transference of a value system placing a premium on the use of violence and self-rule, as indicated by the legalism of states rights—a rallying point of southern cultural affirmation during military reconstruction after the war. The historical complexity and cultural fusion on a regional level concerning an insider-outsider social outlook attributed to southerners is discussed and informs understanding of high levels of violence in the region, generally, and why the Scots-Irish are such a fighting folk.*

Wolfgang, Marvin E., and Franco Ferracuti: Subculture of Violence Theory

Borg, M. J. (1997). The Southern subculture of punitiveness? Regional variation in support for capital punishment. *Journal of Research in Crime and Delinquency, 34,* 25–45.

This study is an interesting application of the subculture of violence theory. The southern region of the United States has been hypothesized to have a penchant for violence. This article follows with that line of thought and asks the question: If southerners are more aggressive in their interpersonal relationships, then to what degree do cultural factors affect their punishment decisions?

Cao, L., Adams, A., & Jensen, V. J. (1997). A test of the black subculture of violence thesis: A research note. *Criminology, 35,* 367–379.

This study is also an innovative application of the subculture of violence theory. In this article, the researchers test the theory's relevance to determining if violent values are widespread among African Americans.

Wolfgang, M. E., & Ferracuti, F. (1967). *The subculture of violence: Towards an integrated theory in criminology.* London: Tavistock.

This is the original work from which this entry is derived. A full account of the research behind the theory is included, and readers will gain a more in-depth understanding of the perspective from which the theory was generated.

8. Anomie and Strain Theories of Crime and Deviance

Agnew, Robert: General Strain Theory

Agnew, R. (1992). Foundation for a general strain theory of crime and delinquency. *Criminology, 30,* 47–87.

In this seminal piece, Robert Agnew outlined the key theoretical assumptions underlying his revision of strain theory. He also distinguished general strain theory from other theoretical approaches. The article paved the way for empirical tests as well as future theorizing.

Agnew, R. (1995). Controlling delinquency: Recommendations from general strain theory. In H. Barlow (Ed.), *Crime and public policy* (pp. 43–70). Boulder, CO: Westview.

General strain theory has unique implications for the control of crime and delinquency. In this chapter, Agnew shows how his theory can be applied to problems in the prevention and control of crime and, ultimately, how it can guide us toward a safer society.

Agnew, R. (2001). Building on the foundation of general strain theory: Specifying the types of strain most likely to lead to crime and delinquency. *Journal of Research in Crime and Delinquency, 38,* 319–361.

Robert Agnew offered his initial statement of general strain theory as a starting point and as a framework for future development. This article illustrates the development of the theory over time. Here, Agnew discusses the possibility that some strains may be more criminogenic than others, thereby adding precision and specificity to the theory.

Agnew, R. (2006). *Pressured into crime: An overview of general strain theory.* Los Angeles: Roxbury.

This book provides a comprehensive overview of general strain theory, discusses the relevance of the theory to key problems in criminology and criminal justice, and examines the existing body of evidence as it relates to the theory's validity. For students who wish to learn more about general strain theory, this short but engaging book provides an ideal resource.

Cloward, Richard A.: The Theory of Illegitimate Means

Cloward, R. A., & Ohlin, L. E. (1960). *Delinquency and opportunity: A theory of delinquent gangs.* New York: Free Press.

In this work, Richard Cloward applied his theory of illegitimate means to explain gang delinquency in the United States. It is considered one of the most important theoretical statements in the strain theory tradition.

Cloward, R. A., & Piven, F. F. (1979). Hidden protest: The channeling of female innovation and resistance. *Signs, 4,* 651–669.

Twenty years after publishing his theory of illegitimate means, Richard Cloward joined with Francis Fox Piven to use this theory to explain how gender-related experiences and opportunities shaped the nature of female deviance.

Cullen, F. T. (1984). *Rethinking crime and deviance theory: The emergence of a structuring tradition.* Totowa, NJ: Rowman and Allenheld.

Francis Cullen was Richard Cloward's doctoral student at Columbia University. For his dissertation, later published as this book, Cullen took Cloward's ideas and applied them to theories of crime and deviance generally.

Cloward, Richard A., and Lloyd E. Ohlin: Delinquency and Opportunity

Agnew, R. (2006). *Pressured into crime: An overview of general strain theory.* Los Angeles: Roxbury.

> *With his general strain theory, Robert Agnew revitalized the work of Robert Merton, Albert Cohen, and Richard Cloward and Lloyd Ohlin. In this book, Agnew provides an up-to-date and readable summary of contemporary strain theory.*

Cullen, F. T. (1984). *Rethinking crime and deviance theory: The emergence of a structuring tradition.* Totowa, NJ: Rowman and Allenhend.

> *Francis Cullen was Richard Cloward's doctoral student at Columbia University. For his dissertation, later published as this book, Cullen took Cloward's ideas and applied them to theories of crime and deviance generally.*

Cullen, F. T. (1988). Were Cloward and Ohlin strain theorists? Delinquency and opportunity revisited. *Journal of Research in Crime and Delinquency, 25,* 214–241.

> *In this essay, Francis Cullen shows that many scholars have assumed that Cloward and Ohlin are merely strain theorists. In so doing, they neglect the most innovative thesis at the core of* Delinquency and Opportunity: *the role of illegitimate means in channeling motivated offenders into one criminal role rather than another.*

Cohen, Albert K.: Delinquent Boys

Cohen, A. K. (1955). *Delinquent boys: The culture of the gang.* New York: Free Press.

> *This is the original treatise that presents the theory discussed herein.*

Lilly, J. R., Cullen, F. T., & Ball, R. A. (2007). *Criminological theory: Context and consequence* (4th ed.). Thousand Oaks, CA: Sage.

> *This book offers an overview of theoretical criminology, including those from Cohen's era as well as more recent theoretical explanations of crime.*

Messerschmidt, J. (2000). *Nine lives: Adolescent masculinities, the body, and violence.* Boulder, CO: Westview.

> *Using more contemporary theories of gender, the author analyzes the relationship between different forms of masculinity and violent delinquent behavior.*

Durkheim, Émile: Anomie and Suicide

Adler, F., Laufer, W. S., & Merton, R. K. (Eds.). (1999). *The legacy of anomie theory* (Advances in Criminological Theory: Vol. 6). New Brunswick, NJ: Transaction.

> *This book provides a detailed examination of anomie, including the changes in its development and application in criminology.*

Emirbayer, M. (1996). Durkheim's contribution to the sociological analysis of history. *Sociological Forum, 11,* 263–284.

> *This article provides a good discussion Durkheim's works and his contributions to the field of sociology.*

Pope, W. (1976). *Durkheim's "Suicide": A classic analyzed.* Chicago: University of Chicago Press.

> *This book provides a useful assessment of Durkheim's findings and discussion in* Suicide *(1897), which is somewhat easier to comprehend than the original work.*

Puffer, P. (2009). Durkheim did not say "normlessness": The concept of anomic suicide for introductory sociology courses. *Southern Rural Sociology, 24,* 200–222.

> *Centered on the variation in defining anomie by introduction to sociology textbooks, this article provides a clear discussion of the concept of anomie that is easy for younger academics to understand.*

Hagan, John, and Bill McCarthy: Mean Streets and Delinquency

Hagan, J., & McCarthy, B. (1997). *Mean streets: Youth crime and homelessness.* Cambridge, UK: Cambridge University Press.

> *This book outlines in detail the development and testing of the theoretical model. The combination of qualitative/ quantitative data sources in multiple locations, longitudinal panel design, and the comparative street/ school samples makes this work one of the most methodologically comprehensive in criminology. Its movement between theoretical integration, generation, and testing provides an exemplary model for research.*

McCarthy, B., & Hagan, J. (1998). Uncertainty, cooperation, and crime: Understanding the decision to co-offend. *Social Forces, 77,* 155–176.

> *In this article, Hagan and McCarthy extend their work by exploring how adversity on the street and connections with potential co-offenders influences street youths' readiness to trust others. This trust, in turn, influences street youths' willingness to collaborate and cooperate with others that increases participation in criminal activity.*

McCarthy, B., & Hagan, J. (2001). When crime pays: Capital, competence, and criminal success. *Social Forces, 79,* 1035–1060.

Hagan and McCarthy build further on their work by examining the roles of human capital, social capital, and personal capital, factors associated with conventional economic success, contribute to the illegal earnings of youth on the street. Here they discover that criminal economic success is more likely for youths who desire wealth (personal capital) and for those with the personal capital characteristic of competence when they are willing to collaborate with others (personal capital), specialize in certain offenses (criminal human and social capital), and enjoy risk taking (personal capital).

Merton, Robert K.: Social Structure and Anomie

Agnew, R. (2006). *Pressured into crime: An overview of general strain theory.* Los Angeles: Roxbury.

Robert Agnew has developed an important extension of social structure and anomie by detailing the diverse strains that may lead individuals into crime. This book provides an introduction to and a summary of the evidence on Agnew's "general strain theory."

Merton, R. K. (1938). Social structure and anomie. *American Sociological Review, 3,* 672–682.

In this classic essay, Robert K. Merton first outlined his theory of social structure and anomie. Those interested in Merton's "classic" anomie theory should start their inquiry with this article.

Messner, S. F., & Rosenfeld, R. (2007). *Crime and the American dream* (4th ed.). Belmont, CA: Thomson Wadsworth.

In this book, Steven F. Messner and Richard Rosenfeld present an important extension of Merton's anomie theory. The authors formulate an "institutional-anomie" theory of crime that explains how the functioning of the major social institutions in society generates and reinforces the anomic features of the "American Dream."

Messner, Steven F., and Richard Rosenfeld: Institutional-Anomie Theory

Merton, R. K. (1938). Social structure and anomie. *American Sociological Review, 3,* 672–682.

Seminal article in which Robert K. Merton first outlined his anomie theory, upon which institutional-anomie theory is built heavily. A must read for those interested in anomie theory.

Messner, S. F., & Rosenfeld, R. (2007). *Crime and the American dream* (4th ed.). Belmont, CA: Thomson Wadsworth.

A highly accessible and relatively short book suitable for those interested in anomie theory and those interested generally in geographic variation in crime or specifically why America exhibits particularly high levels of violence.

Parsons, Talcott: Aggression in the Western World

Cohen, A. K. (1955). *Delinquent boys: The culture of the gang.* New York: Free Press.

Cohen expands on Parsons's 1947 paradigm with his evaluation of the delinquent subculture. This extrapolation is particularly relevant to criminologists because it is considered the first in-depth attempt to explain this phenomenon.

Weber, M. (1905). *The protestant ethic and the spirit of capitalism.* New York: Scribner's.

In this famous text, Weber discusses the evolution and spirit of the capitalist system. While in graduate school in Europe, Parsons translated this text into English. His experience performing this task had a tremendous influence on the way he viewed social processes. Particularly, Weber's concept of "rationalization" continued to exert an influence on Parson's work throughout his adult life.

Stinchcombe, Arthur L.: Rebellion in a High School

Agnew, R. (1992). Foundation for a General Strain Theory of crime and delinquency. *Criminology, 30,* 47–87.

Departing from strain theorists Merton, Cohen, and Cloward and Ohlin, Robert Agnew provides a general overview of strain theory, focusing on the emotional and environmental causes.

Cohen, A. K. (1955). *Delinquent boys: The culture of the gang.* New York: Free Press.

A classic for anyone interested in criminology, youths, and delinquency, Delinquent Boys *develops a theory of subculture that ties together an analysis of social class to micro and macro determinants of delinquency, from individual personality to social structure. Subcultural delinquency simultaneously achieves status among peers while protesting adult systems of authority.*

Merton, R. K. (1938). Social structure and anomie. *American Sociological Review, 3,* 672–682.

Following Durkheim, and arguably the first articulation of strain theory, Robert Merton addresses the impact of social structures on determining deviant and conforming behavior. Merton focuses primarily on culturally defined goals and the structural modes by which those goals are achieved.

Thio, Alex: Relative Deprivation and Deviance

Rushing, W. A. (1972). *Class, culture, and alienation.* Lexington, MA: D. C. Heath.

This book provides data to support the difference between relative deprivation and absolute deprivation.

Thio, A. (1973). Class bias in the sociology of deviance. *The American Sociologist, 8,* 1–12.

This is the original article that discusses the relationship between class bias and deviant behavior.

Thio, A. (1975). A critical look at Merton's anomie theory. *Pacific Sociological Review, 18,* 139–158.

This article critiques Merton's premise that lower-class members of society are more likely to participate in deviant behaviors due to the greater disjunction between their aspirations and opportunities. It also describes the differences between relative and absolute deprivation and the association between deprivation, social class, and deviance.

9. Control Theories of Crime

Briar, Scott, and Irving Piliavin: Delinquency, Commitment, and Stake in Conformity

Hirschi, T. (1969). *Causes of delinquency.* Berkeley: University of California Press.

Hirschi provides the most widely cited version of control theory. He further defines Briar and Piliavin's concept of commitment and adds the remaining three bonds of attachment, control, and belief.

Laub, J. H., & Sampson, R. J. (2003). *Shared beginnings, divergent lives: Delinquent boys to age 70.* Cambridge, MA: Harvard University Press.

The authors examine the Gluecks' data, and apply concepts of control over the life course. We see control theory being integrated into new and exciting theories such as this life-course perspective.

Matza, D. (1964). *Delinquency and drift.* New York: Wiley.

In this classic piece, Matza examines how individuals are typically not "all bad." For many, participation in crime it is not a way of life; rather they drift in and out of this behavior. His study sets the tone for situational inducements into crime.

Gottfredson, Michael R., and Travis Hirschi: Self-Control Theory

Geis, G. (2000). On the absence of self-control for the basis of a general theory of crime: A critique. *Theoretical Criminology, 4,* 35–53.

In this essay, Gilbert Geis offers a critique of Gottfredson and Hirschi self-control theory as it relates to scientific standards. More specifically, he addresses issues of child-rearing and self-control, tautology, opportunity as a concept in self-control theory, how self-control theory deals with white-collar crime, and age and crime, to name only a few.

Goode, E. (Ed.). (2008). *Out of control: Assessing the general theory of crime.* Stanford, CA: Stanford University Press.

This book is a recent edited volume of original essays summarizing Gottfredson and Hirschi's contributions to criminological theory. Specifically, this volume provides a thorough summary of debates and criticisms regarding self-control theory from experts that often have very different opinions.

Marcus, B. (2004). Self-control in the general theory of crime: Theoretical implications of a measurement problem. *Theoretical Criminology, 8,* 33–55.

In this essay, Bernd Marcus suggests that many of the studies testing self-control are seriously flawed and misleading. He argues that the reason for this is due to how self-control has been measured. After reviewing previous measures of self-control, Marcus put forth criteria that must be met for a valid measure of self-control.

Hagan, John: Power-Control Theory

Hagan, J. (1989). *Structural criminology.* New Brunswick, NJ: Rutgers University Press.

This work provides a thorough overview of power-control model, and references many of the early articles that produced the original framework. It also provides other insights into the roles that the social structure and class play in generating criminal outcomes.

Hirschi, Travis: Social Control Theory

Gottfredson, M. R., & Hirschi, T. (1990). *A general theory of crime.* Stanford, CA: Stanford University Press.

This work provides a later version of control theory, which shows how Hirschi's thinking evolved later in his career. Gottfredson and Hirschi acknowledge the stability of offending over time and explain that stability with reference to self-control, which the authors argue is formed in early childhood.

Hirschi, T. (1969). *Causes of delinquency.* Berkeley: University of California Press.

This was the original presentation of Hirschi's social control theory.

Hirschi, T. (2002). *The craft of criminology: Selected papers.* New Brunswick, NJ: Transaction.

This book provides an overview of the work of Hirschi's career and provides further context for social control theory.

Sampson, R. J., & Laub, J. H. (1993). *Crime in the making: Pathways and turning points through life.* Cambridge, MA: Harvard University Press.

Sampson and Laub's theory draws on both social control theory and self-control theory to explain changes in the likelihood of offending over the life course.

Matza, David: Delinquency and Drift

Currie, E. (2004). *The road to whatever: Middle-class culture and the crisis of adolescence.* New York: Metropolitan Books.

A study of delinquency among middle-class youth influenced by Matza's conception of "drift."

Matza, D. (1969). *Becoming deviant.* Englewood Cliffs, NJ: Prentice Hall.

Further development and elaboration of the author's critical perspective on contemporary theories of deviant behavior.

Sykes, G. M., & Matza, D. (1957). Techniques of neutralization: A theory of delinquency. *American Sociological Review, 22,* 664–670.

An early, influential discussion of the key concept of neutralization and its significance for theories of delinquency.

Nye, F. Ivan: Family Controls and Delinquency

Britt, C. L., & Gottfredson, M. R. (Eds.). (2003). *Control theories of crime and delinquency.* New Brunswick, NJ: Transaction.

This collection of papers on social control theory by many different scholars provides a more up-to-date and more diverse view of the theoretical perspective 45 years after Nye's initial explication. It shows how the theory has been developed and applied to different research questions.

Hirschi, T. (1969). *Causes of delinquency.* Berkeley: University of California Press.

Published a decade after Nye's book, Hirschi's book provided a more focused analysis of indirect social controls over juvenile delinquency and extends the analysis of social control beyond the family to the influence of peers, schools, and other outside settings. Hirschi's description is widely regarded as the definitive discussion of indirect social control.

Vold, G. B., Bernard, T. J., & Snipes, J. B. (2002). *Theoretical criminology* (5th ed.). New York: Oxford University Press.

This criminological theory text provides a very succinct yet comprehensive overview of social control theory and the criminological research by which it has been developed and tested. Chapter 10 describes a number of the original contributors to the historical development of social control theory (including Ivan Nye) and evaluates their contributions to the theory.

Reckless, Walter C.: Containment Theory

Hirschi, T. (1969). *Causes of delinquency.* Berkeley: University of California Press.

In much the same fashion of Reckless, Hirschi devises a control theory promoted as being a general theory of crime. Some scholars have noted that Reckless's containment theory laid the foundation for Hirschi's more contemporary, but seminal work.

Martin, R., Mutchnick, R. J., & Austin, W. T. (1990). *Criminological thought: Pioneers past and present.* New York: Macmillan.

In this work, the authors provide very detailed biographical information on Walter C. Reckless from various sources including personal discussions with Dr. Simon Dinitz and Mrs. Martha Reckless.

Reiss, Albert J., Jr.: Personal and Social Controls and Delinquency

Farrington, D. P. (Ed.). (2008). *Integrated developmental and life course theories of offending* (Advances in Criminological Theory: Vol. 14). New Brunswick, NJ: Transaction.

In this book, David Farrington has compiled a number of works that integrate perspectives explaining deviance from the individual, family, peer, school, neighborhood, and community perspectives. Many of the included works suggest that controls at both the personal and societal levels are important in explaining deviance at various phases throughout one's life course.

Hirschi, T. (1969). *Causes of delinquency.* Berkeley: University of California Press.

In this book, Travis Hirschi articulates what later became known as social bond theory. Many of his ideas about the elements of the social bond can be traced (both directly and indirectly) to the personal and social control elements articulated by Reiss in 1951.

McCord, J. (Ed.). (1995). *Coercion and punishment in long-term perspectives.* New York: Cambridge University Press.

Joan McCord has compiled a number of works that examine, longitudinally, the impact of various forms of personal and social controls on delinquency. The impact of both parental and social sanctions, and their effectiveness in reducing delinquency, is examined from a wide variety of theoretical perspectives.

Reiss, A. J., Jr. (1951). Delinquency as the failure of personal and social controls. *American Sociological Review, 16,* 196–207.

In this article, Reiss articulates his ideas about both personal and social controls. This article serves as the foundation of his theoretical perspective articulated here.

Sykes, Gresham M., and David Matza: Techniques of Neutralization

Agnew, R. (1994). The techniques of neutralization and violence. *Criminology, 32,* 555–580.

Agnew's paper is perhaps the most methodologically sound longitudinal study of neutralizations. Using the National Youth Survey (NYS), Agnew showed a significant relation between neutralization and future violent behaviors.

Maruna, S., & Copes, H. (2005). What have we learned from fifty years of neutralization research? In M. Tonry (Ed.), *Crime and justice: A review of research* (Vol. 32, pp. 221–320). Chicago: University of Chicago Press.

Maruna and Copes provide the most comprehensive overview and summary of the theory. In addition they propose a modification of the theory by arguing that neutralization theory is best understood as an explanation of criminal persistence or desistance, rather than initiation.

Maruna, S., & Mann, R. (2006). Fundamental attribution errors? Re-thinking cognitive distortions. *Legal and Criminological Psychology, 11,* 155–177.

Maruna and Mann discuss the policy implications of neutralization theory. In particular, they argue that the world of cognitive-based offender treatment has misunderstood and misapplied the research on offender neutralizations. They suggest a new way forward that is more in line with both the original theory and the latest research in this regard.

Sykes, G. M., & Matza, D. (1957). Techniques of neutralization: A theory of delinquency. *American Sociological Review, 22,* 664–670.

This article is the original formulation of the theory. It is the article that all research on neutralizations is based.

Topalli, V. (2005). When being good is bad: An expansion of neutralization theory. *Criminology, 43,* 797–835.

Topalli expanded the theory to show that people use neutralizations when they violate subcultural norms. He showed that persistent street offenders did not experience guilt when committing serious forms of crime and thus did not neutralize their criminal actions. They did, however, neutralize when they snitched or failed to retaliate when wronged.

Tittle, Charles R., David A. Ward, and Harold G. Grasmick: The Capacity and Desire for Self-Control

Hirschi, T. (2004). Self-control and crime. In R. F. Baumester & K. D. Vohs (Eds.), *Handbook of self-regulation: Research, theory, and applications* (pp. 537–552). New York: Guilford Press.

In this essay, Travis Hirschi agrees that his use of characteristics to describe self-control is incongruent with many of his original arguments. He therefore redefines low self-control as the tendency not to consider the full range of potential costs of a particular act. Although he uses items to measure his redefined version of self-control that are similar to Tittle et al.'s "desire to exercise self-control," the fundamental distinction between capability and desire still exists.

Reckless, W. C. (1967). *The crime problem* (4th ed.). New York: Appleton-Century-Crofts.

Reckless's containment theory proposes that there are two types of controls—inner and outer containment. By focusing on the environmentally influenced desire to self-control, Tittle et al.'s modification of self-control theory is in the spirit of earlier control theories that examined both the importance of inner and outer constraints.

Tittle, C. R. (1995). *Control balance: Toward a general theory of deviance.* Boulder, CO: Westview.

Tittle, Ward, and Grasmick (2004) created the concept "desire for self-restraint" by finding similar themes throughout competing criminological theories. This is a prime example of synthetic integration, a key step for criminology to progress according to Tittle in this book. In addition to providing a solid discussion and defense of synthetic integration, he critiques extant criminological theories, including self-control theory.

Toby, Jackson: Stake in Conformity

Toby, J. (1971). *Contemporary society: An introduction to sociology* (2nd ed.). New York: Wiley.

This was Toby's introduction to sociology textbook. He discusses his stake in conformity theory in the text and further elaborates on the ideas and theories of Talcott Parsons.

Toby, J. (1974). The socialization and control of deviant motivation. In D. Glaser (Ed.), *Handbook of criminology* (pp. 85–100). Chicago: Rand McNally.

In this article, Toby further discusses the role of families as sources of social control and applies Parsons's theories to an understanding of delinquency.

Toby, J. (1979). Societal evolution and criminality: A Parsonian view. *Social Problems, 26,* 386–391.

In this article, Toby argues that the work of his mentor, Talcott Parsons, could be used to understand variations in crime rates across jurisdictions. Parsons was Toby's mentor at Harvard University and wrote many articles elaborating on Parsons's ideas and theories.

Toby, J. (2001). Let them drop out: A response to the killings in suburban high schools. *Weekly Standard,* 6(29), 18–23.

In this article, Toby discusses the suburban school shootings that occurred at Columbine, Santana, and Granite Hills in the context of his stake in conformity theory.

Wooldredge, J., & Thistlethwaite, A. (2002). Reconsidering domestic violence recidivism: Conditioned effects of legal controls by individual and aggregate levels of stake in conformity. *Journal of Quantitative Criminology, 18,* 45–70.

The authors explore the influence of both individual and aggregate level measures of Toby's stake in conformity theory in determining the effectiveness of court sanctions on domestic violence recidivism.

Wells, Edward L., and Joseph H. Rankin: Direct Controls and Delinquency

Rankin, J. H., & Wells, L. E. (1990). The effect of parental attachments and direct controls on delinquency. *Journal of Research in Crime and Delinquency, 27,* 140–165.

The authors re-examine the impact of direct parental controls, indirect parental controls, and the relationship to delinquency. An analysis of the Youth in Transition data finds that while each control is important, the interactions between the variables are weaker than previous studies found.

Rankin, J. H., & Wells, L. E. (2006). Social control theory and direct parental controls. In S. Henry & M. M. Lanier (Eds.), *Essential criminology reader* (pp. 119–128). Boulder, CO: Westview.

This essay chronicles the development of social bond theory, discusses the effectiveness of direct and indirect controls, and focuses on the effects of family controls and policy considerations.

Seydlitz, R. (1993). Complexity in the relationships among direct and indirect parental controls and delinquency. *Youth and Society, 24,* 243–275.

This study tests the linearity of direct and indirect controls of parental attachment on delinquency. Seydlitz discusses the specifics of parental attachment, monitoring, and discipline. The findings conclude that interactions between the variables are gender and age-specific and depend on the type and intensity of direct control utilized.

Wells, L. E., & Rankin, J. H. (1988). Direct parental controls and delinquency. *Criminology, 26,* 263–285.

Rankin and Well propose a new view of direct controls. By reconceptualizing the concept to include regulation, monitoring and punishment, they find a stronger relationship to delinquency than previous studies.

10. Labeling and Interactionist Theories of Crime

Athens, Lonnie: Interaction and Violence

Athens, L. (2003). Violentization in larger social context. In J. T. Ulmer (Ed.), *Violent acts and violentization: Assessing, applying, and developing Lonnie Athens' theories* (pp. 1–42). Oxford, UK: Elsevier Science.

In this article, Athens intended to extend his violentization theory toward the macro-social perspective. Efforts were made to establish the linkage between the micro-level theory and macro-level social characteristics, such as social structure and community culture. With the newly amended theory, Athens expected to counter the criticism that violentization theory fails to see the larger social context underlying violent conduct.

Ulmer, J. T. (Ed.). (2003). *Violent acts and violentization: Assessing, applying, and developing Lonnie Athens' theories.* Oxford, UK: Elsevier Science.

Articles with in-depth discussions of Athens's arguments about the decision process, self-image, and interpreting social experience of violent criminals are gathered in this edited book. The contributors' works enhance Athens's violentization theory and also provide insights on linking Athens's theory to social learning theory and labeling theory in a comparative manner.

Becker, Howard S.: Labeling and Deviant Careers

Becker, H. S. (1963). *Outsiders: Studies in the sociology of deviance.* New York: Free Press.

This is Howard S. Becker's primary work on deviance and, according to his website, is all he has to say on the topic to date.

Bernberg, J. G., Krohn, M. D., & Rivera, C. J. (2006). Official labeling, criminal embeddedness, and subsequent delinquency: A longitudinal test of labeling theory. *Journal of Research in Crime and Delinquency, 43,* 67–88.

This work is a current reexamination of labeling theory as is applies today. The article also references the work of Becker and others that may enhance understanding of labeling theoretical perspective.

Cole, S. (1975). The growth of scientific knowledge: Theories of deviance as a case study. In L. A. Coser (Ed.), *The idea of social structure: Papers in honor of Robert K. Merton* (pp. 175–220). New York: Harcourt Brace Jovanovich.

This article was cited by Howard S. Becker on his website and provides another perspective on the theoretical approach to deviance.

Lemert, E. M. (1951). *Social pathology: A systematic approach to the theory of sociopathic behavior.* New York: McGraw-Hill.

In Social Pathology, *Edwin Lemert developed the concepts of primary and secondary deviance. This distinction was an early statement of how societal*

reaction can stabilize individuals in deviant or criminal careers that otherwise might have been transitory.

Tannenbaum, F. (1938). *Crime and the community.* Boston: Ginn.

This work is considered to have great impact and influence in the formation of labeling theory and thus is essential in the creation of this perspective. In order to more fully understand the concepts that Becker discusses in his work and later studies in which empirical observations and findings are framed under labeling theory, an understanding of the historical foundation of the theory could be useful.

Chambliss, William J.: The Saints and the Roughnecks

Becker, H. (1963). Outsiders: Studies in the sociology of deviance. London: Free Press.

Becker's classic book explains why some people are labeled as deviant and some are not, even for the same acts. The process and outcomes of labeling are explained by Becker.

Macleod, J. (2008). *Ain't no makin' it: Aspirations and attainment in a low-income neighborhood* (3rd ed.). Boulder, CO: Westview.

Originally published in 1987, this is the third installment of Macleod's book that follows white and black adolescents from public housing over a period of 25 years. He explains how both class and race combine to determine one's future.

Reiman, J. (1998). *The rich get richer and the poor get prison: Ideology, class and criminal justice* (5th ed.). Boston: Allyn & Bacon.

Reiman's classic work explains how having money and influence may actually decrease the chances of being arrested, prosecuted, or convicted of a crime. He details how white-collar crime is not taken as seriously as street crime by the criminal justice system.

Cohen, Albert K.: Deviance and Control

Cohen, A. K. (1955). *Delinquent boys: The culture of the gang.* Glencoe, IL: Free Press.

This is Cohen's classic text that established the fundamental elements of strain theory. By building on Merton's theory of anomie and crime, Cohen created a theory of subcultural deviance and also explored the role masculinity plays in delinquency.

Cohen, A. K. (1966). *Deviance and control.* Englewood Cliffs, NJ: Prentice Hall.

> *Deviance and Control provided an overview of deviance theories and allowed Cohen to refine his strain theory. Cohen suggested an integration of role theory, anomie theory, and cultural transmission theory in this text.*

Cohen, A. K. (1997). An elaboration of anomie theory. In N. Passas & R. Agnew (Eds.), *The future of anomie theory* (pp. 54–64). Boston: Northeastern University Press.

> *Cohen's chapter in this book presented an opportunity for him to reflect on the impact of his theoretical work. Cohen also suggested that the choices made by both collectivities and individuals be studied to understand how both become involved in deviant behavior.*

Erikson, Kai T.: Wayward Puritans

Durkheim, É. (1981). *Rules of the sociological method.* New York: Free Press.

> *In this text, Durkheim laid out the thesis that deviance and criminality are an inevitable part of all societies. He stated that not only is deviance ubiquitous, but also it is necessary, within certain tolerance levels, for a healthy society.*

Merton, R. K. (1938). Social structure and anomie. *American Sociological Review, 3*(5), 672–682.

> *This contribution to the sociology of deviance contravened Durkheim and Freud, theorizing that society actually contributed to the deviance of individuals rather than serving to minimize it. This revolutionary theory provided the foundation for a generation of social researchers on deviance and social control.*

Grounded Theory

Bryant, A., & Charmaz, K. (Eds.). (2007). *The SAGE handbook of grounded theory.* Thousand Oaks, CA: Sage.

> *A collection of papers on the history, methods, and ongoing debates of the grounded theory approach by some of the preeminent scholars working within the grounded theory tradition today.*

Charmaz, K. (2006). *Constructing grounded theory.* Thousand Oaks, CA: Sage.

> *Informed by the interactionist tradition, Charmaz offers a reflective and constructionist approach to*

grounded theory methodology that is very much in line with Glaser and Strauss's early work, as well as Strauss's (1993) Continual Permutations of Action. This methodological guide further refines and demystifies the grounded theory method from an interactionist perspective for another generation of qualitative researchers.

Prus, R., & Grills, S. (2003). *The deviant mystique.* Westport, CT: Praeger.

> *Many of those interested in the implications of grounded theory for the study of crime, deviance, and regulation are likely to find that this text is of particular value. Prus and Grills address the matters of people defining deviance and deviants, people's involvements and careers in deviance, their participation in subcultural deviance and solitary deviance, as well as the informal and formal regulation of deviance, the disinvolvement process, and the problematics of studying deviance. Not only do Prus and Grills take the deviance-making process apart piece by piece, but as ethnographers as well as social theorists who built directly on the works of Herbert Blumer, Anselm Strauss, and others in the Chicago tradition of symbolic interaction, Prus and Grills also provide one of the most sustained developments of grounded theory in the literature.*

Strauss, A. L. (1993). *Continual permutations of action.* New York: Aldine de Gruyter.

> *This text stands as a particularly potent testimony to the broader importance of grounded theory for the study of human group life and people's involvements in the many life-words or subcultures in which community life takes place. Strauss attempts to translate the pragmatist philosophical assumptions of Mead and other pragmatists into a "theory of action" and a guide for sociological (specifically interactionist) inquiry and analysis. This text is of great value to those of the human sciences and has much to offer to students of crime, deviance, and regulation as a highly instructive conceptual and methodological resource.*

Heimer, Karen, and Ross L. Matsueda: A Theory of Differential Social Control

Heimer, K. (1995). Gender, race, and the pathways to delinquency. In J. Hagan & R. D. Peterson (Eds.), *Crime and inequality* (pp. 141–174). Stanford, CA: Stanford University Press.

> *In this book chapter, Karen Heimer examines the role of race in the process leading to gender differences in delinquency.*

Heimer, K. (1996). Gender, interaction, and delinquency: Testing a theory of differential social control. *Social Psychology Quarterly, 59,* 39–61.

> *In this article, Karen Heimer employs differential social control theory to generate and test predictions about similarities and differences across gender in the relationship between commitment to reference groups, role-taking, and delinquency.*

Matsueda, R. L. (1992). Reflected appraisals, parental labeling, and delinquency: Specifying a symbolic interactionist theory. *American Journal of Sociology, 97,* 1577–1611.

> *Karen Heimer and Ross Matsueda's differential social control theory is an extension of Ross Matsueda's earlier work, namely his symbolic interactionist theory of the self and delinquency. In this article, Matsueda outlined his symbolic interactionist theory of the self and delinquency as well as subjected the theory to empirical test.*

Matsueda, R. L., & Heimer, K. (1997). A symbolic interactionist theory of role-transitions, role-commitments, and delinquency. In T. P. Thornberry (Ed.), *Developmental theories of crime and delinquency* (pp. 163–213). New Brunswick, NJ: Transaction.

> *In this book chapter, Ross Matsueda and Karen Heimer argue for the utilities of the symbolic interactionist approach in general and their differential social control theory in particular in the study of crime and criminals over the life course.*

Katz, Jack: Seductions of Crime

Cromwell, P. (Ed.). (2010). *In their own words: Criminals on crime* (5th ed.). New York: Oxford University Press.

> *Cromwell's anthology provides an in-depth examination of a broad range of criminal behavior. Through field research that includes firsthand accounts by offenders, the reader gains insight into the motives, methods, and rationalization of criminal behavior.*

Presser, L. (2008). *Been a heavy life: Stories of violent men.* Urbana: University of Illinois.

> *In this book, Lois Presser provides a detailed account of interviews she conducted with men who commit violent crime. Presser's work goes beyond describing the stories of offenders to how these men construct their narratives, how these change, and what it means for our understanding of the people we most fear.*

LaFree, Gary D., and Christopher Birkbeck: Situational Analysis of Crime

Clarke, R. V. (1980). "Situational" crime prevention: Theory and practice. *British Journal of Criminology, 20,* 136–147.

> *Ronald Clarke provides an argument for the use of situational measures of crime, as opposed to a continued focus on dispositional theories of crime. In doing so, he lays the foundation for the development of situational crime prevention techniques.*

Cohen, L. E, & Felson, M. (1979). Social change and crime rate trends: A routine activity approach. *American Sociological Review, 44,* 588–608.

> *Cohen and Felson (1979) lay the groundwork for future opportunity theories. In this work, they assess how an aggregate level of opportunity affects the aggregate crime rate. Later, this idea is taken to the individual level. The theory posits that criminal opportunity exists when motivated offenders and suitable targets converge in time and space in the absence of capable guardians.*

Sutherland, E. H. (1947). *Principles of criminology* (4th ed.). Philadelphia: Lippincott.

> *Making a distinction between dispositional theories of crime/deviance and situational theories of crime/deviance, Edwin Sutherland argues that theorists need to address both. However, criminologists focused mainly on dispositional theories until the 1980s.*

Lemert, Edwin M.: Primary and Secondary Deviance

Braithwaite, J. (1989). *Crime, shame and reintegration.* Cambridge, UK: Cambridge University Press.

> *In this book, Braithwaite presents one of the most noted contemporary labeling theories: the theory of reintegrative shaming. Of particular importance, Braithwaite argues that societal reaction can lead to either more or less offending, depending upon its nature—whether it is "stigmatizing shaming" or "reintegrative shaming."*

Sherman, L. W. (1993). Defiance, deterrence, and irrelevance: A theory of criminal sanction. *Journal of Research in Crime and Delinquency, 30,* 445–473.

Like Braithwaite, Sherman also presents the idea that societal reaction (i.e., intervention) can have negative effects, but it can also have positive or null effects. Intervention are most likely to produce negative effects (i.e., defiance) if the person receiving the intervention is weakly bonded to society and defines the intervention as undeserved or unfair.

Luckenbill, David F.: Stages in Violence

Blumer, H. (1969). *Symbolic interactionism: Perspective and method.* Englewood Cliffs, NJ: Prentice Hall.

Blumer's work provides a good jumping off point for readers interested in a further discussion of symbolic interactionism. This work will help readers struggling with the concepts of microsociology.

Goffman, E. (1967). *Interaction ritual: Essays on face-to-face behavior.* Garden City, NY: Doubleday.

Goffman's essays provide a detailed description of his theory of "face." Luckenbill refers to this work throughout his essay on the stages in violence. Readers interested in learning more about Goffman's analysis of face-to-face interaction should find this work useful.

Matsueda, Ross L.: Reflected Appraisals and Delinquency

Heimer, K., & Matsueda, R. L. (1994). Role-taking, role commitment, and delinquency: A theory of differential social control. *American Sociological Review, 59,* 39–61.

In this article, Heimer and Matsueda extend Matsueda's theory of reflected appraisals. In particular, the authors address how social control— also integral to understanding delinquency from an interactionist perspective—is combined with reflected appraisals of self. They also discuss more fully how social interactions are organizationally structured.

Matsueda, R. L., & Heimer, K. (1997). A symbolic interactionist theory of role transitions, role commitments, and delinquency. In T. P. Thornberry (Ed.), *Developmental theories of crime and delinquency* (pp. 163–213). New Brunswick, NJ: Transaction.

This book chapter builds upon both Matsueda (1992) and Heimer and Matsueda (1994) by exploring how

reflected appraisals and differential social control can be useful in understanding crime over the life course.

Matza, David: Becoming Deviant

Matza, D. (1964). *Delinquency and drift.* New York: Wiley.

In his drift theory, Matza argues that adolescents are neither committed nor compelled to delinquency and that delinquents are not really different from law-abiding youths. Instead, youths drift between conventional behavior and delinquency, often feeling guilt as a result of their delinquent acts.

Matza, D., & Sykes, G. M. (1961). Juvenile delinquency and subterranean values. *American Sociological Review, 26,* 712–719.

Building on their earlier discussion of neutralization theory, Matza and Sykes provide an example of soft determinism in which youths select from among values available in their immediate environment. Youths are exposed to both conventional and subterranean (deviant) values that exist alongside one another, and displays of deviant values often provide greater status than conventional values.

Sykes, G. M., & Matza, D. (1957). Techniques of neutralization: A theory of delinquency. *American Sociological Review, 22,* 664–670.

This essay, published 12 years before Matza's Becoming Deviant, *is considered one of the seminal works in the interactionist perspective. The authors argue that formal social controls, and the guilt that often follows violations of law, are effectively neutralized for delinquents through a variety of justifications and rationalizations.*

Schur, Edwin M.: Radical Non-Intervention and Delinquency

Becker, H. S. (1963). *Outsiders: Study in the sociology of deviance.* New York: Free Press.

Schur based a large portion of Radical Non-Intervention *on Becker's labeling theory. In this book, Becker introduced labeling theory and illustrated how assigning negative labels to juveniles can result in "secondary" delinquency.*

Platt, A. (1969). *The child savers: The invention of delinquency.* Chicago: University of Chicago Press.

The primary thesis in radical non-intervention theory is that the juvenile justice system intrudes too far into the lives of youths. In this book, Platt describes the history of the juvenile justice system, including its political and social origins.

Shelden, R. G. (n.d.). *Resurrecting radical non-intervention: Stop the war on kids.* Retrieved January 5, 2009, from the Center on Juvenile and Criminal Justice: http://www.cjcj.org/files/radical.pdf

It has been more than 30 years since Schur published Radical Non-Intervention. *In this essay, Shelden gives an up-to-date synopsis of the theory and argues that its core concepts remain applicable today.*

Spector, Malcolm, and John I. Kitsuse: Constructing Social Problems

Best, J. (2008). *Social problems.* New York: W. W. Norton.

Spector and Kitsuse sought to provide an introduction to constructionist thinking about social problems. Best has a similar goal but seeks to build on the theoretical developments since Constructing Social Problems *appeared.*

Holstein, J. A., & Gubrium, J. F. (Eds.). (2008). *Handbook of constructionist research.* New York: Guilford.

Constructionist thought has evolved in many directions since Spector and Kitsuse wrote. This collection surveys developments in the constructionist approach across the social sciences.

Jenness, V., & Grattet, R. (2001). *Making hate a crime: From social movement to law enforcement.* New York: Russell Sage Foundation.

Spector and Kitsuse's ideas have inspired hundreds of case studies that extend the constructionist perspective, including many concerned with crimes. Jenness and Grattet's monograph explores constructionist processes in establishing and enforcing hate crime laws.

Sudnow, David: Normal Crimes

Sudnow, D. (1967). *Passing on: The social organization of dying.* New York: Prentice Hall.

Using similar methods, Sudnow takes his concept of "normal" activities and applies it to a medical context. In this book, he looks at how dying is managed by various actors in an urban hospital. He is especially interested in the idea of a normal death, which, like a normal crime, has a pattern to which the actors fit the case, instead of fitting a pattern to a case.

Tannenbaum, Frank: The Dramatization of Evil

Becker, H. S. (1963). *Outsiders: Studies in the sociology of deviance.* New York: Free Press.

In his book, Howard Becker provides an outline of his social reaction theory that was one of the first comprehensive labeling theories developed. Becker's piece focuses on the creation of deviance by social groups and how rule-breakers view themselves differently from the rest of society.

Chambliss, W. J. (1973). The saints and the roughnecks. *Society, 11,* 24–31.

In his piece, William J. Chambliss provides an examination of two groups of males from the same high school who were both involved in delinquent behavior. He examines how the community's perceptions of the groups helped influence the future success of the Saints and the failure of the Roughnecks.

11. Theories of the Criminal Sanction

Becker, Gary S.: Punishment, Human Capital, and Crime

Ehrlich, I. (1974). The supply of illegitimate activities: An economic approach. In G. S. Becker & W. M. Landes (Eds.), *Essays in the economics of crime and punishment* (pp. 68–134). New York: Columbia University Press.

Isaac Ehrlich uses economic choice theory to construct a model of decision-making between legal and illegal behavior. Under the assumption that human beings are rational, Ehrlich argues that individuals compare alternatives on the basis of their expected utility and seek to maximize welfare.

McCarthy, B. (2002). New economics of sociological criminology. *Annual Review of Sociology, 28,* 417–442.

In this essay, Bill McCarthy summarizes the rational choice model and its relevance to the study of criminal behavior. He argues that combining the rational choice model with sociological perspectives provides insight toward our understanding of, and ability to predict, criminal behavior.

Braithwaite, John: Reintegrative Shaming Theory

Ahmed, E., Harris, N., Braithwaite, J., & Braithwaite, V. (2001). *Shame management through reintegration.* Melbourne, Australia: Cambridge University Press.

> *This book offers a revision of the theory that incorporates ideas form shame management, procedural justice and defiance theory.*

Braithwaite, J. (2002). *Restorative justice and responsive regulation.* New York: Oxford University Press.

> *This book discusses the complementary relationship between Ayres and Braithwaite's (1992) theory of responsive regulation, which had initially been applied for business non-compliance, and restorative justice.*

Braithwaite, J., & Pettit, P. (1990). *Not just deserts: A republican theory of criminal justice.* Oxford, UK: Oxford University Press.

> *This book, which followed closely on Crime, Shame and Reintegration, presents a republican theory of criminal justice, which argues against the normative view of justice presented by just-deserts theory.*

Gendreau, Paul, D. A. Andrews, and James Bonta: The Theory of Effective Correctional Intervention

Andrews, D. A., & Bonta, J. (2006). *The psychology of criminal conduct* (4th ed.). Newark, NJ: Anderson.

> *This book can be used as a key reference for effective correctional practices. It provides a foundation for the theories and research that support the principles of effective intervention.*

Andrews, D. A., Zinger, I., Hoge, R., Bonta, J., Gendreau, P., & Cullen, F. T. (1990). Does correctional treatment work? A clinically relevant and psychologically informed meta-analysis. *Criminology, 28,* 369–404.

> *This is the first meta-analysis to test the principles of effective intervention. It is also a classic study providing early support for the principles of effective intervention.*

Gendreau, P. (1996). The principle of effective intervention with offenders. In A. T. Harland (Ed.), *Choosing correctional options that work: Defining the demand and evaluating the supply* (pp. 117–130). Thousand Oaks, CA: Sage.

> *This is a classic article providing an early description of the principles of effective intervention. This article also touches upon principles of ineffective intervention, providing a framework for strategies that have lacked effectiveness in corrections.*

Gendreau, P., Smith, P., & Goggin, C. (2000). Treatment programs in corrections. In J. Winterdyk (Ed.), *Corrections in Canada: Social reaction to crime* (pp. 238–263). Toronto, ON: Prentice Hall.

> *This book chapter provides a reader-friendly description of the principles of effective intervention, including empirical support for the principles.*

General Deterrence Theory

Stack, S. (2001). Publicized executions and the incidence of homicide: Methodological sources of inconsistent findings. In M. A. DuPont-Morales, M. Hooper, & J. H. Schmidt (Eds.), *Handbook of criminal justice administration* (pp. 355–369). New York: Marcel Dekker.

> *Provides the largest review of investigations (N=20) that measure public awareness of executions (most of the 104 investigations on executions and homicide do not measure awareness). Methodological differences among these studies are associated with the extent to which they find any deterrent effect.*

Yang, B., & Lester, D. (2008). The deterrent effect of executions: A meta-analysis thirty years after Ehrlich. *Journal of Criminal Justice, 36,* 453–460.

> *This is the first meta-analysis of the universe of research on the impact of the death penalty on homicide. It covers 95 studies with adequate data published between 1975 and 2006. The average effect size, while not large, is consistent with general deterrence theory. Variation in the methodological features of studies is associated with the effect size reported.*

Gibbs, Jack P.: Deterrence Theory

Pratt, T. C., Cullen, F. T., Blevins, K. R., Daigle, L. E., & Madensen, T. D. (2006). The empirical status of deterrence. In F. T. Cullen, J. P. Wright, & K. R. Blevins (Eds.), *Taking stock: The status of criminological theory* (Advances in Criminological Theory: Vol. 15, pp. 367–395). New Brunswick, NJ: Transaction.

> *Pratt et al. (2006) reveal Gibbs's continuing impact on deterrence research.*

Tittle, C. R. (1980). *Sanctions and social deviance.* New York: Praeger.

> *Tittle (1980) was contemporaneous with Gibbs's deterrence publications and shows the breadth and depth of deterrence scholarship during its heyday in the 1970s and 1980s.*

Tonry, M. (2008). Learning from the limitations of deterrence research. In M. Tonry (Ed.), *Crime and justice: A review of research* (Vol. 37, pp. 279–312). Chicago: University of Chicago Press.

Many deterrence researchers continue to address the issues initially considered by Gibbs, bringing his goal of a deterrence theory closer to fruition. Tonry (2008) is a good example.

Zimring, F. E., & Hawkins, G. (1973). *Deterrence: The legal threat in crime control.* Chicago: University of Chicago Press.

This timely piece provided an illustration of the importance of deterrence research.

Incarceration and Recidivism

Gendreau, P., Goggin, C., Cullen, F. T., & Andrews, D. A. (2000, May). The effects of community sanctions and incarceration on recidivism. *Forum on Corrections Research, 12,* 10–13.

Gendreau et al. conducted a meta-analysis on the impact of incarceration on recidivism. They not only examined custodial versus non-custodial sanctions but also investigated the impact that the length of time served has on subsequent recidivism.

Maurer, M. (1999). *Race to incarcerate.* New York: New Press.

Maurer attempts to explain the multitude of reasons that have lead to the massive increase in the use of incarceration. He discusses multiple sentencing policies, the media, and the political advantage for politicians to be "tough on crime." He also addresses the substantial number of minorities now incarcerated in U.S. prisons. A discussion of the impact of this incarceration boom on subsequent crime rates is also presented.

Nagin, D. S., Cullen, F. T., & Jonson, C. L. (2009). Imprisonment and reoffending. In M. Tonry (Ed.), *Crime and justice: A review of research* (Vol. 38, pp. 115–200). Chicago: University of Chicago Press.

Nagin and colleagues extend Villettaz et al.'s (2006) systematic review of the research on incarceration and crime. Not only do these authors examine custodial versus non-custodial sanctions, but they also review the research on the length of incarceration. Nagin et al. take much care in ensuring that the findings are sound and control for the various factors believed to influence recidivism.

Smith, P., Goggin, C., & Gendreau, P. (2002). *The effects of prison sentences and intermediate sanctions on*

recidivism: General effects and individual differences (User report 2002–01). Ottawa, ON: Solicitor General Canada.

Smith and colleagues expand the 2000 meta-analysis conducted by Gendreau et al. They examine the impact of custodial versus non-custodial sanctions and the length of time incarcerated on post-release recidivism. This meta-analysis is unique as it investigates the impact of multiple moderator variables on the results, such as age, gender, race, risk level, and quality of the research design.

Villettaz, P., Killias, M., & Zoder, I. (2006). *The effects of custodial vs. noncustodial sentences on re-offending: A systematic review of the state of knowledge.* Philadelphia: Campbell Collaboration Crime and Justice Group.

This article provides a systematic review of the current literature on the effects of custodial and non-custodial sanctions. It employs sound methodology so the findings can be viewed with reliability. It also includes studies both within and outside North America.

McCarthy, Bill, and John Hagan: Danger and Deterrence

Jaeger, C. C., Ortwin, R., Rosa, E. A., & Webler, T. (2001). *Risk, uncertainty, and rational action.* London: Earthscan.

This book describes the Rational Actor Paradigm (RAP) and how the principles of this paradigm have been applied in economics, psychology, and sociology. Emphasis on risk assessment in each of the aforementioned disciplines is discussed.

Pratt, T. C., Cullen, F. T., Blevins, K. R., Daigle, L. E., & Madensen, T. D. (2006). The empirical status of deterrence. In F. T. Cullen, J. P. Wright, & K. R. Blevins (Eds.), *Taking stock: The status of criminological theory* (Advances in Criminological Theory: Vol. 15, pp. 367–395). New Brunswick, NJ: Transaction.

This essay traces the empirical history and highlights recent theoretical advances in the area of deterrence. The authors also present findings from a meta-analysis of 40 empirical studies of deterrence.

Nagin, Daniel S., and Raymond Paternoster: Individual Differences and Deterrence

Nagin, D. S., & Paternoster, R. (1991). The preventive effects of the perceived risk of arrest: Testing an expanded conception of deterrence. *Criminology, 29,* 561–588.

This article provides an early example of Nagin and Paternoster's thinking about the conditionally deterrent effects of sanctions. In this article, the threat of informal sanctions are considered in conjunction with more traditional measures of sanction threats typically examined in tests of deterrence theory.

Nagin, D. S., & Paternoster, R. (1993). Enduring individual differences and rational choice theories of crime. *Law and Society Review, 27,* 467–496.

This article focuses on the contributions of expected probability of sanctions, stable individual differences in the propensity to offend, and expected utility in the explanation of offending intentions. It expands on their earlier work by further elaborating the processes by which sanction threats are most salient and how sanction threats may fit into the entire offending decision-making process.

Nagin, D. S., & Paternoster, R. (1994). Personal capital and social control: The deterrence implications of a theory of individual differences in criminal offending. *Criminology, 32,* 581–606.

This article represents the most complete statement of the Nagin and Paternoster theory. It expands on previous work by fully elaborating a theory of offender decision making including attending to sanction threats, life-span developmental issues, and related issues of utility, conscience, and personal and social capital.

Perceptual Deterrence

Matsueda, R. L., Kreager, D. A., & Huizinga, D. (2006). Deterring delinquents: A rational choice model of theft and violence. *American Sociological Review, 71,* 95–122.

Using sophisticated empirical methods and panel data from the Denver Youth Study, this article reports evidence for the two linkages of perceptual deterrence—that individuals who are punished elevate their perceptions of sanction risk, and that offending relates inversely to perceived sanction certainty.

Pogarsky, G. (2007). Deterrence and individual differences among convicted offenders. *Journal of Quantitative Criminology, 23,* 59–74.

This study tested how variation in criminal propensity (operationalized as "self-control") moderated deterrent effects in a sample of convicted offenders in New Jersey's Intensive Supervision Program (ISP) in 1989 and 1990. Offenders' perceptions of the risks and consequences from violating ISP were associated with whether they successfully completed ISP. Moreover, lower self-control did not diminish and, if anything, enhanced these deterrent effects.

Pogarsky, G. (in press). Deterrence and decision-making: Research questions and theoretical refinements. In M. D. Krohn, A. J. Lizotte, & G. P. Hall (Eds.), *Handbook on crime and deviance.* New York: Springer.

This chapter comments on the current state of criminological deterrence research. It identifies areas of intersection between behavioral economics and criminological deterrence and suggests avenues of further investigation to improve our understanding of crime decisions.

Pogarsky, Greg, and Alex R. Piquero: The Resetting Effect

Clotfelter, C. T., & Cook, P. J. (1993). The "gambler's fallacy" in lottery play. *Management Science, 39,* 1521–1525.

In their article, Charles Clotfelter and Philip Cook examine the gambler's fallacy using a lottery experiment. Their findings indicate that rare occurrences are discounted immediately after they occur.

Gibbs, J. P. (1975). *Crime, punishment, and deterrence.* Amsterdam: Elsevier.

In his book, Jack Gibbs discusses the deterrence doctrine, paying particular attention to the wide array of legal and non-legal elements that may be considered deterrents to law violation.

Jacobs, B. A. (1996). Crack dealers and restrictive deterrence: Identifying narcs. *Criminology, 34,* 409–431.

In his article, Bruce Jacobs examines the processes by which drug dealers legitimize their customers. He identifies restrictive deterrence as a process whereby dealers reduce but do not completely refrain from offending following punishment. One type of restrictive deterrence is probabilistic—a reduction of offense frequency based on a law of averages.

Zimring, F. E., & Hawkins, G. J. (1973). *Deterrence: The legal threat in crime control.* Chicago: University of Chicago Press.

In their book, Franklin Zimring and Gordon Hawkins focus on deterrence as the threat of legal punishments. They discuss the background and rationale of deterrence theory, distinguish general and specific deterrence, examine problems with measurement in deterrence research, and outline numerous issues warranting future research.

Rose, Dina R., and Todd R. Clear: Coerced Mobility Theory

Clear, T. R. (2007). *Imprisoning communities: How mass incarceration makes disadvantaged neighborhoods worse.* New York: Oxford University Press.

This book provides an in-depth theoretical foundation for coerced mobility. Clear discusses in more detail how concentrated incarceration undermines the legitimate systems within which offenders are embedded. It also provides a detailed description of community justice.

Sherman, Lawrence W.: Defiance Theory

Bouffard, L. A., & Piquero, N. L. (2010). Defiance theory and life course explanations of persistent offending. *Crime and Delinquency, 56,* 227–252.

This article provides the most recent and most complete test of defiance theory. It also includes a discussion of the link between defiance, labeling, and the life course perspective.

Sherman, L. W. (1993). Defiance, deterrence, and irrelevance: A theory of the criminal sanction. *Journal of Research in Crime and Delinquency, 30,* 445–473.

This article presents Sherman's defiance theory in full along with examples of defiant behavior and a review of the literature on sanction effects.

Stafford, Mark C., and Mark Warr: Deterrence Theory

Pogarsky, G., & Piquero, A. (2003). Can punishment encourage offending? Investigating the "resetting" effect. *Journal of Research in Crime and Delinquency, 40,* 95–120.

This article investigates why punishment experiences may increase the likelihood of offending. The first hypothesis is that committed offenders are more likely to be punished, which is known as the selection account. The second hypothesis asserts that punished offenders believe they would have to be extremely unlucky to get caught again. The article concludes with a discussion of challenges posed to deterrence theory as a result of the "positive punishment effect."

Tyler, Tom R.: Sanctions and Procedural Justice Theory

Tyler, T. R. (1990). *Why people obey the law.* New Haven, CT: Yale University Press.

This book contrasts different perspectives on why people obey the law, explores how people react to their personal experiences with legal authorities, and explains the meaning of procedural justice. It provides a comprehensive analysis of the links among procedural justice, legitimacy, and compliance with the law and legal authorities.

Tyler, T. R. (2003). Procedural justice, legitimacy, and the effective rule of law. In M. Tonry (Ed.), *Crime and justice: A review of research* (Vol. 30, pp. 283–357). Chicago: University of Chicago Press.

Based on Tyler's theory of procedural justice, this article analyzes the process-based model of regulation. It also provides a comprehensive review of previous empirical studies.

Tyler, T. R., & Huo, Y. J. (2002). *Trust in the law.* New York: Russell Sage.

This book explores the deference to legal authorities among minorities. Using empirical analyses, it emphasizes the role of procedural justice and legitimacy in shaping people's willingness to consent and cooperate with legal authorities.

Williams, Kirk R., and Richard Hawkins: Deterrence Theory and Non-Legal Sanctions

Akers, R. L. (1990). Rational choice, deterrence, and social learning theory in criminology. *Journal of Criminal Law and Criminology, 81,* 653–676.

Akers points to the conceptual and theoretical links between deterrence theory and rational choice theory and argues that both are deducible from social learning theory. He further argues that a social learning approach to deterrence offers the greatest promise for advancing an understanding of the deterrence process.

Pratt, T. C., Cullen, F. T., Blevins, K. R., Daigle, L. E., & Madensen, T. D. (2006). The empirical status of deterrence. In F. T. Cullen, J. P. Wright, & K. R. Blevins (Eds.), *Taking stock: The status of criminological theory* (Advances in Criminological Theory: Vol. 15, pp. 367–395). New Brunswick, NJ: Transaction.

This article offers a systematic review and assessment of decades of deterrence studies and identifies directions for further research.

Stafford, M. C., & Warr, M. (1993). A reconceptualization of general and specific deterrence. *Journal of Research in Crime and Delinquency, 30,* 123–135.

> *Stafford and Warr propose a conceptualization of general and specific deterrence that considers the indirect and direct experiences of people with legal punishment and the implications of this conceptualization for such key deterrence issues as "experiential effects."*

Tittle, C. R. (1980). *Sanctions and social deviance.* New York: Praeger.

> *Tittle's book represents one of the first attempts to systematize deterrence theory. In the process, he points to the complexity of the deterrence process, including the possibility that a host of non-deterrence variables may condition the deterrent effects of legal punishment.*

12. Conflict, Radical, and Critical Theories of Crime

Abolitionism

Knopp, F. H., Boward, B., & Morris, M. O. (1976). *Instead of prisons: A handbook for abolitionists.* Syracuse, NY: Prison Research Education Action Project.

> *Knopp et al.'s text provides a description of the practical application of abolitionist ideals. The text details the application of abolitionist ideology to the practice of eradicating prisons.*

Mathiesen, T. (1974). *The politics of abolition.* London: Martin Robertson.

> *Thomas Mathiesen's text provides a strong basis on the concept of abolitionism. Mathiesen, one of the forefathers of abolitionist thought, details the development of the penal reform movement in Scandinavia, a movement that is strongly rooted in abolitionist ideology.*

Anarchist Criminology

Capouya, E., & Tompkins, K. (Eds.). (1975). *The essential Kropotkin.* New York: Liveright.

> *This collection of essays by Peter Kropotkin offers an accessible introduction to the work of one of the founding figures in anarchist theory, and perhaps the most important progenitor of anarchist criminology. Especially notable are the essays "Law and Authority" and "Prisons and Their Moral Influence on Prisoners."*

Ferrell, J. (2001). *Tearing down the streets: Adventures in urban anarchy.* New York: Palgrave.

> *This book blends perspectives from anarchist criminology with a wide-ranging account of contemporary anarchist activism and anarchist social movements, including homeless activists, micro-radio operators, bicycle militants, and those working to "reclaim the streets." The anarchist critique of law is here embodied in an analysis of legal enforcement strategies that are designed to control marginal groups and to protect private economic development at the cost of urban community.*

Bonger, Willem: Capitalism and Crime

Mike, B. (1976). Willem Adriaan Bonger's "Criminality and Economic Conditions": A critical analysis. *International Journal of Criminology and Penology, 4,* 211–238.

> *Mike takes a critical look at how Bonger's interpretation of Marx and the influence of Social Darwinism on his theory, and he further clarifies some of Bonger's arguments through his discussion of the difficulties with Bonger's approach.*

Van Bemmelen, J. M. (1955). Pioneers in criminology. Willem Adriaan Bonger. *Journal of Criminal Law, Criminology, and Police Science, 46,* 293–302.

> *Van Bemmelen discusses the life history of Bonger and helps provide a social context to explain how and why Bonger became a criminologist as well as what influenced his perspective on crime causation.*

Chambliss, William J.: Power, Conflict, and Crime

Chambliss, W. J. (with King, H.). (1972). *Boxman: A professional thief's journal.* New York: Harper & Row.

> *In Boxman, William Chambliss expanded Edwin Sutherland's pioneering research on professional theft. Based on the diaries of a professional safe cracker named Harry King, whom Chambliss befriended during this research on organized crime in Las Vegas, Boxman remains a classic text on professional theft more than 30 years after its publication.*

Chambliss, W. J. (1978). *On the take: From petty criminals to presidents.* Bloomington: Indiana University Press.

> *On the Take constitutes a major contribution to the organized crime literature. William Chambliss argued that the Cosa Nostra or the Mafia was simply a*

smokescreen for a more complex set of social relations between financiers, businessmen, politicians, policemen and organized crime figures. Chambliss concluded that a symbiotic relationship between these individuals is essential for organized crime to survive in America.

Chambliss, W. J., & Seidman, R. B. (1971). *Law, order, and power.* Reading, MA: Addison-Wesley.

Law, Order, and Power is a seminal textbook on law and society. Chambliss and Seidman advanced the conflict perspective beyond a Marxian discussion of law formation to an examination of the processes by which the interests of the rich and powerful are actually translated into law and administration.

Colvin, Mark: Coercion Theory

Alexander, A. D., & Bernard, T. J. (2002). A critique of Mark Colvin's, *Crime and Coercion: An Integrated Theory of Chronic Criminality. Crime, Law and Social Change, 38,* 389–398.

This essay criticized the differential coercion theory for providing vague statements that are inappropriate for empirically testing the propositions of the theory. The authors proposed several statements that capture at least a portion of the theory and more suitable for empirical tests.

Colvin, M. (2000). *Crime and coercion: An integrated theory of chronic criminality.* New York: Palgrave Macmillan.

Integrating several existing perspectives of criminology, Colvin lays out his differential coercion theory in this book with a great emphasis on the role of coercive forces that create social and psychological dynamics that lead to chronic criminality.

Colvin, M. (2003). Crime and coercion. In F. T. Cullen & R. Agnew (Eds.), *Criminological theory: Past to present—essential readings* (pp. 379–386). Los Angeles: Roxbury.

This chapter provides a compact essay for a general understanding of Colvin's differential coercion theory.

Colvin, M. (2007). Applying differential coercion and social support theory to prison organizations. *Prison Journal, 87,* 367–387.

Colvin tested the general premises of the differential coercion and social support theory using the levels of social support in the Penitentiary of New Mexico and coercion felt by the inmates thereof in different time

periods. This study is important to observe how the variables of the differential coercion theory were included in an empirical theory testing.

Unnever, J. D., Colvin, M., & Cullen, F. T. (2004). Crime and coercion: A test of core theoretical propositions. *Journal of Research in Crime and Delinquency, 41,* 244–268.

Using 2,472 middle-school students, this study tested the core propositions of Colvin's differential coercion theory. Supporting the major arguments of the theory, this empirical test reported that participants exposed to coercion in their environments develop social-psychological deficits that lead them to delinquent behavior.

Colvin, Mark, and John Pauly: A Structural Marxist Theory of Delinquency

Colvin, M., Cullen, F. T., & Vander Ven, T. (2002). Coercion, social support and crime: An emerging theoretical consensus. *Criminology, 40,* 19–42.

In this article, Mark Colvin, Francis Cullen, and Thomas Vander Ven propose an integrated theory of crime that addresses the causal role of coercion, a key concept included in the integrated structural Marxist theory of crime.

Simpson, S., & Elis, L. (1994). Is gender subordinate to class? An empirical assessment of Colvin and Pauly's Structural Marxist Theory of Delinquency. *Journal of Criminal Law and Criminology, 85,* 453–480.

This article presents an empirical test of Colvin and Pauly's integrated structural Marxist theory of crime. In addition to testing the core propositions of the theory, Simpson and Elis examine the gender neutrality of the theory.

Convict Criminology

Irwin, J. (2005). *The warehouse prison: Disposal of the new dangerous class.* Los Angeles: Roxbury.

A recent study of a modern prison in California. The author uses the convict criminology perspective in reporting qualitative interviews at length as support for policy changes.

Irwin, J., & Austin, J. (1994). *It's about time: America's imprisonment binge.* Belmont, CA: Wadsworth.

A book that recommends policy changes favored by the Convict Criminology Group. The authors make a strong case for immediate reductions in the nation's prison population.

Newbold, G. (2007). *The problem of prisons: Corrections reform in New Zealand since 1840.* Wellington, New Zealand: Dunmore.

> *The book looks at prison conditions in New Zealand. Special attention is paid to how the prisoners experience different levels of security.*

Ross, J. I., & Richards, S. C. (2002). *Behind bars: Surviving prison.* Indianapolis, IN: Alpha/Penguin.

> *The book demonstrates how the convict criminology perspective can be used to trace the life of an anonymous defendant and convict. The everyman is followed from arrest, through court, jail, prison, and return home to the community.*

Ross, J. I., & Richards, S. C. (Eds.). (2003). *Convict criminology.* Belmont, CA: Wadsworth.

> *This is the book that first defined convict criminology as an emerging theoretical perspective and movement. This co-edited text includes nine autobiographical contributions of ex-convicts professors.*

Terry, C. M. (2003). *The fellas: Overcoming prison and addiction.* Belmont, CA: Wadsworth.

> *Convict criminology perspective used to examine lives of heroin addicts. The ex-convict professor author interviews prisoners he did time with in prison. The book is an in-depth look at what happens to convict heroin addicts in prison and on the street.*

Cultural Criminology

Ferrell, J., Hayward, K., Morrison, W., & Presdee, M. (Eds.). (2004). *Cultural criminology unleashed.* London: Glasshouse/Routledge.

> *This collection of some 25 essays explores issues ranging from domestic violence, virtual grief, and urban symbolism to street fighting, the USA PATRIOT Act, and the multicultural administration of justice.*

Ferrell, J., Hayward, K., & Young, J. (2008). *Cultural criminology: An invitation.* London: Sage.

> *This book offers perhaps the best single overview of cultural criminology as theory, method, and field of study. It includes discussions of cultural criminology in relation to stylistic innovation, media dynamics, everyday experience, and existing criminological theory.*

Presdee, M. (2000). *Cultural criminology and the carnival of crime.* London: Routledge.

> *This innovative book mixes autobiography and historical analysis with accounts of advertising, music, and street crime in developing a cultural criminology attuned to the dangerous dynamics of carnival.*

Currie, Elliott: The Market Society and Crime

Reiner, R. (2007). *Law and order: An honest citizen's guide to crime and control.* London: Cambridge University Press.

> *Reiner analyzes the increase in crime in England linking it to unregulated capitalism, which results in higher poverty, unemployment, inequality, and authoritarian criminal justice control.*

Taylor, I. (1999). *Crime in context: A critical criminology of market societies.* Boulder, CO: Westview.

> *Taylor looks at broad economic changes in Canada and how they have influenced crime and the criminal justice system. He specifically notes how the market economy has negatively transformed contemporary society.*

Young, J. (1999). *The exclusive society: Social exclusion, crime and difference in late modernity.* London: Sage.

> *Young looks at changes in society from being very inclusive and homogenous to very exclusive. He identifies three areas of exclusion: economic, social, and the activities of the criminal justice system.*

Gordon, D. M.: Political Economy and Crime

Box, S. (1987). *Recession, crime and punishment.* London: Macmillan.

> *Stephen Box adds human agency to these structural explanations for the political economy shaping society's reaction to crime. He develops theoretical explanations for why human actors respond more aggressively during periods of economic stagnation.*

Hall, S., Critcher, C., Jefferson, T., Clarke, J., & Roberts, B. (1978). *Policing the crisis: Mugging, the state, and law and order.* London: Macmillan.

> *Hall et al. demonstrate how a moral panic can be constructed and then impact crime control policy.*

Reiman, J. (2004). *The rich get richer and the poor get prison: Ideology, crime, and criminal justice* (7th ed.). Boston: Allyn & Bacon.

> *Jeffrey Reiman provides extensive evidence for how government crime control policy tends to support the*

interest of the capitalist class while providing social control over the poor.

Rusche, G., & Kirchheimer, O. (1968). *Punishment and social structure.* New York: Russell and Russell. [Original work published in 1939]

This is one of the first and more important works for establishing the relationship between the political economic structure and society's response to criminal behavior and deviance.

Greenberg, David F.: Age, Capitalism, and Crime

Ezell, M. E., & Cohen, L. E. (2005). *Desisting from crime: Continuity and change in long term crime patterns of serious chronic offenders.* New York: Oxford University Press.

This statistical study uses three large samples of young offenders tracked over the period of time to assess age-crime patterns and to answer questions about their stability over time. Different theoretical perspectives are tested using sophisticated statistical models and the findings have serious implications for penal policies, such as "three strikes and you're out" convictions.

Pequero, A. R., & Mazerolle, P. (Eds.). (2001). *Life-course criminology: Contemporary and classic readings.* Belmont, CA: Wadsworth.

This reader consists of seminal articles written about theories of crime as it relates to human development and biological maturation. The life-course approach that is being assessed builds on recent trends in psychology and sociology answering the growing demand for integrated theories of crime and age. The reader includes articles by life-course scholars such as Robert Sampson and John Laub, Travis Hirschi and Michael Gottfredson, and Alfred Blumstein, among others.

Sampson, R. J., & Laub, J. H. (Eds.). (2005). Developmental criminology and its discontents: Trajectories of crime from childhood to old age [Special issue]. *Annals of the American Academy of Political and Social Science, 602.*

This special issue provides critical debate on patterns of age and crime across the life course. The debate was inspired by 2003 American Society of Criminology conference session titled "Age, Crime and Human Development: The Future of Life-Course Criminology," chaired by the editors of this issue. Criminal career topics such as onset, continuation, termination and career length are also discussed, along with questions about the suitability of existing

data and prospects of integrating longitudinal and experimental studies.

Left Realism Criminology

Currie, E. (1985). *Confronting crime: An American challenge.* New York: Pantheon.

This book is the first major theoretical and political statement on left realism in the United States. Currie's book is also deemed to be the definitive left-wing response to James Q. Wilson's 1985 right-wing book Thinking About Crime.

Currie, E. (2004). *The road to whatever: Middle-class culture and the crisis of delinquency.* New York: Metropolitan Books.

Historically, left realists have focused mainly on crimes committed by and against inner-city working class people, as well as on the victimization of women in intimate heterosexual relationships. This book constitutes the first attempt to offer a left realist understanding of troubled middle-class youths.

DeKeseredy, W. S., Alvi, S., & Schwartz, M. D. (2006). Left realism revisited. In W. S. DeKeseredy & B. Perry (Eds.), *Advancing critical criminology: Theory and application* (pp. 19–42). Lanham, MD: Lexington.

Born during the years that Ronald Reagan and Margaret Thatcher governed their respective countries, left realism is now seen by many scholars as a marginalized subdiscipline of critical criminology. DeKeseredy, Alvi, and Schwartz show that nothing can be further from the truth and demonstrate that left realism is still important today.

DeKeseredy, W. S., Donnermeyer, J. F., Schwartz, M. D., Tunnell, K. D., & Hall, M. (2008). Thinking critically about rural gender relations: Toward a rural masculinity crisis/male peer support model of separation/divorce sexual assault. *Critical Criminology, 15,* 295–311.

Thus far, there have been only a handful of attempts to develop a critical criminological understanding of violence against women in rural communities. DeKeseredy and his colleagues help fill this gap by offering an integrated theory heavily influenced by left realist thought.

Donnermeyer, J. F., & DeKeseredy, W. S. (2008). Toward a rural critical criminology. *Southern Rural Sociology, 23,* 4–28.

The main objective of this article is twofold: (1) to describe the key reasons for a more fully developed rural critical criminology and (2) to outline some of its key elements. Donnermeyer and DeKeseredy also assert that the left realist square of crime does not have an intrinsic urban bias.

Lea, J., & Young, J. (1984). *What is to be done about law and order?* New York: Penguin.

There are actually quite a few books that could be read on left realism, most of which are edited works by Jock Young, Roger Matthews, or both. However, this co-authored book offers one of the best theoretical statements of British left realism.

Young, J. (1999). *The exclusive society.* London: Sage.

Although he does not explicitly identify himself as a left realist in this book, Jock Young offers a left realist account of how major social and economic transformations that occurred during the latter part of the 20th century have shaped current patterns of crime and highly punitive societal reactions to crime.

Marx, Karl, and Frederick Engels: Capitalism and Crime

Taylor, I., Walton, P., & Young, J. (1973). *The new criminology: For a social theory of deviance.* New York: Routledge.

This book is an important milestone in contemporary Marxist criminology. The authors situate Marxist criminology within the history of relevant social and political thought and then provide a succinct overview (in chapter 7) of Marx and Engels perspectives on crime (as well as a critique of Bonger's interpretation of Marx).

Taylor, I., Walton, P., & Young, J. (Eds.). (1975). *Critical criminology.* New York: Routledge.

The essays compiled in this book provide a number of interpretations of Marx and Engels work, as well as attempt to move beyond their work toward a Marxist criminology. Contributions by the editors, as well as Hirst, Quinney, Platt, and others.

Peacemaking Criminology

Pepinsky, H. E., & Quinney, R. (1991). *Criminology as peacemaking.* Bloomington: Indiana University Press.

Harold Pepinski and Richard Quinney set forth this volume of collected essays as one of the first clear articulations of peacemaking criminology. Substantive topics include homelessness, violence against women, reconciliation, conflict resolution, education, and human rights enforcement.

Wozniak, J. F., Braswell, M. C., Vogel, R. E., & Blevins, K. R. (Eds.). (2008). *Transformative justice: Critical and peacemaking themes influenced by Richard Quinney.* Lanham, MD: Lexington Books.

Wozniak et al. have brought together a collection of essays that celebrate the life and the work of Richard Quinney, father of peacemaking criminology. Topics examine both the critical orientation in Quinney's work as well as his contributions to peacemaking.

Postmodern Theory

Arrigo, B. A., & Milovnaovic, D. (2009). *Revolution in penology: Rethinking the society of captives.* Lanham, MD: Rowman & Littlefield.

The development of postmodernism—including chaos theory, continental philosophy, constitutive thought, and psychoanalytic and cultural studies—is presented as a more holistic assemblage of ideas. This synthesis is then applied to penal philosophy and practice in which the radicalized post-penological self/society duality is described.

Arrigo, B. A., & Milovanovic, D. (Eds.). (2010). *Postmodernist and post-structuralist theories of crime.* Surrey, UK: Ashgate.

This edited volume includes previously published articles by some of the leading international scholars in the field of postmodernist and post-strucutralist criminology. Collectively, the articles represent important reflections on the current theoretical landscape in criminology. For the contributors, this is a landscape in which symbolic, linguistic, material, and cultural realms of inquiry inform the analysis. The volume's substantive sections address: (1) major theoretical developments and integrations (2) critical applications; (3) transformational analyses and attention to marginalized identities; (4) international, transnational, and post-national directions; and (5) postmodern and post-structural criminology's interlocutors. An original introductory chapter situates the assembled articles within relevant philosophical and social theoretical perspectives, and proposes novel future directions in research, practice, pedagogy, and activism.

Arrigo, B. A., Milovanovic, D., & Schehr, R. C. (2005). *The French connection in criminology: Rediscovering crime, law, and social change.* Albany: SUNY Press.

In this book, Bruce Arrigo, Dragan Milovanovic, and Robert Carl Schehr present a thorough guide to postmodernism and its contribution to criminology, law, and social justice. Drawing on the thoughts offered from the 11 most prominent French scholars who have helped develop and advance postmodern theory, the authors conceptualized these insights and applied them to today's most critical crime and justice problems.

Best, S., & Kellner, D. (1991). *Postmodern theory: Critical interrogation.* New York: Guilford Press.

Steven Best and Douglas Kellner methodically analyze postmodern theory in order to assess the strength of its influence and its limitations in application, particularly in regard to social critical theory and contemporary radical politics. A comprehensive overview and critique of the works by the foremost contributors to postmodern thought is provided.

Henry, S., & Milovanovic, D. (1996). *Constitutive criminology: Beyond postmodernism.* London: Sage.

Based on affirmative postmodernism, Stuart Henry and Dragan Milovanovic offer a constitutive approach to understanding criminal behavior. Rather than determining what causes deviancy, the authors are concerned with discerning how human subjects and the social structures that they develop coproduce crime. Topics discussed range from human nature and behavior to justice policy and practice.

Quinney, Richard: Social Transformation and Peacemaking Criminology

Pepinsky, H. E., & Quinney, R. (Eds.). (1991). *Criminology as peacemaking.* Bloomington: Indiana University Press.

This book presents chapters addressing concerns of peacemaking criminology. Chapters are organized into religious, feminist, and critical traditions of peacemaking criminology.

Wozniak, J. F. (2008). Toward a theoretical model of peacemaking criminology: An essay in honor of Richard Quinney. In J. F. Wozniak, M. C. Braswell, R. E. Vogel, & K. R. Blevins (Eds.), *Transformative justice: Critical and peacemaking themes influenced by Richard Quinney* (pp. 141–166). Lanham, MD: Lexington.

Upon review of research and a survey of peacemaking authors, this article delineates elements of a peacemaking criminology theoretical model. The analysis suggests ways this peacemaking theoretical model can be adapted toward future crime research and policies.

Wozniak, J. F., Braswell, M. C., Vogel, R. E., & Blevins, K. R. (Eds.). (2008). *Transformative justice: Critical and peacemaking themes influenced by Richard Quinney.* Lanham, MD: Lexington.

This book outlines the links between peacemaking criminology, critical criminology, social transformation, and transformative justice. Also, it contains chapters on critical and peacemaking criminology inspired by Richard Quinney.

Regoli, Robert M., and John D. Hewitt: Differential Oppression Theory

Colvin, M. (2002). *Crime and coercion.* New York: St. Martin's Press.

Children who are exposed to coercive environments are more likely to develop social-psychological deficits that increase the possibility of their committing crimes.

Hewitt, J. D., & Regoli, B. (2003). Differential oppression theory and female delinquency. *Free Inquiry in Creative Sociology, 31,* 165–174.

Hewitt and Regoli argue that girls commit less delinquency because girls are doubly oppressed. They are oppressed as children and as females.

Kingston, B., Regoli, B, & Hewitt, J. (2003). The theory of differential oppression: A developmental-ecological explanation of adolescent problem behavior. *Critical Criminology, 11,* 237–260.

The developmental-ecological perspective provides a way for understanding how the oppression of children occurs within multiple social contexts.

Spitzer, Steven: Capitalism and Crime

Spitzer, S. (1975). Toward a Marxian theory of deviance. *Social Problems, 22,* 638–651.

An article in which Spitzer develops the essential outlines of his argument linking the structure of capitalism with the nature of social control in capitalist societies.

Spitzer, S., & Scull, A. (1977). Privatization and capitalist development: The case of the private police. *Social Problems, 21,* 18–29.

This article traces the history of policing and its emergence as a profit-making enterprise. It is a good example of the argument that criminal justice institutions increasingly reflect the priorities of the capitalist mode of production.

Taylor, Ian, Paul Walton, and Jock Young: The New Criminology

Ferrell, J., Hayward, K., & Young, J. (2008). *Cultural criminology*. London: Sage.

Whereas its authors do not explicitly state that this perspective is a direct result of The New Criminology, *it nonetheless provides an excellent introduction to cultural criminology and its links to late modernity and capitalism.*

Reiner, R. (2007). *Law and order: An honest citizen's guide to crime and control*. Cambridge, UK: Polity Press.

Understanding the causes of crime and policy responses to it is a complex endeavor no less for academic criminologists and honest citizens. This book will be useful to both.

Turk, Austin T.: The Criminalization Process

Kowalski, B. R., & Lundman, R. J. (2008). Sociologist Austin Turk and policing: Structural reinforcers and reversals of the positional authority of police. *Sociological Forum, 23,* 814–844.

In this essay, Kowalski and Lundman examine Turk's theory at police traffic stops. They conclude that testing of Turk's theory is still in its infancy and has been limited to policing citizens with mixed results. Further tests of Turk's work are recommended.

Lanza-Kaduce, L., & Greenleaf, R. G. (1994). Police-citizen encounters: Turk on norm resistance. *Justice Quarterly, 1,* 605–623.

Addressing the problem of police-citizen conflict, Lanza-Kaduce and Greenleaf develop specific hypotheses about Turk's theory. The authors claim that Turk's theory provides fertile ground for formulating propositions about the likelihood of norm resistance.

Lanza-Kaduce, L., & Greenleaf, R. G. (2000). Age and race deference reversals: Extending Turk on police-citizen conflict. *Journal of Research in Crime and Delinquency, 37,* 221–236.

In this essay, Lanza-Kaduce and Greenleaf extend their research on Turk's theory and explore social deference norms and police-citizen conflict. The spotlight is on race and age of authorities and subjects at domestic violence calls.

Vold, George B.: Group Conflict Theory

Bernard, T. J., Snipes, J. B., & Gerould, A. L. (2010). *Vold's theoretical criminology* (6th ed.). New York: Oxford University Press.

In the latest edition of Vold's seminal work, published 52 years after the first edition, readers can see how group conflict theory fits in the context of several other types of conflict theories.

Vold, G. B. (1958). *Theoretical criminology*. New York: Oxford University Press.

Vold's entire presentation of his group conflict theory was presented in a single chapter of this major text of his, which is a summary and critical assessment of theories of crime.

13. Feminist and Gender-Specific Theories of Crime

Adler, Freda: Sisters in Crime

Chesney-Lind, M., & Pasko, L. (2004). *The female offender: Girls, women, and crime*. Thousand Oaks, CA: Sage.

Meda Chesney-Lind is a leading contemporary feminist scholar whose writings in this work (along with Lisa Pasko) highlight how young criminalized women are disproportionately affected by the United State's punitiveness toward female offenders, despite their relatively small numbers.

Flynn, E. E. (1998). Freda Adler: A portrait of a pioneer. *Women and Criminal Justice, 10,* 1–27.

This 1998 article chronicles Freda Adler's scholarship, including but not limited to feminist criminology.

Hartman, J. L., & Sundt, J. L. (in press). The rise of feminist criminology: Freda Adler. In F. T. Cullen, C. Lero Jonson, A. J. Myer, & F. Adler (Eds.), *The origins of American criminology* (Advances in Criminological Theory: Vol. 18). New Brunswick, NJ: Transaction.

This chapter, based on a series of interviews with Freda Alder, discusses in greater detail the origins of the liberation hypothesis. The chapter also includes more biographical information about a fascinating, influential figure.

Peterson, Rebecca D. (2006). The female presidents of the American Society of Criminology. *Feminist Criminology, 1,* 147–168.

In this article, Peterson relates the personal and professional experiences of the female presidents of the American Society of Criminology. Freda Adler was the third woman to serve in this prestigious role.

Smart, C. (1978). *Women, crime and criminology: A feminist critique*. New York: Routledge.

Smart, who was writing about gender and crime at the same time as Adler, provides a radically different perspective on female criminality. This work provides a good contrast to Adler's work. Smart was one of the outspoken critics of the liberation hypothesis.

Alarid, Leanne Fiftal, and Velmer S. Burton, Jr.: Gender and Serious Offending

Alarid, L. F., & Cromwell, P. (Eds.). (2006). *In her own words: Women offenders' views on crime and victimization.* Los Angeles: Roxbury.

This edited book of contemporary readings by a variety of scholars examines the overlap of female offending and victimization as a function of women's family of origin, peer groups, relationships with men, economic marginalization, and rational choice.

Heimer, K., & Kruttschnitt, C. (Eds.). (2006). *Gender and crime: Patterns in victimization and offending.* New York: New York University Press.

This edited book examines how women's patterns of criminal behavior and victimization are gendered by differences in social interactions and social organizations in daily life.

Bartusch, Dawn Jeglum, and Ross L. Matsueda: Gender and Reflected Appraisals

Heimer, K. (1996). Gender, interaction, and delinquency: Testing a theory of differential social control. *Social Psychology Quarterly, 59,* 39–61.

In this article, Heimer operationalizes three dimensions of role-taking to explain the gender gap. She asserts important implications concerning group social controls and their influence over delinquency by gender.

Heimer, K., & Matsueda, R. L. (1994). Role-taking, role commitment, and delinquency: A theory of differential social control. *American Sociological Review, 59,* 365–390.

Heimer and Matsueda build on the original symbolic interactionist theory put forth by Matsueda. The authors find support for social interactionist theory in the context of competing theories.

Koita, K., & Triplett, R. A. (1998). An examination of gender and race effects on the parental appraisal process: A reanalysis of Matsueda's model of the self. *Criminal Justice and Behavior, 25,* 382–401.

The authors build off of Matsueda's original model of the self and delinquency. Koita and Triplett examine the effects of race and gender on reflected appraisals.

Bottcher, Jean: Social Practices of Gender

Messerschmidt, J. W. (1993). *Masculinities and crime: Critique and reconceptualization of theory.* Lanham, MD: Rowman & Littlefield.

In this book, James Messerschmidt challenges the traditional association between crime and masculinity. In so doing, James Messerschmidt examines gender roles that influence the occurrence and types of crimes in society. This book provides a thorough discussion of the inseparable relationship between gender and crime.

Messerschmidt, J. W. (2004). *Flesh and blood: Adolescent gender diversity and violence.* Lanham, MD: Rowman & Littlefield.

In this book, James Messerschmidt provides the reader with a discussion of how masculine practices may be constructed by both boys and girls and how these social practices are related to both violence and nonviolence. In addition, this book explores the misleading notion of the sex-gender, and gender difference dichotomies.

Renzetti, C., & Curran, D. (1992). *Women, men, and society* (2nd ed.). Boston: Allyn & Bacon.

In this book, Claire Renzetti and Daniel Curran provide the reader with an analysis of gender inequality, addressing how sexism affects both men and women. In addition, this book discusses the consequences of gender inequality and how these consequences can be compounded by other factors such as racism, social class inequality, ageism, and heterosexism.

Broidy, Lisa M., and Robert S. Agnew: A General Strain Theory of Gender and Crime

Agnew, R. (2006). *Pressured into crime: An overview of general strain theory.* Los Angeles: Roxbury.

Fourteen years after the initial presentation of general strain theory, Agnew revisits the theory, assesses related empirical research, discusses added theoretical extensions of general strain theory, and demarcates future directions in this book. The role of gender in general strain theory is discussed at length.

Broidy, L. M. (2001). A test of general strain theory. *Criminology, 39,* 9–33.

This empirical piece tests general strain theory's propositions regarding gender, emotion, and crime. Authored by Broidy, the theoretical piece reviewed here is tested by its original author.

Chesney-Lind, M. (1989). Girls' crime and woman's place: Toward a feminist model of female delinquency. *Crime and Delinquency, 35,* 5–29.

> *This classic piece in feminist criminology addresses two issues: (1) the "generalizability problem," which questions whether traditional theories of crime apply to women and (2) the "gender ratio problem," which questions why women are less likely than men to engage in criminal behavior. The applicability of general strain theory is inferred.*

Ganem, N. M. (2008). *The role of negative emotion in general strain theory.* Saarbrücken, Germany: VDM Verlag.

> *This dissertation systematically investigates the role of negative emotion in general strain theory. A review of the causes and consequences of negative emotions pulls together information from the social psychology of emotion and general strain literature. Multiple emotions are considered, with analyses and discussion focusing on how gender differences in emotion may explain gender differences in criminal behavior.*

Campbell, Anne: Girls in the Gang

Chesney-Lind, M., & Hagedorn, J. (Eds.). (1999). *Female gangs in America: Essays on girls, gangs, and gender.* Chicago: Lake View Press.

> *This Office of Juvenile Justice and Delinquency Prevention (OJJDP)-sponsored reader summarizes past and current studies on female gangs. The reader highlights stereotypes of female criminality, law enforcement surveys that measure gang participation, as well as levels of offending.*

LeBlanc, A. N. (2003). *Random family: Love, drugs, trouble and coming of age in the Bronx.* New York: Scribner.

> *Adrian LeBlanc is a journalist who spent nearly 10 years studying girls in the Bronx. Her observation began in the late 1980s. LeBlanc's contribution is that like Campbell, she delves into the lives of girls and women in order to help the reader understand how a person's choices and opportunity are limited by social forces such as the economy, violence, and the cycle of poverty.*

Miller, J. (2000). *One of the guys: Girls, gangs, and gender.* New York: Oxford University Press.

> *Miller's book presents both a qualitative and quantitative picture of girls in gangs. Miller's insightful interviews of gang girls in Columbus, Ohio,*

and St. Louis, Missouri, helps fill in the gap of quality scholarly research in an oft-overlooked area.

Chesney-Lind, Meda: Feminist Model of Female Delinquency

Bloom, B., Owen, B., & Covington, S. (2003). *Gender responsive strategies: Research, practice, and guiding principles for women offenders.* Washington, DC: National Institute of Corrections.

> *This research report provides an overview of current gender-responsive strategies for correctional intervention with female offenders. Further, this work demonstrates the policy and practices in the criminal justice system that have been developed from feminist criminologists, most notably Meda Chesney-Lind.*

Chesney-Lind, M. (1989). Girls' crime and a woman's place: Toward a feminist model of female delinquency. *Crime and Delinquency, 35,* 5–29.

> *In this article, Chesney-Lind presents a feminist model for delinquency. Through her discussion of patriarchy and victimization, she develops a theory of female crime, which became a major contribution to criminology and guides much gender-responsive research that is conducted today.*

Chesney-Lind, M., & Pasko, L. (2004). *The female offender: Girls, women, and crime.* London: Sage.

> *The book provides an overview of much of the literature on female offending and feminist theories. Special attention is paid to the experience of girls and women in the criminal and juvenile justice systems, the causes of female crime, and the common offenses of women.*

Costello, Barbara J., and Helen J. Mederer: A Control Theory of Gender and Crime

Chapple, C. L., McQuillian, J., & Berdahl, T. A. (2005). Gender, social bonds and delinquency: A comparison of boys' and girls' models. *Social Science Research, 34,* 357–383.

> *In this article, the authors examine whether the social bond is measured similarly and operates similarly for boys and girls. Chapple et al. find that the social bond is invariant across gender, although the effect of peer attachment on decreasing delinquency is stronger for boys than girls.*

Miller, J., & Mullins, C. M. (2006). The status of feminist theories in criminology. In F. T. Cullen, J. P. Wright, &

K. R. Blevins (Eds.), *Taking stock: The status of criminological theory* (Advances in Criminological Theory: Vol. 15, pp. 217–249). New Brunswick, NJ: Transaction.

> *Miller and Mullins argue for an integration of feminist perspectives within traditional theories. They suggest that because boys and girls often give many of the same reasons for offending, traditional theories of delinquency should not be abandoned but rather modified to incorporate gendered paths to delinquency for girls and a greater understanding of the social context of female offending.*

Daly, Kathleen: Women's Pathways to Felony Court

Alarid, L. F., & Cromwell, P. (Eds.). (2006). *In her own words: Women offenders' views on crime and victimization.* Los Angeles: Roxbury.

> *This edited book of contemporary readings extends Kathleen Daly's theoretical pathways of crime approach to a fuller understanding of female offending, particularly as it relates to race/ethnicity and class differences, and as a function of women's family of origin, peer groups, relationships with men, victimization, economic marginalization, and rational choice.*

Daly, K., & Maher, L. (Eds.). (1998). *Criminology at the crossroads: Feminist readings in crime and justice.* New York: Oxford University Press.

> *This edited book reviews three decades of feminist work in criminology, presenting the most important and pivotal works in this area.*

Feminist Criminology. Can be accessed at http://fc.sage pub.com

> *A quarterly journal published by SAGE that focuses on theory and research regarding the gendered nature of crime from a feminist perspective. This is the official journal of the Division on Women and Crime of the American Society of Criminology.*

Freud, Sigmund: The Deviant Woman

Freud, S. (1930). *Civilization and its discontents* (J. Strachey, Ed. & Trans.). New York: W. W. Norton.

> *This book is a must for anyone interested in Freud's view of the world. The work provides a unique look into the effects of society on man from the theoretical lens of psychoanalysis.*

Saguaro, S. (Ed.). (2000). *Psychoanalysis and woman: A reader.* New York: New York University Press.

> *This reader opens with Freud's theory on female sexuality and provides the reader a look at psychoanalysis through the eyes of women. The book includes chapters written by Freud's contemporaries and those who followed him regarding their insights into different aspects of psychoanalysis and its relation to women.*

Young-Bruehl, E. (1990). *Freud on women.* New York: W. W. Norton.

> *This edited compilation provides a look at Freud's theories on female sexuality. The work offers an overview of different materials written by Freud and gives the reader an opportunity to view some of the evolution of his works.*

Hagan, John, and Holly Foster: Stress and Gendered Pathways to Delinquency

Hagan, J., Gillis, A. R., & Simpson, J. (1985). The class structure of gender and delinquency: Toward a power-control theory of common delinquent behavior. *American Journal of Sociology, 90,* 1151–1178.

> *This further reading was selected because it provides the theoretical foundation for the formation of the gendered and age-graded sequential stress theory. It serves as the direct springboard for the formation of the theory discussed in this entry.*

Hagan, J., McCarthy, B., & Foster, H. (2002). A gendered theory of delinquency and despair in the life course. *Acta Sociologica, 45,* 37–46.

> *This further reading was selected because it also provides the foundation for the formation of the gendered and age-graded sequential stress theory. In this article, which discusses the gendered role of delinquency was published the year before the gendered and age-graded sequential stress theory appeared. Thus, it also serves as a springboard to the theory.*

Jang, S. J. (2007). Gender differences in strain, negative emotions, and coping behaviors: A general strain theory approach. *Justice Quarterly, 24,* 523–553.

> *This further reading was selected because it provides one of the most recent empirical investigations of how strains can differ by gender. Since stress, or strain, is an essentially component of Hagan and Foster's theory and because the researchers posit gender differences in reactions to strains, this article was included.*

Moffitt, T. E. (1993). Life-course-persistent and adolescence-limited antisocial behavior: A developmental taxonomy. *Psychological Review, 100,* 674–701.

This further reading was included to direct readers to an alternative view of offending. This cite was mentioned in the entry in the criticisms section. Hagan and Foster do not acknowledge the importance of biology and the role it can play in shaping criminal behavior.

Wright, R. T., & Decker, S. H. (1997). *Armed robbers in action: Stickups and street culture.* Boston: Northeastern University Press.

This further reading was included because it discusses the importance of examining behaviors after crime. Often criminologists do not examine post-crime behavior. Hagan and Foster posit that crime should be considered as an intervening variable between behaviors before and after the commission of a crime.

Haynie, Dana L.: Contexts of Risk

Akers, R. L. (1985). *Deviant behavior: A social learning approach* (3rd ed.). Belmont, CA: Wadsworth.

In this book, Akers presents his social learning theory of delinquency. Building on Sutherland's differential association theory, Akers lays out a theory of how individuals learn delinquency through their interactions with significant others. Friends and parents both play critical roles in the delinquent behavior of adolescents.

Armour, S., & Haynie, D. (2007). Adolescent sexual debut and later delinquency. *Journal of Youth and Adolescence, 36,* 141–152.

This article extends Haynie's previous work on pubertal timing and delinquency. In this piece, the authors try to determine whether becoming sexually active earlier than one's peers is linked to later delinquency. Findings suggest that early sexual activity relative to peers is associated with an increased risk of delinquency later.

Caspi, A., & Moffitt, T. E. (1991). Individual differences are accentuated during periods of social change: The sample case of girls at puberty. *Journal of Personality and Social Psychology, 61,* 157–168.

In this earlier article, Caspi and Moffitt explore three competing hypotheses about the relationship between female puberty and changes in behavior. Their results indicated that the early onset of puberty appeared to increase behavioral problems that existed prior to puberty.

Heimer, Karen, and Stacy De Coster: The Gendering of Violent Delinquency

Belknap, J. (2001). *The invisible woman: Gender, crime, and justice* (2nd ed.). Belmont, CA: Wadsworth.

Belknap provides a comprehensive overview of women as offenders, victims, and criminal justice professionals. This book also re-examines mainstream criminological theories in terms of their applicability to female offending and introduces feminist criminology.

Sutherland, E. H. (1947). *Principles of criminology* (4th ed.). Philadelphia: Lippincott.

This reading offers the original theoretical framework for differential association theory including both the individual-level and structural-level differential social organization—concepts discussed by Heimer and De Coster (1999).

Klein, Dorie: The Etiology of Female Crime

Belknap, J. (2007). *The invisible woman: Gender, crime, and justice* (3rd ed.). Belmont, CA: Thomson Wadsworth.

A widely used and excellent textbook on women and crime, this readable text covers the whole range of the relationship between women and the criminal justice system—as offenders, victims, and employees. There is a good chapter critiquing criminological theories, following the early groundwork laid by Klein and others.

Morash, M. (2006). *Understanding gender, crime and justice.* Thousand Oaks, CA: Sage.

Another excellent basic text about women and crime, though this one employs a postmodernist theoretical approach to understanding the relationships between women and criminal offending, victimization, and working in the criminal justice system.

Rafter, N. H. (Editor-in Chief). (2000). *Encyclopedia of women and crime.* Phoenix, AZ: Oryx Press.

A comprehensive presentation of the key ideas comprising the field of women and crime in encyclopedia format. Though Klein does not appear in this text as a separate entry, her work is recognized in the preface as fundamental to the development of the field.

Koss, Mary P.: The Prevalence and Sources of Rape

Fisher, B. S., Cullen, F. T., & Turner, M. G. (2000). *The sexual victimization of college women.* Washington, DC:

National Institute of Justice. Available from http://www .ncjrs.org/criminal_justice2000/vol_4/04g.pdf

This study examines several aspects of sexual victimization among college women. For example, this article provides sections of the definition of rape, prevalence, and impact. Results from the National College Women Sexual Victimization (NCWSV) are discussed.

Hamby, S. L., & Koss, M. P. (2003). Shades of gray: A qualitative study of terms used in the measurement of sexual victimization. *Psychology of Women Quarterly, 27,* 243–255.

This study used a qualitative focus group method to examine methodological and definitional issues raised in past sexual victimization research. Specifically, terms used frequently in sexual victimization research are assessed.

Kalof, L. (1993). Rape-supportive attitudes and sexual victimization experiences of sorority and non-sorority women. *Sex Roles, 29,* 767–780.

This article explores the hypothesized link between sorority participation and sexual victimization of college women. Rape-supportive attitudes of sorority compared to non-sorority women are also examined.

Koss, M. P. (1993). Rape: Scope, impact, interventions, and public policy responses. *American Psychologist, 48,* 1062–1069.

This article provides an overview of past research in the area of sexual victimization, including scope, impact, and intervention. Several policy implications and suggestions for future research are given.

Koss, M. P., Dinero, T. E., & Cerbel, C. A. (1988). Stranger and acquaintance rape. Are there differences in the victim's experience? *Psychology of Women Quarterly, 12,* 1–24.

This article examines differences between women who experienced sexual victimization from either a stranger or acquaintance. Variables such as number of offenders, violence level, and drug or alcohol use were used as distinguishing factors.

Lackie, L., & De Man, A. F. (1997). Correlates of sexual aggression among male university students. *Sex Roles, 37,* 451–457.

This purpose of this article was to examine characteristics of males who were sexually aggressive. Several variables such as athletic participation, *fraternity participation, sex role stereotyping, and attitudes are tested.*

Testa, M., VanZile-Tamens, C., Livingston, J. A., & Koss, M. P. (2004). Assessing women's experiences of sexual aggression using the sexual experiences survey: Evidence for validity and implications for research. *Psychology of Women Quarterly, 28,* 256–265.

In this article, the revised sexual experiences survey is given to a sample of women to determine the validity of the modified tool. Survey items were assessed to determine the ability to detect several forms of sexual aggression.

Lombroso, Cesare: The Female Offender

Lombroso, C. (2006). *Criminal man* (M. Gibson & N. Hahn Rafter, Trans.). Durham, NC: Duke University Press.

Mary Gibson and Nicole Hahn Rafter are leading scholars of Cesare Lombroso's work. This contemporary translation of Criminal Man *brings new light to Lombroso's classic text.*

Lombroso, C., & Guglielmo, F. (2004). *Criminal woman, the prostitute, and the normal woman.* (N. Hahn Rafter & M. Gibson, Trans.). Durham, NC: Duke University Press.

This new translation of La donna delinquente *incorporates more of the original text that was omitted from* The Female Offender. *Hahn Rafter and Gibson pay particular attention to the matters of sexuality, which were largely ignored in the original and incomplete translation of the text. The translators offer not only a historical analysis of Lombroso's influence but also detail the scientist's context at the time of the text's publication in their introduction.*

Maher, Lisa: Sexed Work

Belknap, J. (2007). *The invisible woman: Gender, crime, and justice* (3rd ed.). Belmont, CA: Thomson.

This book provides an up-to-date summary and review of feminist research on the relationship between gender and crime. This includes recent data and major theoretical explanations of women's participation in crime, women's experiences as victims, and women working within the criminal justice system.

Britton, D. (2000). Feminism in criminology: Engendering the outlaw. *Annals of the American Academy of Political and Social Science, 571,* 57–76.

This article examines the significance of feminist theory and research for criminology. It considers the difference between mainstream and feminist perspectives on crime and identifies emerging trends in feminist criminological research.

Richie, B. E. (1996). *Compelled to crime: The gender entrapment of battered black women.* New York: Routledge.

Richie's study of drug- and crime-involved women serving time is one of the first to offer a comprehensive explanation of how both gender and race shape women's experiences as victims and offenders. Her study offers a compelling explanation of how physical and sexual victimization contribute to women's patterns of offending.

Messerschmidt, James W.: Masculinities and Crime

Messerschmidt, J. (1997). *Crime as structured action: Gender, race, class and crime in the making.* Thousand Oaks, CA: Sage.

A more involved exploration of the theory being used with more explicative cases.

Messerschmidt, J. (2000). *Nine lives: Adolescent masculinities, the body, and violence.* Boulder, CO: Westview.

Application of the theory to life-history interviews with nine young men.

Messerschmidt, J. (2004). *Flesh and blood: Adolescent gender diversity and violence.* Lanham, MD: Rowman & Littlefield.

An analysis of the gendered lives of both male and female adolescents involved in violence. Extends structured action theory into femininities.

Newburn, T., & Stanko, E. (Eds.). (1994). *Just boys doing business? Men, masculinities and crime.* London: Routledge.

An edited volume of papers exploring the intersections of masculinities and crime.

Miller, Jody: Gendered Social Organization Theory

Britton, D. M. (2000). The epistemology of the gendered organization. *Gender and Society, 14,* 418–434.

Traditionally, the theory of gendered organizations has been applied to workplace and professional settings (e.g., Acker, 1990). Miller developed a theory of gendered social organizations. This article by Britton will enrich one's understanding of the early

work in this vein. Here, Britton argues that scholars must be deeply attentive to the significance of organizational context in order to effectively understand and apply this theoretical approach. Both she and Miller demonstrate how being attentive to context enriches our understandings of social phenomena.

Miller, J. (2008). *Getting played: African American girls, urban inequality, and gendered violence.* New York: New York University Press.

This is Miller's most recent foray into gendered social organizations theory, a richly detailed study drawing on interviews with 75 girls and boys. In this book, Miller documents violence experienced by poor urban African American girls, effectively arguing that this violence is deeply rooted in structures of gender, race, and class inequality in the girls' distressed urban neighborhoods.

Zhang, S. X., Chin, K., & Miller, J. (2007). Women's participation in Chinese transnational human smuggling: A gendered market perspective. *Criminology, 45,* 699–733.

The authors do an exemplary job demonstrating how their data about Chinese transnational struggling reveal a gendered process, illuminating the intersection of criminal enterprise and gendered organizations. This article enriches our theoretical understanding of Miller's theory of gendered social organizations.

Miller, Jody: Girls, Gangs, and Gender

Miller, J. (1998). Up it up: Gender and the accomplishment of street robbery. *Criminology, 36,* 37–66.

In this article, Miller examines street robberies among inner-city residents involved in prostitution and drug markets to illustrate both the gendered nature of street life and how violence is marshaled as a resource for both males and females.

Miller, J. (2002). The strengths and limits of "doing gender" for understanding street crime. *Theoretical Criminology, 6,* 433–460.

In this article and subsequent responses, Miller critiques static depictions of masculine and feminine criminality provided by the research literature. Here, Miller asserts that offending differences in criminal offending are a product not so much of individual-level notions of "doing gender" as some have suggested, but also of broader structural considerations that place women in social positions subordinate to men.

Moore, Joan W.: Homeboys and Homegirls in the Barrio

Hughes, E. (1971). Bastard institutions. *The sociological eye: Selected papers* (pp. 98–105). Chicago: Aldine-Atherton.

Moore's most influential mentor was the first to conceptualize gangs within a context of institutionalization.

Klein, M. (1971). *Street gangs and street workers.* Englewood Cliffs, NJ: Prentice Hall.

Klein's approach to Los Angeles gangs argues that process trumps ethnicity and in this regard is diametrically opposed to Moore's perspective.

Vigil, D. (1988). *Barrio gangs.* Austin: University of Texas Press.

This comprehensive treatment of the Mexican American experience owes a great debt to Moore's pioneering work.

Pollak, Otto: The Hidden Female Offender

Anderson, E. A. (1976). The "chivalrous" treatment of the female offender in the arms of the criminal justice system: A review of the literature. *Social Problems, 23,* 350–357.

This reading posits a position opposite to Pollak's assertions about how female offenders are treated by the criminal justice system. In this empirical article, Anderson dispels the myth that the criminal justice system is chivalrous to women.

Chesney-Lind, M. (1997). *The female offender: Girls, women, and crime.* Thousand Oaks, CA: Sage.

This work shows that there is some debate in the field as to whether females receive shorter sentences than male offenders when similar crimes are committed and when prior arrests and convictions are controlled for as Pollak has asserted. Opposite of Pollak's assertions and expectations, Chesney-Lind states that females disproportionately receive harsher sentences for drug offenses than males.

Freud, S. (1933). *New introductory lectures on psychoanalysis.* New York: W. W. Norton.

Freud's work offers a theoretical precursor to Pollak's theory and reveals how women criminals were described by early theorists. This is a pivotal reading.

Heidensohn, F. M. (1968). The deviance of women: A critique and an enquiry. *British Journal of Sociology, 19,* 160–173.

Heidensohn directs readers to alternative views of female offending. She critiques Pollak's assertions, including his failure to explain why some female deviance and criminality surfaces and is processed in the criminal justice system.

Lombroso, C., & Ferrero, W. (1895). *The female offender.* London: Fisher Unwin.

This reading provides another theoretical precursor to Pollak's theory and thus is a pivotal reading.

Smart, C. (1976). *Women, crime, and criminology: A feminist critique.* London: Routledge & Kegan Paul.

Smart provides a critique of Pollak, including his interpretations of the data that he cites to support his viewpoints are flawed.

Thomas, W. I. (1923). *The unadjusted girl.* Boston: Little, Brown.

Thomas is another significant theoretical precursor to Pollak's work.

Rape Myths and Violence Against Women

Wilson, P. (1978). *The other side of rape.* Queensland, Australia: University of Queensland Press.

This book has provided a comprehensive yet detailed study on rape, victims, and perpetrators. Paul Wilson highlights the social stigmatization faced by the victims not only by society but also by the police, lawmakers, and the criminal justice system. His research provides an in-depth report about the risk factors, nature of victimization, and why rape is underreported.

Winkler, C. (2002). *One night: Realities of rape.* New York: AltaMira Press.

This book portrays the nightmare a rape victim has experienced. The author's narrative, ethnography, and radiant observation describes the appalling experience and frustration she underwent in her long fight to seek justice, much of which are due to the myths associated with rape. This book provides researchers with a framework to introspect about victims' experiences with rape, its aftermath, and the processing of the offense in the justice system.

Russell, Diana E. H.: The Politics of Rape

Henderson, H. (2007). Feminism, Foucault, and rape: A theory and politics of rape prevention. *Berkeley Journal of Gender, Law and Justice, 22,* 225–253.

Henderson considers Foucault's views of rape as a violent crime, not a sexual crime, and considers feminist views of rape and power. She argues that self-defense as a mechanism for rape prevention is physical feminism.

Russell, D. E. H. (1998). *Dangerous relationships: Pornography, misogyny and rape.* Thousand Oaks, CA: Sage.

In this book, Russell argues that pornography is a misogynistic endeavor to the detriment of women. She considers the role of pornography as women-hating propaganda and as a cause of rape.

Schwartz, Martin D., and Victoria L. Pitts: A Feminist Routine Activity Theory

Cohen, L. E., & Felson, M. (1979). Social change and crime rate trends: A routine activity approach. *American Sociological Review, 44,* 588–608.

This article was the original discussion of routine activity theory that was published. It outlines what Cohen and Felson theorized regarding why crime rates had increased. This original version of routine activity theory has a macro orientation.

Mustaine, E. E., & Tewksbury, R. A. (2002). Sexual assault of college women: A feminist routine activities analysis. *Criminal Justice Review, 27,* 89–123.

This article was published after the Schwartz and Pitts article and is a further explication of the combination of routine activity theory and feminism. Mustaine and Tewksbury utilize a sample of female college students and explore the relationships between the lifestyles of women and the types of behaviors that increase their risks for sexual assault victimization.

Schwartz, M. D., & DeKeseredy, W. (1997). *Sexual assault on the college campus: The role of male peer support.* Thousand Oaks, CA: Sage.

This book is a much more thorough and in-depth examination of the concepts and theory raised in the Schwartz and Pitts article. Here, one of the areas that is explored more fully is the idea that male college students in certain settings (e.g., fraternities) receive support from their peers for the sexual assault of women. Then, women who live lifestyles that bring them into contact with men belonging to such groups are at greater risk for victimization.

Schwartz, M. D., & Pitts, V. L. (1995). Exploring a feminist routine activities approach to explaining sexual assault. *Justice Quarterly, 12,* 9–31.

This is the original article that is discussed in this entry. It is the first time routine activity theory was combined with feminism in order to explore the concept of target attractiveness. In this article, the authors theorize that one aspect of target attractiveness could be the ease of getting away with the sexual assault of women, in part because women are not likely to report their victimization or because the penalties for this type of behavior are not terribly severe.

Simon, Rita J.: Women and Crime

Adler, F. (1975). *Sisters in crime: The rise of the new female criminal.* New York: McGraw-Hill.

This book explores the increase in women's criminality during the 1970s. The author purports that changes in women's criminality could be attributed to their "emancipation" from the home and their traditional female sex roles. Adler argues that there will be significant increases in women's violent offending, such that women criminals would essentially mimic male criminals.

Messerschmidt, J. (1986). *Capitalism, patriarchy, and crime: Toward a socialist feminist criminology.* Totowa, NJ: Rowman & Littlefield.

Messerschmidt shows how capitalism and patriarchy work together to affect women's criminality. He suggests that women's subordinate position in a capitalist, patriarchal society provides them with limited opportunities for white-collar or employment-related crime. Rather, he argues that women's criminality typically involves petty economic crimes, drug issues, and prostitution. In sum, women engage in crime as a result of economic marginalization or necessity rather than from increased labor force participation.

Pollack-Byrne, J. (1990). *Women, prison, and crime.* Pacific Grove, CA: Brooks/Cole.

This reading explores the nature of women's involvement in the criminal justice system. It specifically examines the idea of chivalry in regards to sentencing women offenders. Moreover, it also investigates the conditions women face in U.S. prisons, such as programming, health care, and violence.

Simon, R. J., & Ahn-Redding, H. (2005). *The crimes women commit, the punishments they receive* (3rd ed.). Lexington, MA: Lexington Books.

This book is the most recent edition of Rita Simon's original Women and Crime. *It provides updated statistics on women in the criminal justice system, from arrest to imprisonment. Moreover, it includes a new discussion of women's criminality around the world in regards to the liberation hypothesis.*

Simpson, Sally S.: Gender, Class, and Crime

Simpson, S., & Elis, L. (1994). Is gender subordinate to class? An empirical assessment of Colvin and Pauly's Structural Marxist theory of crime. *Journal of Criminal Law and Criminology, 82,* 453–480.

In this article, Simpson and Elis examine the basic relationship between class, family, peers, and educational experiences and serious patterned delinquency so as to determine whether the implicit assumption of gender neutrality in Colvin and Pauly's theory holds true. This is an interesting view of the race-class-gender intersection that utilizes an additional structural theory in the analysis.

Simpson, S., & Elis, L. (1995). Doing gender: Sorting out the caste and crime conundrum. *Criminology, 33,* 47–81.

Simpson and Elis contend that the field of criminology tends to view social class as the primary system of stratification. From this point, they systematically link gender and race oppression as moderating ecological variables. Further, these researchers examine how hegemonic masculinities and femininities are played out in work, the family, school, and so forth.

Simpson, S., & Gibbs, C. (2005). Intersectionalities: Gender, race, poverty, and crime. In K. Heimer & C. Kruttschnitt (Eds.), *Gender and crime* (pp. 269–302). New York: New York University Press.

This is a more recent work on intersections in the gender, race, class, and crime nexus. Though this work is similar to other prior works on this topic, it is included due to its recency in publication. It provides the reader with a good overview of Simpson's contentions in most of her research on intersectionalities. This work is also co-authored with Carole Gibbs, another prime researcher on intersectionalities who is often cited conducting similar research.

Smart, Carol: Women, Crime, and Criminology

Cowie, J., Cowie, V., & Slater, E. (1968). *Delinquency in girls.* London: Heinemann.

This book examines the social and psychological variables that are related to female delinquency. The authors observe case studies and focus on age, parents and family background, and psychiatric records.

Konopka, G. (1966). *The adolescent girl in conflict.* Englewood Cliffs, NJ: Prentice Hall.

The author examines at-risk females' behavior by interviewing adolescent girls that were reported to the courts or social agencies. The book includes writings from the females and transcripts from the original interviews.

Pollak, O. (1961). *The criminality of women.* New York: A. S. Barnes.

Author focuses on the manner that women commit crimes, the specific nature of female criminality, the personal attributes of female offenders, and the differences between female offenders and other offenders. The book discusses the underestimation of female crime as well as the biological and cultural components of female criminality.

Steffensmeier, Darrell J.: Organization Properties and Sex Segregation in the Underworld

Acker, J. (1990). Hierarchies, jobs, bodies: A theory of gendered organizations. *Gender and Society, 4,* 139–158.

In this essay, Acker develops a theory of gendered organizations, explicitly articulating how organizational structures, rather than being gender neutral, are built on assumptions about gender. Though not addressing crime or criminal organizations, it provides a useful expansion of the concepts discussed by Steffensmeier.

Britton, D. M. (2000). The epistemology of the gendered organization. *Gender and Society, 14,* 418–434.

Britton's application of gendered organizational theory builds from and refines Acker's. While again not written for a criminological audience, and focused primarily on formal occupations, it outlines important epistemological considerations for studying gender across organizational types, including those involving crime.

Maher, L. (1997). *Sexed work: Gender, race, and resistance in a Brooklyn drug market.* New York: Clarendon Press.

Maher's longitudinal ethnography of a Brooklyn crack economy provides an important look at the impact of gender and race on this specific illicit market. Many of the tenets of Steffensmeier's original theory are supported, while Maher's analysis of the intersection of gender and race further advances this framework.

Zhang, S., Chin, K.-O., & Miller, J. (2007). Women's participation in Chinese transnational human smuggling:

A gendered market perspective. *Criminology, 45,* 699–733.

Zhang et al.'s analysis of women's roles in Chinese transnational human smuggling networks is one of the few explicit efforts to examine the second facet of Steffensmeier's theory, specifically, the variability of gendered exclusionary practices across illicit organizational contexts. The nature of these human smuggling networks appears to provide a unique niche for female smugglers due to organizational facets and market conditions shaping these networks.

Steffensmeier, Darrell J., and Emilie Andersen Allan: A Gendered Theory of Offending

Haynie, D., Steffensmeier, D. J., & Bell, K. (2007). Gender and serious violence: Untangling the role of friendship sex composition and peer violence. *Youth Violence and Juvenile Justice, 5,* 235–253.

This study applies concepts from the gendered paradigm and insights from social influence literature to examine the effect of friendship sex composition on girls' and boys' involvement in serious violence. Findings are consistent with the tenet that girls' focal concerns, femininity norms, and lesser physical strength influence their offending patterns and also that girls' greater prosocial norms influence the behavior of males in their lives.

Maher, L., & Daly, K. (1996). Women in the street-level economy: Continuity or change? *Criminology, 34,* 465–491.

Ethnographic work in New York City demonstrates that the crack cocaine market of the late 1980s and early 1990s was highly gender-stratified with women playing lesser roles in selling and distribution, much like in heroin markets of the 1960s and 1970s. Street-level sex work was a more viable option for women than selling drugs, demonstrating pervasive sexism in the underworld.

Miller, E. M. (1986). *Street woman.* Philadelphia: Temple University Press.

This work highlights how relational obligations and gender norms influence women's pathways into and out of offending.

Zhang, S., Ko-Lin, C., & Miller, J. (2007). Women's participation in Chinese transnational human smuggling: A gendered market perspective. *Criminology, 45,* 699–733.

Interviews with human smugglers are analyzed to understand the extent and nature of women's roles in smuggling operations and gender stratification in illicit enterprises. Gender ideologies about work and caregiving, the importance of social networks, the emphasis on safety, and the limited use of violence offer a niche for women in these operations.

Thomas, W. I.: The Unadjusted Girl

Blumer, H. (1979). *Critiques of research in the social sciences: An appraisal of Thomas and Znaniecki's the Polish peasant in Europe and America.* New York: Transaction.

With this critique of Thomas's writings, Herbert Blumer was able to articulate his theory of symbolic interactionism. Blumer would develop a more precise vision of social action that emphasized less the wishes that Thomas relates and more how social interaction is the essence of all social action. If not for Thomas's scholarship, it is difficult say if Blumer would have been able to develop his theory of symbolic interactionism.

Bressler, M. (1952). Selected family patterns in W. I. Thomas' unfinished study of the Bintl Brief. *American Sociological Review, 71,* 563–571.

This article more clearly states the sources for many of the letters that Thomas cites in his book The Unadjusted Girl. Thomas was less clear about his methodology and how his letters were selected. Bressler shows that he had a larger project, one that reflects his obsession with not only the stories of Polish immigrants but also Eastern Jewish immigrants. The letters were letters to the editor and reflected the need for advice in the new world of America. A theme that fit well with Thomas's general argument that the lives of immigrants would remain disorganized if not provided with expert knowledge.

Merton, R. K. (1995). The Thomas theorem and the Matthew effect. *Social Forces, 74,* 379–422.

Merton traces the history of ideas and the several reasons for why W. I. Thomas's collaborator Dorothy Thomas was not initially cited as well in reference to "definitions of the situation." This is an important article because it shows not only the intellectual history of an idea but also how the Matthew effect leads to the citation of an older and more distinguished scholar over that of the lesser known scholar.

Widom, Cathy Spatz: The Cycle of Violence

White, H. R., & Widom, C. S. (2008). Three potential mediators of the effects of child abuse and neglect on adulthood substance use among women. *Journal of Drug Problems, 69,* 337–347.

> *This article attempts to explain the relationship between childhood victimization and substance abuse in women. It examines whether posttraumatic stress disorder, stressful life events, and delinquency are the casual mechanism through which childhood victimization causes substance abuse in adulthood.*

Widom, C. S. (1992). *The cycle of violence* (NCJ No. 136607). Washington, DC: National Institute of Justice.

> *This report describes Widom's original research and findings. It provides an overview of the research methodology and describes the sample and measures. It also provides detailed findings regarding the effects of abuse on arrests as a young adult.*

Widom, C. S. (2000). Childhood victimization and the derailment of girls and women into the criminal justice system. In J. E. Samuels & J. Thomas (Eds.), *Plenary papers of the 1999 Conference on Criminal Justice Research and Evaluation: Enhancing policy and practice through research: Vol. 3. Research on women and girls in the justice system* (pp. 27–36) (NCJ No. 180973). Washington, DC: National Institute of Justice.

> *This paper outlines the implications for Widom's research for females in the criminal justice system. It provides a review of the research on women, childhood victimization and offending as well as points out key issues regarding the treatment of female offenders who have been victimized.*

Widom, C. S., & Maxfield, M. G. (2001). *An update on the cycle of violence* (NCJ No. 184894). Washington, DC: National Institute of Justice.

> *This report provides results from a 6-year follow-up to the cycle of violence. It provides detailed information regarding the methodology of the follow-up as well as new findings from the follow-up data. It also points out that gender and race are important factors in the cycle of violence.*

Widom, C. S., Schuck, A. M., & White, H. R. (2006). An examination of pathways from childhood victimization to violence: The role of early aggression and problematic alcohol use. *Violence and Victims, 21,* 675–690.

> *This article seeks to provide an explanation for the cycle of violence. It examines whether aggression and alcohol use provide the casual mechanism through which childhood victimization causes violence in adulthood.*

14. Choice and Opportunity Theories of Crime

Brantingham, Patricia L., and Paul J. Brantingham: Environmental Criminology

Felson, M. K. (2002). *Crime and everyday life* (3rd ed.). Thousand Oaks, CA: Pine Forge Press.

> *With his routine activities theory, Marcus Felson provides theoretical support for many of the central tenets of environmental criminology. In this book, Felson emphasizes how everyday actions provide the context for criminal activities.*

Rossmo, D. K. (1999). *Geographic profiling.* Boca Raton, FL: CRC Press.

> *D. Kim Rossmo was Patricia and Paul Brantingham's doctoral student at Simon Fraser University. For his dissertation, later published as this book, Rossmo took the Brantingham's ideas and applied them to criminal investigation and geographic profiling.*

Wortley, R., & Mazerolle, L. (Eds.). (2008). *Environmental criminology and crime analysis.* Portland, OR: Willan.

> *In this collected edition, Richard Wortley and Lorraine Mazerolle bring together scholars who provide the key theories in environmental criminology and brings them up to date with current research.*

Clarke, Ronald V.: Situational Crime Prevention

Clarke, R. V. (2004). Technology, criminology and crime science. *European Journal on Criminal Policy and Research. 10,* 55–63.

> *Clarke draws a stark contrast between traditional criminology and the field of environmental criminology.*

Clarke, R. V. (2008). Situational crime prevention. In R. Wortley & L. Mazerolle (Eds.), *Environmental criminology and crime analysis* (pp. 178–194). Cullompton, Devon, UK: Willan.

> *This is the most recent comprehensive description of the theory and practice of situational crime prevention. The book containing this chapter describes other related theories of crime and prevention.*

Clarke, R. V., & Eck, J. E. (2005). *Crime analysis for problem solvers: In 60 small steps.* Washington, DC: Office of Community Oriented Policing.

> *This manual, available as a PDF file from www.pop center.org integrates Clarke's works with other environmental criminology and shows their practical*

application to policing. This manual, and a companion manual for the British police services, have been translated into 15 languages (also available at the above website). The manual contains the most up-to-date version of situational crime prevention.

Clarke, R. V., & Newman, G. R. (2006). *Outsmarting the terrorists*. Westport, CT: Praeger Security International.

Clarke and Newman take on terrorism, show its "rationality" and how understanding principles of opportunity theory can help prevent terrorist incidents. Not only does this book show how situational approaches can be applied to terrorism, but it also gives a good overview of situational crime prevention and opportunity theories.

Felson, M., & Clarke, R. V. (1998). *Opportunity makes the thief: Practical theory for crime prevention* (Police Research Papers No. 98). London: Home Office, Research Development and Statistics Directorate.

This paper (available for free from http://www .homeoffice.gov.uk/rds/prgpdfs/fprs98.pdf) describes opportunity theories, including situational crime prevention, and provides 10 principles of crime opportunity theory. Though over a decade old, this monograph, written for practitioners, provides a lively introduction to opportunity theories and situational crime prevention.

Cohen, Lawrence E., and Marcus K. Felson: Routine Activity Theory

Felson, M. (2002). *Crime and everyday life* (3rd ed.). Thousand Oaks, CA: Pine Forge Press.

In this book, Felson presents an overview of contemporary routine activity theory, highlighting how everyday aspects of social settings facilitate or inhibit the commission of criminal offenses. This is perhaps the most easily read and digested overview of routine activity theory. Both scholars and laypersons alike will find this book highly informative.

Kennedy, L. W., & Forde, D. R. (1999). *When push comes to shove: A routine conflict approach to violence*. Albany: SUNY Press.

In this book, Kennedy and Forde focus on the ways in which individuals define and consequently respond to everyday confrontations in life. Emphasis is on how and when people do or do not use violent means to respond to and resolve disputes in everyday life.

Miethe, T. D., & Meier, R. F. (1994). *Crime and its social context: Toward an integrated theory of offenders, victims, and situations*. Albany: SUNY Press.

This text draws together issues encompassing those who commit crime, are victims of crime and the variable contexts in which offenders, and victims intermingle to offer an explanation of criminal events that is multifaceted. The core issues of routine activity are emphasized, with the ultimate explanation for criminal events relying on interactions and intersections of the three core theoretical components.

Sacco, V. F., & Kennedy, L. W. (1996). *The criminal event*. Belmont, CA: Wadsworth.

This book emphasizes the event of a crime as the intersection of multiple factors that are necessary for crime to occur. The argument presented emphasizes criminal events as a process, not just a distinct event that is not tied to larger social issues.

Schwartz, M. D., & Pitts, V. L. (1995). Exploring a feminist routine activities approach to explaining sexual assault. *Justice Quarterly, 12,* 9–31.

In this study, Schwartz and Pitts present one of the first attempts to apply routine activity theory to sexual violence. The study emphasizes both victim vulnerability (women's drinking in public frequently) and motivations of offenders (men working to get women drunk so as to victimize them). The study applies feminist principles as well as the core concepts of routine activity theory to the explanation of sexual assault among college students.

Cook, Philip J.: Supply and Demand of Criminal Opportunities

Clarke, R. V. (1980). Situational crime prevention: Theory and practice. *British Journal of Criminology, 20,* 136–147.

This article provides an introduction to the principles of situation crime prevention, a strategy that focuses on thwarting crimes by eliminating criminal opportunities.

Ehlich, I. (1981). The market for offenses and the public enforcement of laws: An equilibrium analysis. *British Journal of Social Psychology, 21,* 107–120.

This article discusses the "demand for offenses" in terms of supply and demand.

Felson, M., & Clarke, R. V. (1998). *Opportunity makes the thief: Practical theory for crime prevention* (Police Research Series No. 98). London: Home Office.

This article provides an overview of opportunity theories and implications for crime prevention.

Wilcox, P., Land, K. C., & Hunt, S. A. (2003). *Criminal circumstance: A dynamic, multicontextual criminal opportunity theory.* New York: Aldine de Gruyter.

This book introduces a multilevel and mulitcontextual theoretical model for how criminal opportunities are created.

Cornish, Derek B., and Ronald V. Clarke: Rational Choice Theory

Clarke, R. V., & Cornish, D. (1985). Modeling offender's decisions: A framework for research and policy. In M. Tonry & N. Morris (Eds.), *Crime and justice: An annual review of research* (Vol. 6, pp. 147–185). Chicago: University of Chicago Press.

This is the original article that describes the contributions from other social sciences and lays out the involvement and event models.

Cornish, D., & Clarke, R. V. (Eds.). (1986). *The reasoning criminal: Rational choice perspectives on offending.* New York: Springer-Verlag.

This book reviews rational choice approaches to studying crime, as well as multiple empirical studies of criminal decision making and relevant theoretical issues.

Crime Hot Spots

Sherman, L., Gartin, P., & Buerger, M. (1989). Hot spots of predatory crime: Routine activities and the criminology of place. *Criminology, 27,* 27–56.

This article is one of the seminal works in the micro-level examination of the distribution of crime within and across neighborhoods. This article also develops routine activity theory as an explanation for the concentration of crime in particular hot spot locations.

Weisburd, D., & Braga, A. (2006). Hot spots policing as a model of police innovation. In D. Weisburd & A. Braga (Eds.), *Police innovation: Contrasting perspectives* (pp. 225–244). New York: Cambridge University Press.

This chapter describes the role of criminological theory and careful empirical study in the development of hot spots policing. The evaluation evidence on the crime prevention effectiveness of hot spots policing is also reviewed.

Weisburd, D., Bushway, S., Lum, C., & Yang, S. (2004). Trajectories of crime at places: A longitudinal study of street segments in the city of Seattle. *Criminology, 42,* 283–321.

This article presents empirical evidence that crime hot spots have generally stable concentrations of crime over time. The research also suggests that a relatively small proportion of crime places belong to groups with steeply rising or declining crime trajectories and that these places may be primarily responsible for overall city trends in crime.

Decker, Scott H., and Richard T. Wright: Decisions of Street Offenders

Katz, J. (1988). *Seductions of crime: Moral and sensual attractions in doing evil.* New York: Basic Books.

This is a prominent work in criminology that focuses on emotional and "foreground" factors in shaping the decisions of persons who partake in certain acts of crime and aggression.

Lofland, J. (1969). *Deviance and identity.* Englewood Cliffs, NJ: Prentice Hall.

Wright and Decker draw from Lofland in developing their theoretical framework and in interpreting the behaviors of active street criminals.

Eck, John E.: Places and the Crime Triangle

Clarke, R. V., & Eck, J. E. (2005). *Crime analysis for problem solvers in 60 small steps.* Washington, DC: Office of Community Oriented Policing Services, U.S. Department of Justice.

This manual was written for crime analysts but can also be used to introduce readers to the crime science perspective. The manual translates the basic principles of environmental criminology into practical analytical strategies (e.g., use of the crime triangle) for crime researchers.

Eck, J. E., & Weisburd, D. (Eds.). (1995). *Crime and place: Crime prevention studies* (Vol. 4). Monsey, NY: Criminal Justice Press.

Crime and Place *is the most popular volume of the* Crime Prevention Studies *series. It contains a collection of chapters dedicated to examining place and crime relationships.*

Wortley, R., & Mazerolle, L. (Eds.). (2008). *Environmental criminology and crime analysis.* Portland, OR: Willan.

This edited volume provides summaries of environmental criminology theories and related contributions. This volume serves as the most complete resource for those interested in the environmental criminology paradigm. Many of the chapters are authored by the original theorists.

Economic Theory and Crime

Bushway, S., & Reuter, P. (2008). Economists' contribution to the study of crime and the criminal justice system. In M. Tonry (Ed.), *Crime and justice: A review of research* (Vol. 37, pp. 389–451). Chicago: University of Chicago Press.

The current chapter is based on this much larger work on the contribution of economists to the study of crime. Those readers interested in more detail should refer to this article.

Coase, R. (1978). Economics and contiguous disciplines. *Journal of Legal Studies, 7,* 201–211.

This chapter lays out general elements of what economists bring to the study of new areas, including crime. Coase is a Nobel Prize–winning economist who helped found the area of Law and Economics.

Miles, T., & Levitt, S. (2007). The empirical study of criminal punishment. In A. M. Polinsky & S. Shavell (Eds.), *The handbook of law and economics* (pp. 453–495). Amsterdam: North-Holland.

This chapter reviews empirical work by economists on the study of criminal punishment. While not explicitly about economic theory, the theoretical approach is made explicit in the empirical approach of the economist.

Tonry, M. (2008). Learning from the limitations of deterrence research. In M. Tonry (Ed.), *Crime and justice: A review of research* (Vol. 37, pp. 279–312). Chicago: University of Chicago Press.

This balanced critique of deterrence research by a non-economist presents some insight into the potential limitations of economic theory when applied to criminal behavior.

Felson, Marcus K.: Crime and Everyday Life

Cohen, L. E., & Felson, M. K. (1979). Social change and crime rate trends: A routine activity approach. *American Sociological Review, 44,* 588–608.

This article is the introduction to routine activity theory and is the foundation of much of environmental criminology.

Eck, J. E., & Weisburd, D. (Eds.). (1995). *Crime and place.* Monsey, NY: Criminal Justice Press.

This volume in the Crime Prevention Studies *series is one of the seminal pieces in empirical research on the influence of place in crime occurrence.*

Felson, Marcus K.: Crime and Nature

Felson, M. (2002). *Crime and everyday life* (3rd ed.). Thousand Oaks, CA: Pine Forge Press.

In this unconventional textbook on crime causation, Felson explains how routine everyday activities set the stage for illegal activities, and how crime can be reduced by simple measures.

Felson, M. (2006). *Crime and nature.* Thousand Oaks, CA: Sage.

This textbook, written for undergraduate courses in criminology and criminal justice, formulates Felson's perspective on crime as outlined in this entry.

Krebs, J. R., & Davies, N. B. (1993). *An introduction to behavioral ecology* (3rd rev. ed.). Oxford, UK: Blackwell.

Felson's Crime and Nature *uses many concepts that have been developed in behavioral ecology, a contemporary branch of biology that explains behavior as a function of ecological and evolutionary mechanisms. This book is generally seen as an accessible introduction to this field of investigation.*

Hindelang, Michael J., Michael R. Gottfredson, and James Garofalo: Lifestyle Theory

Robinson, M. B. (1999). Lifestyles, routine activities, and residential burglary victimization. *Journal of Crime and Justice, 22,* 27–56.

In this article, Matthew Robinson provides a brief summary of lifestyle/exposure and routine activity theories. He also reports the findings from his telephone survey regarding the relationship between victims' lifestyles, routine activities, and residential burglary victimization.

Jeffery, C. Ray: Crime Prevention Through Environmental Design

Jacobs, J. (1961). *The life and death of great American cities.* New York: Random House.

This book introduced the insight that the natural and social environment contributes to crime and deviance, as well as suggested ideas for combating crime by changing the physical environment.

Jeffery, C. R. (1971). *Crime prevention through environmental design.* Beverly Hills, CA: Sage.

This book introduces the idea that it is possible to curtail offending by removing environmental cues that reinforce the offending behavior.

Jeffery, C. R. (1977). *Crime prevention through environmental design* (2nd ed.). Beverly Hills, CA: Sage.

In this edition, Jeffery added major discussion of the biological influences of behavior. He spends much time outlining the influence of the individual's biological makeup on processing input to behavior.

Jeffery, C. R. (1990). *Criminology: An interdisciplinary approach.* Englewood Cliffs, NJ: Prentice Hall.

This work argues for fully integrating biological, social, psychological, and other disciplinary approaches into a single coherent model for understanding behavior and what can be done to prevent crime.

Newman, O. (1972). *Defensible space: People and design in the violent city.* New York: Macmillan.

This book introduces the idea of defensible space, which seeks to create "a physical expression of a social fabric which defends itself." The book offers very specific recommendations on what to change in the environment in order to combat crime.

Wood, E. (1961). *Housing design, a social theory.* New York: Citizens' Housing and Planning Counsel of New York.

This work reports on an evaluation of public housing in Chicago and problems that contribute to crime in that setting. The analysis made early suggestions on enhancing safety by promoting resident surveillance and activity in the area.

Miethe, Terance D., and Robert F. Meier: An Integrated Theory of Victimization

Miethe, T. D., & Meier, R. F. (1994). *Crime and its social context: Toward an integrated theory of offenders, victims and situations.* Albany: SUNY Press.

In this book, the authors demonstrate empirically and conceptually the importance of integrating offender-, victim-, and situation-based theories in one perspective.

Miller, Jody: Gendered Criminal Opportunity

Anderson, E. (1999). *Code of the street: Decency, violence, and the moral life of the inner city.* New York: W. W. Norton.

This book provides a good understanding of both the culture and ideals of normalcy among inner-city residents.

Giordano, P. C., Cernkovich, S. A., & Rudolph, J. L. (2002). Gender, crime, and desistance: Toward a theory of cognitive transformation. *American Journal of Sociology, 107*(4), 990–1064.

This study provides a detailed look at the gender-race-crime interaction. It also works to develop an updated theory of cognitive transformation that is applicable across gender and races.

Jacobs, B. A., & Wright, R. (1999). Stick-up, street culture, and offender motivation. *Criminology, 37,* 149.

This study provides a detailed look at the influence of street culture and norms on the decision to commit crime, in lieu of background risk factors.

Steffensmeier, D. J., & Allan, E. (1996). Gender and crime: Toward a gendered theory of female offending. *Annual Review of Sociology, 22,* 459–487.

This study provides an all-encompassing look at the effect of gender on criminality, including variance over time and general theory.

Suchman, L. A. (1987). *Plans and situated actions: The problem of human-machine communication.* New York: Cambridge University Press.

This book is the first to discuss the concept of situated action. It provides a detailed description of its meaning and application.

Newman, Oscar: Defensible Space Theory

Newman, O. (1972). *Defensible space: Crime prevention through urban design.* New York: Macmillan.

In this book, Newman lays out for the first time, a detailed description of the concept of defensible space. The book contains many photographs, drawings, and blueprints to portray the concept visually.

Newman, O. (1996). *Creating defensible space.* Washington, DC: U.S. Department of Housing and Urban Development.

This volume contains an updated version of Newman's thesis about the relationship between physical space and crime. He explores the concept as it applies to the design of the Five Oaks neighborhood in Dayton, a row house public housing complex in the South Bronx, and dispersed, scatter-site public housing in Yonkers.

Reynald, D. M., & Ellfers, H. (2009). The future of Newman's defensible space theory. *European Journal of Criminology, 6,* 25–46.

This article describes the evolution of the defensible space concept and critiques the ambiguity of key aspects of the concept. The authors show the relationship between the defensible space approach and situational crime prevention theory and routine activity theory.

Osgood, D. Wayne, Janet K. Wilson, Jerald G. Bachman, Patrick M. O'Malley, Lloyd D. Johnston: Routine Activities and Individual Deviant Behavior

Felson, M. (2002). *Crime and everyday life* (3rd ed.). Thousand Oaks, CA: Pine Forge Press.

This book provides a thorough and engaging introduction to routine activity theory. Felson demonstrates that the theory offers a coherent and distinct perspective about crime by showing its relevance to a surprisingly wide range of topics.

Osgood, D. W., & Anderson, A. L. (2004). Unstructured socializing and rates of delinquency. *Criminology, 42,* 519–549.

These authors apply individual-level routine activity theory to explaining rates of delinquency for neighborhoods and schools. They show that this perspective is a useful addition to social disorganization theory.

Osgood, D. W., Anderson, A. L., & Shaffer, J. N. (2005). Unstructured leisure in the after-school hours. In J. L. Mahoney, R. W. Larson, & J. S. Eccles (Eds.), *Organized activities as contexts of development: extracurricular activities, after-school and community programs* (pp. 45–64). Mahwah, NJ: Lawrence Erlbaum.

This chapter discusses the connection between unstructured socializing and delinquency in relation to the students' after-school time use. It reviews evidence about the connection, lays out the developmental trends of time use with age and their association with age differences in delinquency, and considers the policy implications of these themes.

Physical Environment and Crime

Fowler, E. P. (1992). *Building cities that work.* Montreal, QC: McGill-Queens University Press.

The most impressive ideas about crime and physical environment at the community—as opposed to the site level—originated with Jane Jacobs. Fowler provides a test of her idea that short blocks with mixed land use are safer.

St. Jean, P. K. B. (2007). *Pockets of crime: Broken windows, collective efficacy, and the criminal point of view.* Chicago: University of Chicago Press.

Of most value in the above volume is hearing how offenders—drug dealers and robbers—in extremely disadvantaged neighborhoods think about physical environment. They pay attention to what the Brantinghams call crime generators and crime attractors. Although the volume overlooks the contributions of environmental criminology to land-use dynamics, it provides considerable detail on how offenders choose sites and the roles of land use—at least in this type of setting.

Taylor, R. B. (2001). *Breaking away from broken windows: Evidence from Baltimore neighborhoods and the nationwide fight against crime, grime, fear and decline.* Boulder, CO: Westview.

This work seeks to provide a longitudinal test of the incivilities thesis. It raises methodological and theoretical questions and finds some support for some ideas in some versions of the thesis.

Pogarsky, Greg: Behavioral Economics and Crime

Nagin, D. S., & Pogarsky, G. (2003). An experimental investigation of deterrence: Cheating, self-serving bias, and impulsivity. *Criminology, 41,* 167–193.

This article reported on a randomized experiment in which student subjects could cheat on a laboratory task to earn extra money and on which the probability of detection and severity of punishment were manipulated. Among the key results was that cheating was more prevalent among individuals with strong present orientation and who were prone to self-serving bias.

Pogarsky, G. (2007). Deterrence and individual differences among convicted offenders. *Journal of Quantitative Criminology, 23,* 59–74.

This study tested how variation in criminal propensity (operationalized as "self-control") moderated deterrent effects in a sample of convicted offenders in New Jersey's Intensive Supervision Program (ISP) in 1989 and 1990. Offenders' perceptions of the risks and consequences from violating ISP were associated with whether they successfully completed ISP. Moreover, lower self-control did not diminish and, if anything, enhanced these deterrent effects.

Pogarsky, G. (in press). Deterrence and decision-making: Research questions and theoretical refinements. In M. D. Krohn, A. J. Lizotte, G. Penly Hall (Eds.), *Handbook on crime and deviance.* New York: Springer.

This chapter comments on the current state of criminological deterrence research. It identifies areas of intersection between behavioral economics and criminological deterrence and suggests avenues of further investigation to improve our understanding of crime decisions.

Pogarsky, G., Kim, K., & Paternoster, R. (2005). Perceptual change in the National Youth Survey: Lessons for deterrence theory and offender decision making. *Justice Quarterly, 22,* 1–29.

This study advanced and tested a theoretical framework in which perceptions of the certainty of punishment are a function of the offending experiences and consequences of both the actor and others. The findings included the following: (1) Arrests had little effect on perceptions of the certainty of punishment for stealing and attacking. (2) In contrast, offending corresponded with decreases in the perceived certainty of punishment for both offenses. (3) Peer offending produced decreases in the perceived certainty for stealing, but not for attacking. (4) Prior offending experience did not diminish the influence of more immediate offending experience on risk perceptions. (5) Moral inhibition reduced the effects of offending experience on risk perceptions.

Sacco, Vincent F., and Leslie W. Kennedy: The Criminal Event Perspective

Anderson, A. L., & Meier, R. F. (2004). Interaction and the criminal event perspective. *Journal of Contemporary Criminal Justice, 20,* 416–440.

Anderson and Meier used the criminal event perspective to explore how components of the social environment interact together to produce crime or delinquency.

Meier, R. F., Kennedy, L. W., & Sacco, V. F. (Eds.). (2001). *The process and structure of crime: Criminal events and crime analysis.* New Brunswick, NJ: Transaction.

This edited book explores the criminal event perspective in detail from the perspective of a variety of authors. Specific topics include the application of the criminal event perspective to macro studies of crime, using qualitative methods to study criminal events, and the relationship between criminal careers and criminal events.

Pino, N. W. (2005). Serial offending and the criminal events perspective. *Homicide Studies, 9,* 109–148.

In this article, Pino applied the criminal events perspective to understanding serial offending through a focus on the precursors, the event, and the aftermath.

Weaver, G. S., Wittekind, J. E., Huff-Corzine, L., Corzine, J., Petee, T. A., & Jarvis, J. P. (2004). Violent encounters: A criminal event analysis of lethal and nonlethal outcomes. *Journal of Contemporary Criminal Justice, 20,* 348–368.

Weaver et al. explored the contextual factors related to violent encounters, including the type of weapon used, the temporal and spatial characteristics of the event, and the offender and victim characteristics of the event.

Shover, Neal: Great Pretenders

Shover, N. (1985). *Aging criminals.* Thousand Oaks, CA: Sage.

This work uses some of the data used in Great Pretenders *with more specific focus.*

Wright, R. T., & Decker, S. H. (1996). *Burglars on the job: Streetlife and residential break-ins.* Boston: Northeastern University Press.

This work adds additional insight into how streetlife affects criminal decision making.

Wright, R. T., & Decker, S. H. (1997). *Armed robbers in action: Stick-ups and street culture.* Boston: Northeasters University Press.

This work adds additional insight into how streetlife affects criminal decision making.

Stark, Rodney: Deviant Places

Sampson, R. J., & Groves, W. B. (1989). Community structure and crime: Testing social disorganization theory. *American Journal of Sociology, 94,* 774–802.

This article is considered a seminal piece contributing to the social disorganization theory literature. Their study was the first to directly test social disorganization theory. They mentioned problems with past research; these problems consisted of a lack of intervening variables in the model, and reliance on official crime rates. They addressed these issues in their study. They used self-report victimization and offending data. Their sample included 10,905 households across 238 localities in Great Britain. For intervening variables, they created a model that was an extension of Shaw and McKay's original theory.

With this new model, they were able to directly test Shaw and McKay's theory. They found that the results from their study were consistent with social disorganization theory.

Shaw, C. R., & McKay, H. D. (1969). *Juvenile delinquency and urban areas* (2nd ed.). Chicago: University of Chicago Press.

Shaw and McKay developed social disorganization theory. The work that they undertook was unprecedented and was conducted without the use of computers and statistical techniques that we have today. Further, their theory, which was first published in 1942, is still being tested and supported today. They found that rather than individuals themselves being the cause of crime, it is neighborhoods that create criminal conduct. Their work sparked a movement that explored contextual level theories of causes of crime.

Wikström, Per-Olof H.: Situational Action Theory

Wikström, P.-O. (2005). The social origins of pathways in crime. Towards a developmental ecological action theory of crime involvement and its changes. In D. P. Farrington (Ed.), *Integrated developmental and life-course theories of offending* (Advances in Criminological Theory: Vol. 14, pp. 211–245). New Brunswick, NJ: Transaction.

Wikström, P.-O., & Treiber, K. (2009). What drives persistent offending. The neglected and unexplored role of the social environment. In J. Savage (Ed.), *The development of persistent criminality* (pp. 389–420). Oxford, UK: Oxford University Press.

These two chapters give jointly the best overview of how situational action theory conceptualizes and deals with the topic of development and change.

Wikström, P.-O. (2006). Individuals, settings and acts of crime: Situational mechanisms and the explanation of crime. In P.-O. Wikström & R. J. Sampson (Eds.), *The explanation of crime: Context, mechanisms and development* (pp. 61–107). Cambridge, UK: Cambridge University Press.

This chapter presents in detail the foundations of situational action theory and its grounding in social and behavioral science theory.

Wilcox, Pamela, Kenneth C. Land, and Scott A. Hunt: Multicontextual Opportunity Theory

Sampson, R. J., & Wooldredge, J. D. (1987). Linking the micro- and macro-level dimensions of lifestyle-routine

activity and opportunity models of predatory victimization. *Journal of Quantitative Criminology, 3,* 371–393.

This study examines whether micro- and macro-level indicators of opportunity independently influence the likelihood of victimization. Consistent with the main effects of individual and environmental opportunity on crime posited by multicontextual opportunity theory, the findings suggest that both macro- and micro-level indicators of opportunity influence victimization risk.

Wilcox, P., Madensen, T., & Tillyer, M. S. (2007). Guardianship in context: Implications for burglary victimization risk and prevention. *Criminology, 45,* 771–803.

This study uses multicontextual opportunity theory to guide the development of hypotheses predicting the relationship between neighborhood- and individual-level guardianship indicators and their influence on burglary victimization risk. The findings reflect support for the hypothesized moderating effects suggested by multicontextual opportunity theory.

Wilcox Rountree, P., Land, K. C., & Miethe, T. D. (1994). Macro-micro integration in the study of victimization: A hierarchical logistic model analysis across Seattle neighborhoods. *Criminology, 32,* 387–414.

This study examines whether the effects of individual-level opportunity variables on victimization risk vary depending on neighborhood context. Consistent with the interactive effects of environmental- and individual-level opportunity on crime posited by multicontextual opportunity theory, the findings suggest that the importance of individual-level opportunity in explaining victimization varies by neighborhood context.

Wortley, Richard: A Revised Situational Crime Prevention Theory

Clarke, R. V., & Cornish, D. B. (1985). Modeling offenders' decisions: A framework for research and policy. In M. Tonry & N. Morris (Eds.), *Crime and justice: An annual review of research* (Vol. 6, pp. 147–185). Chicago: University of Chicago Press.

In this essay, Ronald Clarke and Derek Cornish argue that crime is the outcome of an offender's rational choice. These authors provide fundamental theoretical groundwork for situational crime prevention by emphasizing offender decision making across all stages of a criminal event.

Cohen, L. E., & Felson, M. (1979). Social change and crime rate trends: A routine activity approach. *American Sociological Review, 44,* 588–608.

> *Lawrence Cohen and Marcus Felson suggest that offending is a function of opportunity when motivated offenders converge in time and space with suitable targets in the absence of capable guardianship. Their routine activity theory underlies using situational crime prevention to disrupt criminal opportunity structures at specific times and places.*

Cornish, D. B., & Clarke, R. V. (2003). Opportunities, precipitators, and criminal decisions: A reply to Wortley's critique of situational crime prevention. In M. Smith & D. Cornish (Eds.), *Theory for practice in situational crime prevention* (Vol. 16, pp. 41–96). Monsey, NY: Criminal Justice Press.

> *Derek Cornish and Ronald Clarke offer a rebuttal to Wortley's (2001) critique of situational crime prevention. In the end, these authors concede to Wortley and update the existing framework for situational crime prevention.*

15. Macro-Level/Community Theories of Crime

Blau, Judith R., and Peter M. Blau: Inequality and Crime

Messner, S. F., & Golden, R. M. (1992). Racial inequality and racially disaggregated homicide rates: An assessment of alternative theoretical explanations. *Criminology, 30,* 421–447.

> *Messner and Golden delineate the various arguments linking racial inequality to race-specific homicide rates. Their results indicate that racial inequality affects both black and white homicide rates, suggesting a generalized disorganizing effect on the total population, rather than on just one racial group.*

Shihadeh, E. S., & Flynn, N. (1996). Segregation and crime: The effect of black social isolation on the rates of urban black violence. *Social Forces, 74,* 1325–1352.

> *This article by Shihadeh and Flynn marked a critical turn in the macro-level research on urban black violence. Their summary of the social disorganization/ social control model informed by the work of William Julius Wilson and of Douglas Massey and Nancy Denton and their empirical analysis of black social isolation highlighted the importance of spatially embedded inequalities.*

Bursik, Robert J., Jr., and Harold C. Grasmick: Levels of Control

Bursik, R. J., Jr., & Grasmick, H. G. (1993). *Neighborhoods and crime.* New York: Lexington.

> *This book furnishes more details on Bursik and Grasmick's levels of control and systemic theory. It also provides useful discussion on how neighborhoods deal with disorder, fear of crime, and gangs and provides examples of community organizing against crime.*

Carr, P. (2005). *Clean streets: Controlling crime, maintaining order, and building community activism.* New York: New York University Press.

> *This book is a close-up examination of a single neighborhood in Chicago and of how levels of control come together there to fight against crime. Carr spent 5 years interviewing neighborhood residents and taking field notes to produce insightful observations about how order is maintained in a modern urban community.*

DeLeon-Granados, W. (1999). *Travels through crime and place: Community-building as crime control.* Boston: Northeastern University Press.

> *This book is an ethnographic travelogue by a criminologist intent on determining how neighborhoods and communities around the United States maintain order. Interesting reading on the topic of communities and crime.*

Rose, D. R., & Clear, T. R. (1998). Incarceration, social capital, and crime: Implications for social disorganization theory. *Criminology, 36,* 441–479.

> *This article extends Bursik and Grasmick's theory to consider in more detail how incarceration, as a form of public control, contributes to social disorganization and a breakdown of social capital. The authors also outline an extension of the theory that considers "feedback" effects of crime and incarceration on neighborhood order.*

Sampson, R. J., Raudenbush, S. W., & Earls, F. (1997). Neighborhoods and violent crime: A multilevel study of collective efficacy. *Science, 277,* 918–924.

> *This article describes collective efficacy and systemic theory in more detail and provides an empirical test using data from Chicago neighborhoods. It is an influential article in the literature on neighborhoods and crime published in one of the leading scientific journals.*

Inequality and Crime

Hipp, J. (2007). Income inequality, race, and place: Does the distribution of race and class within neighborhoods affect crime rates? *Criminology, 45,* 665–696.

Hipp argues that if inequality-crime theories are correct, inequity in the distribution of economic resources within neighborhoods should affect crime rates. He contends that because most theories suggest that the social interaction of residents is an important mechanism by which inequality affects crime, neighborhoods are a preferred unit of analysis than larger aggregates (e.g., cities or standard metropolitan statistical areas).

Reiman, J. (2007). *The rich get richer and the poor get prison: Ideology, class, and criminal justice* (8th ed.). Boston: Allyn & Bacon.

In this classic book, Reiman argues that the "criminal" actions of the economic elite frequently cause as much or more death, destruction, and financial loss as is caused by all "street crimes." Yet, these actions and their perpetrators commonly are not treated as criminal. In contrast, members of the lower class are more likely to be arrested, convicted, and imprisoned than the members of the middle and upper classes, even when they commit the same type of crime. Reiman contends that the criminal justice system operates to preserve and enhance the wealth of the rich, and its function is not really to reduce crime, as many believe.

Walker, S., Spohn, C., & DeLone, M. (2007). *The color of justice: Race, ethnicity, and crime in America.* Belmont, CA: Thomson Wadsworth.

In this accessible book, Walker and colleagues document the extent of racial inequality in crime and criminal justice, review potential explanations of existing disparities, and provide insightful summaries of the state of the research literature on these issues.

Krivo, Lauren J., and Ruth D. Peterson: Extreme Disadvantage and Crime

Bernard, T. J. (1990). Angry aggression among the "truly disadvantaged." *Criminology, 28,* 73–96.

Bernard presents a theoretical model that incorporates psychological data on aggression in order to explain why we should expect to see a relationship between neighborhood disadvantage and violence. This article both complements the major findings of Krivo and Peterson (1996) and posits underlying causal mechanisms that Krivo and Peterson were unable to establish.

De Coster, S., Heimer, K., & Wittrock, S. M. (2006). Neighborhood disadvantage, social capital, street context, and youth violence. *Sociological Quarterly, 47,* 723–753.

In this study using individual-level data, De Coster, Heimer, and Wittrock demonstrate that the effects of living in concentrated disadvantage on violent offending drop out of statistical significance once criminogenic street context variables are added to the model. The authors' findings provide a counterpoint to the findings of Krivo and Peterson (1996) because they suggest that community disadvantage itself might not cause violence once other criminogenic characteristics of the community are taken into account. De Coster and colleagues' contrasting findings might also be the result of using individual-level data versus Krivo and Peterson's aggregate-level analysis.

Wilson, W. J. (1996). *When work disappears: The world of the new urban poor.* New York: Vintage.

In this later book, Wilson expands on his discussion of the world of the urban underclass in The Truly Disadvantaged *by further analyzing the effects of the loss of manufacturing jobs on low-skilled inner-city residents. Of interest to criminologists, he particularly discusses the link between the rise of unemployment and social disorganization and the surge in drug trafficking.*

Negotiated Coexistence

Browning, C. R. (2009). Illuminating the downside of social capital: Negotiated coexistence, property crime, and disorder in urban neighborhoods. *American Behavioral Scientist, 52,* 1556–1578.

This article builds on the negotiated coexistence framework presented in Browning, Feinberg, and Dietz (2004) and applies the model to the case of property crime and disorder. The analyses offer additional empirical support for the negotiated coexistence model—the regulatory effects of collective efficacy on the prevalence of property crime and disorder are diminished as network interaction exchange increase.

Browning, C. R., Feinberg, S. L., & Dietz, R. (2004). The paradox of social organization: Networks, collective efficacy, and violent crime in urban neighborhoods. *Social Forces, 83,* 503–534.

The negotiated coexistence model is described and contrasted with two extant competing perspectives on the joint effects of collective efficacy and social network interaction and exchange. Employing data on violence in Chicago neighborhoods, results of the analyses are consistent with the expectations of the negotiated coexistence model—as network interaction and exchange increase, the beneficial effect of collective efficacy in reducing the prevalence of violence is diminished.

Pattillo-McCoy, M. (1999). *Black picket fences.* Chicago: University of Chicago Press.

Pattillo-McCoy's insightful analysis of a middle-class African American community provides an important foundation for the negotiated coexistence model. Residents of "Groveland" expressed concern about—and attempted to control—the prevalence of crime in their community. Nevertheless, the density of ties between Groveland's more conventionally oriented residents and local gang members inhibited the community's ability to translate strong social control inclinations into effective regulation of local crime.

Racial Threat and Social Control

Blalock, H. M. (1967). *Toward a theory of minority-group relations.* New York: Wiley.

This is the work that got social scientists interested in the social control implications of minority group threat. Some readers may find parts of it to be somewhat technical, but it is essential reading for anyone interested in this perspective.

Chiricos, T., Welch, K., & Gertz, M. (2004). Racial typification of crime and support for punitive measures. *Criminology, 42,* 359–390.

This article develops an alternative micro-level measure of racial threat that directly assesses the extent to which crime is perceived to be associated with African Americans. That perception is implicit, though unmeasured, in macro-level assessments of the relationship between racial composition of place and criminal justice controls.

Liska, A. E. (1992). *Social threat and social control.* Albany: SUNY Press.

Liska provides a readable summary of the origins, propositions, and problems with this perspective. Chapters written by other authors expand the range of potentially threatening "others" that may be subject to fatal, coercive, and beneficent controls.

Sampson, Robert J., and William Julius Wilson: Contextualized Subculture

Morenoff, J. D., Sampson, R. J., Raudenbush, S. W. (2001). Neighborhood inequality, collective efficacy, and the spatial dynamics of urban violence. *Criminology, 39,* 517–559.

This article examines how concentrated disadvantage, structural social disorganization, collective efficacy, and spatial proximity to violence affect homicide rates. It represents a sophisticated test of Sampson and Wilson's ideas about the importance of neighborhood context in explaining violent crime.

Sampson, R. J., & Wilson, W. J. (1995). Toward a theory of race, crime, and urban inequality. In J. Hagan & R. D. Peterson (Eds.), *Crime and inequality* (pp. 37–54). Stanford, CA: Stanford University Press.

This chapter presents the original statement of Sampson and Wilson's theory.

Skogan, Wesley G.: Disorder and Decline

Kelling, G. L., & Coles, C. M. (1996). *Fixing broken windows: Restoring order and reducing crime in our communities.* New York: Free Press.

In this book, George Kelling and Catherine Coles expand on the "broken windows" hypothesis and Skogan's work in Disorder and Decline. *They discuss the increase of disorder in America, the failure of past municipal strategies to deal with disorder, and methods to prevent disorder and crime in neighborhoods.*

Thacher, D. (2004). Order maintenance reconsidered: Moving beyond strong causal reasoning. *Journal of Criminal Law and Criminology, 94,* 101–133.

In this essay, David Thacher discusses the difficulty of establishing the connection between disorder and serious crime with scientific certainty. He argues, however, that the control of disorder is still important.

Wilson, J. Q., & Kelling, G. L. (1982, March). Broken windows: The police and neighborhood safety. *The Atlantic Monthly,* pp. 29–38.

In this essay, James Q. Wilson and George L. Kelling develop the broken windows hypothesis. Disorder and Decline *is a test of the broken windows hypothesis.*

Systemic Model of Social Disorganization

Bursik, R. J., Jr., & Grasmick, H. (1993). *Neighborhoods and crime: The dimensions of effective community control.* New York: Lexington Books.

This book lays out an extensive discussion of the systemic model of social disorganization theory and provides a thorough review of research up to its point of publication.

Sampson, R. J., & Groves, W. B. (1989). Community structure and crime: Testing social-disorganization theory. *American Journal of Sociology, 94,* 774–802.

> *This was among the first empirical studies examining social disorganization theory that included both an adequate number of neighborhoods to empirically test the theory and measures of social disorganization separate from exogenous neighborhood structural features. It is generally considered the classic piece for the systemic model of social disorganization theory.*

Warner, B. D. (2007). Directly intervene or call the authorities? A study of forms of neighborhood social control within a social disorganization framework. *Criminology, 45,* 99–129.

> *This is one of the more recent studies specifically examining the systemic model of social disorganization. It is important because the study distinguishes between direct and indirect forms of social control and examines the relationship of social ties to each.*

Wilson, James Q., and George L. Kelling: Broken Windows Theory

Kelling, G. L., & Coles, C. M. (1996). *Fixing broken windows.* New York: Simon & Schuster.

> *This book was George Kelling's first big follow-up to the original broken windows article. The authors examined the New York City Police Department's experience with broken windows theory and provided several arguments in favor of the effectiveness of this approach.*

Sampson, R. J., & Raudenbush, S.W. (1999). Systematic social observation of public spaces: A new look at disorder in urban neighborhoods. *American Journal of Sociology, 105,* 603–651.

> *This article is a good single source for an empirical test of broken windows theory combined with a discussion of the major weaknesses of the theory and directions for future theoretical development.*

Skogan, W. G. (1990). *Disorder and decline.* Berkeley: University of California Press.

> *This was the first large-scale, widely-read empirical test of broken windows theory. In addition to analyzing disorder's effect on crime, Skogan also addressed the significance of disorder for the entire process of community decline, including structural decay and reductions in property values.*

Taylor, R. B. (2001). *Breaking away from broken windows.* Boulder, CO: Westview.

> *This is probably the most large-scale, comprehensive test of broken windows theory to date. Taylor used both observed and perceived measures of incivilities and employed a longitudinal design. These two strategies allowed for a strict test of the proposition that disorder causes crime over the long run. Taylor's extensive analyses and nuanced conclusions make this a good single source for a better understanding of the strengths and weaknesses of the theory.*

Wilson, William Julius: The Truly Disadvantaged

Sampson, R. J., & Wilson, W. J. (1998). Toward a theory of race, crime and urban inequality. In D. R. Karp (Ed.), *Community justice: An emerging field* (pp. 97–115). Lanham, MD: Rowman & Littlefield.

> *This chapter discusses the implication of Wilson's work to the field of criminology by trying to develop a theoretical perspective to understand the relationship between race and violent crime. This is one of the first significant works to specifically integrate Wilson's The Truly Disadvantaged to criminality.*

Wilson, W. J. (1996). *When work disappears: The world of the new urban poor.* New York: Knopf.

> *Wilson's work from The Truly Disadvantaged was continued in this book. A further understanding of the underclass along with short-term and long-term policy recommendations are incorporated in this piece.*

16. Life-Course and Developmental Theories of Crime

Catalano, Richard F., and J. David Hawkins: Social Development Model

Catalano, R. F., & Hawkins, J. D. (1996). The Social Development Model: A theory of antisocial behavior. In J. D. Hawkins (Ed.), *Delinquency and crime: Current theories* (pp. 149–197). Cambridge, UK: Cambridge University Press.

> *This chapter provides a thorough overview of theoretical foundation and specific propositions contained in the theory. It is the definitive outline of the social development model by its developers.*

Catalano, R. F., Park, J., Harachi, T. W., Haggerty, K. P., Abbott, R. D., & Hawkins, J. D. (2005). Mediating the effects of poverty, gender, individual characteristics, and external constraints on antisocial behavior: A test of the social development model and implications for developmental life course theory. In D. P. Farrington (Ed.), *Integrated developmental and life-course theories of offending* (Advances in Criminological Theory: Vol. 14, pp. 93–123). New Brunswick, NJ: Transaction.

This book chapter provides an empirical examination of some key tenets of the social development model. It also responds to some broader questions surrounding integrated developmental and life-course theories of crime and delinquency.

Criminal Career Paradigm

Blumstein, A., Cohen, J., Roth, J. A., & Visher, C. A. (Eds.). (1986). *Criminal careers and "career criminals"* (Vol. 1: Report of the Panel on Criminal Careers, National Research Council). Washington, DC: National Academy of Sciences.

This report provides an overview of the criminal career framework and discusses research on key dimensions as well as methodological and statistical issues.

Farrington, D. P. (2003). Developmental and life-course criminology: Key theoretical and empirical issues—the 2002 Sutherland award address. *Criminology, 41,* 221–255.

This article provides an overview of key life-course criminology facts and then theoretical explanations of them.

Laub, J. H., & Sampson, R. J. (2003). *Shared beginnings, divergent lives: Delinquent boys to age 70.* Cambridge, MA: Harvard University Press.

This resource consists of quantitative and qualitative data for the longest longitudinal study in the world tracking Boston-area delinquents until age 70.

Piquero, A. R., Farrington, D. P., & Blumstein, A. (2003). The criminal career paradigm. In M. Tonry (Ed.), *Crime and justice: A review of research* (Vol. 30, pp. 359–506). Chicago: University of Chicago Press.

This study updates the Blumstein et al. (1986) report with new literature and issues on criminal career issues.

Farrington, David P.: The Integrated Cognitive Antisocial Potential Theory

Farrington, D. P. (Ed.). (2005). *Integrated developmental and life-course theories of offending* (Advances in Criminological Theory: Vol. 14). New Brunswick, NJ: Transaction.

In this edited book, David Farrington gathers some of the leading experts who, from their perspectives,

present and elucidate their different developmental and life-course theories of offending, many of which were formulated in the last 20 years.

Flannery, D. J., Vazsonyi, A. T., & Waldman, I. D. (Eds.). (2007). *The Cambridge handbook of violent behavior and aggression.* Cambridge, UK: Cambridge University Press.

In this edited book, Flannery, Vazsonyi, and Waldman present a comprehensive and multidisciplinary investigation of aggressive and violent behavior from international leading experts in the field. Many of the chapters constitute a developmental, biological, bio-genetics, and cultural analysis of the risk factors and mechanisms implicated in the origin of violent behavior over the life span.

Gulotta, G. (Ed.). (2002). *Elementi di psicologia giuridica e di diritto psicologico* [Juridical psychology and psychological law]. Milan, Italy: Giuffrè.

Even though this book is mainly for European readers, mostly Italians, it offers an overall view of the theories of offending and looks at how the criminal system responds to prevent and control the onset and development of criminal careers.

Loeber, R., & Farrington, D. P. (Eds.). (2001). *Child delinquents.* Thousand Oaks, CA: Sage.

Child Delinquents is an edited book that permits readers to be up to date with the most recent work on early criminal onset. Loeber and Farrington assemble some of the most interesting investigations on the risk-processes behind the onset, persistence, and aggravation of a criminal career started in childhood.

Thornberry, T. P., & Krohn, M. D. (Eds.). (2003). *Taking stock of delinquency: An overview of findings from contemporary longitudinal studies.* New York: Kluwer Academic/Plenum.

This edited book by Thornberry and Krohn provides readers with an extensive overview of seven of the most significant longitudinal studies in contemporary criminology. The underlying message for researchers is to recognize and appreciate that longitudinal investigation has become a crucial empirical approach to direct theory testing and policy making.

Welsh, B. C., & Farrington, D. P. (Eds.). (2006). *Preventing crime: What works for children, offenders, victims, and places.* New York: Springer.

This book is a project of the Campbell Collaboration Crime and Justice Group. Welsh and Farrington affirm that crime prevention should be rational and based on the best possible evidence—and explain why. Criminal behavior is multidetermined by individual, familial, scholastic, situational, and social risk factors. Multimodal programs, which tackle these dimensions, are proved to be the most effective in the long term.

Giordano, Peggy C., and Stephen A. Cernkovich: Cognitive Transformation and Desistance

Giordano, P. C., Cernkovich, S. A., & Rudolph, J. L. (2002). Gender, crime, and desistance: Toward a theory of cognitive transformation. *American Journal of Sociology, 107,* 990–1064.

> *This is the original article that first presents the foundation of the theory of cognitive transformation. The development and tenets of the theory are also discussed in a clear and concise manner.*

Giordano, P. C., Schroeder, R. D., & Cernkovich, S. A. (2007). Emotions and crime over the life course: A neo-Meadian perspective on criminal continuity and change. *American Journal of Sociology, 112,* 1603–1661.

> *This article presents the new direction of the theory. It describes the additional role of emotions, particularly the emotion of love, as well as the role that cognitions and social bonds play in the desistance process.*

Le Blanc, Marc: An Integrated Personal Control Theory of Deviant Behavior

Farrington, D. P. (2006). Building developmental and life-course theories of offending. In F. T. Cullen, J. P. Wright, & K. R. Blevins (Eds.), *Taking stock: The status of criminological theory* (Advances in Criminological Theory: Vol. 15, pp. 335–364). New Brunswick, NJ: Transaction.

> *Farrington provides a brief overview of Le Blanc's theory along with other developmental and life-course theories of crime. This work is of particular importance because it provides a concise comparison of these theories on key topics such as underlying constructs, age of onset, and desistance.*

Le Blanc, M. (1997). A generic control theory of deviant behavior: The structural and dynamical statements of an integrative multilayered control theory. In T. P. Farrington (Ed.), *Developmental theories of crime and delinquency* (Advances in Criminological Theory: Vol. 7, pp. 215–286). New Brunswick, NJ: Transaction.

> *In this foundational chapter, Le Blanc introduces his integrative multilayered control theory. Le Blanc*

argues that his control theory addresses two deficiencies of traditional control theories: single layered and non-developmental. This chapter is important because it not only provides a description of his entire theory but also details his integrated personal control theory of deviant behavior and places it in the context of his integrative multilayered control theory.

Le Blanc, M. (2005). An integrative personal control theory of deviant behavior: Answers to contemporary empirical and theoretical developmental criminology issues. In T. P. Farrington (Ed.), *Integrated developmental and life-course theories of offending* (Advances in Criminological Theory: Vol. 14, pp. 125–163). New Brunswick, NJ: Transaction.

> *This book chapter serves to expand and clarify Le Blanc's integrated personal control theory of deviant behavior by focusing on the developmental aspect of this theory. Specifically, he addresses the causes of change in deviant behavior overtime by discussing the role of quantitative and qualitative changes.*

Le Blanc, M. (2007). Self-control and the social control of deviant behavior in context: Development and interactions along the life-course. In P.-O. H. Wikström & R. J. Sampson (Ed.), *The explanation of crime: Context, mechanisms, and development* (pp. 195–242). New York: Cambridge University Press.

> *This book chapter can be characterized as an additional expansion and clarification of Le Blanc's earlier works (see Le Blanc, 1997 and 2005). This essay expands on his earlier works by focusing on self-control and how it interacts with other forms of control, including characteristics of the community in which an individual resides.*

Life-Course Interdependence

Ousey, G. C., & Wilcox, P. (2007). The interaction of antisocial propensity and life-course varying predictors of delinquent behavior: Differences by method of estimation and implications for theory. *Criminology, 45,* 313–354.

> *This article summarizes and tests models of antisocial behavior and life-course ties.*

Sampson, R., & Laub, J. (1993). *Crime in the making: Pathways and turning points through life.* Cambridge, MA: Harvard University Press.

> *A classic theory about the effect of antisocial behavior on crime via weakened social ties.*

Wright, B. R. E., Caspi A., Moffitt, T. E., & Silva, P. A. (2001). The effects of social ties on crime vary by criminal propensity: A life-course model of interdependence. *Criminology, 39,* 321–352.

A statement and test of the life-course model of interdependence.

Loeber, Rolf, and Magda Stouthamer-Loeber: Pathways to Crime

Loeber, R., Keenan, K., & Zhang, Q. (1997). Boys' experimentation and persistence in developmental pathways toward serious delinquency. *Journal of Child and Family Studies, 6,* 321–327.

This work extends upon Loeber et al.'s 1993 work by examining whether the pathway model equally applies to chronic offenders (i.e., persisters) and experimental offenders.

Maruna, Shadd: Redemption Scripts and Desistance

Laub, J. H., & Sampson, R. J. (2003). *Shared beginnings, divergent lives: Delinquent boys at age 70.* Cambridge, MA: Harvard University Press.

This work traces the life experiences of 500 delinquent boys into late adulthood. The findings indicate that desistance is shaped by structural routines and strong connections to family and community.

Maruna, S., Porter, L., & Carvalho, I. (2004). The Liverpool Desistance Study and probation practice: Opening the dialogue. *Probation Journal, 51,* 221–232.

Maruna et al. provide a brief overview of the findings from the Liverpool Desistance Study and develop recommendations for how these results can inform probation practice.

Shover, N. (1996). *The great pretenders: Pursuits and careers of persistent thieves.* Boulder, CO: Westview.

Like Making Good, *this work provides a narrative analysis of the life stories of more than 50 persistent thieves. Shover shows how the choice to commit crime is shaped by cultural and social constraints. The work challenges assumptions about the effectiveness of imprisonment as a deterrent.*

Moffitt, Terrie E.: A Developmental Model of Life-Course-Persistent Offending

Moffitt, T. E. (2006). Life-course-persistent versus adolescence-limited antisocial behavior. In D. Cicchetti & D. Cohen (Eds.), *Developmental psychopathology* (2nd ed., pp. 570–598). New York: Wiley.

Moffitt reviews 10 years of research on her dual taxonomy of offending, with particular emphasis on empirical tests of her theory. She provides a comprehensive and up-to-date discussion of the empirical status of the theory and concludes that many of her original postulates are well-supported. She also identifies those postulates that require either theoretical refinement or additional empirical scrutiny.

Nagin, D. S., & Tremblay, R. E. (2005). Developmental trajectory groups: Fact or a useful statistical fiction? *Criminology, 43,* 873–904.

Moffitt's dual taxonomy of offending—and developmental theories at large—has generated significant conversation and heated debate as to the appropriate methodological and analytical techniques to apply. This article is the first of three (printed sequentially in the same volume) in an exchange between (1) Nagin and Tremblay and (2) Sampson and Laub that proves both enlightening and provocative.

Piquero, A. R., & Moffitt, T. E. (2005). Explaining the facts of crime: How the developmental taxonomy replies to Farrington's invitation. In D. P. Farrington (Ed.), *Integrated developmental and life course theories of offending* (Advances in Criminological Theory: Vol. 14, pp. 51–72). New Brunswick, NJ: Transaction.

In this systematic response to David Farrington's 2003 Sutherland Address to the members of the American Society of Criminology, Piquero and Moffitt provide a detailed discussion of how Moffitt's dual taxonomy fits in to the larger landscape of developmental theories of offending behavior and of the contributions and challenges of the theory.

Philadelphia Birth Cohorts, The

Cohen, J., Roth, J. A., Visher, C. A., & Blumstein, A. (Eds.). (1986). *Criminal careers and "career criminal"* (Vols. 1–2). Washington, DC: National Academy Press.

These two volumes were produced by the National Academy Panel on Research on Criminal Careers and include work by major scholars studying crime, measurement, and policy issues related to crime patterns over the life course.

Gottfredson, M. R., & Hirschi, T. (1986). The true value of lambda would appear to be zero: An essay on career criminals, criminal careers, selective incapacitation, cohort studies, and related topics. *Criminology, 24,* 213–234.

This article provides perhaps the harshest criticism of the cohort studies and longitudinal framework used for studying the Philadelphia Birth Cohorts. This is one of a series of papers by these authors, and readers should consult these other works as well.

Sampson, R. J., & Laub, J. H. (1993). *Crime in the making: Pathways and turning points through life.* Cambridge, MA: Harvard University Press.

This award-winning book offers an age-period-specific explanation for criminal careers, or crime over the life course, based on data that were collected by Sheldon and Eleanor Glueck for 500 delinquents and 500 youths not involved in juvenile justice who were followed for many years. The nature of the "Glueck" data differ dramatically from that of the Philadelphia Birth Cohort.

Sampson, Robert J., and John H. Laub: Age-Graded Theory of Informal Social Control

Sampson, R. J., & Laub, J. H. (Eds.). (2005). Developmental criminology and its discontents: Trajectories of crime from childhood to old age. *Annals of the American Academic of Political Science.* Volume 602.

This volume covers the major theoretical and methodological controversies of contemporary life-course criminology with essays from top criminologists.

17. Integrated Theories of Crime

Agnew, Robert: Integrated Theory

Agnew, R. (2005). *Why do criminals offend? A general theory of crime and delinquency.* Los Angeles: Roxbury.

In his complete work, Robert Agnew describes in further detail the particulars of his theory, describes the specific manner in which he believes that his theory can most effectively be tested by future research, and builds on his theory to elaborate the implications that he believes it to have for efforts to control criminal behavior most effectively.

Bernard, Thomas J., and Jeffrey B. Snipes: Variable-Centered Approach

Agnew, R. (2005). *Why do criminals offend? A general theory of crime and delinquency.* Los Angeles: Roxbury.

This book provides another example of a variable-centered approach to theory integration.

Bernard, T. J., & Snipes, J. B. (1996). Theoretical integration in criminology. In M. Tonry (Ed.), *Crime and justice: A review of research* (Vol. 20, pp. 301–348). Chicago: University of Chicago Press.

This reading provides an overview of most of the major integrated theories in criminology and then presents Bernard and Snipes variable-centered approach to integration.

Messner, S. F., Krohn, M. D., & Liska, A. E. (1989). *Theoretical integration in the study of deviance and crime: Problems and prospects.* Albany: SUNY Press.

This book provides an overview of other strategies for constructing integrated theories of crime.

Chamlin, Mitchell B., and John K. Cochran: Social Altruism and Crime

Chamlin, M. B., & Cochran, J. K. (1997). Social altruism and crime. *Criminology, 35,* 203–228.

This is the original theoretical piece. It provides an overview of the logic behind the development of the theory. Moreover, it provides insight into how to test the relationship between crime and social altruism.

Chamlin, M. B., & Cochran, J. K. (2001). Social altruism and crime revisited: A research note on measurement. *Journal of Crime and Justice, 24,* 59–72.

In this article, Chamlin and Cochran delve into the complications and issues surrounding measurement and testing of social altruism theory. Any future tests of social altruism theory would benefit from reading this article.

Chamlin, M. B., Novak, K. J., Lowenkamp, C. T., & Cochran, J. K. (1999). Social altruism, tax policy, and crime: A cautionary tale. *Criminal Justice Policy Review, 10,* 429–446.

This research paper provides the first policy test of social altruism theory. While unsuccessful, the authors provide suggestions for future research, as well as a discussion on what this means for the policy implications of social altruism theory.

Colvin, Mark, Francis T. Cullen, and Thomas Vander Ven: Coercion, Social Support, and Crime

Colvin, M. (2000). *Crime and coercion: An integrated theory of chronic criminality.* New York: Palgrave Macmillan.

Integrating several existing perspectives of criminology, Colvin lays out his differential coercion theory in this book with a great emphasis on the role of coercive forces that create social and psychological dynamics that lead to chronic criminality. A comprehensive understanding of the differential coercion and social support (DCSS) theory requires being exposed to the arguments of Colvin on "coercion" as proposed in this book.

Colvin, M. (2007). Applying differential coercion and social support theory to prison organizations. *Prison Journal, 87,* 367–387.

Colvin tested the general premises of the differential coercion and social support (DCSS) theory using the levels of social support in the Penitentiary of New Mexico and coercion felt by the inmates thereof in different time periods. This study supported the core propositions of the DCSS theory and indicated that it has implications beyond individual criminal behavior.

Colvin, M., Cullen, F. T., & Vander Ven, T. (2002). Coercion, social support, and crime: An emerging theoretical consensus. *Criminology, 40,* 19–42.

Colvin, Cullen, and Vander Ven proposed a new perspective in understanding criminal behavior around the themes of "coercion" and "social support" in this essay that was the basis for the DCSS theory.

Cullen, F. T. (1994). Social support as an organizing concept for criminology: Presidential address to the Academy of Criminal Justice Sciences. *Justice Quarterly, 11,* 527–559.

In this essay, Cullen offered "social support" in both instrumental and expressive forms as an organizing concept for the contemporary approaches against the crime problem in the society. Since the DCSS theory grips "social support" along with "coercion" to explain vicious cycle of chronic criminality, reading Cullen's presidential address is vital for a comprehensive understanding of the DCSS theory.

Cullen, Francis T.: Social Support and Crime

Currie, E. (1997). Market, crime and community: Toward a mid-range theory of post-industrial violence. *Theoretical Criminology, 1,* 147–172.

In this article, Currie lays out what he refers to as a "mid-range" theory of violent crime among post-industrial nations. What is important here from a social support perspective is that he argues that market-based societies (like the United States) tend to emphasize individualism, which systematically undermines key sources of social support—such as education, health care, and welfare—that could conceivably reduce violence in the long term.

Pratt, T. C. (2009). *Addicted to incarceration: Corrections policy and the politics of misinformation in the United States.* Thousand Oaks, CA: Sage.

While Pratt's book is focused most heavily on the collateral consequences of policies emanating from the "control" tradition in criminology, considerable discussion is devoted to how these policies have eroded forms of social support over time in the United States. His discussion of potential correctional reform draws heavily on Cullen's (1994) social support theory both generally (i.e., socially supportive policies outside of criminal justice that may have a significant impact on crime) and specifically related to corrections (i.e., socially supportive approaches such as correctional rehabilitation).

Putnam, R. D. (2000). *Bowling alone: The collapse and revival of American community.* New York: Simon & Schuster.

Although Putnam's work is only peripherally concerned with criminal behavior, his work is relevant here in that his discussion of the breakdown of the American community is rooted firmly in the social capital tradition (a close cousin of social support theory). Drawing from many of the same ideas that influenced Cullen's (1994) work, Putnam outlines the harmful consequences that have emerged as a result of social institutions from education, religion, and politics having all become weakened over time.

Savolainen, J. (2000). Inequality, welfare state, and homicide: Further support for the institutional anomie theory. *Criminology, 38,* 1021–1042.

Savolainen's cross-national study, while rooted explicitly in the institutional anomie perspective, focused on how the effect of economic inequality on levels of lethal violence is most pronounced among nations that are also characterized as having weakened institutions of social protection (i.e., the strength of the welfare state). In short, Savolainen argues that "nations that protect their citizens from the vicissitudes of market forces appear to be immune to the homicidal effects of economic inequality."

Drennon-Gala, Don: Social Support and Delinquency

Cullen, F. T. (1994). Social support as an organizing concept for criminology: Presidential address to the Academy of Criminal Justice Sciences. *Justice Quarterly, 11,* 527–559.

Cullen, another early theorist on social support, provides an alternative theory that builds upon literature in mental health. Reflecting his background in corrections and rehabilitation, Cullen's social support theory suggests that criminal offenders have difficulty ceasing their deviant behavior because they lack the adequate social resources and support mechanisms. He suggests that a society and criminal justice system that is focused on providing offenders with the necessary social supports is not only more likely to reduce crime but also is more benevolent.

Drennon-Gala, D. (1994). *The effects of social support and inner containment on the propensity toward delinquent behavior and disengagement in education.* Unpublished doctoral dissertation, University of Rochester.

Drennon-Gala's dissertation was the original work from which his book, Delinquency and High School Dropouts, *was produced. It provides a detailed description of his theoretical statements, a thorough review of the literature, an in-depth discussion of his methodology, and a comprehensive presentation of his findings.*

Drennon-Gala, D. (1995). *Delinquency and high school dropouts: Reconsidering social correlates.* Lanham, MD: University Press of America.

In this book, Drennon-Gala details his hypothesis regarding social support, inner containment, and social bond theory. After a theoretical explanation, he provides a test of his key propositions and finds that social support and inner containment are strongly related to both disengagement from education and delinquency. He closes with his revised model of social bond theory that includes measures of social support.

Hirschi, T. (1969). *Causes of delinquency.* Berkeley: University of California Press.

In this book, Hirschi presents a comprehensive theoretical review of theories of social control, cultural deviance, and strain. He suggests that control theories have a stronger logical and theoretical framework and presents his own control theory on social bonds and delinquency. Hirschi also tests his theory using survey data from a large sample of adolescents and finds that his theory is shown more support than measures of cultural deviance and strain.

Elliott, Delbert S., Suzanne S. Ageton, and Rachelle J. Canter: Integrated Perspective on Delinquency

Elliott, D. S. (1985). The assumption that theories can be combined with increased explanatory power: Theoretical integrations. In R. F. Meier (Ed.), *Theoretical methods in criminology* (pp. 123–149). Beverly Hills, CA: Sage.

In this piece, Elliott discusses the benefits of developing integrated theories of delinquency. Much of the material is part of an ongoing debate between Elliott and Travis Hirschi.

Elliott, D. S., Ageton, S., & Canter, R. (1979). An integrated theoretical perspective on delinquent behavior. *Journal of Research in Crime and Delinquency, 16,* 3–27.

Elliott and colleagues introduce their integrated theory of delinquency in this article. The key components of the theory (strain, social learning, and social control) are discussed and combined into a comprehensive explanation of individual involvement in sustained delinquent behavior.

Elliott, D. S., Huizinga, D., & Ageton, S. (1985). *Explaining delinquency and drug use.* Newbury Park, CA: Sage.

Elliott and colleagues present information from the National Youth Survey (NYS). This book includes a description of the theoretical framework of the study, the research methodology, and study findings.

Hirschi, T. (1979). Separate and unequal is better. *Journal of Research in Crime and Delinquency, 16,* 34–38.

Hirschi presents arguments against the use of integrated theories in criminology. Hirschi presents the benefits of using a "classical approach" in which components of various pure theories are tested against one another.

Hirschi, T. (1989). Exploring alternatives to integrated theory. In S. F. Messner, M. D. Krohn, & A. E. Liska (Eds.), *Theoretical integration in the study of deviance and crime: Problems and prospects* (pp. 37–49). Albany: SUNY Press.

Part of the ongoing debate on the utility of integrated approaches to delinquency between Hirschi and Delbert Elliott, Hirschi offers additional support for the "competing hypothesis" approach to theoretical development.

England, Ralph W.: A Theory of Middle-Class Delinquency

Cernkovich, S. A. (1978). Evaluating two models of delinquency causation. *Criminology, 16,* 335–352.

In this article, Cernkovich tests competing theoretical perspectives on juvenile delinquency, including one of the assumptions of England's theory that adherence to a hedonistic value system is conducive to delinquency. He finds that both elements of both structural (including subcultural) and control theories interact to explain delinquency likelihood.

Eve, R. A. (1975). "Adolescent culture": Convenient myth or reality? A comparison of students and their teachers. *Sociology of Education, 48,* 152–167.

In this article, Eve tests whether, as England proposed, adolescents have a distinct subculture from adults. He reports that adolescents differ from adults in their commitment to values that condone deviant behaviors, but that adolescent values derive mainly from those of adults.

Miller, J. G. (1970). Research and theory in middle-class delinquency. *British Journal of Criminology, 10,* 33–51.

Miller provides a comprehensive discussion on how criminological theories explain delinquent behaviors committed by middle-class youths. He includes a comparison of subcultural theories, including England's theory, with learning, control, and social disorganization theories.

Felson, Richard B., and James T. Tedeschi: Social Interactionist Theory of Violence

Felson, R. B., & Tedeschi, J. T. (Eds.). (1993). *Aggression and violence: Social interactionist perspectives.* Washington, DC: American Psychological Association.

This edited book is based on a 1991 conference held on SUNY Albany campus titled "Social Interactionist Approaches to Aggression and Violence." Participants were asked to prepare more elaborated versions of their presentations that were published as book chapters. The result is an interesting collection of studies providing social interactionist explanations for different forms of violence, and they also compare and contrast social interactionism with alternative explanations for violence.

Tedeschi, J., & Felson, R. B. (1994). *Violence, aggression, and coercive actions.* Washington, DC: American Psychological Association.

This book presents the social interactionist theory of violence, aggression, and coercive actions in great details. The first part includes a careful examination and critique of traditional theories of aggression based on biological, psychological, and criminological perspectives. In the following parts, the authors present their own theory (social interactionism) and a variety of empirical evidence and logical arguments to support it. They also demonstrate how social interactionism can explain specific forms of aggression like family violence and sexual coercion.

Hagan, John, and Bill McCarthy: Social Capital and Crime

Hagan, J., & McCarthy, B. (with Parker, P., & Climenhage, J.). (1997). *Mean streets: Youth crime and homelessness.* Cambridge, UK: Cambridge University Press.

In this award-winning book, Hagan and McCarthy outline the development and testing of a social capital theory of crime. This rich field study of adolescents living on the streets of Vancouver and Toronto, Canada, identifies the risk factors that forced youths to abandon the security of home for the mean streets of the city. The book provides rich insight into street culture, the criminal social capital that is vital to survival on the street, and policy interventions toward alleviating homeless in North American cities.

McCarthy, B., & Hagan, J. (2001). When crime pays: Capital, competence, and criminal success. *Social Forces, 79,* 1035–1059.

In this article, McCarthy and Hagan extend work on occupational success with an examination of prosperity in illicit activities. They demonstrate the importance of human and social capital to economic success but also the salience of personal forms of capital. Their study reveals that personal capital—including a heightened ambition for wealth, an inclination toward risk-taking, specialized skills, a willingness to cooperate, and competence—play important roles in both legal and illegal prosperity.

McCarthy, B., Hagan, J., & Martin, M. J. (2002). In and out of harm's way: Violent victimization and the social capital of fictive street families. *Criminology, 40,* 831–865.

McCarthy and colleagues identify in this article different types of relationships that are important to people living on the street. They describe "street families" as fictive kin that serve as a source of social capital to homeless youths. Their study reveals that street families provide greater protection against criminal victimization than do other street associations.

Krohn, Marvin D.: Networks and Crime

Krohn, M. D. (1986). The web of conformity: A network approach to the explanation of delinquent behavior. *Social Problems, 33,* S81–S93.

This article is mainly a theoretical argument about the effects of multiplex networks on deviance. Here, Krohn focuses on area status and how urban areas are prone to developing higher crime rates due to social distance.

Krohn, M. D., & Massey, J. L. (1980). Social control and delinquent behavior: An examination of the elements of social bond. *Sociological Quarterly, 21,* 529–544.

> *Krohn introduces his theory of the relationship between networks and deviance in this reading. His main goal is to build on Hirschi's work.*

Krohn, M. D., Massey, J. L., & Zielinski, M. (1988). Role overlap, network multiplicity, and adolescent deviant behavior. *Social Psychology Quarterly, 51,* 346–356.

> *This article establishes more empirical evidence for Krohn's theory. The study examines adolescent's social network multiplexity and the effects on cigarette smoking.*

Krohn, M. D., Stern, S. B., Thornberry, T. P., & Jang, S. J. (1990). *Family processes and initiation of delinquency and drug use: The impact of parent and adolescent perceptions.* Albany, NY: Rochester Youth Development Study, Hindelang Criminal Justice Research Center, University at Albany.

> *This is an empirical study on the effects of parental involvement on adolescent deviance. It concludes that adolescents who have stronger relationships with their parents are less likely to exhibit deviant behavior.*

LaFree, Gary D.: Legitimacy and Crime

Blumstein, A., & Wallman, J. (Eds.). (2000). *The crime drop in America.* Cambridge, UK: Cambridge University Press.

> *This collection of readings represents a variety of explanations of the decline in crime in the United States.*

LaFree, G. D. (1998). *Losing legitimacy: Street crime and the decline of social institutions in America.* Boulder, CO: Westview.

> *In this book, LaFree fully explains institutional legitimacy theory.*

Robinson, T. H. (2003). Towards bridging the gap between micro and macro levels of analysis in criminology. *Dissertation Abstracts International: The Humanities and Social Sciences, 63,* 4101.

> *This dissertation provides an extensive analysis of institutional legitimacy theory. It is not an empirical test of the theory, but it examines the logic and theoretical construction of institutional legitimacy theory.*

Thornberry, Terence P.: Interactional Theory

Jang, S. J. (2002). The effects of family, school, peers, and attitudes on adolescents' drug use: Do they vary with age? *Justice Quarterly, 19,* 97–126.

> *Jang tested interactional theory's developmental hypotheses about changing influence of four interactional variables (attachment to parents, commitment to school, drug-using peers, and pro-drug attitudes) on drug use across the ages of adolescence. While age-varying effects were found, observed patterns were only partly consistent with the theory.*

Krohn, M. D., Lizotte, A. J., Thornberry, T. P., Smith, C., & McDowall, D. (1996). Reciprocal causal relationships among drug use, peers, and beliefs: A five-wave panel model. *Journal of Drug Issues, 26,* 405–428.

> *Analyzing longitudinal data, Krohn and his colleagues estimated a model of interrelationships among peer drug use, peer reactions to drug use, beliefs about drug use, and adolescent drug use. Findings generally support the hypotheses of reciprocal causal relationships among the variables.*

Thornberry, T. P. (1996). Empirical support for interactional theory: A review of the literature. In J. D. Hawkins (Ed.), *Delinquency and crime: Current theories* (pp. 198–235). New York: Cambridge University Press.

> *This article provides an overview of empirical findings about interactional theory. Given the lack of test of the theory's developmental hypotheses, Thornberry focused on studies examining bidirectional relationships among interactional variables.*

Tittle, Charles R.: Control Balance Theory

Braithwaite, J. (1997). Charles Tittle's control balance and criminological theory. *Theoretical Criminology, 1,* 77–97.

> *Braithwaite provides one of the first critiques of control-balance theory.*

Hickman, M., & Piquero, A. R. (2001). Exploring the relationship between gender, control balance and deviance. *Deviant Behavior, 22,* 323–351.

> *Hickman and Piquero apply control-balance theory to explain gender differences in crime.*

Piquero, N. L., & Piquero, A. R. (2006). Control balance and exploitative corporate crime. *Criminology, 44,* 397–430.

Piquero and Piquero apply control-balance theory to the study of corporate crime.

18. Theories of White-Collar and Corporate Crime

Anomie and White-Collar Crime

Clinard, M. B., & Yeager, P. C. (2006). *Corporate crime.* New Brunswick, NJ: Transaction.

This is an updated and well-sourced volume on issues regarding organizational crimes for profit.

Cullen, F. T. (1984). *Rethinking crime and deviance theory: The emergence of a structuring tradition.* Totowa, NJ: Rowman and Allenhend.

Cullen took Cloward and Ohlin's theory and applied it to crime generally, showing the importance of differentiating between various types of deviant adaptation.

Ermann, M. D., & Lundman, R. J. (Eds.). (2002). *Corporate and governmental deviance: Problems of organizational behavior in contemporary society* (6th ed.). New York: Oxford University Press.

A classic reader revealing the nature and harms of upperworld illegality.

Geis, G., Meier, R. F., & Salinger, L. M. (Eds.). (1995). *White-collar crime: Classic and contemporary views* (3rd ed.). New York: Free Press.

A good collection of significant contributions to the white-collar crime literature.

Kwitny, J. (1987). *The crimes of patriots: The true tale of dope, dirty money, and the CIA.* New York: W. W. Norton.

This is a good study of how well-integrated actors pursuing legitimate national objectives may engage in serious misconduct.

Passas, N., & Goodwin, N. (Eds.). (2004). *It's legal, but it ain't right: Harmful social consequences of legal industries.* Ann Arbor: University of Michigan Press.

This collection of essays illustrates the importance of exploring the concept of white-collar crime beyond legal definitions, while at the same time shunning moralistic and subjective positions. It shows how the pursuit of legitimate economic goals by legal organizations generates consequences more socially harmful than what others call "organized crime."

Pontell, H. N., & Geis, G. (Eds.). (2007). *International handbook of white-collar and corporate crime.* New York: Springer.

A recent international collection of contributions to the white-collar crime criminology.

Vaughan, D. (1996). *The* Challenger *launch decision: Risky technology, culture and deviance at NASA.* Chicago: University of Chicago Press.

Excellent case study of organizational deviance analyzed through the lens of the anomie tradition.

Benson, Michael L.: The Collateral Consequences of White-Collar Offending

Conklin, J. E. (1977). *Illegal but not criminal: Business crime in America.* Englewood Cliffs, NJ: Prentice Hall.

This book focuses on the intricacies of various types of business crime, public attitudes toward business crime, and possible mechanisms for control of business crime. The book also discusses specific cases of business crime, as well as offender rationalizations for engaging in such behavior.

Cressey, D. R. (1953). *Other people's money: A study in the social psychology of embezzlement.* New York: Free Press.

Donald Cressey chronicles lengthy prison interviews with incarcerated felons convicted of embezzlement. He contends that three common themes are central to cases of embezzlement for offenders: (1) the existence of financial problems and the opportunity to engage in crime, (2) intricate knowledge of the business environment in order to engage in embezzlement, and (3) rationalizations for engaging in embezzlement.

Capitalism and White-Collar Crime

Cullen, F. T., Cavender, G., Maakestad, W. J., & Benson, M. L. (2006). *Corporate crime under attack: The fight to criminalize business violence* (2nd ed.). Newark, NJ: LexisNexis.

This book examines one of the most famous cases in the history of corporate crime: the trial of the Ford Motor Company for negligent homicide in the design and manufacture of the Ford Pinto automobile. It includes chapters on the history and contemporary status of the law in regards to corporate crime.

Friedrichs, D. O. (2007). *Trusted criminals: White-collar crime in contemporary society* (3rd ed.). Belmont, CA: Wadsworth.

> *This book presents an encyclopedic treatment of the literature on white-collar crime. It covers the history of the concept of white-collar crime, its many different forms and types, theories of white-collar crime, and official reactions to white-collar crime in the criminal justice system.*

Shover, N., & Hochstetler, A. (2006). *Choosing white-collar crime.* New York: Cambridge University Press.

> *This book treats recent developments in white-collar crime. It has particularly good treatments of the effects of globalization on opportunities for white-collar crime and of the differences between elite corporate crime and ordinary white-collar crime.*

Clinard, Marshall B.: The Black Market

Clinard, M. B. (1983). *Corporate ethics and crime: The role of middle management.* Beverly Hills, CA: Sage.

> *Based on interview with officials from Fortune 500 companies, Clinard probes how middle managers view ethics and illegal behavior.*

Clinard, M. B., & Yeager, P. C. (1980). *Corporate crime.* New York: Free Press.

> *In this classic study that updates Edwin Sutherland's* White Collar Crime, *Clinard and Yeager provide systematic empirical information on the extent of corporate illegality. They also develop a framework for understanding why crime flourishes in corporate organizations and explore policies for controlling lawlessness in the upperworld.*

Cressey, Donald R.: Embezzlement and White-Collar Crime

Cressey, D. R. (1973). *Other people's money: A study in the social psychology of embezzlement.* Montclair, NJ: Patterson Smith. (Original work published 1953)

> *The short monograph demonstrates the use of the technique of analytic induction to study the financial violation of trust.*

Cressey, D. R. (1989). The poverty of theory in corporate crime research. In W. S. Laufer & F. Alder (Eds.), *Advances in criminological theory* (Vol. 1, pp. 31–56). New Brunswick, NJ: Transaction.

> *Cressey's iconoclasm is on display in his powerful criticism of the view that corporations can be treated in criminology as human entities because the criminal law so regards them.*

Cressey, D. R. (1990). Learning and living. In B. Berger (Ed.), *Authors of their own lives: Intellectual autobiographies by twenty American sociologists* (pp. 235–259). Berkeley: University of California Press.

> *Cressey, along with 19 other eminent sociologists, offers autobiographical information about his background and his scholarly work.*

Laub, J. H. (1983). Interview with Donald R. Cressey: March 29, 1979. In J. H. Laub (Ed.), *Criminology in the making* (pp. 131–165). Boston: Northeastern University Press.

> *Cressey responds to a series of questions regarding his life, work habits, and his views of various criminological theories.*

Croall, Hazel: Individual Differences and White-Collar Crime

Clinard, M. B., & Quinney, R. (1973). Occupational criminal behavior. *Criminal behavior systems: A typology* (2nd ed., pp. 187–205). New York: Holt, Rinehart and Winston.

> *Clinard and Quinney introduce two typologies of white-collar crime: occupational crime and corporate crime. They discuss the ability of white-collar offenders to use their role as professionals to monitor and define illegality in their behaviors. Specifically, they focus on the role that professional associations play in monitoring and defining illegality.*

Daly, K. (1989). Gender and varieties of white-collar crime. *Criminology, 27,* 769–794.

> *This is another work that questions the stereotype of the white-collar criminal. Daly examines the socioeconomic status of men and women and demonstrates that a majority of the women employed were clerical workers and most of the men were managers or administrators. Also, she raises questions regarding the relationship between gender, social status, and race in which white-collar criminals get caught and prosecuted.*

Sutherland, E. H. (1940). White-collar criminality. *American Sociological Review, 5,* 1–12.

> *Sutherland discusses crimes that include corporate business violations committed by those of the upper-class for the purposes of developing a more comprehensive theory of criminal behavior. He also examines ways in which upper-class offenders can*

shape the law and manipulate the system, thus allowing the elites to influence the administration of the law. For this reason, Sutherland's introduction of the term white-collar crime *into the criminological community purposely generalizes this concept to focus on powerful corporations and elite offenders.*

Geis, Gilbert: Perspectives on White-Collar Crime Scandals

Pontell, H. N., & Geis, G. (Eds.). (2007). *International handbook of white-collar and corporate crime.* New York: Springer.

White-collar and corporate crimes have recently gained international attention and concern. In this recent text, well-known authorities from around the world contribute original chapters regarding numerous issues in white-collar and corporate crime, many of which relate directly to the global economy.

Rosoff, S. M., Pontell, H. N., & Tillman, R. (2010). *Profit without honor: White-collar crime and the looting of America* (5th ed.). Upper Saddle River, NJ: Prentice Hall.

This widely cited book provides a substantive and thorough overview of white-collar and corporate crime that incorporates detailed and rich case histories, social and theoretical analysis, and policy discussion.

Shover, N., & Hochstetler, A. (2006). *Choosing white-collar crime.* New York: Cambridge University Press.

Neal Shover and Andy Hochstetler's thesis regarding the "generative worlds" of white-collar offending and issues of rational choice frame this informed and novel theoretical discussion. It updates an enormous amount of research and provides important and new conceptualizations for understanding a broad range of offenses.

Green, Stuart P.: Moral Theory of White-Collar Crime

Geis, G., Meier, R., & Salinger, L. (Eds.). (1995). *White-collar crime: Classic and contemporary views.* New York: Free Press.

A collaboration of both classic and contemporary literature regarding white collar criminality.

Green, G. (1997). *Occupational crime.* Chicago: Nelson Hall.

Describes white-collar criminality as being largely occupational and used by individuals in their legitimate positions of employment. Examines

criminological theory and its application to specific white collar offenses.

Rawls, J. (1971). *A theory of justice.* Cambridge, MA: Harvard University Press.

Examines the concept of social justice through a politically philosophical framework.

Individual Differences and White-Collar Crime

Piquero, N. L., & Weisburd, D. (2009). Developmental trajectories of white-collar crime. In S. Simpson & D. Weisburd (Eds.), *The criminology of white-collar crime* (pp. 153–174). New York: Springer.

Some of the strongest works in this field arise from a wealth of longitudinal research on a dataset of U.S. federal offenders in the 1970s. Piquero and Weisburd's essay summarizes and further develops this earlier work on white-collar criminal careers.

Shover, N., & Hochstetler, A. (2006). *Choosing white-collar crime.* New York: Cambridge University Press.

Shover and Hochstetler, especially in chapters 3 and 5 of their book, provide a thoughtful analysis of white-collar crime and the factors that influence decision making.

Integrated Theories of White-Collar Crime

Barak, G. (1998). *Integrating criminologies.* Boston: Allyn & Bacon.

This book remains the single most thorough survey of the issues involved in integrated theories of crime, authored by a prominent and prolific critical criminologist.

Friedrichs, D. O. (2010). *Trusted criminals: White collar crime in contemporary society* (4th ed.). Belmont, CA: Wadsworth/Cengage Learning.

The text by the author of this entry is the most comprehensive survey of what is known about white-collar crime and its control. It includes a chapter reviewing virtually all theories—including integrated theories—applied to white-collar crime.

Pontell, H., & Geis, G. (Eds.). (2007). *International handbook of white-collar and corporate crime.* New York: Springer.

This handbook, edited by two leading white-collar crime scholars, includes a number of articles of relevance to integrated theories of white-collar crime.

Schlegel, K., & Weisburd, D. (Eds.). (1992). *White-collar crime reconsidered.* Boston: Northeastern University Press.

This collection of articles, originally papers presented at a conference commemorating Edwin H. Sutherland, includes some important contributions by Braithwaite, Coleman, and Vaughan, on integrated theories of white-collar crime.

Michalowski, Raymond J., and Ronald C. Kramer: State-Corporate Crime

Kauzlarich, D., & Kramer, R. (1998). *Crimes of the nuclear state: At home and abroad.* Boston: Northeastern University Press.

Kauzlarich and Kramer analyze the interaction of state and private entities in facilitating massive environmental crimes spanning many decades, and in doing so both apply and develop concepts relevant to state-corporate crime.

Kramer, R. C., Michalowski, R. J., & Kauzlarich, D. (2002). The origins and development of the concept and theory of state-corporate crime. *Crime and Delinquency, 48,* 263–282.

Kramer et al. chronicle the historical development of the concept of state-corporate crime and discuss its relation to existing criminological theory.

Michalowski, R. J., & Kramer, R. C. (Eds.). (2006). *State-corporate crime: Wrongdoing at the intersection of business and government.* New Brunswick, NJ: Rutgers University Press.

This represents the most recent contribution from the progenitors of the concept of state-corporate crime. In collaboration with a number of researchers, they examine a variety of tragic historical events that resulted from a confluence of organizational forces.

Pontell, Henry N., and Kitty Calavita: Explaining the Savings and Loan Scandal

Black, W. K. (2005). *The best way to rob a bank is to own one.* Austin: University of Texas Press.

Authored by a former savings and loan regulator, this book uses economic and criminological theories to explain how corrupt CEOs and CFOs, with the aid of industry regulators and politicians, perpetrated massive accounting fraud. Special attention is given to Charles Keating.

Rational Choice and White-Collar Crime

Benson, M. L., & Simpson, S. S. (2009). *White-collar crime: An opportunity perspective.* New York: Routledge.

Provides a detailed analysis of how opportunities available within organizational settings shape the criminal choices that white-collar offenders make.

Shover, N., & Hochstedler, A. (2006). *Choosing white-collar crime.* New York: Cambridge University Press.

Details the factors that "bound" or circumscribe the "rational" choice to engage in white-collar crime.

Ross, E. A.: Sin and Society

Borgatta, E. F., & Meyer, H. J. (Eds.). (1959). *Social control and the foundations of sociology: Pioneer contributions of Edward Alsworth Ross to the study of society.* Boston: Beacon Press.

This volume contains versions of two of Ross's major works, each edited to half its original length but retaining substantive content and conclusions, as well as the author's distinctive literary style.

Hertzler, J. O. (1951). Edward Alsworth Ross: Sociological pioneer and interpreter. *American Sociological Review, 16,* 609–613.

This review of Ross's life and achievements contains a complete list of all his published works.

McMahon, S. H. (1999). *Social control and public intellect: The legacy of Edward A. Ross.* New Brunswick, NJ: Transaction.

Sean McMahon's intellectual biography traces Ross's career as an activist and academic. The author discusses Ross's major works and makes extensive use of unpublished lectures, speeches, and essays, as well as Ross's letters and correspondence.

Ross, E. A. (1977). *Seventy years of it: An autobiography.* New York: Arno Press.

Originally published in 1936, this illustrated autobiography gives a spirited account of Ross's life as scholar, traveler, activist, and reporter.

Sutherland, Edwin H.: White-Collar Crime

Geis, G. (2007). *White-collar and corporate crime.* Upper Saddle River, NJ: Prentice Hall.

Considers the developments in the realm of white-collar crime that have followed in the wake of

Sutherland's original work. Discusses definitional issues, research contributions, and the historical background of white-collar crime.

Sutherland, E. H. (1983). *White collar crime: The uncut version.* New Haven, CT: Yale University Press.

The restored full text of Sutherland's pioneering statement on white-collar crime.

Vaughan, Diane: The Normalization of Deviance

Calavita, K., Pontell, H. N., & Tillman, R. (1997). *Big money crime: Fraud and politics in the savings and loan crisis.* Berkeley: University of California Press.

In this study of the savings and loan crisis of the 1980s, Calavita, Pontell, and Tillman analyze how deregulation created a criminogenic environment that fostered the commission of various forms of fraud in the thrift industry. What they characterize as collective embezzlement appears to have resulted, in part, from elastic norms in the industry that normalized deviance within savings and loan institutions.

Kramer, R. (2010). From Guernica to Hiroshima to Baghdad: The normalization of the terror bombing of civilian populations. In W. J. Chambliss, R. J. Michalowski, & R. C. Kramer (Eds.), *State crime in the global age* (pp. 118–133). Devon, UK: Willan.

This study analyzes how international outrage over the terror bombing of civilians at Guernica and other places prior to World War II was transformed into general acceptance and support for such practices, including the use of atomic bombs against Japan, by the war's end. Kramer argues that the socially constructed morality of war goals, the instrumental rationality of military bureaucracies, and the legitimation of state violence through the failures of international law combined to normalize the bombing of civilians within the political culture and war planning organizations of the United States and the United Kingdom.

Pontell, H. N., & Geis, G. (Eds.). (2007). *International handbook of white-collar and corporate crime.* New York: Springer.

This book is an outstanding collection of articles on white-collar and organizational crime by internationally renowned scholars. Diane Vaughan's contribution to this volume is a clear, concise overview of her theoretical strategy; the concepts of situated action and the normalization of deviance;

and the connection between causes and strategies for social control.

19. Contemporary Gang Theories

Bourgois, Philippe: In Search of Respect

DeKeseredy, W. S., Alvi, S., & Schwartz, M. D. (2006). Left realism revisited. In W. S. DeKeseredy & B. Perry (Eds.), *Advancing critical criminology: Theory and application* (pp. 19–42). Lanham, MD: Lexington.

This chapter offers readers and researchers alike an in-depth overview of left realism, which is a major subdiscipline of critical criminology.

DeKeseredy, W. S., & Schwartz, M. D. (2002). Theorizing public housing woman abuse as a function of economic exclusion and male peer support. *Women's Health and Urban Life, 1,* 26–45.

This article includes an integrated theory of woman abuse in public housing that is heavily influenced by Bourgois's empirical and theoretical work on drug dealing gangs in East Harlem.

Lewis, O. (1966). *La vida: A Puerto Rican family in the culture of poverty—San Juan and New York.* New York: Random House.

Prior to the publication of In Search of Respect, *this was the last major ethnographic study conducted in El Barrio, and the culture of poverty theory emerged from this research. This theory is flawed for several reasons, but despite its major shortcomings, it is broadcast locally and nationally by leading radio and television personalities.*

Schwartz, M. D., & DeKeseredy, W. S. (1997). *Sexual assault on the college campus: The role of male peer support.* Thousand Oaks, CA: Sage.

This book includes a comprehensive analysis of the ways in which male peer support contributes to sexual assault on the college campus. Rich with theory, this book also includes a review of large-scale survey data gathered in the United States and Canada.

Waterson, A. (1993). *Street addicts in the political economy.* Philadelphia: Temple University Press.

Using rich ethnographic data gathered in New York City, Waterston provides a critical criminological description of the ways in which street addicts' lives are shaped by broader economic, political, and ideological forces.

Wilson, W. J. (1996). *When work disappears: The world of the new urban poor.* New York: Knopf.

This book is essential reading for anyone interested in developing a rich sociological understanding of the relationship between joblessness and drugs in U.S. urban ghettos.

Gangs and the Underclass

Hagedorn, J. M. (1988). *People and folks: Gangs, crime, and the underclass in a rustbelt city* (2nd ed.). Chicago: Lake View Press.

John Hagedorn's classic ethnographic study of gangs in Milwaukee presents a dramatic look at the structural changes that contributed to gang development and continuity. This book provides a quintessential look at "gangs and the underclass."

Moore, J. W. (1978). *Homeboys: Gangs, drugs, and prison in the barrios of Los Angeles.* Philadelphia: Temple University Press.

Joan Moore's classic book on the lives of Latino gang members in Los Angeles presents an intriguing look at how history, culture, and community structure converge to shape gangs in Los Angeles. The connection between street life and prison for the gangs and their members makes this a particularly interesting read.

Moore, J. W. (1991). *Going down to the barrio: Homeboys and homegirls in charge.* Philadelphia: Temple University Press.

This follow-up to Moore's prior work provides additional insight into the lives of male and female gang members, including their involvement in crime, drugs, and violence. This book provides additional insight into Moore's earlier (1978) work.

Wilson, W. J. (1990). *The truly disadvantaged: The inner-city, the underclass, and public policy.* Chicago: University of Chicago Press.

William Julius Wilson provides an intriguing look at the structural conditions contributing to the development of the "underclass." This classic book provided a foundation for much of the research on neighborhood context and structural disadvantage during the past 2 decades.

Horowitz, Ruth, and Gary Schwartz: Honor and Gang Delinquency

Anderson, E. (1999). *Code of the street: Decency violence, and the moral life of the inner city.* New York: W. W. Norton.

This work extends the idea of normative ambiguity to modern day, inner-city communities. Anderson proposes that individuals in crime-prone, urban neighborhoods have two sets of norms, street and decent, that they utilize depending on where and with whom they are interacting.

Horowitz, R., & Schwartz, G. (1974). Honor, normative ambiguity and gang violence. *American Sociological Review, 39,* 238–251.

This work defines the role of normative ambiguity as it relates to the causes of gang violence. Horowitz and Schwartz explain that gang violence is the result of the interpersonal conflict that arises when a gang member's honor is impugned and the resulting disrespect causes the individual to break from the conventional normative response, thereby responding in a manner that would value criminal and violent behavior.

Jankowski, Martin Sanchez: Islands in the Street

Jankowski, M. S. (2002). Representation, responsibility and reliability in participant-observation. In T. May (Ed.), *Qualitative research in action* (pp. 144–160). London: Sage.

This chapter highlights some of the important elements and responsibilities of a researcher conducting participant-observation, such as that done for Islands in the Street. *Jankowski argues that participant-observers have a tremendous responsibility to the groups they study because there is limited opportunity for reliability of findings to be confirmed since replication is nearly impossible. Because there is rarely replication of participant-observations, groups under study must be represented to the public as accurately and fairly as possible.*

Jankowski, M. S. (2003). Gangs and social change. *Theoretical Criminology, 7,* 191–215.

Jankowski explains how American gangs have responded to environmental and social changes over five different eras and that urban characteristics have a significant impact on structural elements of gang membership. In doing so, he further differentiates gang behaviors from other social actions.

Klein, Malcolm W., and Cheryl L. Maxson: Street Gang Structure and Organization

Spergel, I. A. (1995). *The youth gang problem.* New York: Oxford University Press.

Also considered one of the preeminent gang scholars in the field, Spergel provides an exhaustive and intricate analysis of gangs and gang research. In chapter 6 specifically, Spergel discusses at length gang structure and organization, how it differs across gangs, how it develops and evolves, and the many and varied gang typologies already in existence.

Starbuck, D., Howell, J. C., & Lindquist, D. J. (2001). Hybrid and other modern gangs. *Juvenile Justice Bulletin,* Youth Gang Series. Washington, DC: Office of Juvenile Justice and Delinquency Prevention.

A collaborative piece from a widely published gang researcher and a retired gang unit sergeant, this article calls attention to—and describes the recent proliferation of—a new gang type: the "hybrid" gang. With characteristics such as a mixture of racial/ethnic groups, an amalgam of symbols and graffiti from various gangs, shifting membership patterns, and frequent merging and splintering among gangs, the authors discuss the importance in recognizing this gang type as distinct from the more traditional gangs.

Weisel, D. L. (2002). The evolution of street gangs: An examination of form and variation. In W. L. Reed & S. H. Decker (Eds.), *Responding to gangs: Evaluation and research* (pp. 25–65). Washington, DC: National Institute of Justice.

Utilizing data collected from a large-scale survey of police department and in-depth interviews with gang members in two large cities, this article describes different gang types in terms of their characteristics, organizational dimensions, and criminal versatility. The author also observes a great deal of agreement between the two data sources on many of the organizational and structural features of gangs.

Maxson, Cheryl L.: Gang Migration Theorizing

Klein, M. W., & Maxson, C. L. (2006). *Street gangs: Patterns and policies.* New York: Oxford University Press.

This book is a current and thorough review of the available research on many aspects of gangs. In particular, chapter 1 offers a good summary of the work on prevalence, proliferation, and migration.

Maxson, C. L. (1998). *Gang members on the move: Juvenile justice bulletin.* Washington, DC: U.S. Department of Justice, Office of Juvenile Justice and Delinquency Prevention.

This article is the original explication of Maxson's work on gang migration. It includes more in-depth

findings of the original 1992 study conducted by the University of Southern California.

Maxson, C. L., Woods, K. J., & Klein, M. W. (1995). *Street gang migration in the United States.* Unpublished final report, Los Angeles Social Science Research Institute, University of Southern California.

This unpublished report is the basis for the larger University of Southern California study on gang migration. This report provides a longer treatment of the study methods and findings.

Short, James F., Jr.: Gangs and Group Processes

Decker, S. H., & Van Winkle, B. (1996). *Life in the gang: Family, friends, and violence.* Cambridge, UK: Cambridge University Press.

Scott Decker and Barrik Van Winkle interviewed 100 current members in St. Louis to capture intricate details of gang life. Many of these details illuminate Short's key contention that group processes dictate individual crime and delinquency. A key concept the authors offer is how gang involvement perpetuates a constant threat, which often prompts violence.

Short, J. F., Jr. (1998). The level of explanation problem revisited: The American Society of Criminology 1997 Presidential Address. *Criminology, 36,* 3–36.

In this article, Short calls attention to the level of explanation problem in criminology on the largest of platforms—the 1997 presidential address to the American Society of Criminology. Short acknowledged the importance and advances in individual-level research, but that the field "must be sensitive to context" (p. 28).

Thornberry, T. P. (1987). Toward an interactional theory of delinquency. *Criminology, 25,* 863–891.

Terence Thornberry, the principal investigator of the Office of Juvenile Justice and Delinquency Prevention's longitudinal Rochester, New York, site, introduced a bidirectional model of juvenile delinquency. Thornberry called for a merging of major theories at the three levels of explanation and later went on to write Gangs and Delinquency in Developmental Perspective *(2003) based on the Rochester gang youth.*

Vigil, James Diego: Multiple Marginality Theory

Vigil, J. D. (2004). Gangs and group membership: Implications for schooling. In M. A. Gibson, P. Gandara, & J. P. Koyama (Eds.), *School connections: U.S. Mexican youth, peers, and school achievement* (pp. 87–106). New York: Teachers College Press.

> *This additional work by Vigil further examines the relationship between gang membership and schooling.*

Vigil, J. D., & Long, J. M. (1990). Emic and etic perspectives on gang culture: The Chicano case. In C. R. Huff (Ed.), *Gangs in America* (pp. 55–68). Newbury Park, CA: Sage.

> *This is another work that explains a methodological approach to studying gangs. Utilizing this method, to examine Chicano gangs, it outlines characteristics of gangs and gang members.*

20. Theories of Prison Behavior and Insurgency

Colvin, Mark: Social Sources of the New Mexico Prison Riot

Colvin M. (1981). The contradictions of control: Prisons in a class society. *The Insurgent Sociologist, 11*, 33–45.

> *An early publication on prison riots, in this article, Colvin provides an interpretation of the New Mexico Prison riot from a conflict perspective. It offers a critical analysis of how economic and political changes following World War II altered the relationship between the inmate social structure and administrative control structure.*

Colvin, M. (1982). The 1980 New Mexico prison riot. *Social Problems, 29*, 449–462.

> *In this article, Colvin provides a concise overview of the historical context that led up to the riot at the Penitentiary of New Mexico. An emphasis is placed on how political and ideological influences increased the disorganization of both the administrative control structure and the inmate social system.*

Colvin, M., Cullen, F. T., & Vander Ven, T. (2002). Coercion, social support, and crime: An emerging theoretical consensus. *Criminology, 40*, 19–42.

> *This article provides an overview of how changes in the levels of coercion and support in the environment can influence criminal behavior in general. This theory is applied to the prison environment to explain riots in Colvin (2008, see entry reference section).*

DiIulio, J. (1987). *Governing prisons: A comparative study of correctional management.* New York: Free Press.

> *DiIulio suggests that understanding prison management is most pertinent to explaining prison disorganization and violence. Unlike Colvin, DiIulio suggests that effective prison management can control*

even the most unruly inmate populations and that prison violence is primarily the result of failed management.

Useem, B., & Kimball, P. (1989). *States of siege: U.S. prison riots, 1971–1986.* New York: Oxford University Press.

> *This book provides a narrative review of riots that occurred from 1971 to 1986 in order to examine the historical and contextual factors that encourage prison uprisings. Similar to DiIulio, Useem and Kimball argue that riots are caused primarily by administrative breakdown, not the organization of prisoners. Similar to Colvin, they also place high importance on the historical and political context the preceded the riots.*

Useem, B., & Reisig, M. D. (1999). Collective action in prisons: Protests, disturbances, and riots. *Criminology, 37*, 735–760.

> *This article examines factors that cause riots, protests and disturbances. In particular, it investigates the influence that both managerial practices and inmate organization have on collective action.*

DiIulio, John J., Jr.: Prison Management and Prison Order

DiIulio, J. (1989). Managing constitutionally. *Society, 26*(2), 81–82.

> *A response to Toch's (1989) review (see below).*

Reisig, M. (1998). Rates of disorder in higher-custody state prisons: A comparative analysis of managerial practices. *Crime and Delinquency, 44*(2), 229–244.

> *An empirical test of DiIulio's theory using data from prison employees.*

Stohr, M. K., Loverich, N. P., Menke, B. A., & Zupan, L. L. (1994). Staff management in correctional institutions: Comparing DiIulio's "control model" and "employee investment model" outcomes in five jails. *Justice Quarterly, 11*(3), 471–497.

> *An empirical test of DiIulio's theory using data collected from employees of different jails.*

Toch, H. (1989). Being tough versus being fair. *Society, 26*(4), 84.

> *A response to DiIulio (1989, see above).*

Toch, H. (1989). Review of *Governing Prisons*: A comparative study of correctional management. *Society, 26*(2), 86–88.

> *A book review and criticism of* Governing Prisons.

Useem, B., & Reisig, M. (1999). Collective action in prisons: Protests, disturbances, and riots. *Criminology, 37*(4), 735–759.

An empirical test of administrative control theory and it relevance for inmate collective action.

Giallombardo, Rose: Women in Prison

Casey-Acevedo, K., & Bakken, T. (2001). The effect of time on the disciplinary adjustment of women in prison. *International Journal of Offender Therapy and Comparative Criminology, 45,* 489–497.

The authors present a study of female inmates who spent time in a maximum security prison. They examine adaptation to prison and disciplinary infractions over time.

Greer, K. R. (2000). The changing nature of interpersonal relationships in a women's prison. *Prison Journal, 80,* 442–468.

In this article, the author interviews female inmates to gain insight into the subcultures that exist in women's correctional facilities. Results indicate that women in prison do still form subcultures reminiscent of those found in early research, but the structure of the subcultures seems to be changing.

Maeve, M. K. (1999). The social construction of love and sexuality in a women's prison. *Advances in Nursing Science, 21,* 46–65.

Using interviews with female inmates, the author presents a summary of the development and types of relationships in a women's prison. Findings indicate that relationships in prison generally reflect the types of relationships found outside of prison.

Goffman, Erving: Asylums

Goffman, E. (1959). *The presentation of self in everyday life.* New York: Doubleday Anchor.

In this seminal work by Goffman, he presents a dramaturgical approach to understanding social action. The theatrical metaphor implies that the self develops in response to performing for others and simultaneously observing and responding to the direction others give; social life is literally a stage. It can also be argued that this book forms the basis of Goffman's theory of interaction.

Goffman, E. (1967). *Interaction ritual: Essays on face-to-face behavior.* New York: Doubleday Anchor.

The concept of "face" is defined and shown how it conforms individual behavior into socially acceptable forms. Taken with The Presentation of Self in Everyday Life, *this book is often viewed as another step toward Goffman's theory of interaction order.*

Goffman, E. (1974). *Frame analysis: An essay on the organization of experience.* New York: Harper & Row.

The "frame" metaphor is used to address the individualist dilemma and show how structures (i.e., frames) can organize human experiences. When read with The Presentation of Self in Everyday Life *and* Interaction Ritual, *this book can be seen to round out Goffman's theory of interaction.*

Irwin, John, and Donald R. Cressey: Importation Theory

Irwin, J. (1980). *Prisons in turmoil.* Boston: Little, Brown.

In this book, Irwin traces the historical changes in prison paradigms and discusses how prisoners cope with the hardships of institutional life.

Irwin, J. (2005). *The warehouse prison: Disposal of the new dangerous class.* Los Angeles: Roxbury.

In this book, Irwin discusses how prisons have become a receptacle for incapacitating society's most disadvantaged citizens. He discusses the idea that prisons have lost their capacity to reform inmates.

Irwin, J., & Cressey, D. R. (1962). Thieves, convicts and the inmate subculture. *Social Problems, 10,* 142–155.

In this article, Irwin and Cressey first developed and explained the importation model. The authors describe their model and discuss the three unique prison subcultures.

Kruttschnitt, Candace, and Rosemary Gartner: Women and Imprisonment

Kruttschnitt, C., & Gartner, R. (2005). *Marking time in the golden state: Women's Imprisonment in California.* Cambridge, UK: Cambridge University Press.

This book gives a detailed account of Kruttschnitt and Gartner's study of the California Institution for Women and Valley State Prison for Women.

McCorkel, Jill: Gender and Embodied Surveillance

Gartner, R., & Kruttschnitt, C. (2004). A brief history of doing time: The California Institution for Women in the 1960s and the 1990s. *Law and Society Review, 38,* 267–304.

This article discusses the experiences of women prisoners under a penal discourse of rehabilitation in the 1960s compared to the penal discourse characterized by "get tough" sentiments.

Hannah-Moffat, K. (2004). Losing ground. *Social Politics: State, and Society, 11,* 363–385.

In this article, Hannah-Moffat discusses the results of a study of 144 women parole candidates and their parole board decisions. Decisions and discussions are examined in the broader context of gender-responsive policy and how risk is reframed.

McKim, A. (2008). Getting gut-level. *Gender and Society, 22,* 303–323.

This article discusses penal governance of women in a mandated, community-based drug treatment program.

Pollack, S. (2005). Taming the shrew: Regulating prisoners through women-centered mental health programming. *Critical Criminology, 13,* 71–87.

In this article, Pollack discusses the new women-centered mental health agenda that the Correctional Service of Canada has implemented. Pollack discusses that, despite this progressive rhetoric, these processes still serve to regulate women rather than empower them.

Prison Insurgency Theory

Useem, B., & Goldstone, J. A. (2002). Forging social order and its breakdown: Riot and reform in U.S. prisons. *American Sociological Review, 67,* 499–524.

Their most recent work extends their state-centered theory of collective behavior to look at the role of prison administrators and political officials in breaking down and/or restoring social order inside of prisons. They examine two riots from the 1990s, including one at Rikers Island in New York and the other in private prisons in New Mexico.

Useem, B., Graham-Camp, C., & Camp, G. M. (1996). *Resolution of prison riots: Strategies and policies.* New York: Oxford University Press.

The authors examine the stages before, during, and after prison riots. The authors provide real life strategies for policy makers and prison administrators to prevent and deal with these situations.

Useem, B., & Kimball, P. A. (1987). A theory of prison riots. *Theory and Society, 16,* 87–122.

The authors put forth a theory of prison violence based on the social-psychological variable of

identification. *Moreover, they use identification to explain the intensity and duration of prison riots.*

Useem, B., & Reisig, M. D. (1999). Collective action in prisons: Protests, disturbances, and riots. *Criminology, 37,* 735–759.

In this article, the authors explore riots as well as lesser forms of collective behavior inside of prisons, such as protests, work stoppages, and general disturbances. The authors test whether inmate-balance theory or administrative-control theory provide the best explanation for these actions.

Sykes, Gresham M.: Deprivation Theory

Giallombardo, R. (1966). *Society of women: A study of a women's prison.* New York: Wiley.

Giallombardo's work is a useful contrast to Sykes's work due to her focus on women (versus Sykes's focus on men). Her research also occurred within the same general time frame as Sykes's study, allowing more direct comparisons between the two studies.

Hagan, J. (1995). The "imprisoned society": Time turns a classic on its head. *Sociological Forum, 10,* 519–525.

In this review essay, Hagan revisits Sykes's classic work and discusses the applicability of his perspective several decades later. The evolution of correctional facilities and changes to inmate populations and prison administrators forces consideration of whether the deprivations and cultural adaptations described by Sykes remain fully applicable.

Toch, Hans: Coping in Prison

DiIulio, J., Jr. (1991). Review: Understanding prisons: The new old penology. *Law and Social Inquiry, 16,* 65–99.

A review of Coping: Maladaptation in Prisons *and two other studies carried out during the same time period.*

Summers, R., & Dear, G. E. (2003). The prison preference inventory: An examination of substantive validity in an Australian prison sample. *Criminal Justice and Behavior, 30,* 459–482.

An empirical test of the validity of Toch's prison preference inventory.

Toch, H. (1981). Inmate classification as a transaction. *Criminal Justice and Behavior, 8,* 3–14.

Toch outlines his perspective on inmate classification.

Wright, K. (1988). The relationship of risk, needs, and personality classification systems and prison adjustment. *Criminal Justice and Behavior, 15,* 454–471.

An empirical test of the predictive validity of the prison preference inventory.

21. Theories of Fear and Concern About Crime

Altruistic Fear

Madriz, E. (1997). *Nothing bad happens to good girls: Fear of crime in women's lives.* Berkeley: University of California Press.

In this book, Esther Madriz explores fear of crime among a group of urban women suing qualitative techniques. She details the negative consequences of higher levels of personal fear felt by women, which is relevant to gendered patterns in fear for others. She also discusses women's altruistic fear.

Snedker, K. A. (2006). Altruistic and vicarious fear of crime: Fear for others and gendered social roles. *Sociological Forum, 21,* 163–195.

In this essay, Karen Snedker explores fear for others through qualitative interviews of male and female urban residents. She documents the gender differences in altruistic and vicarious fear and the behavioral consequences of fear for others.

Warr, M., & Ellison, C. G. (2000). Rethinking social reactions to crime: Personal and altruistic fear in family households. *American Journal of Sociology, 106,* 551–578.

In this essay, Mark Warr and Christopher Ellison provide an in-depth quantitative analysis of altruistic fear within the household. They report different types of altruistic fear: spousal and parental. This seminal piece has spurred research on altruistic fear.

Chiricos, Ted: Racial Threat and Fear

Chiricos, T., Hogan, M., & Gertz, M. (1997). Racial composition of neighborhood and fear of crime. *Criminology, 35,* 107–131.

This is the first article by Chiricos and colleagues to address the issue of racial threat. It demonstrates a relationship between the perceived racial composition of neighborhoods and fear of crime. However, it does not include a racial threat measure beyond racial composition.

Chiricos, T., McEntire, R., & Gertz, M. (2001). Perceived racial and ethnic composition of neighborhood and perceived risk of crime. *Social Problems, 48,* 322–340.

This article probably provides the fullest explication of the racial threat thesis. It also presents empirical evidence linking minority presence to victimization risk.

Chiricos, T., Welch, K., & Gertz, M. (2004). Racial typification of crime and support for punitive measures. *Criminology, 42,* 359–389.

This represents probably the most explicit test of the racial threat hypothesis at the individual level. It includes specific, individual-level measures of both the association of minorities with crime and punitive sentiments.

Crawford, C., Chiricos, T., & Kleck, G. (1998). Race, racial threat, and sentencing of habitual offenders. *Criminology, 36,* 481–511.

This article represents Chiricos's first effort to directly measure racial threat. It connects county-level indicators of racial threat with the use of Florida's habitual offender law. The results are somewhat counterintuitive but not inconsistent with the racial threat thesis.

Collective Security/Fear and Loathing

Black, D. (1980). *The manners and customs of the police.* New York: Academic Press.

Black discusses the history of the police and the function of the police and law in contemporary society. He introduced the concept of self-help, which he argues is a decentralized form of social control. When the people are threatened by crime and when people cannot rely on the government for protection, they take individual measures in the form of gun ownership to protect themselves. This concept of self-help is closely related to the concept of informal security.

Waskow, A. I. (1966). *From race riot to sit-in, 1919 and the 1960s.* Garden City, NY: Doubleday.

Elaborating Max Weber's thesis of the state with the monopoly of legitimate use of physical force, Waskow discusses the unique situation of U.S. private gun ownership and its use. He predicted that American society was moving in the direction of a "state" in the Weberian sense in the mid-1960s, with inclination to concentrate the use of physical force in the hands of governmental agencies.

Ferraro, Kenneth F.: Risk Interpretation Model

Ferraro, K. F. (1995). *Fear of crime: Interpreting victimization risk.* Albany: SUNY Press.

This is the work in which Ferraro spells out the foundations for his risk interpretation model.

Hale, C. (1996). Fear of crime: A review of the literature. *International Review of Victimology, 4,* 79–150.

In this article, Hale undertakes a thorough review of the literature regarding fear of crime. While over a decade old, the article still provides a good summary of the theoretical perspectives used to explain fear of crime.

Ricketts, M. L. (2007). K-12 teachers' perceptions of school policy and fear of school violence. *Journal of School Violence, 6*(3), 45–67.

In this article, Ricketts reviews the literature regarding Ferraro's risk interpretation model and its various applications. She then applies the risk interpretation model to explain fear among public school teachers in Kentucky.

Fisher, Bonnie S., and Jack L. Nasar: Fear Spots

Fisher, B. S., & Nasar, J. L. (1992). Fear of crime in relation to three exterior site features: Prospect, refuge, and escape. *Environment and Behavior, 24,* 35–65.

In this work, Fisher and Nasar develop the initial components and mechanisms of fear spots. This work is a cornerstone piece in the greater understanding of fear spots.

Fisher, B. S., & Nasar, J. L. (1995). Fear spots in relation to microlevel physical cues: Exploring the overlooked. *Journal of Research in Crime and Delinquency, 32,* 214–239.

Here Fisher and Nasar further test the construct of fear spots and solidify the importance of subcomponents prospect, concealment, and escape.

Lewis, Dan A., and Greta W. Salem: Incivilities and Fear

Hunter, A. (1978). *Symbols of incivility: Social disorder and fear of crime in urban neighborhoods.* Paper presented at the Annual Meeting of the American Society of Criminology, November 8–12, Dallas, TX.

Hunter is widely credited with being the first to tie the concept of incivility to fear of crime. Hunter contends that minor transgressions of community norms are not fear producing per se yet are able to trigger feelings of fear because people associate these incivilities with criminal activity. The greater the incivility, the more our protective vigilance is aroused.

Lewis, D. A., & Salem, G. W. (1986). *Fear of crime: Incivility and the production of a social problem.* New Brunswick, NJ: Transaction.

It is in this book that Lewis and Salem carefully develop their theory of incivility and fear. The book provides a solid theoretical foundation built upon the Chicago School of Social Disorganization and the victimization perspective. The book also reports Lewis and Salem's empirical findings where they find support for the theory.

Wilson, J. Q., & Kelling, G. L. (1982, March). Broken windows: The police and neighborhood safety. *Atlantic Monthly, 249,* 29–38.

Wilson and Kelling's well-known broken windows theory appeared a few years before Lewis and Salem's book on incivility and fear. Whereas Lewis and Salem provided the theoretical foundation for this general line of inquiry, Wilson and Kelling's metaphorical imagery of a broken window popularized the connection between minor misbehavior and fear of crime among a wide audience.

Perceptually Contemporaneous Offenses

Lane, J., & Meeker, J. (2003). Women's and men's fear of gang crimes: Sexual and nonsexual assault as perceptually contemporaneous offenses. *Justice Quarterly, 20,* 337–371.

Lane and Meeker provide an up-to-date and thorough review of the literature on perceptually contemporaneous offenses. This article also presents empirical evidence that fear of rape and fear of assault are perceptually contemporaneous offenses for both women and men.

Warr, M. (1984). Fear of victimization: Why are women and the elderly more afraid? *Social Science Quarterly, 65,* 681–702.

In this article Mark Warr introduced the concept of perceptually contemporaneous offenses and explained its theoretical importance to the study of fear of crime. This article also provided the first empirical evidence supporting the existence of perceptually contemporaneous offenses.

Skogan, Wesley G., and Michael G. Maxfield: Coping With Crime

Lewis, D. A. (Ed.). (1981). *Reactions to crime: Individual and institutional responses.* Beverly Hills, CA: Sage.

The overarching theme of this volume is the importance of the victimization perspective to understanding different responses to crime. The 11 chapters are organized around three interrelated themes: (1) individual's reactions, (2) political dimensions, and (3) institutional responses.

Lewis, D. A., & Salem, G. W. (1981). *Crime and urban community: Toward a theory of neighborhood security.* Washington, DC: National Crime Justice Reference Service.

The authors compare the victimization perspective and the social control perspective as approaches to the study of the impact of crime on the attitudes and reactions of people. They argue that the social control perspective may be a more useful means to address crime and fear. This perspective focuses on the capacity of community organizations to organize collectively to control signs of disorder that lead to increased fear and crime among large-city dwellers.

Podolefsky, A., & DuBow, F. (1981). *Strategies for community crime prevention: Collective responses to crime in urban America.* Springfield, IL: Charles C Thomas.

The authors use the lens of the social problems approach and the victimization prevention approach to understand responses to crime by community and other groups. They describe who participates in these responses, as well as the types, patterns of, and reasons for different types of collective responses. Their conclusions do not support conventional wisdom that individuals are motivated by fear-related factors to participate in collective efforts; rather participation is linked to the social integration to the neighborhood.

Rosenbaum, D. P. (Ed.). (1986). *Community crime prevention: Does it work?* Beverly Hills, CA: Sage.

The overarching theme of this edited volume is to access a fundamental question that grew out of the War on Crime and Reactions to Crime Project: Do citizen and police initiatives have any effect on fear of crime, crime and incivilities in residential, and

commercial areas. Each chapter presents results from 1 of 11 evaluations of citizen or police strategies that were implemented during 1970s and mid-1980s. After critically assessing the evaluations, Yin in the last chapter concludes that overall intervention did succeed in reducing crime and fear.

Stanko, Elizabeth A.: Gender, Fear, and Risk

Stanko, B. (2004). A tribute to 10 years of knowledge. *Violence Against Women, 10,* 1395–1400.

This article discusses some of the things Stanko has learned over the 25 years of research on women and violence and describes her current view of the world.

Stanko, B. (2007). From academia to policy making: Changing police responses to violence against women. *Theoretical Criminology, 11,* 209–219.

This article discusses Stanko's experience moving from the world of academia into the practitioner world, as well as how her academic history influences her current role working with police.

Stanko, E. A. (1985). *Intimate intrusions: Women's experience of male violence.* London: Routledge & Kegan Paul.

This book is the first major work where Stanko makes the argument that women's experience with men's violence is an "ordinary" part of their lives—that they are legitimately afraid because they are constantly in danger from the men that they know (e.g., spouses, boyfriends, friends, and coworkers) and men that they do not know (e.g., strangers).

Stanko, E. A. (1990). *Everyday violence: How women and men experience sexual and physical danger.* London: Pandora.

This is Stanko's second book, where she interviews both men and women about their experiences with danger and discusses her argument that most people have learned to manage these situations as part of their daily lives.

Index

Entry titles and their page numbers are in **bold**.

Heimer, Karen, and Stacy De Coster: the gendering of violent delinquency, 1:437–439
Helvétius, Claude, 1:88–89, 93
Henggeler, Scott, 2:689
Henry, Stuart, 2:729, 731
Herding culture, 2:866
Heredity, as factor in crime, 1:17, 19, 59–61, 106, 275–277, 354, 380, 2:602–605, 1035–1037. *See also* Biosocial criminology; Criminal biology; **Prenatal influences and crime; Psychophysiology and crime** Raine's research, 2:768–770
Herrnstein, Richard J., 1:xliv, 2:834, 1014–1017
Herrnstein, Richard J., and Charles Murray: crime and *The Bell Curve*, 1:444–447
Hesseling, Rene, 1:162
Heusmann, Rowell, 2:599
Hewitt, John D., 2:781–784
Hibbeln, Joseph, 2:668
Hiday, Virginia Aldigé, 2:609
Hiding places, 1:341
Hilal, Musa, 2:904
Hill, Terrence, 2:715
Hindelang, Michael J., Michael R. Gottfredson, and James Garofalo: lifestyle theory, 1:445, 448–451, 2:675. *See also* Cohen, Lawrence E., and Marcus K. Felton: routine activity theory
   antecedents of lifestyle, 1:449
   background, 1:448–449
   lifestyle and exposure, 1:449–450
   propositions of theory, 1:450
   reassessment of, 1:450–451
Hipp, John, 1:96
Hipsters, 2:917
Hirschi, Travis, 1:xxxvii–xxxix, xliii, xliv, 13, 52, 118, 140, 234–235, 273, 274, 288, 290–291, 371, 403, 445, 470, 527, 529, 2:604–605, 607, 645, 675, 786, 844, 992, 1013. *See also* **Gottfredson, Michael R., and Travis Hirschi: self-control theory; Hirschi, Travis: social control theory**
   A General Theory of Crime, 1:xxxvii–xxxviii, 392, 457, 2:1017
Hirschi, Travis: social control theory, 1:282, 451–457, 514, 2:656, 676, 780
   attachment to friends, 1:454–455
   attachment to parents, 1:453
   attachment to school, 1:453–454
   belief, 1:456–457
   Causes of Delinquency, 1:xxxiii, 451, 453, 514, 2:583
   commitment to conventional goals, 1:455–456
   elements of the social bond, 1:452–453
   empirical research, 1:453–457
   involvement in conventional activities, 1:456
   significance of, 1:451
   street culture, 1:421
Hirst, Paul, 2:578
Historical materialism, 2:579
Hitler, Adolf, 2:685
Hobbes, Thomas, 1:451
Hoek, H. W., 2:735

Hogan, Michael, 1:159
Hogan, Richard, 1:209
Hoke, Scott, 1:283
Hollander, Jocelyn, 1:39–40
Holmes, Oliver Wendell, 1:307
Homel, Ross, 1:232
Home Office Research and Planning Unit, 1:216
Homicides
   seductions of crime, 1:497–498
   stages, 1:569–570
   subculture of violence theory, 2:1025–1029
Homies, 1:366
Homosexuality, female inmates and, 1:366
Homosocial reproduction, 2:883–884
Honor, 1:461–464
Honor, and Southern subculture of violence, 2:865–866
hooks, bell, 2:619
Hooton, Earnest A.: the American criminal, 1:458–460, 521, 2:834
Horney, Julie, 2:595
Horowitz, Ruth, and Gary Schwartz: honor and gang delinquency, 1:461–464
   gang violence defined, 1:461–462
   theories of gang violence, 1:462
   theory and empirical work, 1:463
Horton, Henry, 1:136
Horwood, L. John, 2:647, 649
Hostile attribution model/style, 1:175–176, 269–272
Hot deals (savings and loan crisis), 2:727
Hot spots. *See* **Crime hot spots**
House Banking Committee, 2:725
Howard, John, 1:76
Howard, Kenneth, 2:842
Huesmann, Rowell, 1:176
Hughes, Everett C., 1:80, 383, 407, 2:651, 652
Hughes, Timothy, 1:467
Hugon, Daniel, 2:1036
Human capital, 1:78, 2:788–789
Human nature
   Bentham, 1:89
   selfishness of, 1:451
   Wilson and Herrnstein, 2:1014–1017
Human smuggling, 2:639
Hume, David, 1:89
Hunt, Alan, 1:477
Hunt, Scott A., 2:1008–1011
Hunter, Albert, 1:127, 554, 2:929
Hutchinson, Anne, 1:303
Hyporesponsiveness, 2:603

Id, 1:346
Identity, stripping individuals of, 1:385
Illegitimate means. *See* **Cloward, Richard A.: the theory of illegitimate means**
Illegitimate opportunity structures, 1:30
Image, and defensible space, 2:665
Imitation, 1:24. *See also* Modeling

Law, Moira, **2:**606
Law enforcement, discrimination in, **1:**475
Law Enforcement Assistance Administration (LEAA), **2:**859
Lay, Kenneth, **2:**774
Lazarsfeld, Paul, **1:**407, **2:**749
Lea, John, **1:**546, 549
Lead, toxic effects of, **1:**299–300
Leary, Timothy, **1:**143
Le Blanc, Marc: an integrated personal control theory of deviant behavior, 1:543–546
  constraints, **1:**544
  contextual factors, **1:**544
  control mechanisms, **1:**543–544
  development of personal control, **1:**545–546
  prosocial model, **1:**544
  self-control, **1:**544
  social bonding, **1:**543
  structure of personal control, **1:**544–545
Leclerc, Benoit, **2:**595
Lee, David, **1:**284
Lee, Matthew, **2:**659
Lee, Yoon Ho, **2:**918
Left realism criminology, 1:104–105, **546–549, 2:**938
Legal positivism, **1:**90, 93
Legitimacy. *See* Institutional legitimacy
Legitimate subculture, in prison, **1:**488
Leistico, A. M. R., **1:**429
Lemert, Edwin, 1:22, 80, **2:**616
Lemert, Edwin: primary and secondary deviance, 1:550–552, 2:581, 584
Leniency theory, **2:**724
Lenza, Michael, **1:**209
Leonard, Kenneth, **1:**32
Leopold, Peter, **1:**76
Lester, David, **1:**364
Letkemann, Peter, *Crime Work*, **2:**908
Level of Service Inventory (LSI–adult and youth versions), **1:**360
Levels of control. *See* **Bursik, Robert J., Jr., and Harold C. Grasmick: levels of control**
Levi, Michael, **1:**357, 470
Levin, David, **1:**467
Levine, Harry, **1:**158
Levine, Stephen, **1:**310
Levitt, Steven, *Freakonomics*, **1:**287
Lewis, Dan A., and Greta W. Salem: incivilities and fear, 1:552–555
  empirical test, **1:**554–555
  social control perspective, **1:**553–554
  theoretical development, **1:**553–554
  victimization perspective, **1:**553
Lewis, Helen Block, **1:**113
Lewis, Oscar, **1:**103
Lex talionis ("an eye for an eye"), **1:**76
Li, Spencer, **2:**700
Liberal feminism, **1:**4
Liberation of women, and rising crime rates, **1:**xxxiv, xxxv, 3–5, 133, 222, 413, **2:**849–850, 852
Libido, **1:**346

Life-course criminology, **2:**574
Life-course interdependence, 1:555–557
Life-course-persistent offenders (LCPs), **1:**xxxix, 11, 238, **2:**645–649, 661–662
Life-course theory of crime, **1:**xxxviii–xxxix, 138–140, **2:**948. *See also* **Criminal career paradigm; Sampson, Robert J., and John H. Laub: age-graded theory of informal social control**
Life domains, **1:**16–18
Lifestyle factors, victimization correlated with, **1:**188–190
Lifestyle theory
  Hindelang, Gottfredson, and Garofalo, **1:**448–451
  routine activity theory, **1:**186–192
  Walters, **2:**989–991
Lilly, J. Robert, **2:**617, 844
Limbic psychotic trigger action, **1:**293
Lindesmith, Alfred R., **1:**142, 225
  The Addict and the Law, **1:**143
Linked financing, **2:**727
Lipset, Seymour Martin, **1:**xxxiv
Lipsey, Mark, **1:**240
Lipton, Robert, **1:**33
Liquid ethnography, **1:**252
Liska, Allen, **1:**140, 158, **2:**767
Liu, J., **2:**736
Liu, Jianghong, **2:**668
Lochner, Lance, **2:**700
Locke, Harvey, **1:**424–425
Locke, John, **1:**89
Loeber, Rolf, and Magda Stouthamer-Loeber: pathways to crime, 1:557–560
Loevinger, Jane, **1:**509
Loewenstein, George, **2:**719
Loftin, Colin, **1:**192, **2:**699
Loftland, John, **1:**462
Lombroso, Cesare: The criminal man, 1:xxxii, xli, 58, 59, 307, 335, 352–353, 389, 434, 521, **560–564, 2:**661, 1035
  biography, **1:**561–562
  critiques of, **1:**458–459
  influence of, **1:**476, 560–561, **2:**681
  The Criminal Man, **1:**561, 563
Lombroso, Cesare: The female offender, 1:132, 502, 564, **565–568, 2:**722, 862
  female born criminal, **1:**567–568
  female criminal type, **1:**567
  physical anomalies, **1:**566–567
Long, Janet, **2:**777, 780
Longitudinal studies, **2:**700–701, 708–709, 844
Loock, C. A., **2:**734
Looking glass self, **1:**72
Lopez, Vera, **1:**183
Los Angeles, **1:**131–134, 350–351, **2:**650–653
Lower class, and delinquency, **2:**642–644
Low-level chronic offenders, **2:**648
Lowney, Kathleen, **2:**868
Loyalty/disloyalty, **1:**401, **2:**697–698
Lozoff, Bo, **2:**692
Luciano, Charles "Lucky," **1:**144, 146

National Longitudinal Survey of Youth (NLSY), 1:236, 395, 444–447, 2:853
National Rifle Association, 1:193
National Science Foundation, 1:257
National Youth Survey (NYS), 1:51, 288, 290, 2:581–583, 696
National Youth Survey–Family Study, 1:290
Naturalism, 2:583–584
Natural selection, 1:292, 354
Nature, 1:326–329. *See also* **Environmental toxins theory**
Nature vs. nurture debate, 1:431, 434
Nazis, 1:61, 307, 2:682, 685
Nebbit, Vonn, 1:209
Necessarily included charges, 2:896
Needleman, Herbert, 1:299–300
Negative emotionality, 1:541
Negative opportunity, 1:4
Negativism, 2:894
Negotiated coexistence, 2:657–660
Neighborhoods. *See also* Communities
    broken windows theory, 2:1018–1021
    defining, 2:831–832
    delinquent subcultures, 2:870–873
    deviant places, 2:881–883
    differential association theory, 2:904
    disorder, 2:856, 858
    gendered experience of, 2:638–639
    incarceration policies' effect on, 2:787–791
    intra-neighborhood crime, 2:657–660
    Korbin, 1:507–508
    opportunities offered by, 2:783
    physical environment and crime, 2:712–715
    social control, 1:127, 2:657–660, 927–928
    social disorganization, 1:128, 2:927–928
    truly disadvantaged, 2:1022–1025
Neoliberalism, 1:57
Nervous system. *See* Autonomic nervous system (ANS) theory
Netherlands, 1:1
Nettler, Gwynn, 1:227, 471
Networks. *See* Social networks
Neugebauer, R., 2:735
Neumann, Craig, 1:428
Neuroandrogeny, 1:292–295
Neurobiology, schizophrenia and, 2:816–817
Neurology and crime, 2:661–664. *See also* Autonomic nervous system (ANS) theory
    evidence from traumatic brain injuries, 2:663–664
    policy implications, 2:768–770
    Raine, 2:768–770
    theories, 2:661–663
Neuropsychological factors, 2:646
Neurosis, 1:347
Neuroticism (PEN model), 1:308–310
Neutralization. *See* **Sykes, Gresham M., and David Matza: techniques of neutralization**
Nevin, Rick, 1:299
Newbold, Greg, 1:208, 209, 210
Newburn, Tim, 2:622

New criminologies, 1:xxxiv–xxxv, 46, 249, 2:936–940
New Jersey State Penitentiary, 2:915
New Labor Party, 2:939
Newman, Graham, 1:164
Newman, Oscar: defensible space theory, 1:116, 341, 2:664–667, 753
    Defensible Space, 1:115, 496
New phrenology, 2:711
Newton, Huey P., 1:143
New York City, 1:131–134, 2:857, 1020
Niches, in prison environment, 2:966
Nichols, Charles, 1:478
Nicotine, prenatal exposure to, 2:734
Nightstick law, 2:968
Nisbett, Richard, 2:865–866
Nixon, Richard M., 1:143
Nominee lending, 2:727
Non-custodial sentences, recidivism following, 1:467–468
Non-legal sanctions, 1:185–188, 2:1011–1013
Non-shareable problems, 1:226
Nonviolence, 2:691–692
Normal crimes, 2:895–898
Normal distribution, 1:305, 2:750, 751
Normative ambiguity, 1:461–464
Norström, T., 1:34
North, Oliver, 1:145
Norway, 1:1
Norwegian Association for Penal Reform (KROM), 1:2
Nurture assumption, 1:431–433
Nutrition and crime, 2:667–669, 735–736
Nye, F. Ivan, 1:22, 118, 2:778, 786, 992
Nye, F. Ivan: family controls and delinquency, 2:670–673
NYS. *See* National Youth Survey

Oberholser, Winfred, 1:458
O'Brien, Robert, 1:96
Observational learning, 1:69
Ochsner, A. J., 1:306, 307
O'Donnell, Ian, 1:64
Oettingen, Alexander von, 1:58
Offenders. *See also* Criminals
    continuity in criminal behavior, 2:646
    discontinuity in criminal behavior, 2:646–647
    drivenness of, 1:162–163
    Freudian theory applied to, 1:348
    gender and, 1:29–30, 2:885–888
    persistent, 1:xxxix, 11, 60, 2:846–848, 889–893, 1017
    rationality of, 1:160–161
    serious, 1:29–30
    victims in relation to, 2:634
Office of Juvenile Justice and Delinquency Prevention, 1:84, 352, 2:705
Office of the Comptroller of the Currency, 2:725
Office of Thrift Supervision, 2:725
Ohlin, Lloyd, 1:6, 142, 174, 223, 224, 229, 297, 2:864. *See also* **Cloward, Richard A., and Lloyd E. Ohlin: delinquency and opportunity**
Oklahoma Habitual Criminal Sterilization Act, 1:307
Olson, Bernadette, 1:209